A History of the American People

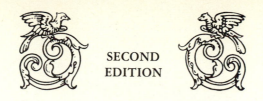

SECOND
EDITION

A History of the American People

Norman A. Graebner
University of Virginia

Gilbert C. Fite
Eastern Illinois University

Philip L. White
University of Texas

McGraw-Hill Book Company

NEW YORK   ST. LOUIS   SAN FRANCISCO   AUCKLAND   DÜSSELDORF
JOHANNESBURG   KUALA LUMPUR   LONDON   MEXICO   MONTREAL
NEW DELHI   PANAMA   PARIS   SÃO PAULO
SINGAPORE   SYDNEY   TOKYO
TORONTO

To our wives:
Laura, June, and Meda

Library of Congress Cataloging in Publication Data

Graebner, Norman A.
  A history of the American people.

  Includes bibliographical references and index.
  1. United States—History. I. Fite, Gilbert
Courtland, date joint author. II. White,
Philip L., joint author. III. Title.
E178.1.G838 1975b   973   74-26671
ISBN 0-07-023885-5 (v. 1)
ISBN 0-07-023886-3 (v. 2)

CIP for the combined vol.
E178.1.G838 1975   973   74-26670
ISBN 0-07-023887-1

A HISTORY OF THE AMERICAN PEOPLE

1234567890 DODO 798765

This book was set in Garamond by Black Dot, Inc. The
editors were Robert P. Rainier, John Hendry, and Annette
Hall; the designer was Ben Kann; the production supervisor
was Joe Campanella. The photo editors were Sam Holmes
and Gabriele Wunderlich.
R. R. Donnelley & Sons Company was printer and binder.

Contents

CONTENTS

CONTENTS

CONTENTS

CONTENTS

CONTENTS

Preface

No person can fully share with others his impressions, his understanding, or his appreciation of the past. Individuals, invariably unique in their psychic makeup and belonging to different generations, regions, races, religions, classes, and political parties, all perceive the past in some distinctive manner. No one can alter the facts of history, but those concerned with the human record, historians among them, ignore some facts, exaggerate the importance of others, and, without necessarily intending to do so, often interpret the past more in accordance with their own preconceptions than in the interest of historical balance. The authors of this text are as susceptible to these prejudices as all mortals, but, like all conscientious historians, we have tried to be as objective as possible while still fulfilling the historian's obligation to reveal the meaning of words and events and their relevance to the present. Where conflicts of interpretation still rage, we have attempted to do justice to each side. But we have not hesitated to exhibit preferences in the choice of interpretations when the evidence, in our judgment, warrants such selections.

Traditionally, textbook writing has emphasized narrative, the construction of an accurate and significant story of what actually occurred. More recently, the search for analysis and greater understanding and insight into human affairs has become an explicit, rather than a largely implicit, aim of the historian, and we have followed this trend. For that reason, this second edition, like the first, is less narrowly narrative and more explicitly analytical than most. We have, furthermore, endeavored to distinguish our text in matters of synthesis, organization, and subject matter. Specialized historical works flow from the nation's presses in an ever-increasing flood—some of them clearly significant, others more significant than clear, still others neither. To keep pace with this outpouring and to incorporate significant new findings into a coherent presentation is a monumental, perhaps an almost impossible, undertaking. Still we hope that we have succeeded better than many in keeping our material historiographically fresh, our chapters digestible in length and internally consistent, and our titles and headings meaningfully descriptive.

Like other contemporary historians, we have attempted to place American history in international perspective. Not only have we recognized the effects of conditions elsewhere in the world upon the history of the American people, but also we have attempted to compare American institutions at certain moments in history with those abroad in order to help the reader see what it means and has meant to live in the United States. We have, moreover, sought to write of the poor and oppressed as well as of the more affluent in American society. Those millions who have lived in the United States without ever becoming members of the nation's dominant middle class have played an unquestionably vital role in our past. But until relatively recent times, historians have tended not only to write *of* the rich and powerful but also to assume that essentially they wrote *for* such people. Even in the late 1960s, when concern for the lives of the poor and oppressed clearly existed, historians found it difficult to uncover adequate sources of information except in secondhand accounts written by people who were themselves neither poor nor disadvantaged. Yet within the limits imposed by these circumstances, we have attempted to write a history of and for all the American people, not merely that minority which supposedly "made history."

We have, in the preparation of this new edition, again resorted to lavish illustration, especially with the unprecedented device of the picture essays, in the conviction that carefully selected illustrations may well be worth many thousands of words. These portfolios document in depth subjects that we suggest but cannot take space to explore as well as central topics that we explicitly discuss. Extended pictorial documents such as these, in this age of visual stimulation,

not only should excite the student's interest but should actually enable him or her to participate, intellectually and emotionally, in each of the experiences being presented. We also believe that full color conveys a much more arresting message than simple black-and-white reproductions, and we have used it where appropriate. All the graphic elements here—the two-color maps and charts, the individual photographs, the picture portfolios, the full-color sections—have been carefully coordinated to dramatize, and indeed to bring to life, the supremely significant and exciting experience of the American people.

Above all, this history of the United States has been designed to teach. Historical processes are always complex, and those who choose to examine the record for guidance must recognize the crucial forces, principles, and tendencies within each episode if their study is to serve any useful purpose. So we have sought to bring what is relevant in history to a generation of Americans that must face the imminent and critical problems of racial injustice, tension, and insurrection; poverty and discontent; crowded cities and violence; and foreign involvements and war that can no longer be shielded from critical and incisive public debate by phrases and slogans that traditionally expressed the ideals, not the realities, of American life. For too long Americans in high places, themselves often oblivious to the conditions blighting the lives of millions, repeated shibboleths that entered easily into American thought without suffering any strain or guilt and without creating any mental disturbance among those who listened. But no longer can Americans speak of freedom and justice in American society as if those ideals exist for all. Demands that the nation conform to its ideals have become too insistent and widespread to be ignored. Any meaningful response to the challenges of today and tomorrow requires understanding as well as good intent. History cannot supply the answers for the country's emotional and economic ills, but it can encourage and assist in the diagnosis, suggest the magnitude of the tasks ahead, and, by interspersing hope with caution, better assure success for the continuing process of change.

This second edition has been made current not only by the inclusion of new material on the 1970s that extends the nation's history into the administration of Gerald Ford, but also by innumerable changes throughout the text. These alterations result in part from new publications, in part from the critical comments of readers and reviewers of the first edition. This new edition is considerably shorter than the first; the reduced size will render the text more useful. Still it presents a full treatment of the American experience, with a superior balance resulting from additions as well as deletions.

An instructors' manual, prepared by John H. Schroeder and Douglas C. Johnston, is available for teachers who use this text.

Historical writing is too dependent on the limits of human knowledge to achieve perfection. This volume, despite the time, patience, and care that have gone into it, cannot emerge without error. Aided by the suggestions of our readers as well as by our own continued examinations of the past, however, we intend to improve each successive edition. Whatever the errors—and for these we take full responsibility—they have been rendered less numerous by the assistance we have received from scholars who have read either sections or all of this book; we have profited greatly from the thoughtful reviews of James M. Banner, Jr., J. Leonard Bates, Don E. Fehrenbacher, Jack P. Greene, Sheldon Hackney, Winthrop Jordan, Thomas A. Krueger, Walter LaFeber, James M. McPherson, Gerald D. Nash, Roderick Nash, James T. Patterson, Earl E. Thorpe, Richard Wade, and Bernard Weisberger. We are also grateful to Donald J. Berthrong, John S. Ezell, Russell D. Buhite, David W. Levy, Robert Shalhope, R. Alton Lee, J. Carroll Moody, David E. Conrad, Duane M. Leach, Thomas H. Buckley, and John R. Ferrell for their incisive and helpful editorial assistance. We express our deep appreciation to John Hendry, Basic Book Editor, and to Annette Hall, Subject-Area Supervisor, for their imaginative and constructive suggestions.

Norman A. Graebner
Gilbert C. Fite
Philip L. White

1

Environment and Heritage

Whatever its faults or virtues, American society is largely the product of interaction between its European heritage and the American environment. Some years ago Americans generally preferred to magnify the differences between themselves and Europeans and to attribute American distinctiveness to factors peculiar to the American experience, particularly that of the frontier. Similarities between America and Europe have come in for reemphasis recently, however, as Africa and Asia, with their own distinctive cultures, have risen to more prominent positions in world affairs. In this perspective Americans have begun to acknowledge again, as they had in the nineteenth century, that their society does indeed derive from the traditions of Western or European civilization. Not just in the ancestry of most of its people but also in language and religion, in social traditions, in ways of making a living, even in its pattern of government, American society reveals its European foundations.

Despite the importance of its European origins, however, society in the New World was to become something more than an extension of Europe. The American environment, both physical and cultural, exerted influences which operated to distinguish American from European culture. It is appropriate, therefore, to begin a history of the United States with some observations both on the American environment and on the evolution of the enduring civilization of which it was and is a part.

WHY STUDY HISTORY?

History is the study of the human record through time. It deals with all aspects of man's adventure—political, economic, social, intellectual, and military. Its foundations lie overwhelmingly in written records—private and public documents, letters, diaries, newspapers, and a variety of other writings. It is by examining and evaluating such materials that historians approach the past. Thus the reconstruction of the human experience demands more than a compilation of the "raw material" contained in the written record. For historians are generally concerned less with the stream of events than with those interrelationships which explain the occurrence of those events and measure their significance.

George Santayana once observed, "Those who do not know the past are condemned to repeat it." Sound practice in any field of human endeavor must rest on the foundation of experience. If personal maturity requires some reflection on yesterday's events, national maturity demands some concern for the lessons of history. Historical processes are always complex, and those who examine the record for guidance must recognize the forces, principles, and tendencies within each episode. History that has meaning and purpose must encompass those elements which determine the subsequent direction and quality of human behavior and achievement. In the words of the Frenchman Jean Jaurès, those who seek the lessons of history must take from the altars of the past "the fire—not the ashes."

Every nation's character is unique. In large measure, therefore, the study of United States history unveils not only the sources of the country's remarkable energy and its material triumphs at home and abroad—but also the roots of those troublesome and ignoble conditions which have ever been the concern of critics and reformers. History can give each generation of Americans an understanding of themselves and suggest guidelines for humane and successful action. Why this therapeutic effect of history has been negligible is clear enough: It is easier to diagnose than to cure. But surely a sound diagnosis is the first step, and a people familiar with their history are less likely than others to suffer the fate against which Santayana warned.

The American Environment

Geological changes affecting the geography of North America have profoundly influenced the course of American history. Paramount in importance among the continent's geographical characteristics is its isolation, shared of course by South America, from the great, interconnected land mass of Europe, Asia, and Africa. Homo sapiens or modern man apparently evolved from hominids or manlike creatures somewhere in the "old" world roughly 200,000 years ago. He lived in fact on each of the old world's three continents. No human beings set foot on American soil until, at the earliest, some twenty thousand years ago. Thus for roughly 90 percent of the period of man's existence on earth the New World had no human habitation.

New World plants and animals differed also from those of the Old World because of the water barrier between the two great land areas. Until the coming of the Europeans America had no cattle, hogs, sheep, or goats. Horses and camels had once inhabited the Western Hemisphere, but had become extinct before the coming of Columbus. Of man's major domestic animals only the dog, fellow immigrant with man from Asia, preceded Columbus to these shores. Cultivation of crops such as wheat, rice, rye, oats, and barley had helped the inhabitants of the Old World to progress from nomadic hunters and food-gatherers to settled tillers of the soil. With the exception of wild rice, none of those crops grew in pre-Columbian America, but corn, a hybrid plant developed by the Indians, had enabled some of them to make the same transition from hunting and food gathering to settled agricultural life.

Those geological conditions which isolated the New World from the Old were not constant. Alternate warming and cooling of the earth have raised and lowered sea level dramatically. In the warm periods glacial ice has melted in such quantities as to raise sea level, perhaps in association with other factors, high enough to inundate about half of North America, including large portions of the South and the Middle West. In such periods forms of tropical life existed on the fringes of the Arctic. On four occasions, the last one some nine thousand years before Christ, cooling of the earth permitted glaciers a mile or two in thickness to blanket the northern half of North America.

The effects of the glaciers stagger the imagination. They swept New England's topsoil out to sea, leaving a rocky and infertile land behind. As if to compensate the region for its loss, however, the glaciers apparently were responsible for endowing it with a vast coastal shelf of relatively shallow water which still provides one of the world's major commercial fishing areas. Farther west the glaciers scooped out the Great Lakes and converted two northward flowing rivers into the Missouri and Ohio River systems as tributaries to the Mississippi.

By holding so much of the world's water supply on land, the glaciers also lowered sea level sharply. In the narrow Bering Strait between Alaska and Siberia there appeared a land bridge linking the Old World and the New. Archaeological and anthropological evidence has established beyond any question that by this bridge man and his friend the dog first emigrated from the Old World to the New.

The First Americans

America's first immigrants, later misnamed "Indians" by Columbus, were in fact Mongolians. Physically they had brown skin, high cheekbones, thin lips, strong chins, and broad faces.

Their hair was straight and black. Culturally they were about at the level of other Old World people of the time. They could make and use fire. They used stone and wood for weapons, such as spears and arrows, and also for tools. They made baskets from plant fiber. Hunting, fishing, and food gathering provided their subsistence.

Gradually the immigrants diffused over all of the Western Hemisphere, including the Caribbean islands. Tropical America from Mexico to Peru was the region in which Indian culture reached its highest levels. The Mayas of Mexico in the millennium following the birth of Christ achieved a high level of political organization, built impressive pyramids, palaces, and temples, did art work which is still striking, and devised a calendar superior to that used until 1752 in the British empire. Several centuries before Columbus, the Mayas suffered conquest by the less-cultured Toltecs from the north, who in turn fell before another northern and still more warlike group, the Aztecs. Two centuries of Aztec predominance terminated with the Spanish conquest achieved by Hernando Cortes between 1519 and 1522.

In northern South America, the Incas, centering in western Peru, were outstanding. They included several million subjects in an absolute theocracy of which the ruling Inca was both high priest and sovereign. The Incas excelled in military, civil, and religious organization, in road building, and in communication. They resisted bravely but at last succumbed to the Spanish invasion of 1531 and 1533 under Francisco Pizarro.

Even the most advanced of the Indian civilizations, however, had notable deficiencies in comparison with European culture when the two first met. By 1492 Europeans had long employed horse-drawn wagons, written languages, and a variety of metal tools and weapons. Although some Indians then made wheeled toys, none used wheeled vehicles. None had yet devised an alphabet, although some were beginning to communicate by pictographs or picture writing. Some had used metal for ornamental purposes and in a few instances for tools or weapons, but in 1492 the American Indians made no important use of metal for practical purposes.

Indian people in what is now the United States were distinctly less advanced than those of Mexico or Peru. Their highest political organizations, loose confederations of tribes, were never very large. In contrast to governments in the tropical regions, those north of the Rio Grande probably never encompassed as many as a million people. Population estimates in fact vary wildly, but whether there were only one million or several times that many inhabitants between the Rio Grande and the 49th parallel (the northern border of the United States) in 1492, population density was still far less than among the Aztecs and the Incas. Building, communication, and the measurement of time were also less advanced. Many tribes cultivated corn and other food crops by means usually learned from their southern neighbors, but others still subsisted chiefly by hunting, fishing, and gathering.

Infinite cultural diversity existed at least in part because of geographical differences. In the heavily wooded eastern region the people slashed or burned trees to make clearings in which to cultivate their corn and a few other crops, but they depended largely on hunting to provide both meat and material for clothing. In the grasslands farther west enormous herds of buffalo afforded meat, clothing, material for bone tools, and even fuel in the form of dried manure chips. Conical tepees constructed of a few poles covered with buffalo hides afforded homes which could be moved easily as the tribe migrated following the buffalo. In the arid Southwest where wood was scarce, adobe construction afforded houses, sometimes multi-storied and organized into pueblos (towns), whose people subsisted chiefly on corn and beans. In the Great Basin area centering in Nevada and Utah still more arid conditions largely precluded agriculture. Consequently people with a minimum of social organization and ever on the verge of starvation wandered widely in search of edible plants and animals. In California acorns enabled people to live without resort to agricultural labor. Farther north along the Pacific Coast salmon and other fish as well as abundant game and wild plants helped delay the advent of agriculture. In Alaska, where Arctic cold severely limited vegetation, Eskimo people devised ice block houses and subsisted by hunting and fishing. Relative isolation fostered linguistic differences as well. There were about two hundred mutually unintelligible Indian languages in the area of what is now the United States.

War was a "principal preoccupation" among many tribes, but others, especially in the Great Basin area, were notably nonaggressive. As among medieval Europeans, war had some of the aspects of sport. Merely touching an enemy in battle or "counting coup" often afforded more prestige than killing him. Wars of conquest were very rare. The usual objectives were prestige, revenge, plunder, the defense of tribal areas, and in some instances, particularly in the Northwest, the capture of slaves. Captives might often experience sadistic torture to test their courage. They might also be adopted by their captors. Intermittent raiding was much more prevalent than sustained warfare.

Values in other matters showed both diversity and similarity. Some tribes, notably those of the Iroquois confederacy, traced ancestry in the female line. Women who headed Iroquois clans not only named men to tribal counsels but could depose them. Nearly all Indians were extremely

A Carolina Indian dance, painted around 1585 by the English artist John White.

Culver Pictures, Inc.

dignified, expressing anger and other emotions much less than is usual for Europeans. Most were also highly individualistic. Coercion of individuals was infrequent, but social pressure for conformity could be strong. Chiefs usually gave advice rather than orders. Dancing, often highly ritualized, was very common. Drums and flutes afforded the principal accompaniment. Most Indians believed that human life was closely linked to all other forms of life, which they respected accordingly. Shamans, or medicine men believed to have supernatural powers, guided them in appeasing or conforming to the will of deities.

Individual ownership in the extreme sense associated with a capitalistic economy was largely alien to the Indians. To them land was not something to be owned but something which existed for their use. Agricultural labor, exclusively women's work in many tribes, tended to be communal. Often its products were held in common for use in accordance with need. Homes, notably the long houses of the Iroquois, were sometimes communal as well. In conspicuous exception to the general rule of indifference to individual ownership, Indians of the Northwest sought eagerly to acquire valued commodities to give away or destroy in highly competitive ostentation, a practice known as "potlatch." For the most part, European sojourners would find repeated occasion to echo the observation of Columbus that "of anything they have, if it be asked for, they . . . invite the person to accept it, and show as much lovingness as though they would give their hearts." Applied to land, this cultural difference was to become a source of endless confusion, misunderstanding, and conflict.

Europe before 1500

Old World civilization, so much of which would cross the Atlantic with the European immigrants, began in the Mediterranean region where Asia meets both Africa and Europe. Irrigation, the plow, controlled reproduction of plants and animals, as well as the use of domesticated animals, permitted production of food in quantities sufficient to free some from agricultural labor and allow them to pursue other specialized occupations. Discovery of smelting techniques made possible the production of bronze, an alloy of copper and tin, harder than either of the others and therefore much more satisfactory for tools and weapons. A similar advance at a later date produced iron. Scholars devised written languages and deduced mathematical principles adequate to solve quadratic equations. Complex political systems evolved. The religion of Judaism took form and at the period from which we begin the measure of time gave rise to Christianity.

In mountainous and infertile Greece during the millennium preceding the birth of Christ ancient civilization reached almost incredible heights. Aided by a network of colonies around the Mediterranean, the Greeks developed a prosperous commerce. The people themselves, rather than a king, a priest, or a military despot, controlled the government. In the "pure" democracy of Athens all men (excluding resident aliens and slaves) could participate in public meetings which chose officers and made decisions on public policy. Almost as epochal as the appearance of democracy were the intellectual and artistic achievements of the Greeks. Pythagoras did fundamental work in mathematics; Democritus made prophetic speculations on atomic theory, Heraclitus on the constancy of change in nature. Hippocrates sought natural rather than supernatural causes of disease. Socrates, the questioner, Plato, the political theorist, and Aristotle, the logician, formed a trio whose works are still central to the study of philosophy. Greek drama still finds an audience. Greek myths and poetry still find readers. In Herodotus the Greeks produced the world's

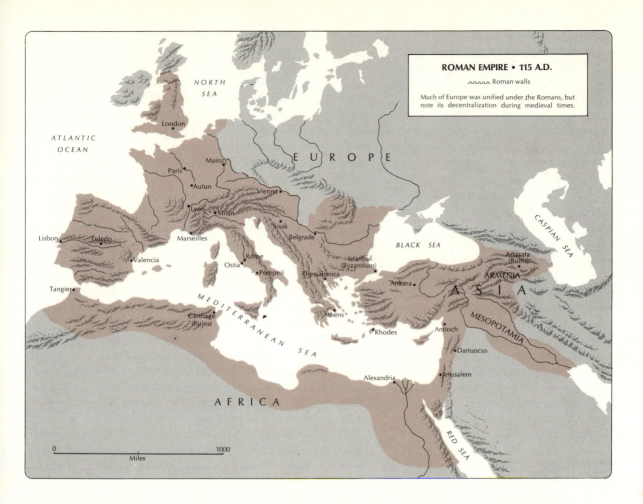

first great historian. Tourists still flock to see the ruins of the Parthenon, surely one of the most beautiful buildings ever designed. Museum goers still marvel at Greek skill in sculpture. Yet for all their positive achievements, the Greeks produced in Sparta the most perfect example of militaristic totalitarianism the world has ever witnessed. Because they failed to unify their fiercely rivalrous states, the Greeks experienced conquest by their Macedonian neighbors some three hundred years before the birth of Christ.

While Greece was waning, Rome was rising. Originally an agricultural people living in the center of the Italian peninsula, the Romans developed a republican or representative form of government rather more practical than the pure,

mass-meeting democracy of Greece. They developed also civic pride, a legal system, administrative efficiency, and military skill which in the millennium centering roughly on the birth of Christ enabled them to create an empire without parallel in the history of the world. From England to Egypt, from Spain to Iraq, Roman authority held sway in the early centuries of the Christian era. During their long ascendancy the Romans built roads superior to those which were built for centuries thereafter. For public spectacles, notably gladiatorial combat, they constructed a coliseum which still stands amid the exhaust fumes and traffic congestion of modern Rome. Christianity, originally a persecuted religion of the poor, of pacifists and nonconformists,

ENVIRONMENT AND HERITAGE

became Romanized in some measure following the conversion of the Emperor Constantine in 313 and the gradual assumption of papal authority by succeeding bishops of Rome. The decline and fall of Rome, as of other great societies of the past, still puzzles historians, but among the more widely cited causes are corruption, extreme economic and social inequality, deficiencies in economic productivity, and replacement of republican government by an army-dominated, imperial autocracy. Such changes largely destroyed civic pride and almost invited "barbarian" invasion.

The invasions which destroyed Rome and ushered in the medieval era continued for several centuries. The "barbarians" themselves were illiterate people from as far north as Scandinavia and as far east as modern Russia. No one knows why they came, but they plundered or conquered from Greece to Spain and from North Africa to Iceland. Venturing as daringly by sea as they did by land, they were also the first Europeans to behold America.

Norsemen who had plundered Ireland and apparently driven the Irish out of Iceland moved on from there to Greenland, Labrador, and Newfoundland. Icelandic and Norwegian sagas and legends, confirmed by archaeological and other evidence, make clear that in 986 Bjarni Herjolfsson, attempting to sail from Iceland to the new colony in Greenland, missed his target and sighted Labrador. In 1001 Leif Eriksson landed at Baffin Island, Labrador, and Newfoundland. Natives killed Leif's brother Thorvald when he returned to Newfoundland or "Vinland," as Leif called it, in 1004–1005, and drove off Thorfinn Karlsefni, whose child, Snorri, was born there about 1009. The last of the Norsemen to visit Vinland were Freydis, sister of Leif, and her husband Thorvard. They left after murdering some of their own party in 1013. No Europeans would return for almost five hundred years.

Conditions in Europe during medieval times (between the fall of Rome and the rise of modern Europe) were such that Europeans developed no interest in America and indeed that even the

best-educated people had no knowledge of its existence. Law and order had disintegrated with Rome's collapse. Long-distance trade understandably declined sharply. Specialization of labor diminished and cities based upon it disappeared. Rome itself shrank from a million to some fifty thousand people. The typical economic unit had come to be the manor, a rural village centered about the fortified home of a nobleman. Peasants bound to the land as serfs farmed the land of the manor lord, paying him in services and commodities for the privilege of protection. The manor lord himself owed "feudal" obligations of many kinds, particularly military, to others of higher rank in a chain of nobles ascending to a king. The ambitions of individual nobles, backed by military force at their disposal, made for constant turmoil and impeded the growth of centralized authority. Christianity, however, extended throughout Europe and its hierarchy, in which authority descended from the Pope to the people through cardinals, archbishops, bishops, and priests, attained wealth and power superior to those of kings. Throughout the medieval Age of Faith, theology preoccupied scholars at the newly instituted universities, inspired the writing of Dante and Chaucer as well as Saint Thomas Aquinas, and the artistic effort which created and adorned the great cathedrals which still distinguish European cities. Religious considerations also encouraged fruitless effort to unify Christendom in a Holy Roman Empire and inspired the major military action of the period, the eight Crusades intended to free the Christian Holy Lands from Muslims who had seized them during their great surge of expansion which followed the inception of their faith in 622.

The renaissance or rebirth of Europe, which set the stage for the third and historically most important discovery of America, was well along by the time of Columbus. Reestablishment of law and order aided by the slow evolution of royal authority had permitted revival of trade and with it the rise of cities populated in part by artisans and merchants. These urban people

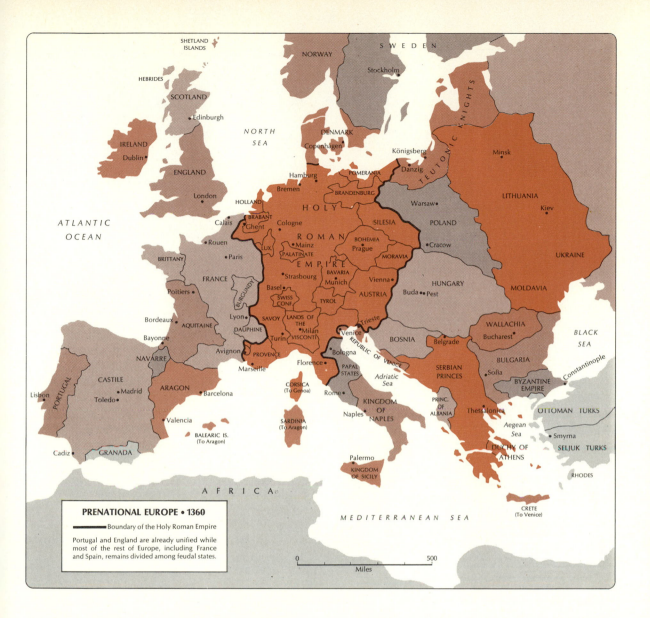

PRENATIONAL EUROPE · 1360

⎯⎯⎯ Boundary of the Holy Roman Empire

Portugal and England are already unified while most of the rest of Europe, including France and Spain, remains divided among feudal states.

0   500

Miles

formed a new class, the bourgeois or middle class, between the landowning nobility and the landworking peasants. Their appearance signified that the economy was in transition from subsistence farming to commercial capitalism, a stage dominated by merchants rather than by landowners, as in the past, or by manufacturers, as in the future. Secular matters in general began to interest people more, concern for salvation less. Art reflected less religious symbolism, more admiration for Greece and Rome, more interest in real human life. Technology advanced. Guns outmoded the bow and arrow and the sword. Arabic numbers replaced Roman numerals. Printing replaced the laborious hand-copying of books. Navigation became more scientific with the invention of the compass, cross-staff, astrolabe, and mechanical clock. The deep-drafted

ENVIRONMENT AND HERITAGE

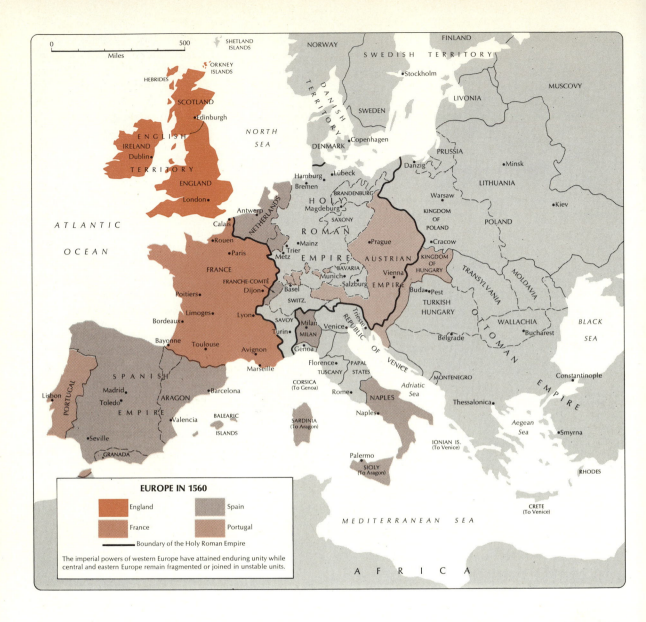

Portuguese caravel made ocean sailing safer than it had been with the older, shallow-draft vessels.

Political circumstances had altered sharply also as "modern" Europe began to emerge from the medieval period. The new middle class, manifesting a national culture, communicating in a national language rather than in the Latin of the church and of Rome, wanted strong national governments. Such governments could provide more security for commerce than had prevailed amid the rivalrous contention of feudal landlords. Strong national governments could also provide freedom from local taxes on the movement of goods, uniformity and simplicity in regulation of commerce, discriminatory policies against foreign competition, and aid in securing favorable conditions abroad. As commerce with foreigners increased, middle-class people became more conscious of their own "national" identity and of the role of the king as the servant of the nation's interest. Accordingly mercantile wealth helped finance the efforts of kings to unify chaotic feudal holdings as integrated national monarchies. Before 1500 there had emerged on the western periphery of Europe four "modern" nations: Portugal, Spain, England, and France. From these nations came the epochal exploration voyages which would transform America, Europe, and the world.

The Age of Exploration

Pursuit of commercial advantage inspired the exploration voyages financed or commissioned by each of the four "new" nations of western Europe. The Crusades, beginning in 1096 and continuing for almost two centuries, had failed ultimately to drive the Muslims from the Holy Land, but they had imparted to the crusaders an avid desire for Asian luxuries, spices to improve the palatability of half-spoiled foods, silks, perfumes, and drugs. Produced in southeast Asia, China, and India, these goods came westward chiefly by sea to the head of the Red Sea or the Persian Gulf. Caravans then carried the cargoes overland to the shores of the Mediterranean, where Italian vessels picked them up and distributed them to European markets. The profits

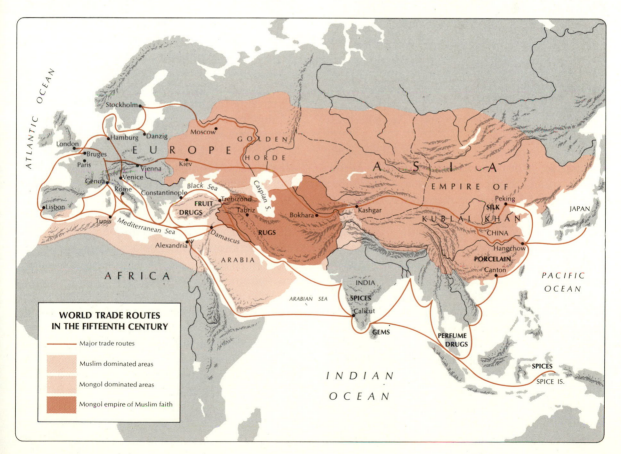

WORLD TRADE ROUTES
IN THE FIFTEENTH CENTURY

— Major trade routes

Muslim dominated areas

Mongol dominated areas

Mongol empire of Muslim faith

of Arab and Italian middlemen greatly increased the price of Asian luxuries for western Europeans, limiting the amount which they could buy and causing a serious drain on their limited supply of gold.

Informed people had known theoretically for centuries that the world was round. Now there was an obvious incentive to achieve direct trade by sea between western Europe and the Orient. By eliminating the middlemen, such a route would indeed lower the price of Asian goods in western Europe. Still more important, merchants who could import more cheaply could undersell the Italians and probably replace them as distributors of Asian items for most of Europe.

Portugal pioneered in systematic exploration. From their voyages along the African coast the Portuguese developed a lucrative trade in ivory, gold, pepper, and slaves and found a water route to Asia as well. On a voyage which began in 1486, Bartholomeu Dias rounded the southern tip of Africa. Vasco da Gama reached India in 1498 and returned with spices and jewels priced far below those secured from the Italians. Soon the Portuguese had set up bases in India and become the principal purveyors of Asian luxuries in Europe.

Spanish exploration began with Christopher Columbus. Born to an artisan family in the Italian commercial center of Genoa, Columbus became a coastal pilot and map maker. In time he became obsessed with the idea of reaching Asia by sailing west across the Atlantic. There was nothing theoretically novel in this. What was unique in Columbus was his determination to do it and his conviction, based on a gross miscalculation of the earth's size, that fewer than 3,000 miles of ocean separated western Europe from eastern Asia.

In the early 1480s Columbus began to seek financial backing for his expedition in Portugal. The Portuguese, however, had more realistic notions than Columbus as to the size of the earth. They turned him down and he left for Spain.

In Spain, Columbus haggled interminably with vacillating authorities. Then in 1492, Ferdinand of Aragon and his wife, Isabella of Castile, who had been struggling jointly to unify Spain, expelled the last of the Moors (Muslims), who had conquered the area seven centuries earlier. Buoyed apparently by this achievement, Ferdinand acceded to Isabella's desire to give Columbus the financial support he needed.

On August 3, 1492, Columbus set sail with three ships and about ninety men. Ten weeks out from Europe, on October 12, the party arrived at an island in the Bahamas which Columbus named San Salvador. Convinced, as he would always remain, that he had found "the Indies," then a common designation for Asia, Columbus applied the misnomer "Indian" to the native population. He kidnapped a few Indians and returned with them to the acclaim of Europe.

Three subsequent voyages of Columbus proved disappointing. He searched for gold, coercing natives to help him, but found little. Columbus also explored the Venezuelan and Central American coast looking for the nonexistent passage which would lead to China or Japan. Discredited by his harsh and inept administration of the areas he had conquered, Columbus sank into disfavor. He died in obscurity in 1506.

Meanwhile the kings of Portugal and Spain disputed how to divide the world between them. In the Treaty of Tordesillas (1494) they ultimately fixed a line of demarcation which put Brazil, the easternmost portion of the Americas, within the Portuguese sphere. This unintended result was not known until 1500 when a Portuguese fleet en route around Africa to Asia accidentally encountered the Brazilian coast.

Amerigo Vespucci, another Italian explorer, denied that Columbus had reached Asia. He had himself sailed along the South American coast to a point south of Buenos Aires in 1501 and 1502. He may have made earlier voyages as well. In any case, Vespucci labeled the area a "New World." A German geographer, Martin Waldseemueller, suggested that the land be named "America" in honor of "Americus Vespucius." The world accepted his suggestion.

Spanish explorations after Columbus's great discovery aimed usually at one of two objectives. The first was to find a passage around or through America to Asia, which, they hoped, would enable Spain to gain a commercial advantage in the Far East such as Portugal had secured in southern Asia. The second objective was to find and exploit the wealth of the New World itself.

Enthusiasm for voyages seeking a westward passage through America to Asia diminished somewhat after the remarkable feat of Ferdinand Magellan. A Portuguese in Spanish service, Magellan found his way through the treacherous straits at the tip of South America which now bear his name. Then he successfully crossed the Pacific to the Philippines, where in 1521 he died in a clash with natives. His crew managed to sail onward, however, to complete, in 1522, the first round-the-world trip. The difficulties and the distance of this voyage made it clear that Europe's trade with the Orient would not pass via the Straits of Magellan.

As their dreams of wealth from Asian commerce faded, the Spanish turned to exploiting American resources. Seeking the source of the silver and gold found among the Indians of the Caribbean, Hernando Cortes, in 1519, led some five hundred men in a Cuba-based invasion of the Aztec domain in Mexico. Aided by superior weapons, by Indian awe of horses, by native enemies of the Aztecs, and by his acceptance among some Aztecs as the god Quetzalcoatl, Cortes vanquished this highly developed Indian civilization. Control over extensive deposits of silver rewarded his efforts. In the 1530s the ruthless Francisco Pizarro achieved still more spectacular success at the expense of another highly developed Indian society, the Incas of Peru. During the remainder of the century, American treasure, mostly silver but some gold as well, poured into Spain. Its effect was to inflate prices, to increase Europe's purchases from Asia, to speed up to Europe's economic growth, to make Spain the envy of her rivals, and to encourage other countries not only to plunder Spanish commerce, but also to join the search for American treasure.

Spanish explorations in what is now the United States were economically unsuccessful. Several expeditions traversed various parts of the Gulf Coast and the Southwest without finding any significant avenue to wealth. Their chief effect was to dot the region with missions whose founders sought to convert the Indians to Catholicism.

Spain's earliest competitor in America was England. English fishermen may in fact have reached Newfoundland in the 1480s, several years before Columbus reached the Bahamas. In 1497 Henry VII authorized a modest venture of one ship and eighteen men under John Cabot, another of the ubiquitous Italians. Cabot found many fish in the Grand Banks area off Newfoundland but no people to confirm his conviction that he had reached China. After several subsequent and equally unsuccessful voyages, the English lost interest.

The French were next. Francis I of France in 1524 employed still another Italian, Giovanni da Verrazano, to seek a passage through North America to the Pacific and China. In this quest Verrazano explored the American coastal line from North Carolina to Maine, including New York Harbor. Further French voyages, delayed because of problems at home, began in 1534 under Jacques Cartier. Between 1534 and 1541 Cartier made three trips up the St. Lawrence River. He dubbed the rapids above Montreal "La Chine" (China) and brought back large cargoes of what he thought to be gold and diamonds. They proved to be fool's gold (a form of iron) and quartz. The French explored no more in the sixteenth century.

Most of the later sixteenth-century exploration was English. Sir Humphrey Gilbert in 1576 published an essay affirming that America was an island (because it had no Asian animals) and that therefore there must be some way around it in the north. Martin Frobisher and John Davis in the 1570s and 1580s attempted in vain to find the elusive passage to the Pacific.

What was the effect of the discoveries of Columbus and da Gama upon the evolution of European society and thus upon the people who would colonize America? Walter Prescott Webb suggested in *The Great Frontier* that the effect was to inaugurate an epoch of prosperity, "the 500-year boom," which strongly influenced the basic features of modern Europe. His critics, on the other hand, have pointed out that the discoveries themselves resulted in part from the rising prosperity in Europe. Clearly, however, the nearly simultaneous discovery of the Americas, of most of Africa, and of economical routes to southern and eastern Asia added enormous momentum to Europe's economic progress.

Development was by no means uniform throughout Europe. The Atlantic countries of western Europe progressed most rapidly. Portugal replaced Italy as the commercial center of Europe following da Gama's voyage, but was not strong enough to protect its Asian empire from interlopers. Spain, largely because of the silver and gold produced in its American colonies, became the wealthiest nation in Europe. By spending its American wealth to buy what it wanted abroad and to meet its great military commitments, Spain did not foster the development of its own rather limited resources. The commercial areas of northern Europe (Netherlands, France, Germany, and England) benefited from American wealth in a healthier manner. Spurred by rising prices resulting at least partly from Spain's expanded purchasing power, these areas increased their productive capacity, especially in woolen and linen textiles, then major items of trade. As their commercial production grew, so did their middle-class population, their urban centers, and their national wealth and power.

In these newly risen commercial areas of northern Europe occurred the great religious upheaval of the early sixteenth century—the Protestant Reformation. The relation between Protestantism and the rise of commercial capital-ism has occasioned much dispute. Max Weber in a celebrated essay, *The Protestant Ethic and the Spirit of Capitalism*, suggested that the Protestant Reformation, by imparting religious sanction to certain economic virtues, such as hard work and thrift, aided the development of capitalism. R. H. Tawney in an equally famous work, *Religion and the Rise of Capitalism*, proposed conversely that the previous development of capitalism strongly influenced the formation of Protestant views. Whichever is more nearly correct, it remains true that the Protestant Reformation was of profound importance in American history, as the vast majority of the early settlers of eastern North America were Protestants from the commercial regions of northwestern Europe.

The first of four major Protestant groups to emerge was the Lutheran. Martin Luther touched off the reform movement in 1517 by challenging what had become a papal fund-raising device—the sale of "indulgences," or remission of punishment for a confessed sin. Unable to reform the Church from within, Luther broke completely with Catholicism. The Lutheran movement which he led affirmed that salvation came from faith, not from good works and observance of the sacraments. Interpretation of the Bible became to Lutherans a matter for the individual rather than the prerogative of the Church. Accordingly Bibles appeared in the language of the people rather than in Latin as heretofore. Lutherans also renounced the Catholic tradition of a celibate clergy and encouraged clergymen to marry. Finally, Lutherans substituted state control of religion for papal control and thereby enhanced the appeal of the movement to those who chafed under a "foreign" papacy. Lutheranism gained ascendancy in north Germany and Scandinavia. Some Lutherans emigrated from these areas to pre-Revolutionary America, but the chief importance of Lutherans for early American history lay in the example which they set for others in breaking away from Rome.

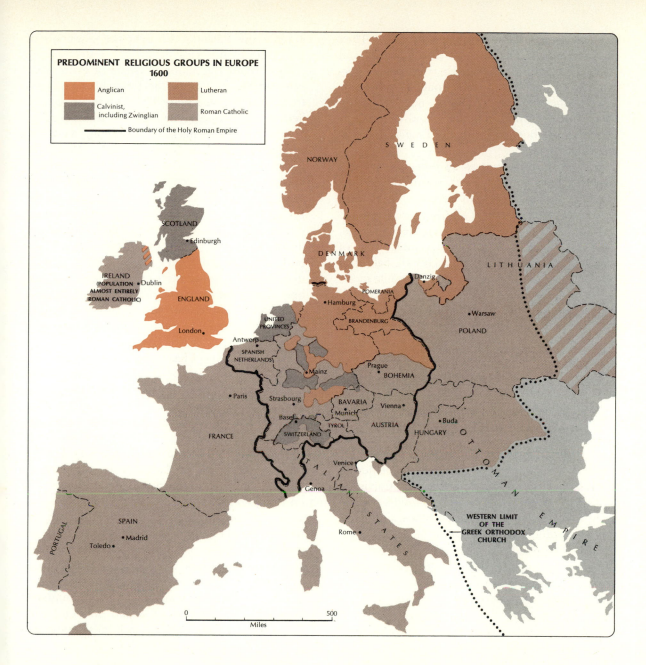

PREDOMINENT RELIGIOUS GROUPS IN EUROPE 1600

- Anglican
- Lutheran
- Calvinist, including Zwinglian
- Roman Catholic
- —— Boundary of the Holy Roman Empire

NORWAY

SWEDEN

SCOTLAND
• Edinburgh

IRELAND
(POPULATION
ALMOST ENTIRELY
ROMAN CATHOLIC)
• Dublin

ENGLAND
London •

DENMARK

LITHUANIA

Danzig •

POMERANIA

• Hamburg

UNITED
PROVINCES

BRANDENBURG

• Warsaw

POLAND

Antwerp •
SPANISH
NETHERLANDS

• Mainz

Prague •
BOHEMIA

• Paris

Strasbourg

BAVARIA

Vienna •

Basel •
SWITZERLAND

Munich •
TYROL

AUSTRIA

• Buda

HUNGARY

FRANCE

Venice •

OTTOMAN EMPIRE

ITALIAN STATES

Genoa •

WESTERN LIMIT
OF THE
GREEK ORTHODOX
CHURCH

SPAIN

PORTUGAL

• Madrid

Toledo •

Rome •

0   500
Miles

The Anabaptist movement, which was to have somewhat more influence on early American history, also had its roots in Germany. In the Peasants' War of 1524, militant poor people tried to end serfdom and the special privileges of nobles and clergy. Luther himself helped to suppress this revolt. In its aftermath many of the lower-class people of north Germany turned to a new religious movement. Because they insisted that baptism was meaningful only to adults and not to infants, adherents of this movement were called Anabaptists, or rebaptizers. They believed in a literal application of biblical teachings. They opposed war, tithes, oaths, a paid ministry, and social inequality. Although rigorously persecuted, Anabaptist beliefs would not die out. They came to early America not only with Mennonites, Amish, Dunkers, and other German groups, but also with the English Baptists and Quakers.

Still more important as an influence in early America were the Calvinists. Calvinism derived from the theology of John Calvin, a Frenchman who wrote his *Institutes of the Christian Religion* in 1536 at Geneva, Switzerland. To the Calvinists, God was less a figure of love and mercy than of majestic power. Man was innately evil. Salvation came to a small minority of the elect while most, in accordance with God's "predestination," were doomed to damnation. The Bible was not merely the word but the law of God, to be rigorously enforced upon a world of sinners by the elect minority assisted by the state. Control of the church, including the selection of a minister and the admission of new members, rested neither with a hierarchy nor with the state but with the local congregation of the elect. Calvinists also glorified work and thrift. The man who achieved success by working hard at his "calling" and saving his money was deemed to enjoy the favor of God. As a corollary, Calvinists tended to see extreme poverty as God's punishment for idleness and self-indulgence. Calvinism spread rapidly, especially among business people in urban centers, becoming in time the dominant theology among the Dutch (Dutch Reformed) and the Scots (Presbyterian). Calvinists were highly important minorities in France (Huguenots), in Germany (German Reformed), and in England (Puritan). Each of these groups, most

notably the Puritans, brought the essentials of Calvinism to America.

Last among the major divisions of Protestantism was the Anglican—the Church of England. Its originator was Henry VIII. To secure a male heir to his throne Henry wanted to divorce his Spanish wife, Catherine of Aragon, who had produced only one surviving child, Mary. To obtain his divorce and control of the vast landholdings of the Church, Henry had himself made head of the Church of England in place of the Pope. His daughter Mary restored Catholicism during her brief reign (1553–1558), but at her death the throne passed to her half-sister, Elizabeth, daughter of Henry's second wife. Illegitimate in the eyes of the Catholic Church, Elizabeth was determined to make England Protestant once more despite her strong personal distaste for many of the ideas and policies associated with Calvinism.

Anglicanism, as Elizabeth I established it, endured as a compromise between Calvinism and Catholicism. Control lay in the English government, but beneath the monarch the old hierarchical pattern of authority descending from bishops remained. The essential features of the ritual of worship were also retained, although English replaced Latin as the language of the service. Clergymen were permitted to marry. Faith was emphasized more than good works as a means to salvation, and the government taxed all to support its church. Many English immigrants to America were loyal supporters of this official church. Others, some Catholics but mostly Calvinists and Anabaptists, chose American exile to escape Anglican pressure to conform. Such immigrants brought with them a profound and enduring bias against a basic element in English society.

Imperial Rivalry

Spain's wealth and power, based so largely on American treasure, inspired rival nations both to prey on Spanish commerce and to seek American colonies in defiance of the Spanish and

Portuguese. At the outset Spain was clearly stronger than her rivals. In addition to Spain itself, the Spanish monarch held the wealthy commercial provinces of the Netherlands plus

Naples and Sicily. While Cortes was conquering Mexico, Spain's ruler became Holy Roman Emperor as well. Until 1556, when again the two offices were separated, the Spanish king could claim the loyalty of much of the area which later became Germany. For two generations after 1580 Spain controlled Portugal. None of Spain's rivals yet possessed significant territories other than their own homelands.

By 1600 Spain had begun to lose ground. Loss of control over the Holy Roman Empire was certainly one factor in Spain's decline. Overcommitment was another. Deeply dedicated to Catholicism, the Spanish government expended inordinate effort, as the Protestant Reformation spread through Germany, the Netherlands, England, and elsewhere, to stamp out what they regarded as intolerably heretical belief. They carried on intermittent warfare not only with Dutch and English Protestants, but also with the Catholic French and the Muslim Turks, each of them major power rivals. Spain's economy, poorly endowed by nature, suffered neglect as warfare preoccupied the nation's ablest leaders and American treasure encouraged heavy purchases from foreigners without increasing Spanish productivity. Yet, despite its declining position, Spain in 1600 remained master of all the Americas. No rival had secured a firm foothold in the New World.

Spain's position even in America had serious weaknesses. Spanish settlements extended as far north as Florida and the pueblo region of the southwestern United States, but everything north of Florida on the Atlantic Coast was still unoccupied and open to penetration. Even in areas where they had settled Spaniards tended to constitute a small ruling class exploiting either the native Indians or imported African slaves. So inadequate was Spanish merchant shipping that the nation regularly granted to one foreign power a monopoly, the asiento, for the importation of African slaves to all its colonies. Even in convoys the Spanish navy could not afford full protection to the treasure fleets which so attracted foreign pirates.

The Dutch began to emerge as a world power during their revolt against Spanish rule (1567–1648). As early converts to Calvinism they lived in dread of attempts by the Spanish to restore Catholicism. They also resented oppressive taxation, the presence of Spanish military forces, and perhaps most of all the alien and authoritarian character of Spanish rule.

In their fight for independence the Dutch employed sea power both to weaken Spain and to enrich themselves. After Portugal became linked to Spain in 1580, the Dutch began to appropriate Portuguese trading posts in Asia. In the hope of finding a way to reach these Asian areas quickly and without skirting Spain, the Dutch dispatched the English explorer Henry Hudson on a voyage to America in 1609. Hudson explored New York Harbor and what is now the Hudson River, which flows into it. Failing to find a passage to Asia, he nevertheless did locate one of the world's finest harbors and a major avenue for penetrating the North American continent. No settlement followed immediately, partly because of a truce the Dutch concluded with Spain that same year.

When war resumed in 1621, the Dutch formed the West India Company to exploit trading and plundering opportunities in America. In 1624 the company set up a fur-trading post, Fort Orange (now Albany), and two years later made the well-known purchase of Manhattan Island.

Trading for furs was the principal business in New Netherland. The Hudson and Mohawk Rivers afforded the Dutch the best natural route into North America between the St. Lawrence and the Mississippi. Dominating that region were the five "nations" of the remarkable Iroquois confederacy. Inveterate enemies of the Algonquian tribes of the St. Lawrence region who cooperated with the French, the Iroquois quickly attached themselves to the Dutch. They became middlemen in the trade between the Dutch at Albany and Indian tribes farther west.

By 1660, however, the situation of New Netherland had become precarious. Infiltrated by English settlers, outnumbered by English

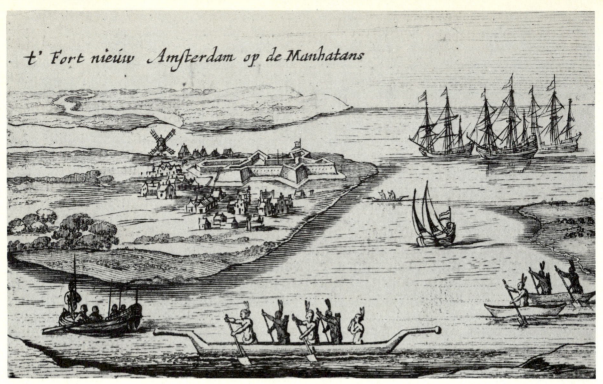

t' Fort nieúw Amsterdam op de Manhatans

A view of New Amsterdam, Manhattan Island, as it appeared around 1628.

The Granger Collection

colonists on both the north and the south, the Dutch outposts depended on the military power of their homeland for defense. That power had forced Spain to grant the Dutch provinces independence in 1648, but was now threatened by both the armies of Louis XIV of France and the naval power of England.

French colonizing efforts failed in Brazil, South Carolina, and Florida at about the middle of the sixteenth century, but farther north the foundation of New France already existed. French fishermen had visited the Grand Banks area off Newfoundland since the voyages of Verrazano and Cartier. To reduce the amount of salt required to preserve their catch, they began drying fish on Cape Breton Island and the Gaspé peninsula. While waiting for their fish to dry, they traded with the Indians. Thus began the fur trade which became the economic foundation of New France. Its basis was the Indian demand for

such European wares as cloth, metal pots, guns, knives, and liquor, combined with the Indian ability to supply furs, chiefly beaver, used in making specially designed hats long in vogue among European gentlemen.

To further that trade Samuel de Champlain founded Quebec in 1608. Population and agricultural settlement in New France followed slowly. By the end of the seventeenth century there were probably thirty or forty European settlers in the English continental colonies for every one in New France. The reasons for the disparity were varied. The government of New France excluded Protestants. Catholic missionaries at times discouraged immigration because they regarded most immigrants an unfortunate influence on their Indian converts. Finally few Frenchmen felt any compulsion to leave their homeland.

Despite the population advantage enjoyed by

the English in America, the French cause was by no means hopeless. In Europe, for one thing, the population advantage was theirs: they outnumbered the English more than two to one. In America most Indian tribes were on their side. So was geography. Without an Appalachian barrier like that which blocked the English path to the interior, the French (Marquette and Jolliet) were on the Mississippi by 1673. By 1682, La Salle had followed the river to the Gulf of Mexico and claimed Louisiana in the name of Louis XIV. The English did have the world's best navy, but the French had the best army. Supremacy in North America as in Europe awaited the outcome of their rivalry.

England at the time of Columbus had proved far too weak to challenge Spain's claim to all of the Americas. During the ensuing century, however, England made dramatic progress in developing export products, extending its commerce, building its naval power, and acquiring technological skill. Encouraged by its growing strength, England challenged Spain with increasing boldness. Henry VIII had defied Spain in divorcing Catherine of Aragon and making England Protestant. Elizabeth I not only restored Protestantism following the Catholic hiatus under her older sister but also after 1577 openly aided the Dutch

revolt against Spain. John Hawkins, an English slave trader, infuriated Spanish authorities by smuggling slaves into their colonies. After the Spanish had destroyed three of Hawkins's five ships, his cousin, Francis Drake, plundered Spanish settlements from Central America southward around the South American continent and north to Mexico before heading homeward across the Pacific. A secret investor in Drake's lucrative enterprise, Elizabeth met Spanish demands that he be punished by conferring knighthood upon him. Angered by perennial Spanish-supported intrigue on behalf of Mary, Queen of Scots, the Catholic claimant to her throne, Elizabeth finally had her rival executed. Philip II of Spain then crowded some seventeen thousand soldiers aboard an enormous invasion fleet and dispatched it for England. As it approached the English coast in 1588, speedy English vessels, employing long-range bombardment instead of the usual boarding technique of naval warfare, wrought havoc on the famed Spanish Armada. A heavy storm then completed the rout and devastation of the Spanish ships. Spain's naval power probably remained greater than that of England for some time, but the defeat of the Armada forecast the end of Spain's superpower status in both the Old World and the New.

Virginia and Maryland

English colonization efforts began even before the defeat of the Spanish Armada. As early as 1578 Sir Humphrey Gilbert, adventurer and companion of pirates if not a pirate himself, began efforts to found a colony among the fishermen at Newfoundland, but he went down with his ship at sea before attaining his goal. His half brother Walter Raleigh, who had worked with him in the Newfoundland venture, then turned his attention to a region which he persuaded Elizabeth, the "Virgin Queen," to designate Virginia in her own honor. Between 1585 and 1587, on Roanoke Island off the coast of North Carolina, Raleigh planted the first of

England's American colonies. Cut off from England for three years (1588–1591) by the outbreak of war with Spain, the colony vanished. Would-be rescuers found only the word "CROATOAN," the name of a nearby island, carved on a doorpost.

Successful efforts to colonize Virginia began at the end of the war with Spain in 1604. Inspired by the financial success of the East India Company (founded 1600), a group of London investors formed the London Company (1605) with the approval of the new monarch, James I. Its aim was to produce a profit by establishing a colony in Virginia rather than by preying—at least immediately—on the Spanish. Three company ships arrived in Virginia in 1607. Instead of going 100 miles inland to avoid "a low or moist place" as instructed, the newcomers founded Jamestown in precisely the kind of terrain they had been warned to avoid. They also neglected to plant sufficient food crops, preferring to look for gold and expecting to be supplied from England. They managed furthermore to antagonize some of the Indians. Consequently with the natives "as fast killing without as famine and pestilence within," a phrase used actually to describe a similar period of suffering later, about half the settlers died before a supply ship reached them in midwinter.

Captain John Smith, surely one of the most remarkable of the great adventurers of the Elizabethan era, came forth to rescue the colony from the chaos of committee rule which the company had prescribed. Smith was only twenty-seven and neither a nobleman nor even a gentleman but essentially a soldier of fortune. While fighting Turks in Hungary, he had been captured, sold into slavery, and then rescued by "fair maidens." Employed by the London Company as military officer for the prospective colony, he had made at least part of the voyage to America in confinement for inciting to mutiny. Upon arrival he busied himself in mapping Chesapeake Bay, which he did with impressive accuracy. Returning to the leaderless and floundering settlement, he took charge. He secured corn from the Indians to alleviate starvation. He put the colonists to work effectively providing their own food, shelter, and protection. Injured in a gunpowder explosion, Smith returned to England in 1609, there to write accounts of his exploits so embroidered with self-praise that until recently they aroused great skepticism, especially as to his rescue by the maiden Pocahontas from execution by Indian captors. What little evidence historians have been able to find, however, corroborates rather than refutes his story.

During the "starving time" (1609–1611) which followed Smith's return to England, the colony of Jamestown almost ceased to exist. When leaders designated by the company failed for one reason or another to get to Virginia in 1609, near anarchy again prevailed. "So lamentable was our scarcity," Virginians later recounted, "that we were constrained to eat dogs, cats, rats, snakes, toadstools, horse-hides and what not; one man out of the misery that he endured, killing his wife, powdered her up to eat her, for which he was burned. Many besides fed on the corpses of dead men. . . ." Sixty-odd survivors were aboard ship, determined to return to England, when relief arrived.

Developments which followed the "starving time" assured the permanence of the colony. Tough governors imposed discipline. Pocahontas married the planter John Rolfe, reflecting improvement in relations with the Indians. Of paramount importance was Rolfe's success in cultivating West Indian tobacco. Europe had learned from the Indians how to use this native American plant, but the variety of tobacco native to Virginia was unsuitable for commercial purposes. Successful growing of West Indian tobacco in Virginia, however, assured the colony's future. Investors poured in more money. Colonists immigrated in great numbers under a "headright" system by which the company allocated 50 acres of land per immigrant to the person who paid the immigrant's passage. Immigrants still died like flies, particularly "servants" who were overworked and underfed in a malarial climate. A surprise Indian uprising in 1622 killed off more than 300, but by 1625 a census showed 1,210 hardy survivors of an immigrant total of several thousand.

Neighboring Maryland within a few years also attracted settlers intent on cultivating tobacco. The impetus to the founding of Maryland came from George Calvert, an investor in the company which founded Virginia and a major figure in the government of James I. Newfoundland was the original focus of Calvert's interest, but despite being farther south than London, its climate, because of prevailing wind and ocean currents, proved too frigid for Calvert's liking.

He began to seek land in the area of Chesapeake Bay. Meanwhile in 1625 he announced his conversion to Catholicism, still a suspect religion in England, resigned from the government, and received the title of Lord Baltimore. The land grant was still not final when Calvert died in 1632, but his son Cecilius secured it before the end of the year. The name Maryland was chosen to honor Queen Henrietta Maria, also a Catholic.

Unlike Virginia, which belonged initially to a corporation, Maryland was a "proprietary" possession of the Calvert family. Corporations had proved troublesome, especially in Massachusetts, and they were based on the mistaken belief that American colonies would be profitable trading posts like those in Asia. Proprietorship correctly identified land as the major source of wealth to be found in English America. The proprietor owned all the land. He granted it to settlers of his choice and derived income from "quit rents," a small but perpetual obligation which freed the payer from other traditional obligations to the landlord.

Economic development in Maryland proceeded rapidly. As in Virginia, tobacco sustained the economy. The example of Virginia, as well as its proximity, helped the new neighbors to minimize troublesome encounters with the nearby Indians and to avoid a "starving time."

Religious and political developments were potentially more turbulent. George Calvert had hoped that Maryland would be a refuge for English Catholics, against whom legal discrimination was severe. Relatively few English Catholics, however, chose to migrate. Those who did constituted essentially a ruling class of large landowners, but they were outnumbered by Protestants even on the *Ark*, which brought the first settlers in 1634. Migration from Virginia did not improve the balance.

New England and the West Indies

New England's settlement, in contrast to that of Virginia, grew out of incentives which were religious and political more than economic. Elizabeth I, although ruling without much reference to Parliament from 1555 to 1603, had maintained "her subjects' love and good affections." Her successor, James I, was well-meaning but offensively pedantic, "the wisest fool in Christendom," and a spendthrift. He believed implicitly in the divine right of kings, a concept widely accepted on the Continent and in an authoritarian church as well. In fact, he thought he could keep his authority in the government only as long as bishops retained similar control of the church. "No bishop," he often stated, "no king." Parliamentary leaders, many of them Puritans, resisted the attempts of James I and his like-minded son, Charles I, to impose revenue measures without consent of Parliament, and protested the refusal of Charles I to convene Parliament from 1629 to 1640. Puritans in general were indignant because Anglican Archbishop William Laud not only blocked religious reforms the Puritans wanted but replaced many of their ministers with more orthodox Anglicans and undertook in general to enforce conformity to unreformed Anglican practices.

This conflict which smoldered through the reign of James I (1603–1625) burst into civil war (1642–1646) under Charles I. The outcome was a Puritan, or Roundhead, victory over the Cavalier forces of the King. However, the Puritans' Commonwealth soon disintegrated into a dictatorship headed by the military genius Oliver Cromwell. After his death, conditions deteriorated so badly that in 1660 the English people, by common consent, restored as king a somewhat chastened representative of the Stuart royal family, Charles II. With him returned the Elizabethan Church of England as the official, state-controlled religion.

Against this English background occurred the settlement of New England and the West Indies. The first effort to colonize New England was in fact a business enterprise much like that which founded Virginia. The Plymouth Company, chartered at the same time as the London Company, put a group of prospective settlers ashore at the mouth of the Sagadahoc River in Maine in 1607. After experiencing one Maine winter these first colonists of "northern Virginia" returned to England's milder climate.

Separatist Pilgrims, a small group of religious extremists who would have no truck with the Anglican Church, proved more determined. Oppressed by laws which required them to attend Anglican services and to hold no other religious meetings, Pilgrims had immigrated to Leyden, in Holland. Unhappy there, they arranged with a group of London merchants to finance their settlement in "northern Virginia." Aiming for the Hudson River, they landed instead in November 1620 on Cape Cod, in the region which Captain John Smith had called "new England."

Even before the Pilgrims disembarked, they had won a place in history. First, they had received a precedent-setting commitment from James I that he would not "molest them": the government would not enforce observance of Anglicanism upon Dissenters in America. When it became clear that they would land outside the bounds of the Virginia Company, some of the numerous non-Pilgrims aboard asserted that in consequence "none had power to command them." To meet this threat of anarchy, Pilgrim leaders drew upon the religious tradition of the "covenant" to write the Mayflower Compact. Its forty-one signers agreed to "combine ourselves together into a civil Body Politick" to make "just and equal Laws . . . for the general Good of the Colony."

Survival was less difficult at Plymouth than at Jamestown. Roughly half of the colonists died in the first winter, but the survivors, instructed by the Indians in corn culture, raised crops successfully thereafter. The larger Puritan colony of Massachusetts soon overshadowed Plymouth, however, and in 1691 absorbed it. Plymouth's final gift to posterity was *Of Plymouth Plantations*,

a superb history written by the wise and virtuous William Bradford, longtime governor of the colony.

The Puritans who followed the Pilgrims to New England were closer to the mainstream of English life. They had long struggled from within to "purify" the Church of England. They wanted to eliminate "Romish" ceremonial traditions, to secure a better-educated clergy, to prevent the appointment of one clergyman to two or more income-yielding parishes (pluralism), and to keep priests from residing outside their parishes (absenteeism). Above all, they wanted local congregations to have more power, the bishops less. The Calvinist background of James I gave them high hopes when he became king, but he supported the bishops fully. He assured Puritans in fact he would "make them conform" or "harry them out of the land."

Easygoing James I in fact did neither. Charles I and Archbishop Laud, however, especially in the period of "personal rule" from 1629 to 1640 when Parliament was not allowed to meet, prompted thousands of Puritans to join the "Great Migration." Most went to the sugar islands of the West Indies, but the twenty thousand or so who chose Massachusetts ensured the success of that colony.

Few still argue, as some historians of the last generation did, that the Puritans came to America to "catch fish" rather than to "praise God," but they did come organized as a business corporation. In 1629 a group of leading Puritans, largely Cambridge-educated and including theologian John Cotton and lawyer John Winthrop, secured controlling interest in the Massachusetts Bay Company. For reasons never satisfactorily explained, the charter omitted the usual specifications as to where stockholders should meet. Consequently, the Puritans took it with them to America in 1630 and eventually made it the constitution of an autonomous Puritan society.

Transformation of the charter into a constitution took only a few years. The colony redefined "freeman" or voting stockholder of the corporation to include adult male members of the Puri-

Of all the groups settling in the New World, none has had more pervasive influence on the American culture than the Puritans—yet no group is more difficult to understand. Science has now undercut dogmatic belief; materialism and concentration on the present moment have eclipsed concern for the spirit; moral certainty has been replaced by confusion. It is difficult to imagine what it was like to be a Puritan, but a look into one aspect of their culture—their religious art— may ease the task.

One of the most vexing problems in dealing with the religious art of the Puritans is that they have told us in no uncertain terms that they would have nothing to do with idolatry and the making of religious images. To read their literature, one would suspect that not a single religious symbol was to be found in all of New England, and yet we know that their burial grounds were filled with image-bearing gravestones. For a supposedly iconophobic people, their ready use of the traditional vocabulary of Paleo-Christian symbols is most surprising. Nevertheless, scholars who never ventured out of their dusty libraries continued to promote the idea of Puritan iconophobia well into the twentieth century.

The function of Puritan religious art in the community is still in many ways perplexing, but we can certainly get some idea of their intense preoccupation with the problems of life, death, and resurrection from even the most cursory glance at the images they created. Visual symbols made a much greater impact upon a society virtually bereft of visual materials than they would today when we are bombarded with visual data from the mass media. A picture or a relief sculpture in the seventeenth and eighteenth centuries was something rare, not an item to be quickly looked at and disposed of like the latest magazine. To understand the attraction of graven images, one must imagine a society without extensive figural art, save in the burial ground.

THE PURITAN HERITAGE

Religious symbols, whether visual or verbal, try to describe the nature of the unknown, and what could be more unknown than the universal mysteries of death and rebirth? That the Puritans created a symbolic art outside the confines of the institutionalized church is most interesting. Notorious organizers, the Puritans institutionalized emotional matters as few other theocentric societies in the seventeenth century ever attempted to do. For example, the profession of sainthood soon became little more than a stylized recitation of a memorized formula rather than the true story of a religious conversion. While these rigid formulas may have quelled the babbling of the merely enthusiastic, they did nothing to assuage the anguish of the religious heart.

The turn from stylized forms of profession within the framework of the church to a deeply symbolic art outside it was an obvious attempt in the face of the awful immensity of death to escape from the rigid rituals of Puritanism. But the turn toward religious art, a stylized form of expression in itself, was not something to be held against Puritanism but something appropriate to it. What began as a radical act to plumb the mysteries of

Among scholarly efforts which have brought new insight into the thought and feeling of the Puritans in recent years is a remarkable eight-year study of New England gravestones, Graven Images, by Allan I. Ludwig (Wesleyan University Press, 1966). This book, which was awarded the John Addison Porter Prize at Yale University in 1964, totals nearly 500 pages of text and photographs, and is an excellent example of how systematic study of artifacts can reveal the past. A sampling of Mr. Ludwig's pictures appears here together with text and captions written especially for this volume.

death and resurrection became, in the end, yet another stylized Puritan ritual. The most interesting feature of this progressive institutionalization of symbols is that it came from the people themselves rather than from the ministerial elite. This could never have happened in Europe. We know, for example, that as soon as monumental sculpture made its appearance in medieval France, it was taken over almost at once by the Church. Not so in New England. The symbols began and ended as wholly popular forms of expression. Hence we can say that the patterns of Puritan life were so strong at every level of society that what almost surely began as a protest against the arid verbalism and rationality of Puritan dogma became itself programmatic and dogmatic. The most mystical symbols, for example, are always found on the geographical periphery of urbane Puritanism, in faraway Chester, Vermont, for example, rather than in orthodox Boston.

Detail of the Susannah Jayne stone, 1776, Marblehead, Mass. The motif, derived from an English emblem book, pictures death triumphant in the sublunary world but encircled by a hooped snake, a Neo-Platonic symbol of the immortality of the soul.

Preceding page, a detail of the Rev. William Whitwell stone, 1781, Marblehead, Mass., and a fine example of eighteenth-century provincial baroque portraiture in coastal New England. That the majority of these portraits were done for ministers does not protect them from a charge of excessive vanity.

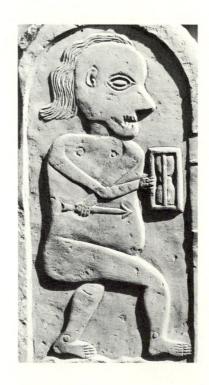

Detail of the left panel of the William Dickson stone, 1692, Cambridge, Mass., attributed to Joseph Lamson of Charlestown. This imp of death carries an arrow and an hourglass, combined symbols of death and time, a theme popular until ca. 1710.

Details of the Strong stone, 1749, South Windsor, Conn.; the Skinner stone, 1753, South Windsor; and the Wolcott marker of 1743 in the same burial ground. Although not in chronological order, the death's head is being transformed into a soul-effigy. Similar transformation took place throughout New England between ca. 1710 and ca. 1750.

Detail of the Sarah Yale stone, 1800, Meriden, Conn., showing a severe linear depiction of the soul-effigy in heaven. The economy of style is characteristic of Connecticut Valley carving influenced by the Neo-Classical style. Many such soul-effigies look like babies, perhaps reflecting the medieval tradition of picturing the soul as a naked baby, indicating its purity and freedom from sin.

tan church. The charter authorized freemen to vote yearly to elect a governor, deputy governor, and an eighteen-member council. After 1634 freemen in each settlement chose deputies to meet with the governor, deputy governor, and council as the "General Court" empowered by the charter to make laws.

Rhode Island was mainly the creation of two brilliant controversialists expelled from Massachusetts for their unorthodox views, Roger Williams and Anne Hutchinson. Williams was a Cambridge-educated clergyman who first offended Massachusetts leaders by denying that the King had any right to grant them Indian lands. Still more offensive to the Puritans was Williams's assertion that government should not concern itself at all with matters of religion. Banished by the General Court, Williams in 1636 bought land from the Indians at Providence and began a new colony. "God," he later wrote in a pamphlet war with his Puritan adversaries, "requireth not a uniformity of religion to be . . . enforced in any civil state; which enforced uniformity . . . is the greatest occasion of civil war, . . . persecution, . . . and . . . hypocrisy." Accordingly, when he secured a charter from Parliament in 1644 to help fend off possible aggression from Massachusetts, it provided for freedom of conscience and full separation of church and state, as well as representative government.

Mrs. Anne Hutchinson, while leading discussions at her home, had gradually come to the antinomian belief, heretical to most Puritans, that scholarly guidance and an individual's "works" mattered little in salvation. What did matter was the inspiration of God's grace bestowed directly upon individuals such as herself. After her faction, including Governor Sir Henry Vane and theologian John Cotton, lost a not entirely fair election in 1637 to orthodox Puritans led by John Winthrop, Mrs. Hutchinson was convicted of heresy and exiled. She then helped found the town of Portsmouth in Rhode Island.

Connecticut too was an offshoot of Mas-

sachusetts, but its founders departed voluntarily and in good religious standing. By 1636 the Reverend Thomas Hooker and others had founded several river towns in the Hartford area. In 1639 the settlers began to govern themselves under what they called "Fundamental Orders." Freemen were to elect a governor yearly, but, as in Massachusetts, a "freeman" meant a Puritan in good standing. A separate colony founded at New Haven by the Reverend John Davenport in 1637 merged with the river towns under royal charter in 1662 to form the colony of Connecticut.

New Hampshire and Maine remained in uncertain status for many years. The Council for New England, a reorganized Plymouth Company which owned all ungranted lands in New England, awarded much of the area to Sir Ferdinando Gorgas and John Mason in 1622. Each tried to colonize and govern the area, but so did neighboring Massachusetts. Finally, in 1677, Massachusetts bought the claims of the Gorgas heirs and thus acquired control of Maine. New Hampshire became a separate royal province in 1679.

West Indian colonies, although they attracted many Puritan immigrants from England, were primarily economic enterprises rather than religious refuges. Caribbean islands which could produce tropical products appeared infinitely more desirable to Europe's rival imperial powers than colonies in the temperate regions of North America. Spain quickly occupied the larger islands, such as Cuba and Santo Domingo, but it usually ignored the innumerable smaller ones. Long the resort of pirates preying upon Spanish commerce, these smaller islands became important in the seventeenth century also as potential producers of sugar, tobacco, cotton, and indigo. By the 1650s England's island colony of Barbados, roughly one-third the size of Rhode Island, had the largest population of any English colony. Oliver Cromwell added Jamaica to England's possessions in 1655. The French and the Dutch also engaged in island grabbing from the Spanish in the same period. West Indian planters, whatever their nationality, usually had their slaves produce for export instead of striving for self-sufficiency. The result was that the West Indies became a major market for food and lumber exporters on the continent of North America.

English Colonization after 1660

Restoration of the monarchy in 1660 ended the turmoil of the Civil War era and enabled the English to devote more attention to external matters, particularly to their rivalry with the Dutch Republic. Benefiting from a commercially strategic location adjacent to the North Sea fisheries and at the mouth of several of Europe's major arteries of river transportation, the Dutch in the seventeenth century had developed fabulous prosperity and a golden age of cultural achievement distinguished by the philosopher Spinoza and by painters including Rembrandt, Hobbema, Hals, and Vermeer. To English economic nationalists, however, what mattered was that Dutch ships carried so much English commerce and that English people wore woolen cloth manufactured in the Netherlands from English wool.

Economic rivalry had already brought on one indecisive Anglo-Dutch War (1652–1654) before the Restoration. Charles II, upon assuming the throne in place of his deposed and beheaded father, magnanimously conferred the Dutch colony of New Netherland upon his brother, the Duke of York. The Duke's naval expedition seized the area from the indignant but incompetent Peter Stuyvesant in 1664, thus inaugurating the second Anglo-Dutch War (1664–1667). At the conclusion of the war the Dutch ceded New Netherland to England. The imperial role of the Dutch on the continent of North America had ended.

Developments in England meanwhile were transforming the nation from a French ally against the Dutch to a Dutch ally against the French. Charles II hoped to restore Catholicism to England, but despite assurance of French support, he refrained from embracing Catholicism himself until almost the moment of his death because of the depth of public opposition to Catholicism. His brother and heir, James, Duke of York, was less cautious; he announced his conversion to Catholicism in 1676. This act, followed by exaggerated revelations of the French commitment, provoked an outbreak of anti-Catholic, anti-French hysteria from 1678 to 1680 over the "Popish Plot."

In these circumstances, Parliament moved to replace James in the line of succession with his Protestant daughter Mary, wife of the Dutch ruler, William of Orange. Charles II prevented Parliament from excluding his brother, who acceded to the throne in 1685. For three years England's anti-Catholic majority tolerated a Catholic monarch. Then in 1688 the King's second wife, also Catholic, bore a son, who took precedence in the succession line over his Protestant half sister Mary. That finished James II. A national consensus such as that which had restored Charles II in 1660 now ousted James II in favor of William and Mary. This Glorious Revolution confirmed both Parliamentary supremacy and a Protestant succession. The deposed King took refuge in France, where Louis XIV vowed to restore him. The ensuing War of the League of Augsburg (1689–1697), which also involved general European resistance to French expansionism, began a century of conflict between England and France for dominant status in Europe and in North America.

England's conquest of New Netherland in 1664 resulted in the creation of several new colonies. For himself, the Duke of York kept as a proprietary possession the area since known as New York. It became a royal province automatically when he became king in 1685. At that time James II also abolished the legislature he had created two years before.

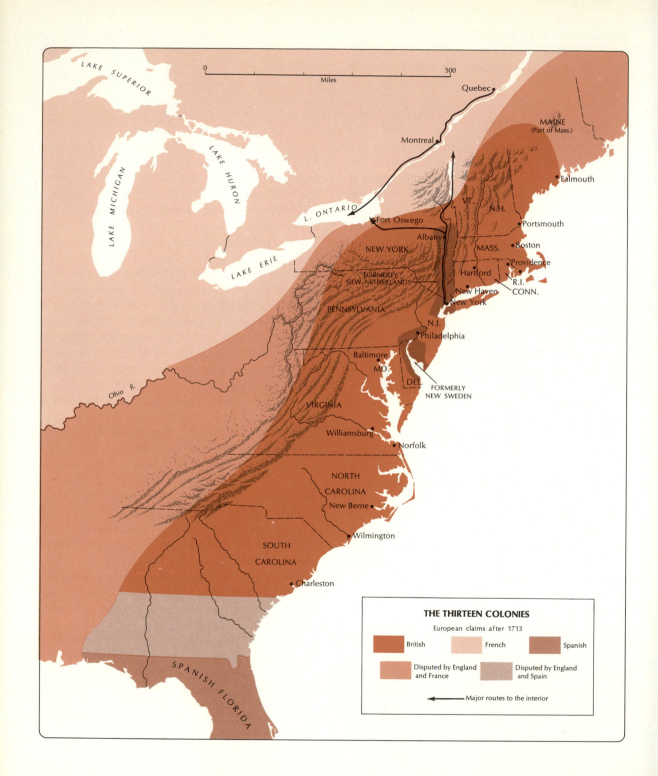

The Thirteen Colonies

By gift of the Duke of York, present-day New Jersey became the possession of Sir George Carteret and Lord Berkeley in 1664. Quakers, including William Penn, were prominent among the bewildering succession of proprietors who bought or inherited parts of the colony. It was divided into East and West Jersey from 1676 until 1702, when the halves were rejoined to form a royal province, which shared its governor with New York until 1738.

Pennsylvania and Delaware, the remaining colonies carved out of New Netherland, became the proprietary possessions of William Penn. Chartered in 1681, Pennsylvania represented the repayment of a debt owed by Charles II to Penn's father, an admiral and wealthy landholder. William Penn, converted apparently while a student at Oxford, was the staunchest of Quakers. He managed nevertheless to maintain the friendship of both Charles II and James II and with their indulgence set out to make his colonies both a "Holy Experiment" and a refuge for victims of religious persecution. A representative assembly secured all legislative authority under Penn's Charter of Liberties (1701), which abolished the customary upper house. Like Roger Williams, Penn believed the Indians were entitled to compensation for their land, and he made such payment to their satisfaction. He then sold land to settlers on relatively easy terms. Pennsylvania grew rapidly. The economy prospered from the sale of lumber and food, especially flour, to the West Indies. Advertising in Britain and in northern Europe produced a flood of immigrants. Prominent among them were the Pennsylvania Dutch (a corruption of *deutsch*, the German word for "German"), many of whom had an Anabaptist religious heritage similar in its essentials to that of the Quakers.

Quaker beliefs were the very foundation of society in Penn's two colonies. The name Quaker originated as a derisive reference to their insistence that one should "tremble at the name of the Lord." George Fox, onetime shoemaker's apprentice, began the movement amid the religious ferment of the English Civil War in 1647.

He believed that the ultimate religious authority was neither a church organization nor even the Bible but an "inner light" by which God made known the path of righteousness to each individual conscience.

Associated with this concept was a dogmatic dedication to equality. Because one person's "inner light" was likely to be as good as another's, Quakers had no paid clergy. They listened respectfully to anyone, man or woman, who felt moved to speak in their ritual-free meetings. They dressed plainly, refused to bow or doff their hats in the presence of presumed social superiors, and addressed everyone, regardless of rank, as "thee" or "thou"— terms customarily reserved for people of inferior status. They were also pacifists. Because they expected to tell the truth at *all* times, they refused to take oaths affirming that they were doing so on *particular* occasions.

The founding of the Carolinas contrasted sharply with that of Pennsylvania. Its guiding spirits were Sir John Colleton, a royalist supporter of Charles I, and Sir William Berkeley, an equally staunch loyalist who was a longtime governor of Virginia (1641–1652, 1660–1677). Colleton and Berkeley together recruited a number of others from the highest circles of the Restoration government to join with them in petitioning the King for a proprietary grant. Charles II acceded to their request in 1663.

North Carolina, already settled by a few migrants from Virginia, quickly became differentiated from its southern sister. A provincial government with an elected assembly began operating in 1665. Because coastal reefs and nonnavigable rivers impeded ocean shipping, North Carolina remained populated chiefly by small farmers and a few slaves. Its principal export for many years was tobacco, often exported illegally by New England smugglers.

South Carolina secured its first settlers from England and the West Indies in 1670. They dwelt downstream from the splendid harbor of Charleston for a decade, but moved there in 1680 after recognizing its advantages. For a time the major export was deer hides obtained in trade with the Indians, but before the end of the century rice had become a major product. Proprietary plans for the colony's political and social systems stood forth starkly in a document called "Fundamental Constitutions," drafted in all probability by John Locke, then secretary to one of the proprietors and later to be famous for a rather different political philosophy. The plan called for a feudal-style hierarchy descending from the proprietors through "landgraves," "caciques," and manor lords to freeholders. Popular resistance prevented its implementation.

Georgia was part of the original Carolina grant, but fear of the Spanish in Florida delayed its development for half a century. Settlement began in 1732 under the leadership of James Oglethorpe. Oglethorpe was a general who had fought against the Spanish and was eager to build a military bastion to confine them to Florida. As head of a Parliamentary investigating group, Oglethorpe had also become aware of the large numbers of noncriminal debtors languishing in English jails. He hoped to give such unfortunates a new start and establish his military bastion as well by settling them as farmers and militiamen in Georgia. The Crown accordingly conferred the land upon him and nineteen others as proprietary trustees until 1753.

Oglethorpe and his colleagues planned meticulously for the development of Georgia. Considerations which seemed plausible in England led them to exclude slaves, to limit land grants to a maximum of 500 acres, to forbid resale of the 50-acre plots awarded the poor, and to ban rum. Although Georgia did afford a refuge for selected indigents and for religious refugees, chiefly German, its settlers stubbornly resisted the pattern of life prescribed for them. By 1752, when the royal government took control of the province, most of the early restrictions had been lifted and Georgia was rapidly becoming indistinguishable from South Carolina.

Conclusion

The New World environment was remarkable perhaps above all else for its isolation from the Old World of Europe, Asia, and Africa. Because of its isolation the American continent had different plants and animals. At least partly for that reason it had also a sparse population of emigrants from Asia, neither well enough organized nor sufficiently advanced in technology to resist expropriation of their abundant land by European intruders. Both the presence of the Indians and the abundance of land were ultimately to exert considerable influence in modifying the life-style of the arriving Europeans.

The intruders were not themselves united, but represented rival national groupings. Different as they were from each other, each of these nationalities bore a basic cultural heritage, in particular a religion, passed on through medieval Europe from Rome, Greece, and the ancient Near East. The Spanish, rewarded by a treasure of American silver for their discovery of the continent, were strong enough initially to keep the hemisphere largely to themselves. Even as the Spanish declined in power, they still held in 1700 almost all of the Gulf Coast and everything southward except Portuguese Brazil. The Dutch, attaining independence from Spain and great power status almost simultaneously in the seventeenth century, put their imprint on New Netherland, which comprised modern New York, New Jersey, Pennsylvania, and Delaware, but lost the region to the English in 1664. France itself by the early eighteenth century had followed its fur traders and explorers to achieve dominance of the two great watersheds that were the heartland of North America. The English by 1700 had taken firm hold of the eastern seaboard from Maine to South Carolina and would soon add Georgia. Thus as the eighteenth century began, the national—and to some extent cultural—heritage of North America was still at issue among the Spanish, French, and English.

SUGGESTED READINGS

American distinctiveness has long fascinated both American and foreign observers. As early as 1782 M. G. St. Jean de Crèvecoeur in his *Letters from an American Farmer* sought to characterize the American, "this new man," for Europeans. In the 1830s another Frenchman, Alexis de Tocqueville, in his *Democracy in America**, found its hallmark to be "equality of conditions." Frederick Jackson Turner, the most popular American interpreter, found frontier conditions, assessed in *The Significance of the Frontier in American History** (1893), to be responsible for American democracy, individualism, and equality. Turner's thesis received careful reassessment in Ray A. Billington, *America's Frontier Heritage** (1966). David Potter in *People of Plenty** (1954) fixed upon wealth as America's most distinctive feature. Louis Hartz in *The Liberal Tradition** (1955) attributed America's liberalism to the absence of a feudal past. Daniel J. Boorstin's trilogy *The Americans** (1958–1973) stressed their practical, nonideological ability to get things done. Michael Kammen in *People of Paradox* (1972) finds American history shot through with contradictions.

On the Indians, G. H. S. Bushnell's *The First Americans** (1968) is brief, readable, and profusely illustrated. W. T. Hagan, *American Indians** (1961) is also brief. *The Indian Heritage of America* (1968) by Alvin M. Josephy, Jr., is more detailed. H. E. Driver's *The Indians of North America* (1961) is still more scholarly. On what the European discovery meant both to the Indians and to the Europeans see Alfred W. Crosby, Jr., *The Columbian Exchange: The Biological and Cultural Consequences of 1492** (1974).

Of the many historians who have dealt with the emergence of modern society in Europe, W. H. McNeill in *The Rise of the West* (1963) has the widest perspective. W. K. Ferguson's *Europe in Transition, 1300–1520*, is superbly organized. The older works of E. P. Cheyney, *The European Background of American History, 1300–1600** (1904) and *The Dawn of a New Era** (1936), are still rewarding. Max Weber's *The Protestant Ethic and the Spirit of Capitalism** (1926), R.

H. Tawney's *Religion and the Rise of Capitalism** (1926), and W. P. Webb's *The Great Frontier* (1952) present interpretations of a challenging nature.

On European explorations Samuel E. Morison, *The European Discovery of America: The Northern Voyages, 500–1600* (1971) has the most readable account of the Norse expeditions and later explorations in the North Atlantic. His *Admiral of the Ocean Sea* (2 vols., 1942) is a superb biography of Columbus. He has also done a shorter study, *Christopher Columbus, Mariner** (1956). D. H. Waters affords fascinating background on the exploration voyages in *The Art of Navigation* (1958). J. H. Parry describes the explorations fully in *The Age of Reconnaissance* (1963); C. E. Nowell does so more briefly in *The Great Discoveries** (1954). On British exploration see David B. Quinn, *England and the Discovery of America, 1481–1620* (1974); A. L. Rowse, *The Expansion of Elizabethan England** (1955); J. A. Williamson, *Sir Francis Drake** (1951). For an overview of the Spanish empire see J. H. Parry, *The Seaborne Empire of Spain* (1966), Charles Gibson, *Spain in America** (1966), and J. H. Elliott, *Imperial Spain** (1963); for the Dutch, C. R. Boxer, *The Dutch Seaborne Empire* (1965); for the French, S. E. Morison's abridgment of the work of Francis Parkman, *The Parkman Reader* (1955) and G. M. Wrong, *The Rise and Fall of New France* (2 vols., 1928). J. H. Elliott examines European thought about America in *The Old World and the New, 1492–1650* (1970).

Among the most useful works on seventeenth-century England are Christopher Hill, *Century of Revolution, 1603–1714** (1961) and *The World Turned Upside Down: Radical Ideas during the English Revolution** (1972); Mildred Campbell, *The English Yeoman* (1942); Lawrence F. Stone, *The Crisis of the Aristocracy, 1558–1641* (1965); Wallace Notestein, *The English People on the Eve of Colonization** (1954); Carl L. Bridenbaugh, *Vexed and Troubled Englishmen, 1590–1642** (1968); William Haller, *The Rise of Puritanism** (1938); Michael Walzer, *The Revolution of the Saints* (1965).

On the early English settlements one of the outstanding works is W. F. Craven, *The Southern Colonies* in the Seventeenth Century (1949). Philip Barbour's *Three Worlds of John Smith* (1964) recounts the career of one of the world's great adventurers. On Plymouth S. E. Morison has edited William Bradford's classic *Of Plymouth Plantations* (1952), but see also George Landon, *Pilgrim Colony* (1966) and on family life John Demos, *A Little Commonwealth** (1970). The harsh view of Puritanism in such older works as J. T. Adams, *The Founding of New England** (1921), has fallen before a flood of more sympathetic works including Perry Miller's highly theological *Orthodoxy in Massachusetts** (1933), *The New England Mind: The 17th Century** (1939), and *Errand into the Wilderness** (1956); Edmund S. Morgan's more comprehensible *Visible Saints** (1963) and his study of John Winthrop, *The Puritan Dilemma** (1958). See also David D. Hall, *The Faithful Shepherd* (1972); R. E. Wall, Jr., *Massachusetts Bay* (1972); D. B. Rutman, *Winthrop's Boston* (1965) and

*American Puritanism** (1970); Larzer Ziff, *Puritanism in America* (1973); G. L. Haskins, *Law and Authority in Early Massachusetts* (1960); Sumner C. Powell, *Puritan Village* (1963). On Rhode Island see Ola Winslow's *Master Roger Williams* (1957) and E. S. Morgan, *Roger Williams* (1967). *Younger John Winthrop* (1966) by R. C. Black III depicts the early years of Connecticut. Bernard Bailyn has analyzed early New England economic history in *The New England Merchants in the Seventeenth Century** (1955). Among the better works on the Middle Colonies are G. B. Nash, *Quakers and Politics* (1968); F. B. Tolles, *James Logan* (1957); W. F. Craven, *New Jersey and English Colonization of North America* (1964); L. H. Leder, *Robert Livingston* (1961). On the West Indies see C. L. Bridenbaugh, *No Peace beyond the Line* (1972), and Richard Dunn, *Sugar and Slaves* (1972).

*indicates availability in paperback.

2

The Silent Revolution

During the 169 years which elapsed between the founding of Jamestown and the signing of the Declaration of Independence, what historian Charles M. Andrews called a "silent revolution" gradually transformed English colonial society. Fighting the Indians, borrowing from them, adjusting to wilderness conditions, the immigrants began to lose some of their Old World characteristics and to adopt new patterns of living. Unlimited expanses of unoccupied land fostered a prosperity unparalleled for the common man in Europe's experience and largely precluded the development of a landowning nobility like that which dominated Europe. Because the aristocrats themselves stayed home, middle- and even lower-class immigrants were able to build a new social order quite different from that of most regions of Europe, where aristocratic traditions, carried over from feudalism, remained strong. Ironically, American prosperity fostered also the development of two forms of involuntary labor unknown in England—indentured servitude and black slavery, both of which helped

to populate the colonies and to alleviate the chronic scarcity of labor which so handicapped those eager to found plantations for large-scale agricultural production. The religious freedom which Britain accorded the colonies attracted particularly those whose beliefs were unpopular, even persecuted, in the Old World, and produced a society far more radically Protestant than was England itself. The distinctiveness of American society appeared also in the status of women and children, in education, in science, and especially in the arts. By 1776 Europeans had long since recognized the uniqueness of American society and, ignoring profound differences among people of different provinces, had begun to lump them all together as Americans. The colonists themselves, however, still thought of themselves primarily as British subjects of particular provinces. In fact they were in some measure becoming more English culturally on the eve of the Revolution. Not until the period of the Revolution itself were the colonists to begin to sense the unity long attributed to them by Europeans.

Unpredictable at first, relations between the settlers and the Indians before long began to follow a pattern which would repeat itself from the Atlantic to the Pacific through a period of two and a half centuries. It began in Virginia. Powhatan, the first Indian leader with whom the English had to deal, was an empire builder who had brought a number of Virginia tribes more or less firmly under his influence. He welcomed the few intruders at Jamestown as potential allies against his enemies, allies whose metal weapons, especially guns, would be very helpful. The marriage of his daughter Pocahontas to John Rolfe cemented an alliance which preserved peace until after his death in 1618. After that time the arrival of more and more tobacco-mad settlers, appropriating more and more land, led to the Indian "massacres" of 1622 and 1644, each of which killed several hundred settlers. There was no "body count" among the Indians, but by 1669 retaliatory killing, reinforced by smallpox and demoralization, had reduced Powhatan's confederacy of perhaps nine thousand people to about two thousand survivors. These survivors, their own culture almost extinguished, paid tribute to their conquerors and served them as scouts against more distant tribes. Virginia experienced more Indian trouble in the 1670s and on the eve of the Revolution, but these later troubles related closely to political and military developments to be discussed in the following chapter.

New England's experience with Indians differed from Virginia's in significant ways despite a fundamental similarity. A smallpox epidemic, initiated by itinerant coastal traders, had killed off most of New England's Indian population before the arrival of the Pilgrims in 1620. An English-speaking native named Squanto, enslaved by an earlier trader but then ransomed and returned to America, helped the Pilgrims survive by teaching them to plant corn. Trade initially proved beneficial to both. Trouble began with the arrival of the Puritans, who tended to regard the Indians as agents of Satan and their land as belonging properly to those who would develop it. The murder of a wandering trader in 1633 led to the Pequot War (1637), in which Puritans and their native allies set fire to the Pequot fort and then massacred those who fled to avoid being burned to death. Few Pequots survived. In 1675–1676 Indians rose up again to resist Puritan land grabbing. In King Philip's War they destroyed a number of frontier settlements and killed off an appreciable proportion of New England's adult male population. Ultimately starvation among the Indians helped the united New Englanders to prevail. King Philip was killed; his wife and son were sold into West Indian slavery. New England had no more trouble with its natives.

New York's Indians, unlike those of Virginia or New England, included both Algonquian and Iroquois tribes. The coastal Algonquians, like their relatives both north and south, at first traded with the Europeans, in their case, the Dutch, and then between 1641 and 1645 attempted to destroy the invaders' settlements. They did indeed wreak havoc in the lower Hudson Valley before the Dutch rallied to defeat them. In the Mohawk Valley of central New York, however, the powerful Iroquois preserved both their territory and their culture into the Revolutionary era. They were able to do so not only because of their useful role in trade with western tribes but also because their interior location long placed them beyond the reach of Europeans.

Quaker Pennsylvania had no such sorrowful problems as the earlier colonies had. Penn's fair-minded land policy helped. So did the success of missionary efforts. No major outbreak of violence occurred until non-Quaker settlers began crossing the Appalachians on the eve of the Revolution.

In the lower South the Indians confronted not only English settlers in the Carolinas and Georgia but also the Spanish missionaries based in

Florida and, after 1699, the French traders based first at Biloxi, then at Mobile, and after 1718 at New Orleans as well. Resentment over the business practices of the South Carolina traders led in 1716 to the Yamasee War, in which Cherokee tribes helped the Carolinians defeat the Yamasees and the Creeks. After that no major outbreak occurred. Intense demand for labor, however, led Indians to capture and sell rival tribesmen into slavery and to act as slave catchers, tracking down and returning escaped slaves for a reward. The Creeks and the Cherokees especially preserved their identity throughout the colonial period, as did the Iroquois, but most coastal tribes by 1700 had gone the way of the Pequots and Powhatan's confederacy.

Spanish and French occupation in areas which would become the United States was less devastating to Indian culture than was British settlement. In areas where money was to be made, the Spanish had proved utterly ruthless in exploiting and in some cases even exterminating the Indians. In the region from Florida to California, however, the Spanish found no silver or gold and consequently permitted the missionaries to prevail to a greater extent than elsewhere. Throughout the region Spaniards brought not only Christianity but also horses, sheep, and a variety of devastating European diseases, particularly smallpox. The Pueblo Indians of the Southwest rose up successfully to expel them in 1680, but the Spanish came back in the 1690s and remained. In language, religion, and other aspects of culture, they left an indelible imprint.

French occupation was far more beneficial and less harmful than that of either the Spanish or the British. The major explanation for the difference is that the French were primarily traders rather than settlers. They intended to use trade to overcome the British in the contest for dominance over the entire Mississippi and Great Lakes watersheds. Had they succeeded in defeating the British, one can suspect that the ensuing settlement would ultimately have brought the same result as in the British colonies.

At the opening of the eighteenth century, the French were moving to implement their plan of control. By 1750 they had fortified trading posts not only at Biloxi, Mobile, and New Orleans on the Gulf Coast, but also at points such as St. Louis (Cahokia) along the Mississippi and its tributaries, and on the Great Lakes at Green Bay, Michilimackinac (between Lakes Michigan and Huron), Detroit, and Niagara. On the whole the French supplemented the Indian economy through trade without threatening to dispossess the Indians or to destroy their culture. Their chief problem in dealing with the Indians was that British goods, offered by Iroquois as well as English traders, were both better and cheaper.

Trade with Europeans, even if through Indian intermediaries, profoundly altered the life-style of all eastern tribes. They became very dependent upon European traders for guns, metal knives and hatchets, pots and pans for cooking, and woolen cloth for blankets and clothing. They developed a great desire also for European liquor and ornamental finery. Furs were the principal items which the Europeans would accept in trade. Consequently the Indians devoted more and more time to trapping, or after trapping the fur-bearing animals of their region to extinction, to trading for them with other Indians farther west. The greatest impact of the Europeans on the Indians, however, was depopulation brought on by smallpox and other European diseases. Estimates on this score are still not very firmly based, but the most recent evidence suggests that in what is now the United States diseases brought from Europe may have reduced the Indian population by several million.

The Indian impact upon European culture has attracted less attention, but it was significant. Europeans began smoking tobacco. Sooner or later all areas of Europe began also to cultivate potatoes, native to Latin America, as a cheap dietary staple. Oddly enough it was nineteenth-century European immigrants who initiated widespread use of the potato in the United States. Europeans also acquired syphilis from the Indians, a partial retaliation for smallpox.

Indian influence was also important in differentiating American from English and other European cultures. The earliest and most striking point of differentiation was the use of corn. Among frontier settlers in general and the poor in particular corn quickly replaced wheat as the basic food. It required less preparation of the soil, less labor in harvesting, no immediate harvesting when ripe, and no expensive milling (not to mention transportation to and from a mill) to be prepared for consumption, and it yielded about twice as many bushels per acre. While Europeans considered it unfit for human consumption, and for the most part still do, the average American farmer made it his chief sustenance as it had long been for the Indian population. The presence of the Indians brought to the surface the racial and cultural prejudice latent in the European settlers as in most human beings and made it a guiding feature of public policy and private behavior. Fighting the Indians also differentiated American from European conceptions of warfare. Among Europeans, as largely among Indians themselves, warfare had limited objectives and observed conventional rules. Warfare between the American settlers and the Indians, however, too often sought either to terrorize or to exterminate and employed any means appropriate to those grisly ends.

The Southern Economy

Economic development in the Southern colonies differed markedly from both European experience and that in the northern colonies. Below the Mason-Dixon line, which separates Pennsylvania from Maryland, a longer growing season permitted cultivation of crops which could not be grown commercially in the North or in Britain. A wide coastal plain abounding in natural waterways provided Southerners with both favorable conditions for tillage and inexpensive avenues of transportation. Thus Southern settlers could expect to market their large crops cheaply and without competition from producers in Britain itself or in the Northern colonies. Accordingly, those Southern settlers who could afford to do so invested heavily both in land and in bound laborers to produce a staple agricultural commodity for export. The plantation became a characteristic feature of the Southern economy.

Tobacco, produced largely in the Chesapeake Bay area, was the most important plantation crop and by far the most important of all American exports throughout the colonial period. The European market for tobacco had grown rapidly despite much intense opposition to the Indian habit of smoking. In the 1630s Britain was importing as much as 3 million pounds of American tobacco yearly; by the 1670s roughly 14 million pounds; by the 1770s about 100 million pounds. Meanwhile the Caribbean region had just about abandoned tobacco in order to concentrate on sugar, a product even more in demand.

Securing land was the first step in becoming a tobacco planter. Throughout much of the seventeenth century, men of wealth could claim 50 acres for each immigrant whose passage they had paid. By exploiting this headright law, often corruptly, many men built up extensive holdings. Purchasing from the government or even from speculators was also relatively easy. "Every person," a traveler claimed in 1759, "may with ease procure a small plantation, can ship his tobacco at his own door, and live independently." He exaggerated, of course, but many immigrants were able to save enough as laborers or tenants to purchase land. By 1760 thousands of such small farmers were competing with the great planters in raising tobacco for export.

Whatever the extent of his landholdings, a tobacco planter remained a "one-hogshead man," able to produce only one or two hogsheads of cured tobacco yearly, unless he could secure bound laborers. Most free persons simply would not long remain agricultural laborers

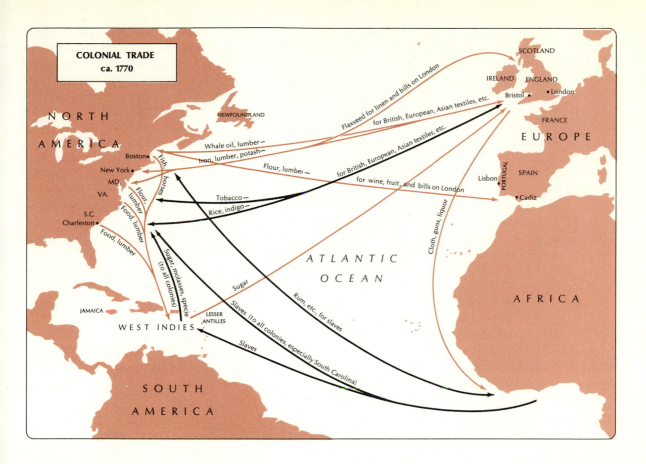

COLONIAL TRADE
ca. 1770

SCOTLAND

IRELAND ENGLAND

Bristol • London

FRANCE

EUROPE

NORTH AMERICA

NEWFOUNDLAND

Flaxseed for linen and bills on London

for British, European, Asian textiles, etc.

Whale oil, lumber—

Iron, lumber, potash—

for British, European, Asian textiles, etc.

Boston•

Fish, horses

New York •

MD.

VA.

Flour, lumber —

for wine, fruit, and bills on London

Lisbon •

PORTUGAL

SPAIN

• Cadiz

Flour, lumber

Tobacco—

Rice, indigo—

S.C.

Charleston •

Food, lumber

Food, lumber

Cloth, guns, liquor

ATLANTIC
OCEAN

AFRICA

Sugar, molasses, specie
(to all colonies)

Sugar

Slaves (to all colonies, especially South Carolina)

Rum, etc., for slaves

JAMAICA

WEST INDIES

LESSER
ANTILLES

Slaves

SOUTH
AMERICA

when they could so easily become landowners. From this need arose, first, the large-scale importation of indentured servants from Europe and, later, of black slaves from Africa, both to be considered in detail in a later section.

British regulation was an important factor in the development of the Tobacco Coast. From 1660 one of Britain's famous Navigation Acts made tobacco an "enumerated" commodity, one which could be sent only to British ports. Initially American production was expected only to supply the British market, but by the eve of the Revolution, Britain was reexporting 60 to 70 percent of its tobacco imports from America, sometimes over 90 percent. Thus, while Americans produced the world's supply of tobacco, the British sold it to foreign markets.

Debt was a major problem for nearly all tobacco planters. "Debts had become hereditary . . . for many generations," wrote planter Thomas Jefferson, "so that the planters were a species of property annexed to certain mercantile houses in London." Probably not even the planters themselves understood clearly why this was so, but overproduction was certainly one cause. By oversupplying the world market, Chesapeake planters repeatedly depressed the price of their product. Neither crop-destroying riots nor restrictive legislation, both of which the British condemned, could solve the problem. Planters often overestimated both their income from tobacco sales and their ability to sell imported items to their poorer neighbors at a profit. To make payments on the resulting debts, they had to ship still more tobacco, thus further depressing the price.

Diversification followed naturally from the poor prospects in tobacco culture. George Washington, a particularly acute businessman, turned to speculating in Western lands and to making cloth. Robert Carter, another wealthy planter, leased most of his lands to tenants whom he required to grow wheat for export. He also invested in various manufacturing endeavors. Despite such efforts, however, tobacco still made up 75 percent of the value of the Tobacco Coast exports as late as 1775.

In the Lower South, the first settlers hoped to establish plantations, but they had trouble finding suitable crops. While they were experimenting, an export economy based on deer hides, cattle, naval stores, and lumber developed. Deer hides, secured in trade with the Indians, were used extensively in Europe for clothing and long remained an important export. Frontier "crackers" (so called from the noise of the whips they used) drove cattle from the wild lands of the interior to seaboard slaughterhouses which prepared meat for export. Lumbering, often a side-line industry for those who were clearing land for agriculture, enjoyed a vast market, although competition from frontier settlers in every colonial region kept prices low. On the eve of the Revolution, lumber products ranked behind only tobacco, wheat flour, rice, and fish in export value.

Naval stores (tar, pitch, turpentine, and resin) became significant exports from the Carolinas after Britain began to subsidize their production during the War of the Spanish Succession (1702–1713). Before the Revolution, however, production had declined considerably.

Rice became the export staple of the Lower South within a few years after the introduction of superior seed from Madagascar in 1695. Parliament normally taxed rice imports into Britain heavily to favor domestic grain growers. In addition, Britain enumerated rice, thus requiring, as with tobacco, that it be exported only to British ports so that British rather than American merchants could derive the major profit from selling it to foreign consumers, chiefly in northern

Indigo culture in colonial South Carolina.   *Mark Hewlett*

Europe. After 1730 Americans could sell rice directly to southern Europe, but roughly 60 percent of the crop still went via Britain to northern Europe. Because rice production required heavy investment in labor and machinery, only very wealthy individuals could become rice planters. Unlike tobacco planters, colonial rice producers did not oversupply the market and thus continued to enjoy ample returns throughout the eighteenth century.

After 1748 indigo joined rice as a major plantation product in the Lower South. When properly processed, the indigo plant produced a blue-violet dye which was widely used in the British textile industry and by farm families which produced their own cloth. The Lower South could usually secure two crops of indigo yearly, as compared to four or more in the Caribbean area, but preoccupation with sugar in the British West Indies pushed out indigo as it had tobacco. When war with France (War of the Austrian Succession, 1740–1748) interrupted the supply from the French islands, Britain began to subsidize production in its continental colonies. Instructed by Eliza Lucas, who had emigrated from the West Indies, Carolina planters produced indigo profitably from 1748 until the Revolution.

Unlike the Tobacco Coast, which had no port city and was indeed an exclusively rural society, the Lower South developed a true metropolis, the city of Charleston, South Carolina. Large ships could not reach individual plantations as they did along Chesapeake Bay, but came to Charleston as a point of transshipment. Merchants in Charleston, as in other colonial ports, often acted as agents for British merchants, selling imported items, chiefly textiles and slaves, and buying rice, indigo, or other commodities for export. Their compensation for such services was a commission, usually about 5 percent, on both sales and purchases.

The Northern Economy

Similar to old England in climate, New England could not produce the highly valued semitropical products which sustained the plantation system in the South. Grain growing on family farms, the basis of a prosperous economy in the Middle Colonies, failed in New England to produce sufficient surplus for export. Rugged terrain, rocky soil, blights, or "blasts" which often reduced wheat yield, a scarcity of navigable waterways—all contributed to deny New England an agricultural staple.

Still, most New Englanders lived in rural villages. Unlike the settlers in other sections, they gained title to their land, except in New Hampshire, by grants from a representative legislature, rather than from an appointed governor. In the seventeenth century, groups of settlers, often church congregations, received town grants which they settled in a communal pattern. Houses clustered around a village "common," and each family worked strips of land in communal fields. This system helped sustain a sense of community and aided development of churches, schools, and militia, but it also involved irksome restrictions on individuals and wasted time coming and going to the fields. In the eighteenth century, when Indian dangers no longer helped to sustain it, the communal system of settlement yielded to integral family farms. Even then rural New England remained remarkable for its "pleasing uniformity of decent competence." It was a society in which extreme wealth was as rare as dire poverty.

Most small farmers in New England, or elsewhere in the colonies for that matter, were obliged from childhood "to practice twenty different employments with equal dexterity" in order to make a living. To gain cash income the farmer might sell some of his agricultural surplus locally, but he needed also to become a wintertime lumberman, a tavern keeper, teamster, carpenter—whatever his own talents and the needs and opportunities of his community suggested. Conversely the lawyer, doctor, miller, blacksmith—virtually all craft and professional people—had to moonlight as farmers or in some other work to support their families. Only in the cities was it feasible to specialize in one kind of endeavor.

Northern farms were similar in many respects. They were small, generally under 100 acres, and only partly cleared. Corn was the chief staple for food, and wheat for sale, but farmers grew a variety of other cereals and vegetables as well— although no potatoes until late in the eighteenth century. In an age when everyone thought alcohol essential to health and strength, an apple orchard enabled the family to substitute homemade hard cider for "store-boughten" rum. A few sheep and a patch of flax provided the raw materials for homemade linsey-woolsey (linen-woolen) clothing. A few cattle kept the family in milk, butter, and cheese. Hogs, generally turned loose to "get their living in the woods," provided most of the meat. Methods were about the same as those of medieval or even biblical times. Oxen rather than horses were the usual beasts of burden; horses were much faster, but too expensive. Indentured servants and slaves were very few, but young men and boys provided some farm labor while saving money to marry and start farms of their own. Productivity per acre was scandalously low by European standards, but output per man and the general standard of living were undoubtedly higher.

Frontier opportunities lured many westward. Settlers could achieve handsome rewards by investing some capital and several years of labor in clearing cheap wilderness land for sale. Even "squatters" who lacked capital with which to buy land could sell "betterments" which they had made in land to which they had no title. Lumbering also afforded particularly remunerative employment in at least some frontier areas. Finally, productivity per acre on freshly cleared land was likely to be about double what it was in older areas. Because of such opportunities, westward migration often attracted the most enterprising young residents of older communities.

Fishing rather than farming sustained seaboard New England and paid for most of the region's imports. In 1770 the exports of New England's fishing industry exceeded the combined value of the rice and indigo produced on the plantations of the Lower South. Only tobacco and wheat flour were more valuable American exports. Dried cod and other fish caught in the Grand Banks area off Newfoundland were New England's major export staple, but whale oil (for lamps) and whale fins (for corsets) brought additional income. Far from being enumerated, New England fish were excluded from the British market at the behest of British fishermen. Consequently New Englanders sold their fish to southern Europe or to West Indian planters as food for their slaves.

From fishing, New Englanders moved easily into commerce and manufacturing. In marketing their fish they found a demand for shipping services and consequently began to carry cargo wherever anyone was willing to pay them to take it. Often they could be persuaded even to sell their ships, as they could replace them cheaply at home. New Englanders thus became not only traders and carriers but important manufacturers of ships. By the time of the Revolution, American ships constituted nearly one-third of the British merchant marine.

Rum manufacturing was a New England enterprise which grew directly out of the marketing of fish in the West Indies. Molasses, the raw material for rum, was itself a by-product of sugar refining. British sugar producers made their molasses into rum and sold it widely in Britain and in America. The French government, however, responded to the pleas of French brandy producers by banning the exportation of rum from its sugar islands to France. Consequently the French islands found themselves with vast amounts of molasses for which there was little demand. New Englanders, supplying fish to the sugar planters, chose often to invest their income in cheap French molasses. Some of it they sold in the colonies as molasses. Much of it they made into rum. Some went into New England's slave trade. Most remained in the colonies, where employers used it as a liquor ration for their workers, fur traders bought it for resale to the Indians, and tavern keepers found it the most popular alcoholic beverage of the poor.

Competition in commerce turned many New England merchants from import-export ventures to manufacturing. They agreed with Henry Laurens of Charleston, who complained in 1755 that there were in all the colonies "too many Tradeing Men . . . in proportion to the business of the Country." Some turned to making rum or building ships. The Browns of Providence began to manufacture expensive candles from the spermaceti found in whale heads. Capitalists in Lynn, Massachusetts began to "put out" leather to piece-rate workers who made shoes in their own homes. In such ventures New Englanders were in the vanguard of American economic development.

Manufacturing faced many obstacles in the American colonies. British policy was one. Britain wanted America to concentrate on producing what Britain needed or could sell to the rest of the world, chiefly extractive industry products with low profit margins. From income derived in this way Britain expected Americans to buy relatively high-priced manufactured goods— Asian and continental European as well as British in origin—from merchants in Britain. Accordingly Parliament enacted measures (the Woolens Act, 1699; the Hat Act, 1732; the Finished Iron Products Law, 1750) designed to restrict colonial manufacturing. Governors also received royal instructions to veto legislative measures intended to foster manufacturing.

None of these measures was rigidly enforced, partly because conditions in America tended in any case to discourage extensive growth in manufacturing. Imported commodities commanded higher prestige. High transportation expenses enabled local artisans to undersell distant producers. Labor was expensive, hard to keep, and usually deficient in skill.

Scarcity of money, both for investment and for consumer expenditure, was also a problem. The Americans did acquire some gold and silver in trade with the West Indies, but they almost invariably sent it off to England to pay debts or to import manufactured goods. Hence they needed another medium of exchange. Most colonies used commodities for money, but only Virginia and Maryland did so with much success. In those colonies, receipts for tobacco deposited at government warehouses served very well. Massachusetts in the 1690s began to buy war supplies by issuing "bills of credit," or promises to pay later from future tax revenues. Other colonies did this in later wars. In peacetime, several provinces turned to "land banks," which created paper money to be lent to landowners who gave mortgages on their property as security. In the Middle Colonies, such paper money was relatively stable in value. In Rhode Island, however, deliberate inflation led to a Parliamentary ban (1751) on land banks and on legal tender bills of credit throughout New England.

Large landholdings were rare in the settled areas of the North, except for the Hudson Valley of New York. There much of the best land was in the possession of a few major landlords determined to hold their estates for their heirs in perpetuity. Even as late as 1772, a royal governor of New York endorsed such landholdings as tending "to create subordination and counterpoise, in some measure, the general levelling spirit." By then, however, most new land grants were going to speculators whose aim was not to establish perpetual, tenant-operated estates but to accumulate quick profits from sales to ordinary settlers.

In the Middle, or "Bread," Colonies, extending from New York to Delaware, rich farmlands lay adjacent to excellent natural waterways, affording cheap transportation. Accordingly, farmers in this region produced wheat for export. Millers, although not all as ingenious as Oliver Evans, whose Pennsylvania mills were almost entirely automated, added to the grain's value by transforming it into flour. Only in occasional years of crop failure in Britain, however, would

Parliament allow Americans to market their wheat and flour in the mother country. The major markets for American producers were the West Indies and southern Europe.

Immigrants: White and Black

Immigrants who peopled England's North American colonies came primarily from England itself, from other British possessions, from continental Europe, and from Africa. England itself provided probably more than half of the immigrant total. In fact until late in the seventeenth century, nearly all the immigrants came from England. A large proportion of them, especially those who chose New England, were people of middle-class background—artisans, merchants, shopkeepers, landowners—impelled to leave by the religious and political turmoil which sparked the Puritan Great Migration. Of those who chose Virginia or Maryland many were younger sons of landed families destined for difficult times in England by traditions which gave the eldest son possession of all his father's land (primogeniture) and forbade its division (entail). Most immigrants, however, were poor people, their lives disrupted by the transition from medieval agriculture emphasizing subsistence farming to a capitalistic system stressing large-scale production of wool for England's leading industry or of food for a growing urban population. Even those who had employment suffered from price inflation brought on by the influx of American treasure while their own wages, fixed by justices of the peace who were often their employers, increased little. The countryside abounded with "sturdy beggars" who had left their villages in search of work. Local authorities, fearful that they might require public assistance or might resort to crime, could and often did return them in custody to their original communities. Until about 1670 such circumstances created an illusion of overpopulation and official encouragement of emigration despite the fact that England's total population was then not much more than half that of modern London.

"Indentured servitude" was the means by which thousands of England's poor became American colonists. Because free persons would not remain agricultural laborers when they could so easily acquire land, the London Company at a very early date sent over poor orphan children to be bound to the planters as apprentices. From this beginning there evolved the tradition of indentured (contractual) servitude. Shippers transported poor Englishmen to the Tobacco Coast and sold them to planters. The planter's payment not only compensated the shipper for providing passage but also entitled the planter to a 50-acre headright for each immigrant whose service he bought. The indentured servant then worked for the planter for a period of from four to seven years to buy back his freedom.

Indentured servitude was a hard lot. Although most entered upon it voluntarily, some were kidnapped off the streets or out of taverns. Some twenty thousand were convicts, transported to rid the country of them. "Transportation" and fourteen years of servitude was long an alternative to execution for those convicted of certain crimes in England. Some such convicts oddly "did chuse to be hanged ere they would go thither, and were." Passage to America was often an ordeal of overcrowding, inadequate food, decimation by dysentery, typhus, or smallpox. Labor along the Tobacco Coast was even more deadly during the first few decades. Harshly disciplined, overworked, and undernourished in a depressingly humid climate, perhaps as many as half succumbed to malaria, typhoid fever, or some other ailment before they gained their freedom. Those who did survive found it increasingly difficult to obtain land except in the backcountry where transportation problems largely precluded profitable production of tobacco. By 1666 three of every four Virginians either were or had been indentured servants. An alarming proportion of the population consisted of rootless men who bore the planter oligarchy no great love.

Changing circumstances in the second half of the seventeenth century altered the pattern of migration. England became more prosperous; fewer Englishmen chose to leave. Demand for servants in Virginia declined because of both increasing longevity and a decline in the price of tobacco attributable primarily to oversupply of the world market. Consequently as the Middle Colonies and the Carolinas began to compete with the Tobacco Coast and New England for settlers, most of the new arrivals came from outlying British areas (Scotland, northern Ireland, and the British West Indies), from continental Europe, and from Africa.

Immigrants from the British territories came for varying reasons. In the British West Indies the profitability of sugar culture led to the engrossment of the limited land by planters of great wealth. Smaller planters sold out and left for the Carolinas to secure larger landholdings. In northern Ireland after 1718 Scottish Presbyterians who had settled on lands confiscated from Catholic rebels in the period of the Glorious Revolution found their rents much higher and their tenure less secure following the expiration of their initial thirty-year leases. That set off a mass migration which, by the time of the Revolution, had brought perhaps a quarter of a million Scotch-Irish Presbyterians to the American colonies, particularly to the backcountry of Pennsylvania and the South. Depressed economic conditions spurred emigration from the lowlands of Scotland early in the eighteenth century. On the eve of the Revolution an agricultural transformation such as England had experienced in the previous century set off the emigration of whole communities from the impoverished Scottish Highlands.

Germans were by far the most numerous of colonial America's immigrants from continental Europe. William Penn's advertisements attracted many. French invasion drove out others. By 1720 recruiting agents traversed the countryside signing up immigrants, most of whom sold themselves or some member of their family into servitude upon arrival to pay the cost of their passage. Most such "redemptioners" settled in Pennsylvania, where by 1770 they made up about one-third of the population. The only other continental Europeans to emigrate to England's colonies in any numbers were French Huguenots, Protestants subject to severe repression in Catholic France. Most of them were middle-class individuals who paid their own way and assimilated rapidly.

African immigrants, however unwillingly, far outnumbered all other groups except the English. A passing Dutch warship, John Rolfe wrote in 1619, "sold us twenty negars." This arrival of blacks at Jamestown, it is worth noting, preceded that of the Pilgrims at Plymouth by one year. Considered as indentured servants rather than slaves, some blacks acquired freedom, property, and even the right to vote. Gradually, however, the white population began to impose slave status upon imported blacks. By the 1660s Virginia laws had declared that imported Negro laborers and the offspring of all slave women would be slaves for life.

No known evidence explains clearly why Virginia made blacks slaves rather than indentured servants. Part of the explanation is historical. Slavery had long existed among West African blacks as it had in some parts of Europe until about the time of Columbus, chiefly to provide domestic servants rather than workers for commercial enterprise. After the discovery of America, a great market for slaves developed in the mines and the plantations of the Spanish and Portuguese colonies. Capitalizing upon this new market, coastal tribes in West Africa began to capture and sell greatly increased numbers of their inland neighbors in order to enlarge their own purchases of European goods, chiefly textiles, weapons, and liquor. Thus, by the time the first blacks arrived in Virginia, a century of precedent existed elsewhere in the Americas for fixing slave status upon those blacks offered for sale as workers.

Prejudice and economic interest also contributed to fixing slave status upon Virginia Negroes. As the name Negro suggests (*negro* is Spanish for "black"), what impressed Europeans most about the West Africans was the darkness of their skin. Whatever the psychological explanation, this difference in color, plus marked cultural differences, created for many Europeans an initial prejudice against blacks and with it a desire for a social system which would hold them permanently apart as an inferior caste. Slave status served that purpose. Slavery, moreover, provided economic advantages for planters. Not only did slaves serve for life rather than only a few years, but their progeny were similarly bound, not free as was the case with offspring of indentured servants.

Despite the economic advantages they offered, Negro slaves did not become a major factor in the development of the Tobacco Coast until the eighteenth century. Initially, when most new arrivals died within a short time, the cheaper indentured servants were a better buy despite their short term. Furthermore, for most of the seventeenth century, the Dutch had been the principal purveyors of slaves, and British policy discouraged purchasing from them. Late in the century, the British replaced the Dutch as the world's leading slave sellers, but until the end of the century the trade was monopolized legally by the somewhat complacent Royal Africa Company. The opening of the slave trade to free competition at the end of the century greatly increased the supply and reduced the price.

"Negro men," merchant Henry Laurens frequently reminded his British correspondents on the eve of the Revolution, were "the most certain Article" for Charleston's market. Indigo planters, Laurens observed in 1755, had secured "such large Sums" for their crops that they were "all mad for more Negroes." At that time Charleston imported about two thousand slaves annually; in 1773 the figure had soared to nearly eight thousand, and blacks outnumbered whites in the province by about six to four. In Georgia, where the trustees had barred slavery until 1749, Negroes by 1770 were roughly half of the population. In North Carolina, where problems of navigation impeded the growth of the plantation system, only about 35 percent of the people were black. Virginia was about 40 percent black, Maryland 30 percent. For the colonies as a whole blacks were about 20 percent of the population as compared to 11 percent in the 1970s.

North of the Mason-Dixon line blacks constituted a far lower proportion of the population. In Pennsylvania, Quaker principles as well as a climate unsuitable for semitropical commodities discouraged slaveholding. Blacks were about 2 percent of the population. Farther north economic circumstances were also unpropitious, but New York was about 18 percent black. Many Northerners who bought slaves, it has been suggested, sought them as status symbols more than as a source of profit.

Mortality among Negro slaves was remarkably low in England's continental colonies. No detailed study of that subject yet exists, but a careful assessment of the slave trade as a whole has shown that only about 5 percent of the Africans brought to the Americas came to what is now the United States. Roughly 95 percent went to the West Indies and Latin America. Yet so great was the difference in the survival rate that those areas now have only about 70 percent of the hemisphere's black population while the United States has about 30 percent.

The American Social System

Social tension was probably higher in colonial America than in most other areas of the world because the pattern of immigration had thrown together not only a number of different European culture groups but three different races. The turbulence of Indian-white relations should need no more elaboration, but troubles arising out of the racial and cultural differences between black and white deserve some comment. Negroes, more than 90 percent of them slaves, understandably harbored their own grievances against white society. Rigid discipline and constant surveillance minimized opportunities for planned uprisings, yet they occurred. In 1739 twenty whites and about twice as many blacks lost their lives in a slave insurrection in South Carolina. New York City experienced one uprising in 1712 and in anticipation of another in 1741 began a frenzy of executions (twenty-nine blacks and four suspected whites) which ended only when the coerced confessions began to implicate people of "known credit, fortune and reputation." Fear of such interracial violence was a constant feature of life in areas of large Negro population as well as on the Indian frontier.

Discrimination was more rigorous than in the West Indies or Latin America, partly at least because there was no such scarcity of white women as had fostered interracial intimacy in the tropical regions. Most white people, including such intellectuals as Franklin and Jefferson, believed Negroes to be inherently inferior in intelligence. A few Quakers such as Anthony Benezet, who had actually taught Negro children, knew better, as did the distinguished Virginia planter William Byrd, who affirmed as a commonplace that "very bright talents may be lodged under a very dark skin."

Relations among the differing European ethnic groups were good enough generally to excite admiration, but there was tension. Here, wrote the admiring French observer Crèvecoeur, "the poor of Europe have by some means met together" and "individuals of all nations are melted into a new [breed] of men." Intermarriage had indeed occurred extensively, but it was also true that isolated ethnic islands remained— Dutchmen in New York's Hudson Valley, Germans and Scotch-Irish in Pennsylvania, Highland Scots in North Carolina, among others. Ethnic slurs and cultural conflicts kept an edge of tension in relations among such groups and between each of them and the dominant English. This would seriously impede unity against the British in the Revolution.

To many Europeans what seemed most remarkable about colonial America was the opportunity which it afforded to middle- and lower-class people to better their station in life. For Europe's rural poor, struggling for survival usually with insecure tenure on land inadequate to meet a family's subsistence needs, the remarkable ease with which one could gain access to an ample expanse of highly productive land was a powerful incentive for emigrating to America. In sharp contrast to the situation in most areas of Europe, only some 20 percent of the white men in the colonies in the period of the Revolution did not own land. A large proportion of landless individuals were young men who would become landholders before they died. In the growing cities America's high wage scale was also a lure. Crèvecoeur exaggerated in claiming that an American workman would get "four or five times more than he can get in Europe." However, the general scarcity of labor did keep the wage level in America appreciably higher than in Europe.

Poverty of course existed. Slaves and indentured servants knew it. In the Southern backcountry, "poor whites" also made their appearance early. A traveler in the Carolinas noted Irish immigrants living on "what in England is given to the Hogs and Dogs." In Virginia during the Revolution, a Frenchman observed "miserable huts . . . inhabited by whites, whose wan looks and ragged garments bespeak poverty." The northern colonies too had poor inhabitants, rural squatters and urban laborers, although apparently fewer relatively than the South.

Middle-class immigrants could usually better their circumstances in America. Even the richest men in colonial America, it is true, were hardly more than well-to-do by European standards, but many had risen far. Virginia's "great families" of the eighteenth century sprang mostly from "ambitious younger sons of middle-class families." The "most opulent families" in New

York's mercantile and landed aristocracy, avowed a contemporary, "have risen from the lower Rank of People." Fully one-third of the rich merchants who made up the New York chamber of commerce at the time of the Revolution were self-made men.

Ancestry, except in the case of Negroes, clearly had less to do with status in America than it did in Europe. There were no inherited titles. The governors who stood at the apex of colonial society usually returned to England within a few years; they did not found American families. In some provinces a few great families continued to be prominent for generations, but in comparison with Britain, status seemed to adjust quickly to either the acquisition or the loss of wealth.

Deference to those of higher station was a central requirement in a traditional etiquette of class relations. Governors were abjectly humble in addressing correspondence to the king or even to his major ministers. Leading American land-

A colonial housewife spinning wool.   The Granger Collection

owners or merchants were ostentatiously polite in addressing governors. They in turn expected artisans, shopkeepers, and farmers to be appropriately servile in the presence of "gentlemen" like themselves. Even the "middling sort" felt themselves entitled to "proper" respect from the very poor, especially from apprentices, indentured servants, and slaves. In comparison with Europe, however, this "Great Law of Subordination," as historian Carl Bridenbaugh called it, was suffering a decline, a fact attested by the grumbling of European gentlemen who found themselves addressed as equals by ordinary Americans whom they encountered in their travels. New Englanders in particular were frequently criticized for what many outsiders called their "leveling" tendencies.

The influence of frontier conditions upon early American society remains a matter of historical dispute. In many instances, as argued earlier, the frontier clearly afforded great economic opportunity. Frederick Jackson Turner, in a famous essay of 1893, argued that the "perennial rebirth" of civilization in the wilderness helped develop American democracy, equality, individualism, and nationalism. Other historians have questioned these points, stressing the leadership of urban dwellers, and identifying less salutary influences of the frontier. William Byrd, one of the first gentlemen of Virginia, thought the easy subsistence afforded in the backcountry South tended to "discharge the men from the necessity of killing themselves with work" but allowed them to keep "many sabbaths" every week. With reference to law and order on the frontier, Byrd mentioned that a backcountry magistrate who had ordered a drunk put into the stocks "was for his intemperate zeal carried thither himself, and narrowly escaped being whipped into the bargain." There were many frontier squatters, of whom Pennsylvania's Scotch-Irish were only the most notorious, who disregarded land titles quite often in the self-righteous conviction that it was "against the laws of God and Nature, that so much land should be idle while so many Christians wanted it to labour on.''

Women led rather different lives in America than in England. No English woman was either a slave or an indentured servant, compelled by the lash to do gang labor in the fields. No English woman had to be quite so self-sufficient as the frontier housewife who had largely to make what she needed or do without. Spinning wool or flax into yarn, weaving yarn into cloth, making cloth into clothing were principal occupations of most American farmwives. The American woman could depend less on others to provide home furnishings, to care for the ill or the injured, to impart either religious or secular training. She was herself more likely than her husband, although less likely than her English counterpart, to be illiterate. By English standards she married early (usually in her early twenties), bore more children (usually at least five), lost fewer of them to infant diseases or other causes, indulged them more, watched more of them ultimately leave the community for better opportunity elsewhere, and was more likely to live long enough to enjoy some of her very numerous grandchildren. Colonial American women occasionally began businesses of their own, but still more often continued those, including large plantations and major mercantile or manufacturing establishments, inherited from a deceased husband.

Legally a married woman in the colonies as in England had almost no identity. Her husband could ''discipline'' her. He could do as he pleased with her property. Consequently among wealthy families the father was likely to make a careful contractual agreement with the father of the prospective groom regarding his daughter's dowry before the young man proposed matrimony. Widows with property and especially those with children often negotiated their own marriage contracts before remarrying. Divorce was possible only in New England and little used there. ''Elopement'' with a third party was a common means of terminating an unhappy marital alliance.

Sex mores were distinctly pre-Victorian. Although skirts were long and full, necklines were at some distance from the neck. Those whom we politely call ''illegitimate children'' were then simply bastards. They were numerous. Premarital chastity was expected of middle- and upper-class girls, but those of lower social status, especially indentured servants and slaves, were fair game for males of all classes. Kept mistresses were rarer than in England, except perhaps among Southern slaveholders, but even in the South where slavery invited such a practice it was far less common than in the West Indies. Prostitutes were becoming common in the port cities before the Revolution, but they were never so conspicuous as in London.

Religion in Colonial America

Religion in colonial America was highly unusual by European standards. Of the three hierarchical forms of Christianity which dominated Western Europe—Catholicism, Lutheranism, and Anglicanism—only Anglicanism was a major force in the American colonies. Even the Anglicans, however, were only about as numerous in eighteenth-century America as Congregationalists and Presbyterians, both of whom practiced a representative system of church government. Quakers and Baptists, the remaining religious

groups of considerable importance in pre-Revolutionary America, were so individualistic and egalitarian as to condone almost no religious authority at all. Thus hierarchical religions had far less importance in America than in Europe as a whole.

Equally remarkable by European standards was the absence of government support for religion in several colonies. In Rhode Island the dominant Baptists and Quakers enforced separation of church and state, as did the Quakers in

Pennsylvania and Delaware. New York and New Jersey included so many religious groups that none was ever strong enough to secure support as broad as the Anglicans had in the southern colonies and Congregationalists in New England (except Rhode Island). In those colonies the law required everyone to pay taxes to support the dominant church. In New England, however, both Anglicans and Baptists won the right to have their tax payments for the support of religion diverted to their own churches.

Anglicanism itself was different in America. An episcopal or bishop-governed church in England, the Anglican Church in America functioned until after the Revolution without a bishop. Parish priests in England received lifetime appointments from a government-controlled hierarchy, usually on the nomination of major local landholders. In America, the vestrymen of individual parishes hired and fired parish priests at will. In England, church offices were often sinecures conferred on a political patronage basis, and the appointees were in some instances flagrantly immoral. Despite some criticism of "fox-hunting parsons" in the South, neither evil was widespread in the colonies. In England only Anglicans could hold civil or military office or attend a university. In America they did not enjoy such exclusive privileges.

Despite the hostility of Dissenters, Anglicanism did strengthen its position as the eighteenth century progressed. Its Society for the Propagation of the Gospel, chartered in 1701, founded charity schools and did missionary work among Indians and Calvinists. About 1760 Anglicans established a "mission" at Harvard's doorstep and built a pretentious residence which fearful Congregationalists expected would become "the Bishop's Palace." Anglicans helped found King's College (later Columbia) in New York in 1754, and in 1749 the Philadelphia institution which later became the University of Pennsylvania. Closely linked to British authority, Northern Anglican clergymen in particular inculcated "the great Principles of Loyalty and Submission to Government" and denounced

"republican mobbish principles" and "servile compliance" to popular will. They also sought appointment of a bishop for the colonies, although Southern Anglicans, enjoying vestry control of their churches, opposed it.

Calvinism was much stronger in America than in all but a few areas of Europe. Its followers consisted not only of Puritans and Presbyterians, the two leading denominations on the eve of the Revolution, but also of Dutch Reformed, German Reformed, and French Huguenots. Furthermore, Baptists in increasing numbers embraced Calvinism's concept of predestination, while Anglicans were adopting Calvinist practices of congregational control.

Calvinism incurred criticism for various reasons. New England Puritans persecuted Baptists and Quakers for their beliefs. They executed twenty "witches" in Salem, Massachusetts, in 1692. Their insistence upon the depraved nature of man and the predestination of most for damnation also incurred criticism. Yet there was much to admire in Calvinism as it was practiced in New England. Its glorification of work and thrift helped New Englanders maintain an outstanding place in American business leadership for generations. Puritan zeal for education aided New England to attain enduring intellectual eminence. Despite the difficulty of reconciling Calvinist concepts of predestination with social equality and representative government, it is apparent that New England was a spearhead of progress in these matters as well.

Quakers, originally members of a radical lower-class denomination, became increasingly prosperous, and in some respects conservative, in the eighteenth century. In Pennsylvania successful merchants rather than struggling artisans or farmers seemed to typify the movement. Instead of zealously seeking converts, Quakers tended to expel those who were insufficiently orthodox. Nonetheless, it was the Quaker commitment to human equality which produced the only significant opposition to slavery.

Baptists, while tending to adopt the theology of middle-class Calvinists, remained chiefly a lower-class denomination. Charles Woodmason, a profoundly biased Anglican clergyman, denounced backcountry Baptist preachers as "ignorant wretches, who cannot write" and compared a Baptist communion service to "a Gang of frantic Lunatics broke out of Bedlam."

Religious revivals, which subsequently became a permanent part of American culture, swept the colonies in a Great Awakening during the generation preceding the Revolution. Leaders of the Awakening sought by emotional exhortation to enable individuals to experience "conversion," a sense of mystic communion with God accompanied by new dedication to Christian values. Theodorus Frelinghuysen, a German-born minister of the Dutch Reformed Church, began the movement with prayer meetings in New Jersey during the 1720s. William Tennent, a Presbyterian immigrant who had studied at the University of Edinburgh in Scotland, inspired and trained many future revivalists of distinction at the "Log College" which he founded at Neshaminy, Pennsylvania, in 1736. The most outstanding preacher in the movement was George Whitefield, an associate of John Wesley in the English revivalist movement, which ultimately split off from the Anglican to become the Methodist Church. Whitefield made many trips to America and preached with great success under the auspices of every major denomination.

New England's Jonathan Edwards was the Awakening's outstanding intellectual advocate. His narrative of the *Conversion of Many Hundred Souls* reported his success as a revivalist. Later he published a distinguished essay *Freedom of the Will*. Through these and other writings Edwards became the principal defender of the emotional aspects of the revival and perhaps America's foremost theologian.

In the South, the Presbyterians, Methodists, and Baptists all played major roles in the revival. Presbyterian Samuel Davies, later president of Princeton, enjoyed great success in Virginia between 1748 and 1758. Methodist Devereux Jarratt and Baptists Shubal Stearns and Daniel Marshall were "reviving" portions of the South on the eve of the Revolution.

The effect of the Great Awakening on American society is difficult to establish. Clearly it inspired the founding of several notable institutions of higher learning to train more ministers: Presbyterian Princeton (1746), Baptist Brown (1764), Dutch Reformed Rutgers (1766), and Congregationalist Dartmouth (1769). Yet the Awakening was at the same time anti-intellectual, for it exalted mystic enthusiasm, even that of the uneducated, as a path to religious understanding superior to the legalistic scholarship of erudite ministers. The Awakening was also highly divisive. Many "settled ministers," enjoying tax support as the official religious leaders in their communities, resented the disruption of their complacency by uneducated but enthusiastic itinerants. Religious freedom became an issue in New England when Congregational authorities jailed revivalists for unauthorized preaching or for refusing to pay taxes to support an "unconverted" minister. Anglican leaders created similar problems in Virginia.

The least tangible but perhaps most important of all the effects of the Awakening was its erosion of ancient traditions of social deference on the part of the poor toward those of superior wealth and power. Newly converted "saints" of lower-class background found in their conversion new confidence to challenge the traditional prerogatives of their social superiors who remained unconverted. It is significant that Baptists and Methodists, denominations favored by the lower classes, began at the time of the Awakening the rise in membership which, in little more than a generation, would make them the most numerous American religious groups.

At the other extreme from the revivalist movement was a school of thought called "Deism" to which, in fact, the revival was in some measure a reaction. Intellectuals in the late seventeenth century had come to believe that there were "natural laws" not only in astronomy, physics, and other physical sciences, but in fields such as religion and government as well. These individuals believed that through exercise of his reason man could discover the natural laws of religion as well as of science. Deism, the "natural" religion which resulted, postulated an omnipotent God who required virtuous living and allocated rewards and punishments accordingly after death. Deists rejected divine revelations, even the divinity of Christ, along with biblical astronomy. While the doctrines of Deism and natural law were losing popularity in Europe on the eve of the Revolution, their acceptance by American Revolutionary leaders is strikingly evident in the best-known passages of the Declaration of Independence.

Education, Arts and Science

Educational practices in the American Colonies were generally much like those in England. Primary responsibility for educating children lay, as it did in England, with the family. Middle-class parents might send their children to private schools or perhaps hire private tutors, as the very rich did. To train children for the professions as well as in various artisan crafts, parents arranged to apprentice them to serve and learn from an established "master," usually for a period of seven years. Religious denominations maintained charity schools for the children of the poor. These traditions worked best in areas where both population and cash incomes were relatively high. In the colonial South, where the population was widely scattered and cash incomes were low, they served very badly. For slaves the traditional practices did almost nothing; very few Southern planters made any efforts to teach their slaves to read and write.

Only in New England did government assume a significant role in education. New England's Puritan leaders were fully convinced of the value of education. In addition to founding a college-preparatory Latin School in 1635 and Harvard College in 1636, both essentially private institutions, Puritan leaders in 1642 enacted a law requiring all parents to see that their children could read well enough to understand religious principles and capital laws. In 1647 Massachusetts enacted a statute which required each town of fifty families to operate an elementary school and each town of a hundred families to maintain a grammar or secondary school in which youth might be "fitted for the university." Precisely how well the towns met these obligations remains a matter of dispute, but they did fix an unprecedented public duty. Illiteracy was rare among New England men but perhaps as high as 40 percent among the women. Elsewhere it was still more common.

Pressure for curriculum reform at the secondary level was strong in the generation preceding the Revolution. Under attack was the old preoccupation with Latin and Greek, which were useful chiefly in preparing for ministerial careers. The curriculum preferred by the reformers featured subjects which would help students to earn a secular living.

College education was more easily attainable in colonial America than in England itself. The basic reason was that America had more colleges, thanks to the Great Awakening and to the fact that England imposed fewer restrictions on the educational activities of dissenters in the colonies than it did in England. Most students in the seventeenth century aimed to be ministers, but in the eighteenth century more prepared for secular careers. The curriculum was always predominantly secular.

Painting was the first of the arts in which Americans attained recognition abroad. Benjamin West of Pennsylvania, aided by Philadelphia merchants, studied in Europe and won great acclaim in London, even from George III, despite West's undisguised sympathy for the American Revolution. Boston's John Singleton Copley, unlike West, did many of his best paintings in America before he settled in England in 1774. Both painted chiefly portraits and historical subjects. Each was outstanding at that time for his realism. Most painters who worked in the colonies were immigrants trained in Europe. Those who patronized them wanted principally portraits, sometimes with extravagant costumes and backgrounds to suggest high status, but often, especially in New England, with a realistic emphasis on individuality, including indications of one's profession or trade. Religious and mythological subjects, despite their popularity in Europe, found almost no market in colonial America.

Music in the classical tradition had little place in colonial life. Wealthy gentlemen in a few large cities organized chamber music societies in the generation preceding the Revolution, but most of the musicians were European immigrants and the works they performed were those of European composers.

Religious music encountered opposition among Calvinists, who considered it to be an emotional distraction from the intellectual pursuit of religious understanding. Thus Puritan New England tolerated no religious music except unaccompanied psalm singing. Even hymns, which began to gain popularity during the Great Awakening, aroused much protest. Among Anglicans and many of the German sects, religious music found ready acceptance.

Folk or popular music suited the taste of most Americans. The songs themselves were usually traditional European tunes, although American variations in the words were frequent. Before the Revolution urban Americans were enjoying ballad operas, forerunners of modern musical comedies, particularly *The Beggar's Opera*, a London production of 1728 which employed many old folk tunes in a bawdy satire of English life.

Theater encountered great opposition from the Puritans in Northern urban centers while the rural character of society made it uneconomic among the more tolerant Anglicans of the South. Like their English antecedents who had stamped out theater in England during the Civil War,

Northern Puritans tried to bar performances by the few traveling theatrical companies which came from England more frequently after 1750. By devious means such as billing their plays as "Moral Dialogues" and calling their theaters "schoolhouses," the thespians slowly gained acceptance in the major cities, especially Philadelphia, which had become quite cosmopolitan by the 1760s.

Creative writing also suffered from Puritan disapproval. Despite the examples of eighteenth-century English novelists, no colonial American wrote a novel. Particularly dogmatic Puritans disapproved even of reading novels, although poetry met their favor. Indeed, New England Puritans suffered what Moses Coit Tyler called a "lust of versification." Most of these versifiers, Tyler concluded, "it was a charity to call amateurs in the art of poetry." Representative of such work is Michael Wigglesworth's best-selling *Day of Doom*, which Tyler characterized as a "grim, pathetic, horrible" rendition of the "hideous dogmas" of the Puritan creed. Much more appealing to modern taste is the work of Edward Taylor, unpublished until this century and Anne Bradstreet. Theological disputation, history, and private diaries or journals were forms of literature which enjoyed general approval. Rhode Island's founder, Roger Williams, engaged Quaker and Puritan alike in pamphlet warfare equally remarkable for its ideas and its scurrility. In the eighteenth century, New England ministers such as John Wise (*Churches Quarrel Espoused*, 1710; *Vindication of the Government of the New England Churches*, 1717) and particularly Jonathan Mayhew (*A Discourse Concerning Unlimited Submission*, 1750) gave a somewhat more political cast to their disputatious essays. Jonathan Edwards, on the other hand, became more abstractly philosophical in his famous *Freedom of the Will* (1754).

History became less theological and more political. Cotton Mather's *Ecclesiastical History of New England* (1702) was representative of the God-centered history of the preceding century. In a more modern vein Virginia's Robert

Beverly wrote *The History and Present State of Virginia* (1705) to refute the aspersions of English authors upon his province. William Byrd sought to amuse his fellow aristocrats with an account of the peculiar mores of the backcountry in his *History of the Dividing Line* (1738). William Smith and Thomas Hutchinson wrote accounts of political history in their respective provinces (New York and Massachusetts).

Late in the colonial period, three men wrote personal narratives of distinction. The saintly Quaker John Woolman forecast in his *Journal* (1774) that "when our minds are thoroughly divested of all prejudice in relation to difference of colour, . . . I believe it will appear that a heavy account lies against us as a Civil Society for oppressions committed against people who did not injure us." In an entirely different spirit, the "irrepressibly indignant" Charles Woodmason, an Anglican parson, recorded his contemptuous but fascinating views of life in the backcountry of the Carolinas. Finally, the all-round genius Benjamin Franklin produced the first classic of American literature, his *Autobiography*.

Architecture in America followed English fashions, although both castles and cathedrals were conspicuously absent. In the seventeenth century, colonists of English background built homes which, like those of rural England at the time, were quite medieval in structure—steep-roofed, gabled, often with an overhanging second story. They looked quite different, however, because Americans used wood (clapboard and shingles) for walls and roof, whereas the English, less abundantly supplied with forests, usually made exterior walls of plaster and roofs of thatch (straw). In the eighteenth century both Britain and America adopted the English, or Georgian, variant of Renaissance style which featured classical symmetry, columns, and pediments. Before the Revolution, frontier dwellers were beginning to rely largely on primitive log cabins (notched logs) or more substantial block-houses (squared timbers), neither of which had much place in Europe. Plain, multipurpose "meeting houses" served for religious assemblies in the seventeenth century, but before the 1750s Americans had begun building steepled Georgian churches patterned after London's St. Martin-in-the-Fields (1721).

Science attracted gentlemen amateurs in America as it did in Europe. Harvard still accepted Ptolemaic or earth-centered astronomy as late as 1670, and Yale even longer, but Boston merchant Thomas Brattle made observations of Halley's comet which the great Isaac Newton cited in his *Principia Mathematica*. Harvard professor John Winthrop IV carried out astronomical work respected in Europe. James Logan of Philadelphia and his protégé, John Bartram, were the most successful of many amateur botanists who sought to inform curious Europeans about America's vegetation. Connecticut's Jared Eliot, in his *Essays on Field Husbandry* (1748–1759), tried to communicate to American gentlemen some of the enthusiasm for agricultural improvements then so common among the English. European interest in the "noble savage" stirred New York's Cadwallader Colden to make an anthropological inquiry into *History of the Five [Iroquois] Indian Nations* (1727). The ubiquitous Benjamin Franklin gained international recognition for his *Experiments and Observations on Electricity* (1751).

Conclusion

By the eve of the Revolution a distinctive and in many ways a distinctly un-English society had emerged in England's continental American colonies. Abundant land enabled American families to work larger plots than most Europeans could and thus to enjoy a higher standard of living. A chronic shortage of labor kept wages above European standards, but had led also to the importation of impoverished Europeans as indentured servants and black Africans as slaves.

Early Architecture
in America

From the time of the first settlements until the late nineteenth century, Europe naturally exerted the main influence on architectural styles in America. Most of the settlers were Europeans, and they considered themselves as such until the end of the Colonial period. After the Revolutionary War, European traditions continued as the foundation of much American culture, including its architecture.

Despite its European origins, however, something distinctive and characteristic did emerge in the development of architecture in America. In selecting from the range of traditional European architectural styles, Americans stressed certain elements. They altered the European forms as they adapted them to American environments and to American building materials. To the interested observer, American architectural developments can yield insights into the history of the national culture as a whole.

The kitchen of the Bryant-Cushing House in Norwell, Mass. (left), for example, incorporates English design and methods, but at the same time mirrors the austerity and simplicity of New England Puritan life of the seventeenth century. Other American architectural developments have reflected the flourishing of the Southern plantation economy, the desire for elegance which supplanted austerity as New England prospered, and the attempt of the American founding fathers to fashion the nation on the classic models of ancient Greek democracy and the Roman republic.

The sampling of American architectural history on the pages which follow was selected with assistance of Denys Peter Myers of the Historic American Buildings Survey, a

division of the National Park Service which, since 1933, has documented over 13,000 historic buildings and has done much to encourage their preservation. With a few noted exceptions, the photographs here are from the Survey collection on file at the Library of Congress.

Among the early traditions in American building were simplicity and the use of building materials which came easiest to hand. The New England of the Puritans made simplicity a virtue in itself, but this tendency was reinforced by the hard facts of what was still very close to frontier living: skilled workmen were in relatively short supply and money was required for elaborate building.

The McIntire Garrison House in York, Me. (left, above), probably built about 1707, accurately represents New England style during the first one hundred years of the settlement. The overhanging second story was an English mode. Like most New England houses of the period, the abundant forests of the area provided the wood for its construction. The use of brick in New England did not become widespread until later in the eighteenth-century.

Log cabins did not predominate in early American settlements, but some appeared in the Delaware River Valley built by Swedes who had similar dwellings in their home country. The example at left, below, is near Darby, Pa.

The traditions of simplicity and use of native materials are exemplified in the Kaufman House and barns near Oley, Pa., built between 1727 and 1762 (far right, below), the finest-known example of a Pennsylvania-German farm group in the Oley Valley. Pennsylvanians often built with stone because of its easy availability.

Early colonial building in the backwoods and at the mountain frontiers of the South included buildings as simple as those prevalent in the North, but the buildings which stand today and characterize the time and place are the manor houses of the great plantations. Built on enormous tracts of land granted by the Stuart monarchs, these manor houses had a grandeur not generally achieved in the North until much later. The early manor houses, grand though they were, did share a relative absence of ornamentation and a feeling of austerity. Bacon's Castle in Surry County, Va., built before 1676 (right, above), has the clustered chimney flues typical of Jacobean architecture, as does Stratford Hall in Westmoreland County (far right, above), which has also the typically Jacobean central hall with wings forming an H-plan. Abundance of clay in Virginia fostered brick as a building material, as did the great wealth of the planters who imported workmen especially to build their houses.

By the middle of the eighteenth century, most parts of settled America were ready for new and more elegant forms. Ascetic Puritan strictures had lost their hold, and in the North and South prosperous planters, merchants, sea captains, and traders looked to England where designers like Sir Christopher Wren, James Gibbs, and Robert Adams had in the late seventeenth and in the eighteenth centuries fostered and refined Renaissance influences in English architecture. Characteristic of their work were balanced façades and classical decorative devices, spacious interiors, and fine stairways. With the rise of this style, called "Georgian" after the contemporaneous line of English kings, brick came increasingly into use in New England, but craftsmen there also used wood to duplicate the effect created in stone in English Georgian buildings.

By no means the most elegant doorway of the period, but typical in its style, is that of the manse built in 1742 by the Reverend Ebenezer Gay in Suffield, Conn. (left). Classical pilasters support a broken scroll pediment, while wood, cut to look like stone, provides a frame for the door. The Chase-Lloyd House (right, above) was built in Annapolis, Md., between 1769–1771. The façade has the characteristic symmetrical organization in three parts with a central pavilion. The third-floor window echoes the arch of the Palladian doorway.

Following the Revolutionary War, the Georgian styles of the period developed into what came to be called Federal style, which had as one of its distinguishing characteristics an even greater preoccupation with ornament. The Nightingale Brown House, built in Providence, R. I., in 1792 (right, below), with its ornate "widow's walk," Palladian window, and decorative porch with balustrade provides a fine example of the Federal style.

The Georgian style had an equal impact on the South. Typical of the many Georgian mansions built before the Revolution is Westover, the Byrd mansion (below), built between 1730 and 1734 in Charles County, Va. Symmetrically placed outbuildings were commonly associated with many Southern houses. (In the case of Westover, these originally stood free of the main house.) The high-hipped roof also appeared frequently in Southern mansions of the period. Note the similarity of the doorway, with its broken scroll pediment, to the humbler version of the same design employed by the Reverend Ebenezer Gay on the preceding page.

The fortunes which enabled the building of such great Southern mansions rested on a foundation of slave labor. The design of slave quarters, usually humble, varied from plantation to plantation. An early nineteenth-century slave dormitory at Keswick in Powhatan County, Va., appears at left; its interior had a central circular chimney containing several fireplaces, and slaves slept in a circle around the chimney with their feet toward the fires.

Although Georgian design concepts persisted in the Federal style after the Revolution, the first great break with the Georgian manner came in the 1790s. As America sought a pattern for its government, a general interest in the old Roman republic stirred. In the planning of Washington, leaders like Thomas Jefferson sought a monumental Roman style. An upsurge of interest in the ancient Greek style of building followed shortly upon this passion for Roman things.

The American Greek Revival began, according to most architectural historians, in 1798, with the building of Benjamin Latrobe's Bank of Pennsylvania; by the 1820s, it dominated. According to Talbot Hamlin, the Greek Revival was "in the widest sense a popular movement deeply emotional, and despite its classic guise, deeply romantic."

Starting in the middle-Atlantic seaboard region, the Revival spread to all quarters of the nation. An inseparable part of the mythology of the antebellum South, it spawned great plantation houses like Milford, the Governor Manning plantation in the Pinewood vicinity of South Carolina (above). Careful and elegant detail characterizes the portico of the 1850 Robert A. Grinnan House in New Orleans, (right).

The Greek Revival, predictably, greatly affected buildings of a public character, such as the Second Bank of the United States (left, above), built in Philadelphia between 1818 and 1824 from a design by William Strickland. Pride in handsome appearance extended also to many of the factory buildings of the young republic, such as the Crown and Eagle Mills (left, below) begun in the 1820s. This mill is partly supported by an arch over the Mumford River in North Uxbridge, Mass. Here, as in the Wiscasset, Me., County Court House some vestiges of late Federal style still persist. That the North fell equally under the influence of the Greek Revival is evidenced by the Congregational Church at Cornwall, Conn. (far right, above); the William F. Keuhneman House in Racine, Wisc. (far right, below); and the interior of the Campbell-Whittlesey House in Rochester, N.Y. (right).

From Maryland southward a warm climate permitted production of crops which could not be grown commercially in England and fostered the growth of the plantation system, which employed bound labor to achieve large-scale agricultural production for export to the mother country. North of Maryland farmers produced wheat and other crops, also grown in England, with the result that they had to look elsewhere for a market, chiefly to southern Europe and the West Indian sugar plantations. New England, not well endowed for farming, sold fish from the nearby Grand Banks to the same markets. The northern colonies made progress in the development of both commerce and manufacturing, but in conformity with British policy all the colonies tended to import most of their manufactured goods from Britain and to pay for them in less valuable raw products. The result was a highly unfavorable balance of trade or, more specifically, deep indebtedness to Britain.

A distinctive social and intellectual pattern emerged also. Racial variety and racial strife were prominent as whites struggled to wrest land from the Indians and labor from Negro slaves. Calvinist and Anabaptist religious views, confined largely to bourgeois and lower-class minorities in Europe, dominated the northern colonies and strongly influenced the Anglican South. A Great Awakening in the generation preceding the Revolution made American religion much more emotional and less intellectual in character. No hereditary nobility developed in America, and traditions of social deference were breaking down more rapidly than in Europe. New England began to provide public support for education. Colleges were more numerous than in England. There was little memorable achievement in the arts or the sciences although two American painters, Benjamin West and John Singleton Copley, did win fame in London.

SUGGESTED READINGS

In the growing body of literature in which Indians receive close attention the following are outstanding: Alden Vaughan, *New England Frontier: Puritans and Indians, 1620–1675** (1965), pro-Puritan; Douglas Leach, *Flintlock and Tomahawk: New England in King Philip's War** (1958) and *The Northern Colonial Frontier, 1607–1763* (1966); W. F. Craven, *White, Red, and Black: Seventeenth Century Virginians* (1971); A. W. Trelease, *Indian Affairs in Colonial New York* (1960); George Hunt, *Wars of the Iroquois** (1940); V. W. Crane, *The Southern Frontier** (1929). In *The Savages of America* (1953) R. H. Pearce analyzes how Americans perceived the Indians. *Red, White and Black** (1974) by Gary B. Nash considers race relations in early America with particular attention to Indians.

Colonial economic history is a somewhat neglected field. Among the few outstanding works are W. T. Baxter's *The House of Hancock* (1945), which explains how "bookkeeping barter" enabled merchants to do business without money; J. B. Hedges's *The Browns of Providence Plantations* (1952); G. M. Waller's *Samuel Vetch, Colonial Enterpriser* (1960); Bernard Bailyn's *The New England Merchants in the Seventeenth Century* (1955); H. A. Innis's *The Cod Fisheries* (1940); and Virginia Harrington's *The New York Merchant on the Eve of the Revolution* (1935).

Black history has traditionally attracted chiefly those historians interested in the nineteenth century, but some notable works with an earlier focus have appeared. On African history, J. D. Fage, *Introduction to the History of West Africa* (1959) is short and to the point. Philip Curtin in *The African Slave Trade* (1969) has provided fascinating statistics. W. D. Jordan's *White over Black** (1968) studies the development of Anglo-American attitudes toward blacks with fascinating detail and profound insight. D. B. Davis's *The Problem of Slavery in Western Culture* (1966) supplements Jordan usefully on many points. J. H. Bennett, Jr., in *Bondsmen and Bishops* (1958) affords unique insight into the life of slaves on a West Indian sugar plantation. L. J. Greene reports well on *The Negro in Colonial New England** (1942). Edgar McManus has written comprehensively in *Black Bondage in the North* (1973). G. W. Mullin's *Flight and Rebellion* (1972) deals with Virginia. J. W. Blasingame has studied black mores in *The Slave Community* (1972).

European immigration of the colonial period has also received relatively little attention. However, A. E. Smith's *Colonists in Bondage* (1947) is superb on indentured servitude as a means of immigration. There are also excellent studies of particular ethnic groups such as J. G. Leyburn's *The Scotch-Irish* (1962); I. C. C. Graham's *Colonists from Scotland* (1956); and F. Klees's *The Pennsylvania Dutch* (1950).

Middle-class democracy prevailed before the Revolution, according to Robert E. Brown in *Middle Class Democracy and the Revolution in Massachusetts* (1955) and (with his wife, B. Katherine Brown) *Virginia, 1705–1786: Democracy or Aristocracy?* (1964). J. T. Main sees the situation somewhat differently in *The Social Structure of Revolutionary America* (1965), as does C. S. Synor in *Gentlemen Freeholders* (1952) (called *American Revolutionaries in the Making* in paperback). L. W. Labaree relates class to ideology with great insight in *Conservatism in Early America* (1948).

City and town have also intrigued colonial historians. Carl L. Bridenbaugh's *Cities in the Wilderness* (1938) and *Cities in Revolt* (1955) study all aspects of colonial urban life. Ola Winslow's *Meetinghouse Hill* (1952) deals with New England towns in general, as does Michael Zuckerman's *Peaceable Kingdoms** (1970). Charles Grant's *Democracy in the Connecticut Frontier Town of Kent** (1961) studies one in particular as also does K. E. Lockridge, *A New England Town** (1970). J. T. Lemon's study affirms that southeastern Pennsylvania was *The Best Poor Man's Country* (1972). P. J. Greven, Jr., used Andover, Massachusetts for his *Four Generations** (1970). John Demos studied Plymouth family life in *A Little Commonwealth* (1970).

Several contemporaries left outstanding observations of colonial life. Crèvecoeur's *Letters from an American Farmer** is a classic inquiry into American character. *Gentleman's Progress* (edited by C. L. Bridenbaugh, 1948) records the views of a Scottish traveler. German immigrant Gottlieb Mittelberger described his *Journey to Pennsylvania* (edited by Oscar Handlin and John Clive, 1960). L. B. Wright and M. Tinling edited *The Secret Diary of William Byrd* (1941) with its observations on Virginia and North Carolina. R. J. Hooker edited *The Journal of Charles Woodmason* (1953), which has indignant accounts of life in the Carolina backcountry.

S. E. Mead's *The Lively Experiment* (1963) is a good introduction to American religious history. Perry Miller's examination of the thought of *Jonathan Edwards* (1949) supplements Ola Winslow's biography (1940). W. G. McLoughlin's *Isaac Backus** (1967) is an excellent biography of a major Baptist leader. His *New England Dissent* (2 vols., 1971) adduces vast information on the struggle to separate church and state. S. C. Henry is competent on the great *George Whitefield* (1957). L. J. Trinterud's *The Forming of an American Tradition* (1949) is excellent on Presbyterianism. Alan Heimert views the Awakening very favorably in his controversial *Religion and the American Mind* (1966). W. M. Gewehr's *The Great Awakening in Virginia* (1930) is still the best of several regional studies. M. L. Starkey's *The Devil in Massachusetts* (1949) deals popularly but reliably with the uproar over witches. W. J. Frost recounts the increasing conservatism of *The Quaker Family in Colonial America* (1973).

On education, Bernard Bailyn's *Education in the Forming of American Society* (1960) conceives its subject as the means by which culture is transmitted across generations and surveys the relevant literature. On secondary education Robert Middlekauf's *Ancients and Axioms* (1963) is authoritative. L. A. Cremin explores educational ideas before 1783 in *American Education* (1971).

Among books which deal generally with colonial American cultures, D. J. Boorstin's *The Americans: The Colonial Experience** (1958) and Max Savelle's *Seeds of Liberty** (1948) are outstanding. L. B. Wright's *The Cultural Life of the American Colonies** (1957) focuses on thought and the arts. Michael Kraus's *The Atlantic Civilization* (1949) puts American culture in a European setting.

Several excellent volumes distinguish the scanty literature on the arts in colonial America. Hugh Morrison relates American to European architecture superbly in *Early American Architecture* (1952). Alan Gowan's *Images of American Living* (1964) has interesting suggestions concerning the history of furniture as well as architecture. J. T. Flexner in *First Flowers of Our Wilderness* (1947) and *The Light of Distant Skies* (1954) finds American distinctiveness reflected in American painting.

*indicates availability in paperback.

British versus American Authority

Political institutions in colonial America became different in some measure from their British models in the generations after Jamestown, chiefly as a result of continuing contention between imperial authorities and representatives of the colonial people. British officials sought to enforce regulations designed to make the colonies economically beneficial to Britain. To help them attain that end they sought also to preserve as much as possible of the power inherent in the ancient prerogatives of the king. In the seventeenth century British authorities found inspiration in the absolute monarchy of France, where no legislature met from 1614 to 1789. Accordingly, in the 1680s London tried to eliminate the popular assemblies previously granted. The Glorious Revolution in 1689 put a stop to that. Indeed the new regime in Britain promptly extended to America the principles of representative government which the Glorious Revolution established in Britain itself. In America, however, greater power for representative legis-

latures meant also greater freedom from British authority. To put the point another way, reducing the ancient prerogatives of the king diminished the capacity of his governors in the colonies to enforce British rule.

For several generations after 1689 British leaders refused to recognize the dilemma posed by what many called the increasing ''independency'' of the colonial legislatures. At last in the 1750s they began to take a harder line. They tried, largely in vain, to compel the legislatures to accept royal instructions as absolutely binding. Then, prompted by the pressure of debts from the Seven Years' War, which had driven the French out of America, Parliament attempted to levy taxes upon the Americans for revenue rather than for trade regulation as had been the case with all previous taxes imposed by Parliament upon the Americans. At first the British pledged to use the revenue only for the defense of the colonies, but after 1767 they frankly professed their intention to use the income to pay those provincial officials previously dependent upon the colonial legislatures for their salaries. By 1774 this effort to undermine provincial autonomy, added to grievances over western land policies, fear of favor to the Anglican Church, and ·discriminatory measures for the enforcement of commercial regulations, had pushed the Americans to the brink of rebellion.

Seventeenth-Century Crises

The original charter of the Virginia Company had conveyed to settlers the king's commitment that they would "enjoy all Liberties . . . as if they had been abiding . . . within . . . our Realm of England." In that spirit the company provided in 1618 that two "burgesses" elected freely by the inhabitants of each plantation (settlement) should act with the appointed governor and his council as a general assembly "to make and ordaine . . . lawes." The assembly began to do so in 1619. When James I nationalized the company in 1624, following revelations of appalling abuses, he discontinued the assembly. However, Charles I permitted it to function again from 1629 even though he did not allow Parliament itself to convene during the next eleven years.

Nathaniel Bacon's dramatic rebellion against Governor Sir William Berkeley illustrates the character of the political system as it operated later in the century. Berkeley was a reactionary, whose views stand starkly revealed in his famous observation: "I thank God, *there are no free schools* [in Virginia] *nor printing* . . . ; for *learning* has brought disobedience, and heresy, and sects into the world, and *printing* has divulged them. . . . God keep us from both!" In 1676, Berkeley, exercising his constitutional authority, had permitted no legislative election for fourteen years. Overproduction of tobacco had depressed prices and incomes. The government had reinstituted a poll tax, a fixed sum for each man, which compelled "the poorer sort . . . [to] pay as deeply to the publick as he that had 20,000 acres." To Nathaniel Bacon, a young, Cambridge-educated immigrant whose high status had gained him appointment to the Governor's Council, it appeared that "all power and sway is got into the hands of the rich, who . . . , having the common people in their debt, have always curbed and oppressed them." He saw little hope of improvement, as appeals had to be directed "to the very persons our complaints do accuse."

What sparked the rebellion, however, was Berkeley's refusal to authorize offensive action against the Indians. Buffeted by advancing settlers on the one hand and Iroquois incursions on the other, the local Indians had recently killed perhaps three hundred Virginia frontiersmen. Responding to clamor for an attack which would "spare none" of the natives, Bacon made himself "General by Consent of the People" and in defiance of Berkeley set out after Indians. A newly elected legislature, denounced by a Berkeleyite as consisting of men "lately crept out of the condition of servants," provided for increased popular participation in local government. Then Bacon contracted dysentery and died. Berkeley regained power even before the arrival of a relief expedition from England. He undid most of the reforms, executed a number of Bacon's followers, and confiscated their property. He would, a contemporary charged, have "hanged half the country" had Charles II not recalled him in 1677.

Far more important than Bacon's brief rebellion were the revolutions in three American provinces which accompanied the Glorious Revolution (see Chapter 1) in England. Both Charles II (1660–1685) and James II (1685–1688) hoped not only to increase royal power at home but also to consolidate a number of colonies into large administrative units, to be governed without a representative assembly by a Crown-appointed governor and council. Like their relatives in England, however, the American colonists were determined to resist such absolutist efforts. Preventing the forceful imposition of Catholicism was another goal as important to the king's American subjects as it was to those in England itself. Aware that France had offered to help restore Catholicism to Britain, many Americans feared that appointees of James II would collaborate with French authorities in Canada to impose Catholicism upon them. Consequently when the Glorious Revolution sent James II fleeing to France for support, frightened colonials in Massachusetts, New York, and Maryland overthrew their existing governments to assure not only representative government but also their Protestant faith.

Massachusetts had most to lose from the policies of James II. During the Puritan Civil War, Massachusetts had made itself virtually independent of British authority. According to Edward Randolph, a royal investigator, the people not only ignored commercial regulations but insisted that "legislative power . . . abides in them solely." Consequently, in 1684 Charles II revoked the Massachusetts charter, and in 1686 James II threw the colony along with the rest of New England into the Dominion of New England, a new administrative unit to which he later added New York and New Jersey. Sir Edmund Andros, appointed by James II as first Governor of the Dominion, was to rule with the aid of an appointed council but without an elected assembly. He had done so for three years when news of the Glorious Revolution inspired the populace to overthrow and arrest him. Under the new monarchs, William and Mary, Massachusetts in 1691 received a new charter. It provided for an elected assembly and allowed the assembly a role in selecting the Governor's Council. Royal appointment, however, replaced election of the governor. Property ownership replaced church membership as the major qualification for voting.

New York responded to the news of the Glorious Revolution by calling a popular convention which elected Jacob Leisler, a German-born militia captain, as commander in chief. Exaggerating the dangers both of subversion and of invasion, Leisler ruled rigorously until a governor appointed by William and Mary arrived. Leisler's insistence on seeing evidence that the new governor was the agent of William and Mary rather than of James II occasioned a delay in surrendering power which allowed his numerous enemies to "gratifye the malice of their party" by persuading the inebriate governor to rush him to the gallows for "treason." William and Mary did restore a legislature in New York, but provincial politics remained embittered for years by the conflict between Leislerians and their aristocratic opponents, who had always disdained Leisler and his followers as "men of meane birth sordid Education and desperate Fortunes."

Maryland, where a Catholic minority ruled a Protestant majority twenty times its size, was overdue for revolution. In fact, unsuccessful insurrections had occurred in 1659, 1676, and 1681. Protestants deeply resented what they referred to as the Catholic proprietor's "partiality . . . towards those of the Popish Religion." There were grievances on other points as well. Unfortunately for the proprietors in England, their messenger carrying the authorization to proclaim William and Mary King and Queen died en route. Without the authorization the proprietor's agents declined to make the proclamation and thus enhanced the credibility of rumors about Catholic plotting. John Coode, a Protestant agitator, led the forcible overthrow of the proprietary authorities and summoned a popular convention to institute a new government. The Calverts did not regain political control until 1715, after the conversion of Benedict Calvert to Anglicanism. The Church of England enjoyed government support in Maryland from 1702.

England's Glorious Revolution was of enormous importance for Americans as well as British history. In both America and England it barred imposition of Catholicism. It also established the principle that without consent of Parliament the king could not raise taxes, make or suspend laws, create new seats in the House of Commons, or refuse to call elections within a fixed time. To the Americans it appeared that these same principles should govern the relations between their Crown-appointed governors and the elected assemblies. In America such principles tended to strengthen not only the representative legislatures in dealing with appointed governors but also American (legislative) as opposed to British (gubernatorial) authority.

British Political Theory and Practice

Outstanding works of political theory in seventeenth-century England influenced thought on both sides of the Atlantic. Thomas Hobbes's *Leviathan* (1651) argued that the savage nature of man required him to surrender absolute and irrevocable power to his monarch in order to avoid chaos. Puritan John Milton in *Areopagitica* (1644) denounced censorship as "hindering . . . the discovery that might yet further be made, both in religious and civil wisdom." James Harrington's *Commonwealth of Oceana* (1656) argued that political power tends to follow wealth and that accordingly England should become a constitutional republic dominated by owners of large landed estates. Most radical of the major theorists was John Lilburne, leader of the Civil War Levelers. Lilburne asserted that "every man and woman . . . are equal and alike in . . . authority" and that none could exercise authority unless by "mutual consent." The most influential work was John Locke's second treatise *Of Civil Government* (1690), which argued in terms to be paraphrased in the Declaration of Independence that officials who try to exert "absolute power over the lives, liberties, and estates of the people . . . forfeit the power the people have put into their hands." In such circumstances, he believed, the people "have a right" to create a new government "such as they shall think fit" to provide for their own security and the protection of their property.

Popularized versions of some of the more radical of these theories, especially Locke's, received wide attention in the colonies beginning in the 1720s. Chief among the popularizers were John Trenchard and William Gordon, whose *Independent Whig* and *Cato's Letters* appeared in London between 1719 and 1723. Calling themselves "Real Whigs" and "Commonwealthmen" (after the Puritan victors in the Civil War), they helped to rally support for Whiggish principles which were resisted by Tory supporters of royal authority.

In practice, Britain's monarch continued to dominate imperial administration prior to the American Revolution despite the Glorious Revolution's restrictions upon his power. He commanded the armed forces, conducted diplomacy, and appointed not only all civil, military, and judicial officers but also the bishops who ruled the Anglican Church. In Parliament, as in the empire as a whole, there was still a general expectation, supported by Anglican doctrine, that people would normally accede to the wishes of the king. Opposition smacked of disloyalty. On the other hand, the beheading of Charles I and the expulsion of James II suggested strongly that the monarch had better exercise his powers with discretion.

Parliament's two houses, the House of Lords and the House of Commons, were by no means equal in strength. The hereditary nobles and the Anglican bishops who composed the House of Lords had lost even the power to amend money bills; they had to accept or reject those which the House of Commons passed. However, many of the great nobles who sat in the House of Lords received appointments as major ministers (administrative officers) of the Crown, and in that capacity they were among the political managers who controlled the House of Commons and ran the empire.

So great were the powers of the House of Commons that "management" or control of the House was the chief responsibility of the king's major ministers. Only the Commons could im-

Charleston, South Carolina, around 1760.

pose the new taxes required to meet rising expenditure needs, an especially critical function in wartime. The Commons had also gained the right to specify how tax funds should be expended. Thus, to get both the needed revenue and the authority to spend it, the king required majority support in the House of Commons.

Until the American Revolution, the king's ministers had always won him such support. The general custom of deference to the king's wishes explains this in part, but there were other factors of importance. While each county chose two members of Parliament under a rather wide suffrage, more than three-quarters of the members represented special borough constituencies. Boroughs were infinitely varied, but most were so constituted that great families of the nobility, those which normally provided the king's ministers, could control the elections, as indeed they did. Members of Parliament who desired royal appointments for themselves, for relatives, or for friends were also loath to offend the king by opposing his ministers. Lastly, both George I and George II chose particularly able managers who avoided crises and allowed great autonomy

not only to the colonies but also to the counties at home.

Two practical principles guided the king's ministers in ruling the empire. First was the imperialist view succinctly stated by one administrator, that "Every Act of Dependent Provincial Governments ought . . . to Terminate in the Advantage of the Mother State, unto whom it owes its being, and Protection." Second was the still more practical economic theory later to be called mercantilism. As enunciated by Thomas Mun in *England's Treasure by Forraign Trade* (1664), the theory affirmed that "The ordinary means . . . to encrease our wealth . . . is by forraign trade, where in wee must ever observe this rule; to sell more to strangers yearly than wee consume of theirs in value." Legally of course the American colonists were not "forraigners," but for economic purposes quite often they were. The king's ministers, advised by a Board of Trade which included representatives of the business community, designed imperial policies with these goals in mind. To enforce their policies they relied very largely on the colonial governors.

Colonial Government

Colonial governors administered three kinds of colonies: corporate, proprietary, and royal. In the corporate, or self-governing, colonies the

people elected their own governors, and their laws were not subject to "disallowance" by the King's Privy Council. After 1691 only Connecticut and Rhode Island enjoyed government in this pattern. Proprietary families appointed governors in Maryland after 1715, and in Pennsylvania and Delaware; but by 1752 what would now be called nationalization had transformed all the others—each of them private ventures at the outset—into royal provinces.

Royal commissions which appointed governors and "instructions" issued in the king's name theoretically fixed the constitutional systems of the eight royal provinces. In each case the rules required the governor to summon an "assembly of freeholders," meaning landowners, which alone could impose taxes. The governor, however, was to hold and to spend the revenue raised. The governor not only could summon the assembly when he chose, but also could adjourn it to a specified time, postpone it for an indefinite period, or dissolve it and call a new election at his pleasure. In addition, he possessed an absolute veto, one which could not be overridden. His instructions required him to use it against all measures which conflicted with the laws of England, impaired the royal prerogative, restricted the sale of slaves or the dumping of convicts, or aided the growth of manufacturing. In addition, governors were required to veto measures in several categories if they failed to include a "suspending clause" making them effective only after approval by the king's Privy Council. Finally, the royal governor had to send all new colonial laws to England for possible disallowance by the Privy Council.

Still other powers of the governor were important. He commanded the colonial militia, granted lands, appointed and dismissed judges, sheriffs, and justices of the peace. Theoretically he could appoint to vacant parishes ministers licensed by the Bishop of London.

On paper the powers of the royal governors seemed more than adequate to enforce imperial policy; in practice the elected assemblies made it increasingly difficult. Governors found it harder and harder to manage their assemblies as effectively as the king's ministers managed the House of Commons. Governors lacked the prestige of royal birth and usually even that of noble status. They were also ordinarily outsiders and as such subject to colonial resentment. The people whom they sought to govern included a high proportion of militant dissenters not imbued with the Anglican doctrine of nonresistance. Protestant dissenters tended instead to believe that political authority should be representative, as it was in their churches, rather than appointive. Certainly more free adult males could qualify to vote in the colonies than in England, probably at least 50 to 75 percent, although the proportion actually voting was usually rather low. Colonial assemblies, furthermore, consisted largely if not entirely of county representatives, and thus were not dominated by members from special constituencies controlled by great families, as was the case in England.

Aided by such factors, colonial assemblies became more and more assertive. New York's relatively new Assembly in 1711, for example, demanded that the appointed Council, which was the upper house of the legislature, must accept or reject the Assembly's money bills without amendment, putting the Council in a position analogous to that of the House of Lords in England. When the Council pointed out that the governor's commission placed no such restriction upon its powers, the Assembly retorted that it had "the inherent Right . . . to dispose of the Money, of the Freemen of the Colony" because it was based upon the "free Choice and Election of the People; who ought not to be divested of their Property (nor justly can) without their Consent." The Assembly prevailed— as, sooner or later, did those of the other provinces when they chose to press the point.

Their exclusive right to initiate tax measures was the basic weapon with which the assemblies won more powers. Britain expected the governors to persuade their assemblies to authorize collection of certain taxes for a number of years, if not in perpetuity, and to allow the governor to hold the money, spend it, and secure an audit. In practice, however, the assemblies often limited the duration of their tax measures to only one year, thus assuring frequent legislative sessions and a strong bargaining position. Taking advantage of the governors' revenue needs, especially in wartime, the assemblies in time took control of the power to authorize expenditures and to make the audit, as had the House of Commons in England. Unlike the House of Commons, however, the American assemblies, rather than leave tax funds in the custody of the executive, had also by 1760 taken physical possession of the revenues raised.

Making the colonial treasurer an agent of the assembly rather than a subordinate of the governor was only one of several ways in which the assemblies surpassed the House of Commons in gaining control of administration. They sometimes named commissioners to administer public works projects, named militia officers, and instructed agents or lobbyists employed to look after the colony's interests in London. At times they also used their control over the salaries of provincial officers to influence decisions, although by 1760 many such officials were deriving their income from official fees or from the British Treasury.

Assembly spokesmen always denied any intention to "wrest the Government . . . out of his Majesty's hands," but administrative officers of the Crown thought otherwise. "If they shall be allowed to go on without some remedy to put a stop to them," one official observed in 1727, "a resolve of the House of Representatives [assembly] will in time be look't on as of more force than his Majesty's positive Command, or even perhaps of an Act of Parliament if it be not accompanied with sufficient force to put it in Execution."

Two courses of action were open to the British to combat the assertiveness of the assemblies. One, urged by a governor in 1713, was that Parliament "settle" a revenue, meaning impose a tax upon the province, so that the governors thereafter would not need to depend upon the assembly for revenue. The Board of Trade endorsed the recommendation, but Parliament, respecting tradition, declined to honor it.

Rumors of another approach reached the colonies in 1745. According to a veteran legislator, "A bill is prepared to be brought in this parlement . . . Commanding all Governors Councel Assemblys . . . to . . . adhere to all . . . Instructions . . . as they shall git transmited . . . from the King and his privee Councel." "If such Act Doe pas in a Law," he continued, it "stricks Emediately at the Liberty, of the Subject and Establish arbetrary pour [power] . . . in America." He concluded correctly, however, that Parliament would probably "not Doe things so rash; for in the preparing Slavery to us would give a presedent and hand it against themselves." By choosing neither to tax the provincials, so that governors would no longer be dependent upon their assemblies, nor to order compliance with royal instructions, Parliament allowed the assemblies to go on increasing their authority. Each successful encroachment brought a greater degree of independence from British control.

Executive control of the judiciary remained much greater in the colonies than it was in Britain. The assemblies were successful in taking from the governors the power to create courts, but the more important power of removing judges from office remained with the governors to be exercised at their discretion. British judges had gained permanent, or "good behavior," tenure at the beginning of the eighteenth century, thus ending the threat of executive interference.

Freedom to criticize the government, in the colonies as in Britain, meant only the absence of prior restraint and did not preclude subsequent punishment if the words employed did, in the opinion of the judge, foster "an ill opinion of the government." The famous case of John Peter Zenger in 1736 made clear that American juries would not enforce that law to stop criticism of unpopular British officials.

Zenger was a New York newspaper publisher who printed caustic criticisms of Governor William Cosby, written by former Chief Justice Lewis Morris. Cosby was a generally unpopular governor who had removed Morris from office for rendering a decision which reduced the Governor's income. Under English law the function of the jury in Zenger's case was merely to determine whether or not Zenger had published the material in question. Zenger's lawyers, James Alexander and Andrew Hamilton, persuaded the jury, however, that making *truthful* accusations against an oppressive government was a right essential to protecting liberty and property. Accepting this argument, the jury acquitted Zenger. Thus it appeared that Americans would not punish those who criticized unpopular officials, but, as Alexander himself affirmed, "to infuse into the minds of the people an ill opinion of a just administration, is a crime that deserves no mercy." Provincial assemblies continued to see themselves as "just" and construed "parliamentary privilege" so as to allow them to punish their own critics.

Local government in the colonies generally followed English patterns. In rural areas outside New England, counties were the administrative units. Appointed sheriffs were the chief law-enforcement officers, but justices of the peace, also appointed, were still more important. Together the justices could impose taxes as well as make expenditures and pass laws. In their administrative capacity they supervised local officers such as overseers of the poor. As judges they enforced both civil and criminal law. Governors nominally appointed sheriffs and justices of the peace, but in doing so they followed the recommendations of the local elite, as presented by one or both of the county's representatives in the assembly.

Towns rather than counties were the important units of local government in New England. Annual town meetings, representing nearly all the men of the community, chose the town's officers and passed local laws. The town was also the unit represented in the legislature, although with a more restricted suffrage.

Metropolitan centers enjoyed only those powers which the provincial government saw fit to bestow upon them. "New York City's" charter of 1731 provided for an elected council. However, the mayor and other officers were to be appointed by the governor. Philadelphia's charter gave the city so few privileges that its citizens created a host of voluntary organizations to meet the city's needs. Boston retained its "town meeting" government rather than seek such a charter.

Contest for a Continent

While the colonial assemblies bickered endlessly with their governors, France and Britain contested for control of North America. The War of the League of Augsburg (1689–1697), growing out of the Glorious Revolution, began the contest. Seaborne New Englanders captured Port Royal in Nova Scotia, but failed to take Quebec. The peace terms of 1697 restored Port Royal to France.

Five years later the rivals were at it again in the War of the Spanish Succession (1702–1713). Britain's major objective was to prevent the union of France and Spain, which became a threat when an heir to the throne of France became ruler of Spain. New Englanders again seized Port Royal and once more failed to take Quebec. South Carolinians plundered Spanish colonial commerce and destroyed several Gulf Coast missions, but failed to capture the fort at St. Augustine, Florida. In Europe the victories of the Duke of Marlborough enabled the British to achieve their basic war aim and to gain firm title to Nova Scotia (also called Acadia), Newfoundland, and Hudson Bay. From Spain, Britain gained the asiento, the privilege of selling a fixed number of slaves in the Spanish colonies yearly, plus the right to send one merchant ship to trade there each year.

During the generation of peace which followed 1713, France prepared assiduously for the

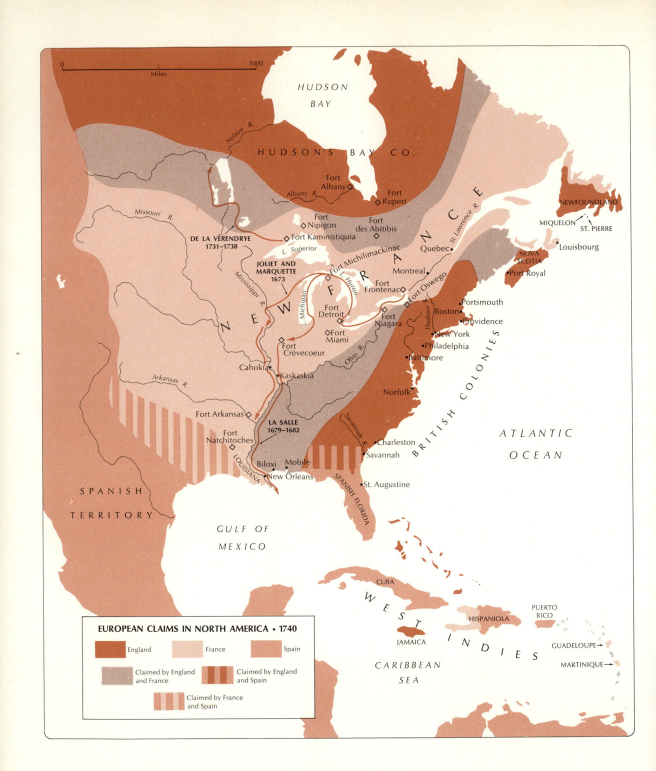

0   1000
Miles

HUDSON'S BAY CO.

Nelson R.

Albany R.

Fort
Albany

Fort
Rupert

Fort
Nipigon

Fort
des Abitibis

NEWFOUNDLAND

MIQUELON
ST. PIERRE

Fort Kaministiquia

Missouri R.

DE LA VÉRENDRYE
1731–1738

L. Superior

Fort Michilimackinac

St. Lawrence R.

Quebec

Louisbourg

NOVA
SCOTIA

Port Royal

JOLIET AND
MARQUETTE
1673

Mississippi R.

N   E   W

L. Michigan

L. Huron

Montreal

Fort
Frontenac

Fort Oswego

Portsmouth

Boston

Hudson R.

Fort
Detroit

F   R   A   N   C   E

Fort
Niagara

Providence
New York

Fort
Miami

Fort
Crèvecoeur

Ohio R.

Philadelphia

Baltimore

Arkansas R.

Cahokia

Kaskaskia

Norfolk

B   R   I   T   I   S   H   C   O   L   O   N   I   E   S

ATLANTIC

OCEAN

Fort Arkansas

LA SALLE
1679–1682

Savannah R.

Charleston

Fort
Natchitoches

LOUISIANA

Biloxi   Mobile

New Orleans

Savannah

SPANISH FLORIDA

St. Augustine

SPANISH

TERRITORY

GULF   OF

MEXICO

CUBA

W   E   S   T

PUERTO
RICO

HISPANIOLA

GUADELOUPE

JAMAICA

I   N   D   I   E   S

MARTINIQUE

CARIBBEAN

SEA

EUROPEAN CLAIMS IN NORTH AMERICA · 1740

England   France   Spain

Claimed by England   Claimed by England
and France   and Spain

Claimed by France
and Spain

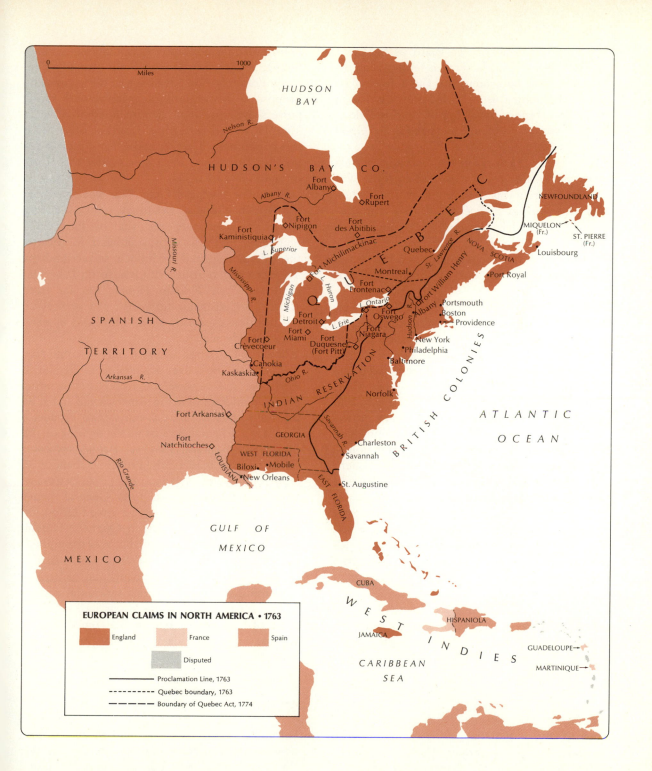

EUROPEAN CLAIMS IN NORTH AMERICA · 1763

England
France
Spain
Disputed
—— Proclamation Line, 1763
----- Quebec boundary, 1763
– – – Boundary of Quebec Act, 1774

HUDSON BAY

Nelson R.

HUDSON'S BAY CO.

Albany R.

Fort Albany
Fort Rupert
Fort Nipigon
Fort des Abitibis
Fort Kaministiquia
L. Superior
Fort Michilimackinac
Quebec
NEWFOUNDLAND
MIQUELON (Fr.)
ST. PIERRE (Fr.)
Louisbourg

Missouri R.

Mississippi R.

QUEBEC

NOVA SCOTIA

Montreal
St. Lawrence R.
Port Royal

SPANISH

L. Michigan
L. Huron
Fort Frontenac
Fort Ontario
Fort Oswego
Fort William Henry
Portsmouth
Boston
Providence

TERRITORY

Fort Detroit
L. Erie
Fort Niagara
Hudson R.
Albany
New York

Fort Miami
Fort Crevecoeur
Fort Duquesne (Fort Pitt)
Philadelphia
Baltimore

Cahokia
Kaskaskia
Ohio R.

Arkansas R.

INDIAN RESERVATION

Norfolk

BRITISH COLONIES

ATLANTIC OCEAN

Fort Arkansas

GEORGIA

Savannah R.

Fort Natchitoches

WEST FLORIDA

Charleston

Savannah

LOUISIANA

Biloxi
Mobile
New Orleans

EAST FLORIDA

St. Augustine

Rio Grande

GULF OF MEXICO

MEXICO

CUBA

WEST INDIES

HISPANIOLA

JAMAICA

GUADELOUPE

CARIBBEAN SEA

MARTINIQUE

0   1000
Miles

BRITISH VERSUS AMERICAN AUTHORITY

[75]

next round in America. To guard its St. Lawrence lifeline to Canada, France built an imposing fortress at Louisbourg on Cape Breton Island. That country also founded New Orleans in 1718 and extended its string of outposts along the Mississippi and Ohio Rivers and in the Great Lakes region.

War began again in 1739, initially against Spain, but in the 1740s it evolved into the War of the Austrian Succession, in which Britain sought to prevent France and Prussia from dismembering Austria. Intrepid New Englanders seized Louisbourg, but in Europe the fighting was indecisive. Consequently the peace terms of 1748 restored all conquests, including Louisbourg.

Six years later the great imperial contest culminated in the Great War for the Empire (also called the Seven Years' War and the French and Indian War). In 1753 France had begun to construct a line of forts southward from Lake Erie across western Pennsylvania. Virginia's Governor Robert Dinwiddie first sent a youthful surveyor, George Washington, to warn off the French from territory claimed by his colony, and when that failed, Dinwiddie sent Washington to beat the French to the strategic site of modern Pittsburgh. Washington surprised and defeated a small French contingent near what is now Uniontown, Pennsylvania, but surrendered soon after to a superior French force. However ingloriously, he had begun a major world war, upon which the fate of the continent depended and from which would arise one of history's most significant revolutions.

Meanwhile in the Albany Conference (1754) representatives of several colonies sought to allay the concern of the Iroquois over French military preparations. Thirty wagonloads of gifts boosted Iroquois morale somewhat, but the conference achieved little else. Pennsylvania's Benjamin Franklin took advantage of the occasion to propose an intercolonial legislature with taxing powers and a president general appointed by the king. However, authorities from the other provinces, denounced by Franklin for "their weak noodles," declined even to consider this "plan of union."

For three years the Great War went badly for the British. General Braddock, sent over from Britain to recapture the site of Pittsburgh, blundered into a disastrous ambush. Montcalm, the brilliant leader of the French, seized the New York frontier outposts of Oswego on Lake Ontario and Fort William Henry, not far from Albany. Indian raids terrorized the settlers on the frontier, especially those who lived in western Pennsylvania.

William Pitt, confident that only he could save the empire, took over leadership in Britain in 1757. He did reverse the tide. Concentrating Britain's military effort in America and India, he provided chiefly financial support to Frederick the Great of Prussia to sustain the fighting on the European continent. In 1758, British successes on the frontier induced the French to abandon all their forts in Pennsylvania; the great fortress of Louisbourg also fell. In 1759 General James Wolfe, still in his early thirties, forced Montcalm to accept a crucial contest at Quebec. Though both generals died, the British forces triumphed. By the end of 1760, New France was in British hands. The terms of peace concluded at Paris in 1763 transferred all France's continental American possessions east of the Mississippi as well as much of India to the British. To compensate its ally for losing Florida to Britain, France gave Spain Louisiana.

Wartime Aggravations

How to restore the American provinces to what was presumed to be proper "dependence" had begun to concern the Board of Trade even before the Great War began. Instructions to a new governor of New York in 1753 charged that "in open violation of our said commission and instructions," the Assembly had taken over "the disposal of public money, the nomination of all officers of government, the direction of the militia . . . which by our said commission and instructions we have thought fit to reserve to our governor only." Accordingly the King required the Governor to inform the Assembly of "our high displeasure" and to "enjoin them for the future to pay to our said commission and instructions due obedience." Specifically the King wanted the Governor to secure, "without limitation" by the Assembly on how he might spend it, a "permanent revenue" adequate to meet normal expenditures of the province. Soon after his arrival, however, the Governor committed suicide, and the Assembly, even while expressing its "Abhorrence of . . . groundless Imputations of Disloyalty," continued to make annual rather than permanent provision for the support of the government.

During the war Britain had seen fit to avoid contention with the colonies, not only over such matters as obedience to royal instructions but also over contributions to the war's cost. Rather than antagonize the assemblies by heavy financial demands, Pitt arranged for the British government to feed and arm the provincial forces, and he promised compensation to the provinces even for such costs as clothing and pay for their own military forces. The policy preserved harmony and aided the buildup of the empire's forces, but it also helped to saddle the British taxpayers with a gigantic debt while Americans remained relatively debt-free.

Trade with the enemy, on the other hand, offended Pitt's sense of patriotism. At the expense of much colonial ill will, he tried mightily to suppress trade-as-usual between the American continental colonies and the French West Indian sugar islands. Such trade was important to the Americans both to provide a market for their produce and to secure cheap molasses (see Chapter 2) and sugar. Consequently they connived to continue it through such means as fraudulent flag-of-truce vessels purportedly exchanging prisoners. When Pitt used naval patrols

to stop the traffic, a typical merchant wrote "Dam them all," for he found his "Sugar Trad is Entirely Ruined."

Boston's famous quarrel with "writs of assistance" had its inception in the same situation. General writs of assistance, good for the period of a king's reign, were virtual hunting licenses authorizing customs officers to enter any premises during daylight in search of evidence of illegal importation. When the death of George II in 1760 necessitated the issuance of new writs, Boston merchants retained James Otis, an attorney who had been disappointed in his desire for major appointive office, to challenge their legality. Although Otis lost his case against what he called "instruments of slavery" unauthorized by Parliament, his argument proved very popular with Boston's radicals.

Anglican zeal in the course of the war also dismayed American Dissenters. The chief source of their concern was a new Archbishop of Canterbury, Thomas Secker. Secker raised "a great clamor" among Congregationalists by establishing a missionary post at Harvard's doorstep and impeding their missionary work among the Indians. He tried to get a bishop appointed for the colonies, but the King's ministers chose not to stir up that particular hornet's nest.

British efforts to reestablish the binding character of royal instructions, which they had temporarily abandoned at the beginning of the war, reappeared as early as 1759. A high official had informed him, wrote Benjamin Franklin from London in that year, that the government would attempt to secure what Franklin called "absolute Subjection to . . . Instructions." "The King in Council," Franklin quoted his informant as saying, "is *the Legislator* of the Colonies, his Majesty's Instructions . . . are the *Law of the Land.*"

Virginia's Two-Penny Act of 1758 afforded an opportunity to test the new policy. To alleviate the hardship following a drought which had cut tobacco production and tripled its price, the Legislature provided in the Two-Penny Act that during the next year all obligations fixed in tobacco could be paid at the rate of 2 pence per pound of tobacco, roughly the previous price, rather than at the much higher current price or in tobacco itself. Thus, in effect, the Two-Penny Act repealed an earlier law requiring Anglican parsons to be paid a fixed amount of tobacco to be secured by taxation in each community. The Governor's instructions required him to veto repeal measures lacking a "suspending clause" which made them effective only after approval by the Privy Council. To serve its purpose, however, the Two-Penny Act had to take effect at once, not a year or so later when the dilatory Privy Council might get around to considering it. Accordingly, the Governor ignored his instructions and approved the Two-Penny law despite the omission of a suspending clause. A year later, after the law had served its purpose, the Privy Council disallowed it, censured the Governor for approving it, and threatened to recall him if he did not observe his instructions "punctually" thereafter. There the affair might have ended with no great animosity, had it not been for a few avaricious parsons.

Seeking to triple their income for 1758, several parsons brought suit alleging that, because it conflicted with the King's instructions, the Two-Penny Act was void from the outset rather than only from the time of disallowance. Had the courts upheld this argument, royal instructions would henceforth have bound Virginians tightly. However, the Privy Council, doubling as the empire's top appellate court, declined to hear an appeal from a decision adverse to the parson by a Virginia court. Only in one instance did a parson win his case in a local court. In that case, a hitherto obscure young lawyer named Patrick Henry exclaimed that a king who voided acts beneficial to the people "degenerated into a Tyrant, and forfeits all right to his subjects' obedience." Moved by Henry's oratory the jury awarded the parson not the £288 which he had sought but only 1 penny. In a pamphlet war on the subject, legislative leader Richard Bland argued that to accept "royal Instructions" as law to be obeyed "without Reserve" would "strip us of all the rights . . . of British Subjects, and . . . put us under . . . despotic Power."

George III, acceding to the throne in 1760, found the idea of a tough new imperial policy to his liking. Obstinate and unimaginative, the young monarch, aged twenty-two, was also deeply conscientious and determined to make more of his constitutional powers than had his immediate predecessors, George I and George II. He ousted the popular William Pitt and altered his policies; he hounded John Wilkes into exile to silence his radical criticism. To manage the empire's affairs he relied often upon his own favorites, sometimes men of limited ability and brief political experience. He himself became chief among the nation's "borough-mongering" politicians. Although he acted within the unwritten British Constitution as most of his subjects then conceived it, his determination to reduce the colonies to "absolute obedience," says British historian J. H. Plumb, "made his presence on the throne . . . a national disaster."

Regulation of Settlement and Trade

Always resentful of intruding settlers, the Indians were not so ready as their French allies to surrender the Ohio Valley to the British. Goaded by Britain's commander Jeffrey Amherst, who discontinued gifts to the Indians as unworthy "purchasing [of] good behavior," the Ottawa chieftain Pontiac began his famed rebellion in 1763. Despite Amherst's contemptuous conviction that no fort commanded by a British officer could be endangered by "such a wretched enemy," Pontiac's Indians captured one after another until only Forts Pitt (Pittsburgh), Detroit, and Niagara remained. Indian enthusiasm soon waned, however. By the end of 1765 negotiations which committed the British to resume gift giving had restored peace.

Even before learning of Pontiac's rebellion, British authorities in London had determined to station an army of some eight thousand men in the American West. Why they wished to do so remains uncertain. Ostensibly the object was to protect the settlers from the Indians, and vice versa. Historians have thought it odd, however, that this force was vastly greater than that deemed necessary before the war to protect the colonists against both the Indians and the French. Another object of the move, in the words of a British official, was "to retain the Inhabitants of Our ancient Province in a State of Constitutional Dependence," suggesting that Britain wanted the troops available for use in enforcing British policies to which Americans objected. Whatever the rationale for the action, the British subsequently cited the protective function of the troops as one justification for imposing unprecedented Parliamentary taxation upon the colonies.

Slowing the advance of Western settlement, whether or not the troops were there to help achieve it, was an important objective of the British. The usual haphazard migration into Indian country in violation of agreements, rather than after careful negotiation of new treaties, was sure to bring warfare with its heavy costs and disruption of the Indian trade. Furthermore British mercantilists were eager, as they saw it, to keep the settlers "within the reach of the . . . commerce of this kingdom." Those who settled beyond the Appalachians, the British believed, would be forced by transportation expenses to "ingage in the . . . manufacture of those articles . . . which they ought to take from the mother country."

To achieve the desired restriction of Western settlement, Britain issued the famous Proclamation of 1763. Enlarging upon a wartime policy of 1761, the proclamation banned settlement and land grants beyond the crest of the Appalachians for an indefinite time and ordered those already settled in that area "forthwith to remove themselves." However, the British were never able to enforce the proclamation as effectively as

Pontiac had in the summer before it appeared. Between 1768 and 1770 the empire's Indian agents, Sir William Johnson in the north and John Stuart in the south, negotiated agreements allowing the extension of settlement farther into Indian country.

Restrictions of colonial economic activity following the war evoked resentment and resistance just as they had during the war. After only a brief respite, the British navy resumed its antismuggling patrol of colonial ports. Customs officers, apparently pressed to produce revenue to help meet Britain's postwar debt crisis, announced in 1764 that they would no longer accept bribes (usually a penny or less per gallon) on the importation of foreign molasses, but would collect the steep legal duty of 6 pence per gallon. Vehement protests led Parliament in 1764 to reduce the tax to 3 pence. Two years later Lord Rockingham's ministry lowered it to just 1 penny but applied it to imports from British as well as foreign islands. Molasses traders and distillers thereafter had little economic basis for complaint.

Regulations contained in the Sugar Act of 1764 also stirred resentment among American merchants. The law (also called the American Act and the Revenue Act of 1764) banned export to any European port outside Great Britain of iron, lumber, hides and skins, whale fins, potash, and pearl ash—all significant items in the colonial export trade. The effect of the law, as with the enumeration of tobacco and other products much earlier, was to assure that British, rather than American, merchants would profit from any sale of those commodities to Europeans. To tighten enforcement procedures, the Sugar Act required the accused to prove full compliance with the detailed provisions of the law. It also immunized the accuser from assessment of either damages or court costs if the accused were found innocent. Added to the traditional rule that customs officers receive a third of the proceeds from the sale of ships and cargoes confiscated for smuggling, these provisions provided strong incentive to make arrests.

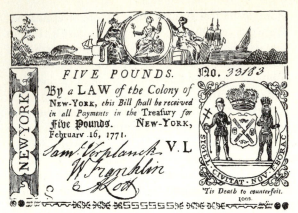

A New York five-pound note, issued in 1771. The small print under the seal at lower right says "'Tis death to counterfeit."

Culver Pictures, Inc.

Despite this obvious encouragement to indiscriminate prosecution, these provisions proved ineffective. Intimidation, bribery, and anti-British juries seem to have diminished the enthusiasm of customs officers for prosecution. In New England between 1765 and 1767 there were only six seizures and one conviction.

Controversy over enforcement of commercial regulations became more intense after 1767 when "Champagne Charlie" Townshend, then Britain's chief financial officer, instituted drastic reforms. Townshend's program included Parliamentary authorization for the hated writs of assistance, juryless vice-admiralty courts with jurisdiction over cases involving alleged evasion of customs duties, and creation of an American Board of Customs Commissioners at Boston.

Still so underpaid that "without bribery and corruption, they must starve," agents of the new customs board sought both income and official favor by seizing the sloop *Liberty* belonging to John Hancock, a wealthy Boston merchant who was a leader of the opposition to British policy. At Hancock's trial in a vice-admiralty court, his attorney, John Adams, pointed out that in Britain Hancock would have been entitled to a trial by jury. "Is there not in this . . . ," Adams demanded, "a Brand of Infamy, of Degradation, and Disgrace, fixed upon every American? Is he not degraded below the rank of Englishman?" The customs men were less zealous thereafter, but in 1770 the unwelcome troops whom they had requested for their protection fired on a Boston mob, killing a free Negro, Crispus Attucks, and four others in "the Boston Massacre."

British regulation of paper money also stirred resentment. Virginia, a latecomer to such experimentation, made unsound issues during the war with the result that British creditors complained of being paid in depreciated money. Instead of regulating the issuance of paper money so that its value would remain constant, a misguided Parliament required in the Currency Act of 1764 that the colonies retire all outstanding issues of legal tender paper money and make no more. The effect was to reduce the supply of money and further aggravate a postwar recession. Even more annoying to many Americans was Britain's insistence that their laws for the issuance of paper money which was not legal tender must include a suspending clause, making them effective only after approval by the Privy Council.

Taxation

Resentful as Americans were over royal instructions and regulatory measures, taxation was the issue which brought their relations with Britain to a crisis. At the conclusion of the war Britain faced a national debt which was double its prewar size. Riotous resistance greeted its new domestic taxes. In the colonies, by contrast, the provincial governments had relatively insignificant debts and the tax burdens imposed were very modest. Nearly everyone in Parliament except William Pitt assumed that Parliament had every right to tax the colonists for revenue as it did many of the

King's domestic subjects who had no representation in its chamber. They also assumed that it would be fair to do so.

Most Americans thought otherwise. They naturally wanted to avoid increased taxes, and many of them shared the fear of the ringleader of Boston's radicals, Sam Adams, that a body in which Americans had no representation might be tempted to impose "new taxations upon us" without limit. Most agreed as well with the Virginia Legislature that "it is essential to British Liberty that Laws imposing taxes on the People ought not to be made without the Consent of Representatives chosen by themselves." To colonial legislators generally it was crystal clear that their powers derived from their exclusive right to initiate revenue measures upon which the British governors depended to sustain necessary programs. Few felt any disposition to allow Parliament to deprive them of the basis of their power. Many agreed with William Pitt that submission to imperial trade regulations was "the price that America pays . . . for her protection." That price, estimated at £2 million yearly in 1766, seemed to many to justify economically the colonies' continued exemption from Parliamentary taxation for revenue.

Nevertheless, Parliament's Sugar Act of 1764, in addition to its regulatory and enforcement provisions, imposed colonial import taxes designed to raise revenue "for defraying the expenses of defending, protecting, and securing" the colonies. Molasses, sugar, textiles, and wines were among the items taxed. All the colonies protested. Consumption of the taxed items declined; smuggling increased. The trickle of revenue, roughly £20,000 yearly, made little impression on Britain's national debt of £130 million.

To supplement the meager revenue of the Sugar Act, the King's chief financial officer, George Grenville, determined to impose a stamp tax. Such taxes, long employed in Britain, legally required that stamps purchased from the government be fixed on various items offered for sale. Grenville's plan was to tax newspapers, legal documents, and several other items. Colonial agents whom he consulted offered mild objections, but Parliament nonetheless enacted the law in 1765 by a large majority. To appease the Americans, the law provided that its revenue, expected to run about £100,000 yearly, would be "appropriated to the Defense of the Colonies and . . . never be drawn out of them" to England.

Much to the surprise even of colonial officials, resistance to the Stamp Act vastly exceeded that evoked by the Sugar Act of 1764. In all the provinces mobs intimidated officials who showed any disposition to enforce the law. Lieutenant Governor Thomas Hutchinson of Massachusetts, who privately disapproved of the law, saw his splendid mansion go up in smoke. His more fortunate counterpart in New York, Cadwallader Colden, lost only his coach, burned with his effigy on top. Merchants organized an effective nonimportation movement against Britain. Delegates from nine provinces met in a Stamp Act Congress which declared that because Americans were not and could not conveniently be represented in Parliament, "no Taxes ever have been, or can be Constitutionally imposed on them, but by their respective Legislature[s]."

Pressed by British merchants whom the nonimportation movement was hurting, Parliament in 1766 repealed the Stamp Act without having carried it into effect in any of the continental colonies. Over the objections of William Pitt, who had endorsed the American position, Parliament enacted at the same time a Declaratory Act affirming its "full power . . . to bind the colonies . . . in all cases whatsoever."

Repeal of the Stamp Act assuaged Americans, but Britain's tax troubles brought renewed contention in 1767. Nearly desperate for revenue, a new ministry headed by Charles Townshend persuaded Parliament to impose taxes on lead, glass, paint, and tea imported into America. Such "external," or import, duties, Townshend believed, would be less offensive to Americans than "internal," or excise, taxes such as the Stamp Act. Unlike Grenville, Townshend intended to use the revenue for "support of the civil government" in the colonies in order to reduce the dependence of the governors upon the assemblies.

Accompanied by the authorization of writs of assistance and the creation of the American Board of Customs Commissioners mentioned on p. 80, the Townshend Duties of 1767 again provoked organized resistance. In a "Circular Letter," Massachusetts legislators urged that all the colonies "harmonize with each other" in opposing such taxes. They also defied a demand from London to rescind the letter. When Virginia's governor dissolved the Legislature, its members met informally to institute another nonimportation movement. In New York mobs clashed twice with British troops as Parliament suspended the Legislature for refusing to provide for the troops in accordance with the directive it had received from Parliament.

Again Britain ended the crisis by concessions. The meager revenue from the Townshend Duties was not worth the trouble and the economic damage of another nonimportation agreement. Consequently, on March 5, 1770, the day of the Boston Massacre, Parliament repealed all the Townshend Duties except the tax on tea. The tea tax remained, at the insistence of Lord North, the head of still another British ministry, to uphold the "supremacy of Parliament." American patriots continued their boycott of British tea and increased their smuggling of tea from Holland.

A Tempest over Tea

Despite the bitter quarrels with Britain during the 1760s, the task of uniting Americans of different classes, cultures, and provinces was monumental. To an English traveler at the end of the preceding decade, it had seemed that differences "of character, of manners, of religion, of [economic] interest" were so great among Americans that "were they left to themselves, there would soon be a civil war from one end of the continent to the other; while the Indians and Negroes would, with better reason, impatiently watch the opportunity to exterminate them altogether." In 1771, several North Carolinians lost their lives in a battle pitting forces of the governor against backcountry "Regulators," vigilantes whose major grievance was the exploitative corruption of local officials appointed by the Governor. In South Carolina the absence of local law-enforcement agencies in the backcountry forced vigilante groups to take up arms against organized bandits. Pennsylvania frontiersmen beset by Indians demanded a militant policy which was resisted by the Quaker majority, while bitter factionalism split the legislative leaders. Tenant farmers in New York's Hudson Valley rose up against their landlords during the Stamp Act crisis. Violence occurred also in several border quarrels. That such a disparate and contentious people did in the 1770s achieve a measure of unity was in large measure the consequence of Lord North's policies on tea.

All was not quiet for the British before Lord North's tea policy of 1773 ended the lull which followed the repeal of the other Townshend Duties in 1770. South Carolina outraged the King's ministers by appropriating money to help pay the considerable debts of John Wilkes, the most virulent of the King's domestic critics. By special instruction, Britain tried to restore the governor's lost control over expenditures, but Assembly resistance brought instead a total cessation of legislation in 1771. When Crown officers in Massachusetts announced in 1772 that they would thereafter receive their pay from the British rather than from the provincial treasury, Boston's town meeting under the leadership of Sam Adams created a Committee of Correspondence to publicize complaints against Britain. In Rhode Island a mob led by a prominent merchant burned the British custom ship *Gaspee* after it ran aground. When the British sent a commission to investigate, Virginians took offense at the intervention in local law enforcement and urged that committees of correspondence link all the colonies together in resistance.

Thus it was a still-simmering controversy which Lord North brought to a boil in 1773. One of his aims was to aid the East India Company, still the empire's agent in India. Its principal source of income was the sale of tea, which bore an import tax of 12 pence a pound on importation into Britain. Because of that high tax many Englishmen drank smuggled Dutch tea or else did without, just as the Americans were doing because of Parliament's refusal to end the Townshend tax of 3 pence a pound on tea imported into the colonies. Lord North's Tea Act of 1773 provided that, for all tea reexported from Britain to the colonies, the company would receive a refund of the 12-penny British import tax. The law reduced the price of British tea in the colonies so that, despite the Townshend Duty tax, the East India Company agents could still undersell smuggled Dutch tea. Lord North intended thus to help the company sell surplus tea at a profit and, in effect, to bribe the Americans to end their boycott and thus accept the principle of Parliamentary taxation. Had he been willing to forego the second point, he could have achieved the first and maintained the same revenue pattern by ending the Townshend tax and making the refund on the British tax only 9 instead of 12 pence.

American resistance to Lord North's cheap tea was surprisingly uniform. New York and Philadelphia sent it back. Charleston locked it in a warehouse. The resistance resulted not only from the Townshend Duty tax but also from favoritism in the selection of agents to monopolize sale of the bargain tea. In Boston the consignees included two sons of Loyalist Thomas Hutchinson, who had by then become governor.

What would happen to Boston's tea depended on the outcome of a battle of wits and will between Hutchinson and the radical forces led

To the Public.

THE long expected TEA SHIP arrived laſt night at Sandy-Hook, but the pilot would not bring up the Captain till the ſenſe of the city was known. The committee were immediately informed of her arrival, and that the Captain ſolicits for liberty to come up to provide neceſſaries for his return. The ſhip to remain at Sandy-Hook. The committee conceiving it to be the ſenſe of the city that he ſhould have ſuch liberty, ſignified it to the Gentleman who is to ſupply him with proviſions, and other neceſſaries. Advice of this was immediately diſpatched to the Captain; and whenever he comes up, care will be taken that he does not enter at the cuſtom-houſe, and that no time be loſt in diſpatching him.

New-York, April 19, 1774.

Notice of arrival of a tea ship in New York, 1774. It announces that the ship's captain will be allowed to "come up" (come ashore) to obtain "provisions and other necessaries" for his return voyage, but that he will not be allowed to "enter at the customhouse" (because to do so would obligate him to pay the British tax on his tea cargo).

Grace Swayne

by Sam Adams. To forestall the patriot mob, Hutchinson had customs men board the tea ship before it reached dockside. They officially "entered" the ship and fixed the obligation to pay the tax. Hutchinson then allowed the ship to dock and to be seized by the patriot mob who demanded that the ship be returned to England. Backed by British warships, Hutchinson refused to allow it to leave. On December 17 the tea would become liable to seizure and public sale for nonpayment of duties. On December 16, when Hutchinson again refused to allow the ship to return to England, Adams's men unloaded its tea into Boston Harbor.

Boston's Tea Party evoked what Franklin

called "great Wrath" in Britain. American sympathizers dwindled. Parliament retaliated with laws which Bostonians called the "Intolerable Acts." The Boston Port Act of 1774 closed the port by naval blockade until payment was made for both the tea and the tax. A Quartering Act authorized the army to billet troops in privately owned buildings and to secure certain supplies from the colony. The Administration of Justice Act permitted British officers accused of crimes in Massachusetts to transfer their trials to Britain to escape provincial prejudice. The Massachusetts Government Act authorized the king to appoint members of the Governor's Council to serve indefinitely; it banned town meetings except for annual elections and made other changes designed to "take the executive power from the democratic part of the government." Finally, the Quebec Act, having nothing to do with the Tea Party, aroused many Americans by permitting no representative assembly in the former French province, by granting the Catholic Church a favored position, by recognizing French laws which had no provision for jury trials in civil cases, and by attaching to Quebec all the frontier territory north of the Ohio River.

Summoned by New York and Philadelphia, a Continental Congress met in Philadelphia to consider how to help the beleaguered Bostonians. Delegations representing the anti-British faction in every colony except Georgia attended. With one vote for each delegation, the Congress defeated by one vote a plan of reconciliation drafted by Joseph Galloway of Pennsylvania. Instead it endorsed the defiant Suffolk Resolves (named for Boston's county), which Galloway branded a "complete declaration of war." After defining the American constitutional position in the words of John Adams, the Congress urged each colony to create an "Association" binding its people as in a covenant neither to export to Britain nor to import or consume British goods. It urged local committees to expose violators as "enemies of American liberty." South Carolina forced a grudging exemption of rice from the ban on exports, and Virginia won a year's delay for growers of tobacco. Before agreeing to adjourn, the members of the Congress determined that they would meet again in May 1775. As the members departed in October 1774, Charles Thomson, secretary of the Congress, wrote Benjamin Franklin in London, "We are on the brink of a precipice." Before Franklin had received the letter, George III had concluded: "Blows must decide."

Conclusion

Between the Glorious Revolution and the end of the Great War for the Empire each of Britain's continental American colonies made great strides toward both representative government and provincial autonomy. The measure of their success was the power of their elected assemblies vis-à-vis the appointed governor (elected only in Rhode Island and Connecticut) upon whom the British depended principally to exercise control. According to their commissions and instructions, the governors possessed great power, but the assemblies—by virtue of exclusive control over the initiation of revenue measures—had made the governors subservient to them in many respects. In fact, in some ways they enjoyed greater power over the governors than Parliament held over the king and, quite contrary to the British experience, assemblies increasingly resisted "management" by the governor and his agents. Even before the Great War for the Empire, authorities in Britain had recognized the extent to which the mother country had lost control of the provinces and had determined to do something about it. The war, while it delayed implementation of their ideas, demonstrated still more clearly the dimensions of the British dilemma: they could neither compel the Americans to pay what they considered a fair share of the war's costs nor prevent them until the very end of the war from carrying on trade with the enemy.

Britain tried essentially two tactics to restore its control over the colonies. First was the demand, reinforced by royal disallowance of important colonial laws, that governors and their legislatures carry out literally the king's instructions, most of them unchanged for generations and highly authoritarian in tone. That effort, dangerous in its implications for representative government in Britain itself, was largely a failure. More nearly in accord with British constitutional conceptions was the assertion that Parliament possessed unlimited authority to bind the colonies and hence not only could legislate for them, as it had done at times in the past, but also could impose taxes upon them. Recognizing that Parliamentary taxation would eviscerate their assemblies, thus negating both their representative government and their autonomy, Americans resisted by every means at hand, even boycotts and mob violence. Their tactics brought repeal of all the taxes except those of the Sugar Act and a tea tax. When Parliament in the Tea Act arranged to combat an American boycott of British tea by subsidizing the sale of the taxed tea at bargain prices, Bostonians dumped a cargo in the harbor rather than allow a stubborn governor to have it offered for sale. On this issue the revolutionary die was cast.

SUGGESTED READINGS

Bacon's Rebellion receives very favorable treatment in T. J. Wertenbaker's *Torchbearer of the Revolution* (1940) while W. E. Washburn's *The Governor and the Rebel** (1957) defends Governor Berkeley. D. A. Lovejoy provides a detailed study of *The Glorious Revolution in America* (1972). It does not supplant entirely, however, the earlier paperback (1964) with the same title presenting brief essays and documents edited by M. G. Hall, L. H. Leder, and M. G. Kammen. See also L. G. Carr and D. W. Jordan, *Maryland's Revolution of Government* (1974).

George Bancroft's *History of the United States* (6 vols., 1883–1885) and G. O. Trevelyan's *American Revolution* (4 vols., 1909–1912) popularized a Whig interpretation of the period sympathetic to British and American advocates of more representative government and hostile to "Tory" George III. L. B. Namier in *England in the Age of the American Revolution* (1930) and *The Structure of Politics at the Accession of George III* (rev. ed., 1957) convinced his generation that no Whig-Tory division of consequence existed. Robert Walcott in *English Politics in the Early Eighteenth Century* (1956) found Namier's major conclusion applicable to his period as well. However, J. H. Plumb in *The Origins of Political Stability: England, 1675–1725* (1967) and Geoffrey Holmes in *British Politics in the Age of Anne* (1967) both insist that Whig-Tory conflict was the focus of politics at the beginning of the century. Less argumentative are Basil Williams's *The Whig Supremacy* (rev. ed., 1962); J. B. Owen's *The Rise of the Pelhams* (1957); A. S. Foord's *His Majesty's Opposition, 1714–1830* (1964); Peter Thomas's *The House of Commons in the Eighteenth Century* (1973); and H. C. Mansfield, Jr.'s *Statesmanship and Party Government* (1965), a study of opposing views on the desirability of party government.

On British politics in the Revolutionary era Ian Christie's brief *Crisis of Empire* (1966) synthesizes recent scholarship effectively. More specialized works of value include John Brooke's *The Chatham Administration* (1956) and (with Namier) *Charles Townshend* (1964); Bernard Donoghue's *British Politics and the American Revolution. The Path of War, 1773–1775* (1964); B. D. Bargar's *Lord Dartmouth and the American Revolution* (1965); F. B. Wickwire's *British Subministers and Colonial America, 1763–1783* (1966); D. M. Clark's *The Rise of the British Treasury* (1960); John Shy's *Toward Lexington: The Role of the British Army in the Coming of the American Revolution* (1965); J. M. Sosin's *Whitehall and the Wilderness* (1961) and *Agents and Merchants* (1965); M. G. Kammen's *A Rope of Sand: Colonial Agents, British Politics, and the American Revolution* (1968) and *Empire and Interest* (1970).

On British colonial administration the last volume of C. M. Andrew's *The Colonial Period of American History* (4 vols., 1934–1938) is a standard source. O. M. Dickerson's *The Navigation Acts and the American Revolution* (1952) found that Americans objected more to the means of enforcement than to the Navigation Acts themselves. T. C. Barrow's *Trade and Empire:*

The British Customs Service in Colonial America, 1660–1775 (1967) found that the service was ineffective and that measures to improve it were significant contributions to the Revolution. S. N. Katz's *Newcastle's New York* (1968) shows the interlocking of British and provincial politics. In *Salutary Neglect* (1972) James Henretta finds that British administrators looked to America chiefly for patronage jobs for loyal followers.

To see colonial government in American perspective, J. P. Greene's *The Quest for Power: The Lower Houses of Assembly in the Southern Royal Colonies* (1963) is invaluable. It largely supersedes L. W. Labaree's long standard *Royal Government in America* (1930). On Pennsylvania politics, see T. Thayer, *Pennsylvania Politics and the Growth of Democracy* (1952); W. S. Hanna, *Benjamin Franklin and Pennsylvania Politics* (1964); James Hutson, *Pennsylvania Politics* (1972); and B. H. Newcomb, *Franklin and Galloway* (1972). On New York see Patricia Bonomi, *A Factious People* (1971). L. W. Levy's *Legacy of Suppression* (altered to *Freedom of Speech and Press* in paperback, 1960) drastically changes old ideas concerning the evolution of freedom of expression. L. H. Leder's *Liberty and Authority* (1968) attempts to qualify Levy's dire conclusions. M. P. Clarke's *Parliamentary Privilege in the American Colonies* (1943) illustrates the use and abuse of that great legislative power.

Ideological issues upon which the British and American majorities differed stand forth in varying perspectives in such works as Bernard Bailyn's *Ideological Origins of the American Revolution* (1966) and *The Origin of American Politics* (1968); J. R. Pole's *Political Representation in England and the Origins of the American Republic* (1966); and Clinton Rossiter's *Seedtime of the Republic* (1953) (partially reprinted in paperback as *American Colonies on the Eve of Independence*).

Max Savelle's *Origins of American Diplomacy* (1968) shows the background of the colonial wars. Howard Peckham's *The Colonial Wars, 1689–1762** (1964) af-

fords brief treatment of their military aspect. So does D. E. Leach, *Arms for Empire* (1973). J. H. McCallum (ed.), *The Seven Years War** (1968), condenses Parkman's volumes on that conflict.

To see the American Revolution from outside one should consult R. R. Palmer's *The Age of the Democratic Revolution* (1959); Crane Brinton's *The Anatomy of Revolution** (rev. ed., 1952); Hannah Arendt's *On Revolution** (1963); and R. W. Van Alstyne's *Empire and Independence** (1965). Imperial perspective characterizes L. H. Gipson's *The Coming of the Revolution** (1954); C. M. Andrew's *The Colonial Background of the American Revolution** (1931); C. H. Van Tyne's *Causes of the War of Independence* (1922); and Esmond Wright's *Fabric of Freedom** (1961). More American in tone are Merrill Jensen's massive synthesis, *The Founding of a Nation* (1968); E. S. Morgan's brief *Birth of the Republic** (1953); B. Knollenberg's *Origin of the American Revolution** (1961); C. L. Bridenbaugh's *Mitre and Sceptre* (1962); A. M. Baldwin's *The New England Clergy and the American Revolution* (1928); Carl Ubbelohde's *Vice-Admiralty Courts and the American Revolution* (1960); B. W. Labaree's *The Boston Tea Party** (1964); Pauline Maier's *From Resistance to Revolution* (1972); J. A. Ernst's *Money and Politics in America, 1755–1775* (1973); and A. M. Schlesinger, Sr.'s *Prelude to Independence* (1958). Schlesinger emphasizes class division among Americans in *The Colonial Merchants and the American Revolution* (1918). Herbert Aptheker's *The American Revolution** (1960) is a Marxist synthesis.

Biographical studies of value include John C. Miller's *Sam Adams* (1936); Gilbert Chinard's *Honest John Adams* (1933); Carl Van Doren's massive *Benjamin Franklin* (1938); V. W. Crane's shorter *Benjamin Franklin and a Rising People** (1959); J. T. Flexner's *George Washington: The Forge of Experience* (1965); Robert Meade's *Patrick Henry* (1957); and Bernard Bailyn's, *The Ordeal of Thomas Hutchinson* (1974).

*indicates availability in paperback.

Independence

Forced by British intransigence to choose between total submission and violent resistance, most Americans chose to fight. Initially they fought chiefly to compel Britain to acknowledge that Parliament had no authority to tax them for revenue. A year of fighting, however, helped persuade the majority in the resistance movement that it would be better to seek full freedom from Britain. On July 4, 1776, the Continental Congress announced its intention to the world in the Declaration of Independence. Dedication to the goal of independence sustained the Revolutionaries through eight years of ravaging warfare, years in which the British sought first to subdue the North and then, after that hope was shattered by Burgoyne's surrender at Saratoga, to restore their authority at least in the South. The surrender of Cornwallis at Yorktown ended that illusion. French assistance to the Americans was invaluable in attaining victory; but in negotiating the peace, the Americans found British ideas as to the new nation's territorial extent more generous than those of France. To avoid making the United States a dependency of France, Britain surrendered all its territory south of the Great Lakes.

Significant changes in the pattern of life accompanied the Revolution. New state governments derived their power from the people rather than from a king and sought to serve the people's interests. Liberated from British restrictions, American trade took new directions. Americans sought also to foster manufacturing, to reestablish viable monetary systems, to accelerate development of the wilderness. Exclusion from Britain's mercantilist system, however, coupled with the loss of confidence in paper money because of wartime inflation, caused considerable economic disruption, even temporary hardship. Slavery, the compulsory support of religion, and property qualifications on the right to vote were among the targets of reform efforts which enjoyed varying degrees of success. The people also gave clear evidence that their provincial loyalties, while still very strong, had suffered in competition with their new American identity and pride.

War was clearly imminent in Massachusetts by late 1774. Special militia forces called "Minute Men" trained conspicuously for speedy action. They flocked to the scene when the British destroyed artillery which they had brought to the outskirts of Boston, but offered no resistance. In their turn, American militiamen seized war material in a British fort at Portsmouth without opposition. In open defiance of General Thomas Gage, now the appointed governor of Massachusetts as well as British commander in chief in America, the colonial legislature transformed itself into a revolutionary "Provincial Congress."

General Gage was in a most awkward position. The people, he explained, "are not held in high estimation by the Troops, yet they are numerous, worked up to a Fury, and not the Boston Rabble but the Freeholders and the Farmers of the Country." In Britain, authorities remained convinced that New Englanders would back down in the face of force and that the "better sort," especially in the Middle and Southern Colonies, would lend decisive support to the British position. They rejected Gage's appeal for more troops. George III, insisting that "Great Britain cannot retract," rebuffed as well Gage's suggestion that he suspend the coercive laws. Urged on by the King, Lord Dartmouth, Secretary of State for the Colonies, instructed Gage to "arrest and imprison the principal actors . . . in the provincial Congress," even though such a step might constitute a "signal for hostilities."

Dartmouth's instructions, hedged with injunctions that Gage use his own discretion, reached the General on April 14, 1775. Exercising his discretion, Gage made no immediate effort to seize the insurgent leaders. Instead he waited until the Provincial Congress in session at Concord had adjourned and then, on April 18, dispatched a force of some seven hundred men on a night march to seize war material stored there.

Gage's expedition did not catch the Americans off guard. Boston silversmith Paul Revere, acting for the local Committee of Safety, carried word to John Hancock and Samuel Adams at Lexington. A British patrol captured Revere before he reached Concord, but a companion, Dr. Samuel Prescott, got through with the warning to remove the supplies. When the British reached Lexington at dawn, about seventy Minute Men awaited them on the common. Major John Pitcairn, commanding an advance force of the British troops, ordered his men to surround and disarm them. Militia Captain John Parker had instructed his men to withdraw when firing started. Who began it, whether British or American, no one knows. Pitcairn's troops, however, rushing on out of control, killed eight and wounded ten militiamen. One British regular was wounded. The engagement, concluded a recent historian, approximating contemporary American estimates usually considered exaggerated, was "less a battle . . . than an hysterical massacre at the hands of badly disciplined British soldiers."

The British forces moved on to Concord and began destroying what few supplies remained. A clash there killed two Americans and three English regulars. As the British returned to Boston, militiamen firing from every kind of concealment killed about seventy and wounded about two and a half times that number while suffering only ninety-five casualties themselves. Next day Lord Percy, commander of the 1,200 troops dispatched to assist what remained of the original force of 700, prophesied in revision of an earlier opinion that the "insurrection here" would not "turn out so despicable as it is perhaps imagined at home."

News of the events at Lexington and Concord flew quickly in all directions. Within a day or two, some twenty thousand outraged Americans had assembled at Cambridge to put a stop to the various atrocities of which most believed the British guilty. At Boston, Gage's force of about four thousand became a dangerously isolated garrison. The nucleus of an American army had sprung into existence.

Western New Englanders also responded quickly to the news of Lexington. Ethan Allen and Benedict Arnold, rival rather than joint commanders, captured a precious stock of artillery from the pathetic garrison of the moldering Fort Ticonderoga. They took Crown Point as well.

Delegates to the Second Continental Congress convened at Philadelphia just three weeks after Lexington. The Congress "adopted" the army besieging Gage at Boston, arranged to raise additional troops, issued $2 million in bills of credit to pay military costs, and made George Washington of Virginia commander in chief. In addition, Congress created a post office system and assumed control over Indian affairs.

Moderates, led by John Dickinson of Pennsylvania, were still in control, however. They squelched the efforts of more radical delegates, including Benjamin Franklin and John Adams, to call for independent governments and an intercolonial confederation. Instead, congressional moderates dispatched the so-called Olive Branch Petition humbly beseeching the King "to procure us relief."

Despite the suppliant tone of the petition, even the moderates were determined to keep up forceful resistance until the British abandoned their contention that no limits whatever restricted Parliament's power to bind the Colonies. Congress rejected almost with contempt the not-very-conciliatory proposal Lord North had pushed through Parliament in February, which promised only to exempt from British taxation all colonies which made financial provisions satisfactory to Parliament for their own defense and civil government. In a "Declaration of the causes and necessities of taking up arms," Congress made clear American determination. Drafted by Dickinson and Thomas Jefferson, the declaration boiled with indignation at Parliament's "intemperate rage for unlimited domination" and at its presumption in undertaking to "give and grant our money without our consent." "In our own native land," the document concluded, "in defence of the freedom that is our birthright, . . . for the protection of our property, . . . against violence actually offered, we have taken up arms. We shall lay them down when hostilities shall cease on the part of the aggressors, and all danger of their being renewed shall be removed, and not before."

Severing the Tie

At Boston, meanwhile, General Gage, reinforced by 1,000 troops and three major generals—William Howe, John Burgoyne, and Henry Clinton—determined to make a frontal assault on the Americans threatening the city from Bunker Hill across the bay on Charlestown peninsula. Three times Howe led the English regulars against the American positions. On the third try the Americans ran out of ammunition and, after some hand-to-hand combat, retreated in good order, having suffered only moderate losses. Howe's casualties were 226 killed and 828 wounded—in all, nearly half of his attacking force. As Clinton observed, "Another such [victory] would have ruined us." Had Gage fol-

lowed Clinton's suggestion to land troops behind the Americans at the bottlenecked base of the peninsula, the result might have been significantly different. When General Washington assumed command and brought Ticonderoga's cannon onto Dorchester Heights on the other side of Boston, the British quietly departed for Canada accompanied by over a thousand American Loyalists.

A contest for Canada was also under way. Congress in 1774 had invited Canadians to join in rebellion against Britain, but no resistance movement of significance materialized. Sir Guy Carleton, commanding the British forces in Canada, hoped to raise Loyalist forces among

French Canadians, but he too was largely disappointed. British strategists, however, agreed that the Hudson-Champlain waterway afforded, as Burgoyne put it, "precisely the route that an army ought to take" in order, with a naval blockade, to isolate and subdue intransigent New England. Even before the evacuation of Boston, Lord Germain, successor to Dartmouth as Secretary of State for the Colonies, had approved Howe's plan to occupy New York in force, link up with another major British force from Canada on the Hudson-Champlain waterway, and invade New England from the west.

Americans, unencumbered by the necessity of transporting men and supplies across 3,000 miles of ocean, beat the British to the punch. Under the command of Richard Montgomery, a former British officer, Americans captured Montreal in November. Montgomery and Benedict Arnold, who with great hardship had brought another force through the Maine wilderness, jointly attacked Quebec on New Year's Eve, with disastrous results. Montgomery was killed, Arnold badly wounded, over a third of their force captured. Smallpox and the expiration of enlistments completed the ruin of the invading force amid the rigors of the Canadian winter. Reinforcements arrived for both sides in the spring, but their relative numbers made it clear that the invading force of 1776 would move south, not north.

During the winter of 1775–1776, increasing numbers of Americans became convinced that complete independence from Britain was desirable. British actions helped them toward that conclusion. In March 1775, the New England Restraining Act barred New Englanders from the Grand Banks fisheries and confined their trade to the British Isles and the West Indies. Parliament applied similar restrictions to most of the other colonies in April. George III refused to consider the Olive Branch Petition and charged that the Americans were trying to establish "an independent empire." In the Prohibitory Act of December 1775, Parliament barred all trade with the rebellious Colonies and ordered their ships confiscated. With news of the Prohibitory Act came rumors that the British had arranged to hire foreign mercenaries, professional soldiers with an awesome reputation for ruthless plunder. In fact, Britain concluded treaties for 18,000 troops from German principalities in January 1776, after negotiations for 20,000 Russians fell through.

Common Sense, an anonymously published pamphlet written by immigrant Thomas Paine, electrified Philadelphia in January, about a month before Americans learned of the Prohibitory Act and the employment of mercenaries. The son of a Quaker corset maker, Paine had come to Pennsylvania, with recommendations from Benjamin Franklin, after experiencing both economic and marital failure in England. Dubbing George III "the royal brute of Britain," Paine ridiculed the very concept of hereditary monarchy and of a royal family sprung from "a French bastard [William the Conquerer] . . . with an armed banditti." It would be absurd, he argued, for a continent—North America—to be "perpetually governed by an island." "England," he warned, "consults the good of *this* country no farther than it answers her *own* purpose." Appealing to what would later be called isolationist sentiment, he reminded Americans that while dependent upon Britain they could never "steer clear of European contention, but would always be involved in European wars." Furthermore, only by declaring their independence, he concluded, could Americans secure foreign aid in their struggle against Britain.

Congress, reconvening at Philadelphia in September of 1775 after a six-week recess, began to take tentative steps toward independence. Before the end of 1775, it had created a navy, appointed a committee to sound out "friends" abroad, and welcomed a French agent bearing informal assurances of assistance. In March 1776, Congress sent Silas Deane to Europe to purchase war supplies. It also authorized privately owned vessels to prey on British commerce. In May, France decided to provide assistance in the guise of sales from the fictitious Hortalez Company,

The cartoon, first published in 1768, warns that England's inept administration is cutting off her own colonies and she will soon be a hopeless cripple. Taxes and interference with colonial self-government were the major problems. Sugar and stamp acts, import-export quotas and duties, and other levies drove the American colonies to a common bitter resentment of King George's government.

Benjamin Franklin probably designed this tragic cartoon for London's *Political Register,* a monthly journal. The Latin banner, "Give a little something to Bellisarius," alludes to a brilliant general of the Roman Empire who was reduced to begging in his old age. Further explanation reads: "The colonies being severed from [Great Britain] she is seen lifting her eyes and mangled stumps to heaven; her shield, which she is unable to wield, lies useless at her side; her lance has pierced New England; the laurel branch has fallen from the hand of Pennsylvania; the English oak has lost its head, and stands a bare trunk." The moral: "The ordaining of laws in favor of *one* part of the nation, to the prejudice and oppression of *another,* is certainly the most erroneous and mistaken policy.... The whole state is weakened, and perhaps ruined forever!"

In 1764, new taxes were levied in the form of a Sugar Act. James Otis of Massachusetts wrote an eloquent pamphlet on the rights of the colonies (following page, left, above). Though the pamphlet was aimed at maintaining relations with England, a basic American principle was asserted here. "[No legislature can] take from any man part of his property without his consent.... No parts of His Majesty's dominions can be taxed without their consent; every part has a right to be represented...."

The following year, England passed a Stamp Act requiring that tax stamps be attached to every newspaper page, all official documents, wills, deeds, marriage, birth, and death certificates, every legal paper of any kind. As the starting date approached, newspapers announced their own deaths. Throughout the thirteen colonies, resentment and retaliation grew. Protest groups, the Sons and Daughters of Liberty formed to harass government officials and to boycott merchants who supported England (following spread, right). Women refused to buy imported cloth and other goods. The handwritten warning on the next pages appeared the day the first shipment of tax stamps arrived in New York. Those who sold stamps were burned in effigy and, in some cases, were tarred and feathered.

Library of Congress

Documents of Revolution

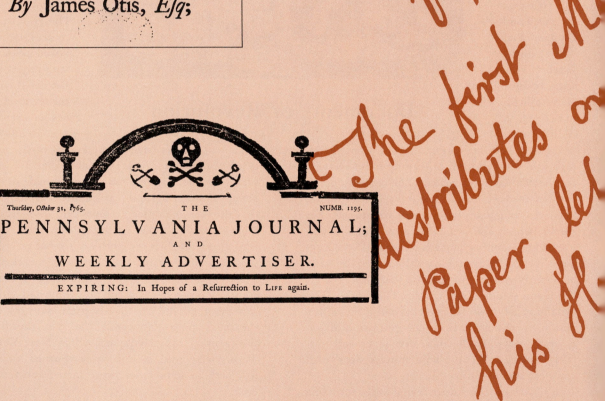

THE

RIGHTS

OF THE

British Colonies

Aſſerted and proved.

By James Otis, *Eſq*;

202

Thurſday, *October* 31, 1765.　THE　NUMB. 1195.

PENNSYLVANIA JOURNAL;
AND
WEEKLY ADVERTISER.

EXPIRING: In Hopes of a Reſurrection to LIFE again.

nat either—
es use of Stampt
take Care of
Persons, & Effects.
Vox Populi;
We will

WILLIAM JACKSON,

an IMPORTER; at the

BRAZEN HEAD,

North Side of the TOWN-HOUSE,

and Opposite the Town-Pump, i

Corn-hill, BOSTON.

It is defired that the SONS and
DAUGHTERS of LIBERTY,
would not buy any one thing of
him, for in fo doing they will bring
Difgrace upon themfelves, and their
Pofterity, for ever and ever, AMEN.

Liberty and Property vindicated, and
the St--pm-n burnt.

A

DISCOURSE

OCCASIONALLY MADE

On burning the Effige of the

ST -- PM - N.

IN

NEW-LONDON,

IN THE COLONY OF

CONNECTICUT.

Center and near left: Courtesy of the New-York Histori-
cal Society, New York City
Far left, above and below: New York Public Library, Rare
Book Division
Top: Massachusetts Historical Society
Above: American Antiquarian Society

The colonies formed militia, Committees of Correspondence, undercover governments, and harassment groups. The British used troops to maintain civil order, to protect shipments from England, and to search for and seize arms. A number of serious incidents occurred, including the Boston Massacre in March 1770: troops fired into an unruly mob, killing five.

These pictures, as Harold Murdock has pointed out in *The Nineteenth of April* (Houghton-Mifflin, 1923), show another incident which has become glorified as the Battle of Lexington; it was not, in fact, a battle at all. On April 19, 1775, British troops marching to Concord encountered a group of colonial militiamen on the common at Lexington. The colonials were ordered to lay down their arms and disperse. As they did so a musket went off on one side or the other; the British reacted by firing into the group, killing eight. The picture above was made just after the incident by a Connecticut Minuteman, Amos Doolittle. It shows accurately that the colonials dispersed and did not fire back.

Art and patriotism, however, soon began to alter history. An 1830 drawing (right, above) shows six Minutemen firing back while two others reload. In 1855, only a few men disperse while many more return fire (right, center). The 1886 painting (right, below) is completely fictitious. Here resolute

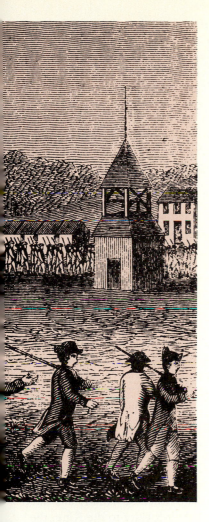

Minutemen stand firm and fight a battle that never occurred.

The British continued to Concord where they did find a battle:
By the rude bridge that arched the flood,
Their flag to April's breeze unfurled,
Here once the embattled farmers stood,
And fired the shot heard round the world.

conducted by a remarkable secret agent, the playwright Caron de Beaumarchais.

Efforts to postpone a declaration of independence came chiefly from the Middle Colonies, especially Pennsylvania. Under Dickinson's leadership, Pennsylvania had continued to observe meticulously the constitutional contention that the colony, although immune from the authority of Parliament, was subject to the king. To overcome the reluctance of such moderates as Dickinson to sever the last bond of empire by renouncing loyalty to King George III, Samuel and John Adams persuaded Congress to resolve, on May 15, that royal authority of every kind "should be totally suppressed." Organized militants in Philadelphia were in fact beginning to organize a new government for Pennsylvania and would surely do so more rapidly, it was clear, if the opponents of independence continued to drag their feet.

Virginia pushed the question to a showdown. On May 15 Virginia's Revolutionary Legislature had instructed its congressional delegation to introduce a resolution endorsing independence, foreign alliances, and the preparation of a plan for intercolonial confederation. As introduced by Richard Henry Lee on June 7, the resolution included the declaration, "That these United Colonies are, and of right ought to be, free and independent states." Dickinson secured a three-week delay, during which a committee headed by Thomas Jefferson of Virginia and including Franklin, John Adams, Robert R. Livingston, and Roger Sherman was to draft a declaration. Other committees were to consider confederation of the Colonies and foreign alliances.

Congress returned to the question of independence on July 2. Dickinson again sought delay; but when the decisive vote took place, he and two other Pennsylvania moderates stayed away, and one other joined the militants. Consequently, by a 3-to-2 margin, Pennsylvania cast its vote for independence. All the other delegations also endorsed independence—except for that of New York, which declined to vote on the ground that it had not received instructions from its government.

Jefferson's draft declaration of independence, however, was not yet in a form satisfactory to Congress. For two days the delegates cut and polished the declaration. They struck out a somewhat strained passage blaming the King for the existence of slavery but made no other changes of importance. Then on July 4, Congress unanimously approved the declaration. On July 8 the crowd which heard the first public reading built a bonfire in celebration and cast into it the king's coat of arms, which had rested symbolically over the door to the statehouse in which Congress met.

What the declaration said (see Appendix for full text) was nothing new to the many Americans who had resisted British authorities for so long. Rather it represented a consensus in support of the Whiggish doctrines expressed by John Locke (see p. 69) almost a century before. Jefferson merely condensed the popular ideas to two sentences and changed the list of natural rights from "life, liberty, and property" to the somewhat less specific "life, liberty, and the pursuit of happiness." Because Americans had so long emphasized their loyalty to the King, the major thrust of the declaration was to justify breaking that final tie by attributing to George III oppressive acts "which may define a tyrant . . . unfit to be the ruler of a free people." In addition, the declaration made clear to the British people the determination of Americans to resist the efforts of "their legislature to extend an unwarrantable jurisdiction over us."

Victory in the North

Prospects for American independence were not good in July 1776. While Congress was voting to fight for independence on July 2, Sir William Howe was landing on Staten Island with an army of 34,000 men. Washington had a growing but only half-trained army of some 20,000 to oppose him. In Canada, General Carleton, also enjoying overwhelming superiority, prepared to move south to join Howe and thus isolate New England. Beset by personal and provincial jealousies and plagued, too, by both Tory and Indian supporters of the Crown, a rudimentary American national government prepared to stave off invasion by a nation four times its size in population, which had proved itself in the Seven Years' War the greatest of the world powers.

But for Benedict Arnold, disaster might well have overtaken the Americans in 1776. Recovered from the leg wound he had received at Quebec, Arnold spent the summer frantically building warships to contest the British advance over Lake Champlain. Because of the greatly superior mobility of waterborne forces, Carleton had to take time to do the same, and not until October was he sufficiently confident of superiority to proceed. Carleton destroyed Arnold's fleet in battles at Valcour Island and Split Rock but decided that the imminence of winter prevented further offensive effort and accordingly withdrew to Canada. Had Carleton been as successful as Howe, the British strategy for the isolation of New England might well have worked in 1776.

Sir William Howe could perhaps have crushed the Revolution in 1776 without assistance from Carleton. The Americans, anticipating that New York would be the British target after the evacuation of Boston, rashly committed themselves to defend the virtually indefensible city. Washington placed troops not only on Manhattan Island but also at Brooklyn Heights on Long Island. He would not repeat Gage's mistake at Boston in failing to occupy the commanding Dorchester Heights. But neither was Howe disposed to repeat the mistake of Bunker Hill. He flanked the entrenched American positions at Brooklyn Heights and captured two major generals with a large body of troops. Washington himself led a relief force across the East River onto the tiny pocket of Long Island remaining in American hands; fortunately Howe, despite the urging of subordinates, declined to press his advantage. The warships under his brother, Admiral Lord Richard Howe, appeared indeed to be capable of preventing Washington's escape, but, under cover of a rainy night and a foggy morning, New England fishermen ferried the American troops back to Manhattan Island, out of a tight trap into a looser one.

Howe again proved dilatory, and once more Washington and the American cause escaped disaster. After some skirmishing at Harlem Heights, Washington at last got his men onto the mainland, except for a garrison of about three thousand at Fort Washington near the upper end of Manhattan, which Howe captured. Howe's subordinate, Lord Cornwallis, then pursued Washington across New Jersey to the Delaware River. But instead of pushing on in the hope of destroying Washington's dwindling and demoralized army, the British in mid-December followed European convention by dispersing their forces as town garrisons for the winter.

Washington could not afford to be conventional. He needed a victory to revive American morale. "These are the times that try men's souls," wrote Thomas Paine in the first of his *Crisis* pamphlets. "The summer soldier and the sunshine patriot will, in this crisis, shrink from the service of their country; but he that stands it *now*, deserves the love and thanks of man and woman." New Jersey and Pennsylvania militiamen came forth. Beaten army units from the Canadian and the New York disasters responded to Washington's call. Crossing the ice-filled Delaware on Christmas Day, Washington surprised a garrison of German mercenaries—Hessians—at Trenton on December 26 and captured over nine hundred men.

Somewhat overconfident because of his victory, Washington remained in Trenton and soon found himself confronted by a superior force under Cornwallis. Slipping southward around Cornwallis's camp during the night of January 2, 1777, Washington marched north to Princeton, where he defeated a small British force before moving on to the mountains of Morristown. There the terrain made his position unassailable while the location enabled him to threaten British communications across New Jersey. Cornwallis accordingly drew back to New Brunswick. Washington's daring and unconventional campaign had freed most of New Jersey from British occupation. But it had done more. As a British observer wrote: "A few days ago they had given up the cause for lost, . . . now they are all liberty mad again. . . . They have recovered [from] their panic and it will not be an easy matter to throw them into that confusion again."

One reason for the apparent lack of British aggressiveness in 1776 was the belief that a mere show of force might end the rebellion. In that expectation, the Howe brothers were authorized to deal with the Americans, but only to the extent of accepting submission and issuing pardons. A congressional committee did meet with Admiral Howe on Staten Island during the battle for New York, but only to make it clear that Congress meant what it had said in the Declaration of Independence.

In the campaign of 1777, the British made mistakes fully as damaging as those of the previous year. Howe abandoned his earlier plan to move up the Hudson, join the Canadian army, and then turn in overwhelming force against New England. Instead he planned to pacify the purportedly Tory-ridden province of Pennsylvania. George Germain, Britain's chief war minister, approved the change. Washington met Howe's army at Brandywine Creek, well west of Philadelphia, but the British flanked the Americans as they had on Long Island, and Washington was fortunate to get away. In October Washington launched another attack against the main body of Howe's troops at Germantown, just north of Philadelphia. It also failed. Howe wintered comfortably with his mistress and his liquor in Philadelphia, while the Americans endured great hardship at nearby Valley Forge.

General John Burgoyne meanwhile had lost an army. Having replaced Carleton, Burgoyne set off southward from Canada during June into the New York wilderness. His entourage included British, German, Canadian, and Indian fighting men, nearly 8,000 in all. Another force of nearly 2,000, mostly Indians and Tories, moved eastward through the Mohawk Valley under Colonel Barry St. Leger to meet Burgoyne in Albany. Tough fighting with New York militiamen and fearful rumors spread by Benedict Arnold prompted St. Leger's Indians to depart, leaving him little choice but to do the same.

Burgoyne toiled on through the wilderness. He took undermanned Fort Ticonderoga on July 5, but General Philip Schuyler slowed his progress by felling trees and diverting streams in his path. Seriously short of draft animals and provisions, Burgoyne sent off a 700-man foraging party to seize supplies at Bennington, Vermont. New England militiamen, aroused by the murder of Jane McCrea by Burgoyne's Indians, had joined General John Stark in great numbers. They killed or captured virtually all the foraging party and much of the relief party sent to rescue it.

After Bennington, Burgoyne had only two hopes. One was to crush the opposing American forces in a major battle. His own dwindling supplies and the rapidly increasing numbers of Americans in arms against him dictated speedy action if he chose that course. His other hope was that General Sir Henry Clinton, whom Howe had left with a considerable army at New York, might rescue him. On September 19 Burgoyne attacked the American army, now commanded by Horatio Gates, a onetime major in the British army who had resigned and emigrated to Virginia in 1772 because his inferior social standing precluded further advancement in the British army. The battle at Freeman's Farm near Saratoga was inconclusive, but Burgoyne's casualties were 600, compared with only 300 for the Americans. Learning that Clinton was on the move, Burgoyne decided to wait, in the hope that Gates would divert much of his force to meet Clinton. Gates declined to do so.

Three weeks later, his men on half rations, Burgoyne dismissed suggestions that he retreat and took the offensive again. In the battle of

Bemis Heights (or the second battle of Freeman's Farm) on October 7, during which Benedict Arnold again distinguished himself for valor, Burgoyne lost another 700 men, more than four times the American loss. By October 12, Burgoyne's 5,000 survivors were surrounded by a force several times as large. He surrendered under terms—never honored—which called for the return of his men to England.

After Saratoga, Britain virtually abandoned hope of conquering the North. The South, considered more important, more dependent economically, and more loyal, seemed a better target. British strategists also believed that the scattered population and the high proportion of blacks would make the South an easier mark. In the North the new strategy would consist of naval blockade and coastal raids.

Detail from The Surrender of General Burgoyne, *by John Trumbull.*   Yale University Art Gallery

Managing a World War

France, relegated to inferior status by Britain in the Seven Years' War, had recognized almost from that war's conclusion the prospect that American resentments might present an opportunity to humble Britain and enhance its own relative status. "It is our duty," wrote Foreign Minister Vergennes, "to seize every possible opportunity to reduce the power and greatness of England." Accordingly, as early as March 1776, he began to provide the Americans with war supplies. Burgoyne's surrender gave Vergennes the evidence, for which he had been hoping, that the Americans might succeed. He quickly concluded both a Treaty of Amity and Commerce and a military alliance. The terms of the alliance bound each party to make peace only with the other's consent. France renounced any claim to continental territory east of the Mississippi and received American endorsement for efforts to capture British sugar islands. The stated purpose of the alliance was to secure American independence. Thus from June 1778, Britain was again at war with its ancient and most formidable foe.

Spain found the American Revolution convenient to its purposes as well. Although they contributed money to the American cause after 1776, the Spanish would neither make an alliance nor even recognize American independence. Spanish leaders had what proved to be well-founded apprehensions over the security of their trans-Mississippi territories and the dangerous example of republican revolution being given their own colonies. Gibraltar, however, was a major concern to Spain. When Britain declined to yield it in return for Spanish neutrality, Spain concluded an alliance with France (Aranjuez, 1779), pledging a joint invasion of England and no peace until Gibraltar was won. A great French-Spanish fleet put to sea for the invasion in the summer, but its bungling commanders seemed no more anxious to attempt a landing than the British were to attack at sea. Some anxious moments followed in England, however, before the effort was abandoned.

Vergennes assiduously sought to maintain Britain's isolation. In previous world wars of the eighteenth century Britain had always enjoyed the advantage of a continental ally. To preclude that possibility in the War of the American Revolution, France arranged in 1779 to terminate an incipient war between its Austrian ally and Prussia. With French support, the Netherlands resisted British pressure to curtail shipment of war supplies to the allies, and in consequence, Britain declared war on the Netherlands at the end of 1780. Again with Vergennes's encouragement, neutral nations set about in 1780 forming a League of Armed Neutrality, intended to compel Britain to permit neutrals to trade freely with its enemies. While the League members were never firmly united, the very existence of the League reminded Britain of still another danger in the isolation which its superpower status and Vergennes's diplomacy had forced upon it. Without an ally, Britain from the end of 1780 was fighting a naval war with France, Spain, and the Netherlands while struggling also to suppress the American Revolution and to avoid serious offense to a hostile League of Armed Neutrality which encompassed much of the rest of Europe.

Civilian leaders in the Continental Congress experienced baffling difficulties in conducting both war and diplomacy, but in contrast to revolutionaries in some other countries, they kept ultimate authority in their hands and exercised it well. To the Carlisle peace commission sent out by Britain in 1778, at the time of the French alliance, Congress made clear that there would be no reunion with Britain on any terms, that its demands were independence and the withdrawal of British troops. After futile attempts to bribe several congressmen and then to appeal over their heads to the people, the Carlisle commissioners went home empty-handed.

Washington, more outstanding in character than in military skills, continued to retain and to deserve the confidence which Congress had originally placed in him. After Saratoga, General Thomas Conway, Dr. Benjamin Rush, and others touted Gates as a replacement for Washington, but the "Conway Cabal," or conspiracy against Washington, was apparently little more

than the muted mutterings of a minority of dissidents. Appointment of the able Nathaniel Greene as Quartermaster General solved the supply problems, which had been acute at Valley Forge in the winter of 1776–1777. Failure to gratify individual ambitions for promotion frequently evoked resentment, notably in the case of Benedict Arnold. His unsuccessful effort to betray the fort at West Point on the Hudson River to the British in 1780 was, at least in part, the result of Congress's failure to take what he regarded as sufficient notice of his distinguished record.

Financing the Revolution was the most crucial responsibility of Congress. In the first five years (1775–1780) of the Revolutionary struggle, Congress financed the war by issuing paper money. In that period "Continental" paper money provided about 81 percent of the national revenue. Borrowing from individual Americans provided 11 percent, while the states supplied about 3 percent and foreign loans 4 percent. Unlike the old colonial governments, Congress could not tax to redeem its paper money. The states, which were supposed to redeem it on a prorated basis, declined to do so. Some in fact could not. As a result Continental currency ultimately depreciated in value. Indeed, by 1779 its value was so slight that Congress decided to issue no more. It redeemed $120 million at one-fortieth of face value in 1780, but another $71 million became worthless. In effect this depreciation in value was simply a disguised form of taxation, one which sustained the Revolution in its most critical stages.

Collapse of the paper money produced an acute financial crisis. After a winter of deprivation at Morristown in 1779–1780, two Connecticut regiments from Washington's army demonstrated on May 25, to demand full rations and five months' back pay. In January 1781, Pennsylvania troops marched off to negotiate with Pennsylvania's government for better treatment. New Jersey troops also mutinied. By a combination of concessions, persuasion, and a few executions, the mutinies were put down, but it was obvious that the embryonic nation desperately needed a new financial base.

To solve the problem, Congress early in 1781 turned to Robert Morris, a Philadelphia merchant with long experience in Congress. As head of a new Department of Finance which lasted until 1784, Morris experienced some failures, but he achieved minor miracles. He failed to win state authorization for Congress to impose an import tax which he and other nationalists had favored. He did not pay the army on schedule until the end of the war in 1783. But he used the army pay policy to induce the states to respond more favorably to congressional "requisitions," and in fact secured some $2 million in that manner. He raised $4 million in new loans from abroad, mostly from France, and pared expenditures to the approximate level of income. He improved the efficiency of supply operations for the army and in 1781 at Philadelphia established, largely with government capital, the first commercial bank in American history, the Bank of North America. He used the bank effectively to stretch the government's resources. When Morris quit in 1784, the government was solvent. Suspicion that Morris had used his office to benefit his own business interests and those of his friends was widespread, but—at least with reference to his own fortune—the charge was apparently without foundation.

War costs, including state expenditures, from 1775 through 1783 amounted to about $163 million. Of this the states expended about half, roughly $78 million, although the United States in 1790 assumed $18 million of this amount. Paper money paid a little over one-fourth, or $46 million; domestic borrowing less than one-fifth, $28 million; and foreign loans still less, $10.5 million.

Victory in the South

British strategy after Saratoga was to maintain a naval blockade and carry out harassing raids in the North while making a major effort to subdue the South. Sir Henry Clinton, successor to Howe as British commander, moved from Philadelphia to New York to be in a better position for coastal raiding but French land and sea forces, based firmly in Rhode Island after 1780, helped to frustrate his plans. Tories and Indians in 1778 committed massacres in the Wyoming Valley of Pennsylvania and at Cherry Valley in New York. General John Sullivan drove them back and devastated much of the Iroquois country, although he did not push on to their base at Fort Niagara. From Detroit, Colonel Henry ("Hair-buyer") Hamilton, widely believed to have paid bounties for American scalps, had fostered raids on Ohio Valley settlements. Militiaman George Rogers Clark, with authorization from Virginia's government, captured not only the British frontier outposts of Kaskaskia and Vincennes in 1779 but even Hamilton himself. Detroit remained in British hands, however, and at the end of the war the British were still strong on the northwestern frontier.

Even the war at sea produced embarrassments to Britain in the years after Saratoga. The tiny American navy was no real threat, but in isolated engagements John Paul Jones and John Barry spectacularly bested British seamen. Naval vessels also captured nearly two hundred British merchant ships, while privateersmen (privately owned, profit-seeking vessels) caught several times as many. Britain, too, had to divert some of its blockade vessels to strengthen its defenses against the sizable naval might of France and Spain.

In the South, Britain initially enjoyed more success. In the fall of 1778, Clinton sent off a force from New York which easily captured Savannah. With the subsequent fall of Augusta, royal government returned to Georgia. In 1780 Clinton himself seized Charleston and with it the entire defending American army of 5,000 men. Clinton wrote hopefully of recovering everything north to the Hudson River unless "a superior fleet shews itself, in which case I despair of ever seeing peace restored to this miserable country."

Immediately ensuing events made Clinton's hope seem reasonable. Congress sent Horatio Gates, hero of Saratoga, to repel the British, but at Camden, South Carolina, Gates suffered a shattering defeat at the hands of Lord Cornwallis. South Carolina irregulars also suffered at the hands of Banastre Tarleton. But rallying frontier riflemen on October 7 surrounded a Tory detachment of about one thousand men at Kings Mountain and killed or captured the entire force. Daniel Morgan, by effectively faking the usual flight of militiamen, killed or captured most of Tarleton's attacking force at Cowpens near Kings Mountain early in 1781. Nathaniel Greene, Washington's choice to replace Gates, kept pressure on Cornwallis as did guerrilla forces under Francis Marion, Thomas Sumter, Andrew Pickens, and others. Abandoning hope of restoring British authority in the interior, Cornwallis moved toward the relative safety of the coast and thence northward to Virginia. By the end of summer the invaders in the lower South were confined to narrow enclaves at Charleston and Savannah.

In Virginia, Cornwallis was about to encounter the superior fleet which Clinton had dreaded. To conquer the Lower South, Cornwallis believed he had first to subdue Virginia, from which supplies and reinforcements came. Benedict Arnold, now in Britain's service, was already raiding widely over Virginia on Clinton's orders but with a relatively small body of troops. Cornwallis's arrival and reinforcements increased the British army in Virginia to over 7,000. Opposing them was a small body of regular American army men, "Continentals," and growing numbers of those whom Cornwallis contemptuously dismissed as "peasantry," all under command of "the boy," the twenty-four-year-old Marquis de Lafayette, a French volunteer who had become a trusted subordinate of Washington. Lafayette could offer no resistance as Cornwallis moved to Yorktown near the mouth of Chesapeake Bay and began to build a fortified base for his contemplated campaign. Clinton, characteristically indecisive, disapproved Cornwallis's plan, but—anticipating that George Germain was about to oust him in favor of Cornwallis—did nothing to impede his rivalrous subordinate.

Responding to repeated American pleas, France had sent a large fleet to the West Indies under Admiral de Grasse. His instructions were "to detach a portion" of his fleet "to cooperate in any undertaking which may be projected by the French and American generals." The British felt sure that the need to protect French and Spanish possessions and commerce in the Caribbean would severely limit the number of ships which de Grasse could spare. The British believed that it would be only twelve or fifteen of his twenty-eight warships. Accordingly, they employed several of their ships in convoying merchant fleets to England; one carried the British naval commander, Admiral Rodney, home to England for treatment of gout. His subordinate, Admiral Sir Samuel Hood, had only fourteen ships when he sailed north to meet Admiral Thomas Graves at New York, there to await the anticipated arrival of the French fleet. Since Graves proved to have only five serviceable warships, the combined British fleet numbered only nineteen. Still unknown to the British was the fact that de Grasse was bringing north his entire fleet of twenty-eight ships. In addition, a French squadron of some strength lay at Newport, Rhode Island.

Washington had wished to aim the great French-American attack against Clinton at New York, but Count de Rochambeau, commander of the French expeditionary force in America, argued that trapping Cornwallis would be less difficult. De Grasse also preferred to make Cornwallis the target, and Washington acquiesced. De Grasse arrived at the Chesapeake on August 30, putting ashore some three thousand French troops to help Lafayette prevent Cornwallis's escape. On September 5, Graves and Hood arrived with their combined fleets under the command of Graves. Despite their astonishment at being so badly outnumbered, they gave battle. The British fleet under Admiral Graves emerged more badly damaged than the French and consequently returned to New York for repairs. During the battle, eight French warships from Rhode Island had arrived, thus increasing French superiority and eliminating any prospect that Cornwallis could escape by sea.

By land, Cornwallis's situation rapidly became equally hopeless. Washington and Rochambeau had faked the attack on New York which Clinton had long anticipated and were well on the way to Virginia before Clinton realized their aim. By September 24, Cornwallis with an army of 8,000 faced French and American forces of more than twice that number. On October 18, after enough resistance to demonstrate its futility, he surrendered. In the South as in the North, Britain's effort to subdue the Colonies had ended with the loss of an entire army.

Peace and Independence

After Yorktown, Britain abandoned all hope of suppressing the American Revolution. Early in 1782, Parliament acknowledged the situation and authorized peace negotiations. Lord North, so long the agent of royal intransigence, at last resigned, as he had often sought to do in the past. Negotiation of peace fell to the Earl of Shelburne, a reform-minded conciliator, who envisioned unrestricted trade between America and Britain as a boon to both.

To capitalize on the conciliatory spirit of Britain's new leaders, the American representatives felt compelled to violate instructions from Congress which required them to consult the French at every step. "We can depend upon the French," John Jay observed, "only to see that we are separated from England, but it is not in their interest that we should become a great and formidable people, and therefore they will not help us to become so." Learning that Vergennes had arranged secret talks with the British, Jay persuaded his colleagues in Paris, Franklin and John Adams, to do the same. Vergennes was somewhat taken aback to discover that the British and Americans had agreed upon peace terms without consulting him, but he found the fact convenient in persuading a reluctant Spain to abandon the war without gaining Gibraltar. When the British offered Spain Florida (East and West) plus the Mediterranean island of Minorca, the Spanish agreed to forget Gibraltar and conclude the peace which became official on January 20, 1783.

For the United States, the terms of the Peace of Paris were generous. The thirteen former Colonies gained explicit recognition of their independence. Britain agreed to fix the northern border approximately where it still remains instead of at the Ohio River, the Canadian border fixed in 1774 by the Quebec Act. In the West, where Spain and France had hoped to confine their ally east of the Appalachians, Britain yielded all it had; the Mississippi became the border with Spain. In the South, the United States failed to gain access to the Gulf of Mexico, as both modern Florida and an ill-defined strip running westward to the Mississippi were acknowledged to be Spain's. Tenacious bargaining by John Adams gained for Americans the "right" to fish in the Grand Banks and the "liberty" to dry fish on unsettled adjacent shores. On the troublesome issue of debts owed by Americans to British subjects, the negotiators agreed that the United States should impose "no lawful Impediment" to their recovery. They pledged that Congress would "recommend" to the states restoration of confiscated Loyalist property. George III choked at the word "independence" when he announced the terms in Parliament, but he consoled himself by arguing that "knavery seems to be so much the striking feature of its [America's] inhabitants that it may not in the end be an evil that they become Aliens to this Kingdom."

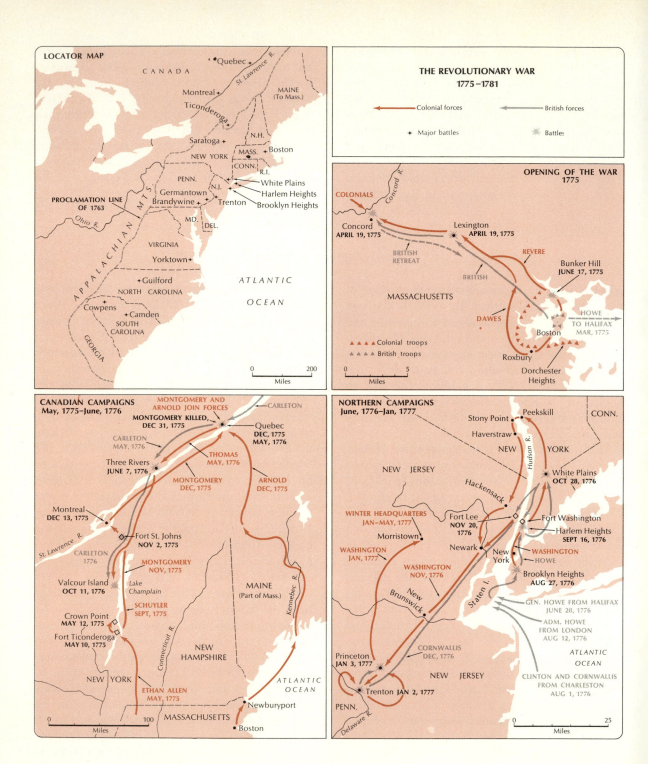

LOCATOR MAP

CANADA

- Quebec
- Montreal
- Ticonderoga

St. Lawrence R.

MAINE
(To Mass.)

N.H.

Saratoga +

NEW YORK

MASS.
- Boston

CONN.

R.I.

PENN.

N.J.

PROCLAMATION LINE
OF 1763

Germantown
Brandywine

Trenton

White Plains
Harlem Heights
Brooklyn Heights

MD.

DEL.

Ohio R.

A P P A L A C H I A N   M T S.

VIRGINIA

Yorktown +

+ Guilford

NORTH CAROLINA

Cowpens +   + Camden

SOUTH
CAROLINA

GEORGIA

ATLANTIC
OCEAN

0 _____ 200
Miles

THE REVOLUTIONARY WAR
1775–1781

→ Colonial forces   → British forces

+ Major battles   ✳ Battles

OPENING OF THE WAR
1775

COLONIALS

Concord R.

Concord
APRIL 19, 1775

Lexington
APRIL 19, 1775

BRITISH
RETREAT

BRITISH

REVERE

Bunker Hill
JUNE 17, 1775

MASSACHUSETTS

DAWES

Boston

HOWE
TO HALIFAX
MAR, 1775

Roxbury

Dorchester
Heights

▲▲▲▲ Colonial troops
▲▲▲ British troops

0 _____ 5
Miles

CANADIAN CAMPAIGNS
May, 1775–June, 1776

MONTGOMERY AND
ARNOLD JOIN FORCES

CARLETON

MONTGOMERY KILLED,
DEC 31, 1775

CARLETON
MAY, 1776

THOMAS
MAY, 1776

Quebec
DEC, 1775
MAY, 1776

Three Rivers
JUNE 7, 1776

MONTGOMERY
DEC, 1775

ARNOLD
DEC, 1775

Montreal
DEC 13, 1775

St. Lawrence R.

Fort St. Johns
NOV 2, 1775

CARLETON
1776

MONTGOMERY
NOV, 1775

Valcour Island
OCT 11, 1776

Lake
Champlain

SCHUYLER
SEPT, 1775

Crown Point
MAY 12, 1775

Fort Ticonderoga
MAY 10, 1775

Connecticut R.

NEW YORK

ETHAN ALLEN
MAY, 1775

NEW
HAMPSHIRE

MAINE
(Part of Mass.)

Kennebec R.

ATLANTIC
OCEAN

Newburyport

MASSACHUSETTS

Boston

0 _____ 100
Miles

NORTHERN CAMPAIGNS
June, 1776–Jan, 1777

Stony Point

Peekskill

CONN.

Haverstraw

NEW YORK

Hudson R.

NEW JERSEY

Hackensack

White Plains
OCT 28, 1776

WINTER HEADQUARTERS
JAN–MAY, 1777

Fort Lee
NOV 20,
1776

Fort Washington

Morristown

Harlem Heights
SEPT 16, 1776

WASHINGTON
JAN, 1777

Newark

New
York

WASHINGTON
HOWE

WASHINGTON
NOV, 1776

New
Brunswick

Staten I.

Brooklyn Heights
AUG 27, 1776

GEN. HOWE FROM HALIFAX
JUNE 28, 1776

ADM. HOWE
FROM LONDON
AUG 12, 1776

CORNWALLIS
DEC, 1776

Princeton
JAN 3, 1777

NEW JERSEY

ATLANTIC
OCEAN

CLINTON AND CORNWALLIS
FROM CHARLESTON
AUG 1, 1776

PENN.

Trenton JAN 2, 1777

Delaware R.

0 _____ 25
Miles

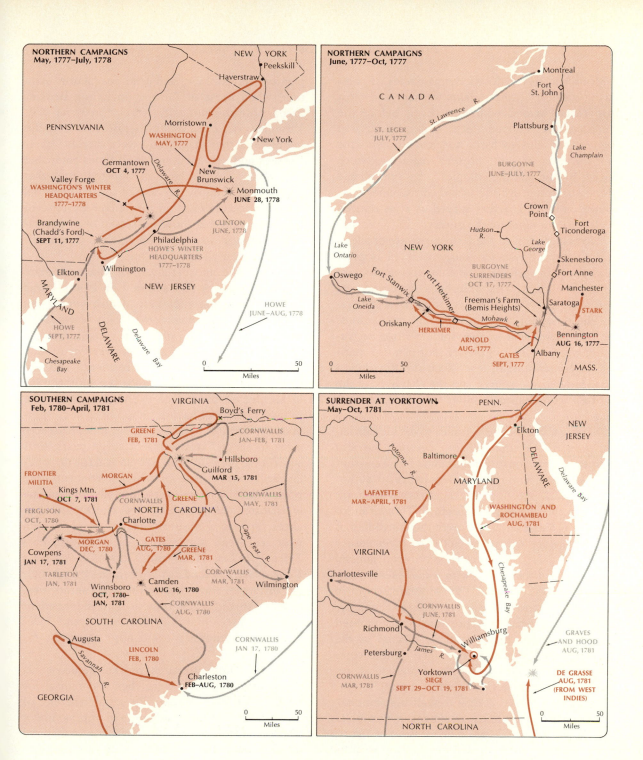

NORTHERN CAMPAIGNS
May, 1777–July, 1778

NEW YORK
Peekskill
Haverstraw
PENNSYLVANIA
Morristown
WASHINGTON MAY, 1777
New York
Germantown
OCT 4, 1777
New Brunswick
Valley Forge
WASHINGTON'S WINTER
HEADQUARTERS
1777-1778
Monmouth
JUNE 28, 1778
Brandywine
(Chadd's Ford)
SEPT 11, 1777
CLINTON
JUNE, 1778
Philadelphia
HOWE'S WINTER
HEADQUARTERS
1777-1778
Elkton
Wilmington
MARYLAND
NEW JERSEY
HOWE
JUNE–AUG, 1778
HOWE
SEPT, 1777
DELAWARE
Delaware Bay
Chesapeake
Bay
0   50
Miles

NORTHERN CAMPAIGNS
June, 1777–Oct, 1777

Montreal
Fort St. John
CANADA
ST. LEGER
JULY, 1777
St. Lawrence R.
Plattsburg
Lake Champlain
BURGOYNE
JUNE–JULY, 1777
Crown Point
Fort Ticonderoga
Hudson R.
Lake George
Skenesboro
Fort Anne
Lake Ontario
NEW YORK
Oswego
Fort Stanwix
Fort Herkimer
BURGOYNE
SURRENDERS
OCT 17, 1777
Manchester
Saratoga
STARK
Lake Oneida
Oriskany
Freeman's Farm
(Bemis Heights)
Mohawk R.
HERKIMER
ARNOLD
AUG, 1777
Bennington
AUG 16, 1777
GATES
SEPT, 1777
Albany
MASS.
0   50
Miles

SOUTHERN CAMPAIGNS
Feb, 1780–April, 1781

VIRGINIA
Boyd's Ferry
GREENE
FEB, 1781
CORNWALLIS
JAN–FEB, 1781
FRONTIER
MILITIA
Hillsboro
MORGAN
Guilford
MAR 15, 1781
Kings Mtn.
OCT 7, 1781
CORNWALLIS
GREENE
CORNWALLIS
MAY, 1781
FERGUSON
OCT, 1780
NORTH
CAROLINA
Charlotte
MORGAN
DEC, 1780
GATES
AUG, 1780
GREENE
MAR, 1781
Cornwallis
MAR, 1781
Cowpens
JAN 17, 1781
TARLETON
JAN, 1781
Winnsboro
OCT, 1780–
JAN, 1781
Camden
AUG 16, 1780
CORNWALLIS
AUG, 1780
Cape Fear R.
Wilmington
SOUTH
CAROLINA
CORNWALLIS
JAN 17, 1780
Augusta
Savannah R.
LINCOLN
FEB, 1780
Charleston
FEB–AUG, 1780
GEORGIA
0   50
Miles

SURRENDER AT YORKTOWN
May–Oct, 1781

PENN.
Elkton
NEW JERSEY
Potomac R.
Baltimore
MARYLAND
DELAWARE
Delaware Bay
LAFAYETTE
MAR–APRIL, 1781
WASHINGTON AND
ROCHAMBEAU
AUG, 1781
VIRGINIA
Chesapeake Bay
Charlottesville
CORNWALLIS
JUNE, 1781
GRAVES
AND HOOD
AUG, 1781
Richmond
Williamsburg
DE GRASSE
AUG, 1781
(FROM WEST
INDIES)
Petersburg
James R.
Yorktown
SIEGE
SEPT 29–OCT 19, 1781
CORNWALLIS
MAR, 1781
NORTH CAROLINA
0   50
Miles

INDEPENDENCE

"Mobs will never do to govern states or command armies," John Adams warned, and most Americans agreed with him. Even before the decision for independence, Congress advised several colonies to form new governments for the duration of the "present dispute between Great Britain and the colonies." By 1780 all had done so, except Rhode Island and Connecticut, whose colonial charters served as constitutions well into the nineteenth century.

No state followed the British pattern of allowing its constitution to consist only of popular traditions. In each state the constitution was a set of written rules. This difference, however, was not new. Each colony, whether by royal charter, by the governor's commission and instructions, or otherwise, had known some written instrument which at least in theory set forth its superior, or constitutional, law. What the Revolution changed was the source and the character of the written constitutions under which Americans lived.

Virginia, first of the colonies to decide officially upon full separation from Britain, was also first to adopt a constitution. Framed by a convention which also acted as a legislature, it authorized annual election of the governor by joint ballot in the bicameral legislature. Though shorn of the veto and all power over the convening of the legislature except to call it to meet earlier than scheduled, the governor retained general executive authority and, with some reservations, held the power to make appointments both in the judiciary and in local government. The upper house of the legislature, previously an appointed council, now became popularly elected as the lower house had always been. The right to vote, applicable only in the choice of legislators, remained confined to owners of property.

Virginia's great constitutional innovation— one which evoked much comment in Europe as well as in America—was a declaration of rights. Its principal author was George Mason, wealthy planter, slaveholder, and land speculator. At a time when most of Europe, including Britain, based political authority largely on royal will, Virginia proclaimed that power derived from the people and that magistrates were merely "their trustees and servants, and at all times amenable to them." The declaration asserted, too, that people should enjoy freedom of speech, that "all men are equally entitled to the free exercise of religion," and that those possessed of a "permanent common interest with . . . the community" should be allowed to vote.

By far the most radical of the new state constitutions was that adopted by Pennsylvania during the summer of 1776. Contravening the traditional requirement that only owners of property could vote, the new constitution extended the suffrage to all men over twenty-one who had at least one year's residence and had paid taxes. Very limited executive authority lay in an elected council of twelve members. The judges, instead of having "good behavior" (permanent) tenure to assure their independence, were to serve fixed terms of seven years, thus subjecting them in time to removal for unpopular decisions. These provisions, concentrating power in the state's traditionally unicameral legislature and providing few checks and balances, appeared absurdly radical to gentlemen who had read such works as Montesquieu's *Spirit of the Laws* (1748) and William Blackstone's *Commentaries on the Laws of England* (1765–1769). According to these highly regarded authorities, only a "mixed" government with independent power sources for "aristocratical" and "democratical" interests could hope to escape tyranny.

Several other features of the Pennsylvania constitution of 1776 were then too radical for widespread acceptance. The establishment of free schools and the elimination of imprisonment for debt were goals which would not be attained in that generation. There were no property qualifications fixed for holding office, and the religious qualifications were so vague as to send one zealous radical into opposition moaning: "[F]arewell Christianity when Turks, Jews, infidels, and what is worse Deists and Atheists are to make laws for our State." Included in the original draft of the constitution, but omitted from the approved document, was the still-radical affirmation that "an enormous Proportion of Property vested in a few Individuals is dangerous to the Rights, and destructive to the Common Happiness, of mankind; and therefore every free State hath a Right by its Laws to discourage the possession of such Property." What the radical Pennsylvanians wanted was a government highly responsive to majority opinion—without the checks of an independent executive and judiciary upon the will of the people's representatives. This had been the direction of political evolution in the British empire, including the colonies, and would ultimately result in the modern British system. In the United States it would continue for some time to represent the characteristic aspiration of radicals. For the most part, however, as one observer noted in 1776, "the poorer commonalty, having hitherto had little or no hand in government, seem to think it does not belong to them to have any." Partly for this reason and its converse, that "the rich, having been used to govern, seem to think it is their right," Pennsylvania's radical constitution of 1776 survived only until 1790.

European political philosophers had long affirmed that people who had overthrown an oppressive government might, through the formation of a new "social contract," institute a new government. No one had indicated at all clearly how it should be done. In most of the new American states, Revolutionary legislatures presumed to act for the people in drafting new constitutions. Only six bothered to ask specific authorization from the people to do so. None, until Massachusetts did so in 1778, offered the people an opportunity to ratify the state constitution before it went into effect.

In Massachusetts the people were determined to take a direct role in the reformulation of their social contract. In 1776, when the Legislature asked authority from the people to write a constitution, most towns responded favorably. Concord, however, resolved testily: "A Constitution alterable by the Supreme Legislature is no Security at all to the Subject against . . . Encroachment" by the government upon his "Rights and Privileges." When the towns came to consider the Legislature's draft constitution in 1778, they rejected it overwhelmingly, partly because of dissatisfaction with various provisions, but also because it was the Legislature's product.

Legislators were content to go along with a provisional government operating more or less under the old colonial charter, but "Constitutionalists" in western Massachusetts demanded that the Legislature "call a special convention of Delegates from each Town . . . , for the purpose of forming a Bill of rights and a Constitution." Claiming that without a constitution there was no proper "Foundation" for the administration of justice, they closed the courts, thereby preventing legal action to collect debts. In 1779 the towns voted more than 2 to 1 for a special convention to write a constitution.

Whom would the convention represent? "The only moral foundation of government," John Adams observed, "is the consent of the people," but he confessed perplexity as to how far to "carry the principle." In the end, Massachusetts scrapped traditional property qualifications and allowed all freemen over twenty-one to vote for both convention delegates and approval of the constitution. Paradoxically, the constitution drafted by the convention and ratified by the adult freemen of the towns in 1780 reimposed a property qualification of £60 on voting for legislators. Such conservative features evoked much opposition and even required some juggling of the returns to support the decision for ratification. Nevertheless, in its constitutional difficulties between 1776 and 1780, Massachusetts, at the insistence of its people, had worked out a method by which people could indeed secure a form of government reflecting their wishes and endow it with their explicit consent. Nationalists intent upon instituting a new government for all the American people would ultimately profit from the example.

Separation of governmental powers appealed strongly to the people of Massachusetts. The assumption behind the idea was essentially that minority interests, particularly the wealthy, deserved an opportunity to block acts of potentially unreasonable legislative majorities. Massachusetts' constitution of 1780, drafted by the erudite John Adams, empowered the people rather than the legislature to choose the governor and endowed him with a veto power. A two-thirds vote in each house, however, could override the veto. Judges did not serve fixed terms but enjoyed permanent, or good behavior, tenure. To assure representation of the wealthy in the upper house, its membership was limited to those who owned land worth £300 or personal property worth £600.

Common to all the new state constitutions were a number of fundamental concepts. Among these were the assumptions that government derived its authority from the people and that its function was to serve their interests. Equally universal was the assumption that governmental powers were limited: that individuals possessed fundamental rights which governments must respect. Short terms of office reflected the determination to keep government highly responsive to popular will. South Carolina gave members of its lower legislative chamber two-year terms, but elsewhere they were one year or less. For the aristocratic upper houses, terms were generally longer, as much as five years in Maryland. Governors served terms of three years in New York and Delaware, two years in South Carolina, but only one year elsewhere. Local government, as in the past, enjoyed only a limited autonomy. Major local officials, especially in the cities, were generally not elected, but were state appointees.

Much of the early disagreement among Americans focused on the relative merits of separation of powers as opposed to legislative supremacy. Legislative supremacy, the perennial thrust of the colonial years, was at first more popular than separation of powers. Although no other state went as far as Pennsylvania, eight states authorized their legislatures to select governors; nine denied the governor a veto; and the same number gave the legislature a share of the appointive power. Yet the new constitutions revealed considerable respect for separation of powers. Eight states gave judges tenure during good behavior; three others gave them very long terms. All the states except Pennsylvania had governors who enjoyed some independence as well as bicameral legislatures, in which the upper house was designed to represent the wealthy or the "aristocratical" element.

Special privileges for those who owned property aroused further debate. Several states—notably South Carolina, New Jersey, Maryland, and Massachusetts—fixed property qualifications so high as to exclude all but the wealthy from holding major offices. Other states imposed no such restrictions at all. Land holding qualifications for voting remained in force in nine states, often at a higher level for the upper than for the lower house of the legislature. Only New Hampshire, North Carolina, and Georgia followed Pennsylvania's example in substituting payment of taxes for landownership as a prerequisite for voting. In North Carolina and Georgia, a compulsory poll tax theoretically qualified all free adult males to vote. Few as they were, these breaches in the wall of suffrage restriction, according to one leading authority on the subject, "were the most important in the entire history of American suffrage reform." They were, of course, in keeping with the basic ideology of the Revolution, which recognized all the people, not merely the owners of property, as the source of political authority.

Merely by waging a successful war for independence Americans had profoundly altered the course of their economic development. Trade became much freer. Americans could now send their exports wherever there was demand for them. Major products no longer needed to go only to Britain as enumerated commodities. American ports became open to ships of all nations. Imports could come directly from continental Europe or Asia rather than through the hands of middlemen in Britain as they had done previously. Americans were free as well to issue paper money and to create banks to foster economic development.

Independence produced fundamental changes in landownership as well. Either Congress (for ceded Western lands) or state governments (for lands not ceded) took over the titles to public lands from the British Crown or British proprietary families. If the American governments initially followed policies rather more favorable to speculators than to settlers, it is also true that they, more than the British, attempted to foster the rapid extension of settlement, partly as a means to increase government revenue by speedy sales. Public lands became in fact a source of great public wealth which governments used to reward Revolutionary soldiers and ultimately to subsidize schools and other desirable enterprises.

State governments, although generally disposed to favor speculators, pursued policies inimical to aristocracy. New York ended the rights of its manor lords to representation in the legislature. States sold frontier land very cheaply to innumerable speculators who then competed with each other to resell it quickly for profit. Prices one-fifth to one-twentieth of those prevailing in older areas operated powerfully both to lure settlers to frontier regions and to diffuse landownership still more widely and thus combat aristocracy.

Resale of lands confiscated from Tories contributed also to the decline of the aristocracy. In every state, wealthy supporters of the Crown had held enormous landed estates which the Revolutionary governments seized and sold to patriots. In New York, fifty-nine Tories suffered losses averaging over 40,000 acres each. It was often patriot speculators rather than small farmers who bought these confiscated lands, but such owners usually sought a speculative profit by retailing small parcels to settlers rather than creating large, tenant-operated estates to be held by their descendants forever.

Freedom from British restrictions encouraged the development of American industry. Gentlemen formed private societies to promote manufacturing and to subsidize individual enterprises. Artisans beseeched state governments to impose high taxes on imports of items which they manufactured, so that they might enjoy a competitive advantage. Such tariff measures also appeared desirable to combat America's unfavorable balance of trade by reducing the drain of gold and silver from the country. Impressed by these arguments, many Northern states passed tariff measures and thus, in contrast to Britain's prewar policy, encouraged the development of new manufacturing enterprises. States which lacked important manufactures, however, chose usually to allow such goods to be imported from abroad without heavy taxation. By so doing, they undermined the tariff protection available to American producers in other states.

Independence was advantageous for American economic growth, but it carried a high price in the short run because Britain now excluded Americans from the many benefits they had previously enjoyed under the British mercantilist system. New England suffered most. Britain barred American fish from the British West Indies, with the result that New England exports of cod in the late 1780s were 43 percent less than they had been before the war. Discriminatory taxes or outright bans hurt other New England products as well. Exclusion of American ships from British West Indian ports was a severe blow to New England shipping. Frequent suspensions of these regulations by authorities in the British West Indies, as well as outright smuggling, brought some relief.

For the Middle Atlantic region the problem of readjustment was less acute. The staple exports of wheat and flour continued to find a West Indian market, although their importation was limited legally to British ships. Britain reduced its importation of American iron, but domestic American consumption apparently increased sufficiently to keep the furnaces in operation.

Southerners suffered considerably. About thirty thousand slaves reportedly disappeared from Virginia and twenty-five thousand from South Carolina during the war, taken by the British in many instances as a form of confiscation. Even without the benefit of the prewar enumeration policy, Britain managed to retain its major role as processor and distributor of American tobacco, but a domestic consumption tax in Britain itself somewhat reduced the market. France arranged to do its purchasing of tobacco through a national monopoly. These developments tended to reduce the world price and consequently the producers' income. Indigo planters, deprived of their prewar British subsidy, found they could not compete with West Indian producers.

Americans themselves greatly aggravated their economic difficulties in 1784 by importing vast quantities of goods from Britain on credit. Hampered by the shortage of acceptable money, as well as by the British restrictions on their export trade, American merchants experienced great difficulty, first in selling the imported items, and then in making enough export shipments to pay for them. To reduce their interest costs on debts to British firms, many American merchants, unable to find commodities acceptable to Britain, arranged to send gold and silver instead. This practice aggravated the already-serious shortage of money.

Scarcity of money became in fact the most serious manifestation of a severe postwar depression. One root of the difficulty lay in the depreciation of continental paper money during the war. Hurt by the depreciation of paper money, many men of wealth subsequently opposed additional issues. Unfortunately, by 1784 gold and silver, which had been derived chiefly from British and French army expenditures and foreign loans, were no longer flowing into the economy rapidly enough to offset the rate at which they were being exported. As the money supply dwindled, prices, already depressed by export problems, fell still further. Between 1784 and 1788, wholesale commodity prices in Philadelphia and Charleston declined about 25 percent. Farmers found it difficult to meet fixed mortgage payments, buy imported commodities, or even pay their taxes.

Pressures for the issuance of paper money grew accordingly. Farmers in particular sought the issuance of land bank notes, or money created by the state on the security of land mortgages. Seven states acceded to such pressures in 1785 and 1786. Some, notably South Carolina and New York, repeated the generally favorable experience of the years before the Revolution. Rhode Island and North Carolina, however, horrified creditors. They made their paper money legal tender, the offer of which legally discharged a debt even if the payment was refused. They failed to make adequate provision for redemption so that the value of the currency diminished rapidly. Such records stiffened resistance to paper money in other states, most notably in Massachusetts.

Violence broke out in Massachusetts in the wake of seemingly honorable but unfortunate decisions by the Legislature. In contrast to the Continental Congress, Massachusetts legislators determined to redeem the wartime paper money at the value which it had when issued, even though the currency had subsequently depreciated greatly. This decision more than doubled the state debt. The legislators resolved, furthermore, to repay the state debt quickly rather than inconvenience creditors and disgrace the government by delaying settlement. For much of the revenue to repay its debt, the state relied upon a poll tax—a fixed sum charged against all males over sixteen. To encourage payment of both taxes and private debts, the state law provided, as was usual in other areas as well, that the property of delinquents might be seized and sold to make good their obligations. They might even be jailed if their estates proved insufficient to meet such obligations.

Poor people in rural Massachusetts unquestionably suffered under these policies. Property seized and sold to pay debts brought far less than its value in normal times. Seizures sometimes deprived men of the means of their livelihood. Men with dependent families went to jail for inability to pay small amounts. Towns hit by depression were often unwilling to pay the expenses of a delegate to the state Legislature and thus went unrepresented while the Legislature, in which wealthy communities were somewhat overrepresented, ignored petitions for paper money and stay laws. Denied relief and facing continued oppression both by seizure of their property and by incarceration for debt, the poor took matters into their own hands. By mob action they prevented the meeting or forced the adjournment of the courts, which were the instruments of their oppression. When insurgents under a former Revolutionary captain, Daniel Shays, attempted to seize arms from an arsenal at Springfield, militia forces killed four men and put the rest to flight. Despite the wrath of such onetime radicals as Samuel Adams, who felt that "the man who dares rebel against the laws of a republic ought to suffer death," all the Shaysites condemned to death ultimately gained pardons, including Daniel Shays himself. The legislative session of 1787, while it still held out against

Commonwealth of Maſſachuſetts.

By His EXCELLENCY

JamesBowdoin,Eſq.

GOVERNOUR of the COMMONWEALTH of

MASSACHUSETTS.

A Proclamation.

WHEREAS by an Act paſſed the ſixteenth of February inſtant, entitled, " An Act deſcribing the diſqualifications, to which perſons ſhall be ſubjected, which have been, or may be guilty of Treaſon, or giving aid or ſupport to the preſent Rebellion, and to whom a pardon may be extended," the General Court have eſtabliſhed and made known the conditions and diſqualifications, upon which pardon and indemnity to certain offenders, deſcribed in the ſaid Act, ſhall be offered and given ; and have authorized and empowered the Governour, in the name of the General Court, to promiſe to ſuch offenders ſuch conditional pardon and indemnity :

I HAVE thought fit, by virtue of the authority veſted in me by the ſaid Act, to iſſue this Proclamation, hereby promiſing pardon and indemnity to all offenders within the deſcription aforeſaid, who are citizens of this State ; under ſuch reſtrictions, conditions and diſqualifications, as are mentioned in the ſaid Act : provided they comply with the terms and conditions thereof, on or before the twenty-firſt day of March next.

GIVEN at the Council Chamber in Boſton, this Seventeenth Day of February, in the Year of our LORD. One Thouſand Seven Hundred and Eighty Seven, and in the Eleventh Year of the Independence of the United States of AMERICA.

JAMES BOWDOIN.

By His Excellency's Command,
JOHN AVERY, jun. Secretary.

BOSTON : Printed by ADAMS & NOURSE, Printers to the GENERAL COURT.

A proclamation of amnesty, dated February 17, 1787, for participants in Shays' Rebellion.   The Granger Collection

paper money and stay laws, lowered the tax burden and exempted both household goods and tools of one's trade from seizure and sale for debt. A general improvement in economic conditions during the next few years helped to alleviate discontent.

Social Change

Social changes of fundamental importance accompanied the American Revolution, just as they have other major revolutions in world history. Perhaps the most important change, although one difficult to characterize clearly, was the awakening of the "inferior sort," who then rose to challenge the traditional dominance of society by a landed and mercantile elite. Pennsylvania's radical constitution and Shays' Rebellion were merely two examples of the new activism inspired among previously deferential classes by the rhetoric of liberty and the experience of coercing "gentlemen" insufficiently supportive of the Revolution.

Symbolizing the change was the exodus of at least 60,000 and perhaps 100,000 Loyalists, a greater number relatively than fled the later revolution in France.

By no means were all Loyalists upper-class in status. In the backcountry many recent immigrants were Tories because they retained strong British feeling. Others in the backcountry resented local patriot landlords or the eastern patriot establishment more than they did the agents of George III. For the most part, however, those who left were people more afraid of the revolutionary ideas of representative government and its social implications than of British traditions of monarchical and aristocratic authority. Most such exiles were from the middle states and the South, very few from New England. Their departure for Canada, the British West Indies, or Britain itself made it easier for the Revolutionary Whigs to continue implementing their ideas.

Slavery was a standing affront to the ideology of the Revolution, and consequently came under strong attack at the conclusion of the war. In the North, slavery served no important economic function and was unnecessary as a means of assuring white supremacy; blacks were relatively few. New York, although smaller in total population than either Pennsylvania or Massachusetts, had by far the largest Negro population of any Northern state (21,000 in 1780); but even in New York the proportion of blacks in the population was only about one in ten. Therefore the consideration uppermost in the minds of most Northern Revolutionary leaders with reference to slavery was its contradiction of the moral foundation of the Revolution—the concept that all men are equally entitled to liberty.

Still, elimination of slavery in the North came gradually. The prospective state of Vermont barred slavery in its constitution of 1777. In the case of Quock Walker in 1783, the Chief Justice of Massachusetts affirmed that slavery was "inconsistent with our . . . constitution," whose first article began: "All men are born free." Pennsylvania in 1780 was the first state to provide for gradual abolition. New York failed to enact a gradual abolition law in 1785 only because of disagreement over whether or not free blacks should be entitled to vote. By that time all Northern states except New York and New Jersey had acted to end slavery. The laggards did so ultimately in 1799 and 1804.

Equality, however, did not keep pace with freedom in the North. The assumption of black inferiority was virtually universal, and from it sprang laws not only against Negro voting but also against miscegenation and Negro immigration. Custom confined blacks largely to menial jobs and to segregation in churches and schools.

In the Southern states, where one in every three or four people was a Negro and slavery was basic to both the economy and the social system, human rights won still less recognition. Southern libertarians, such as Patrick Henry, recognized the clear conflict between their principles and the ownership of slaves. Many freed their slaves under the provisions of state laws designed to encourage that practice, but others, including Henry, were "drawn along by the general Inconvenience of living without them." In the Lower South, where plantation agriculture was comparatively more prosperous and slaves relatively more numerous than in Virginia, manumission was less popular. All the Southern states except Georgia had by 1786 prohibited or severely restricted the importation of slaves, but revulsion against the institution of slavery was perhaps less important in accounting for this development than fear for the maintenance of white supremacy and concern over the balance of payments. Even before the Revolution, most Southern colonies had sought to restrict the importation of Negroes, but on behalf of British

Art in America: 1660–1860

Painting in America began as early as the 1600s, as far as we know from the earliest-dated painting so far located, but, presumably, pictures were painted even earlier. These early paintings of the seventeenth century were portraits, works of art with utilitarian purposes, albeit the utility was psychological rather than overtly practical. The tradition of portraiture which already existed in Great Britain reinforced this emphasis, and, indeed, portraiture remained the principal art form in the American colonies until the time of the Revolution and even afterward.

By the end of the first decade of the eighteenth century, professional portraitists from both Britain and the continent began to supercede the early artisan painters and brought at least a measure of professional competence to the art. The styles of painting naturally reflected those practiced in Europe, although at first at least, a certain lag occurred in the arrival of successive aesthetic approaches to portraiture. Only in the 1740s did the colonies begin to produce native-born

The portrait above of Alice Mason by an unknown artist, was painted in New England in the second half of the seventeenth century. The flat, patterned, decorative style of Elizabethan portraiture of almost 100 years earlier typifies most early New England portraiture, which was created by talented but anonymous and relatively untrained artisans.

Above: Artist unknown, Alice Mason, *1670, oil. Adams National Historic Site.*

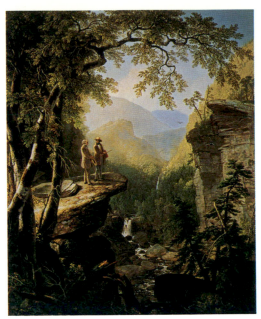

As a tribute to Thomas Cole after his death, fellow landscape painter Asher B. Durand painted him in his favorite Catskills, communing with their mutual friend and interpreter of nature William Cullen Bryant.

artists who could compete successfully with their European-born-and-trained colleagues. Thus the earliest professionals who arrived usually remained as "big fish in a small pond," while those Europeans who arrived during and after the mid-eighteenth century tended to draw what patronage they could and depart. By the 1760s America had begun to produce master portraitists, especially in the person of John Singleton Copley, who could certainly rival any European visitors and could actually compete on an international level.

During the same decade, aspiring American artists began to reverse the trend and migrate to Europe, primarily to London, for their artistic education. Some, like Copley and Benjamin West, remained abroad. Others, like Charles Willson Peale, learned their craft and returned to America to become the leading painters at home. Still others, like Gilbert Stuart, became highly successful in Europe but returned to America after practicing abroad for a number of years.

Even into the early years of the nineteenth century, portraiture reigned supreme. But by the 1820s there had grown up in America a patron class with time, money, and interest enough to become collectors and to give encouragement to American painters who wished to go beyond the limits of portrait painting. Fortunately, in the domains of landscape and still-life painting, artists such as Thomas Cole, Asher B. Durand, and Raphaelle Peale were able to meet this challenge successfully, and in landscape painting particularly, a school of painters responded to the romantic interpretation of nature already being defined by the poet William Cullen Bryant among others. The glorification of the American landscape continued well into the mid-nineteenth century, but nature could stand for the handiwork of God, too, as embodied in the complex allegories of Thomas Cole. American artists' attempts at interpreting the Old Masters' themes, however, found little response in their native land, despite the acknowledged talents of such painters as Washington Allston and John Vanderlyn; even the interpretation of American historical events could find little patronage although John Trumbull was widely acclaimed and eventually patronized by the national government.

In the mid-1840s, American art had visibly begun to outgrow the dependence upon English cultural forms that had lasted despite two wars with the mother country. Patronage shifted from a few wealthy individuals to the growing middle class which demanded artistic forms easily understood and easy to respond to. Thus, by 1850 genre painting, the depiction of everyday scenes, dominated American art, and William Sidney Mount had become the most revered of American artists. His interpretation of distinctly American scenes and subjects further insured his success for this was a particularly nationalistic period in America's cultural development. Indeed, the art of midcentury can be characterized as democratic, nationalistic, and optimistic in its outlook.

The selection, text, and captions in this and succeeding fine-arts sections are by William Gerdts. Formerly curator of the Norfolk Museum of Arts and Sciences, Curator of Painting and Sculpture at the Newark Museum, and Associate Professor and Gallery Director at Johns Hopkins University, Mr. Gerdts currently lectures at Johns Hopkins, serves as vice-president of a New York City art gallery.

Eastman Johnson, a later genre painter who studied in Düsseldorf, grafted upon the American genre scene the detailed, anecdotal, and sentimental style of that art center. Düsseldorf, in fact, superseded London in the mid-nineteenth century as a training center for American artists.

Eastman Johnson (1824–1906), Old Kentucky Home, Life in the South, 1859, oil on canvas. Courtesy of the New-York Historical Society, New York City.

When professional portrait painters began to arrive in the Colonies, they came not only from Great Britain, but, as in the case of Justus Englehardt Kühn, from the Continent as well. In his interpretation of Eleanor Darnall (right), Kühn projects her into a fantasy world of elegant nobility far removed from her actual surroundings. Kühn probably drew upon some engraving source for his background, costume, and pose, and this is certainly the case in the portrait by a New York limner (below, left), for which the engraving has been located (below, right). Such painters naturally tended to simplify their engraving source in order to handle the complex problems of composition and modelling, and, of course, the color interpretation was original. Although such a practice may suggest plagiarism today, it was an honored basis for Colonial portraiture practiced even by such outstanding professionals as John Smibert and John Singleton Copley.

Artist unknown, John Van Cortlandt, *ca. 1731, oil on canvas. The Brooklyn Museum, Dick S. Ramsay Fund.*

G. Kneller, Engraving by I. Smith, The Lord Buckhurst and Lady Mary Sackvil Sister, *mezzotint. Courtesy of the Waldron Phoenix Belknap, Jr. Research Library of American Painting at the Henry Francis du Pont Winterthur Museum.*

Justus Engelhardt Kuhn (*unknown*–1717), Eleanor Darnall, *cs.* 1710, *oil on canvas. From the Collections of the Maryland Historical Society.*

John Smibert (1688–1751). Francis Brinley, 1731, oil on canvas. The Metropolitan Museum of Art, Rogers Fund. 1962.

With the arrival of John Smibert in New England, first in Newport, R.I., and then in Boston, the Colonies gained a portraitist of considerable power and reputation. Smibert was called upon to portray many of the leading citizens of Massachusetts in his baroque style using massive form and strong characterization; the Portrait of Francis Brinley *(above) gains further interest from its background which depicts one of the earliest painted views of Boston.*

John Singleton Copley (1738–1815), Paul Revere, 1765–1770, oil on canvas. Courtesy of the Museum of Fine Arts, Boston. Gift of Joseph W., William B., and Edward H. R. Revere.

The tradition of incisive realistic portraiture founded by Smibert in Boston reached its culmination just before the Revolution in the portraiture of native-born John Singleton Copley. Copley's subjects included leading merchants, statesmen, ministers, and fellow-artists such as Paul Revere, here shown in an informal, working portrait, as were several other Copley subjects, perhaps in deference to the Puritan glorification of work.

Benjamin West (1738–1820)
Penn's Treaty with the Indians, *ca.* 1771, *oil on canvas*
Courtesy of the Pennsylvania Academy of the Fine Arts

Many of the painters of the late Colonial period and of the early Republic accepted the need to paint portraits for a livelihood but hankered after subjects in the grand tradition: classical, religious, or historical events. Benjamin West was one of these. He left America in 1760 and settled permanently in London where he achieved great success as one of the leading history painters of his day. A stout defender of the American Revolution, West remained faithful to his Colonial background in two other ways: he taught dozens of younger American aspirants, and he often depicted scenes from Colonial history such as Penn's Treaty with the Indians *(above). John Trumbull, one of West's pupils, undertook one series of subjects that West, as history painter to George III of England, could not, namely, the history of the American Revolution (right, above). Many years later Trumbull enlarged four of these spirited late-eighteenth-century scenes to decorate the rotunda of the Capitol building. Thomas Sully of Philadelphia, America's leading portraitist of the early nineteenth century, made occasional forays into the field of historical painting, here joining the scores of other professional artists memorializing the first American President (right, below).*

John Trumbull (1756–1843), Battle of Bunker's Hill, 1786, oil on canvas. Yale University Art Gallery.

Thomas Sully (1783–1872), The Passage of the Delaware, 1819, oil on canvas. Courtesy of the Museum of Fine Arts, Boston, Gift of the Museum Owners.

Gilbert Stuart (1755–1828), General Henry Knox. *Courtesy of the Museum of Fine Arts, Boston. On Deposit by the City of Boston.*

rles Willson Peale (1741–1827), Family Group, 1773, *oil on canvas. Courtesy of the New-York Historical Society, New York City.*

…en Copley left the Colonies, the mantle for …listic portraiture fell upon the Philadelphian, …arles Willson Peale, who added, in some of his …st paintings, an emphasis upon sympathetic …ily interrelationships (above). The realistic …trait style of the Federal period was soon …erseded, however, by the vivid, bravura brushwork …d color of Gilbert Stuart (left). Stuart, a pupil …Benjamin West, had great success in London and …blin before returning to America in 1792 and …cticing in New York City, Philadelphia, and …shington, and finally settling in Boston in 1805. …le, meanwhile, had fathered "America's first family" …rtists. His sons, Rembrandt, Rubens, Titian, and …haelle Peale became noted painters, the first an …ortant portraitist, and the last, the finest still-life …nter in America in the early nineteenth century …ht).

Raphaelle Peale (1774–1825), Melons and Morning Glories, 1813, *oil on canvas. Courtesy of National Collection of Fine Arts, Smithsonian Institution. Gift of Paul Mellon.*

Thomas Cole's fame, in his own time, lay in his allegorical series of paintings. These series depended upon the contrasts of two, three, four, or five separate canvases in which the artist stated his two major themes: the transience of civilization against the permanence of nature and the insignificance of man against the greatness of nature. Cole's allegories were popular here because they related to the New World itself.

Above: Thomas Cole (1801–1848), The Departure. *Courtesy of the Corcoran Gallery of Art.*
Below: Thomas Cole, The Return. *Courtesy of the Corcoran Gallery of Art.*

The 1820s witnessed rise of interest in the depict. of nature and of ma relationship to it. Thom Cole was our first gr landscapist. In his in pretation of the Oxbow of Connecticut River (rig above), he concentrates on unusual aspects of nature, c trasting its stormy and ser elements. The belief in, love of, the American landsc continued well into the mia of the nineteenth century Jasper Cropsey's Autumn the Hudson River where r. blazing color and benefic light illuminates the scene an almost visionary man (right, below). Altho painted in England, this u typifies what has been ter the "Hudson River" schoo paint.

Thomas Cole (1801–1848), The Oxbow (the Connecticut River near Northampton), 1846, oil on canvas. The Metropolitan Museum of Art. Gift of Mrs. Russell Sage, 1908.

Jasper Francis Cropsey (1823–1900), Autumn on the Hudson River, 1906. National Gallery of Art, Washington, D. C. Gift of the Avalon Foundation.

John Vanderlyn and Washington Allston, on the other hand, both trained in the study of the Old Masters. Represented here by classical and religious subjects, respectively, both were admired by connoisseurs in Americ but neglected by the general public. Vanderlyn's study of and relationship to French Neo-Classicism and Allston's kinship with Titian and the sixteenth-century Venetian brought both artists much recognition in Europe, but the painting was too foreign for the American public.

..lliam Sidney Mount specialized in
..icting scenes of farm and country life on his
..ive Long Island (right). His clearly
..derstandable and humorous genre paintings
..n him great success, independent as they
..e of European study or subject. His works,
..d their western equivalent, the river life
..es (above) of the St. Louis artist George
..eb Bingham, were further popularized
..ough the engraving medium which enabled
..ts after the paintings of these artists to be
..g in thousands of homes.

Opulent color and a sense of wealth, abundance, and optimism—nowhere more fully depicted than in the still-life painting of the day—characterized American painting at midcentury. This is particularly true of the work of Severin Roesen, one of the many refugees from the European revolutions of 1848, who fled the persecution of the Old World for the abundance of the New. Indeed, American painting of the period came to picture a vision of a new Eden, of man's second chance on earth as the American Adam. The fullest expression of this "Adamic vision" appears in the tropical landscapes of Frederic Church, where uncorrupted man lives in peace and serenity with the richness and fullness of nature. Thus, in Church's paintings, man and nature coexist in total rapport, contrasting with the earlier, dark and dramatic allegories of Church's teacher, Thomas Cole.

Above: Severin Roesen (unknown–1871), Still Life: Flowers, *oil on canvas. The Metropolitan Museum of Art, Charles Allen Munn Bequest; Fosburgh Fund, Inc., Gift; Mr. and Mrs. J. William Middendorf II, Gift; and Henry G. Keasbey Bequest, 1967.*

Below: Frederick E. Church (1826–1900), View of Cotopaxi, *1857, oil on canvas. The Art Institute of Chicago.*

slave sellers the Privy Council had consistently voided colonial laws designed to achieve that end.

Religious customs also altered after the Revolution. Belief in freedom of religious opinion as a "natural" or God-given right was coming to be generally accepted. State-enforced religious conformity, based to some extent on the assumption that God would reward or punish whole societies according to the extent to which its members observed His will, was losing ground.

Massachusetts, over much opposition, held to the old tradition. By far the most controversial feature of the state's constitution in 1780 was the article dealing with religion. The constitution expressly assumed that happiness and good order in society "depend upon piety, religion and morality" and that "these cannot be generally diffused . . . but by . . . public worship . . . and . . . public instruction." It authorized the Legislature, therefore, to require towns to provide "at their own expense, . . . for the support of public protestant teachers of piety, religion and morality." Compulsory attendance "upon the instructions of the public teachers," with provisions for exceptions based on conscience and convenience, was to be authorized at the Legislature's discretion. The constitution did guarantee to towns the right to "elect" their public teachers or ministers and to contract with them on the matter of support. As had been true before the Revolution, individuals could earmark their religious support payments for their own sect or denomination, if they actually attended its "instructions."

Virginia, by way of contrast, was in the vanguard of the new movement for religious freedom. Thomas Jefferson drafted a "Statute of Religious Liberty" during the Revolution, but it was not enacted until 1785. Its preamble castigated the "impious presumption" by which "fallible and uninspired men, have assumed dominion over the faith of others." Compelling a man to make payments "for the propagation of opinions which he disbelieves," the statute affirmed, "is sinful and tyrannical." The law then provided specifically that "no man shall be compelled to frequent or support any religious worship . . . nor . . . suffer on account of his religious opinions." Rather, "all men shall be free to profess" their beliefs and "the same shall in no wise diminish, enlarge or affect their civil capacities." In this new spirit, reinforced by patriotic sentiment, the Church of England lost its "establishment," or government support, in all the Southern states. Legal qualifications designed to exclude Catholics from voting and holding office declined almost to the vanishing point.

Drastic reorganization of the Church of England was necessary to permit its continuance in America after the Revolution. A group of Anglican (Church of England) clergymen from Connecticut dispatched the Reverend Samuel Seabury to England in 1783 to seek consecration as a bishop and thus to become administrative head of the Church in America in place of the Bishop of London. The English bishops refused to consecrate Seabury when he would not swear allegiance to the British Crown, but he secured consecration from dissident bishops in Scotland. Parliament acceded in 1787 to the consecration of two other American bishops. Thus the American Episcopal Church secured the three bishops necessary for the consecration of others and for its perpetuation.

Reorganization was less troublesome for other religious groups. The handful of priests who served America's 24,000 Catholics received authorization from Rome to elect one of their number as bishop. The choice fell upon Father John Carroll, a Jesuit, who was consecrated Bishop of Baltimore in 1790 at ceremonies which took place in London. American followers of the English evangelist John Wesley organized the Methodist Episcopal Church in 1784 under the leadership of Francis Asbury, even though Wesley himself remained nominally a member of the Church of England for several more years. One of the modifications from Anglican practice enabled Asbury, in effect, to designate himself a bishop. Congregationalists, Baptists, and Quakers placed so much authority in local congregations or individual members that they needed no reorganization to establish American control. Presbyterians, organized in a representative system of church government, likewise needed no change, although they did become markedly less deferential to Scottish Presbyterian authorities than they had been.

Nationalistic feeling became apparent also among artists, poets, musicians, and intellectuals in general. John Trumbull of Connecticut, studying in the London studio of Benjamin West, whose historical paintings had so glorified the history of Britain, began there in the early 1780s a series of paintings celebrating the American struggle against British rule. "The greatest motive I . . . have for engaging in . . . painting," he wrote, "has been the wish of commemorating the great events of our country's revolution." William Billings, onetime Boston tanner, composed music with patriotic themes. Another John Trumbull of Connecticut, a lawyer related to the painter, achieved great popularity in 1782 with *M'Fingal*, an epic poem satirizing the British and their Tory supporters. Noah

Webster, later to achieve immortality through his dictionary, urged reform of British spelling with the object of establishing "a *national language*." "As an independent people," he argued, "our reputation abroad demands that in all things we should be federal; be *national*; for if we do not respect *ourselves*, we may be assured that *other nations* will not respect us."

Historical writing, largely provincial in its focus before the Revolution, now began to reflect a national spirit. Foremost among the nationalist historians was David Ramsay, a South Carolina doctor. In his perceptive *History of the American Revolution*, published in 1789, Ramsay noted that before 1775:

> the bulk of the people in the interior country were unacquainted with their fellow citizens [in other regions]. A continental army, and Congress composed of men from all the States, . . . disseminated principles of union among them. Local prejudices abated. By frequent collision asperities were worn off, and a foundation was laid for the establishment of a nation.

Still the United States in the mid-1780s was merely a loose confederation of nearly sovereign states, not yet a nation.

Conclusion

Britain's dogmatic insistence upon the right of Parliament to bind Americans in any way it chose invited violence. It began at Lexington under circumstances which convinced many Americans of the barbarity of the king's troops. Initially, Americans fought only to compel restitution of what they regarded as "our former just and unalienable Rights and Privileges," but British intransigence led them in 1776 to declare their independence and to solicit French assistance in attaining it.

Successive British plans for crushing colonial resistance failed. The British captured New York in 1776, but they proved unable to destroy Washington's army or—thanks to Washington's timely victory at Trenton—to demoralize the

resistance forces. Their plan to isolate and subdue New England failed with the surrender of Burgoyne's Canadian-based army at Saratoga in the fall of 1777. A campaign to regain the South, complicated by French naval and military cooperation with the Americans, ended when a similar disaster overtook Cornwallis at Yorktown in 1781. Capitalizing on the desires of a new British ministry to avoid driving the Americans into complete dependence on France, astute American diplomats gained at Paris in 1783 more generous territorial limits for an independent "United States" than the French or the Spanish had desired.

During the Revolution and the early postwar years the American people altered their society profoundly. They based their state governments upon the will of the people and, through provisions for frequent elections with a relatively wide suffrage and reasonably fair apportionment of legislative seats, arranged to keep them representative. Economically, independence brought not only great opportunities for the future but also severe temporary hardship, chiefly the result of America's exclusion from the British mercantilist system and the wartime loss of confidence in paper money. Putting the Revolutionary ideology into practice helped to undermine old traditions of deference, to begin the elimination of slavery in the North, and to extend religious freedom.

SUGGESTED READINGS

John Shy's *Toward Lexington* (1965) characterizes the British army effectively for the period before 1775. The best treatment of the war itself is Don Higginbotham's *The War of American Independence* (1972). H. H. Peckham's *The War for Independence** (1958) is concise and reliable. It attributes less to French assistance than does W. M. Wallace's *Appeal to Arms** (1951). John R. Alden in *The American Revolution** (1954), extensively altered in *A History of the American Revolution* (1969), puts military events in their political context. Eric Robson's *The American Revolution** (1955) presents a British scholar's provocative analysis of factors affecting the outcome. Piers Mackesy defends the much-criticized Lord George Germain and emphasizes naval aspects of *The War for America* (1964). Defense of Germain is also the hallmark of *The American Secretary* (1963) by G. S. Brown. John C. Miller's *Triumph of Freedom** (1948) is a fast-moving narrative, as is Lynn Montross's *Rag, Tag, and Bobtail* (1952). A. B. Tourtellot in *Lexington and Concord** (1959) recounts those battles vividly. In *Rebels and Redcoats** (1957), G. F. Scheer and H. F. Rankin weave contemporary accounts into a flowing narrative. H. S. Commager and R. B. Morris (eds.) in *The Spirit of Seventy-six* (2 vols, 1958) present contemporary accounts in a topical arrangement.

More specialized studies are also abundant. Ira Gruber, *The Howe Brothers and the American Revolution* (1972), blames their crucial lack of aggressiveness on a desire to effect reconciliation. David Syrett shows the limiting role of *Shipping in the American War* (1972). John R. Alden gives a full account of *The South in the Revolution* (1957). G. A. Billias has edited appraisals of several of *George Washington's Generals** (1964) and of *George Washington's Opponents** (1969). North Callahan appraises *Daniel Morgan* (1961); Theodore Thayer, *Nathanael Greene* (1960). W. B. Willcox makes a psychological inquiry into the failure of Sir Henry Clinton in *Portrait of a General* (1964). D. S. Freeman's seven volumes (1948–1957) on Washington are difficult; J. T. Flexner's recently completed four-volume work is much more enjoyable.

The battle of Saratoga is the focal point of S. D. Patterson's *Horatio Gates* (1941). S. E. Morison's biography *John Paul Jones** (1961) is as reliable as it is readable. M. F. Tracy's *Prelude to Yorktown* (1963) concerns the war in the South. H. A. Larrabee's *Decision at the Chesapeake* (1964) stresses the epochal importance of the naval battle of Yorktown. Paul H. Smith in *Loyalists and Redcoats* (1964) recounts Britain's failure to secure maximum support from their potential fifth column.

The Continental Congress (1941) by E. C. Burnett is a scholarly record of that often slighted legislative body. Lynn Montross's *Reluctant Rebels* (1950) is a reliable popularization of the same subject. E. J. Ferguson's *Power of the Purse* (1961) is a superb analysis of the nation's financial problems viewed in the context of the conflict between nationalism and states' rights. C. L. VerSteeg in *Robert Morris* (1954) makes clear the remarkable achievement of the nation's first finance minister. On the most famous of the enactments of the Continental Congress, Carl L. Becker's *The Declaration of Independence* (1922) is a classic. David Hawke's *A Transaction of Free Men* (1964) traverses the same ground with a little less ideological and more political emphasis. A. O. Aldridge's *Man of Reason* (1959) is the best study of Thomas Paine available. S. F. Bemis's *Diplomacy of the American Revolution** (1935) remains unchallenged in essentials, although R. B. Morris's *The Peacemakers* (1965) greatly embellishes the story. E. S. Corwin's *French Policy and the American Alliance of 1778* (1916) is an admirable monograph modified slightly by Alexander DeConde's *Entangling Alliance* (1958). G. Stourzh in *Benjamin Franklin and American Foreign Policy* (1954) supplements both V. W. Crane's

Benjamin Franklin and a Rising People* (1954) and Carl Van Doren's biography (1938) in recounting Franklin's long and varied diplomatic career.

Jackson T. Main's work, especially The Upper House in Revolutionary America (1967), Political Parties before the Constitution (1973), and Sovereign States, 1775–1783* (1973), largely supersedes such earlier works as Rebels and Democrats* (1955) by E. P. Douglass and The American States during and after the American Revolution (1924) by Allan Nevins. Chilton Williamson's American Suffrage (1960) is authoritative on state actions to extend the right to vote. M. L. Starkey's A Little Rebellion (1955) is a good account of Shays' Rebellion.

Social and cultural change in the Revolutionary era is another topic on which historians have not yet reached a clear consensus. J. F. Jameson in The American Revolution Considered as a Social Movement (1926) scratched the surface provocatively. E. B. Greene's The Revolutionary Generation (1943) is more descriptive than analytical. C. W. Van Tyne's The Loyalists in the American Revolution (1902) has never been surpassed overall, although W. H. Nelson's The American Tory (1961) is an interesting essay. R. R. Palmer in The Age of the Democratic Revolution (1959) compares American and French treatment of those who stood by the old regime. Wallace Brown's The King's Friends (1965) and The Good Americans (1969) provide detailed information on Loyalist refugees. Jack Sosin's The Revolutionary Frontier, 1763–1783 (1967) describes wartime changes in the West. A. Zilversmit's The First Emancipation (1967) attributes the ending of slavery in the North to ideological considerations.

*indicates availability in paperback.

Forging a National Unity

During the Revolution Americans encountered major difficulties in reaching agreement on the amount of authority to be delegated to a national government. Only after bitter and interminable debates could they form the constitutional basis for a confederation with even minimal authority. They achieved victory and even fixed far-reaching policies to deal with Western territories with their makeshift government, but within a few years after victory it was apparent to all that the wartime constitutional system could not survive without drastic change.

During the war popular determination to resist British domination had created voluntary enforcement agents for congressional policies in every community. With peace and independence secured, people began to think again of more narrowly personal interests and to fear for both their individual liberties and the rights of their own state governments. The Confederation's financial crisis deepened as the states ignored requisitions and Congress lacked power to im-

pose taxes to repay its war debt. Merchants and artisans demanded help in meeting foreign competition, but because the Confederation was without any power whatever to regulate foreign or domestic commerce, they were forced to look to the states for assistance in establishing favorable terms of trade.

Persuaded that representative government and freedom for ordinary people were secure only in small states, many Americans regarded the prospective disintegration of the Confederation complacently. Nationalists, however, were determined to weld all the American states together into a powerful and prestigious nation. Failing in repeated efforts to strengthen the Confederation, they at last determined to replace it entirely with a new federal union. In the spirit of the Revolution, they were equally determined that the new government would represent the people as a whole, that it would reserve important powers to the component states, and that it would afford safeguards to assure the people that they need not fear oppression. By brilliant tactical leadership they brought about a constitutional convention, drafted a satisfactory instrument for a strong federal government, and persuaded popular conventions in the states to give it their endorsement.

The Confederation of American States

During the Revolution, unity of the American states was essential to the attainment of independence. "We must indeed all hang together," Benjamin Franklin is reported to have said, "or most assuredly we shall all hang separately." The Continental Congress, an assembly of delegates from the Revolutionary organizations in each colony, assumed the task of providing that unity in pursuit of independence. Its authority for several years derived not from a constitution, nor even from a treaty, but from widely recognized necessity. As early as 1775, however, a few farsighted patriots directed their endeavors toward perpetuating the Union of the states.

Fixing the basis for Union proved much more troublesome than writing constitutions for the states themselves. All the states had revised their constitutional systems by 1780, but there was then still no agreement on a permanent Union among them. In 1775 Franklin had proposed in the Continental Congress "Articles of Confederation and Perpetual Union," patterned after the plan which he had submitted to the Albany Conference twenty-one years before. Not until a year later, however, did Congress begin preparation of such a plan. Prompted by the same Virginia resolution which had cleared the way for independence, Congress established a committee to consider the matter of Union.

A tentative plan, largely the work of Pennsylvania's reluctant revolutionary, John Dickinson, emerged from the committee on July 12, 1776, after a month of "warm disputes." These disputes resumed in Congress itself and continued into the fall of 1777 before the Articles of Confederation gained congressional approval. The Articles would not become effective, however, until endorsed as well by each of the states. That proved still more difficult.

Western land claims were the major stumbling block. Six states which had no claims to Western lands (Maryland, Delaware, Pennsylvania, New Jersey, New Hampshire, and Rhode Island) had tried to win authority for Congress to fix western borders for those states which, according to their original charters, had extensive and often overlapping territorial claims. The seven landed states blocked this action, but Maryland refused to ratify the Articles of Confederation until the landed states made a satisfactory concession. Deadlock prevailed from 1777 until 1781, while the Continental Congress continued to operate without a formal constitutional foundation.

Virginia was the chief target of the states without Western land claims. Largest of the states by far, Virginia then included what is now West Virginia and Kentucky and claimed all the area north from the Ohio River to Canada as well. Speculators from Maryland and Pennsylvania were convinced that their aspirations would suffer in competition with rivals from Virginia if that state kept control of all the land it claimed. Consequently, they lobbied assiduously for common or national control of the West so that speculators from all states would be treated impartially. Early in 1781, while Cornwallis's campaign in the South was still proceeding well, Virginia decided for "the good of the country" to cede to the United States the lands which it claimed north of the Ohio River. The cession had to be renegotiated at some length between 1781 and 1784, but Maryland, prodded by French agents who were eager at that time to foster American unity, accepted the initial act as sufficient to warrant ratification. The Articles of

Confederation became the Constitution of the United States on March 2, 1781.

Endorsement of the Articles of Confederation by all the states gave a legal foundation to the basic pattern of government which had been evolving informally. In that pattern Congress was the only federal agency of government. There was neither a chief executive nor a national system of courts. Congress itself represented state governments rather than people. The governments of the states chose from two to seven delegates, instructed them, and paid them. However many delegates it sent to Congress or whatever its population, each state had only one vote. Whereas Congress could support the Army, conduct foreign relations, borrow money, and make "requisitions" against the states, it was unable to tax, regulate foreign or domestic commerce, enforce its will by any means other than the Army. Limited as its powers were, the Congress could increase them only by amendment of the Articles, a procedure requiring the unanimous consent of the states.

During the war the obvious necessity for cooperation enabled Congress to get things done, but as the war drew slowly toward its successful conclusion, the cooperative spirit faded. Attendance at congressional sessions fell off. Some states failed for a time even to name delegates. The morale of those who attended and attempted to conduct business sagged badly. The Congress, moaned one delegate, was "responsible for everything, and unable to do anything." Without any "visible head," the government of the United States lacked strong executive leadership and, as one patriot observed, could impart to Europeans "no very favorable opinion of our stability, wisdom, or Union."

Congress and the West

Despite its general weaknesses, Congress achieved spectacular success in fixing guidelines for Western development. Definite policies for land distribution and government were necessary because of the steady westward advance of population, especially into Kentucky and Tennessee. Daniel Boone had cut his "Wilderness Road" in 1775, opening the Kentucky lands of speculator Richard Henderson to settlers from Virginia. By 1790, Kentucky had more than seventy thousand people and was clamoring for separation from Virginia as a new state.

Tennessee developed somewhat less rapidly. Richard Henderson had brought about the settlement of Nashville, first as a self-governing community and then (after 1782) as part of North Carolina. When North Carolina ceded the area of Tennessee to the United States in 1784, settlers in the Watauga area (northeastern Tennessee) formed the prospective state of Franklin, under the leadership of John Sevier, and sought admission to the Union. North Carolina revoked its cession in 1787, however, and continued to assert authority over the area of Tennessee until 1790, when the final cession occurred. Tennessee by then had some thirty-five thousand inhabitants.

How would Congress deal with Western problems? As early as 1779, it had resolved that lands which might be ceded to it by the states "shall be . . . formed into distinct Republican states, which shall become members of the federal union, and have the same rights of sovereignty, freedom and independence, as the other states." Such a moral commitment, however, did not solve the problem of securing the cession of Western lands by several reluctant states or providing for the settlement and early government of lands which had been ceded.

All the states which had claims to the area north of the Ohio River (Massachusetts, New York, Connecticut, and Virginia) had ceded their claims to the United States by 1786, although Connecticut until 1800 kept title to the northeastern section, or the "Western Reserve," of the future state of Ohio. South of the Ohio River, however, the record was less impressive. Virginia retained title to the area of Kentucky until it became a state in 1792. North Carolina, as just noted, did not finally surrender the Tennessee area until 1790. South Carolina ceded its narrow strip across the top of modern Alabama and Mississippi, but Georgia, claiming all the rest of Alabama and Mississippi except the Spanish portions along the Gulf Coast, refused to surrender its title until 1802. Thus, only the area north of the Ohio River, plus South Carolina's tiny cession, became subject to the control of the United States in the Confederation period.

Policies designed to develop the national domain appeared in a number of land ordinances passed by Congress. First of these was the Ordinance of 1784, drafted largely by Thomas Jefferson. Its major effect was to recommit the Congress to the principle that new states would be formed from the area and admitted to Congress "on an equal footing" with the others. The Ordinance of 1785 aimed to raise revenue from the sale of newly ceded Western lands. It applied to all such lands whose titles had been purchased from the Indians and required that the areas be surveyed in township lots 6 miles square, with each township subdivided into thirty-six lots or "sections" of 640 acres (1 square mile) each. Half the townships were to be sold as townships; the others in lots of 640 acres. Sales were to be conducted by auction but without credit and at prices no less than $1 per acre. These terms discriminated against small farmers, who were not likely to have $640. The terms were much more suitable to speculators, from whom Congress hoped to secure substantial income quickly. Congress defeated a proposal to reserve one lot in each township to provide a subsidy for the religion favored by the township's majority, but it did reserve one section to subsidize public schools.

Not until 1787, on the eve of its extinction, did the Congress provide in any detail for the government of its Western territories. It acted under the prodding of speculators who saw to it that the provisions of the law were framed "for the accommodation of . . . [absentee] purchasers" as well as "inhabitants." In place of the self-government which Jefferson had envisioned for the settlers, the Northwest Ordinance of 1787 provided that, until the population reached 5,000, the government should consist of a governor, secretary, and judges, all appointed by Congress. When the population reached 5,000, the people could elect an assembly, but the governor appointed by Congress was to exercise an absolute veto. The people could also send a voteless delegate to Congress. Only when the population had reached 60,000 could the people of the area qualify for self-government and all other privileges of statehood. Because Easterners looked with horror on the prospect of a Confederacy nearly dominated by frontier "depravity," the number of new states to be carved out of the Northwest Territory was fixed at from three to five, instead of the ten which Jefferson had suggested. Jefferson's proposed ban on slavery, however, was included, along with other guarantees of civil liberties. The law required new states to allow duty-free use of their navigable waterways by citizens of other states forever.

Speculation ran rampant in the Northwest from the beginning. Behind the Northwest Ordinance itself lay the lobbying efforts of a group of New Englanders organized as the Ohio Company, with the Reverend Manasseh Cutler as their chief spokesman. By 1788 Cutler and his associates had purchased a large acreage and had founded Marietta, Ohio. The Scioto Company, organized by Treasury official William Duer and apparently including some members of Congress, secured an option to purchase 5 million acres. Poet Joel Barlow, an overenthusiastic agent of the Scioto Company in Paris, "sold" some of this not-yet-purchased land to Frenchmen, several hundred of whom then emigrated to the United States. The Scioto Company never exercised its option to buy and, in fact, within a few years became bankrupt. The French im-

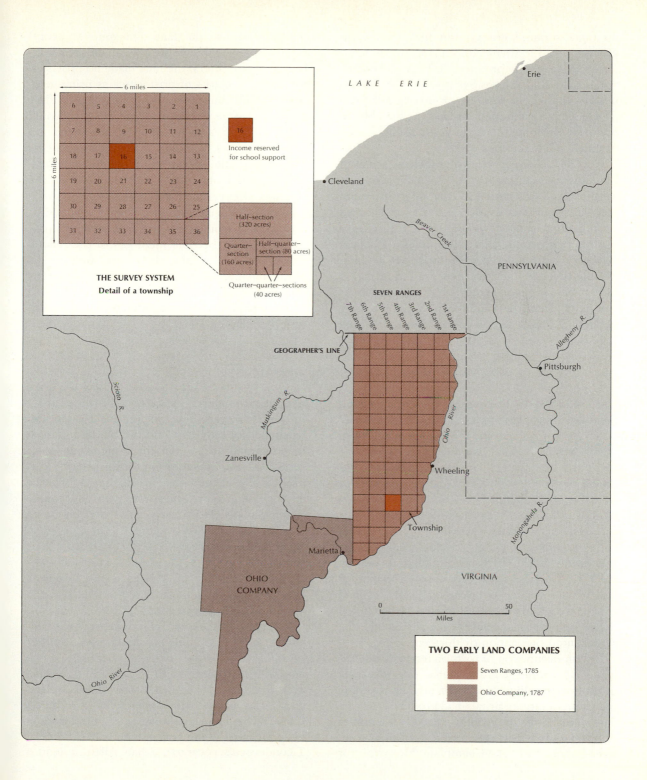

THE SURVEY SYSTEM
Detail of a township

6 miles

6	5	4	3	2	1
7	8	9	10	11	12
18	17	16	15	14	13
19	20	21	22	23	24
30	29	28	27	26	25
31	32	33	34	35	36

16
Income reserved
for school support

Half-section
(320 acres)

Quarter–
section
(160 acres)

Half-quarter–
section (80 acres)

Quarter–quarter–sections
(40 acres)

LAKE ERIE

Erie

Cleveland

Beaver Creek

PENNSYLVANIA

Allegheny R.

SEVEN RANGES

7th Range
6th Range
5th Range
4th Range
3rd Range
2nd Range
1st Range

GEOGRAPHER'S LINE

Pittsburgh

Muskingum R.

Scioto R.

Zanesville

Ohio River

Wheeling

Township

Monongahela R.

Marietta

OHIO
COMPANY

VIRGINIA

Ohio River

0   50
Miles

TWO EARLY LAND COMPANIES

Seven Ranges, 1785

Ohio Company, 1787

migrants suffered greatly, but ultimately Congress donated to them land such as they thought they had bought before they left France. Another speculator, John Cleves Symmes of New Jersey, bought and settled land which included the site of Cincinnati, although he was never able to purchase the entire million acres for which he originally contracted.

Few laws in all American history have had such fundamental significance as the land ordinances of the 1780s. At a time when few interests bound the American states together, the ordinances expressed a national consensus concerning a common property and its development. The land allocation system, fixed with the emphasis upon raising revenue quickly, benefited speculators rather than ordinary settlers, but future changes would in some measure redress the balance. Meanwhile, as Jefferson noted, the poor would continue to use the land "in spite of everybody." Envisioning a society of independent, landowning farmers, the laws made no provision for such hallmarks of aristocracy as primogeniture, entail, quitrents, or feudal dues. They assumed instead that ordinary people would purchase land and would owe no obligation whatever to its purveyor once their payments had been made. Repudiating colonial subjugation such as Britain had sought to fix upon the colonies forever, the laws spelled out how, with temporary safeguards to the interests of absentee speculators, frontier territories across the continent would "become members of the federal union" on an "equal footing" with the original states. Finally, the Northwest Ordinance of 1787 was the first act of the government of the United States looking toward the extinction of the institution of slavery.

Inadequacies of the Confederation

Successful as it had been in winning independence from Britain and fixing Western land policy, the Confederation was unsatisfactory in many ways. It was particularly unsuited for peacetime diplomacy. Unable to regulate commerce or to enforce its will upon individuals or states on any matter, the Confederation could neither promise reciprocal concessions nor threaten commercial retaliation. In England, John Adams after 1785 could only fume in frustration as the British continued to occupy forts on American territory, fixed commercial policies harmful to American interests, declined to send a diplomatic representative to the United States, and inquired condescendingly whether he represented one nation or thirteen.

British occupation of forts on territory officially ceded to the United States was the most inflammatory diplomatic difficulty confronting the Confederation. Britain had promised to evacuate "with all convenient speed" a number of posts strung along the northern frontier from Lake Superior to Lake Champlain. However, for reasons never clearly established, perhaps chiefly to preserve peace with the Indians, Britain determined not only to retain these forts but even to recapture any which the Americans might seize. As moral justification for this treaty violation, Britain alleged that the Americans were not keeping their treaty obligations regarding confiscation of Loyalist property and the debts owed by Americans to British subjects. The Confederation could not compel the states to alter their confiscation policies, nor could it force individuals to pay their debts. Neither could Congress itself assume the obligations, for it lacked the means to make payments.

Foreign encouragement of separatist tendencies in Western regions constituted another problem which the Confederation Congress was ill-equipped to handle. Vermont, still operating in the 1780s as an unaffiliated state on land claimed by New York, depended heavily upon Canada's St. Lawrence River as its major avenue of commerce. When Levi Allen, Tory brother of Ticonderoga's cocaptor, Ethan Allen, sought a commercial treaty with Britain on behalf of Vermont, a Privy Council committee recommended that Vermont and other frontier areas be encouraged to maintain their independence and "to form Treaties of Commerce and Friendship with Great Britain." Britain made some commercial concessions to Vermonters but had made no treaty when the Allens lost control to a faction more disposed to join the other American states.

In the Ohio-Mississippi Valley, Spain more than Britain was the fomenter of separatist sentiment. Because commercial transportation was confined so largely to natural waterways, most of the American West depended upon Spanish-held New Orleans at the mouth of the Mississippi River for its access not only to foreign but even to American markets. Spain, fearing for the security of its sparsely settled territory from Louisiana eastward into Florida, hoped to slow the westward movement of Americans or at least induce Westerners to set up independent, and consequently fairly weak, governments.

In pursuit of this policy, Spain closed the Mississippi to Americans at the end of the war. Through its Minister, Diego de Gardoqui, Spain suggested to American Secretary of State John Jay in 1784 that if the United States would give up its claim, derived from the peace treaty with Britain, to use the river, Spain would make commercial concessions in its domestic market to the United States and renounce its not-very-serious claim to the area northward from its Gulf coast settlements to the Tennessee River. Jay was willing, as was the commercially depressed North, but the South considered surrendering the claim to Mississippi navigation too high a price to pay for a commercial treaty. Because the five Southern states had enough votes to bar the 9-vote majority necessary to ratify a treaty, none was concluded. Resentment in the South and West continued to sustain separatist feeling.

Fostering prosperity was a still more important function in which the performance of the Confederation was inadequate. Although laissez-faire ideas were not unknown in America even before the publication of Adam Smith's attack upon mercantilism in *The Wealth of Nations* (1776), such ideas were still new and radical in the 1780s. Most people who engaged in commerce, including seaboard farmers, urban artisans, as well as merchants, were still mercantilists. As such they expected and desired a government which, like Britain's, would actively aid the accumulation of wealth by private individuals. They wished the government to impose regulations and to pay subsidies which would aid them to achieve an excess of exports over imports, thus leading to a net inflow of gold and silver from which the economy as a whole would benefit. Lacking any power over foreign or domestic commerce as well as any authority to tax, the Confederation could do virtually nothing to fulfill these mercantilistic expectations. The state governments attempted to do what was expected of them, but their small size and lack of unity on foreign trade policies were serious handicaps, especially in dealing with Great Britain, an economic colossus which still held a commanding share of American trade. Import taxes imposed by one state, for example, often succeeded less in reducing purchases of the imported items than in diverting their importation to a neighboring state. Accordingly, many seaboard farmers, as well as most urban artisans and merchants, clamored for a stronger central government.

Depressed conditions in commerce, once blamed largely on inadequacies of the Confederation, had in fact, begun to improve before a new government replaced the Confederation. Freed from British restrictions, Americans began after the war to develop new trading relations with Asia, especially China, as well as with continental Europe. Enterprising merchants, aided by co-operative local officials, found ways to circumvent British restrictions on the West Indian trade. American producers recovered from the disruptions of war; in some states reliable paper money helped to alleviate the scarcity of specie. Yet American merchants, still wedded to mercantilist ideas and forced to compete with foreigners who had the assistance of strong mercantilist governments, understandably demanded a government which could render similar advantages to them. The depression, whatever its causes and despite considerable recovery in the late 1780s, intensified this desire.

Events such as Shays' Rebellion (p. 111), attributable in part to the depression, helped to build sentiment favorable to a stronger federal government. Although few reasonable people really feared a "federal Shays," men of wealth recognized the desirability of a federal structure which could act quickly and decisively in such a crisis. Many also viewed with favor the prospect of a central government which might bar the inflationary paper money issues and the stay laws which some states had passed at the insistence of clamoring debtors. Exploiting such sentiments, nationalists viewed the occasion of Shays' Rebellion as a moment "very favorable . . . for increasing the dignity and energy of [the federal] government." One even expressed the fear that "the Insurgents will be conquered too soon."

Such rational and self-interested bases for dissatisfaction with the Confederation may have counted for less than the emotions of an emerging nationalism. American gentlemen engaging in overseas trade and those who read newspapers full of foreign "intelligence" were acutely aware that Europeans expected America to become, not a unified and powerful nation, but a geographic expression—an area full of insignificant, "petty," and anarchic states. Among the Revolutionary elite the American identification arising out of the struggle with Britain had not only replaced British loyalty but had weakened their earlier self-conception as provincials as well. Consequently there was great demand for an *American* government worthy of respect. Washington's reaction to Shays' Rebellion affords an illustration. "I am mortified beyond expression," he wrote, "that . . . we [Americans] should by our conduct verify the predictions of our transatlantic foes and render ourselves ridiculous and contemptible in the eyes of all Europe." To his former aide, Alexander Hamilton, there was also "something . . . contemptible in the prospect of a number of petty states, with the appearance only of union, jarring, jealous and perverse, . . . weak and insignificant in the eyes of other nations." For such men, incipient national pride was among the most profound reasons for dissatisfaction with the weak Confederation.

Nationalist Reform Efforts

Repaying the money which it had borrowed to support the war was the only function of importance, except for the administration of Western lands, which Congress retained after the conclusion of peace. Accordingly, nationalists tried to make the most of it. They attempted to increase the Confederation debt by taking over those incurred by states in support of the war and to use this repayment obligation as justification for amending the Articles of Confederation to confer a limited power of taxation upon the federal government. With that precedent established, nationalists hoped to expand federal powers and transform the weak confederation into a truly national government.

Much of the opposition to the nationalist program came from individuals rather more parochial in outlook and more democratic in conviction than the nationalists. Subsistence farmers in the backcountry could expect little from a stronger national government, other than increased taxes. They neither knew nor cared how Americans were regarded in Europe. Many people of the "middling sort" shared the conviction of the aristocratic Gouverneur Morris that "the great and wealthy . . . will necessarily compose the legislative body" of the federal government. But, unlike Morris, they desired consequently to minimize federal power and retain maximum authority in the state legislatures, in which men of their own class could better afford to serve. Many shared the belief, widespread in Europe, that only in small states could liberty and representative government flourish and that governments of large states tended inevitably toward tyranny.

Nationalist efforts to confer a limited taxing power upon the Confederation began in 1781, even before Yorktown, and continued into 1786. "Requisitions" to the states had proved inadequate either to redeem the Confederation's Continental paper money or to meet the general revenue needs of the government. Many states found it extremely difficult to secure the gold and silver with which to meet their requisitions. Most were reluctant to part with what little specie they had, especially to pay requisitions in full when it was clear that some other states would not do so. States in which there were few creditors of the federal government were especially reluctant to part with specie, since they could be sure it was not coming back but would wind up in other states. Those states which had made great war expenditures of their own naturally felt that some priority was due their own creditors. It soon became clear that, unless Congress gained some taxing authority, the function of repaying its war debts would be transferred to the states. Superintendent of Finance Robert Morris, an early leader of the nationalist movement, asserted in 1781 that the "political existence of America" depended on adoption of a plan to allow Congress to collect an "impost," or duty, of 5 percent on all imports. The income from such a tax, in fact, would have paid only the interest on the federal debt, but Morris had plans for additional federal taxes if the impost won approval.

Reaction to the impost plan was generally favorable, but it foundered on that provision of the Articles of Confederation which specified that amendments would become effective only when "confirmed by the legislatures of every state." By midyear, 1782, only one state had not approved the plan. Gripped by radicals who saw in the impost "the Chains Rivotted" and a

"Yoke of Tyranny" poised, tiny Rhode Island refused its assent. A congressional delegation began a journey to Rhode Island to reason with the legislators there but abandoned the trip upon learning that Virginia had repealed its endorsement.

Realizing that the case for American unity would weaken still more with the end of the war, Morris and his coterie of nationalists made another strong effort to gain taxing authority during 1783 while peace negotiations were in progress. Morris himself thought that, even without amending the Articles of Confederation, Congress could impose taxes on the ground that authority to spend implied power to collect revenue. Capitalizing on discontent within the army, especially among officers to whom Congress could not make good its compensation commitments, the Morris group encouraged the issuance of ominous pronouncements from Washington's camp at Newburgh, New York. Washington himself, however, squelched his more aggressive subordinates, including General Gates, so that the "Terror of a mutinying Army" lost some of its effectiveness as a pressure tactic. Suspected always of self-interested economic motives as well as indifference to public opinion, Morris resigned in 1784 in the hope that "the People will . . . more easily believe when they hear Truth from some other Quarter."

Federal taxing authority seemed close to realization again in 1786. Except for New York, all the states had then approved it in one form or another. Under the leadership of Governor George Clinton, New York finally agreed to allow the federal government to tax imports at 5 percent, but only under conditions which included state control of collections. Congress considered New York's conditions unacceptable. Pennsylvania, at the other extreme, held out for conferring a far wider range of taxing authority upon the federal government. Thus, even though all the states desired some form of taxing authority for the federal government, it gained none because it could not secure the required unanimity in support of one specific proposal.

Truly ruinous conditions in Confederation finance, attributable to the absence of taxing power, seemed to presage disintegration of the federal Union. Total Confederation income in 1785 and 1786 amounted to less than one-third of the interest charges on its debts. Congress managed to pay the interest on debts due Holland but defaulted completely on its obligations to France. State governments more and more met the interest payments on federal securities held by their own citizens. The general expectation was that ultimately all war costs, those incurred by state governments as well as by Congress, would be lumped together and apportioned by an agreed-upon formula among the states for payment.

Holders of federal securities strongly preferred payment by the federal government rather than by the states. This reflected the fact that

those who had been both willing and able to back the Revolutionary cause with money were generally American nationalists. But there were economic considerations as well. Whereas Congress was committed to pay its obligations at face value in specie, the states, in many instances, preferred to redeem securities at their depreciated market value—rarely as much as half of face value—and in paper money, or at least something less valuable than specie. Many speculators purchased securities at their depreciated market value in the hope that they would ultimately be redeemed at a higher rate. Such men constituted a pressure group which favored the creation of a stronger federal government with taxing powers, but the scarcity of surviving evidence makes it impossible to determine which speculators invested most in federal securities in the 1780s or how extensive their influence upon political developments was.

By appealing to considerations of commerce rather than of finance, the nationalists were ultimately able to secure a convention to reconsider the nature of the American Union. Demands for such a convention had been frequent from 1780 onward, as nationalists felt more and more poignantly the weaknesses of the Confederation. The leadership in arranging a convention came initially from the South. Commissioners from Virginia and Maryland met at Alexandria, Virginia, in March 1785, to consider common problems relating to the navigation of Chesapeake Bay and the Potomac River. After moving from Alexandria to the spacious grounds of Washington's estate, Mount Vernon, the conferees not only agreed on joint administration of the Potomac but urged upon their respective legislatures steps such as uniform commercial regulations and currency, which were at least suggestive of economic union. Prompted by James Madison, a youthful legislator who had previously served in Congress, Virginia then invited all the states to a convention at Annapolis, Maryland, to consider commercial matters of common interest.

Madison's Annapolis convention, meeting in

The Pennsylvania State House—later renamed Independence Hall—where the Constitutional Convention opened in May 1787.

September 1786, failed in its stated purpose but achieved a larger one. Four states, including the host state of Maryland, sent no representatives. Delegates from four other states arrived only after the convention had concluded. Thus only New York, New Jersey, Pennsylvania, Delaware, and Virginia were actually represented at Annapolis. Their twelve delegates thought it useless to consider commercial problems in view of the limited attendance, but instead approved an appeal drafted by New York's Alexander Hamilton for a new convention to meet in Philadelphia on May 14, 1787. Hamilton's resolution asserted that unspecified "defects in the System of the Federal Government" had placed the United States in a "critical" situation "calling for an exertion of the united Virtues and Wisdom of all the Members of the Confederacy." The appeal urged all states to send "Commissioners" to Philadelphia "to take into Consideration the situation of the United States" and "to devise such further provisions as shall appear to them necessary to render the constitu-tion of the Federal Government adequate to the exigencies of the Union."

Hamilton's appeal for a convention to meet at Philadelphia proved popular in nearly every state. Congress had declined in 1786 to submit to the states the elaborate plans for strengthening the federal government which had been worked out under the leadership of Charles Pinckney of South Carolina. Its refusal resulted, however, not from disinclination to increase federal power but from despair over what might follow after the rejection of the plans for want of unanimity. Early in 1787, Congress cautiously endorsed the proposed Philadelphia convention "for the sole and express purpose of revising the Articles of Confederation and reporting [suggested changes] to Congress and the several legislatures" for their consideration. Five states had already named delegates. Except for Rhode Island, the others did so subsequently. In view of the requirement of unanimous consent to amend the Articles of Confederation, even Rhode Island's aloofness was disheartening.

The Grand Convention

Fifty-five men participated in the Convention which John Adams called "the greatest single effort of national deliberation that the world has ever seen." Preeminent among them was the former commander in chief, George Washington, whose popularity was so great as almost to assure public acceptance of the work of the Convention. As presiding officer, however, Washington took little part in the debates. Benjamin Franklin, the first American to achieve high distinction in the world at large, was also present, but at eighty-one he was too aged to do more than encourage harmony and compromise. Intellectual leadership in the deliberations fell largely to younger men, notably James Madison, who had done so much to secure a convention, and James Wilson, a Scottish immigrant who practiced law in Pennsylvania and later sat on the Supreme Court. Gouverneur Morris, an aris-tocrat blessed with literary skill as well as an incisive mind, was also to make significant contributions. Alexander Hamilton, the brilliant young New Yorker who shared with Madison major responsibility for the calling of the Constitutional Convention, held such extreme views on national power and executive authority that he was largely without influence in the deliberations. At the other extreme, Luther Martin, the garrulous, bibulous, but brilliant attorney general of Maryland, argued interminably in defense of states' rights. Notable absentees were John Adams and Thomas Jefferson, both abroad on diplomatic missions, as well as Samuel Adams and Patrick Henry, then devotees of states' rights. Massachusetts' delegation did not include Adams, while Henry, selected by Virginia, "smelt a rat" and declined to attend.

Several characteristics of the Convention delegates stand out. The members were relatively young: their average age was forty-two. But their level of experience was high. Nearly three-fourths had served in Congress, and most had worked in state government as well. Over half were lawyers. A substantial number had lived abroad or at least in a state other than that which they represented. Few lived in the backcountry. Most were from seaboard areas and enjoyed comfortable incomes. A handful, including Washington, were men of great wealth, with investments primarily in land. The most significant fact concerning the delegates, however, was that all but four were nationalists.

Enthusiasm, if measured by attendance, was not commensurate with the importance of the task. Scheduled to begin May 14, 1787, at the Pennsylvania State House, the Convention did not secure a quorum until May 25. Rhode Island never sent a delegation, and New Hampshire's spokesmen did not arrive until late in July, by which time two of New York's three members had gone home in disgust.

Agreement on a number of important questions came quickly. No one opposed the selection of Washington as presiding officer. Not everyone agreed with Madison that the Convention would "decide forever the fate of Republican Government," but all felt great respect for the seriousness of the undertaking. No one objected seriously to the suggestion that sessions be secret so that the members could express themselves openly, change positions with less embarrassment, and enjoy freedom from outside pressure. "Leaks" were, in fact, remarkably few during the four-month convention, a reflection perhaps of the importance the delegates assigned to the privacy of their discussions. While the early arrivals were waiting for the laggards, Gouverneur Morris suggested that the states with large populations "should unite in refusing to the small states an equal vote," but the Virginians feared with good reason that such an effort would produce "fatal altercations between the large and small States." Accordingly, the dele-

gates agreed readily that each state, regardless of its size, should have one vote.

Disagreement came quickly enough. The Virginia Plan, worked out in advance by James Madison and introduced by Governor Edmund Randolph on behalf of the Virginia delegation, was too strongly nationalistic for many delegates. A prefatory resolution, suggested by Gouverneur Morris, stated that no mere "treaty" among the states would be sufficient but "that a national government" with a "supreme Legislative, Executive, and Judiciary" should be established. Although many delegates objected to these ideas, only Connecticut voted against the resolution. The Virginia Plan itself assumed that the Articles of Confederation, "the treaty," would be abandoned for a completely new constitution. The Virginia Plan provided also a bicameral legislature whose lower house would be elected directly by the people with representation apportioned among the states according to population. Its upper house was to be chosen by the lower house from candidates nominated by state legislatures, but again the number of representatives from each state would vary with population. The legislature would choose a chief executive. Power to veto legislative enactments absolutely, such as colonial governors had possessed, was to repose not in the executive alone but in a Council of Revision which included a number of judges as well as the chief executive. The Virginians provided also for a federal court system, including a supreme court. Madison wished as well to endow the federal government with power to veto any act of a state legislature and to use force against a recalcitrant state. As he conceived it, the Virginia Plan would provide "a due supremacy of the national authority" and yet "not exclude the local authorities whenever they can be subordinately useful."

Opposed to the Virginia Plan were both the antinationalist minority and the representatives of smaller states. The antinationalists, who wished to retain the essential features of the Confederation, tilting the power balance in favor

The Making of the Constitution

Eleven years after the Declaration of Independence, most men felt the Articles of Confederation insufficient to meet America's needs, especially for the development of trade and the economy. An amending convention was called in Philadelphia in May of 1887 (following page). George Washington presided; fifty-five state leaders were delegates. Opposition quickly arose over central issues: states' rights versus strong central government; rural agricultural interests versus urban business interests.

After four months of debate and hard-won compromise, the result was not amendment of the Articles but a new document: the Constitution of the United States. It established three branches of government, their method of selection and their powers; it permitted national taxation; and it provided the framework for America's future growth. Nine of the thirteen states had to ratify the Constitution before it could become effective.

In these contemporary cartoons, ratification appears as the raising of pillars for a federal edifice. Although New Hampshire was the crucial ninth state to ratify, populous Virginia and New York were also essential. After great debate, Virginia came tenth and exerted an irresistible pull on New York, which feared the economic consequences of remaining outside the Union. Agricultural North Carolina and Rhode Island, which had boycotted the convention, lagged behind. North Carolina ratified in 1789. Rhode Island's foundation was good; ratification in 1790 restored its shattered column.

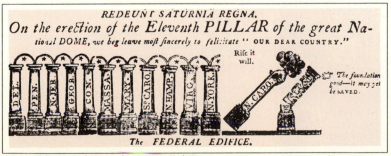

*Those in favor of a strong national government included James
Madison (above, right) and Alexander Hamilton (above, left), who
together had succeeded in calling the amending convention. Benjamin
Franklin (far left, center) served as an elderly advisor. James Wilson
(far left, above) led nationalist debate along with Madison. Aristocratic
Gouverneur Morris (far left), representing Eastern financial and
commercial interests, felt governments should naturally be in the hands
of "the great and wealthy."*

*Minority leaders at the convention forced major concessions
from the nationalist majority. George Mason (above) feared the
loss of individual rights and later voted against ratification in
Virginia. William Paterson (above, left) proposed the "New
Jersey Plan" for confederation amendments. Oliver Ellsworth
(above, right) of Connecticut and John Dickinson of Delaware
(right) fought for equal representation of small states in the
national legislature. Luther Martin (above, far right), Attorney
General of Maryland, opposed a federal court system.*

of the states, were so few as to be almost impotent. The more significant opposition came from delegates of small states, who insisted upon equal representation for all states. Delaware, New Jersey, and New York opposed representation proportional to population even in the lower house. Maryland and Connecticut joined them in the small-state effort to eliminate this principle from the higher chamber, but the proposition carried by a vote of 6 to 5.

Spokesmen for the small states and the antinationalists did not give up. The early discussions and votes had occurred in the committee of the whole, a parliamentary device to permit free discussion and nonbinding votes. Before the Convention proper took up the Virginia Plan as amended by the committee of the whole, William Paterson of New Jersey presented a "federal" plan, known ever since as the New Jersey Plan, reflecting the views of the minority.

Mere modification of the Articles of Confederation was the gist of the New Jersey Plan. Significantly, however, the modifications all tended to strengthen the federal government, giving it limited power not only to tax and to regulate commerce but even to coerce states. Acts of Congress and treaties were to be "supreme law," and there was to be a supreme court of rather narrowly limited jurisdiction. The minority suggested that Congress choose an executive whose powers would not include the veto. The United States under the New Jersey Plan would remain, however, a confederation of limited powers representing not people but strong state governments, each with an equal voice. When the delegates in committee of the whole were asked on June 19 to choose between the Virginia and New Jersey Plans, the vote was 7 to 3 (New York, New Jersey, and Delaware) in favor of the nationalists, with Maryland's delegates evenly divided.

From June 19 to July 2, the Convention debated final approval of those provisions of the Virginia Plan relating to representation in the legislature. The proposal that the lower house should be elected by the people and the upper house by state legislatures won easy acceptance. But whether the vote of each state in the legislative chambers should be equal or in proportion to population was a more divisive issue. After much acrimonious debate, a vote of 6 to 4, on June 29, determined that representation in the lower house would be in proportion to population. Still more bitter debate followed until July 2, when the proposal to give the states equal representation in the upper chamber lost on a tie vote, 5 to 5. John Dickinson, onetime opponent of independence and draftsman of the Articles of Confederation, gave cogent expression to the determination of the small states. On behalf of Delaware, Dickinson observed that the small states were "friends to a good national government; but we would sooner submit to a foreign power than . . . be deprived of an equality of suffrage in both branches of the legislature, and thereby thrown under the domination of the larger states."

To prevent what appeared to be an imminent breakup of the Convention, moderate nationalists determined to make a concession to the small-state delegates. Over the opposition of Madison and Wilson, the Convention agreed to refer the dispute to a compromise committee, which it then packed with small-state and moderate delegates. The committee recommended representation proportional to population in the lower house, but an equal vote for each state in the upper house. It was subsequently agreed that members of the upper chamber should have their votes counted individually, rather than having them collectively cast one vote for their state as was done in the Continental Congress and in the Convention. The Convention approved the compromise on July 16, by a 5-to-4 vote, with Pennsylvania, Virginia, South Carolina, and Georgia in opposition, Massachusetts evenly split, and New York absent. Although first suggested by Dickinson, the provisions resolving the controversy between the small and the large states subsequently acquired the designation Connecticut Compromise, apparently because Connecticut delegates, including

Oliver Ellsworth, who "preferred doing half the good we could, rather than do nothing at all," were especially prominent among its supporters.

Disagreement over slavery arose out of the decision to apportion seats in the House of Representatives according to population. Delegates from Georgia and South Carolina thought slaves should be counted as people in the apportionment procedure. Seven other delegations thought they should not. Congress, however, was to have the power to apportion "direct taxes" among the states in relation to population, the best index of wealth available. In this instance, delegates from the major slave states thought slaves should not be counted. The solution, carried over from an agreement in the Confederation Congress in 1783, was to count three-fifths of the slaves for purposes of both representation and taxation. Population figures would come from a federal census to be taken every ten years.

Strengthening Federal Authority

Once they had gained assurance of equal representation for each state in one chamber of the legislature, delegates from the small states became much more amenable to nationalist suggestions for strengthening the new Union. In relative harmony, the delegates proceeded to remedy each of the four major deficiencies of the Confederation, giving the government power to tax, to regulate commerce, to secure amendment without unanimous consent, and to enforce federal policies. In endowing the new government with so much more power, they agreed also on the wisdom of providing safeguards against oppression by dividing authority among distinct legislative, executive, and judicial branches of government in accordance with the theory of separation of powers. It was assumed as well that the new government would possess no powers at all other than those which they put down in writing.

The authority to tax bore a number of qualifications. The delegates required that measures of taxation originate in the House of Representatives, to which the people would elect members directly, but they imposed no barrier to the amendment of tax measures by the Senate, which would represent state governments. They required, in addition, that taxes be "uniform throughout the United States" and that they be imposed in order to pay debts, to provide for the common defense or the "general welfare."

Southerners, their economy heavily dependent upon exports, insisted that export taxes should be barred. Four states objected, but the measure carried, partly because such taxes would, in any case, have violated mercantilist principles by tending to reduce sales abroad. Ambitious planters from the Lower South, anxious to increase their labor supply, secured, in addition, a provision limiting to $10 each the tax which might be imposed upon imported slaves. Except for the provision concerning the apportionment of "direct taxes," no other restriction limited the power of Congress to "lay and collect taxes."

Congress received power to regulate commerce "with foreign nations, and among the several States, and with the Indian tribes." Authority to regulate commerce wholly within any state remained, by implication, with the government of the state. Additional restrictions on the federal government's authority over commerce arose out of conflicting sectional interests. Northern mercantilists were eager for federal "navigation acts" which would favor American over foreign ships, both in coastal and in overseas trade. Southerners, major exporters but not shipowners, wished foreign ships to be admitted without discrimination so that the South could benefit from greater competition among shipowners. Despairing of a total ban on navigation acts, Southerners sought instead the requirement of a two-thirds vote in each house of Congress to enact such measures, a provision which would have given them what amounted to a veto power. Another important compromise occurred, however, as Southerners abandoned their efforts to restrict navigation acts in exchange for Northern agreements not to ban the importation of slaves before 1808 or to tax imported slaves more than $10 each. The earlier Northern agreement to prohibit export taxes may have helped put Southerners in a conciliatory frame of mind. The provisions concerning slavery, supplemented by a rigid requirement for the return of fugitive slaves from one state to another, offended the "religious and political prejudices" of many Northern delegates, but to Southerners they were important enough, as one delegate put it, to determine "whether the southern states shall or shall not be parties of the Union."

Amendment of the Constitution, impossible in practice under the Articles of Confederation, became possible, though not easy, under the provisions of the new document. Congress could propose an amendment by a two-thirds vote in each house. Alternatively (under an option never yet employed), Congress could call a special constitutional convention if so requested by the legislatures of two-thirds of the states. However proposed, amendments would become effective only when approved by three-fourths of the states, either in special ratifying conventions or through their legislatures, whichever Congress specified. Exempted from the amendment provisions—deemed to be inviolate—were those assuring an equal vote to all states in the Senate and barring interference with the importation of slaves before 1808. Thus minority interests fixed the price of union for the majority.

How to enforce federal authority, almost impossible under the Confederation, was another crucial question for the Convention. Madison's proposal in the Virginia Plan—that Congress be authorized to veto state laws in conflict with the "Articles of Union" and to employ force against recalcitrant states—won little support. Ultimately, the delegates awarded some measure of enforcement authority to each of the three branches of the proposed federal government. To Congress, the delegates awarded power "to make all laws necessary and proper for carrying into execution the foregoing [enumerated] powers, and all other powers vested by this Constitution in the government of the United States, or in any department or office thereof." In addition, Congress could "provide for calling forth the militia [state military forces] to execute the laws of the Union, suppress insurrections and repel invasions."

To the Presidency, an office created with an eye to securing, among other objectives, a more effective execution of the laws than had been forthcoming from congressional committees, the delegates awarded sweeping, although less specific, enforcement authority. "Executive power" belonged to the President, but it was not defined. The Constitution obligated the President to "preserve, protect, and defend the Constitution" and to "take care that the laws be faithfully executed," without specifying or restricting what means he might employ. The President could make recommendations to Congress on any matter whatever; he also held supreme command of the Armed Forces which Congress might provide, including the militia of the states when called into federal service.

In a new federal judiciary the delegates reposed additional enforcement power. Antinationalist Luther Martin, seeking to avert the creation of a federal court system, proposed a provision binding state courts to void any provisions of state laws or constitutions which conflicted with the federal Constitution, federal laws, or treaties. While binding state judges to give priority to federal over state law, Martin's proposal, known subsequently as the "supreme law clause," left to the state courts the crucial decision as to whether or not there was conflict between the two. Elsewhere, however, the Constitution provided for a United States Supreme Court and such inferior federal courts as Congress "may from time to time . . . establish." Furthermore, the Constitution defined the federal judicial power as extending "to all cases . . . arising under this Constitution," the laws, and treaties of the United States. Some nationalist delegates construed these words as granting to federal courts the power to review the decisions of state courts whenever they involved interpretations of a federal law, a treaty, or the Constitution itself. This opinion, however, was far from universal.

With these changes the Convention had provided for an extremely powerful government. Its Congress could enact laws bearing directly upon individuals. A Supreme Court could interpret their meaning with finality, and a chief executive to whose command Congress could commit the militia forces of the states was obligated to enforce them.

Furthermore, new restrictions upon the states supplemented those taken over from the Articles of Confederation, the chief effect of which had been to exclude the states from diplomatic matters. States could no longer coin money, issue paper money in the form of bills of credit, or make anything legal tender except gold and silver. The restrictions on money stemmed from recent efforts of some states to assist debtors by inflationary measures. Another provision prohibited state laws "impairing the obligation of contracts." Here the aim was to bar "stay laws" postponing the due date of debts. In addition, a state could not, without consent of Congress, tax shipping or impose duties on imports or exports, "except what may be absolutely necessary for executing its inspection laws." Thus the new constitution had weakened state governments while it strengthened federal power.

Separation of Powers

The doctrine of separation of powers, although still controversial in detail, held the confidence of the Convention more than did legislative supremacy. Among the earliest votes of the Convention was one which determined that the new government not only should be national, meaning stronger than the Confederation, but also should include legislative, executive, and judicial branches rather than only a legislature as was the case under the Confederation.

Distrust of a simple legislative majority, reflected chiefly in the creation of an independent President and judiciary, dictated also that the legislature, which the delegates continued to designate as "Congress," should be divided into two houses, as had been the rule in all the Colonies except Pennsylvania. The House of Representatives, its members apportioned among the states in proportion to population and popularly elected every two years, appeared to the Convention to be the "democratical" branch essential to give fair representation to the people. The Constitution neither fixed nor barred property qualifications or other restrictions on the right to vote, except to say that in each state the legal qualifications for the electorate should be the same as those required to vote for "the most numerous branch of the State Legislature." The Senate, its members chosen as each state legislature determined and for six-year terms, appeared to the delegates as analogous to the governors' councils of colonial days or to the British House of Lords as the agent of the "aristocracy," but in fact it represented the states. Like the bodies upon which it was patterned, the Senate was to share in certain executive functions from which the lower chamber was excluded, specifically, confirmation of major executive appointments and the rendering of "advice and consent" in the conclusion of treaties.

Despite the disfavor with which most delegates viewed legislative supremacy, Congress received most of the essential powers with which the Convention endowed the new government. Among them in addition to its enforcement authority, power to tax, to regulate foreign and interstate commerce, and to initiate constitutional amendments were authority to provide for the Armed Forces and to declare war. Furthermore, Congress alone could authorize the expenditure of public funds. Every congressional measure was subject to veto by the President, but contrary to the rule which had prevailed in the Colonies, the veto was not absolute but could be overridden by a two-thirds vote in each of the two houses. Constitutional provisions for impeachment also permitted Congress to remove from office the President or any other federal official judged guilty of "treason, bribery, or other high crimes and misdemeanors."

What should be the power and role of the President? To be truly independent of Congress, James Wilson suggested, he should owe his election to the people. But the majority felt strongly that the people were unqualified to judge the merits of candidates from states other than their own. Election by Congress, as proposed in the original Virginia Plan, would invite intrigues which were generally undesirable and would almost certainly limit the President's independence. Ultimately the delegates settled the question, perceived by one member as the "most difficult of all on which we have had to decide," by authorizing each state legislature to provide for the selection of presidential electors equal in number to the total of the state's representatives and senators. The electors were to vote for two individuals, at least one of whom must be from another state. The candidate receiving a majority vote was to become President; the second ranking man, Vice President. If no candidate received a majority, the House of Representatives, with one vote for each state's congressional delegation, was to make the choice from among the top five candidates. The delegates assumed that, after Washington had retired from the office to which he would be a virtually unanimous choice, the large states would control what would amount to nominations under the electoral college system and that normally no one would receive a majority in the electoral college. Consequently, the selection from among the five leading contenders would be made in the House of Representatives, with all the states entitled to one vote. Thus the method

of selecting a President represented yet another compromise between the large and small states.

Like the royal governors and the British monarch, the President under the new Constitution would bear the immediate responsibility for executing laws. "The executive power," states the first sentence in the Constitution dealing with the Presidency, "shall be vested in a President of the United States of America." Congress and the Supreme Court, as indicated previously, each held some enforcement authority but by implication each had to rely upon the President to carry out its decisions, if they required administrative action or if they should be resisted.

As chief administrative officer, the President received additional authority of a more specific nature. With the consent of the Senate, he could appoint all major "officers of the United States." He could "require the opinion, in writing, of the principal officer in each of the executive departments." The delegates also charged the President, in the pattern of his earlier counterparts, to advise the Congress on what they called the "state of the Union," to make recommendations "as he shall judge necessary and expedient," and to call special sessions of Congress "on extraordinary occasions." Unlike the colonial governors, the President lacked not only the absolute veto but also control over legislative sessions. The Constitution required Congress to convene yearly on a day fixed by law and to terminate its session at a time fixed by mutual consent of the two houses. Again in the pattern of the British monarchy, the President received the power to pardon, to command the Armed Forces, and, with the advice and consent of the Senate and the approval of two-thirds of its members, to make treaties with foreign powers. His four-year term of office was long enough to frighten those accustomed to annual election, but it afforded the people every four years an opportunity, unprecedented among major nations, to remove a Chief Executive whose conduct had not met their approval.

The provisions for a United States Supreme Court and such inferior courts as Congress might wish to create also bowed in the direction of separation of powers. The Constitution by no means stated explicitly that the Supreme Court could invalidate acts of Congress, but leading nationalists, such as Madison, assumed that the judges would void any law "violating a Constitution established by the people themselves." In contrast to the fixed terms of judges in some of the states, federal judges were to enjoy the independence afforded by good behavior tenure after appointment by the President and confirmation by the Senate.

Policy for the Western territories came under the scrutiny of the Convention at about the same time that the Confederation Congress enacted the Northwest Ordinance of 1787. Gouverneur Morris, spokesman for Eastern men of commerce, stated that he wished to fix the "rule of representation" in such a manner as "to secure to the Atlantic States a prevalence in the National Councils." More in keeping with the spirit of the Northwest Ordinance, James Wilson insisted that "the majority of the people, wherever found, ought in all questions to govern the minority." He justified this sentiment pragmatically by affirming that the majority "not only have the right [to govern the minority], but will avail itself of it whether we will or no." The Convention chose not to fix policy on this point, but left it to Congress by providing only that "New States may be admitted by the Congress into this Union."

Ratification

How could the delegates put the new Constitution into effect? The Confederation Congress, in sanctioning the Convention, had referred to its purpose as that of "revising the Articles of Confederation." Disregarding the requirement of unanimous consent for amendment of the Articles, the Convention delegates provided that, when approved by conventions in nine states, their Constitution would become effective within the ratifying states. Ratification by the state legislatures was unacceptable to the nationalists because, as Madison put it, approval by the legislatures would give the document the aspect of a treaty, whereas endorsement by popular conventions would make it truly "a *Constitution*." At New York the moribund Confederation Congress bestirred itself to consider the document produced so secretly at Philadelphia. After unrecorded, but apparently bitter debate over the merits of the work, Congress decided without opposition on September 28 to transmit the proposed Constitution to the states "in conformity to the resolves of the Convention"—but without any indication of approval.

In several states ratification came easily. Conventions in Delaware on December 7, New Jersey on December 18, and Georgia on January 2, 1788, approved the Constitution without dissent. Delaware and New Jersey were dependent economically upon larger neighbors. Georgia, still small in population, wanted help against the Indians on its frontier. Connecticut, dependent like New Jersey upon neighbors for much of its commerce, endorsed the Constitution on January 9 by a 3-to-1 margin (128 to 40). Maryland, strong but squeezed between two much larger states, defeated the opponents of ratification on April 26 by 63 to 11. South Carolina, despite some inconsistent misgivings over the limited protection afforded both civil liberties and the slave trade, approved on May 21 (149 to 73).

In crucially important Pennsylvania, one of the largest and most prosperous states, ratification came quickly but not without a struggle. To prevent the Legislature from summoning a ratifying convention, opponents of the Constitution deliberately stayed away from the legislative chamber so that, for lack of a quorum, the majority favorable to a convention could not act. To secure a quorum, advocates of the Constitution seized two opponents, enough to secure a quorum, and, while compelling their attendance, proceeded to set the election of convention delegates at a date too early to permit the opposition to organize effectively and publicize its views. Pennsylvania's convention gave a quick endorsement on December 12 by a vote of 46 to 23, but the tactics of victory embittered the opposition.

Massachusetts, another critical state, proceeded more deliberately to a narrower victory for the nationalists. Both Samuel Adams and John Hancock, as well as numerous Shaysite delegates to the state convention, were skeptical. Solid support among the artisans of Boston, plus hints of high federal office for John Hancock, helped to persuade enough of the doubters, including both Adams and Hancock, to produce on February 6, 1788, a decision favoring the new Constitution.

By June 1788, eight states had endorsed the Constitution, and conclusive deliberations were about to begin in New Hampshire, Virginia, and New York. In February New Hampshire's towns had sent to the state convention a majority of delegates with instructions to reject the Constitution. Proponents of ratification secured an adjournment until June and by that time their agreement to recommend twelve amendments had reduced resistance. New Hampshire ratified the Constitution by a vote of 57 to 47.

Government under the new Constitution could have begun after New Hampshire's actions, but it appeared essential to include both Virginia and New York. Virginia, largest of the states in both area and population, had pushed the nationalist cause with great vigor at the deliberations in Philadelphia, but in the state as a whole, antinationalist sentiments found both able advocates and popular support. Patrick Henry, George Mason, and Richard Henry Lee, in particular, worked assiduously against acceptance of the document, which they regarded as dangerously insufficient in provisions to protect the liberties of the people. Supporters of the Constitution included the venerated Washington, James Madison, Edmund Randolph (despite early waverings which led him to withhold his signature from the document at Philadelphia), and a young Richmond lawyer, John Marshall, who was later to amplify the Constitution greatly as Chief Justice of the United States Supreme Court. To blunt Henry's demand for the addition of a bill of rights *before* ratification, Madison ultimately pledged to work for such amendments *after* ratification, "not because they are necessary [under a government possessing only delegated powers], but because they can

Title page of the first book edition of The Federalist, *1788.*   The Granger Collection

T H E

FEDERALIST:

A C O L L E C T I O N

O F

E S S A Y S,

WRITTEN IN FAVOUR OF THE

NEW CONSTITUTION,

AS AGREED UPON BY THE FEDERAL CONVENTION,
SEPTEMBER 17, 1787.

IN TWO VOLUMES.

V O L. I.

N E W - Y O R K:

PRINTED AND SOLD BY J. AND A. M^cLEAN,
No. 41, HANOVER-SQUARE.
M, DCC, LXXXVIII.

produce no possible danger, and may gratify some gentlemen's wishes." Whether or not because of this concession, Madison's forces won approval of the Constitution on June 25, by an 89-to-79 majority.

In New York, as in New Hampshire, prospects for approval at first appeared dim. New York City was solidly favorable, but followers of Governor George Clinton, representing suspicious upstate farmers fearful of the new Constitution and its backers, held a majority of the convention seats. Some of them wavered, however, in face of evidence that the new government would take effect with or without New York's participation. A vote to approve the document only if it were amended in several ways, chiefly to protect civil liberties, lost (31 to 29). Ratification finally carried on July 26, 1788, by a vote of 30 to 27.

Historians have long attributed New York's ratification to the persuasive efforts of Alexander Hamilton and John Jay in the convention and to *The Federalist*, a series of newspaper essays written by Hamilton, Jay, and Madison, but the evidence indicates that neither the essays nor the oratory persuaded the skeptics. What brought a sufficient number of the opponents to change sides was the desire to be part of the new American nation which was taking shape, the fear that New York City would join even without the rest of the state, and the expectation that amendments protecting civil liberties would be added after the new Constitution had gone into effect.

Advocates of the Constitution had also helped their cause somewhat by calling themselves "Federalists," a term with popular connotations, instead of "nationalists," which frightened those concerned over states' rights. Opponents of ratification, less skilled in public relations, became known as "Antifederalists."

Flat rejection of the Constitution occurred in only two states. North Carolina voted no by more than a 2-to-1 margin (184 to 84) in July 1788, but when the new federal Congress in 1789 proposed amendments which ultimately became the Bill of Rights, North Carolina held a second convention, which voted 194 to 77 to join the Union. Rhode Island remained adamant. It had sent no delegates to the Convention, and it refused to call a ratifying convention, staging instead a popular referendum, in which the advocates of ratification refused to participate. In 1790 a ratifying convention at last brought the reluctant Rhode Islanders into the Union by the narrow margin of 34 to 32.

Conclusion

Nationalists, who had become increasingly discontented with the Confederation after the conclusion of peace, eventually had their way. After failing in repeated efforts to strengthen the Articles of Confederation, the critics ultimately secured in 1787 a Constitutional Convention dominated by men determined to create a stronger national government. Reflecting a growing sentiment for the separation of powers rather than weak central government as the surest safeguard against oppression, the Convention proposed to replace the supreme legislature of the Confederation with a government consisting of distinct legislative, executive, and judicial branches. Fear of excessive restriction upon the freedom of individuals and state governments evoked much opposition to this plan, especially among backcountry farmers; but the general desire among the people to establish the foundations of a powerful nation, plus the nationalists' agreement to add a bill of rights, ultimately brought the states to accept the new Constitution. Thus a mere confederation of nearly sovereign states at last became a nation.

Conflict has raged bitterly among historians over interpretation of the Confederation period as a whole. One side, looking back to John Fiske's *The Critical Period of American History* (1888), sees American unity, political stability, and economic development each in jeopardy until rescued by the adoption of the Constitution. Another side, best exemplified in Merrill Jensen's *The New Nation** (1950), stresses the successes of the Confederation and condemns those who wished to change it as antidemocratic. C. P. Nettels in *The Emergence of a National Economy* (1962) depicts an economy much less robust than that which Jensen describes. E. J. Ferguson's *The Power of the Purse* (1961) is sympathetic to the nationalists who sought to strengthen American unity. R. B. Morris in *The American Revolution Reconsidered* (1967) attempts to reach a balanced judgment and in so doing echoes in some measure B. F. Wright's *Consensus and Continuity* (1958), which dwelt on what united Americans rather than divided them.

Until the twentieth century, amateur historians generally as nationalist as John Fiske wrote of the Constitutional Convention chiefly to glorify its members and its product. Something of that spirit survives in the works of twentieth-century professionals such as Charles Warren, *The Making of the Constitution* (1926), and Clinton Rossiter, *1787: The Grand Convention* (1966). More objective, factual records of what occurred have appeared also, notably Max Farrand's *The Framing of the Constitution** (1913) and Carl Van Doren's *The Great Rehearsal** (1948). Overshadowing these works for most of the century was the hostile interpretation of the Convention which arose in the progressive era. Reacting against Supreme Court decisions which made the Constitution a bar to effective regulation of business, J. Allen Smith argued that *The Spirit of American Government** (1907) as embodied in the Constitution was one of opposition to majority rule. Charles A. Beard, experimenting with the newly imported economic interpretation of history, suggested in *An Economic Interpretation of the Constitution** (1913) that economic motives had guided the Founding Fathers in writing a Constitution to serve their individual and class interests. Despite the inadequacy of the evidence sustaining Beard's conclusion, it gained a wide following until overthrown by the combined efforts of R. E. Brown in *Charles A. Beard and the Constitution* (1956), Forrest McDonald in *We the People* (1958), and especially E. J. Ferguson in *The Power of the Purse* (1961). Gordon Wood's *Creation of the American Republic* (1969) puts the American political ideas in an international context. F. W. Marks III in *Independence on Trial* (1973) looks at the writing of the Constitution in diplomatic perspective.

Somewhat incidentally the progressive attack upon the Constitution produced an upsurge of interest in its contemporary opponents, the Antifederalists. J. T. Main portrays them sympathetically in *The Antifederalists** (1961), as does R. A. Rutland in the *Ordeal of the Constitution* (1966). Linda G. Depauw, studying the New York ratifying convention in *The Eleventh Pillar* (1966), shows high appreciation for Antifederalist efforts.

The Bill of Rights, the Antifederalists' price for approval of the Constitution, is the subject of several significant studies: R. A. Rutland's *The Birth of the Bill of Rights** (1955) and Irving Brant's *The Bill of Rights* (1965). Brant considers subsequent interpretations, as well as the history of the adoption of the amendments. Leonard Levy's *Origins of the Fifth Amendment* (1968) ranges well back into English history for perspective on the right of the accused against self-incrimination.

Biographical studies are particularly good sources on the Constitutional Convention. Best is Irving Brant's *James Madison: Father of the Constitution* (1950). Others of value include Charles P. Smith's *James Wilson* (1956); Clinton Rossiter's *Alexander Hamilton and the Constitution* (1964); R. A. Rutland's *George Mason* (1961). For a collective portrait, see Rossiter's *1787: The Grand Convention* (1966) or Nathan Schachner's *The Founding Fathers* (1954).

The Federalist papers, essays by Madison, Hamilton, and Jay in support of ratification, are available in innumerable editions, most notably that of J. E. Cooke. W. U. Solberg has compiled a wide-ranging selection of documents with a valuable introduction in *The Federal Convention and the Formation of the Union** (1958). W. B. Gwyn's *The Meaning of Separation of Powers* (1965) examines the history of that idea in the seventeenth and eighteenth centuries.

*indicates availability in paperback.

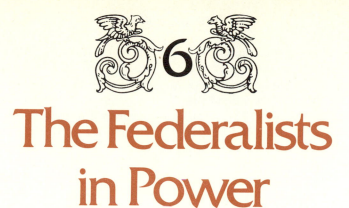

6

The Federalists in Power

Federalist leaders, having gained popular endorsement of the new United States Constitution, won as well the opportunity in 1789 to inaugurate the new government which it prescribed. George Washington was everyone's first choice for president; his fellow Federalists secured overwhelming majorities in the first Congress. Together they acted quickly and competently to create the federal edifice for which the people had given their mandate.

Nearly every Federalist objective, however, antagonized some portion of the population. Federalists construed the Constitution broadly to increase federal authority, thus alarming those who feared for states' rights. They repaid the national and state debts in such a manner as to enrich speculators concentrated in a few Northern cities, thus alienating both Southern planters and Northern farmers. They imposed unpopular internal, or excise, taxes and used the Army to crush resistance to their collection. In foreign policy, they infuriated radical republicans who were pro-French by concluding a treaty which

seemed almost to ally the United States with Britain against the French. Consequently, long before Washington left office the new nation had become deeply and dangerously divided. From these deep divisions, however, arose organized political parties, ultimately a major asset in the functioning of democracy despite their often undecorous and occasionally frantic conduct.

John Adams, elected as a Federalist in preference to Republican Thomas Jefferson in 1796, further alienated Republicans. He pursued an undeclared naval war with France. Furthermore, amid near hysteria over fears of Republican subversion in the interest of France, his Federalist supporters passed a Sedition Act and used it to jail leading critics of the administration. In the Virginia and Kentucky Resolutions, Republicans defiantly threatened to employ state power to prevent enforcement of what they regarded as an unconstitutional law. Thus as the election of 1800 approached, the stability if not the very existence of the new federal union seemed in jeopardy.

Would the federal government work any better under the Constitution than it had under the Articles of Confederation? There was some reason to doubt that it would. Both as individuals and in private groups, Americans had long demonstrated a great capacity to evade or to resist governmental policies inimical to their interests. Their new state governments had operated generally with the necessary support and observance of law, but it was not at all clear that the new federal government would be deemed worthy of respect or that it would have the capacity to enforce obedience to its policies by assertive individuals, groups, and especially the zealously autonomous states.

Returns from the first election under the Constitution in 1788 were encouraging. Federalists swept everything. Washington became president without opposition. Only two Antifederalists, both from Virginia, won Senate seats. In the House of Representatives, Federalists outnumbered the opposition 7 to 1. Rhode Island

Washington delivering his inaugural address in Federal Hall, New York City. Culver Pictures, Inc.

and North Carolina, it is true, had not participated, but there were already indications that each would soon terminate its resistance.

Less encouraging was the tardiness of congressmen in reporting for work. March 4, 1789, was the day fixed for the opening of Congress, but not until April 6 was there a quorum in both houses. Another three weeks elapsed before Washington could receive official certification from Congress of his election and complete the journey from Virginia to the temporary capital at New York. At last on April 30, federal officials staged the first presidential inauguration amid ceremony reminiscent of that with which the king began sessions of the British Parliament.

Ceremony and official titles indeed produced the first significant division in Federalist ranks. What underlay these seemingly trivial disputes was the desire of some to endow the President and other high federal officials with an aura of authority and dignity such as that which surrounded Britain's monarch and nobility. A majority of senators thought that the President should be addressed by some such designation as "His Elective Majesty"; they themselves would have liked to be called "Honorable." Such individuals approved the very formal receptions ("levees"), which President Washington initiated, and encouraged the public celebration of his birthday just as the king's birthday had been observed before the Revolution. Other Federalists and most Antifederalists regarded such practices as aristocratic and unbecoming to republican society. Reflecting this democratic spirit, the House of Representatives barred the conferring of the titles desired by the Senate. It became customary instead to address the Chief Executive simply as "Mr. President" and to introduce him with equal simplicity as "The President of the United States."

Eager to consolidate public support behind the new national government, Federalists under the leadership of Representative James Madison gave high priority to a bill of rights, which so many had urged in the ratifying debates. "If we can make the Constitution better in the opinion of those who are opposed to it without . . . abridging its usefulness in the judgment of those who are attached to it," Madison believed, "we act the part of wise and liberal men to make such alteration." On September 25, 1789, Congress approved twelve prospective amendments incorporating many of the eighty substantive changes included in the 210 amendments recommended by the ratifying conventions. Ten amendments received the endorsement of three-fourths of the states and became part of the Constitution in 1791. As Madison and other Federalists then construed the amendments, they in no way diminished the powers intended to be granted to the United States. Rather they provided only reassurance that individual liberties would be respected and that "powers not delegated to the United States . . . , nor prohibited . . . to the States, are reserved to the States respectively, or to the people."

Still seeking to reassure states' rightists without unduly weakening the federal government, the Federalist Congress, in the Judiciary Act of 1789, created a federal court system which bore all the aspects of compromise. On the one hand, it left to state courts original jurisdiction in many cases involving enforcement of federal law. This actual increase in the jurisdiction of state courts was highly gratifying to those who had feared that the state tribunals would be entirely supplanted by the new federal courts. On the other hand, as authorized by the Constitution, Congress created thirteen federal district courts and three circuit courts in addition to the Supreme Court established by the Constitution. Federal district courts were to have exclusive jurisdiction over certain types of cases, such as those dealing with import regulations. Circuit courts, consisting of two Supreme Court justices sitting with one district judge, were to have some original jurisdiction and in addition to hear appeals from district courts. The key provision of the law, however, was that section authorizing the Supreme Court to hear appeals from the decisions of

state as well as inferior federal courts whenever the case involved interpretation of the United States Constitution, federal laws, or treaties. This afforded reassurance to the nationalists that state courts would not block enforcement of federal law.

The checks and balances required by the theory of separation of powers proved troublesome at the outset. In providing that the president should make treaties "by and with the advice and consent of the Senate," the Constitutional Convention apparently intended that the Senate should participate in forming policy, much as members of the colonial councils had shared executive responsibility with the provincial governors before the Revolution. Washington had other ideas. In August 1789, while framing instructions relating to a treaty with the southern Indians, the President appeared in the Senate chamber, occupied the presiding officer's chair, and with Vice President Adams as his reading clerk set forth several treaty provisions for which he desired Senate approval. After reading each question, the Vice President inquired of the assembled Senators: "Do you advise and consent?" When Senator Robert Morris tried to refer the questions to a committee, the President lost his temper. The Senate had its way, however, although it did agree to report within three days. But thereafter the President, when it suited him, afforded the Senate no opportunity at all to offer advice in the preparation of treaties. His policy became a precedent, which in effect eliminated the Executive's obligation to seek the *advice* of the Senate in negotiating treaties. The Senate's role became only that of expressing or denying consent, for which the Constitution requires a two-thirds vote.

Still more troublesome was the division of responsibility between the legislative and executive branches on questions of revenue. Except for the crisis years under Robert Morris, the Confederation Congress had never been willing to entrust so crucial a function as management of the Treasury to a single executive but had always insisted upon an executive board which Congress itself supervised very closely. Only with great reluctance did Congress in 1789 accede to the arguments of James Madison that in the interest of efficiency a Treasury Department should be created and should be headed by a single executive.

Slighting the theory of separation of powers, Congress included in the law the provision that the Secretary of the Treasury should report to Congress and respond to congressional inquiries directly rather than through the President. Fearing acutely the influence of the Secretary of the Treasury upon the exercise of its power to initiate revenue measures, the House of Representatives insisted that the Secretary was not to report in person, but only to prepare reports for its consideration. Behind these seemingly excessive fears lay the knowledge that in Britain it was the head of the Treasury who was emerging as the nation's chief executive or Prime Minister. Ambitious Alexander Hamilton, first Secretary of the Treasury, was also well aware of this development.

Hamilton's Economic Program

Federalist economic policies, largely but not entirely Hamilton's, had profound significance not only for the nation's economic future, but also for the development of organized political opposition. One of the most controversial Federalist triumphs in the formulation of national economic policy concerned the payment of Revolutionary debts, both state and federal. When the new government assumed power in 1789, the United States owed nearly $12 million to foreign sources, chiefly Dutch and French, and $44 million to its own citizens. Under the Confederation, the Congress had proved incapable of meeting even the interest obligations on these sums. Consequently state governments had taken up the burden, even though their own debts amounted to about $25 million. Under the Constitution, however, the states could no longer tax imports although the federal government had an almost unlimited authority to tax. Clearly changes were in order.

Hamilton's suggestions for dealing with the debts came to Congress, at its request, in a detailed "Report on Public Credit" (1790). Hamilton's plan had three principal objectives. Foremost among them was the elevation of the power and prestige of the federal government over that of the states. Hamilton sought to serve that objective by demonstrating that the federal government could and would repay the entire Revolutionary war debt, both state and federal, at full face value. Another of Hamilton's objectives was to make federal securities a major investment opportunity for the wealthy, in the expectation that "moneyed men" who made such investments would help to maintain a powerful national government to protect their capital. His third intention was to alleviate the chronic money shortage by greatly increasing the value of federal securities, which might then serve, at least among the wealthy, as a form of money which would not depreciate.

Hamilton's "funding" proposal to redeem all *federal* securities at full face value rather than at the depreciated market rate aroused extensive controversy in Congress. Antifederalists and other Hamiltonian opponents had little objection to paying the foreign debt ($12 million) at full face value in order to bolster American prestige, but they wished to pay the domestic debt ($44 million) at something nearer the market value. By reducing the amount of the debt, payment at market value would also lower the tax burden necessary to repay it and avoid paying windfall profits to speculators. Speculative purchases had indeed concentrated nearly all the federal debt in the hands of a tiny minority of rich men whom Hamilton's policy would afford an enormous profit. As one critic expressed it, Hamilton's policy would "make noblemen and nabobs of a few New York gentlemen, at the expense of all the farmers in the United States."

Since four-fifths of the federal debt belonged to people in the North, Southerners were particularly hostile to Hamilton's plan.

Under these circumstances Madison, as a Virginia congressman, had little choice but to oppose Hamilton. He demanded that some part of the payment at full face value go to the original holders of the securities. His aim purportedly was to see that justice was done to the "hardy veterans" whose needs had forced them to sell at a fraction of face value the securities issued to them in payment for military service. Madison's measure, which would have been very difficult to administer, lost (36 to 13). Congress then accepted Hamilton's "funding" program.

Even more controversial was Hamilton's plan for the "assumption" of most of the *state* debts by the federal government, again at full face value rather than at the market price. The effects would be to enhance still further the relative prestige of the federal government and to detach more of the "moneyed men" from financial dependence upon state governments. Hamilton argued that all those who had lent money to finance the Revolution, whether they had lent to the federal or to the state governments, should be repaid on equal terms. Madison objected, declaring that since 1783 some states had repaid far more of their debt than others. In this category were the Southern states, except South Carolina. Thus another sectional split occurred. The South, except for South Carolina, backed Madison in proposing that the debts be assumed as they had existed in 1783. But the North, on the whole, backed Hamilton in favoring "assumption" as of 1790, when the total state debt was scarcely half of what it had been at the earlier date.

Bitter sectional division deadlocked the Congress for half a year. Utterly irrelevant diatribes on the slavery question lent heat to the dispute. Virginia's Antifederalist Senator Richard Henry Lee declared that he would prefer to dissolve the Union rather than submit, as he put it, to the rule of an "insolent northern majority." Meanwhile, Northern speculators, betting on Hamilton, went south to buy up depreciated state securities from those who believed the measure would be defeated. After North Carolina joined the Union, its Antifederalist congressmen changed the balance in the House of Representatives, making it 31 to 29 against assumption. Already negotiations for a compromise which would pass the measure were in progress.

What has been called "the compromise of 1790" had something for everybody. Virginians wanted the national capital located permanently on the Potomac; they desired assurance that the clearing of state accounts would be pushed to a conclusion; and they hoped to see the relaxation of rigorous accounting standards which had limited the acceptance of Virginia's claims. They achieved each objective. States with small debts or none wanted a compensating federal handout; they received it. Certainly the most famous of these political bargains was the transfer of the capital from New York, first to Philadelphia for ten years, and then to a site on the Potomac which President Washington would choose. Secretary of State Jefferson, recently returned from a long sojourn abroad, had a hand in completing the arrangements whereby the debts would be assumed and the capital moved. When assumption proved very unpopular, Jefferson claimed that Hamilton had duped him, but the evidence indicates that Jefferson, consulting closely with Madison, almost certainly knew what he was doing. So did Hamilton.

The Bank, Manufactures, and Taxes

Hamilton attached great importance to the establishment of a central bank, to be patterned after the privately controlled Bank of England.

The capital which stockholders invested in such a bank, both in specie and in government securities, would provide backing for the issuance of a considerably greater quantity of paper money. The bank would also serve the government as a depository of public funds, a lender, and a convenient agency for the collection of taxes and the transfer of funds from one area to another. Somewhat more controversial was the role of the bank as a regulatory agency. By returning paper money of lesser banks for redemption in specie or government securities, Hamilton's bank would be capable of embarrassing, or even breaking, banks which issued paper money in amounts greatly in excess of their hard money reserve.

Hamilton's "Report on a National Bank" (1790) quickly created another sectional division from which there emerged a constitutional precedent of major importance. Southerners on the whole preferred state-chartered banks, if any, and found no clause in the Constitution authorizing the federal government to charter business corporations of any kind. In the House of Representatives, 19 of 20 votes opposing passage of the bank bill came from Southerners, while 36 of 39 in favor were cast by Northerners. The constitutional objections which Madison and others had raised caused Washington, in considering whether or not to approve the measure, to ask for written opinions not only from Hamilton and Attorney General Randolph but from Secretary of State Jefferson as well.

The crux of the matter was the interpretation to be given the paragraph in the Constitution which enumerates the powers of Congress. It concludes that Congress shall have power "to make all Laws which shall be necessary and proper for carrying into Execution the foregoing Powers." Jefferson argued that this should be construed literally, that a federally chartered bank was not necessary to execute any specifically granted power and was therefore unconstitutional. Hamilton urged to the contrary that "*necessary* often means no more than needful, . . . useful, or conducive to," and that because a bank had a "natural relation" to tax collection, trade regulation, and defense, it was constitu-

tional. Neither line of argument persuaded Washington, but because the matter was of more consequence to Hamilton's Treasury Department than to Jefferson's Department of State, he signed the bill.

Despite the political controversy which surrounded its inception, Hamilton's Bank was highly successful. In chartering the Bank for twenty years, Congress had pledged itself to create no rival institutions. Accordingly, the Bank enjoyed a privileged, in some respects a monopolistic, status. Private investors, mostly Northerners, purchased its stock—except for the 20 percent reserved to the government—and controlled the Bank's management by naming twenty of its twenty-five directors. The stockholders received handsome returns on their investment, but it was true also that the Bank served the government well, so well that Jefferson, despite his original argument that the Bank was unconstitutional, continued it without protest when he became president in 1801.

Hamilton's famous "Report on Manufactures" (1790) appeared in response to a request from the House of Representatives for a plan to promote manufacturing and thus help the United States become "independent of other nations for essential . . . supplies." To encourage investment in manufacturing, Hamilton urged high import taxes (protective tariffs) on manufactured goods, government subsidies, special patent rights for inventors of labor-saving machinery, and tax-free importation of raw materials.

Several nonpolitical handicaps were more important than limited congressional cooperation in impeding the industrial movement in general. Among these were the lack of experienced management and labor; the scarcity of capital; and, perhaps above all, the existence of profitable alternative activities. Particularly after 1793, when warfare became general in Europe, commerce and shipping attracted much liquid capital. Land remained an attractive investment as prices for farm products and lumber rose. Thus Hamilton's "Report on Manufactures" helped to establish a goal and identify the means to attain it, but the 1790s saw little permanent progress in the development of manufacturing.

Taxation commanded very early attention from Congress. The Tariff Act of 1789 was in fact the first law enacted by the new government. Recognizing that states could no longer tax imports to protect their artisans and other manufactures from foreign competition, the measure did afford some "protection" to American producers in the form of import tax rates as high as 15 percent on such items as coaches, gunpowder, paint, and glass. Madison thought the federal government was obligated to afford some protection since the states could no longer do so under the Constitution. The major thrust of the measure, however, was to bring in revenue from low taxes on the importation of items which Americans did not produce, such as coffee, tea, wine, sugar, and molasses. Tariffs remained the basic source of federal revenue for the next two generations.

To encourage the further development of American shipping, Congress passed the Tonnage Act of 1789. Ships entering American ports were obligated to pay 50 cents per ton if they were foreign-owned and foreign-built, 30 cents if foreign-owned but American-built, and only 6 cents if both American-owned and American-built. Import taxes were also to be reduced 10 percent on all items imported on American ships. Other provisions effectively barred foreign ships from the coastal trade. Southern agricultural exporters, considering competition from foreign shipping to be in their interest, resisted these policies unsuccessfully. During the next generation, while the American economy remained deeply committed to overseas trade and coastal shipping, these provisions helped the infant nation to become a major maritime power.

Hamilton's whisky excise tax was by all odds the most controversial of the Federalist tax measures. Hamilton had urged a license tax for distillers of whisky and a tax per gallon on their product. For many Americans this tax

was intolerable. Many distillers were trans-Appalachian farmers who could not sell grain in competition with Eastern farmers because of the high cost of transportation across the mountains. By making their grain into whisky, they reduced its volume while increasing its value, thus improving their competitive position for Eastern sales. With little cash income, such individuals deeply resented the taxes even though they might, in time, be passed on to the consumers by a general price increase. Western farmers, mostly Antifederalists, also objected to being taxed by a strong national government to help pay rich Eastern speculators who held the lion's share of the national and state debts which Hamilton had arranged to redeem on such generous terms. To make matters worse, until the law was amended in 1794, individuals accused of violating the act could not be tried in state courts but only in one of the relatively few federal courts, usually in a major city far from the offender's home.

Resistance smoldered for several years until it finally reached a crisis in 1794. By then, mobs were intimidating tax collectors, as they had done before the Revolution, and interfering with court proceedings. In one instance, a mob captured the Army forces protecting a Treasury official. While the Whisky Rebellion occurred in many backcountry areas, particularly in the South, it was in the Pittsburgh area of western Pennsylvania that resistance was most flagrant. Here the enforcement of federal authority against popular local resistance faced its first genuine test. Acting upon its constitutional authorization to "provide for calling forth the Militia [of the states] to execute the Laws of the Union," Congress in 1792 had empowered the President, "whenever the laws of the United States shall be opposed, or the execution thereof obstructed, in any state, by combinations too powerful to be suppressed by the ordinary course of judicial proceedings, or by the powers vested in the [federal] marshalls . . . to call forth the militia of such State . . . to cause the laws to be duly executed." The only restrictions upon the President's discretion were that there be certification by a federal judge that the normal law-enforcement methods were inadequate (eliminated in 1805), and that the President first issue a proclamation calling upon those in resistance to desist.

Urged on by the militant Hamilton, President Washington acted vigorously to end the Western defiance of federal authority. On August 7, 1794, he issued the required proclamation stating: "I, George Washington, President of the United States, do hereby command all persons being insurgents . . . to disperse and retire peaceably to their respective abodes." When resistance continued after September 1, the deadline he had announced, the President called for 13,000 militiamen and set out for western Pennsylvania. The President soon returned to Philadelphia, but Hamilton stayed with the Army and sought out the ringleaders of the rapidly dissipating resistance movement. Twenty hapless insurgents fell into Army hands and suffered the indignity of a parade down the main street of Philadelphia and some time in jail. Two received sentences of execution for treason, but the President pardoned them.

Revenue from Hamilton's whisky excise was never as high as expected, and collection costs (about 15 percent) were excessive, but in a broader perspective the tax was a major success. It provided opportunity to demonstrate that the federal government indeed had the capacity, founded in public support, to collect whatever excise taxes it chose to enact. Even before the crushing of the Whisky Rebellion, Congress had subjected several other commodities to similar taxation and would continue to do so at its discretion without fear of violent resistance by organized groups.

Hamilton's triumph was short-lived. By 1795 he had resigned. The widespread resentment against his programs and his domination of Congress, plus suspicions of financial favoritism, though largely unwarranted, had limited his usefulness. Even in retirement, however, Hamilton would command the loyalty of many dedicated Federalists, including Cabinet members and Congressmen.

Western Problems

Many Eastern Federalists were only slightly less reluctant than the Indians to see American settlement extend westward. Landowners and employers themselves, they feared that rapid settlement of the West would lower land values and increase the cost of labor in their section. Since Western areas were normally Antifederalist, such migration would increase the relative political strength of the Federalists' congressional opposition as well. On the other hand, Western lands north of the Ohio River were a national asset which would produce revenue only as settlement advanced.

Federalist land laws reflected more concern for federal revenue than for aiding settlers to secure homesteads. The first land law in 1796 provided for the sale of large blocks of land at what might be called wholesale rates. No purchase was to include less than 640 acres (one section) or to be sold at less than $2 per acre. Family farms were then usually about 100 acres, and the going price of frontier land sold by state governments or private speculators, who had secured title from states, was generally under $2. In 1795 Georgia, because of corruption in the Legislature, had sold 30 million acres of superior land in the Yazoo area of Mississippi at about 1½ cents per acre. In addition to the other obstacles to the purchase of federal land by ordinary settlers under the 1796 law, only two offices were provided at which purchases could be made, one at Pittsburgh, the other at Cincinnati. Credit was limited to one year. When Congress altered the law in 1800, it reduced the minimum purchase to

320 acres, allowed four years to pay, and increased the number of land offices to four. These were only small steps toward enabling ordinary settlers to buy land directly from the government. Congress declined to provide "preemption rights"—a provision that squatters be given a prior right to purchase land on which they had settled before the government offered it for auction to the highest bidder.

Indians were another major deterrent to the advance of settlement into the Old Northwest, the chief area actually at the disposition of the United States government. There an informal alliance of the British and the Indians constituted a perennial threat. British leaders told the Indians, in disregard of the peace treaty of 1783, that there was no British-American boundary line and seemingly invited the Indians to help them fix one well to the southeast of the Great Lakes. Britain instructed its first Minister to the United States to seek the creation of an "Indian barrier state" in the Northwest Territory, but American hostility to the idea forced him to drop it quickly. However, one British official or another continued to talk of renegotiating the British-American boundary, of military adventures aimed at dismembering the Union, and of overt assistance to the Indians in resisting the encroachment of American settlement.

Federalist efforts to cope with the Indians of the Northwest met with two humiliating defeats. In 1790 President Washington sent General Josiah Harmar into northwestern Ohio to chastise Indians who had been raiding frontier settlements in areas purportedly ceded to the United States by treaties signed during the 1780s (Fort Stanwyx, 1784; Fort McIntosh, 1785). Harmar destroyed some Indian villages but had to retreat expeditiously after he fell into an ambush near the present site of Fort Wayne. General Arthur St. Clair, territorial governor for the Northwest, equalled Harmar's humiliation in 1791 on the banks of the Wabash near the present Ohio-Indiana border. The exasperated President turned next to General Anthony Wayne, who met with greater success. In 1794 his well-trained forces devastated a band of Indians supported by Canadian militia at Fallen Timbers, almost within earshot of the British Fort Miamis on the Maumee River, not far from present-day Toledo. Wayne avoided conflict with the British regulars, who in turn disappointed Indian expectations by taking no offensive action. At the ensuing peace conference, held at Fort Greenville in 1795, the chastened Indians agreed, in exchange for gifts and the promise of annuities, to open new territories to American settlement. The memory of Fallen Timbers helped to secure peace for many years on the northwestern frontier.

Despite all obstacles, Western settlement proceeded rapidly during the 1790s. Overriding Federalist anxieties concerning Western "barbarism" and democratic propensities, Congress admitted three new states to the Union during the decade: Vermont (1791), Kentucky (1792), and Tennessee (1796). Their combined population was only 5 percent of the national total in 1790 but had risen to 9 percent by 1800. Ohio and the western regions of New York, Pennsylvania, and Georgia were also gaining population at a very rapid rate.

Bearing out Federalist fears, several new states not only opposed the national administration but also made democratic innovations in their constitutions. Frederick Jackson Turner, historian of the frontier, undoubtedly exaggerated when he wrote that because the "wind of Democracy blew so strongly from the west," Eastern states imitatively liberalized their constitutions; yet Vermont was the first state to impose neither property-holding nor tax-paying requirements for voting. In Kentucky confusion over land titles, plus the feeling that all who were obliged to serve in the militia should be entitled to vote, led to the abandonment of the traditional property qualification for voting. Tennessee also opened the vote to adult males without property or tax-paying qualifications. The next Western states to be admitted (Ohio, 1803; Louisiana, 1811) reverted, however, to tax payment as a qualification for voting.

Problems arising from the wars of the French Revolution involved the United States in recurring diplomatic crises during Washington's second administration. The French Revolution in its initial phase (1789–1792) merely substituted limited for absolute monarchy; accordingly it met with great approval in Britain as well as in the United States. However, in its second phase (1792–1795), the French Revolution eliminated monarchy and established a republican form of government marked by extreme instability, the famous Reign of Terror, and territorial aggressions inspired by republican ideology and intense nationalism. These developments led to the rise of a reactionary spirit in Britain based on fear of both republican subversion and French invasion. After 1793 Britain, together with much of the rest of Europe, was at war with France.

Bound to France by the "perpetual" alliance of 1778, the United States faced difficult decisions when radical French republicans engulfed Europe in war. Most Americans endorsed the republican ideology, but the Reign of Terror and a campaign against religion within France, added to the military aggressions abroad, encouraged second thoughts and altered sympathies, especially among the more aristocratic Federalists. American egalitarians, however, were likely to agree with Jefferson, who was willing to see "half the earth devastated" to ensure the "liberty of the whole." The half of the earth which Jefferson was willing to see destroyed apparently did not include the United States, for as Secretary of State from 1790 to 1793 he favored American neutrality. Actually, the very small American naval and military forces made the involvement of the United States seem of little potential benefit to France, while a neutral United States, possessing a large merchant fleet, could afford France badly needed ocean transportation, presumably immune from British seizure.

How to announce American neutrality was still another question over which Jefferson and Hamilton differed. Jefferson argued that, by implication from its constitutional authority to declare war, Congress was the proper source for such a proclamation. Hamilton insisted that as a practical matter the President should have such authority. Washington agreed with Hamilton and accordingly issued a proclamation of neutrality on April 22, 1793.

A pamphlet war followed. Anticipating opposition, Hamilton acted quickly to defend Washington's proclamation with essays published under the pseudonyms "Pacificus" and "Americanus." In meeting the largely moral arguments of those who favored a pro-French policy, although not a declaration of war on the enemies of France, Hamilton denied that the United States had any obligation to support France. It was also doubtful, he warned, that France would win its war against the rest of the Continent. Furthermore, the woeful state of the United States Navy made it clear that the nation could not make its aid effective in Europe even if it chose to support the French. Hamilton denied, finally, that the United States owed any debt of gratitude to France or that the cause of France was the cause of liberty.

To Madison, as to most other opponents of the administration, the proclamation appeared "a most unfortunate error." Writing to Jefferson, Madison asserted further, "It wounds the national honor, by seeming to disregard the stipulated duties to France. It wounds the popular feelings by a seeming indifference to the cause of liberty. And it seems to violate the . . . Constitution by making the Executive Magistrate the organ . . . of the nation in relation to war and peace." Urged on by Jefferson, Madison soon published articles under the name "Helvidius," seeking to refute Hamilton's arguments in support of the President's action.

Widespread sympathy for France meanwhile encouraged that nation's exuberant young diplomat Edmond Charles Genêt to take actions which threatened, as Washington put it, to involve the United States in "war abroad and . . . anarchy at home." Calling himself "Citizen" Genêt, the new minister arrived in Charleston, South Carolina, shortly before the issuance of Washington's proclamation. He began at once to equip French privateers to operate from American ports against British shipping and set up French prize courts to dispose of captured British vessels. He took steps as well to organize Americans into military units to march against Spanish Florida and Louisiana. While Genêt had little success in the latter effort, he ultimately sent out twelve privateers which captured some eighty British ships. Belatedly, the administration secured his promise to cease such actions, which did indeed threaten to involve the United

States in war with Britain, but the widespread popular sympathy for France encouraged Genêt to break his word. He transformed a captured British merchant vessel into the privateer *Petite Democrate*, and sent it to sea in violation of his promise. The administration requested his recall and secured congressional enactment of a tough neutrality law in 1794 barring exactly those practices in which he had engaged. In France there was no difficulty over Genêt's recall, for his faction (the Girondins) had lost control. The new government in fact ordered his arrest. Rather than return to an uncertain fate, Genêt remained in the United States and became in time the son-in-law of New York's longtime governor and Antifederalist leader George Clinton.

Jay's Treaty

War with Britain still seemed imminent at the end of 1793, despite the elimination of Genêt. Britain had no desire, while engaged in a crucial conflict with France, to take on another belligerent, even one so inconsequential in strength as the United States. As usual in major European wars, Britain's "big navy" status threw that country into controversies with any neutral nation which engaged heavily in commerce and shipping. The United States, despite its very recent emergence from colonial status, was already a major maritime power. Its shipowners and merchants had jumped at the opportunity when France, at the outset of war, opened to neutral ships the trade between the French West Indies and France—a commerce from which foreigners had formerly been excluded. Under its "Rule of 1756," to the effect that trade not open in time of peace could not be opened in time of war, Britain captured some 250 American ships engaged in such trade, although about half were subsequently released.

Ship seizures by the British were by no means the only prominent American grievance against England. Along the Canadian border the British still occupied American territory and aided the

Indians to resist expulsion. Washington feared that the British Navy would soon resume the impressment of American seamen into its service, as it had a few years earlier at the time of a war scare with Spain. American merchants were convinced, in addition, that their increased troubles with Algerian pirates in the Mediterranean region were an intended result of a British-Portuguese treaty which reduced Portuguese naval patrols. Continued commercial discrimination by the British against Americans rankled, as did Britain's refusal to pay compensation for slaves removed during the Revolution.

Madison had argued in the *Federalist* Number 10 that nations, like individuals, pursued interests of their own with little respect for the interests of others. For that reason, wrote Madison, the United States could protect its commercial interests abroad only with retaliatory navigation acts. As early as 1789 Madison introduced measures into Congress to confer special privileges on American shipping. He soon discovered, however, that the Washington administration preferred to rely on British friendship and import duties. Facing Hamilton's opposition, Madison's program languished. But early in 1794, backed by Jefferson's report of December 1793, on the unfavorable state of American commerce, Madison introduced a series of resolutions to erect barriers against British imports until Britain accepted a reciprocal trade policy. Hamilton again seized the initiative by proposing a diplomatic rather than a congressional resolution of the perennial British-American conflict over trade, now encompassing massive ship seizures, and western posts.

With little hesitation Washington dispatched Chief Justice John Jay, an Anglophilic Federalist of high prestige and extensive diplomatic experience, on a special mission to London. Jay faced several hazards in his forthcoming negotiations with the British. The South and West remembered him unfavorably as the diplomat who had

John Jay in 1786, about eight years before his great diplomatic mission to London.   The Granger Collection

attempted, a few years earlier, to sacrifice Mississippi navigation for Eastern commercial advantage. Ardent republicans, with their emotional commitment to France, would oppose any concession whatever to Britain.

Federalist sympathy for Britain, on the other hand, weakened Jay's position in London. Jay's instructions included the suggestion that he consult with representatives of other neutral nations concerning collective action to resist British interference with their trade. Britain was apparently unwilling to make any concession at all to dissuade the United States from cooperating in such an endeavor. Hamilton, however, made it clear to the British that major concessions were unnecessary. Hamilton not only was pro-British, but also was determined to prevent any interruption of Anglo-American trade, the major source of the import tax revenue which so largely financed the government. To some extent Hamilton also appears to have thought that as Secretary of the Treasury he could properly exercise power over diplomatic and other governmental decisions far removed from the responsibilities of his own department. Whatever his rationalization, Hamilton informed the British that the Cabinet had considered participation in an armed neutrality movement and decided against it. This information probably induced the British to take a tougher line in their negotiations with Jay, although Jay himself was not disposed to push the British very hard.

After negotiating from June to November, Jay sent home a draft treaty with the apologetic affirmation that "to do more was not possible." He had, of course, attained the major Federalist objective: he had preserved peace. Merely by concluding a treaty with Great Britain, he had also elevated American prestige. The British, in addition, agreed to evacuate forts which they occupied on American soil, although they had determined on that course without reference to Jay. Their fur traders still had unrestricted access to American territory, and they faced no limitations on the sale of weapons to the Indians. The treaty made no reference to American claims relating to slaves removed by the British during the Revolution, but it was equally silent on the payment of compensation to exiled Tories. Pre-Revolutionary debts, claims arising out of British ship seizures, and the disputed northeastern boundary were referred to special commissions.

Americans gained some commercial advantages. Britain agreed to treat Americans as favorably as any other foreigners in its home market, an improvement over previous conditions, and to admit American ships to India. In Article XII, the treaty provided for the admission of American ships into the British West Indies, but on such restrictive conditions (see next paragraph) that the Senate threw out the entire article. Britain made no concessions whatever on the touchy subjects of neutral trading rights and impressment of American seamen.

Anticipating uproarious protest from Republicans, the Federalists kept the terms of Jay's treaty secret as long as they could. After its submission to the Senate, however, its details leaked out and denunciations began in earnest. "Archtraitor" was among the milder epithets hurled at Jay. Hamilton was stoned while attempting to defend the treaty. Most of the denunciations came from radical republicans, who rightly regarded the treaty as distinctly more pro-British than pro-French. Even Federalists objected to Article XII. It provided for admission into the British West Indies of American ships under 70 tons ("canoes" according to Madison), but it bound Americans in return to carry no molasses, sugar, coffee, cocoa, or cotton to any foreign port. Such a policy would have banned one of the most profitable activities of American shipowners in carrying West Indian products to Europe. It would have cut off the export of American cotton which, following the invention of Eli Whitney's cotton gin in 1793, was already beginning a meteoric rise in production. Rubbing salt in the wound, Article XII also would have committed the United States to permit the importation of West Indian products in British ships. Even after eliminating Article XII, the Federalists in 1795 could secure not one

vote more than the two-thirds majority required for Senate approval.

Still the treaty was not law. President Washington, deeply angered by Britain's seizure of American ships, deliberated from June until August before finally affixing his signature. He did so only after receiving from the British some captured correspondence of Secretary of State Randolph, which indicated that he was engaged in some manner of intrigue with the French. Subsequent research has vindicated Randolph of anything more than indiscretion, but Washington, construing the evidence in the perspective suggested by his Federalist advisers, deemed it necessary to dismiss Randolph, a longtime friend, and to sign the treaty to make clear that the United States had not become a satellite of France.

For the House of Representatives the treaty was still not final. Despite Washington's impolitic admonition that the Constitutional Convention had intended the House to have no role in treaty making, the House reiterated a demand to see papers relating to the treaty before it would agree to appropriate funds necessary to its implementation. Washington refused, thereby establishing a major precedent, and the House, under mounting pressure from the interested parties, fell into line with the tie-breaking vote of its Speaker.

While Jay's treaty convulsed the United States in political wrangling, Thomas Pinckney of South Carolina in 1795 concluded a far more satisfactory agreement with Spain. American grievances against Spain related chiefly to the southwestern frontier. Border claims overlapped, and the Spanish provided the Indians with supplies and encouragement to resist the advance of American settlement. Still more important, Spain controlled the outlet of the Mississippi, upon which much of the American West depended for access to markets. Manuel de Godoy, who dominated Spain's government, wanted mutual territorial guarantees and an alliance, but Pinckney, citing American determination to avoid entanglement in European affairs, declined. Instead he secured—almost without reciprocal concessions—permission for Americans to use the Mississippi, including for at least three years the port of New Orleans. Spain also recognized the 31st parallel, the extreme American claim, as the border with Florida and pledged to restrain Indian attacks. Whether these Spanish concessions owed more to worry over a possible Anglo-American alliance or to fear of attack on Spain's possessions by American frontiersmen remains disputed. In any case Godoy ignored his obligations until 1798, when renewed danger of both an Anglo-American alliance and aggression by frontiersmen induced him to keep his earlier commitments.

Political Parties

To the Founding Fathers, political parties, or "factions," as they called them, appeared too dangerous to be desirable. Like many modern Americans, they were unable to see clearly that such organizations, especially if highly competitive, could improve the functioning of democracy. Parties define the policy alternatives between which voters must choose; they identify, even if vaguely, the will of the majority; they provide a measure of discipline with which to implement majority wishes; and finally, when evenly matched, they tend to keep government reasonably honest, efficient, and responsive to popular will.

What the Founding Fathers saw instead amid the political turmoil of their time was the divisive influence of parties. Washington in his Farewell Address branded the party spirit as the "worst enemy" of popular government. To him it seemed partisanship would be likely to produce "geographic discrimination," or a sectional alignment of parties, thus threatening to disrupt the Union with separatist movements. Madison wrote in *The Federalist*, Number 10, of class division, or the "unequal distribution of property," as a more likely cause of "factions," but, like Washington, he considered their existence undesirable, even if inevitable.

When political parties began is still a matter of dispute. "Progressive" historians see the conflict of interests between classes as the principal basis of political division and argue that such a cleavage existed from pre-Revolutionary times onward. According to this notion, farmers, artisans, and laborers formed the bulwark of the radical Whig opposition to Britain during the Revolutionary struggle, of the Antifederalist movement against ratification of the Constitution, and of the Jeffersonian Republican party which opposed Hamiltonian Federalism. Conversely, in this view, the upper classes, especially the large landholders and merchants of seaboard areas, appear to have been for the most part conservative Whigs or even Tories during the Revolution, and Federalists thereafter.

At least two considerations emphasized by "Consensus" historians contravene this theory. In the first place, it is clear that many individuals and even large groups resist such easy categorization. Urban artisans, for example, were chiefly radical Whigs during the Revolution but became Federalists at least temporarily during the ratification controversy. Furthermore, the very concept of a political party implies some measure of organization. Prior to the 1790s such political organizations as did exist never transcended the state level, unless one considers the Revolutionary patriots themselves as a party. Even within the states in which coherent voting blocs did exist before the 1790s, only a small proportion of qualified voters bothered to go to the polls.

Nationally organized political parties, most authorities agree, arose in the 1790s. Hamilton's debt, taxation, and banking programs aroused many rich Southern planters as well as ordinary farmers, who charged that they favored wealthy merchants in Northern cities. To dedicated agrarians, whether rich planters or small farmers,

Hamilton's program threatened to transform a rural American paradise into a commercialized, urban society, peopled less by self-reliant, land-owning farmers than by cringing, dependent, slum-dwelling workers. Devotees of states' rights worried over Federalist tendencies to augment national power. Advocates of equal political rights deplored Federalist hostility to the ideology of the French Revolution and found in Federalist admiration for aristocratic Britain an indication of the objective of their program.

Three events of 1791 presaged the appearance of an organized opposition party. Jefferson and Madison persuaded Philip Freneau, sometimes called "the poet of the Revolution," to establish the *National Gazette*. Its function was to do verbal battle with John Fenno's *Gazette of the United States*, which, with the aid of both private and public subsidies arranged by Federalists, had castigated Republicans vigorously since 1789. In lieu of outright subsidies, Freneau received a sinecure in Jefferson's Department of State. Until he fled Philadelphia during the yellow fever epidemic of 1793, Freneau's paper built up Jefferson as assiduously as it attacked Hamilton.

Thomas Paine's *Rights of Man* appeared also during 1791 in an American edition with an introductory endorsement by Jefferson. Paine vigorously defended the French Revolution against the British attack embodied in Edmund Burke's *Reflections on the Revolution in France*, but Jefferson's endorsement, published without his knowledge, referred to Paine's work as an answer to "political heresies which have sprung up among us." Informed Americans, including the Vice President, construed this as a reference to John Adams's *Discourses on Davila*, which had recently deplored the "mistake" of the French in concentrating authority in a supreme legislature rather than creating a "balanced" government with powers divided among legislative, executive, and judicial branches.

Suspicious Federalists also interpreted the Northern tour of Jefferson and Madison in 1791 as an organizing effort, although it seems in fact to have been chiefly a "botanizing" vacation.

Thomas Paine.   Culver Pictures, Inc.

What Federalists had suspected in 1791 became reality in 1792. Republicans did indeed begin to organize. They did so chiefly in Congress under Madison's leadership and in opposition to Hamilton's program. Jefferson, holding office as Washington's secretary of state, kept his opposition to Hamilton's program largely within the Cabinet until 1793, when he resigned and retired to Monticello. Despite these indications of a strong disinclination to lead, it was always Jefferson whom both Federalists and Republicans considered to be the chief of the opposition.

Washington's popularity was still so great in 1792 that the Republicans planned no campaign against his reelection, but they considered Vice President Adams, "the monarchical rubbish of our government," highly vulnerable. With John Beckley, clerk of the House of Representatives, as their liaison man, Madison and Jefferson arranged to run New York's Antifederalist Governor, George Clinton, against Adams. Adams won reelection with 77 electoral votes to Clinton's 50, but the Republicans drew encouragement from their respectable showing.

Party lines hardened appreciably between 1792 and 1796. Congressional Republicans kept Hamilton under fire until he resigned in 1795. By then, however, it was foreign policy rather than Hamilton's economic measures over which differences were sharpest. Jay's treaty, which ended the threat of war with Britain, deeply offended the Republican partisans of France. Even before that controversy reached its climax, Washington had rejected further efforts at impartiality and resolved: "I shall not . . . bring any man into any office of consequence knowingly whose political tenets are adverse to the measures which the general government are pursuing." To do otherwise, he had concluded, "would be a sort of political suicide."

When Washington announced in his Farewell Address of 1796 that he would not accept another term, Republicans eagerly put forth Thomas Jefferson as their consensus candidate to succeed him. The Federalists had little trouble agreeing on John Adams. Hamilton, however, disliked Adams so strongly that he schemed to divert the votes of Southern Federalists from Adams to South Carolina's Thomas Pinckney, who—because of the popularity of his treaty with Spain—had been the party's vice-presidential choice. The Constitution had invited such intrigue by failing to require separate elections for the two offices; it merely provided that electors should vote for two men and that the man with the highest electoral vote should be president while the vice presidency should go to the man who placed second. None of the candidates campaigned in the modern sense. In fact, only eight of the sixteen states provided for a popular vote in choosing electors; the rest permitted their legislatures to appoint them. The outstanding campaign document was Washington's Farewell Address, which Hamilton helped him compose. With Republican admiration for France in mind, Washington cautioned against "passionate attachments" in foreign policy as well as against partisan division along sectional lines.

Sectional division such as Washington had feared was clearly evident in the results of the election of 1796. Adams, with 71 electoral votes to Jefferson's 68, had won every vote north of Pennsylvania plus a scattering elsewhere, largely in the upper South. Jefferson had won the two new Western states (Kentucky and Tennessee) and nearly all of the South, but nothing in the North save Pennsylvania. New England Federalists, with some knowledge of Hamilton's scheme to throw the election to Pinckney, cut the South Carolinian so severely that he received only 59 votes, thus allowing Jefferson to become vice president. Southern Republicans, on the other hand, failed to give full support to New York's Aaron Burr, the Republican vice-presidential choice. He ran 20 votes behind Jefferson.

An Undeclared War

John Adams, like Washington, had secured a major place in American history before he became president. He was an outstanding leader of the Revolutionary movement, both in Massachusetts and in the Continental Congress; with Franklin and Jay, he negotiated the remarkable treaty which secured American independence. He was also the principal author of the respected Massachusetts constitution of 1780. His nonpartisan selection as vice president under Washington, even though he considered it "the most insignificant office that ever the invention of man contrived," testified to the high esteem in which he was held.

As President, John Adams suffered from too close adherence to his own rather dogmatic political philosophy. In its simplest terms, that philosophy held that rich and poor alike, reflecting the evil nature of man, engage in a perpetual, self-interested struggle for political dominance. The function of government in general, but of the Chief Executive in particular, was to prevent either group from gaining full power to impose its will. The fact that throughout much of his administration the Federalists controlled the Senate, the "aristocratical" branch of the government, while the Republicans dominated the House of Representatives, or "democratical" branch, probably helped to confirm the President in his conclusion. What he failed to perceive (understandably, in view of the very recent emergence of political parties and their presumed impermanence) was that to be an effective leader the President must be master of his party.

Alexander Hamilton, not John Adams, was the effective leader of the Federalist party through most of Adams's administration. Not only congressional leaders, but even members of the President's Cabinet gave first loyalty to Hamilton when his views and those of the President conflicted. Adams complicated this problem by spending long periods at his home in Massachusetts, so that there was some validity to the observation of Treasury Secretary Oliver Wolcott that he and two other Cabinet members "govern this great nation."

Whether or not to declare war on France was the major external problem of Adams's administration. France had construed Jay's treaty— particularly America's silent acceptance of Britain's seizure of American ships carrying cargo for France—as aligning the United States with Britain in the continuing war between the two great powers. In reprisal, French ships operating in the Caribbean and in American coastal waters captured over three hundred American merchant ships during the year preceding July 1797. The absence of American naval power encouraged the French to expect no effective retaliation.

War with the United States, however, had no part in France's plans. The recovery of Louisiana (ceded to Spain in 1763) was one French objective. Another was to keep the United States neutral so that American merchant ships could carry cargoes to France with presumed immunity from British seizure. Another French hope was to see the Federalist "Anglo-men" replaced by pro-French Republicans in control of the American government. War with the United States would serve none of these objectives. Still more important for France were European considerations. Although French armies had ringed the nation with satellites from Belgium to Italy, France had conquered neither Austria nor Britain. These goals took priority.

Because peaceful relations between the United States and France would clearly serve the interest of both nations, Adams decided to send a mission to Paris, much as Washington had done in sending Jay to London in 1794. The three-man delegation included Charles C. Pinckney, brother of the Federalist vice-presidential candidate of 1796; John Marshall, a Virginia Federalist; and Elbridge Gerry, a Republican friend of the President from Massachusetts. They were greeted by the French with demands that they disavow anti-French statements of the President, promise a $12 million loan, and donate $250,000 to various French officials before negotiations could even begin. While such demands were not entirely unprecedented, they were offensive, especially to Adams. He thought seriously of asking Congress to declare war but decided wisely to wait until the French had alienated their Republican supporters in the United States. To foster that objective Adams readily agreed to congressional demands that he make public the commissioners' report. Published with "X," "Y," and "Z" substituting for the names of the French agents, the documents evoked a great outburst of national indignation. In its wake, Congress created a Department of the Navy, authorized construction of more warships, and increased the Army to 10,000 men. Without seeking a declaration of war, the President sent the Navy in search of French warships.

The undeclared or "quasi-war" with France widened the split between the Hamiltonian "High Federalists" and the President's more moderate following. Hamiltonians wanted a declaration of war "to enable us," as one Senator put it, "to lay our hands on traitors." Hamilton himself wanted to seize Florida and Louisiana from Spain, then an ally of France, and to cooperate with the British in liberating Latin America and capturing the Caribbean colonies of France. At Hamilton's insistence, Congress tripled the Army. Adams persuaded Washington to accept nominal command of the Army, but Washington insisted that Hamilton be made second in command and authorized to manage the Army until real need for Washington's services arose. Thus President Adams had to bestow effective command of an Army about to be greatly enlarged upon the chief opponent of his defensive strategy, a factional leader to whom even major Cabinet members gave higher loyalty than to the President. Adams reluctantly accepted Washington's terms, but he did not hurry to recruit men for Hamilton's Army.

Fortunately for Adams, the French began to reconsider their policy. Even before the end of 1798, the expanding American Navy had largely cleared American coastal waters of French privateers and in the next two years would carry the war into the West Indies at a considerable cost to the French in warships. Vastly more serious to

the French was the devastation suffered by their navy at the hands of Britain's Horatio Nelson in the Battle of the Nile during August 1798. To Napoleon Bonaparte, coming to power in France in 1799, it seemed clear that restoration of peace with the United States was desirable so that France could use neutral American ships to combat Britain's blockade. Even before Napoleon assumed control, however, Adams had received assurances from the French government that a new American mission would be met "with the respect due to representatives of a free, independent, and powerful nation," the precise words Adams had used in fixing the only condition under which he would send another mission. To the consternation of the Hamiltonians, Adams accepted the French assurances. A commission consisting of diplomat William Vans Murray, Chief Justice Oliver Ellsworth, and North Carolina Governor William R. Davie ended hostilities with the highly satisfactory Convention of 1800. The treaty helped to cool domestic political hostilities as well.

A Constitutional Crisis

At the height of the undeclared war both Federalist factions agreed on a program of repression aimed at their Republican opponents. Some Federalists believed "a great body of domestic traitors" would abet a French invasion of the United States, as subversives had done in European areas which had fallen under French control. Should a French conquest occur, a Federalist warned, "We must receive a constitution from Paris, as the Dutch and the Swedes have been compelled to do," and submit to a puppet government headed by such an arch-Francophile as Vice President Thomas Jefferson. Such exaggerated fears afflicted only a few, but many Federalists shared Hamilton's worry that if French conquests continued, the "United States might be left alone to Contend with the Conquerors of Europe." Why Republicans in such

circumstances remained sympathetic to France and opposed increased military expenditures was difficult for Federalists to comprehend.

Federalists also feared Republican radicalism in domestic matters. Should Republicans gain control of the federal government, their dedication to states' rights, many Federalists felt, might well jeopardize the still-precarious federal Union. The unorthodox religious views of Republican leaders spawned fears of atheistic, antireligious programs like those of the French republicans. Republican opposition to "aristocracy" appeared to some Federalists a threat to traditional property rights.

To combat Republican radicalism, the Federalists in 1798 enacted four important laws. One, a Naturalization Act, extended the residence requirement for citizenship from five years to fourteen. Its objective was to prevent immigrants, for the most part prospective Republicans from voting in crucial upcoming elections. An Alien Enemies Act, passed with Republican support, provided for dealing with enemy aliens in time of war. An Alien Act, limited to the remaining two years of Adams's term, authorized the President, even without a declaration of war, to deport any alien whom he judged "dangerous to the peace and safety of the United States." John Adams never employed this power, but hundreds of aliens, mostly French, left voluntarily, some primarily for business reasons. Last but most important of the new laws was the Sedition Act, a law designed to suppress Republican criticism of the Federalist administration in advance of the presidential election of 1800. It too was to be in force for only two years.

In theory, the Sedition Act actually increased freedom to criticize the government. Contrary to English tradition, the law permitted the accused to secure acquittal by proving the truth of his accusations. In addition, it required the government to show malicious intent and authorized the jury to decide not only whether the accused had made the criticisms but also whether they constituted seditious libel. In permitting the jury rather than the judge to decide the extent of libel, Congress followed the example of the British Parliament which had made the same provision in 1792.

In operation, the Sedition Act was harshly repressive. Its terms provided a fine and imprisonment for anyone who published "false, scandalous, and malicious writing" tending to bring the government "into contempt or disrepute." This seemed to posterity a flat violation of the First Amendment to the Constitution, which states that "Congress shall make no law . . . abridging the freedom of speech, or of the press." However, it is now clear that this guarantee applied at the time, as in the English common law, only to prior restraint and not to subsequent punishment. Accordingly, Federalist prosecutors, often aided by Federalist judges, convinced Federalist juries that the words of

leading Republican critics of the Adams administration did warrant punishment. Congressman Matthew Lyon of Vermont was fined and jailed for telling his constituents that the President engaged in a "continual grasp for power" and that he had an "unbounded thirst for ridiculous pomp." Editors of four of the nation's five leading Republican newspapers were convicted and punished for similar allegations.

Republicans refused to be intimidated. Their criticism continued undiminished. Considering seditious libel a matter for state rather than federal prosecution, Kentucky's Legislature adopted a resolution drafted secretly by Vice President Jefferson, affirming that each state could "judge for itself . . . the mode . . . of redress" when the "general government assumes undelegated powers." Later it specifically endorsed "nullification" as the "rightful remedy." A Virginia resolution drafted by Madison referred to the "duty" of the state to "interpose" its authority to prevent the federal government from exercising "powers not granted" in the Constitution. Virginia also asked other states to join in declaring both the Alien and the Sedition

A political cartoon of 1798, depicting the fight in Congress between Roger Griswold (with cane) and Matthew Lyon. Lyon was victimized by the Sedition Act as well as by Griswold's cane. The Granger Collection

He in a trice struck Lyon thrice
Upon his head, enrag'd sir,

Who seiz'd the tongs to ease his wrongs,
and Griswold thus engag'd sir.

Congress Hall,
in Philad.ª Feb. 15, 1798.

Acts unconstitutional. Most states ignored the appeal, but some affirmed in rebuttal that the nation's Supreme Court should make such determinations. Thus the Virginia and Kentucky Resolutions made the nature of the federal Union as well as the question of freedom of the press an important issue in the presidential contest of 1800.

Conclusion

As the election of 1800 approached, Federalists could take considerable satisfaction from their achievements. Confounding foreign skeptics of both America's political capacity and its republican ideology, they had established a powerful federal government, more powerful indeed than their opponents believed the constitution warranted. They had gained the firm allegiance of the "moneyed men" of the commercial Northeast, but at the price of alienating the agricultural interests, especially in the South and West. Wayne's victory at Fallen Timbers plus the Jay and Pinckney Treaties had greatly improved conditions for Western settlement.

Under John Adams, successful naval action in an undeclared naval war with France had won the nation more respect abroad at the expense of still deeper division at home. The Republican party, born out of opposition to Federalist domestic policies, grew increasingly vehement in reaction to anti-French aspects of Federalist foreign policy. To suppress criticism of their program through the period of the election of 1800, the Federalists passed the Sedition Act of 1798 and in highly partisan prosecutions jailed several of their more outspoken Republican critics. Thus the nation faced no shortage of issues in 1800 as the Republicans sought to substitute Thomas Jefferson for John Adams as the nation's leader.

SUGGESTED READINGS

John C. Miller's *Federalist Era** (1960) is comprehensive, reliable, and delightful. The most important supplement to it is L. D. White, *The Federalists* (1948), an appreciative study of how the Federalists created and operated a new national government. Bray Hammond's *Banks and Politics** (1957) esteems Hamilton highly for his success with the first Bank of the United States. L. D. Baldwin in *Whiskey Rebels* (1939) deals competently with that challenge to the new government's authority.

Washington's diplomatic difficulties are the subject of several good studies. S. F. Bemis is outstanding in both *Jay's Treaty* (rev. ed., 1962) and *Pinckney's Treaty* (rev. ed., 1960). Alexander DeConde's *Entangling Alliance* (1958) recounts the problems arising from the "permanent" alliance with France. A. H. Bowman's *The Struggle for Neutrality* does the same with a Jeffersonian slant. P. A. Varg's *Foreign Policies of the Founding Fathers* (1963) and Felix Gilbert's *To the Farewell Address** (1961) discuss Washington's policies in relation to American ideology. Louis M. Sears in *George*

Washington and the French Revolution (1960) has given a year-by-year account of the American's reactions to the news from France. A. P. Whitaker is authoritative on the southwestern frontier in *The Spanish-American Frontier, 1783–1795* (1927) and *The Mississippi Question, 1795–1803* (1934). A. L. Burt considers the problems on the northern frontier in long-range perspective in *The United States, Great Britain, and British North America* (1940). J. P. Boyd in *Number 7* (1964) accuses Hamilton of acting secretly and improperly to alter American foreign policy in favor of Britain even before Jay's treaty. C. R. Ritcheson's *The Aftermath of Revolution* (1969) affords new insight into Jay's treaty from a British perspective. J. A. Combs in *The Jay Treaty* (1970) puts it at the center of political contention.

Biographies which overlap the Washington administrations are not only numerous but also highly important source materials. In addition to those cited previously, see Broadus Mitchell's *Alexander Hamilton* (2 vols., 1962), very favorable to Hamilton; John C.

Miller's *Alexander Hamilton: Portrait in Paradox* (1959), both critical and appreciative; Gerald Stourzh's *Alexander Hamilton and the Idea of Republican Government* (1970); Dumas Malone's *Jefferson and the Ordeal of Liberty* (1962), carefully balanced, a segment of a major multivolume work; Merrill Peterson's *Thomas Jefferson and the New Nation* (1970); Ralph Ketcham's *James Madison* (1971); Irving Brant's *James Madison: Father of the Constitution* (1950); Frank Monaghan's *John Jay* (1935); W. E. A. Bernhard's *Fisher Ames* (1965); Richard W. Welch, Jr.'s *Theodore Sedgwick, Federalist* (1965); and M. R. Zahniser's *Charles Cotesworth Pinckney* (1967).

Hamilton's famous reports are in J. E. Cooke (ed.), *The Reports of Alexander Hamilton** (1964).

No consensus is yet evident among historians on the emergence of political parties. Charles A. Beard in *Economic Origins of Jeffersonian Democracy** (2d ed., 1940) saw continuity between the Antifederalists and the Jeffersonian Republicans and assumed that persisting class differences underlay such political rivalry. Alfred F. Young in *The Democratic Republicans of New York* (1967) sees essential continuity in New York from radical Whigs to Antifederalists to Republicans on the one hand and from conservative Whigs to Federalists on the other, nevertheless taking exception to Beard on many points. Noble Cunningham has studied the organization of the Republicans in *The Jeffersonian Republicans: The Formation of Party Organization** (1957). He denies the existence of the continuity asserted by Beard and Young. He insists also that party organization began in Congress under Madison's leadership and filtered down from there to the states. Other works of importance on the topic include J. T. Main's *Political Parties before the Constitution* (1973): Paul Goodman's *The Democratic-Republicans of Massachusetts* (1964); Carl E. Prince's *New Jersey's Jeffersonian Republicans* (1967); J. E. Charles's *The Origins of the American Party System* (1956); W. N. Chambers' *Political Parties in a New Nation* (1963), largely a synthesis of earlier studies; Morton Borden's *Parties and Politics in the Early Republic** (1967), similar to Chambers' work, but shorter; M. J. Dauer's *The Adams Federalists** (1953); H. M. Tinkcom's *Republicans and Federalists in Pennsylvania* (1950); Staughton Lynd's *Antifederalism in Dutchess County* (1962); E. P. Link's *Democratic-Republican Societies* (1942); J. M. Banner's *To the Hartford Convention* (1970); Richard Buel, Jr.'s *Securing the Revolution: Ideology in American Politics, 1789–1815* (1972); Patricia Watlington's *The Partisan Spirit: Kentucky Politics, 1779–1792* (1972); R. R. Beeman's *The Old Dominion and the New Nation, 1788–1801* (1972); S. C. Patterson's *Political Parties in Revolutionary Massachusetts* (1973); Van Beck Hall's *Politics without Parties: Massachusetts, 1780–1791* (1972). In a class by itself is Richard Hofstadter's *The Idea of a Party System* (1969), which studies the gradual acceptance of organized opposition to the administration as legitimate.

On the undeclared war the best accounts are Alexander DeConde, *The Quasi-War** (1966), Bradford Perkins, *The First Rapprochment* (1955), and A. H. Bowman's *The Struggle for Neutrality* (1974).

J. M. Smith's *Freedom's Fetters* (1956) is a full and fascinating account of the Alien and Sedition Acts, but it needs to be supplemented by Leonard Levy's *Legacy of Suppression** (1960) for long-range perspective on the evolution of the legal concept of freedom of speech. The best source on the Virginia and Kentucky Resolutions is Adrienne Koch's *Jefferson and Madison: The Great Collaboration* (1950).

On John Adams and his administration generally, see M. J. Dauer, *The Adams Federalists* * (1953); S. G. Kurtz, *The Presidency of John Adams** (1957); Page Smith, *John Adams* (1962), a very personalized biography; J. R. Howe, *The Changing Political Thought of John Adams** (1966); Zoltan Haraszti, *John Adams and the Prophets of Progress** (1952).

* indicates availability in paperback.

7

The Jeffersonian Ascendancy

What Thomas Jefferson called "the Revolution of 1800" ousted the Federalists from national power for all time. Saddled with public resentment of the tax burden required by their military preparations, suspected of "aristocratic" or even "monarchical" tendencies, insufficiently sensitive to the views of the agrarian majority, intolerant of criticism, the Federalists lost a bitterly contested election in 1800 and never did as well thereafter. Jefferson and his ideological heirs in the Republican party controlled the government for the next generation. In their hands the government no longer showed such particular solicitude for the wealthy Northeastern merchants as Hamilton had. Rather it was the nation's farmers and planters whom the government sought to serve. Yet what the farmers and planters wanted was not so much overt assistance from the federal government as maximum authority for state governments to meet the varying needs of particular communities and maximum freedom for individuals to pursue their own interests without special advantages afforded to any. Consequently, under Jeffersonian leadership the federal government gave little positive aid to the party's supporters. Moderate and pragmatic, the Republicans merely diluted Federalist nationalism with states' rights, mercantilism with laissez-faire. In foreign affairs, Jefferson accepted his good fortune when Napoleon presented him with the opportunity to buy Louisiana; but in his efforts to compel warring Britain and France each to allow America to trade freely with the other he not only failed but evoked dangerous domestic strife as well.

When James Madison succeeded Jefferson, European civilization as a whole was in great turmoil. Napoleon's conquests encompassed nearly all of Europe. Only two nations offered any hope for the continent's redemption from the conqueror's rule: Britain, supreme at sea since Trafalgar and protected by the English Channel from Napoleon's armies; and Russia, seemingly secured by its peripheral position and its vastness. To Napoleon the independence of each was an irresistible challenge.

From the very outset, Madison's administration was necessarily preoccupied with the defense of American honor and trade against offensive measures enforced by Britain and France in their economic warfare. Insults and injuries multiplied while American indignation mounted and the economy suffered. American reprisals as well as the actions of the belligerents restricted the nation's business. The country became bitterly divided over the proper American response and at last plunged into an unpopular and potentially disastrous war with Britain, a war which neither belligerent really wanted. Despite incredible mismanagement in the early stages of the war, the nation emerged at its conclusion with its territory intact, more strongly united than ever, and enjoying for the first time international recognition as a nation of consequence.

"The Revolution of 1800"

Amid the furor over the Alien and Sedition Acts and the squabbling among Federalists over the termination of the quasi-war with France, the nation prepared for the election of 1800. The Federalists had won a victory of landslide proportions in the congressional elections of 1798 when near hysteria over the French menace gripped the nation, but thereafter the party alienated many voters. Hence, the election seemed likely to be close.

Hamilton's enlarged Army was proving a serious addition to the political burdens which the Federalists already bore. Many voters shared the Republican fear that its purpose was to "arm one half of the people, for the purpose of keeping the other in awe." Such fears did not diminish when the President used federal troops in Pennsylvania to arrest an ex-Federalist, John Fries, for leading a mob which liberated men jailed for tax dodging. The taxes imposed to pay for the Army served also, as one contemporary observed, to "carry reason and reflection to every man's door, and particularly in the hour of election."

The Hamilton and Adams wings of the Federalist party continued to fight each other. Adams dismissed two Hamiltonians from his Cabinet: Secretary of State Timothy Pickering and Secretary of War James McHenry. Hamilton, having failed to persuade the dying Washington to oppose Adams, tried again to throw the Presidency to the party's vice-presidential candidate, this time South Carolinian Charles Cotesworth Pinckney of XYZ fame, a brother of the nominee of 1796. Hamilton showed little regret when Republican Aaron Burr secured and published a copy of a pamphlet in which he had severely criticized the President.

Since each state voted at a time of its own choice, the outcome of the election long re-

Aaron Burr.　　　　　　　　　*The Granger Collection*

mained in doubt. Aaron Burr moved the Republicans ahead with a brilliant organizing effort in New York City, which gave his party a majority in the state legislature. This transferred New York's 12 electoral votes, which Adams had won in 1796, to Jefferson's column. Adams picked up strength elsewhere, however, and in time it became clear that South Carolina's 8 votes would be decisive. Despite the candidacy of Charles Cotesworth Pinckney on the Federalist ticket, South Carolina's legislators, influenced in some measure by patronage promises held out on behalf of the Republicans by still another Pinckney, Senator Charles Pinckney, gave the state's vote and thus the election to the Republicans. Jefferson and Burr, the vice-presidential choice, had 73 votes each while Adams had 65 and Pinckney 64. In the congressional elections Republicans scored an overwhelming victory, reversing the Federalist tide of 1798.

Because each of the Republican electors had voted for both Jefferson and Burr, an electoral college tie left it to the old House of Representatives elected in 1798 to choose between them. With one vote for each state's congressional delegation, as the Constitution requires, Jefferson, on the first ballot, gained eight votes, one short of the necessary majority. For thirty-five ballots the Federalists held firm for Burr, while trying to exact policy commitments from Jefferson as a price for ending the stalemate. Then Delaware's only congressman, Federalist James A. Bayard, announced his intention to switch to Jefferson. In the end no Federalist voted for Jefferson, but some did abstain, with the result that Jefferson was properly chosen on the thirty-sixth ballot. Before the next election, the Twelfth Amendment of the Constitution, providing separate balloting for president and vice president, ruled out the danger that such a problem would recur.

Thomas Jefferson, author of the inspirational affirmation that "all men are created equal," leader of a party considered, in the North at least, to be that of the "middling sort," possessed full credentials as an American aristocrat.

His mother's family, the Randolphs, was one of Virginia's most distinguished. Jefferson himself owned thousands of acres of land and over a hundred slaves. He had received a classical education from tutors and at William and Mary College. He knew several languages and was a lawyer, an inventor, and an amateur architect of distinction. He played the violin and wrote a book of intelligent commentary, *Notes on Virginia* (1785), on the economy and society of his native state. Like many other educated gentlemen of his time, he eschewed orthodox Christianity for Deism, the religion of reason. Like most Southern planters, he never allowed his perpetual burden of debts to restrict his gracious style of living.

Politically, Jefferson had much in common with the nation's farmers. In contrast to Hamilton's zeal to foster manufacturing, Jefferson intended to foster agriculture. "Those who labour in the earth," he had written in his *Notes on Virginia*, "are the chosen people of God." He favored assistance to commerce so that surplus agricultural commodities might be sold abroad; but rather than aid manufacturing, he believed Americans should "let our workshops remain in Europe" and thus avoid the growth of cities whose mobs he considered a menace to "pure government." To serve the interests of ordinary farmers, Jefferson believed, as they did, that what was needed was not Hamiltonian mercantilism but "a wise and frugal government, which shall restrain men from injuring one another, shall leave them otherwise free to regulate their own pursuits." In particular, Jefferson wished to limit the role of the federal government. He considered state governments "the most competent administrations for our domestic concerns and the surest bulwark against antirepublican tendencies."

Recognizing the problem of reconciling majority rule with minority rights, Jefferson made qualified commitments to both. On the one hand, he demanded "absolute acquiescence in the decisions of the majority, the vital principle of republics, from which there is no appeal but to force, the vital principle and immediate parent of despotism.'' On the other hand, he insisted that the will of the majority ''to be rightful must be reasonable; that the minority possess their equal rights, which equal law must protect, and to violate would be oppression.'' In his list of the ''essential principles of our Government,'' he gave first place to ''Equal and exact justice to all men.''

Jefferson's belief that his election effected a revolution in 1800 has often struck historians as greatly exaggerated. They have tended to emphasize instead how little really changed. Indeed, there was none of the drastic change or violence which people normally associate with revolutions. Jefferson made no effort to undo Hamilton's funding of the national debt or the assumption by the federal government of the state debts. The Bank of the United States, which he had originally opposed as unconstitutional, Jefferson condoned as President because his Secretary of the Treasury found it useful. His federal appointees were, on the whole, slightly lower in social status than Federalist appointees had been, but the standing of ''gentleman'' was still nearly prerequisite to selection.

Nevertheless, a number of important changes had occurred. A rival leader had ousted the nation's Chief Executive. In contrast to most parts of Europe where only violence could produce such a change, Americans had achieved it legally, peacefully, by means of an electoral process prescribed in a written Constitution. The new leader's party had also gained firm control of the national legislature. Contemporaries recognized clearly that political power had shifted from the commercial Northeast to the rural South and West. Any consideration of secession in the next two decades would center in the Northeast, not in the South and West as it had in the Federalist era. To say that government by agents of farmers and planters had replaced that by representatives of a mercantile aristocracy would be an oversimplification, yet such a generalization contains elements of truth too important to overlook. Younger Federalist leaders

would try to compete with the Jeffersonians in appealing to the newly awakened electorate of ''middling'' status, but for Federalists generally the aristocratic image of federalism established in the 1790s would prove an insuperable handicap.

Jefferson made specific policy changes of some importance as well. His brilliant Secretary of the Treasury, Albert Gallatin, reduced by nearly one-half the considerable national debt which the Federalists had left, doing so chiefly by reducing the size of the Army. In Republican eyes, the Army was not only excessively expensive and potentially oppressive but also a source of *federal* power. They preferred to rely on militia forces, which were not only part-time and hence cheaper but also in normal times under *state* control. Republican economies also permitted repeal of the hated whisky tax. Reluctant to offend Federalist converts to Republicanism, Jefferson resisted pressure from his supporters for wholesale removals from the federal service, but when making new appointments, he did seek to ''afford Republicans a proportionate share'' of federal jobs. There had been only 6 Republicans among 600 federal employees when he took office; by 1803, Republicans enjoyed a slight majority.

Social traditions which appeared aristocratic or monarchical also underwent change. Instead of proceeding in stately dignity as had kings, colonial governors, and earlier presidents to deliver formal addresses to the legislature, Jefferson sent written messages to Congress to be droned out by a clerk. The procedure ended for a century a somewhat ''monarchical'' custom; in addition, it enabled Jefferson to avoid calling unnecessary attention to his weakness in speaking. He also ended the very formal ''levees'' of the Federalist era and prescribed a much less formal code of etiquette to govern official social affairs. Privately, the President continued to entertain lavishly, but he shocked some foreign dignitaries by receiving them in very casual attire.

Freedom to criticize federal officials broadened after the Sedition Act controversy but in ways which added little to Jefferson's stature. Throughout his presidency, Jefferson clung to the Blackstone conception that freedom of the press meant only the absence of prior restraint. His objection to the Sedition Act, although he never made it public at the time, was that it was a *federal* restraint unauthorized by the Constitution. "While we deny that [members of] Congress have a right to control freedom of the press," Jefferson wrote, "we have ever asserted the right of the states . . . to do so." Accordingly, Jefferson refused to extend the expiring Sedition Act and of course pardoned his followers still in jail for violating it.

Eager to conciliate the opposition, Jefferson made no effort to quell criticism for some time. By 1803, however, the attacks had become so intense that he thought it desirable to act in order to restore "credibility" to the press. He suggested privately to the Governor of Pennsylvania that "a few prosecutions of the most prominent offenders would have a wholesome effect in restoring the integrity of the presses." Prosecutions followed in the courts of several states, but only one resulted in a conviction, and that was overturned on appeal.

Three significant conclusions emerged from these controversies. New York's Legislature put into a widely copied statute the argument used by Alexander Hamilton in defense of one of Jefferson's critics: that "with good motives" a person might safely publish truth "though reflecting on government, magistracy, or individuals." The United States Supreme Court, hearing an appeal on another case, held (*United States v. Hudson*, 1812) that federal courts could not try common law (nonstatutory) crimes, such as seditious libel, but only those defined in the Constitution or in acts of Congress. Finally, the Republicans, like the Federalists before them, seem to have found that tolerating even the most offensive criticism may be less painful than trying to suppress it.

Quite contrary to their basic commitment to minimize federal functions, the Republicans tried to increase them in several areas. Despite their general animosity toward the Army, the Republicans in 1803 created the United States Military Academy at West Point. Within a few years it had developed into the nation's first college of engineering, and for generations its graduates provided the nation's best-trained engineers, widely employed in private industry as well as in government service. Despite his early opposition, Jefferson in 1806 approved the appropriation of federal funds for constructing the "national road" which ultimately extended from Baltimore into Illinois. Treasury Secretary Gallatin in 1808 submitted to Congress an elaborate plan for a national network of roads and canals, but Republican orthodoxy prevailed. The impetus such a program would have given to the nation's economic growth had to await another generation.

Jefferson and the Judiciary

Federalists remained firmly entrenched in the federal judiciary as the Jeffersonian era began. Republicans, dedicated to the idea that majority will should prevail, were not pleased by the prospect that, in accordance with the theory of separation of powers, Federalist judges enjoying lifetime tenure might in some instances deny the majority what it wished. Moreover, those Republicans who were most firmly dedicated to states' rights looked upon federal courts not only as unnecessary but also as a positive threat to the power of state courts and an unwanted agency for bending the people of any state to the will of the "general" government.

Foremost among the Federalists ready to battle Republicanism from their judicial stronghold was Chief Justice John Marshall, appointed by President Adams at the very end of his term. Although Marshall had opposed the Sedition Act, he was otherwise a highly orthodox Federalist, fully determined to establish the independent power of the judiciary, to sanctify the rights of ownership, and above all to make national authority superior to that of the states. While these views by themselves assured clashes between the President and the Chief Justice, the two men, although fellow Virginians, distant cousins, and both normally quite amiable, detested each other as well.

Their first clash involved the Judiciary Act of 1801, a lame-duck measure of the outgoing Adams administration. In anticipation of a big increase in the work load of federal courts, the law provided for sixteen new federal judges. In addition, it relieved the Supreme Court justices of the duty of sitting on regional circuit courts. Because the Constitution states explicitly that federal judges "shall hold their offices during good behavior," Jefferson could not replace the Federalists whom Adams had appointed to the new posts. However, the Constitution also states: "The judicial power of the United States shall be vested in one Supreme Court and in such inferior courts as the Congress may from time to time . . . establish." On the theory that what Congress could do it could also undo, the Republicans repealed the law creating the new positions and restored the provisions of the Judiciary Act of 1789, which required Supreme Court justices to serve on regional circuit courts in addition to their other duties. Marshall tried to persuade some of the victims to challenge the Republican measure in the courts, but none chose to do so.

Meanwhile Marshall was deliberating the famous case of *Marbury v. Madison* (1803). Marbury had received one of the very last of President Adams's "midnight" appointments, that of justice of the peace in the District of Columbia. His commission had been signed, sealed, but not delivered, an oversight of the outgoing Secretary of State, John Marshall. Jefferson, who regarded such appointments as "an outrage on decency," ordered his Secretary of State, James Madison, not to deliver the commission. Marbury then asked the Supreme Court to issue

an order, a "write of mandamus," requiring Madison to do so. The Court ordered Madison to "show cause" why he should not deliver the commission, but Madison declined to do that as well.

Marshall thus found himself in an acute constitutional quandary. Section 13 of the Judiciary Act of 1789 authorized the Court to issue such orders to "any . . . persons holding office under the authority of the United States." However, the court must ultimately rely upon the President to enforce its orders. Marshall had every reason to believe Jefferson would ignore a Supreme Court order directing him to compel Madison to do what he had already ordered Madison not to do.

Marshall's decision extricated his Court brilliantly from the dilemma. First, he scolded the administration for refusing to honor what he declared was a valid appointment and thus violating "a vested legal right." Then he concluded that his Court really lacked jurisdiction. To reach that conclusion, Marshall construed Section 13 of the Judiciary Act of 1789 as adding to the *original* (as opposed to the appellate) jurisdiction of the court. As the Constitution fixes the original jurisdiction of the court with finality, the law in question appeared "not to be warranted by the constitution." Accordingly, Marshall refused to order Madison to deliver Marbury's commission and avoided revealing the impotence of his Court to enforce such an order. To support his conclusion, Marshall's decision included a classic affirmation that, since the Constitution is the "fundamental . . . law of the nation," the courts must refuse to enforce acts of Congress which conflict with it. Although this proposition was to be important only once again before the Civil War, it assumed fundamental importance after that time.

Modern scholars make two major criticisms of Marshall's decision. First, by present standards it is improper for the Court to state a conclusion on the merits of a case over which it has no jurisdiction. Second, it appears that the intent of Congress in passing the Judiciary Act was not to add to the original jurisdiction of the Supreme

Court, but merely to empower the Court to issue writs of mandamus on matters within its existing jurisdiction. In this view Marshall held void a valid law.

Eager to make the federal judiciary more responsible to the popular will, the Republicans in 1803 began to remove highly partisan Federalist judges by impeachment proceedings. The Constitution, while assuring federal judges tenure "during good Behaviour," also provided for their removal by impeachment proceedings for "Treason, Bribery, or other high Crimes and Misdemeanors." Normally advocates of literal construction of the Constitution, the Republicans in this instance wished to construe the language loosely, as Hamilton did in justifying the national Bank. Their first target was federal Judge John Pickering of New Hampshire. As Pickering was both an alcoholic and insane, the Republicans had little trouble convincing a majority in the House to impeach him and getting the required two-thirds vote in the Senate to remove him.

Next the Republicans turned to Judge Samuel Chase, the Maryland Federalist who as presiding judge had helped to jail several Republicans under the Sedition Act. Recently he had denounced the Republicans from the bench for instituting "mobocracy." The House impeached Chase, but the Senate vote, despite the Republican majority of 25 to 9, fell 4 short of the 23 necessary for a conviction. Impeachment, Jefferson concluded, was "a farce which will not be tried again." The occasion thus served to reinforce the independence of the federal judiciary, but it also persuaded federal judges to restrain their partisan impulses in public. Although the Republicans never succeeded in making the *federal* judiciary more responsive, they did achieve that result in many states by providing that judges would serve for fixed terms rather than during "good behavior."

Doubling the Nation's Size

Expansion of America's territory seemed to Jefferson and his contemporaries only a matter of time. Britain's power made northward extension of the nation's borders unlikely, but Spain's weakness marked both Florida and the vast Louisiana Territory as potential targets. While Jefferson was winning the Presidency, Spain had reluctantly agreed in a secret treaty of 1800 to return Louisiana to France. The actual transfer of control, delayed by Napoleon's failure to keep his part of the bargain, occurred in 1802, after Spain had secured Napoleon's promise never to sell the region. Intending to use the territory to produce food for the French sugar plantations on Santo Domingo (modern Haiti and the Dominican Republic), Napoleon planned to occupy it in force as soon as he had crushed the revolutionary regime of Toussaint L'Ouverture and his fellow blacks on the island.

Jefferson's reaction to the news, despite his reputation as pro-French, was highly bellicose.

He informed Napoleon indirectly that, as three-eighths of the United States depended upon New Orleans for access to markets, this country must consider the nation which possessed it "our natural and habitual enemy." "The day that France takes possession of New Orleans," he added, "we must marry ourselves to the British fleet and nation."

Informed that money would probably influence Napoleon more than threats, Jefferson arranged to send James Monroe on a mission to Paris with authorization to offer $10 million for New Orleans and Florida. Jefferson assumed that France had secured West Florida, the coastal region between modern Florida and Louisiana, but the Spanish, as the President later discovered, thought otherwise. Should Napoleon decline to sell, Monroe was to proceed to England to discuss the implementation of Jefferson's earlier threat.

Fortunately for the United States, even

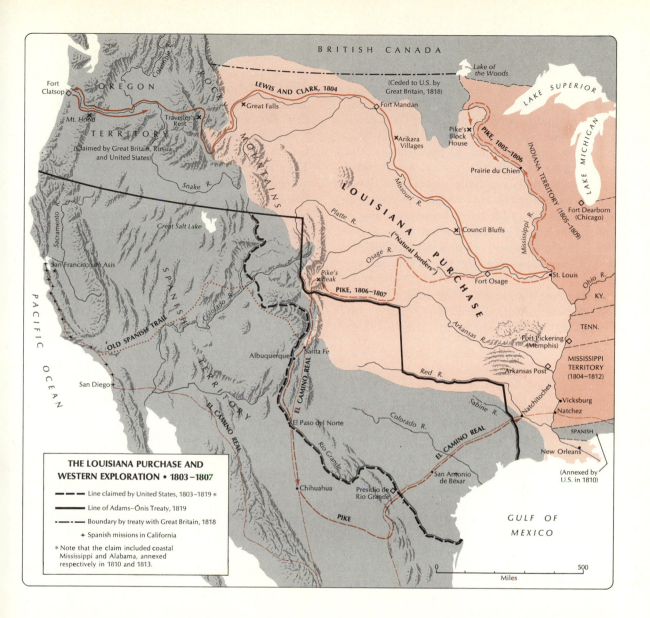

THE LOUISIANA PURCHASE AND
WESTERN EXPLORATION · 1803–1807

– – – Line claimed by United States, 1803–1819 *
——— Line of Adams–Ónis Treaty, 1819
–··–··– Boundary by treaty with Great Britain, 1818
+ Spanish missions in California

* Note that the claim included coastal
Mississippi and Alabama, annexed
respectively in 1810 and 1813.

though the French captured Toussaint L'Ouverture, the blacks of Santo Domingo, aided by tropical diseases, utterly destroyed the army which Napoleon sent to subdue them. Consequently, Napoleon determined to abandon his American plans and return his attention to Europe. Thus, even before Monroe's arrival, he had suggested to the somewhat startled American Minister, Robert R. Livingston, that the

United States buy all of Louisiana. Although Monroe had authorization to offer only $10 million for New Orleans and Florida, he and Livingston quickly agreed to Napoleon's price of $15 million for all Louisiana. Jefferson, too, readily accepted the price, but he worried about constitutional authorization for such a purchase. Unfounded rumors that Napoleon might change his mind pursuaded him that "the less we say about constitutional difficulties respecting Louisiana the better." Congress agreed; it appropriated the money in 1803 without protest.

Precisely what the United States had bought remained in doubt. American officials believed they had bought everything from the Rio Grande to the Perdido River, the present western border of Florida. Spain insisted, to the contrary, that the purchase included no coastal region other than that of what is roughly modern Louisiana. Jefferson did not choose to press the American claim aggressively, for he was convinced that in time both East Florida (modern Florida) and West Florida (coastal Alabama, Mississippi, and part of Louisiana) "cannot fail to fall into our hands."

Always interested in Western exploration and development, Jefferson had made arrangements for an exploratory expedition into the Pacific Northwest even before the Louisiana Purchase. Its commanders were Meriwether Lewis, who had been Jefferson's private secretary, and William Clark, brother of Kentucky's Revolutionary hero, George Rogers Clark. Between 1803 and 1806 Lewis and Clark journeyed up the Missouri River, across the Rocky Mountains, down the Columbia River to the Pacific, and back again. Their trip strengthened the nation's claim to the northwestern territory—an area also claimed by Britain and Spain. The expedition also brought back information of interest to scholars and useful for fur traders and future settlers. For reasons which still remain mysterious, James Wilkinson, the territorial governor of Louisiana, sent Zebulon Pike to explore the source of the Mississippi in 1805–1806 and the Arkansas River in 1806–1807, but Pike's report was neither very reliable nor as useful as that of Lewis and Clark.

Reelection and the Burr "Conspiracy"

Early portents for Jefferson's reelection were favorable. The Republicans after 1800 did well in state elections; they gained in the congressional contest of 1802. The popular Louisiana Purchase of 1803 did nothing to reverse the trend. Jefferson's conciliatory attitude and moderate policies also evoked a generally favorable response. It is clear, furthermore, that partisan competition was bringing more of the "middling sort" to vote. Shaking off the "habit of subordination" which had long kept them from challenging their "betters," such people came forth to help repudiate Federalism. To one old Federalist the explanation for the popularity of the Jeffersonians was that "The democrats [Jeffersonians] being men of inferior birth and breeding can more easily mix with the rabble. . . . They affect, with their dress and manners, to regard themselves of the Plebian order, and condescend to a familiarity of intercourse with the vulgar from which gentlemen would revolt."

Arguing that Easterners "cannot reconcile their habits, views, and interests with those of the South and West," diehard New England Federalists, early in 1804, began a secessionist movement aimed at creating a "Northern Confederacy." Chief instigator of the movement was Timothy Pickering, whom Adams had ousted as Secretary of State for opposing his peace policy. Hamilton refused to assist in bringing New York into the movement, but the Republican Vice President, Aaron Burr, was more cooperative. Anathema to Jeffersonians for his conduct in the contest of 1800, Burr determined to court Federalist support in his campaign for governor of New York.

For the secessionists as for Federalism in general the election of 1804 was a disaster. With Hamilton's help, the Republicans turned back Burr's effort to become governor of New York. Jefferson, running for the presidency against Charles C. Pinckney of South Carolina, lost only Connecticut and Delaware. His electoral margin, equaled by George Clinton in defeating his fellow New Yorker Rufus King for the vice presidency, was 162 to 14. In the new Congress,

Republicans outnumbered their opponents about 5 to 1.

Burr blamed Hamilton for his defeat. Capitalizing on the growing vogue for dueling, he demanded "satisfaction" of Hamilton for alleged aspersions made during the campaign. Hamilton agreed to a duel, intending to fire without aiming to kill, but Burr did aim to kill and succeeded. Ostracized in the East as a result, Burr fled westward toward still more degradation.

Precisely what Burr intended to accomplish in the West no one has ever been able to determine. He sought $500,000 from the British for what they believed was another secessionist scheme. He plotted with General James Wilkinson, Jefferson's territorial governor of Louisiana, who was himself deeply involved in suspicious dealings with the Spanish. Whether the new political base which Burr sought was to be on American territory or Spanish, within the United States or outside it, nobody yet knows. In any case, Wilkinson betrayed him as the two were about to join forces. Burr fled southward from his Ohio River camp toward Spanish Florida, but was captured in Alabama.

At Burr's subsequent trial for treason two important constitutional developments occurred. First, Chief Justice Marshall, intent on embarrassing the President, tried to compel Jefferson to appear and testify. Jefferson refused to go to Richmond, where the trial took place, but he provided documentary evidence. His actions fixed precedents as to the extent of "executive privilege" in dealing with courts. Marshall did succeed, however, in frustrating the President's ambition to hang Burr. He did so by defining treason narrowly. The Constitution states that treason "shall consist only in levying war against them [the United States], or in adhering to their enemies, giving them aid and comfort." It specifies further, "No person shall be convicted of treason unless on the testimony of two witnesses to the same overt act, or on confession in open court." Reversing their usual roles in constitutional construction, Jefferson sought to have these words interpreted broadly, while Marshall became quite literal. He acquitted Burr because the government could not produce two witnesses to an overt act of treason. In doing so he altered an earlier opinion which he himself had written holding that "all those who perform any part however minute, or however remote from the scene of action, and who are actually leagued in the general conspiracy, are to be considered traitors."

Freedom of the Seas

The defense of American rights at sea troubled Jefferson throughout both his terms of office. Barbary pirates operating from the North African states of Morocco, Algiers, Tunis, and Tripoli were most bothersome in his first term. American independence had not only excluded United States ships from the protection which Britain routinely purchased for vessels belonging to the king's subjects, but it also led Britain to encourage piracy directed at American ships to hinder the development of a major maritime rival. Payment of tribute to the pirates had always troubled Jefferson, and in 1801 he indignantly rejected a demand from the Bashaw of Tripoli that payments be increased. In the ensuing war, American bombardment of Tripoli and assistance to an insurgent movement led to a negotiated settlement advantageous to the United States. American tribute and ransom payments for captured seamen continued until 1816 but at a more favorable rate than those paid by other powers.

By the time the Tripolitan War had ended, Jefferson was in more serious trouble arising from American determination to carry on commerce with both Britain and France during the Napoleonic Wars. After the collapse of his American enterprise, Napoleon turned his ambitions again to Europe and by 1805 had made himself master of much of the Continent. In the same year a British fleet commanded by Horatio Nelson crushed French naval power at the battle of Trafalgar. With Britain unable to challenge Napoleon on land and the French incapable of overcoming Britain's advantage at sea, each side, both the "tiger" and the "shark," turned increasingly to economic warfare, attempting to weaken the enemy by reducing its trade. As the chief neutral carriers, American ships fell victims in ever large numbers to the measures of economic warfare imposed by each belligerent.

Britain's first significant act of economic war affecting the United States was a court decision of 1805 involving the American ship *Essex*. Between 1800 and 1805 the British had observed the rule fixed by their courts in the case of another American ship, the *Polly*. The *Polly* decision held that American ships carrying cargo from the French West Indies to France, a trade from which French policy had excluded them in peacetime, were not subject to seizure if they had first gone to an American port and cleared the cargo through an American customs office. Under that doctrine American shipowners had established a flourishing "reexport" trade, profitable to them and helpful to Napoleon. The *Essex* ruling jeopardized that trade by upholding seizure of such cargoes when the Americans could not prove that the shipment had been intended for the United States.

Blockade orders enforced by each belligerent added to the woes of American shipping. In 1806, Britain instituted a partial blockade of French-controlled ports; the Orders in Council of 1807 made it all-inclusive. Accordingly, American ships attempting to run the blockade were subject to seizure. Napoleon's policy, set forth in the Berlin decrees of 1806 and the Milan decrees of 1807, closed continental ports to British ships, a blow to Britain's export economy, and further declared Britain itself under blockade. The Milan decrees called for seizure of any neutral ship bound to or from a British port. Although French seizures of American ships

actually exceeded Britain's between 1807 and 1812, the long-range figures for the period from 1803 to 1812 are 917 British seizures and 558 French.

British seizure of seamen from American ships, commonly referred to as "impressment," aroused still more American indignation. Impressment alone was in fact sufficient cause for war. Behind the British policy lay a need for naval manpower which, especially before Trafalgar, was often desperate. Britain's traditional method of recruiting, dispatching "press gangs" from shorthanded vessels into port cities to shanghai men in sufficient numbers to meet the need, was offset by the high rate of desertion, especially in American ports. Repelled by the British navy's brutal discipline, abominable food, and deplorable conditions, sailors deserted in droves to take jobs in the growing American merchant marine, in which conditions were better and the pay some three to five times as high. By 1812 about half the sailors on American ships plying foreign markets were British.

Eager to combat the rise of a rival merchant marine as well as to meet its naval manpower needs, Britain encouraged impressment from American ships at sea. Even when the sailors taken in such instances were actually British subjects, the offense to American sovereignty was great. Adding to the offense, Britain not only refused to respect naturalized American citizenship, but seized many native Americans. In the decade before 1812, between 4,000 and 6,000 Americans, mostly native citizens, were impressed into the British navy.

The crowning indignity occurred in 1807. Several British deserters had enlisted for service aboard the new American warship *Chesapeake*, after the United States had rejected Britain's efforts to recover them by diplomatic means. When the *Chesapeake* put out to sea, the British navy's *Leopard* demanded permission to search the ship for British deserters. Commodore James Barron of the *Chesapeake* refused, whereupon the *Leopard* fired, killing three Americans and wounding eighteen. After Barron's capitula-

A Humanist Leader

Thomas Jefferson, the nation's third president, was a leader whose capabilities, broad range of interests, and intelligence have been virtually unmatched in United States history. During his two terms as president, from 1801 to 1809, Jefferson demonstrated his talents as scholar, diplomat, legislator, natural scientist, practical economist, lawyer, political author, farmer, inventor, architect, landscape designer, university founder, educator, and advisor to the state and national governments. His inquiring mind and constant energy produced innovations that significantly shaped the development of all these areas of endeavor in America.

This watercolor portrait by Robert Field (above) shows Jefferson in his early sixties, at the time of his presidency.

Before the Louisiana Purchase was completed, Jefferson persuaded Congress to appropriate $2,500 for a forty-three-man expedition headed by Capt. Meriwether Lewis (above) and William Clark (top) to explore the Missouri and Columbia Rivers and the Pacific northwest. From 1803–1806, they mapped the terrain, recorded details of Indian life, and closely observed the natural resources. Their journals were encyclopedic as the page at right proves.

The American Philosophical Society, founded in
1743 by Benjamin Franklin, was the first body to
collect and investigate scientific knowledge. Jefferson
supplied data, specimens, ideas, and reports, and
served as Society president from 1797 to 1815.

Two Missouri bears (above) were shipped from a
western expedition by Zebulon Pike. Jefferson startled
Washington by keeping them on the White House
lawn before he donated them to the Society. The western
bird (below) was painted from specimens returned by
Lewis and Clark by Charles Willson Peale, one of
the most brilliant members of the Society. In the 1822
self-portrait at right, Peale reveals his own vast
collection of natural history specimens: live and stuffed
animals, plants, minerals, and the bones of a
mastodon Peale excavated in upstate New York in
1801.

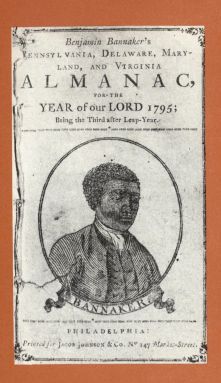

Benjamin Bannaker's
PENNSYLVANIA, DELAWARE, MARY-
LAND, AND VIRGINIA
ALMANAC,
FOR THE
YEAR of our LORD 1795;
Being the Third after Leap-Year.

BANNAKER.

PHILADELPHIA:
Printed for Jacob Johnson & Co. Nº 147 Market-Street.

The son of slaves and largely self-educated, Benjamin Bannaker has been called "a black Benjamin Franklin" in tribute to his intellect and achievements. He surveyed land to lay out Washington, D.C., published highly accurate almanacs based on his own astronomical observations and calculations, and was an accomplished engineer, naturalist, and musician. In 1791, Bannaker wrote asking Jefferson to reconcile his slaveholding with his libertarian philosophy.

Jefferson sincerely opposed slavery as an institution. He represented slaves in court, argued that children of slaves were born free, created a Virginia law forbidding further importation of slaves, and insinuated nonslavery clauses into the Northwest Ordinance. Nevertheless, he held about 150 slaves which he had inherited. He felt "to give liberty, or rather, to abandon persons whose habits have been formed in slavery is like abandoning children." Although he replied to Bannaker, "No body wishes more than I do to see such proofs as you exhibit, that nature has given to our black brethren talents equal to those of other colours of man, and that the appearance of a want of them is owing merely to the degraded condition of their existence both in Africa and America . . . ," he suspected in other writings that "the blacks . . . are inferior to the whites in the endowments both of body and mind."

Since his youth, Jefferson had eagerly investigated American Indian life and customs. He questioned travelers and traders from the West, sought out Indian visitors and local tribesmen in the East, and compiled extensive word lists of many Indian languages.

One important mission of the Lewis and Clark expedition was to establish good relations with the tribes they encountered. All chiefs received medals (right) showing President Jefferson and the hands of an Indian and white man clasped in "Peace and Friendship" under a crossed pipe and hatchet. They also received an American flag and a military uniform coat, hat, and feather.

The Osage chiefs on the opposite page were portrayed by Charles Balthazar Julien Fevret de Saint-Mémin. His technique satisfied Jefferson's passion for accuracy: first he traced the profile directly from the subject—a kind of physionotrace— then added colors and detail in crayon.

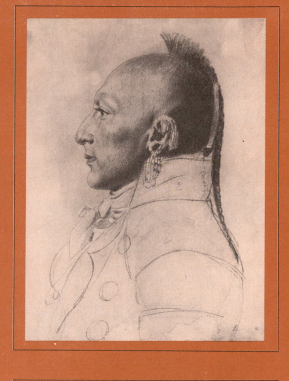

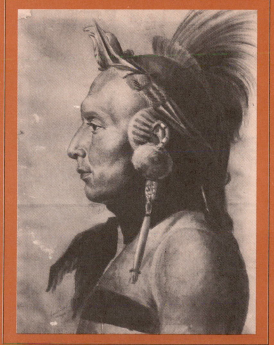

Left, above: Courtesy of the New-York Historical Society, New York City
Left, below: Courtesy of the American Museum of Natural History
Right, all pictures: Courtesy of the New-York Historical Society, New York City

Jefferson constantly applied his wide knowledge of
science and mechanics to solving practical problems.
A prolific inventor, he filled his home with devices of
his own design, including a swivel chair and
America's first dumb-waiter. He also designed a central
heating plant. Two notable inventions are shown here.
The mould-board plow (above) was easier to handle
and turned a deeper furrow than those in general use.
A polygraph with two pens (below) helped to ease the
problem of his enormous correspondence: as he wrote
with one pen, the other traced an exact copy on a
second page.

Architecture was one of Jefferson's deepest interests.
After traveling to France with the French architect
Charles L. A. Clérisseau, Jefferson extensively remodeled
and enlarged Monticello (right). Greatly influenced
by the temples of antiquity, he helped to foster the
Roman revival in America.

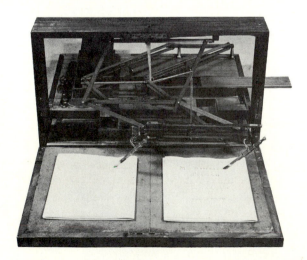

Above and below: Thomas Jefferson Memorial Foundation
Right: Bradley Smith, Photo Researchers

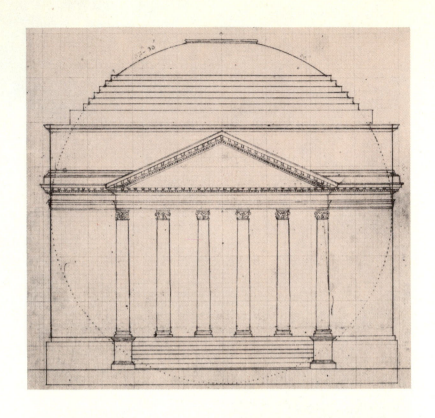

house "Bremo" in Fluvanna
unty, Va. (left, below),
ws the quiet elegance typical of
erson's influence on residential
gns. Of all his architectural
ects, the greatest was the
lding of the University of
ginia. He designed and
ervised its construction during
last years. Jefferson's drawing
the library rotunda (left, above)
bines the classic columns and
an Parthenon dome he so much
ired. The unusual serpentine
s (right) border the campus
ks. The impressive symmetry
sweep of his campus design are
ent on the next page.

above: University of Virginia Library,
scripts Division
below: Library of Congress
Library of Congress
ing page: George Cserna

tion, the British removed four men: one British deserter; two American Negroes who had deserted after enlisting voluntarily in the British navy; and an American who had "deserted" after suffering impressment.

Rather than yield to the outraged demand for war, Jefferson persuaded Congress to enact an embargo. Hastily drafted and promulgated at the end of 1807, the embargo barred departure of American ships for any foreign port. In justification of the prohibition, Jefferson argued that "our commerce is so valuable to them [Europeans] that they will be glad to purchase it when the only price we ask is to do us justice." The embargo did hurt the British, who had taken nearly half of all American exports in 1806, but it hurt Americans too. The index of farm prices fell from a previous high of 106 in 1805 to a low of 71 in 1808. Cotton exports fell to about one-fourth of the average of the previous five years. Many Americans, particularly Federalists, regarded the consequences of the embargo as worse than impressment and ship seizures which it was designed to combat. Evasion and even defiance were common, especially in the Northeast, where sympathy for Britain was strong.

Unpopular as it was in the Northeast, Jefferson's embargo did not seriously threaten the election of Secretary of State James Madison as his successor. Seizing eagerly on Washington's precedent, Jefferson declined a third term, commenting later on his great relief "on shaking off the shackles of power." The Federalist presidential ticket of Pinckney and King, which had won only 14 electoral votes in 1804, now got 47, but Madison won 122. Clinton remained Vice President. The Federalists made no gains in the Senate and, despite doubling their strength in the House of Representatives, still were outnumberd there by nearly 2 to 1.

Before leaving office, Jefferson acquiesced in the repeal of the embargo and the enactment of the Non-Intercourse Act of 1809. A compromise pleasing to neither the advocates of war nor those who merely wanted the embargo repealed, the Non-Intercourse Act banned both import and export trade with either Britain or France. However, it authorized the President to restore trade with France or Britain if either power ceased to violate American maritime rights. On its face the Non-Intercourse law seemed strong, but in fact it would afford Madison little leverage against the British.

James Madison

James Madison, like his older friend and frequent collaborator Thomas Jefferson, was a Virginia planter of aristocratic status, deeply dedicated to public service. His family was neither so prominent nor so wealthy as Jefferson's, but Madison had enjoyed a tutored education in the classics and further study, including a year of postgraduate work, at Princeton. Anglican in background, Madison disavowed sectarianism during his stay at Presbyterian Princeton, where he showed great interest in theology, as well as in philosophy, science, and public law. Princeton had been a hotbed of anti-British sentiment while Madison was there, but what seems to have done most to heighten the young scholar's politi-

cal concern was what he called the "hell-conceived principle of [religious] persecution" which his fellow Anglicans were then pursuing against the revivalist denominations in Virginia. Together with Thomas Jefferson, he played a major part in ending that state's support of religion and establishing a greater measure of religious freedom. During the Revolution, Madison served first in the Virginia Legislature and then in the Continental Congress, taking a leading role in each.

Like his predecessors in the Presidency, James Madison had secured his place in history before becoming Chief Executive. Along with Hamilton, Madison deserves primary credit for bringing about the Constitutional Convention of 1787. No man was more influential than he in determining at that Convention what manner of government would serve best to create "a more perfect Union." In the struggle over ratification of the Constitution in Virginia, Madison's leadership was instrumental in defeating the opposition forces. His contributions to *The Federalist* rank still among the best American writings in political science. In the first Congress no man did so much as James Madison in shaping the innumerable suggestions for constitutional amendments into the ten proposals which became the Bill of Rights. Finally, it was Madison even more than Jefferson who gave the initial guidance in the formation of the Republican party, the first political party in the United States.

The prospects for Madison's Presidency appeared mixed as he assumed office. In terms of experience he was supremely qualified. To his impressive earlier record he had added eight years as Secretary of State, during which time he had been a principal consultant of President Jefferson. His popular wife, Dolley, had already become the leader of Washington society. Yet Jefferson's embargo had revived the seemingly moribund Federalist opposition, and within Madison's own party extreme partisans continued to regard his moderation with distrust. Perhaps most serious of the new President's handicaps were certain of his own characteristics. Small in stature, relatively frail and shy, he lacked what one critic called "commanding talents." Because he was less forceful than his predecessor, Madison was less successful in overcoming the Republican dogma which affirmed that the President should merely execute policies fixed by Congress rather than fix them himself.

Controversy over Commerce

What most Americans wanted when Madison took office was a policy which would compel the two major belligerents, Britain and France, to permit Americans to carry on business as usual with both. How seriously belligerent restrictions on neutral trade affected American prosperity is difficult to determine. One rough indicator was the yearly value of American exports. From the beginning of the wars in Europe in 1793 until the imposition of severe commercial restrictions in 1807, the value of American exports, including reexports of French West Indian products, had quadrupled. From 1807 until the American declaration of war in 1812, the highest yearly total (1810) was more than one-third below that of 1807. The declining volume in the American reexport of French West Indian products accounted for much of the reduction. American policies, such as the embargo and nonintercourse laws, were also partially responsible.

In the South and West where commercial farmers depended heavily upon such exports for their income, resentment against Britain, in particular, ran high. "The necessity . . . of resisting the British orders and forcing our way to those markets where there is a demand [for American products]," stated a Kentucky senator, "must be evident to every one."

Even more serious than the detriment to American economic interests was the affront to American pride. Impressment was clearly the most offensive British action in this respect, but after the *Chesapeake* incident of 1807 it became less inflammatory. Since Napoleon no longer challenged their naval supremacy, the British slacked off on impressment, but they neither renounced the practice nor stopped it entirely.

Ship seizures were also very offensive. As early as 1807, the British consul in New York observed that it was "highly grating to the Feelings of an independent Nation to perceive that . . . every Ship coming in or going out of their Harbours [is] examined vigorously in Sight of the Shore by British Squadrons stationed within their Waters." To Americans only one generation removed from the Revolution, the idea of British squadrons enforcing British regulation of American trade was entirely too reminiscent of what Congressman John C. Calhoun referred to as "the colonial state to which again that power is endeavoring to reduce us." In such circumstances, particularly as the British persistently and haughtily rejected American protests, Americans began to advocate what they envisioned as a second war for independence. The fact that such a war, as a British leader observed, would virtually ally "this favourite child of freedom . . . with the oppressor of the world" was a consequence which concerned many Federalists but few Republicans. For most Republicans immediate concern for American honor and trade obscured the potential menace of Napoleon's unbounded ambition for imperial power.

When President Madison took up his duties in 1809, Americans could trade legally with neither Britain nor France but could, under the Non-Intercourse Act, conduct commerce with neutrals. The American price for restoring free trade with Britain was the latter's renunciation of impressment and the termination of Britain's interference in American trade with French-controlled areas of Europe. Britain regarded this price as too high. The British Admiralty valued impressment as a policy which might again prove necessary in an emergency to fill the crews of the Royal Navy. To give immunity from British seizure to American ships carrying products to France would not only benefit the French economy but also stimulate the growth of the American merchant marine as a rival to Britain's in the world carrying trade. Indeed the American merchant marine doubled its size between 1802 and 1810. Finally, the British were in no great rush to secure repeal of the Non-Intercourse Act because it operated to their benefit. France, because of its inferior naval status, could not secure American goods from neutral ports, but Britain's naval superiority enabled British merchants to conduct an extensive business with Americans at neutral sites.

Thus, far from yielding to American demands, Britain greeted the Madison administration with proposals of its own. Anticipating that Americans might perceive Napoleon as a threat to American as well as to European security, the British early in 1809 presented terms designed to make the United States their nonbelligerent ally against France. Specifically, the British government suggested that the United States end all restrictions on trade with Britain but retain the ban on trade with France. London went so far as to ask authorization for British ships to seize American vessels trading with France in violation of American law.

To elicit American approval of its proposals, Britain relied upon its youthful, inexperienced, and very pro-American Minister to Washington, David Erskine. In April 1809, Erskine concluded an executive agreement with the United States, promising revocation of the British Orders in Council insofar as they restricted American trade with France in return for resumption of American trade with Britain. Madison had committed the United States to keep nonintercourse in effect against France, thus meeting Britain's terms except for that authorizing the British to enforce American law against American ships. Anticipating British acceptance of the agreement, many Americans dispatched ships for Britain, and the nation in general had concluded joyfully that the controversy with England had been resolved without resort to war. Then, apparently because the agreement put enforcement in American rather than British hands, the Tory ministry rejected it.

In selecting a replacement for the now discredited Erskine, the British redoubled American indignation. The new British Minister in Washington was Francis James Jackson. He conducted himself so offensively that the Madison Administration soon refused even to accept communications from him. Britain recalled him early in 1810, but he remained in the United

States for almost a full year, during which time he encouraged and even subsidized Federalist attacks upon the Administration.

Changing policy again, Congress enacted, in May 1810, a law known since as Macon's Bill Number Two, immortalizing its not-very-enthusiastic sponsor, Nathaniel Macon, chairman of the House Foreign Affairs Committee. The new law meekly reopened trade with both Britain and France but promised to reward the belligerent which ended its restrictions upon American trade by reimposing nonintercourse against the nation's enemy if it failed to do the same. Napoleon accordingly instructed his Foreign Minister, the Duc de Cadore, to inform the Americans that his Berlin and Milan decrees would be revoked with reference to the United States, effective November 1. Though incensed by Napoleon's earlier seizure of American vessels, Madison proclaimed on November 2 that nonintercourse would take effect against Britain at the end of three months unless that country, too, repealed its obnoxious restrictions on American trade. In reality, Napoleon had no intention of abandoning his Continental System, but wished only to cause Great Britain to relax its Orders in Council or to see his enemy incur increased troubles, perhaps war, with the Americans if it refused to do so. Madison may well have suspected Napoleon's insincerity, but the Cadore letter afforded a welcome opportunity to increase the pressure on Britain. "It promises us, at least," the President wrote, "an extrication from the dilemma of a mortifying peace, or war with both the great belligerents."

Meanwhile, the British economy had begun to experience serious dislocations. A general depression prevailed after July 1810. It was most acute among manufacturers producing for export and may have owed as much to increasing productive capacity as to French and American interference with sales. Spurred by domestic depression, the government increased the issuance of "licenses" for trade with Napoleon's Continent. In doing so, the British abandoned their efforts to impose scarcities on Napoleon in order to keep up sales, income, and employment in Britain. The government also licensed reexport of commodities secured from the Western Hemisphere, thus benefiting the British merchant marine and merchants as well as manufacturers. To Americans the licensing system was particularly infuriating because it permitted British subjects to trade with their enemy while denying that opportunity to neutral Americans. Licensing had transformed the Orders in Council from an anti-French to an anti-American policy.

Madison's resumption of nonintercourse with Britain early in 1811 aggravated Britain's economic difficulties. The United States had long afforded Britain its best market, buying not only more than continental Europe but as much as one-third of all British exports. Hard-pressed British manufacturers, ably organized by the Whig opposition, clamored insistently that the Tory government repeal its Orders in Council to permit American trade with Napoleon's Europe. If the Orders were repealed, there was good reason to hope that the United States would resume importation from Britain. Such resumption would afford short-run relief to British manufacturers and reduce the incentive for Americans to develop their own manufacturing establishments and thereby secure economic independence from Britain.

Throughout 1811 the Tory government refused to repeal its Orders in Council. The leaders persuaded themselves that the repeal would bring too much economic benefit to France and would, in addition, tend to undermine Britain's traditional dominance of the seas by giving the American merchant marine a competitive advantage. They discounted not only the likelihood of war with the United States but also the risk involved should it occur. Finally, a new administration repealed the Orders in Council on June 23, 1812. Unfortunately, the United States had lost its patience a few days before.

By 1812, many Americans had come to the conclusion that there must be war with Britain—if not with France as well. Indignation over the restrictions on American commerce was undoubtedly the major force contributing to the war fever. But in considering how the United States might help itself and hurt its enemy in the event of war, Americans focused their attention on the northern and southern frontiers.

In the South, some had long cast covetous eyes on Spanish Florida. Jefferson had failed to validate his wishful contention that the Louisiana Purchase included West Florida, but by 1810 Spain, occupied by Napoleon's' forces since 1808, was in no position to resist determined American action. When Americans living in the Baton Rouge area of Spanish West Florida revolted successfully in 1810, Madison quickly proclaimed West Florida part of the United States. With congressional encouragement, Madison sent General George Mathews, a former Governor of Georgia, to arrange a similar takeover of East Florida in 1811. Since Americans were relatively less numerous in that area, however, the military action partook far more of an aggressive invasion than of internal insurrection. Although Mathews occupied much of modern Florida, Madison, embarrassed by the general's lack of subtlety, recalled him and promised to restore Spanish control. Spain retained control of its fort on Mobile Bay as well.

In the North, Americans sought territorial gain more to hurt Britain than to help themselves. "If the English do not give us the satisfaction we demand," Thomas Jefferson had stated privately at the time of the *Chesapeake* crisis of 1807, "we will take Canada." In the years that followed, more and more Americans of all sections came to realize that seizing Canada was the only way in which the almost impotent United States could retaliate against British insults to American honor and interference with American trade.

For the frontier dwellers of the Northwest, there was an additional incentive to seize Canada. With British encouragement a talented Shawnee chieftain, Tecumseh, had organized tribes both north and south of the Ohio River for offensive action. While Tecumseh was organizing in the south, William Henry Harrison, territorial governor of Indiana, collected a large force of frontiersmen with the aim of striking first. At Tippecanoe Creek on November 7, 1811, the Indians, led in Tecumseh's absence by his brother, the Prophet, surprised Harrison, but he beat off their attack, destroyed the village which was their headquarters, and retired. No war resulted, but Tippecanoe deepened the conviction among Northwestern frontiersmen that Indian attacks would plague them as long as the British remained in Canada.

At sea as well as in the Southwest and the Northwest, Americans were beginning to do more than make diplomatic representations and enforce retaliatory economic measures. When Macon's Bill Number Two reopened American trade with France, Britain had resumed an active patrol of the American coast. The Royal navy not only seized vessels bound for France but also began again to impress seamen from American ships. Early in 1811, the British warship *Guerrière* aroused a storm of indignation by stopping a coastal vessel just outside New York Harbor and impressing a native American. A United States Navy frigate, the *President*, put to sea with orders to protect American trade. In May 1811, it exchanged fire with the *Little Belt*, a smaller British vessel which the Americans mistook for the *Guerrière*. To the American public, the death of nine British seamen and the wounding of twenty-three others aboard the *Little Belt* avenged the loss in the *Chesapeake* incident of 1807 far more satisfactorily than the offer of compensation belatedly brought by the new British Minister.

America's more belligerent attitude became still clearer when the new Congress elected in 1810 convened in November 1811. The election had brought no more than the usual turnover, but dynamic new leaders, dubbed "War Hawks" by their opponents, quickly took control. Chief among them was the new Speaker of the House of Representatives, Henry Clay of Kentucky. Youthful, vigorous, and fiercely nationalistic, Clay had argued in the Senate in 1810 for forceful resistance to "British slavery." Now he stacked the House committees, especially Foreign Affairs and Military Affairs, with fellow War Hawks. The Senate was less bellicose, but the President and Secretary of State James Monroe—whom Madison had chosen to replace the incompetent and politically disloyal Robert Smith—were no less determined than Clay's War Hawks. Monroe's private discussions with the House Foreign Affairs Committee led one member to conclude, "The present session [of Congress] will not be closed, without an *arrangement*, or an actual *war* with Great Britain."

Congress began to prepare for war. It authorized an increase in the regular Army, which then had less than 6,000 men (although 10,000 were authorized) to a total of 35,000 officers and men. In addition, Congress provided for 50,000 state militiamen to be called into service at the President's discretion. Naval expansion, although appealing to the opposition Federalists, roused ancient Republican prejudices and appeared futile to many in view of Britain's unsurpassable advantage. Consequently Congress defied Clay's leadership by refusing to increase the nation's naval forces.

On April 1, 1812, Madison took another step toward war. To place American ships beyond the clutches of the British navy should hostilities begin, the President recommended that Congress enact a sixty-day embargo. He had every intention of seeking a declaration of war at the end of that period if the British had not in the meantime altered their Orders in Council to permit American trade with French-controlled ports. Congress, understanding fully the President's intention, quickly enacted the measure on April 4, specifying, however, that it continue ninety days rather than sixty.

Less than two months later the British Minister, Augustus Foster, made clear to Secretary Monroe where the British stood. On May 27, Foster permitted Monroe to read a dispatch from the British Foreign Secretary, Viscount Castlereagh, which stated explicitly that even if France should exempt the United States from the operation of its commercial restrictions, Britain would decline to do so. On June 1, 1812, the President's war message went before Congress.

In his war message, the President identified five grievances against Britain. First was impressment, the continuing affront to American sovereignty by the removal of the seamen, often native Americans, from United States ships at sea. Second was the British naval patrol off American ports which harassed commerce. Third was the improper enforcement of blockade restrictions in Europe. Item five was the accusation that the British had encouraged Indian warfare.

The heart of the message was in Madison's fourth point. In it the President called attention to Castlereagh's position that Britain would not except the United States from commercial restrictions. Then, with the Orders in Council as well as the licensing of British trade with Napoleon's domains in mind, he charged: "It has become, indeed, sufficiently certain that the commerce of the United States is to be sacrificed, not as interfering with the belligerent rights of Great Britain; not as supplying the wants of her enemies, which she herself supplies; but as interfering with the monopoly which she covets for her own commerce and navigation. She carries on a war against the lawful commerce of a friend that she may the better carry on a commerce with an enemy."

Congressional reaction to the President's request revealed a dangerous division in national feeling. Opposition centered strongly in the Federalist party and in the Northeastern section of the country. Not a single Federalist in either house voted in favor of war. Although nine Federalist opponents of war were Southerners, all the rest (thirty-one) were from the Northeast.

Among Republican congressmen from that section, only the Pennsylvania delegation gave a strong vote for war. From New Jersey northward, nearly half of the Republicans, as well as all the Federalists, voted against war. On the other hand, Republicans of the South and West gave overwhelming support to the declaration.

Reasons for opposing the war were varied. Some Federalists still believed that the Republicans were puppets of France acting to aid the French dictator. Others thought that an alliance with Britain to overthrow Napoleon would be a wiser and more honorable course. Federalist merchants thought war would be more ruinous to their trade than Britain's restrictive economic policies were; still other Federalists believed that continued negotiation would in time bring Britain to reason. Among Republican opponents of the declaration, the most common objection was to its timing. Many who lived adjacent to Canada or in undefended seaports preferred to prepare the nation more adequately for war before beginning hostilities.

The declaration of war passed the House of Representatives 79 to 49 and the Senate 19 to 13. It became official on June 18, 1812, two days after Castlereagh announced in Parliament his government's intention to repeal the Orders in Council. Napoleon, meanwhile, with an army of 600,000 men, had invaded Russia, his last significant continental opponent.

A Mere Matter of Marching

To conquer Canada—and thus punish Britain or induce London to change its policies—appeared to many Americans in 1812 as "a mere matter of marching." Canada indeed seemed vulnerable. Regular army forces available for its defense numbered approximately 7,000, as opposed to 12,000 in the growing United States Army. Excluding Indians and slaves, Canada's population was only about one-sixth that of the United States. The loyalty of many of its people, notably the French Canadians and recent immigrants from the United States, was doubtful. The Indians would support the British, but their aid was never wholly reliable.

Severing the St. Lawrence lifeline was the surest way to conquer Canada. Seizure of Montreal, situated on the north bank of the river, would almost certainly win the war. Accordingly, the capture of Montreal became the major strategic goal in American military planning. Kingston, situated at the eastern end of Lake Ontario, became a secondary target, while other invasions were slated to occur along the Niagara River and from the isolated frontier outpost of Detroit.

For the capture of Montreal, Madison relied at first on Henry Dearborn, a general whose principal qualification was seniority. In November, nearly six months after the declaration of war, Dearborn finally put his army in motion, but at the border the militia forces balked, refusing on constitutional grounds to take offensive action outside the country. Thus ended the threat to Montreal in 1812.

There was more action to the west, but no better results. General William Hull, an aging veteran of the Revolution and territorial governor of Michigan, was in charge of the force which was to invade Canada from Detroit. By aggressive action Hull might have achieved decisive victories before the British, Canadian, and Indian forces consolidated against him. He dallied indecisively, however, worrying particularly over his long line of communications, which was indeed jeopardized both by Indians and by British naval superiority on Lake Erie. When it appeared that the brilliant British commander Isaac Brock was about to launch an attack upon Detroit with the support of a large body of Indians, Hull surrendered ignominiously without firing a shot. The British had already captured Fort Michilimackinac, the frontier fort at the head of Lake Huron, and the Indians had massacred the garrison of Fort Dearborn at the site of modern Chicago. Thus the abortive American invasion of Canada from Detroit culminated in the virtual loss of Michigan.

On the Niagara frontier incompetent leadership was also in evidence. Stephen Van Rensselaer, a Federalist aristocrat, managed to commit some of his men to offensive action, but others balked at a crucial stage, with the result that the British captured many of the more aggressive Americans. Van Rensselaer had the good sense to resign. His successor, a regular Army general named Alexander Smyth, although adept at composing bombastic proclamations, proved unable to manage the logistical problem of getting his men across the river. The Niagara campaign of 1812, however, did inflict one severe loss on the enemy. General Isaac Brock, captor of Detroit, fell dead from American rifle fire during an engagement at Queenston Heights.

American efforts to conquer Canada continued to go badly in 1813 despite some initial success. An amphibious raid on York (Toronto) destroyed or captured strategic naval supplies. However, the American troops stirred up great civilian animosity by plundering and allegedly setting fire to government buildings. Winfield Scott cleared the Canadian bank of the Niagara River, allowing several ships which had been bottled up just above Niagara Falls to join the American fleet on Lake Erie under Oliver Hazard Perry. Yet by the end of 1813, the British had not only reestablished themselves on the Canadian side of the river but had captured Fort Niagara on the American side and ravaged all the American settlements between the two lakes, including the future metropolis of Buffalo.

General James Wilkinson, successor to Dearborn as leader of the campaign against Montreal, proved fully as ineffective. He advanced reluctantly down the St. Lawrence toward Montreal until November 11 when a small British force humiliated a portion of his army at Chrysler's farm. Wilkinson then gave up the offensive.

Meanwhile, Perry, a twenty-eight-year-old naval officer, had created a fleet with which to

Huzza for our Navy!

Another 15 minutes Job.

Being the 8th Naval Victory in which John Bull has been obliged to douce his flag, to the invincible skill of American Tars.

CHARLESTON, SUNDY MORNING, SEPT. 19th, 1813.

We have the satisfaction of announcing to the public that the United States sloop of war ARGUS is in the offing, with the British sloop of war BARBADOES her prize in company, taken after a desperate engagement of 15 minutes, carried by boarding.

Capt. Allen, of the Argus, has just come up, and we have conversed with a midshipman who states that she was taken off Halifax, but it was deemed expedient to proceed to this place for the purpose of escaping the British blockading squadrons. He also states that the captain, R. P. Davies, of the Barbadoes was killed, and the vessel was commanded the most part of the action by the 1st Lieut. Savage.

British loss, 97 killed and wounded. American loss, 12 killed and wounded. The Argus rates 16 and carries 20 guns, the Barbadoes rates 28 and carries 32 guns. She had previously captured, Aug. 22, the James Madison of 14 guns.

☞ This is the second Engagement in which Captain ALLEN has signalised himself, as he was 1st Lieu't. of the U. States, was in the Engagement with the Macedonian, took Command of her and brought her into port.

This broadside of September 19, 1813, proudly announces that "the invincible skill of American tars" carried the day against the British Navy in a Canadian campaign. *The New-York Historical Society*

challenge British control of Lake Erie. Displaying great personal heroism, he captured the entire British fleet in a battle near Put-in-Bay. "We have met the enemy," he reported, "and they are ours: two ships, two brigs, one schooner, and one sloop."

Perry's victory persuaded Henry Proctor, the British commander in the western region, to abandon Detroit and retreat up the Ontario peninsula before waterborne American forces cut off his escape. Tecumseh, Britain's Indian ally, opposed the decision, but acquiesced on Proctor's assurance that they would ultimately stand and fight. General William Henry Harrison, hero of Tippecanoe, pursued Proctor up the Thames River. In the battle of the Thames near Moraviantown, Ontario, Harrison's riflemen quickly routed Proctor's outnumbered forces. Tecumseh's Indians, unwilling to retreat farther, bore the brunt of the fighting in which Tecumseh himself was killed.

In two years of offensive effort the United States had accomplished little. As 1814 began, Montreal was as secure as it had been at the outset of hostilities. At Niagara the Americans occupied no Canadian territory, but had experienced devastating raids. In the West, Harrison had achieved the only conquest; at the end of 1813, he still held a small area of Canada adjacent to Detroit. Thus, after two years of war, the United States had managed only to wound the British lion slightly in the tail.

Resisting British Invasion

Napoleon's crushing defeat at Leipzig in October 1813, following his disastrous retreat from Moscow that previous winter, presaged the end of war in Europe. In March 1814, the allies occupied Paris and sent Napoleon into exile. Napoleon's elimination ended Britain's needs to restrict American commerce with France and to impress seamen from American ships, root causes of the American declaration of war; but it also freed the major portion of Britain's military resources for use against the United States. The British public demanded that the government use these resources to punish the Americans for what Britains regarded as an attempted stab in the back while they fought Napoleon in Europe. "They thirst for a great revenge," wrote diplomat Albert Gallatin from London, "and the nation will not be satisfied without it."

American capacity to deny Britain its "great revenge" appeared much in doubt at the beginning of 1814. Madison's record in choosing generals and Cabinet members inspired little confidence. The militia forces which would carry much of the defensive burden afforded ample reason for doubting their ability to repulse the armies which had beaten Napoleon. Federalist New England still appeared more hostile to Madison than to Britain. New Englanders not only were supplying enemy forces but also were considering secession.

Britain's American war plans for 1814 had several objectives. One was to tighten the blockade of the United States coast and ravage selected coastal cities. In the North, the British planned to invade and occupy the major base or bases which threatened Montreal. In the South, they would seize New Orleans and either establish an independent government in that region or return all Louisiana to Spain.

Britain's blockade was effective. The United States, despite its great merchant marine, was not a strong naval power when the war began. Republicans had done nothing to increase the seagoing Navy beyond the sixteen ships they had inherited from the Federalists. These vessels, notably the *Constitution* under Isaac Hull and the *United States* under Stephen Decatur, did shock the British by gaining decisive victories in single-ship encounters. Such individual victories served chiefly to give American morale a needed lift. By the summer of 1814, Britain's navy of some six hundred ships had destroyed, captured, or bottled up all the American warships except the *Constitution*, thus imposing a tight blockade upon the entire American coast. Even New England, previously exempted by reason of the British desire to encourage secessionist sentiment, now had its commerce throttled. The reduction of revenue from import taxes by more than one-half so intensified the financial crisis that Madison called a special session of Congress to deal with it. American privateers captured some thirteen hundred British merchant ships and even attacked towns in the British Isles, but they did not divert the British navy from its blockading function.

Ravaging coastal areas of the United States brought the British some success. Raids in New England and along Chesapeake Bay provided income to British commanders from the sale of plunder and encouraged still bolder ventures. Admiral Sir Alexander Cochrane and General Robert Ross together planned to attack Washington, to strike a blow at American morale, and then Baltimore, to bag a fortune in merchandise. Ross captured Washington with ease and burned both the Capitol and the White House in August 1814. At Baltimore, however, Senator Samuel Smith organized effective defenses and, with the aid of the artillery in Fort McHenry, held off the British raiders. Ross himself was killed. Baltimore attorney Francis Scott Key, observing the bombardment of his city as a prisoner on a British vessel, dashed off at its conclusion the verses which, set to the music of a popular English melody, "Anacreon in Heaven," became "The Star-Spangled Banner."

In Canada, Sir George Prevost had received orders to take either Sackets Harbor or Plattsburgh. To assist him in the project, Britain dispatched some twelve thousand veterans of the campaigns against the French in Spain. Prevost chose to strike first at Plattsburgh, where American General George Izard, with a force of 6,000, was building fortifications. Meanwhile the Secretary of War ordered Izard and the bulk of his army to the Niagara front, where severe but inconclusive fighting had recently occurred. Izard's departure left only some fifteen hundred men to hold Plattsburgh against Prevost's army of about fifteen thousand.

Prevost experienced no trouble in reaching Plattsburgh, but upon arriving he observed a fleet of four warships and ten gunboats anchored in the bay. Noted always for his caution, Prevost decided to wait for the appearance of the Royal navy. On September 11, both Prevost and the newly arrived British naval force attacked. On land British regulars had little trouble with the American defenders, but the American naval commander, Lieutenant Thomas Macdonough, had so arranged his anchors that he could swing his ships around when one side was badly battered and bring fresh guns into action. By doing so successfully in mid-battle, Macdonough won a brilliant and highly important victory. His success persuaded Prevost to march his splendid army back to Canada without taking Plattsburgh.

The capture of New Orleans was by far the most serious of the injuries which Britain hoped to inflict upon the United States. If they succeeded at New Orleans, the British intended not only to deprive the United States of the Louisiana Territory but also to reimpose restrictions on the use of the Mississippi River, an action which would have detrimental effects as far to the north and east as Pittsburgh.

Fortunately, local military efforts prior to 1814 had strengthened the American position along the Gulf of Mexico. General Wilkinson had occupied Mobile, a probable invasion site which the United States had failed to secure when it annexed the rest of Spanish West Florida in 1810. Early in 1814 Andrew Jackson, commander of the Tennessee militia, killed over five hundred Creek Indians at Horseshoe Bend on the Talapoosa River in eastern Alabama and compelled the Creeks to abandon a large portion of Georgia and a still larger segment of Alabama. Jackson also invaded Spanish East Florida to cut off the supply of weapons to the Indians through Apalachicola. These actions effectively deprived the British of Indian assistance such as Tecumseh had supplied in the North.

While Jackson concerned himself with Florida, the British assembled a huge invasion force in the West Indies. Jackson expected the British to attack Mobile, a considerably easier target, but the British chose New Orleans, partly, it appears, because of Admiral Cochrane's desire to loot a major port. With great effort and some good fortune, the British managed to get General Sir Edward Pakenham's army of about nine thousand across shallow Lake Borgne, up an unguarded bayou, and onto one of the few expanses of solid ground amid the swamps which surrounded the city. The route was difficult for infantry and still more so for artillery, in which the British proved fatally weak.

At dawn on January 8, 1815, the British attacked Jackson's motley force of about five

One of many engravings depicting the Battle of New Orleans. American pride fairly bristles in the engraving's statistics about this battle with the British, ". . . in which 3 of their most distinguished Generals were killed, & several wounded, and upwards of 3,000 of their choicest Soldiers were killed, wounded, and made Prisoners, &c."

thousand, which included regulars, militia, Negroes, Indians, and pirates. The attackers moved forward across level ground raked by superior American artillery toward mud ramparts behind which Jackson had arranged four ranks of riflemen prepared to fire in turn. Before midmorning, two thousand British bodies strewed the field, while behind the ramparts fewer than ten Americans lay dead. General Pakenham and several of his chief subordinates were among those killed. Five weeks later, a British diplomat arrived in New York with a tentative peace agreement which British and American representatives had signed in Belgium on Christmas Eve, two weeks before the battle.

From the outset the War of 1812 had seemed destined to end in a negotiated settlement. On learning of the American declaration of war, Britain had instructed its commanders to exercise "all possible forebearance towards the Citizens of the United States," with the hope that the United States would end the war when news of the repeal of the Orders in Council arrived. In August 1812, Madison himself had expressed America's willingness "to accommodate all differences." His major condition for the immediate restoration of peace was that the British agree informally to end impressment. Should the British agree to do so, Madison had pledged that the United States would bar the employment of foreigners on American merchant ships. The British, however, still feared that to renounce impressment would render Great Britain incapable of securing adequate manpower for the Royal Navy. Accordingly, the war went on.

In the fall of 1812, the presidential election had afforded another opportunity to end the war. Federalists, strong in the commercial areas of the Northeast and bitterly opposed to "Mr. Madison's war," named no candidate of their own but supported Mayor De Witt Clinton of New York City, a dissident Republican. Appealing chiefly to the "peace" vote, Clinton carried nearly all the Northeast. Madison, committed to continue the war, carried all the South and West in addition to Pennsylvania, Vermont, and part of Maryland. He won reelection with 128 votes to Clinton's 89. Again the war continued.

Russian mediation offered yet another hope for peace in 1813. Upon receiving Czar Alexander's offer, Madison dispatched Treasury Secretary Albert Gallatin and Federalist Senator James Bayard of Delaware to join John Quincy Adams, the American Minister to Russia, for talks in St. Petersburg. Suspecting that the Czar would be less than impartial on such issues as neutral rights and impressment, the British declined to participate. They did offer to negotiate directly.

Peace negotiations began at Ghent, Belgium, in August 1814. The British, having disposed of Napoleon and wishing to punish the Americans before concluding peace, were in no hurry. They first suggested the creation of an Indian barrier state west of Ohio, the surrender of extensive territory along the Canadian border, and the extinction of the "liberty" which Americans had enjoyed since the Revolution to dry fish on British territory adjacent to the Grand Banks. After the sack of Washington, and while they still anticipated the capture of New Orleans, the British suggested that each nation retain the territory which it occupied at the end of hostilities.

After the Battle of Plattsburgh, however, a number of developments led Britain to soften its terms. The Duke of Wellington, when offered the opportunity to duplicate his European victories in America, replied: "That which appears to me to be wanting in America is not a general, . . . but a naval superiority on the lakes." He suggested further that "the state of military operations" warranted no territorial demands on the part of Britain. Madison also strengthened the American bargaining position by publishing the original British terms, a breach of diplomatic etiquette which served the President's purpose by producing a highly belligerent reaction from the American public. Furthermore, in the attempted reordering of Europe at the Congress of Vienna, Britain was experiencing troubles with its erstwhile allies; there were even ominous rumblings from conquered France. Because of all these circumstances, supplemented by domestic financial strain and general war-weariness, Britain's cabinet decided to end the war without concessions from the Americans and without awaiting the outcome of the attack on New Orleans. Their peace commissioners found the American negotiators (Gallatin, Bayard, Adams, Clay, and Jonathan Russell) quite amenable to such a solution.

What the British and the Americans agreed to on Christmas Eve, 1814, was to stop the fighting and to restore their prewar borders. The United States, however, retained the former Spanish territory of Mobile, which it had claimed before the war. Since neutral rights and impressment had become less urgent issues with the elimination of Napoleon, the treaty made no reference to them. It left for future commissions the troublesome questions concerning the fisheries, British navigation of the Mississippi, the northern boundary of the Louisiana Purchase, and the border between Maine and New Brunswick (uncertain since 1783).

To the American public these provisions were eminently satisfactory. Three days after the first copy reached Washington, the Senate ratified the treaty on February 17, 1815, by a unanimous vote.

Jefferson, Madison, and their Republican followers altered the course of the new nation, but in a sense they also steadied it. Having organized the nation's first political party, they put American democracy to the test by outpolling the incumbent Federalist President, John Adams, in a bitterly divisive climate. Adams and his supporters yielded the government to the Jeffersonians despite their deep fear that their opponents would destroy the federal system and make America a satellite of France. The Jeffersonians in fact did neither, but pursued instead a highly successful policy of reconciliation. American democracy had passed its first big test so easily that few people since have recognized even the possibility of failure. As agents for the nation's planters and farmers, the Republicans made American society less elitist and more egalitarian, less mercantilistic and more favorable to laissez-faire, less nationalist and more disposed to exalt states' rights.

In foreign affairs the warfare between England and France posed insuperable problems for the world's leading neutral carrier, but the situation also brought some benefit to the United States. The vagaries of international relations enabled Jefferson to double the nation's size by purchasing Louisiana from France. Britain degraded the new nation by seizing seamen from its ships at sea and by preventing Americans from trading with France while "licensing" its own nationals to do so. When protracted negotiation failed to produce any change in Britain's offensive policies, the Republicans declared war. They went to war partly to gain access to continental European markets, partly to secure western territory from which Indians had received supplies and encouragement to resist western settlement. They went to war also as Republicans, traditionally anti-British and deeply fearful that submission to British infringements of American sovereignty discredited not only the American nation but also the republican principles upon which its government was founded.

Militarily a standoff, the war nevertheless brought significant advantages to the United States. Wartime chastisement of the Indians at the hands of Harrison and Jackson enabled frontier settlement to proceed more rapidly both in the North and the South. The United States occupied and retained the Gulf Coast region between modern Florida and Louisiana. Federalist secessionist scheming ceased. Still more impressive, however, was the elevation of American prestige. To have reached a draw, whatever the reasons, with such a great power as Britain and to have crushed an invading British army so thoroughly as Jackson did at New Orleans were remarkable achievements for a fledgling nation. As the London *Times* observed, the Americans' first war with Britain made them independent; the second made them a formidable power.

SUGGESTED READINGS

The most recent survey of the Jeffersonian era is Marshall Smelser's *The Democratic Republic, 1800–1815** (1968). However, the basic source remains the majestic work of Henry Adams, *A History of the United States of America during the Administrations of Thomas Jefferson and James Madison* (9 vols., 1889–1891). Numerous paperback abridgments of his work are available. L. D. White in *The Jeffersonians** (1951) continues the superb administrative history begun in *The Federal-*

ists. Alexander Balinky's *Albert Gallatin* (1958) criticizes the fiscal theories and policies of Jefferson's financial expert.

On Jeffersonian philosophy see Adrienne Koch, *The Philosophy of Thomas Jefferson** (1943) and *Jefferson and Madison: The Great Collaboration** (1950). C. M. Wiltse's *The Jeffersonian Tradition in American Democracy** (1935) considers the Jeffersonian heritage of values as does Merrill Peterson's *The Jeffersonian*

Image in the American Mind* (1960). Norman Risjord examines the views of extreme Jeffersonians in The Old Republicans (1965).

On political parties in the age of Jefferson, Noble Cunningham's The Jeffersonians: Party Operations, 1801–1809 (1963) is the only major study to focus on the national Republican party. D. H. Fischer, The Revolution of American Conservatism (1965) finds Federalism very much alive and adopting Jeffersonian tactics and rhetoric in order to survive after 1800. Linda Kerber, Federalists in Dissent (1970), shows why they abominated Jefferson. J. M. Banner traces the path of Massachusetts Federalists in To the Hartford Convention (1969). In a more bipartisan spirit J. S. Young points up in The Washington Community, 1800–1829 (1966) the decline in presidential leadership and the confusion and insignificance of the federal government. See, also, the works on parties listed in the previous chapter.

Federal courts began to loom large in Jefferson's time. Among the best studies of their role are Richard Ellis, Jeffersonian Crisis: Courts and Politics in the Young Republic (1971); E. S. Corwin, John Marshall and the Constitution (1919); R. K. Faulkner, The Jurisprudence of John Marshall (1968). See also Leonard Levy's Jefferson and Civil Liberties: The Darker Side (1963), which finds its subject less than perfect in his support of libertarian values.

Indians and the frontier continued to demand national attention. Reginald Horsman's The Frontier in the Formative Years, 1783–1815* provides the best overview of frontier developments for the period. Horsman's Expansion and American Indian Policy, 1783–1812 (1967) explores the formation and execution of policies intended to "civilize" the Indians whether they liked it or not. B. W. Sheehan in Seeds of Extinction (1973) examines both the civilization effort and removal of the Indians in a more intellectual context. For the army outlook on the matter see F. P. Prucha, The Sword of the Republic: The United States Army on the Frontier, 1783–1846 (1969). On frontier land speculation and problems arising from it see C. P. Magrath's Yazoo (1966). On exploration B. De Voto edited The Journals of Lewis and Clark* (1953) in one sparkling volume.

On the Louisiana Purchase the major works are E. W. Lyons' Louisiana in French Diplomacy (1934); A. P. Whitaker's The Mississippi Question (1934); George Dangerfield's Chancellor Robert R. Livingston of New York (1960); Irving Brant's James Madison: Secretary of State.

Precisely why the United States declared war on Britain in 1812 still perplexes historians. Henry Adams thought maritime grievances, particularly ship seizures and impressment of American seamen, were responsible. So also did A. L. Burt in The United States, Great Britain, and British North America (1940). J. W. Pratt expounded a tentative hypothesis in The Expansionists of 1812 (1925) to the effect that expansionists in the South and West wanted war because it was the only way in which they could drive out the British and Spanish upon whom their Indian enemies depended. Pratt's thesis found wide acceptance until the 1960s, when "national honor" became the key phrase. It tied in closely with the maritime grievances emphasized long before. Bradford Perkins's Prologue to War* (1961) stands out among the new works, but there is much merit also in R. H. Brown's The Republic in Peril (1964), which ties the war to concern for Republican ideology, and in Louis N. Sears, Jefferson and the Embargo (1927); in Reginald Horsman's The Causes of the War of 1812 (1962); Patrick F. T. White's A Nation on Trial* (1965), very brief; and L. S. Kaplan's Jefferson and France (1967).

On the military history of the war H. L. Coles has written briefly but perceptively in The War of 1812* (1965); he begins with a good account of the conflicting views as to the origins of the war. John K. Mahon has provided a good professional account of military developments in his War of 1812 (1972). A. T. Mahan's Sea Power in Its Relation to the War of 1812 (2 vols., 1905) is a scholarly effort to show the need for a big navy. Theodore Roosevelt's Naval War of 1812 (1882) is colorful.

For more information on the peace negotiations consult Bradford Perkins, Castlereagh and Adams (1964) and the biographies listed below for Adams, Clay, and Madison.

Biographies are among the most important works in this period. Dumas Malone's study of Jefferson, now complete through 1809 in five volumes, and Irving Brant's on Madison are among the outstanding biographies of this generation. Other good ones include the one-volume works on Jefferson and Madison cited in Chapter 6 plus Raymond Walters, Jr., Albert Gallatin* (1957); S. E. Morison, Harrison Gray Otis (1969); S. F. Bemis, John Quincy Adams and the Foundations of American Foreign Policy (1949); C. M. Wiltse, John C. Calhoun: Nationalist (1944); Bernard Mayo, Henry

Clay (1937); C. F. Eaton, *Henry Clay and the Art of American Politics* (1957); G. G. Van Deusen, *The Life of Henry Clay** (1937). On Aaron Burr, Nathan Schachner is favorable in his *Aaron Burr* (1937) while T. P. Abernethy is hostile in *The Burr Conspiracy* (1954). Faun Brodie's *Thomas Jefferson* (1974) tries to substantiate the ancient charge that Jefferson fathered several slave children by Sally Hemings, half-sister of his deceased wife.

*indicates availability in paperback.

Consensus and Conflict, 1815-1828

"We are all Republicans, we are all Federalists." With these words Thomas Jefferson had suggested in 1801 that what Americans agreed upon was more fundamental than what they had recently disagreed upon so stridently. In his first term Jefferson had done much to restore goodwill between the two political parties, but thereafter the difficulties with Britain, culminating in the War of 1812, again had poisoned the dialog of American politics. New England Federalists defied the Republican administration, sought to frustrate its war aims, and even considered seceding from the Union. Yet within a few years after the end of the war, the Federalists allowed their national organization to die out and loudly proclaimed their dedication to Republican principles. Monroe's administrations (1817–1825) eased the final hours of the expiring Federalists by adopting much of their program and appointing some former Federalists to help administer the government. To some it appeared that an era of nonpartisan "good feelings" had at last ar-

rived and even that the Republican party might peacefully disband as the entire nation basked contentedly in patriotic and prosperous euphoria.

Still conflict would not cease. Extreme Jeffersonians carried on a bitter warfare against those whom they considered Federalist wolves in Republican sheep's clothing and fumed in frustration over important Supreme Court decisions rendered by that unreconstructed Federalist, Chief Justice John Marshall. In the debates preceding the Missouri Compromise the question of slavery's future showed for the first time its capacity to divide national opinion bitterly along geographic lines. Rivals for the designation as Republican candidate to succeed Monroe jockeyed intently for political advantage. Still more heated rivalry focused on the presidency after 1824, when no presidential candidate received an electoral majority, and the House of Representatives chose John Quincy Adams, who had run second, rather than Andrew Jackson, who had led in both popular and electoral votes.

Jackson and his followers worked almost incessantly after 1824 to unseat Adams and in 1828 won a clear mandate to inaugurate a new era in American political history.

The Demise of the Federalist Party

"Mr. Madison's War" had seemingly imparted new life to the Federalist party, but as if possessed by a death wish too strong to be denied, the Federalists transformed their opportunity into the occasion for their destruction. Because of their great sympathy for the British, the Federalists stopped little short of treason in their opposition to the American war effort. Not only did they refuse to allow militia forces in the states which they controlled to join the invasion of Canada; they also threw every impediment in the way of regular Army recruitment. Rich Federalists declined to buy government securities to help finance the war; some lent funds to Britain instead. Many New England Federalists engaged in illegal trade with the enemy. In fact, New Englanders supplied most of the food which sustained General Prevost's army in Canada.

Federalist hostility to the war reached its climax in the Hartford Convention of 1814. The Massachusetts Legislature, dominated by Federalists, proposed a convention of delegates from the New England states to consider revision of the federal Constitution. Meeting at Hartford, Connecticut, in December 1814, official delegates of Massachusetts, Connecticut, and Rhode Island, plus representatives of local groups in Vermont and New Hampshire, debated in secret for three weeks. Early in January 1815, after repudiating those delegates who urged secession, the Convention declared in words much like those which Madison had used in the Virginia Resolutions of 1798, that each state had a duty "to interpose its authority" to protect state sovereignty and the liberties of the people from unconstitutional acts of the federal government. The delegates proposed several constitutional amendments limiting federal power and warned that if the national government declined to act on these suggestions, to conclude peace, or to provide more effectively for New England's defense, another convention would meet with instructions to act "as the exigency of a crisis so momentous may require."

Significant as these declarations seemed to the delegates who composed them, they had become ridiculous even before they could be presented to the President. Committee members designated by the Massachusetts Legislature were en route to Washington for "negotiations" when news of the peace concluded at Ghent arrived at the Capitol. Buoyed by the news from New Orleans as well as that from Ghent, the President laughed on learning in February 1815 what the Hartford Convention had wrought.

As a national political party the Federalists scarcely survived the Hartford Convention. Already branded as advocates of aristocracy, party members now carried the additional political burdens of near disloyalty in wartime and intent

A political cartoon lampooning the Hartford Convention. It shows Connecticut, Massachusetts, and Rhode Island plotting to leap into the arms of King George III, who says encouragingly: "O, 'tis my Yankey boys! Jump in my fine fellows; plenty of molasses and Codfish, plenty of goods to Smuggle; Honours, titles and Nobility into the bargain. . . ."   Media Features

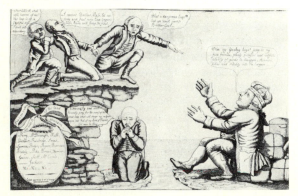

to disrupt the Union. In the wave of nationalist sentiment which followed the peace, Federalists retained little hope of success at the national level. They remained strong for many years in coastal areas from Maryland northward, but even with Senator Rufus King of New York, a supporter of the recent war, as their candidate for president in 1816, they carried only three states—Massachusetts, Connecticut, and Delaware. They did not try again.

Postwar Nationalism

Albert Gallatin, perspicacious as always, observed in 1816 that the War of 1812 "has renewed and reinstated the national feelings which the Revolution had given." The people, he noted, "are more American; they feel and act more like a nation." Republican leaders in Congress, yielding to the Federalists their traditional parochialism and dedication to states' rights, provided ample evidence that Gallatin was right.

A peacetime national Army, so offensive to Republicans before they came to power, seemed eminently desirable to those who controlled the national government at the end of the war. Madison recommended a force of 20,000. Congress approved 10,000, about four times the number actually in service before the war.

Naval power also began to appear in a new light. Reversing their prewar position, the Republicans maintained a postwar Navy about double the strength in manpower of that which existed before the war. Following the conclusion of the war, the administration dispatched a naval expedition under Stephen Decatur to free American prisoners held by Barbary pirates and to induce Algiers, Tunis, and Tripoli to cease their depredations against American commerce. His victories over the Algerians enabled Decatur to achieve both goals.

On the question of a national bank some leading Republicans also changed their views. In 1811, when the twenty-year charter of Hamilton's original Bank expired, Republicans in Congress had refused to renew it. Jeffersonian constitutional scruples were largely responsible. Freed from the regulating influence of the national Bank, state-chartered private banks, joined by a host of new ones, greatly expanded their issuance of paper money and their lending. By the autumn of 1814 banks everywhere except in New England had ceased to pay specie (gold or silver) in meeting their obligations. While their obligations had grown, their supply of specie had declined. The reduced confidence in paper money, together with the wartime curtailment of imports and the high level of government spending, produced the most severe inflation of the nineteenth century. With regional variation, prices rose as much as 50 to 90 percent.

To combat these inflationary pressures, the Republican administration asked Congress in 1815 to re-create a national bank. Following the lead of its legislative sponsor, South Carolina's Republican War Hawk, John C. Calhoun, Congress chartered the second Bank of the United States in 1816. Kentucky's Henry Clay, who had found constitutional objections to renewing the first Bank's charter in 1811, now found none. The government, as before, provided one-fifth of the Bank's capital and named one-fifth of its directors.

Protective tariff duties for America's infant industries were still another manifestation of postwar Republican nationalism. To establish greater economic independence of Great Britain, nationalists in Congress sought to tax imports of manufactured goods severely to provide a competitive advantage to new American enterprises and thus spur their growth.

By later standards, the tariff which the Republicans enacted in 1816 was not highly protective. On cotton and woolen cloth, the duty was 25 percent until 1819 and 20 percent thereafter. To combat cheap Asian cloths, however, all cottons were to be taxed at a value of no less than 25 cents per yard, thus increasing the percentage of tax on the cheaper cloth. Iron, paper, leather, and hats also received protection. Federalists in Congress favored the new tariff (25 to 23); Republicans did so by a 2-to-1 majority. The principal Federalist opponents were import merchants. Republican opponents feared that price-raising taxes would burden the agricultural interests which were a major component of the Republican coalition. The tariff proved so popular, however, that in 1818 Congress increased the protection for iron and postponed a planned reduction of the textile tariff until 1826.

Federal aid for improving transportation—"internal improvements" in the parlance of the times—was another major nationalist objective. With few exceptions interregional commerce, upon which the development of a truly national economy depended, was feasible only for those who had access to navigable rivers or coastal shipping. Local governments bore the basic responsibility for roads; in most instances they were not built but "cut." Often they amounted to little more than ax-hewn paths through the forest. Their inadequacy impeded commercial development and proved to be an obstacle to efficient military operations as well.

Calhoun's proposal for federal aid for internal improvements narrowly passed Congress early in 1817. It allocated for that purpose the "bonus" of $1.5 million which the national Bank was required to pay the government for its charter. Madison vetoed the bill. Although he favored federal aid to provide better transportation, he believed an amendment to the Constitution alone could confer the required authority. Precedents for such action, including federal aid to the "national road" in Jefferson's administration, he dismissed as "insufficient."

Postwar Republican foreign policy remained highly nationalistic, but its major achievements came several years later.

The New Republican Leadership

James Monroe, a critic once charged, "hasn't got brains enough to hold his hat on." Yet in a long career which began with service in the Revolutionary Army, Monroe had been a trusted protégé of Jefferson and a close associate of Madison. In 1811, when Madison dumped Robert Smith, his unfortunate choice as Secretary of State, he offered the post to Monroe, then governor of Virginia. In the protracted diplomacy which ultimately concluded the War of 1812, Monroe proved himself a reasonably competent Secretary of State. In addition, he occasionally took over the War Department when incompetence there reached intolerable levels. It surprised no one, therefore when Madison endorsed his fellow Virginian to be his successor.

Monroe's only rival for the succession was a Cabinet colleague, Treasury Secretary William H. Crawford of Georgia. Huge, handsome, affable, and ambitious, Crawford was a native Virginian who had grown up on the Georgia frontier. He had served as senator, wartime Minister to France, and Secretary of War (1815–1816) before becoming Secretary of the Treasury. In the Republican congressional caucus which met in March 1816, fifty-four were for Crawford and sixty-five for Monroe. In the presidential election, Crawford supported Monroe against Federalist Rufus King, whom Monroe defeated with 183 electoral votes to 34. Crawford, however, insisted that his showing in the caucus marked him as first in line to follow Monroe.

Henry Clay was one of several party leaders strongly disposed to challenge Crawford's succession. Tall, ungainly, and unattractive in appearance, aggressive, spirited, and meddlesome in manner, Clay was, like Crawford, an émigré Virginian, a frontier dweller, a duelist, and an ebullient extrovert. After serving in the Kentucky Legislature and the United States Senate, Clay entered the House of Representatives in 1811 and almost immediately became Speaker and a principal leader of the War Hawks. After serving creditably on the commission which concluded the treaty of Ghent, Clay declined Madison's invitation to become Secretary of War and instead returned to consolidate his position in Congress. Ardently nationalistic, Clay had always supported tariff protection and federal aid for internal improvements, both endorsed overwhelmingly by his constituents. Believing appointment as Secretary of State to carry with it an implicit designation as heir apparent to the presidency (it had for Madison and Monroe), Clay in 1816 aspired openly to that position in Monroe's Cabinet.

John C. Calhoun, Clay's colleague in Congress, was still abler in sheer intellectual capacity and only slightly less ambitious. Descended from Scotch-Irish immigrants who had settled on the South Carolina frontier, Calhoun was tall, elegant, with piercing eyes and strong face, "a cast iron man." He had received a degree from Yale; at Litchfield, Connecticut, he had studied law in Tapping Reeve's law school, the first in the United States. Calhoun had helped to push the nation into war with Britain and during that contest supported the war effort so assiduously that one observer referred to him as "the young Hercules who carried the war on his shoulders." After the war he outdid all other nationalists in his zeal for military preparedness, reestablishment of the national Bank, internal improvements legislation, and a protective tariff.

For the top position in his Cabinet Monroe chose none of the major congressional leaders, but picked instead the brilliantly eccentric John Quincy Adams. Adams was superbly qualified by extensive diplomatic experience to be Secretary of State, but political considerations had influenced the appointment. Adams was a Northerner, and Northerners in general were becoming extremely resentful not only of the "Virginia dynasty" of presidents but also of Southern domination of the Republican party and the government. Monroe was eager not only to appease such sentiment but to reconcile Federalist New England to Republican rule and to end partisan rivalry for all time. Choosing as Secretary of State a man who was a New Englander, a former Federalist, and the son of a former Federalist president, seemed likely to further these aims, even though Monroe did not expect Adams to become president.

Clay and Crawford were deeply disappointed. Declining to become either Secretary of War or Minister to Britain, Clay remained Speaker of the House and used his influence to resist the administration. Crawford stayed on as Secretary of the Treasury—a "worm" John Quincy Adams complained, "preying upon the vitals of the Administration from within its body." Calhoun, his nationalism as yet undiminished, became Secretary of War. All four looked ahead to 1824 and the election of Monroe's successor. So did admirers of "the Hero of New Orleans," Andrew Jackson.

Westward Migration and the Panic of 1819

Westward migration was another conspicuous feature of the immediate postwar years. People rushed westward for several reasons. Horseshoe Bend and the battle of the Thames had weakened the Indians. Treaties in the wake of those victories opened vast new areas for settlement. In the South cotton prices two or three times higher than before the war lured settlers west-

School-House.   Emigrants to the West.

Westward migration: from an early nineteenth-century geography schoolbook.

The Granger Collection

ward to gain new land which was cheaper, more productive, and often better situated with reference to water transportation than that which was available in the older regions. North of the Ohio River the climate, by precluding cotton production, made opportunities much less spectacular, but the soil was splendid, the terrain level, and access to overseas markets much better than that of the upland regions of Virginia, Maryland, and Pennsylvania. Still another factor contributing to the westward movement was the abundant supply of inflated paper money. With it buyers purchased land from the federal government in 1819 at a rate five times that of 1811.

Westward migration brought several new states into the union before the Panic of 1819 slowed the movement. Louisiana became a state in 1812. Mississippi entered the Union in 1817, Alabama in 1819. In the North the flood of migrants brought statehood to Indiana in 1816 and to Illinois in 1818.

Then came the Panic. In 1819, American exports dropped one-fourth from the level of 1818, due chiefly to a worldwide economic decline. Cotton exports, which had been the chief support of the preceding boom, declined by one-third. British merchants, themselves hard-pressed, began to curtail credit to American importers and to increase pressure for the immediate repayment of existing debts. American imports also fell off markedly.

Severe deflation of a badly inflated paper currency was another causal factor. After the demise of the first Bank of the United States in 1811, state-chartered private banks had multiplied rapidly and flooded the country with inadequately backed paper money. One of the objectives which led to the chartering of the second Bank of the United States in 1816 was the eventual resumption of specie payment throughout the nation and the reestablishment of public confidence in the paper money with which the nation's business was conducted.

Unfortunately, under its original leadership the second Bank bungled its assignment. Madison's choice to head the Bank was William Jones, a Philadelphia merchant and former Cabinet member. As head of the Bank, Jones seemed more intent on encouraging inflation, especially in the West and South (where it was most serious but also most popular), than on assuring its control. The Bank itself was on the verge of bankruptcy when Jones resigned early in 1819.

Jones's successor, Langdon Cheves, a former congressional War Hawk from South Carolina, aimed to redeem the Bank and use it for its intended purposes. Cheves pursued both efficiency and deflation with a vengeance. By 1820 he had reduced the Bank's own currency by half and its loans by one-fourth. This restored the financial health of the Bank itself but forced such a severe contraction of the currency and loans of other banks that "the people were ruined." The downturn inaugurated by the decline of European purchasing became a major depression which lasted into the early 1820s. The Bank itself became "the monster," hated by many private bankers for its competition and its regulatory actions, hated by the people for enriching its own stockholders while impoverishing the nation through its deflationary policies. As early as 1819, public hostility toward the Bank evoked a constitutional crisis which brought the institution under the scrutiny of John Marshall's Supreme Court.

John Marshall stands preeminent over all the men who have served as justices of the United States Supreme Court. Marshall dominated the Court as no other man has done. His Court's decisions on major cases invariably strengthened the authority of the federal government rather than that of the states and upheld "vested" private rights against public control.

Born in a log cabin in the Virginia Piedmont in 1755, Marshall came to maturity at the beginning of the Revolution. He served in the Continental army for several years and, as he later expressed it, became "confirmed in the habit of considering America as my country and Congress as my government." His major historical achievements began when John Adams made him Chief Justice. Before the War of 1812 he had set judicial landmarks in *Marbury v. Madison* (1803), affirming the power of the Court to void acts of Congress; in the Burr treason trial (1807), defining treason; and in *Fletcher v. Peck* (1810), establishing the power of the Court to void state laws. In the postwar years Marshall rendered still more judgments of major importance.

McCulloch v. Maryland, the Bank case of 1819, was one of the most significant in Marshall's tenure. Maryland and several other states, reflecting popular animosity toward the Bank, attempted to prevent it from operating within their borders by imposing high and discriminatory taxation upon it. When the Maryland branch of the National Bank refused to pay the tax, the state sued the Bank cashier, James McCulloch. Early in 1819 the case reached the Supreme Court on McCulloch's appeal from an adverse decision in the Maryland courts.

Marshall's decision affirmed three major principles. First, he took exception to the somewhat incidental contention of Maryland's counsel that the federal government derived its power from the states and that only they were "truly sovereign." "The government of the Union," Marshall asserted, ". . . is, emphatically and truly, a government of the people." It was not from the state governments but from the popular ratifying conventions, he declared, that "the constitution derives its whole authority." Next, Marshall explicitly upheld the authority of the federal government to create the Bank. The decision hinged upon the interpretation of that portion of the Constitution which states that Congress shall have power "to make all laws which shall be necessary and proper for carrying into execution" any of the previously listed powers, such as power to tax or to regulate commerce. For achieving an end or objective "within the scope of the Constitution," he stated, "all means which are appropriate, which are plainly adapted to that end, which are not prohibited, but consist with the letter and spirit of the Constitution, are constitutional." Finally, Marshall ruled that Maryland could not tax the Bank. The American people, as he put it, "did not design to make their government dependent on the states." The national government, he added, "though limited in its powers, is supreme within its sphere of action." Since Congress could constitutionally create a bank, no state could properly tax its operation because "the power to tax involves the power to destroy."

States' rightists came into conflict with Marshall also on the question of the Supreme Court's power to hear appeals from state courts. Spencer Roane, an ardently orthodox Republican, was Marshall's major antagonist in this struggle. As chief justice of Virginia's top court, Roane contended that although state courts were bound by the Constitution to void state laws which conflicted with any portion of federal law, the decision of the state court should be final. Roane lost one round on that issue in *Martin v. Hunter's Lessee* (1816). In *Cohens v. Virginia* (1821) Marshall stated that in order for the federal government to be effective in exercising its granted powers, it must have authority to review the decisions of state courts whenever they involved interpretation of federal law. That indeed seemed the obvious intent behind the constitutional provision that the jurisdiction of the Supreme Court should extend to *all* cases arising under the Constitution, federal statutes, or treaties.

Gibbons v. Ogden (1824) voided a New York State law which had granted to Robert Fulton and his backer, Robert R. Livingston, a monopoly on the operation of steamboat service between New York and New Jersey. Although Marshall shrank from denying the states any role at all in regulating interstate commerce, he ended the monopoly in question because it conflicted with an act of Congress authorizing *any* vessels licensed by the federal government to engage in coastal shipping.

Marshall's defense of vested private rights was almost as controversial as his exaltation of federal power. In *Fletcher v. Peck* (1810) he had ruled not only that his Court could void state laws in conflict with the Constitution but also that state laws altering property rights previously conferred by the state came under the Constitution's ban on state actions "impairing the Obligation of Contracts." In the Dartmouth College case of 1819 Marshall extended his earlier ruling. The case arose out of controversy between Republicans and Federalists for control of the college, established by royal charter in 1769. The Republicans, who dominated the state government, sought by state law to transform the private college, run by Federalist trustees, into a public institution whose management would then be in Republican hands. Exceeding even the position taken by alumnus Daniel Webster on behalf of the trustees, Marshall held that the original charter constituted a contract which the Legislature could not alter. The effect of this ruling was to bar state legislatures from changing the terms of charters which they had bestowed, usually by separate and lenient laws, on new business corporations. Republicans took offense at the impairment of majority rule.

States and Localities

Despite the nationalistic atmosphere of the postwar years, the United States remained a remarkably decentralized nation. States and localities, exercising a high degree of autonomy, performed functions of enormous importance to the people. Among the matters with which they concerned themselves were economic development, education, national defense, law enforcement, public welfare, and the electoral processes.

Economic development was a matter of major concern to state and local governments. Many states established inspection systems for export products to maintain a good reputation—and a good price—for the state's products in foreign markets. These products traveled to market over roads which were maintained in most instances by local governments in conformity with state laws. Payments occurred normally in money issued by state-chartered banks. In addition, states fostered economic growth by issuing generous charters of incorporation to manufacturing and other business concerns, by granting tax concessions, by investing in private enterprises which needed extra capital, or even by launching state enterprises in canal or road construction, banking, or commercial production of various commodities.

Education, traditionally the responsibility of family, church, or the apprentice system, became more a matter of public concern. New England had long required towns to provide schools at public expense, but elsewhere schools had generally lacked extensive government support. New York State, for example, granted aid to the towns for schools in the 1790s, but state assistance for public schools had real impact on education only after 1812. Even then tuition payments rather than public funds bore most of the burden, and the period of attendance for most children was brief. Nevertheless, in the postwar years local and state governments were slowly beginning to follow New England's example in providing public support for education.

To most Americans even after the War of 1812, defense appeared a joint responsibility of the national Armed Forces and the state militia. In accordance with federal law, each state maintained and trained a militia force, of which the governor was commander in chief. Although the War of 1812 had demonstrated glaring deficiencies in the militia system, it remained unchanged after the war and figured prominently in national military planning.

Law enforcement, particularly of state laws in criminal cases, was primarily in the hands of local officials. Welfare likewise rested on state laws enforced by local officials. In many areas the major concern in administering welfare programs was the limitation of costs to local taxpayers. Accordingly, newcomers of doubtful solvency might legally be "warned out" or, if they became welfare clients, might be "transported" back to the localities from which they came. Often transportation was a major expenditure of local welfare programs. Welfare officers, sometimes called "Poor Masters," could "bind out" children of indigent families as servants; in some areas they sold adults as laborers. In the 1820s the poor commonly accepted virtual confinement in self-sustaining county poorhouses, often termed "workhouses," as a condition for receiving aid. Such institutions commonly housed insane people as well as those merely incapable of self-support.

Finally, states and localities were political units of major importance. States decided who could and who could not vote. They fixed the powers and duties, more often the latter, of local governments. Their legislatures chose United States senators and, in many states until the 1820s, cast the state's electoral vote for president as well. For these reasons, as well as because of the state's major role in economic matters, state elections were the chief focus of political interest. For that reason political parties organized far more effectively at the state than at the national level.

Missouri Compromise

North-South differences over the future of slavery produced a dangerously divisive conflict in 1819 when Missouri sought admission to the Union. Approximately six thousand of the territory's sixty thousand inhabitants were slaves. In accordance with Missouri's prevailing sentiment, the proposed state constitution recognized and protected slavery. When the bill to admit Missouri came before Congress, however, Representative James Tallmadge of New York proposed an amendment requiring that Missouri be admitted only if it agreed to bar the admission of more slaves and to free all children of slaves when they reached the age of twenty-five. The Tallmadge amendment passed the House with Northern support, but failed in the Senate, where the South was still in control.

Tallmadge, wittingly or not, had saddled Congress with perhaps the most dangerous issue in its brief history. Northern congressmen possessed both the power and the determination to block Missouri's admission as a slave state. Southern congressmen, on the other hand, affirming "state sovereignty" with eloquence and passion, denied that Congress could properly bind the prospective state of Missouri with reference to slavery. When Senator Rufus King of New York, the defeated Federalist candidate for the presidency in 1816, began to exploit the issue, Madison expressed to President Monroe the suspicion that King was concerned less with human rights than with "dividing the Republicans of the North from those of the South" to help Federalists return to power.

This burgeoning sectional controversy brought forth numerous proposals for compromise. Senator James Barbour of Virginia argued that Congress should link the admission

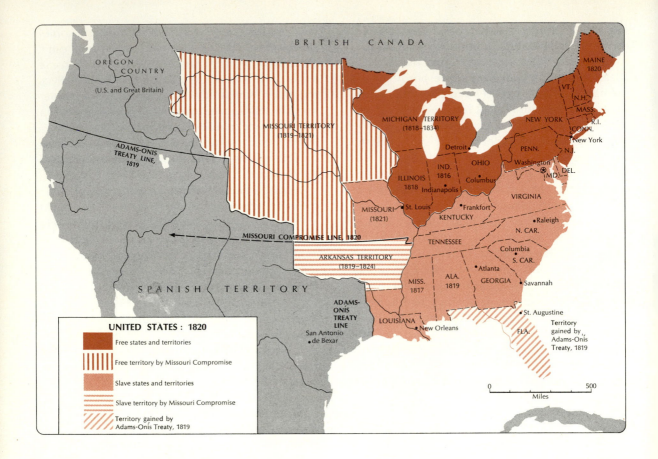

UNITED STATES : 1820

- Free states and territories
- Free territory by Missouri Compromise
- Slave states and territories
- Slave territory by Missouri Compromise
- Territory gained by Adams-Onís Treaty, 1819

of Missouri to that of Maine, then seeking separation from Massachusetts, so that the nation's traditional balance between free and slave state Senators would be preserved. When that proved insufficient to satisfy Northern opponents of slavery, Senator Jesse B. Thomas of Illinois suggested that the proslavery forces agree to bar slavery forever from the remainder of the Louisiana Purchase north of a line corresponding to the southern border of Missouri (36°30′ north latitude). Because the Louisiana Purchase was so much wider in the north than in the south, the proposal presaged a predominance of free states over slave states unless the nation acquired more territory to the south.

Pushed along by Speaker Henry Clay's tireless persuasion, Congress, in March 1820, endorsed a three-point compromise. Missouri would enter

as a slave state. Maine would enter as a free state to preserve the sectional balance in the Senate. Slavery would be forever barred from the Louisiana Purchase north of 36°30′.

Another Missouri controversy ensued when Missouri included in its constitution a clause prohibiting the entrance of free blacks. That clause clearly conflicted with the provision of the United States Constitution which assures the citizens of each state "all Privileges and Immunities of Citizens" residing in other states. Under pressure from Speaker Henry Clay the Missourians agreed never to exclude the citizens of any state on terms which defied the Constitution. That concession secured Missouri's admission in 1821, although the legislature later restricted the movement of free blacks into the state.

Whatever their motives in the Missouri debates, Northern spokesmen had failed to break up the Republican coalition that had placed three Virginians in the White House. The controversy had, however, seriously frayed many cords holding the old Jeffersonian alliance together. Most congressmen had refused to argue the Missouri issue on sectional grounds. Southerners still hoped to avoid the necessity of defending slavery and its expansion; the vast majority of Northerners were not yet prepared to condemn the institution, at least not in public debate. Yet the fact that a minority of Northern writers and politicians would employ the question of Missouri statehood to defy the national leadership demonstrated that neither the unity of the Republican party nor indeed that of the nation itself could be assumed. The Missouri controversy was, as Jefferson characterized it, "a fire bell in the night." He was an accurate prophet when he warned that "a geographical line" dividing the nation on a matter of moral principle, "once conceived and held up to the angry passions of men, will never be obliterated."

The Diplomacy of John Quincy Adams

In dealing with other nations, President Monroe relied heavily on the advice of John Quincy Adams, unquestionably the most accomplished secretary of state in the nation's history. Adams scarcely fitted the stereotype of the diplomat. He was approximately fifty years old when he assumed his Cabinet duties in 1817, short and bald, with a belligerent demeanor and an affliction which caused his eyes to run incessantly. But in those qualities of mind that mattered, Adams was superbly prepared for the tasks of diplomacy. His interest in the country's external relations began a quarter century earlier when he publicly defended George Washington's highly controversial foreign policies. It propelled him into long periods of service abroad, including extended stays in St. Petersburg and London, where he acquired a realistic grasp of diplomatic limitations. For him diplomacy had one major purpose: to serve the interests of the United States, which he saw largely in geographical terms.

As secretary of state, Adams sought first to resolve a series of disputes with England, for he understood well that continued security for the United States hinged on good relations with that country. As early as the peace negotiations of 1782, his father, John Adams, had sought the elimination of fortifications from the Canadian-American frontier. The younger Adams, in turn,

had pressed the British for such an agreement at Ghent in 1814, but again without success. Still undaunted, Adams repeated the offer in a note of March 1816. The British government, now hoping to avoid any naval race with the United States on the Great Lakes, accepted Adams's overture. The result was the Rush-Bagot Agreement of April 1817, which limited British and American naval armaments on the lakes to those required to enforce customs regulations. This treaty was the first reciprocal naval disarmament agreement in modern history.

During the following year Adams managed to achieve extensive American fishing rights off the Labrador and Newfoundland coasts. Of equal significance was the new Secretary's effort to define the long northern boundary of the Louisiana Purchase. In the Convention of 1818, he negotiated the line from the Lake of the Woods westward along the 49th parallel to the Rocky Mountains. West of the Rockies, however, British interests were still too demanding to permit a settlement which Adams would accept. The British claimed the Columbia River as the boundary between the Rockies and the Pacific. Adams, who was greatly interested in acquiring a usable port on the western shore, had been made aware by New England seamen that the turbulent Columbia would never fill that need. He understood also that the Strait of Juan de Fuca and

Puget Sound, both north of the Columbia but south of the 49th parallel, constituted one of the world's largest and safest harbors. For these reasons, Adams would settle for no less than the extension of the boundary along 49° to the Pacific. When the British negotiators proved intractable on this point, Adams agreed to a policy of joint occupation with Britain of the country west of the Rockies for a period of ten years, an arrangement which either nation could terminate on one year's notice.

Adams's next diplomatic achievement, perhaps his greatest, came in 1819 in the Adams-Onis Treaty. The United States had acquired West Florida, the narrow coastal region between Mobile and New Orleans, in the period of the War of 1812, but modern Florida, then called East Florida, was still under Spanish rule. The region had become a problem for the United States government simply because Spain was too plagued with troubles elsewhere to maintain order in the colony. For years British adventurers in Florida had armed and incited Indians to conduct raids north of the Florida boundary. In 1818 General Andrew Jackson forced the Florida issue to a crisis. Carrying out his instructions to punish the Seminoles for their destruction of American lives and property, Jackson pursued a band of Indians into Florida, where he captured and executed two British agents as well as two Indian chiefs. Spain protested the action; Jackson's enemies in Congress and the Cabinet, led by Clay and Calhoun, demanded that the general be dismissed. Adams, however, defended Jackson and reminded the Cabinet that Spain had an obligation to keep order in its empire. If Spain could not, then it had no choice but to cede Florida to the United States. Lord Castlereagh, Britain's celebrated Foreign Minister, agreed with Adams. The Spanish weakness was so obvious that the Madrid government opened negotiations with the United States and by the Adams-Onis Treaty, signed in February 1819, ceded Florida to the United States. At the same time the Washington government assumed the claims of United States citizens against Spain, which totaled approximately $5 million.

Meanwhile Adams's negotiations with the Spanish Minister turned to the still-undefined boundary between Spanish Mexico and the southwestern United States. Spain hoped to push the line eastward and northward as far as possible; Adams, on the other hand, sought a boundary which would bring much of Texas into the United States. After weeks of proposals, counterproposals, and threats to break off negotiations, Adams achieved, in the treaty of February 1819, a transcontinental boundary that left to Spain the vast region stretching from Texas to California, but ceded to the United States Spain's claim to the Pacific Northwest.

Latin American Independence and the Monroe Doctrine

Adams's opportunities for action in foreign affairs stemmed not alone from Spanish weakness in Florida but also from that nation's precarious position throughout the Western Hemisphere. Napoleon's invasion of Spain in 1808 had terminated Madrid's effective control of the Spanish empire. Provisional *juntas* established by Spain's ruling classes claimed jurisdiction over Spanish America, but by 1812 their New World influence was purely nominal. Freed of Spanish commercial restrictions, the now-independent regions of Latin America opened their commerce to the world. Yankee shippers entered South American ports in large numbers. When war broke out again after 1814 between Spain and the rebellious colonies, struggling South America looked to the United States for economic, moral, and military support.

Strong pressure arose for American guardianship of Latin American independence. Congressman Henry Clay, in particular, denounced the American government for neglecting the cause of liberty. But Monroe and Adams would not be stampeded. They recognized the preference of the people of the United States for Latin American independence, but they refused to commit the nation to a policy of involvement before the European powers had revealed their intentions or the patriots of Latin America had demonstrated their capacity to establish their independence and maintain a semblance of order. Adams doubted that the people of Latin America were capable of self-government. Nor did Adams have any interest in antagonizing Spain while the Florida issue remained unsettled. Thus the administration urged circumspection.

Nevertheless, the Monroe administration seemed bound to recognize the independence of Latin America. With the ratification of the transcontinental treaty and the final annexation of Florida in 1821, the administration lost its former hesitancy over possible Spanish reaction to American recognition policies. Also, before the end of 1821, Latin American patriots had all but destroyed Spanish influence in the hemisphere. Monroe recognized these developments in a special message to Congress on March 8, 1822. He declared that Chile, the United Provinces of the Plata (Argentina), Peru, Colombia, and Mexico were fully independent and thus could claim recognition by other nations.

Meanwhile, British trade and investment in Latin America had confirmed England's interest in the continued independence of the former Spanish empire. When in 1823 an invading French army successfully restored Ferdinand VII to his full royal prerogatives in Spain, Britain's new Foreign Minister, George Canning, suspected that France might attempt to restore the Spanish empire as well. It was possible, moreover, that France might use its influence in Spain to lay the foundation for another French empire in America. In this crisis the troubled Canning turned to Richard Rush, the American Minister in London. He suggested that Britain and the United States issue a joint declaration disavowing any territorial ambitions in Latin America but warning Europe against intervention unless that

intervention should come from Spain itself. Rush, although highly flattered by this recognition of America's growing importance, insisted on referring the matter to Washington unless Britain recognized the independence of the Latin American nations immediately. This Canning refused to do. Instead, he delivered a secret warning to Paris. The French government responded in its "Polignac Memorandum" with satisfactory assurances that it had no intention of dispatching an expedition to the New World. Thus Canning, by unilateral action, had resolved the immediate challenge to British policy.

Monroe received Rush's dispatches during October 1823. The President, who looked with favor upon the Canning proposal, sought the advice of his old friend Jefferson, in quiet retirement at Monticello. Jefferson warmly endorsed the idea. So did James Madison. But Secretary of State Adams had convictions of his own. The Russian Minister had recently warned the Secretary that his government would not recognize Latin American independence and would support any French invasion of the former Spanish empire. Adams refused to be frightened. He doubted that France intended armed intervention in Latin America; moreover, the British navy was powerful enough to prevent it. In fact, Adams suspected that Canning's overture was aimed less at obtaining United States diplomatic support than at preventing, through the mutual disavowal of territorial ambitions, future United States expansion into Texas and the Caribbean. Adams had already warned Madrid that the United States would not tolerate the transfer of Cuba, still held by Spain, to any other European power. Thus when the Cabinet met on November 7, Adams proposed that the United States stand unilaterally. "It would be more candid, as well as more dignified," said Adams, "to avow our principles explicitly to Russia and France, than to come in as a cock-boat in the wake of the British man-of-war."

Monroe, although still hesitant to take a stand against the Holy Alliance (the reactionary league of European powers headed by Russia, France, and Austria), favored a dramatic statement in behalf of the Greeks, then in revolt against Turkey. In Congress, Webster had taken up the popular Greek cause. Adams, on the other hand, argued strongly against any American meddling in the affairs of Europe. "The ground that I wish to take," he told the Cabinet, "is that of earnest remonstrance against the interference of the European powers by force with South America, but to disclaim all interference on our part with Europe."

This concept of two worlds Monroe embodied in his celebrated message to Congress on December 2, 1823. The so-called Monroe Doc-trine declared specifically that the American continents were no longer open to European colonization and that the United States would regard any European intervention in the affairs of nations in the Western Hemisphere as a threat to its peace and safety. On the other hand, Monroe assured the nations of the Old World that the United States would not interfere with their dependencies in the New World or involve itself in matters purely European. Clearly the United States had committed itself to the status quo in the Atlantic. But it was obvious to all that the British navy was the force which would most dissuade European adventures in Latin America.

The Election of 1824

Democracy, if measured by the proportion of people exercising the franchise, grew rapidly in the United States during the first quarter of the nineteenth century. The increase in voter turn-out reflected in part the relaxation of state restrictions on voting and in part the decision of voters at last to exercise legal rights long held. Of the original thirteen states, New Hampshire, Pennsylvania, New Jersey, Maryland, North Carolina, and Georgia had adopted the principle of universal manhood suffrage before the War of 1812. Still it seems clear that after 1800 the extension of voting privileges alone could not account for the increase in those actually casting ballots in state and local elections. Voter par-ticipation rested less on legal changes than on changes in habit. Eighteenth-century American society was deferential; Americans generally ac-cepted the leadership of the landed and business elites and had little interest in contesting the established political and social order by resort to the ballot. After 1800, however, the direct ap-peal of the Jeffersonians to the political instincts of the masses, added to the continuing two-party rivalry between Jeffersonians and Federalists, gradually destroyed the older elitism and en-couraged men both to select and then to pass judgment on their political leaders.

Nonpartisan or even antipartisan sentiment during Monroe's "era of good feelings" con-tinued to discourage popular participation. There was minimal interest in the presidential election of 1820, when Monroe won reelection without opposition and with only one dissenting vote in the electoral college. By then all leading political figures professed to be Republicans. By tradition Republican members of Congress had met in caucus to make their party's presidential nomination. The nominating caucus could func-tion properly, however, only as long as it repre-sented a party consensus. By 1824 that consensus no longer existed. A number of powerful politi-cal figures clearly intended to seek the pres-idency. Moreover an increasingly politicized population clamored for a voice in the decision. More and more states transferred to the voters the choice as to how the state's electoral vote for president would be cast. As the contest of 1824 approached, several state and regional favorites announced that they would not feel bound by a congressional caucus nomination if the choice did not fall upon them. Consequently an open scramble for the presidency developed, and from it there emerged in time a revitalized two-party system and still wider popular participation in the electoral process.

The presidential campaign of 1824 seen as a footrace, with candidates Adams, Crawford, and Jackson toeing the mark. Henry Clay (who ran fourth) is shown out of the race at right, scratching his head. *The Granger Collection*

William H. Crawford of Georgia, Secretary of the Treasury, won the endorsement of the Republican congressional caucus, but only one-third of the Republican congressmen had attended. As early as 1822 Tennessee's General Assembly had endorsed Andrew Jackson. In 1823 a Republican legislative caucus in South Carolina had proposed John C. Calhoun, Secretary of War. When a Pennsylvania state convention in 1824 named Jackson for president and Calhoun for vice president, Calhoun decided to settle for the second spot. Meanwhile, Henry Clay, advocate of what he called the "American system" of tariff protection for industry and federal aid for improved transportation, had won the support of Kentucky, Missouri, Louisiana, and Ohio. In the Northeast the American system was popular, but its favored spokesman was not Clay of Kentucky but John Quincy Adams of Massachusetts, then Secretary of State.

In the four-way presidential contest Jackson showed the greatest strength. He gained 99 electoral votes, chiefly from the West and South. Adams ran second with 84 electoral votes, chiefly from New England and New York. Crawford carried three states (Georgia, Virginia, and Delaware) with 41 electoral votes. Clay trailed with 37 votes from Kentucky, Missouri, and Ohio.

Jackson also led in the popular vote with 153,544 to 108,740 for Adams.

Ignoring Jackson's superior appeal to the electorate, Adams determined to make a bid for election in the House of Representatives, where each of the twenty-four states would have one vote. This was the method of election provided by the Constitution when no candidate had a majority. Adams needed six states—all those carried by Clay and Crawford—in addition to the seven he had gained in November. Two Western or Southern states, added to his November total of eleven, would give Jackson the victory. Clay, as Speaker, was in a powerful position to control the House election, and he favored Adams over Jackson. Clay's decision to support Adams, followed by Adams's own success in lining up several key House delegations, deprived Jackson of a majority. The House, on February 9, 1825, elected Adams on the first ballot. To his own seven, Adams added Clay's three states of Missouri, Ohio, and Kentucky, as well as three states that had voted for Jackson in 1824—Louisiana, Maryland, and Illinois. The price of victory came high, for Jackson's followers would claim throughout the next four years that Adams and Congress had betrayed the will of the voters.

From the day of his inauguration, Adams faced the hopeless task of prolonging an era of nonpartisan rule without strong congressional or personal support. His only hope of conciliating the many personal factions in Washington lay in the creation of a broad national program and in the careful selection of his Cabinet. With Clay and Jackson in his administration, Adams might have sustained a semblance of nonpartisan government. But Jackson would accept no appointment, and Clay could not enter the Cabinet without inviting charges of a "corrupt bargain." Clay, in supporting Adams's bid for the presidency, had neither demanded nor received the promise of a high-level appointment. However, when Adams selected Clay for the State Department as the most experienced Western man available, he alienated the Jacksonian faction completely.

Adams, having been unable to achieve unity in his administration, turned to the task of creating an acceptable national program. To protect and enlarge the national interest in liberty and property—the twin foundations of American constitutionalism—Adams favored a strong federal government capable of directing the nation's power and resources. His concern for a program of internal improvements binding together a great continental republic, supported by moderate protection for American industry, expressed his belief in nationalism and the Federalist tradition.

Unhappily for his domestic program, the President had little support in Congress. The refusal of many senators to approve Clay's nomination as Secretary of State presaged strong opposition at the outset. Vice President Calhoun, who dominated the Senate, was never a spokesman for the administration. Webster, like Adams a former Federalist, might have served the administration well as its spokesman in the House, but Adams distrusted Webster too much to assign him that role. If the Republican party remained the nation's only organized party, it

did not belong to Adams. From the beginning of Adams's administration, the forces of Jackson, Calhoun, and Crawford coalesced against the executive leadership. By 1826 this new coalition, calling itself the Democratic Republican party, captured control of the House of Representatives. Congress, under no pressure from the White House or a pro-Adams populace, was able largely to ignore the President's program. At his urging, Congress did provide about $2 million for such internal improvements as road construction and harbor improvements, a sum twice the amount spent for the purpose in all previous administrations combined. But the lawmakers disappointed the President by refusing to consider an integrated system of internal improvements for the country as a whole.

Adams, always conscientious in the performance of his duties, refused to ignore the troublesome problem of Indian removal. When Georgia had ceded its Western lands in 1802, the federal government had agreed to extinguish all Indian titles within that state and turn the Indian lands over to the people of Georgia. What made the fulfillment of this obligation difficult was the fact that the Cherokees and Creeks of Georgia had achieved a high state of organization and culture. Their investment in agricultural production alone was too great to make their removal easy or peaceful. But Georgians, anxious to enter the rich cotton lands of the Indians, pressed the federal government to negotiate the necessary treaties of removal.

When Adams entered the Presidency in March 1825, he found on his desk the Treaty of Indian Springs, already approved by the Senate. Adams signed the document despite the warning of the United States Indian agent in Georgia that the treaty had been negotiated with only a small portion of the Creeks and Cherokees. Soon a delegation of Indians appeared at the White House, demanding a new treaty. A compromise Treaty of Washington, signed in January 1826, provided that the Indians cede only their lands east of the Chattahoochee River, or about two-thirds of the territory included in the Treaty of Indian Springs. Georgia's Governor George N. Troup rejected the compromise and proclaimed his intention to have the full area claimed by the state surveyed in preparation for white settlement. Adams tried to dissuade Troup from surveying land not included in the treaty of 1826, warning him that the federal government would protect the rights of the Indians. But the Georgia Governor informed the Secretary of War that, if need be, Georgia would call out the militia to defend its interests. Although Adams recognized Indian rights, neither he nor Congress was willing to use force to protect them. Finally in November 1827, the Creeks ceded all their Georgia lands and prepared to move. The problem of the Cherokees remained unsettled.

Despite his special aptitude for foreign affairs, Adams as President could not sustain the successes of his earlier years. When he attempted to cement better commercial relations with the new nations of Latin America, an obstructionist Congress frustrated his aim while the British forged ahead.

The Jacksonian Triumph

No less than the presidential election of 1824, that of 1828 evolved into a contest between Adams and Jackson. The second contest, like the first, turned less on issues than on personalities. Jackson had never opposed the Clay-Adams program. His own political and social ideals were for the most part unknown, but he had somehow become identified with the aspirations of the common people. Politicians and editors across the country had rallied to his standard; so, too, had the masses. Whereas Adams chose to ignore the new forces for political change, the Jacksonians embraced them eagerly.

In Martin Van Buren, Jackson acquired an accomplished political strategist. A small, balding man with muttonchop whiskers and a disarming personality, Van Buren held a commanding position in New York politics as head of the "Albany Regency," a group of orthodox Republicans with influence throughout the state. Van Buren, careful both in his timing and in his measuring of Jackson's appeal, waited until late in 1826 to put his New York machine behind the candidacy of the Tennesseean. Equally astute politicians in other states quickly fell into line. The new Democratic coalition was a strange one. Within its ranks were men who had seldom in the past agreed on national policies but were now committed to a single movement. For this new order of politicians, Jackson's great personal popularity and his opposition to Adams were his essential assets. Not only were there more voters in the late 1820s than ever before, but also there existed among Southern planters and Northern farmers, among urban artisans, tradesmen, and members of the growing middle class everywhere, enough convergence of interest to permit their inclusion within a single political movement. Still any program that would satisfy such divergent elements was elusive. In the debates of the twenties, spokesmen of the new Democratic party divided on every important issue. What gave the party some intellectual unity, however, was the vague, if traditional, preference of both the liberal-democratic elements of the North and the states' rightists and Jeffersonian philosophers of the South for less, rather than more, centralization of federal authority.

Perhaps no issue of the Adams years better illustrated the failure of the Jacksonians to agree on public policy than did the tariff. The tariff of 1824, with additional duties on wool and hemp to broaden its appeal to the North and the West, constituted a moderate increase over the tariff of 1816. Calhoun, as a spokesman for American nationalism, voted for the measure, whereas Webster did not. However, Calhoun's tariff views had already entered a period of transition.

He had defended earlier tariffs solely as measures of national defense, but in 1824 the country was scarcely in danger of war. Most South Carolinians, moreover, had never shared Calhoun's enthusiasm for the tariff and had never ceased to oppose it. Early in 1827, protectionists introduced a higher tariff on wool, designed to raise the tariff on imported woolens from 33$^{1}/_{3}$ percent to about 50 percent of actual value. Webster, now under the influence of the rapidly expanding industrial interests of New England, drove the measure through the House, but South Carolina's states' rightists were incensed. In the Senate, Vice President Calhoun, now enlisted in the defense of Southern rights, broke a tie by casting the deciding vote against the bill. Thereafter, antitariff South Carolinians took refuge in Jackson's candidacy, for the fact that Jackson had already selected Calhoun for the vice presidency offered them some assurance that he favored tariff reduction.

When Congress met in December 1827, the advocates of protection—having formulated their plans at a tariff convention which had met at Harrisburg, Pennsylvania, during the previous summer—doubled their efforts to commit Congress and the President to higher schedules. Adams passed the burden of conciliation to Congress. There the Jacksonians responded to the demand for tariff increases with a measure designed to gratify both farmers and manufacturers in the states of Pennsylvania, New York, Ohio, Kentucky, and Missouri, where the political balance of power lay. Under the leadership of Silas Wright, a Van Buren lieutenant, they offered firm protection for iron, hemp, raw wool, and whisky (by taxing imports of molasses from which New Englanders made rum). New England, sure to be Adams country politically, received no favors, nor did the South, which was equally firm for Jackson despite its antitariff views. Manufacturers of woolen cloth, chiefly New Englanders, suffered a lowering of their protection. Yankee shipping and distilling inter-

ests found materials they imported more expensive. Southerners voted for the provisions offensive to New England, hoping to turn New Englanders against the bill as they might have done had they not bragged too early of their cleverness. In any case a scattering of New England votes provided the victory margin. Denounced elsewhere as a "tariff of abominations," the measure nevertheless improved Jackson's prospects in the middle states.

After 1826 the Jacksonian forces in Congress determined to destroy Adams. Behind the oratory of the brilliant, if erratic, John Randolph, they harassed the President and his partisans in every conceivable way. They charged the administration with extravagance and corruption. They accused Adams of attempting to perpetuate his power by building up a vast patronage, although the President actually refused to reward even his closest friends with political office. Once begun, tirades of abuse spilled over into the campaign of 1828, making it one of the most bitter in the nation's history. When Adams heard charges of corruption and incompetence, his supporters replied in kind, accusing Jackson, among other things, of gross immorality in connection with his slightly irregular marriage to his beloved Rachel.

Long before November 1828 it was clear that the Jacksonians were carrying the nation before them. Adams appeared secure only in New England; elsewhere his political strength was in doubt. With Jackson and Calhoun, as running mates, assured of victories in the South and West, Adams needed both New York and Pennsylvania if he were to be reelected. When the ballots were counted, it was disclosed that Jackson had swept Pennsylvania and everything to the west and south of it, with the exception of 6 Maryland electoral votes. Jackson had captured 20 of New York's 36 votes as well. Adams had held New England, New Jersey, and Delaware. Jackson led in electoral votes, 178 to 82; in popular votes, 647,276 to 508,064.

While Jackson's triumph at the polls was profound, its meaning was less than clear. What notions of government and what policies had triumphed? As a national organization, the Democratic party had electioneered more for Jackson than for a program. Yet for Adams himself, defeat spelled the end of federalism. "I fell, and with me fell," he complained, ". . . the system of internal improvement by National means and National Energies. The great object of my Life therefore as applied to the Administration of the Government of the United States, has failed." In part Adams was correct. Jackson's election was indeed more than a personal triumph. In some measure it had been a triumph in principle. Many of those in both North and South who led the fight against Adams had questioned the continuing trend toward centralization. For Randolph and Taylor, for the old Jeffersonians, as well as for Van Buren and many of the New York Democrats, the new President represented the promise of less government.

Jackson's election marked the end of nonpartisan politics at the national level, a development encouraged by the country's democratic structure. The election neither inaugurated the rise of the common man nor brought an end to aristocracy in America, but it created for the common citizen national political machinery through which he could register his preferences and thus influence public policy. If the parties of Jackson and Adams had not displaced the political habits and personal allegiances of the past, they had laid foundations for national party structures which might encompass existing and future party organizations in the states, the cities, and even the villages. In overthrowing the nonpartisan tradition so dear to Monroe and Adams, the Jacksonians had employed new techniques of campaigning whereby politicians might bid successfully for popular support. In short, the Jacksonians, in guiding and sustaining the political revolution of the 1820s, left to the American people a vehicle for making their democracy effective.

SUGGESTED READINGS

Several good books deal with the decline of the Federalists and the nonpartisan "era of good feelings." The best overall treatment is in George Dangerfield, *The Awakening of American Nationalism** (1965), which updates and alters somewhat in interpretation his earlier *Era of Good Feelings** (1952). J. M. Banner treats the Massachusetts Federalists quite sympathetically in *To the Hartford Convention* (1969). Shaw Livermore analyzed on a national scale *The Twilight of Federalism* (1962). Harry Ammon's biography of *James Monroe* (1971) also affords national perspective on the period.

Two good books on nationalism are P. C. Nagel, *One Nation Indivisible* (1964), and Clinton Rossiter, *The American Quest* (1971).

On economic developments good studies are also numerous. Bray Hammond's *Banks and Politics in America** (1957) pushes its conclusions very hard but

undoubtedly has revised many previous estimates. George R. Taylor's *The Transportation Revolution* (1951) is really a general economic study of outstanding quality, omitting only agriculture, which is treated in the companion volume by Paul W. Gates, *The Farmer's Age* (1960). M. N. Rothbard's *The Panic of 1819* (1962) deserves notice. Recent preoccupation with economic growth is reflected in two perceptive works covering this period: D. C. North's *The Economic Growth of the United States, 1790–1860** (1961) and Stuart Bruchey's *Roots of American Economic Growth** (1965). No modern work has yet surpassed F. W. Taussig's *Tariff History of the United States** (8th ed., 1931).

On the frontier and the Indians the works by Sheehan and Prucha, cited in chapter 7, remain important. Overall perspective distinguishes Dale Van Every, *The Final Challenge: The American Frontier,*

1804–1845 (1964), although it suffers in comparison with F. J. Turner's *The Rise of the New West* (1906). J. D. Barnhart's *Valley of Democracy* (1953) is the work of a dedicated Turnerian; it concerns the Ohio Valley. So also does Richard Wade's path-breaking *The Urban Frontier** (1959). Public land policies concern R. M. Robbins in *Our Landed Heritage** (1942) and M. J. Rohrbaugh in *The Land Office Business* (1968). Other works of value relating to western development include T. P. Abernethy, *The South in the New Nation* (1961); L. K. Mathews, *The Expansion of New England* (1919); L. D. Stilwell, *Migration from Vermont* (1937); R. C. Buley, *The Old Northwest* (2 vols., 1950); P. D. Jordan, *The National Road* (1948); Ronald Shaw, *Erie Waters West* (1966); L. C. Hunter, *Steamboats on Western Rivers* (1949); L. D. Baldwin, *The Keelboat Age on Western Waters* (1941); Carter Goodrich, *Government Promotion of American Canals and Railroads* (1960). Richard Slotkin regrets the influence of frontier mythology in *Regeneration through Violence* (1973).

The works on Marshall cited in the preceding chapter are relevant. In addition there are two good studies of Justice Story: G. T. Dunne, *Justice Joseph Story and the Rise of the Supreme Court* (1970) and James McClellan, *Joseph Story and the American Constitution* (1971).

State studies of great merit are also available. In a series concerned with the role of the state in economic development, Oscar and Mary Handlin's *Commonwealth: A Study of the Role of Government in the American Economy: Massachusetts, 1776–1861* (1947) and Louis Hartz's *Economic Policy and Democratic Thought: Pennsylvania, 1776–1861* (1948) are particularly valuable. D. R. Fox's *The Decline of Aristocracy in the Politics of New York** (1919) is a minor classic.

Outstanding among books on major political devel-

opments of the 1820s are Glover Moore, *The Missouri Controversy, 1819–1821** (1953), and Robert Remini, *Martin Van Buren and the Making of the Democratic Party* (1959) and *The Election of Andrew Jackson** (1963).

The best account of John Quincy Adams's diplomacy is S. F. Bemis's Pulitzer prize study, *John Quincy Adams and the Foundations of American Foreign Policy* (1949), but see also Bradford Perkins's *Castlereagh and Adams* (1964). P. C. Brooks's *Diplomacy and the Borderlands: The Adams-Otis Treaty of 1819* (1931) is the standard account of that episode. The classic study of the origins of the Monroe Doctrine is Dexter Perkins's *The Monroe Doctrine, 1823–1826* (1927). For a differing approach to the Monroe Doctrine see E. H. Tatum, Jr.'s *The United States and Europe, 1815–1823: A Study in the Background of the Monroe Doctrine* (1936). On the Latin American background see A. P. Whitaker's excellent *The United States and the Independence of Latin America, 1800–1830** (1941), as well as J. H. Powell's *Richard Rush: Republican Diplomat* (1942). Two other valuable studies are C. C. Griffin's *The United States and the Disruption of the Spanish Empire* (1937) and J. A. Logan, Jr.'s *No Transfer: An American Security Principle* (1961). Armin Rappaport has edited a useful anthology, *The Monroe Doctrine** (1964).

In addition to the studies of Adams, Clay, Calhoun, and Jackson cited in Chapter 7 and Ammon's *Monroe* (cited above), the best biographies for the period are G. M. Caper's *John C. Calhoun: Opportunist* (1960); M. L. Coit, *John C. Calhoun** (1950); C. M. Fuess, *Daniel Webster* (2 vols., 1930); R. N. Current, *Daniel Webster and the Rise of National Conservatism** (1955); J. T. Horton, *James Kent: A Study in Conservatism* (1939). *indicates availability in paperback.

9

Jacksonians and Whigs

For the throngs who crowded into Washington on March 4, 1829, Andrew Jackson's inaugural symbolized the final triumph of democracy. Jacksonians had characterized their assault on Adams and Clay as a contest between those who trusted and those who feared the common man; thus the masses interpreted Jackson's election as a victory of their own. Twenty thousand gathered at the Capitol to see their hero take the oath of office. Only when he had finished reading his inaugural address did they press forward to grasp the new President's hand. Before his well-wishers could surround him, Jackson retreated through the building to a waiting horse. Thousands followed him up Pennsylvania Avenue, and with muddy boots, pushing and shoving, they pursued the disappearing figure into the White House. Friends saved the general from being trampled to death by blocking the way while he escaped through the south door. They rescued the White House and its costly furnishings by placing tubs of punch on the lawn; there,

noisily but safely, gathered the masses who had come to celebrate, until they drifted away again to the farms and villages whence they had come. Conservatives who observed the antics of the crowd were incredulous. Margaret Bayard Smith recalled, "Ladies and gentlemen only had been expected at this levee, not the people en masse. But it was the People's day, the People's President and the People would rule."

Who was this man who had captured the imagination and support of the American people? Born of Scotch-Irish immigrant parents on the western Carolina frontier in 1767, young Jackson experienced the British invasion of the Carolina backcountry during the American Revolution. Following the war, he read law and was admitted to the North Carolina bar in 1787. The next year he moved to Nashville, Tennessee, where he soon emerged as a prosperous lawyer, farmer and slave owner, politician, and judge. Appointed a major general in the state militia in 1802, Jackson rose to a stormy national prominence. His victory over the British at New Orleans in January 1815 and his successful campaigns against the Indians made him a national hero and established his potential as a presidential candidate. Jackson—tall, erect, with lean, sharp features—was strong-willed, intolerant, and contentious. His hot temper and keen sense of personal honor drew him into numerous fights and brawls. He was a man of action, not a clear or deep thinker. In his inaugural address, he outlined his principles, but he failed to advance any specific program.

The New Administration

Jackson faced the necessity of welding his great following into an effective political force. Unlike Adams, Jackson was a majority president. But what was the majority will? Behind his election was no single program generally understood and accepted by party spokesmen. Instead, Jackson was trapped in a conflict of philosophies and personalities among the top men in his victorious coalition. Vice President John C. Calhoun, representing the extreme states' rights side of the Jeffersonian tradition, had argued his case in the *South Carolina Exposition* of 1828. The document's approval by the South Carolina Legislature had made it official state doctrine. Defying the "Tariff of Abominations," Calhoun had told the nation that no state need tolerate policies that enriched one section or class at the expense of another. Should the rights of a state be violated by a sectional majority in Congress, he warned, then that state, acting singly under the compact theory of government, might employ its sovereign power to nullify the law in question. Not since Jefferson's and Madison's Virginia and Kentucky Resolutions of 1798 had the states' rights position been so explicitly drawn. Thus Jackson began his administration under circumstances which presaged conflict with his own Vice President.

Calhoun's elimination as a key member of the administration came quickly, but not over the question of political philosophy. Shortly before Jackson's inaugural, Senator John H. Eaton of Tennessee, already designated Secretary of War, married Mrs. Margaret O'Neale Timberlake, the daughter of a Washington tavern keeper and widow of a Navy purser. The new Mrs. Eaton was reputedly a woman of extraordinary beauty and intelligence but also of questionable morals. For Floride Calhoun, Mrs. Eaton's presence in Washington society was intolerable. In pointedly snubbing Mrs. Eaton, she set a precedent followed by a number of Cabinet wives. Jackson became incensed at this treatment of Mrs. Eaton, whose maligning he associated with that suffered in the 1828 campaign by his own wife Rachel, now dead. When Calhoun sided with Floride, he opened a rift with Jackson that would never be healed.

Calhoun's rapid downfall opened for Martin Van Buren a broad avenue to power and influence. Jackson had revealed his debt to the New Yorker by making him Secretary of State, and Van Buren was no less determined than Calhoun to control the presidential succession. Van Buren's open defense of Mrs. Eaton won him the President's gratitude and esteem, and he pressed this early advantage to the fullest. Jackson, finding his Cabinet divided and worthless, turned increasingly to a group of unofficial advisers known as the "kitchen cabinet." Prominent in this group were Van Buren and editors Amos Kendall and Isaac Hill. Van Buren's prestige and power were further enhanced when the President assigned him the management of the federal patronage.

In 1829 the concept of "rotation in office" was not new. The practice of rewarding political friends with public offices had begun as early as Jefferson's presidency. But Jackson rationalized the spoils system as an agency of democracy. Rotation in office, with appointments going generally to members of the victorious party, would not only democratize the federal service but also render it more representative of the nation's citizenry. Too many federal offices, Jackson believed, had become mere family sinecures and havens for aristocrats. To him the federal government required no specially trained bureaucracy. "The duties of all public offices are . . . so plain and simple," he said, "that men of intelligence may readily qualify themselves for their performance." Thus encouraged, hundreds of deserving Democrats beseiged the White House to state their claims. Van Buren filled key positions with men of his own choice—usually politicians who had served the party well. This permitted him to strengthen both the national party organization and his own influence in that organization. Yet Jackson and Van Buren showed restraint. Under Jackson's presidency perhaps no more than 10 percent of the public offices changed hands. Nevertheless, federal patronage became for the first time an essential element in the creation and maintenance of a democratically based political party. Patronage, moreover, gave party leaders the power to enforce party discipline on important national issues.

Webster and Hayne

Jackson's first annual message of December 1829 disappointed the South, for the President failed to promise tariff reform. Southern leaders now turned to the West, offering that section a freer land policy in exchange for its support on tariff reduction. It was this incipient alliance between the South and West that frightened New England protectionists and set the stage for the celebrated Webster-Hayne debate of January 1830.

Senator Samuel A. Foot of Connecticut quite innocently opened the way for the debate when he offered the Senate, in December 1829, a resolution designed to restrict public lands sales to those lands already offered by the government at the minimum price of $1.25 an acre. Whatever Foot's motivation, the resolution, if accepted, would have curtailed Western growth. Senator Thomas Hart Benton of Missouri accused Foot of attempting to retard westward expansion and thus sustain a ready supply of cheap labor in the Eastern factory towns. Such bluntness was characteristic of the man. Born in North Carolina in 1782, this Missourian had moved as a young lawyer to Tennessee and then in 1815 to St. Louis. After his election to the United States Senate in 1820, he became a strong Jacksonian. In the Senate, Benton concerned himself with the interests of Western pioneers, favoring not

only preemption—the granting to squatters on public lands the first option to buy the lands they occupied—but also "graduation." As early as 1824 he proposed that the price of unsold government land be lowered 25 cents; after that, he proposed lowering the price even further.

Benton's reaction to the Foot resolution aroused Robert Y. Hayne of South Carolina, who now committed the South to the extremely liberal program of selling the public lands to the states in which they were located. Daniel Webster detected in this offer a special threat to his region, for neither free land nor tariff reduction would serve the interest of his industrialist constituents. Webster's only hope of alienating the West from the South lay in exposing the South's ideological peculiarities. Having gained the floor, Webster ignored the question of Western lands and instead pointed his attack at South Carolina and its doctrine of state sovereignty. Hayne, forced by sectional pride to reply, retreated to the theories of Calhoun, defending eventually the doctrine of nullification itself. His argument was simple and clear: ". . . though the States have surrendered certain specific powers, they have not surrendered their sovereignty."

Webster now had the opportunity for which he had been waiting—to tear down Calhoun's *South Carolina Exposition* point by point. His arguments were essentially those of John Marshall. Challenging the concept of state sovereignty, Webster charged that the people, not the states, were sovereign. Webster rolled on, hour after hour, in what was perhaps the greatest American oration on record, his deep, rich voice and well-turned phrases sometimes amusing and always delighting the packed galleries. For those who saw and heard the "Olympian," this was an experience to remember, for never before had the Senate been so thoroughly exposed to Webster's commanding presence and intellect.

The clarion appeal of Webster's second reply to Hayne—"Liberty *and* Union, now and forever, one and inseparable!"—resounded across the nation as it subsequently reverberated through American history. Van Buren found Webster's words pleasing, for the New Englander's theories, like his own, pointed not to minority rights, as Calhoun would have preferred, but to majority rule. Nor was Webster's nationalism displeasing to Jackson. Whatever the President's views toward states' rights, he never questioned the sovereignty of the federal Union. Not long after at a Jefferson Day Dinner, in the presence of Calhoun, his Vice President, Jackson threw out a direct challenge to the champion of states' rights. "Our Federal Union" he declared in a toast which left Calhoun shaken, "—it must be preserved." The South Carolinian, his hand trembling with emotion, responded in his turn: "The Union—next to our liberty most dear. May we always remember that it can only be preserved by distributing equally the benefits and the burthens of the Union." Both men had taken their stands: Jackson for the nation and majority rule; Calhoun for the Constitution and minority rights. The two would meet again.

Van Buren and Jackson

Van Buren's ultimate advantage over Calhoun lay not only in his superb relations with Jackson but even more in his genuine acceptance of the new democratic order. Whereas Calhoun looked to the checks and balances of the Constitution, placed there to protect minority rights, Van Buren accepted majority rule without qualification, with all its opportunities and dangers. Although Calhoun's assets as a political and intellectual figure were remarkable, his philosophy of government was entirely too sectional and particularistic to attract a sizable national or party following.

Jackson shared Van Buren's faith in democracy and hoped to follow policies which conformed to the popular will. By instinct a Jeffersonian, he was suspicious of the centralizing tendencies of the federal government. Yet he believed strongly that the federal government must be dominated by the President, the only official elected by *all* the people. A conservative in things economic, he entered the White House with an abiding fear of speculation. Having been driven into bankruptcy by his own early financial extravagances, he viewed the boom of 1819, based on easy credit. and the panic which followed, as a national expression of his own folly. As President, Jackson opposed measures that might encourage easy profits based on financial manipulation, speculation, and the use of credit. To that end he favored an economical government that would serve only the general interest. In his first annual message, he pledged the ultimate liquidation of the national debt.

Congress put Jackson and Van Buren to the test in April 1830, when it passed a bill authorizing the federal government to purchase stock in a Kentucky corporation designated to build a turnpike from Maysville to Lexington. Jackson's Western advisers urged him not to veto the bill, for the West favored internal improvements. Though the Maysville road lay within one state, it was part of a projected interstate system. But Van Buren argued against the measure, persuading the President that the time had come to terminate all federal aid to private corporations.

George Catlin painted the Plains Indians from life between 1830 and 1836, a time when much of the West was unknown and unexplored. Working in a huge area between the Mississippi and the Rocky Mountains, ranging from the northernmost United States to the Mexican Territory, he documented in pictures and words the leaders, ceremonies, and lifeways of most of the major tribes. In George Catlin and the Old Frontier, biographer Harold McCracken has written, "It can be said with justice and justification that no other artist or writer in the field of the North American Indian and the Old West has had as long and broad an influence as George Catlin."

George Catlin and the Indian Documents

Catlin's accomplishment grew not only from his skill and adventuresome tenacity but from his success in achieving rapport with his subjects and gaining their cooperation — a success which was the result of his real respect for the Indians and their way of life. "I love a people," he wrote, "who have always made me welcome with the best they had . . . who are honest without laws, who have no jails and no poor houses . . . who worship God without a Bible, and I believe that God loves them also . . . who are free of religious animosities . . . who have never raised a hand against me or stolen my property, where there was no law to punish either . . . and, oh! how I love a people who don't live for the love of money."

In his travels among some forty-eight tribes, Catlin did portraits of hundreds of chiefs, braves, women, and children. At Fort Pierre in South Dakota, where he painted Ha-Won-Je-Tah, The One Horn, First Chief of the Sioux (near left, below), he had to overcome objections of medicine men who feared their chief would not be able to sleep at night because he had been depicted with his eyes open. But Catlin's persuasiveness and the hitherto-unseen charm of realistic painting soon made it an honor to be painted, and his subjects sat for him in the order of their importance in the tribe. Others in this sampling include Stu-Mick-O-Sucks, The Buffalo's Back Fat, Head Chief of the Blackfeet (right), and Osceola (far left, below), whom Catlin painted after the great Seminole leader had been imprisoned.

All portraits courtesy of Smithsonian Institution

While Catlin deliberately sought to record the lives of tribes which had been little touched by the white man, he was also bitterly aware of the harm the white man was doing to the Indian. From the Southeast the Choctaw, Chickasaw, Creeks, Cherokees, and Seminoles were driven west of the Mississippi into Oklahoma "territory" along a "Trail of Tears." The Sauk were driven from their villages in Illinois despite a futile war led by Black Hawk, whose portrait by Catlin is shown at right, above. The print directly above, not by Catlin, shows the Sauk being fired upon as they attempted to return to their homes. At right, below, are Catlin's two views of Wi-Jun-Jon, Pigeon's Egg Head, son of an Assiniboin chief, before and after he went to Washington to meet President Jackson. Catlin learned that after his return Wi-Jun-Jon's description of the East was so unbelievable to the tribe and his conduct so unbecoming that he was considered a liar and a disgrace and eventually was killed.

Catlin's emotions at what he saw happening are reflected in his writing about the Indian: "I have seen him set fire to his wigwam and smooth over the graves of his fathers . . . with tears of grief sliding over his cheeks, clap his hand in silence over his mouth, and take the last look over his fair hunting grounds. . . . I have seen this splendid juggernaut rolling on and beheld its sweeping desolation, and held converse with happy thousands living as yet beyond its influence, who have not yet been crushed, nor yet have dreamed of its approach. . . . I have stood amidst these unsophisticated people and contemplated with feelings of deepest regret the certain approach of this overwhelming system, which will inevitably march on and prosper, until reluctant tears have watered every rod of this fair land."

Above and below: Courtesy of Smithsonian Institution

Jackson's veto message not only denounced the Maysville road project as too local in nature but also questioned the constitutionality of all public programs at federal expense. The veto message, though a lasting triumph for Van Buren, began a process of alienation which gradually drove Jackson's Western advisers out of his inner circle.

Eventually the President decided to end the factionalism within his administration. In 1831 he persuaded his entire Cabinet to resign, thus removing the Calhounites. The President then sent Van Buren to London as United States Minister and Eaton to Madrid, where Mrs. Eaton scored a series of new personal triumphs. The President built his new Cabinet around Edward Livingston of Louisiana as Secretary of State, Lewis Cass of Michigan as Secretary of War, and Roger B. Taney of Maryland as Attorney General. Calhoun, embittered by this turn of events, now sought revenge. His moment came in January 1832, when, as presiding officer of the Senate, he cast the deciding vote against Van Buren's nomination to London. But when Calhoun boasted that he had finally disposed of his rival, Benton retorted, "You have broken a minister, and elected a Vice President." Van Buren, already in London for five months, returned to the United States in June 1832 to enter that year's canvass as Jackson's running mate. Calhoun resigned the vice presidency. Elected to the Senate by a compliant South Carolina Legislature, he was back in Washington in December to defend the interests of the South against any further assault from Congress or the administration.

Indian Removal

For the moment a further clash between Jackson and Calhoun appeared remote, for Jackson, in defending Georgia's rights to its Indian lands, assumed an extreme states' rights position. In 1827, the year that the Creeks ceded their Georgia lands, the highly civilized Cherokees signaled their defiance by adopting a constitution declaring themselves to be an independent, sovereign nation. A year later, when the discovery of gold in the Cherokee nation brought an influx of miners, the Georgia Legislature responded by making all whites in the Cherokee Territory subject to the laws of the state and warned that after June 1, 1830, all Cherokee laws would be considered void. Chief Justice Marshall, in a case brought by a missionary (*Worcester v. Georgia*), upheld the Cherokee laws, but the administration ignored the decision. Jackson had no interest in defending Cherokees. Georgia went on unhindered to annihilate the Cherokee political structure and deprive the Indians of their lands. The Indians held out a few years longer, but by 1838 the great majority had moved to Indian Territory west of the Mississippi.

During Jackson's presidency, population pressures along the Mississippi Valley frontier produced dozens of treaties whereby the Indians were compelled to cede their lands and join the westward trek to designated areas across the Mississippi. The "trail of tears" proved to be costly for all these tribes in loss of life and property. The Chickasaws and Choctaws agreed to leave their tribal homes in Alabama and Mississippi and join the Creeks and Cherokees in Indian Territory. The Florida Seminoles were far less amenable. Several chiefs signed a treaty in 1832 which sent some tribesmen to the West. Chief Osceola resisted, however, and, aided by the fastness of the Everglades, chopped up and eluded United States military forces sent against him. When captured in 1842 he had cost the nation millions of dollars. Even then, several thousand of his fellow Seminoles refused to leave the Everglades and continued to reside there.

The effort at Indian removal produced another tragic episode in the story of Chief Black Hawk of the Sauk and Fox. Black Hawk's people

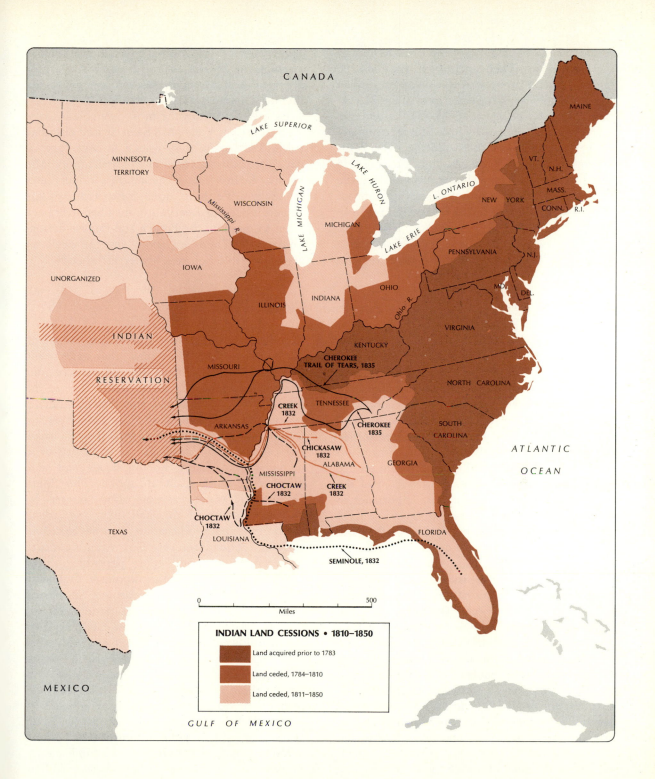

CANADA

LAKE SUPERIOR

MINNESOTA
TERRITORY

WISCONSIN

LAKE MICHIGAN

MICHIGAN

LAKE HURON

L. ONTARIO

MAINE

VT.

N.H.

MASS.

CONN.   R.I.

NEW YORK

LAKE ERIE

PENNSYLVANIA

N.J.

IOWA

UNORGANIZED

INDIAN

RESERVATION

ILLINOIS

INDIANA

OHIO

MD.   DEL.

Ohio R.

VIRGINIA

MISSOURI

KENTUCKY

CHEROKEE
TRAIL OF TEARS, 1835

TENNESSEE

NORTH CAROLINA

ARKANSAS

CREEK
1832

CHEROKEE
1835

SOUTH
CAROLINA

CHICKASAW
1832
ALABAMA

GEORGIA

MISSISSIPPI

CHOCTAW
1832

CREEK
1832

ATLANTIC

OCEAN

CHOCTAW
1832

LOUISIANA

FLORIDA

TEXAS

SEMINOLE, 1832

Mississippi R.

0   500

Miles

INDIAN LAND CESSIONS • 1810–1850

Land acquired prior to 1783

Land ceded, 1784–1810

Land ceded, 1811–1850

MEXICO

GULF OF MEXICO

JACKSONIANS AND WHIGS

[247]

resided at the confluence of the Rock River and the Mississippi. When squatters in 1831 entered the region and proceeded to tear up the Indian crops, Black Hawk retreated across the Mississippi, only to be harassed by famine and the more warlike Sioux. Driven by desperation and hunger, Black Hawk recrossed the river to his original home in Illinois. So long had the Old Northwest been free of Indian troubles that the presence of this destitute and starving band of Indians sent waves of terror across Illinois, Indiana, and even Michigan Territory. The Illinois militia converged on Black Hawk's straggling villagers, following them up the Rock River into the wilderness of southern Wisconsin. Finally catching the Indians as they attempted to escape across the Mississippi, the troops massacred them, including women and children.

By the midthirties the most desirable lands of the Mississippi Valley had been cleared of Indian titles. Tribesmen now resided in new "permanent" homes beyond the Mississippi. John Quincy Adams judged the nation's Indian policy in 1837: "We have done more harm to the Indians since our Revolution than had ever been done to them by the French and English nations before. . . . These are crying sins for which we are answerable before a higher jurisdiction."

The Tariff and Nullification

If Jackson refused to face Georgia on the question of Indian rights, he did not hesitate to oppose South Carolina on the issue of nullification. This time it was ostensibly the tariff that led to the clash between Jackson's nationalism and Calhoun's doctrine of state sovereignty. Jackson's second Cabinet had no more interest than the first in tariff reform. Any sharp downward revision of the high tariff of 1828 would reduce federal revenues and delay the payment of the national debt, a matter of utmost importance to Jackson. Van Buren hoped to avoid a tariff debate, fearing it would break the North-South alliance which he wished to maintain. But South Carolina was impatient and would tolerate no further delay. That state, traditionally one of the most prosperous of the nation, had never fully recovered from the Panic of 1819. In South Carolina's interest Calhoun had deserted Clay's old assertion that the tariff served all sections and economic interests equally. By raising the price of manufactured products artificially, the tariff placed the South at an economic disadvantage in its quest for profits. By the twenties, the South generally had fallen behind the North in wealth, population, immigration, and productivity; and the fact that the South Carolina planter aristocracy had been one of the South's richest and proudest made that state's economic decline all the harder to bear. More than other states of the South, South Carolina attributed its economic problems to federal policies rather than to the general weaknesses in the Southern economy.

Still, depression and tariff alone cannot explain the unreasoning fear of federal power which possessed South Carolina's tidewater aristocracy, that remarkably homogeneous and able group for which Calhoun spoke. The South Carolina tidewater was not cotton country. Its two chief crops of rice and luxury sea island cotton enjoyed good markets and never ceased to bring adequate returns. This region's concern centered on a second, more pervading, threat from the North—that of abolitionism. Only with slave labor could the planters around Charleston wrest profits from their disease-ridden swamps. The Northern preachments on racial equality which followed the Missouri debates, limited as they were, exceeded what hard-pressed South Carolinians would tolerate. Charleston had witnessed the effects of such doctrine in the well-planned revolt of 1822, conceived and led by Denmark Vesey, a free black of the city. This revolt was crushed without disaster only because a black conspirator, indebted to a kind master, revealed the plot. Nat Turner's black rebellion of 1831 never crossed the boundaries of Virginia, but again it sent waves of fear through the Carolina tidewater. Even as South Carolinians battled the tariff of 1827, the American Colonization Society requested federal funds to aid it in exporting to Africa those blacks who desired to go. Congress quickly tabled the petition, but the mere existence of the request demonstrated the full vulnerability of the South to federal power. Calhoun's *South Carolina Exposition* of 1828 responded to this Southern fear of Northern power and hostility toward slavery.

Clay unwittingly forced the nullification issue on South Carolina in July 1832, when he drove a new tariff measure through Congress. This bill, passed with the aid of Southern as well as Western votes, eliminated the worst excesses of the Tariff of Abominations, but it maintained high schedules on iron and textiles and revealed a strong protariff consensus in the Congress. Even a number of representatives from South Carolina voted for the measure. For the nullifiers, however, the tariff of 1832 was a direct challenge. Led by Calhoun, they carried the elections that fall and called a state convention in late November, which declared the tariff law to be "null, void, and no law, nor binding upon the State, its officers or citizens." The ordinance further forbade federal officials to collect customs within the state after February 1, 1833, and threatened secession if the federal government chose to employ force.

Jackson met the nullification issue head on. His famous proclamation to the people of South Carolina, stern, yet kind, revealed Jackson's frontier nationalism at its best. The doctrine that a state could nullify a law of Congress that it did not like, he said, defied the letter and spirit of the Constitution and was incompatible with the existence of the Union. The President appealed to the doctrines of Marshall and Webster:

> The Constitution of the United States, then, forms a *government*, not a league; and whether it be formed by compact between the States or in any other manner, its character is the same. . . . Because the Union was formed by a compact, it is

said the parties of the compact may, when they feel themselves aggrieved, depart from it; but it is precisely because it is a compact that they can not. A compact is an agreement or binding obligation.

No state, declared Jackson, had the right to secede. The federal government had the authority not only to pass laws but also to enforce them.

Jackson's warning merely exacerbated the crisis. The South Carolina Legislature called for volunteers to defend the state even as Jackson prepared to dispatch an army to Charleston to collect the customs. Fortunately for both sides in the quarrel, the overwhelming majority of Americans favored peace and drove the extremists into isolation. Not one state answered South Carolina's call for a national convention or supported its doctrine of nullification. Jackson's nationalism had clearly captured the nation's sentiment.

Henry Clay, ever the great conciliator, accepted the responsibility for bringing the crisis to an end. Jackson himself had recommended tariff reform, suggesting in his December message to Congress that protection be "limited to those articles of domestic manufacture which are indispensable to our safety in time of war." Clay, working with Calhoun, now seized the issue and secured a compromise measure designed to reduce all tariffs over a ten-year period to a uniform level of 20 percent. This satisfied the nullifiers, who, after all, had centered their attack on the previous tariff. Meanwhile, Jackson asked Congress for a measure that would fully authorize him to use the land and naval forces of the United States to compel states to comply with federal law. Late in the session Congress passed both the tariff and the Force Bill. On March 2, 1833, as his first term ended, Jackson signed both measures into law. South Carolina's reassembled convention, in repealing its nullification measure, accepted the compromise tariff but threw down another meaningless challenge to Jackson by nullifying the Force Act. The nullifiers had demonstrated that a single determined state could alter national policy; they had demanded tariff reform and achieved it. Jackson, however, had demonstrated that no state could defy federal authority without facing the country's military power. This was the essential lesson which the crisis had taught, though it was clear from the nullifiers' boasts of victory that they had not learned it.

The Bank War

These battles were merely prelude to that struggle which above all others illustrated the philosophical inconsistency in Jacksonian Democracy—Jackson's war on the Second Bank of the United States. Except for Clay, the issue might have remained dormant, at least until 1836, when the Bank's charter would expire. But Clay, nominated for the presidency by the National Republican party in December 1831, believed that he could force the issue on the Democratic party and turn it into a winning cause. The President, Clay assumed, could not sign or veto a measure to recharter the Bank without alienating powerful factions in the Democratic party.

Two major strains in Jacksonian thought opposed the Bank—agrarian and democratic. The agrarians feared banks generally because of their role in speculation. They opposed the Bank of the United States especially because it wielded almost absolute control over the nation's credit structure. For the urban-centered democratic radicals the issue at stake was social and economic democracy. The Bank, as a public corporation, symbolized the power and advantage of the nonproducing classes over the farmers and laborers who created wealth with their hands. The collapse of the credit and paper money system in 1819 had convinced such men as Thomas Hart Benton that the government should restrict itself to hard money, dealing only with gold and silver. In this spirit, a group of Philadelphia workingmen in 1829 blamed their hard times on the "too great extension of paper credit." Their committee reported that banking and paper money created the foundation for an artificial inequality of wealth. Such views spread rapidly through the Eastern cities, giving rise to new organizations which favored hard money. One was the radical faction of the Democratic party in

New York—the "Locofocos." Distrustful of bank notes, hard money advocates demanded that the federal government reduce all circulating medium to gold and silver and require deposit banks to stop issuing and receiving notes.

That the Bank of the United States was a powerful institution no one would deny, least of all its able president, Nicholas Biddle. After assuming his duties in 1823, Biddle had used his Bank's authority to restrain state banks in their extension of credit, thereby strengthening the nation's banking and currency structure. Nonetheless, this regulatory power, however judiciously applied, was the Bank's undoing. Returning prosperity, feeding on a new burst of Western expansion, had created a new, aggressive, entrepreneurial class. The older economic order rested on wealth—accumulated chiefly from commerce—which its owners could invest in new enterprises. In the age of Jackson the older reliance on accumulation was too slow and limited. For the new investors, the key to success was credit; and the looser the restrictions on state banks, the greater their power to extend it. Although credit expansion could lead to inflation and eventual collapse, it could also build fortunes and develop communities. For new-breed enterprisers, claiming also to be Jacksonians, the chief barrier to easy credit was the Bank of the United States, citadel of the nation's traditional, conservative business, representing established rather than speculative wealth.

Overwhelmingly, Jacksonian anti-Bank warriors were the spokesmen of the new enterprise, but their phraseology was that of agrarians and workingmen. They accused the Bank of tyranny and oppression; they identified it with special privilege and monopoly. In their praise of honest work, they identified themselves with the urban and rural lower classes, although, as rising capitalists representing the new enterprise, they pursued wealth and economic power as much as the Bank men did. Whatever their claims to class interest, these Jacksonians were no more concerned with human rights than were the Bank's defenders.

Biddle, conscious of the wide support which the Bank of the United States enjoyed among conservatives generally, including such old Jeffersonians as Madison and Gallatin, received his initial shock when Jackson questioned the Bank's constitutionality in his first annual message of December 1829. Then as pressure against the Bank slowly accumulated, Benton, in February 1831, launched a vigorous attack on the Bank, based on class antagonism. The Bank, he said, was too powerful to be tolerated by a government of free and equal laws. "It tends," he charged, "to aggravate the inequality of fortunes, to make the rich richer, and the poor poorer; to multiply nabobs and paupers." As the Jackson press took up the cry, Biddle went to Clay and Webster for support. Still hoping to avoid a political debate over the Bank's merits, Biddle took confidence from Jackson's refusal to attack the Bank in his annual message of December 1831. But Clay, distrustful of Jackson and Van Buren, decided to take charge of the issue by introducing recharter petitions in both houses of Congress during January 1832. Biddle had no choice but to support Clay's action.

The pro-Bank forces easily pushed the recharter bill through Congress, but they reckoned without the President's veto. On July 10, 1832, Jackson declared the Bank unconstitutional, unnecessary, and dangerous to liberty. Favorable Supreme Court decisions, he said, did not establish the Bank's constitutionality. Whether the Bank was *necessary* and *proper* under the enumerated powers of the federal government was a matter for Congress and the President—not the Supreme Court—to decide. Jackson found it neither necessary nor proper. The Bank conferred exclusive privileges upon a small minority of the American people in the realm of banking and finance. The benefits derived from this powerful monopoly and the rising value of its stock accrued not to the millions of Americans whose money backed its credit structure but to the stockholders. To Jackson the Bank was a monster, manipulating paper money and credit so as to bring artificial and ill-gotten wealth to its managers, supporters, and beneficiaries.

Jackson's Reelection

Unable to carry the recharter bill over the President's veto, the Bank men took the issue into the election of 1832. Clay, nominee of what had become known as the National Republican party, campaigned mainly on the Bank question. Jackson was pleased to run with Van Buren as the people's champion against the "monster" Bank. For the first time in American history, both leading candidates received the endorsement of popular national conventions, a practice in keeping with the growing democratic tendencies of the time. This contest witnessed, as well, the broader use of new campaign techniques such as political cartoons and parades.

Another novel feature of the election of 1832 was the appearance of the Anti-Masonic party, the first "third" party to run a candidate in an American presidential election. This party emerged in 1826 when the body of a New York bricklayer named Morgan, who had divulged the secrets of his lodge, was discovered floating on the Niagara River. The resulting Anti-Masonic movement, led by such notable New York political figures as William H. Seward and Thurlow Weed, elected a number of local officials. The party never extended much beyond New York and New England. In 1831 its national convention nominated William Wirt for the presidency. Jackson swept the November election. He carried more popular votes than Clay and Wirt combined, and enjoyed a large majority in the electoral college—Jackson, 219; Clay, 49; and Wirt, 7. Clay's attempt to win the presidency on the Bank issue had proved a miserable failure.

Death of the Bank

Encouraged by his resounding victory, Jackson moved to kill the Bank before Biddle could organize his vast economic and political resources to push yet another recharter bill through Congress. The Bank remained the darling of the National Republican party, many leading businessmen, and much of the press. With the reduction of the national debt to the point of extinction, federal receipts, symptomatic of a booming economy, piled up in the vaults of the Bank and further extended its power to lend and thus control the nation's money market. Jackson planned to cripple the Bank by depriving it of the government deposits, but conservative members of the Cabinet refused to support this policy. Finally the exasperated Jackson named Attorney General Taney, who shared his anti-Bank views, to the Treasury. In September 1833, the President announced that thereafter the federal government would deposit its funds in selected state banks (named "pet banks" by Jackson's enemies).

Jackson's direct assault on the Bank provided Biddle with the excuse he needed to bring renewed pressure on Congress. Using the removal of federal funds as justification for a general contraction of the Bank's credit structure, Biddle soon produced bankruptcies and general economic decline across the nation. Petitions poured into Congress, demanding either restoration of the deposits or immediate recharter of the Bank. Jackson held firm. Meanwhile, Biddle overreached himself. To destroy Jackson, he had contracted credit more rapidly than the President's decision warranted, injuring many of his own political sympathizers in the process. After Congress adjourned in 1834, friends of the Bank forced Biddle to relax the Bank's credit. Business responded quickly, demonstrating that the Bank, in its ability to manipulate the na-

tion's currency, had even more economic power than its enemies charged. With the expiration of its federal charter in 1836, Biddle secured a new one from the state of Pennsylvania. The Bank continued to exist as a state bank until shattered in the Panic of 1837.

With the Bank's decline, the anti-Bank forces revealed their fundamental disagreements. The agrarians, as well as urban radicals, attached their continuing assault on the rich and powerful to a hard money policy. But their program had no chance against the unparalleled speculation of the mid-thirties, now no longer restrained by the Bank's stabilizing influence. State banks, old and new, flooded the country with bank notes and credit. Even the deposit banks were caught up in the inflationary spiral which mounted relentlessly to its crest in 1836. Hard money men looked on aghast, while Jacksonian enterprisers who had joined them in killing the Bank wallowed in the profits of the credit system.

Henry Clay subjected the country's financial health to further hazards when he pushed a "distributing" or "deposit" bill through Congress. By January 1835, Jackson had achieved one of the major objectives of his administration—payment of the national debt—and thereafter federal surpluses continued to mount. Clay wanted to distribute a large portion of this money to the states, where it could be used to finance internal improvements. His deposit bill, passed in 1836, was a partial triumph for his American System. Altogether, beginning early in 1837, the United States government distributed some $37 million in federal money to state treasuries. Lavish state spending now broadened the nation's speculative base.

Alarmed by the runaway inflation, especially evident in the selling prices of Western lands, Jackson in July 1836 issued through his Secretary

Andrew Jackson: The Man and the Legend

Courtesy of the New-York Historical Society, New York City

"The most roaring, rollicking, game-cocking, horse-racing, card-playing, mischievious fellow . . . the head of rowdies hereabouts . . ." in his youth, Andrew Jackson's origins contained all the ingredients of what had not then but would later become a native American "success story." Born in the Carolina hills, defiant prisoner of the British at thirteen, Jackson studied law, and at twenty-one went adventuring in Tennessee as public prosecutor. A career as Representative and then Senator from Tennessee followed quickly—he appeared in Washington with his hair in "a queue down his back tied with an old eel skin." Then his state appointed him judge of the superior court, and he returned home temporarily. But it was as an indomitable fighter, scourge of Indians and the British, "Old Hickory," that Jackson's image acquired its ultimate rough-hewn grandeur, and it is as a romanticized, but superheroic commanding general that Asher Durand, after a work by John Vanderlyn, painted this portrait in 1828, the year Jackson became President.

Jackson's often harsh militancy did not go entirely uncriticized. During the campaign of 1828, charges and counter-charges—some substantiated, most not—flew between Jackson and Adams partisans. Below, the "coffin handbill," widely circulated during the election year, condemns Jackson for ordering the execution of six militiamen accused of mutiny in 1815. At the left, Jackson raises his sword to strike off the ears of a dissenting Congressman. The unidentified man that Jackson hangs below could well be Everyman: the caption warns that if Jackson is elected, "you will be HANGED." Popular sentiments like those expressed at the right, however, won the day.

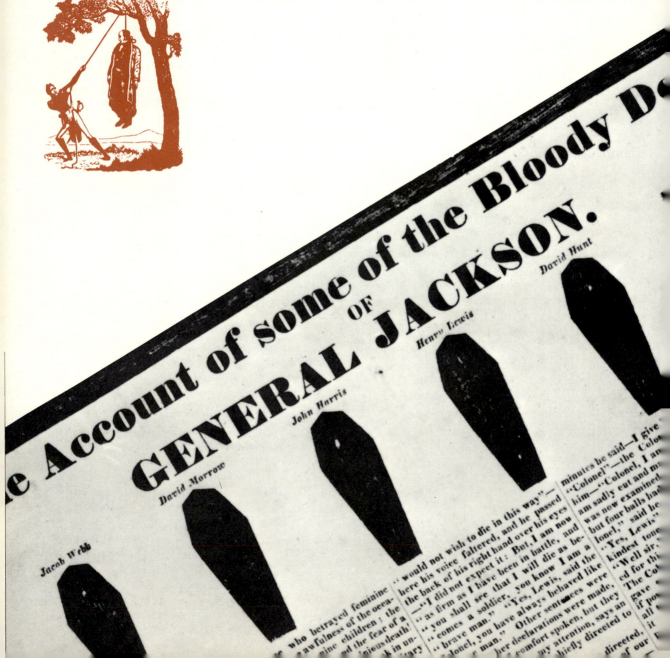

e Account of some of the Bloody De
OF
GENERAL JACKSON.

Jacob Webb   David Morrow   John Harris   Henry Lewis   David Hunt

Jackson Forever!

The Hero of Two Wars and of Orleans

The Man of the People!

HE WHO COULD NOT BARTER NOR BARGAIN FOR THE

PRESIDENCY!

although " *A Military Chieftain*," valued the purity of Elections and of ...s, MORE than the Office of PRESIDENT itself! Although the gre... ...ift of ...s countrymen, and the highest in point of dignity of any in the w...

BECAUSE

It should be derived from the

PEOPLE!

...Law...! No Black Cockades! No Reign of Terror! No Standing A... ...Navy Officers, when under the pay of Government, to browbeat, or

KNOCK DOWN

...olutionary Characters ... our Representatives while in the discharg... ...their dut...? To the Polls then, and vote for those who will support

OLD HICKORY

All pictures: Courtesy of the New-York Historical Society, New York City

AND THE ELECTORAL LAW.

Jackson roundly defeated John Quincy Adams (left) in 1828, after gaining more popular votes but losing the 1824 election to him in the House.

John C. Calhoun (right) fought Jackson most bitterly over the issue of states' rights.

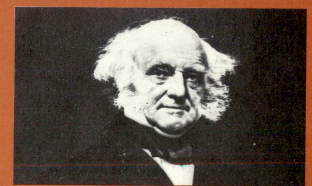

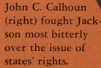

A strong administrator, Jackson found himself surrounded by unusually capable, if not always agreeable, statesmen. The architect of Jackson's campaign, Martin Van Buren (right) served as Secretary of State and succeeded Jackson as President. The ambitious Henry Clay (right, below) often clashed with the chief executive, as did Daniel Webster (below), who, however, joined Jackson in arguing against nullification.

This early daguerrotype was taken in 1844, a year before Jackson's death. All the photographs here necessarily present their subjects in their later years.

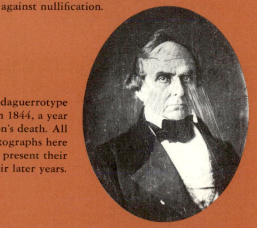

Personal scandals marred both Jackson's rise to political power and his presidency. Tongues wagged continuously over both his wife, Rachel, above, and Peggy Eaton. Mrs. Jackson had supposedly not been divorced when Jackson married her, a circumstance still remembered upon her death one month after his presidential election. Calhoun's wife, Floride, led the gossip about Peggy Timberlake, who married Jackson's Secretary of War, John Eaton, at the President's urging only after reputedly bearing Eaton two children. Jackson defended the Eatons and even called a Cabinet meeting to discuss Peggy's vindication. Still, Washington remained outraged.

The satirical Robert Cruikshank drawing at the right, "The President's Levee, or All Creation Going to the White House," appeared in England in 1841. Jackson never escaped mockery in his role as "the people's President."

Robert Cruikshank fec.

of the Treasury the famous Specie Circular, specifying that henceforth all public lands be paid for in specie, or in notes redeemable in specie. Since state banks did not have specie to loan, this order greatly reduced the credit available and curtailed land sales. But Jackson's action came too late. The uncontrolled speculation, encouraged by the banking policies of the middle thirties, contributed heavily to the Panic of 1837. The American people had paid a heavy price for Jackson's destruction of the Bank of the United States.

Politics and the Election of 1836

Jackson's reelection in 1832 had demonstrated the remarkable success of his party managers in building a political machine to exploit the sentiments of an egalitarian society. All actions of the Democratic party were aimed at the voters, and none more so than the Bank veto message itself. Its language was designed to influence, not Congress, but the people—to win support outside of Congress by arousing bitter emotions against Bank supporters. Behind the veto message were Jackson's personal advisers who cared little for constitutional arguments but recognized the essential fact that a democratic system placed political power in the masses, not the classes. Such key Democrats in Washington as Amos Kendall and Martin Van Buren were effective simply because they understood the necessary role of the electorate in a democratic society. Organization, not individual talent, was the key to Jacksonian politics, for it elevated the function of politics above the individual. The Jacksonians saw correctly that an organization built on specialization and interchangeability would be more effective than one based on unique, or even superb, talent.

Jackson's opponents recognized this trend toward impersonality and large-scale organization in the Democratic party. In their experience it had been men, not organization, that mattered. Great men, acting as individuals, had given the Republic its early leadership and direction; superior men, Jackson's opponents believed, must continue to govern it. The Bank of the United States embodied their idea of elite leadership. Jackson's veto message disturbed them, not because the President had exceeded his authority, but because he had ignored Congress and aimed his words at the electorate. As Webster complained in his reply: "The message toils through all the commonplace topics of monopoly, the right of taxation, the suffering of the poor, the arrogance of the rich, with as much painful effort, as if one, or another, or all of them, had something to do with the constitutional questions." For men like Webster and Biddle, Jackson, by appealing to lower-class prejudices, had broken tradition, debauched common sense, and endangered the natural social order.

Using the charge of "executive usurpation," Jackson's enemies attempted to build an alliance against him to defeat him and his adherents. The new Whig party, built largely around the old National Republicans, accepted Clay's American System as its creed. In 1834 it had carried a censure of Jackson through the Senate. Unable to agree on a candidate in 1836, the Whigs named three sectional favorites, hoping to split the electoral vote and deprive the Jacksonians of a majority in the electoral college, and then perhaps win the election in the House of Representatives. In the Southwest, they made a powerful bid for the conservative Democratic vote by naming Judge Hugh Lawson White, the popular Tennessee senator and onetime Jackson supporter who had joined the rebellion against Jackson's Bank policies. In the North the Whigs relied chiefly on aged General William Henry Harrison, the hero of Tippecanoe, although Webster was their man in Massachusetts.

Van Buren was the choice of the Democrats; Richard M. Johnson of Kentucky gained the second spot. The successor to the "throne" of the Democrats' "King Andrew" won easily in the November presidential sweepstakes, despite bitter denunciation from the Whigs. White carried Tennessee; Webster took Massachusetts, but only by a very narrow margin; Harrison revealed surprising strength, carrying seven states. But the three Whigs in aggregate received only 124 electoral votes, compared with 170 for Van Buren.

What for Americans was the significance of the Jacksonian triumph? Was Jacksonian Democracy what it claimed to be—a great crusade against privilege conducted in behalf of the poor? The very successes of the Democratic party, it would appear, required nothing less than a consistent program, clearly conceived, that served the needs of its mass constituency. Basing their appeal on emotion, the Jacksonians drew sharp contrasts between the virtues of equality, honesty, frugality, and hard work—which they allegedly represented—and the vices of corruption, plutocracy, privilege, inequality, and indebtedness, which they attributed to the Second National Bank. But the Jacksonian appeal, anchored to the notion of class conflict, was always divorced from action. Jacksonian policies created no more class feeling among the broad middle ranks of American society than did the programs set forth by the Whigs. The Bank's destruction demoralized the aristocrats; it eliminated the brakes on inflation; and it stimulated the new, speculative enterprise. It contributed nothing to the urban masses, the farmers, and the frontiersmen. New York's Democratic politicians and its Wall Street bankers emerged from the Bank war as the only certain victors.

Whigs and Democrats

More than the party of Jackson, the Whigs perpetuated both the Jeffersonian emphasis on gentility and the Hamiltonian faith in federal supremacy and power. Fundamentally the Whig party was composed of former National Republicans—the followers of Adams and Clay. But another significant element in the Whig coalition was the Anti-Masons, whose program of the early thirties had been hardly distinguishable from that of the National Republicans. Henry Clay and Daniel Webster were both recognized leaders of the party, although even Webster's New England friends granted the party's titular headship to the popular and remarkable Clay.

In Northern states, the Whig party encompassed much of the talent, wealth, and business experience of the large and growing cities. The Democratic party attracted the support of the small farmers, workingmen, and disadvantaged. But these groups were only the extremes of the political spectrum. Neither party found its essential support and leadership among these elements but among the great middle and lower-middle classes. Here was waged the real struggle for power. The same socioeconomic groups which provided leadership for the Whig party did so for the Democratic party as well. Democratic leaders were little less wealthy than their Whig opponents; often they were the more ambitious and avowedly materialistic enterprisers. Not even the rank and file of party supporters divided markedly along income lines. Conservatives who feared a mass electorate discovered that the masses had property interests of their own and that they harbored hopes and ambitions which scarcely separated them in outlook from men of wealth. Such attitudes reflected the realities of existence in a rapidly expanding nation where opportunities for profit were widespread. It was not strange that the two parties, forced to appeal in large measure to the same socioeconomic groups, differed little in programs, techniques, and even rhetoric.

In both North and South, the balance of party strength was exceedingly precarious. Only in New England was one party, the Whig, clearly dominant. In the pivotal Middle Atlantic states, combined returns from 1832 to 1852 gave the Democrats a plurality of less than 1 percent; yet New York and Pennsylvania went Whig in 1840 and again in 1848 and brought victories to the only two Whigs elected to the White House. The Northwest became a predominantly Democratic region after 1840, but the Whigs retained strongholds in the commercial centers bordering the Great Lakes and the Ohio. The South as a whole cast over three million votes in the elections of 1836, 1840, 1844, and 1848. The overall Whig majority in the four elections was 66,000 votes, or slightly more than 2 percent of the total. In the South Atlantic states, Democrats predominated. In Virginia and Georgia the Democratic party was strong in the western districts, the Whigs in the tidewater. In the Carolinas, the backcountry tended to be Whig; the tidewater, Democratic. The south central area, which furnished much of the nation's leadership, was evenly balanced. Kentucky and Tennessee were bulwarks of the Whig party, whereas the Gulf states were normally Democratic. Across the Mississippi in Louisiana, Arkansas, and Missouri, the rich planting areas along the Mississippi, Arkansas, and Missouri Rivers were Whig; the backcountry tended to be Democratic.

The chief areas of Southern Whig strength coincided with the districts occupied by the great planters, but the ties that bound the Whig party together were urban. Here, as in the North, the core of Whig power and influence lay in the merchant class with its allies—bankers, lawyers, and editors. If the leading planters, especially outside South Carolina, were Whig, it was not primarily because of their wealth but because of their community of interest with the merchants and their need for banking and transportation facilities. The Southern cities were not large, but they were influential and the only mercantile centers the South possessed. Most Southern Whigs who sat in Congress were not planters; they were lawyers aligned with business interests. All Whig issues other than internal improvements enjoyed considerable popularity in the South. For the sugar planters of Louisiana, the hemp growers of Kentucky, and the iron manufacturers of Virginia and Maryland, it was the tariff that mattered. For Southern men of wealth generally, the Whig party's opposition to Jacksonian radicalism appeared to be a source of genuine security. Southern bankers, merchants, industrialists, lawyers, and planters thus had their own party, which competed successfully in the South with the Jacksonians.

The Van Buren Presidency

Unlike his seven predecessors in the White House, Van Buren enjoyed no reputation earned in diplomacy or war. His career had been one of politics, but so uncanny was his ability to turn every opportunity into personal advancement that his friends referred to him as "the Little Magician." Emerging victorious from every conflict of Jackson's early presidency to become Vice President in 1833, he no longer faced any opposition in 1836 as heir to the Democratic party leadership. Van Buren's popularity among party chieftains was axiomatic; such shrewdness and perspicacity would serve him well in the White House. Unwilling to create any sharp break with

the Jacksonian past, Van Buren retained John Forsyth as secretary of state; placed Joel Poinsett, another Jacksonian, in the War Department; and reserved the postmastership for Amos Kendall, the amazingly artful manager of Jackson's "kitchen cabinet."

As early as February 1837, Thomas Hart Benton had warned the incoming President that the nation had reached the verge of financial collapse. *"You will soon feel the thunderbolt,"* he predicted. Yet Van Buren entered the White House still preferring to ignore the signs of the times. Unfortunately for the new administration, prophets of doom had ample evidence. Bankers had extended credit far beyond the nation's specie supply. Land purchases, as well as road and canal construction, had become increasingly speculative, outstripping the needs of existent markets at home and abroad. Late in 1836 a succession of British bankruptcies forced these companies to throw their American securities on the market, thus increasing the flow of specie across the Atlantic. It required but a few major business failures in the United States during the spring of 1837 to reveal the gap between paper credits and hard money. During May, New York banks stopped all specie payments; soon banks across the nation followed that city's example. By fall depression stalked the land. Land prices collapsed; markets evaporated.

For the next several years, the United States endured one of its worst depressions. Thousands of unemployed tramped the streets of Northern towns and cities looking in vain for work; canal and road building nearly ceased; and farm prices dropped to disastrous levels. Cotton, for example, declined from 15 to 6 cents a pound between 1836 and 1842. Not until 1843 did conditions begin to show major improvement.

Only one depressed group—the farmers—attracted much governmental attention. In his special message on the economic crisis, Van Buren in 1837 attributed the nation's distress to those speculative investments which outran its needs. What gave the American economy its ultimate security and its promise of commercial recovery, he said, were its resources and industry, especially its production of the great staple crops. This agricultural interest Van Buren would defend. To assure land to actual settlers at moderate prices and at the same time keep the agricultural communities compact, the President favored Benton's system of "graduated" land prices. This system would permit the government to reduce the price of lands previously opened for sale but not settled because of their apparent inferiority. Van Buren believed that only by discouraging settlers from moving ahead in search of more attractive lands could frontier outposts be transformed into prosperous and stable communities.

Van Buren's determination to defend the farmers' interests led him to support the pre-emption principle as well. Squatters on empty lands, he believed, should not be deprived of their improvements by speculators or men with greater resources. Still preemption laws, he feared, tended to injure public regard for federal authority, for they protected those who had broken the law by squatting on public lands. For Van Buren the only land policy ultimately acceptable was one of cash sales to those ready to move onto the land. Congress enacted no major land legislation during the Van Buren presidency.

Banking Reform

Behind the Panic of 1837 lay a discredited banking structure. Radicals attributed the collapse to the paper system; conservatives, among them Nicholas Biddle, blamed Jackson's refusal to recharter the national Bank. Van Buren had three choices before him. He could restore the big Bank; he could rely on an improved and regulated system of state banking; or he could accept the hard money program of separating federal fiscal policies from banks. From the beginning of the panic, Van Buren's analysis of the crisis revealed his Jacksonian views. The spec- ulative craze, he reminded the nation, had driven men from productive to unproductive pursuits, encouraging them to live luxuriously on fancied riches. The banking system, uncontrolled, had encouraged the extravagance, but the creation of a new national Bank, he said, would only raise the old menace of "a concentrated moneyed power, hostile to the spirit and threatening the permanency of our republican institutions."

Van Buren's solution to the nation's banking problem took the form of his "Independent Treasury" proposal. This plan, embodying his hard money views, would sever all governmental relations with banks and hold all federal funds in subtreasuries kept under direct government control. This removal of federal funds from the business of the nation would deny those who controlled the credit structure the power to reap unearned profits from the investment of the public's money. Conservative Democrats—those who favored either a national Bank or a system of state banks—fought Van Buren's Independent Treasury plan; not until 1840 did the bill pass Congress. By thus applying the doctrine of laissez-faire to the operation of the nation's banks, Van Buren forced state legislatures to devise their own needed banking reforms. Taking as a model New York's Free Banking Act of 1838—a statute which threw open the business of banking to free competition under general restrictions—the nation moved after 1840 toward a general consensus on the banking question. State banks would continue to provide credit for a rapidly expanding economy, but henceforth state laws rather than a national Bank would impose necessary limits on their activities.

The Taney Court

When Chief Justice John Marshall died in 1835, his personality had towered over the Supreme Court for more than a third of a century. Justice Joseph Story, who had served with Marshall for over twenty years, doubted that the Court could survive Marshall's death. Jackson soon compounded Story's fears and those of conservatives generally by naming Roger B. Taney to the chief justiceship. Born into a Federalist family of Maryland, Taney had long since deserted his Federalist heritage. His willingness as Secretary of the Treasury to execute Jackson's final assault on the Bank had made that clear. To Whig leaders, the new Chief Justice, unlike his brilliant predecessor, had neither the formal training nor a self-acquired legal reputation to fit him for the robe of justice. The Senate had once rejected Taney's appointment to the Supreme Court; only the Democratic sweep of 1836 permitted the Jacksonians to carry his confirmation against determined Whig opposition. Yet the Supreme Court under Taney lost neither its distinction nor its importance. His major decisions revealed knowledge of law and society.

Van Buren inherited more than a new Chief Justice. Because Jackson had appointed three new justices and Van Buren was himself able to appoint two more in 1837, Democrats completely dominated the Supreme Court. Although they never rendered decisions as political partisans, their outlook toward an expanding, democratic nation steered them markedly away from the assumptions and purposes of the Marshall Court. Taney appreciated Marshall's nationalism, but he was determined to protect the states in the proper performance of their obligations. Better than Marshall, he understood the essentials of a changing America and saw that an unrestrained and federally protected commerce and industry would create serious political and legal problems, whether those problems reached the Court or not. Enough issues did reach Taney to provide material for a series of remarkable decisions.

For Taney the contract clause, which Marshall had converted into a drastic limitation on the states, required redefinition. His opportunity came early in the Charles River Bridge case of 1837. At stake was the validity of a Massachusetts law which had chartered a new corporation, the Warren Bridge Company, and granted it permission to build a bridge across the Charles River. This new bridge would compete with the Charles River Bridge, built under a charter granted fifty years earlier. Story, in favoring the previous charter and thus the Charles River Bridge, reverted to the doctrine of the Dartmouth College case. But Taney, speaking for the Court's majority, upheld the new Massachusetts law. In granting a state the right to "devest vested rights,"

Taney insisted that the states had the liberty to manage their own internal affairs. The state had duties as well as rights, said Taney, and no federal restrictions should prevent the states from performing their duties, especially those of protecting the well-being of their citizens. Conservatives feared that the Taney decision would encourage a general assault on private property. Instead, it kept the dead hand of the past from preventing the improvements required by a growing nation.

Again the Taney Court demonstrated its social and economic realism when it upheld the right of the state bank of Kentucky to issue bank notes. The Marshall case of *Craig v. Missouri* (1830) had denied that power to Missouri on the ground that the Constitution prohibited states from emitting bills of credit. When the Court faced the issue in *Briscoe v. The Bank of Kentucky* (1837), it rejected the strong nationalism of the earlier Court in its decision to facilitate the nation's access to paper money.

Thirdly, the Taney Court modified Marshall's noted decision which granted the federal government exclusive control of interstate commerce, even in areas where Congress had not yet acted. In 1837 the Court, in *New York v. Miln,* upheld a New York law demanding special reports from ship captains regarding all passengers entering New York Harbor. The Court argued that the state, in the interest of protecting its citizens, had the right to impose such obligations on ship captains engaged in interstate commerce. Ten years later, in the License cases (1847), Taney reaffirmed his defense of state regulation of commerce. Yet when Massachusetts and New York imposed taxes on passengers entering those states, a badly divided Court, in the Passenger cases of 1849, declared the state laws unconstitutional as an unreasonable interference with interstate commerce. In its major decisions the Taney Court did not overturn the precedents established by Marshall, but it encouraged the process by which the Supreme Court adapted constitutional law to the complexities of American life.

Log Cabins and Hard Cider

During their years of wandering through the political wilderness, the Whigs learned much from the party of Jackson. If Americans wanted democracy, they could have it with hands overflowing, for Whigs had discovered the advantages of running popular candidates, avoiding issues—at least divisive ones—and appealing to the emotions, not the intelligence, of the electorate. The continuing depression after 1837 gave the Whigs an initial advantage over the Jacksonians. In General William Henry Harrison of Ohio, the Whigs had an ideal candidate. Although born in Virginia, Harrison was a man of the frontier. As an Indian fighter he had achieved a reputation for courageous leadership at the Battle of Tippecanoe; as a general he had won additional renown for heroism in the War of 1812 in the Northwest. His political experience included the governorship of the Indiana Territory from 1801 to 1813 and membership in the House of Representatives from 1816 to 1819 and the Senate from 1825 to 1828. Yet Harrison possessed no firm or generally known views on political and economic questions.

Clay, the party's perennial favorite and logical candidate, confronted Whigs with a difficult choice. The Whig nominating convention which met at Harrisburg in December 1839 revealed the power of New York and its new Whig leadership headed by Thurlow Weed, editor of the *Albany Evening Journal.* This wire-puller extraordinary, supported by the able William H. Seward and Horace Greeley of the *New York Tribune,* convinced Whig delegations that Clay could not carry the essential states of New York and Pennsylvania. Having scuttled Clay's nomination in the interest of party victory, the convention managers pushed through the nomination of

HARRISONIAN

BALL ROLLING.

WILLIAM HENRY HARRISON THE FARMER OF NORTH BEND.

KEEP THE

RALLY!

A General Meeting

Will be held at the Old COURT ROOM, [Riey's building]

On Saturday Evening,

The 18th instant, at early candle light.   A punctual attendance is requested.

MESSRS. DAVIS, BOTKIN, KEATING

And others, will address the Meeting.

July 17, 1840.   **R. P. TODD,** *Chairman*
                                      Vigilance Committee.

*A broadside of the 1840 election campaign. William
Henry Harrison is shown with the symbolic log cabin
and barrel of hard cider.*   *The Granger Collection*

Harrison. For the vice presidency the convention selected John Tyler of Virginia, largely to
mollify Clay's friends in the South. To oppose
Harrison, the Democrats at Baltimore in May
1840 nominated Van Buren for reelection.

If the Whigs had slighted questions of national
policy in 1836, they avoided such topics with a
vengeance in 1840. Convinced that victory was
paramount to principles, they submitted but one
issue to the public—the need for a change.
Unburdened by Clay and Webster—men who
represented wealth and ideas—in their front
ranks, Whigs could herald their candidate as a
man of simple American virtues. Behind their
slogan of "Tippecanoe and Tyler too" they

began their assault on the emotions of the American people, receiving a special windfall when a
Baltimore American editor charged that Harrison
would have been content with a pension, a log
cabin, and a barrel of hard cider. The Whigs
accepted this challenge, claiming that they were
indeed the party of hard cider and log cabins—
the true representations of democracy. Although
Harrison was well-to-do and lived in a large,
spacious home overlooking the Ohio River, the
Whigs bewildered and amused the voters with
the trappings of the unsophisticated, honest,
frontier life which their candidate supposedly
characterized. The campaign was set to music,
much of it with the frenzy of a revival.

In their denunciation of executive authority
the Whigs claimed the support of Jefferson, for
Jefferson had challenged Hamilton's principle of
the strong president. Harrison informed an immense throng at Dayton, Ohio, that "the Auge-
an stables of Van Burenism can be cleaned only
by a Jeffersonian broom." Webster conveniently
forgot his early Federalist affiliations and avowed
himself a "Jefferson Democrat." At Saratoga,
New York, in August, Webster repeated the old
charges, now standard for the Whigs, that the
administration favored the rich and injured the
poor by refusing to shield American wages with a
protective tariff. Similarly the subtreasury,
charged Webster, lowered wages and prices,
hurting the workingmen while aiding their creditors. "While his rich neighbor . . . is made
richer," said Webster, ". . . he, the honest and
industrious mechanic, is crushed to earth; and
yet we are told that this is a system for promoting
the interests of the poor!"

For such appeals to democratic passions the
Jacksonians had no answer. In victory the Whigs
carried every section of the nation. They not
only cut heavily into the regions of Democratic
successes in 1836 but also augmented their majorities in areas where their superiority was
already well established. In Connecticut, Rhode
Island, Vermont, and Delaware, they carried
every county. They won all but one of Massachusetts' fourteen counties. They captured

normally Democratic Maine and almost doubled their vote in New Hampshire, although still failing to carry the state. They won New York and Pennsylvania, both traditionally Democratic. They swept the Northwest, with the exception of Illinois. South of the Ohio, they captured the areas of Whig strength—Maryland, North Carolina, Kentucky, Tennessee, Georgia, and Louisiana. They carried Mississippi by a narrow margin for the first and only time. Only in Tennessee and South Carolina did the Democrats make gains over 1836. The popular vote was close, 1,275,000 to 1,129,000, but Harrison won 234 electoral votes to 60 for Van Buren.

The Whigs in Power

Having swept their hero, William Henry Harrison, into the White House, after being battered in Congress and at the polls for a dozen years, the Whigs could anticipate a rosier future. Indeed, Whig leaders interpreted Harrison's victory as a major triumph for Whig principles and assumed that the old soldier would hand over control of policy to the party's established mentors. Webster, a master of style, prepared for Harrison an inaugural address which the President-elect rejected in favor of one he had written—based on Roman history. Harrison prevailed upon Webster to take the State Department, but Clay controlled the other Cabinet posts. Having refused a Cabinet appointment for himself, Clay prepared to manage the Whig party from his seat in the Senate. Determined to present his own program to Congress as quickly as possible, he persuaded Harrison to call a special session for May 1841.

Harrison did not live to face the Clay-controlled Congress. On April 4, 1841, a month after his inaugural, Harrison died. Thus John Tyler (1790–1862), a Virginia gentleman, became the first vice president to move into the presidency. A lawyer with wide political experience, having served in the House of Representatives and the Senate and as governor of Virginia, Tyler assumed Harrison's title and duties, keeping the Cabinet intact. Clay, still hopeful of dominating the administration, presented his full-blown Whig program to Congress, only to discover that Tyler not only had a mind of his own but also that the President was a believer in the Jeffersonian states' rights principles of 1798.

Clay selected the question of a national bank as a test of strength, assuming that his control of Congress would force Tyler to submit or leave the party. Tyler had no objection to a national bank, provided that it preserved the principle of states' rights by limiting its branches to only those states which gave their consent. When Clay rammed a bank bill through Congress, Tyler vetoed it, declaring that it did not meet his requirements. Clay responded in September 1841 with a second bill, one designed specifically to satisfy the President's constitutional scruples. This the President also vetoed. Thereafter Clay's fury, and that of his followers, knew no bounds. Flaming effigies of Tyler appeared across the nation. The President was mystified by the Whig hysteria. To him, his vetoes revealed neither inconsistency nor bad faith. The Whigs had known his opposition to the American System when they nominated him. But so incensed were the congressional Whigs over Tyler's apostasy that by 1842 they no longer made any effort at political reconciliation. Southern Whigs stood as a bloc behind Clay and his program. A Southern Whig, Willie P. Mangum of North Carolina, presided at the caucus which read Tyler out of the party. Clay resigned his Senate seat in March 1842 to campaign for the presidency.

Having already disposed of Van Buren's Independent Treasury in August 1841, but unable to restore a national bank, the Whigs embarked on a move to increase the tariff. In Whig minds the problem of a tariff had become associated with the matter of public lands. For a decade Clay had sponsored the movement to distribute the proceeds from land sales among the states, for such a step would reduce federal income and make an alternative source of income—for example, an increased tariff—more attractive. The West had long advocated a general preemption law for the public domain. During 1841 both distribution and preemption bills were steered through Congress and became law. The Preemption Act granting squatters the right to purchase public land at the minimum rate of $1.25 per acre was cordially received in the West, but that same section roundly denounced distribution as a disguise for the assumption of state debts. In December 1841, Lewis F. Linn of Missouri introduced a bill to repeal those sections of the land act which provided for the distribution of public land revenues.

Eventually, as a sop to the West, the Whigs attached the antidistribution provision to the tariff bill under consideration. Even then the compromise tariff of 1842 narrowly passed in the Senate, 24 to 23. It declared that distribution would be suspended when the rate of duty reached 20 percent. Since tariff duties were already above that figure, no distribution of land revenue occurred under this law. The vote on the measure revealed no clear intersectional split. The Northeast was solidly behind it. Elsewhere the Whigs captured the votes they needed in Louisiana, Kentucky, and the older Northwest. The tariff of 1842 was the last of the Whig legislative triumphs. George McDuffie of South Carolina opened the tariff debate again in December 1843 by introducing a bill for tariff reduction. The Whigs upheld their measure, but the tariff issue was still not settled.

Webster's Diplomacy

The Whig desertion of Tyler's administration in 1842 placed Secretary of State Webster in a dilemma. New England Whigs who distrusted Tyler urged him to resign. But Webster had gained deep satisfaction from his first administrative appointment, and he had no desire to follow in the footsteps of Clay. Tyler, for his part, had made it clear that he desired Webster to remain in the Cabinet. Finally, Webster had inherited the pro-British proclivities of the Federalists; the opportunity to effect an improvement in American relations with Great Britain was irresistible.

By 1842, a series of unresolved conflicts had pushed United States–British relations to the breaking point. During the Canadian rebellion of 1837, Washington had failed in its efforts to prevent the people of New York and Vermont from siding openly with the Canadian rebels, shipping supplies, harboring refugees, and even furnishing them with a small steamer, the *Caroline*. When a band of loyal Canadians in 1840 crossed the Niagara River and burned the vessel—the British government admitting its part in the affair—latent anti-British sentiment in the Northeast became fully aroused. At the same time, London antagonized the South by openly attacking slavery. This conflict reached a crisis in 1842 when British officials in the West Indies refused to return blacks who had seized their slave ship, the *Creole*, and sailed it to the Bahamas. Democrats, to whom Britain had always appeared aristocratic, arbitrary, and overbearing, demanded that the Tyler administration exact satisfaction for every American grievance.

To Webster cordial United States relations with Britain seemed the key to both the nation's security and its economic well-being. The British government, equally disposed toward peace, dispatched Lord Ashburton to Washington in the spring of 1842 to negotiate the settlement of another lingering issue, the northeastern boundary separating Canada from the United States. Ashburton's instructions restricted him to protecting a land route from Quebec to Halifax, a strategic necessity confirmed by the War of 1812.

Webster could not negotiate a successful compromise with Ashburton until he had won approval for such an agreement from the state of Maine. This was not a simple matter, for Maine claimed almost the entire disputed area. Webster did not lack arguments favoring concession. The historian Jared Sparks had drawn from memory a red line across a map of the Northeast, ostensibly duplicating a line he had seen on a map in the French archives which Sparks assumed to have been Franklin's original of 1782. Sparks' line conceded most of the disputed area to the British. This map Webster revealed privately to the Maine commissioners, who then agreed to compromise. Freed of unreasonable domestic demands, Webster now sought a realistic settlement with Ashburton. Working through the hot Washington summer, they produced a treaty which granted the United States about 7,000 of the 12,000 square miles of disputed land. The Webster-Ashburton Treaty provided as well for the extradition of criminals from Canada to the United States and for British-American cooperation in suppressing the slave trade.

Webster next faced the task of securing public approval for his work. Using secret service funds of the State Department, he hired a persuasive journalist to secure the support of key Maine editors, men who could be troublesome if they chose to attack the treaty. The Secretary argued that the treaty served the best interests of the United States by resolving the outstanding issues between Britain and the United States and thus avoiding war. Long before the Senate received the treaty, the nation had overwhelmingly accepted Webster's peaceful alternative. In the Senate Benton charged that the Whig administration had sold out the interests of the South and West to those of the Northeast. But the red line map persuaded the Senate as it had the Maine commissioners: the final vote for the treaty was 39 to 9.

Conclusion

By 1840 Jackson and Clay, two powerful, yet attractive, political opponents, had established the country's first genuine two-party system. If the two-party tradition had its inception in early struggles between Federalists and Antifederalists over ratification of the Constitution, or in arguments between Alexander Hamilton and Thomas Jefferson over the domestic (and later the foreign) policies of the United States, it did not become a continuous, nationwide encounter until the 1830s. The Whig organization, like that of the Democrats, reached from the Boston waterfront to the great plantations of Louisiana. Each party maintained a network of partisan newspapers; each confronted the electorate at every level of political activity with a stream of candidates, orators, pamphlets, broadsides, and parades. Thousands of people converged on endless political rallies to listen for hours to speakers of national consequence—or perhaps simply to enjoy the outing. It was not strange that voters, aroused by such incessant campaign-ing, turned out in numbers on election day.

Still the political issues in conflict seldom matched in clarity and forthrightness the zeal with which party spokesmen proclaimed them. For politics represented a struggle for power, not a crusade for righteousness. Clay's American System embodied a recognizable Whig program, but the Whig Harrison won the White House by ignoring it. Jacksonians, too, had their prefer-ences, tending to favor lower tariffs and to show distrust of governmental centralization. Still for Democrats and Whigs alike, their broad, national constituencies of varying individual and regional concerns compelled a high level of pragmatism and equivocation. Indeed, the national parties were actually confederations of state and city parties, stitched together every fourth year to nominate and elect a president. What mattered fundamentally was the sensitivity of local barons to regional interests, and the Democratic party's chief claim to power lay in the superiority of its local organizations.

Glyndon G. Van Deusen's *The Jacksonian Era 1828–1848** (1959) contains a judicious, moderately pro-Whig survey of the Jackson years. In addition to the biographies of Webster and Calhoun listed in the bibliographical essay of Chapter 8, several studies of excellent quality portray the careers of other important leaders in the Jackson years: Carl B. Swisher's *Roger B. Taney** (1936); W. N. Chambers's *Old Bullion Benton: Senator from the New West* (1956); Elbert B. Smith's *Magnificent Missourian: The Life of Thomas Hart Benton* (1958); and Russell B. Nye's *George Bancroft: Brahmin Rebel** (1944).

On Indian removal the standard work is Grant Foreman's *Indian Removal: The Emigration of the Five Civilized Tribes* (1932). U. B. Phillips's *Georgia and States Rights** (1902) presents the Georgia side of the Supreme Court controversy. The best exposition and defense of Calhoun's role in nullification is Charles M. Wiltse's *John C. Calhoun: Nullifier* (1949). Also useful on Southern motivation is C. S. Sydnor's *The Development of Southern Sectionalism** (1948). Largely superseding previous studies of nullification is W. W. Freehling's *Prelude to Civil War: The Nullification Controversy in South Carolina, 1816–1836** (1966).

Two volumes which interpret Jackson as a symbol of the new democracy are J. W. Ward's *Andrew Jackson: Symbol for an Age** (1955) and H. C. Syrett's *Andrew Jackson: His Contribution to the American Tradition* (1953). A. M. Schlesinger, Jr., in *The Age of Jackson** (1945), interprets Jacksonian Democracy as a genuine democratic movement taking its egalitarian spirit and program from the urban radicals of the Northeast.

Critical of the Jacksonian leadership on bank and economic policy is Bray Hammond's *Banks and Politics in America from the Revolution to the Civil War** (1957). Another important effort to explain Jacksonianism is Marvin Meyers's *The Jacksonian Persuasion** (1957). Richard Hofstadter's essay on Jackson in his *The American Political Tradition** (1948) views the Jacksonians as ambitious, incipient capitalists. Edward Pessen's *Jacksonian America: Society, Personality, and Politics** (1969) is an excellent synthesis of historical opinion on political and social aspects of the period.

On the Van Buren years, and especially the Panic of 1837, R. C. McGrane's *The Panic of 1837** (1924) remains the standard work. On land policy, see R. G. Wellington's *The Political and National Influence of the Public Lands, 1826–1842* (1914). On the Taney Court see Swisher's *Roger B. Taney** (1936). The election of 1840 is described well in R. G. Gunderson's *The Log Cabin Campaign* (1957). Two satisfactory biographies of William Henry Harrison are Freeman Cleaves's *Old Tippecanoe* (1939) and J. A. Green's *William Henry Harrison* (1941).

Existing volumes reveal much that is essential on questions of party strength and affiliation. An excellent study of the parties in each section can be found in F. J. Turner's *The United States, 1830–1850: The Nation and Its Sections* (1935). Charles McCarthy's *The Antimasonic Party* (1903) remains the standard account of that political movement. In addition, such volumes as E. M. Carroll's *Origins of the Whig Party* (1925); A. C. Cole's *The Whig Party in the South* (1913); and G. R. Poage's *Henry Clay and the Whig Party* (1936) relate much of that party's history. Charles G. Sellers, Jr., in "Who Were the Southern Whigs?" *American Historical Review*, LIX (January 1954), identifies Whig leadership in the South more with the merchants and lawyers of the urban centers than with the planter aristocracy. Lee Benson in *The Concept of Jacksonian Democracy** (1961) challenges the older view that the Whigs and Democrats can be differentiated by class and wealth.

For the Tyler years the best study available is O. P. Chitwood's *John Tyler: Champion of the Old South* (1939). Another excellent account of Tyler's leadership can be found in R. J. Morgan's *A Whig Embattled: The Presidency under John Tyler* (1954). For Webster's diplomacy both C. M. Fuess's *Daniel Webster* (2 vols., 1930) and R. N. Current's *Daniel Webster and the Rise of National Conservatism** (1955) are excellent. Special monographs that contain accounts of the Webster-Ashburton negotiations are A. B. Corey's *The Crisis of 1830–1842 in Canadian-American Relations* (1941) and W. D. Jones's *Lord Aberdeen and the Americas* (1958).
*indicates availability in paperback.

10

The Mind and Culture of America, 1815-1860

Having solidified its political and economic freedom from Europe in 1815, the United States moved rapidly toward the achievement of cultural independence as well. Trends in literature, the arts, education, religion, and social reform during the early nineteenth century testified to the continuing differentiation of American society. Those two generations which separated Ghent from the crisis of 1860 witnessed intellectual triumphs at once impressive and pervading.

Although Americans generally were accused of being excessively materialistic, they by no means ignored things of the mind and the spirit. And in their cultural and intellectual life they searched for and achieved a strong individuality. During the pre-Civil War years, a major private and community effort introduced public education at the elementary level and made secondary school and college courses available for increasing numbers of students. The proliferation of new religious bodies indicated a deep interest in religion, even as Puritanism continued to decline. Outstanding writers and artists did much to raise literature and the fine arts to high levels of competence, and they made a conscious effort to concentrate on American themes. Numerous reform movements reflected America's restless experimentalism—its hope as well as its discontent.

Late in the eighteenth century, the Frenchman Michel de Crèvecoeur, who spent nearly half his life in America, had asked the question "What then is the American, this new man?" Foreigners who traveled extensively in the United States between 1815 and 1860 agreed on the existence of certain special American characteristics and disagreed on the presence of others, but were unanimous in the belief that Americans differed markedly from their European ancestors.

America's preeminent trait was the habit of hard work. It took tremendous energy and labor to clear the forests, to establish farms, to build towns. This trait became so deeply embedded in the American character that even when there was no economic necessity to toil, most Americans felt a social compulsion to perform useful labor. Far from the dishonor that it brought to the European aristocrat, work, in America conferred a distinct nobility. And Americans who worked hard expected a comfortable standard of living. Indeed, European observers charged that Americans were excessively materialistic, and that, as James Buckingham wrote, they displayed "an inordinate love of gain." It was easy and natural to be materialistic in a land where so many people experienced considerable economic success.

The great natural wealth of the United States, the widespread well-being among its people, inspired in most Americans a pronounced optimism and confidence in the future. They believed firmly that better things were yet to come—and within their own lifetime. A second American trait, then, was the belief in progress. This spirit probably sprang from the undeniable observation that, as Charles Dickens wrote, "There is no other country on earth which in so short a time has accomplished so much." Americans were proud—even boastful—and they unabashedly scorned other political and social systems. One American with less politeness than forthrightness, in addressing the Englishwoman Frances Trollope, referred to her homeland as a contemptible little country and then "placed his feet upon the chimney-piece, considerably higher than his head, and whistled Yankee Doodle."

Americans felt a deep commitment to liberty, democracy, and equality for white men. Democratic institutions they generally considered far superior to Old World political systems. The vast majority of people took a vital interest in the success of their government, believing that both their material and their political interests would be best served by a democratic system. The expansion of suffrage and fuller public participation in the political life of the nation in the early nineteenth century testified to this belief.

Practicality became another American hallmark. Americans had little interest in speculation or abstraction, in philosophical or theoretical inquiries. "Immediate practical results," wrote one foreign traveler, "are more attractive for the American mind, although not exclusively, than the charms of imagination."

Americans may have been democratic, equalitarian, optimistic, self-reliant, materialistic, individualistic, hospitable, generous, restless, and versatile. But they also possessed other, less desirable, traits, such as lack of culture, race prejudice, tolerance of political corruption, easy resort to physical violence, heavy drinking, and a certain uncouthness demonstrated by tobacco chewing and indiscriminate spitting. The Englishman William Cobbett wrote that at a Harrisburgh, Pennsylvania, tavern he had seen several fine, well-dressed young men who were "everything but sober. What a squalid, drooping, sickly set they looked in the morning," he added. Another writer described a man in a tavern who "took a large roll of tobacco out of his pocket, and taking an immense quid, he rolled it about in his mouth and squirted about the saliva in all directions, without paying much regard to who might come in contact with it."

Americans displayed an abiding faith in education as a means of lifting the nation's cultural level and guaranteeing free, democratic institutions. Thomas Jefferson had declared that the best way to prevent tyranny would be "to illuminate, as far as practicable, the minds of the people at large." He sought tax support in vain for elementary schools in Virginia but was responsible in large measure for founding the University of Virginia. George Washington had recommended the establishment of a national university. Such demands for public-supported education were backed by the clergy, publicists, and workingmen.

During the pre-Civil War period, the principle of free, tax-supported schools gradually gained acceptance throughout much of the northern United States. The first step toward a system of public education was the establishment of free schools for pauper children. Poor people, however, resented having to declare that they were impoverished before their children could attend school tuition-free. For years proponents and opponents of free public education fought a lively battle over tax-supported common schools. Properted interests which balked at higher taxes, people without children, and those who doubted the importance of universal education generally opposed free schools. One North Carolina legislator represented the sentiments of the latter group when he declared, "I hope you do not conceive it at all necessary that *everybody* should be able to read, write and cipher." Despite such opposition, by the 1850s the principle of free public schools had won the day throughout much of the North. Local taxes, some state aid, and grants of land by the federal government provided the major financial support for free public schools. In the South, tuition schools and private tutors were more common, although during the 1840s the rudiments of a public school system came into existence.

Only a few black children enjoyed the benefits of formal education. During the first half of the nineteenth century, some free blacks in the North attended separate schools, occasionally integrated schools. In the South fear of an educated black population prompted the states to pass laws against education for blacks. Most free blacks who received any education at all attended private schools or received tutoring.

Much of the educational progress made during the pre-Civil War years was attributable to Horace Mann, who became state superintendent of education in Massachusetts in 1837. He worked untiringly for better-trained teachers, improved textbooks, and modern buildings and equipment. He started the first state-supported normal school for teacher training at Lexington, Massachusetts, in 1839. "In a republic," Mann wrote, "ignorance is a crime."

Despite increased financing, improved supervision and organization, and stronger educational leadership, the condition of most public schools was far from ideal. Funds available for buildings and equipment were insufficient. Women staffed the schools because they constituted the only labor pool available and willing to work for the low wages offered. The chief courses in grade schools were reading, writing, and arithmetic, with occasional excursions into spelling, geography, composition, and history. Teachers read the Bible regularly and everyone expected the schools to teach such principles as faith, industry, charity, and democracy. The most common textbooks were McGuffey's Readers and Noah Webster's blue-backed spellers. (Webster also compiled a famous *Dictionary*, published in 1828, which was the most authoritative reference work by an American on the English language.)

Children who attended school at all usually stopped with the elementary grades, but some citizens demanded that the system extend upward to include secondary and college education. Private academies, chartered by the hundreds in both North and South, provided most of the secondary education in the late eighteenth and early nineteenth centuries. Their greatest development came between 1820 and 1840; by 1850, there were 6,085 academies in the United States, with a total enrollment of 263,096 students. Academies, often established by religious groups, relied on private funds and tuition, although in some cases they received state aid. The academies at first existed largely to prepare students for college, but the 1830s saw a rising demand for the inclusion of more so-called practical subjects. Algebra, botany, United States history, and other new subjects gradually entered the curriculum alongside Latin and Greek. Girls as well as boys attended the general academies. Some female academies existed after 1800 for daughters of the well-to-do.

Whatever their value, academies did not meet the growing insistence on an upward extension of the public school system. Even at the height of the academy movement, many people demanded public, tax-supported high schools which would educate poor and rich alike. Boston established the first high school in 1821, and other cities soon followed. Progress was slow, but by 1860 a reported 321 high schools were operating in the United States, more than half of them in Massachusetts, New York, and Ohio. As late as 1860 there were almost no public high schools in the South. Although the high school movement was only in its beginning stages between 1820 and 1860, it had firmly established the principle of public secondary education and set the course for the democratization of American education which was to follow.

Before 1800, only a few well-known institutions—Harvard, Yale, William and Mary, and Princeton—all of which had been established by religious groups, offered the opportunity for a college education. Their primary purpose was to train ministers. Early in the nineteenth century, however, Americans began to argue for public-supported universities. Congress had granted land to the new Western states to help finance universities, and, by the time of the Civil War, the foundations of the state university system had been laid.

Despite the growing number of state universities—among them Indiana, Michigan, and Wisconsin—most of the colleges before the Civil War were organized and supported by religious denominations. Connecticut Wesleyan and Emory were Methodist, Oberlin was Congregationalist, Georgetown was Catholic. Among the new female seminaries after 1820 were Emma Willard's Troy (New York) Female Seminary, Mary Lyon's Mount Holyoke Seminary in Massachusetts, Elmira College in New York, and Rockford Seminary in Illinois. These institutions trained many of the leading teachers of the time, but their instruction remained largely at the seminary, not the college, level. Oberlin and several Western state universities were the only college-level institutions providing genuine coeducation before 1860.

Expansion and improvement characterized professional and technical education in the pre-Civil War years. The apprentice system survived, but an increasing number of doctors and lawyers received formal instruction in the new schools of law and medicine. Harvard opened its law school in 1817. Baltimore started the first dental college in 1839. After 1862, the land-grant colleges provided agricultural and mechanical education.

While education made great gains at every level, progress was not uniform throughout the nation. Many poor whites in the Southern mountain regions, Western settlers, and Eastern laborers could neither read nor write. In parts of the South, a third of the white population in 1850 was illiterate. Although the situation was better in the West, a resident in Illinois wrote in 1831 that "many adults, especially females, are unable to read or write . . . ." But because of widespread improvement in educational opportunities, scarcely 5 percent of the American adult white population was illiterate in 1860.

Education in its broadest sense was not confined to formal schooling; people learned much from newspapers, magazines, books, and public lectures. The first American lyceum was organized at Boston in 1826 to promote "the general diffusion of knowledge." Organized by local groups, lyceums sponsored lectures and discussions on science, literature, and other topics in hundreds of local communities. Even people in isolated areas could hear Horace Greeley, editor of the *New York Tribune*, Wendell Phillips, or Ralph Waldo Emerson.

Newspapers and magazines also served to diffuse knowledge and ideas among the people. In the 1830s alone, the number of newspapers increased from 800 to 1,400 and sales tripled. By the 1840s, even small towns published weekly newspapers. An increasing number of cities had dailies. Circulation rose rapidly after 1830 as papers became cheaper and more interesting. In 1833, Benjamin H. Day began to publish his *New York Sun* at 1 cent a copy. Horace Greeley established the *New York Tribune* in 1841 and fought for reforms varying from abolitionism to vegetarianism. Two significant newspapers published by Afro-Americans were *Freedom's Journal* and the *North Star*.

Magazines provided further information on many aspects of American life. The *North American Review*, founded in Boston in 1815, and *Niles' Weekly Register*, started in Baltimore in 1811, were the only magazines with national circulation. Periodicals which dealt with literature, the arts, and some contemporary social and political questions were the *North American Review*, *Amer-*ican *Monthly Magazine* of Boston, the *Knickerbocker* of New York, and the *Southern Literary Messenger*, published at Richmond and edited for a time by Edgar Allan Poe. *Harper's Magazine* (1850) and *Atlantic Monthly* (1857) carried a variety of materials on cultural and political subjects. *Godey's Lady's Book* (1830) was the forerunner of modern women's magazines. Founded by Louis A. Godey and successfully edited for many years by Sarah Josepha Hale, this journal catered to every feminine interest. Mrs. Hale strongly advocated feminine health and hygiene, and urged better education for women, including education in medicine.

Page detail from an 1843 issue of Godey's Lady's Book. Media Features

Science and Invention

Advances in science and technology were closely associated with greater educational opportunities and broader diffusions of knowledge. During the pre-Civil War years, the United States produced a number of thoroughly creditable natural scientists and some inventors who gained international recognition. Asa Gray, who began his teaching at Harvard in 1842, made distinguished contribu-

Cyrus McCormick's *"improved reaper"* of 1847.

The Granger Collection

tions in botany; Louis Agassiz, who immigrated to the United States in 1846, did important research in both geology and zoology. At Yale, J. D. Dana published his *System of Mineralogy* (1837), a book which became standard in its field. Even more famous was Yale's geologist Benjamin Silliman. Already the country's leading universities were actively engaged in basic scientific research. Joseph Henry developed important theories about electricity. J. J. Audubon, whose bird paintings became world-famous, made distinguished contributions to ornithology. Significant gains also were made in medical research, especially in the field of anesthetics. Ether was first used in an operation at Massachusetts General Hospital in 1846.

By the 1830s and 1840s, a new scientific spirit prevailed throughout the United States. Many people detected a connection between democracy and science. One editor wrote in 1840, "Democracy is the cradle of science and only an unfettered mind can expand to its utmost."

Scientists exchanged ideas and cooperated in advancing scientific knowledge. Some five hundred delegates attended the first chemical convention in 1831; and in 1844, the first national scientific congress met in Washington. Senator Robert J. Walker told the participants that "scientists could make this country the greatest and freest nation of the world."

Already known as a practical people, Americans readily applied their scientific knowlege to everyday purposes. President Fillmore declared in 1852 that "we live in an age of progress. . . . The inventive talent of our country is excited to the highest pitch. And the numerous applications for patents for valuable improvements distinguish this age and its people from all others." Perhaps the outstanding technological achievements after 1830 included McCormick's reaper, John Deere's plow, and other farm implements; Charles Goodyear's process of vulcanizing rubber; Elias Howe's invention of the sewing machine; Samuel Colt's revolver; David Alter's production of oil from coal; and Samuel F. B. Morse's invention of the telegraph. Americans also gained recognition for their machine tools and scientific instruments. The inventive genius of Americans was recognized at the London Exhibition in 1851, when McCormick, Colt, and Goodyear won prizes. After using an American-built locomotive, the Pasha of Egypt exclaimed: "God is great, but those Yankees are very near perfection." A quick estimate of the technological advance can be gained from patent records: between 1820 and 1860 the number of patents granted for inventions rose from 155 to 4,357.

Literature in the Young Republic

Between 1820 and 1860, American writers produced a rich and distinctive literature. When Edward Channing, soon to become editor of the *North American Review*, and Richard Henry Dana read the manuscript of William Cullen Bryant's "Thanatopsis," in 1817 Dana exclaimed: "No

one on this side of the Atlantic is capable of writing such verses." Such an observation was understandable in 1817, but times were changing. New York already had two outstanding literary figures, Washington Irving (1783–1859) and James Fenimore Cooper (1789–1851). It soon attracted Bryant from Massachusetts. Irving published his humorous *History of New York by Diedrich Knickerbocker* in 1809. A decade later his noted *Sketch Book* gave readers such unforgettable characters as Rip Van Winkle and Ichabod Crane. Cooper's literary themes centered on the West, which he romanticized highly. *The Pioneers, The Last of the Mohicans,* and *The Prairie,* all published in the 1820s, won a wide reading public. Bryant, having moved to New York in 1825, became editor and part owner of the *Evening Post.* He had earlier published his *Poems* (1821), which included "Thanatopsis" and "To a Waterfowl."

Despite the talent centered in New York, New England dominated the literature and thought of the period. Henry Wadsworth Longfellow (1807–1882), James Russell Lowell (1819–1891), and Oliver Wendell Holmes (1809–1894) were clustered in Cambridge. Not far from them resided John Greenleaf Whittier (1807–1892), Nathaniel Hawthorne (1804–1864), Herman Melville (1819–1891), Ralph Waldo Emerson (1803–1882), and Henry David Thoreau (1817–1862). Longfellow settled in Cambridge to become professor of modern languages at Harvard in 1835. Within the next quarter century, he poured out a stream of poetry which placed him among the nation's top literary figures. His *Ballads and Other Poems* (1841) included "The Village Blacksmith" and "The Wreck of the Hesperus." These poems were followed by *Evangeline* (1847) and the *Song of Hiawatha* (1855). Whittier rivaled Longfellow in popularity. His sentimental poems and ballads, such as "The Old Burying Grounds," "The Barefoot Boy," and later "Snow-Bound," brought him fame. Oliver Wendell Holmes, medical doctor and poet, sought to destroy the confining influences of theology. He symbolized the collapse of New England Calvinism in "Wonderful One-Hoss Shay."

In his novels, Nathaniel Hawthorne described the sense of ghostly decay in Salem. Two of his most famous books were *The Scarlet Letter* (1850),

in which he dealt with the effects of adultery on his characters, and *The House of the Seven Gables.* Herman Melville astonished his readers with realistic tales of the sea. In his masterly novel *Moby Dick* (1851), he struck at the optimism and blandness of the many intellectuals who denied the existence of evil. Walt Whitman (1819–1892) was the poet of individualism, democracy, and physical freedom; he wove these themes through his *Leaves of Grass,* first published in 1855.

New England may have dominated the literature of the period, but it never monopolized it. Edgar Allan Poe, whose horror tales of torture, murder, and insanity revealed his genius as well as his own instability, was born in Boston but lived out most of his life in Richmond, New York, Philadelphia, and Baltimore. William Gilmore Simms of South Carolina produced eighty-two volumes of verse, novels, criticism, and history. Henry Timrod and Paul Hamilton Hayne were other leading Southern writers.

Ralph Waldo Emerson's writing and thought had a universal character. Tired of the rush and discipline of urban life, he quit the ministry of his Boston church and withdrew to the freer air of Concord, Massachusetts, in 1834. Those who saw industrialism as a threat to individual freedom had two choices: they could escape in flight or they could work for reform. Emerson chose to flee. "Let the countrymen beware of cities," he warned. "A city is the paradise of trifles." But a more important reason for Emerson's retreat to Concord was his search for oneness with God. He had deserted Puritanism for Unitarianism, but even the latter's liberality could not contain him.

Emerson, in search of a more personal religion, settled on German transcendentalism. Here was an order of truth that transcended all external evidence. There was something in the "involuntary soul," the "absolute being" of the German thinkers that captivated Emerson. Another stimulus for him also emanated from the Quaker notion of the "inner light," which he seemed to experience on his strolls about Concord. If men could find this universal soul within themselves, they could cast off the tawdry pressures of life about them and know God. Emerson broke with the past when he concluded that God was not a person, but an impersonal force that pervaded all nature.

To achieve inner independence required time and solitude. Emerson bought a wooded lot at Walden Pond where he could devote his leisure hours to reading and contemplation. "In the woods," he wrote, "we return to reason and faith. . . . Standing on the bare ground—my head bathed by the blithe air and uplifted into infinite space,—all mean egotism vanishes. . . . I am part or parcel of God." At Concord, Emerson spun out the essays that vexed some and delighted others. *Nature* (1836) expressed most of the themes on which he dwelt for the remainder of his life. He published volumes of essays in 1841 and 1844, and his *Poems* in 1847.

Henry Thoreau was Emerson's true disciple and friend. Like Emerson, Thoreau cared little for the social virtues, and he found no merit in hard work or accumulation of goods. He rebuked the material forces transforming American society. "Trade," he said, "curses everything it touches." In 1845, Thoreau constructed a hut at Walden outside Concord. In *Walden* (1854), he made it clear, however, that he had sought to discover the true meaning of life. "I wanted to live deep and suck out all the marrow of life, to live so sturdily and Spartan-like as to put to rout all that was not life. . . ." Margaret Fuller ranked with Thoreau in the transcendentalist movement. She propagated many of the transcendentalist ideas in the *Dial*, which she edited in the 1840s.

Other Boston intellectuals found their escape to discovery at Brook Farm. George Ripley, at one time a Boston preacher, had purchased the farm at West Roxbury, 9 miles from the city. Converted to the new ideas of associationism, he decided to turn his farm into a model community. Beginning in 1841, building was added to building, member to member, until by the mid-

forties Brook Farm boasted over a hundred associates. Ripley, ably assisted by his wife Sophia, directed the work, the relaxation, and the study with singular devotion and energy. The members farmed, danced, argued, studied, and occasionally traveled to Boston for a concert or lecture. Brook Farm was a paradise for intellectuals, but it was little else. The experiment soon failed.

Much of the nation's literary taste after 1830 veered toward history. A new school of historians—William H. Prescott, John Lothrop Motley, George Bancroft, Jared Sparks, and Richard Hildreth, all New Englanders—produced distinguished volumes. Sparks published twelve volumes of *The Life and Writings of George Washington* between 1834 and 1837. Bancroft's *History of the United States*, based on the author's thesis that God had directed the course of history to its culmination in the American experiment, began to appear in 1834. In 1838, Prescott published his classic narrative, *The Reign of Ferdinand and Isabella*, soon to be followed by his additional books on Spain and the Spanish empire. Motley's volumes on the Dutch Republic, like Prescott's works on Spain, revealed extraordinary scholarship and literary skill. These writers represented the romantic, nationalistic school of history. More objective and less influenced by romantic nationalism was Richard Hildreth who published, in 1849, his three-volume *History of the United States of America*, which covered the period to 1789. Francis Parkman's trip to Oregon in 1845 resulted in his first book, *The Oregon Trail*, published the next year; six years later appeared *The Conspiracy of Pontiac*. Parkman here revealed his unusual talents of description and narration, which enlivened his whole series on France's role in North America.

Declining publication costs and the increase in school and public libraries provided a growing opportunity for people to become familiar with the great volume of literature and history being written after 1830. Between 1825 and 1850, some 550 libraries of all types sprang up in the United States.

Little of the nation's wealth and energy encouraged the fine arts in the early national period. Painters could find few patrons for their works. However, by 1820 wealthy merchants, cities, and even the federal government spent large sums on painting and sculpture. The principal demand in the early nineteenth century was for portraits, but the country's two greatest portrait painters, Charles Willson Peale and Gilbert Stuart, had died in 1827 and 1828, respectively. John Trumbull, another distinguished portrait painter, lived another fifteen years, but he was better known for his historical works, including the *Battle of Bunker Hill* and the *Declaration of Independence*.

English artistic influences declined by 1820. Artists uninterested in European imitation turned instead to subjects and techniques which expressed the strength, nationalism, and independence of America. During the two decades after 1830, a new group of landscape painters chose the Hudson River region and the White Mountains as subjects to display their nationalistic pride on canvas. Together these artists became known as the Hudson River school. Thomas Doughty of Philadelphia painted the very popular *Peep at the Catskills* while Thomas Cole, Asher B. Durand, and John F. Kensett produced excellent landscape paintings. The frontier regions and beyond attracted some of the period's leading painters. George Caleb Bingham's striking *Fur Traders Descending the Missouri* became a classic. George Catlin (1796–1872) painted Indian scenes as well as individual portraits, while Alfred Jacob Miller (1810–1874) made scores of sketches and watercolors of Indians, fur trappers, and other Western subjects. (See pages 241–245 and page 293.)

Hiram Powers (1805–1873) won international acclaim for his *Greek Slave*. Otherwise American sculpture of this period was not notable. John Rogers (1829–1904) depicted everyday existence with extraordinary skill in such pieces as *Checker Players* and *Town Pump*. But most American sculptors who came to prominence after 1800 had spent long periods in Europe, where they were heavily influenced by neoclassicism. Among them were two outstanding female sculptors, Harriet Hosmer and Edmonia Lewis. Architecture, too, was dominated by European modes, mainly the Greek style. The Bank of North America in Philadelphia, a number of state capitols, and many Southern mansions reflected the classic Greek form.

Religious and secular music expressed the sentimental character of American life in the pre-Civil War years. Lowell Mason (1792–1872), banker, writer and compiler of hymns, teacher, and president of Boston's Handel and Haydn Society, wrote such familiar religious songs as "Nearer, My God, to Thee" and "My Faith Looks Up to Thee." Mason promoted music teaching in the schools. Revival songs remained popular.

Sentimental ballads, such as Henry Russell's "A Life on the Ocean Wave," won a wide audience. Stephen Foster (1826–1864) popularized another type of folk music and became one of the most famous songwriters in American history with such plantation melodies as "Old Folks at Home," "My Old Kentucky Home," and "Old Black Joe." Of far greater cultural significance were the Negro spirituals which reflected the spirit and hope, as well as the trials, of slavery in the South. European musical tastes appeared; New York, Philadelphia, and other cities had opera companies and symphony orchestras, although a busy, mobile people denied them the needed public support. The United States produced no serious American composers before 1860.

Americans viewed themselves as religious people, and their religion was primarily Protestant Christianity. Deism and other forms of religious rationalism found little acceptance in the early nineteenth century, when most people preferred a warmer, more personal faith. Religion was by no means an individual matter, however; it permeated almost every facet of society. Americans looked upon Christianity as the promoter and sustainer of moral rectitude and political liberty. They saw the three as inextricably bound together.

In the 1790s, it had seemed to many that there was no future for religion or the church in the new Republic. John Marshall declared that the church was "too far gone ever to be revived." But the skepticism and indifference so characteristic after the Revolution gave way to religious revival after 1800. Under the influence of evangelical preaching, religious teaching in the colleges, and the leadership of some outstanding clergymen, Protestantism experienced a notable

A revivalist, or camp, meeting at Eastham, Massachusetts, in 1842.   Media Features

and unexpected renewal and expansion. Moreover, when the separation of church and state became final—Massachusetts abolished taxes for church support in 1833—churches throve as never before on private contributions.

At the beginning of the nineteenth century, Congregationalism was the leading denomination in New England. In the Middle Atlantic states, the Dutch Reformed, Episcopalians, Quakers, and Presbyterians were the dominant religious bodies. South of the Potomac, the Episcopalians held a predominant position, especially among the upper classes, but in some communities they were being overtaken by the Presbyterians. Large numbers of Catholics occupied the belt from Maryland northward to New York. Except for the Quakers, most services of these eastern denominations were ritualistic and formal, qualities which did not fulfill the more emotional religious needs of people in the rapidly growing West. There the Methodists and Baptists predominated, joined later by the Disciples of Christ and other such evangelistic sects.

Revivalism emerged as one highly significant development in American religious history during the second quarter of the nineteenth century. The great revivals of the early years of the century had declined in the East. But the movement soon arose in the West, and continued intermittently among the more evangelistic denominations such as the Baptists, Methodists, and western Presbyterians. Charles G. Finney, a New Englander reared in western New York and licensed to preach by the Presbyterians in 1824, was the greatest revivalist of the pre-Civil War era.

Some Americans preferred a more intellectual approach to their religion. In New England, Unitarians abandoned the tenets of Calvinism, rejected the Trinity and other traditional Christian beliefs, and preached the goodness of man, a loving God, religious joy, and the importance of good works. William Ellery Channing and Lyman Beecher were among the great Unitarian preachers whose influence went far beyond their pulpits. Universalism did not differ greatly from Unitarianism in its theology, but the acceptance of universal salvation as preached by the Universalists was confined largely to country districts of New England. Altogether, those with some Protestant allegiance may have totaled 7 million by 1850.

Membership in the Roman Catholic Church made rapid gains, especially after 1830. Most of the increase resulted from German and Irish immigration. Boston, Philadelphia, New York, and Baltimore drew many Irish Catholics, and in the 1840s a large German Catholic emigration extended as far west as Missouri and Wisconsin. Between 1830 and 1850 the number of Catholics rose from approximately 600,000 to 3,500,000. They did not, however, escape periodic criticism, discrimination, and charges of un-Americanism. Following a dispute over public support for Catholic schools in New York City, a strong nativist movement began in the late 1830s which led to the Know-Nothing Movement in the 1850s. The nativists demanded tight restrictions on immigration and naturalization to discourage the influx of Catholics.

The intense interest in religion resulted also in the formation of some new religious movements. Alexander Campbell organized a new denomination commonly called "Christians" or "Disciples of Christ." They favored local autonomy in church government and declared that their only creed or guide was the New Testament. In the early 1830s, William Miller, a New Englander with a Baptist background, began to preach the Second Coming of Christ, predicting that Christ would return on March 21, 1843. By the late 1830s, he had won thousands of supporters. However, when Christ did not appear then or on subsequent dates, Miller and his followers gave up the idea of an immediate Second Coming. In 1846 they organized the Seventh Day Adventist Church, observing the Jewish Sabbath rather than Sunday as the day of worship. After Miller's death in 1849, Ellen G. White led the movement.

Spiritualism attracted many people who resided in western New York, a center of religious radicalism and revivalism. The Fox sisters near Palmyra in 1847 began to hear rapping and knocking noises, which purportedly were sounds from the spirit world. Many people became convinced that one could commune with the dead. Scores of books and pamphlets popularized this notion. Spiritualism fascinated many Americans, but it never evolved into an organized body of believers.

Western New York was the home of Joseph Smith, founder of Mormonism. The son of poor parents, Smith and his family settled near Palmyra, New York, in 1815. As a boy, Smith experienced visions, and in 1827 he declared that an angel had revealed to him the location of golden plates which contained sacred writings. Smith said that he dug up the plates and, during the next three years, translated them. This *Book of Mormon*, which was printed at Palmyra in 1830, purported to be the history of settlements in America by refugees from the Tower of Babel and Jerusalem. After centuries of fighting, only Mormon, his son Moroni, and a few others remained. The records were supposedly buried by Moroni, who predicted that a prophet would finally discover them. Many accepted the *Book of Mormon* as a spiritual guide and Smith as a prophet. Through intense missionary effort the Church of Latterday Saints soon won thousands of converts.

Black Americans had considerable interest in religion and, after being rejected by most white congregations, formed their own churches. The African Methodist Episcopal Church spread rapidly among free blacks in the North during the early nineteenth century. Even more attractive to blacks in subsequent years were the many Baptist congregations which they organized and supported. Southern whites opposed the organization of free black congregations; consequently Negro church bodies in the South made only minor progress before the Civil War. Nevertheless, many black Americans found solace in religion.

During the 1830s and 1840s, Americans developed a remarkable concern for social and humanitarian reform. Spurred by religious and democratic zeal, people believed that a new Canaan might be built here on earth. Churches and religious leaders called attention to the need of temperance, better care for the insane, improved prison conditions, education, international peace, and the abolition of slavery.

Historically, Americans had appeared to be hard drinkers, consuming large quantities of rum, hard cider, brandy, wines, and whisky. Nothing in Puritanism forbade drinking intoxicating liquors, and even the clergy drank freely. But in the late eighteenth century, strong voices attacked intemperance. Timothy Dwight, who became president of Yale in 1795, associated sobriety with godliness and sought to restrict student drinking. After 1800, revivalist religion inspired increasingly active support for the temperance movement. Opponents of liquor argued that there was a direct connection between drinking and crime and pauperism, while others complained that the social cost of caring for excessive drinkers was needlessly high. Lyman Beecher, a leader of New England's temperance movement, declared that "intemperance is the sin of our land." By the 1820s, the time seemed ripe for an organized effort against liquor and the liquor traffic.

Temperance advocates formed the American Society for the Promotion of Temperance in 1826; by 1834 the society claimed a million members. Soon thereafter a split developed between those who favored only temperance and those who insisted on total abstinence. Beginning in the late 1830s, the drive for complete prohibition tended to overshadow the less radical demand for temperance. An outpouring of literature attacked the use of liquor. T. S. Arthur's *Ten Nights in a Bar Room* was the most dramatic and influential piece of antiliquor literature. By the 1840s, prohibition forces had made great gains, and in 1851, under the leadership of

Neal Dow, Maine legislators passed the first statewide prohibition law.

Prisoner abuse wounded the conscience of reformers. Humanitarians found the dirty, overcrowded jails and the mistreatment of prisoners revolting. If criminals were to be reformed, it seemed evident that better buildings and improved administration of prisons were necessary. In addition to better buildings, reformers demanded the reduction of physical punishment, the separation of the sexes, and the introduction of religious teaching in the prisons.

The English practice of imprisonment for debt was still widely followed in America during the early nineteenth century. In 1816, for instance, New York City jails alone held some 2,000 debtors, many of whom owed less than $25. People could be, and were, imprisoned for debts of only a few cents. Reformers argued that imprisonment for debt was not only inhumane, but that a debtor could not possibly pay his obligation so long as he was confined. At last, in 1821, Kentucky outlawed imprisonment for debt, and during the next forty years most states made the debtors' prison illegal.

Reformers also directed their concern at the plight of the mentally ill. Prior to 1800, most insane persons were cared for by relatives who did little more than tie them up or lock them in a room. In some cases, insane persons were held in jail. In the early nineteenth century, however, reformers called for at least some degree of psychiatric treatment and state care for the mentally ill. But progress toward construction of special, tax-supported hospitals for the insane made slight headway. In 1840, most mental patients still received only private care. Dorothea Dix of Massachusetts took the lead in improving the care of mental patients. Miss Dix reported in 1843, after investigating conditions in her state, that she had seen insane persons "in *cages, closets, cellars, stalls, pens! Chained, naked, beaten with rods, and lashed into obedience.*" She campaigned from state to state on behalf of state-supported institutions for the mentally ill. By 1860 many of the states had appropriated funds to establish mental hospitals.

The vision of international peace did not escape the reformers. The Quakers were among the most vocal critics of war, but ministers of other denominations also denounced it. Antiwar arguments usually flowed from the teachings of Christ. As was true with most reform movements, peace advocates formed associations to promote their ideas and demands. In 1828 one group met in New York City to organize the American Peace Society. During subsequent years scores of books and articles advocated peace, but pacifism won few adherents in the United States.

The Role of Women

While women played an important role in the achievement of humanitarian reform, they were interested as well in expanding their own freedoms. Many observers believed that women received greater respect and better treatment in America than anywhere else in the world, but as late as the early nineteenth century women lived under numerous legal and social restrictions. Most Americans would restrict women to the home, limiting their special role to that of wife and mother. Women were considered the guardians of morality, piety, culture, and general social stability. Their legal status reflected their basic position in society. Married women had no legal control over property or wages, no right to guardianship over their children in the event of divorce or desertion by a husband. They could not vote. As late as 1850 some states permitted a husband to beat his wife "with a reasonable instrument."

Growing numbers of women rejected this traditional role of subservience and discrimination, demanding equal rights. An outstanding feminist leader was Francis Wright, a Scotswoman who emigrated to the United States in 1818. She horrified most Americans by advocating not only more social and legal freedom but also greater sexual freedom for women, including extramarital sexual relations. Her radical ideology, influenced by the French Revolution, alienated most middle-class Americans because of its "infidelity." She conveyed her ideas in the press and from the rostrum. This made her seem even less conventional, for any woman's appearance on a public platform was shocking.

Other women who worked effectively for equal rights were Sarah Grimké, whose *Letters on the Equality of the Sexes* (1838) was the first significant feminist tract; Margaret Fuller, author of *Woman in the Nineteenth Century* (1845), which called for full freedom for women; Lucretia

Susan B. Anthony. *The Granger Collection*

Mott, a Philadelphia Quaker; Elizabeth Cady Stanton; and Susan B. Anthony. Stanton and Mott were among organizers of the first woman's rights convention in Seneca Falls, New York, in 1848. This noted gathering asserted that men and women were created equal; it demanded the same social, economic, and political rights for both sexes, including the right to vote. During the years which followed, several states passed laws extending the property rights of married women and giving them some legal control over their children.

Women gradually entered the professions and broke new paths to greater independence. Elizabeth Blackwell in 1848 became the first trained woman doctor in the United States; Antoinette Brown in 1853 received ordination as a Congregational minister; and Mary Ann Shadd, a free Negro, edited a newspaper for fugitive slaves who had escaped to Canada. Other women forged careers as missionaries, writers, actresses, and teachers. But women did not win the right to vote until after the Civil War.

Conclusion

During the pre-Civil War years, most Americans were highly nationalistic—proud of their country, its institutions, and its material progress. They recognized weaknesses in American society, but believed them entirely correctable. Indeed, Americans demonstrated a deep concern for improving the quality of national life as they set out to eliminate such evils as ignorance, poverty, and injustice. Education and religion they considered two of the most effective levers for raising the level of society. Although Americans generally were not directly involved in the fine arts and literature, some of its painters and writers won international acclaim. The abiding concern of many people for various reforms amply demonstrated the perennial American dissatisfaction with social conditions, as well as the willingness of Americans to experiment in their quest for greater justice and a better life.

SUGGESTED READINGS

One of the best interpretations of the American character is Arthur M. Schlesinger's "What Then Is the American, This New Man," *American Historical Review*, XLVIII (January 1943). Concentrating on the 1830s and 1840s, Carl Russell Fish has discussed and analyzed American social and intellectual life in *The Rise of the Common Man* (1927), while in *Young America, 1830–1840* (1949), Robert E. Riegel has dealt with a single decade. *The Growth of American Thought* (2d ed., 1951) by Merle E. Curti has excellent material on the country's intellectual trends during these years. Ralph Gabriel's *The Course of American Democratic Thought* (2d ed., 1956) is very good on this subject.

Developments in pre-Civil War education can be followed in H. G. Good's *A History of American Education* (1956). Carl Bode in *The American Lyceum: Town Meeting of the Mind* (1956) provides a good discussion of the development of the lyceum.

The standard survey on American religion is William Warren Sweet's *The Story of Religion in America* (1950 ed.) See also Sweet's *Religion in the Development of American Culture, 1765–1840* (1952). Timothy L. Smith emphasizes the role of revivalism in social reform in *Revivalism and Social Reform in Mid-nineteenth Century America* (1957). Two other excellent studies of religious manifestations are Charles A. Johnson's *The Frontier Camp Meeting* (1955), and *The Burned-over District** (1950) by Whitney R. Cross. On nativism, see Ray A. Billington's *The Protestant Crusade** (1938). For a discussion of pre-Civil War journalism, students should consult volumes I and II of Frank L. Mott's *A History of American Magazines* (1937) and his *American Journalism: A History of Newspapers in the United States through 250 Years, 1690–1940* (1941).

There are a number of excellent studies on American literature for the years before the Civil War.

These include volume II of Vernon Louis Parrington's *Main Currents in American Thought** (1927), which is a classic. Also very good is Van Wyck Brooks's *The Flowering of New England, 1815–1865** (1940 ed.) and his book on *The Times of Melville and Whitman* (1947).

For accounts of art in American life consult Oliver W. Larkin's *Art and Life in America* (1949) and Eugene Neuhaus's *The History and Ideals of American Art* (1931). Neil Harris emphasizes art as a profession in *The Artist in American Society: The Formative Years, 1790–1860* (1966), while Lillian B. Miller shows how Americans encouraged the fine arts in *Patrons and Patriotism: The Encouragement of the Fine Arts in the United States, 1790–1860* (1966). On music see Gilbert Chase's *America's Music* (1955).

The best survey of reformism is Alice Felt Tyler's *Freedom Ferment: Phases of American Social History to 1860** (1944). Specific reform movements are dealt with by John A. Krout in *The Origins of Prohibition* (1925); Blake McKelvey in *American Prisons: A Study in American Social History Prior to 1915* (1936); and Merle E. Curti in *The American Peace Crusade* (1929). On the struggle for women's rights see Eleanor Flexner, *Century of Struggle: The Women's Rights Movement in the United States* (1968); William L. O'Neill, *Everyone Was Brave: The Rise and Fall of Feminism in America* (1969); Gerda Lerner, *The Black Woman in White America* (1972); and Anne F. Scott, *The Southern Lady* (1970).

*indicates availability in paperback.

11

The Northern Economy, 1815-1860

During that half century which separated the War of 1812 from the American Civil War the country expanded on every front—in population, agriculture, transportation, industry, even territory. Never before had it been more true that the United States was a land of opportunity. The new agricultural and urban frontiers, with their momentary hardships, did not necessarily exert a leveling influence on American society, for each new settlement encouraged and recognized its own aristocracy of wealth, education, and personal distinction. But if the new regions of settlement in the great Mississippi Valley did not create a uniquely American society, they did create the foundations of abundance. Even at that the exploitation of new frontiers curtailed rather than increased per capita productivity in the United States, for it directed much of the nation's energy into pursuits that did little to improve economic efficiency. Per capita income during the 1830s, despite the decade's major economic boom, rose only about 0.6 percent

annually. Not until after 1840 did the American people create the urban, technological, and financial bases of genuine economic growth. Only then did the country enter the industrial age and begin to expand its per capita production at an ever-increasing rate. The country's slowly rising standard of living was sufficient to excite the envy of most foreigners. When Jenny Lind, the famous Swedish singer, arrived in the United States in 1850, she looked at the crowds and exclaimed: "How well dressed everybody is— have you no poor people in America?"

Until 1860 agriculture was the leading economic activity in the United States. Farmers were important to the economy because they produced food for the growing urban population. In 1850 the average farmer of the United States could feed himself and four city dwellers. Agriculture also supplied most of the raw materials for the developing industries. This was especially true for the South with its large staple production of cotton and tobacco. Meat-packing, flour milling, and textiles were among the manufactures which depended on agriculture for their raw materials. Despite the predominance of agriculture, the country after 1840 presented a reasonably well-balanced economy. Commerce, industry, mining, transportation, and services all grew swiftly and contributed to the country's substantial economic growth.

Thus long before the Civil War the burgeoning complexity of the American economy had created an unprecedented interregional dependence. Never before had the economy been as truly national, with the South furnishing raw materials for Northern industry, the Northeast supplying the South and West its manufactured products, and the West exporting both foodstuffs and the products of its growing cities. Still the Southern and Northern economies, one overwhelmingly agricultural with a unique labor system, the other balanced between agriculture and industry, were sufficiently different that for reasons of organization and understanding they can be studied separately. This chapter focuses on economic developments in the North; the following chapter, on the special qualities of Southern economic and social life.

Population Growth and New Settlements

In 1815 the United States was largely undeveloped economically, its rich natural resources still awaiting exploitation by farmers and businessmen. To develop this abundant natural wealth the country required a rapidly growing population which, in turn, would create unprecedented opportunities for labor, capital, and entrepreneurial skill. In 1800 the United States contained only 5.3 million people, but by 1860 it claimed more than 31 million. Of the total population in 1860, about 26.9 million were whites and 4.4 million, blacks. Most of the latter were slaves.

Besides the high birthrate an endless stream of immigrants from Europe to American shores, especially after 1840, added to the population. In the peak year of immigration before the Civil War—1854—nearly 428,000 foreigners arrived. They came chiefly from Ireland, Germany, and, later, the Scandinavian countries. The potato famine in Ireland in the 1840s, added to political difficulties, low wages, heavy taxes, and general lack of economic opportunity, caused many Europeans to leave their homelands and migrate to the United States. Many of the Irish immigrants remained in the growing Eastern cities, but they also provided much of the cheap labor used between 1830 and 1860 to construct the canals and railroads. Germans and Scandinavians spread over the Middle West, settling in both cities and rural areas. The evolution of more liberal land laws encouraged the rapid westward march of settlement. The land laws of 1800 and 1804 enabled settlers to purchase land directly from the federal government, but these measures also encouraged speculation. In 1820 Congress abandoned the credit system, lowered the amount of land a person could buy to 80 acres, and reduced the price to $1.25 an acre. Although national land laws made it increasingly easier for farmers to acquire land, some members of Congress sought additional measures to serve the interests of those willing to till the soil. The Preemption Act of 1841 was designed especially to protect actual and potential squatters against speculators who might outbid them when land was put up for sale at public auction. Thereafter those concerned most directly with national land policy insisted that the federal government, under the homestead principle, give actual settlers 160 acres of public land. Not until 1862 did Congress incorporate this principle into law.

After 1820 settlers continued to flow into the unoccupied prairies of the great Mississippi Valley. The Panic of 1819 slowed the movement for a half decade; thereafter it quickly reached flood tide until halted again by the crash of 1837. By

1850 much of the Old Northwest had been occupied. Another heavy migration pushed west and south into Kentucky, Tennessee, Alabama, Mississippi, Louisiana, and even Texas. What lured the settlers was not only the attraction of land, but also improved roads, steamboats on the rivers, governmental control over the Indians, and the old habit of pioneering.

Northern Agriculture

General farming, which involved a combination of crops and livestock, prevailed throughout the Northern states during the pre-Civil War years. Corn was the dominant crop. The soil and climate in the region from Pittsburgh to Iowa were so ideally suited for corn that a distinct "corn belt" developed in the eastern part of this region as early as the 1840s. Wheat ranked second among Northern crops. In the 1820s and 1830s, western New York and Pennsylvania and eastern Ohio dominated American wheat production. But like corn, wheat growing moved rapidly westward to the prairies of southern Michigan, northern Indiana and Illinois and southern Wisconsin. Northern farmers also raised oats, barley, rye, and flax, as well as fruits and vegetables, in abundance.

Livestock provided some income on most Northern farms, for cattle, hogs, and sheep usually found ready cash markets. Livestock was driven to distant markets long before efficient transportation made it profitable to ship wheat or other bulky products over long distances. Cincinnati and Chicago became important packing centers in the 1840s and 1850s and provided additional outlets for hogs and cattle. Dairying was important throughout the Northern states. Before 1860 commercial dairying was concentrated mostly in New England and the Middle Atlantic states, especially New York.

Agriculture's rapid march westward to the Mississippi and beyond by 1860 caused the decline and readjustments of farming in the Northeast. After canals and railroads reduced the cost of transportation, farmers in New England and the Middle Atlantic states could not compete in grain and meat production with the larger and more productive farms in the West. Conse-quently, farmers in the Northeast ceased to produce wheat, corn, hogs, and wool commercially, and concentrated on dairying, fruit growing, vegetable farming, and other specialties which they marketed in the nearby cities. But even major adjustments of production could not save many farmers in the Northeast.

Growing mechanization of farm operations was a significant reason for the increased output of Northern farms. In 1800 only a few crude implements, such as plows and harrows, used power provided by oxen or horses. Most farm labor was performed by hand tools not greatly different from those used by the Romans. Corn, for example, was planted, cultivated, and harvested entirely by hand. During the next half century, new and improved machines became available for many important phases of farm production. By 1819 Jethro Wood of New York had invented a successful iron plow, but John Deere's steel plow gradually replaced it in the late 1830s and afterward. The steel plow cleaned itself more readily and was strong enough to break the tough prairie sod. In 1833 Obed Hussey, and a year later Cyrus McCormick, built reapers, which within a few years reduced the labor necessary for harvesting small grains. Threshing machines began to replace the flail in the 1840s.

Greater production flowed also from the greater application of science to farming. By the 1830s, agricultural reformers urged farmers to conserve their soil, to rotate their crops, and to use fertilizer. Some farmers adopted improved practices, but most Northern farmers exploited their soil without much concern for long-range productivity. Of the three factors of production —land, labor, and capital—land was the cheap-

During Andrew Jackson's lifetime American folk art rose and
flourished as it never had before. This creative expression
of untutored painters is a self-conscious record of
particular faces, scenes, and events. By
describing these in great detail —
one of the most common
characteristics of the

Folk Art as History

self-taught artist's work — the
painter serves as the social historian of his
time and place. His observations about his society
make him a particularly useful critic and commentator.
The examples of folk art shown here are among the most telling documents
in an art that flourished from the end of the Revolution to the eve of the
Civil War. During this period, the faces and manners of the rising middle
class were illustrated by painters of comparable status and background. In
performing a useful service that was much in demand, the self-taught painter

Terrence J. Kennedy, Political Banner, ca. 1840. New York State Historical Association, Cooperstown, N.Y.

The nineteenth-century political banner on the previous page, approximately five feet in diameter, encompasses the dominant elements of American life a midcentury. Industry, commerce, politics, and agriculture appear symbolically in this canvas by young Terence J. Kennedy of Auburn, N.Y. The eagle from the nation's seal stands zealous guard over the composite scene. The three-masted schooner and the side-wheeler sailing choppy seas at left center; the train towpath, bridges, and canal at right center; and the anvil and bodkin in the foreground—all serve as concrete reminders of the prosperous nation's business and trade. Agrarian interests are demonstrated in the livestock, plow, and rake set around a pond fed by a waterfall. This idealization accurately reflects the inventiveness, the excitement, the prosperity that prevailed

became a respected and important member of his cultural community, and his work constitutes a small mirror reflecting the appearance, possessions, and attitudes of many nineteenth-century Americans. Folk art fulfills this function admirably. Were aesthetic virtue the criterion for the works selected here, the portraits of the tire-maker as manufacturer, the sign-painter as artisan, and the pedlar as merchant would not appear; but as detailed illustrations of man's work in the new republic, they provide valuable information.

This brief glimpse of American folk art reveals only a fragment of a vast record kept in rural areas and in small towns by great numbers of naïve painters whose talents ranged from the mediocre to the sublime. Except for Lockport on Erie Canal, *a watercolor (right), all the paintings in this portfolio are oil on canvas.*

The folk paintings on the following pages are accompanied by text and captions writt especially for this volume by Mary Black. Mrs. Black is co-author with Jean Lipman American Folk Painting (Clarkson Potter, 1967) and is Director of the Museum American Folk Art in New York Ci

The first spadeful of dirt for the Erie Canal was turned at Rome, N.Y., 1817; "De Witt Clinton's ditch" opened to commerce in 1825. Trade goo and agricultural products moved along the water road providing a new li between the business enterprises of the northeast and the gateway to pione land

The change in grade from Lake Erie to Albany was chiefly made up a down the water steps at Lockport. These are portrayed in the naïve a romanticized watercolor by Mary Keys, which is probably based on the pri after a painting by George Catlin published in Cadwallader Colden's 18 Canal Memo

Right: Mary Keys Lockport on the Erie Canal, 1832. Munson-Williams-Proctor Institute, Utica, N

A portrait of the New York town of Eagle Mill
dramatically illustrates the change that took
place in the Northeast after 1820. Rich and
productive farmland surrounds the settlement to
which a new mill has given its name. The
factory, situated along a stream from which it
receives its power, is connected to the surrounding
homes, stores, and churches by a two-lane
covered bridge.

*Attributed to T. Wilson, Eagle Mills, N.Y., ca. 1845. Abby Aldrich
Rockefeller Folk Art Collection, Williamsburg, Va.*

Towns and factories lay beyond the heart of town
where houses, hotels, shops, and churches testify to the
work and pleasure of domestic life. Joseph Hidley was
a lifelong resident of Poestenkill, N.Y., the village that
became his favorite painting subject. Between 1830
and his death forty-two years later he worked as an
artist and also learned taxidermy and cabinet making.
In Hidley's picture of Poestenkill (left) the landscape
and the people remain the same while the seasons and
the vantage point change.
More often than not the craftsman lived in the
heart of town. The chairmaker, David Alling of
Newark, N.J., lived and worked in the attractive
commercial and residential buildings seen below. Two
of Alling's ladder-back chairs are set before the shop
and office doors.

Left: Joseph H. Hidley, Poestenkill, N.Y., ca. 1855. The Metropolitan Museum
of Art. Gift of Edgar William and Bernice Chrysler Garbisch, 1963. Above: Artist unknown, House and Shop of David Alling, Newark Chair Maker, 1777–1875, ca.
1830. The Newark Museum, Purchase 1939, Thomas L. Raymond bequest.

The three genre scenes here show the rise of industry and the increase of traffic along the nation's newly developed roads.

Often the man who became an established folk artist began life as an apprentice in sign or carriage painting. In a scene painted by an unknown artist about 1845, a painter and two assistants work on a sign that illustrates the predominant Northeastern sentiments toward support of the Union over the individual state's rights. At left, an assistant mixes oil with paint on a slab while another at the right stands ready to lay out broad areas of color. The proprietor, distinguished from the workers by his dress, is the craftsman who letters and illustrates the political sign with a portrait of the first President. Even fifty years after his death, Washington's likeness epitomized the nation's government.

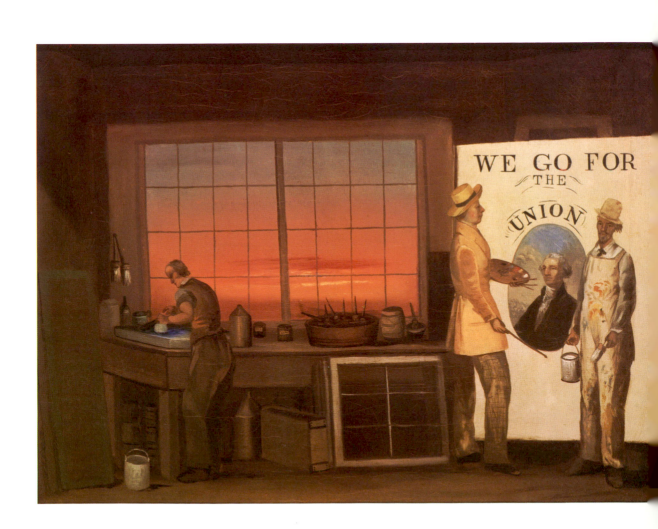

Right, above, a blacksmith and his two apprentices are shown in a California shop. An impressive and instructive array of blacksmithing tools surrounds the hand-operated bellows. The owner presides over his anvil in top hat, leather apron, and shirtsleeves, while the two workers wear derbies which may provide protection against flying objects, sparks, and scraps of iron. The painter, H. M. T. Powell, worked in California in the mid-1850s after traveling there along the Sante Fe trail.

Another small businessman was the Yankee peddler (right, below). Here he displays his goods in a country kitchen already amply stocked with produce and trader's goods. Part of the traveling merchant's stock hangs along the sides of his cart outside at the farmhouse door.

Artist unknown, We Go for the Union, ca. 1845; and above: H. M. T. Powell, Blacksmith Shop, ca. 1855. National Gallery of Art, Washington, D.C. Gift of William and Bernice Chrysler Garbisch. Right, below: unknown, Yankee Pedlar, ca. 1845. Collection of IBM Corporation.

our citizens of the new republic are commemorated here in portraits that capture not
only their features but also their prosperity and
industry. Maxwell B. Chace (left) was a sea
captain or ship owner. His vessel probably
appears in the background, and the chart in his
hand may indicate that New York is the ship's
home port. An unidentified Indiana merchant
(right) records in his ledger the artist's name,
R. B. Crafft, and the approximate date of the
painting, August 16, 1836. A physician in the
New York town of Pine Plains, Cornelius
Allerton (below) had his interest in horse-raising
illustrated in the figure of a miniature saddle
horse on the table beside him. William Whipper
(right, below), son of a black house servant and
her white employer, was apprenticed as a
carpenter and joiner in his youth. The tiny
gold saw on his watch chain indicates his trade
and his success at the lumber trade. A free
negro, Whipper became a leader in the
abolitionist movement.

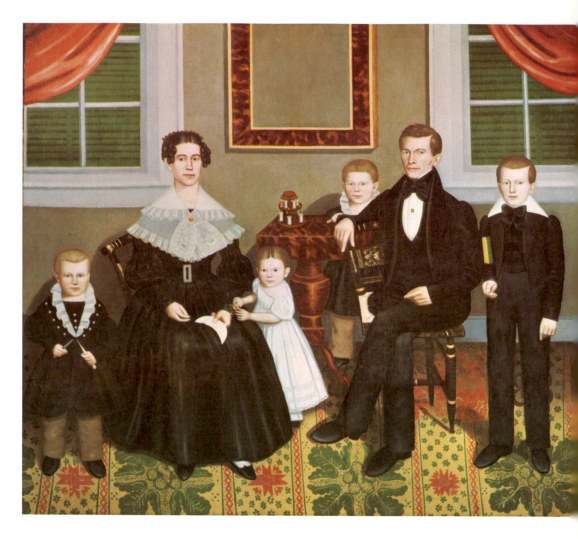

Painted in southern New England only five years apart, these two family portraits illustrate the prosperity and comfort of small-town life. Although the panic of 1837 brought ruin to many families, no hint of crisis mars these insights into family life. Joseph Moore, his wife, their two children, an the orphaned children of Mrs. Moore's sister pose in their best suits and dresses against a colorful living room furnished with possessions now owned along with the portrait, by the Boston Museum. The house at 12 Pleasant Street in Ware, Mass., appears as it did in 1839 when the artist, E. S. Fie was living with his in-laws on the same street.

Nathan Starr was a munitions maker in Middletown, Conn., where the family had manufactured arms since the end of the Revolution. The younger Starr children play at battledore and shuttlecock while their older sister watches them complacently. The wide-flung door shows the scene beyond, a view that includes the Starr factory located on the Connecticut River. The artist, Ambrose Andrews, began his career as an itinerant painter. By the 1850s he had learned to paint in academic style and exhibited at the American Art Union and the National Academy.

Left: Erastus Salisbury Field, The Family of Joseph Moore, 1839. Courtesy of the Museum of Fine Arts, Boston, M. and M. Karolik Collection. Above: Ambrose Andrews, The Children of Nathan Starr, 1835. Mr. and Mrs. Nathan C. Starr, New York.

Edward Hicks, The Residence of David Twining, 1787; *ca.* 1846. *Abby Aldrich Rockefeller Folk Art Collection, Williamsburg, Va.*

One of four versions known of the Quaker painter's boyhood home, Edward Hicks reconstructed this scene from memory. The farm appears here as it did when he first went to live with the Twinings as a child of three. No painter captured the abundance and the beauty of eastern Pennsylvania with greater skill than Hicks. The soft golden light, pink-tinged skies, and hazy distances accurately record the look of its prosperous fields. Serenity fills the air, in contrast to the excitement of the uneasy truces between the ideal and the real worlds in his Peaceable Kingdoms. Orphaned as a child, Hicks was apprenticed to a carriage-maker when he was only thirteen, then progressed to signs. When he was twenty-one, he turned from a life that had been easy and undisciplined to become a Quaker and eventually a Quaker preacher.

The ewe and suckling lamb, familiar from his Kingdoms and his several versions of the Birthplace of William Penn, appear in all four Twining farm scenes. Although a plowman stands behind a team of horses in every farm scene but one that Hicks painted, only in this painting is the plowman black. Mary Twining Leedom and her husband are set in poses borrowed directly from the engraving that inspired Hicks's paintings of Washington crossing the Delaware.

Twining Farm is incisive painting. But instead of a unified composition on a single theme, here a clear staccato beat draws the eye from scene to scene. The mare with foal and cow with calf at left background are vignettes inspired by newspaper or almanac reproductions of John Anderson's woodcuts. The animals at either side, the well with a sweep handle, and an apple press for cider are typical Buck's County fixtures.

Many of the tedious and time-consuming jobs required to maintain life in frontier communities were shared labors that became entertainment for the participants. In an art in which static scenes are the rule, the exceptions are interesting. In the painting Flax Scutching (following spread), Linton Park depicts a lively scene in which a whole community takes part in the conversion of flax to linen thread. Armed with paddles and dressed up by western Pennsylvania standards, the group engages in scutching the flax over upright boards set into the ground. The scene is almost Flemish, but translated to American soil and placed against a background of pioneer cabins. Park was a lumberjack and his trade is reflected in the piles of logs and the neatly felled tree in the foreground.

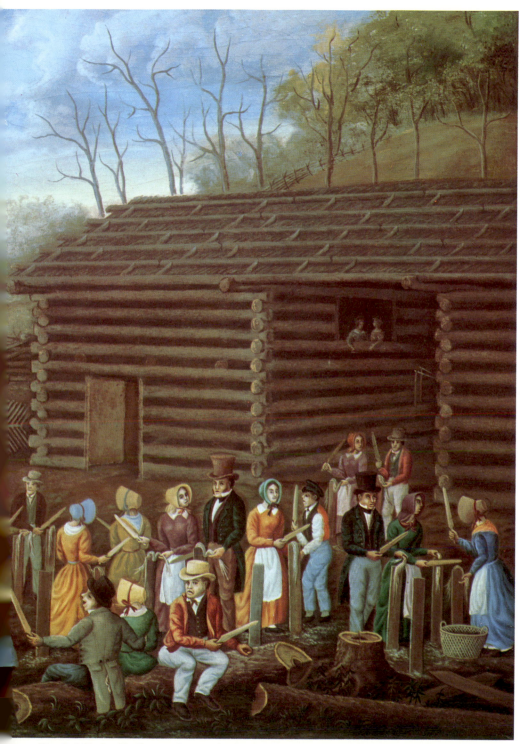

Linton Park, Flax Scutching Bee, *ca. 1860. National Gallery of Art, Washington, D.C. Gift of Edgar William and Bernice Chrysler Garbisch.*

A. Tapy, The Neigh of an Iron Horse, *1859. Collection of Edgar William and Bernice Chrysler Garbisch, New York.*

This scene fittingly ends an era in which romanticism gave wa
technology. The terrified horse gallops away from a toy-sized train a
trundles across the pastoral landscape. The streaming mane and tail of
horse repeat the arc of the railroad cars as they round a tr

est. Thus it appeared good sense to exploit the land, at least temporarily, rather than apply expensive labor or capital in the form of fertilizer or soil-conservation practices.

Perhaps the most fundamental change which occurred in Northern agriculture before the Civil War was the gradual shift from self-sufficient to commercial farming. Pioneer farmers produced much of their own food, made some of their clothing, and manufactured such items as furniture, utensils, and soap. But as transportation improved and towns developed, farmers turned more and more to production for sale rather than for home use. By the 1850s, commercial agriculture flourished as far west as Illinois and southern Wisconsin.

Transportation and Communication

Fundamental to the country's economic advance was a reasonably efficient transportation system. By 1860 a network of roads, canals, and railroads bound the nation, especially the Northern section, into an economic whole. Improved transportation permitted lower freight rates, facilitated the movement of raw materials and finished products, expanded markets, and greatly stimulated industrial growth. Traffic on the rivers, lakes, and coastal waterways increased markedly, but failed to keep pace with the railroads.

The construction of turnpikes (usually built by private corporations which charged fees to those who traveled over them) represented one of the earlier efforts to improve overland transportation. Between 1790 and the 1820s, private and public agencies constructed thousands of miles of dirt and crushed-rock roads in New England, New York, Pennsylvania, and to a lesser extent, in the Southern states. The Cumberland, or National, Road was the nation's most famous turnpike. Begun in 1811 as a federal project, it ran from Cumberland, Maryland, to Wheeling, West Virginia, on the Ohio River, and by 1840 had reached Vandalia, Illinois.

The expansion of river traffic also provided new avenues for trade and commerce. Rafts, flatboats, and barges carried people, as well as large amounts of freight, well into the nineteenth century. The development of a successful steamboat by Robert Fulton in New York in 1807 opened a new era in river traffic. In 1811, Nicholas J. Roosevelt sent a steamboat from Pittsburgh to New Orleans; within a few years steamboats were plying the Ohio, Mississippi, Missouri, and many lesser rivers.

But neither turnpikes nor steamboats could meet the transportation needs of countless new communities. By 1815, a strong demand arose for the construction of canals. In New York, Governor De Witt Clinton took the lead in arguing for a state-financed canal which would connect Albany on the Hudson to Buffalo on Lake Erie. Such a water connection would give New York City a distinct advantage over Philadelphia and Baltimore in the competition for Western trade. In April 1817, the New York Legislature authorized construction of the canal; eight years later, the last part of the 363-mile waterway was opened for business. Although the canal had cost the state slightly more than $7 million, it was an immediate financial success. It infused western New York with new economic life, and engaged New York City in commerce originating as far west as northern Ohio. The Erie Canal revealed, too, how a state could contribute to general economic development by providing public credit for such an enterprise. The success of the Erie sparked a nationwide movement to construct canals.

Between 1826 and 1834 the "Pennsylvania System" connected Philadelphia and Pittsburgh by a canal at a cost of more than $10 million. Other seaboard states from New England to Virginia spent millions to develop successful canal systems. Ohio and other western states also turned to canal building. By 1840, the United States had 3,326 miles of canals, but the Canal

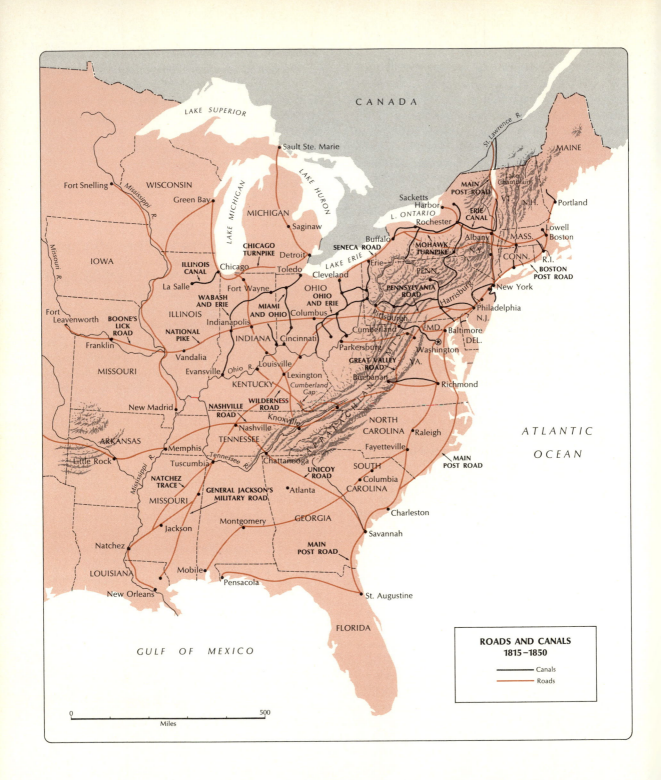

CANADA

LAKE SUPERIOR

Fort Snelling

Sault Ste. Marie

WISCONSIN

Green Bay

LAKE MICHIGAN

LAKE HURON

MICHIGAN

Saginaw

IOWA

CHICAGO
TURNPIKE

Detroit

ILLINOIS
CANAL

Chicago

Toledo

Cleveland

L. ONTARIO

Sacketts
Harbor

Rochester

ERIE
CANAL

MAINE

Lake
Champlain

VT. N.H.

Portland

Albany

Lowell
Boston

MASS.

Buffalo

SENECA ROAD

LAKE ERIE

Erie

MOHAWK
TURNPIKE

N.Y.

CONN.

R.I.

La Salle

Fort Wayne

WABASH
AND ERIE

ILLINOIS

MIAMI
AND OHIO

OHIO
OHIO
AND ERIE

Columbus

PENN.

PENNSYLVANIA
ROAD

Pittsburgh

Harrisburg

New York

BOSTON
POST ROAD

Fort
Leavenworth

BOONE'S
LICK
ROAD

Missouri R.

NATIONAL
PIKE

Indianapolis

INDIANA

Cincinnati

Cumberland

MD.

Philadelphia

N.J.

Baltimore

DEL.

Franklin

Vandalia

Parkersburg

Washington

Mississippi R.

MISSOURI

Evansville

Ohio R.

Louisville

GREAT VALLEY
ROAD

Buchanan

VA.

Lexington

KENTUCKY

Cumberland
Gap

Richmond

New Madrid

NASHVILLE
ROAD

WILDERNESS
ROAD

Knoxville

APPALACHIAN MTS.

NORTH
CAROLINA

Raleigh

ARKANSAS

Nashville

TENNESSEE

Fayetteville

MAIN
POST ROAD

Little Rock

Memphis

Tennessee R.

Chattanooga

UNICOY
ROAD

SOUTH

Columbia

Tuscumbia

NATCHEZ
TRACE

CAROLINA

ATLANTIC

OCEAN

MISSOURI

GENERAL JACKSON'S
MILITARY ROAD

Atlanta

Charleston

Jackson

Montgomery

GEORGIA

Savannah

Natchez

LOUISIANA

Mobile

MAIN
POST ROAD

New Orleans

Pensacola

St. Augustine

FLORIDA

GULF OF MEXICO

ROADS AND CANALS
1815–1850

——— Canals

——— Roads

0   500
Miles

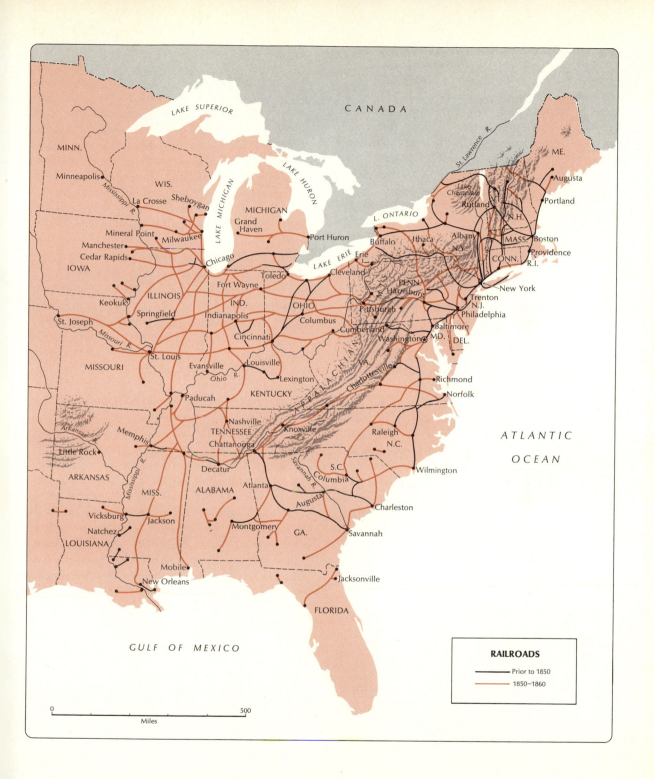

CANADA

LAKE SUPERIOR

MINN.

Minneapolis

WIS.

La Crosse   Sheboygan

Mineral Point   Milwaukee

Manchester

Cedar Rapids

IOWA

Keokuk

Springfield

St. Joseph

MISSOURI

MISSOURI

St. Louis

Evansville   Louisville

Paducah

Memphis

Little Rock

ARKANSAS

Vicksburg

Natchez

LOUISIANA

New Orleans

Mobile

LAKE MICHIGAN   LAKE HURON

MICHIGAN

Grand Haven

Chicago

Fort Wayne

IND.

Indianapolis

ILLINOIS

Cincinnati

Toledo

Port Huron   LAKE ERIE

Cleveland

OHIO

Columbus

Cumberland

KENTUCKY

Lexington

Nashville

TENNESSEE

Chattanooga

Decatur

ALABAMA   Atlanta

MISS.

Jackson

Montgomery

GA.

Augusta

L. ONTARIO

Buffalo   Ithaca   Erie

Lake Champlain

Rutland   VT.

N.H.

ME.

Augusta

Portland

Albany

N.Y.   MASS.   Boston

CONN.   Providence

R.I.

New York

Trenton
N.J.

PENN.   Harrisburg   Philadelphia

Pittsburgh

Baltimore

Washington   MD.   DEL.

VA.

Charlottesville

Richmond

Norfolk

Raleigh
N.C.

S.C.

Columbia   Wilmington

Knoxville

Charleston

Savannah

APPALACHIAN

St. Lawrence R.

Mississippi R.

Missouri R.

Ohio R.

Savannah R.

Arkansas R.

ATLANTIC

OCEAN

Jacksonville

FLORIDA

GULF OF MEXICO

RAILROADS

Prior to 1850

1850–1860

0   500

Miles

THE NORTHERN ECONOMY, 1815–1860

[307]

Age had largely run its course. High construction and maintenance costs, poor management, winter losses from freezing, and the developing competition from railroads combined to bring the Canal Era to a close. Yet, while they operated, canals made a substantial contribution to the nation's economic development by reducing freight rates and opening new areas for settlement. Moreover, the canals, especially the Erie, reduced economic self-sufficiency and encouraged regional specialization and a more integrated economy.

In the long run, railroads answered the transportation problem most effectively. The first railroad chartered in the United States was the Baltimore and Ohio, organized in 1827. Still, successful railroading required a practical steam locomotive. Following experiments with steam locomotives in England during the 1820s, the Charleston and Hamburg Railroad of South Carolina became the first railway in the United States to use a steam engine to pull a train of cars. This was in January 1831. Early railroads were crude and often dangerous affairs: the rails were made of wood with a strip of iron attached, and wood-burning locomotives spit sparks, which frequently caused fires along the track and even ignited the clothes of passengers. Harriet Martineau reported after one railroad trip: "I found that my own gown had thirteen holes in it; and in my veil, with which I saved my eyes, more than could be counted." Early cars were modeled after stagecoaches, and tied together with chains, making a train ride a jerky, rough, and generally uncomfortable experience.

Railroading made slow progress during the 1830s, increasing from 73 to only 2,818 miles in the decade ending in 1840. Following 1840, however, track mileage expanded rapidly, especially in the 1850s. By 1860 the United States led every nation in the world, with more than 30,000 miles of operating railroads. More than two-thirds of the total railroad mileage was in the North and West, a development which tended to unite the economic interests of those regions. Although private individuals furnished much of the capital to finance railroad building by investing in company stocks and bonds, state governments and local communities also provided much of the money for construction. The federal government underwrote some construction cost with land grants. In 1850 Congress gave 3,736,000 acres of land to the Illinois Central to help finance construction of that line between Chicago and New Orleans. This was the first of many federal land grants designed to encourage railroad building. Because of their economy, speed, and dependability, railroads by 1860 had triumphed over all other means of transportation.

The telegraph and an enlarged postal system spurred American economic growth with improved communication. Samuel F. B. Morse invented a successful telegraph and managed the construction of the first line between Baltimore and Washington in 1844. When telegraphic communication reached the West Coast in 1861, most of the nation had telegraph service. Congress increased the number of post offices from only 75 in 1890 to 28,498 by 1860. The Pony Express, inaugurated in April 1860, provided the speediest mail service between the Mississippi Valley and the West Coast, requiring about a week. But it was a financial failure and lasted only about eighteen months.

Shipping and Overseas Trade

Overseas commerce added new markets and encouraged, by the demands it placed on shippers, many significant improvements in ocean transportation. Responding to the need for scheduled sailings between the United States and England, a group of New York merchants in 1817 established the Black Ball line with four fast ships, each to make three runs per year. Through its twelve scheduled trips each year between New York and Liverpool, the line hoped to command much of the passenger and "fine freight" traffic. By the 1840s several companies offered American businessmen and travelers scheduled sailings weekly. Meanwhile these lines had introduced larger, faster ships with more comfortable accommodations.

American ocean sailing reached its final and most dramatic phase with the launching of the famed clipper ships in the 1840s. These magnificent vessels, varying from 2,000 to 4,000 tons and carrying over an acre of sail, set unheard-of records for speed. Donald McKay, the noted New England ship builder, brought the long, narrow, high masted clippers to their ultimate superiority with his *Surprise*. On its maiden voyage the *Surprise* reached California in ninety-six days, reducing by almost half the normal sailing time between New York and San Francisco. Yet from the beginning the clipper ships were doomed. Even during the fifties the steam-power vessels began to replace them, and had taken over much of the ocean transportation by 1860.

Although less important than before the War of 1812, foreign trade continued to be extremely significant in the total economy. Between 1812–1820 and 1856–1860, the average annual value of American foreign trade rose from about $186 million to $616 million, more than tripling in forty years. Exports consisted almost entirely of staple agricultural products. Cotton was the country's most valuable export. Between 1815

The famed clipper ships, whose heyday coincided with the California gold rush in the 1850s, could make the New York–San Francisco run in 90 to 100 days.

and 1860 it totaled more than half the value of American shipments abroad.

Industry and the Rise of the Factory System

In creating new markets, the rapid expansion of agriculture stimulated manufacturing. The greatest industrial development occurred in the Northeast, but manufacturing expanded substantially as far west as Chicago. In some Northern communities manufacturing accounted for more income than farming as early as 1850.

Fortunately, the United States was in a favorable position for potential industrial development. It had abundant supplies of raw materials, such as coal, iron ore, timber, and agricultural commodities. Rivers provided waterpower to run the mills. The United States had access to Western European technology, and Americans possessed the ingenuity to develop laborsaving machines to replace hand and animal power. Furthermore, prominent Americans, such as Washington and Hamilton, actively promoted manufacturing as national policy.

Manufacturing grew slowly before the War of 1812. At that time most industrial production was in the handicraft stage, carried on in households or in small establishments which employed few workers. There were some larger mills producing flour, lumber, textiles, and iron, but the true factory system had not yet appeared.

Francis C. Lowell and his associates first introduced the factory system at Waltham, Massachusetts, in 1814. The Boston Manufacturing Company established by Lowell brought all phases of textile manufacturing—spinning, weaving, and dyeing—together under one management. By installing the latest machinery, including the power loom, Lowell developed the mass production of cotton cloth. Within a few years enterprising businessmen established scores of textile factories; industrialists quickly applied factory techniques to the production of lumber, shoes, flour, men's clothing, leather, wagons and carts, and iron goods.

Each year recorded countless advances in technology and with them the introduction of new, heavier, and more basic industries. The substitution of anthracite coal for charcoal in iron manufacturing, accompanied by improved methods in the processing of pig iron, revolutionized the iron industry. Among other important technical advances in the industrial revolution was the introduction of the interchangeability of parts. This process called for the production of precision-built parts which could be fitted together to make the final product. Eli Whitney, a manufacturer of guns, was one of the first to use this method. Invention of the sewing machine by Elias Howe in 1846 and the development of such machine tools as turrets and lathes were among other significant developments which aided the manufacturing process. By 1860, America's 140,433 manufacturing establishments were turning out products valued at nearly $2 billion. Most of this production was in New England and the Middle Atlantic states. By the time of the Civil War, the United States ranked fourth, possibly second only to Great Britain, in manufacturing, and was already well on the way to becoming the world's leading industrial power.

This industrial expansion would not have been possible without a great increase in the market for manufactured goods. Demand was as essential as supply. The market for industrial commodities grew because of the expanding population, rising real incomes, declining costs of transportation, and the wider distribution of products. Moreover, specialization developed in both the wholesale and retail trades.

From colonial times onward American manufacturers and their political spokesmen had demanded tariff laws to protect domestic products against cheaper imports. Tariff advocates argued that the newer, smaller, and less efficient manufacturing firms in the United States could not compete successfully with the better-established plants in Europe, especially in England. Hamilton and other Federalists had favored a protective tariff in the 1790s, but the demands became particularly strong following the War of 1812 when cheap English textiles and iron goods flooded the American market. Henry Clay was among the leading politicians who insisted that the home market must be protected for the benefit of both industry and agriculture. In response, Congress raised the tariff rates on textiles, iron bars and manufactures, and other commodities in 1816. Congress raised rates in 1824 and again in 1828. But with growing opposition to protection in the South, Congress lowered tariff rates slightly in 1832; and the highly controversial "compromise of 1833" provided the reduction of duties gradually over the next nine years. The Whigs reversed the downward trend and raised rates in 1842. After the Democrats returned to office, they passed the Walker tariff in 1846 which provided for a general lowering of duties. In 1857 Congress reduced tariffs even further. The contribution of the tariff laws to industrial development is not certain, but the tariff remained an important political issue.

The Industrial Workers

Industrialization revolutionized the position of workingmen in American economic life. In 1800, most workers gained their living from agriculture or from specialized employment as skilled craftsmen who had learned their trade by the apprentice system. During the next half century, however, many craftsmen and the sons and daughters of American farmers entered factories as members of the growing army of wage earners. Between 1820 and 1860, the number employed in manufacturing rose from about 350,000 to 1,930,000. By the latter year more than 18 percent of gainfully employed workers were in industry.

Industrial growth may have been hindered by the lack of skilled labor, but, generally, the supply of workers was adequate. The early textile factories recruited their laborers from nearby farm communities and often employed entire families. Child labor was common, and children as young as seven or eight years old worked long hours. Women provided much of the labor for the early textile factories. To attract young, unmarried women operatives, the Boston Manufacturing Company established boardinghouses near its factories where the company provided food, shelter, and supervision. However, the attempt to establish this kind of industrial society gave way to the demand for greater profits. Nevertheless, women workers played a key role in the country's early factory development.

Although factory wages were higher in America than in Great Britain, they were not much above subsistence levels. A factory in Paterson, New Jersey, reported in 1828 that men made $5, women $2.37, and children $1.37 weekly. By the early 1850s, male factory workers and common laborers made no more than about $6 a week in most parts of the country. The *New York Tribune*

claimed in 1851 that a minimum budget for a family of five in New York was $10.37 a week, so it is clear why several members of a family sought employment. Skilled craftsmen earned wages of $10 to $15 a week. Industrial laborers usually worked from twelve to sixteen hours a day. America was pictured as a land of opportunity, but laborers were often harassed by unemployment, hard times, and outright poverty.

To protect their interests, some skilled craftsmen organized even before 1800. The modern labor movement in the United States dates from

Working at a loom in a Massachusetts cotton mill, about 1850.
The Granger Collection

1827, when workingmen organized the Philadelphia Mechanics' Union of Trade Associations. To that time there had been no attempt to bring the individual craft unions or associations of workingmen together into a larger body. Union organization was limited largely to skilled artisans in the cities of the Northeast; unions had made little headway among factory workers, because of lack of interest and opposition from employers. In 1828, labor organized the Workingmen's Party and established the *Mechanics' Free Press,* the country's first labor paper, to promote labor's goals.

During the years after 1827, workers advocated a broad program of reform. Besides opposing child labor and favoring the ten-hour day, labor groups demanded free public schools, abolition of imprisonment for debt, laws to exempt tools from seizure for debt, improved court procedures, and destruction of monopoly. Of these issues, they considered the ten-hour day and free public education most essential. Agitation by labor parties and pressure from the rising trade unions in the middle 1830s finally established the ten-hour day in many kinds of employment. The federal government adopted the ten-hour day for its employees in 1840.

During the 1830s workers turned to more vigorous trade union activity. They formed scores of local unions in such cities as Baltimore, New York, and Philadelphia. Sometimes they struck to achieve their demands. Workers organized the National Trades Union in 1834, and two years later boasted a union membership of an estimated 300,000. Attempts to form an effective national labor organization failed, although

South Street, Manhattan, New York City, in 1828: ". . . a forest of masts and flapping sails."

workers won one important victory. In 1842 the Supreme Court of Massachusetts in *Commonwealth v. Hunt* asserted that workers had the legal right to organize unions and to strike in favor of the closed shop.

Organized labor's progress in the prosperous mid-1830s came to an abrupt halt with the Panic of 1837. Under the impact of widespread unemployment, when jobless workers were literally begging for food, most of the trade unions simply disappeared. This demise of unionism encouraged a variety of reformers and idealists to advance their solutions for labor's problems. Between the late 1830s and early 1850s, agrarianism, associationism, and cooperation all had their supporters. George Henry Evans of New York, who argued that the public land was a gift of nature and should be free for all men, formed his Agrarian League in 1840. Evans envisioned the establishment of self-sufficient communities where farmers and craftsmen would labor together in peace and harmony.

Associationist reformers favored industrial associations, called phalanxes, where people could live together and work at tasks which interested them. They formed several phalanxes during the 1840s, among them Brook Farm near Boston, but they all failed within a short time from lack of interest among laborers. A third reform movement among workers was the establishment of producer and consumer cooperatives. Many cooperatives appeared in the 1840s, but collapsed quickly because of inadequate capital, poor management, and the absence of a cooperative spirit among workers.

Most of the schemes advanced to help labor in the 1840s were aimed at basic changes in society which would permit workers to escape the wage system. Since none of the plans proved successful, workers turned back to trade union activity in the 1850s to strengthen their bargaining position with employers. By 1856 the cigar makers, iron molders, silversmiths, and printers had all formed national unions. While workers failed to secure many of their demands, they contributed to such basic reforms as public education and abolition of imprisonment for debt, and laid a base for the modern labor movement.

Urbanization, Economic Trends, and Living Standards

Industrial and commercial expansion laid the foundation for rapid urban development throughout the North. The number of people living in communities of 2,500 or more increased more rapidly than the population as a whole. Between 1820 and 1860 the nation's total population rose 226 percent; meanwhile urban population increased 797 percent. In 1820 only two American cities had more than 100,000 people; by 1860 eight cities had reached that size, and New York had passed the million mark. Superficially at least, the Northeast, with its impressive urbanization, had attained economic maturity. By the fifties, its great cities changed imperceptibly year after year. Yet never before had they so completely controlled the commercial, financial, and business structure of the country.

New York City was the financial emporium of the nation. Visitors were amazed by the mansions of its business aristocracy along Fourth and Fifth Avenues, the impressive hotels, A. T. Stewart's famed shopping center, Wall Street with its stock exchange and banks, and the East River with its wharves teeming with coaches, horses, wagons, baskets, and boxes, its forest of masts and flapping sails, its steam ferryboats, and its majestic ships heading out to sea. Broadway was jammed with omnibuses, coaches, phaetons, gigs, and carriages. New York also had its share of low life. Five Points, the city's slum and vice quarter, was notorious the world over.

Midwestern urban centers gave leadership and direction to that region's economic evolution. Strung out along the routes of commerce, they created the markets which pushed the agricultural frontier toward the Mississippi and beyond.

Pittsburgh, standing at the gateway to the Ohio Valley, had developed substantial industry by the 1840s. The city's belching furnaces, its smoke-blackened bricks, and the din of its factories reminded the British traveler of Glasgow or Birmingham. Cincinnati, 300 miles downstream, was the leading metropolis on the Ohio and the largest city of the West. St. Louis, far to the west, was another pulsating river metropolis, a depot on the Mississippi second only to New Orleans. The commercial activity along its levee filled travelers with wonder. As far as the eye could see the docks were piled high with barrels of flour, bags of corn, hogsheads of tobacco, and the products of American industry. By 1860 the population of St. Louis, like that of Cincinnati, was approaching 200,000.

New urban centers along the shores of the Great Lakes reflected even more the revolutionary changes of the 1850s. Cleveland, Detroit, Chicago, and Milwaukee were all tiny villages in 1840; a decade later all had between 15,000 and 30,000 inhabitants. Chicago, despite its extreme youth, was already in 1840 the most promising city of the West. Its promoters boasted attractive stores, beautiful, if unpaved, streets, sidewalks, an excellent hotel, a theater, several churches, stone houses, a foundry, sawmills and flour mills, wagon and coach shops, printing establishments, brick factories, three daily newspapers, and a post office. Emigrant parties passed through almost daily, drifting onto the surrounding prairies. Chicagoans worked with a strange sense of urgency. "Every one in the place seemed in a hurry," one visitor recalled, "and a kind of restless activity prevailed which I had seen no where else in the West, except in Cincinnati." Chicago's citizens could well exude optimism, for the city's geographical position made it the natural gateway to the West. By 1860, 100,000 people resided there.

This growth of cities brought cries of anguish from agrarians who believed that urban life was corrupt and sinful. Writing in the *Ohio Farmer* in 1855, one reporter said: "Oh how fearful a thing is a city! How full of sin and sorrow." But such warnings failed to slow the drift of farm youth into the urban centers.

Although agriculture, transportation, and industry expanded greatly and conditions among many classes of workers improved, the country between 1815 and 1860 suffered from periods of depression and economic stagnation. The worst panics occurred in 1819, 1837, and 1857, while the most prosperous years were those immediately following the War of 1812, the middle 1820s, the middle 1830s, and the early 1850s. Depressions usually followed unrestricted speculation in land and internal improvement enterprises.

Panic engulfed the nation in the spring of 1837 when the federal government eliminated credit purchases and demanded specie payment for land. This broke both the orgy of speculation and confidence in the circulating bank notes. The depression which followed the Panic of 1837 was long and hard. Farm prices dropped to disastrous levels, businesses went bankrupt, internal improvement projects collapsed, and thousands of laborers lost their jobs. Horace Greeley, editor of the *New York Tribune*, estimated that at least 200,000 were unemployed in New York City alone in January 1838. Public soup kitchens kept the most destitute from starving.

There was a brief return to better times, especially in 1845, but only after the discovery of gold in California in 1849 did the country experience a sustained period of prosperity. Again it was land speculation, easy credit, large investments in railroads, and increased exports which stimulated the economy. But in 1857, the bubble once more burst. Hard times reflected the lower farm prices, the drop in land values, the curtailment in railroad building, and the extensive unemployment. Full recovery came with the Civil War.

Despite the fluctuations of the business cycle, most Americans had achieved a higher standard of living in 1860 than they had experienced a half century earlier. Real income per capita, that is, income in dollars of constant purchasing power, rose about 50 percent between 1815 and 1860, much of this gain coming after 1840. Americans generally had better food and housing than other people of the world.

Sharp class distinctions still characterized American society. A great gulf separated the common laborer or factory worker who made his $6 a week from the rich merchant, landowner, or industrialist. New York City alone had some twenty millionaires in 1845, and when John Jacob Astor died in 1848, he left an estate valued at $20 million. Rich New Yorkers lived in magnificent homes, rode in fine carriages, and traveled abroad, while thousands of the poor existed in ground-level slums or in damp, filthy cellars. The vast majority of people lived between these extremes of wealth and poverty.

Conclusion

By 1860 Americans residing in the North had developed a well-balanced, productive, and expanding economy. Agriculture was still their principal economic activity, but commerce and manufacturing, accompanied by urbanization, had made extensive gains. Manufacturing, banking, and shipping were concentrated in the Northeast, and enterprising businessmen in that section provided capital, industrial goods, and services to the agricultural and increasingly industrial West.

As Northern Americans viewed their lengthening railroad lines, their smoking factories, their productive farms, and their rising business centers in the 1850s, it was not strange that they viewed the future with optimism and assurance.

SUGGESTED READINGS

Agriculture in the pre-Civil War Northern economy has been best covered by Paul W. Gates's *The Farmer's Age: Agriculture, 1815–1860* (1960) and Percy W. Bidwell and John I. Falconer's *History of Agriculture in the Northern United States, 1620–1860* (1925). On federal land policy consult Roy M. Robbins's *Our Landed Heritage: The Public Domain, 1776–1936** (1942) and Malcolm Rohrbough's *The Land Office Business* (1968).

The best single volume on transportation is George R. Taylor's *The Transportation Revolution, 1815–1860** (1951), which also contains excellent material on industry, labor, and finance. The history of the Erie Canal has been best told by Ronald E. Shaw in *Erie Water West: A History of the Erie Canal, 1792–1854* (1966). The important role of canals in the country's economic growth has been ably discussed in Carter Goodrich (ed.), *Canals and American Economic Development* (1961). The role of pre-Civil War railroads can be surveyed in the popular *The Story of American Railroads* (1947) by Stewart H. Holbook, but more serious students should consult specialized studies of particular lines such as *The Story of the Baltimore and Ohio Railroads, 1827–1927* (2 vols., 1928) by Edward Hungerford. One of the best railroad histories is Paul W. Gates's *The Illinois Central Railroad and Its Colonization Work* (1934). The overall impact of the railroads on the economy has been assessed in a series of discussions edited by Alfred D. Chandler, Jr., in *The Railroads: The Nation's First Big Business** (1965). Two important aspects of communication have been considered by Robert L. Thompson in *Wiring a Continent* (1947) and LeRoy R. Hafen in *The Overland Mail, 1849–1869* (1926). The westward march of urbanization is traced by Richard C. Wade in *The Urban Frontier: The Rise of Western Cities, 1790–1830* (1959).

The fullest account of industrial development before the Civil War is volume I of V. S. Clark's *History of Manufactures in the United States* (1929). Taylor's *The Transportation Revolution, 1815–1860*, cited above, has some excellent chapters on early nineteenth-century industry. On specific industries see Caroline F. Ware's *The Early New England Cotton Manufacture* (1931) and Arthur H. Cole's *American Wool Manufacture* (2 vols., 1926). The best general account of technological achievements for the beginning student is John Oliver's *History of American Technology* (1956). Thomas C. Cochran and William Miller's *The Age of Enterprise** (1942) is an excellent survey of business development.

Also of great value is Stuart Bruchey's *Roots of American Economic Growth** (1965).

The most complete history of labor in the pre-Civil War years is volume I of John R. Commons's *History of Labour in the United States* (1918). An excellent short account is Norman J. Ware's *The Industrial Worker, 1840–1860** (1924). See also Joseph G. Rayback's *A History of American Labor** (1959).

There are several good books which deal wholly or in part with pre-1860 immigration. They include Marcus Lee Hansen's *The Atlantic Migration, 1607–1860** (1940); Carl Wittke's *We Who Built America* (1939); and George H. Stephenson's *A History of American Migration, 1820–1924* (1926).

Domestic trade and commerce can be followed in Taylor's *The Transportation Revolution*, but much greater detail is provided in parts 2 and 3 of volume I, *A History of Domestic Trade and Commerce in the United States* (2 vols., 1915) by Emory R. Johnson and associates. Lewis E. Atherton's *The Southern Country Store* (1949) and *The Pioneer Merchant in Mid-America* (1939) are excellent. On the tariff Frank W. Taussig's *The Tariff History of the United States** (8th ed., 1931) is old but still useful.

A most valuable and stimulating book which emphasizes cotton exports as a factor in America's pre-Civil War economic growth is Douglass C. North's *The Economic Growth of the United States, 1790–1860** (1961). Of first-rate importance on the role played by the government in financing economic growth are Nathan Miller's *The Enterprise of a Free People: Aspects of Economic Development in New York State during the Canal Period, 1792–1838* (1962) and Carter Goodrich's *The Government and the Economy, 1783–1861** (1967).

*indicates availability in paperback.

12

The Antebellum South

While a widely diversified economy based on agriculture, commerce, industry, and finance developed in the North before 1860, the antebellum South remained primarily agricultural. Not only did farming in its varied forms predominate at the expense of industrial and urban growth, but also a large proportion of Southern wealth came from four chief staple crops— cotton, tobacco, sugar, and rice. Cotton was the South's major source of income and the entire country's primary export product during the pre-Civil War years. By the 1840s Southerners were boasting that "cotton was king." At the same time the South depended heavily on slave labor, and as time passed the Cotton Kingdom became a slave kingdom as well.

Cotton had been raised for home use during the colonial period, but it had never become as significant a commercial crop as tobacco, rice, or indigo. But during the eighteenth century tech-

nical advances in the British textile industry increased the demand for cotton. These successive advances, each filling a need to maintain the technological balance between spinning and weaving, included John Kay's flying shuttle in 1733, James Hargreaves's spinning jenny and Richard Arkwright's water frame in the 1760s, and Edmund Cartwright's power loom in the 1780s. The invention of the cotton gin by Eli Whitney, a graduate of Yale who was residing near Savannah, Georgia, in 1793, provided a relatively cheap and efficient device to process raw cotton for the expanding British market. Encouraged by a good market and ideal conditions of soil and climate, hundreds of farmers in upland South Carolina and Georgia turned to cotton production after 1790. During the next half century the expansion of cotton production in the United States was phenomenal.

Population in the South which totaled about 11 million on the eve of the Civil War, fell into rather distinct social and economic classes. At the top of the scale stood the small aristocracy of large planters. In 1860 there were 2,292 planters who owned more than one hundred slaves, and 10,658 who held over fifty. However, the wealth of this small group gave them social prestige and political power far beyond their numbers. Slightly below the large planters in social and economic status were the lesser planters who had fewer slaves and farmed less land; in 1860 there were 35,616 planters who had twenty to fifty slaves. Professional men and the few business and industrial leaders were also in this general class. Most of the people in the Old South were in the middle or lower-middle class and were mainly yeoman farmers, skilled mechanics, and tradesmen. The so-called plain people of the Old South owned very few slaves, in many cases none at all. They raised a wide variety of crops and livestock and were largely self-sufficient. Below the yeoman farmers were the poor whites, the free blacks, and finally the slaves.

Poor whites, living generally in isolation on the least productive soils, had been largely bypassed by civilization. Some had managed to acquire small patches of land, but countless numbers existed perennially as squatters. Known variously as "crackers," "hillbillies," and "clay eaters," they spent much of their time in hunting and fishing. Some raised vegetables, planted some corn, and claimed ownership of a few head of livestock which roamed freely through the woods. Their crude huts, usually of one room, abounded with towheaded children and lean hound dogs. The men were often gaunt and emaciated, with sunken eyes, yellow skin, and poor teeth, having degenerated under the enervating assault of inadequate diets, unyielding environments, and malaria, hookworm, and pellagra. Suffering as they did from feelings of inferiority, they often fled with their dogs at the sight of a stranger. One traveler approached the

home of an unsuspecting family to be greeted at the door, he recalled, "with the barking of dogs, the squealing of pigs, and the vociferating lungs of about a dozen children who bawled out, mama, mama, here's a man."

Still lower on the social scale were the free blacks. In 1850 some 228,000 of these resided in the fifteen slave states. Most were concentrated in the towns and cities of the Upper South, although many lived in the environs of New Orleans. Approximately half the free blacks were mulattoes because masters often liberated the mulatto children of slave mothers. Such Southern free blacks as William T. Johnson, John Chavis, Lunsford Lane, Thomas Day, Thomy Lafon, and Jehu Jones achieved some notability. Johnson, a resident of Natchez, Mississippi, operated three barber shops, owned several hundred acres of land, loaned money, and even held title to eight slaves. Yet whatever success such men achieved was won against serious racial and legal impediments. Southern laws and customs kept most free blacks in a social, economic, and political status only slightly higher than that of the slaves. Laws required free blacks to obtain licenses to preach or own firearms, to register with the proper courts, and to pay special taxes. They could not vote; nor could they testify in court against a white man. Increasingly they suffered from general social discrimination. By midcentury there was simply no satisfactory place for the free black in the Southern social order.

Another quarter million free blacks lived in the North. Among those who achieved positions of respect and even distinction before 1860—as did such slaves as Phillis Wheatley and Jupiter Hammon—were Crispus Attucks, Benjamin Banneker, Harriet Tubman, and Frederick Douglass. Still, law and custom throughout the North degraded free blacks and severely limited their political and economic activities. Despite the North's professed opposition to slavery and its rhetoric of freedom, the Northern states refused to grant blacks the social equality accorded to other citizens. Throughout the North prejudice against blacks ran deep; in many areas they received no guarantees of citizenship or personal safety. Some free blacks lived in constant, vigorous protest against the denial of their rights as well as the institution of slavery itself.

At the bottom of the Southern class structure stood the slaves. Their numbers rose rapidly to meet the demand for field hands. Between 1800 and 1860 the slave population rose from 857,000 to 3,838,000. Most of the slaves were owned by a relatively small proportion of Southerners. Of the approximately 1,400,000 white families in the South in 1860, only 383,635 were owners of slaves. This meant that two-thirds to three-fourths of the families had no proprietary interest in slavery. Despite its rather sharp class distinctions, Southern white society was not rigid or fixed. Many prominent Southerners who began life in humble circumstances became wealthy or achieved positions of political leadership. Andrew Jackson, Henry Clay, and Jefferson Davis all came from families of plain people.

The Cotton Kingdom

Once the production of cotton became profitable, its expansion knew no bounds. Between 1815 and 1859, cotton output in the South jumped from 209,000 to 4.5 million 400-pound bales. The United States became the world's leading cotton producer. Southern farmers and planters rushed westward to find new and fertile land. By 1860, Mississippi, with a production of 1,202,207 bales, had become the nation's leading cotton state.

Although many small farmers raised cotton to obtain a ready cash income, large-scale production on well-organized plantations became more characteristic. Developed to produce tobacco and rice during the colonial period, the plantation system was a capitalistic type of farm organization, in which slaves or indentured workers produced a staple cash crop. Plantation agriculture was characterized by heavy investments in land and labor. The largest cotton planters had thousands of acres of land and several hundred slaves, and could produce hundreds of bales of cotton a year. Typical of the large planters was Stephen Duncan, who lived near Natchez. In 1850 he had more than one thousand slaves and an income from cotton, after deducting expenses, of $169,354. Frederick Stanton, also of Natchez, had a slave force of 444 on his three plantations. He produced 3,054 bales valued at $122,000 in 1858.

Within the so-called Cotton Kingdom existed the subkingdoms of rice and cane sugar. These important cash crops were raised almost exclusively on large plantations and were confined to limited geographic areas. The rice culture was concentrated along the coasts of Southern Carolina and Georgia, where the tidal flow furnished the water necessary to flood the fields. Huge rice estates developed, boasting thousands of acres and from 200 to 500 slaves. One large planter, Thomas Allston, owned a 4,257-acre plantation on the Savannah River in Georgia; his land, slaves, and other property were valued at $527,081 upon his death in 1862. Rice production demanded a large capital investment. Land, slaves, and milling machinery required such huge sums that only those with substantial financial backing could enter the business. Rice culture declined somewhat in the 1850s as higher cotton prices drew land and slaves into cotton production.

Sugar cane cultivation thrived mostly in Louisiana along the Mississippi River north of New Orleans, an area which boasted some of the largest plantations in the South. The capital requirements for sugar production ran as high or higher than those for rice. Land and labor were expensive. In addition, planters required costly machinery to grind the cane and process sugar. However, the largest plantations produced as much

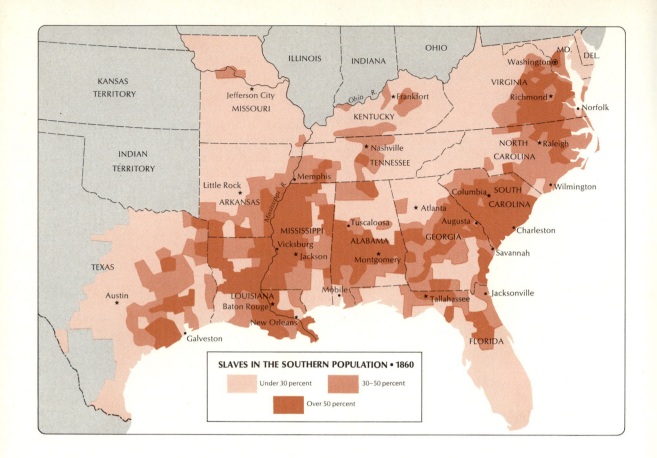

SLAVES IN THE SOUTHERN POPULATION • 1860

Under 30 percent

30–50 percent

Over 50 percent

as 1,000 tons of sugar annually with good profits.

Large planters concentrated on cash crops for the commercial market. Cotton went from plantations to dealers in New Orleans, Mobile, Augusta, or Charleston, who, in turn, shipped it on to England or to New England manufacturers. Factors or commission merchants in these and other cities arranged for credit, sold the cotton, and purchased goods and supplies ordered by the planter. New York merchants, with offices in the South, bought and sold much of the cotton. Thus Southern planters sold their products outside the region and imported most of their supplies. Concentrating capital and labor on the production and sale of a staple crop brought sufficient income, especially at times of high prices, to render the home production even of foodstuffs undesirable.

Slavery

Many Americans in the late eighteenth century believed that slavery might eventually die out, but the heavy demand for labor in the expanding staple economy of the South fastened the "peculiar institution" firmly on the region. Most of the work associated with the production of staple crops involved simple tasks which the untrained black men, women, and children could perform though many continuously resisted. When slaves were not working the fields, they cleared new

Sale of Estates, Pictures and Slaves in the Rotunda, New Orleans

The Slave Economy

When the British journalist J. S. Buckingham toured the South in the early 1840s, he witnessed the New Orleans scene above and included it in his book *The Slaves of America.* Slaves were being sold at auction in the same rotunda with paintings, parcels of land, and other valuables. This estimation of slaves as property rather than men was later defended most staunchly by Confederate President Jefferson Davis, who maintained that abolition constituted the first step in an attack on all private property in both the North and the South.

With slaves selling for as high as $1,800, depending on the tides of the economy, the great Southern planters had enormous capital investments in slaves. A Natchez planter, Stephen Duncan, owned more than one thousand slaves, and by 1860, 2,292 planters owned more than one hundred; 10,658 held over fifty; and 35,616 held between twenty and fifty. In proportion to the total number of Southern families the percentage of slaveholders was not major—about one quarter—nevertheless they dominated the political and economic scene. This dominance was one factor in preventing the industrialization of the South, and it greatly stimulated the growth of slavery—from 857,000 in 1800 to about four million in 1860.

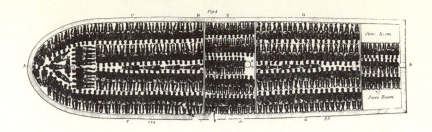

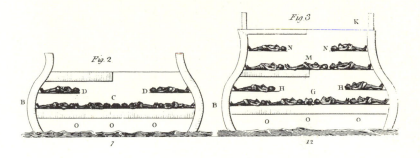

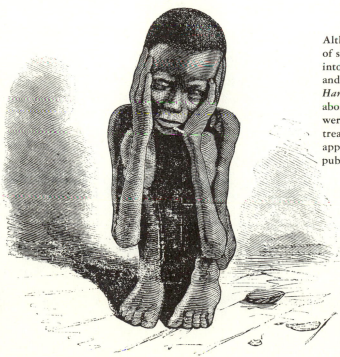

Although the Constitution forbade the importation of slaves after 1808, some 250,000 were smuggled into the country before 1860. The shipboard scene and the squatting slave boy at the left appeared in *Harper's Weekly* in 1860 after daguerreotypes made aboard the bark *Wildfire* off Key West. That slaves were considered merely cargo and that inhumane treatment was intentional becomes immediately apparent in the plans drawn for a slave ship and published in London in 1808 (above).

The big cash crops raised for export in the South required vast amounts of hand labor. Above, Northern magazine illustrations of the period show sugar harvesting in Louisiana (left), rice cutting in South Carolina (center), and cotton being borne to the gin. At the left, cotton is prepared for the gin at Smith's plantation on Port Royal Island in South Carolina in 1862. Timothy O'Sullivan took this photograph during Union occupation of the island.

While the South relied on hand labor, the North advanced not only in industrialization but in the application of machinery to agriculture. The Alexander Anderson woodcut (below) shows harvesting with a cradle, a method increasingly supplanted by the reaper developed by Cyrus McCormick. First demonstrated in 1831, the improved 1848 model appears at far right. By this time the Virginia-born McCormick had moved his factory to Chicago where he supplied machines for the booming farm frontier. McCormick sold a thousand reapers in 1851; by 1857 the number was twenty-three thousand. Many competitors strove to make farm machinery do more and do it better, with the result that they were frequently in court suing for patent infringements. The old hand method of threshing wheat with a flail (bottom) was also mechanized. At right is the J. I. Case Company's threshing machine of 1848.

1848

Threshin

J. I. CASE,

Having purchased of H. A. Pitts the right to manufacture Pitts' Patent Separator, and having added several importan Tread Power Threshing Machine, with a very superior article of eith years, and devoted my particular attention to improving and perfecting they manufactured east or west.

TERMS OF PAYMENT.

TREAD MACHINE.

Fifty dollars on delivery of machine (freight or ware-house charges if any;) seventy-five dollars on the first day of November; one hundred dollars on the first day of January; and sixty-five dollars on the first day of October following—all with interest.

LEVER MACHINE.

Fifty dollars on delivery of machine (freight and ware-house charges if any,) seventy-five dollars on the first day of November; ninety dollars on the first day of January; and the balance on the first day of October following—all with interest.

A deduction of ten per cent. on all sums over fifty dollars paid down for either machine.

The great and increasing demand f and put in Steam Power. For the last three y Buffalo, and hope in future to be able to supply best of mechanics. I have formerly purchased my castings from othe good castings, and sometimes poor. Having my own Furnace, I shall against expense and loss from breakage of bad castings. I am manufactur

IMPROVED WEMPLE
PITT'S PA

As manufactured by J. A. Pitts, of Buffalo, (also Machines. Some of the above Machines will be geared and others with drum cylinder, and $325 with Iron cylinder. I will also have for

IMPROVED TWO

with Separator; price $200 without wagon for the horse-power, and $ Wheat in a day, or twice that quantity of Oats. The Lever Power Ma described Machines, I will suggest the necessity of your forwarding you you will confer a favor on him, his neighbors and myself, by inducing

CASTINGS FURNISHED FOR ALL

A. C. Sandford, Printer,

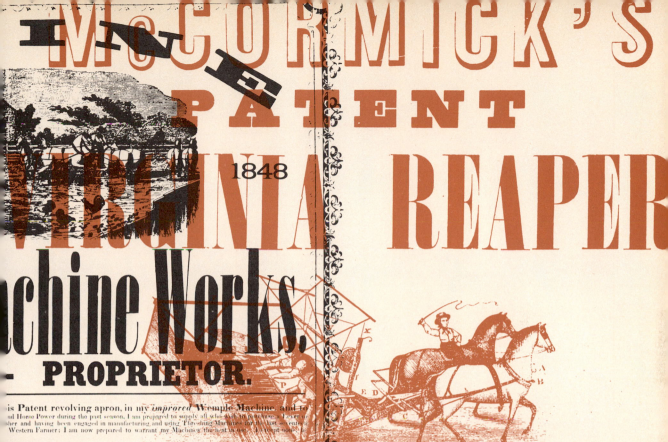

McCORMICK'S PATENT VIRGINIA REAPER

1848

WISCONSIN ... chine Works,

— PROPRIETOR.

...is Patent revolving apron, in my *improved* Wemple Machine, and to ... nd Horse Power during the past season, I am prepared to supply all who wish to purchase. Lever ... her and having been engaged in manufacturing and using Threshing Machines for the last seventeen ... Western Farmer; I am now prepared to warrant my Machines the best in use. ...

From the Wisconsin Farmer.

The above cut represents one of M'CORMICK'S PATENT VIRGINIA REAPERS, as built for the harvest of 1848. It has been greatly improved since that time, by the addition of a seat for the driver; by a change in the position of the crank, so as to effect a direct connection between it and the sickle, (thereby very much lessening the friction, and wear of much of the machinery;) by dispensing altogether with the lever and its fixtures;) by board ribs on the reel ... operates ... instead of the round ones;) by a sheet of zinc on the platform, (which very much lessens the labor of ... by an increase ... size ... and strength of the wheel of the machine, and by improvement made on the cutting apparatus ... west. To those who are acquainted with the work of these machines, it is unnecessary to say anything in their praise. We believe these machines take the precedence of all others whenever they can be procured. We are ... by those who have used them that they are the most profitable machines that can be used, both for the employer and the employed—that one machine has saved over $1200 during the season of threshing.

Mr C. also keeps on hand and for sale, the most approved kinds of Power. His Separators are the best in use. Mr C. has been a practical thresher ... fifteen years, and knows how to get up thresh... chines just right. We would advise all interested ... give him a call or examine his machines, before purchasing elsewhere. We have ...

... BROWN,

OF ASHLAND, OHIO,

induced me to enlarge my Establishment, attach an Iron Furnace. ... ders I have received for Machines; but I have now the largest and most commodious shops west of ... er is all of the best quality, seasoned perfectly, and put together in a workmanlike manner, by the ... Agent for the sale of the above va... (manufactured by C. H. McCormick ... ber saving machine, ... Counties of Seneca, Sandusky, E ...

WITH CLIMAX HORSE POWER,

SEPARATOR,

...ron ... Ashland and Wayne, would respectfully inf... the farmers of those counties, that he is prepared to furnish th... ...rvin Hughes, of Kenosha,) with important improvements on both... ...nt the fancies of all purchasers. My price for either of the above Machines, at the shop, is $345 ... th the above Reapers on very liberal terms.

READ POWER MACHINE.

... Machine, if well attended in good grain, will thresh and clean nicely from 2 ... ng and cleaning, in the best manner, all that can be got to it. Should you wish either ... season. If you know of any one in your vicinity who wishes to purchase a Threshing M ... the above territory will be visited, ... archasing elsewhere. ...nt will be ready to give any information relative to ...

...RY, AND REPAIRING DONE ON SHORT NOTICE. ...aper, by addressing him at Ashland, Ashland County, Ohio.

Advocate Office, Racine.

Although the daguerreotype and subsequent photographic processes had been in use for twenty years before the Civil War, there is scant photographic record of the institution of slavery, little to show us how slaves lived, dressed, and looked. The group of slaves above were photographed on a Virginia plantation in 1862, shortly after the arrival of Union forces. At this period of the war, those slaves who joined up with Union armies were officially considered "contraband," or confiscated property of war.

land and built fences. On the large plantations they worked under a white overseer. While some slaves labored as field hands, others did more specialized work. Dressed in coarse clothing and barefooted much of the year, the slaves lived in cheap cabins near the master's house. They usually ate cornmeal and salt pork, supplemented by greens, vegetables, and fruits in season from their own small gardens.

The Southern states all had harsh slave codes, which they enforced with increasing rigor after the rise of abolitionism. It was lawful to mistreat and even to whip or beat slaves; and it was illegal to teach them to read or write or permit them to own property. No slave, for example, could smoke, laugh, or talk loudly in public, be out after curfew, buy liquor, or assemble in groups of more than five unless a white person was present. The letter of the law, fortunately, was generally harsher than its application. But whether the slaves were contented or miserable, they were locked in a closed system of servitude from which no escape was possible except by the will of their owner or flight, which involved great risk. The master's legal rights over the slaves were embodied in state law and protected by the Constitution and the courts.

Concentrations of slaves developed in staple-crop areas. To meet the demand for labor on new plantations, especially in the lower Mississippi Valley, Southerners developed a lively internal slave trade, one of the most abusive features of the slave system. Thousands of slaves from Virginia, Kentucky, and Tennessee found themselves on plantations in the Lower South. During the inflationary period following the War of 1812, healthy, serviceable hands in Alabama and Mississippi brought as much as $1,000 to $2,000.

The profitability of slave labor was a controversial question among antebellum Southerners; thereafter it provoked disagreement among historians and economists as well. Its profitability for individual planters was important enough, but much more significant was the effect of slavery on the entire Southern economy. Recent research seems to indicate that slavery's influence on the overall economic development of the South was unhealthy. The South's emphasis upon staple-crop agriculture—made possible largely by slave labor—caused manufacturing and urbanization to develop much more slowly than in the North. Southerners invested a large portion of their capital in slaves, leaving relatively little money for investment in industry and transportation. Furthermore, most plantation profits flowed out of the region to pay for food and manufactured goods as well as the costs of marketing, insuring, and shipping.

Furthermore, the presence of both a large slave class and many self-sufficient, low-income whites greatly reduced the Southern market for manufactured goods. The concentration of wealth in the hands of a minority tended to keep purchasing power low. Without a heavier regional demand, Southerners felt little incentive to manufacture for local markets. Slavery was part and parcel of a conservative economic and social system which resisted change and diversification. Finally, the slave system itself had unfavorable psychological effects on both blacks and whites.

Yeoman Farming

Yeoman farmers generally grew tobacco or cotton as a cash crop along with grain and livestock. Small family-type farms raised most of the South's tobacco. Because of the large amount of labor required to produce tobacco—planting, cultivating, worming, picking, and curing—most producers had only 2 or 3 acres under cultivation, but the income per acre was high, often reaching $50 or $60 annually. Following the American Revolution, tobacco production shifted westward from Virginia and Maryland into parts of Kentucky and Tennessee. Among the South's leading cash crops—cotton, sugar, tobacco, and rice—tobacco ranked third in value in 1855.

Corn was the South's most important grain crop. Almost every farmer, planter, or yeoman raised some corn. This was a subsistence rather than a money crop. Southern farmers ate corn bread, corn pone, mush, hominy, and grits, or fed it to poultry and livestock. Some Southerners converted corn into whisky. Yeoman farmers, mainly in the Upper South, also grew wheat,

as well as small amounts of oats, flax, and rye. Hemp was a major crop in Kentucky.

Most Southern farmers, especially those in the Upper South, raised livestock. Cattle raising was a major enterprise in the border states, and by 1860 the South had 55 percent of the nation's cattle, excluding milk cows. The slave states also had more swine than any other section; horses and mules were plentiful; and farmers raised some sheep. Livestock was abundant in the South; its general quality was low.

Southern Transportation, Commerce, and Manufacturing

Southern economic growth languished not only because of that region's emphasis upon agriculture, but also because of its slow, inefficient transportation. The South had its navigable rivers, but it lagged behind the North in the construction of roads, canals, and railroads. Much of the South remained isolated. The few railroads in the South made little progress before 1860. Charleston businessmen were among the first to advocate construction of a railroad to bring Western trade to their port. The Charleston and Hamburg Railroad reached Hamburg, across the river from Augusta, Georgia, a distance of 136 miles in 1833. It was then the longest railway in the world. Richmond, Chattanooga, Nashville, Memphis, and New Orleans had railroads of their own, but large regions of the South had no rail transportation even in 1860.

Most of the South's staple agricultural commodities moved into national or international commerce before 1850 by river. The Mississippi, particularly, carried cotton from Tennessee, Mississippi, and Louisiana, sugar and cotton from Louisiana, and tobacco from Tennessee and Kentucky. In the late antebellum years, railroads captured some of this traffic, but farmers and planters continued to rely heavily upon river transport until the Civil War.

Southern commerce revolved around the export of staple crops and the importation of manufactured goods. Large planters sold their cotton and sugar through factors, or commission merchants, at the leading Southern ports, but small farmers usually disposed of their meager surpluses at the country store. When the storekeeper had collected a sufficient supply of farm commodities, he forwarded the produce to urban markets. Planters and small farmers, as well as local townsmen, bought manufactured goods shipped in from the North or from Europe.

American foreign trade depended heavily on Southern products. Cotton was the chief American export in the pre-Civil War years. The value of cotton exports increased from $121.5 million in the five years 1816–1820 to $744.6 million in the period 1856–1860. Between 1821 and 1860, cotton provided 46 to 63 percent of the country's total exports. The income from cotton sales abroad paid for imported manufactures and for much of the capital invested by foreigners in internal improvement projects. Cotton exports produced considerable wealth, but only a small part of it flowed back into the South. Too much of the Southern effort brought huge profits to New York and New England manufacturers, merchants, and shipowners.

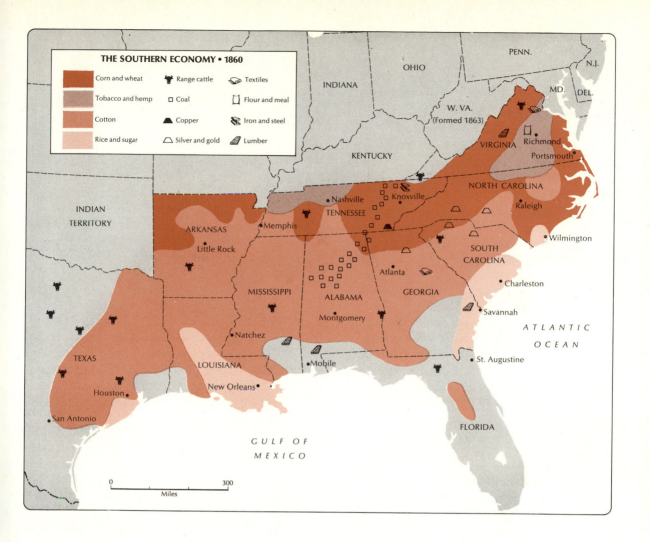

THE SOUTHERN ECONOMY · 1860

Corn and wheat	Range cattle	Textiles
Tobacco and hemp	Coal	Flour and meal
Cotton	Copper	Iron and steel
Rice and sugar	Silver and gold	Lumber

PENN.

OHIO

N.J.

INDIANA

MD. DEL.

W. VA. (Formed 1863)

VIRGINIA

Richmond

Portsmouth

KENTUCKY

NORTH CAROLINA

Nashville

Knoxville

Raleigh

TENNESSEE

Memphis

INDIAN TERRITORY

ARKANSAS

Little Rock

Wilmington

SOUTH CAROLINA

Atlanta

Charleston

MISSISSIPPI

ALABAMA

GEORGIA

Montgomery

Savannah

Natchez

ATLANTIC OCEAN

TEXAS

LOUISIANA

Mobile

St. Augustine

Houston

New Orleans

San Antonio

FLORIDA

GULF OF MEXICO

0   300
      Miles

Manufacturing, which would have given the South a balanced economy, made slow progress in the pre-Civil War period. The region had some distinct advantages for industrial development, including raw materials, especially cotton, the potential for cheap labor, and waterpower. But the unfavorable circumstances outweighed the favorable factors. The competition from the cotton industry for capital and labor, an inadequate transportation system, and prejudice against manufacturing on the part of many leading Southerners all retarded industrial growth.

Consequently, by 1860 the South turned out a mere 8 percent of the value of American manufactured products. The chief Southern manufactures were flour, lumber, tobacco, and textiles. Most plants were small and employed limited amounts of capital and labor. William Gregg of Charleston, who established a cotton mill at Graniteville, South Carolina, in 1846, was one of the few Southerners who developed successful industries in the South. The South's largest iron manufacturer was the Tredegar Iron Works at Richmond.

THE ANTEBELLUM SOUTH

Abolitionism and the Defense of Slavery

No reform movement in the pre-Civil War period aroused so much emotion as the crusade to abolish slavery. Most Americans in the late eighteenth and early nineteenth centuries deplored slavery and hoped that somehow it might be abolished. Even some Southerners voluntarily freed their slaves. To a generation nurtured on Revolutionary principles slavery was inconsistent with liberty, incompatible with the rights of man, and contrary to Christianity. But while many Southerners opposed slavery in principle, very few freed their slaves because of the economic and social dilemmas which large numbers of free blacks might create in Southern society. Slavery was an evil, but for many it seemed a necessary one.

While Southerners wrestled with their problem of race, Northerners moved to abolish slavery, if not necessarily discrimination. By 1804, all the states north of the Mason-Dixon line had arranged for immediate or gradual abolition. In 1808, Congress declared the foreign slave trade illegal. The freeing of slaves by law in the North and by voluntary action in the South increased the number of free blacks who faced discrimination, in both sections. Concerned over the status of free blacks, a group met in Washington, D.C., early in 1817, to form the American Colonization Society for the purpose of colonizing blacks in Liberia. But colonization efforts, both as a means of removing free blacks from the United States and as an antislavery effort, failed miserably. Most free Negroes did not wish to emigrate but wanted instead decent treatment and better economic opportunities in America. "The Colonizationists want us to go to Liberia if we will," wrote one free black; "if we won't go there, we may go to hell."

Meanwhile, a full-fledged abolitionist movement spread throughout the North. Ministers, editors, politicians, and others—white and black—began to condemn what they considered a brutal evil. In 1821, Benjamin Lundy, a Quaker, established a newspaper, the *Genius of Universal Emancipation*, at Mount Pleasant, Ohio, and through its columns demanded immediate emancipation of slaves without any compensation to the owners. By the early 1830s, an increasing number of Northern newspapers and magazines attacked slavery sharply.

One man who gained a particularly dominant position in the growing abolitionist campaign was William Lloyd Garrison. Born in Massachusetts in 1805, Garrison grew up in poverty and went to work as an apprentice printer at thirteen. After serving his seven-year apprenticeship, this pious and ambitious youth quit the printing trade and associated himself with a number of reform newspapers. In 1829, he went to Baltimore to become editor of the *Genius of Universal Emancipation*, then published in that city. While in Baltimore, Garrison was jailed for libel when he assailed a shipowner who had agreed to transport a planter's slaves to Louisiana. Bitter and indignant over his imprisonment, Garrison moved to Boston where on January 1, 1833, he began to issue his new antislavery paper, the *Liberator*.

An intense moralist, Garrison could be neither moderate nor compromising in his stand on this great moral and social evil. He wrote that he would speak out against it regardless of the consequences. "I will be as harsh as truth and as uncompromising as justice . . . I will not retreat a single inch, and I WILL BE HEARD," he wrote in the first issue of the *Liberator*. Garrison denounced the gradual emancipation which many abolitionists favored and called for immediate freedom for the slaves. He attacked slavery as immoral. He vilified slave owners. Within a short time, other effective abolitionists joined the crusade against slavery. Among them were Lewis and Arthur Tappan, New York businessmen; Theodore Weld, a partially trained minister and reformer who organized antislavery sentiment at Lane Seminary in Cincinnati and throughout the West; Wendell Phillips, a Boston lawyer and lecturer; Presbyterian minister Henry Ward Beecher; and Elijah P. Lovejoy.

INJURED HUMANITY;

BEING

A Representation of what the unhappy Children of Africa endure from those who call themselves CHRISTIANS.

he husband and wife, after being sold
ferent purchasers, violently separated ;
ably never to see each other more.

en slaves are purchased by the plant-
ey are generally marked on the breast
a red hot iron.

epresentation of a slave at work cru-
ccoutred, with a Head-frame and
-piece to prevent his eating—with
and Spurs round his legs, and half a
d weight chained to his body to pre-
s absconding.

manner of fixing the slaves on a
to be flogged, which is also occa-
laid flat on the ground for severer
ment.

The Abolitionists

During the first half of the nineteenth century the cause of abolition challenged American morality. At issue was the disparity between the realities of slavery and the nation's avowed ideals—the ideals of freedom, equality, and humanity as professed by a preponderantly Christian people. This early antislavery broadside, published in New York, appeals directly to Christian conscience in its detailed descriptions of the horrifying maltreatment of blacks at the hands of slave masters.

Continuing evidence of the inhumanity and unworkability of slavery as an institution was provided by the sometimes violent protests of blacks themselves. The revolt aboard the slave ship Amistad in 1838 (following page, above) commanded national attention and brought ex-President John Quincy Adams to the successful defense of its leaders before the United States Supreme Court. Uprisings took place as well on American soil, two of which were represented in lurid and sensational newspaper illustrations of the time (following page, center and below). The middle cut comes from a contemporary account of the Nat Turner insurrection in Virginia in 1831 which took the lives of fifty-seven whites. The bottom cut purports to represent the massacre of whites by Indians and blacks in Florida during 1835 and 1836—but it is notable that the printer has lifted several pieces from the Nat Turner woodcut to create his "illustration."

The manner of yoking the slaves by the Mandingoes, or African slave merchants, who usually march annually in eight or ten parties, from the river Gambia to Bambarra ; each party having from one hundred to one hundred and fifty slaves.

The Log-Yokes are made of the roots of trees, so heavy as to make it extremely difficult for the persons who wear them to walk, much more to escape or run away.

A front and profile view of an African's head, with the mouth-piece and necklace, the hooks round which are placed to prevent an escape when pursued in the woods, and to hinder them from laying down the head to procure rest.—At A is a flat iron which goes into the mouth, and so effectually keeps down the tongue, that nothing can be swallowed, not even the saliva, a passage for which is made through holes in the mouth-plate.

An enlarged view of the mouth-piece, which, when long worn, becomes so heated, as frequently to bring off the skin along with it.

A view of the leg-bolts or shackles, as put upon the legs of the slaves on shipboard, in the middle passage.

An enlarged view of the boots and spurs, as used at some plantations in Antigua.

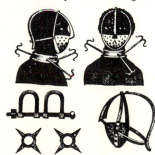

Another method in which the poor victims are placed to be flogged.

HORRID MASSACRE IN VIRGINIA.

Massacre of the Whites by the Indians and Blacks in Florida.

The American Anti-Slavery Society, formed in Philadelphia in 1833, and one of the important forces in the cause of abolition, used the popular almanac to disseminate its propaganda, and its illustrations frequently reflect the fact that abolition was by no means popular among many Northerners. The antislavery printing press of E. P. Lovejoy was set upon and destroyed by mobs three times, in New York, Ohio, and Illinois (right, above). Almanac cuts depicted the brutal punishment of a slave (right, center) and the destruction of a Northern school for black girls (right, below) among other racist activities. According to the caption for the last, "When schools have been established for colored scholars, the law makers and the mob have combined to destroy them—as at Canton, Connecticut, at Canaan, New Hampshire . . . and Zanesville and Brown County, Ohio . . ."

ANTI-SLAVERY

ANAC,

1840,

BISSEXTILE OR LEAP-YEAR, AND THE 64TH OF AMERICAN INDEPENDENCE. CALCULATED FOR NEW YORK; ADAPTED TO THE NORTHERN AND MIDDLE STATES.

Slave State — *Free State*

Outstanding among Abolitionist leaders were the escaped slave, Frederick Douglass (left) founder and editor of The North Star, *and William Lloyd Garrison (left, below),* editor of The Liberator. *Garrison was uncompromising: "On this subject," he wrote, "I do not wish to think, or speak, or write, with toleration." Douglass wrote: "I base no man's right upon his color and plead no man's rights because of his color. My interest in any man is objectively in his manhood and subjectively in my own manhood."*

Among the important black Abolitionists was the Reverend Samuel Cornish (far right, above), pastor of the First Presbyterian Church of New York, who, with James Forten and John Hilton, in 1830 established an annual meeting at which blacks could consider means of improving their condition. With the pioneer black editor John Russwurm, Cornish published the newspaper Freedom's Journal. *Sojourner Truth (near right) was one of many blacks who wrote on the conditions of slaves. Henry Highland Garnett (far right, below) advised slaves, "The diabolical injustice by which your liberties are cloven down, neither God nor angels, or just men command you to suffer for a single moment."*

Wm. Lloyd Garrison.

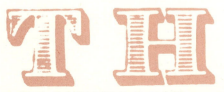

THE LI

VOL. I.]

WILLIAM LLOYD GARRISON

BOSTON, MASSACHUSETTS.]

OUR COUNTRY IS THE WOR

SLAVES
HORSES &
OTHER CAT-
TLE TO BE
SOLD AT
12 OC.

RA TOR.

SAAC KNAPP, PUBLISHERS. [NO. 22.

UNTRYMEN ARE MANKIND. [SATURDAY, MAY 28, 1831.

The Underground Railroad, described at right in a mock advertisement in the Western Citizen in 1844, was not a railroad at all but a system by which opponents of slavery helped fugitive slaves escape to Canada by providing them with hiding places along the way. Harriet Tubman (far right), a Maryland slave who escaped in 1849, became a famous "conductor" on the railroad, helping more than 300 slaves to freedom during the next ten years. The drawing above shows Leon Green, a slave who escaped by hiding in a chest which was shipped to the North.

LIBE[RTY]
NEW ARRANGE[MENT]

The improved and splendid Locomotives, Cla[y] and Lundy, with their trains fitted up in the best s[tyle of] accommodation for passengers, will run their r[egular] trips during the present season, between the bord[ers of] the Patriarchal Dominion and Libertyville, Upper C[anada.] Gentlemen and Ladies, who may wish to improve [their] health or circumstances, by a northern tour, are re[spect-] fully invited to give us their patronage.

SEATS FREE, *irrespective of color*

Necessary Clothing furnished gratuitously to s[uch as] have *"fallen among thieves."*

LINE.

NIGHT AND DAY.

"Hide the outcasts—let the oppressed go free."—*Bible.*

☞For seats apply at any of the trap doors, or to conductor of the train.

J. CROSS, *Proprietor.*

N. B. For the special benefit of Pro-Slavery Police cers, an extra heavy wagon for Texas, will be furnished, whenever it may be necessary, in which they be forwarded as dead freight, to the "Valley of Ras-;" always at the risk of the owners.

☞Extra Overcoats provided for such of them as afflicted with protracted *chilly-phobia.*

Frederick Douglass, an escaped slave who in 1847 founded the newspaper *North Star* in Rochester, New York, became the leading Negro abolitionist. Douglass received the able and determined support of other black abolitionists such as William Wells Brown, Henry Highland Garnet, David Walker, Sojourner Truth, Harriet Tubman, and Charles Lenox Remond.

As abolitionist sentiment spread, local antislavery societies sprang up throughout the North. In December 1833, the year England abolished slavery in all of its colonies, a group of abolitionists met in Philadelphia to form the American Antislavery Society. The abolitionist movement now shifted from individual and group criticism of slavery to a widely organized effort for national reform. Yet the extreme and uncompromising abolitionists met bitter resistance. Garrison was dragged through the streets of Boston in 1835, as opponents sought to silence him; and Elijah P. Lovejoy of Alton, Illinois, was shot and killed in 1837 when he tried to defend his abolitionist press from a mob. Such incidents, however, only transformed the victims of the attacks into martyrs to the cause of abolition.

The Nat Turner rebellion, which occurred in southeastern Virginia in August 1831, added to the fears of Southerners who were already disturbed over the growing attacks on slavery. Turner, a lay preacher, led some seventy fellow slaves in a major revolt which resulted in the death of over fifty whites before he and his followers met defeat and death. Turner was hanged. Fear of other slave revolts caused Southerners to harden their position in favor of slavery.

Following the Missouri Compromise, the various assaults on slavery prompted Southerners to justify their "peculiar institution" more vigorously and openly. In the previous century the South had abandoned the natural-rights theory of man and the Christian concept that every individual had equal worth in the eyes of God. Now Southerners developed a theory of society characterized by permanent class distinctions—

the so-called mud-sill theory. Professor Thomas Cooper of South Carolina wrote in 1835: "We talk a great deal of nonsense about the rights of man. We say that man is born free, and equal to every other man. Nothing can be more untrue: no human being ever was, now is or ever will be born free." Governor James H. Hammond of South Carolina declared that "in all social systems there must be a class to do the menial duties, to perform the drudgery of life. . . . Such a class," he continued, "you must have or you would not have that other class which leads progress, civilization, and refinement. It constitutes the very mud-sill of society and of political government."

Having rejected the liberal democratic principles of the Declaration of Independence, defenders of slavery advanced a series of arguments to vindicate their position. They declared that both history and religion supported slavery and pointed to Greek and Roman civilizations to prove their point. They quoted the Bible, especially the Apostle Paul, who advised slaves to obey their masters. Moreover, proslavery advocates argued that slaves were better off than what they termed the "wage slaves" of the North who labored long hours under unhealthy conditions for low pay and then found themselves compelled in their old age to shift for themselves. "White slaves," Governor Hammond called them. Slavery was a regional and national good; the North as well as the South, declared slavery's proponents, profited from the products of slave labor. The crusade against slavery was nothing less than an attack on the whole principle of private property.

As the controversy over slavery raged, the ardent proslavery and antislavery groups hardened their positions to the point where compromise on specific issues involving slavery became increasingly more difficult. Abolitionists declared slavery an absolute evil; defenders of the institution called it an absolute good. Both sides had raised a fundamental moral question— the rightness or wrongness of slavery—which would soon engulf them in a bitter quarrel, terminable only with slavery's demise in civil war. Meanwhile the blacks would protest against their plight even as they contributed much to the nation with their toil, idealism, folktales, and spirituals.

Party Politics and Slavery

For the vast majority of Americans in the early 1840s the federal Union appeared durable enough. A troubled minority could see that there were issues on the political horizon that would defy compromise through the American democratic process, but such issues had not as yet reached the forefront of national life. For a full generation the important questions confronting the nation had been economic—the tariff, internal improvements at federal expense, the National Bank, land policies, and distribution of the proceeds from Western land sales to the states. On none of these great economic issues did any region stand as a bloc; in all areas there were minorities dissenting from the majorities. On some questions congressmen deserted their parties and voted the economic interests of their constituents; on others they hewed to the party line. So divided were regional and party loyalties that each new measure created its own congressional coalition.

One issue—slavery—possessed the power to alter this varied political pattern and drive men into sectional blocs. Unlike other public issues, slavery was a sectional phenomenon, moral as well as economic in nature. As an undemocratic and inhumane institution, slavery had, by the thirties, aroused a determined abolitionist movement in the North, but it was largely a religious movement and one which looked to education and persuasion, not political power, as the chief elements in its crusade for human freedom. As long as slaveholders recognized no moral necessity to free their slaves and enjoyed the protection of Southern laws, there could be no clear relation between the growth of abolitionist power in the North and the demise of slavery in the South. Slavery, unlike the other evils of American society, lay outside the jurisdiction of federal action—except in the District of Columbia.

Abolitionists discovered this Achilles' heel in the Southern armor as early as 1835 and flooded Congress with petitions demanding the elimination of the slave trade from the nation's capital. The constant movement of chained Negroes through the streets of Washington bound for the Southern states shocked Northern sensibilities. But for the South the presence of slaves in the capital was a matter of principle, a symbol of the national acceptance of the slave system and thus a condition to be retained in the face of abolitionist pressures.

On December 1837, John C. Calhoun rose again to the South's defense. In an effort to commit his Democratic party to the Southern cause, he introduced a series of resolutions into the Senate which would deny Congress the right to receive petitions against slavery. His argument began with his well-known concept of the Union—that it was a compact among sovereign states. Each state enjoyed the right to determine the nature of its own institutions. It was the duty of the federal government to guarantee the security of local institutions against attack by other states or citizens. Any interference with slavery in the District of Columbia, therefore, would be an unwarranted assault on the institutions of the slaveholding states. By a vote largely sectional, Calhoun carried his resolutions in the Senate. In January 1840, the House added the so-called 21st Rule to its standing resolutions; this obligated that body to table automatically all petitions relating to slavery.

The South had won the first round in its struggle to protect its "peculiar institution," but at an enormous price. In their effort to squelch all discussion of slavery in Congress, Southern leaders had merely redoubled the determination of Northern antislavery advocates and permitted them to enlist new converts to their cause. For John Quincy Adams, now a member of the House, the "gag rule" was nothing less than tyranny. He opposed it in session after session, employing every device to antagonize those who favored it. Southern extremists belabored Adams; they attempted to expel him; but they fought in a losing cause. By 1844 the abolitionists had achieved sufficient unity among the Northern delegations to endanger Southern control of the gag issue. In December, on Adams's motion, the House rescinded the measure.

Slavery, as an issue demanding reform, entered the halls of Congress readily enough. But Garrisonian abolitionists denied the feasibility of organizing an antislavery party, believing such a move both inexpedient and unnecessary. Yet there were abolitionists, especially in the Old Northwest, who believed that political action might help remove the curse of slavery without challenging the Constitution or endangering the Union. During 1839 politically minded abolitionists organized the Liberty party and inaugurated their assault on the established party system of the nation. Antislavery delegates met at Albany, New York, in April 1840, to nominate James G. Birney, a Kentucky abolitionist, for the presidency of the United States. This first convention adjourned without creating a platform. But in 1843, when the new party named Birney again, it prepared an elaborate platform which spelled out its ambitions. Slavery, it charged, created an "impoverished and embarrassed condition" in the South, as well as a "withering and impoverishing effect" on the free states. The platform condemned the federal government for protecting slavery and the slave trade in the District of Columbia; it demanded that federal officials no longer interfere with efforts of the free states to prevent the recapture of fugitive slaves.

Undoubtedly the antislavery politicians of the North responded to motivations primarily moral. Yet their constant references to the "slave power" suggested that their opposition to the South was partly economic and political. For too long, they charged, Southerners had dominated the federal government through their influence in the Democratic party. As a third-party movement, the Liberty party generated little numerical strength, but by the early forties it had gained the balance of power in several Northern states where the Democratic and Whig parties were almost equal in voting power.

In Calhoun's conservative doctrines the sectional issue was joined. How could the South as a minority section defend its slave system as well as its predominantly agricultural interests? Southern fears were real. By the forties the South's population numbered scarcely two-thirds that of the North; its control of the House of Representatives was irrevocably gone. In spinning out his political philosophy of state sovereignty, Calhoun sought to protect the South against majority rule, whether the North's political thrust should be against Southern social institutions or economic interests. Calhoun regarded the Northern urban centers as the chief threats to Southern power and influence. "To distribute power . . . in proportion to population," he warned, "would be, in fact, to give the control of government, in the end, to the cities, and to subject the rural and agricultural population to that description of population which usually congregate in them, and, ultimately, to the dregs of the population." For the moment, the South's security rested on the ability of Southern politicians to bargain successfully with Northern leaders within the two national party organizations. Already a small minority of Southerners wondered whether the everlasting struggle for Northern support was worth the effort. For them safety ultimately required escape from the Union.

Although the Republic was young in years, the ties that bound it together were many, varied, and strong. Tradition itself was a powerful force. Perhaps the American people, unlike the nations of Europe, lacked a cultural homogeneity, a unique language, and an ancient past. But they were nevertheless a nation. Only a few decades separated the generation of the 1840s from the common achievements that had launched the new nation and nurtured its development. Abraham Lincoln could speak with truth of the "mystic chords of memory, stretching from every battlefield and patriot grave to every living heart and hearthstone all over this broad land." For the vast majority of Americans, the Union was the symbol of a revered past and the hope of a brilliant future.

American loyalty rested on an unshakable belief in the superiority of America's democratic institutions. Nationalism must ultimately express itself in the political state, and for a democracy this demands that the state be subject to popular control and employ its authority in the public interest. The American political system was admirably suited to foster nationalism, especially after Jefferson and Jackson had rendered assurances that the government would seek the welfare of the average citizen.

American nationalism was derived, secondly, from a sense of mission. One widespread article of faith insisted that this nation was the special instrument for achieving not only the material prosperity and expanding power of the American people but also the moral elevation of the entire globe. If men were really capable of self-government, declared Robert J. Breckinridge of Kentucky in 1837, then "no mortal power can estimate the height and grandeur waiting to receive us—nor compute the depth and thoroughness of that tremendous change which the influence of our spirit must operate throughout the world." What mattered was that the

Republic have time to achieve its promise of greatness. "May our happy union not be torn asunder," wrote Henry Wheaton, the distinguished American diplomat, "even before we have gathered its best fruits in the successful cultivation of science and letters, under the shadow of its protecting wings; and before we have produced any works of art or genius to command the admiration and envy of posterity. . . ."

For many men of business, the essence of nationalism lay not in democracy and America's mission but in the economic guarantees of the Constitution; to them, the foundations of American nationalism were material as well as emotional. The Constitution underlay the entire business structure of the nation. In that document of law and order, merchants and industrialists found the values and requirements essential to the business community. It bound the states together under one law and made possible a national market. It forced the fulfillment of contracts and protected property rights against the onslaught of radicalism. Only the national government, created by the Constitution, could promote foreign markets. It alone could negotiate favorable commercial treaties, protect American shipping and property abroad, improve harbors, maintain lighthouses, control the national currency, and secure protective tariffs.

Geography and national economic ties created additional material bases of American nationalism. Americans were proud of the immense extent of their country, and they sensed, too, that its geography was peculiarly designed to achieve national greatness. The United States in the forties had developed a genuinely national economy based on a regional division of labor. New England and the Middle Atlantic states were devoted principally to commerce and industry. This region satisfied the demands for manufactured goods in the other areas of the

Bales of cotton on a Charleston, South Carolina, wharf in the days when cotton was perhaps the strongest tie of Union.
The Bettmann Archive

nation and required the foodstuffs and raw materials of the Lake regions and the South. The Northwest was predominantly agricultural, finding its markets in both the East and the South but its source of manufactured goods and capital in the East. The South engaged chiefly in the production of staples and depended on other sections for most of its food, its markets, its capital, and its manufactures. The heavy flow of commerce along the rivers, canals, and the Great Lakes, as well as the Atlantic and Gulf Coasts, merely reflected the tendency toward a regional division of labor. This interlocking of the nation's economic interests prompted Joseph P. Bradley, a justice of the New Jersey Supreme Court, to declare that agriculture, industry, and commerce constituted "an indissoluble bond which unites and keeps *us* together as one nation, one people." Improved transportation, added the nationalists, would help to annihilate distance and strengthen the ties of Union.

Economic interdependence created a powerful bond of union. Just as the Western rivers tied together the whole Mississippi Valley and rendered disunion unthinkable, so cotton united the New England countinghouses and the great Southern plantations in one community of interest. "Cotton thread holds the Union together," confided Raph Waldo Emerson to his journal, "unites John C. Calhoun and Abbott Lawrence. Patriotism for holidays and summer evenings, with music and rockets, but cotton thread is the Union."

National churches and national political parties constituted two final forces encouraging national unity. By 1845, however, the leading churches had broken along sectional lines. When the General Convention of the Methodist Church suspended a Georgia bishop for owning slaves, the national body divided, and the Methodist Episcopal Church South came into being. In that same year, the mission societies of the Baptist Church split into Northern and Southern groupings, and the Presbyterian Church embarked on its bitter sectional struggle. Politicians proved more successful than churchmen in holding their national organizations together. Victory demanded that the parties remain united, inasmuch as a divided party was doomed at the polls. For that reason, the Whig and the Democratic parties struggled to conceal the growing conflicts between North and South. The politicians' task was to seek out candidates and principles that would cause men to ignore sectional differences in the interest of political success. No party can face all the issues; many are self-contradictory. Victory requires a party to soften or avoid those issues that might alienate some essential element in the party coalition and to feature those with some national appeal. For that reason the parties, under devoted leadership, were the nation's strongest ties of union. The churches might divide, sectional differences might deepen, extremists might become more demanding, but as long as the two parties remained national in scope, forcing their leaders to compromise all divisive issues which confronted the nation, the Union was safe.

Conclusion

By 1860 the South had developed a special and different type of society. Agriculture was the principal foundation of the region's economy, and cotton had become the leading crop. Cotton exports were tremendously important in the nation's overall development because they earned millions of dollars in foreign exchange—capital—which the country needed for rapid economic growth. But most of the wealth of the South was concentrated among relatively few people in that region, or flowed into the hands of Northern shippers and manufacturers. Moreover, Southerners neglected the development of industry, finance, and transportation which would have given them a balanced and more profitable economy.

While slaves provided much of the labor in the South, their position in society gave rise to a strong abolitionist movement which threatened the peace and unity of the nation. But as late as the early 1850s, the ties of union seemed stronger than the divisions between South and North over slavery and national economic policies. Whether national unity could be preserved was the major challenge facing party leaders after 1850.

SUGGESTED READINGS

The best survey of the history of the Old South is Clement Eaton's *The Growth of Southern Civilization, 1790–1860** (1961). The most complete treatment of Southern agriculture is Lewis C. Gray's *History of Agriculture in the Southern United States to 1860** (2 vols., 1933). Gates's *The Farmer's Age*, cited, at the end of the previous chapter, has several excellent chapters on agriculture in the South. A standard work on agriculture and slavery is U. B. Phillips's *Life and Labor in the Old South** (1929). There are several good state studies of pre-Civil War agriculture. These include John M. Moore's *Agriculture in Ante-bellum Mississippi* (1958) and C. O. Cathey's *Agricultural Developments in North Carolina, 1783–1860** (1956).

The picture of the institution of slavery presented by Phillips in *American Negro Slavery** (1918) has been greatly modified by John Hope Franklin in *From Slavery to Freedom** (1956); Stanley M. Elkins in *Slavery: A Problem in American Institutional and Intellectual Life** (2d ed., 1968); and Kenneth M. Stampp in *The Peculiar Institution** (1956). On slavery in Southern cities see Richard C. Wade's *Slavery in the Cities of the South, 1820–1860** (1964). Some of the most important studies on the economics of slavery have been reprinted in Harold Woodman's *Slavery and the Southern Economy** (1966). *Time on the Cross, the Economics of American Slavery* (1974), by Robert W. Fogel and Stanley L. Engerman, is a study of slavery based on computer techniques.

On cotton production see Matthew Hammond's *The Cotton Industry* (1897) and William E. Dodd's *The Cotton Kingdom* (1919). For special crops consult Joseph C. Robert's *The Story of Tobacco in America** (1949); J. Carlyle Sitterson's *Sugar Country: The Cane Sugar Industry in the South, 1759–1950* (1953); and James F. Hopkins's *A History of the Hemp Industry in Kentucky* (1951). Two excellent books which deal with the yeoman farmers are Blanche Henry Clark's *The Tennessee Yeoman, 1840–1860* (1942), and *Mississippi Farmers* (1945) by Herbert Weaver. Of great value is F. L. Owsley, *Plain Folk of the Old South* (1949). W. K. Scarborough details plantation management in *The Overseer* (1966).

The abolitionist campaign is most fully covered in Louis Filler's *The Crusade against Slavery** (1960) and Dwight Dumond's *Abolitionism** (1961). *The Antislavery Impulse, 1830–1844** (1933) by Gilbert H. Barnes is good, but less comprehensive. On the black abolitionists see Benjamin Quarles's *Black Abolitionists* (1969). The biographies of abolitionist leaders add much to a better understanding of the movement. See Merton L. Dillon's *Elijah P. Lovejoy, Abolitionist Editor* (1961); B. P. Thomas's *Theodore Weld: Crusader for Freedom* (1950); Walter M. Merrill's *Against Wind and Tide: A Biography of William Lloyd Garrison* (1963); Gerda Lerner's *The Grimké Sisters from South Carolina: Rebels against Slavery* (1967); and Benjamin Quarles's *Fred-*

erick *Douglass** (1948), which deals with the leading Negro abolitionist.

The Southern reaction to abolitionism is discussed adequately by William S. Jenkins in *Pro-Slavery Thought in the Old South* (1935).

Party leaders, in and out of Congress, ignored the slavery question until the late 1830s, when abolitionist groups raised the issue of slavery and the slave trade in the District of Columbia, where Congress held political jurisdiction. Charles M. Wiltse in *John C. Calhoun: Nullifier* (1949) relates Calhoun's success in passing the "gag rule"; S. F. Bemis in *John Quincy Adams and the Union* (1956) traces the successful abolitionist efforts to rescind the tabling resolution in the House of Representatives.

Several available studies analyze in detail the nature and purpose of Southern sectionalism. C. S. Sydnor's *The Development of Southern Sectionalism, 1819–1848** (1948) is a standard work on the subject. Still rewarding is Robert R. Russel's *Economic Aspects of Southern Sectionalism 1840–1861* (1924). On Calhoun's important role see C. M. Wiltse's *John C. Calhoun: Sectionalist, 1840–1850* (1951). Emphasizing the intellectual and psychological aspects of Southern sectionalism are Jesse T. Carpenter's *The South as a Conscious Minority, 1789–1861* (1930); W. J. Cash's *The Mind of the South** (1941); Clement Eaton's *The Mind of the Old South** (1964); and J. H. Franklin's *The Militant South, 1800–1861** (1956).

*indicates availability in paperback.

The Continental Empire

In 1845 much of Illinois and Wisconsin was still an unoccupied wilderness, and the westward-moving frontier was creeping across Iowa and Missouri. To the west, the prairies rolled on for several hundred miles before they became lost in that high, level expanse known as the Great Plains. Except for groves and patches of willow and cottonwood that marked the course of the Missouri, Platte, Arkansas, and their tributaries, the region was one continuous grassland, its thick covering of prairie grass in the east gradually thinning out into clumps of buffalo grass and sagebrush on the high, parched plains to the west. This continental grassland experienced wide extremes in temperature and rainfall, with long, cold winters followed by hot summers. Over the plains roamed the great nomadic Indian tribes—Sioux, Blackfoot, and Crow to the north; Pawnee, Cheyenne, Arapaho, Kiowa, and Comanche to the south. The millions of buffalo that grazed the plains provided the Indians with their immediate necessities of life—food, clothing, tepees, thread, and fuel. Buffalo hunting was the major economic endeavor of the wandering tribes. Mounted on their wiry ponies—descendants of the imported Spanish horses—the plains Indians were among the greatest horsemen in the world. Trappers, traders, and explorers had long regarded the region as barren and dangerous for white habitation. For American frontiersmen and pioneers of the forties, the Great Plains were an interminable barrier separating the Mississippi Valley frontier from the Rockies and the silent world beyond, which beckoned with promises of wealth and adventure.

St. Louis first gained distinction as the great emporium of the trans-Mississippi frontier through its control of the Rocky Mountain fur trade. From this village on the Mississippi the early fur traders, such as Manuel Lisa, attempted after 1804 to exploit the newly discovered beaver country in the Rockies. From there in 1823 William Henry Ashley dispatched the first group of "Mountain Men" up the Missouri. These trappers combed the Upper Yellowstone and spread southward through South Pass, a wide, gently sloping opening through the Rockies (which they discovered in 1824), to the beaver country of the Green River. Each year the Mountain Men gathered at a designated rendezvous. There they acquired fresh supplies and sent their pelts on the long journey by pack train and riverboat to St. Louis. In 1826 one of their number, Jedediah Smith, followed the Colorado River southward and westward around the Great Bend to the Mojave villages, and from there traversed the Mojave Desert into southern California. Other explorer-trappers blazed new trails: Kentuckian Sylvester Pattie, crossing the Southern deserts from the Rio Grande, reached San Diego in 1828; two years later, Tennesseean Ewing Young opened the Old Spanish Trail from Sante Fe to Los Angeles. By the forties, countless trappers had pierced successive ranges of the Rockies, crossed the deserts beyond, blazed trails through the Sierras, viewed the Bay of San Francisco, and wintered at Monterey. These men charted routes and water holes which permitted them to cross and recross a wilderness of awesome grandeur and dimension. Some who entered the coastal valleys chose to remain.

Meanwhile, St. Louis had drawn the Mexican province of New Mexico into its trading empire. Santa Fe, the provincial capital, was a mere speck in a vast, enchanting world of plains and deserts broken only by cacti, brightly colored mesas, occasional mountains and canyons, and Indian pueblos. Yet this sleepy village of adobe huts scattered along the Rio Grande was the central market for the province's 40,000 inhabitants who looked in vain to Mexico City, 1,000 miles to the south, for manufactured goods. Even more significant, in the town resided people who had silver, gold, and furs to exchange for products of Yankee factory and mill. The vision of a profitable prairie commerce between St. Louis and Santa Fe was not lost on American traders. By the early forties, hundreds of men were involved in a traffic that carried goods valued at several hundred thousand dollars annually. The famed Santa Fe Trail had become the major highway of commerce and travel across the Southern plains.

Texas

But the pioneers who inaugurated the expansionist movement of the forties did not enter the great wilderness of the Rockies but rather the prairies of east Texas. As early as the 1820s these Americans had decreed that one day Texas would force the country into a major decision. Moses Austin, a New Englander with business interests that carried him to Missouri, obtained a large grant of land in Texas from the Mexican government in 1821. When he died shortly thereafter, his son Stephen F. Austin assumed control of the grant and, by offers of free land, encouraged hundreds of American families to settle on his holdings. Responding to Mexico's liberal land policies, Americans surged into Texas in overwhelming numbers and in a decade came to dominate much of the province. As early as 1830 the Mexican government recognized the danger of Anglo-American power in Texas and attempted to stop the invasion. It was too late. Mexico lacked the power to guard its distant frontier. Nor could Mexico City enforce its

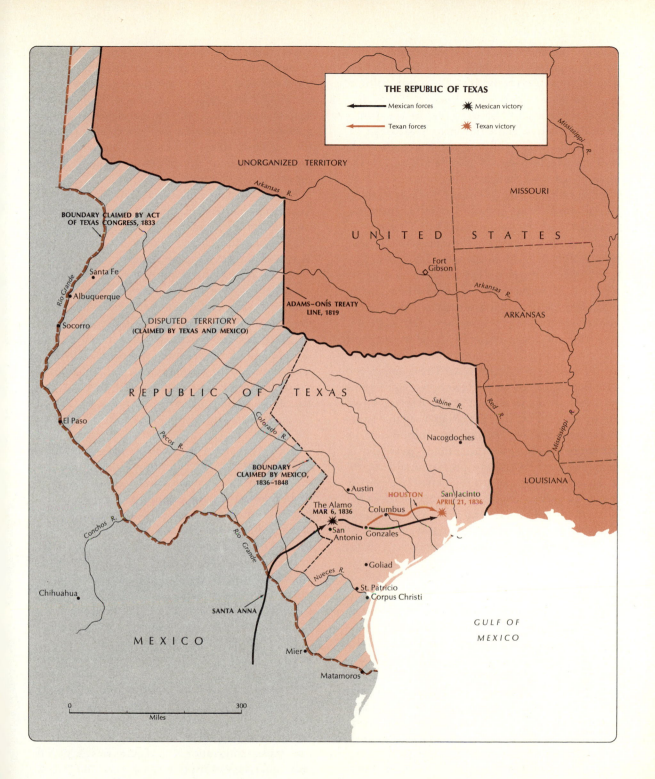

THE CONTINENTAL EMPIRE

abolition decrees against the determination of Southerners to import slaves into Texas, where frontier conditions were ideal for cotton culture. By 1834 the American colony in Texas had 20,000 settlers plus 2,000 slaves. In the sometimes destructive clash of cultures Mexican officials could not even protect the rights and property of the Mexican population against the pressures of the condescending intruders.

Increasingly the Texans, their ranks strengthened by an influx of colorful frontiersmen like Sam Houston and Davy Crockett of Tennessee and the Bowie brothers of Louisiana, became defiant of Mexican rule. The crisis came in 1835 when the president of Mexico, Antonio López de Santa Anna, proclaimed a new constitution for Mexico which terminated the former pioneer-controlled government of Texas. Thereupon the American emigrants established their own provisional government. Santa Anna now marched his army of 3,000 into Texas and closed in on San Antonio, where fewer than 200 Texans had barricaded themselves in the Alamo, refusing to surrender. During March 1836, Santa Anna assaulted the Alamo and wiped out its defenders. Meanwhile the Texans persisted in their independent course, proclaiming a republic. Santa Anna, to recapture control of events in Texas, moved eastward, driving the settlers before him. Sam Houston and his Texas volunteers waited at the San Jacinto River and on April 21 fell on Santa Anna's forces, capturing the general and securing from him the promise to recognize the independence of Texas.

Mexico's government refused to grant recognition to the new nation. Independent nevertheless, Texans drew up a constitution and elected Sam Houston president. President Jackson, fully aware of the Mexican charges of United States complicity in the Texas revolution, hesitated to recognize the Lone Star Republic, much less annex it. Not until March 3, 1837, the day before he left office, did Jackson extend diplomatic recognition. Southern spokesmen for cotton and slavery saw in the annexation of Texas an opportunity to extend the area of both, for the Texas

government had legalized slavery within that country's borders. But the South faced the determined opposition of antislavery forces led by John Quincy Adams. Adams's final speech against annexation in July 1838 succeeded in terminating the annexation movement, thereby forcing Texas to resolve its foreign and domestic problems without the benefit of United States power or leadership.

By 1842 Britain and France had recognized the Texas republic and hoped together to preserve its independence against pressures building in Mexico and the United States. An independent Texas, producing cotton, sugar, and tobacco, and acting as a buffer to American expansion, would serve British and French interests, but neither power could influence Mexican policy toward granting recognition. Still, during the early forties the Texas republic faced neither internal nor external crises, and many Texans no longer wished to terminate their independence through annexation to the United States. It was Southern politicians who dragged the Texas question into the realm of American political life.

With Webster's resignation from the State Department in 1843, President Tyler found himself surrounded by personal friends—most of them Democratic and Southern. He had not lost his political ambition and was determined to make a bid for a second term. To build the needed political influence without a party, however, the President required a powerful issue. He found it in Texas. During October 1843, he instructed Abel P. Upshur, his new secretary of state, to negotiate a treaty of annexation with the Texan minister in Washington. Before Upshur could complete this negotiation, he died in a naval accident. Tyler then made Calhoun secretary of state.

Now the Texas issue moved into even more powerful hands. Behind Calhoun's leadership, Southern Democrats saw the issue as an opportunity to strengthen their own political fences. For these annexationists, Texas was a purely sectional issue—a program to expand the plantation system and increase Southern power in Congress. Andrew Jackson's celebrated letter to Aaron V. Brown in 1843 accused the British of ambition and intrigue in Texas and raised the question of British abolitionist influence. For the South the destruction of slavery in Texas would constitute a special danger.

Secretary of State Calhoun began to promote annexation with the sectional fervor expected of him. He opened treaty negotiations with Texas, admitting to Richard Pakenham, the British Minister in Washington, that slavery was the controlling motive in his annexationist diplomacy. But having cast the issue into a sectional mold, Calhoun could not carry his treaty through the Senate.

If Tyler could not control the Texas issue, neither could the Southern Democrats. A new coalition of agrarian Democrats, centering in the lower Midwest, with allies in the Southwest and the East, gradually captured the issue by nationalizing it. The leaders in this expansionist movement were such key Democratic politicians as Lewis Cass of Michigan, Stephen A. Douglas of Illinois, Edward Hannegan and Jesse Bright of Indiana, William Allen of Ohio, Robert J. Walker of Mississippi, James Buchanan of Pennsylvania, Daniel Dickinson and William L. Marcy of New York. These men cared nothing for the expansion of slavery. They favored annexation, Douglas said later, "upon broad national grounds, elevated far above, and totally disconnected from the question of slavery." Even before the Democratic Convention at Baltimore in May 1844, they had pushed Calhoun aside and taken control of the Democratic party.

The Election of 1844

Van Buren approached the campaign of 1844 still titular head of the Democratic party and confident of another nomination. State Democratic conventions across the country generally favored him and committed more than half the convention delegates to support his candidacy. But the New Yorker revealed his strong antislavery leanings by faltering on the annexation issue. He announced to the press on April 27 that he regarded Texas annexation, for the moment at least, inexpedient and dangerous. At Baltimore the new party managers moved to deny Van Buren the nomination, convinced that he could not carry the country against Clay. Their control became clear when they engineered the adoption of the "two-thirds rule." When the voting for candidates began, those pledged to Van Buren gave him a clear majority on the first ballot. But the Van Buren nomination was doomed, for they could never command two-thirds of the votes. On the other hand, the Van Burenites could prevent the nomination of his enemies Buchanan and Cass. James K. Polk of Tennessee appeared on the eighth ballot. A stampede during the ninth gave him the unanimous vote of the convention.

Polk was a devout Jacksonian and a known devotee of Van Buren. He had favored Texas annexation but had not engaged in any of the intrigue that overthrew the New York machine. The convention offered the vice presidency almost unanimously to Silas Wright, a close associate of Van Buren in New York, who declined it. It then went to George M. Dallas, a colorless Democrat of Pennsylvania. The fact that Wright had been chosen for the vice presidency and that he was principal author of the expansion plank in the Democratic platform indicated how completely Texas served merely as a catalyst to achieve a revolution in leadership within the Democratic party. For Wright's views on Texas coincided with those of Van Buren.

Whig conservatives, North and South, felt threatened by the Texas issue. Annexation, they feared, would endanger peace with Mexico. Their chief concern, however, was for the Union and for the success of their party. They recalled bitterly four futile years in power that had produced little but the tariff of 1842. Now Texas was again placing the Whig program in jeopardy. Clay himself summarized well the Whig stand on Texas in a letter to the *National Intelligencer* in May 1844, "I consider the annexation of Texas, at this time, without the assent of Mexico, as a measure compromising the national character, involving us certainly in a war with Mexico, probably with other foreign powers, dangerous to the integrity of the Union, inexpedient in the present financial condition of the country, and not called for by any general expression of public opinion." Thoroughly united behind their popular nominee, the Whigs anticipated Clay's election, and a thorough Whig regime. Their platform did not equivocate on matters of economic policy. Having gained confidence since 1840, they chose to give the American people a choice of philosophies as well as candidates.

Texas dominated the campaign. Democratic editors and politicians transformed the question of expansion into that significant expression of American nationalism known as "manifest destiny," which implied that this country was destined by the will of Heaven to achieve territorial eminence. The doctrine attributed the country's inevitable growth to a homogeneous process emanating from certain unique qualities in American civilization—the energy and vigor of its people, their idealism and faith in their democratic institutions (enhanced in the forties by the dramatic achievements of the past), and their obligation to extend "the area of freedom" to their less fortunate neighbors. Such notions, preached by Democratic orators from every

stump in the land, helped the Democrats upset Whig calculations and gain both the White House and control of Congress. The popular vote gave Polk a narrow margin: 1,337,000 to 1,299,000. The electoral vote was 170 for Polk and 105 for Clay. So confident had the Whigs been of victory that they were disconsolate in defeat. Horace Greeley's *New York Tribune* charged the Democrats with corruption in buying votes, especially those of the newly arrived immigrants in New York City. Clay lost New York with its 36 electoral votes by a margin of 5,000.

Polk's victory pointed to the immediate annexation of Texas. When Congress convened in December 1844, the Democratic leadership brought a joint resolution of annexation before both houses. Convinced that Mexico would react violently to annexation, Senator Benton proposed negotiation with Mexico, prior to any congressional action, for the purpose of defining the boundary. By January 1845, however, the Missourian had agreed to immediate annexation, with the question of the boundary to be left to future diplomacy. The House passed the resolution for annexation late in January; at the end of February, by a narrow vote of 27 to 25, the Senate approved an amended resolution. Tyler, anxious to proceed under the authority granted by Congress, directed the American chargé in Texas, on March 3, to invite Texas to join the Union. Texas responded favorably to the American invitation and entered the Union when Congress approved its new constitution the following December.

Polk's Domestic Policies

Polk was in many respects an unlikely president. He possessed no unique qualities of mind, body, or spirit. Neither in personality nor appearance was he conspicuous. Yet his political experience as speaker of the House of Representatives and governor of Tennessee had been long and deep, giving him a knowledge of party behavior as

thorough as that of any of his contemporaries. Polk's election to the White House brought the new Democratic leadership into power. Both in Congress and in the Cabinet, the expansionist element reached new heights of influence and remained the core of the Democratic organization—thus wielding major influence over national policy—until the eve of the Civil War. As a group, these men were Jacksonian in philosophy; moderate on the question of slavery; generally expansionist in outlook; devoted to the party and the Union, recognizing, as did the conservative Whig leadership, that the Union would not long survive any breakup of the two national parties along sectional lines.

Polk entered the White House determined to achieve tariff reduction and reestablishment of the Independent Treasury. On the tariff issue Polk had the full support of Calhoun and the Southern Democrats. Assured of the required backing, Polk included tariff proposals in his message of December 1845. Submitted to Congress by Secretary of the Treasury Robert J. Walker, the new tariff bill contained duties levied by value which were bitterly opposed by the New England industrialists. Webster, now back in the Senate, led the attack on the Walker bill, but he failed to break the Democratic ranks. The vote on the Walker tariff revealed an almost straight party alignment. The New England and Middle Atlantic states voted overwhelmingly against the measure (18 to 4), but Jacksonians of the South and West (23 to 9) tied the vote at 27 to 27. The affirmative vote of Vice President Dallas decided the issue. The new law cut the general level of duties to about 20 percent.

That same session of Congress, again on an almost straight party vote, reestablished the Independent Treasury. After the abolishment of the earlier Independent Treasury system in 1841, the federal government had deposited its money in state banks. Now the new law divorced the government from private banking and established subtreasuries for the deposit of federal funds which again placed the national Treasury on a specie basis. While the Walker tariff was still before Congress, the Whig opposition faced yet another test in the Rivers and Harbors bill of 1846. Overwhelmingly supported by the West, this measure passed Congress in July 1846. Polk vetoed the measure as requiring too large an appropriation for the nation, then at war with Mexico; an effort to carry the bill over his veto failed. Democratic opposition to the high tariff and internal improvements had been dictated essentially by Jacksonian traditions. Still votes in Congress constituted major victories for the Southern Democrats. For Northern antislavery editors and politicians, Whig and Democrat, this was sufficient proof that Polk had sold out to the slave power.

Such charges were false. What characterized American politics as late as 1846 was not the force of sectionalism, revolving around the issue of slavery, but rather the strength and determination of the nation's two major parties to resist sectional pressures in the interest of preserving both their organizations and their philosophies of government and economics intact. The struggle for power between Whigs and Democrats was too intense and long-standing to disappear before issues that did not touch the economic well-being of most Americans. Slavery as a moral issue had entered the nation's consciousness, no longer to be submerged, but even the bitter sectional animosities which it generated scarcely touched the membership or the positions of the two major parties on the immediate political questions facing the American people.

Congressional voting on the key economic measures of the decade revealed the extent to which the parties held firm, and those Whigs and Democrats who wavered from established party positions did so, not because of sectional pressure, but because of regional economic self-interest. On such central issues as the National Bank, the tariff, distribution and land policy, over 90 percent of Democrats usually voted with their party; among the Whigs about 80 percent of the party membership generally followed the party line. Both parties had moderates who broke occasionally, but not one member of Congress voted consistently against the established position of his party. Most Southern Whigs were as loyal to national Whig policy as the Whigs of New England. Even on the Texas issue party lines held firm, with the Whigs, including the Southern Whigs, almost unanimously opposed to annexation. Only on the issue of internal improvement, so universally demanded by the Western states, was there a general absence of party cohesion.

Oregon and California

Texas annexation did not terminate the American impulse to expand. "The Rio Grande," predicted the *Baltimore American* in March 1845, "has no more efficacy as a permanent barrier against the extension of Anglo-Saxon power than the Sabine possessed. The process by which Texas was acquired may be repeated over and over again." The rhetoric of manifest destiny, proclaimed so freely by Democratic politicians and editors during the debates over Texas, suggested that the United States would extend ultimately over the entire North American continent. But those who identified American destiny with the creation of a continental empire rarely bothered to define either the precise imperial boundaries they desired or the means whereby they intended to achieve them.

When restless frontiersmen broke through the Rocky Mountain barrier, they entered a vast empire of mountains, deserts, and forests to which the United States had only partial title. To the Oregon country north of 42°, the United States had the old Spanish claims acquired in the Louisiana Purchase. But above the Columbia River, the United States still found itself in conflict with the expanding British empire, which pushed southward from Canada with the Hudson's Bay Company in the vanguard. Britain's claims to the region, based on actual occupation, were strong; for as late as 1845 the Hudson's Bay Company had complete possession of the entire country north of the Columbia. British officials readily conceded all claims to Oregon south of the river. Thus the 300 miles of shaggy coast between the mouth of the Columbia and the 42d parallel still composed the total uncontested frontage on the Pacific possessed by the United States in 1845. And because this coast was totally devoid of harbors for ocean commerce, no administration would accept the perennial British proposal for a permanent division of the Oregon country along the Columbia River.

Long before 1845, an enlarging American presence in Oregon was affecting the region's destiny. New England merchants had brought Oregon into the China trade as early as 1787, when they commissioned Captain Robert Gray and the *Columbia* to visit the Oregon coast in search of sea otter skins. From that moment onward, the trade grew to impressive proportions, almost solely through Boston enterprise. This highroad of commerce offered profits and excitement— rounding the Horn, bartering for furs in Oregon, trading for tea and silk in Canton. By the forties the traffic had declined, but through the decades it had impressed that stretch of coast from the Columbia River to the Strait of Juan de Fuca on the minds of Yankee seamen.

During the thirties other Americans entered Oregon to transform that wilderness into a promising outpost of American civilization. Earlier diplomats and traders had seen that only permanent American settlements would dislodge the Hudson's Bay Company from its monopoly of trade and occupation. Convinced of this, one Yankee, Hall Jackson Kelley, established a society in 1831 to encourage emigration to Oregon. His campaign advertising the opportunites for merchants, farmers, and missionaries in that distant land prompted Nathaniel J. Wyeth, a young adventurer, to demonstrate the feasibility of overland migration to Oregon. Wyeth's efforts opened no avenues to easy riches, but Jason Lee, a Methodist missionary who accompanied Wyeth in 1834, remained in the Willamette Valley and there established a tiny but permanent American settlement. And in 1836 the American Board of Foreign Missions sent Dr. Marcus Whitman, a Presbyterian, to the eastern

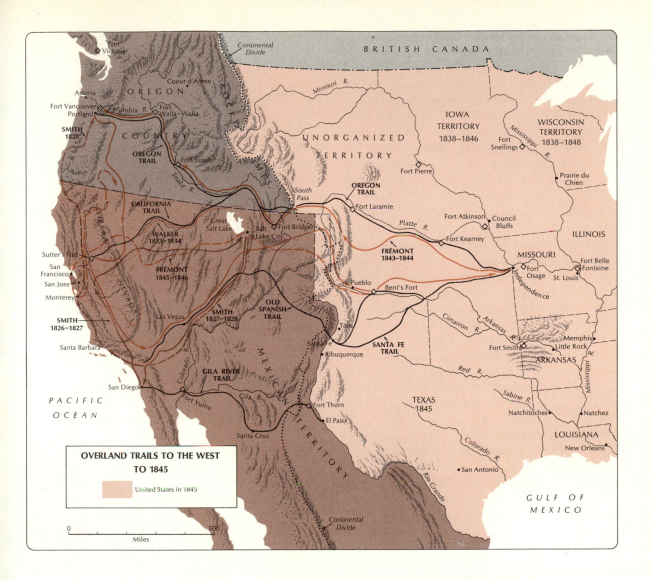

Oregon country. Whitman, accompanied by his young bride, reached Oregon after a long, hard journey and immediately established missions among the Cayuse, Nez Percé, and Flathead Indians. These missionary ventures encouraged the Catholic Church to enter the field. It dispatched Father Pierre-Jean de Smet of the Catholic University in St. Louis to the Oregon country, where in 1841 he established the mission of Sacré Couer.

These missionaries were the vanguard of a great inpouring of settlers. After 1842 the Midwest, awakening at last from its long depression, began to swarm. Oregon—praised by travelers, books, and pamphlets for a decade—attracted a thousand emigrants in 1843 and a similar number the following year. Arriving often by riverboat at the St. Louis waterfront, pioneers purchased equipment and supplies, headed for the staging areas to the west, and there joined caravans for the long, arduous summer and autumn journey over the Oregon Trail. By 1845 these emigrants had sealed the fate of Oregon.

Beyond the Rockies south of 42° the United States had no claims at all. Stretching from the mountains to the Pacific Coast was the Mexican province of California, still remote and exposed after seven decades under Mexican rule. Its fewer than ten thousand people were almost lost in a narrow strip touching the sea. Franciscan missions—a score of them, nestled snugly in well-chosen valleys along the coastal ranges, thoughtfully spaced about a day's travel apart— bore evidence of better days. By the 1840s, these venerated establishments were crumbling. Stripped of their landed possessions in 1835 by the Mexican government, their priestly commissions superseded by civil authority, they had suffered an inevitable decline. The wasting away of the missions precipitated a general economic decline, for the old Spanish-American mission, like the medieval manor, had been the center of the provincial economy. Economically, the California of the forties was not golden. It presented a picture of desolation.

Politically, the province showed even less promise. Travelers after 1840 agreed that it was drifting beyond the grasp of the central Mexican government. San Francisco's Presidio overlooking the Golden Gate was in ruins; two of its four walls had crumbled. Its garrison consisted of one officer and one soldier. The *Times* of London observed in 1845 that to conquer all California would be akin to occupying a desert island.

Yet California, like Oregon, had captured the Yankee imagination. Long before the Mexican Republic opened its ports to world shipping, Boston vessels had frequented the California coasts in search of sea otter. With the news of

Mexican independence in 1822, Boston mercantile houses dispatched their ships to acquire hides in California. By the late thirties many Yankees originally brought to California by the hide trade had decided to remain; residing in the tiny villages along the California coast—Yerba Buena, Monterey, Santa Barbara, Los Angeles, and San Diego. Boston's exciting commerce with California stands commemorated in Richard Henry Dana's *Two Years before the Mast* (1840), an American adventure classic.

Other Americans moved into California overland. National boundaries were meaningless in that vastness west of the mountains, and hunters and trappers, pushing relentlessly onward, never hesitated in their drive toward the Pacific. By 1840, both the fur and Santa Fe trades had long since passed their peak. Each year increasing numbers of American trappers and traders, finding their earlier profits disappearing, pushed into California, never to return. Pioneers who crossed the plains after 1842 often turned southward, leaving the Oregon Trail and following newly discovered routes across the Great Basin and the Sierras into northern California. From John Sutter's post on the American River they fanned out along the lower Sacramento, converting it into an Anglo-American valley. John Charles Frémont's published account of his second exploring expedition in 1844 deepened American interest in Mexican California. His account, which was widely read, stressed those qualities of the Golden West that mattered—the disheveled state of California's government and economy under Mexican rule and the limitless commercial and agricultural possibilities which that region, under a more enterprising people, would hold for the future.

The Oregon Settlement

American pioneers who pushed into the Oregon country in 1845 weakened the British hold north as well as south of the Columbia. Migration to

Oregon that year totaled 3,000 and doubled the population of the Willamette Valley. As early as July 1843, the settlers of the Willamette Valley met at Champoeg and there established a provisional government for the Oregon Territory. Obviously the pioneering movement emphasized the need for a permanent territorial settlement. Oregon enthusiasts, meeting in Cincinnati during July 1843, proclaimed United States rights to all the territory from California to Alaska. Throughout the Midwest the "whole of Oregon" became the popular cry. Western politicians took up the issue to solidify their position within the Democratic party. The Baltimore convention in 1844 embodied these Western demands in the platform. Unfortunately, the claim to all of Oregon up to the Alaska line at 54°40', while appealing politically, was untenable diplomatically.

Although one thing seemed certain—the United States would move northward from the Columbia—Polk discovered quickly that the Democratic campaign promise of 54°40' had destroyed his freedom to negotiate a reasonable settlement of the Oregon question. To insist on 54°40' meant war, Benton observed; to recede from it would abandon the platform and expose the administration to political attack. Convinced privately that a settlement at 49° would satisfy all American interests in the Northwest, Polk offered that traditional line to Britain in July 1845. Pakenham, the British minister in Washington, questioned the details and rejected the offer outright. The President, determined to run no further risk of an intraparty clash, terminated the Oregon negotiations.

When the Twenty-ninth Congress met in December 1845, there was little indication that within six months the settlement of the Oregon boundary would be assured. Polk's message to Congress promised extremists of his party that he would not weaken again. It no longer mattered that the American title to territory north of the Columbia was far from conclusive—and to lands above the 49th parallel, practically nonexistent. It had become, wrote John L. O'Sullivan of the *New York Morning News,* "our manifest destiny to occupy and to possess the whole of the Continent which Providence has given us." To

James Polk, in a photograph by Mathew Brady.

54°40' proponents that seemed to settle the issue.

Such expansiveness was already doomed by the patent interests of American commerce. Robert Winthrop of Massachusetts defined the objective of New England in the Oregon country. "We need ports on the Pacific," he declared in January 1846. "As to land, we have millions of acres of better land still unoccupied on this side of the mountains." Travelers agreed that the Columbia was dangerous for large ships and almost inaccessible for considerable periods each year. But the Strait of Juan de Fuca, ran the common judgment, was easy of access, safe, and navigable at all seasons and in any weather. Commercial realists argued, moreover, that the United States could acquire the strait and all the excellent inlets to the east of it with a settlement at the 49th parallel. Granting Vancouver Island to Great Britain would secure this nation's maritime objectives and still not deny England the navigation of the Strait of Juan de Fuca, a right which London would not relinquish peacefully.

By January 1846, the movement for compromise in the United States had effectively challenged the hold of extremists on American policy. Throughout the commercial East, writers condemned them for engaging in war talk to advance their political fortunes and for purposely keeping the Oregon question in a ferment to prevent its peaceful solution. Merchants complained that Western threats of war were already hampering United States commerce over the world, for no whaler or East India merchantman would venture freely onto the high seas with a war against Britain in the offing. "This will all do famously for the valley of the Mississippi, where they have all to gain by a war and nothing to lose," grumbled Philip Hone, the noted New York merchant and diarist. "But we on the seaboard must fight all, pay all, and suffer all."

In Congress the movement for compromise had the support of two powerful Democratic factions: the Van Burenites, led in the Senate by John A. Dix of New York and Benton of Missouri; and the Southern wing, led by Calhoun. United Whig support assured the eventual triumph of the compromise movement. As early as February 1846, Calhoun planned to introduce a resolution advising the President to reopen negotiations with England for a settlement at 49°. By then it had become obvious that a settlement at the 49th parallel would receive a two-thirds vote in the Senate. The *New York Herald* described this strange political alignment well: "The chivalry of the West goes hot and strong for 54-40 while the ardent South, and the calculating East, coalesce, for once, on this point, and quietly and temperately call for 49."

Polk still refused to defy the Western Democrats. But his personal dilemma did not prevent the British from entering the diplomatic vacuum. In 1845 the Hudson's Bay Company moved its main depot from Fort Vancouver to Vancouver Island. This surrender of the Columbia was the key to the Oregon settlement. To British officials American pioneers, although still south of the Columbia, endangered the peace and threatened to disrupt the fur trade. Convinced of the need to compromise, the London government sought only an equitable distribution of ports. Lord Aberdeen, the British Foreign Minister, had made that clear as early as September 1844, when he wrote: "I believe that if the line of the 49th degree were extended only to the waters edge, and should leave us possession of all of Vancouver's Island, with the northern side of the entrance to Puget's Sound; and if all the harbors within the Sound, and to the Columbia, inclusive, were made free to both countries, . . . this would be in reality a most advantageous settlement."

In the spring of 1846, Aberdeen offered such a treaty to the United States, extending the 49th parallel to the coast, but leaving all of Vancouver Island in British hands. Polk passed the responsibility to Congress. Senate approval came promptly. Benton passed final judgment on the 49th parallel: "With that boundary comes all that we want in that quarter, namely, all the waters of Puget's Sound."

The Mormons and the Great Basin

One significant migration of the forties—that of the Mormons—did not terminate in either Oregon or California but in the region of Great Salt Lake on the eastern fringe of the Great Basin. Unlike those who entered the Great West determined to carry American institutions with them, the Mormons chose Mexican territory purposely to escape American officials and traditions.

That the Mormons would face the hostility of American society was assured by both the history and the nature of their religion. Mormonism spread rapidly from New York into the Western Reserve of Ohio and there, at Kirtland, Joseph

Smith, its founder, developed the pattern of community life that came to characterize his movement. Facing economic difficulties in the wake of the Panic of 1837, the Mormons migrated to Independence, Missouri. There they aroused the animosity of the frontier settlers, who viewed them as Yankee abolitionists. Seeking a more tolerant environment, they moved back across the Mississippi in 1839 and established a settlement at Nauvoo on the Illinois bank of that river. Here Smith built a theocracy, and his tightly regulated community soon outstripped its river rivals in commerce and prosperity.

Smith faced trouble again when he announced a revelation that sanctioned polygamy, a practice in which he and other Mormon leaders were already involved. In 1843, when he ordered the destruction of a press operated by his monogamous opponents, civil authorities arrested him and his brother Hiram for illegal destruction of property. After being freed, the two men were arrested again on a similar charge and placed in the county jail at Carthage, where a mob surrounded the building and shot the two Mormon leaders in their cell. Brigham Young, who now assumed leadership of the church, attempted to avenge these deaths. This brought open war with settlers of the vicinity, forcing the Mormons to choose either to give up their unique communal and social practices or to move.

Through the years the Mormons had augmented their numbers through successful missionary activity in the Northern states as well as in England. When Brigham Young made his decision in 1846 to take his flock to the West, his resources—a hardy, determined people and an ample treasury—were sufficient to promise success. The Mormons crossed into Iowa and spent their first winter near Council Bluffs on the Missouri. Early in 1847 Young, with a small vanguard, pushed out along a route (later known as the "Mormon Trail") which crossed the plains to the north of the Platte. In late June his party reached the basin of the Great Salt Lake. There Young established a settlement where the "Saints" at last could avoid harassment from the "Gentiles." He gave it the descriptive title of Deseret. The Mormon migration of 1848 brought the total number of people in this new Zion to 5,000. Young's selection of this economically unpromising region satisfied certain necessary requirements of his group, especially that of escaping those community and legal pressures which warred on the practice of polygamy. Partially because the new Canaan lay in Mexican territory, but particularly because the environment was inhospitable, Young hoped that other pioneers would continue to move on to Oregon or California.

This experiment might have failed without the leadership and the sense of community which Young brought to the Mormon settlement. With the power to determine all land, economic, and religious policy, Young and his associates were able to organize their people for survival. They ruled out all practices which promoted individualism at the expense of the majority. Permitting no land speculation, they put the community's limited land and water resources to maximum use by establishing small, irrigated, intensely cultivated farms. They found a ready market for their crop surplus among migrants traveling to California; the trade added wealth to their community, and their presence at the edge of the desert added immeasurably to the security of the trail.

Despite the heavy flow of outsiders through the Salt Lake settlement, Young succeeded in protecting his polygamous, theocratic society from direct interference by a monogamous, democratic nation. With the Treaty of Guadalupe Hidalgo in 1848, the United States acquired the Great Basin; two years later Congress organized Deseret as Utah Territory. Even then Brigham Young, as the new territorial governor, was able to maintain his rigid, but shrewd and reasonable, control of both civil and spiritual affairs in the dozens of Mormon communities now scattered over the region.

Polk turned to the question of California with considerable resolution during the summer and autumn of 1845, for this challenge, unlike that of Oregon, was not encumbered by politics. In California, however, the United States had no legal claim. The acquisition of this Mexican province required bargaining with its owner, and in 1845 the chance of negotiations with Mexico appeared slight indeed. That nation had never recognized the independence of Texas and had warned the United States repeatedly that annexation would mean war. Scarcely a month had elapsed after Polk's inauguration when Mexico severed diplomatic relations. The gesture was futile, for Mexico could not escape the power and determination of the Polk administration simply by ignoring it. In July the President ordered General Zachary Taylor with a detachment of American troops to take up a position on the Nueces River, the historic southern boundary of Texas. His intention, however, was to underwrite Texas' claims to the Rio Grande. At the same time the Secretary of the Navy instructed Commodore J. D. Sloat, commander of the United States fleet in the Pacific, to occupy San Francisco should Mexico declare war on the United States.

California began to disturb the Polk administration in the fall of 1845. There were rumors of British designs on the Bay of San Francisco. Thomas O. Larkin, a Monterey merchant and Polk's recently appointed secret agent in California, informed Secretary of State Buchanan that the British and French governments were maintaining consular posts in Upper California, although neither nation had any ostensible commercial interests there. The British consul resided on a ranch 50 miles from the coast. "Why they are in the Service their Governments best know and Uncle Sam will know to his cost," Larkin warned as early as July. Buchanan reported his fears to Louis McLane, United States minister at London: "I need not say to you what a flame would be kindled throughout the Union should Great Britain obtain a cession of California from Mexico."

Only by acquiring California could Polk terminate the European threat. Throughout the autumn months of 1845 the President pursued a dual program designed to gain the province without war. Through his agent Larkin he prepared to annex the region should it, like Texas, establish its independence. Then, having been assured that the Mexican government would again accept an American commissioner, Polk, in November 1845, dispatched John Slidell of Louisiana to the Mexican capital. Through Slidell he hoped to settle the Texas boundary and purchase California. Polk authorized Slidell to offer up to $25 million for the region westward from Texas to the Pacific. When Slidell failed to influence the Mexican government, Polk dispatched General Taylor and his army to the Rio Grande, thus occupying territory now claimed by the United States as part of Texas. By May 1846, Polk's entire Mexican policy of acquiring California peacefully had failed. California had not achieved its independence, and Mexico had refused to sell. Moreover, when the President placed Taylor on the Rio Grande, he created a critical situation wherein a few scattered shots in a distant wilderness could involve the United States in war.

For this declining state of affairs Mexico could not escape all responsibility. Its resentment of American energy and expansionism, especially as revealed in the Texas movement for independence, was understandable. Unfortunately, this drove Mexican leaders into policies that could only produce bitter frustration and anger within the United States. Texans especially could forget neither the cruelties of Santa Anna which followed in the wake of the Alamo nor the atrocities perpetuated in the early forties by occasional Mexican raids against isolated Texas villages. American officials could not accept as reasonable the bitter Mexican reaction to Jackson's recognition of Texan independence in 1837 and the complete breakdown of satisfactory United States–Mexican relations which followed. But Mexican politicians had found it profitable politically to abuse the neighbor to the north, and by the mid-forties Mexican opinion against the United States was inflamed beyond control. Two successive Mexican governments, in 1845 and 1846, simply dared not recognize Slidell when the issues he represented were Texas and California.

Some magnanimity within the Polk administration toward Mexico might have prevented war. Mexico had broken diplomatic relations, but had not resorted to force. Time favored a return to normal diplomacy. American security, meanwhile, was not endangered. But in the balance against peace was the pressure of American public sentiment as well as a measured acquisitiveness toward California.

By May 1846, Polk was determined to have war. His rationale for declaring it was the Mexican government's refusal to pay the claims of United States citizens against Mexico. These claims, totally legitimate, were another reflection of the chaotic state of Mexican politics. In 1839, the Mexican government had awarded American claimants a settlement of $2 million for property destroyed in Mexico. But no payment followed. Some Americans suggested during the autumn of 1845 that the United States assume the Mexican debts in exchange for California; Buchanan included such a proposal in his instructions to Slidell. Claims were no cause for war. Yet Polk, on May 9, 1846, informed his Cabinet that he intended to ask Congress for a declaration of war over claims alone. Secretary of the Navy Bancroft disapproved, preferring that the President wait until Mexico had committed some act of open hostility. That evening news arrived in Washington that, on April 25, a detachment of Mexicans had crossed the Rio Grande and fired on a company of United States dragoons. With Cabinet approval, Polk now prepared his war message, charging that Mexico had "invaded our territory and shed American blood upon the American soil." On May 13, two days after it received the President's message, Congress recognized the war and authorized Polk to accept 50,000 volunteers.

Taylor's exposed position on the Rio Grande gave the Whigs little choice but to support the President's request for volunteers, but after they had time to reconsider Polk's aggressive decisions, they turned the Mexican War into a serious political burden for the Democratic administration. Webster's apprehension rang through speech after speech: "The people . . . appear to me to demand, and with great reason, a full, distinct, and comprehensive account of the objects and purposes of this war of invasion." Several Northern legislatures, especially those of Massachusetts and Vermont, accused Polk of conducting a war of conquest designed to strengthen the "slave power" at the expense of the free states. Most Whigs in Congress limited their attacks to decisions of the Polk administration; they realized that there was no slaveholders' conspiracy.

Military Action in Mexico

General Taylor took the offensive against Mexico even before Congress had approved the war resolution. Having won minor engagements at Palo Alto and Resaca de la Palma, he followed the fleeing Mexicans southward across the Rio Grande and on May 18, 1846, occupied Matamoros. Emboldened by these successes, Taylor left Matamoros in June and advanced slowly toward his major target—Monterrey, the major trading and transportation center of northeast Mexico. As Taylor approached the city in September, his engineers reported that the city's terrain gave an overwhelming strategic advantage to the defenders. After a council of war, Taylor decided to assault the city directly, while General William Jenkins Worth with 2,000 men

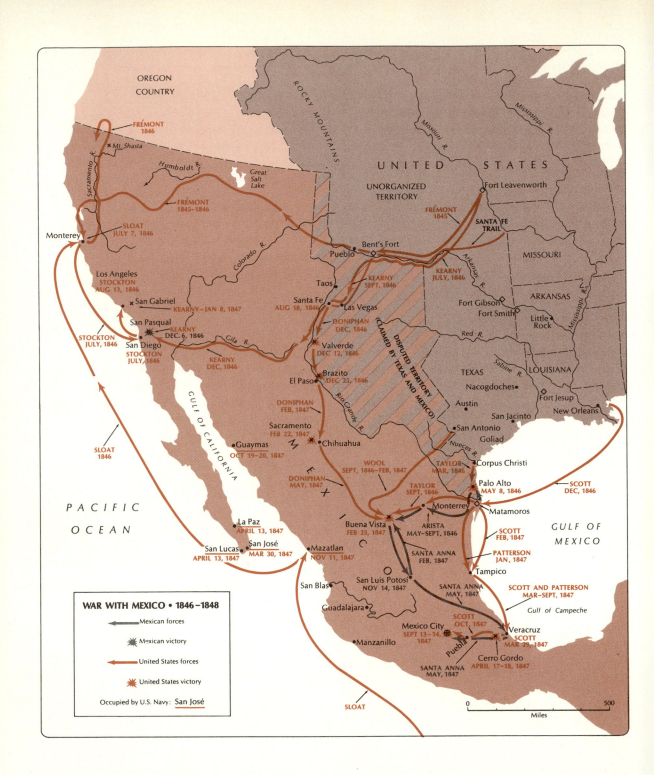

WAR WITH MEXICO • 1846-1848

Mexican forces

Mexican victory

United States forces

United States victory

Occupied by U.S. Navy: San José

flanked the defenses and gained control of Saltillo Road, thus cutting off supplies and blocking the only avenue of retreat. Worth's maneuver was a total success; several days of intense fighting gave him control of the Saltillo Road and permitted him to enter Monterrey from the west. Meanwhile Taylor, using his artillery with good effect, assaulted the city from the northeast. As the two American forces converged on the heart of the city, General Pedro de Ampudia surrendered, hoping to limit the destruction. Taylor's leniency permitted the Mexican army to evacuate. In November the American invasion forces occupied Saltillo. Shortly thereafter, reinforcements reached Saltillo from San Antonio, and General Taylor prepared for a showdown with the Mexican army.

Polk was not delighted with Taylor's victories, for Whig managers were openly grooming Taylor for the party's nomination in 1848. During the autumn of 1846, Polk decided to transfer the main thrust of the American offensive to a direct assault on Mexico City through Vera Cruz. For this expedition he reluctantly selected another Whig, General Winfield Scott. To concentrate its limited resources on the Mexico City campaign, the administration ordered Taylor to establish a defense line and hold it. Convinced that Taylor's army was vulnerable, Santa Anna, having recently returned to Mexico and taken command of the Mexican army, moved northward with 20,000 men to capture or annihilate the American forces near Saltillo. During February 1847, he struck Taylor's defenses at Buena Vista. But after one fierce day of battle, Santa Anna withdrew to San Luis Potosi. This retreat brought the north Mexican campaign to a close.

Polk's early instructions to the Pacific fleet confirmed his determination to have California in American hands at the conclusion of any war against Mexico. In May 1846, the President ordered Colonel Stephen W. Kearny to prepare a force of frontiersmen at Fort Leavenworth for an expedition against New Mexico and California. Kearny advanced along the Santa Fe Trail and occupied Santa Fe in mid-August without

firing a shot. Kearny faced no resistance even when he claimed the region for the United States. Late in September 1846, when Kearny set out for California, that province was already falling into American hands. Early in July, John Charles Frémont, on another Western exploring expedition, had supported the Bear Flag revolt at Sonoma which delared the independence of California. Several days later, on July 7, Commodore Sloat occupied Monterey, running up the American flag. Three days later, a naval force took possession of San Francisco Bay. During August, Commodore Robert F. Stockton, who had replaced Sloat, joined forces with Frémont to establish American control in Los Angeles and San Diego. Believing the region secure, both men then returned to northern California; but during September the Californians revolted and regained control of Los Angeles. Kearny, hearing of the revolt while still in the desert, fought his way into California and met Stockton at San Diego. Stockton, now reinforced, retook Los Angeles. In January 1847, all California was under American control.

These easy successes in Mexico and California presaged brilliant victories for Scott's expedition in central Mexico. During March 1847, Scott's invasion forces invested the city of Vera Cruz, and they captured it on March 27. To avoid yellow fever in the lowlands, Scott set out immediately along the main road to Mexico City. Santa Anna, having recovered from his defeat at Buena Vista, rushed southward to meet Scott's advance at Cerro Gordo pass, and when Scott reached the pass in mid-April, he found Santa Anna in complete command of the highway. American engineers, however, discovered a route leading off to the Mexican left; over this Scott sent a division under David Twiggs. Placed under fire by direct and flanking attacks, the Mexicans retreated, Santa Anna himself narrowly escaping capture. On May 6 Scott occupied Puebla. Here he prepared his final advance to Mexico City, still 75 miles to the west. Early in August, American forces entered the beautiful Valley of Mexico, flanked the Mexican defenses, and on August 20 cut up the Mexican army in two major battles—Contreras and Churubusco. At Churubusco the advancing Americans faced withering fire from the San Patricio Battalion, composed of American deserters. But

Santa Anna lost a third of his effective troops in the two battles, and Mexico City lay only 3 miles away. Such victories deep in Mexican territory encouraged Americans to ponder the conditions of peace.

The Treaty of Guadalupe Hidalgo

From the beginning of the war, Polk's three-pronged invasion of Mexican territory had an essentially diplomatic purpose—to gain by force what his administration had once hoped to achieve by diplomacy alone. It was Mexico's continued diplomatic resistance to Polk's wartime objectives that compelled Washington officials to escalate the war. Had the President desired merely to guarantee the status quo ante bellum, he need not have gone to the expense of a total conquest of Mexico.

Polk and his advisers viewed the ports of San Francisco and Monterey as the chief attractions in California. In June 1846, Samuel Hooper, a Marblehead merchant, reminded the administration that a settlement at the 32d parallel would secure Los Angeles and the Bay of San Diego. Should the United States acquire these as well as the northern ports, he continued, "it would insure a peaceful state of things through the whole country and enable [the Americans] to continue their trade as before along the whole coast." Thereafter, the administration looked to San Diego. Bancroft, Secretary of the Navy, assured Hooper that the government would accede to New England's wishes. "If Mexico makes peace this month," he wrote in June, "the Rio del Norte and the parallel of 35° may do as a boundary; after that 32° which will include San Diego." From that moment until the end of the war, the territorial aims of the Polk administration were limited to the three California ports. Still Polk dared not announce these war aims publicly. The principle of territorial indemnity, under which the President hoped to acquire California, was acceptable only to those

Americans who placed the responsibility for the war on Mexico.

Polk understood from the beginning that the Mexican government, even in defeat, would balk at his boundary proposals. Convinced that no Mexican administration could long remain in power if it ceded territory, unless it received sufficient funds to support an army, Polk, in August 1846, sent a request to Congress for $2 million to assist in overcoming the chief obstacle to peace—"the adjustment of a boundary between the two republics." The President was careful not to hint at the boundary he desired, but some members of Congress assumed logically that the President was after territory on the Pacific. The bill passed the House of Representatives but was talked to death in the Senate during the final minutes of the session.

Despite Mexico's obvious reluctance to negotiate, Polk grasped at the hope that the American victories of February and March 1847 might compel the Mexican government to admit defeat and accept his peace terms. To maintain secrecy, the President entrusted his new peace efforts to the private diplomatic mission of Nicholas P. Trist, chief clerk in the Department of State and onetime private secretary of President Jackson. Trist, departing quietly from Washington in mid-April, carried with him instructions to negotiate for no less than the entire coast of California to San Diego. Proceeding to Vera Cruz, he joined Scott on the road to Puebla. Not until after the battle of Churubusco, in August, did Santa Anna agree to an armistice. Even then the terms he offered Trist suggested that he sought a respite, not a peace. When Santa Anna shortly

California State Library

Opening the West

The American West from Missouri to the Pacific was opened up and joined to the United States between the 1830s and the 1850s. It took many thousands of courageous, hardy people and an expansionist war to do the job. In the 1830s trappers and hunters pushed through Indian lands and established major trails. The 1840s saw waves of settlers in Conestoga wagons follow the same trails in search of land and business opportunities. Gold and silver discoveries brought miners and prospectors. Stage coach lines and the Pony Express kept developing communities together in the 1850s. The telegraph and railroads arrived in the 1860s. But the importation of Chinese laborers to work for the railroads and in the mines — such as those shown above who were part of a crew prospecting for gold in Auburn Ravine in 1852 — had already laid the groundwork for the severe racial problems that emerged in the West during later decades.

The members of the Church of Jesus
Christ of Latter-Day Saints or Mormons,
formed a distinct wave of settlers. Driven
out of Illinois for their religious beliefs,
their communal life, and their polygamy,
in 1847 they followed the Oregon trail
past Fort Laramie, then turned southwest
toward the Great Salt Lake in Utah.
Their migration by ox-wagon and hand-
cart and their subsequent prosperity in
the West were firmly guided by
Brigham Young (above). Young became
governor of the Utah Territory before
statehood. Seventeen wives survived him.

In 1848 gold was discovered at Sutter's Mill and the frantic rush to California began. By 1852 ships jammed San Francisco harbor as this three-part panoramic daguerreotype by William Shew illustrates (below). Indeed, so many ships were abandoned when even their crews deserted them for the gold fields, and so great was the demand for buildings to house expanding businesses that boats at the wharves were actually converted into stores as this possibly imaginative drawing indicates (right).

Right: Courtesy of the New-York Historical Society, New York City
Below, left, center, right: History of Photography Collection, Smithsonian Institution

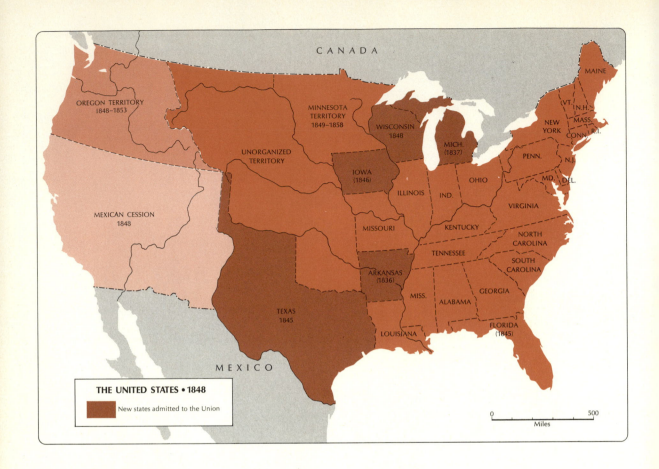

CANADA

OREGON TERRITORY
1848–1853

MINNESOTA
TERRITORY
1849–1858

WISCONSIN
1848

MICH.
(1837)

MAINE

VT. N.H.
MASS.
NEW
YORK
CONN. R.I.

N.J.

PENN.

MD. DEL.

UNORGANIZED
TERRITORY

IOWA
(1846)

ILLINOIS

IND.

OHIO

VIRGINIA

MEXICAN CESSION
1848

MISSOURI

KENTUCKY

NORTH
CAROLINA

TENNESSEE

SOUTH
CAROLINA

ARKANSAS
(1836)

MISS.

ALABAMA

GEORGIA

TEXAS
1845

LOUISIANA

FLORIDA
(1845)

MEXICO

THE UNITED STATES • 1848

New states admitted to the Union

0   500
Miles

broke the armistice, Scott made his final assault on the Mexican capital, taking Molino del Rey, after a hard battle, on September 8. Five days later his forces stormed the fortress of Chapultepec. On September 17 the American Army occupied Mexico City.

Still there was no peace. Polk's initial purpose of exerting vigorous, if limited, pressure on the Mexican government—just enough to gain his precise territorial objectives—ended in miscalculation simply because no Mexican government would deal with agents of the victorious United States. By the autumn of 1847, the fear that the instability of the Mexican governments might indefinitely prolong an expensive war convinced members of the expansionist press that the United States had no choice but to meet its

"destiny" and annex the entire Mexican Republic. In December, the *New York Evening Post* charged that the Mexican people did not possess the elements to exist independently alongside the United States. "Providence has so ordained it," the *Post* continued, "and it is folly not to recognize the fact. The Mexicans are *Aboriginal Indians,* and they must share the destiny of their race." During December and January, with Congress in session, Democratic orators seized control of the all-of-Mexico movement and carried this burst of expansionism to unprecedented heights of extravagance. What destroyed the new movement abruptly was the work of Trist in Mexico.

When it appeared that Trist, in his armistice negotiations of August 1847, might settle for less than his instructions demanded, Polk asked for his recall. But unknown to Washington, the elusive Mexican government made what appeared to be a serious overture to Trist and begged him to remain in Mexico to negotiate a settlement. Trist thereupon ignored his instructions to leave and during the month of January 1848, negotiated the Treaty of Guadalupe Hidalgo, signed on February 2, 1848. In this treaty, Mexico accepted the Rio Grande as the division between Texas and Mexico and ceded all of New Mexico and California to the United States. Trist's final line of demarcation across California joined the mouth of the Gila River at the Colorado with a point on the Pacific one league south of San Diego Bay. For this Mexican Cession, the United States agreed to pay $15 million and to assume the claims of American citizens against Mexico. The treaty failed to protect the economic and social status of the Mexican population against the great numbers of United States citizens who soon invaded the region. Polk dismissed Scott and rejected Trist, but he accepted the treaty with both hands, for it brought both peace and the boundary settlement that he desired.

Conclusion

So completely was the nation's responsible leadership of the forties governed, ultimately, by the quest of clearly perceived objectives that its achievements proved to be both permanent and complete. For in gaining 1,300 miles of frontage on the Pacific, the United States had acquired what a full generation of seamen, merchants, and travelers had declared to be essential for the nation's future development as a Pacific power. Polk, boasting to Congress of his diplomatic achievements, pointed not to new empires of land beyond the Rockies but only to the great harbors which his administration had annexed along the distant coast.

Already in 1848 the United States was potentially the most powerful country bordering the great Pacific Ocean. This fact alone established the basis of new far-flung interests that would require the defense of diplomacy, if not war. Earlier in 1844, in the Treaty of Wanghia, the nation had secured its trading privileges in China. From the acquisition of San Francisco Bay and Puget Sound, it was but a small step to Commodore Matthew C. Perry's expedition to Tokyo Bay in 1853 to open the ports of Japan to American commerce. The immediate challenge to American power in the Pacific lay at home, however, for the nation could not make that power effective until it had linked the villages of California and Oregon with the population centers of the East. Washington looked to Central America, where the American interest in an isthmian canal collided with that of Britain. The Clayton-Bulwer Treaty of 1850 resolved the British-American conflict over territory, but it shelved the canal issue in the process, for both nations denied themselves the right to control or fortify unilaterally any canal which they might build.

That American sense of mission aired so fully in the debates over Texas, Oregon, California, and Mexico found another outlet in the great revolutions sweeping through Europe in 1848. The proponents of manifest destiny in Congress responded to the February Revolution in France with demands that the United States somehow guarantee its success, yet with nothing stronger or more dangerous than a congratulatory resolution. This new crusade for liberty was stimulated even further by the dramatic events in Hungary, where the Magyars under their colorful leader, Louis Kossuth, fought to cast off the yoke of Austrian Hapsburg rule. Kossuth's cause collapsed in 1849 before an invasion of Czarist troops, but the Hungarian's subsequent visit to the United States in December 1851, turned into a triumphal procession. Yet Kossuth soon discovered, as did European revolutionaries generally, that American sentiment, whatever its appeal to democratic idealism, was no more a measure of United States policy in Europe than it had been a guide for American expansion across the continent.

SUGGESTED READINGS

Most notable as a survey of Anglo-American encroachment on the Great West is Ray A. Billington's *The Far Western Frontier, 1830–1860** (1956). Two older, but still highly rewarding, studies of the Far West are Cardinal Goodwin's *The Trans-Mississippi West, 1803–1853* (1922) and L. R. Hafen and C. C. Rister's *Western America* (1941). On the early trappers are three exciting works: H. M. Chittenden's *The American Fur Trade of the Far West* (3 vols., 1902); Bernard De Voto's *Across the Wide Missouri** (1947); and R. G. Cleland's *This Reckless Breed of Men: Trappers of the Southwest* (1950). *Exploring the Great Basin* (1963) is a dramatic account. Also rewarding is R. L. Duffus's *The Santa Fe Trail* (1930).

David M. Pletcher's *The Diplomacy of Annexation* (1973) covers with extensive research the entire range of American expansion in the 1840s.

On the annexation of Texas the standard work is Justin H. Smith's *The Annexation of Texas* (1911), supplemented by later studies, especially that of J. W. Schmitz, *Texas Statecraft* (1945). On Texas independence and after are W. C. Binkley's *The Texas Revolution* (1952) and J. M. Nance's massive volumes, *After San Jacinto* (1963) and *Attack and Counter-Attack* (1964). Texas' role in European diplomacy is carefully analyzed in Ephraim D. Adams's *British Interest and Activities in Texas, 1838–1846* (1910).

Albert K. Weinberg's *Manifest Destiny: A Study of National Expansionism in American History** (1935) has long remained the basic study of the American expansionist rationale. Two recent and more critical studies of American expansionism in the 1840s are Frederick Merk's *Manifest Destiny and Mission in American History** (1963) and *The Monroe Doctrine and American Expansionism, 1843–1849* (1966). Norman A. Graebner's *Manifest Destiny** (1968) challenges the concept that manifest destiny was a determining factor in American expansion.

The political background of the 1844 presidential election is discussed in two brief monographs, Oscar D. Lambert's *Presidential Politics in the United States, 1841–1844* (1936) and C. N. Paul's *Rift in the Democracy** (1951). Charles G. Sellers, Jr.'s *James K. Polk:*

Continentalist, 1843–1846 (1966) is an admirable and detailed account. Joel H. Silbey's *The Shrine of Party: Congressional Voting Behavior, 1841–1852* (1967) makes clear the extent to which the parties resisted sectional pressures in the 1840s.

For American migration into Oregon the standard account is O. O. Winther's *The Great Northwest: A History* (1947). This is now supplemented by D. O. Johansen and C. M. Gates's *Empire of the Columbia* (1957). A survey of early American activity in California can be found in R. G. Cleland's *From Wilderness to Empire* (1944). George R. Stewart's *Ordeal by Hunger: The Story of the Donner Party* (1936) is the standard account. Linking the far-flung activities along the distant frontier during 1846 to American expansionism is Bernard De Voto's exciting *The Year of Decision, 1846** (1943). N. A. Graebner's *Empire on the Pacific* (1955) sees American expansion to the Pacific as a search for ports. Frederick Merk's *The Oregon Question: Essays in Anglo-American Diplomacy and Politics* (1967) includes key articles published over a period of several decades.

Several standard works relate the early history of the Mormons and their migration to Utah. W. A. Linn's *Story of the Mormons* (1902), Nels Anderson's *Desert Saints** (1942), and especially L. H. Creer's *The Founding of an Empire* (1947) are excellent accounts. For a biography of Joseph Smith see F. M. Brodie's *No Man Knows My Story* (1945). On the economics of the Utah settlements see L. J. Arrington's outstanding *The Great Basin Kingdom: An Economic History of the Mormon People** (1958).

Justin H. Smith's *The War with Mexico* (2 vols., 1919) is highly nationalistic. Largly critical of Polk is Glenn W. Price's *Origins of the War with Mexico: The Polk-Stockton Intrigue* (1967). Excellent biographies of the war's leading generals are Holman Hamilton's *Zachary Taylor: Soldier of the People* (1946) and C. W. Elliott's *Winfield Scott* (1937). Pressures on the Polk administration to annex all of Mexico are delineated well in John D. P. Fuller's *The Movement for the Acquisition of All Mexico, 1846–1848* (1938).

* indicates availability in paperback.

14

The Impending Crisis

Continental expansion threatened party allegiances that had held for a generation. So even was the balance of regional economic interests that party leaders had generally settled for far less than they wanted. But the political climate was changing. Ambitious politicians in Northern commercial and industrial districts were growing impatient. National policies, they charged, were out of step with progress, and progress was now measured in terms of cities, industries, and transportation facilities. Jacksonians, they said, had no right to hold back the nation. Adding to their bitterness was their recurring pattern of failure. Whereas they were forced to compromise or suffer defeat on every issue, Southern Democratic opponents of governmental paternalism always seemed to have their way. The conclusion was momentous. For some

Northern editors and politicians the real impediment to progress in the nation lay in a rising slave power and the national government's alleged subservience to it.

Under such circumstances a powerful minority of Americans could not view California as a legitimate national asset to be acquired by whatever means came to hand. Except for its abolitionists, even the North had accepted the annexation of Texas as a national gain. Expansion to the Pacific, however, would extend jurisdiction of the hated slave power into a region freed by Mexican law and create additional pockets of Southern Democratic influence. On two counts —one moral and one political—Northern sectionalists determined to guarantee California's freedom in advance or prohibit its acquisition entirely.

During the brief debate of August 1846, on the $2 million appropriation bill requested by Polk to aid him in negotiating peace with Mexico, one little-known member of Congress stumbled into immortality. David Wilmot, representative from Pennsylvania and a zealous member of the Van Buren wing of the Democratic party, moved to amend the administration measure by adding the proviso that "neither slavery nor involuntary servitude" should ever exist in any territory acquired from Mexico, "except for crime, whereof the party shall first be duly convicted."

The Wilmot Proviso was more than an effort to limit slavery to the South; it was an expression of political revolt. The powerful Van Buren faction had been on the verge of open rebellion against the national Democratic leadership ever since Van Buren had been deprived of the party's nomination in 1844. By opposing the expansion of slavery into California, they could not only weaken Southern dominance in the party but also embarrass Polk. Jacob Brinkerhoff of Ohio heralded the North's wide acceptance of the Proviso "as offering unmistakable indication that the day is past when subserviency to Southern dictation is made the standard of political orthodoxy."

Still Southern reaction to the Proviso lagged. Calhoun believed it a Northern issue and that the responsibility for limiting its effect on national politics lay with the North itself. His confidence in the moderate Democrats of the North was not totally misplaced, for they not only had joined the South in determining national economic policies but also had risen to the defense of the South on matters of slavery. Yet how long could they be trusted? Antislavery forces, with heavy Northern Democratic support, had carried Wilmot's initial proposal through the House of Representatives.

In February 1847, when the administration introduced another appropriation bill to enhance its negotiating power with Mexico, Calhoun determined to base the defense of Southern rights in the territories on the Constitution itself. He reminded the Senate that, if the North successfully excluded slavery from the territories, it would end the balance between the sections. He issued a stern warning to the North: "The day that the balance between the two sections of the country . . . is destroyed, is a day that will not be far removed from political revolution, anarchy, civil war, and widespread disaster." Calhoun insisted that all states had equal rights to the territories, including the right of importing slaves into them. Congress, therefore, as the agent of all the states, had no right to legislate slavery into or out of the territories. Although Calhoun's resolutions never came to a vote, Virginia's Legislature adopted his arguments in a series of resolutions, as did also Democratic conventions and mass meetings in Mississippi, Alabama, and South Carolina.

Democratic spokesmen around Polk searched frantically for an acceptable compromise, for they were bent on national expansion. The President and Secretary of State Buchanan favored extension of the Missouri Compromise line to the Pacific, but Lewis Cass, leader of the administration forces in the Senate, produced the celebrated alternative of popular sovereignty in his letter of December 1847 to A. O. P. Nicholson. Under Cass's plan, people of all sections would move freely into the new territories. When any new region had sufficient population to warrant a territorial legislature, that legislature would decide the region's pro- or antislavery status.

Popular, or squatter, sovereignty became the official program of moderate Democrats of the North and West. For them the assurance of free territories lay in the simple fact that Northern farmers and businessmen possessed far greater numerical strength and mobility than slaveholders did. Southern adherents of Calhoun saw popular sovereignty for what it was. Cass's doctrine, charged the *Charleston Mercury* in January 1848, was merely a device to transfer political control in the territories from Northern congressional majorities to "mongrel" territorial populations consisting largely of Northerners. Southern moderates insisted that popular sovereignty conformed to the views of Calhoun, for both denied Congress the right to control slavery in the territories. But in mid-January 1848, D. L. Yulee of Florida introduced a resolution in the Senate declaring that neither Congress nor a territorial legislature had the constitutional right to exclude slavery from any territory of the United States. Despite its outward appeal to the national spirit of moderation, popular sovereignty was a potentially disruptive question, as dangerous to Democratic unity as the Wilmot Proviso itself.

The Election of 1848

Moderates still controlled both the Whig and Democratic parties as the country prepared for the 1848 election. Polk's Democratic party, which gathered at Baltimore in May, nominated Cass of Michigan. Heavy and indolent, Cass was hardly the man to arouse enthusiasm. The platform was a bundle of platitudes condemning all efforts to meddle with the subject of slavery.

Whig leaders, called together at Philadelphia in June, were likewise prepared to pay any price for party unity and an electoral victory. Their choice was General Zachary Taylor. Already in 1847, Taylor had won the support of key Whigs who recognized the minority status of their party and the desirability of nominating a popular military hero. Taylor's political views were sufficiently unknown to make him available for a party that hesitated to assume a positive stand on any but a few Whig economic issues. For vice president, the Whigs nominated Millard Fillmore of New York, former leader in the House of Representatives. With Taylor's nomination, Whigs could anticipate a successful campaign. Old Zach was the man of the hour.

But the cost of Taylor's nomination came high, for the popular general was a Southerner from Louisiana and the owner of slaves. Having failed to dictate their party's platform or its candidate, antislavery Whigs were ready to revolt. The Northern rebellion gained momentum during the summer of 1848 with the bolt of free-soil Democrats of New York from the Democratic convention. These Van Buren Democrats had launched an organized political move-ment based on the Proviso. When the Democratic convention nominated Cass and accepted his platform of popular sovereignty, they left the party, taking with them Martin Van Buren.

In mid-August such diverse antislavery elements of the North as the New York "Barnburners," New England abolitionists, "Conscience Whigs," and Liberty men gathered at Buffalo. In idealism and seriousness of purpose, no political convention in American history had ever equaled this one. The platform presented a

This detail of a lithograph, which appeared in the presidential election year of 1848, portrays General Zachary Taylor as "The Hero of Buena Vista." Candidate Taylor won handily. The Granger Collection

broad program for the North—free territories for free men of the North, river and harbor improvements along the Great Lakes, tariffs for Northern industry. The delegates knew that success demanded harmony; when the committee on nominations presented the name of Martin Van Buren, a happy pandemonium broke loose. Despite its ephemeral nature—it was dead by 1852—the so-called Free-Soil party was an organization of major significance, for it was the first party to weld the economic aspirations of Northern industry, commerce, and agriculture to the idealism of the antislavery cause.

Taylor defeated Cass by a popular vote of 1,360,000 to 1,220,000, and his electoral majority was even more impressive. His victory, however, was scarcely reassuring. In the South, Whig orators campaigned for Taylor as a slaveholder, a man whom the South could trust; in the North, they portrayed him as a proponent of the Wilmot Proviso. Thus in victory any positive decision on the slavery issue would break up that party completely. Van Buren carried not a single state, but his 291,000 votes in New York undoubtedly provided Taylor his narrow margin in that crucial state.

The Compromise of 1850

On March 4, 1849, the responsibility for resolving the thorny question of slavery in the Mexican Cession fell to President Taylor and the Whig leadership in Congress. Sectional quarrels had prevented every congressional effort to establish civil government in New Mexico and California. Momentarily this mattered little, for the Anglo-American population in the vast regions acquired by the Treaty of Guadalupe Hildalgo was still small enough to exist satisfactorily under military rule. But James Marshall's discovery of gold in the Sacramento Valley during January 1848 sparked a rush to the gold fields. Within weeks, thousands of people moved toward California—some overland by covered wagon, others by ship around Cape Horn, and still others across the jungle-ridden Isthmus of Panama. By December 1849, California's population had reached 100,000, far more than the minimum required for statehood.

Taylor hoped to avoid a sectional conflict by disposing of the statehood issue quickly and quietly. Permanent removal of the sectional issue, Taylor naïvely believed, required only that California and New Mexico prepare state constitutions and apply for admission to the Union as free states. By October 1849, the Californians had framed a constitution and—without even awaiting congressional approval as required by federal statute—elected state officials as well as a congressional delegation. The President promptly recommended California's admission as a free state.

Unfortunately, the President could isolate the California issue from neither the contentiousness of Congress nor the fears of the South. There were in 1849 fifteen slave and fifteen free states, giving the South equality in the Senate. The admission of California as a free state would destroy this equilibrium irretrievably. Thus when Congress reconvened in December 1849, the Southern leadership was defiant. The parties were so splintered that caucuses meant nothing. Not until Christmas could the House elect a Speaker.

Such a crisis called for political compromise. In the waning days of January 1850, Henry Clay presented a series of resolutions designed to settle the controversy between free and slave states. These would admit California under its free constitution; establish territorial government over the rest of the Mexican Cession without regard to slavery; redraw the Texas boundary to exclude all of New Mexico but compensate Texas by the federal assumption of its public debt; abolish the slave trade in the District of Columbia, but guarantee slavery there unless the people of Maryland and the District consented to its abolition with just compensation to the owners; pass an effective fugitive slave act; and assure the South that Congress would not interfere with the domestic slave trade. Thus did Clay seek to combine all outstanding issues into one "Omnibus bill."

Jefferson Davis of Mississippi drew a packed gallery on February 13 when he launched the Southern attack. But the main thrust came from Calhoun, so near death and so weak that his final plea for the Union had to be read by another. The Senator's reply to Clay's resolutions came on March 4, 1850. Like Davis, Calhoun saw that the real danger to the South resulted from the gradual upsetting of the old balance between the sections. Once—in the days of Washington and Jefferson—the South had felt secure in the Union. Now the North with its augmented numbers was on the verge of creating a consolidated government to pursue its own advantage. Northerners demanded that all new territories be carved eventually into free states. Against such aggression, the South asked for simple justice—equal rights for Southerners in the territories, faithful return of fugitive slaves, end of agitation on the slavery question, and an amendment to restore the guarantees of the Constitution. Without such assurances, Calhoun concluded, the Union was fraught with peril.

The North, in the person of Daniel Webster, entered the debate on March 7. But Webster, much to the chagrin of abolitionist firebrands, remonstrated with both sections to forgive and forbear in the interest of national harmony. In May a Senate committee reported out a compromise package based on Clay's resolutions. But senatorial opposition died hard, and President Taylor threw his influence solidly against the compromise. Clay and his supporters could make little progress against such pressure. Taylor's death in July, like the death of Calhoun, removed an element of opposition. Fillmore's accession to the Presidency so changed the atmosphere in Washington that passage of the compromise was assured. When the original bill failed of passage in July, moderate Democrats, led by popular sovereignty advocate Stephen A. Douglas, promoted the legislation piecemeal, and Democratic votes quickly carried the component bills through Congress. During September, Congress completed its work on the Compromise of 1850.

In the five individual measures which formed the Compromise, Congress admitted California as a free state; it organized New Mexico as a territory under the principle of popular sovereignty, asking Texas at the same time to relinquish its western boundary claim to the Rio Grande in exchange for $10 million from the federal government; it organized Utah as a separate territory; it abolished the slave trade in the District of Columbia; and, lastly, it passed a new Fugitive Slave Act which placed federal enforcement agencies at the disposal of slaveholders. Any Negro accused of being a runaway slave lost the right of trial by jury and even the right to testify in his own behalf; a federal judge or commissioner could remand him to slavery on the presentation of merely an affidavit by any man claiming to be the owner. The law required federal marshals to uphold the act and levied heavy penalties against anyone who assisted a slave to escape. For Southerners the Fugitive Slave Act was no more than due legal recognition of their property rights and their only compensation for the admission of California as a free state. Avoiding the moral issue of slavery, the Compromises of 1820 and 1850 had settled the status of that institution on every square foot of United States soil.

The elections of 1850 soon demonstrated that the Whig party would pay a heavy price for its role in the settlement. In Massachusetts the antislavery Whigs, with some Free Democratic support, overwhelmed the conservatives in the autumn elections. The coalition-controlled Legislature replaced Webster with antislavery Democrat Robert Rantoul and voted a six-year term to Charles Sumner. New York replaced conservative Democratic Daniel Dickinson with another opponent of the Compromise, Hamilton Fish. Ohio sent Benjamin Wade, a bitter enemy of the Fugitive Slave Act, to the Senate, where he joined another antislavery Ohioan, Salmon P. Chase, elected two years earlier.

Some Southern leaders castigated the Compromise with savage fury to prevent its acceptance in the South. Thanks in large part to Georgia's cool but decisive action, however, the diehards were frustrated. When a state convention was called for December 1850, to consider the California bill, Georgia's newly organized Union Democrats, ably supported by Union Whigs, waged a vigorous campaign for the Compromise and were rewarded with a smashing election victory. Packed with Union delegates, the convention proceeded to adopt the famous "Georgia platform," which represented the moderate Southern position. It upheld the Compromise but warned the North that any infringement of this settlement, including modification of the Fugitive Slave Act, would terminate in disunion. State after state in the South now accepted the finality of the Compromise.

The Election of 1852

Only the Compromise could keep the old Whig party united. Yet it was so unpopular among Northern Whigs that no one even remotely associated with the Fugitive Slave law could win Northern support. What was for Southern Whigs the last measure of forbearance was for the North totally unacceptable. In 1852 Southern Whigs secured a campaign platform affirming the Compromise only to alienate countless Whigs in the North. Widespread distrust of the Whig candidate, General Winfield Scott, among the party faithful left the Whig standard in shreds. Thurlow Weed admitted gravely, "There may be no political future for us."

Democratic unity and success in 1852 was not without irony. The Democratic party had borne the brunt of the extremism in both North and South in the campaign of 1848. Even after the passage of the Compromise of 1850, there was doubt that the national organization could recover its dissident elements. The split in the Southern Democracy seemed complete, but the crushing defeat of Southern extremists at the hands of the Unionists in 1851 drove them back into the Democratic fold. Both Democratic factions in the South realized finally that they required the support of Northern Democrats and that they could secure it only through party regularity. On the Compromise platform, the united Democratic party of the South rejoined the national Democracy in 1852. Simultaneously as Northern sentiment shifted toward compromise, the vehemence of the Free-Soilers subsided. In New York, the core of the revolt of 1848, a process of fusion was well under way in 1851. In that year, a reunited Democratic organization swept most of the state offices. By the campaign of 1852, the restoration of harmony seemed complete. In June antislavery Democrats accepted the party's nomination of Franklin Pierce of New Hampshire. When the Compromise plank was nailed firmly to the Democratic platform, that party became the only remaining power for moderation in the nation.

Behind Pierce, the Democratic party won a landslide victory, as Scott carried only four states—Massachusetts, Vermont, Tennessee, and Kentucky. Pierce, youthful and handsome at forty-nine, a general in the Mexican War and a lawyer, nevertheless lacked the qualities of forcefulness and resiliency demanded of a successful president. Such powerful Cabinet members as Secretary of State William L. Marcy and Secretary of War Jefferson Davis dominated his administration. From conviction as well as from strong personal friendship for a number of Southern leaders, Pierce tended to accept the views of Southern Democrats on sectional questions.

Washington had seldom appeared more placid than during Pierce's first year in office. The new President in his inaugural praised the Compromise of 1850 as the guarantee of the country's continuing peace and prosperity. Yet those months of quiet were merely the calm before another storm. By 1854 the promise of sectional peace had evaporated before the moral issue of slavery.

Abolitionist organizations in the North had never accepted the Compromise. The tiny minority of abolitionists in Congress led by Joshua R. Giddings of Ohio maintained an assault on the South from their privileged position in the nation's capital. An especially stirring attack on slavery was Harriet Beecher Stowe's abolitionist novel, *Uncle Tom's Cabin*, published in 1852. Mrs. Stowe knew something about slavery from her previous residence in Cincinnati; as a member of a well-known and distinguished family of New England Calvinists, she had fully imbibed the doctrines of abolitionism. If Uncle Tom and her other characters scarcely resembled real people, their tortured existence made an indelible impression on Northern readers. Within a year of its publication, *Uncle Tom's Cabin* had sold over three hundred thousand copies. There was sufficient realism in Mrs. Stowe's description of slavery's evils to render the book the most influential that had yet appeared in the nation's history.

Slavery became persistently relevant to the North through the operation of the Fugitive Slave law. Nothing could have been better designed to keep the slavery issue alive than the hunting of fugitives through the Northern streets and countrysides. Many Northern abolitionists simply refused to obey the hated law. In 1851 a Unitarian minister led a Syracuse mob in the rescue of a fugitive slave named Jerry McHenry and afterward sent him on his way to Canada. That same year a Boston crowd rescued a runaway named Shadrach and arranged his escape to Canada. All the legislatures of New England, as well as those of Pennsylvania, Ohio, Indiana, Michigan, and Wisconsin, passed "personal liberty laws" which, in one form or another, forbade judges to assist Southern claimants and extended to Negroes claimed as slaves the rights of habeas corpus and trial by jury. These laws placed the burden of proof on the pursuer. In 1859 these laws drew a strong rebuke from the United States Supreme Court in the case of *Ableman v. Booth*, which reversed a decision of the Wisconsin Supreme Court favorable to the rescuer of a black. Meanwhile abolitionist Whigs and ardent Free Democrats never relaxed their efforts to reforge the Free-Soil party. What these men needed above all was another territorial issue.

135,000 SETS, 270,000 VOLUMES SOLD.

UNCLE TOM'S CABIN

FOR SALE HERE.

AN EDITION FOR THE MILLION, COMPLETE IN 1 Vol., PRICE 37 1-2 CENTS.
" " IN GERMAN, IN 1 Vol., PRICE 50 CENTS.
" " IN 2 Vols., CLOTH, 6 PLATES, PRICE $1.50.
SUPERB ILLUSTRATED EDITION, IN 1 Vol. WITH 153 ENGRAVINGS,
PRICES FROM $2.50 TO $5.00.

The Greatest Book of the Age.

Stephen A. Douglas of Illinois unwittingly supplied the territorial issue which led to the disruption of the old national parties. The "Little Giant" was ambitious, his ultimate goal being the presidency of the United States; and he had a program for building political fences in Illinois. His plan called for a transcontinental railroad laid westward from Chicago.

The national administration revealed its interest in such a project in 1853, when the War Department sent out engineers to survey the four feasible routes under consideration. The first was the northern route from Chicago to Puget Sound. The second was the central route from Chicago or St. Louis to San Francisco. The third and fourth routes would have tied the Far Southwest to the South through either Memphis or New Orleans. Powerful voices around Pierce favored the two southern routes because, first, they presented fewer engineering problems and, second, they traversed Texas and New Mexico, regions already organized and at least partially settled. To strengthen the claims for a southern route, Secretary of War Davis prevailed upon the President in 1853 to dispatch James Gadsden to Mexico to secure from Santa Anna, for $10 million, what became the Gadsden Purchase, a strip of land south of the Gila River in New Mexico lying athwart the proposed southern route. For Davis and the South the effort—though a success—was vain. In 1854 a congressional committee, under Douglas's prodding, recommended a single rail link between Chicago and San Francisco.

Because of the heavy drift of settlers from Missouri and Iowa into Nebraska Territory, Douglas decided to combine his great Western project with the organization of that territory. As chairman of the Committee on Territories, he proposed a bill in January 1854 to organize the area without respect to slavery. Immediately a number of Southern leaders, political and ideological heirs of Calhoun, reminded Douglas that he needed at least four Southern votes to get his Nebraska bill out of committee. Unless slavery were permitted to enter the new territory, the votes would be withheld. Trapped between Western pressures for enactment and the need for Southern votes, Douglas offered a bill to organize the whole of unorganized Louisiana Territory, leaving the question of slavery "to the desire of the people residing therein, through their appropriate representatives." Douglas believed that his doctrine of popular sovereignty would exclude slavery from the territories. The Calhounites came to the same disturbing conclusion; with administration support they forced Douglas to offer a substitute bill creating two territories, Kansas and Nebraska, and including a specific repeal of the line of the Missouri Compromise. It was generally believed that Kansas, being adjacent to Missouri, a slave state, would vote in slavery but that Nebraska would be free.

The Kansas-Nebraska bill gave abolitionists in Congress a long-awaited opportunity. Douglas had not only resurrected the question of slavery in the territories but was now applying it to regions immediately at hand—not the deserts of New Mexico a thousand miles from the frontiers of the Midwest. For years Chase, Giddings, and Sumner had awaited the issue that would permit the creation of an antislavery party capable of sweeping the North and controlling the nation. On January 24, 1854, Chase and his colleagues issued a document attacking the Kansas-Nebraska bill "as a gross violation of a sacred pledge; as a criminal betrayal of precious rights; as part and parcel of an atrocious plot to exclude from a vast unoccupied region immigrants from the Old World, and free laborers from our own states, and to convert it into a dreary region of despotism, inhabited by masters and slaves." The paper accused Douglas of bad faith and demagoguery in overthrowing the Compromise of 1850. The effect was electric: indignation reached from Maine to Iowa. Throughout the North, antislavery politicians, clergymen, and editors attacked Douglas's bill with vituperation seldom witnessed in American politics.

Despite all this opposition, political maneuvering forced the Kansas-Nebraska bill through Congress. Perhaps political bargains were decisive factors. The final measure, passed in May 1854, corresponded closely to Douglas's original bill; it organized both Kansas and Nebraska territories divided at the 40th parallel, permitting the people of those territories to be "perfectly free to form and regulate their domestic institutions in their own way." Popular sovereignty had eliminated the Missouri Compromise line.

Reaction to the Kansas-Nebraska Act

Throughout the North and Northwest, fusion meetings of Conscience Whigs and Free and Free-Soil Democrats began to forge a new sectional party. Joseph Warren, editor of the *Detroit Tribune*, called a convention at Jackson, Michigan, with the following appeal: "Our proposition is that a convention be called irrespective of old party organizations, for the purpose of agreeing upon some plan of action that shall combine the whole anti-Nebraska, anti-slavery sentiment of the State, upon one ticket." In July, fifteen hundred enthusiasts attended a mass meeting at Jackson, adopted a free-soil platform, and gave their new party the name "Republican." This old Jeffersonian designation quickly swept the North.

Southern extremists prepared to meet this new challenge to their interests, but they faced resistance everywhere. The vast majority of people residing in the South had not desired the Kansas-Nebraska Act. Many Southern editors condemned its introduction; it would become the rallying cry, they knew, for another antislavery agitation. But as the South felt the sting of Northern charges, Southern editors and politicians appealed for sectional unity behind Douglas's measure. At issue now was the vindication of principle. Impressed by the determination of Democrats to defend Southern equality in the territories, many Southern Whigs went over to Douglas without hesitation.

With the slow demise of the Whig organization, many Unionist Whigs embraced the nascent Know-Nothing party. This party's native American platform appealed to traditional American prejudices against foreigners, especially Catholic foreigners. In opposing the election of Catholics to office and favoring more stringent requirements for naturalization and citizenship, the Know-Nothings possessed a special appeal to highly conservative Americans. Indeed, many conservative Whigs hoped that the Know-Nothing party would succeed the old Whig organization. In 1854 and 1855 the party revealed great vitality and energy, especially in New England, New York, Pennsylvania, Maryland, and the Ohio Valley—wherever the tides of Unionism ran strong. Yet as a political organization the Know-Nothings had no future, for that party's antiforeign, anti-Catholic bias antagonized the vast majority of voters.

In the fall elections of 1854, the Democratic party lost 350,000 votes and carried only two of the Northern states holding elections. In Pennsylvania, the Whig–Know-Nothing fusionists carried the state legislature and sent twenty-one anti-Nebraska men to Congress, losing only four seats. In Massachusetts, the Know-Nothing–Free-Soil coalition elected the Governor and gained control of the Legislature. Anti-Nebraska men captured New York, New Hampshire, Maine, Ohio, and Indiana. In Illinois, the Know-Nothings and Republicans gained control of the Legislature and elected five out of nine candidates to Congress. This upsurge of Know-Nothings and Republicans almost eliminated the Whig party from national politics. The future lay with the anti-Nebraska parties, especially the newly organized Republicans. Kansas presented the occasion for their ultimate success.

Perhaps the majority of those who entered Kansas Territory in 1854 and 1855 viewed it as a typical American frontier to be exploited in the interest of profit. Among them were ordinary farmers, businessmen, and speculators who had no interest in any sectional struggle for control of the territories. Whatever their motives in moving to Kansas, however, most Northerners in the Territory opposed slavery expansion. Some, indeed, had received assistance from antislavery emigrant societies. To offset this influence, pro-Southern leaders in Missouri prepared to control Kansas by flooding it with slaveholders, proslavery sympathizers, and border ruffians.

From the beginning, Northern farmers and merchants who settled around Lawrence and Topeka amounted to a probable majority of the Kansas population. To manage the political evolution of Kansas Territory in accordance with federal procedures, President Pierce dispatched Andrew H. Reeder to Kansas as territorial governor. When Reeder called a general election early in 1855, large numbers of Missourians, whether needed or not, crossed into Kansas to cast illegal votes and assure both the election of a proslavery legislature and the establishment of slavery in the Territory. The free-soil elements were incensed. They sent delegates of their

choosing to a constitutional convention at Topeka and there framed a free-state constitution. The two governments began to maneuver for advantage.

An explosion was inevitable. Whether Kansas bled or not was less important historically than that the Republican party was entering its first national campaign and desperately needed an issue. Kansas alone could keep alive the free-soil appeal on which the party had been built. After violence erupted in Kansas in 1855, Northern and Republican editors had their cause, and they interpreted events in that unhappy territory to suit their own political requirements.

In May 1856, the ''sack of Lawrence'' was an episode of high excitement in the story of ''Bleeding Kansas.'' A federal marshal, determined to arrest the free-state leaders in Lawrence, gathered a posse which attacked the village in a clear and inexcusable case of frontier outlawry. The mob destroyed Lawrence's two ''free'' presses and the unoccupied Free State Hotel, and it damaged some shops and houses. There were two human casualties, both accidental and both Southern. Thereafter Kansas settled down to a desultory guerrilla warfare in which dozens of men were ultimately killed. The struggle was not merely over the slavery issue but over the location of county seats and the direction of internal improvements, all of which had some bearing on rising land values. But to writers seeking to inflame the Northern imagination, terror stalked the land. Throughout the North, antislavery editors called mass meetings to encourage emigration to Kansas to save it and the North for freedom.

Bleeding Kansas eventually led to violence on the floor of Congress. A tense audience jammed the Senate on May 19, 1856, to hear Charles Sumner's diatribe on the ''Crime against Kansas.'' He denounced as sacrilege and robbery the South's effort to seize Kansas. Then he turned to a personal vilification of his chief opponents in the Senate, the aged Andrew Pickens Butler of

A political cartoon of 1856, depicting Brooks's assault on Sumner.
                                    The Granger Collection

SOUTHERN CHIVALRY — ARGUMENT versus CLUB'S.

South Carolina and Douglas of Illinois, concluding with a lengthy tirade against the state of South Carolina. What Sumner's speech was unable to accomplish in arousing Northern sentiment on the slavery and Kansas questions Preston S. Brooks achieved shortly thereafter. This tall, amiable, and popular congressman from South Carolina, a kinsman of Butler, brooded two days over the printed speech. Then, on the morning of May 22, he entered the Senate chamber and found Sumner alone at his desk. He quickly accused Sumner of publishing a libel against his state and his relative, and, with this, he proceeded to rain blows on Sumner's head with his cane. From the Northern press, pulpit, and platform, "Bully" Brooks was now attacked as a symbol of Southern depravity. The incident, declared the *New York Times*, "aroused a deeper feeling in the public heart of the North than any other event of the past ten years." Kansas had come to symbolize all the questions in conflict.

The Election of 1856

Less than one month after the stirring events of May 1856—the "sack of Lawrence," Sumner's speech, and Brooks's assault—the Republican National Convention met at Philadelphia. Some delegates were old Free-Soil party leaders of 1848; others were newcomers from Whig ranks. Wilmot himself reported out the brief platform. It demanded the immediate admission of Kansas as a free state, and a federally supported railroad to the Pacific. For its candidate, the party chose John C. Frémont, a man of no political experience. Frémont was not a strong candidate, but his moderation and broad reputation as a man of action made him eminently suitable.

Events elsewhere aided the Republican cause. As long as the nation had supported four parties—Democratic, Whig, Republican, and Know-Nothing—the Democratic party with its national organization was impossible to defeat. In June, the Democrats met at Cincinnati and nominated James Buchanan as a gesture of conservatism and devotion to national unity. But the Whig party had been eliminated. In New England, New York, and Ohio, most Whigs had now joined the Republican party; in Maryland and Tennessee they remained in the Know-Nothing party, also known in 1856 as the American party. Elsewhere in the South, they either drifted into the Democratic ranks or acted with the Americans. When the American party convention nominated Millard Fillmore and refused to repudiate its Kansas-Nebraska platform of 1855, Northern delegates withdrew, declaring that they could not support a party which so flouted Northern opinion. Most entered the Republican ranks. The Know-Nothing party thus became sectional, its strength limited to Southern conservatives and Unionists who preferred the American party to the Southern Democracy.

With two parties all but eliminated in 1856, the campaign was reduced to a race between Frémont, representing a strong sectional coalition, and the Democrat Buchanan, leading the only remaining national party. When the ballots were counted in November, the Democratic party had held firm enough in the North to win. Buchanan received 174 electoral votes to 114 for Frémont. With the aid of conservative Whig votes, the Democratic party carried Pennsylvania, New Jersey, Indiana, Illinois, and California. Frémont carried all of New England, New York, and the entire Lake region, plus Iowa. The Republican party had revealed power and energy in those areas of the North which were expanding most rapidly in wealth and population. In the South the Know-Nothings carried Maryland; elsewhere the Democratic party was in control.

James Buchanan entered the White House in March 1857, backed by a Democratic party whose continued unity rested on its ability to avoid any specific interpretation of popular sovereignty. Douglas claimed that the first settlers in a territory, through local or territorial governments, could exclude slavery. This would prevent, almost from the outset, the movement of slaves into a new region. Southern Democrats insisted that a territory could not make this decision until it wrote its principles into a state constitution. Douglas and other party leaders simply refused to face this issue during the 1856 campaign, but Southern leaders knew that Buchanan favored their interpretation. They also knew that playing with such political dynamite might blow up the party. At that moment, the Supreme Court was considering a case involving the Missouri Compromise which promised to settle forever the question of slavery in the territories. Southerners anticipated a pro-Southern decision.

In March 1857, Chief Justice Taney read his famed decision in the case of *Dred Scott v. Sanford.* Dred Scott, born a slave in Missouri, had been taken by his owner, an army surgeon, to Illinois and then to Minnesota Territory, a territory freed of slavery by the Missouri Compromise. When Scott returned to Missouri, abolitionists persuaded him to sue for freedom on the ground that his temporary residence in Minnesota made him free. When the Missouri Supreme Court rendered a decision against Scott, the stage was set for the highest court in the land to determine the matter of slavery in the territories. Speaking for the majority, Taney argued that the constitutional authority of Congress to make all needful rules and regulations for the territories did not extend to the prohibition of slavery. Since the right of property in the form of slaves was distinctly and expressly affirmed by the Constitution, any congressional or territorial regulation which prevented slaveholding was void. Congress, moreover, had the further obligation to protect such property.

For both the Republican and the Democratic parties, the Dred Scott decision was tragic. It rendered the basic plank of the Republican platform unconstitutional. At the same time it confronted Southern Democrats with their last fateful decision. They could seek the South's future security either in the legality of Southern rights in the territories or in the continuance of the national Democratic party. They could not do both. Democratic unity demanded that Calhoun's doctrines remain buried. But the Dred Scott decision eased the path of Southern extremists who insisted that the future of Southern society rested on the hopeless question of slavery expansion. Western proponents of popular sovereignty, led by Douglas, refused to accept the principle that slavery might exist in the territories until statehood. For them, popular sovereignty was both the embodiment of frontier democracy and the only doctrine that would render the Wilmot Proviso, and thereby the Republican party, unnecessary.

Buchanan was extremely anxious to rid the nation of the divisive Kansas issue, and he sought to do so by bringing the region into the Union as a state. To this end, he dispatched Robert J. Walker to Kansas to arrange the necessary constitutional convention. When Walker arrived in Kansas, he saw that local lawlessness, rivalry, and speculation would make the functioning of popular sovereignty all but impossible. He warned Southern leaders in the territory that any Kansas constitution not submitted to the people of Kansas would be rejected by Congress. Since the Free-Soilers had by 1857 lost confidence in Kansas democracy and refused to take part in the election of delegates to the constitutional convention, the convention which met at Lecompton was completely pro-Southern. Predictably, the meeting adopted a frame of government protecting existing slave property. It gave the people of the Territory no choice but to ratify the constitution with or without the *further* introduction of slavery. Walker refused to accept either the constitution itself or the conditions of ratification.

What was to be done about Kansas was now up to the President. Under heavy Southern pressure, he repudiated Walker and committed both his administration and the Democratic party to the Lecompton constitution. The President wanted to dispose of the question promptly, and he felt that if the majority of Kansans opposed slavery, they would soon right matters there. When the Kansas convention, with administration approval, submitted the constitution for ratification, the Free-Soilers boycotted the election and permitted the constitution to pass.

Buchanan at first tried argument and patronage to break up the congressional anti-Lecompton bloc. Finally he realized that only a compromise would pass Congress. William H. English of Indiana, an administration Democrat, then proposed a House and Senate conference. The resulting English bill would resubmit the constitution to the people of Kansas. If the Kansans accepted the constitution, they would receive statehood and a federal land grant. If, on resubmission, the residents rejected the constitution, the admission of Kansas as a state would be delayed until the population had reached the minimum required for a congressional seat. This move broke the ranks of the anti-Lecompton Democrats (led by Douglas) and permitted the bill's passage. But Kansans rejected the terms offered by Congress.

Lincoln and Douglas

In Illinois, Abraham Lincoln prepared for the senatorial canvass of 1858, determined to drive home the wedges already splintering the Democratic party. Born in Kentucky on February 12, 1809, Lincoln had spent most of his boyhood in the wooded country of southwestern Indiana. In 1830, his family moved on to Illinois. For several years he worked as a rail-splitter, storekeeper, and postmaster in the tiny village of New Salem on the Sangamon River. In 1836 he entered the practice of law and during the following year moved to Springfield, the new capital of Illinois. During the next twenty years, he developed into one of the most successful lawyers in the state. As an old-line Whig he remained endlessly active in Illinois politics. But until 1858 his efforts had won few successes—some local and state offices and one term in the United States House of Representatives. Lincoln's Whig views had failed to capture much support on the Illinois frontier, and his fundamental conservatism had dictated a marked hesitancy on the slavery question. Not until the Kansas-Nebraska Act gave that issue

special significance did Lincoln seize it as a proper subject for debate. He was soon in the vanguard of Douglas's opposition in Illinois.

Lincoln, distinguishing clearly between slavery and its extension, took his stand on tradition and the law. As a moderate free-soiler, he attacked popular sovereignty as totally illogical. "What better moral right," he asked, "have thirty-one citizens of Nebraska to say that the thirty-second shall not have slaves than the people of the thirty-one States have to say that slavery shall not go into the thirty-second State at all?" Then Lincoln posed the core appeal of the Wilmot Proviso. "The whole nation," he said, "is interested that the best use shall be made of these Territories. We want them for homes of free white people. This they cannot be, to any considerable extent, if slavery shall be planted within them." Lincoln was no abolitionist, but like most free-soilers, he was willing to call slavery a moral wrong. His moderate condemnation of slavery, in contrast to Douglas's official attitude of unconcern for that institution, gave him support among antislavery groups where Douglas had none.

For Lincoln, seeking national recognition, Douglas in 1858 was an ideal opponent, for the Illinois Democrat was the leading candidate for the Democratic presidential nomination in 1860. During the early weeks of the campaign, Lincoln pursued Douglas around Illinois to avail himself of the latter's larger crowds. Finally, in July, Lincoln challenged Douglas to a joint debate. Lincoln surmised that Douglas, if forced to publicly defend his views of popular sovereignty, must alienate either the voters of Illinois or his supporters in the South. Douglas had struggled to avoid this dilemma. He had refused to question either the Cincinnati platform of 1856 or the Dred Scott decision. After the Lecompton de-

Stephen A. Douglas, from a daguerreotype by Mathew Brady.   *The Granger Collection*

bate of 1858, he continued to offer the South what he had in the past—an equal chance in the territories. Douglas accepted Lincoln's challenge with understandable reluctance.

In Freeport's dusty square, on August 27, Lincoln posed the essential question haunting Douglas and the Democratic party: "Can the people of a United States territory . . . exclude Slavery from its limits prior to the formation of a state constitution?" Douglas responded with a tone of impatience: "I answer emphatically . . . that in my opinion the people of a Territory can, by lawful means, exclude slavery from their limits . . . slavery cannot exist a day or an hour anywhere, unless it is supported by local police regulations." Douglas had stated his Freeport Doctrine a year earlier at Springfield and repeatedly in Congress.

Douglas won the senatorial race in the Illinois Legislature later that year, but Lincoln saw the lasting significance of the debates. No longer could Douglas hold his party together. In their exchanges Lincoln and Douglas raised questions fundamental to all governmental action. How was the nation to terminate its historical involvement in the human tragedy of slavery? Whatever the depth of the American predicament, it was obvious to Lincoln that the nation could not escape indefinitely the obligation to resolve it. In June 1858, he reminded a Springfield audience that the conflict over slavery would not cease "until a *crisis* shall have been reached and passed. 'A house divided against itself cannot stand.' I believe this government cannot endure permanently *half slave and half free.*"

Lincoln did not believe that the division would of necessity be ended with the sword. If Kansas remained free, he insisted, the entire slave structure would ultimately crumble. This doctrine permitted him to speak the language of peace and moderation and simultaneously promise the triumph of Northern principles. Whatever Lincoln's peaceful intent, however, freedom's victory still required no less than a constitutional amendment or the unconditional surrender of the slaveholders to the antislavery demands of the North. Such capitulation would require some deep conviction among Southern planters that slavery had become a material liability. As late as 1860 that conviction was not apparent. Possessing no realistic formula for achieving the peaceful elimination of slavery in the teeth of the South's determination to maintain it, neither Lincoln nor any other antislavery politician could present the nation with any genuine alternative but civil war to indefinite coexistence with slavery. Clearly the choices before the nation were scarcely reassuring.

The Vincible South

For the American people, the fifties were an expansive decade, whether measured by material progress at home or new dreams of empire abroad. No aspect of national life failed to respond to the great economic boom that roared along, ever upward, until 1857, when speculation and the overextension of credit again brought the nation's wealth-seekers to earth. Meanwhile, the acquisition of California in 1848 had by no means terminated the quest for new lands to annex. Cuba proved to be as enticing as it was elusive. Throughout the fifties, Democratic orators, North and South, proclaimed a crusade of annexation, denying that Spain had the right to hold the island in subjection when American destiny seemed so apparent. In October 1854, the United States Ministers to Spain, England, and France submitted to the Pierce administration the so-called Ostend Manifesto, demanding that the United States acquire Cuba by war if not by purchase. But neither they nor the proponents of manifest destiny in Congress could discover the occasion for converting their territorial ambitions into policy. Nor were the filibustering activities of William Walker in Nicaragua between 1855 and 1857 any more productive of expansion. The fifties passed, despite all the claims to destiny, without any territorial gains other than the Gadsden Purchase.

Whatever their common hopes, interests, and ambitions—and they were legion—the North and the South in the fifties stood apart as two civilizations, increasingly distinguishable by almost every measure of human existence. Life in the North was competitive, energetic, and realistic. Here was a civilization in ferment, revealing an astonishing expansive power and mobility: crowded cities marked by opulence and poverty; mill towns, villages, and farms—all centers of an amazing productivity; pioneers and railroads building new communities in the West; river and lake steamers jammed with people on the move; German and Irish immigrants in search of new homes; popular commercial entertainment featuring P. T. Barnum and Jenny Lind. No less spectacular was the world of the intellect, subjecting every aspect of American civilization to close scrutiny. Here was a world of scholars, essayists, novelists, poets, and reformers.

Like the North, the South had its commercial and marketing centers, its villages and farms. But the uniqueness of its culture centered in its great plantations. Tradition, stability, and contentment were the hallmarks of Southern civilization—at least for the minority who enjoyed its advantages. Here was a world of magnificent mansions, of outdoor kitchens and slave quarters; of Creoles, Negroes, and mulattoes; of steamboats, cypress swamps, and crowded wharves; of cotton and tobacco; of hominy and corn pone; of gander pullings, hoedowns, and camp meetings; of gambling and dueling; of style and elegance; of poverty and repression; of violence and honor. This was a strange world, romantic and self-conscious, knowing its faults but unwilling, from fear and insecurity, to admit their existence. It was a civilization out of touch with reality. Even its future in a democratic nation was problematical, for it was not democratic.

The South did not lack its defenders who praised its elitism as the essence of its grandeur and the source of its strength. Constructing a sectional self-consciousness was an arduous task, but aggressive editors, clergymen, and politicians pursued that goal relentlessly. Their control of the Southern churches, press, and other media allowed them to build a Southern spirit. Southern writers carried the proslavery arguments of Calhoun forward to their logical conclusions. George Fitzhugh went so far as to declare in his *Sociology for the South* (1854) that slavery was preferable to all other forms of labor. "Free Society!" exclaimed one Southern editor. "We sicken of the name! What is it but a conglomeration of greasy mechanics, filthy operatives, small-fisted farmers, and moonstruck theorists? All the Northern and especially the New England states are devoid of society fitted for well bred gentlemen."

Cotton created another article of faith. Its rapid expansion in the forties and fifties gave it an appearance of strength. David Christy's *Cotton Is King* (1855) furnished the statistics and the arguments to render plausible the kingship suggested by the title. As late as 1861, Senator Hammond of South Carolina could declare: "I firmly believe that the slave-holding South is now the controlling power of the world; that no other power would face us in hostility. Cotton, rice, tobacco, and naval stores command the world. . . . The North without us would be a motherless calf, bleating about, and die of mange and starvation."

Buchanan's presidency furthered the illusion of Southern power. Douglas's Freeport Doctrine was not reassuring, but under Buchanan, the South still determined the nature of national policy. Buchanan's administration was an anomaly. "Old Buck" had been nominated and elected as a member of the conservative machine that had managed the Democratic party since Polk's election in 1844. Although a Pennsylvanian, he had as President surrounded himself with Southern advisers, had accepted the Southern view of the territories, had vetoed Northern economic legislation, and had perpetuated Southern prestige in national councils far beyond

existing Southern power if measured by population. Most Southerners did not care to ponder what would occur when he retired from the White House.

Abolitionism had touched the South's defenses, but slaveholders generally took refuge in the fact that the attacks on their institutions came from outsiders who really knew nothing about their section. Suddenly, in 1857, a North Carolinian, Hinton Rowan Helper, dealt the South's moral and economic defenses a crushing blow. That year Helper, a non-slaveholding white who had come to detest slavery, published *The Impending Crisis of the South*, in which he sought to prove statistically that the Southern slave system had limited the South's economic growth. Only through the destruction of the slave system could the South enter the American race for wealth on terms equal with the North. Here was an antislavery argument from the pen of a Southerner, aimed not at the immorality of the slaveholding minority but at the economic self-interest of the majority.

Why did the South's free population permit the planting aristocracy to commit the entire section to the defense of the slave system? Men sometimes react irrationally in the face of real or imagined dangers, and the emotion-ridden Southerners of the fifties were no exception. Perhaps poorer non-slaveholding whites were too much caught up in the slave system to understand that they were its victims. If slavery hobbled their freedom, they were not conscious of it. Slavery, after all, gave status to the poor whites and even to those free farmers who were not poor. Would not an emancipated black be a more formidable competitor than a slave? Most of those who doubted the morality or economic soundness of the slave culture had simply left.

Southern men of affairs—especially those in the Whig tradition—often desired nothing more than to mine coal, manufacture iron, build railroads, and spin cotton in Dixie, and they saw clearly that the achievement of such goals required both government-financed internal improvements and Northern markets. Their tragedy—and that of the nation—lay in their unwillingness to preserve their political associations with Northerners who shared their nationalism but who also identified themselves, largely as Republicans, with the cause of free soil. Though not slaveholders themselves, Southern lawyers and businessmen were often bound economically to those who held the slaves. Unwilling to break openly with their fellow Southerners on the issue of slavery and slavery extension, they demanded in vain that conservatives of the North discard the antislavery component in their program. It was the failure of the non-slaveholding elements in the South to contest the leadership of the planter minority that permitted the latter to become the arbiters of the South's destiny.

Southern complacency received another rude shock in October 1859. Backed by the moral and financial support of well-known Northern antislavery men, John Brown and a small band of men seized the federal arsenal at Harpers Ferry, hoping by this bold stroke to begin a general slave revolt and insurrection throughout the Southern countryside. Should that purpose fail, Brown hoped to conduct a guerrilla war from the hills of western Virginia. Brown was captured, tried, sentenced by a Virginia court, and hanged a month later. But if Brown was dead, his spirit marched on. Henry Thoreau compared Brown's execution to the crucifixion of Christ, and Ralph Waldo Emerson wrote that Brown had made "the gallows as glorious as the Cross." Overnight, abolitionists established Brown as the martyr of the age.

The South was visibly shaken. John Brown's raid was an irresponsible attack from the North that no Southerner could ignore. It suddenly came home to many that Northern abolitionism, in preaching a crusade against slavery, jeopardized Southern society itself. If the North could not control its abolitionists, the South had no defense except secession.

The Republican Triumph

At Charleston in April 1860, Democratic politics reached an impasse. Douglas and his supporters had tried in vain to change the Democratic convention site to another city, for Charleston was the nerve center of Southern extremism. Southern Democratic leaders had narrowed the choices confronting the convention to rule or ruin. Rather than accept Douglas and Southern inequality in the territories, they would create a Southern-rights party with a candidate and platform of its own. They were assured the support of the galleries and of the Buchanan forces who agreed with them that Douglas must be rejected.

Before the convention could reach the nominating process, it broke up over the platform. No amount of accommodation could close the gap between the Southern demand for full federal intervention in behalf of the almost-nonexistent slave property in the territories and the new Douglas compromise which suggested vaguely that the question of slavery extension be left to the Supreme Court. Convinced by the first ballot that they could not control the convention, Southerners refrained from voting.

After Northern votes determined the platform, the Alabama delegation marched out of the hall, followed closely by the delegations from Mississippi, Louisiana, South Carolina, Florida, and Tennessee, along with scattered delegates from Arkansas, Missouri, Georgia, Virginia, and Delaware. The dominant proslavery leadership of the South now stood together in defiance of the North. Meanwhile, the convention maneuvered to bring the defiant Southerners back. In the interest of party harmony, the New York delegates blocked an easy Douglas nomination by insisting that he receive two-thirds of the votes of the entire convention, not merely two-thirds of those remaining. As Douglas failed repeatedly to obtain more than a bare majority of the ballots, the hopelessly deadlocked conven-

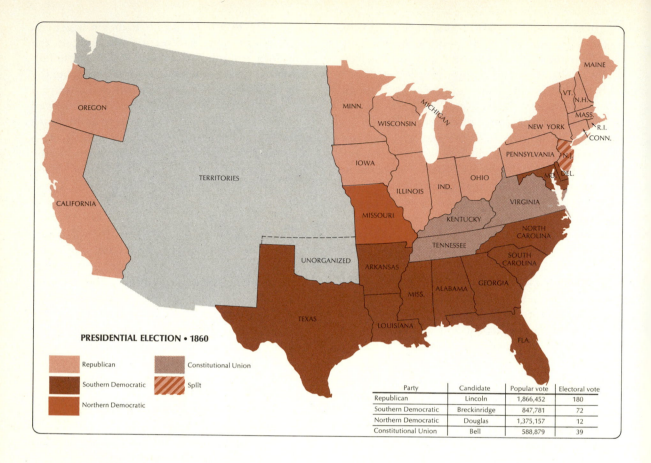

PRESIDENTIAL ELECTION · 1860

Republican

Southern Democratic

Northern Democratic

Constitutional Union

Split

Party	Candidate	Popular vote	Electoral vote
Republican	Lincoln	1,866,452	180
Southern Democratic	Breckinridge	847,781	72
Northern Democratic	Douglas	1,375,157	12
Constitutional Union	Bell	588,879	39

tion voted to reassemble again at Baltimore in June.

At the Front Street Theater in Baltimore, the Douglas men were firmly in control, but tension reappeared as the Southern delegations entered the convention, reiterating their sectional demands. When the balloting started and the Southerners had still not secured the withdrawal of Douglas, one Southern delegation after another left the theater and congregated at Market Hall, there to be joined by delegates from New York, Pennsylvania, Oregon, California, and Missouri. Douglas swept what was left of the convention and won the nomination. The bolters named John C. Breckinridge of Kentucky for the presidency. A Southern convention which met at Richmond endorsed his nomination. The

party had split into sectional factions. But the South had paid the greater price because it had more to lose. Whatever happened to Douglas, the North would triumph.

Republicans faced the campaign of 1860 confident and united. Much had happened in four years to increase Republican strength. Old Whig managers—Seward, Weed, and Lincoln—had modified the party's idealism and broadened its economic program to appeal to every economic interest in the North. By 1860 the Republican platform asked for tariff increases, homesteads, internal improvements, and a transcontinental railroad. The major task confronting the party managers, gathered at Chicago in May 1860, was to find a presidential candidate acceptable both to the party's idealistic crusaders and to its conservative free-soilers and newcomers, who had assumed much of its control. Seward had been too long identified with the extremists; Edward Bates of Missouri, the other front-runner, was too conservative and Whiggish. Abe Lincoln, a novice in national politics who stood between the extremes, became the compromise choice.

Although Republican enthusiasm gave the 1860 campaign a guise of excitement, the near certainty that Lincoln would win made much of the campaigning seem irrelevant. Lincoln's task, and that of his party, was to convince the North that its interest in free soil was safe only in Republican hands and that popular sovereignty in Democratic hands was really no defense of Northern rights and principles at all. In his Cooper Union address of February 1860, Lincoln had developed further his arguments in behalf of free-soilism. It was the *wrongness* of slavery, he said, that aroused the Northern opposition to its expansion. How could Douglas and the Northern Democrats really prevent slavery's expansion if they refused to call it wrong? Only those who insisted openly that slavery was immoral, Lincoln argued, possessed the determination to contain it. Republican editors and orators centered their condemnation of Douglas on the Cooper Union theme.

Douglas bore the burden not only of holding his Northern Democratic constituency but also of reassuring the South that it had nothing to fear from his election. In the political climate of 1860 this purpose proved impossible of achievement.

In the North, Douglas could say nothing in behalf of popular sovereignty to prevent Democrats from bolting in droves to the Republican party. In the South, he battled his enemies on the issue of disunion, but few Southern Democrats were inclined any longer to support him.

Lincoln carried the entire North in November; yet he was a minority president, polling scarcely 40 percent of the popular vote. Both the Republican and Democratic parties increased their voting percentages over 1856. Lincoln increased the Republican vote by 120,000 in Pennsylvania, by 30,000 in New Jersey, by 45,000 in Indiana, and 76,000 in Illinois. Douglas ran a strong second to Lincoln in the popular vote (1,375,157 to 1,866,452) but carried only one state—Missouri. The Constitutional Union party, organized in 1860 to capture the conservative Unionist vote, adopted no platform on slavery. That party's wide appeal in the Unionist border states permitted its nominee, John Bell of Tennessee, to carry Virginia, Kentucky, and Tennessee. Breckinridge carried the remaining slave states. Lincoln's victory, however, did not result from the Democratic schism. Had all his opponents agreed on one candidate, he would still have pocketed all his states but California and Oregon, leaving him 21 electoral votes above a majority. Lincoln's victory resulted rather from the fact that he carried, albeit by narrow margins, those heavily populated regions of the Northeast and the Great Lakes where political and economic power had been accumulating for a decade.

The Secession Crisis

Southerners studied the November election, unsure of the proper course to follow. Breckinridge's vote in the South was no evidence of overwhelming secessionist sentiment, and it is doubtful if the majority of the people in the region ever favored the breakup of the Union. Southern moderates reminded the South that Lincoln had been elected without any violation

of the Constitution, and they inquired bluntly how Lincoln's presidency could injure their section. Lincoln had obligations to the Constitution and could override the will of neither Congress nor the Supreme Court. With the support of Northern Democrats, the South could prevent the passage of a Republican program, for the Republican party had won control of neither house. Even if Republican principles held in the territories, the South could hardly lose what it never possessed. Southern Unionist editors warned that secession was less a remedy for the South's problems than the guarantees of the Constitution were.

But the Unionists were no match for their Southern opponents in exploiting crisis psychology. Such effective clichés as "Black Republicanism" and "Northern aggression," plus the threatening tone of Northern speeches and editorials, strengthened the hand of the Southern extremists. After years of expounding the doctrines of Southern rights, South Carolina fire-eaters had at last found the occasion for uniting the South in a confederacy of its own. On December 20, 1860, a convention at Charleston unanimously voted to dissolve "the Union now subsisting between South Carolina and the other states under the name of 'the United States of America.'" Elsewhere in the South, leading politicians urged delay to give the Republican leadership a fair trial, but they were pushed aside by the excitement of the day. "The people are run mad," reported Alexander Stephens of Georgia. "They are wild with passion and frenzy, doing they know not what." By February 1, 1861, Georgia, Alabama, Mississippi, Florida, Louisiana, and Texas had left the Union. On February 4, delegates from the seceded states met at Montgomery, Alabama, and quickly organized the Confederate States of America, with Jefferson Davis of Mississippi as president and Stephens as vice president. Even the radicals who dominated the conventions conceded the basic political truth that the secession was the work of an organized minority. This being true, their victory was never complete, for throughout the South, partisans of the Union continued to exist.

President Buchanan, in Washington, faced the secession crisis a deserted man. In his December message he denied the legality of secession. The Founding Fathers never intended to implant in the Constitution the seeds of its destruction. He had taken an oath to execute the federal laws, he declared, and no human power could absolve him from that obligation; he would continue to collect revenues and hold federal property in the seceding states. But Buchanan disclaimed all authority to use coercion. It was Congress's obligation, he said, to reestablish the proper relation between the seceding states and the federal government. At the President's suggestion, Congress accepted the challenge to frame compromise measures, the Senate creating for this purpose its Committee of Thirteen under John J. Crittenden of Kentucky, and the House its Committee of Thirty-three under Thomas Corwin of Ohio. Crittenden's formula became the basis of the compromise maneuvers in Congress, although his own committee refused to accept it. This plan took the form of a series of constitutional amendments which would reestablish the Missouri Compromise line of 36°30′, with slavery prohibited north of the line and protected to the south of it; deny to Congress the right to interfere with slavery in the states where it existed, as well as in the District of Columbia; protect the domestic slave trade from congressional action; compensate owners for fugitive slaves lost because of violence; and guarantee the South that no future amendments would alter the first five provisions.

While the moderates of North and South, in Congress and out, searched for a compromise, the crisis deepened. As one Southern state after another left the Union, state troops in each seized federal forts and arsenals, customhouses and post offices, naval vessels and revenue cutters, and even a United States mint. All that remained under federal control in the South by January 1861, was Fort Sumter at Charleston, Fort Pickens at Pensacola, and Forts Taylor and Jefferson off the southern coast of Florida. Buchanan dispatched a merchant vessel, *Star of the West,* to supply Fort Sumter, but when its captain faced fire from the shore batteries in Charleston Harbor, he quickly withdrew. Thereafter, Republican leaders noted shrewdly, any opposition to a vigorous and uncompromising stand against the South could be condemned as abject cowardice.

Searching for an adequate party response to the challenge of secession, Republican leaders gradually united on a firm stand in opposition to both disunion and compromise. In speeches and caucuses, they declared their disapproval of Southern rebellion. In Congress, they organized to defeat the compromise measure, demanding that the South return to the Union before any concessions even be considered. They refused to surrender the free-soil plank of the Chicago platform. Whenever any of the Republicans wa-

vered, observed one correspondent, "he [was] shot down in an instant by his comrades." The Republican minority moved from one anticompromise victory to another. When the final vote on the Crittenden compromise came before the Senate early on the morning of March 4, 1861, Crittenden himself moved to offer, as a better solution, the proposals of the peace conference which had met in Wasington during February. But Southern senators disagreed and united with the Republicans to overwhelm the substitute, 28 to 7. Then the Senate rejected the original Crittenden proposals, 20 to 19, with all the Republican votes cast on the negative side.

Conclusion

Republican leaders rejected compromise in part because it was politically dangerous, in part because it would serve no useful purpose. Free-soilism as embodied in the Chicago platform defined the Republican party's distinguishing purpose; to discard it would threaten the party with annihilation. It was a purpose, moreover, which the vast majority of Republicans took seriously. To the Republican party, the South and not the North was in error. The total responsibility for reforging the Union peacefully, therefore, lay with the secessionists.

Clearly the Southern states would not return except on their own terms. They demanded guarantees which no Northern faction, least of all the Republicans, would grant them. This state of the Southern mind—and it was crucial to the events of 1861—would not lend itself to a simple or conclusive explanation. Undoubtedly Southern secessionist attitudes were an expression of fear. At stake, many believed, were both the slave system and whatever economic security the South enjoyed. For the planters, large and small, slavery represented an established labor system and a huge capital investment. To desert slavery under moral presure, moreover, would require an admission of past error. Thus national unity in

1861 rested on the North's willingness to permit the South to resolve the slavery issue in its own time and fashion. Lincoln, indeed, assured Stephens in December 1860, that he would not interfere with slavery where it enjoyed the protection of the Constitution. Yet Lincoln added: "You think slavery is right and ought to be extended, while we think it is wrong and ought to be restricted. This, I suppose, is the rub."

What magnified Southern fears—and resentments—were the antics of some Northern abolitionists. *De Bow's Review,* published in New Orleans, complained of them in 1860: "Misanthropy, hypocrisy, diseased philanthropy, envy, hatred, fanaticism, and all the worst passions of the human heart . . . continue to be the ruling characteristics of the New England Yankees." For some Southerners Clay's economic program, now the possession of a powerful Northern party, was a special threat to Southern agrarianism. Repeatedly in the fifties Southern leaders —and some historians in later years—pointed to the South's vulnerability to Northern economic power and policy. Still many lawyers and businessmen of the South had no interest in slavery and states' rights or any fear of tariffs and internal improvements. Economic and social tradition, however, had wedded them not only to the South's planter-dominated power structure but also to the extremists who rationalized that structure. The refusal of the Southern Unionists to defend their section against the growing power of extremism was the key to the secession movement. When a minority of extremists bound the future of Southern civilization to the elusive quest for equality in the territories (there were two slaves in Kansas in 1860), it could only split the Democratic Party and invite a Republican victory. Even then the disorganized conservatives were powerless to counter the ensuing, highly organized secessionist movement. Southern hopes and fears for the future—both tied to slavery—had been exaggerated, but they had gripped the emotions of sufficient numbers to determine the course of the South's behavior. Those who knew better had lost control.

SUGGESTED READINGS

Moderately pro-Southern is Avery Craven's *The Coming of the Civil War* (1942; rev. ed., 1957). Craven has distilled this volume's basic themes in his *Civil War in the Making, 1815–1860* (1959). Dwight L. Dumond reveals more sympathy toward the abolitionists in his *Anti-Slavery Origins of the Civil War* (1939). Allan Nevins has covered the years from 1847 to 1861 magnificently in four volumes.: *Ordeal of the Union* (2 vols., 1947) and *The Emergence of Lincoln* (2 vols., 1950). Thomas J. Pressley in *Americans Interpret Their Civil War* (1954) dwells on the historic problems of Civil War causation.

Many useful volumes provide material on the successive events from 1846 to 1860. C. B. Going's *David Wilmot: Free-Soiler* (1924) includes a full account of the authorship of the Proviso. On the Free-Soil movement see T. C. Smith's *The Liberty and Soil Parties in the Northwest* (1897). Holman Hamilton's scholarly account of the Compromise of 1850, *Prologue to Conflict* (1964), supersedes all previous efforts. R. H. Shryock's *Georgia and the Union in 1850* (1926) relates the political response of an important Southern state. On the Kansas-Nebraska issue, P. O. Ray's *The Repeal of the Missouri Compromise* (1909) has been superseded, in large measure by J. C. Malin's *The Nebraska Question, 1852–1854* (1953). Roy F. Nichols has analyzed the pressures of Southern politicians on Douglas in "The Kansas-Nebraska Act: A Century of Historiography," *Mississippi Valley Historical Review*, XLIII (September 1956).

On the issue of Bleeding Kansas, the standard account is J. C. Malin's *John Brown and the Legend of Fifty-six* (1942). Stressing again the frontier nature of the Kansas conflict is Paul W. Gates's *Fifty Million Acres: Conflicts over Kansas Land Policy, 1854–1890* (1954). Allan Nevins's *Frémont: Pathmaker of the West* (1939) is a brief, well-written biography. Roy F. Nichols's *The Disruption of American Democracy* (1948) is a brilliant Pulitzer prize study of the Buchanan years. Two good volumes on the Dred Scott case are Vincent C. Hopkins's *Dred Scott's Case* (1951) and C. B. Swisher's *Roger B. Taney* (1935). Eugene H. Berwanger's *The Frontier against Slavery* (1967) traces in detail the anti-Negro prejudice of the Old Northwest and the Far West. Allan Nevins's *The Emergence of Lincoln* (2 vols., 1950) contains excellent chapters on Northern and Southern life and thought in the late fifties. The best study of Southern society and politics in the 1850s is Avery Craven's *The Growth of Southern Nationalism, 1848–1861* (1953).

Perhaps the most judicious, yet highly sympathetic, study of Lincoln in the fifties in Don E. Fehrenbacher's *Prelude to Greatness: Lincoln in the 1850s* (1962). Lincoln's role in the 1860 campaign is analyzed in R. H. Luthin's *The First Lincoln Campaign* (1944). For the South's experience in that election, see Ollinger Crenshaw's *The Slave States in the Presidential Election of 1860* (1945). A brief volume on the 1860 campaign is N. A. Graebner's (ed.), *Politics and the Crisis of 1860* (1961).

From the viewpoint of the North the two standard volumes on the secession crisis are David M. Potter's *Lincoln and His Party in the Secession Crisis* (1942) and Kenneth M. Stampp's *And the War Came: The North and the Secession Crisis* (1950). Northern attitudes toward compromise receive incisive treatment in R. G. Gunderson's *Old Gentlemen's Convention* (1961). On the South and secession is D. L. Dumond's *The Secession Movement, 1860–1861* (1931). A good companion study is U. B. Phillips's *The Course of the South to Secession* (1939).

* indicates availability in paperback.

15

The Civil War

During the critical winter of 1860–1861, President-elect Abraham Lincoln remained quietly in Springfield, Illinois, where he played host to numerous visitors and wrote occasional letters of encouragement to front-line Republicans. Lincoln agreed with the core of Republican leadership that the party should avoid a split on the divisive issue of slavery in the territories. During the debate on the Crittenden compromise, Lincoln pleaded with one member of Congress to defeat it. "Prevent, as far as possible, any of our friends from demoralizing themselves and our cause by entertaining propositions for compromise . . . ," he wrote, "on that point hold firm as with a chain of steel." Lincoln's private views, circulated freely among Republicans in Congress, brought the majority solidly to his support.

Yet, so forceful were the demands for compromise from such powerful Republicans as William H. Seward of New York that Lincoln, to avoid alienating any faction of his party, adopted an official silence on all matters of sectional conflict. To the throngs that greeted him along his route to Washington, he spoke of the great issues engulfing the nation but refused to commit himself to any position touching the sectional conflict. Even his Republican friends were dismayed at his lack of forthrightness. Arriving in Washington, Lincoln assured a delegation of aspiring peacemakers that the Republic's future depended not upon him but upon the nation's willingness to obey the Constitution.

As the time for Lincoln's inauguration approached, thoughtful men wondered if he was prepared to face the grave responsibility of office. His past career held few clues. His inaugural address on March 4, 1861, gave expression to his nationalism but suggested no specific course of action. Under no circumstances would he recognize the secession movement. The ordinances of secession, he said, were "legally void" and any resistance to federal authority was "insurrectionary or revolutionary, according to the circumstances." He would execute federal laws in all the states. "In *your* hands," he said to the South, "and not in mine, is the momentous issue

Abraham Lincoln on June 3, 1860, shortly after accepting the Republican nomination for President.

of the civil war. The Government will not assail you. . . . [But] I hold that, in contemplation of universal law and the Constitution, the Union of these States is perpetual." His constitutional powers obligated him "to hold, occupy, and possess the property and places belonging to the Government, and to collect the duties and imposts." Lincoln begged the South to submit to the electoral decision of 1860.

Lincoln's approach to the South was conciliatory and reassuring. He pledged his respect for slavery in the Southern states and agreed to enforce any workable fugitive slave law. Between the North and South, a cordon of border states suspended in indecision served to muffle the friction between the extremes. By sidestepping a crisis, Lincoln might hold these states in the Union while gaining time to permit a resurgence of Unionist sentiment in the seceded states.

One issue challenged Lincoln's policy of watchful waiting. The President had made it clear that he intended to hold Fort Sumter in Charleston Harbor, as well as the three Florida forts still in Northern hands, as symbols of the unbroken Union. Unfortunately, however, Fort Sumter quickly became a point of honor for both sections. South Carolina warned the administration that it would regard any Northern attempt to supply or strengthen the garrison as an act of aggression. While the President permitted events to drift during March, Republican Congressmen fumed. If Lincoln vacillated on this question, predicted one critic, "The South will proclaim him a Damned fool, and the North a damned Rascal." The President was not stampeded. He withheld relief until the garrison at Sumter had approached the point of starvation, and even then he informed the Governor of South Carolina that the ship carried provisions only. Throughout the crisis he remained passive, neither withdrawing nor reinforcing the Sumter garrison. Impatient Southerners fired the first shot. On April 12, batteries lining the mud flats and sand dunes around Charleston sent shells bursting over Fort Sumter. After thirty-four hours of constant bombardment, the Union commander, Major Robert Anderson, surrendered the fort.

Preparations for War in the North

As the news of Fort Sumter's capitulation resounded across the nation, few failed to grasp its meaning. Emerson was among those who recalled its volcanic impact: "At the darkest moment in the history of the republic, when it looked as if the nation would be dismembered, pulverized into its original elements, the attack on Fort Sumter crystallized the North into a unit, and the hope of mankind was saved." If the South would fight for its independence, the North, resorting to arms, would make its stand for the Union. Lincoln's call on April 15 for 75,000 troops sent the Upper South of Virginia, Arkansas, Tennessee, and North Carolina into the Confederacy. Virginia's western counties refused to bolt, however, and in 1863 entered the Union as the state of West Virginia.

What mattered in 1861 was not only the North's determination to reforge the Union but also its apparent power to do so. Of the nation's thirty-four states, twenty-three were free. Omitting the two divided states, Missouri and Kentucky, the North had a population of 20,700,000; the Confederacy, only 9,100,000, of whom over 3,600,000 were blacks. But the greatest disparity in power lay in industrial productivity. The North's industries in 1860 employed 1.3 million workers; those of the South, a mere 110,000. The annual production of New York's factories alone was four times that of the entire South. In 1860, the South possessed less than a third of the nation's 31,000 miles of railroad track. The South, moreover, had few financial resources; even its banking and foreign exchange had centered in New York.

Whatever its advantages in size, wealth, and population, however, the North was totally unprepared for war. During the three preparatory months between the Sumter crisis and the assembling of Congress in July 1861, Lincoln employed his emergency powers to inaugurate the long and tedious process of organizing the North for the coming struggle. His purpose in calling for 75,000 militia, he said, was simply to repossess federal property and execute the laws of Congress. To meet the South's deepening resistance, however, Lincoln eventually engaged in actions that exceeded his presidential authority and recognized the existence of war. During April he instituted a blockade of the entire Southern coast which the Confederacy, possessing no navy, could not easily neutralize. Then, early in May, he called for additional recruits for the regular Army, exercising a power vested solely in Congress. Lincoln readily admitted that he exceeded his authority but, as he explained in his message of July 4: "These measures, whether strictly legal or not, were ventured upon, under what appeared to be a popular demand, and a public necessity; trusting . . . that Congress would readily ratify them." Congress responded, first by passing a resolution legalizing the President's decrees, and then in late July issuing a call for 500,000 volunteers, initially for a period of up to three years, and then for the duration of the war.

Lincoln's first call for militia, suggesting a war of only three months, set off a wave of enlistments throughout the North. This expectation of a short war, along with the speed of mobilization, created massive confusion. In addition, the nucleus of the Northern military establishment was the regular Army of the United States, which numbered, in 1861, only 13,000 officers and men. By July 1862, the demands of war forced Congress to strengthen both the militia and the regular Army. It called the militia into active service and provided for the drafting of "all able-bodied male citizens between the ages of eighteen and forty-five" into the militia.

Under this law, the actual drafting remained a function of the states.

Not until March 1863, did Congress pass a national conscription act which declared all able-bodied male citizens between the ages of twenty and forty-five subject to military service. The conscription law provided exemptions for the physically and mentally unfit as well as for the occupants of certain federal and state offices. A draftee, moreover, could either hire a substitute or buy an exemption for $300. In operation the conscript system was ineffective. Under the act only 46,000 entered the Northern armies; another 118,000 bought substitutes. The law, basically unjust, met resistance everywhere.

As early as 1861, Northern Negroes offered their services to the Union. Nothing, it seemed, would have so completely committed the nation to granting blacks first-class citizenship as contributions to the Union on the field of battle. But Washington officials hesitated to challenge racial prejudices among Northern soldiers and refused to accept blacks into the Union armies. Many Northerners—Lincoln among them—were convinced that Negroes would make poor soldiers. Lincoln rejected black regiments offered by Indiana, not only, he said, because such action might turn many citizens in the border states against the North, but also because the Negro equipment would ultimately fall into the hands of the rebels. Only when Northern enthusiasm for the war began to wane in 1862 and enlistments fell off did the administration agree to the recruitment of blacks for Union armies.

The South Faces War

Southern leaders approached their war for independence convinced that they could equal the Northern effort and successfully defend their cause. To maintain a political division already established, the South could remain on the defensive, forcing the North to commit greater quantities of manpower and equipment. The South also had long harbored a more intense martial spirit than the North had. Many of the best students at West Point had been Southerners, and large numbers of these men now resigned their federal posts and returned to take command of Confederate forces. Well-stocked federal arsenals in the South fell into Confederate hands and gave the Southern troops, at least initially, an adequate supply of excellent military equipment. The North's material advantage, if potentially overwhelming, was scarcely noticeable in 1861.

Faced with the necessity of raising an effective army, the Confederate Congress authorized the recruiting of 400,000 men for three years or the duration of the war. The fact that the legislation was confused, permitting Southerners to enter the Confederate armed forces through a variety of arrangements and for widely varying periods of time, seemed to make no difference. The rush to enlist was so overwhelming that the South faced no immediate problem in creating an adequate fighting force. In fact, the numbers of men available far exceeded the South's capacity to train and equip them.

Unfortunately for the South, this enthusiasm was short-lived. Those most devoted to Southern independence volunteered first; thereafter, soldiers entered the Confederate ranks with steadily decreasing eagerness. When one-year enlistments began to expire in the spring of 1862 and no promises of bounties or other special benefits could produce sufficient reenlistments, the Confederate Congress imposed a draft. The first law of April 1862 subjected all able-bodied Southerners between the ages of eighteen and thirty-five to military service. In September, the upper age limit reached forty-five, and in February 1864, fifty. Exempted occupations and the privilege of hiring substitutes kept large numbers of able-bodied Southerners out of the armed forces.

With their armies organized and ostensibly prepared for battle by the summer of 1861, both North and South were spoiling for a fight. During July, Confederate General P. G. T. Beauregard brought a large Confederate force north to the rail junction of Manassas (Bull Run), scarcely 20 miles from Washington. Unable to resist further the Northern demands for victory, General Irvin McDowell, the commander at Washington, sent his raw troops, followed by a mass of spectators who streamed out of the city, against the Confederate positions. Through the morning hours of July 25, the Union forces advanced well against the Southern defenses. Then suddenly the tide of battle turned. Beauregard received some needed reinforcements; the Confederates counterattacked with a series of effective jabs and quickly threw the Federals into general retreat. Unable to regroup, the soldiers joined the flight of the civilians into Washington. Beauregard's forces were too disorganized to pursue. This permitted McDowell's successor, thirty-five-year-old George B. McClellan, to remain undisturbed in Washington until the next spring (1862) while he reorganized the capital defenses.

By contrast, nothing was quiet that winter of 1861–1862 in the West. In January 1862, James A. Garfield's Union forces met and defeated a Confederate army near Prestonburg in eastern Kentucky. Later that month the able Union commander George H. Thomas defeated a Confederate force at Mill Springs. These victories gave the Union control of routes through eastern Kentucky into Tennessee. To the west were three far more important routes of transportation that penetrated deeply into Confederate territory—the Cumberland, Tennessee, and Mississippi Rivers. Two important forts, Henry and Donelson, both located near the Kentucky-Tennessee line, guarded the Tennessee and Cumberland routes. Ulysses S. Grant, with a western army, moved south along the Tennessee in February 1862, intent upon their capture.

Grant, a West Point graduate of mediocre record and a veteran of the Mexican War, had only recently returned to active duty, helping to organize the Illinois volunteers. His modesty, self-assurance, and concern for detail quickly demonstrated his leadership qualities. Grant took Fort Henry on February 6, after a minor engagement. He then transferred his small fleet to the Cumberland and ten days later, after heavy fighting, captured Fort Donelson and, with it, 12,000 Confederate prisoners of war. The Confederates under Albert Sidney Johnston now gave up their exposed position at Columbus on the Mississippi and withdrew to the area below Nashville.

Grant moved his forces southward along the Tennessee to Pittsburg Landing near the Mississippi border. Before he could plan an advance against the new Confederate positions, Johnston threw his men forward against the surprised Northern troops, centering his attack on the Union positions at Shiloh Church, 3 miles west of Pittsburg Landing. The isolated Union soldiers retreated in panic until stopped by Northern calvary and guided back to the front. There they helped to turn the tide of battle for the Union forces. On that first day, the Confederates lost Johnston, their commanding general, who suffered a leg wound and bled to death. His successor, Beauregard, recently transferred from the East, withdrew his forces, keeping them intact for another campaign. Thus the first phase of the war in the West closed with Union armies holding most of Kentucky and much of Tennessee.

The War in Virginia: 1862

By the early spring of 1862, the war was a year old, and McClellan's army at Washington was three times as large as the nearest Confederate force at Manassas. Yet Union armies in the East

THE CIVIL WAR
1861–1865

Locator map

+ Major battles

Union states

Confederate states

Major railroads

CANADA

ME.

MICHIGAN

NEW YORK

VT. N.H.

MASS.

CONN. R.I.

PENNSYLVANIA

N.J.

OHIO

Gettysburg
(Cemetery Ridge)
(Devil's Den)

INDIANA

Sharpsburg

MD. DEL.

Harper's Ferry

ILLINOIS

Winchester

Washington

McDowell

Manassas

KANSAS

MISSOURI

Chancellorsville

Fredericksburg

Ohio R.

Prestonburg

W. VA.

* The Wilderness

Cold Harbor

Spotsylvania

Williamsburg

KENTUCKY

Fort
Donelson

Appomattox

Richmond

Yorktown

Mill Springs

VIRGINIA

OKLAHOMA

Fort
Henry

Nashville

TENNESSEE

NORTH CAROLINA

ARKANSAS

Shiloh

Murfreesboro

Chattanooga

Corinth

Chickamauga

SOUTH
CAROLINA

Columbia

ATLANTIC
OCEAN

Mississippi R.

MISSISSIPPI

Lookout Mtn.

Missionary
Ridge

Peach Tree
Creek

ALABAMA

Atlanta

GEORGIA

TEXAS

Vicksburg

Jackson

Port
Gibson

LOUISIANA

FLORIDA

GULF OF MEXICO

*West Virginia was admitted as a
state to the Union, June 20, 1863.

0   100   200

Miles

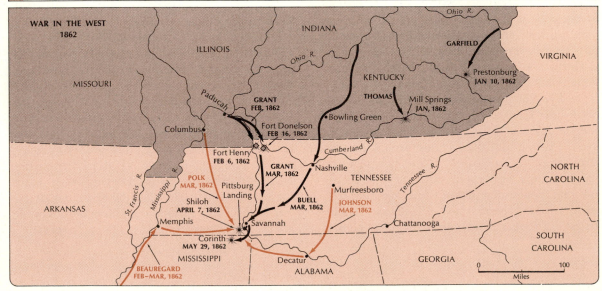

WAR IN THE WEST
1862

Ohio R.

ILLINOIS

INDIANA

GARFIELD

MISSOURI

Ohio R.

KENTUCKY

VIRGINIA

Prestonburg
JAN 10, 1862

Paducah

GRANT
FEB, 1862

THOMAS

Mill Springs
JAN, 1862

Columbus

Fort Donelson
FEB 16, 1862

Bowling Green

Fort Henry
FEB 6, 1862

Cumberland R.

GRANT
MAR, 1862

Nashville

TENNESSEE

NORTH
CAROLINA

St. Francis R.

POLK
MAR, 1862

Pittsburg
Landing

Murfreesboro

JOHNSON
MAR, 1862

Mississippi R.

Shiloh
APRIL 7, 1862

BUELL
MAR, 1862

Tennessee R.

ARKANSAS

Memphis

Savannah

Chattanooga

SOUTH
CAROLINA

Corinth
MAY 29, 1862

MISSISSIPPI

Decatur

GEORGIA

BEAUREGARD
FEB–MAR, 1862

ALABAMA

0   100

Miles

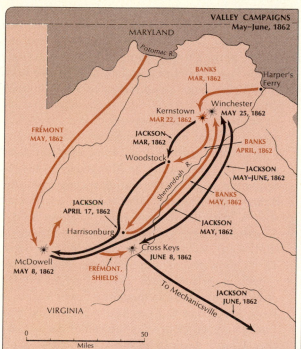

VALLEY CAMPAIGNS
May–June, 1862

MARYLAND

Potomac R.

Harper's Ferry

BANKS MAR, 1862

Kernstown MAR 22, 1862

Winchester MAY 25, 1862

FRÉMONT MAY, 1862

JACKSON MAR, 1862

Woodstock

BANKS APRIL, 1862

JACKSON MAY–JUNE, 1862

Shenandoah R.

JACKSON APRIL 17, 1862

BANKS MAY, 1862

JACKSON MAY, 1862

Harrisonburg

Cross Keys JUNE 8, 1862

McDOWELL MAY 8, 1862

FRÉMONT, SHIELDS

To Mechanicsville

JACKSON JUNE, 1862

VIRGINIA

0 — 50 Miles

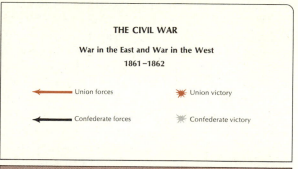

THE CIVIL WAR

War in the East and War in the West
1861–1862

→ Union forces   ✳ Union victory

→ Confederate forces   ✳ Confederate victory

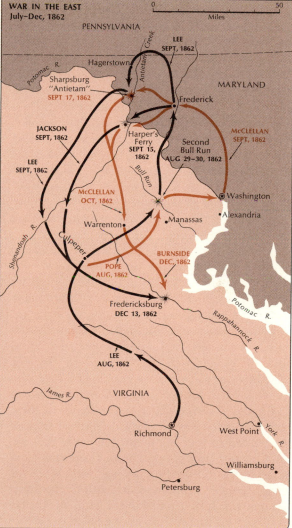

WAR IN THE EAST
July–Dec, 1862

0 — 50 Miles

PENNSYLVANIA

LEE SEPT, 1862

Potomac R.

Hagerstown

Antietam Creek

Sharpsburg "Antietam" SEPT 17, 1862

Frederick

MARYLAND

JACKSON SEPT, 1862

Harper's Ferry SEPT 15, 1862

McCLELLAN SEPT, 1862

LEE SEPT, 1862

Second Bull Run AUG 29–30, 1862

Shenandoah R.

McCLELLAN OCT, 1862

Bull Run

Washington

Warrenton

Manassas

Alexandria

Culpeper

POPE AUG, 1862

BURNSIDE DEC, 1862

Fredericksburg DEC 13, 1862

Rappahannock R.

Potomac R.

LEE AUG, 1862

James R.

VIRGINIA

Richmond

West Point

York R.

Williamsburg

Petersburg

FIRST BULL RUN, JULY, 1861
PENINSULAR CAMPAIGNS
May–July, 1862

Bull Run

McDOWELL JUNE, 1861

First Bull Run JULY 21, 1861

Washington

BEAUREGARD JUNE, 1861

Manassas

MARYLAND

DEL

VIRGINIA

JACKSON JUNE, 1862

Mattaponi R.

Pamunkey R.

Potomac R.

Rappahannock R.

McCLELLAN MAR–APRIL, 1862

Chesapeake Bay

Mechanicsville

SEVEN DAYS JUNE 25–JULY 1, 1862

Fair Oaks

Richmond

LEE

West Point

Malvern Hill

Harrison's Landing

Yorktown MAY 4, 1862

Petersburg

Williamsburg MAY 5, 1862

McCLELLAN JULY, 1862

James R.

Fort Monroe

Norfolk

0 — 50 Miles

THE CIVIL WAR

had not fought one major battle. While the Union commander drilled, organized, reorganized, wrote lengthy reports, assembled equipment, demanded additional troops, inspected, and held conferences with his subordinates, Lincoln pressed for action by becoming his own strategist—a better one, some historians insist, than any of his generals.

Under the President's prodding, McClellan moved, but not against Manassas. Instead he placed his huge army on a flotilla and sailed to the mouth of the James for a strike at Richmond. By May he had established his base at Fort Monroe. He took Yorktown on May 4 and continued toward the Confederate capital with perhaps 100,000 effectives. At Richmond McClellan faced the South's two greatest generals, Robert E. Lee, now the commander of all Confederate forces, and Thomas J. ("Stonewall") Jackson. Unlike Grant, Lee had graduated from West Point with distinction. During the Mexican War, General Winfield Scott had assigned the young captain to his personal staff; thereafter, Lee had served as superintendent of West Point. Handsome, cultured, possessing a fine character and an excellent mind, Lee in 1861 had so high a reputation that he could have had the command of Union forces in the field. But moved by a deep devotion to Virginia, Lee had cast his lot with the South. For the defense of Richmond in 1862, Lee had 85,000 men.

Quite cognizant of McClellan's immense caution, Lee dispatched Jackson into the Shenandoah Valley with 16,000 men to threaten Washington via Harpers Ferry. The ruse succeeded, for it brought 45,000 Union troops into the valley. Having deprived McClellan of these possible replacements, Jackson hurried back to Richmond to join Lee in the defense of the city. McClellan began his final move against the Confederate capital on June 25, and for a week the action raged in individual battles, the most bloody on July 1 at Malvern Hill. McClellan managed his forces well, but he failed to capture Richmond.

Thereafter Republican leaders in Congress distrusted McClellan, doubting his capacity to lead. McClellan moreover had made it plain that he favored a war of moderation against the South, limited to punishing the South's military forces, not its civilian population. When General John Pope, having demonstrated some military capabilities in the West, announced that he favored a vigorous prosecution of the war, Lincoln appointed him to the Eastern command.

After brief preparations, Pope moved against the Confederate army at Manassas. In several disjointed engagements during August 1862, the Army of the Potomac suffered a series of flank attacks from the dashing J. E. B. Stuart's Confederate cavalry. The second battle of Manassas (Bull Run) occurred on August 29 and 30, 1862. The Union forces suffered from the lack of command organization. Lee closed in on the retreating enemy, administering heavy losses. In June, McClellan had met Lee at Richmond with almost 100,000 troops; by the end of August, the only Union soldiers within 100 miles of Richmond were in full retreat. In this crisis, Lincoln sought another general and turned once more to McClellan.

Meanwhile, in a move to free Maryland of Union control, Lee crossed the Potomac on September 5, 1862, and occupied Frederick, Maryland. McClellan moved out to keep his forces between Lee's army and the capital. Lee wanted Harpers Ferry because it was the gateway from the Shenandoah Valley into Maryland. To take the river crossing, Lee divided his forces, sending Jackson with 25,000 men to capture Harpers Ferry while he proceeded to Hagerstown. Jackson met with perfect success at Harpers Ferry and took 11,000 prisoners, but Lee, dangerously exposed with the Potomac at his rear, decided to withdraw into Virginia. Before he could do so, McClellan, on September 17, threw the Union army against him near Sharpsburg in the war's bloodiest engagement yet—the battle of Antietam. Lee retreated into the Shenandoah Valley.

McClellan, still reacting slowly, crossed the Potomac late in October and by November 7 had massed his army near Warrenton. But before McClellan could make another thrust at Lee's forces, Lincoln replaced him with General Ambrose E. Burnside. Burnside's tenure was brief. In mid-December he struck Lee's forces at Fredericksburg. His numerical advantage over Lee was 114,000 to 72,000, but the Confederate forces held such superior battle positions that Burnside sent wave after wave of experienced Union troops against the Confederates in vain. By nightfall, when the Union forces finally withdrew, they left behind almost 1,300 dead and 9,600 wounded, approximately twice the Confederate losses. Fredericksburg marked the low point in Northern morale. In twenty months the North had managed to organize a magnificent army, but no general seemed capable of using it to advantage. Battles had produced casualties in abundance, but no victories. Lincoln faced an increasingly critical Congress. In this new crisis, Lincoln sent for "Fighting Joe" Hooker. To Hooker's remark that the country needed a dictator, Lincoln replied, "Only those generals who gain successes can set up dictators. What I now ask of you is military success, and I will risk dictatorship."

The War Congress

Lincoln could hardly dispose of the South's challenge to the Union before he had established a working majority in Congress. Despite the political and military crisis of 1861 and 1862, Congress was not inclined to defer to the Executive. Democrats who had fought the Republican party throughout its brief history found it difficult, even in wartime, to accept the leadership of a Republican president. Supported by a united Republican majority, Lincoln might have ignored the Democratic opposition. But neither pressures of war nor requirements of party cohesion could eliminate the conflicts which separated Republican moderates from the party's more determined antislavery elements, led by the powerful Thaddeus Stevens of Pennsylvania, Charles Sumner of Massachusetts, Zach Chandler of Michigan, and Benjamin F. Wade of Ohio.

Republican strategy toward the South evolved slowly. When the fighting began in 1861, the Republicans in Congress seemed to agree with Lincoln that the war should be fought solely to force the South back into the Union. Such agreement over war aims soon evaporated. Lee's initial military successes made it clear that only a total Northern effort would bring an acceptable peace. This realization prompted Republican Radicals in Congress—those who spoke for the party's antislavery wing—to demand a more intensive conduct of the war, aimed not only at the destruction of Southern military power but also at the elimination of slavery. The early enthusiasm for the war among many Northern antislavery leaders had stemmed in part from their anticipation that it would settle the slave question forever. Charles Francis Adams had observed, "We cannot afford to go over this ground more than once. The slave question must be settled this time once for all." As the war proceeded, Northern antislavery forces became increasingly militant. They assaulted everyone who appeared to favor a return to the Union as it had been.

Lincoln accepted reconstruction of the Union as the one estimable goal which Northern power could achieve. This limited objective he phrased over and over again. "The sooner the national authority can be restored," he said, "the nearer the Union will be to the Union as it was. . . . My paramount object in this struggle is to save the Union." Lincoln hated slavery, but he shared the conservative conviction that it was the racial aspect of the slave question, not slavery itself, that tormented the nation. Had the slaves been indistinguishable by color, slavery would have vanished in some previous age. Recognizing his limited power to remake Southern society or enforce the principle of equality in the South, the President hesitated to touch the slave issue at all.

But Lincoln could not escape the Radicals. During 1862, they began to abuse him for his moderation, to condemn him for maintaining a Cabinet of conservatives who, with him, seemed to think the Union more important than emancipation, and to accuse him of aiding the enemy with his conduct of the war. To secure an immediate and vigorous pursuit of victory, Congress in December 1861, created the Congressional Committee on the Conduct of the War. Led by Senator Wade, the committee challenged both the administration's military policies and its choice of commanders. Above all, it demanded the unlimited employment of Northern resources to punish the South.

To reduce the South's capacity to fight, the Radicals pushed through Congress a series of confiscation acts. The first measure of August 1861 provided merely for federal seizure of all property used for insurrectionary purposes. In the second Confiscation Act of July 1862, the federal government condemned to forfeiture the property of the country's enemies—that is, those supporting the rebellion. Slaves of such Southerners, moreover, were to be liberated. It authorized the President, thirdly, to employ blacks, even freed slaves, in the Union forces. Lincoln felt that the second Confiscation Act was too drastic and prepared a veto message explaining his disapproval, which he placed on the record. But when Congress agreed not to extend the property foreiture beyond the life of the accused, Lincoln signed the measure. Except for its revelation of a hardening congressional attitude, the act had little immediate consequence.

Wartime Measures of Government

Congress faced the need of financing a major war with a depleted treasury. Its members assumed, in 1861, that Secretary of the Treasury Salmon P. Chase would recommend a system of wartime taxes. Instead, he announced that the federal government would rely on deficit financing through borrowing. This announcement so completely unnerved the nation's financial circles that it produced a banking crisis and forced New York banks to suspend specie payments in December 1861. But Chase persisted in his borrowing policies and commissioned Jay Cooke and Company as the sole agent for the sale of United States bonds. Cooke quickly disposed of the entire issue, largely to bankers and men of wealth. At the same time Chase turned to Congress which, in July 1862, imposed an excise tax on the manufacturers and sellers of a wide variety of civilian goods. Congress had merely to increase the rates to augment federal revenues. Still the income from loans during four years of war exceeded $2.2 billion as compared to $667 million from taxes.

Pursuing yet another course, Congress passed a legal tender act in February 1862, which provided for an issue of $150 million—later increased to $450 million of which $432 million was issued—in United States notes, known as "greenbacks." War financing demonstrated forcefully the country's need of a national banking system and a national bank note currency. Congress, pressed by Chase, established such a system in February 1863, modifying it in June 1864. This act provided for the creation of banks under federal charters with a required capital of $50,000 to $200,000, at least one-third of which had to be invested in government bonds. The National Bank Act permitted banks to issue the new National Bank notes.

Placed in control of Congress by the fact of Southern secession, the Republican majority embarked on the Whig program which the powerful Jacksonian coalition had earlier denied the country. The Democratic party had terminated a long period of protectionism with the Walker tariff of 1846. Another Democratic Congress pushed the tariff further downward in 1857. With the recovery of prosperity, most Northern industrialists were content with the existing tariff structure. But Lincoln in 1860 had made a special appeal to the depressed Pennsylvania iron regions by citing his long adherence to Clay's American System. Mounting deficits of the federal government, moreover, indicated the need for additional revenue, and in February 1861, shortly before Buchanan left office, the Republicans passed the Morrill tariff, which, in general, returned the nation to the tariff levels of 1846. The act of July 1862, granting as it did specific advantages to many items produced in the United States, was decidedly protective. Another act of June 1864 compensated Northern industrialists for their wartime taxes. Manufacturers had achieved so favorable a position in national life that they could obtain almost any tariff level they regarded essential. When the war ended in 1865, duties of 100 percent were common; the general average of 47 percent was double that of 1857.

For a decade, sectional jealousy had negated every congressional effort to create a transcontinental railroad. Freed of Southern opposition, the wartime Congress passed its first transcontinental railroad bill in July 1862. This act created two lines—the Union Pacific, charged with the task of building a railroad westward from Omaha, and the Central Pacific, instructed to build eastward from San Francisco Bay across the Sierras until the two lines met. To facilitate the construction, the federal government not only authorized a right-of-way and protection from Indians, but also granted the railroads millions of acres of public lands and inaugurated special bond issues.

Throughout the fifties Northern editors had heralded the homestead principle of free land as a great boon for all Americans, especially the economically depressed. Buchanan had vetoed the Homestead bill of 1860, largely at the insistence of a disapproving South, which could anticipate no benefits from the measure. But on May 20, 1862, a determined Republican Congress passed the Homestead Act, which granted 160 acres of unoccupied public domain to homesteaders in return for the payment of nominal fees. Full title required five years of actual residence. For city workers without capital the Homestead Act created no ready alternative to intolerable urban conditions.

During 1862, Congress also passed the Morrill Act, which established a national land-grant system of higher education. Behind this measure were years of agitation by Jonathan Baldwin Turner, a Midwest college professor who saw the need for large numbers of "industrial colleges" to meet the demands of expanding industry, financed in part by federal grants of land to the states. Justin S. Morrill of Vermont steered the program through the House in 1858 and the Senate in 1859. Buchanan vetoed the measure, partly because of constitutional scruples. Finally in July 1862, Congress passed the bill again; with Lincoln's signature it became law. The new act granted each state 30,000 acres of public land for each of its senators and representatives in Congress. Since the grants were only a stimulus, individual states were expected to carry the burden of university building themselves.

Emancipation

Whatever Lincoln's private views toward the object of the war, the logic of the times drove him inexorably toward the Radical goal of emancipation. As President, Lincoln shouldered responsibilities that the Radicals refused to recognize. His conservatism on matters of slavery was dictated not only by his sincere constitutional scruples but also by his determination to hold the border states—Delaware, Maryland, Kentucky, and Missouri—within the Union. In accordance with his limited goal of reforging the nation, Lincoln had informed Congress in July 1861 that he would not permit the war to "degenerate into a violent and remorseless revolutionary struggle." Only when most segments of Northern opinion seemed to support emancipation did Lincoln take up the cause. Even then, he did so with extreme reluctance. For Lincoln, it was always the nation that mattered. He stressed this theme in his famed Gettysburg Address. Soldiers had given their last full measure of devotion, he declared, "that this nation, under God, shall have a new birth of fredom. . . . "

Lincoln reached his great decision on emancipation in the autumn of 1862. In April, a congressional proclamation had abolished slavery in the District of Columbia. During June, a similar act had ruled slavery out of the territories. Lincoln in late summer drafted the Emancipation Proclamation, read it to his Cabinet, and awaited a decisive Union victory. Scarcely a decisive victory, Antietam, in September, was enough for the purpose. Lincoln proclaimed that unless the rebel states returned to the Union by January 1863, all slaves in those states, or portions of states, under arms against the federal government would be given their freedom. On January 1, 1863, informed that none of the Southern states had complied, Lincoln declared the decree in force.

In large degree, Lincoln's proclamation was a war measure designed to bring blacks into the Union forces. Congress had already authorized the President to enlist Negroes as soldiers. In August 1862, the War Department instructed General Rufus Saxton, military governor of the South Carolina Sea Islands, to raise five regiments of black troops. Early in 1863 these troops engaged in a series of successful raids into Georgia and Florida. Lincoln now seemed convinced that black regiments would assure Union success. "The bare sight of 50,000 armed and drilled black soldiers upon the banks of the Mississippi," he wrote War Governor Andrew Johnson of Tennessee, "would end the rebellion at once." Lincoln's judgment of emancipation as a war measure was sound. After January 1863, the formation of Negro units was so rapid that eighteen months later the President could acknowledge the presence of 150,000 black men in the Union forces.

As a freedom document Lincoln's proclamation was an empty gesture. It freed no slaves. The exclusion of blacks in the loyal slave states brought a gibe from the *London Spectator:* "The principle is not that a human being cannot justly own another, but that he cannot own him unless he is loyal to the United States." In short, the Emancipation Proclamation freed those slaves beyond the reach of its effect—and freed none under the authority of the federal government. The North ignored the discrepancy. Thus Lincoln, despite himself, became the Great Emancipator.

Gettysburg, Vicksburg, and Chattanooga

As late as the spring of 1863, the Civil War in the East had produced little but military stalemate. Lee and Jackson had won a series of tactical victories, based largely on superior generalship and imagination, but they had not disposed of the Northern armies. Even while they punished the Union forces in battle after battle, the enemy army grew larger, both comparatively and absolutely.

Despite appalling Union casualties at Fredericksburg, Lee, with 60,000 men, still faced a Union army far larger than his own. Hooker, with 130,000 men under his command, decided to attack, striking Lee's army from the direction of Chancellorsville. Lee responded by sending Jackson with 30,000 men against Hooker's right, catching O. O. Howard's forces by complete surprise and driving them back. Meanwhile Lee, with his reduced forces, awaited Hooker's assault. The attack came on May 1, 1863, and continued for five days. Unable to dislodge Lee's forces, Hooker withdrew, blaming his officers for the Union failure. One incident blurred the Confederate victory at Chancellorsville—the accidental death of Stonewall Jackson. Hooker's powerful army was still intact, and Lincoln recognized the continuing Northern advantage. He instructed Hooker to harass Lee's communications, adding some critical advice, "I think *Lee's* army, and not *Richmond,* is your true objective point. If he comes toward the Upper Potomac, follow on his flank, and on the inside trace, shortening your lines, whilst he lengthens his. Fight him when the opportunity offers. If he stays where he is, fret him, and fret him."

After Chancellorsville, Lee, somewhat contemptuous of his Northern antagonist, decided upon a bold advance into Pennsylvania. Hooker moved northward, keeping his army between Lee and the capital. But before the two forces could engage again, Lincoln replaced Hooker with General George G. Meade, a West Point graduate who had performed well as a subordinate officer in the Virginia campaigns. As Lee's advance troops approached Gettysburg on July 1, they engaged detached cavalry and infantry units of the Union army. Following this opening skirmish, Lee and Meade quickly brought their full strength into battle. The Confederates, approaching from west and northwest in ever-increasing numbers, drove the Union forces toward the southeast, where they took up a position on Cemetery Hill at the southern edge of Gettysburg. Lee took up his position along Seminary Ridge, stretching north and south 1 mile to the west of Cemetery Ridge.

On the second day of the battle, General Richard S. Ewell led a Confederate assault against the Union's right but failed to dislodge Meade's forces. On the third day Lee, gambling on one supreme effort, ordered General George E. Pickett to pierce the Union center—an almost impossible assignment inasmuch as Pickett's men could not reach the Union forces on Cemetery Ridge without charging across a half mile of open ground. Supported by furious cannonade, Pickett moved his men forward into a succession of withering artillery and infantry volleys. The Confederates were cut to ribbons, and on the fourth day the battlefield was silent, for Meade refused to countercharge. Lee packed up his forces and began a long, orderly retreat to Virginia.

Meanwhile Union successes in the West brought added distinction to U. S. Grant, whose primary objective in early 1863 was the capture of Vicksburg on the Mississippi. Grant's assault on the city relied in part on the North's unchallenged naval supremacy. A combined Union Army-Navy operation under the command of Admiral David G. Farragut ran the forts along the lower Mississippi during April 1862 and occupied New Orleans. In June, Farragut took a flotilla up the Mississippi but failed to capture Vicksburg, the powerful fortress which commanded a hairpin curve on the river. General William T. Sherman attempted to approach Vicksburg from the north through the swampy Yazoo Delta in December but found it hopeless. The only remaining approaches to the city were from south and east.

Embarking on his most imaginative and successful maneuver of the war, Grant took his army to Milliken's Bend north of Vicksburg, where the Union fleet transported it across the Mississippi. Grant then marched his troops south of Vicksburg through Louisiana's marshes and swamps, while the Union craft ran the batteries at Vicksburg. By the end of April 1863, the vessels were ready to transport Grant's army across the river into Mississippi at Bruinsburg. In a series of thrusts northward he defeated portions of the Confederate forces, taking Jackson, the Mississippi capital, on May 14. Five days later, having encompassed the only avenues of retreat from Vicksburg by land or water, Grant settled down to a siege of the city. For six weeks the opposing armies faced one another at distances of 600 yards or less. By July the situation within the city had become desperate. On July 4, John C. Pemberton surrendered his entire force of 30,000 men. The South could not afford such losses. After Vicksburg the Union fleet at last

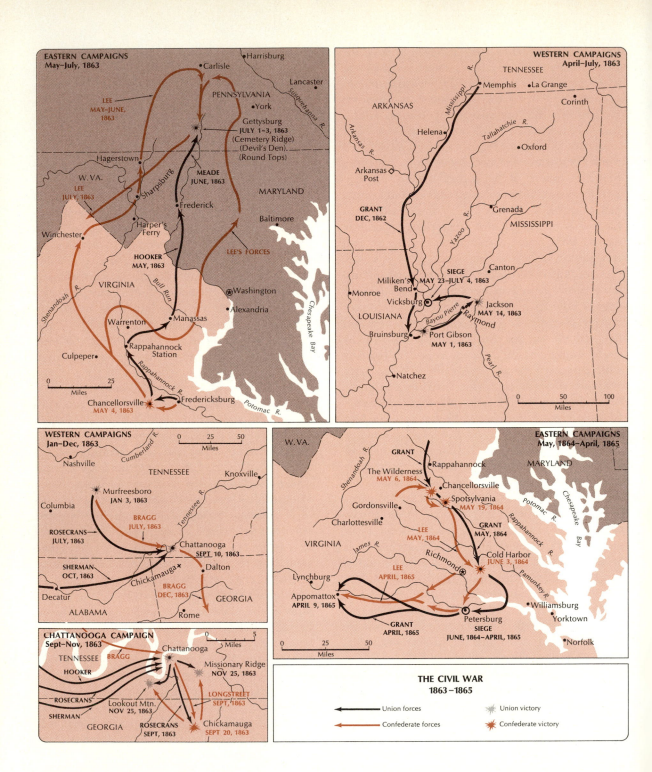

EASTERN CAMPAIGNS
May–July, 1863

Harrisburg
Carlisle
Lancaster
LEE
MAY–JUNE,
1863
PENNSYLVANIA
York
Susquehanna R.
Gettysburg
JULY 1–3, 1863
(Cemetery Ridge)
(Devil's Den)
(Round Tops)
Hagerstown
W. VA.
LEE
JULY, 1863
Sharpsburg
MEADE
JUNE, 1863
Frederick
MARYLAND
Harper's
Ferry
Baltimore
Winchester
Shenandoah R.
Washington
HOOKER
MAY, 1863
LEE'S FORCES
Alexandria
VIRGINIA
Bull Run
Warrenton
Manassas
Chesapeake Bay
Culpeper
Rappahannock
Station
Rappahannock R.
0   25
Miles
Chancellorsville
MAY 4, 1863
Fredericksburg
Potomac R.

WESTERN CAMPAIGNS
April–July, 1863

TENNESSEE
Mississippi R.
Memphis
La Grange
ARKANSAS
Corinth
Helena
Tallahatchie R.
Oxford
Arkansas R.
Arkansas
Post
GRANT
DEC, 1862
Grenada
MISSISSIPPI
Yazoo R.
SIEGE
MAY 23–JULY 4, 1863
Canton
Miliken's
Bend
Monroe
Vicksburg
Jackson
MAY 14, 1863
LOUISIANA
Bayou Pierre
Raymond
Pearl R.
Bruinsburg
Port Gibson
MAY 1, 1863
Natchez
0   50   100
Miles

WESTERN CAMPAIGNS
Jan–Dec, 1863

0   25   50
Miles
Nashville
Cumberland R.
Knoxville
TENNESSEE
Columbia
Murfreesboro
JAN 3, 1863
BRAGG
JULY, 1863
Tennessee R.
ROSECRANS
JULY, 1863
Chattanooga
SEPT 10, 1863
SHERMAN
OCT, 1863
Chickamauga
Dalton
Decatur
BRAGG
DEC, 1863
GEORGIA
ALABAMA
Rome

CHATTANOOGA CAMPAIGN
Sept–Nov, 1863

0   5
Miles
TENNESSEE
BRAGG
Chattanooga
HOOKER
Missionary Ridge
NOV 25, 1863
ROSECRANS
LONGSTREET
SEPT, 1863
Lookout Mtn.
NOV 25, 1863
SHERMAN
GEORGIA
ROSECRANS
SEPT, 1863
Chickamauga
SEPT 20, 1863

EASTERN CAMPAIGNS
May, 1864–April, 1865

W. VA.
GRANT
Shenandoah R.
Rappahannock
MARYLAND
The Wilderness
MAY 6, 1864
Chancellorsville
Spotsylvania
MAY 19, 1864
Gordonsville
Chesapeake
Bay
Charlottesville
Potomac R.
GRANT
MAY, 1864
LEE
MAY, 1864
VIRGINIA
James R.
Richmond
Cold Harbor
JUNE 3, 1864
Rappahannock R.
Lynchburg
LEE
APRIL, 1865
Pamunkey R.
Appomattox
APRIL 9, 1865
Williamsburg
Yorktown
GRANT
APRIL, 1865
Petersburg
SIEGE
JUNE, 1864–APRIL, 1865
Norfolk
0   25   50
Miles

THE CIVIL WAR
1863–1865

→ Union forces
→ Confederate forces
✳ Union victory
✶ Confederate victory

moved freely on the Mississippi from its mouth to the Ohio.

Grant now shifted his chief operations toward Confederate armies protecting Alabama and Georgia. In June 1863, after several months of preparation, General William S. Rosecrans had moved his Union forces toward Chattanooga, headquarters of the defending Confederate army. During September he managed to take the city without a battle. But Lee, seeing the importance of protecting the heartland of the South, dispatched 11,000 men by rail to strengthen the defenses outside Chattanooga. There on the field of Chickamauga, Confederate forces defeated Rosecrans and drove him back into Chattanooga. The battle had been exceedingly costly to both sides. Confederates controlled the rail lines into Chattanooga and occupied Missionary Ridge and Lookout Mountain above the city.

Grant now came to Rosecrans's support. While Union detachments opened up the Tennessee River for transportation of food, Sherman moved from Memphis. Grant was ready by November 23 to send his 60,000 men into battle. Sherman struck the Confederate right at Missionary Ridge; Hooker's two corps advanced against the Confederate left at Lookout Mountain, carrying the height against little opposition. After two days, Confederate forces were still concentrated on Missionary Ridge, where Sherman could not dislodge them. That afternoon two divisions under George H. Thomas moved out to relieve Sherman by taking the Confederate positions at the foot of the ridge. Having achieved this, without orders but simply caught up in the spirit of battle, they swept up the ridge, dislodged the Confederate forces, and carried the crest. Tennessee had been cleared of Confederate forces.

Grant in Command

Union victories at Gettysburg, Vicksburg, and Chattanooga during 1863 set the stage for the overwhelming Union successes that were to follow. Even if the Western campaigns had not shown Grant to be a great military strategist, they proved his tenacity. Long convinced that ruthless conduct of the war would bring the Confederacy to terms, the President on March 9, 1864, presented Grant with a commission as lieutenant general and gave him command of all Union armies. Recognizing the necessity of invading Virginia, capturing Richmond, and destroying Lee's army, the new commanding general opened his Virginia campaign in May 1864, by pushing the Army of the Potomac across the Rapidan to the west of Fredericksburg. There in the heavily wooded and tangled "Wilderness" where he could neither plan the battle nor even control his troops, Grant met Lee's army in what quickly disintegrated into a terrible slaughter. Grant lost an estimated 18,000 of his 118,000 troops. He knew, however, that he could afford

such losses better than could Lee, who left 10,000 men in the Wilderness. Grant, instead of retiring, continued his pursuit. The two armies met again at Spotsylvania Court House in a second battle of immeasureable ferocity, then pushed on to Cold Harbor. Here Grant threw three corps against Lee's strong intrenchments, suffered 12,000 casualties, and achieved nothing. It was the greatest blunder of Grant's Virginia campaign. In one month of campaigning Grant had lost 55,000 men, a number almost the equivalent of Lee's entire army. Unlike Lee, however, Grant had access to almost unlimited manpower, food, and supplies. Lee's tactical achievements could not offset the heavy damage to his Army of Northern Virginia.

Grant now crossed the James in a move against Richmond from the south. Between June 15 and 18 the Union forces assaulted Petersburg. Before they could move forward, Lee arrived with his army, saving Petersburg and Richmond for the moment. Grant used a month of comparative

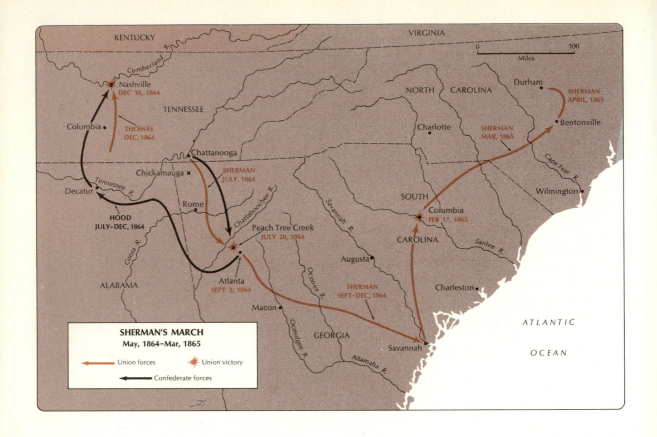

SHERMAN'S MARCH
May, 1864–Mar, 1865

→ Union forces   ✴ Union victory
→ Confederate forces

inaction to mine the Confederate position. On July 30, a mammoth explosion within Confederate lines set off another massive assault. Never had Lee's soldiers fought as valiantly as they did on that day. Lee remained in control of Petersburg and Richmond. After weeks of bloody fighting, the war in Virginia settled down to a long siege. "Hold on with a bulldog grip," Lincoln instructed his general in August, "and chew and choke as much as possible." Grant, meanwhile, directed his war of attrition against other Southern fronts.

At Chattanooga, Tennessee, Sherman commanded a magnificent army of 98,000 facing 53,000 Confederates under Joseph E. Johnston. Johnston engaged Sherman in a series of defensive maneuvers, avoiding a major battle as he fell back toward Atlanta. Johnston's replacement, J. B. Hood, exposed his forces at Peach Tree Creek only to take a whipping on July 20 which forced his retreat to Atlanta. Sherman's forces surrounded Atlanta and cut off the flow of supplies; Hood withdrew on September 1; Sherman occupied the city the following day.

Sherman now cut the railroad line to Chattanooga to protect his rear, ordered all civilians out of Atlanta, and burned the city. On November 10, 1864, he began his famous march to the sea. Sherman's four army corps moved toward Savannah on four roads, covering a band 60 miles in width. The devastation along the route of travel was complete, including bridges, railroads, and rolling stock, as well as homes and villages. Turning northward after the capture of Savannah, Sherman invaded the Carolinas. Fortunately the city of Charleston, center of the rebellion, was not along the route of travel. But the Union forces entered Columbia, South Carolina's capital; before they left, the city had burned.

Grant's attention had meanwhile turned to the stategic and agriculturally rich Shenandoah Valley of Virginia. In September 1864, he dispatched Philip Sheridan to follow Jubal A. Early's Confederate forces, recently retired from the environs of Washington, into the Shenandoah Valley and to devastate the area. Sheridan defeated the Confederates at Winchester on September 19 and then proceeded to fight his way down the valley in a series of minor engagements. Sheridan's forces scattered out across the rich valley, destroying everything—crops, livestock, buildings, railroads, and bridges. By October they had reduced one of the South's most productive farmlands to a desolate waste. At the end of 1864, although Grant had not yet disposed of Lee's army, Sherman was moving northward through the Carolinas, and Sheridan had returned from his Shenandoah venture to join Grant in a final thrust against Lee and Richmond, the Confederate capital.

Seward's Diplomacy

Diplomacy assumed major significance in 1861, for the country's future would be determined not only on the battlefield but also in the leading chancelleries of Europe. To forestall European interference in this nation's internal affairs after the fall of Fort Sumter, Secretary of State William H. Seward denied officially that a state of war existed between North and South. But Washington became disturbed in May 1861, when Britain, recognizing the existence of the Northern blockade of the South, issued a declaration of neutrality, a move duplicated by France, Spain, the Netherlands, and Brazil. This was an acknowledgment of Southern belligerency and suggested the possibility of further recognition of the Confederacy. Seward immediately warned the British and French that any diplomatic recognition of the Richmond government would mean war with the United States. British economic interests lay overwhelmingly in Northern commerce and agriculture. Still London desired Southern cotton and permitted the South to buy freely the products of British mills and shipyards, including such highly effective commerce raiders as the *Alabama*.

Conscious of the importance of European goodwill, the Confederate government, in November 1861, commissioned two distinguished Southerners, James M. Mason and John Slidell, to carry the Southern quest for recognition to London and Paris. At Havana they took passage for Europe on a British merchant vessel, the *Trent*. One day out, the packet was confronted by the United States warship *San Jacinto* under Captain Charles Wilkes. A search party removed the two Confederate envoys with their two secretaries and took them to Boston, where, as political prisoners, they remained in Fort Warren. Throughout the North the exultation elevated Wilkes to the stature of a hero. But when Palmerston, the British prime minister, received the news, he flew into a rage. "You may stand for this," he told the British cabinet, "but damned if I will!" Seward recognized the justice in the British position and gave up the case on principle. Wilkes had erred especially in removing the prisoners to the *San Jacinto* instead of taking the *Trent* into port for adjudication. Mason and Slidell, who had suspected correctly that they might serve the Confederate cause better in a Northern prison than in Europe, were sent on their way.

During the critical months before Antietam both England and France, convinced that the North could not win, seriously considered intervention to stop the bloodshed and the interminable assault on their neutral rights, as well as to regain access to Southern cotton. Seward exerted relentless pressure on both European governments, assuring them that the Confederate cause would ultimately fail. McClellan's success at Antietam produced sufficient doubt in

London to forestall any immediate decisions for involvement. In November 1862, the British cabinet made its final decision to observe strict neutrality in the American Civil War; the French government followed the British lead.

Lincoln's Emancipation Proclamation, although designed at least partially to influence European attitudes toward the Union cause had little influence on European sentiment and none on European action. Thus Seward's diplomatic success lay less in British economic interests and liberal sentiment than in an established diplomatic tradition. Many nations in the past had undergone internal revolution. Such uprisings had succeeded and failed, but the record demonstrated that when a major government was threatened, no external power could intervene diplomatically without running the risk of war. The United States itself had recognized this danger in its decisions favoring nonintervention in the revolutions of Latin America, Greece, and Hungary.

Lincoln refused to involve the United States in France's Mexican venture. When, in 1861, Louis Napoleon dispatched an army to Mexico, ostensibly to collect debts, and began to interfere openly in the internal affairs of that Latin American country, Seward ignored Mexico's appeal to the Monroe Doctrine. Instead, he warned Napoleon that France could not determine the political structure of Mexico because Mexican resistance would be effective.

Even when France, in 1864, established Maximilian of Austria as the Emperor of Mexico, Seward continued to avoid any open American commitment to Mexican independence. Both Lincoln and Seward recognized the need of hoarding the country's energy to preserve the Union, and they refused to dissipate American resources in involvements abroad to defend principles which they knew must succeed or fail on their own. Eventually Napoleon found the financial and military price of his Mexican involvement so burdensome that in 1866 he withdrew what was left of his army and permitted Maximilian to die before a Mexican firing squad.

Problems of the Confederacy

Southerners had overestimated the power of "King Cotton." Cotton had dominated the prewar export trade of the United States; without it, predicted the secessionists, the mills of England and France would lie idle. So confident was the South of the power of cotton to force European recognition of its interests that it instituted an embargo early in the war to force British and French intervention. Next, the South resorted to crop curtailment, producing only 1 million bales in 1862, or about one-third the crop of the previous year. Finally Southerners destroyed hundreds of thousands of bales to assure scarcity in Europe and keep cotton out of Northern hands. Too late, the South discovered that cotton was only a normal, not a miracle, weapon. Because of the heavy export of cotton in previous years, that commodity in 1861 was a glut on the British market. When Confederate policy eventually produced extensive hardship in the mill districts of England, British workingmen turned against the South for creating the shortage. Whatever Southern hopes for European intervention remained after Antietam were shattered by the Confederate disasters at Gettysburg and Vicksburg in July 1863.

Southern leaders never succeeded in creating an efficient administration. President Davis, although completely devoted to the Confederate cause, suffered from ill health and a lack of magnetism and vitality needed to sustain the Southern war effort. By 1862, many leading secessionists had begun to ridicule his leadership. Eventually the entire Confederate government came under bitter criticism from the Southern press.

Southern weakness was economic as well as political. The South tried to meet the economic challenge of war by refining the art of blockade running and eventually by expanding its own industrial production. But it lacked the enterprise, skilled labor, and resources to build the massive capacity demanded by modern war. Still the Confederacy lost no battles because of shortages in arms and ammunition. For this the credit must go to Josiah Gorgas, the Confederacy's chief of ordnance. Through his encouragement, the Richmond government established arsenals and foundries in key areas of Alabama, Georgia, and South Carolina, as well as a huge powder mill at Augusta. The most conspicuous industrial success, however, was the conversion of the Tredegar Iron Works at Richmond into an astonishingly productive munitions plant.

In obtaining adequate quantities of food and clothing the South was far less successful. The region lacked textile industries, and the shoe and uniform factories eventually established never satisfied the demand. Southern railroads were always short of equipment, and the South could not maintain its existing roadbeds. As the war progressed, rail service suffered from broken ties, flat wheels, dilapidated cars, and powerless locomotives.

Confederate finances reflected the South's lack of production. In four years that government raised only $25 million in liquid capital. Its accumulation each year was only twice what the federal government spent each day. This scarcity of gold and silver forced the Confederacy to manufacture paper money in vast amounts, creating an inflation which became worse. By 1865, the value of the Confederate dollar was equal to 1 cent in gold. The South, by destroying its cotton, had denied itself the sale of its one commodity which might have built up necessary credits in Europe.

Despite its manifold weaknesses, the Confederacy created an army that reached 260,000 men in 1863—one of the most effective fighting forces in modern history. Through four grueling years, the Richmond government managed a prodigious military effort and resisted until much of the South had been systematically devastated. Although the Southern command structure might have profited from innovation, Lee, Jackson, and others inspired their soldiers to unsurpassed feats of courage. Almost one hundred thousand Confederates died in battle, a sacrifice in relation to population greater than any European nation had ever sustained in war. Men and women, working heroically behind the lines, sustained the Southern cause.

Yet morale inevitably slumped as the promise of victory receded. Perhaps most people of the South had opposed the secession movement; little in subsequent Confederate experience could convince them that the struggle for Southern independence was other than a dreadful mistake. Those who carried the war's military and civilian burden chafed under the inefficiency of the Confederate government. They resented laws which exempted many from military duty, especially slaveholders who had the requisite number of slaves engaged in food production. By 1864 soldiers in the South were deserting by the thousands. Southern governors, under the doctrine of states' rights, continued to undermine the entire Confederate war effort. By 1864 the whole system of supply had broken down. Lee went to Richmond to express his concern. His impressions of the government he recorded for his son: "I visited Congress today and they did not seem to be able to do anything except to eat peanuts and chew tobacco while my army is starving. I told them the condition my men were in and something must be done at once but I can't get them to do anything, or they are unable to do anything. When this war began I told these people that unless every man should do his whole duty they would repent it, and now—they will repent it."

Life behind the Northern lines bore little resemblance to that in the Confederacy. Northerners could not escape the emotional onslaught of the war's death and destruction, but the North maintained the offensive and thus escaped the terrible presence of an invading enemy. One Illinois soldier, in August 1863, reminded relatives at home of their good fortune. "I allmost sicken," he admitted, "at the thought of this war ever reaching the homes of my family and friends. I think I would be willing to . . . sacrifice my life on the soil of the Southern States to shield the soil of Illinois from the dreded tramp of an army. . . . You should be the last people to murmer at the war tax. If you could travel with the Army of the Cumberland a few days you would learn that the inhabitants of those States pay all they possess and pay it in a few hours. Women and children cry but to no avail." The North's ultimate advantage lay in its capacity to meet the demands of total war. The *New York Times* reported in 1864 that the people of the North were better fed, clothed, and sheltered than ever before in the nation's history.

Northern business responded quickly to the Confederate challenge. Still, the War Department's almost limitless need for goods and equipment created unprecedented pressures. Whether the government procured uniforms, munitions, or food, it soon found itself paying premium prices for second-rate merchandise. Compounding the problem and multiplying the opportunities for profiteering were state expenditures for the local volunteer forces. By bidding against the War Department for supplies and equipment in both the United States and Europe, state agents drove prices skyward at a prodigious rate, creating an orgy of waste, fraud, and speculation. The appointment of Edwin M. Stanton as Lincoln's second secretary of war in early 1862 brought a modicum of order into the federal procurement system, but the problems of profiteering and corruption proved particularly intractable.

Special governmental and private agencies ministered to the health and comfort of Union troops. The United States Sanitary Commission, a civilian auxiliary to the medical bureau of the War Department, was by far the most important agency engaged in the work of sanitation and hospitalization. Women like Louisa Schuyler in New York and Mary Livermore in Chicago led the Commission's efforts to raise money and secure the necessary food and medical supplies in what was the first large-scale activity undertaken by women outside the home. Many private groups established military hospitals, staffed them with volunteer nurses, and effectively supplemented the efforts of the government in caring for the wounded. The noted Clara Barton was a volunteer nurse in the Virginia campaigns. Much of the service went beyond medical care to include the supplying of books, magazines, and even financial assistance.

Almost every branch of manufacturing in the North responded to wartime requirements and new protective tariffs. The cotton textile industry suffered as a result of the war, but the woolen industry expanded to take its place. There was a steady increase in the output of coal, iron, and oil, the three major extractive industries. The arms industry, which before the war could manufacture only 22,000 weapons a year, reached a capacity of 5,000 rifles per day by 1865. Every Northern city sprouted new industries, but the most spectacular advances in production came from the application of new machines and processes to industries already established.

Agriculture produced enough to satisfy the needs of the Union armies and to offset the poor harvests of Europe. Between 1859 and 1862 England's importation of American grain increased fiftyfold. Such unprecedented pressures on American agriculture accelerated the development of the Great Lakes country. By the

The Documented War

The Civil War—America's grimmest, dirtiest, most bitter test—became the world's first exhaustively documented conflict. Reporters and correspondents wrote millions of words; uncountable pages of orders, plans, official papers, letters, and memoirs appeared; countless sketches, paintings, and engravings were made. But above all, there were photographs. Hundreds of thousands of tintypes, daguerreotypes, and wet plate negatives recorded every facet of the struggle. For the first time an entire country truly *saw* a war.

Our primary impression of the Civil War is a visual one created by Alexander Gardner, Timothy H. O'Sullivan, and George W. Barnard; by the photographers supervised by Mathew Brady; and by hundreds of lesser known cameramen. Their images are as stark and compelling today as they were then, when the nation tore open its own flesh and bled for four agonizing years.

Library of Congress

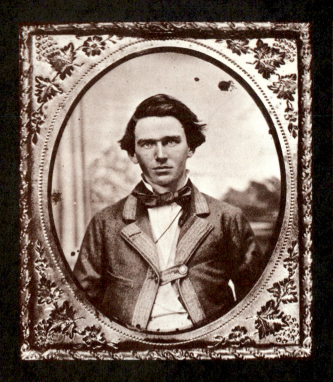

Civil War officers were often professionals, but the soldiers were ordinary men and boys who first volunteered and later were drafted from cities, farms, and plantations. For the first time families had pictures to remind them of the men at war. These photographs of Confederates (this page) and Federals (opposite) typify the many thousands sent home from training camps and the front. Usually inexpensive but durable (and therefore mailable) tintypes such as these measured about 2 × 3½ inches. Blacks, who fought valiantly for the North, encountered bitter hatred in the South. When captured, they were considered contraband, or war booty, rather than prisoners.

The South could never bring itself to arm Negroes, even when it desperately needed troops, but the Union Army had segregated black regiments from 1862 onward. Valiant soldiers, they comprised almost 20 percent of Federal troops by war's end.

Confederates Advancing to the Capture of ...

Many famous illustrators covered the war for newspapers and magazines. Field artists Alfred and William Waud drew vivid sketches such as these as the basis for engravings in *Harper's Weekly*.

Clara Barton formed the Red Cross during the Civil War but field hospitals and doctors were few. An injured limb almost surely meant amputation under primitive conditions. Anaesthesia and antiseptic precautions were generally lacking. Infection and disease killed twice as many on both sides as died in battle.

Captured soldiers fared even worse. Conditions in Northern and Southern prison camps were horrendous, as attested to by the condition of many who survived the ordeal.

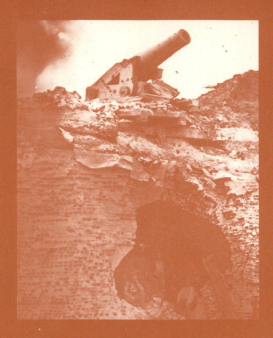

The war was dirty, grim, grinding. New machines, new fighting techniques wreaked a physical devastation unseen before. For the first time commanders relied on reducing civilians to despair and crippling every kind of production as well as on crushing the enemy's military force. Pounding artillery, rockets, torpedoes, siege, unrelenting assault all aimed at one goal: destruction.

More men died in the Civil War than the total of all of America's other wars. The human damage was irreparable; the human attitudes remained unchanged.

sixties, Chicago had become the largest primary wheat market in the world.

From 1862 until 1865 the North's commercial and industrial leaders enjoyed an uninterrupted spree. Materialism triumphed, bringing a new commercial and financial preeminence to New York. "Every man worships the dollar, and is down before his shrine from morning to night," wrote the famous British visitor, Anthony Trollope, in 1862. Secretary of the Treasury Chase in 1864 found leading businessmen of New York more concerned over the stock market than news from the front.

Northern labor, unorganized economically or politically, was no match for those who controlled the nation's business and governmental policies. Unsupported by congressional action, wages lagged behind prices. The average wartime wage stood a full 43 percent above the prewar level, but the more rapidly climbing prices reduced real wages to about two-thirds of their 1861 level. Industrialists fought the tendencies of skilled labor to organize. Congress demonstrated its open hostility in 1864 when it created a Bureau of Immigration and authorized the importation of semi-indentured labor. Labor in general supported the war effort, but revealed its resentment toward federal policies by occasionally battling conscription and refusing reenlistment. Such latent bitterness toward the maldistribution of economic rewards erupted in a series of draft riots in New York City during July 1863.

Republican war policies faced their only unrelenting opposition in the lower Middle West. Douglas, before his death in 1861, warned his fellow Westerners that in war there could be no neutrals—only patriots and traitors. Still many Western Democrats never ceased to oppose the Republican administration and its wartime policies. These "Copperheads," as the Republicans called them, condemned the confiscation acts, Emancipation Proclamation, conscription laws, violations of freedom of the press, and especially the "abolitionist fanaticism" to which they at-

tributed the war's prolongation. Although Republican policies, if not the Republican party, satisfied general Northern sentiment, Lincoln could not ignore what appeared to be pro-Southern sympathies in the North. Much of the criticism directed at the war effort verged on the disloyal. Lincoln was never reluctant to use Executive power to harness Northern freedom of expression. Under his orders federal officials often held prisoners without showing cause.

The civil liberties case of Clement L. Vallandigham was the most spectacular of the war. In May 1863, in a speech at Mount Vernon, Ohio, this Democratic politician and outspoken critic of Lincoln's leadership accused the President of avoiding compromise and needlessly prolonging the bloodshed. Vallandigham advocated resistance only through debate and the ballot, not through acts of insurrection. Nevertheless, General Ambrose E. Burnside, then commander of the Department of the Ohio, accused him of "declaring sympathies for the enemy" and had him arrested. The military commission found Vallandigham guilty and sentenced him to close confinement for the duration of the war. Lincoln, very embarrassed by the overwhelmingly sympathetic response of many Northerners to the Ohioan's appeals for liberty, commuted Vallandigham's sentence from close confinement to banishment behind Confederate lines. Later Vallandigham escaped from the South and took up his residence in Windsor, Canada, where he continued his assault on the Republican leadership. Finally in 1864 he reentered the United States and campaigned openly for the Democratic party. The Supreme Court in February 1864 refused to take under consideration the Vallandigham issue. But in a similar case, that of L. P. Milligan, who was arrested in Indianapolis in October 1864, the Supreme Court in the famous decision of *ex parte Milligan* (1866) declared that Milligan's trial by a military commission was illegal, since no actual invasion had occurred and civil courts had not been relieved of any of their functions.

Lincoln's conduct of the war enjoyed little support in Congress, the press, or the Republican party leadership. Most Republicans felt no obligations of loyalty to the President. Their open rejection of Lincoln's leadership had a strong political motivation. Long-term Republican power hinged on the party's ability to exploit its wartime advantages in making further inroads among the North's Democratic constituency. To demonstrate their fundamental agreement on wartime objectives, Republicans and War Democrats combined early in the war to form the Union party. Yet even this maneuver failed to strengthen the Republican cause. Democratic victories in 1862, reducing the Republican majority in the House from 35 to 18, reminded Radicals that except for the absence of Southerners they would have lost control of Congress completely. Dissaffected Radicals blamed Lincoln's caution for their failures. By 1864 they were prepared to desert the President for one of their own number. During May they met in Cleveland, heaped their customary abuse on Lincoln, and nominated John C. Frémont for the presidency on a Radical platform.

In his fierce struggles with Radicals, Lincoln moved with the skill of a master craftsman. Always sensitive to public trends and the demands of a restless nation, he could shift from secrecy and procrastination to firmness and decision when the occasion demanded. Often by recourse to stories and good humor he would disarm obstreperous callers at the White House and dismiss them later with their questions unanswered. If congressional heads would not conform to his leadership, there were powerful weapons in the presidential arsenal which he could and would employ. Behind the scenes Lincoln's agents maneuvered, lining up support with executive patronage. Before any other candidate could enter the field, Lincoln had assured his own renomination. When the regular Republican convention met at Baltimore in June, Lincoln received every vote recorded and then picked his own candidate for the vice presidency—Andrew Johnson, a War Democrat from Tennessee.

To capitalize on the growing war-weariness, the Democrats postponed their convention until late August and then, at Chicago, nominated the popular war hero, George McClellan. The Democratic platform referred to "four years of failure to restore the Union by the experiment of war" and demanded an end to hostilities at the earliest possible moment advantageous to the restoration of the Union. McClellan, however, repudiated the peace platform and emphasized only the need for restoring the Union. He campaigned purely as a war leader, attacking Lincoln and his administration, not for their objectives, but for their failure to achieve them.

Lincoln's chances brightened as the election approached. In September, Sherman entered Atlanta. Republicans won victories in Maine and Vermont. Frémont withdrew from the race, and a last-minute Radical convention to replace Frémont with another candidate failed to materialize. Thereafter Radicals had no alternative but to support Lincoln.

The President's reelection in 1864 demonstrated how inconsequential his personal popularity actually was. With the South out of the Union, he received but 52 percent of the popular vote. Powerful Democratic minorities in New York, Pennsylvania, Ohio, Indiana, and Illinois indicated that the Democratic party was far from dead, even in the North. McClellan carried only three states—Kentucky, Delaware, and New Jersey—but he had secured almost half the ballots. The campaign did make clear, however, that those Northerners who believed the war unjust were too insignificant numerically to either encourage the South or influence the North.

The War's End

The spring of 1865 saw the hopes of the South fade and collapse. Sherman was moving northward from Columbia through the Carolinas. Outside Petersburg the Confederates continued to resist. Finally on April 1, Union troops broke Richmond's defenses and entered the ruined city. Grant trapped the remnants of Lee's ragged army at Appomattox Court House. Grant had sent to Lincoln Sheridan's telegram stating that if "the thing is pressed I think that Lee will surrender." The President replied characteristically, "Let the *thing* be pressed." It was Lincoln's final military order. Whatever Lincoln expected of the peace, he did not live to mold it. Five days after Lee's surrender, on the evening of April 14, the President attended Ford's Theater in Washington. There John Wilkes Booth entered his box and fired a bullet into his brain. Lincoln lingered through the night, then died. He had saved the Union, but the task of national reconstruction belonged to others.

Lincoln four days before he was shot.   The Granger Collection

Conclusion

For the victorious North the Civil War constituted a bloody divide between an older America which was agricultural, rural, humanitarian, and personalized and a new America which was industrial, urban, secular, and institutionalized. The trend toward large-scale organization of American life had been well under way before the war began; the required mobilization for victory merely accelerated the process. Fundamentally what shaped the new nation was the need to create a huge army; to feed and clothe it; to supply it with munitions; to organize its sanitation, finance, and medical services; to provide it with efficient transportation; and to develop popular support to sustain it. Such a broad national effort required the coordination of goals and acceptance of national direction. It trans-

formed an inchoate country, once guided by individual effort without regard to public interest, into a more disciplined nation, increasingly subject to national planning and control. It shifted the emphasis of human behavior from individualism to cooperation, for the interest in victory was public, not private. The nation emerged from the war an incipient industrial giant, pulsating with crude energy already seeking new outlets. But the problems of peace, unlike the challenges of war, called less for engines of creation and destruction than for specific attitudes of mind, such as tolerance and understanding. And somehow for the United States in 1865, the latter attributes proved to be more elusive than the capacity for amassing strength. The destruction of Southern military and political resistance on the battlefield lay well within the competence of Northern power. Whether that power, once leashed, could transform Southern traditions of race and society in accordance with Northern purpose remained to be seen.

SUGGESTED READINGS

Undoubtedly the soundest one-volume study of the Civil War period is J. G. Randall and David Donald's *The Civil War and Reconstruction* (rev. ed., 1961). Two monumental histories of the Civil War, both detailed and dramatic, are Allan Nevins's *The War for the Union* (4 vols., 1959–1971) and Bruce Catton's *The Centennial History of the Civil War* (3 vols., 1961–1965). Perhaps the best introduction to the life of Lincoln is Benjamin P. Thomas's *Abraham Lincoln: A Biography* (1952). The most comprehensive study of Lincoln in existence is by Carl Sandburg, *Abraham Lincoln: The Prairie Years** (2 vols., 1926) and *The War Years** (4 vols., 1939). A more balanced, yet thorough, study of Lincoln is J. G. Randall's *Lincoln: The President** (4 vols., 1945–1955). (The final volume was completed by R. N. Current.) David Potter's *Lincoln and His Party in the Secession Crisis** (1942) and R. N. Current's *Lincoln and the First Shot** (1963) discuss Lincoln's actions in the Fort Sumter crisis.

Bruce Catton's three volumes, *Mr. Lincoln's Army** (1951), *Glory Road** (1952), and *A Stillness at Appomattox** (1953), constitute a highly readable history of the Northern campaigns in the East. Catton's *This Hallowed Ground** (1956) is a vivid one-volume summary. Even more detailed and analytical, with greater emphasis on the Western campaigns, is Kenneth P. Williams's *Lincoln Finds a General* (5 vols., 1949–1959). T. H. Williams's *Lincoln and His Generals** (1952) is briefer but more vivid. The best military accounts of the Confederacy are the seven classic volumes by Douglas S. Freeman: *R. E. Lee: A Biography* (4 vols., 1934–1935) and *Lee's Lieutenants* (3 vols., 1942–1944). Two excellent volumes on the common soldier, North and South, are Bell I. Wiley's *The Life of Billy Yank** (1952) and *The Life of Johnny Reb** (1943).

T. H. Williams's *Lincoln and the Radicals** (1941) stresses the Radical drive for power, whereas David Donald in *Lincoln Reconsidered** (1956) cites evidence of humanitarian motivation in the Republican demands for victory. For a full discussion of emancipation see Benjamin Quarles's *Lincoln and the Negro* (1962) and John Hope Franklin's *The Emancipation Proclamation** (1963). On Civil War diplomacy, North and South, see E. D. Adams's *Great Britain and the American Civil War* (2 vols., 1925) and Frank L. Owsley's *King Cotton Diplomacy* (1931; 2d ed., 1959). Dexter Perkins's *The Monroe Doctrine, 1826–1867* (1933) covers Mexican problem during the Civil War.

On life behind the Confederate lines, the standard work is E. M. Coulter's *The Confederate States of America, 1861–1865* (1950). Also see Clement Eaton's *A History of the Southern Confederacy** (1954). For two brief but judicious accounts see Charles P. Roland's *The Confederacy** (1960) and Frank Vandiver's *Basic History of the Confederacy** (1962). The problems of leadership and administration are portrayed in Burton J. Hendrick's *Statesmen of the Lost Cause: Jefferson Davis and His Cabinet* (1939). R. W. Patrick in *Jefferson Davis and His Cabinet* (1944) is less critical of Davis. On problems of conscription in the South, see A. B. Moore's *Conscription and Conflict in the Confederacy* (1924). Wartime Washington is described in detail in Margaret Leech's *Reveille in Washington, 1860–1865** (1941). See also W. Q. Maxwell's *Lincoln's Fifth Wheel: The Political History of the United States Sanitary Commission* (1956); M. E. Massey's *Bonnet Brigades, American Women and the Civil War* 1966); and R. V. Bruce's *Lincoln and the Tools of War* (1956), revealing Lincoln's interest in weapons development. Two excellent studies of Northern railroads are Thomas Weber's *The Northern Railroads in the Civil War* (1952) and G. E. Turner's *Victory Rode the Rails* (1953). Two outstanding studies of Copperheadism are Wood Gray's *The Hidden War** (1942) and Frank L. Klement's *The Copperheads in the Middle West* (1960).

H. J. Carman and R. H. Luthin trace *Lincoln and the Patronage* (1943). On Lincoln's Cabinet there are several volumes of great value: Burton J. Hendrick's *Lincoln's War Cabinet** (1946); David Donald (ed.), *Inside Lincoln's Cabinet: The Civil War Diaries of Salmon P. Chase* (1954); B. P. Thomas and H. M. Hyman's *Stanton: The Life and Times of Lincoln's Secretary of War* (1962); and R. S. West, Jr.'s *Gideon Welles* (1943).
*indicates availability in paperback.

16

Postwar Reconstruction

Robert E. Lee's surrender at Appomattox Court House in April 1865 opened a new era in the history of the United States. Politically and morally, the nation could never return to the lost world of Lincoln's first inaugural. Wars generally achieve more than the mere separation of the quick from the dead. Essentially they comprise the means whereby those who direct a country's policies can employ the force of mass destruction to achieve what they believed impossible through compromise and agreement alone. The American Civil War was no exception. John Quincy Adams had once prophesied that the major interests in conflict between the slave and the free states could best be resolved through limitless application of Northern industrial and military might on the battlefield. Victory had come hard for the North, but it had eliminated, at least for the moment, the South's traditional influence in American national life.

But the revolution wrought by Northern arms had been moral as well as political, for the Union victories had placed the Southern slave system on the road to oblivion and now confronted the Republic with the inescapable challenge of creating a new role for the blacks in American society. Thus the Republican leadership in 1865 faced two fundamental and related questions: Under what conditions would it permit the South to reenter the Union? How could it, at the same time, translate emancipation into social, economic, and political equality for the freed slave? The national experience decreed against any permanent alienation of the South from its historic role in the nation's life. But on the question of the Negro's future in Southern society, there were no hopeful precedents. Whatever the sincerity of their moral purpose, Northern leaders would soon discover that practical measures for refashioning the South would depend less on coercion than on the continuing factors of Southern conviction, interest, and tradition.

Its power of resistance destroyed, the South awaited the North's conditions of peace and contemplated the task of rebuilding its ruined economy. Although a small minority of Southern businessmen had succeeded in accumulating capital, the South generally was impoverished. Emancipation had wiped out the South's investment of more than $2 billion in slaves. Confederate securities totaling $1 billion fell worthless with the collapse of the Richmond government. Inflation, added to the economic dislocation and destruction of war, had eliminated the South's banking capital, disorganized its currency and credit structure, and undermined its commerce and industry. Union forces had systematically eliminated the South's transportation system.

Areas which had experienced the full ravages of war lay desolate and helpless. Invading armies, whether fighting or foraging, generally managed to ruin whatever they touched, and by 1865 Union forces had penetrated large areas of the

South. The destruction of the countryside that separated Alexandria from Richmond and Charlottesville reminded travelers that Virginia had carried the chief burden of war. Across the Blue Ridge Mountains, General Philip Sheridan had, it seemed, fulfilled his promise to denude the Shenandoah Valley. Likewise the valley of the Tennessee carried the scars of invading Union soldiers. One English traveler recalled, "The trail of war is visible throughout the valley in burnt-up gin-houses, ruined bridges, mills, and factories, of which the gable walls only are left standing, and in large tracts of once cultivated land stripped of every vestige of fencing." Ultimately no areas of the South suffered more thoroughly than those which experienced the fury of Sherman's campaigns through Georgia and the Carolinas. The general estimated Georgia's loss from war at $100 million, most of it wrought by deliberate waste and destruction. But this was merely prelude to the retribution which Sherman's army exacted of South Carolina. Carl Schurz reported in 1865 that the northward route followed by Sherman "looked for many miles like a broad black streak of ruin and desolation—the fences all gone; lonesome smoke stacks, surrounded by dark heaps of ashes and cinders, marking the spots where human habitations had stood; the fields . . . wildly overgrown by weeds, with here and there a sickly looking patch of cotton or corn cultivated by negro squatters."

Added to its physical and psychological burdens, the South faced the necessity of integrating 4 million freedmen into its economic, political, and social structure. Many problems lay ahead, but blacks regarded emancipation as a time of celebration. Deserting the plantations, many entered the cities in search of employment and educational opportunities. But freedmen wanted and needed far more opportunity, equality, and respect than the nation was willing to give. Thus the transition from slavery to freedom, from rural to urban life, could be neither swift nor

Richmond, Virginia, 1865.   *The Granger Collection*

easy. Southern whites, determined to preserve their traditional way of life, often resorted to violence to drive blacks off the roads. Freedmen who reached the cities crowded endlessly into urban pockets and Union "contraband camps," established specifically to sustain them through a period of relocation. Countless thousands died of disease and exposure.

The loss of black agricultural labor completed the disintegration in the Southern plantation system, forcing many former masters into the fields to maintain themselves and their families. The rural South revealed the decay and neglect of war, and those who turned to agricultural production in 1865 faced shortages in labor, livestock, and equipment.

Incorporating freed blacks into Southern white society under favorable conditions emerged in 1865 as the central challenge of Southern Reconstruction. The problem, aggravated by the issue of race, was rendered even more complex by the slave tradition which had barred the vast majority of Southern blacks from all educational, political, and business experience. Negro leaders attempted to close the gap between reality and promise by assuming the task of black education. They received some needed aid from Northern religious bodies, as well as from the Freedmen's Bureau. Established by Congress in March 1865, the Bureau assigned some abandoned lands to freedmen, defended them in controversies with whites, and provided food and clothing for those without employment. Under the leadership of General Oliver O. Howard the Bureau favored some form of governmental guardianship over blacks; still the program remained too conservative and limited to record any lasting achievements.

Presidential Reconstruction

Lincoln desired freedom for slaves; he never anticipated equality for blacks in American society. For him the overriding challenge of postwar reconstruction was restoration of the Union. He was convinced that a moderate Republican program could induce the powerful ex-Whig minority of the South to join the Republican party, true heir of the Whig tradition in the North, and thus reconstruct the old Whig party under the Republican banner. Lincoln suspected that most Southern Whigs had never favored the secession movement; now they seemed the best hope for leading the Southern states back to their former allegiance.

Lincoln announced his conditions for Southern restoration in his proclamation of December 8, 1863. He offered amnesty to those who would take an oath of loyalty to the Union and accept all federal laws regarding slavery. He specifically denied amnesty only to high-ranking military, political, and diplomatic officials of the Confederacy and to those who had left Congress and the federal service to join the Southern cause.

When one-tenth of the voters of any seceding state took the oath of allegiance, that state could, upon presenting a constitution, republican in form, reenter the Union. Lincoln acknowledged the sole right of Congress to recognize elected representatives of the restored states.

Republican Radicals in Congress noted correctly that the President's plan offered no guarantees of civil rights to Southern blacks and that it assigned to the Executive rather than to Congress the power to determine conditions and processes of Reconstruction. Congress threw down the gauntlet to Lincoln in July 1864, when it passed a bill introduced by Senator Benjamin F. Wade of Ohio and Representative Henry Winter Davis of Maryland, which imposed more stringent requirements on the South. The Wade-Davis bill provided that Reconstruction would begin when a *majority* of white male citizens of a Confederate state took the oath of allegiance to the United States. These voters would elect delegates to a state constitutional convention who would, in turn, take a second oath that they had never voluntarily given support to the Confederacy. The bill increased the number of Southern leaders who would be barred from voting or holding office. Lincoln killed the measure with a pocket veto and pressed forward with his own moderate program. Meanwhile Louisiana, in accordance with Lincoln's proclamation, had adopted a new constitution. Congress adjourned on March 4, 1865, without recognizing the new state government.

Many Radicals—disturbed by Lincoln's course—openly professed relief at his death in April 1865. Vice President Andrew Johnson's wartime condemnation of the South had convinced Radicals that he shared their views on Reconstruction. As Wade assured the new President, "Johnson, we have faith in you. By the gods, there will be no trouble now in running the government."

But the struggle for control of federal policy now became more intense, for Johnson, no less than Lincoln, insisted on Executive control. The new President, like his predecessor, was determined to direct federal action toward the creation of a postwar political alignment which would reflect his antebellum political preferences. Those preferences, if momentarily clouded, reflected every phase of the new President's experience in politics. From his unpromising start as an illiterate tailor and local politician in Greenville, Tennessee, Johnson had climbed the rungs of Tennessee politics as a Jacksonian Democrat and a natural enemy of slaveholding Whigs. Entering the United States Senate as an outspoken Unionist, Johnson had condemned the secession movement and remained in the North until Lincoln sent him back to Tennessee as military governor. By the spring of 1865 Lincoln had convinced his Vice President that a harsh Reconstruction policy would fail. As President, Johnson not only accepted Lincoln's Cabinet but also recognized the Southern state governments established under Lincoln's plan. He hoped to return the South speedily to control of its own destiny. Never an opponent of slavery or friend of the Negro, Johnson had no desire to use

federal power in defense of black freedom. He accepted emancipation as a by-product of war, but freedmen were not his concern. He thus limited his purposes for the South to the creation of new governments, which he hoped would rest on Democratic power. Lincoln had sought the reforging of the prewar Whig party; Johnson pursued the vision of a reborn Democratic party based on Jacksonian principles.

Johnson proceeded to implement his own Reconstruction program through Executive action. On May 29 he issued a proclamation of amnesty for those who would take an oath of allegiance to the Union. He extended Lincoln's exclusion list, however, to include persons who had involuntarily participated in the rebellion and those whose taxable property exceeded $20,000. He hoped this would eliminate the upper-class Whigs from Southern politics. Lincoln had recognized Virginia, Tennessee, Louisiana, and Arkansas. Johnson appointed a new Governor for North Carolina and ordered him to call a convention for the purpose of creating a new state constitution. Then in June 1865, he applied the procedure to the other states of the South. Before Congress met in December, all former Confederate states except Texas had formed constitutions and elected governments. All except Mississippi had ratified the Thirteenth Amendment, which became law in December, officially abolishing slavery.

Johnson had prepared the South for readmission to the Union, but he failed to create a new agrarian utopia. The Whigs whom he opposed became the new power in Southern politics. During 1865 they won no less than eight governorships, eleven senatorships, and thirty-six seats in the House. Outside of Texas and South Carolina, Whigs captured almost nine-tenths of the congressional seats. In addition, they gained control of several Southern state legislatures and constitutional conventions. Clearly Lincoln had estimated the realities of Southern politics far more accurately than Johnson had.

What undermined and eventually defeated the President's moderate program were the actions of the Southern states themselves. Assuming generally that the elevation of blacks would result in the South's social and economic degeneration, the Johnson governments resorted to so-called Black Codes in an effort to return the South to its prewar status of economic stability and racial subjugation. These codes were designed essentially to force blacks back to the land and hold them there with annual contracts and the restriction of property rights. Some states even forbade freedmen to seek employment outside agriculture, except with special permission. Three states—Florida, Mississippi, and Texas—passed laws which established the principle of race discrimination in the use of railroads. These laws illustrated the Southern determination to limit the black presence through policies of segregation. Threatening the Negro with fines and imprisonment for every deviation from social and moral standards established by white society, the Black Codes severely limited the freedman's civil and economic rights and sometimes reduced him to a condition of peonage. Clearly the South had rejected the implications of emancipation.

Triumph of the Radicals

When Congress met in December 1865, its Radical leadership was determined to end the President's control of Southern Reconstruction. Wade complained as early as July: "We have in truth already lost the whole moral effect of our victories over the rebellion, and the golden opportunity for humiliating and destroying the influence of the Southern aristocracy has gone forever." To make matters worse, the President accepted Black Codes without a murmur, and on December 18 rationalized them in a special message to Congress as measures designed "to confer upon freedmen the privileges which are essential to their comfort, protection, and security." The President's stand on white rule in the South elevated the question of black rights to a central position in the struggle for power between Congress and the Executive.

Johnsonians supported the concept of racial inequality. Radicals demanded a status for blacks, including the right to vote, which most Americans would not accept. To conservatives such demands for black equality, being unreasonable, simply camouflaged a variety of Radical purposes which had no relation to black rights at all. Obviously the black vote represented political power to those who could control it. And the claim that the Radicals befriended the freedmen only to exploit them carried enough truth to be convincing. Negro enfranchisement would break the economic and political influence of former Southern rebels; Radicals such as Thad Stevens never concealed their desire to punish the "traitors." Negro suffrage, moreover, would assure continued ascendancy of the Republican party and permit that party to complete its dual objective of underwriting a new status for freedmen and protecting business interests in the North with additional tariffs, subsidies, and internal improvements. Such motivations Stevens, among others, readily admitted.

Perhaps hypocrisy abounds wherever men pursue ideals. Yet Radicals possessed their share of forthrightness and sincerity. They had led the Republican party's antislavery crusade before and during the war; their previous concerns would demand no less than an effective postwar program of civil rights for freedmen. Radical Republicans thought they had won the right to determine federal policy. And it was because Johnson's program of Reconstruction threatened to deny them the moral and political fruits of victory that they prepared to challenge his leadership.

In December 1865, the Radicals, with support from moderates, established a Joint Committee on Reconstruction to study all Reconstruction proposals and recommend to Congress those they believed appropriate. Twelve of its fifteen members were Republican, but the moderates, who dominated the committee, denied that its creation was a repudiation of Johnson. Many members of Congress still hoped to avoid a clash with the President. Much depended upon Johnson's attitude toward freedmen, and he soon defied congressional opinion by vetoing two measures framed to extend federal protection to them. Arguing that Congress had no right to impose its will on Southern states without their concurrence, the President vetoed the Freedmen's Bureau bill of February 1866, through which Congress intended to extend and strengthen the wartime agency. Congress responded with a resolution proposing that no reconstructed state be admitted to the Union without congressional recognition. While Congress debated this measure, Johnson, addressing a crowd at the White House, denounced Stevens, Sumner, and Wendell Phillips by name as traitors to the American government. Such intemperance drove congressional moderates into Radical ranks and completed the break between Johnson and Congress.

By April 1866, Congress had achieved sufficient unity to challenge the President openly. Early that month it passed a Civil Rights Act over his veto. This law for the first time defined citizens as all persons born in the United States, except untaxed Indians. It stated further that citizens "of every race and color" should have equal legal and property rights. Then on April 28 Congress received the long-awaited report of the Joint Committee. The report accepted the Radical view, as argued by Stevens and Sumner, that the Confederate states, by waging war against the United States, had reduced themselves to mere territories and as territories could reenter the Union only under conditions established by Congress. In June the Joint Committee reminded Congress that it dared not abandon the freedmen before it had guaranteed them their rights as citizens.

To place provisions of the Civil Rights Act beyond recall, the committee proposed the Fourteenth Amendment, which Congress adopted promptly. This amendment extended guarantees of citizenship and civil rights to freedmen. Specifically, it declared that all persons born or naturalized in the United States and subject to its jurisdiction were citizens of both the United States and the state in which they lived. The amendment further declared that no state could deny any citizen equal protection of the laws. Nor could any state "abridge the privileges or immunities of citizens of the United States . . . [or] deprive any person of life, liberty, or property, without due process of law." The amendment called for the reduction of a state's congressional representation in the same proportion that it denied qualified voters the franchise—a provision which Congress never enforced. The Fourteenth Amendment barred most high Confederates from public office, unless approved by a two-thirds vote of Congress. Finally, it outlawed the debt incurred by the Confederacy. Only when a state had ratified the amendment could it reenter the Union. Johnson denounced the amendment as a contravention of states' rights and urged the Southern states to reject it. Ten of them did, three unanimously, and it was temporarily defeated.

This conflict over civil rights set the stage for the bitter congressional campaign of 1866. Late in August, Johnson left Washington on a speaking tour which carried him as far west as Chicago and St. Louis. His effort proved disastrous. His speeches were vulgar, vindictive, and self-righteous; in violent language he denounced Congress and his enemies for subverting the government. He had fought treason in the South, he said; he was now prepared to fight it in the North. Having dissipated much of his Republican support, he found himself seeking salvation in the Democratic party, which was again upholding the principle of white rule in the South and black inequality in the North. Republican campaigning turned Johnson's affiliation with Democrats into a political liability. Radicals accused the President of attempting to return the government to the enemies of the Union and the Negro. Those who rejected the Radical program, declared Stevens, could join Copperheads and rebels. During the campaign, the Republicans "waved the bloody shirt" to keep alive the wartime hatreds and to identify the Democratic party with treason. This appeal to war patriotism proved eminently successful. Congressional elections in 1866 saw a Radical tidal wave which gave the Republicans control of every Northern state legislature, every contested governorship, and shortly thereafter two-thirds working majorities in the House of Representatives and the Senate.

Congressional Reconstruction

When Congress met in December 1866, the Radicals possessed essential control of Reconstruction. To reconstruct the South on the foundation of racial equality, Radicals had to slow the process of reunion, force the South to discard its Black Codes, and establish political and legal bases of civil rights and black suffrage. This effort to secure an acceptable place in Southern life for the freedmen constituted the core of Radical legislation.

Two years after Appomattox Congress launched its full program of Reconstruction. It declared its basic will in the First Reconstruction Act of March 1867, a measure affirming that "no legal State governments or adequate protection for life or property" existed in any of the eleven states of the former Confederacy except Tennessee. Passed over a presidential veto, the act declared all Johnson governments illegal. To establish Radical control, the Reconstruction Act divided the South into five military districts, each to be placed under a military commander charged with preserving law and order. The act provided that, when a state constitutional convention, chosen under black and white suffrage, had framed a constitution in conformity with the federal constitution, that constitution could be submitted to Congress for its approval. When the state received acceptance and adopted the Fourteenth Amendment, it would gain representation in Congress.

Radicals feared that Johnson might subvert the program through his refusal to enforce the laws. To limit the President's power over the execution of policy, Congress, in March 1867, supported the First Reconstruction Act with two additional measures. The Tenure of Office Act forbade the President to remove civil officers approved by the Senate without first obtaining the Senate's consent. The Command of the Army Act required the President to issue military orders only through the General of the Army, U. S. Grant. Radicals resorted to these extraordinary invasions of Executive authority specifically to prevent Johnson from securing control of the military arm of the government and using it to thwart their Reconstruction program. Not satisfied even with these restrictions, some members of Congress believed that success of the Radical design demanded nothing less than Johnson's removal from office.

In February 1868, Johnson attempted to replace Secretary of War Edwin Stanton with General U. S. Grant. The Committee on Reconstruction now had a pretext to place an impeachment resolution before the House. This body quickly voted to bring the President to trial before the Senate. By early March the House had drawn up eleven articles, ten of which referred to the Tenure of Office Act. Article 10 accused the President of attempting, through his intemperate harangues, to bring Congress into contempt and disgrace. On March 5, Chief Justice Chase organized the Senate as a court of impeachment. In a trial of two months' duration, the prosecution made a vigorous and determined effort to convict Johnson. The critical vote of May 16, on the final article of impeachment, was 35 to 19, failing by one vote to achieve the necessary two-thirds majority. Although he had earlier denounced every Reconstruction measure, Johnson now abandoned his official opposition and appointed able military officers over the five military districts, permitting Radical Reconstruction to move forward uninhibited.

Simultaneously with its successful defense of the First Reconstruction Act against Executive encroachment, Congress sustained the program's constitutionality against the adverse decision of the Supreme Court in the case of *ex parte Milligan* (1866). In this decision the Court had held that continuance of military rule as practiced in Indiana during the war was an unconstitutional usurpation of power in an area where civil courts were open. The fact that courts were open in the South in March 1867 challenged the constitutionality of the First Reconstruction Act even before its passage through Congress. When *ex parte McCardle*, a similar case already on the Court's schedule, threatened to put the new law to the test, Congress passed a measure over the President's veto which withdrew appellate jurisdiction from the Court in matters of habeas corpus. The Court bowed to this legislation, not wishing to challenge Congress so directly. By July 1868, enough states had ratified the Fourteenth Amendment to put that constitutional guarantee of civil liberty into effect.

Reconstruction in the South

No Republican effort at civil reform could have prevented the opposition and resentment of those who in 1860 had preferred disunion and war to any serious alterations in Southern institutions. To scornful Southerners Yankee "carpetbaggers" who invaded the South were adventurers bent on plundering that section under the guise of civil reform. "Scalawags," Southern whites who aided carpetbaggers, were simply traitors to the traditions and best interests of the South. Blacks, usually ignorant and illiterate, emerged as the dupes whose votes their white protagonists exploited for private advantage.

Northerners who played a role in Reconstruction politics entered the South for a variety of reasons. Some, as Union soldiers, had been attracted by the Southern climate; others came with capital, or perhaps with no more than energy, to rebuild the Southern economy. Among them were travelers, missionaries, and agents of the Freedmen's Bureau. If some were opportunists, most were either genuine humanitarians or simply ordinary Northerners in search of an honest living. Carpetbaggers who entered Reconstruction governments were probably motivated less by a desire to capitalize on the sudden invasion of Northern political power than by a desire to guide the South back into the Union and restore its access to Northern markets and capital.

Southern scalawags also were a complex and varied group. Among their numbers there were opportunists in search of advantages that temporary and unanticipated political power might bestow. Some were among the South's most distinguished citizens, but many came from the yeoman farmer class. Southern ex-Whigs especially found an alliance with Republicans in Reconstruction governments both natural and promising. Scalawags were the least stable element in the Southern-Radical coalition. They were determined, as were many carpetbaggers, to put the war-torn Southern economy on the road to recovery. If the price of restoring the South to its rightful place in the Union was acceptance of Radical rule, the scalawags regarded the bargain a good one. But as Southerners they had no genuine interest in extending civil and political rights to blacks.

Every Reconstruction government rested ultimately on Negro suffrage, although blacks themselves controlled none of them. Blacks sat in all the state legislatures but seldom achieved high executive positions. In South Carolina, however, blacks outnumbered whites in the Legislature; they occupied such positions as lieutenant gover-

Several blacks served in Congress during Reconstruction. Left, Senator Blanche Kelso Bruce of Mississippi, an escaped Virginia slave, served from 1875 to 1881. Middle, John Mercer Langston was representative from Virginia in 1890–1891. Right, Robert B. Elliott, representative from South Carolina, served two terms in Washington.

nor, secretary of state, treasurer, speaker of the House, and associate justice of the state Supreme Court. Mississippi, Louisiana, and Florida also elected blacks to high state offices. Altogether fourteen blacks represented the South in the United States House of Representatives; H. R. Revels and Blanche Kelso Bruce, both from Mississippi, served in the United States Senate. Blacks developed some leadership, but in general carpetbaggers and scalawags dominated Southern Reconstruction governments. Blacks seldom demanded more than equal political and civil rights. To gain their ends in cooperation with Southern whites, they made no effort to build a black party or operate outside the Radical political organization. Newly enfranchised freedmen did not always use their power wisely or effectively. Without property, experience, or education, they were easily intimidated and misled by Republicans and Democrats alike.

Radical rule began in the South with the calling of state conventions to form new constitutions for the Southern states. These conventions, dominated by Radicals, were derided by their enemies as "black and tan" conventions. Pro-Johnson Southern whites heaped enough abuse on them to cast doubt on the seriousness of the entire constitution-making process. One

newspaper editor termed the South Carolina convention the "maddest, most infamous revolution in history." Actually the Southern conventions made generally modest innovations. Delegates to several conventions proposed land laws designed to break up large estates, but all such measures failed to secure the necessary support. The new constitutions proclaimed the principle of equal rights before the law but remained vague on questions of racial segregation in education and public conveyances; many avoided such issues completely. They made no effort to disenfranchise former Confederate sympathizers or to establish restrictions on officeholding that went beyond those listed in the Fourteenth Amendment. On the other hand, they removed antebellum discriminations on regional representation, especially in Virginia, North Carolina, and South Carolina. They increased the rights of women and provided for improved systems of taxation, more equitable codes of law, and broader opportunities in education. The convention of South Carolina, the special target of Democratic abuse, produced the first genuinely democratic constitution in that state's history, one notably different from that state's prewar constitution with its upper house based on wealth.

Whatever their determination to rule well, the

new governments could not have escaped the charges of corruption and failure brought against them by Southern whites momentarily deprived of political power. Unfortunately, too, the record of Southern Reconstruction often justified the accusations. The incompetence, dishonesty, and inexperience of new officeholders produced corruption everywhere, with South Carolina and Louisiana creating the poorest records of all. Governor Henry C. Warmoth of Louisiana reputedly pocketed $100,000 one year, on a salary of $8,000. The South Carolina Legislature once paid over $200,000 for furniture not worth $18,000; it voted its speaker $1,000 to cover his losses in a horse race. Under the heading of "supplies," the Legislature voted itself perfumes, wines, whisky, watches, and carriages. Such loose expenditures sent state debts soaring. The South Carolina debt tripled between 1868 and 1871. In 1872, the total state indebtedness of the eleven former members of the Confederacy was $132 million. Such a record seemed to condemn Radical rule and forecast the ultimate failure of the Republican experiment.

Yet the full account was not that dismal, and the carpetbaggers, scalawags, and blacks alone could not be blamed for all the corruption, extravagance, and vulgarity which existed. Radical governments faced the same challenges of social disorganization and economic expansion which exerted pressure on governmental integrity everywhere in the nation. The Whisky Ring in St. Louis and the Tweed Ring in New York stole millions during the postwar decade. Much of the Southern indebtedness resulted less from waste than from expenditures for roads, public works, education, poor relief, and social welfare. Many governments which followed Reconstruction were no more honest than those of the Reconstruction period. Some repudiated their state debts and compelled investors to bear the losses. Radical governments, whatever their weaknesses, wrote into the record a considerable body of social and economic legislation destined to stand the test of time. Even the new constitutions long survived the return of white rule.

The Election of 1868

Reconstruction again dominated national politics in the presidential election of 1868. The Republican Convention met at Chicago on May 20, several days after the failure of the impeachment proceedings against President Johnson. By a unanimous vote on the first ballot, it chose General Ulysses S. Grant as its presidential candidate and, for the vice presidency, Schuyler Colfax of Indiana. Grant served the needs of the Republican party admirably, for, as a popular war hero and strategist of victory, he simplified the Republican task of capitalizing on the lingering emotions of patriotism generated by the Civil War. Grant, moreover, held no political principles or notions of executive leadership which would challenge congressional Reconstruction.

The Republican platform contained a strong endorsement of Radical Reconstruction. On the question of black suffrage the Republicans hedged. Some Northern states had not granted voting rights to blacks within their borders and did not intend to do so. Republican leaders, therefore, dared not make suffrage for blacks a forthright party issue. The Republican platform advocated lower taxes, encouragement of immigration, payment of the national debt, and pensions for veterans.

To challenge the Republicans on the central issue of Reconstruction, the Democratic party nominated New York's war governor, Horatio Seymour, a persistent critic of Radical Reconstruction and Negro suffrage. The party's strongly worded anti-Reconstruction platform accused the Republican Congress of subjecting the ten Southern states "to military despotism and negro supremacy." Republicans rallied against the Democratic attack. Waving the bloody shirt, Oliver P. Morton of Indiana, a leading Radical, termed Seymour's nomination a "declaration of the renewal of the rebellion." A Democratic victory, Morton warned, would return the South to the enemy and halt the work of Reconstruction. In the South, Union League clubs organized the black vote for Republicans.

Handicapped by such Republican electioneering, the Democratic party hoped to capture the Western farm vote on the currency question. Much of the Republican economic program, including banking and tariff legislation, had been designed to serve the nation's expanding business interests. The grain-producing Middle West exhibited increasing discontent at this Republican favoritism and demanded relief from declining farm prices. Many debtors believed that higher prices could be brought about by inflating currency through an expanded use of greenbacks. But Congress in the Funding Act of 1866 had adopted a deflationary program by retiring wartime greenbacks: $10 million in the first six months and $4 million or less per month thereafter. This contraction of the currency during a time of falling prices produced a storm of protest and forced Congress in 1868 to suspend the policy of contraction. Responding to this sentiment, the Democratic party advocated the "Ohio Idea," proposing that the creditors of government be paid in greenbacks except when they expressly demanded payment in gold or silver. The Republicans based their hard money appeal to the West on Unionist sentiment,

reminding farmers that the redemption of government obligations, which had been contracted to preserve the Union, in anything but gold repudiated those debts. Having deftly neutralized the Democratic appeal to Western debtors, the Republican party again made Radical Reconstruction the central issue.

Grant won a solid victory and carried twenty-six states, leaving Seymour only eight. The general won 53 percent of the popular vote. His success in the North was impressive enough, but he also carried Tennessee and five of the former Confederate states where black suffrage had been imposed—North Carolina, South Carolina, Florida, Alabama, and Arkansas.

Clearly Republicans had a heavy stake in the Southern black vote. To assure it in the future, they lost their recent hesitancy and in December 1868 submitted the Fifteenth Amendment, which declared: "The right of the citizens of the United States to vote shall not be denied or abridged by the United States or by any state on account of race, color, or previous condition of servitude." Congress added enforcement measures which reenacted the Civil Rights Act of 1866 and provided penalties for violations of the Fourteenth and Fifteenth Amendments. Virginia, Mississippi, Texas, and Georgia ratified the new amendment as a condition for representation in Congress. By March 1870, the measure had been put into general effect throughout the nation.

The Grant Regime

The Grant administration is well remembered for its scandal. Still the nation's progress in business, transportation, and agriculture was scarcely influenced by the corruption in the federal government. Many of the policies that mattered had been adopted by previous Republican Congresses: the protective tariff; the national banking system; the new currency based on National Bank notes; subsidies for internal improvements; the Homestead law; grants of land,

timber, and mineral resources to railroads and other private industries. It was a narrow program; to its critics it seemed to serve only the lords of the earth.

To meet the varied needs of all, the federal government required determined and dedicated national leadership. Many congressional Radicals who had given direction and purpose to Republican policy, especially in the area of Southern Reconstruction, had by 1869 either died, retired, or lost office. New leaders emerged to take control of the party. These were, in many instances, the bosses of the powerful Republican state machines in the North, organization men for whom political office represented opportunity for power and wealth, not service or reform. The spoils system was the essence of their authority; to sustain it they corrupted the federal civil service. In policy matters these "Stalwarts" were, above all, spokesmen of the status quo. Typical of their breed was Senator Roscoe Conkling of New York.

During the war years Washington had grown accustomed to political corruption, and after Appomattox the quest for special favors continued unabated. The opportunities presented by the "Great Barbecue," national riches spread by a generous government, brought a flood of wealth seekers into the capital. Railroad builders, financiers, business agents, and promoters profited handsomely from lucrative land grants and government contracts, special tariffs, hard money decisions, and a wide range of public expenditures. Even before Grant's presidency, the direct relation between business and government was bordering on the scandalous. Clearly the times called for vigorous White House leadership, and Grant, popular and independent, appeared eminently qualified to meet the challenge.

Yet Grant lacked the experience, knowledge, and character to protect either Congress or the White House from those who would prey on the government. Had Grant possessed the talent to consult with and learn from others, he might still have surrounded himself with men of integrity who could have educated him. But his ability to analyze and judge, a deficiency which he readily admitted, made him an easy victim for the coarser politicians who, by showing deference, could gain his ear and slowly and deliberately urge their ideas upon him until he accepted them as his own. Unable to impose high standards of honesty on the men around him, Grant permitted the White House to become the focus of governmental corruption.

Grant's presidency reflected the materialism of the day. Already, during the immediate postwar years, businessmen had showered this Union hero with lavish gifts. Grant saw no need to curtail the flow after he entered the White House. After years of poverty, he accepted with both hands favors thrust upon him—without ever suspecting the price to the country of the reasonable requests which he granted. It was the President's infatuation with wealth that made possible such episodes as the "Black Friday" gold scandal of September 1869. Having convinced the President that he should not release gold from the federal Treasury, Jay Gould and "Diamond Jim" Fisk, two particularly unscrupulous business adventurers, set out to corner the gold market. Eventually Grant released enough gold to break the price, but not before countless businessmen, unable to acquire sufficient gold at a reasonable price to meet their obligations, were ruined.

Foreign Affairs

Not even in the realm of foreign affairs could Grant avoid charges of corruption. The West Indian island of Santo Domingo had won its independence from Spain in 1865. Shortly after Grant entered the presidency, a group of promoters convinced him that the United States should annex the island. Strangely enough, the Dominican leaders themselves were so thoroughly convinced that they could best solidify their economic and political status on the island through American control that Grant's representative was able, during a visit late in 1869, to negotiate a treaty of annexation. Grant attempted to force the treaty through the Senate, only to face the determined opposition of Foreign Relations Committee Chairman Charles Sumner, who denounced the annexation as a private deal to exploit the island's riches. Because the President failed to secure ratification of this treaty, he deprived Sumner of his chairmanship.

This episode did not prevent Secretary of State Hamilton Fish from negotiating with Britain the Treaty of Washington in 1871. Since 1869, American and British representatives had debated the question of the *Alabama* claims. United States officials insisted that England compensate this nation for losses suffered by Union shipping at the hands of Confederate cruisers built or armed in British shipyards during the Civil War. Washington diplomats presented claims amounting to some $19 million; to this Senator Sumner added indirect losses which he thought obligated Britain to pay the United States $2 billion. Complicating the issue of claims were British-American disputes over the boundary line through the San Juan Islands in the Pacific Northwest and the matter of fishing privileges off Canada's eastern coast. The Treaty of Washington assigned the question of *Alabama* claims to a five-man commission, which awarded the United States $15 million in damages. The German Emperor arbitrated the boundary line through the San Juan Islands, upholding in general the claims of the United States. Not until 1877, however, did a three-man commission settle the fisheries dispute. It awarded Britain $5 million for additional concessions made to American fishermen along the Canadian coast. The Treaty of Washington and the resulting settlements were important in at least two major respects: they constituted a victory for the principle of arbitration, and they indicated a growing feeling of goodwill and cooperation between the two leading Atlantic powers. This treaty was one of the few distinct accomplishments of Grant's administration.

But Secretary Fish gained another success when he resisted domestic pressures to involve the United States in the affairs of Cuba. The Cuban revolt against Spain, erupting in 1868, aroused widespread sympathy in the United States. Members of Congress demanded that the administration aid the cause of Cuban liberty by recognizing the belligerency of the insurgents. Fish convinced the President that involvement would not serve the national interest of the United States. The Secretary met another crisis in 1873 when Spaniards captured the *Virginius,* a Cuban ship flying the American flag, and shot fifty-three passengers and members of the crew, some of them Americans. This time Fish obtained an apology and an indemnity from Spain and again averted serious trouble.

The Liberal Republicans

For those who expected much of Grant, the failures of his presidency were appalling. Young Henry Adams became disillusioned early. "That two thousand years after Alexander the Great and Julius Caeser," he wrote in 1869, "a man like Grant should be called . . . the highest product of the most advanced evolution, made evolution ludicrous. . . . The progress of evolution from President Washington to President Grant was alone enough to upset Darwin." So thoroughly had the Republican party under Grant lost its capacity for direct and efficient performance that many of its most thoughtful leaders wondered if it had outlived its usefulness.

By 1870 many Republican partisans were in open revolt against their national leadership. The demand for reform soon spread to such key leaders as Carl Schurz and Charles Francis Adams, as well as Republican editors, such as Horace Greeley of the *New York Tribune* and Edwin L. Godkin of the *Nation.* When it became clear that the Stalwarts would gain Grant's renomination, reform-minded Republicans met at Cincinnati on May 1, 1872, to organize the Liberal Republican party. They advocated a program of tariff and civil service reform to halt the plunder of the government, and an end to military rule in the South. No longer did old free-

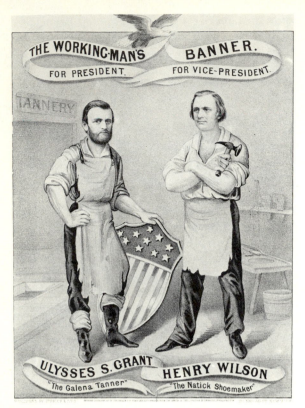

Ulysses S. Grant and his running mate, as depicted in an 1872 campaign poster.

The Granger Collection

old abolitionists with a difficult choice. As idealists they abhorred the low state to which Grant and the Stalwarts had reduced the federal government. Most abolitionists, however, were still concerned over the welfare of the freedmen; they saw that the Liberal Republican program of sectional reconciliation would be achieved only at the price of Negro rights. Frederick Douglass, the black abolitionist, termed the Liberal Republican movement dangerous to the Negro cause and concluded that, whatever its faults, the Republican party "has within it the only element of friendship for the colored man's rights." Most old abolitionists accepted Douglass's reasoning and supported Grant's reelection campaign.

To defeat Grant, Liberal Republicans needed the full support of the national Democratic party. But Greeley, who was selected over Charles Francis Adams as the Liberal Republican standard-bearer, had been a lifelong critic of Democrats and during previous campaigns had waved the bloody shirt with apparent enthusiasm. Still the Democratic party, if it would recover its lost position in national politics, had no choice but to endorse Greeley. This action reinforced the posture of regular Republicans as the nation's only black protagonists. Gerrit Smith summarized such sentiments well when he declared that the "anti-Slavery battle is not yet fought out—and, until it is, we shall need Grant's continued leadership." Meanwhile Grant, who had swept the Republican Convention in June, faced little organized opposition. In victory, he lost only six states, none in the North. His majority of 700,000 popular votes was nothing less than a landslide.

soilers care to fight for Negro rights. Continued Republican interference in the South, Greeley warned, would merely force Southern Whigs into Democratic ranks and terminate abruptly all rights the blacks had won. Liberal Republicans in May 1872 brought pressure on Congress and secured passage of a general amnesty act pardoning all but a few hundred Confederates who had held federal offices at the time of secession.

Liberal Republican moderation confronted the

More Corruption

Having been vindicated at the polls, public officials who supported Grant now pushed corruption to the point of open scandal. Lavish congressional handouts to railroad builders had included land worth more than $300 million; promoters

drew exorbitant profits from collusion in the negotiation of construction and equipment contracts. Congress had granted sizable loans to the Union Pacific and the Central Pacific; thereafter these railroads battled to prevent Congress from establishing conditions of repayment. The Crédit Mobilier, a construction company organized to enable Union Pacific stockholders to profit from construction contracts, distributed stock to key members of the House and Senate. A congressional investigation in the autumn of 1872 implicated such leading Republicans as Vice President Schuyler Colfax and Senator James W. Patterson of New Hampshire. A year later the same Congress not only voted itself a salary increase of 50 percent, from $5,000 to $7,500, but also made it retroactive for two years. So great was the popular outrage that Congress repealed the "Salary Grab Act."

No less dramatic were new scandals within the administration itself. During the spring of 1875, Grant's third Secretary of the Treasury, Benjamin H. Bristow, uncovered the Whisky Ring, a combination of St. Louis distillers and federal revenue agents who had defrauded the government of millions of dollars of internal revenue. When the investigation reached a member of the White House staff, Grant became defensive. The President's prestige, committed fully to the defense, kept his crony out of prison. Another major scandal rocked the administration that year, with the resignation of Secretary of War W. W. Belknap. For five years Belknap had received illicit payments totaling more than $24,000 from a corrupt post trader at Fort Sill in Indian Territory. The House brought impeachment charges against the Secretary, but when Grant accepted Belknap's resignation, the Senate refused to proceed with the trial. By 1875 the spoils system had so undermined the civil service that Grant abandoned the competitive system.

The End of Reconstruction

Had the country's prosperity continued, the Stalwart Republicans might have withstood the challenge of another presidential campaign. The well-publicized failures of Grant's first term had not prevented the general's sweep in 1872. But thereafter factors more pervading than scandals undermined the Stalwart position. After 1873, Grant and his supporters faced the discontent of a depressed nation. Ambitious businessmen and promoters, caught up in the postwar speculative spirit, had overextended the country's railroads as well as its agricultural, commercial, and industrial capacity. So inflated had the economy become through credit expansion that the failure in September 1873 of Jay Cooke, financier of the Northern Pacific Railroad, was sufficient to send the national economy tumbling into a five-year depression.

Hard on the heels of the crash came a wave of Democratic victories in the 1874 election. This election revolutionized the composition of the House of Representatives, turning a two-thirds Republican majority into a Democratic majority of seventy. In the Senate, Republicans maintained a narrow majority. Democrats broke the Republican hold in Pennsylvania, Ohio, and Massachusetts; coalitions of Democrats and Grangers threatened Republican dominance in several prairie states.

In the South, race prejudice continued to undermine the entire Republican effort. Prejudice had an economic base; its easiest victories were among low-status whites whose only claim to distinction was the color of their skin. Oldline Whigs shared the general belief in white supremacy, but their social and economic security reduced their fear of black equality. They eventually accepted Negro suffrage and the principles of the Fourteenth Amendment. Democratic leaders faced the choice of competing with Republicans for the black vote or resorting to demagoguery in an effort to drive blacks out of politics and to rebuild the Southern Democratic party on lower-class white votes. They made the latter decision, exerting whatever pressure the destruction of white and black resistance demanded. Through such clandestine organizations as the Ku-Klux Klan, founded at Pulaski, Tennessee, in 1866, and Knights of the White Camellia, formed at New Orleans in 1867, they used violence and intimidation to weaken Radical control of Southern blacks.

Washington, faced with the weapons of illegal coercion, rejected the use of federal power to enforce the Fourteenth and Fifteenth Amendments. Blacks had long been a weak reed upon which to build political power and a program of civil rights in the South. Without land, the former slaves lacked the economic independence they required to resist political intimidation. But the causes of Radical failure in the South ran deeper. Racism and the general public disinterest in the plight of blacks everywhere undermined Radical influence even in the North. Liberal Republicans, joined by Northern businessmen, became convinced as early as 1872 that Negro rights held less promise for the Republican party and the nation than did a new political alignment between Northern Republicans and

A freedman being expelled from a railroad car at Philadelphia in 1856.

The Granger Collection

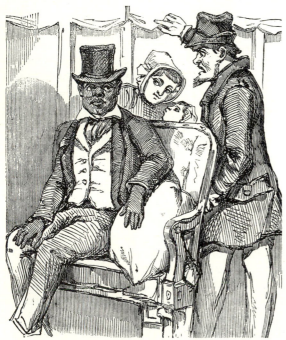

NEGRO EXPULSION FROM RAILWAY CAR, PHILADELPHIA.

Southern conservatives, whether ex-Whigs or Democrats. Yankee investors and promoters with Southern interests preferred the stability that would come from conservative white rule to the instability perpetuated by faltering Reconstruction governments.

Faced with their forthcoming loss of the House when Congress reconvened, the Republicans, on March 1, 1875, passed another Civil Rights Act which guaranteed equal rights to blacks in hotels, public conveyances, amusement centers, and juries. Through measures such as this the Republican party hoped to maintain some semblance of control over social evolution in the South.

But already the Supreme Court had begun to curtail federal encroachment on the traditional rights of the states. The important Slaughterhouse Cases of April 1873 grew out of Louisiana legislation which gave monopoly privileges to a single slaughterhouse in certain parishes of the state. Those denied business as a result of this monopoly, granted under corrupt conditions, charged that it violated the Fourteenth Amendment by taking their property without due process of law. The Supreme Court, however, decided that the Louisiana law did not violate the Fourteenth Amendment and declared that Congress had not intended to expand federal power to "the entire domain of civil rights heretofore belonging exclusively to the States." In *United States v. Reese* (1876) the Court limited the federal government's right to enforce suffrage in cases involving race and color. Thus Southern states gained the legal right to set special prerequisites, such as poll taxes, to restrict black suffrage. In 1883, the Supreme Court declared the Civil Rights Act of 1875 unconstitutional on grounds that the federal government had no right to protect civil rights against the actions of individuals or organizations. This decision set the stage for *Plessy v. Ferguson* in 1896, which permitted segregation on railroads if facilities available for Negroes were equal. Three years later, the Court extended the "separate but equal" concept to schools. The Supreme Court, upholding states' rights, had returned to the South the power to govern its race relations. Tennessee passed the first Jim Crow law in 1875, which separated the races on railroads and streetcars. The retreat from Radical Reconstruction had turned into a disorderly flight.

The Election of 1876

Encouraged by its victories in 1874 and the mounting failures of the Grant administration, the Democratic party entered the campaign of 1876 with high expectations. Beginning with Tennessee in 1869, all the states of the South except Louisiana, South Carolina, and Florida were again under Democratic control. Democrats, like Republicans, differed on many of the national economic issues, but for their presidential candidate they agreed readily on Samuel J. Tilden. This wealthy New York lawyer, as governor of his state, had led an assault on Tammany Hall, the core of New York's political corruption, and had sent its head, "Boss" Tweed, to the penitentiary. For Tilden's running mate the Democrats chose Thomas A. Hendricks of Indiana. The platform called for "immediate reform" in broad areas of American political and economic life. It demanded an end to Radical Reconstruction. It attacked the protective tariff; denounced Republican financial policies, especially excessive spending; demanded that public lands be reserved for actual settlers; and called for civil service reform.

Despite the Republican record, Stalwarts favored Grant's renomination. Many Republican businessmen, however, were tired of corruption and preferred new leadership. The "Half-breeds," moderates who opposed the Stalwarts but had not bolted to the Liberal Republicans in 1872, favored James G. Blaine, former Speaker of the House. Unable to nominate Grant but bitterly opposed to Blaine, the administration forces accepted Rutherford B. Hayes as a compromise candidate. Hayes's record as reform governor of Ohio made him equally acceptable to Republican moderates and liberals. Expressing pride in the party's history, the Republican platform warned that the Democratic party "was

the same in character and spirit as when it sympathized with treason." Republicans declared that they were "sacredly pledged" to enforce the Thirteenth, Fourteenth, and Fifteenth Amendments and protect all citizens in the enjoyment of their rights. On economic questions, the party promised a sound currency, tariff adjustment, and opposition to further land grants to large corporations. The Greenback party, responding to the discontent of Northern debtors, nominated New York industrialist and philanthropist Peter Cooper on a platform that demanded inflation through greater issues of paper money.

In November, the initial returns gave Tilden a 250,000-vote plurality, and even Republican journals conceded his election. He had carried Connecticut, New York, New Jersey, and Indiana, as well as the entire South, and had 184 uncontested electoral votes. Hayes had 166. But the voting in Louisiana, South Carolina, and Florida—the three Southern states still under carpetbag rule—had been grossly irregular, permitting Republican officials there to claim Republican victories. If Hayes could get the 19 votes of these three states, he would have 185 electoral votes, or a majority of 1. There was also one disputed vote from Oregon.

The contest quickly shifted to the three Southern states where the returns were in dispute. Amidst charges and countercharges of graft, corruption, and vote stealing, both Democrats and Republicans claimed victory. Early in December the Republican electors from Louisiana, Florida, and South Carolina met in their capitals and cast their votes for Hayes, while Democratic electors balloted for Tilden. Both sets of returns were then transmitted to Washington. What votes would be counted and by whom? The

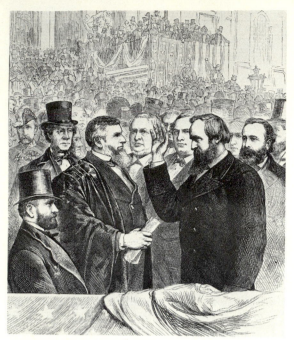

The inauguration of President Rutherford B. Hayes,
March 4, 1877.

Constitution stated that "the President of the Senate shall, in the presence of the Senate and House of Representatives, open all the Certificates and the Votes shall then be counted." But it did not specify who would do the counting. If the president of the Senate—a Republican—should make the count, he would give the disputed ballots to Hayes; if representatives of the House did the counting, Tilden would get the votes.

Congress created a special electoral commission of fifteen men, made up of five from each house of Congress and five Supreme Court justices, to pass judgment on the contested election returns. Among its members were seven Republicans, seven Democrats, and one Independent. When Justice David Davis, the Independent, refused to serve, the Republicans received the fifteenth membership. The commission refused to look behind the returns and, ignoring the irregularities on both sides, gave all the contested votes to Hayes. There was much uneasiness in the country between December 1876, and March 1877; there was even some talk of renewed civil war, but moderate and conservative views prevailed. Hayes's election received official recognition on March 2, 1877, only two days before Grant was to leave office.

Hayes's victory resulted from what scholars have called the Compromise of 1877. Republican leadership, victors in the contested election, faced the necessity of forestalling possible violence and a Democratic filibuster in the House against the completion of the count. Republicans turned to Southern conservatives. To win their support, Hayes had only to promise certain economic benefits—federal aid for flood control, harbor improvements, and railroad subsidies—along with the termination of federal efforts to protect blacks against political and social discrimination. The nation's economic interests played a major part in winning support for the Compromise of 1877.

Hayes had never favored Radical Reconstruction, and he believed, like Lincoln, that the future of the Republic hinged on a new coalition of conservatives, North and South. Nor did he object to the distribution of some federal largess in the South. At the same time, Southern leaders admitted that the "solid South" was not very solid and that the union of ex-Whigs and Democrats within the Democratic party, achieved under the pressure of white-supremacy propaganda, was only a marriage of convenience. During December it became clear that many Southerners would support Hayes, thus assuring an uneventful inauguration. The Compromise of 1877 gave Republicans the presidency and conservative Southern whites dominance over the Negro, plus economic benefits such as federal aid for railroad construction. In April 1877, the new President withdrew the remaining Union troops—now only token forces—from the states of Louisiana, Florida, and South Carolina and thus officially terminated the era of Radical Reconstruction.

For Republicans Reconstruction had been a successful political venture. Their new coalition with Southern conservatives assured the continued triumph of American industrial capitalism. The Republican party had failed in the South, but this mattered little. In the North, Republicans had employed their varied emotional and economic appeals with such effectiveness that the loss of the South to the Democrats scarcely endangered their control of Congress or the White House. Despite the Democratic resurgence in the North after 1872, the Republican party held its own in New England and the Middle states. In the teeming Great Lakes region and in the rapidly expanding West, Republican mastery was complete. Ultimately it was the party's identification with the Union that gave it the unchallengeable advantage of respectability. In many areas of the Midwest, Brand Whitlock later recalled, "it was natural to be a Republican; it was more than that, it was inevitable that one should be a Republican; it was not a matter of intellectual choice, it was a process of biological selection. The Republican party . . . was a fundamental and self-evident thing, like life, and liberty, and the pursuit of happiness, or like the flag, or the federal judiciary. . . . It was merely a synonym for patriotism, another name for the nation."

Only in their effort to bring civil rights to the South had the Republicans failed. Emancipation had neither revolutionized Southern society nor seriously altered the Negro's place in Southern life. Although blacks voted in many parts of the South until the 1890s, their votes after 1876 were usually controlled by conservative whites. Throughout the "black belt" of the South, upper-class whites attached the majority of blacks to the land as tenant farmers or sharecroppers; thereafter, perennial poverty and indebtedness would keep them economically immobile, socially segregated, and politically inert. From such conditions the freedmen had no escape except to federal protection, but the Supreme Court had already severely limited federal jurisdiction in civil rights cases, and the Republican party, having reaped its rewards elsewhere, had lost most of its interest in the problems of the South. What remained to give the Negro, if not immediate comfort, at least ultimate hope, were the Fourteenth and Fifteenth Amendments—the lasting monuments to black rights surviving amid the ashes of Radical Reconstruction.

SUGGESTED READINGS

The tragic view of Reconstruction, highly critical of both the Radical leadership in the North and the Negro-dominated governments in the South, found its first major expression in W. A. Dunning's *Reconstruction: Political and Economic** (1907). This general approach to Reconstruction continued in Walter L. Fleming's *The Sequel of Appomattox* (1919); and Robert S. Henry's *The Story of Reconstruction* (1938). That this view is still much alive is made clear in E. M. Coulter's *The South during Reconstruction* (1947) and Hodding Carter's *The Angry Scar* (1959).

Much of the newer writing treats Reconstruction with sympathy. The first major contribution to this school was W. E. B. Du Bois's *Black Reconstruction in America** (1935). Three superb studies of Reconstruction, all moderately pro-Radical, are Kenneth M. Stampp's *The Era of Reconstruction* (1965); John Hope Franklin's *Reconstruction: After the Civil War** (1961); and Rembert W. Patrick's *The Reconstruction of the Nation** (1967). James G. Randall and David Donald's *The Civil War and Reconstruction* (rev. ed., 1961) is remarkably balanced in judgment.

Among the older pro-Johnson studies are Howard K. Beale's *The Critical Year* (1930) and George Fort Milton's *The Age of Hate: Andrew Johnson and the Radicals* (1930). Many of the postwar studies of Johnson have been critical. Three examples of the new writing are E. L. McKitrick's *Andrew Johnson and Reconstruction** (1960), LaWanda and J. H. Cox's *Politics, Principle, and Prejudice, 1865–1866* (1963); and W. R. Brock's *An American Crisis: Congress and Reconstruction** (1963).

Useful biographical studies of Reconstruction are B. P. Thomas and H. M. Hyman's *Stanton: The Life and Times of Lincoln's Secretary of War* (1962); R. N. Current's *Old Thad Stevens* (1942); F. M. Brodie's *Thaddeus Stevens* (1959); and H. L. Trefousse's *Benjamin Franklin Wade* (1963). A careful analysis of abolitionist attitudes toward Reconstruction is James M. McPherson's *The Struggle for Equality: Abolitionists and the Negro in the Civil War and Reconstruction** (1964).

On the Northern invasion of the South after the war see Otto H. Olsen's *Carpetbagger's Crusade: The Life of Albion Winegar Tourgée* (1965). Also valuable on this theme are Martin Abbott's *The Freedmen's Bureau in South Carolina, 1865–1872* (1967) and James E. Seften's *The United States Army and Reconstruction, 1865–1877* (1967). On the Negro in the South during Reconstruction see V. L. Wharton's *The Negro in Mississippi, 1865–1900** (1947) and Otis A. Singletary's *The Negro Militia and Reconstruction** (1957).

Two books which develop the issues and personalities of the 1868 campaign are C. H. Coleman's *The Election of 1868* (1933) and Stewart Mitchell's *Horatio Seymour* (1938). Viewing Grant's leadership through the eyes of a leading Cabinet member is Allan Nevins's *Hamilton Fish: The Inner History of the Grant Administration* (1936). Earle D. Ross's *The Liberal Republican Movement* (1919) is old but sound. Martin B. Duberman's excellent biography *Charles Francis Adams** (1961) and G. G. Van Deusen's *Horace Greeley** (1953) analyze the campaign roles of two leading Liberal Republicans.

Paul H. Buck's *The Road to Reunion. 1865–1900** (1937) analyzes superbly the forces that brought Reconstruction to an end. One factor, the Ku-Klux Klan, is discussed in S. F. Horn's *The Invisible Empire* (1939). Volumes that deal thoughtfully with the dilemma of the blacks following Reconstruction are C. Vann Woodward's *The Strange Career of Jim Crow** (1953) and *Origins of the New South, 1877–1913** (1951), and G. B. Tindall's *South Carolina Negroes, 1877–1900** (1952). Paul H. Haworth's *The Hayes-Tilden Disputed Presidential Election of 1876* (1906) is still rewarding. More recent interpretations of the 1876 election are Harry Bernard's *Rutherford B. Hayes and His America* (1954) and especially C. Vann Woodward's *Reunion and Reaction: The Compromise of 1877 and the End of Reconstruction** (2d ed., 1956).

*indicates availability in paperback.

17

Industrial Expansion and the Age of Big Business

In the thirty years after Appomattox, the industrial revolution transformed American life. Between 1860 and 1894, the United States advanced from fourth to first among the manufacturing nations of the world. This rise to industrial preeminence, with its many ramifications throughout American life and society, was the most significant national development between the Civil War and the Great War of 1914. Business and industrial leaders created a truly modern America. Transcontinental railroads, deep mines, smoking factories, spurting oil wells, and huge lumber mills all testified to the economic growth and power of the young industrial giant.

In 1859, America's 140,433 industrial establishments produced some $2 billion worth of products; in 1914, 275,791 establishments turned out products valued at more than $24 billion. Before the Civil War agriculture had been the leading producer of wealth, but by 1890 industry had replaced farming as the most important sector of the economy. Between 1860 and 1914 industrial production rose at a rate of about 5.38 percent annually. No nation before or since has equaled the American record in producing and distributing goods.

This burst of industrial activity was no new development but rather the acceleration and intensification of trends already in existence. The production of basic raw materials and manufactures had grown rapidly during the 1840s and 1850s, creating the basis of an industrial economy.

Economic historians disagree on the precise effect of the Civil War on the country's industrial development. Some evidence indicates that the total industrial output was not immediately greater, as a result of war, than it would have been had peace prevailed. The war actually hurt certain industries, such as cotton textiles, and ruined most Southern industry. Nonetheless, the Civil War established a base for productive facilities and capital formation, both of which facilitated postwar industrial expansion. Moreover, it furnished the springboard from which many businessmen jumped into successful industrial careers.

The Civil War had other consequences. The agrarian South was banished from federal councils, and national affairs came under the control of those who favored industrial development. The victorious Republicans maintained a close alliance with big business. And the government did not simply provide a favorable atmosphere for entrepreneurs; it supplied them with direct and indirect assistance. Banking and business groups received high tariffs, a stable national banking system, and the *de facto* gold standard after 1878. Railroads profited from direct aid through grants of federal land. Federal land policies permitted industrial interests to monopolize much of the nation's natural resources, such as timber and minerals. A munificent government, in short, distributed valuable resources to private business in a generous—almost profligate—manner.

In addition, the federal and state governments encouraged industry indirectly by refusing to restrict or regulate business and by restraining labor with troops and court injunctions. Farm and labor demands for restrictions on monopoly behavior fell on the deaf ears of a government which heard only the voices of big business.

Even more fundamental to America's industrial expansion was the availability of abundant natural resources. The United States had vast quantities of coal, iron ore, oil, copper, lead, zinc, limestone, salt, sulfur, and other minerals, as well as lumber. Coal and oil were especially important as sources of power for manufacturing and transportation. Waterpower, particularly in the Northeast and South, provided another source of energy. During the late nineteenth century American industry shifted from animate power, furnished by men and animals, to inanimate power, furnished by engines and machines. The Mesabi Range in Minnesota contained huge stores of iron ore, the essential raw material for industrial development.

Natural resources, without technology to transform them into goods and commodities, have little value. It was improved machinery and new techniques of production, along with the division of labor and better organization of men and materials, that enabled United States industrialists to assume their commanding lead in the output of manufactured products during the late nineteenth century. Standardization and interchangeability of parts, for example, were fundamental to mass production. After 1900 assembly line techniques dominated such industries as farm machinery, machine tools, and automobiles. The Bessemer process for manufacturing steel and the practical application of electric power were notably important technological achievements. Inventions such as the telegraph, telephone, typewriter, cash register, and adding machine were also of inestimable value in business expansion.

The United States had not only adequate natural resources and technical know-how but also a sufficient supply of both common and skilled labor. Much of the labor force in manufacturing, mining, and transportation was recruited from the millions of immigrants who arrived after the Civil War; many other workers drifted into the industrial centers from farms where they were no longer needed. The rapidly increasing population played a dual role in the expanding economy; it provided both a labor supply and a market for mass-produced goods.

Industry required capital to build factories, to buy machines, and to purchase raw materials; the United States again possessed what it needed. Much of the money invested in shipping and commerce before the Civil War flowed into manufacturing during and after the war. Furthermore, personal and corporate profits were plowed back into individual businesses to purchase better machines and underwrite expansion. Finally, industrialists borrowed large amounts of capital abroad.

Leadership and organization played major roles in the rise of American business. After the Civil War, the corporate structure became the common means of organizing large-scale businesses. The corporation could gather almost limitless amounts of capital; it was permanent; and it possessed advantages before the law as a legal person. Thus, it was an ideal instrument through which to organize and operate huge industrial, transportation, and mining enterprises.

That business leadership which emerged during these years contributed greatly to America's industrial record. Edward H. Harriman and James J. Hill in railroading, John D. Rockefeller in oil, Andrew Carnegie in steel production, Philip D. Armour in meat-packing, and J. P. Morgan in banking were among the scores of industrial and business giants.

Some of the nation's leading entrepreneurs were ruthless operators, often outright scoundrels and thieves. Cornelius Vanderbilt, a shrewd, vain, uncouth transportation baron who controlled the New York Central Railroad, once reputedly declared of one of his actions: "Law! What do I care about the law? Hain't I got the power?" Men of this kind were indeed "robber barons." On the other hand, men such as John D. Rockefeller, Andrew Carnegie, and James J. Hill may aptly be called "industrial statesmen." They were vigorous and sometimes ruthless, but they demonstrated great skill and ability in organizing facilities to produce and distribute goods. They thought in expansive, world-spanning terms, and they efficiently organized men and materials on a scale never before known. They made fabulous personal fortunes while they contributed to the nation's economic expansion.

Another national asset was the popular desire for economic betterment. Americans believed —and still believe—in economic progress, in the personal profit motive, and in the principle of unlimited accumulation. They believed that economic success stemmed from hard work and thrift, and these virtues they cherished with almost religious fervor.

Transportation and Communication

Industrialism required efficient transportation; in the United States, an expanding railroad network met this need. The years from 1870 to the early twentieth century might accurately be labeled the "Railroad Age." In 1860, the United States had 30,626 miles of railroads. The New York Central, the Erie, and Pennsylvania, and the Baltimore and Ohio had blanketed the Northeast and penetrated the Midwest. The railroad system in the South was less developed, but on the eve of the Civil War it contained some 10,000 miles of track. Between 1860 and 1890 some 135,000 miles of track were constructed; by 1914 the United States boasted a rail network of 252,105 miles, more than that of all Europe.

The new transcontinental railroads after 1865 accounted for the rapid expansion in total mileage. Railroad enthusiasts had argued for direct rail connections between Chicago and the Pacific Coast before the Civil War, but it was not until after Congress chartered the Union Pacific and Central Pacific lines in 1864 that construction began. The nation's first transcontinental railroad was completed on May 10, 1869, when the two lines—the Union Pacific building west from Omaha and the Central Pacific moving east from San Francisco—joined near Ogden, Utah.

Meanwhile, the Northern Pacific, which had been chartered in 1864, ran into financial difficulty and was not completed until 1883. In the Southwest, the Southern Pacific and the Atchison, Topeka and Santa Fe reached the California coast in 1881 over track either owned or leased. In 1893, James J. Hill completed his Great Northern line from St. Paul to Puget Sound. Meanwhile railroad building in the South lagged. Still, by 1890 that section had more than 50,000 miles of operating railways.

Because the transcontinentals and other Western roads penetrated unsettled regions where there was little production, the railroad turned to the federal government for financial assistance or, more specifically, land grants. Following a grant to the Illinois Central in 1850, the Union Pacific received the first direct federal land grant in a bill of 1862. Congress liberalized the charter in 1864, granting the railroad ten alternate sections of land on each side of the track, or a total of 12,800 acres for each mile constructed. Besides this, the company received a 400-foot right-of-way, plus free timber and other building materials from the public domain. Congress made even more generous land grants to the Northern Pacific.

After 1871 land grants were discontinued; but between 1850 and 1871, the federal government gave away about 175,350,000 acres of land to the railroads. Since the railroads failed to fulfill some of the construction agreements, the final total was approximately 131,350,000 acres. The sale of land substantially underwrote much of the railroad construction. So strong was the popular demand for railroads that they also received local

assistance. To bring a railroad through their communities, hundreds of cities and counties purchased railway bonds (often mortgaging their future for many years) or made outright contributions of property and cash. Although government land grants and public loans received much attention, most of the capital for railroad building came from private sources. Railroad companies sold millions of dollars' worth of stocks and bonds to domestic investors, and additional millions' worth to foreigners, especially the British.

Users soon lodged complaints against the railroads. Rebates paid to special shippers, high rates, and discriminatory charges provoked bitter criticism from farmers, small merchants, and general reformers. The powerful political influence of the railroads—gained through distribution of free passes to influential citizens, payment of retainers to lawyers, and sometimes outright bribery—also came under attack.

But even as the criticism mounted, railroads introduced many basic physical improvements and reduced freight and passenger rates. They introduced larger, more powerful, and faster locomotives, laid heavier steel rails, and by 1886 had adopted a standard gage of 4 feet 8 1/2 inches on most lines. The Westinghouse air brake, perfected in 1887; automatic couplings to connect cars; and a variety of special tank, livestock, and refrigerator cars all increased the efficiency of railroad transportation. Rates declined substantially. The drop was greatest in the East and on main lines where competition was acute, but some reduction occurred on the smaller and more isolated roads as well.

This national railroad system profoundly influenced American life. Railroads pushed the rapid settlement of the West: they advertised for immigrants, sold land to settlers on credit, and hauled people to their new homes at reduced rates. They opened up the Rocky Mountain region to large-scale mining development, established bases for future cities, and made possible the growth of industrial and agricultural specialization. As enormous consumers of iron and steel, railroads had a direct effect upon the growth of those basic industries. As early as 1883, the railroads divided the country into four time zones and thus gradually eliminated the chaos created by some sixty-eight different local times.

Railways affected the overall economic development of the nation. Completion of an efficient transportation system provided American industrialists and farmers with a nationwide market and joined the various sections of the country together into an economic whole. Goods produced in Boston, for example, could now be sold easily in Chicago, St. Louis, or Denver. Southern cotton, Wisconsin lumber, and Colorado minerals could be shipped to distant factories for processing and sale. In other words, railroads provided a cheap, rapid, and efficient means to transport raw materials and finished products. Without such transportation the American industrial revolution could not have occurred.

Other means of transportation contributed to the country's industrial growth. Pipelines became important in the movement of oil from fields to refineries during the 1870s. The later evolution of the motor car depended upon the development of a practical internal combustion engine in the 1860s. Many experiments followed this achievement, but not until the 1890s did Charles and Frank Duryea, Henry Ford, Henry Leland Olds, and other pioneers build successful automobiles. In 1904, a large caravan of automobiles, arriving at the St. Louis Exposition from the East Coast, signaled the new era in transportation. The most successful passenger car was Henry Ford's Model T, which he first produced on a mass basis in 1909.

American business and industry depended heavily on improvements in communication. The postal system expanded and added new services. City delivery was inaugurated in 1863, special delivery in 1885, and rural free delivery in 1896. The first transcontinental telegraph went into operation in 1861; Cyrus Field completed an improved transatlantic cable in 1866. After numerous experiments by different inventors, Alexander Graham Bell sent his first telephone message on March 10, 1876, to his assistant, Thomas Watson. His terse words, "Come here, Watson, I want you," began a new era in communications. American Bell Telephone Company received its charter in 1880. The number of Bell telephones increased from 50,000 to more than a million between 1880 and 1902. These developments in communications became absolutely essential for large-scale and complex business transactions.

Major Industries

American factories turned out a great variety of commodities, but four basic manufactures exceeded all others in importance: food and kindred commodities, textiles, iron and steel, and lumber. By 1914 these four industries accounted for 54 percent of the value of all United States manufactures. Flour milling, meat-packing, sugar refining, and processing of canned and preserved goods were the chief food industries. Charles A. Pillsbury introduced new methods of milling the hard spring wheat of the Upper Midwest and developed a huge milling industry. Philip D. Armour became one of the nation's leading meat-packers. He established Armour and Company in Chicago in 1870 and was among the first to integrate the slaughtering, packing, storage, and shipping processes and to extend his operations to the manufacture of by-products— glue, oleomargarine, fertilizer, and soap. When Armour died in 1901, he left a fortune of some $50 million.

Important industries developed around canned goods, sugar, tobacco, and whisky. Starting with only a few pounds of tobacco at the close of the Civil War, James B. Duke, a poor North Carolina farm boy, and his brother devel-

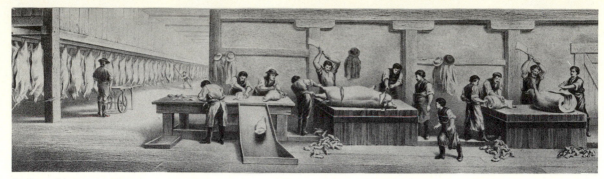

Pork packing, around 1873.

oped a large tobacco business. The Dukes began to manufacture cigarettes in 1881 and soon introduced machines to replace handworkers. By 1889, they produced about half the cigarettes sold in the United States. In 1890, Duke organized several competing tobacco companies into the American Tobacco Company.

The value of manufactured and processed food reached $4,816,700,000 in 1914, more than double the figure of 1899. Such an increase emphasized the needs of a growing urban population and the decline in self-sufficiency, even among farmers. It proved that industrialization need not be retarded by food shortages for nonfarm workers.

Textiles ranked second to food commodities in value of products, although the industry employed more workers than any other branch of manufacturing. One of the country's oldest industries, textile manufacturing was, by 1900, a widely distributed and mammoth business, its 22,995 plants turning out $3,494,615,000 in products. By World War I, the United States was a major exporter of cotton manufactures.

Iron and steel, with their many semifinished and finished products, ranked third, behind foodstuffs and textiles. Industrialization required a foundation of iron and steel, and the United States assumed a commanding world lead in their production during the generation after the Civil War. By 1914, the 17,719 iron and steel establishments in the United States, whose annual output was valued at approximately $3.2 billion,

employed more than a million workers. Pig iron production rose from less than 1 million tons in 1860 to about 33 million in 1914; steel output increased from a mere 19,643 long tons in 1867 to 37 million on the eve of World War I. The United States surpassed Great Britain in pig iron production by the 1880s; by 1900 American production of steel was twice that of England.

The modern industrial revolution had to wait upon the discovery of a structural metal that was hard, tough, malleable, abundant, and cheap—that is, steel. Tougher and less brittle than cast iron, it provided a structural material for many industrial purposes, and its production, along with the use of steampower in manufacturing and transportation, ushered in the era of modern industry.

Most responsible for developing the American steel industry was Andrew Carnegie. Emigrating to Pennsylvania from Scotland in 1847 when he was only twelve, young Carnegie obtained his first job in a cotton mill at $1.20 a week. When only twenty-four, Carnegie became superintendent of the Western Division of the Pennsylvania Railroad. Ambitious, hardworking, and daring, Carnegie invested small sums in various businesses, but soon concentrated his investments in bridge- and ironworks.

In 1873, Carnegie organized the Edgar Thompson Steel Works, and despite the panic of that year, moved ahead by installing the latest and most efficient equipment for making iron and steel. He organized extremely effective production and managerial teams and set out to integrate his operations by gaining control of raw materials and transportation. Carnegie purchased extensive coal deposits and numerous coke ovens. Next he obtained his own supply of iron ore and then purchased railroads and freighters to carry the ore from Lake Superior to Pittsburgh. Carnegie now had his own mills, his own supply of coke and iron ore, and his own transportation. Thereafter the steel industry and Carnegie's personal fortune faced no visible limits.

Petroleum, one of the fastest-growing and most important industries, provided opportunities for the fabulous business and industrial career of John D. Rockefeller. Born in western New York in 1839, the son of a patent medicine salesman and trader, Rockefeller at fourteen moved with his family to Cleveland, Ohio. Employed at the age of sixteen by a commission firm for $15 a month, Rockefeller saved a few dollars and, in 1859, formed a partnership with Maurice B. Clark to deal in meats, hay, and grain on a commission basis.

That year Edwin L. Drake drilled the nation's first oil well near Titusville in western Pennsylvania. At that time, the chief product refined from crude oil was kerosene for lamps. In 1863, Rockefeller made some investments in oil refining, a growing business in Cleveland; two years later, he sold his commission business and devoted his full energies to the oil industry. An energetic, thrifty, careful operator who watched every detail of his enterprise, Rockefeller soon became a major figure in the oil refining industry. In 1870 he formed the Standard Oil Company.

Like other industrialists of the period, Rockefeller sought to integrate and control all phases of petroleum production and distribution. Through purchase and consolidation of competing properties, he gained control of approximately 90 percent of the oil refining business by 1890. To make his operations more self-sufficient, Rockefeller manufactured his own barrels, built his own warehouses, established his own draying service, and acquired pipelines to free himself from the railroads. He manufactured hundreds of by-products: lubricants, waxes, paints, varnishes, and other petroleum derivatives. He created a distribution network to deliver products directly to consumers. Eventually he sold large quantities of petroleum products overseas.

In a day when industrial and transportation tycoons became rich beyond most people's imagination, Rockefeller acquired a fortune which had no equal. By 1913 his wealth amounted to some $900 million, nine times that of Cornelius Vanderbilt at the time of his death in 1877 and twice the figure for which Carnegie sold out in 1901.

Industrial advance relied on new markets generated by technological advances. Kerosene lamps and internal combustion engines became heavy users of petroleum products; the railroads increased demands for iron and steel; and meatpacking benefited from the invention of the refrigerator car. There were direct relationships, although not always clear, among improved technology, increased production, rising incomes, and expanded consumption.

Location of American Manufacturing

Although American manufactures were widely distributed geographically, the two leading regions of production were the Middle Atlantic states—New York, New Jersey, and Pennsylvania—and such North Central states as Ohio, Indiana, Illinois, Michigan, and Wisconsin. By 1914, the Middle Atlantic states produced 33 percent, and the eastern North Central states 27 percent of the value of the nation's industrial output. New England continued to be a major industrial area, but its importance relative to other sections declined in the late nineteenth century. One of the most remarkable postwar developments in manufacturing occurred in the upper Middle West, an area chiefly agricultural at the time of the Civil War. Illinois, and Chicago in particular, became the center of the farm machine and meat-packing industries. Ohio was second only to Pennsylvania in the output of iron.

The South lagged far behind the North in industrial development. The Civil War had been highly destructive of Southern manufacturing, and that troubled economic region did not make substantial industrial gains until a generation after 1865. The South lacked capital, managerial experience, and skilled labor. Still the area had a favorable potential for industry with plentiful raw materials such as cotton, coal, iron ore, petroleum, and lumber; a vast supply of cheap labor, needing only training and experience; abundant waterpower; a mild climate; and friendly state governments. By 1880, important leaders in the South were making a conscious effort to promote manufacturing. Henry W. Grady, editor of the *Atlanta Constitution*, argued that the South's economic progress depended upon industrial development.

Despite the natural advantages and the active promotion of manufacturing, however, Southern industry developed slowly until after 1880. The value of Southern manufactures was only 6.3 percent of the nation's total that year, compared with 9.9 percent thirty years earlier. But gradually the development of large-scale industry

gained momentum. Major Southern industries included cotton textiles, iron, coal, oil, lumber, phosphates, cottonseed oil, and tobacco. Cotton textile production became one of the South's leading industries, outdistancing the Northern mills in the output of coarser cloth. By 1909, the South produced about 40 percent of the country's cotton goods. The South's iron and steel industry centered in the region of Birmingham, which was ideally located in relation to iron ore and coal supplies. Millions of board feet of lumber were cut annually from Southern forests.

Before 1900, most of the oil industry was concentrated in Pennsylvania, New York, Ohio, Indiana, and West Virginia, but after the great Lucas gusher at Spindletop, Texas, in 1901, the center of oil activity began to shift toward the Southwest. Oil booms in Texas, Oklahoma, and Louisiana within the next few years quickly expanded the nation's production. The drilling, transportation, and refining of oil gave the South one of its leading industries. When judged in absolute terms, the South made a fair record in manufacturing before World War I, but in comparison with the Northeast and the Great Lakes states, the region, with a few exceptions, dropped further behind than it had been before the Civil War. In 1909, the sixteen Southern states produced only 12.8 percent of the value of manufactured products, although that region had 32 percent of the population.

Consumer Distribution

Mass production of manufactured commodities after the Civil War compelled changes in distribution. Better transportation and improved means of exchange provided a ready supply of manufactured goods almost everywhere. Consequently, the consumption of homemade articles rapidly declined as more people purchased their canned goods, clothing, shoes, and butter at commercial retail outlets.

Although the general store remained common in rural areas, important changes in retail dis-

tribution appeared after 1860. Following the establishment of A. T. Stewart's New York department store in 1861, similar stores were founded by R. H. Macy in New York, Marshall Field in Chicago, and John Wanamaker in Philadelphia. These stores sold many types of goods, with different departments specializing in certain commodities. The mail-order house, combining the functions of wholesaler and retailer, developed during the late nineteenth century. Montgomery Ward & Company was founded in 1872, and Sears, Roebuck & Company in 1886. Chain stores represented another innovation in retail distribution. The Great Atlantic and Pacific Tea Company, or the A & P, began operations in 1859 and, by 1914, had some three thousand stores. F. W. Woolworth's 5 and 10 cent stores, first established in 1879, became familiar to hundreds of towns and cities by the end of the century.

The advertising and promotion of brand-name goods as a means of increasing sales developed after 1865. Many such commodities were advertised on a national basis—Dr. Lyon's tooth powder, Ivory soap, Pillsbury flour, Singer sewing machines, and scores of other products. One of the biggest advertisers was the patent medicine industry, and among its most famous nostrums, which became household words in America, was Lydia Pinkham's female compound. By 1900, advertising itself had become big business; in the twentieth century it would become a vital part of the American way of life.

Monopoly

Large-scale business and industry produced a high degree of consolidation and, in some cases, outright monopoly. This trend, apparent by the 1880s, became increasingly pronounced later. By 1905, 11 percent of the nation's industrial establishments controlled more than 80 percent of the capital, employed 72 percent of the workers, and produced 79 percent of the manufactured products. As the trend toward concentration intensified, a growing demand arose among farmers, workers, small businessmen, and some intellectuals to curb this unrestricted economic power.

Combinations in transportation and industry grew rapidly after 1870 for a number of reasons. The corporate form of business organization itself was a permissive factor. Multi million-dollar enterprises could have been neither easily nor conveniently financed and managed by individual proprietors or partnerships. Furthermore, the technological revolution made possible and necessary large business units; and improved transportation permitted a single large firm to sell its products in national, and even international, markets. Moreover, many business leaders believed that larger industries were more efficient, although this was by no means always true. Carnegie summed up this idea when he wrote in 1900: "Now, the cheapening of all these good things . . . is rendered possible only through the operation of the law, which may be stated thus: cheapness is in proportion to the scale of produc-tion." The basic economic advantages of large-scale production included a reduction of unit

The first Ivory Soap advertisement—December 1882.

THE "IVORY" is a Laundry Soap, with all the fine qualities of a choice Toilet Soap, and is 99 44-100 per cent. pure.

cost, the manufacture of by-products, and specialization in both production and management.

But the dominant reason for business and industrial combination was the desire to reduce competition and increase profits. Many businessmen believed that excessive and destructive competition resulted from an overexpansion of productive facilities and that by coordinating and combining firms in a particular business, say refining, they could adjust output to market demand and prevent price reductions to unprofitable levels. Although businessmen gave lip service to the principle of competition, they sought to eliminate or reduce it in their practical business affairs.

Techniques of consolidation and monopoly differed. The most elementary method for reducing competition lay in simple business agreements in regard to prices, production, and service among several rival firms. In the early 1870s, businessmen turned to the pool as a more effective way of curbing competition. The railroads had already hit upon the pool as a favorite means of reducing competition, and before 1890, pools existed in the meat-packing, gunpowder, barbed wire, and other industries. Although pools were more compelling than simple agreements, they tended to break down under competitive conditions.

The trust ushered in an enforceable type of combination much more suited to the desires of businessmen who wanted to eliminate competition. The Standard Oil Trust, formed in 1879 by John D. Rockefeller, was the nation's first industrial trust. Stockholders of companies and firms assigned the voting stock of their businesses to a group of nine trustees, among whom Rockefeller was the principal figure. The stockholders received trust certificates, which drew dividends but had no voting power. This gave the trustees complete control of all the companies which entered the agreement. After this combination, the Standard Oil Trust controlled most of the country's refining facilities, much of the pipeline network, and other related companies. The success of the Standard Oil Trust set a pattern for consolidations in cottonseed oil, linseed oil, whisky, lead, cordage, sugar, and other commodities.

As a form of monopoly the trust lasted scarcely a decade. In the late 1880s, outside businessmen brought actions in state courts against several of the leading trusts on the grounds that they violated common law principles in regard to restraint of trade and monopoly.

With the decline of the trusts, outright mergers became more popular, but the most effective type of business consolidation was the holding company, a corporation which sought to reduce competition by purchasing control of competing firms. Between 1897 and 1902, some of the nation's most important businesses emerged under the holding company arrangement—the Standard Oil Company, reorganized under a New Jersey charter of 1899, the United States Steel Corporation, International Harvester Company, and the Northern Securities Company. By 1905, a high degree of concentration and consolidation had been achieved in oil, steel, farm machinery, sugar, and many other industries. As one poet exclaimed:

> Let us corner up the sunbeams
> Lying all around our path;
> Get a trust on wheat and roses;
> Give the poor the thorns and chaff.
> Let us find our chiefest pleasure
> Hoarding bounties of today,
> So the poor shall have scant measure
> And two prices have to pay.
>
> We will syndicate the starlight,
> And monopolize the moon,
> Claim a royalty on rest days,
> A proprietary noon;
> For right of way through ocean's spray
> We'll charge just what it's worth;
> We'll drive our stakes around the lakes—
> In fact, we'll own the earth.

Many common people harbored a deep prejudice against the concentration of economic power in pools, trusts, and other types of business consolidation. But opposition in the late nineteenth century was spasmodic, disorganized, and ineffective, whereas business interests were aggressive and much better united than their opponents.

Businessmen capitalized upon the American tradition which held that government restrictions or legal restraints on business were contrary to the best interests of the entrepreneur and to the economy as a whole—the doctrine of laissez-faire. They argued that the nation was served best when competition operated without interference. Success was a sign of better management and greater efficiency, not a result of undesirable business practices. The destruction of some firms and monopoly control by others merely bore out the laws of natural selection and the survival of the fittest, biological concepts formulated by Charles Darwin in *The Origin of Species* in 1859. This analogy between biology and society, perfected by Herbert Spencer, the English philosopher, came to be called "social Darwinism."

Social Darwinism provided businessmen with scientific and sociological justification for opposing government regulation and maintaining a favorable status quo. Carnegie once declared that, while competition might hurt the individual, it was best for society in general because it ensured "the survival of the fittest in every department." Protestantism buttressed, and indeed enhanced, the economic notion of laissez-faire. Great wealth could be interpreted as a mark of divine favor; poverty, on the other hand, must result from laziness or sin. Many business leaders emphasized the Protestant virtues of thrift, industry, and sobriety to which they laid their success.

Despite widespread economic, religious, and philosophical support for laissez-faire principles, some men took strong exception to unfettered economic freedom, advocating government regulation and control of big business. In *Progress and Poverty* (1879), Henry George, a journalist and social reformer, attacked the system of holding land for speculative gain and proposed a single tax to deprive landowners of any unearned increment which accrued when social progress, rather than personal contribution, caused property values to rise. George's single-tax idea did not gain many adherents, but his book was widely read because of its lucid attack on the economic order of the day. It had a special appeal to college students. Edward Bellamy advocated nationalized industry in *Looking Backward* (1888); Henry Demarest Lloyd, in *Wealth against Commonwealth* (1894), bitterly attacked laissez-faire, social Darwinism, and classical economics as existing merely to justify predatory business practices.

Beginning of Government Regulation

The antitrust movement to curb business and industrial consolidation, which developed after 1870, grew not from particular theories of political economy but from a pragmatic effort to solve definite problems and to correct specific abuses. Few critics wanted to change the American system in any basic way. They hoped only to expand government control and regulation to protect the small and the weak against exploitation by the few.

Midwestern farmers, as well as important elements of the business community, singled out the railroads in their first widespread and well-organized attack on big business. The farmers had wanted railway lines extended to their communities, but by the early 1870s they complained bitterly against high and discriminatory rates and other harmful railroad practices. The Grange, the country's most important farm organization, supported by other independent and antimonopoly parties then beginning to thrive in the Midwest, supported demands for state regulation. Chicago business interests joined the crusade. In 1871 and 1873, Illinois laws set freight and passenger rates and regulated the charges for grain storage in warehouses. Minnesota, Wisconsin, and Iowa, among other states, passed similar "Granger" laws. Most of these statutes attempted to establish maximum rates either by specific legislation or by action of a railroad commission.

Unfortunately, the Granger laws were not very effective. The railroads exploited every type of propaganda and political pressure to nullify the legislation or get it repealed. Their highly successful campaigns had, by the late 1870s, resulted in the revocation or weakening of most restrictive measures. Meanwhile, the railroads attacked the laws in court, charging that such regulations violated the Fourteenth Amendment, which declares that no state shall "deprive any person of life, liberty, or property without due process of law." Corporations were persons under the law, and railroad attorneys argued that restrictive laws denied the companies full property rights. In *Munn v. Illinois* (1877), the Su-

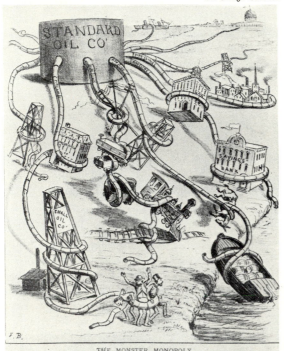

"The Monster Monopoly": An 1884 political cartoon attacking Rockefeller's Standard Oil Company.

The Granger Collection

THE MONSTER MONOPOLY.

preme Court upheld an Illinois law of 1871 designed to regulate warehouse rates for grain storage. In the opinion of Justice C. J. Waite, when "one devotes his property to a use in which the public has an interest, he, in effect, grants to the public an interest in that use, and must submit to be controlled by the public for the common good." But in the Wabash case of 1886, the Supreme Court held that states could not control railroads engaged in interstate commerce since the Constitution granted this function to the federal government. Few railroads operated in only one state.

Even as farm and other groups pressed for state control of railroads and other large-scale enterprise, Congress was considering federal action to curb abuses in interstate transportation. In 1874, the House of Representatives passed the McCrary bill, which called for a federal commission to regulate rates. Although this and subsequent measures failed in the Senate, some congressmen and senators continued to force the issue. By the 1880s, even some of the railroads themselves favored regulation as the only means available to reduce cutthroat competition. After the House and Senate reconciled their differences, the Interstate Commerce Act became law on February 4, 1887.

This act forbade discrimination in rates among localities, provided that all rates be "reasonable and just," made it illegal to charge more for a short haul than for a long haul, and outlawed rebates and pooling. An Interstate Commerce Commission of five members appointed by the President was to administer the law. But the law did not give the Commission power to regulate rates, and if the Commission challenged the reasonableness of a rate, it had to prove its contention in court. The federal courts were then in no mood to impose any genuine regulation on the railroads. In the Maximum Freight Rate case, ten years after the creation of the Commission, the Supreme Court still held that the Commission had no power to set rates. Nevertheless, the Interstate Commerce Act made a significant beginning toward effective regulation.

Understandably, the initial demand for government regulation of big business had focused on the railroads—the biggest business of the day and the most likely to have a direct effect upon the lives of many people. However, before Congress passed legislation to bring railroads under control, a broad antitrust movement had developed to deal with growing monopolies in oil, steel, and other industries. Although President Cleveland never gave strong support to government regulation, he expressed a popular feeling when he said in 1887 that "Corporations, which should be the carefully restrained creatures of the law and the servants of the people, are fast becoming the people's master." Both the Democrats and Republicans recommended regulation of trusts in their platforms of 1888. Finally, in July 1890, Congress passed the Sherman Antitrust Act.

The Sherman Antitrust Act made illegal "every contract, combination in the form of trust or otherwise, or conspiracy, in restraint of trade or commerce among the several states or with foreign nations." Secondly, it declared, "every person who shall monopolize, or attempt to monopolize, or combine or conspire with any other person or persons, to monopolize, any part of the trade or commerce among the several States, or with foreign nations, shall be deemed guilty of a misdemeanor." The government could bring criminal and civil suits against violators of the act, who might be fined a maximum of $5,000 or sentenced to a year in jail, or both.

The Sherman Antitrust Act did not effectively deter industrial consolidation and monopoly. In fact, more mergers and a greater degree of business concentration occurred after the law was passed than before. Why? In the first place, the law itself was vague. It left the definition or interpretation of monopoly or restraint of trade to the courts, which usually adopted the business point of view. In the E. C. Knight case of 1895, for example, the Supreme Court held that the American Sugar Refining Company had not violated the Sherman Antitrust law although the company controlled about 98 percent of the nation's sugar refining. For more than a decade the federal government made no serious attempt to enforce the law, and it remained a dead letter on the statute books until Theodore Roosevelt became president in 1901.

Conclusion

Between 1865 and 1900, the United States changed from a predominantly agricultural nation to the world's leading industrial power. In the process, scarcely any phase of American life went untouched. Improved communications and transportation stimulated and encouraged national unity, and the mass production and distribution of consumer goods brought about greater standardization and uniformity in tastes and styles. Industrialization stimulated the rapid growth of urbanization, as the burgeoning industries drew both local farmers and immigrants from abroad to jobs in urban factories. This concentration of population created many problems which plagued the industrial centers into the twentieth century. Most importantly, America's industrial revolution effected an increase in wealth and standard of living. Between 1859 and 1909, the average annual per capita income in dollars of constant purchasing power rose from $285 to $482, an increase of nearly 100 percent.

SUGGESTED READINGS

The best general history of the late-nineteenth-century industrial economy is Edward C. Kirkland's *Industry Comes of Age: Business, Labor and Public Policy, 1860–1897** (1961). Older but still useful is Ida M.

Tarbell's *The Nationalizing of Business, 1878–1898* (1936). Matthew Josephson presents a lively but extremely critical account of business leadership in *The Robber Barons: The Great American Capitalists, 1861–1901** (1934). Part of Thomas C. Cochran and William Miller's *The Age of Enterprise** (rev. ed., 1961) furnishes a good interpretation of the period. Samuel P. Hays traces the ways in which different groups responded to industrialism in *The Response to Industrialism, 1885–1914** (1957).

Railroads and their contribution to the nation's economic development have been studied in detail. The beginning student should start with John Moody's *Railroad Builders* (1919). Other general studies include *Railroad Leaders, 1845–1890* (1953) by Thomas C. Cochran; Edward C. Kirkland's *Men, Cities, and Transportation: A Study in New England History, 1820–1900* (1948); and John F. Stover's *The Railroads of the South, 1865–1900* (1955). Among the best studies of individual lines or systems are Richard C. Overton's *Burlington West* (1941); James B. Hedges's *Henry Villard and the Railways of the Northwest* (1930), and *History of the Union Pacific* (1923) by Nelson Trottman. Some of the best data on railroad history can be found in the biographies of railroad leaders: J. G. Pyle's *The Life of James J. Hill* (2 vols., 1917); Oscar Lewis's *The Big Four: The Story of Huntington, Stanford, Hopkins, and Crocker* (1938); Julius Grodinsky's *Jay Gould* (1957); and George Kennan's *E. H. Harriman* (2 vols., 1922).

On industrial development see Witt Bowden's *The Industrial History of the United States* (1930); V. S. Clark's *History of Manufactures in the United States* (1929), vol. II; and the short, lively survey by Burton J. Hendrick, *The Age of Big Business* (1919). Industrial expansion in the South has been covered by Broadus Mitchell and G. S. Mitchell in *The Industrial Revolution in the South* (1930). Growth of large-scale corporate enterprise can be traced in the following business histories and biographical studies: Burton J. Hendrick's *The Life of Andrew Carnegie* (2 vols., 1932); Allan Nevins's *Study in Power: John D. Rockefeller, Industrialist and Philanthropist* (2 vols. 1953); Ralph W. and Muriel E. Hidy's *Pioneering in Big Business, 1882–1911: History of the Standard Oil Company* (1955); William T. Hutchinson's *Cyrus Hall McCormick* (2 vols., 1930–1935); and J. W. Jenkins's *James B. Duke* (1927). For a survey of technological advances see John W. Oliver's *History of American Technology* (1956), as well as studies on inventions such as Richard N. Current's *The Typewriter and the Men Who Made It* (1959) and H. C. Passer's more general *The Electric Manufacturers, 1875–1900* (1953).

There are several excellent studies on monopoly and attempts at government control of big business. Among the useful older works are John Moody's *The Truth about the Trusts* (1904); Myron W. Watkins's *Industrial Combinations and Public Policy* (1927); and Charles R. Van Hise's *Concentration and Control* (1912). Newer studies of antitrust policies are Clair Wilcox's *Public Policies toward Business* (1960) and Hans B. Thorelli's *Federal Antitrust Policy* (1955). Gabriel Kolko argues in *Railroads and Regulation, 1877–1916* (1965) that the movement in favor of regulation was basically of a conservative character.

Edward C. Kirkland has examined the ideas of businessmen in *Dream and Thought in the Business Community, 1860–1900** (1956), while Sigmund Diamond views the public attitude toward rich business leaders in *The Reputation of the American Businessman* (1955). Richard Hofstadter is excellent in discussing *Social Darwinism in American Thought, 1860–1915** (1944).

*indicates availability in paperback.

Labor, Immigration, and Urbanization

The industrial revolution meant a great deal more to American society than the building of factories and the production of goods. It profoundly affected the life and opportunities of workingmen; it attracted millions of immigrants to American shores; and it set the conditions for the rise of an urban nation.

Between the Civil War and World War I, wage earners struggled to adjust to the factory system and to win a larger share of the fruits of industrialism. They sought to improve their position by organizing into unions to increase their bargaining power with employers. Workers also looked to both state and national governments for legislation favorable to labor. Although many laborers worked long hours for low wages and under rather unfavorable conditions, by the early twentieth century the position of workingmen had improved substantially.

Meanwhile, millions of immigrants streamed to America. Many of these newcomers went to Midwestern farms, but the great majority of them settled in the nation's growing industrial and commercial centers. The immigrants were city builders. With a steady flow of aliens into American cities, and the internal movement of Americans from the farm to the city, the United States rapidly developed into a predominantly urban nation. By 1920 slightly more than half of the total population lived in what the Census Bureau classed as urban communities. This shift from a primarily agricultural nation to one principally industrial and urban was one of the most fundamental developments in the history of the country.

Early in the nineteenth century the great majority of workers were engaged in some phase of agriculture, but between 1860 and 1910 the total labor force in agricultural pursuits declined from 60 percent to only 31 percent. During that same period those employed in manufacturing establishments rose from 18 to 28 percent. As more and more workers entered factories, where they were dependent upon wages for their income, they lost any remaining self-sufficiency—in terms of producing their own food and clothing or as independent skilled craftsmen.

In the late nineteenth century, hours remained long, wages low, and conditions of work difficult, especially when judged by modern standards. For example, in 1890 the average workweek for industrial laborers was about 58 hours while average earnings were only 21 cents an hour. Twenty years later, the average workweek had dropped to 54.6 hours, and hourly pay had risen to 28 cents. However, averages were deceiving. The workweek for many factory workers was much longer, reaching 72 hours in the iron and steel industry. In 1900 the average annual wage for workers in manufacturing was $435. Despite this seemingly low figure, real wages had risen about 48 percent between 1860 and 1890.

Several industrial developments revolutionized the position of workingmen: the emergence of large corporations, which employed hundreds and even thousands of workers; the increasingly interstate character of business; and the rapid mechanization of industry. The growing use of machines and the division of labor in factory production at first threatened, and then finally destroyed, the historic position of skilled craftsmen. Although the labor market expanded rapidly, most of the demand centered on semi-skilled and unskilled wage earners.

Huge corporate businesses greatly altered the relationship of wage earners to their employers. When industry was in the hands of small individual enterprises or partnerships, there could be a close relation between workers and management. By its very nature and organization, however, the large corporation was impersonal. Moreover, the corporation was primarily interested in profit making, and the personal needs of workers received only secondary consideration. Industrialists considered labor a commodity to be purchased at the cheapest possible price. The manager of one New England textile factory expressed the common attitude: "I regard my workpeople just as I regard my machinery. So long as they can do my work for what I choose to pay them, I keep them, getting out of them all I can."

Wage earners faced other dilemmas. The growing number of immigrants tended to depress wages; and the passing of the frontier late in the century, with the vanishing prospect of acquiring good farmland, either free or at cheap prices, ended any hope that factory or potential factory workers could move west. Few workers actually migrated from the factory to the farm; Western lands did not provide a real safety valve for urban and industrial discontent. Nevertheless, the fact that the possibility of leaving industrial employment and seeking land existed may have had some effect in maintaining better working conditions and higher wage standards in America than in Europe.

Problems which faced industrial wage earners in the "Age of Big Business" emphasized the need for unified action by the workers, but labor lacked unity in its own ranks. Labor leaders and their followers could reach no agreement on either basic objectives or the means of achieving them. Some leaders hoped to escape the wage system through cooperatives or some type of general social or political reform; others insisted that the labor movement should concentrate primarily on higher wages and shorter hours. Many hesitated to desert the dream of self-employment and therefore refused to regard their present state as permanent.

Organization of the National Labor Union in 1866 was labor's first attempt to form a genuine national union. Throughout its short existence the National Labor Union emphasized two major objectives: the eight-hour day and inflation. Beginning in 1867 the NLU devoted its attention to the money question. The idea of inflation was pleasing to workers who sought credit to establish producer and consumer cooperatives. Forming cooperatives, many felt, would be a practical way to escape the wage system. William H. Sylvis, who became president of the NLU in 1868, declared: "We must adopt a system which will divide the *profits* of labor among those who produce them." The Iron Molders Union, in which Sylvis was a prominent leader, established several cooperatively owned foundries in 1866, but these enterprises failed. In 1872 the NLU entered the political arena, and when its efforts failed, the union collapsed and disappeared.

Of more importance was the Noble Order of the Knights of Labor. Organized in Philadelphia in 1869 by Uriah S. Stephens, the Knights was a national organization of secret membership which attempted to bring together all workers into one big union. Although most of the early members consisted of skilled trade unionists, the union was open to unskilled, semiskilled, men, women—any individual who was "working for wages or who at any time worked for wages," without regard to sex, color, race, or position.

The major or "first principles" of the Knights of Labor included education "to create a healthy public opinion on the subject of labor"; a legislative program of benefit to workingmen; and mutual benefit societies and cooperatives. The Knights were not interested in any class struggle. They hoped to create a new order of society through cooperative effort whereby organized labor might escape what Stephens called "wage slavery."

The Knights grew very slowly because of both hard times following the Panic of 1873 and employers' strong opposition to unionization.

To protect their interests, workers staged a series of bitterly fought strikes during the late 1870s. Perhaps the most publicized conflicts were the Great Railroad Strikes of 1877, which began in July against the Baltimore and Ohio Railroad at Martinsburg, West Virginia. Following a second 10 percent wage cut, the workers stopped trains from moving either east or west pending the restoration of their wages. After two days 200 federal troops closed in and broke the strike. Meanwhile the strike had spread to other cities and to other railroads. In Pittsburgh, a strike against the Pennsylvania Railway created a violent situation in which a pitched battle between troops and the strikers left twenty-six persons dead. Labor unrest in 1877 was not confined to the East. At the very time troops were restoring law and order in Pennsylvania, radical labor activity developed in California under the leadership of Denis Kearney. This organized agitation focused on the Chinese, who, Kearney charged, worked for lower wages and took jobs from native Americans. A violent anti-Chinese demonstration swept San Francisco on July 23, 1877. It lasted for two days and destroyed $100,000 worth of property. Later in 1877, Kearney was elected president of the Workingmen's party on a platform which demanded unity among workingmen, opposition to the Chinese, and destruction of land and financial monopolies.

The first national assembly of the Knights of Labor, now confident enough to give up their secrecy, took place early in 1878. The Knights reiterated their faith in education, cooperation, and legislation, but the Order now broadened its demands to attract wider support. It urged the reservation of public lands for actual settlers, the establishment of a federal bureau of labor statistics, the abolition of the contract labor system, and the acceptance of the eight-hour day.

In 1879 the Knights of Labor entered a new phase of its history. To that time the various assemblies had clung to the first principles and had avoided strikes. But in that year Terence V. Powderly replaced founder Stephens as Grand Master Workman. Although Powderly advised caution in matters of strikes, the Knights became more aggressive. Several local strikes were successful, but labor lost most of the important disputes. However, successful strikes against both the Union Pacific in 1884 and Jay Gould's Wabash; Missouri, Kansas and Texas; and Missouri Pacific Railroads in February and March of 1885 brought a flood of members into the union's ranks. Hundreds of locals emerged within a few months. Between 1885 and early 1886, membership in the Knights increased from 111,395 to 729,677. These successes gave labor a false sense of power, for the fundamental weaknesses of the Knights soon became evident. In March 1886, another strike against Gould's southwestern railroads revealed where the real economic power lay. Gould brought in strikebreakers and refused to negotiate any of the disputed points. In time the employees capitulated on every issue.

Despite the prominence of strikes and boycotts in the activities of the Knights of Labor after 1880, Powderly and other leaders continued to emphasize the desirability of cooperatives. Organized labor established scores of cooperative enterprises between 1884 and 1887, including mines and foundries. But most of the businesses were small and of brief existence. Some labor cooperatives succumbed to bitter competition from private enterprise; others failed because of inefficient management and lack of capital. Never again did American labor make cooperatives a major objective.

The cooperatives' failure and the loss of important strikes were the two most obvious reasons for the decline of the Knights of Labor from more than seven hundred thousand to about one hundred thousand between 1885 and 1890. But there were even more fundamental factors which caused the gradual extinction of the Order. In the first place, the Knights lacked unity and solidarity. The Knights proved that it was impossible to weld so many different kinds and classes

of labor into a single effective organization. The organization suffered most of all from a growing lack of support among the skilled workers in the trade unions who had little faith in the prospect of one big union or of escaping the wage system. Also, the violence associated with the Haymarket Riot in Chicago in May 1886 hurt the Knights of Labor as well as the entire labor movement. This unfortunate incident grew out of a strike against the McCormick Harvester Works in Chicago and resulted in the death of four people.

Meanwhile, a basically different type of labor organization was emerging. The new movement was based on the conviction that the best hope for workingmen lay in strong, independent trade unions. In the late 1870s and early 1880s, trade unions experienced a marked revival following their heavy losses after 1873. Leaders such as Samuel Gompers and Adolph Strasser of the Cigarmakers were trade union leaders who opposed the political approach of the National Labor Union and rejected the one-big-union policy of the Knights as impractical and unrealistic. Gompers and Strasser believed in a simple wage-conscious philosophy which held that trade unions should be strengthened essentially to bargain effectively with employers rather than to serve as a stepping-stone to self-employment. This type of wage consciousness rejected cooperatives, greenbackism, socialism, and other general reforms which were designed to replace the wage system. This type of unionism sought simply increased bargaining power for workers within the existing capitalistic framework.

In December 1886, delegates claiming to represent more than 300,000 trade union members met in Columbus, Ohio, to form the American Federation of Labor. The preamble of the AF of L constitution declared that workers must combine for "mutual protection and benefit." Samuel Gompers became the first president, and from 1886 until his death in 1924, he was the driving force behind the growth and development of the AF of L. It was this short, stocky, immigrant cigar maker of Dutch-Jewish ancestry

Dynamic applications of technology between the Civil War and World War I enabled the United States to settle its frontiers and to become a leading industrial power. There were two major human results: a mammoth wave of immigration into the country, and the first widespread organization of working men into labor unions. Immigration and unionization inevitably affected each other.

Twenty-three million foreign-born came to America between 1860 and 1910 in a movement which reached progressively higher levels: 2.8 million in the 1870s, 5.2 million in the 1880s, 8.8 million from 1900 to 1910. Prior to 1890 a majority of the immigrants came from Great Britain, Germany, and the Scandinavian countries, and many of them, spurred on by aggressive advertising of railroads and the states, settled on the cheap farm lands of the West. When most of the cheap and free lands were taken, the next wave of immigrants, from Middle Europe, Italy, and Russia for the most part, settled in or near the growing industrial centers. The handsome Italian family above, photographed by Lewis W. Hine as they prepared to debark at Ellis Island in New York in 1905, was a part of this wave.

The increasing flow of new immigrants provided the labor and much of the intellectual talent that made the United States an industrial leader among the nations of the world. But their presence in large numbers also tended to depress wages. In 1890 the average work week was 58 hours (72 hours in the iron and steel industry) and average earnings were 21 cents per hour. By 1900 the average annual wage for manufacturing workers was $435. As individuals, the workers had little chance of making themselves heard by the increasingly impersonal managements of industry which could easily dip into the pool of immigrant labor to replace the worker who asked too insistently for higher wages. In this situation, labor could find strength only in organization.

For many immigrants, such as those shown on deck in New York harbor in 1906 (following spread, left), the move to the United States proved an exhausting physical and psychological ordeal. It began in crowded steerage quarters aboard ship, and in many cases ended when the immigrant was tagged to be sent off to an inland destination. In between periods of quarantine, red tape, strange surroundings and tongues, and physical and mental tests assaulted the senses. On the following page, immigrants receive physical tests at Ellis Island (above) and undergo intelligence tests (below). At the right, an Italian family photographed by Lewis Hine searches the pier for their lost baggage.

George Eastman House Collection

The New American and Organized Labor

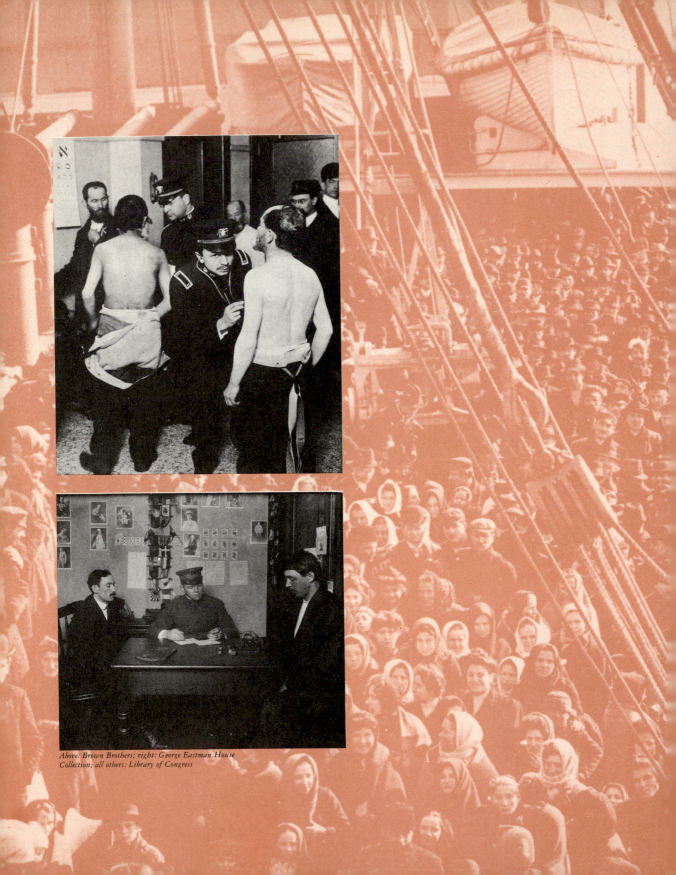

Above: Brown Brothers; right: George Eastman House
Collection; all others: Library of Congress

Leaders in the labor movement in the three decades following the Civil War interested themselves in a wide range of measures which would benefit all of labor, rather than concentrating on wage gains for workers in specific crafts and trades. William H. Sylvis (above, left), president of the National Labor Union, in 1868, believed, "We must adopt a system which will divide the profits of labor among those who produce them." Uriah S. Stephens (above, center) organized the Knights of Labor in 1869 as a secret organization in the hope of bringing about a new order of society through cooperative effort. Terence Powderly (right) who took leadership of the Knights in 1879, stood against secrecy for the Knights, for caution in strikes, and for labor sharing the benefits of production through cooperatives. Here Powderly is introduced at the tenth annual convention of the Knights in 1886 by delegate Frank J. Farrell. Women delegates also came to the 1886 convention of the Knights (above, right). Many early unionists supported women's rights and suffrage.

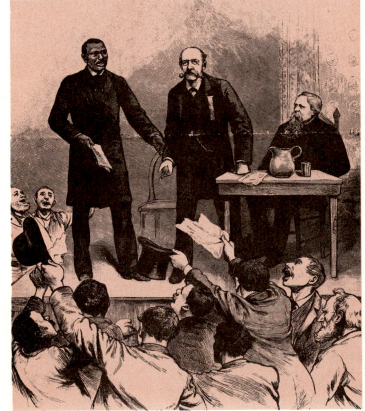

In response to a 10 percent wage cut, railroad workers in 1877 staged strikes across the country which soon became violent. The cavalry charged demonstrators in Chicago, (below) and rioters burned the Lebanon Valley Bridge (far right). But the Knights declined after 1885, and for the balance of the century, workers lost most of their disputes. The 1892 strike against the Carnegie Steel Works at Homestead, Pa. (right), was among the most bitterly fought defeats.

Above: Culver Pictures, Inc.; below: Library of Congress

The International Workers of the World led one of the most widely
publicized strikes of the period before World War I in Lawrence,
Mass., in 1912. Above, Massachusetts militia confront the striking
Lawrence textile workers. Protesting a reduction in wages, the
strikers clashed with police when management attempted to reopen
the struck mills. One woman was killed, and nationwide sympathy
for the strikers created such pressure on management that they got
their increases. The police car below, used in the Cincinnati strike
of 1910, symbolizes the violence that recurred again and again in
labor disputes.

who set the tone and direction of the organization.

Having abandoned any idea of escaping the wage system, the AF of L moved primarily to increase the power of individual trade unions so they could bargain more effectively with employers. Only if bargaining failed would the union resort to strikes and boycotts as a means of exerting economic pressure on management. The AF of L unions levied dues on their members to build up strike funds and provide other benefits. The AF of L placed its emphasis upon immediate and practical goals such as higher wages, shorter hours, and better working conditions. Since the union leadership believed primarily in economic action, it strongly opposed any affiliation with political parties. Instead, the AF of L rewarded friends and punished enemies at the polls. Gompers and most AF of L leaders opposed as well any alliance or affiliation with radical or revolutionary groups.

Organization of the AF of L was the genuine beginning of the modern labor movement. For the next half century it was the principal representative of organized workers in the United States, although, because of internal dissension, the failure of some strikes, and the hard times which followed the Panic of 1893, membership grew slowly. In 1898 the Federation could claim only 265,000 members, not many more than a decade earlier. But after the return of prosperity in 1899, membership increased rapidly. By 1914 the AF of L boasted 2,021,000 members, or about 79 percent of organized labor.

Despite its apparent success, the AF of L failed to organize workers in the principal mass-production industries such as coal, oil, and steel. Furthermore, many unions becoming established in the late 1880s disappeared before the bitter opposition of employers and the hardships of the depression of the 1890s. For example, in June 1892, a strike by Amalgamated Association of Iron and Steel Workers against the Carnegie Steel Workers at Homestead, Pennsylvania, failed completely. After considerable bloodshed from the fighting between workers and Pinkerton detectives, the Governor called out the state militia to restore order and break the strike.

Labor lost another important industrial conflict in the Pullman strike of 1894. The Pullman Company had recently cut wages; and when it refused to negotiate any of the differences with its employees, the local unions voted to strike. The company retaliated with a lockout. The American Railway Union, representing some 150,000 railroad workers and headed by Eugene V. Debs, urged arbitration between the company and the Pullman workers. When Pullman rejected this suggestion, the ARU voted to handle no more Pullman cars. When company officials fired employees for okaying that decision, whole crews would quit, tying up the train. By early July most Midwestern lines were affected.

Violence and damage to property in the first days of July prompted actions which finally defeated the strikers. On July 2 railroad officials obtained a federal district court injunction prohibiting any interference with the mails or the transportation of goods in interstate commerce. Then President Cleveland sent in federal troops on the pretext that local and state authorities could not maintain order. These federal actions completely crushed the strike. Governor John P. Altgeld of Illinois, a friend of labor, heatedly protested the dispatch of federal troops to Chicago, but the President insisted that he was obligated to keep the mails moving and to preserve law and order. In the aftermath Debs and several associates were indicted for violating the court injunction, and the ARU president was sentenced to six months in jail.

A small, but hard-core, radical labor movement existed in the United States between the Civil War and World War I, but it never achieved a significant following. Made up of Socialists, Anarchists, and Syndicalists, the radicals called for fundamental changes in the American industrial and labor system. Organized in 1877, the Socialist Labor party attempted to infiltrate the trade union movement. The Socialists made very little headway, however, until the 1890s, when Eugene V. Debs emerged as the movement's principal leader. He proposed a program of public ownership of basic industries and transportation, abolition of the wage system, and a number of more moderate reforms. By 1901 Debs had united most of the Socialists into the Socialist Party of America.

Some Radicals considered Debs too conservative, and in June 1905, they gathered in Chicago to organize the Industrial Workers of the World. Headed by William D. ("Big Bill") Haywood, a onetime farmer, miner, and labor organizer, the IWW advocated direct and violent action to overthrow the capitalistic system. One basic IWW statement declared that workers and employers had nothing in common, that "between these two classes a struggle must go on until the workers of the world organize as a class, take possession of the earth and machinery of production and abolish the wage system." The IWW set out to organize miners, migratory farm and lumber workers, immigrant textile workers, and others who had been largely ignored by the established trade unions. But the extreme radicalism of the IWW had only limited appeal, and the organization probably never had more than 60,000 members. The idea of overthrowing the capitalistic system and establishing a socialist state never gained much support among workers. It was contrary to American middle-class concepts and traditions. The vast majority of American laborers considered the Socialist attack on private property not only bad economically but also un-American.

Government and Labor

Although the American Federation of Labor sought its main objectives through trade union action, labor as a whole gained substantial benefits from both state and national legislation between 1865 and World War I. Union leaders usually gave their support to labor legislation, but most of the political pressure came from middle-class reformers. This was especially true during the progressive movement after 1900.

The federal government inaugurated an eight-hour day on public works in 1868, set up a Bureau of Labor Statistics in 1884, and abolished contract labor in 1885. In 1903 Congress created a Department of Commerce and Labor. A separate Department of Labor gained full Cabinet status in 1913. Congress passed a federal employer's liability law in 1908 which provided compensation for certain government employees in case of accidental injury. In 1914 a section of the Clayton Antitrust Act forbade court injunctions in labor disputes unless they were necessary "to prevent irreparable injury to property." The La Follette Seamen's Act of 1915 did much to improve the wages and working conditions of men on American merchant vessels. The next year the Adamson Act established an eight-hour day for the nation's railroad workers. Congress passed the Keating-Owen bill in 1916 forbidding the interstate shipment of mine products produced by children under sixteen and products from factories which hired children under fourteen. This effort to protect children failed. In 1918 the Supreme Court declared the law unconstitutional.

Meanwhile some states passed even more significant labor legislation. By 1916, when the Keating-Owen bill passed Congress, some thirty-seven states had enacted child-labor laws. Often these were tied to compulsory school attendance. A number of states also tried to limit the hours of work in certain dangerous occupations or among specific classes of workers. As early as 1874 Massachusetts passed an effective measure limiting the work of women and children in factories to ten hours daily. In 1896 Utah enacted a law which restricted work in mines to eight hours a day. Oregon in 1903 passed a law regulating the hours of work for women; the

Supreme Court upheld this law in 1908 in the case of *Muller v. Oregon.* A New York law providing a ten-hour day for bakers succumbed in *Lochner v. New York* in 1905, but later the Supreme Court relaxed its position on this question. Labor would have received more benefits from state and federal lawmakers if the courts had not declared many laws unconstitutional.

Immigration

Some problems of labor in the late nineteenth century flowed directly or indirectly from the quickening tide of immigration. Millions of European immigrants eagerly sought jobs in mining, manufacturing, and transportation at wages which were little above the subsistence level. It was easy for employers to resist demands for wage increases so long as penniless immigrants required immediate employment. Despite the rapid expansion of industry after the Civil War, there was a constant surplus of labor, and during long periods of depression in the 1870s and 1890s unemployment and underemployment were extremely high. Even so, wages were better in the United States than in Europe, and most immigrants lived better in America than they had as peasants in Europe.

In the half century between 1860 and 1910, some 23 million foreigners migrated to America. As had been true before the Civil War, most of them came in search of better economic opportunities. But there were new forces at work in both the United States and Europe which interacted to attract ever-increasing numbers of immigrants. In the first place industry needed more labor—preferably cheap labor. Consequently, many agencies encouraged Europeans to migrate to America. At the same time, conditions in Europe stimulated immigration as farmers and farm laborers in England, Ireland, the Scandinavian countries, and Germany experienced frequent periods of crop failures, low prices, and hard times.

The same pattern of immigration established before the Civil War continued generally until 1890, with the main body of immigrants arriving from northern and western Europe. In the 1880s about 72 percent of all immigrants came from those parts. Hundreds of thousands of Scandinavians and Germans settled on Midwestern farms as well as in such cities as Milwaukee, Chicago, and Cincinnati. Most immigrants from England and Ireland remained in the eastern seaboard cities. Very few immigrants settled in the South, because that section of the country would provide neither the agricultural nor the industrial opportunities which they were seeking.

By 1890 the tide of immigration from northern and western Europe began to decline, and the so-called old immigration, the nationals who had historically peopled America, was soon replaced by the "new immigration" from southern and eastern Europe. What produced this shift, in large measure, was the broadening of economic opportunity in northern and western Europe and the greater accessibility of eastern and southern Europeans to ports of embarkation. The change which took place can best be seen in the figures. Between 1881 and 1890 only 18 percent of American immigrants originated in the countries of southeastern Europe; in the decade from 1891 to 1900 this number reached 71 percent. The chief sources of the new immigration were the Austro-Hungarian empire, Italy, and Russia, in that order. But thousands of Greeks, Syrians, Poles, and Orientals also arrived. Most immigrants from eastern Europe were Catholics, but among them were thousands of Jews.

Although the new immigrants were a rural, peasant people, most of them settled in the growing industrial centers of the Northeast and Midwest rather than on farms. It was this multitude of Italians, Russians, Austrians, Croatians, Bohemians, Hungarians, and Poles which supplied the cheap labor for America's industrial revolution. By the early 1900s they had taken

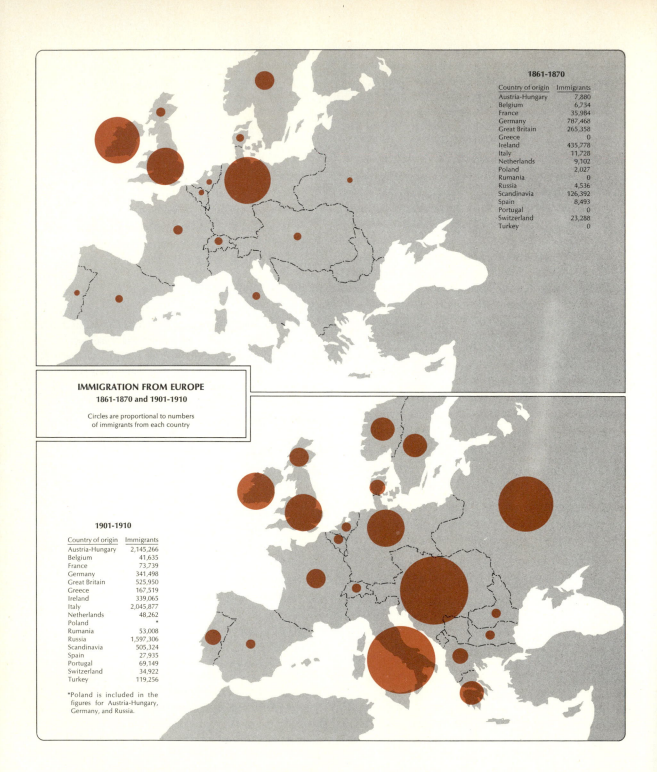

IMMIGRATION FROM EUROPE

1861-1870 and 1901-1910

Circles are proportional to numbers
of immigrants from each country

1861-1870

Country of origin	Immigrants
Austria-Hungary	7,880
Belgium	6,734
France	35,984
Germany	787,468
Great Britain	265,358
Greece	0
Ireland	435,778
Italy	11,728
Netherlands	9,102
Poland	2,027
Rumania	0
Russia	4,536
Scandinavia	126,392
Spain	8,493
Portugal	0
Switzerland	23,288
Turkey	0

1901-1910

Country of origin	Immigrants
Austria-Hungary	2,145,266
Belgium	41,635
France	73,739
Germany	341,498
Great Britain	525,950
Greece	167,519
Ireland	339,065
Italy	2,045,877
Netherlands	48,262
Poland	*
Rumania	53,008
Russia	1,597,306
Scandinavia	505,324
Spain	27,935
Portugal	69,149
Switzerland	34,922
Turkey	119,256

*Poland is included in the
figures for Austria-Hungary,
Germany, and Russia.

over most of the jobs in mines, textile mills, and certain other manufacturing industries. The new immigrants were overwhelmingly industrial workers and city builders.

In America the immigrant contribution had always been great. This was no less true of those who arrived in the late nineteenth century than of those who had immigrated earlier. Yet by the 1870s, many settled Americans moved to restrict immigration. Denis Kearney's campaign against the Chinese in the late 1870s resulted in passage of the Chinese Exclusion Act of 1882. The same year Congress forbade the entrance of certain undesirables—convicts, lunatics, idiots, and those who might become public charges. These laws were selective and did not satisfy those who demanded a more general restriction. From time to time, there had been sporadic outbursts of nativism in American history; in the late 1880s, nativists saw something sinister and dangerous in the influx of Italians, Slavs, Jews, and others from southern and eastern Europe. The American Protective Association, organized in 1887, focused chiefly on Catholics, but it worked to curb the influx of all foreigners. Critics of unlimited immigration argued that these new immigrants were clannish and refused to assimilate as quickly or completely as those from northern and western Europe did.

By the 1890s Congress could no longer ignore the demand for immigration restriction. In 1897 lawmakers passed a measure, sponsored by Senator Henry Cabot Lodge of Massachusetts, which required a literacy test of all immigrants. This bill was aimed at southern and eastern Europeans, among whom illiteracy was high. President Cleveland vetoed the measure. But the relentless drive for immigration restriction continued. Finally, in 1917 Congress passed a law over President Wilson's veto which denied admittance to aliens over sixteen who could not read English or some other language. The head tax was raised to $8. The law of 1917 represented a definite turn in American immigration policy. It was the first major step toward strict limitation, replacing the concept of selection which had been designed to keep out only certain specified groups such as the Chinese.

Urban America

In 1860 the United States was predominantly rural. Most people were engaged in agriculture, and about 80 percent of the population actually resided on farms or in small villages. Only 20 percent lived in towns and cities of 2,500 or more, the census definition of an urban area after 1880. New York alone in 1860 had more than 1 million people, and only eight cities could boast more than 100,000. Thereafter the transition from a rural to a predominantly urban nation was especially remarkable because of its speed. By 1900 urbanization, with all of its benefits, problems, and prospects for a fuller life, became the mark of modern America.

The changing physical landscape reflected the shift to an urbanized society. Railroad terminals, smoking factories, skyscrapers, apartment houses, streetcars, electric turbines, department stores, and the increased pace of life were all signs of an emerging urban America. Indeed, the vitality, dynamic quality, variety, and restless experimentalism in society centered in the urban communities where the only constant factor was change itself.

Urbanization did not proceed uniformly throughout the nation. New England and the Middle Atlantic states contained the highest percentage of city dwellers. In the older Middle West the growth of cities such as Chicago, Milwaukee, Cleveland, and St. Louis measured the importance of urbanization in that region. The three West Coast states also experienced rapid urban growth. In the South urbanization developed much more slowly, although by 1910 the expansion of transportation, commerce, and industry had greatly increased the population of older cities such as New Orleans and stimulated the growth of new urban centers such as Birmingham. However, the South remained predominantly rural. Only somewhat more than 20 percent of the population in that region was urban by 1910.

In some regions the urban impact had a depressing effect upon the surrounding rural communities. Much of New England in the late nineteenth century presented a discouraging picture of abandoned farms and sickly villages as people forsook the countryside and rushed to the larger towns and cities. Commenting on a nearly deserted Vermont village, one observer wrote: "The church was abandoned, the academy dismantled, the village lived on one side of the broad street, and he who owned the farm on the south lived on the other, and they were the only inhabitants." In Ohio and Illinois hundreds of townships lost population in the 1880s.

The Pull of the City

In 1871 a Milwaukee editor wrote that sooner or later "the young man in the country . . . will be sucked into one of the great [urban] centers of life." And so it was in the late nineteenth century, as country and village boys filled the roads and highways on their way to the cities. What created the irresistible pull of the cities? First of all, the city had always been the nerve center of civilization. This was true no less in ancient Greece or medieval Europe than in the United States. Cities normally provided a wide variety of services; they were the cultural, religious, educational, and entertainment centers; and perhaps most important, cities provided many types of economic opportunity for restless and ambitious individuals. Undoubtedly, people migrated from farms to towns and cities more because they believed they could improve their economic position than for any other reason.

Indeed, the Rockefellers, Carnegies, Vanderbilts, and other tremendously rich Americans in the late nineteenth century made their money in city-based businesses. These successes convinced many farm youths that in the city any achievement was possible. Streams of success literature emphasized this thesis.

Both the concentration of population and the accumulation of wealth in the cities made possible many social and cultural advantages not found in the more isolated rural communities. Only large towns and cities supported libraries, theaters, opera, music conservatories, art galleries, and other cultural and educational institutions. Probably most urbanites ignored these cultural opportunities because of disinterest or lack of money, but their availability added greatly to the city's attractiveness. Increasing numbers of country people considered the Saturday trip to town, the country fair, a meeting of the literary society, occasional picnics, and other rural amusements much less exciting than a dramatic production, a musical, or even a prizefight staged in the cities. Urban communities had better schools, churches, newspapers, and medical services. City living, in short, promised not only higher living standards but also greater cultural, educational, and recreational enjoyments. As one observer wrote, one could "shop better, . . . dress more fashionably, . . . give parties more conveniently, . . . get better concerts, and see more sights."

Problems of Urbanization

Rapid urbanization created a host of difficult problems. What blighted city life for many was the absence of adequate housing. Unable to afford individual houses or good apartments, newcomers crowded into cramped and filthy tenements, which were built in large numbers after the 1880s. Tenements were usually four to six stories high, with each floor divided into several family units consisting of two to four poorly ventilated and dimly lit rooms. The following description of life in New York was common enough: "The man, his wife, and three small children shiver[ed] in one room through the roof of which the pitiless winds of winter whistled. The room was almost barren of furniture; the parents slept on the floor, the elder children in boxes, and the baby was swung in an old shawl attached to the rafters." Although conditions in the tenements were well known, it was not until Jacob Riis published his book *How the Other Half Lives* in 1890 that widespread public attention was drawn to the economic, social, and political problems arising from slum conditions.

Millions of new urbanites suffered from a lack of such public services as running water, garbage disposal, and general sanitation. As late as the 1870s, hogs ate the refuse in the streets. Sewage was often dumped in the closest river or lake without any precautions to guard the general health. It was not uncommon for several urban families to rely on a single water outlet. The danger of fire was always present. The congestion which resulted from the heavy concentration of population created severe problems for horse-drawn transportation. City life demanded faster and more efficient transit. Also, candles and kerosene lamps were unsuited for urban living.

At best, these and other problems in American cities were only partially solved before 1914. Some of the needs for housing were met by new apartments as well as additional houses in the growing suburbs. Meanwhile most of the urban poor were crammed into an ever-growing number of dirty and dangerous dwellings. By 1900 there were some 43,000 tenements in New York City occupied by approximately 1.5 million people. To meet transportation needs, cities built brick and asphalt streets and instituted more efficient types of public transportation. By the

These two ragamuffins, photographed in the late 1880s by Jacob Riis, "didn't live nowhere."

The Jacob A. Riis Collection, Museum of the City of New York

turn of the century, overhead railways, cable cars, and subways were hauling the urban multitudes. The construction of central water systems, often owned and operated by the cities themselves, provided a more adequate and safer water supply. Cities alleviated the problem of waste and sewage disposal by burning garbage and introducing filter and treatment plants. Yet sewage continued to be a problem, polluting rivers, lakes, and other natural receptacles. In 1880 the *Chicago Times* reported that the city was enclosed by "solid stink."

Electric lights met the needs for urban lighting. Although artificial gas remained the basic source of city light well into the 1880s, advances in electrical technology brought a rapid shift to electric lights. First introduced in Cleveland in 1879 by a brilliant engineer, Charles F. Brush, arc lamps soon spread to other cities. More important was the incandescent lamp patented by Thomas A. Edison in 1880. Central power stations provided the increasing demands for electric power.

Crime harassed the urban populations. Most large cities had their quota of pickpockets, petty thieves, swindlers, confidence men, robbers, and even murderers. Criminals often concentrated in the slum areas where gangs of hoodlums operated, untouched by the law. Prostitution flourished openly. Criminal and illegal activities often continued with the tacit approval of city and police officials. In 1874 the *Chicago Tribune* charged that the feeble effort to stamp out prostitution amounted to a "co-partnership of Chicago with harlotry." Adequate law enforcement against crime remained elusive.

Urban crowding affected people's behavior and attitudes in many ways. Race prejudice was strong in most cities, particularly against blacks and Orientals. Even some national groups such as Italians and Irish suffered from various types of discrimination. Such exclusiveness was apparent in housing and in public accommodations.

Corruption and Reform in City Government

Urbanization placed limits on good government. As Josiah Strong wrote: "To administer the affairs of a village of 1,000 inhabitants is a simple matter requiring only ordinary intelligence; the government of a city of 100,000 is much more complicated; while that of a city of 1,000,000 or of 5,000,000 demands expert knowledge, ability and character of the very highest order." Unfortunately not enough concern, knowledge, or character was present in late-nineteenth-century cities to provide honest and efficient government. Scandalous conditions involving dishonest elections, political graft and corruption, and police payoffs characterized the political life of many large cities.

One of the worst aspects of city government was the close and often corrupt relation between city officials and businessmen who stood to profit either from special licenses and franchises or from lax enforcement of the laws. Politicians maintained political machines with the financial support of business interests who paid them handsomely for street railway, electric lighting, and other public utility franchises, from which they in turn reaped huge profits. After investigating conditions in St. Louis, "Muckraker" Lincoln Steffens wrote of Colonel Ed Butler, the city's political boss: "His business was boodling. . . . It involves, not thieves, gamblers, and common women, but influential citizens, capital-ists, and great corporations. For the stock-in-trade of the boodler is the rights, privileges, franchises, and real property of the city, and his source of corruption is the top, not the bottom, of society."

Urban bosses also gained support for their political machines from newly arrived immigrants and other low-income groups who were willing to exchange their votes for such considerations as jobs, coal, groceries, and other favors. City bosses often assisted these helpless people when others ignored them; but, as a result, the immigrants became easy prey for ward bosses whose job it was to round up votes at election time.

City after city became trapped in the web of corrupt governmental administration. One of the most notorious examples of dishonest government was the Tweed Ring in New York City. Born in New York in 1823, William M. Tweed was a rough, congenial, unscrupulous fireman who rose to become president of the Board of Supervisors. Once he had gained political control in New York in 1868, Tweed set out to enrich himself and his friends. The Ring awarded city contracts at ridiculously high prices to printing, paving, and other companies in which they had an interest. The city treasurer, a member of the Ring, paid millions of dollars in fictitious bills. The Ring forced contractors to pad their claims and then pocketed the excess millions. Although Tweed, his power broken, died in jail in 1877, New York fell periodically under boss control during the rest of the nineteenth century. In many other cities the situation was little better.

Inefficient and dishonest city government did not go unchallenged. During the 1880s and 1890s reformers organized civic federations, municipal leagues, and other groups to fight for good government. Urban reformers demanded a competitive civil service and stressed the need for better governmental organization. For the cities required better charters, reduced control by state governments, new methods of administration, restructuring of governments to make them more efficient and responsive to the wishes of majorities, as well as honest elections. Many cities adopted the short ballot; others placed more power in the hands of the mayor; some replaced the old mayor-council system with the commission type of government. First introduced in Galveston, Texas, in 1901, following a devastating flood, the commission plan provided for a commission, usually of some five members, which decided all major questions of policy.

THE "BRAINS"

THAT ACHIEVED THE TAMMANY VICTORY AT THE ROCHESTER DEMOCRATIC CONVENTION.

"The 'Brains'": An 1870 cartoon of "Boss" Tweed by Thomas Nast. The Granger Collection

Other municipalities adopted the city-manager plan. This called for a manager to handle the day-to-day administration, under the general supervision of a commission or council.

Urban Life

Most American cities grew haphazardly, without any particular plan or design. The streets were often narrow and crooked; building codes were poorly enforced, permitting a variety of structures to be built in the same area. Cities often retained no open spaces for recreation; they were dirty, unkempt, congested, and often ugly. The variations in architectural forms, elevated trains, dusty streets, laundry hanging from windows, and crude advertising displays gave cities a depressing appearance. The contrasts in physical appearance among different areas of the same city were astonishing. The run-down slum areas of New York, for example, seemed especially ugly contrasted with the palatial homes of a Vanderbilt, Jay Gould, or William Rockefeller.

The elegant residences on Fifth Avenue, which in some cases had cost several million dollars, reflected conspicuous expenditures both inside and out. As transportation facilities improved, many middle-class residents moved to the mushrooming suburbs.

Class lines, based chiefly on income and standard of living, were sharply drawn in urban communities. The rich occupied fine offices in the new business centers and enjoyed the theater, opera, world travel, and lavish parties. In 1897 the Bradley Martin ball in New York cost an estimated $369,200. In 1900 Andrew Carnegie's personal income approached $23 million, and the wealthy Chicago merchant Marshall Field reputedly earned $700 an hour. Millions, on the other hand, worked for as little as $300 or $400 a year, and shopgirls in New York earned $5 to $6 a week. The poor had their cheap amusements which included the "workingman's club," or saloon. Most Americans, generally identified as middle class, lived between these extremes.

The plight of the poor was serious; it did not go unnoticed. As cities became larger and problems multiplied, social and philanthropic organizations attempted to help those unfortunates who, for some reason, could not provide the necessities of life for themselves. Private agencies, church groups, and local governments organized relief programs and participated in recreational and educational work. Social services for the urban poor often centered in settlement houses—refuges in the midst of the slums where social workers provided leadership and assistance to those overwhelmed with social prob-

lems. Some fifty settlement houses appeared after 1890 in Northern and Western cities, the most famous being Hull House, established by Jane Addams on Chicago's South Halstead Street in 1889.

Urbanization compelled the decline of individualism, the decrease in self-sufficiency, and the growth of interdependence. Unlike country people, who still retained a considerable amount of independence, city residents relied on others for most of their basic needs— their jobs, their housing, their food and entertainment. At the same time, life in the city was more impersonal. Some functions previously reserved to the family and home were assumed by the factory, school, and social or recreational agencies. Urbanization thus amounted to more than a mere transfer of people from farms and villages to cities. It instituted a completely new way of life.

Conclusion

Although workers made economic gains in the late nineteenth century, upward mobility was difficult for most laboring men, as well as for their children. Yet their economic progress was sufficient to sustain their faith in the American system of enterprise. Moreover, the prospect of better conditions that could be found in Europe

attracted millions of immigrants to the United States. The nation's growing wealth and economic power became by the end of the 1800s concentrated in the cities, and this development, in turn, caused social and economic problems to emerge which would make themselves felt in urban America far into the twentieth century.

SUGGESTED READINGS

Satisfactory histories of immigration include Carl Wittke's *We Who Built America* (1939); George H. Stephenson's *A History of American Immigration, 1820–1924* (1926); and Maldwyn A. Jones's *American Immigration** (1960). Oscar Handlin's *The Uprooted* (1951) shows the emotional and psychological impact of emigration on those who left their European homes and came to the United States. The strong feelings against foreigners and Catholicism have been excellently described by John Higham in *Strangers in the*

Land: Patterns of American Nativism, 1860–1925* (1955).

The most complete history of labor in this period is all of volume II and parts of volumes III and IV of *History of Labor in the United States* (1918) by John R. Commons and others. Henry Pelling has looked at the American labor movement from the British viewpoint in *American Labor** (1960).

Norman J. Ware's *The Labor Movement in the United States, 1860–1895** (1929) deals mostly with the

Knights of Labor. On the American Federation of Labor, see *The AF of L in the Time of Gompers* (1957) by Philip Taft. The best biography of Gompers is Bernard Mandel's *Samuel Gompers: A Biography* (1963). For the radical labor movement see David A. Shannon's *The Socialist Party of America** (1955) and Paul F. Brissenden's *The I.W.W.: A Study of American Syndicalism* (2d ed., 1950). Black labor has been treated in Charles H. Wesley's *Negro Labor in the United States, 1850–1925* (1927). For a general survey of labor history during this period see the pertinent chapters in Joseph G. Rayback's *A History of American Labor** (1966).

Conflicts between labor and management have been examined in detail in Donald L. McMurry's *The Great Burlington Strike of 1888* (1956); Louis Adamic's *Dynamite: The Story of Class Violence in America* (rev. ed., 1934); and Almont Lindsay's *The Pullman Strike** (1942). The best discussion of wages up to 1890 is Clarence D. Long's *Wages and Earnings in the United States, 1860–1890* (1960).

The best introduction to urban development in the late nineteenth and early twentieth century is *The Urbanization of America, 1860–1915* (1963) by Blake McKelvey. Charles N. Glaab has included a number of useful readings on specific aspects of urbanization during this period in *The American City: A Documentary History** (1963). Details of urban development can best be obtained in the histories of individual cities. See Bessie L. Pierce's *A History of Chicago* (3 vols., 1937–1957); Blake McKelvey's *Rochester: The Flower City, 1855–1890* (1949); and Bayrd Still's *Milwaukee* (1948).

Corruption in urban political affairs has been graphically discussed by Lincoln Steffens in *The Shame of the Cities** (1904); M. R. Werner in *Tammany Hall* (1928); and S. J. Mandelbaum in *Boss Tweed's New York* (1965). Life in the city slums has been well described by Jacob Riis in *How the Other Half Lives** (1890). The development of the ghetto is covered by Gilbert Osofsky's *Harlem: The Making of a Ghetto, Negro New York, 1890–1930** (1966) and Seth M. Scheiner's *Negro Mecca: A History of the Negro in New York City, 1865–1920* (1965).

*indicates availability in paperback.

19

Frontier Expansion and Agriculture, 1865-1890

At the close of the Civil War most of the vast region of plains, mountains, and deserts between Kansas City and San Francisco remained unsettled. Here was the "last frontier," more than 1 billion acres awaiting the miner, farmer, rancher, lumberman, and businessman. Exploitation of the West's tremendously rich natural resources had only begun in 1865; thereafter pioneer Americans settled this last frontier with breathtaking speed. Within a single generation after the Civil War almost all of the Great West, as it was known to contemporaries, had been occupied. The Director of the Census wrote in 1890 that "the unsettled area had been so broken into by isolated bodies of settlement that there can hardly be said to be a frontier line."

Western history of the late nineteenth century centers on the acquisition and development of land, minerals, lumber, water, and other resources. People rushed into the region by the tens of thousands in the hope of gaining a share of the wealth. Mines, ranchlands, farmlands, and timber, as well as speculative business ventures, lured men and capital from all over the world. The story of the settlement and exploitation of the last frontier gripped the interest and imagination of Americans more firmly than any other aspect of their history and left enduring traditions.

Reasons for Rapid Settlement

Several important factors contributed to the rapid settlement of the unoccupied West after 1865. The mining boom which drew thousands of Forty-niners into California was duplicated many times by the Fifty-niners and their followers in Nevada, Colorado, Idaho, Montana, and elsewhere. During and after the Civil War, men rushed to previously isolated and unsettled regions in search of gold and silver. News of one mining strike after another advertised the Great West as had no previous event. Development of the range cattle industry during the 1870s publicized additional opportunities in the West.

New transportation facilities speeded the settlement of the trans-Mississippi frontier. Not only did stage and freight companies extend their lines, but railroads between 1870 and 1890 penetrated almost every section of the West. Moreover, the federal government contributed to the rapid movement of population through generous land policies for farmers; land grants to railroads, which encouraged speedier construction; and restrictions on the movement of Indians. Indians generally did not block westward settlement after 1870.

Finally, the strong desire for land probably outweighed all other factors in bringing the frontier to an end. Between 1865 and 1900 settlers rapidly occupied the prairie plains, the Pacific Northwest, and most of the good land in California and the Rocky Mountain region. Altogether then, the immense wilderness west of Iowa and Missouri succumbed to a series of separate, but interdependent, frontiers. Miners, cattlemen, railroad builders, and farmers hastily overran that great undeveloped region, settled it, and brought it into an integral economic, political, and social relationship with the rest of the nation.

The Mining Frontiers

Between 1858 and 1875 eager prospectors swarmed over the mountains and deserts of the American West, searching for gold and silver. A decade after the rich strikes in California, restless miners located new wealth in Nevada, Colorado, Idaho, and Montana. By the 1860s prospectors were singing:

Farewell, old California, I'm going far away.
Where gold is found more plenty,
In larger lumps, they say.

Early in 1859 John S. Gregory, an experienced gold miner from Georgia, and George H. Jackson, a former California miner, found gold in paying quantities west of Denver in the vicinity of Central City. Reports of these riches brought a flood of prospectors to the region around Denver and Boulder, and by the summer of 1859 an estimated hundred thousand people were feverishly seeking their fortunes with pan and sluice box.

At about the same time, miners entered Gold Canyon in western Nevada. They found small amounts of the precious metal, but their claim also contained large amounts of blue-gray quartz which proved to be rich in silver. Henry T. P. Comstock bluffed his way into a share of the claim, giving his name to the fabulous silver deposits known as the Comstock lode. Reports of the discovery in June 1859 brought the usual rush of prospectors and speculators to the new bonanza. Gold Hill and Virginia City quickly became bustling, boisterous, and flourishing mining towns. Miners and prospectors seemed forever on the move in search of new strikes. Soon big strikes were located in Idaho and Montana. The last major gold rush occurred in the Black Hills of Dakota, mostly around Custer City and Deadwood.

It was placer mining which drew the prospectors to the widely scattered diggings of the Far West. This type of mining required little equipment and simple techniques. Besides a pack of supplies to meet personal requirements, a miner needed only a pan and a shovel. Panning for gold was slow, hard work, and most prospectors profited no more than a few dollars a day. Some miners, however, received as much as $500 for a day's work.

Life in the mining camps was transient, crude, rough, and sometimes dangerous. Men lived in tents, cabins, wagon boxes, and even in the open during the initial rush. Prices of necessities in the mining camps were fabulously high, with flour sometimes selling for 85 cents a pound and potatoes for $27 a bushel. The camps swarmed not only with miners, but with speculators, traders, saloon keepers, teamsters, and prostitutes. Vice and violence flourished. Mark Twain, who as a young man worked on the Virginia City, Nevada, *Enterprise,* wrote that murder, robberies, assassinations, and knifings were the order of the day. Twain said that "to be a saloonkeeper and to kill a man was to be illustrious" in Virginia City. In a single twenty-four-hour period one "woman was killed by a pistol shot, a man was brained with a sling shot," and another man was "disposed of permanently." The red-light district was large and well populated, and it was said that an energetic and thrifty girl could make more money than a hardworking miner. Despite the lawlessness, prospectors organized mining districts to register and protect claims, and miners' courts and vigilante groups maintained a degree of law and order. Miners dispatched justice quickly by whipping or hanging, thus eliminating the need of holding culprits for trial in so-called leaky jails.

The economy of these mining communities was highly unstable and fluctuated with the success or failure of the miners to find new gold or silver. More stable conditions came to prevail as large companies moved in heavy equipment to process the ore, hired labor, and provided business for merchants, professional men, and other permanent settlers. Social conditions became stabilized in most mining communities within a short time, and circumstances such as those Mark Twain described at Virginia City did not survive. Permanent settlers usually gained control and soon established newspapers, schools, churches, libraries, lodges, and other institutions common to the settled East and Middle West.

These widely scattered mining frontiers exerted a powerful influence on the settlement and development of the West. The repeated mining strikes familiarized Americans with the vast region between the Missouri River and the Pacific Ocean and advertised the area's tremendous resources. Trading posts and cities sprang into existence to provide miners with supplies. Towns such as Sacramento, Walla Walla, Salt Lake City, Denver, and Helena were among those which developed as supply centers. The rapid occupation of new areas created a strong demand for better and faster transportation—stage and freight lines, steamboats, and especially railroads.

Moreover, the rush of people into previously unoccupied areas hastened political organization throughout the West. Colorado, for example, became a territory in 1861, only two years after the initial gold rush, and Idaho and Montana gained separate territorial status in 1863 and 1865 respectively. The mining frontiers affected Western agricultural development. The high prices of food in the isolated mining camps caused many emigrants to take up farming—often more profitable than panning for gold. Agriculture soon became firmly established in many remote regions of the West, and farmers discovered that irrigation and proper techniques made possible abundant agricultural production in the semiarid and arid West. In addition, the output of some $1.5 billion in gold between 1860 and 1890 permitted the United States to go on a *de facto* gold standard in 1879. Meanwhile the production of $901 million in silver raised the money question, the most important political issue in the late nineteenth century. Finally, the Western mining industry created a class of new-rich businessmen such as George Hearst of California and William A. Clark of Montana, who made vast fortunes and spent it on everything money could buy.

Western Ranching

Development of the range cattle industry advertised the West and contributed to the closing of the frontier by the 1890s. Cattle raising had always been an important frontier enterprise in the United States. Herds of 1,000 head were not uncommon in Ohio in the 1830s, and the "prairie cattle kings" of Illinois and Indiana developed large operations during the 1840s and 1850s. Meanwhile ranching had also become a substantial business in Texas.

Several major factors contributed to the establishment and growth of the Western range cattle industry after 1865. By the 1850s some ranchers in Idaho, Wyoming, and Montana regions along the trails to Oregon maintained herds of several hundred head. The discovery of gold and silver throughout the West provided additional markets for livestock producers. Cattlemen could now sell beef to miners, Army posts, and railroad builders, as well as emigrants traveling west.

More important, however, was the discovery that the semiarid plains and valleys of the West provided excellent natural conditions for large-scale cattle raising. The short grama and buffalo grasses on the Great Plains were especially nutritious, and they retained most of their value even after drying up in the late summer and fall. Most of the region between the Texas Panhandle and the Canadian border was in the public domain and could be grazed at little or no cost. Thus ranchers could profit handsomely from the stocking of the central and northern plains if markets could be found for increased quantities of beef. Many of the cattle needed to stock these ranges came from Texas.

During the Civil War, the market for Texas cattle had been effectively severed by the Union blockade. Consequently, the number of cattle rose rapidly, and by 1865 prices dropped to as little as $4 and $5 per head. At the time there was no rail transportation between Texas and the Midwest. If Texans, therefore, could drive their cattle to the nearest railroad in Missouri or Kansas, they might sell them for as much as $20 or $30 a head. Although some cattle were driven from Texas to Illinois in the 1840s, the "long drive" northward from Texas to Kansas and beyond did not begin in a systematic way until 1866. That year some 260,000 head were driven northward, mostly to Sedalia, Missouri.

In 1867 Joseph G. McCoy, a wealthy and prominent cattle dealer of Springfield, Illinois, visited Kansas and decided to make the little village of Abilene on the Kansas Pacific Railroad a shipping point for Texas cattle. When this news reached Texas, cattlemen drove about 35,000 head to Abilene later that year and twice that many in 1868. During the next few years cattlemen drove thousands of cattle north to such cow towns as Newton, Wichita, and Dodge City in Kansas, Kearney and North Platte in Nebraska. Stories and legends developed around the alleged glamour of trailing herds from Texas up the Chisholm Trail and other routes, but cattle driving was neither easy nor exciting. The life of a cowboy was dirty and hard. Black as well as white cowboys rode the ranges and followed the herds.

By 1880 the stage was set for a tremendous boom in the Western cattle business. The ranges had been stocked from Texas to Montana. Hunters had killed millions of buffalo for their hides in the 1870s, reducing this source of competition for grass on the public domain. At the same time, soldiers had brought the Indians under stricter control. Furthermore, prices for beef rose, and markets expanded rapidly in both domestic urban centers and foreign countries. Railroad transportation had been extended into much of the Western country, making it easier and more convenient to market cattle from widely dispersed ranges.

Speculation, large-scale operations, the influx of Eastern and foreign capital, and typical Western optimism characterized the range cattle boom of the 1880s. In the early years of the decade, newspaper accounts, magazine stories, and books advertised the favorable prospects for ranching and gave the impression that large profits awaited almost any investor.

By the middle 1880s both small and large ranches dotted the Western plains and valleys. The Swan Land and Cattle Company near Cheyenne, Wyoming, typified some of the big outfits in that area. Financed by Scottish capital, this company owned and controlled thousands of acres of land, ran an estimated 100,000 head of cattle, and was worth about $4 million in 1883. The XIT ranch in the Texas Panhandle was even more extensive. Organized by a Chicago syndicate and supported by foreign capital, the XIT ranged around 110,000 head of cattle over millions of acres, and by 1886 was valued at more than $5.5 million.

The Western range cattle industry reached its height between 1882 and 1886. Its very success, however, led to the decline of free-range ranching. Overexpansion of the cattle business had two closely related and unfortunate effects. The ranges became so overstocked that cattle suffered from a shortage of grass. Moreover, the greatly increased numbers caused a sharp and disastrous price decline. In 1884 Western cattle brought about $5.60 a hundred pounds in Chicago; a year later the price dropped to $3.50. Soon prices went even lower because of the decrease of foreign markets.

Most cattlemen did not provide winter feed and shelter for their livestock; thus they suffered heavy losses during the periodic hard winters on the Plains. The great blizzard of January 1887, following a hot, dry summer, killed thousands of cattle. Low prices and hard winters caused many companies to go bankrupt. Another, more pervading problem for the cattlemen was the penetration of dirt farmers onto the Great Plains in the late 1880s. These "sodbusters," with titles to their lands, broke up much of the former range and forced cattlemen to contract their operations. The day of the free range was for the most part gone. To meet these challenges, cattlemen adjusted and reorganized their operations. They grew hay and forage for winter feed, furnished winter protection for their cattle, bought or leased their own lands, and fenced them. Thus Western ranching existed on a more stable basis by 1900.

The range cattle industry was highly important in settling the last frontier. It was another source of favorable publicity. Cattlemen were the first to demonstrate the value of the semiarid Great Plains. Ranching, like mining and railroading, attracted Eastern and foreign capital into the West to further the region's economic development; it stimulated railroad building and helped to open up the country. Finally, the ranchers' frontier created legends about the American West reflected in movies and novels that continued unabated almost a century later.

The Western Agricultural Frontier

At the end of the Civil War, the Western edge of farm settlement followed a rough line which angled southwestward from near St. Paul, Minnesota, to somewhat west of Fort Worth, Texas, and then south to the Rio Grande. There were tongues of settlement farther west, but not many farmers had ventured beyond Topeka, Kansas, or a few miles west of Omaha, Nebraska. Much of the unsettled area of southwestern and western Minnesota, northwestern Iowa, eastern Dakota, and eastern and central Nebraska and Kansas contained fertile soil and usually received enough rainfall to raise adequate crops. Beyond this Western prairie area, beginning at about the

98th or 99th meridian and extending to the base of the Rocky Mountains, were the Great Plains, a vast semiarid region whose farming potential was yet unknown in 1865. Farther west the Mormons had become successful farmers around Salt Lake City by the 1850s and 1860s. There were also major agricultural communities in California and Oregon. Most of the country between Kansas City or Omaha and the Pacific Coast, however, still awaited the settler's plow. But the desire for land was strong. Within a generation after the Civil War the best lands had been settled.

In 1865 a farmer could obtain public land by purchase or preemption, or by acceding to the provisions of the Homestead Act of 1862. The government sold much public land directly. Under preemption a settler could obtain a quarter section (160 acres) of land by fulfilling certain residence and improvement requirements and then paying $1.25 an acre. The Homestead Act permitted a citizen who was twenty-one years of age, or a person who had declared his intention to become a citizen, to file an entry at a government land office on 160 acres of the public domain. The only cost was a small filing fee. The settler was required to make improvements and live on the land for five years, after which the government would grant him full ownership. If the homesteader did not want to wait five years to obtain title, he was permitted to pay $1.25 an acre after a specific time, and he would then receive his land title, known as a "final patent." Westerners had worked for many years to obtain this legislation. Many people considered free land a great victory for democracy because it gave more citizens an economic stake in society. Although the democratic aims of the law were not entirely realized, the Homestead Act helped thousands of settlers become established farmers, especially in Minnesota, Dakota, Nebraska, and Kansas.

Other land laws included the Timber Culture Act of 1873, the Desert Land Act of 1877, and the Timber and Stone Act, passed in 1878. Of these measures the only one of much interest to farmers was the Timber Culture Act. Under this law a person could enter an additional 160 acres of government land, and the only requirement, except a filing fee, was the planting of 40 acres of trees on the land. This requirement was later reduced to 10 acres. The Timber Culture Act sprang from the conviction that trees grown on the Western prairies and Great Plains would reduce the winds, increase the moisture, and improve the climate for agriculture. It also permitted Western farmers to acquire larger acreages. The Desert Land Act was designed to promote irrigation in the arid West. A person could file for 640 acres in certain Western states and territories by paying down 25 cents an acre, and after irrigating part of the land and paying an additional dollar an acre, he would receive full title within four years. Ranchers took advantage of the measure to gain control of large acreages at cheap prices. The Timber and Stone Act permitted a person in some Western states and territories to buy 160 acres of land for $2.50 an acre. The land was to be "unfit for cultivation," contain no valuable minerals, and be used largely for its timber and stone.

What speeded the settlement of the West after the Civil War were the railroads. People continued to make their way westward in wagons, but railroads provided fast and comparatively cheap transportation into many remote areas. The Union Pacific joined Chicago and San Francisco in 1869, the Santa Fe reached western Kansas in 1870, and the Northern Pacific arrived at Bismarck, Dakota, in 1873. These and other main and branch lines not only provided transportation, but they also carried on vigorous promotional campaigns and advertised the West's economic opportunities. Railroad companies hoped to attract immigrants both to sell their own lands and to promote business along their lines.

During the first decade after the Civil War, most settlers moved into the rich prairie lands of southwestern and western Minnesota, eastern Dakota, and as far west as central Nebraska and Kansas. In Minnesota and Dakota, wheat was the major crop; pioneers in Nebraska and Kansas generally relied on corn. Farm operations were very small; after years of effort most frontier farmers did not cultivate more than 30 or 40 acres of crops or own more than a few head of livestock. Their annual incomes often did not exceed $100 in cash.

While crops were good and prices favorable, Western farmers were able to extract a fair living. But since most of them had little or no capital reserve, one or two poor years could spell disaster. In the middle 1870s, settlers from Minnesota to south-central Kansas suffered terribly because of drought and grasshopper devastations. After grasshoppers had destroyed his crops, one typical farmer in western Minnesota wrote that, unless outside help came soon, he and his family faced starvation.

When farmers pushed onto the Great Plains in the 1880s and occupied central Dakota, western Kansas and Nebraska, eastern Colorado, and northwest Texas, they found geographic conditions which demanded change and adjustment. East of the 98th meridian, settlers found enough timber for building and wood for fuel. But when they moved to the treeless prairie-plains frontier, they were compelled to build their houses of sod and burn twisted hay or dried buffalo and cow manure for fuel. Water was another problem on the Great Plains. Wells often had to be drilled 100 or 200 feet deep. Farmers adopted windmills as a source of power. The need for fencing was met by the use of barbed wire, introduced in the 1870s.

The sod house, barbed wire, and the windmill were tangible evidences of the changes required for successful settlement on the Great Plains frontier. However, they were not as important as the adjustment in farm organization and agricultural practices. Because of limited and irregular moisture, farmers adopted drought-resisting crops; they obtained better results by summer fallowing their land, which meant leaving part idle each year so that it would store up moisture; they built up reserves of feed for dry periods; and they sought more land than a quarter sec-

tion, which was not enough in a semiarid region. Farmers who did not make the proper adjustments failed; those who organized their farming practices to fit the geography of the area had a much better chance to succeed.

During the 1870s and 1880s farmers occupied one frontier after another in the West. Thousands of settlers went to Oregon and Washington, as well as to California. Even the arid Rocky Mountain region drew many farmers, who developed and improved irrigation practices and made some desert areas highly productive. By the late 1880s there remained unsettled in the West very little good agricultural land which could be farmed without irrigation. One previously restricted area remained unexploited. That was Oklahoma. The eastern part of this region had been reserved for the Five Civilized Tribes, which included the Cherokee, Choctaw, Chickasaw, Seminole, and Creek; certain plains tribes had been settled on the western section after the Civil War. By the late 1880s various groups exerted strong pressure to open Oklahoma to white settlement. After years of agitation, the government opened the unassigned lands in central Oklahoma.

Facing more land seekers than available quarter sections, the government adopted a new method of distribution—the land run. Prospective settlers camped near the border of the new territory. The run began at noon on April 22, 1889. One contemporary wrote: "Along the line as far as the eye could reach, with a shout and a yell the swift riders shot out, then followed the light buggies or wagons and last the lumbering prairie schooners and freighters' wagons, with here and there even a man on a bicycle and many too on foot,—above all a great cloud of dust hovering like smoke over a battlefield. It was a wild scramble, a rough and tumble contest filled with excitement and real peril." In a single day, Guthrie and Oklahoma City grew from virgin prairie to towns of several thousand citizens, and the farm lands were claimed under government land laws within a very short time.

Between 1860 and 1900 waves of settlers es-

This house of one settler disappearing into the horizon of the Great Plains, recorded in this early Geological Survey photograph emphasizes the almost unreal vastness of what was, between 1860 and 1900, the stage for a whole series of historic dramas. Here the advancing white man displaced the Plains Indians as well as the Indian's principal economic resource—the buffalo. Here for a period of not much more than twenty-five years a vast open range existed, inviting the cattle industry to expand and flourish on the free grass of government land from Texas to Montana. Here in the late 1870s a new boom developed, as farmers began a great western migration. Barbed wire, first manufactured in America in 1874, enabled the farmer to protect his crops from roving cattle—and also enabled the great cattle barons to fence, for their own use, huge areas of the public domain.

The open range closed at last, and by the 1890s the best of the frontier lands had been occupied. Settlers came from the eastern states, both northern and southern, from Germany, Russia, England, France, Switzerland, Belgium, Canada and the countries of Scandinavia. Between 1860 and 1900, 1,414,276 new farms were established in the nineteen Western states and territories, and 400,000,000 acres of farming land, most of it west of the Mississippi, were added to the total American acreage under cultivation.

Settling the Frontier

The story of Western expansion also became the story of brutal encroachment of the white man upon the lands held by the Indian, an encroachment which the Indian resisted in many bloody battles before he succumbed. Government bounties encouraged the killing of Indians in Minnesota. According to the Museum of the American Indian, "amounts up to $100 per scalp were paid, regardless of age or sex, and friendly Indians were often raided by professional 'bounty hunters' for the reward." A section of the Minnesota General Orders of 1863 (above and below) displays one such offer and payment.

While the most effective body of public opinion supported settlement of what had been Indian land,

THE DAILY GRAPHIC

An Illustrated Evening Newspaper

VOL. VII.   NEW YORK, FRIDAY, MARCH 12, 1875.   NO. 626.

vice will have to arm, equip
own expense, and will be
ate of one dollar and fifty
n of twenty-five dollars will
h scalp of a male Sioux de-

some white people protested the invasion. The front
page of the New York *Daily Graphic* protests the
white trespass into the Black Hills of Dakota, the site
of the last major American gold rush. The caption
quotes the Indian as saying, "The Black Hills are mine,
and the United States have promised to protect me
against the invasion. If you keep not your word with
me, why should I keep mine with you? The villainy
you teach me I will execute, and it shall go hard but I
will better the instruction."

Indian resistance cost settlers' lives, but by 1890 it
was almost entirely broken. The photograph at the
right shows the victims of the Battle of Wounded Knee
being gathered for burial.

URER.   403

for Office,   25 00
                      25 00
                       3 12
                      30 00
                      33 75
litary Laws,   10 00
Lead,   -   61 80

Far left: The New-York Historical Society, New York City; left, above and below: Courtesy of the Museum of the American Indian, Heye Foundation; above: Smithsonian Institution, National Anthropological Archives, Bureau of Ethnology Collection

THE S. D. BUTCHER DOCUMENT

Solomon Devoe Butcher created one of the most important records of frontier life. Starting in 1886 and continuing, with interruptions, for some twenty years, Butcher wrote and photographed the history of Custer County, Nebraska. Butcher's pictures depict the culture of the sod house, a form of building which the settlers used in the absence of cheap, readily available wood. The sod was cut into 18 inch strips and laid like bricks, providing a home that was warm in winter and cool in summer, but hard to live in during extended periods of rain. The pictures from Butcher's collection here and on the pages that follow, are reproduced through the courtesy of the Nebraska Historical Society and with the assistance of Harry E. Chrisman, who in 1965 secured the republication of the rare *Pioneer History of Custer County,* and Purcell Publishing Co., whose *Sod Walls,* by Roger Welsch, is based largely on the Butcher collection. The Chrisman sisters in Custer County, 1886, appear below. The photograph at left shows a typical dugout which used the contour of the land to provide several of its walls. The following spread, above, shows a photograph taken by Butcher in 1904 of the new town of Comstock, Nebraska, when wood was more available and had replaced sod as the most common building material. By contrast, the 1888 farm, with corn planted up to the homesteader's front door, utilizes the older sod construction.

All pictures on these and following pages: S. D. Butcher, Nebraska State Historical Society

tablished some 1,141,276 new farms in the nineteen Western states and territories. These Western farmers more than any other group brought the frontier to an end.

Retreat of the Indians

Pressure from the advancing white men's frontiers finally forced the Western Indians into restricted areas. Here, in the trans-Missouri West, was enacted the final chapter in the long history of Indian retreat before onrushing settlers. However, the Western tribes did not surrender easily. Before peace reigned on the Indian frontier in the 1890s, the Indians had fought many bitter and costly battles with the United States Army. In this struggle power overruled justice.

At the end of the Civil War there were approximately 275,000 Indians west of the Mississippi River. Among the major tribes were the Sioux, Crow, and Blackfeet in the North; the Cheyenne and Arapaho on the Central Plains; the Comanche, Kiowa, and Apache in the Southwest; and the Ute, Snake, and Bannock in the Great Basin. The Five Civilized Tribes occupied what later became the eastern part of Oklahoma. Many lesser tribes lived in widely scattered areas elsewhere throughout the Great West.

The Treaty of Fort Laramie in 1851 had provided territorial boundaries for a number of the plains tribes, including the Sioux, Cheyenne, and Arapaho. However, the whites' desire to open portions of Kansas, Nebraska, and Dakota to settlement and to eliminate all Indians from Iowa and Missouri soon challenged the Fort Laramie agreements. Moreover, the influx of prospectors into the Cheyenne and Arapaho lands around Pikes Peak in 1859 aroused bitter Indian hostility. The steady pressure of whites against the dwindling Indian landholdings and the destruction of the wild game convinced many Indian leaders that they must rely on force to protect their lands and their way of life.

During the 1860s Indians and whites clashed in a series of bloody conflicts. In 1862 the Sioux attacked the Minnesota frontier, destroying property and killing more than 450 whites before they lost to Colonel H. H. Sibley's forces. Two years later the Cheyenne and Arapaho brought death and destruction to the Colorado frontier. Striking back fiercely at the Indians, the Colorado militia led by Colonel J. M. Chivington attacked Chief Black Kettle of the Southern Cheyenne and about five hundred Cheyenne and Arapaho camped at Sand Creek in southeastern Colorado in November 1864. Within a few hours, almost the entire camp had been shot, knifed, or beaten to death. Intermittent fighting continued during the next two or three years.

Some army commanders believed that the so-called Indian problem could be solved only through complete submission or extermination. On the other hand, many Easterners, including senators and congressmen, argued that the problems of Indian-white relations could be solved by enticing the Indians to accept smaller areas of land and encouraging them to give up their nomadic ways. Such a policy, they believed, would reduce friction and maintain peace by separating Indians from white settlements. But how could the federal government restrain Indians who were accustomed to roam over large areas? And how could it make whites understand that the Indians had fundamental rights to land assigned to them?

At a council on Medicine Lodge Creek in October 1867, the Kiowa, Comanche, Cheyenne, and Arapaho tribes agreed to reservations on the Southern plains. The next year, by a second Treaty of Fort Laramie, the Sioux accepted a permanent reservation west of the Missouri River in Dakota. These treaties did not restore peace. Rejecting their chiefs' decision to cede away millions of acres of land, angry Cheyenne and Arapaho warriors ravaged the Texas and Kansas frontiers in 1868. The Army responded vigorously to these depredations, and in November, Colonel George A. Custer defeated Chief Black Kettle and his followers on the banks of the Washita near the Texas border. The Indian raids continued, nevertheless, and it was not until June 1875, after six or seven years of intermittent fighting, that the Indians were completely beaten in Texas. Defeated, humiliated, and broken, they were forced back to remain on their reservations.

Settlers rushing into the Black Hills in 1875 and 1876 violated the Treaty of Fort Laramie and aroused the worried Sioux. Chiefs Crazy Horse and Sitting Bull began to collect arms and warriors near the Little Big Horn in Montana. Faced with another uprising, the Army again prepared for action. In the spring of 1876, several military groups moved against the recalcitrant Sioux. At the Little Big Horn, Custer stumbled into a far superior Indian force which wiped out his entire force of 265 men.

But this victory only postponed Indian defeat. Within a few months the Sioux had surrendered to the military power of General Alfred H. Terry. The Sioux war of 1876 ended Indian resistance in the North except for several sporadic outbreaks in subsequent years. In the Pacific Northwest, the remarkably elusive and capable Chief Joseph and his Nez Percé followers surrendered in 1878 after nearly two years of intermittent fighting against much larger United States armed forces. Among two of the less known, but highly effective, military units which helped to provide frontier defense were the Negro Ninth and Tenth Cavalry regiments.

The immediate solution of the Indian problem had been primarily a military one. Meanwhile the Indians had been weakened by whisky, disease, and destruction of the buffalo. Forced mostly into barren and unproductive areas, the Indians had no choice but to give up their independence and accept government support.

Although most whites supported military action against the Indians, harsh army tactics pricked the consciences of many Americans. By the late 1870s and early 1880s, the Indians' plight received widespread attention. In 1881 Helen Hunt Jackson presented a highly emotional and somewhat distorted account of the relations between the federal government and the Indians in her book *A Century of Dishonor.* She attributed most of the wrongs to a lack of government planning combined with public unconcern for Indian welfare. Other reformers and humanitarians joined the crusades against government Indian policies.

Eventually Washington responded. As early as 1871 Congress had abandoned the policy of dealing with Indian tribes through formal treaties. This action tended to break down tribal organization and authority. This policy of destroying tribal organization and fitting Indians into white society culminated in the Dawes Act in 1887. Sometimes called the Indian Emancipation Act, this law gave the President authority to order surveys of Indian reservations and to allot land to individual Indians. The head of each family was to receive 160 acres and each minor child 40 acres. An unmarried Indian over eighteen years of age was to receive 80 acres. Indian land holders were to become citizens of the United States. To keep unscrupulous whites from cheating Indian owners out of their land, the Dawes Act forbade Indians to sell or alienate their holdings before twenty-five years. This provision was modified in the Burke Act of 1906, which gave the Secretary of the Interior discretionary power to lessen the time period required of Indians before they could gain title to their land. The Dawes Act did not apply to the Five Civilized Tribes in Oklahoma, who opposed the breakup of tribal authority and control. However, after 1897 they, too, were compelled to accept individual allotments.

It soon became apparent that the Dawes Commission, charged with carrying out the purpose of the Dawes Act, could not make successful farmers out of Indians or fit them into a white-dominated economy. Much of the Indian land was poor and nonproductive. Moreover, Indian lands were in time fragmented and divided through inheritance and sale, driving thousands of Indians into stark poverty. Reservation Indi-

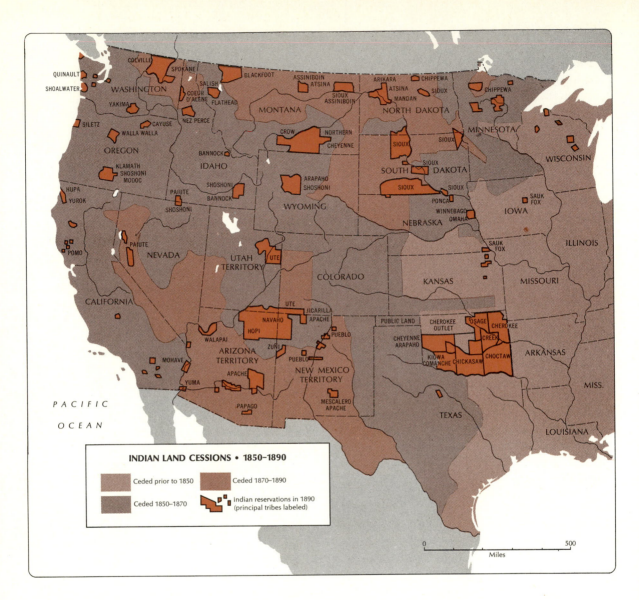

INDIAN LAND CESSIONS · 1850-1890

- Ceded prior to 1850
- Ceded 1850-1870
- Ceded 1870-1890
- Indian reservations in 1890 (principal tribes labeled)

0 ___ 500
Miles

ans were never properly assimilated into the mainstream of America's national life. The economic and social problems of Indians persist even in the twentieth century.

End of the Frontier

Rapid westward migration brought the frontier to an end in one long generation after 1865. Settlement of the West exerted important influences on American life. Westerners demanded statehood for the newly settled regions west of the Missouri River. After Nebraska became a state in 1867 and Colorado in 1876, no states entered the Union until 1889. Then within the space of several years ten states were added. These were the Dakotas, Washington, and Montana in 1889; Idaho and Wyoming in 1890; and Utah in 1896, after Congress insisted that the Mormons abandon polygamy. Oklahoma achieved statehood in 1907; New Mexico and Arizona, five years later.

Twelve new states after 1867 gave the West a degree of political power far out of proportion to its population. Most Western states did not grow at the rate of those settled earlier and, consequently, their equality in the United States Senate gave them an undue amount of political influence.

Furthermore, the exploitative nature of the economy which developed in the mining and lumber industries stimulated a high degree of labor unrest. The Industrial Workers of the World, formed in 1905, was strongest around the mines and lumber camps and represented one of the most radical political and economic movements in United States history. The economic problems and natural hazards associated with Western farming, particularly on the Great Plains, intensified the agrarian discontent which climaxed in the Populist movement of the 1890s. Despite the purported individualism and independence of Westerners, they faced problems which encouraged the growth of governmental powers and functions. For example, in the arid and semiarid regions people demanded federal aid for irrigation because the cost of large-scale dams and ditches was more than individuals or even private corporations could successfully undertake. In 1902 Congress passed the Newlands Act, which provided federal aid for irrigation projects.

Not only did the dramatic settlement of the last frontier carry important political and economic implications for the nation, but also it encouraged the creation of a distinctive literature. Aspects of Western life became the subject matter for some of the country's most popular writers, including Bret Harte, Samuel Clemens (Mark Twain), Hamlin Garland, Willa Cather, and Ole Rölvaag. In *A Son of the Middle Border,*

Hamlin Garland related the pioneering history of his own family, which settled finally on the black prairies of Dakota. Garland recorded in most vivid terms the droughts, snowstorms, poverty, monotony, and cultural barrenness of Western farm life. He emphasized these themes again in *Main-Travelled Roads.* But the most powerful novel dealing with pioneer life was Ole Rölvaag's *Giants in the Earth.* This was the story of a Norwegian family which settled in Dakota in the 1870s. Per Hansa and his wife Beret were the story's central figures, symbols of thousands of pioneers who struggled to build homes on the inhospitable Dakota frontier. Western pioneer life contributed something as well to the nation's music and poetry. Plaintive cowboy songs, such as "Bury Me Not on the Lone Prairie" and "The Dying Cowboy," eventually became popular in all parts of the country.

In 1890 the Director of Census wrote that, in the traditional sense, there was no longer any frontier in the United States. This was not true in the strict sense, because there were still extensive unsettled public lands available. Indeed, more homesteads were filed after 1890 than before that date. But most of the unsettled lands were in the semiarid or arid parts of the West and were unproductive without irrigation. Thus the Director was correct when he implied that most of the good land which could be dependably farmed under conditions of natural rainfall was gone.

Three years later historian Frederick Jackson Turner declared that the census statement "marks the closing of a great historic movement." He then explained that "up to our own day [1893] American history has been in a large degree the history of the colonization of the Great West. The existence of an area of free land," he continued, "its continuous recession, and the advance of American settlement westward, explain American development." Turner believed that continuous contact with the frontier over a period of nearly three centuries had deeply affected the American character. He argued that the frontier had contributed to "a

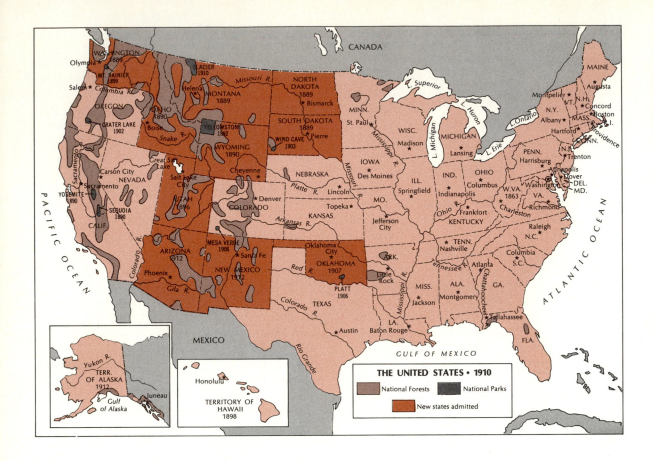

The United States · 1910

THE UNITED STATES · 1910	
National Forests	National Parks
New states admitted	

composite nationality for the American people," that it had promoted democracy, and stimulated independence and individualism. He also attributed such traits as materialism, practicality, and an inventive turn of mind to frontier experiences. Although other historians later challenged the so-called Turner Thesis, for the next generation Turner's ideas had a marked effect upon historical writing and even on public thinking and action.

Trends in American Farming

In the half century after 1860, American farmers settled more land than their forefathers had since the first landing at Jamestown in 1607. Much of this expansion was associated with settlement of the Western prairies and the Great Plains. Between 1860 and 1910, farm acreage more than doubled and the number of farms jumped from about 2 million to nearly 6.5 million. But, despite this tremendous expansion of agriculture,

industry grew even more rapidly and by 1900 had passed farming as the chief producer of wealth in the United States. Nevertheless, agriculture continued to be of tremendous importance in the nation's overall economic development.

Farm production made phenomenal gains. In 1859 the output of corn, the nation's leading grain crop, was 838 million bushels; a half century later it reached more than 2.5 billion bushels. In that same period, wheat production jumped from 173 million to 657 million bushels, an increase of nearly 300 percent. The per capita output of wheat rose from 5.5 bushels in 1859 to 8.6 bushels in 1899. The production of cotton rose from 4.5 million to 10.6 million bales—of 500 pounds each—between 1859 and 1909, while the number of hogs, cattle, horses, and other livestock increased rapidly. Thus abundant production of food and fiber assured the American people an adequate, high-protein diet, and a liberal supply of raw materials for manufacturing.

This expansion of agricultural output would have been impossible without the phenomenal improvements in farm technology which occurred after 1865. In the years after the Civil War, improved plows, manufactured by John Deere and James Oliver, and better harrows, grain drills, cultivators, mowers, and other machines came into widespread use. But the greatest advances were made in harvesting and threshing equipment for small grain. The McCormick reaper was a great improvement over the sickle or scythe for cutting grain, but models sold before the Civil War still required men to rake the grain off the cutting bar and tie it into sheaves. The development of the self-binder, which cut and bound the grain in a single operation, greatly reduced the need for manpower in harvesting. In 1878 John F. Appleby invented a successful twine binder, which soon replaced wire for tying the grain bundles. The horse-drawn twine binder removed the last obstacle to large-scale harvesting of wheat and other small grains. By the late nineteenth century improved threshing machines were powered by steam engines in many areas. Better machines greatly increased the efficiency of farm labor. A wheat grower in 1896 with the latest equipment could produce, with the same time and effort, eighteen times as much wheat as his forefather did in 1830.

Other factors helped increase agricultural output. Improved plant and livestock breeds, better tillage methods, irrigation, the use of more fertilizer, and the policies of the federal government all combined to increase farmers' efficiency. The United States Department of Agriculture, created in 1862 and given full Cabinet status in 1889, distributed seeds, promoted the planting of new and improved crops, and in general sought to better farming practices. Also in 1862 Congress passed the Morrill Act, which provided land grants for new agricultural and mechanical colleges. The Hatch Act of 1887 established federal experiment stations.

Sectional Developments

Agricultural expansion produced varied regional patterns. From Ohio to eastern Nebraska a "corn-hog belt" developed, one of the most productive cereal and livestock empires in the world. Although Ohio ranked first in corn production in 1849, Illinois and Iowa became the leading corn states after the Civil War. In the Western prairies and Great Plains, wheat became the principal cash crop.

Southern agriculture suffered severely during the Civil War, and not until the early seventies did farming in the South recover its prewar position. Southern planters and large farmers faced adjustment from slave to free labor. For a time planters employed freedmen for wages, but a shortage of cash and the lack of experienced workers forced them to abandon this effort. Although there was widespread discussion about distributing land to newly freed blacks, and many freedmen hoped to obtain 40 acres and a mule, Washington never implemented this program. As it turned out, the freedmen remained landless and had nothing to sell except their labor. Landowners, on the other hand, were short of capital and labor, and this presented the problem of bringing landowners and landless workers to-

Picking cotton on a Mississippi plantation around 1870.
The Granger Collection

The general status of black farmers in the South did not improve with time. It made little difference whether they were day laborers, tenant operators, or owners. By 1910 Mississippi, for example, recorded 164,488 of its 274,382 farmers as blacks. Of these blacks only 24,949, or some 15 percent, owned land. Nevertheless, black families grew almost 40 percent of the nation's cotton crop. Total income for a black family was often no more than $100 to $200 a year, and that largely in the form of store credit.

Cotton remained the South's leading crop. By the late 1870s production exceeded the prewar high of 4.5 million bales annually, and output advanced rapidly in succeeding years. In 1909 production reached about 10.7 million bales, or more than three times what it had been forty years earlier. In 1899 cotton accounted for some 32 percent of the value of all Southern crops. Mississippi had been the nation's leading cotton state in 1860, but production shifted westward after the Civil War; by 1889 Texas ranked first.

Other Southern cash crops were tobacco, sugar, and rice. Virginia and Maryland, which had historically been the major tobacco-producing states, lost that leadership to Kentucky and Tennessee. After 1890 the cigarette industry's demand for bright flue-cured tobacco stimulated production in North Carolina, where the soil and climate were ideally suited for this type of tobacco. Between 1859 and 1909 tobacco production more than doubled. Rice production moved westward. Louisiana, Texas, and Arkansas replaced South Carolina as the center of rice output. Sugarcane grown for commercial purposes was still largely confined to Louisiana.

After 1865 most American agriculture shifted to a strictly commercial basis, meaning that farmers produced crops primarily for the commercial market rather than for their own use. They sold their commodities for money and bought manufactured goods. This involved greater specialization. Many farmers raised only one cash crop such as wheat, cotton, corn, hogs, or dairy products. American farmers had always produced some surplus for sale, but now produc-

gether into some sort of productive and profitable arrangement. The sharecrop, or tenant, system was the result.

Sharecropping operated on a somewhat standard formula. Under this arrangement the landowner received one-third of a crop for the use of the land and the tenant or sharecropper received one-third for his labor. The remaining one-third was divided between the landlord and tenant to defray the costs of machinery, fertilizer, and other items necessary to produce the crop. There were very few cash tenants in the South; most worked on a share basis. Sometimes tenancy was a means to ownership, but not often. For the most part, both black and white sharecroppers and tenants found themselves engulfed in a system of economic dependency, low incomes, and perpetual debt from which they could not escape.

tion for the market became the chief end of farming. These changes rendered the individual farmer increasingly vulnerable to economic forces beyond his control.

It was the abundant productivity of American farms that assured the nation's population an adequate supply of high-protein food at reasonable prices. Moreover, farm products provided the raw materials for some of the nation's largest manufacturing establishments, notably cotton textiles, meat-packing, and flour milling. Agricultural surpluses, moreover, made up the majority of American exports. In 1860, for instance, some 82 percent of the nation's total exports consisted of farm products; fifty years later farmers still provided more than half of American shipments overseas. Exports of cotton, wheat, and meat were particularly important.

Farm Problems

Despite the heavy production of farm commodities and their immeasurable economic contribution to the nation as a whole, individual farmers wrestled with many difficult problems in the late nineteenth century. The twenty-year period which followed the early 1870s was one of gradually declining prices, which reached their lowest point in 1894. The result was increasing debt, growing tenancy, and general hard times for many farmers.

Farmers suffered from a poor bargaining position in their competition with other major elements in the economy. Farmers could control neither the prices of their own commodities nor those of the manufactured goods which they bought. Dealers in wheat or cotton, for example, set the price of those commodities on the basis of world conditions, total demand, and other factors. The farmer sold at the offered price or made no sale at all. On the other hand, the farmer purchased machinery and other manufactured commodities at the asking price or got along without them. Any bargaining that occurred was not between equals but between sellers who controlled their prices and farmers who did not. In economic language, farmers exchanged raw and unprocessed products for finished manufactured goods. Farmers operated on an individual, competitive basis; other groups in the economy combined to reduce or eliminate the depressing effect on prices which competition tended to create.

It was the relation between farm and nonfarm prices which troubled the farmer. If cotton brought 10 cents a pound and a plow cost $50, it would take 500 pounds to buy a plow. But if cotton dropped to 5 cents and the price of the plow remained the same, it would take 1,000 pounds, or twice as much, to buy the same implement.

Most farmers in the late nineteenth century, however, did not recognize their basic position of weakness in the economy. They refused to admit that they suffered from surplus production. Farmers argued that they were not prosperous because the exactions of big business, bankers, and land monopolists squeezed the profits out of farming. Agricultural spokesmen blamed high transportation charges, excessive interest rates, a deflationary monetary policy, and disposal of the public domain to railroad, timber, and mining monopolies for their plight.

Many farmers complained of unfair railroad practices. They charged that rates were both unreasonably high and discriminatory and that service was poor. They denounced the railroads, too, for their lobbying and outright bribery. Although freight rates dropped substantially after 1870, farmers continued to view railroads as a major cause of their difficulties. Many farmers believed themselves ruthlessly exploited by agents of the farm machine, fertilizer, cotton-seed oil, beef, and other trusts.

Agricultural producers were equally, if not more, disturbed by inadequate credit facilities and high interest rates. Interest charges on real estate mortgages were seldom less than 6 percent, often 8 to 10 percent, before the turn of the century. In 1890 one farmer wrote that Nebraska had three crops: "One is a crop of corn, one a crop of freight rates, and one a crop of interest." Once a farmer had mortgaged his property, a poor crop, bad management, or low prices could bring financial stringency and foreclosure. Hard times and foreclosures increased tenancy throughout the country, from 25 to 35 percent between 1880 to 1900. Most farm states taxed real property disproportionately. While businessmen might hide their stocks and bonds from the tax assessor, land and livestock were always visible. Finally, agricultural producers faced the destructive and unreliable forces of nature. Grasshoppers, hailstorms, or searing drought often destroyed crops. Experiencing the ravages of nature, low prices, increasing debts, and even declining social prestige, farmers became restless and discontented.

Farm Revolt: The Grange

Unable to solve their problems individually, farmers resorted to joint efforts. They observed the economic benefits which organization brought to industry. Formed in 1867 by Oliver H. Kelley of Minnesota as the first nationwide farm organization, the Patrons of Husbandry, or the Grange, sought to advance the lot of farmers through education, cooperation, and social improvement. This secret organization admitted women to full and equal membership.

At first the Grange grew slowly, but price declines after 1871 aroused farmers to militant action against monopolies. By 1874 the Grange boasted a membership of 800,000. Although the Grange was nonpolitical, individual Grangers joined various independent, reform, and anti-monopoly parties which flourished in the Midwest during the 1870s. Several Midwestern states after 1871 enacted so-called granger laws to regulate railroad and elevator rates, but these efforts at state control proved ineffective. (See Chapter 17.)

Meanwhile, Grange members sought direct economic benefits by forming cooperatives to reduce the cost of supplies and marketing. They established many consumer cooperatives in the 1870s, as well as creameries, elevators, and other producer and marketing cooperatives. These efforts generally failed from inefficient management, insufficient credit, or lack of a true cooperative spirit among farmers.

Between 1874 and 1880 Grange membership dropped from some 800,000 to 150,000. This decline followed the failure of the cooperatives, the return of better times, internal dissensions, and the inability to win permanent political victories. The Grange continued as a national farm organization, but its emphasis shifted to social and educational improvement.

The Greenback Movement

The Grange program did not resolve the problem of low prices and farm debt. During the 1870s a growing number of farmers sought to cure their ills with currency inflation. Farmers accepted the quantity theory of money, which held that commodity prices rose and fell in relation to the amount of currency in circulation—the more dollars in circulation, the higher the commodity prices. Therefore, they argued, agricultural prices could be raised if the federal government would put more paper currency, or greenbacks, into circulation. Debtors were especially concerned with the money problem. Debts incurred during periods of high prices were especially difficult to repay when prices fell.

In 1865, the greenbacks in circulation totaled $433 million. Despite pressure from inflationist groups, the Grant administration followed a deflationary policy. By 1870 the greenback circulation had dropped to $356 million. Some currency expansion followed the Panic of 1873, but Grant vetoed a bill which would have raised the total to $400 million. Angered by this decision, the inflationists turned to political action. They launched the Greenback political movement at a meeting in Indianapolis in November 1874; two years later the Greenback party ran Peter Cooper, the elderly New York philanthropist, for president on a platform which called for greatly expanded issues of paper money.

Failing to win much popular support in 1876, the Greenbackers widened their appeal to both farmers and workers. Besides currency expansion, they advocated taxation of national bonds, a federal income tax, exclusion of Chinese immigration, restriction of working hours in industry, and abolition of child labor. On this platform, the Greenback party polled approximately a million votes in midterm elections of 1878 and elected at least fifteen congressmen. In the presidential campaign of 1880, James B. Weaver of

"The Grange Awakening the Sleepers," a newspaper cartoon of 1873. Criticising the system of secret rebates, it shows the American farmer trying to rouse the public against the railroad "menace."

Iowa polled 308,000 votes. With better times in the early 1880s, the Greenback movement declined.

The Farmers' Alliance

After 1880 farm unrest continued unabated. Deflationary monetary policies, exactions by industrial trusts, railroad abuses, and environmental conditions sustained farm protest. In Texas numerous farmers' clubs carried the burden of agricultural dissatisfaction. In 1879 they organized the statewide Texas Alliance, which stressed social objectives and cooperative buying and selling. In 1886 the Alliance demanded inflation, higher taxes on land held for speculation, the regulation of interstate commerce, and heavier taxes on railroad property. Grievances varied from community to community, but these demands reflected a general concern of farmers over land policies, transportation, and an adequate supply of currency.

The driving force behind the Texas Alliance was C. W. Macune, who set out to extend the organization throughout the entire South. By 1888 most Southern farm organizations had united into what was commonly called the Southern Alliance. Black farmers were banned from the white units, so in 1888 they established the Colored Farmers' National Alliance. By 1890 the white and black alliances may each have had as many as 1 million members.

At the same time discontented farmers in the North formed new protest groups. In 1880 Milton George of Chicago, editor of the *Western Rural,* organized the Northwestern, or Northern Alliance. Spreading out from Illinois, the Northern Alliance recruited approximately 400,000 members by 1887, with the largest and most militant membership in Kansas, where drought and low prices had stimulated seething unrest among farmers. The Northern Alliance pushed reforms in land, transportation, and money. Demands for strict government regulation of the railroads soon gave way to appeals for government ownership. Alliance members advocated free and unlimited coinage of silver as a means of raising prices and helping debtors. The Alliance insisted that public lands be distributed only to actual settlers. Finally, it favored an income tax and revised patent laws.

Strongly organized in both North and South, agricultural spokesmen still faced the task of bringing the Northern and Southern Alliances together into a single national organization. A meeting at St. Louis in December 1889 made an effort to unite the two groups. The leaders reached agreement on some common objectives, including the free and unlimited coinage of silver, government ownership of transportation and communication, abolition of national banks, and a graduated income tax. The Southern Alliance advanced what was known as the "subtreasury plan" to improve marketing conditions and inflate the currency. Farmers could deposit products such as cotton and wheat in subtreasuries and receive a loan in paper money equal to 80 percent of the value of the stored commodities. This system, by design, would permit farmers to hold their crop when prices were low. Moreover, the loans issued against the produce would expand the currency and have a general inflationary effect. Although the Northern and Southern Alliances were unable to achieve a single organization, they agreed on a number of basic principles designed to increase farm income. As late as 1890 two decades of farm protest had achieved meager results.

Conclusion

That quarter century of dynamic national growth which ended in 1890 witnessed the settlement of the vast public domain. So varied and dramatic was the final headlong rush into the Great West that it left an indelible mark on the country's heritage. Beyond the more bizarre qualities of the last frontier was the slow, sometimes painful task of reducing much of the region to the plow. This expansion of American agriculture was essential for the development of a balanced national economy. But many farmers were not prosperous and suffered from a variety of hard economic disadvantages. By 1890 they had brought their economic problems before the nation. While they had sought to solve some of their difficulties through self-help, mainly by increasing productivity and establishing cooperatives, many farmers had concluded that only through political action could they secure the rightful fruits of their labor and investment. As the following chapter will demonstrate, farmers became extremely active in the midterm elections of 1890 and continued to press their programs into the presidential election of 1896. Undoubtedly, the farm revolt which began in the nineties was to a large degree responsible for compelling the old political parties to recognize the major economic and social problems confronting the nation in the late nineteenth century.

SUGGESTED READINGS

The best general survey of the trans-Mississippi West is L. R. Hafen, W. Eugene Hollon, and C. C. Rister's *Western America* (1970). All the general histories of the American West also devote a good deal of attention to that region during the period of settlement and growth after the Civil War. Ray Allen Billington's *Westward Expansion* (3d ed., 1967) is the most comprehensive treatment. The best interpretation of the impact of the frontier on American life and culture is Billington's *America's Frontier Heritage** (1966).

General studies which deal with different areas of the trans-Mississippi West include C. C. Rister's *The Southwestern Frontier, 1865–1890* (1947); W. E. Hollon's *The Southwest: Old and New** (1961); Robert G. Athearn's *High Country Empire** (1960); O. O. Winther's *The Pacific Northwest* (1947); L. J. Arrington's *Great Basin Kingdom** (1958), which considers the Mormons; and Earl S. Pomeroy's *The Pacific Slope* (1965). *The Sod-House Frontier, 1854–1890* (1937) by Everett Dick is a delightful social history, mainly of the Nebraska and Kansas frontier. In *The Great Plains** (1931), W. P. Webb has discussed the problems of settling that region. William L. Katz treats black Americans in *The Black West* (1971).

Land policies have been carefully treated by Roy M. Robbins in *Our Landed Heritage** (1942) and E. Louise Peffer in *The Closing of the Public Domain* (1951). An excellent study of the Western territories is Earl S. Pomeroy's *The Territories and the United States, 1865–1890* (1947).

The best survey of Western mining is Rodman Paul's *The Mining Frontiers of the Far West, 1848–1880** (1963). Another excellent account is William S. Greever's *The Bonanza West: The Story of the Western Mining Rushes, 1848–1900* (1963). See also Watson Parker's *Gold in the Black Hills* (1966),

The Western cattle industry has been adequately treated in E. E. Dale's *The Range Cattle Industry* (1930); Ernest S. Osgood's *The Day of the Cattleman** (1929); and Louis Pelzer's *The Cattlemen's Frontier* (1936). On Western agriculture see Gilbert C. Fite's *The Farmer's Frontier, 1865–1900** (1966).

W. T. Hagan presents an excellent brief survey in *American Indians** (1961). There are histories of many Indian tribes which deal in some way with the problems of the red man and government policy relating to him. Among the better works are *A Sioux Chronicle* (1956) by George E. Hyde; Donald J. Berthrong's *The Southern Cheyennes* (1963); and E. C. McReynolds's *The Seminoles* (1957). On the Indian wars see P. I. Wellman's *The Indian Wars of the West* (1954); C. M.

Oehler's *The Great Sioux Uprising* (1959); E. I. Stewart's *Custer's Luck* (1955); and R. G. Athearn's *William Tecumseh Sherman and the Settlement of the West* (1956). *The Military Conquest of the Southern Plains* (1963) and *The Buffalo Soldiers: A Narrative of the Negro Cavalry in the West* (1967) by William Leckie are important contributions. On government Indian policy consult E. E. Dale's *The Indians of the Southwest* (1949); Henry Fritz's *The Movement for Indian Assimilation, 1860–1890* (1963); and Loring B. Priest's *Uncle Sam's Stepchildren: The Reformation of the United States Indian Policy, 1865–1887* (1942). The fight for reform can best be traced in Robert W. Mardock's *The Reformers and the American Indian* (1971). No student should miss Dee Brown's *Bury My Heart at Wounded Knee* (1970).

Fred Shannon's *The Farmer's Last Frontier: Agriculture, 1860–1897** (1945) is the best and most complete history of late-nineteenth-century farming. Among the best regional studies of agriculture are *From Prairie to Corn Belt* (1963) by Allan G. Bogue; Hiram M. Drache's *The Day of the Bonanza: A History of Bonanza Farming in the Red River Valley of the North* (1964); and *Sugar Country: The Cane Sugar Industry in the South, 1753–1950* (1953) by J. Carlyle Sitterson. There is valuable material on Southern agriculture in H. H. Donald's *The Negro Freedman* (1952); R. B. Vance's *Human Geography of the South* (1932); and A. F. Raper and I. D. Reid's *Sharecroppers All* (1941).

For the development of farm mechanization see Leo Rogin's *The Introduction of Farm Machinery in Its Relation to the Productivity of Labor in the Agriculture of the United States during the Nineteenth Century* (1931); and R. M. Wik's *Steam Power on the American Farm* (1953).

The best brief treatment of agriculture's basic economic problems is found in Theodore Saloutos's "The Agricultural Problem and Nineteenth Century Industrialism," *Agricultural History*, XXII (July 1948). Farm problems and the causes of agrarian discontent are also considered by Shannon in *The Farmer's Last Frontier*, cited above; in John D. Hicks's *The Populist Revolt** (1931); and Theodore Saloutos's *Farmer Movements in the South, 1865–1933** (1960). Accounts of the farmers' revolt are numerous. Besides the works of Hicks and Saloutos, readers should see Solon J. Buck's *The Agrarian Crusade* (1919) and *The Granger Movement** (1913).

*indicates availability in paperback.

20

Politics, Policies, and Personalities, 1877-1896

President Hayes's narrow election in 1876 established another link in the long chain of Republican political control during the post-Civil War period, a control which, except for Grover Cleveland's two nonconsecutive terms, extended into the twentieth century. The Republicans not only dominated the Presidency; they also kept strict control of the United States Senate, where they held a majority in all but four years during the forty-four-year period from 1868 to 1912. During two of those four years, 1883–1885, the Senate was tied. In the House of Representatives, however, the two parties were almost evenly divided, with the Republicans in control twenty-four of the forty-four years. Thus the period between the Civil War and World War I can properly be called "the Republican era."

Yet, until 1896, the Republicans were not as strong as they appeared. During the late nineteenth century, the popular vote split almost evenly, and in two presidential elections, in 1876 and 1888, the Republicans actually received a minority of the popular ballots, winning the Presidency only by carrying the states with large blocs of electoral votes. In 1880 the Republicans won with a plurality of about one-tenth of 1 percent of the popular vote. Except for 1 two-year period, the Republicans failed to control the Presidency, the Senate, and the House simultaneously between 1877 and 1897. Any implementation of a party program was thus extremely difficult, and legislative stalemate often characterized the perennial Republican-Democratic struggle for control of national policy.

Party Politics

With good reason Americans have viewed the last quarter of the nineteenth century as a dreary period politically, a time when mediocre party leaders failed to contend with the burgeoning problems of the nation—industrialization, urbanization, proper disposition of the country's natural resources, and labor-management relations. Politicians seemed dedicated to spoils rather than service. Lord Bryce, an Englishman, wrote that "neither party has any principles, any distinctive tenets. Both have traditions. Both claim to have tendencies. Both have certainly war cries, organizations, interests enlisted in their support. But these interests are in the main the interests of getting or keeping the patronage of the government."

Politics remained closely allied with business. The Republicans generally were more successful than the Democrats in winning support from businessmen and industrialists. Republican programs favored major business interests—a protective tariff for manufacturers; a liberal disposition of natural resources to railroads and timber and mining companies; the gold standard for bankers and moneylenders. Republicans held a strong grip on the Middle Western farm vote; they controlled the votes of Northern veterans and recently freed blacks; and, once in office, they could count on the support of thousands of state and federal officeholders. They obtained votes even of many workingmen.

Besides capitalizing on their own strength, the Republicans made every effort to identify the Democratic party with disloyalty in the South, graft and corruption in the North. The Democrats, often divided on key issues, labored under both the stigma of dishonor and disloyalty and the lack of attractive leaders. Only in the solid South did the Democrats maintain firm and consistent control. After Hayes withdrew all remaining federal troops in 1877, the Southern states maintained a strong Democratic majority.

Throughout the North the Republican party successfully expanded and consolidated its political power at both the state and national levels. By organizing its sources of strength and taking advantage of Democratic divisions, the Republican party assumed a truly dominant position by 1896, when William McKinley won the presidency by a substantial margin.

Major issues during the late nineteenth century were the tariff, currency and banking, civil service reform, immigration restriction, internal improvements, and government regulation of big business. The two parties differed radically over tariffs, but on other issues their positions scarcely varied. As Lord Bryce observed, the two parties "were like two bottles. Each bore a label denoting the kind of liquor it contained, but each was empty." The major battles took place within the parties. Western Republicans, for example, demanded cheap money and inflation, while Eastern party leaders favored the gold standard. Party attitudes and actions on such questions, however, seem relatively unimportant when contrasted with the vital issues of poverty, civil rights, maldistribution of wealth, urbanization, and economic growth that went unnoticed by self-seeking politicians. Still for most Americans of the late nineteenth century questions of tariff and inflation were desperately important.

The Hayes Administration

Once in the White House, Rutherford B. Hayes quickly restored dignity and respectability to an office badly tarnished by the graft, corruption, and cronyism of the Grant administration. The son of an Ohio farmer, Hayes (1822–1893) attended Kenyon College and Harvard University, after which he entered the Ohio bar in 1845. He joined the Republican party a decade later.

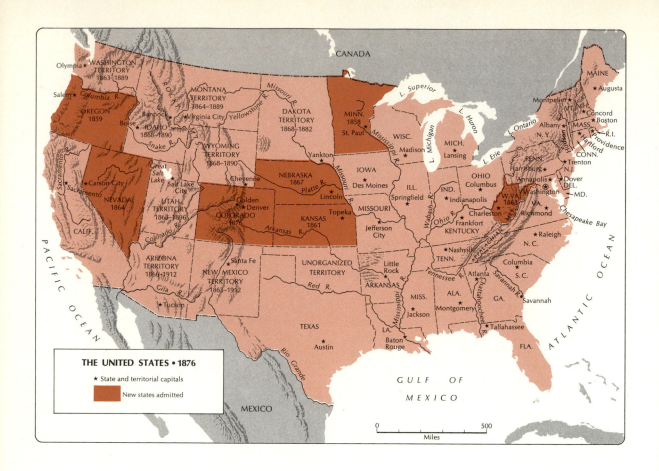

THE UNITED STATES · 1876
★ State and territorial capitals
New states admitted

Hayes performed capably during the Civil War and received a battlefield commission as a major general of volunteers. Elected to the House of Representatives in 1864, he served one term before returning to Ohio for two successive terms as governor. His third gubernatorial victory in 1875 came at a time of marked Republican unpopularity and earned him considerable national prestige. Honest and dignified, Hayes was neither brilliant nor magnetic.

Hayes assumed the presidency under severe handicaps. The Republican party was sharply divided between the Stalwarts and moderates. The Stalwarts, represented by such powerful machine politicians as Senator Roscoe E. Conkling of New York, opposed civil service reform and Hayes's policies toward the South. Along with other spoilsmen in the party, Conkling contemptuously referred to the President and his supporters as "Halfbreeds."

Hayes's withdrawal of the remaining federal troops from the Southern states threatened to restore white rule throughout the South. In April 1877, federal garrisons withdrew from Columbia, South Carolina, and from New Orleans, Louisiana. The carpetbag Republican governments in those states disbanded, and the Democrats assumed control. The Republican phase of political reconstruction was at last closed.

Yet the problem of black civil rights remained unsolved. Federal protection to voters still existed in the Enforcement Acts of 1870 and 1872. These Force Acts, designed to prevent voter intimidation, directed federal marshals, deputy marshals, election supervisors, and the federal courts to protect the civil rights of blacks. Southern whites, however, favored the elimination of all federal interference with elections; in Congress Democrats sought to repeal or nullify the Enforcement Acts. They attached "riders" to appropriation bills denying pay to federal election supervisors and attempted in other ways to weaken national power to protect black voting rights. But President Hayes vetoed these measures. In 1879, the Supreme Court upheld the constitutionality of the federal elections laws, but, in 1882, the removal of certain enforcement features rendered the laws impotent.

Once the South again fell under "Bourbon," or conservative, white rule, many blacks lost their right to vote, especially if they tried to vote Republican. In the plantation-sharecrop areas, blacks continued to exercise their franchise after the withdrawal of federal troops, but economic pressures usually enforced a vote for the conservative Bourbon Democratic candidates. Despite growing restrictions on black voting after 1877, the general Southern denial of black franchise did not take place until the 1890s and the final repeal of the federal election statutes in 1894.

Skirting the Southern questions, Hayes moved to bring at least modest reform to the civil service. The growing functions and responsibilities of the federal government demanded better-trained civil servants to handle the expanding public business. To meet this need, reformers such as Representative Thomas A. Jenckes of Rhode Island, George W. Curtis, and Carl Schurz argued for legislation which would provide competitive examinations for government employees. In 1871, Congress authorized the President to establish a Civil Service Advisory Board, which would prescribe rules and regulations for certain classes of government workers. Hayes favored civil service reform and, in his first annual message, recommended that appointments be made on the basis of merit rather than political connections. But the 1871 law was ineffective and Congress failed to pass any general civil service legislation.

No less than other presidents in the late nineteenth century Hayes faced the troublesome money question. He favored "sound money," which meant the gold standard. During the hard times of the seventies farmers and debtors demanded inflation. Congress resisted this pressure and in 1875 passed the Resumption Act, which directed the Secretary of the Treasury to redeem all United States notes in coin, beginning January 1, 1879. Hayes instructed his Treasury secretary, John Sherman, to carry out this policy, which placed the country on a *de facto* gold standard. Angry at this action, the inflationists argued for currency expansion through the printing of more greenbacks or the coinage of silver. In 1878, Congress passed the Bland-Allison Act over Hayes's veto. This measure directed the Treasury to purchase $2 to $4 million worth of silver monthly and coin it into silver dollars. This provision did not satisfy the inflationists but merely contributed to growing differences within the Republican party.

At the same time, the country experienced social and economic unrest. As noted earlier, the great railway strikes of 1877 and the anti-Chinese movement in California reflected deep dissatisfaction with social and economic conditions. But Hayes thought only of maintaining law and order and ignored the real issues at stake.

Garfield and Arthur

President Hayes gave the country a clean and somewhat more efficient government than Grant, but he provided no real leadership.

Moreover, his emphasis upon civil service reform annoyed the party spoilsmen who longed for the free-wheeling days of the Grant administration. Consequently, as the election of 1880 approached, Roscoe Conkling, John A. Logan of Illinois, and other Stalwarts attempted to nominate Grant for a third term. Through thirty ballots Grant led, but the anti-Grant faction in the convention rallied behind James A. Garfield of Ohio, who finally won the nomination. To placate the Stalwarts, Republican leaders chose Chester A. Arthur of New York as the vice-presidential candidate. The Democrats nominated General Winfield Scott Hancock, a veteran of both the Mexican and Civil Wars, and W. E. English of Indiana. The election of 1880 was an unexciting affair, the only distinguishing issue being the Democratic endorsement of a tariff for revenue only and the Republican championing of protection. Both parties advocated sound money and civil service reform. Helped along by returning prosperity, Garfield squeaked by with an extremely narrow popular majority of 7,368 votes.

A native of Ohio and a Disciples of Christ minister, Garfield had served as president of Hiram College and as a major general in the Union Army before entering the House of Representatives in 1863. Garfield's administration was short and tragic. Shot after only four months in office by Charles J. Guiteau, a disappointed office seeker, he died on September 19. This second presidential assassination in less than twenty years deeply shocked Americans who had believed that their political system had progressed beyond such crime and fanaticism. Guiteau was executed for his crime within less than a year.

Inaugurated on September 20, 1881, President Arthur showed a reasonable understanding of the American political system when he declared: "Men may die but the fabrics of our free institutions remain unshaken." A lawyer by profession, the tall, heavily built, distinguished-appearing, new Chief Executive at least looked like a president. He had been active in the Republican party since its founding and held a number of appointive positions. Despite his close association with the spoils system, Presi-

dent Arthur took his duties seriously and provided a dignified and honorable administration.

Garfield's assassination, the pressure from federal appointments, and the scandals in various branches of the government service all emphasized the need for civil service reform. Under the leadership of Democratic Senator George Pendleton of Ohio Congress had been working on a civil service bill since 1881. Public support and the influence of the National Civil Service Reform League, combined with Arthur's backing, brought passage of the Pendleton Act on January 15, 1883. Both Republicans and Democrats supported the measure, which provided for a Civil Service Commission of three members appointed by the President. This Commission was to administer competitive examinations to determine the fitness of government employees.

During Arthur's administration the tariff again emerged as a lively issue. Democrats demanded lower rates, whereas industrialists urged high protective duties. But in the Arthur years government revenues, derived largely from the tariff, far exceeded expenditures, reaching as much as $145 million by 1882. This drew money out of circulation and created a scarcity of circulating medium in the economy. Critics of the tariff argued that lower rates would not only reduce prices and the cost of living but would also lower the surpluses in the federal Treasury. In 1882 a congressional commission recommended lower tariff duties, but the definitely protectionist Tariff Act of 1883 left the overall duties approximately where they had been.

Treasury surpluses tempted the government to more liberal expenditures. In 1882, over Arthur's veto, Congress passed an $18,743,000 rivers and harbors bill to finance public works in about five hundred different localities where, not coincidentally, federal expenditures for public improvements sometimes provided the bases for very effective local political organizations—a clear case of "pork barrel." Congress also increased veterans' pensions. By 1883, pension expenditures had risen to $66 million, compared with only $27 million in 1878. This crude type of social security went to thousands of veterans. With good reason the Grand Army of the Republic (organization of the Union veterans) remained a powerful element in the Republican party.

Arthur failed to dodge the question of Chinese immigration. After 1850, thousands of Chinese had entered the United States to work in California and other Western states on the railroads, around the mining camps, and in the growing cities. Job competition and race prejudice encouraged the rising sentiment against Chinese immigration. So effective was the pressure that in May 1882 Congress passed the Chinese Exclusion Act.

The Democratic Cleveland

Despite Arthur's altogether respectable administration, few favored his renomination in 1884. The Republicans instead turned to James G. Blaine, perhaps the most colorful and popular Republican of his generation. Born in 1830, Blaine went to Congress in 1862, and until his death in 1893, he devoted his energies to public life. He was Speaker of the House from 1869 to 1875, then Senator from Maine. In 1881, he served briefly as Garfield's Secretary of State. A contender for the presidency during several conventions, in 1884 this popular idol could no longer be denied the nomination, although some Republican liberals—nicknamed "Mugwumps" —protested. The Republican convention named a Stalwart, John A. Logan, as Blaine's running mate. The Republican platform called for a protective tariff, extension of civil service reform, establishment of a national bureau of labor, pensions for Union veterans, and reservation "as far as possible" of public lands for actual settlers.

In Chicago, the Democrats united behind Governor Grover Cleveland of New York. Born in New Jersey in 1837, Cleveland as a young man went to Buffalo where he read law and entered practice. Having become assistant district attorney, he won election for sheriff in 1869. After serving as mayor of Buffalo for one year, Cleveland became Governor of New York in 1882. Despite some opposition from leaders of Tammany Hall, Cleveland emerged in 1884 as the Democratic party's standard-bearer on an early ballot. The ticket gained good sectional balance with the selection of Thomas Hendricks of Indiana for Vice President. The Democrats promised to "revise the tariff in a spirit of fairness to all interests," to work for "honest money" and "honest civil service reform," to oppose monopoly, and to achieve equality for all citizens.

Issues meant little in this exciting campaign of 1884. As a contest of personalities, the campaign became undoubtedly one of the dirtiest in American history. The Democrats—joined by the Mugwumps who had bolted the Republican party—accused Blaine of public dishonesty and tied him to the so-called Mulligan Letters. In 1869, when Blaine was Speaker of the House, he had helped to obtain a land grant for the Little Rock and Fort Smith Railroad and subsequently, along with Warren Fisher of Boston, had sold the road's nearly worthless bonds. Although Blaine denied that he had profited from these dealings, a series of letters kept by Fisher's bookkeeper, James Mulligan, cast doubts on Blaine's integrity. On one note Blaine had written, "Burn this letter." Charged with using his official position for personal benefit, Blaine found his position compromised.

Smarting under attacks of this nature, the Republicans searched for scandal in high Democratic ranks. They were not compelled to look very far. In July 1884, the *Buffalo Evening Telegraph* reported on some of bachelor Cleveland's earlier escapades with an attractive Buffalo widow, Mrs. Maria Halpin. When a child was born to Mrs. Halpin in 1874, she had named

Cleveland as the father. Although no absolute proof of Cleveland's paternity existed, he had not denied the possibility. Thereafter the Republicans declared Cleveland a man of lax morals, unfit for the Presidency.

In the final days of the campaign, Blaine and his key supporters blundered badly. In New York, where the contest was close, Blaine lost Catholic support when one of his backers, the Reverend Samuel D. Burchard, referred to the Democrats as the party of "rum, Romanism, and rebellion." Moreover, Blaine's attendance at a dinner sponsored by New York millionaires John Astor, Jay Gould, and others, as well as their private discussions regarding campaign funds, provided Democratic writers with exciting copy. Critics pictured "Belshazzar Blaine" living in luxury while working people starved.

In a narrow victory Cleveland, who received only 23,000 more votes than Blaine, won New York's 36 electoral votes by a plurality of 1,167. This gave him a total of 219 votes in the electoral college compared to 182 for Blaine. Cleveland undeniably won on the strength of independent, Mugwump support, assisted by the general hard times and business stagnation which Democrats blamed on the Republicans. People voted for Cleveland less because of his stand on major issues than because they believed him honest. Despite the valiant image which his supporters attempted to fashion, Blaine remained for many less than trustworthy.

Cleveland's views regarding the role of government in social and economic affairs were conservative. In general, he held a negative concept of government, a narrow view of presidential powers, agreeing with those conservative Bourbon Democratic spokesmen of business and industry who favored honest and economical government. He had little knowledge of, or interest in, the needs of agriculture and labor. Hard-working, honest, independent, and above all, courageous—one supporter said he was loved "for the enemies he has made"—he lacked tact, imagination, and a personality which appealed to the masses. And he was stubborn. A short, 250-pound man with a droopy mustache, Cleveland appeared every bit as solid and uncompromising as he actually was.

With a capable and conservative Cabinet—including two Southerners, L. Q. C. Lamar of Mississippi, Secretary of the Interior, and Augustus H. Garland of Arkansas, Attorney General—the new President faced the old issues—pensions, land policies, the tariff, and money. In addition, at least two emerging problems demanded national attention: Indian policy and the federal regulation and control of monopolies.

Cleveland faced a widespread clamor for further civil service reform. The Mugwumps, who had supported Cleveland on this issue, expected him to reduce the role of party politics in federal appointments. Cleveland firmly believed that only qualified persons should be named to public office and that appointments should not be made, as he put it, "solely as a reward for partisan service." But he discovered that his party was hungry for spoils. Most Democrats agreed with the senator who defined reform as turning Republicans out of office and "putting honest Democrats in their places." Before the end of Cleveland's administration most government jobs had been filled with loyal Democrats. But Cleveland did advance the cause of civil service reform by extending civil service regulations to cover several thousand additional federal workers.

Pensions for Civil War veterans proved nettlesome. The Arrears of Pensions Act of 1879 had opened the way for widespread graft as veterans and claims agents pressed dishonest demands. Many "invalid" pensioners were actually in perfect health. The Pension Bureau attempted to evaluate the claims fairly and justly and to weed out fraudulent claims, but a veteran turned down by the Bureau might prevail upon his congressman or senator or introduce a special bill granting him a pension. In the middle 1880s, Congress passed hundreds of these bills, and by 1885, some 325,000 Civil War veterans were on the pension rolls.

Anti-Chinese Prejudice

The rise of anti-Chinese prejudice in the last half of the nineteenth century exemplifies the way lack of common understanding breeds fear, hatred, and violence and how a minority group may become a social scapegoat.

Sizeable numbers of Chinese immigrated to America during the early 1850s in response to the discovery of gold in California. Almost immediately Caucasian miners persecuted them, burning their tents and driving them away from many mining districts. Between 1850 and 1870 a Foreign Miner's License Tax, which was levied almost exclusively against the Chinese, raised more than $5 million, but the Chinese were excluded from the rich mining areas.

Many Chinese in California became fishermen and day-laborers in vineyards, lumbercamps, and factories and on the construction crews building the transcontinental railroad. By 1866 the Central Pacific Railroad had hired 6,000 Chinese, many of whom the railroad itself had imported from China.

But when depression struck in the early 1870s, the smouldering resentment against the Chinese flared into violence. Labor leader Denis Kearney, head of the Workingman's Party, led a "Chinese Must Go" campaign, and riots and assaults against people and property were widespread. Legislation was passed to tax, harrass, and humiliate the Chinese, and in 1882 Congress passed an act prohibiting the entry of Chinese laborers for ten years, legislation which became even harsher in the years to follow.

During the 1870s a San Francisco firm sold this cartoon showing a symbolic Irishman and a Chinese devouring Uncle Sam.

Attitudes toward the Chinese in post–Civil War publications ranged from fascination to contempt, but the latter predominated. At the time of the Gold Rush, immigration to America from China cost only $15 — three to five times less than the cost from Europe, although later the fare rose to $50. The numbers of Chinese entering the United States increased continuously until the passage of the Exclusion Act. Between 1861 and 1870 the total was 64,301, and in the following decade it reached 123,201.

Much was made of the fact that the Chinese were not Christians, and even Bret Harte stressed it in the lyrics he wrote for the popular song, "The Heathen Chinee," a song which helped perpetuate a pejorative stereotype of the Chinese (following page). Another example of the extreme prejudice against the Chinese appears in the advertising of George Dee, manufacturer of the "Magic Washer," who used the Kearney slogan intact. It was a measure of the state of public opinion that Dee felt free to display this prejudice so openly. Thomas Nast's cartoon (following page, right, below) reflects the workingman's fear of the competition from cheap Chinese labor in the shoe industry. The Chinese manufactured shoes in more than seventy California factories, and the first time New England saw Chinese labor came when 100 Chinese strike breakers were imported by a North Adams, Mass., shoe manufacturer in the 1870s.

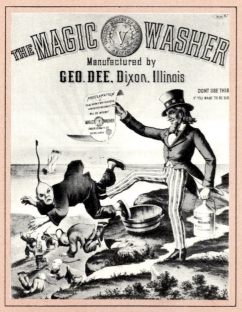

Near right: Arnold Genthe, courtesy California Palace
of the Legion of Honor
All others: Library of Congress

THE NEW
ISSUE
THE CHINESE-AMER
QUESTION

Under the leadership of Denis Kearney (inset), the Workingman's Party helped to pass California legislation making a corporation liable to a fine of $100 to $1,000 if it hired a Chinese. The law was declared unconstitutional, but anti-Chinese riots like this one at Rock Springs, Wyoming, added to the pressure on Congress which resulted in the Exclusion Act of 1882. Commenting on exclusion, Calvin Lee wrote, "One wonders whether history would have been different if more Chinese had accepted Christianity, . . ."

From The American West by Lucius Beebe and Charles Clegg.

Disgusted with what he considered a raid on the public treasury and skeptical of anything which bordered on welfare legislation, Cleveland vetoed a substantial number of private pension bills when he found obvious fraud. Although Americans generally supported Cleveland in this stand, congressmen, individual veterans, and their official organization, the Grand Army of the Republic, loudly criticized the President's penny-pinching attitude. Cleveland's veto of a general pension bill aroused additional criticism.

Western land administration also caused President Cleveland deep concern. For a time after the Civil War, the federal government distributed lands as if they were limitless. False entries, perjured witnesses, and dishonest surveys had, according to Land Commissioner William A. J. Sparks, enabled land monopolies "to rob the government of its lands." This situation challenged Cleveland's sense of honesty and fair play, but government control would arouse the animosity of Westerners and their Eastern financial backers, who demanded access to the area's resources. Whatever Cleveland's weaknesses, he did not lack courage. He ordered Secretary of the Interior L. Q. C. Lamar and Commissioner Sparks to protect the public domain. Altogether they restored some 81 million acres of land to federal control. Cleveland took a more sympathetic attitude toward Indian rights. He opposed the encroachments of white settlers on Indian lands and supported the Dawes Act of 1887.

Enlargement of the Navy, begun by Arthur, continued under the Cleveland administration. Cleveland's Secretary of the Navy reorganized the Department and let contracts for a number of small naval vessels, five cruisers, and the battleships *Texas* and *Maine*—which became famous at the time of the Spanish-American War. Other bipartisan action of the period included passage of the Interstate Commerce Act in 1887 designed to curb railroad abuses. (See Chapter 17.)

Cleveland's major concern was the tariff. He had become convinced that tariff rates were too high and contained serious inequities. He objected to the current tariff law on two grounds. In the first place, the rates brought in much more revenue than was needed. Federal surpluses, he said, encouraged unnecessary government expenditures and waste. Furthermore, Cleveland considered the duties to be an unjust tax upon consumers because they added to the price of daily necessities. He argued that it burdened the farmer while it subsidized the manufacturer.

Cleveland devoted his entire annual message to Congress on December 6, 1887, to the tariff. Referring to it as a "vicious, inequitable, and illogical source of unnecessary taxation," the President called for immediate tariff revision. Early in 1888, Representative Roger Q. Mills of Texas introduced a tariff reform bill calling for lower rates on several articles and placing many items on the free list. The Mills bill passed the House on July 21, but the Republican Senate defeated it. Cleveland failed to resolve the tariff issue, but he had stirred up bitter political animosities.

The Election of 1888

Despite the political uproar over the tariff, the Democrats renominated Cleveland on the first ballot in 1888. The party platform condemned the Republicans for blocking tariff reform and praised Cleveland for a faithful and able administration. The Republicans, meeting at Chicago, chose Senator Benjamin Harrison of Indiana as the party standard-bearer. They selected Levi P.

Morton of New York for vice president. The central issue in the campaign emerged when the Republicans announced their uncompromising support of "the American protective system."

Cleveland's opposition to the tariff brought an unprecedented torrent of money into the campaign. Never before had business and industrial interests played such an open and aggressive political role in a presidential contest. Protectionists raised large campaign funds and used every tactic to defeat Cleveland. They called Cleveland a "standing menace" and pressed industrialists and businessmen for campaign contributions in almost brutal fashion. One eager party worker suggested, "I would put the manufacturers of Pennsylvania under the fire and fry the fat out of them." When all else failed, Republican strategists sought to buy votes. "Divide the floaters into blocks of five and put a trusted man with the necessary funds in charge . . . and make him responsible that none get away," wrote the Republican treasurer. The Democrats simply did not have such sources of support.

Still the election was close. Although Cleveland actually won a popular majority of more than 100,000 votes, he lost some key states, including New York and Indiana. His electoral vote was 168 compared with 233 for Harrison. The Republicans showed increased strength in all parts of the country except the South, a situation which inspired such triumphant chants as:

> Down in the cornfield,
> Hear the mournful sound.
> All the Democrats are weeping,
> Grover's in the cold, cold ground.

Cleveland's administration had been largely negative; but it had effectively defied special interests and had strongly supported honest and efficient practices in government. In practice Cleveland had accepted the support and the policies of conservative Eastern Democrats who controlled the party machinery and whose primary interests lay in low taxes and opposition to any government interference in the economy. Judged by the standards of honesty, economy, and efficiency rather than in terms of twentieth-century reform, Cleveland was probably the strongest President of the late nineteenth century.

Harrison and the Republicans

Benjamin Harrison (1833–1901), a prominent lawyer from Indianapolis, was the grandson of General William Henry Harrison. He had served with distinction in the Civil War, moved up in Indiana Republican politics, and in 1881 entered the United States Senate. Personally cold and unresponsive to all but his family and very closest friends, Harrison was nonetheless sincere, earnest, and capable.

For the first time since 1875, under Harrison the same party controlled both houses of Congress and the Presidency. Understandably voters who had been promised much expected the Republicans to produce results. The Fifty-first Congress met in December 1889, under the leadership of "Czar" Thomas B. Reed of Maine, the powerful Speaker of the House. By means of his power to give or withhold recognition of House members, to appoint the Rules Committee, and to ignore what he considered dilatory motions, Reed ran the House with an iron hand. Under Reed's leadership in the House and with such powerful figures as Allison and Sherman in the Senate, the Republicans passed more important legislation than any Congress since the Civil War.

Many Republicans considered their first and most important business to be that of removing Democrats from federal office; they did so, utterly contemptuous of the civil service reforms they had promised. The Republican administration replaced thirty-two thousand of the fifty-five thousand fourth-class postmasters within eighteen months. Harrison appointed young Theodore Roosevelt to the Civil Service Commission, but Roosevelt found himself helpless to stop the trend, especially when the President refused to resist party demands.

During the campaign, the Republicans had promised liberal pensions to Civil War veterans.

Corporal James Tanner, Commissioner of Pensions and former GAR lobbyist, insisted that the party fulfill its election pledges. Tanner liberalized some pension payments by administrative action, and in 1890, Congress passed the Disability Pension Act, which added many old soldiers to the pension lists. Widows of veterans also received more liberal payments. This legislation sent expenditures for pensions from $88,842,000 in 1890 to $139,812,000 in 1895. In the long run, the total cost of pensions exceeded the expense of the Civil War itself. The Republicans had reduced the Treasury surplus, but they had accomplished this through greater expenditures rather than lower tariffs or reduced taxes.

Republican leaders interpreted their victory of 1888 as a popular mandate to revise the tariff upward. In his annual message to Congress on December 3, 1889, President Harrison called for a revision of both the schedules and the administrative features of the tariff law. Representative William McKinley of Ohio, chairman of the Ways and Means Committee, introduced a measure which raised rates on manufactured goods to the highest level in the nation's history. Average duties reached nearly 40 percent of the value of the goods. In some cases the rates were so high as to practically eliminate imports. The new measure, which became law in October shortly before the elections of 1890, reflected vividly the political power of those who benefited from the protective system.

Meanwhile, Congress wrestled with silver legislation, a matter of vital concern to the West and South. Indeed, the free coinage of silver was becoming the nation's most controversial political question. The unsatisfactory Bland-Allison Act of 1878, which provided for some silver coinage, had pleased no one. The law had not measurably inflated the currency. As hard times enveloped the West and South during the late 1880s, farmers demanded inflation through the free and unlimited coinage of silver.

The old Mint Act of 1792 provided for coinage of both gold and silver at a ratio of approximately 16 to 1. This assumed that gold was sixteen times more valuable than silver. But after 1834 the federal government coined little silver, and in 1853 it discontinued the minting of all silver coins except the dollar. In 1873 Congress removed even the silver dollar from the coinage list. Few paid any attention to this law because the commercial value of enough silver to coin a dollar was worth slightly more than 100 cents in gold, and so people who had silver sold it commercially. During the 1870s, however, the new Western silver mines greatly increased the production of silver, and by 1877 the 371.25 grains of silver necessary to mint a dollar was worth only 90 cents in gold on the commercial market. Silver producers now wanted to mint their silver into dollars but faced the Coinage Act

"The Silver Sun of Prosperity": An 1890 cartoon praising the Sherman Silver Purchase Act.

The Granger Collection

of 1873. Farmers who saw the coinage of millions of silver dollars as a means to inflate the currency teamed up with the silver miners to demand free and unlimited coinage of silver at a ratio of 16 to 1 with gold. The law of 1873 demonetizing silver they now denounced as the "Crime of '73," and pictured it as a dastardly scheme of bankers to deflate the currency, to the detriment of farmers and workers. So strong was the free-silver sentiment in Congress by 1890 that protectionists could not pass the McKinley tariff without free-silver support. Thus, in return for Western support of the McKinley tariff, the protectionists accepted a silver coinage bill. The Sherman Silver Purchase Act, passed on July 14, 1890, provided for the government purchase of 4.5 million ounces of silver per month, with payment in Treasury notes redeemable in coin, either silver or gold.

Congress also dealt with the important question of antitrust legislation in 1890. With bipartisan congressional support, the Sherman Antitrust Act became law on July 2. (See Chapter 17 for a full discussion of government regulation of business.) Despite its general ineffectiveness, the Sherman Act marked the beginning of an attempt by the federal government to curb monopoly.

Although the Harrison administration showed little concern over worsening economic conditions and rising discontent among Western farmers, some of its policies received Western approval. North and South Dakota, Montana, and Washington became states in 1889; Idaho and Wyoming followed in 1890. The opening of the Oklahoma Territory in 1889 saw thousands of people rush for the coveted land; early in 1890, some 11 million acres became available for settlement in the Sioux reservation of South Dakota. Defying those Westerners who favored the rapid exploitation of timber resources, Congress passed the Forest Reserve Act of 1891, which authorized the President to withdraw timberlands for public entry.

Passage of pension, silver, tariff, and antitrust legislation marked the Fifty-first Congress as one of the most active on record. Moreover, it spent more money than any previous peacetime Congress. Outlays for public improvements, naval construction, pensions, and other functions of government increased federal spending under Harrison by about a hundred million dollars annually. Conservative critics labeled it the "billion-dollar Congress," to which Speaker Reed reputedly answered, "Isn't this a billion-dollar country?" The Republican program may have been popular with party leaders, but in the midterm elections of 1890, the people expressed their displeasure. Only 88 Republicans returned to the House of Representatives against 235 Democrats. The Senate remained Republican by 8 votes, but responsible party government ground to a halt. The tariff more than any other issue had produced a major Republican defeat.

Discontented farmers contributed to the Republican debacle. During the summer of 1890 state Farmers' Alliances organized People's or Independent parties in Kansas, Nebraska, and the Dakotas. Having become convinced that farmers could expect nothing from either the Republicans or the Democrats, farmers in these states determined to make a clean political sweep. The most bitter and vigorous campaign occurred in Kansas, where Mary Elizabeth Lease, "Sockless" Jerry Simpson, and William A. Peffer berated the economic royalists and the "bloodhounds of money." Mrs. Lease reportedly urged farmers "to raise less corn and more hell." Despite the lack of funds and proper political organization, farmers won some spectacular victories. Kansas elected Peffer to the United States Senate; voters in South Dakota sent James H. Kyle to the Senate. In the South protesting farmers moved to take over the Democratic party. "Pitchfork" Ben Tillman won the governorship in South Carolina, and Thomas E. Watson of Georgia went to the House of Representatives with the backing of discontented farmers. When Congress met in

1891, at least fifty congressmen were members of, or sympathetic to, the Farmers' Alliance.

Obviously President Harrison and the Republicans were in deep trouble.

Freedmen and Civil Rights

One of the most emotional and controversial issues in the Fifty-first Congress was the attempt to guarantee voting rights to Southern blacks through federal power. Although relations between whites and blacks in the South had not—by the standards of the day—been intolerable in the 1880s, blacks still suffered from social, economic, and political discrimination. For example, there were thirty-nine blacks in the South Carolina Legislature in 1877–1878, only six in 1890–1891. The Supreme Court's decision in 1883 declaring the Civil Rights Act of 1875 unconstitutional undermined black efforts to achieve even minimum civil rights.

In his annual message to Congress in December 1889, President Harrison spoke out on behalf of black civil rights, but he failed to recommend any specific measures to reach this goal. Then in June 1890, Representative Henry Cabot Lodge of Massachusetts introduced his Federal Elections bill to give national officers supervisory power over federal elections in the South under specified conditions. Southerners violently attacked this so-called Force Bill, designed to protect black voting rights, charging that it would destroy states' rights and individual liberty. Nevertheless, on July 2, the House passed the Lodge bill by a vote of 155 to 149.

Despite some enthusiastic Republican support, however, including that of North Carolina Negro Congressman Henry P. Cheatham, the Senate laid the measure aside to take up the tariff question. Congress considered the federal election law at the next session, but neither President Harrison nor the Republican Congress pushed the measure with any determination. Early in 1891 Congress dropped it from consideration.

This debate on federal intervention in Southern elections frightened those Southerners who believed that blacks should have no effective voice in politics. Even the feeble efforts in the Fifty-first Congress to protect black rights provoked Southerners to take additional steps to disfranchise black voters. In 1890, shortly after Congress considered the Lodge bill, Mississippi amended its constitution to assure whites that the vast majority of blacks would not note. Other states quickly followed Mississippi's example and enacted poll taxes, required black voters to interpret sections of the Constitution, and took other effective means to deny them suffrage. Some Southern states added so-called grandfather clauses to their constitutions which limited black suffrage to those whose ancestors had the right to vote in 1867. What brought disfranchisement specifically after 1890 was the fear that the fusionist movement between Southern white Populists and blacks would give the latter the balance of power in Southern politics. Additional political exclusion of blacks came with passage in the Southern states of the white primary. Senator Ben Tillman of South Carolina said later: "We have done our level best [to disfranchise blacks]. . . . We have scratched our heads to find out how we could eliminate the last one of them. We stuffed ballot boxes, we shot them. We are not ashamed of it." So effective was the disfranchisement that the number of registered black voters in Louisiana dropped from 130,334 in 1896 to 1,342 in 1904.

By 1901 the last Negro of the post-Reconstruction period had been removed from Congress. George H. White, a black representative from North Carolina, did not even run in 1900 because he knew his cause was hopeless. When the Judiciary Committee quietly buried White's antilynching bill in January 1900, this black Congressman spoke prophetically to his colleagues. "This . . . is perhaps the Negroe's temporary farewell to the American Congress," he said, "but let me say, . . . he will rise up some day and come again."

The Election of 1892

Local and state successes in the election of 1890 convinced an increasing number of farmers that the time had come to form a national third party which would protect the interests of agriculture. Following several preliminary meetings, delegates met in Omaha in July 1892 to nominate candidates and launch their campaign. Declaring that "we meet in the midst of a nation brought to the verge of moral, political, and material ruin," the delegates complained that "corruption dominates the ballot box, the Legislatures, the Congress, and touches even the ermine of the bench."

The platform of the People's, or Populist, party called for the unlimited coinage of silver; government ownership of railroads and telephone and telegraph lines; a system of postal savings banks; a graduated income tax; and an increase in the amount of circulating currency to at least $50 per capita. Additional resolutions recommended the Australian, or secret, ballot; the initiative and referendum; a single term for president; and the direct election of senators. The convention favored a shorter workday for industrial laborers, denounced contract labor, and expressed opposition to the use of Pinkerton detectives in breaking strikes. The Populists nominated James B. Weaver, a Civil War veteran, former congressman, and a tested leader of the farm movement from Iowa, for president, and James G. Field of Virginia for vice president.

Only the spirited and energetic activity of the Populists enlivened an otherwise dull and uninspiring campaign in 1892. Although President Harrison had made many enemies, there was no practical alternative to his renomination. The Republicans chose Whitelaw Reid as his running mate. Like the Republicans, the Democrats did not have a very appealing list of possible candidates. However, Cleveland, who still had strong support in the East, won the nomination on the first ballot. As a sop to discontented Westerners, Adlai E. Stevenson of Illinois received the nomination for vice president. Neither Cleveland nor Harrison took to the stump in what was probably the cleanest campaign since the Civil War.

In the final voting, Cleveland won a smashing victory with 277 electoral votes to 145 for Harrison and 22 for Weaver. Cleveland surprised even the Democrats by carrying such states as Illinois, Wisconsin, and California, although his election reflected a widespread dissatisfaction with the Harrison administration rather than general approval of Democratic promises. Weaver's popular vote of 1,040,886 was highly encouraging to the Populists. He carried four states and won some electoral votes in others.

Cleveland's Second Administration

Discontented farmers and workers expected little sympathy from Grover Cleveland. Henry Clay Frick of the Carnegie Corporation wrote shortly after the election: "I am very sorry for President Harrison, but I cannot see that our interests are going to be affected one way or another by the change in administration." Cleveland appointed a conservative Cabinet which contained no one sympathetic with the plight of agriculture and labor. In his inaugural address the President promised to maintain "a sound and stable currency" and labeled free silver a dangerous "heresy."

Two months after Cleveland took office on March 4, the Panic of 1893 rocked the nation's economy and ushered in a prolonged depression. Bankruptcies and panic selling on the New York Stock Exchange during the last days of the Harrison administration presaged trouble. On May 5 the previously sound National Cordage Company failed. In rapid succession scores of other businesses and industries closed their doors. A withdrawal of gold by foreign countries, which threatened the gold standard, and a decline in railroad investment contributed to the collapse. Perhaps more important still was the long depression and low purchasing power in the agricultural and labor sectors of the economy.

Cleveland believed that the country's "unfortunate plight" stemmed largely from the Sherman Silver Purchase Act of 1890, which caused a drain on the Treasury's gold reserve. At the President's urging Congress repealed the act in October 1893. The gold supply continued to decline. The Treasury now sold bonds to acquire sufficient gold to replenish the reserve. One of the two issues sold in 1894 was purchased by J. P. Morgan and Company at a handsome discount. Following sharp criticism for trafficking with Wall Street bankers, the Treasury early in 1896 sold a $100 million bond issue to the general public.

While Cleveland had preserved the gold standard, he had aroused bitter political opposition. Democrat William Jennings Bryan said that the people owed Cleveland the same gratitude that a passenger would to "the trainman who has opened a switch and precipitated a wreck." Cleveland's monetary policy did not restore confidence; nor did it improve economic conditions. The President soon entered another political tussle when he urged Congress to lower tariff rates. The Wilson-Gorman tariff, passed in 1894, lowered rates slightly. The law not only failed to please the President but also aroused opposition in other quarters. One of the most notable features of the Wilson-Gorman bill was the inclusion of an income tax demanded by Western and Southern agrarians.

While congressmen and senators argued over the money and tariff issues, hard times gripped every part of the country. Unemployed men drifted from place to place in search of work or relief. Some citizens thought that the federal government should sponsor work relief projects to help jobless men. Jacob S. Coxey, a well-to-do Ohio businessman and reformer, dramatized this demand in the spring of 1894 when he led a march of unemployed men to Washington in support of his Good Roads bill. This measure, already introduced in Congress, called for the Treasury to issue $500 million in legal tender currency for road construction. This bill supposedly would provide employment and inflate the currency. But troops arrested Coxey for walking on the Capitol lawn, and Congress ignored his demands. Thereafter "Coxey's Army" drifted out of the capitol.

Unemployment and reduced wages for those still working produced widespread labor strife by 1894. The most spectacular conflict between management and organized labor was the Pullman strike with its important political consequences. (See Chapter 18.) Cleveland's actions further alienated workers from the Democratic administration. Cleveland's antilabor attitude and his support for the gold standard when farmers wanted free silver and inflation, coupled with the general depression, spelled disaster for the Democratic party. In the midterm elections of 1894, the Republicans gained a heavy majority in the House of Representatives and nearly won control of the Senate. Soon the conservative position of the Supreme Court would anger the discontented.

In the case of *Pollack v. Farmers' Loan and Trust Company* in 1895 the Court struck down the income tax provision included in the Wilson-Gorman tariff. On every hand it seemed to an increasing number of farmers and workers that the government was dominated by special interests unsympathetic to the masses of citizens.

As depression and hard times persisted, the issue of free and unlimited coinage of silver came to overshadow all other political issues. The free-silver movement was not limited to the Populists or other so-called radicals. Large elements in both the Republican and Democratic parties demanded monetary inflation. For years an advocate of inflation, Senator Henry Moore Teller of Colorado led a growing free-silver faction in the Republican party, and Congressman William Jennings Bryan of Nebraska rapidly gained leadership of Western and Southern inflationist Democrats. One of free silver's most effective spokesmen was William H. Harvey, whose small book *Coin's Financial School* (1894) sold thousands of copies.

As the presidential election of 1896 approached, the money question threatened to sweep all before it. The Republican Convention

William Jennings Bryan at the Democratic National Convention, 1886.

Culver Pictures, Inc.

met in June at St. Louis. The party was split on the silver issue but the gold standard faction was clearly in control. Delegates sang:

Gold, gold, gold,
I love to hear it jingle.
Gold, gold, gold,
Its power is untold.

For the women they adore it,
While the men try hard to store it;
There is not a better thing in life than
Gold, gold, gold.

After the delegates voted down a Teller amendment to the platform calling for free silver, the convention adopted a plank calling for bimetallism which really meant the gold standard. Again the Republicans pledged allegiance to tariff protection. They then nominated William McKinley of Ohio to head the ticket and named Garret A. Hobart of New Jersey as their vice-presidential candidate. McKinley had the powerful backing of Marcus A. Hanna, a wealthy Cleveland industrialist who had spent a great deal of time and money to assure his friend's nomination. Born in 1843, McKinley served four years in the Union Army, after which he read law and practiced at Canton, Ohio. He was not brilliant or sophisticated, but he worked hard, had a friendly manner, and inspired confidence. He served in the House of Representatives most of the time between 1876 and 1891. In the latter year he became governor of Ohio.

While the free-silver forces fought a losing battle within Republican ranks, they were gradually acquiring control of the Democratic party. Cleveland's devotion to the gold standard and his alignment with conservative Eastern industrial and banking interests had caused him to lose most of his earlier support in the agrarian West and South. One critic said the country needed something besides "a government of brains, belly and brass." When the delegates assembled for their nominating convention at Chicago in July, the silver forces were clearly in control. All they needed was a fearless, articulate leader. The silverites found their man in thirty-six-year-old William Jennings Bryan.

Bryan was raised in a conservative, fundamentalist Illinois home. He completed college, read law, and then settled down to practice at Jacksonville in 1883. In 1887 he moved to Lincoln, Nebraska. Bryan had a keen interest in politics and ran successfully for the House of Representatives in 1890. During his two terms in Washington he became widely known for his discussions of the tariff and his stand for free silver. A dedicated agrarian, Bryan fought entrenched privilege with all his energy.

Bryan's greatest asset as a politician was his ability as a public speaker. During the Democratic convention, when the delegates were debating the money question, he electrified the huge crowd by concluding a ringing speech in favor of free silver with the words: "You shall not press down upon the brow of labor this crown of thorns, you shall not crucify mankind on a cross of gold." This powerful address helped to win him the nomination on the fifth ballot. To appeal to the conservative interests, the Democrats nominated Arthur Sewall, a wealthy Maine businessman, for vice president. The platform demanded free and unlimited coinage of silver, a tariff for revenue only, and an income tax. It favored stricter regulation of corporations and opposed court injunctions in labor disputes.

Bryan's nomination and the free-silver plank in the Democratic platform placed the Populists in a most difficult position. If they ran a Populist candidate, the free-silver split would assure McKinley's election. If, on the other hand, they supported Bryan, the Populists would probably be absorbed by the Democratic party and lose their separate identity. After some heated arguments at their convention in July, the Populists decided to fuse with the Democrats and nominate Bryan. But to maintain some degree of party independence, they named Thomas E. Watson of Georgia as their vice-presidential nominee. The gold standard Democrats refused to back Bryan and nominated John M. Palmer of Illinois and Simon B. Buckner of Kentucky for president and vice president respectively.

McKinley had hoped to campaign primarily on the tariff question, but free silver eliminated every competing issue. Bryan carried on a whirlwind speaking tour and sharply denounced Republican economic policies, which, he declared, plundered the great mass of citizens. He argued that free silver would liberate the economy and restore prosperity. Bryan traveled more than 18,000 miles and made some six hundred speeches. Refusing to stump the country in competition with Bryan, McKinley staged a "front porch" campaign under the guidance of Marcus Hanna, a masterful political organizer. The Republicans employed hundreds of speakers and distributed tons of literature. They pictured McKinley as a solid, dependable, capable leader, and the "Advance Agent of Prosperity." Bryan, on the other hand, they presented as an un-American radical, whose election would threaten the country's very foundations. The campaign was bitter and highly emotional. When the votes were counted on November 3, McKinley polled 7,104,779 to Bryan's 6,502,925. Bryan carried most of the South and West; McKinley won a majority in the Northeast.

Several factors accounted for Bryan's defeat. McKinley's campaign was highly organized and backed by a minimum of $3 million. Bryan probably spent less than $300,000. Moreover, Bryan's free-silver arguments appealed neither to workers, who feared higher food prices, nor to the more prosperous farmers. Both urban workers and Midwest farmers were actually attracted by McKinley's protective tariff arguments. Bryan, carrying the Democratic burden for the depression, was unable to counteract the Republican resurgence which had begun in 1894. Bryan was no doubt the strongest candidate the Democrats could have named in 1896. No Democrat could have won.

The McKinley-Bryan contest was the most important political campaign between 1860 and 1912. It produced the sharpest class conflict of any election in that half century. To a considerable extent, silver and gold were symbols, one representing agriculture, the other industry and commerce. Industrialism won; from that point onward the power of agriculture in the councils of the nation declined rapidly.

McKinley's election destroyed the farm movement which had been such a potent political force during the previous quarter century. Yet, the Populists and other farm groups had made an important and lasting contribution to American political and economic life. Congress later adopted many of their ideas for reform, including the income tax, parcel post, postal savings, and stricter regulation of big business. Their discussion of the money question stimulated new banking and currency legislation. Populist support for the initiative and referendum, direct primaries, and direct election of senators did not pass unnoticed.

Some writers have accused the Populists of being provincial, nativist, anti-Semitic, and irrational, motivated by a threatened loss of status in American society. These critics have maintained that the Populists opposed industrialism and attempted to restore some earlier agrarian ideal. But these interpretations are far from conclusive. Perhaps they are not even important. The real significance of the Populists lay in their identification of economic abuses in both the agricultural and industrial sectors of the economy and in their effort to correct them through government action.

Conclusion

Both the Republican and Democratic parties built viable, effective political organizations in the post-Civil War years, but the Republicans generally dominated the national scene. Even without distinguished leadership, they skillfully welded together support from business and industry, veterans, government workers, farmers, and even workingmen. Much of the Republican power rested on strong local and state organizations which could deliver the vote in crucial elections. Yet Republican control was tenuous. The Democratic victory of 1892 indicated how rapidly and dramatically party fortunes could change. Neither party developed a program which satisfied the needs and desires of all its members.

By the early 1890s, the winds of political discontent were blowing within both major parties. Despite the excitement aroused by pensions, civil service, and the tariff, many Americans had come to view these as sham issues, irrelevant to the nation's basic needs. Leadership and policies which allied government with business and industrial interests, at the expense of workers and farmers, appeared less and less satisfactory. While the growing concentration of industrial and financial power threatened both political and economic democracy, politicians could not or would not act to preserve egalitarian ideals. Nor would they deal with unattended problems—conservation of the nation's natural resources, control of excessive wealth and economic power, conditions of employment among the nation's workers, and the plight of farmers in the West and South. Nevertheless, there was still a strong underlying demand for reform which finally forced national action early in the twentieth century.

SUGGESTED READINGS

There are some especially good chapters on late-nineteenth-century political history in H. Wayne Morgan (ed.), *The Gilded Age: A Reappraisal** (1963), which modify the interesting but unbalanced *The Politi-cos, 1865–1896** (1938) by Matthew Josephson. An important aspect of Republican policy in the South has been discussed by Vincent P. DeSantis in *Republicans Face the Southern Question: The New Departure Years,*

Art in America: 1865–1905

Nineteenth-century painting in the post-Civil War period generally reflects the pessimism and melancholy which characterized the age in general. The Civil War proved the all-too-bitter truth that the dream of America as new Eden was false and that America could experience a holocaust as great as corrupt Europe had ever produced. Allied to this in the later nineteenth century was the accumulation of great collections of antiques and Old Master's paintings by the nouveau riche who were interested in achieving "instant culture" and a correspondent lessening of support for native, contemporary American art.

Sculpture first felt this impact. While the neoclassic school continued to produce its marmoreal allegories, gods, and goddesses until the end of the century and even beyond, the meaning of such works for Americans greatly diminished as the concept of the United States as a second Greek democracy proved illusory. Sculpture continued to thrive in America, however, and in one area, that of city and state military monuments, at least, the Civil War provided a great springboard for sculptural production.

The Hudson River School continued to flourish with its exploration of American scenery in meticulously rendered detail, but the most successful artists to employ this stylistic approach were painters such as Frederic Church, who applied his talent to the interpretation of the grandiose scenery of the North American West, and Albert Bierstadt, who painted unexplored South America. New currents were entering into American landscape painting, however, particularly from France, where the more personal and more lyrical interpretations of nature inspired such American artists as George Inness.

The great triumvirate of American painters of the period included Thomas Eakins, Winslow Homer, and Albert Pinkham Ryder. The first two were the

---

Hiram Powers was the first American sculptor to achieve international prominence. His sculpture of The Greek Slave, *above all, embodied the neoclassic ideals derived from a study of the art of antiquity and applied to a contemporary allegory where it had an appeal that was sentimental, religious, and moral.*

Death on a Pale Horse *is
unique among the works of
Albert Pinkham Ryder: his
largest painting and a very
personal conception relating to a
friend who committed suicide
after losing at a race track. Even
here, however, we have the
private vision, the simplified
forms, the dark pallette, and the
thick paint so typical of Ryder.*

*greatest American realists of the century, the former applying his prodigiou
talents to create incisive, intimate interpretations of people and figures. Th
approach and his sad, monochromatic pallette justly has earned Eakins th
cognomen, "the American Rembrandt." Homer was one of the greatest painter
of the sea, and, while the most successful of these three artists, like Eakins, h
divorced himself from contemporary society. Even more isolated from the li,
around him, Ryder retreated into an imaginary fantasy world, sometim
drawn from the depths of his mind, sometimes reinterpreting Biblical and li,
erary themes, but always in a very personal way.*

*The greatest artists working in America during this period had little conta
with American society, unlike their pre-Civil War predecessors. Other America*

painters divorced themselves even further from their native milieu and became expatriates, following in the footsteps of the Benjamin West and John Singleton Copley but for very different reasons. James A. M. Whistler spent his whole artistic life in Paris, London, and Venice, producing works variously influenced by the French realist Courbet, the English Pre-Raphaelites, and the newly discovered Japanese art, but ultimately, in the highly refined sensibility of his "art for art's sake" credo, creating a body of work very individual, modern, and almost abstract. John Singer Sargent became the greatest portraitist of his era, painting the likenesses of the internationally and socially prominent and affluent, first in France, then in England. French Impressionism influenced the work of both these painters, but it was Mary Cassatt who became a member of that group of French artists devoted to the study and depiction of light, color, and atmosphere. Miss Cassatt spent her entire artistic career in France, but other American artists, such as Childe Hassam, studied there and then returned to America to introduce these more colorful and happy aspects into American art at the very end of the century.

Devoted to the style and principles of such painters as Claude Monet, Childe Hassam, among other painters so influenced, introduced Impressionism to America. Indeed this approach became so popular here that a group of artists, Hassam among them, gathered together to form "The Ten," which became a sort of Impressionist academy.

Left: Childe Hassam (1859–1935)
The Stewart Mansion, New York City
Santa Barbara Museum of Art. Gift, Preston Morton Collection.

Augustus Saint-Gaudens (1848–1907), Adams Memorial, 1891, *bronze. Rock Creek Cemetery, Washington, D.C.*

The reaction to neoclassicism in sculpture took the form of heroic, bronze historical monuments. Augustus St. Gaudens was the greatest of these late-nineteenth-century sculptors. His great Civil War monuments —that of Colonel Shaw in Boston and the Farragut and Sherman statues in New York (right, above)— were not so much inspired by sculpture of antiquity as by that of the Renaissance, and this period in American sculpture is often referred to as the "Renaissance Revival." A more personal, private, almost mystical note can be sensed in St. Gaudens' memorial to Mrs. Henry Adams. But St. Gaudens was hardly the only accomplished sculptor of the period. His best-known contemporary was Daniel Chester French who rose to rapid fame with his Minute Man (right, below). The work had a stirring, patriotic appeal, but, a close look reveals its direct derivation from the Apollo Belvedere transformed into an American subject and interpreted in the medium of bronze.

Above: Augustus Saint-Gaudens (1848–1907)
General William Tecumseh Sherman Memorial, 1892–1903, bronze
Central Park, New York City.
Right: Daniel Chester French (1850–1931)
The Minute Man, 1874–1875, bronze
Concord, Mass.

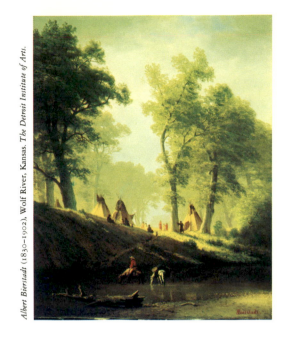

The techniques of the Hudson River School, reinformed by study at the great German art center of Düsseldorf, inspired the painting of Albert Bierstadt, the most famous interpreter of the scenery of the American West. Far from the urban centers of the East and remote from national conflict, the Adamic vision could survive, and Bierstadt's enormous canvases commanded prices not only astronomical but beyond any sums previously paid to American painters. Thomas Moran, a slightly younger painter of the West, based his style instead upon that of the English painter, James Mallord Turner, and thus brought a new sense of dashing brushwork and brilliant color to his equally large Western canvases. Going beyond Bierstadt, Moran sought romantic interpretation, beyond factual accuracy, a feeling popular enough to influence the founding of the National Parks system to protect the natural monuments he was immortalizing.

Thomas Moran (1837–1926), Grand Canyon of the Yellowstone, 1893–1901, oil on canvas National Collection of Fine Arts, Smithsonian Institution. Gift of George D. Pratt.

George Inness (1825–1894)
Peace and Plenty, 1865, oil on canvas
The Metropolitan Museum of Art. Gift of George A. Hearn, 1894.

George Inness completely abandoned the Hudson River meticulousness of his youth and instead, after studying the art of Corot, Rousseau, and other French Barbizon painters, created more generalized yet more poetic landscapes in which topography was of distinctly minor interest. The art of Inness's middle years, from the mid-1850s to the mid-1870s was solid, massive, and dramatic (right). About the time of his move to Montclair, N.J., in 1878, his style became increasingly delicate and feathery until all details disappeared in a soft, generalized, and harmonious atmosphere, merging figures, animals, shrubbery, and trees (above). In this, Inness followed the development of his French predecessor, Corot.

George Inness (1825–1894), Trout Brook, 1891, oil on canvas
Collection of the Newark Museum, Purchase Members Fund, 1965.

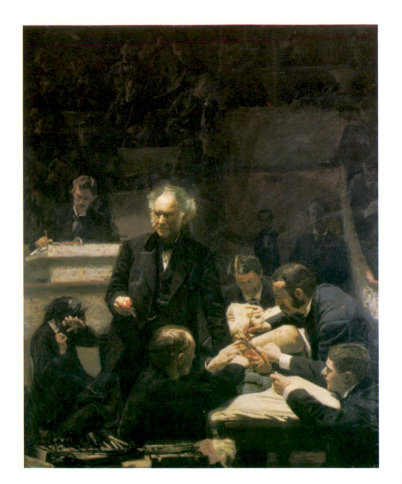

Left: Thomas Eakins (1844–1916), The Gross Clinic, 1875, oil on canvas. Courtesy of the Jefferson Medical College of Philadelphia. Below: Thomas Eakins, The Concert Singer—Portrait of Weda Cook, 1892, oil on canvas. Philadelphia Museum of Art. Right: Thomas Eakins, Salutat, 1898, oil on canvas. Addison Gallery of American Art, Phillips Academy, Andover, Mass.

One of the greatest realists of the nineteenth century, Thomas Eakins was the best figure painter that America produced. The academic French artist, Gerome, with whom he studied, imbued him with a sense of form and structure; and the intense, moving realism of such seventeenth-century Spanish artists as Ribera also impressed him deeply. Eakins' feeling for form and anatomy and his interest in character and individuality in portraiture were never more magnificently and graphically expressed than in his The Gross Clinic (left), which shocked and horrified his contemporaries in its lack of sentiment and uncompromising realism.

Most of Eakins' sitters and subjects, even in his portraits, were friends and relatives, and it is not surprising that he often endows them with a sympathetic, rather intimate melancholy (right). Eakins' pallette was dark and sombre—in his portraits as well as his figure studies. Both a painter and teacher of anatomy, Eakins could study and depict the unclothed human form most naturally in the fighting ring (far right) and the swimming hole. These vigorous and masculine paintings emphasize the solid, powerful forms of his subjects in a completely unposed, nonartificial way.

Left: Winslow Homer (1836–1910), Long Branch, New Jersey, 1809, oil on canvas. Courtesy of the Museum of Fine Arts, Boston, Charles Henry Hayden Fund. Below: Winslow Homer, Northeaster, 1895, oil on canvas. The Metropolitan Museum of Art. Gift of George A. Hearn, 1910.

Right: Winslow Homer, Canoe in Rapids, *1897, water color on paper. Courtesy of the Fogg Art Museum, Harvard University, Louise E. Bettens Fund. Below: Winslow Homer,* The Fox Hunt, *1893, oil on canvas. Courtesy of the Pennsylvania Academy of the Fine Arts.*

If Eakins was America's finest realist figure painter, Winslow Homer was our greatest realistic painter of nature. Even his earlier work conveys the freshness, airiness, and naturalness of the outdoors where man and nature sympathetically join (left, above). Increasingly, however, after the early 1880s, Homer's art became more sombre and more powerful, and the human figure either more monumental and rugged in his battle against the forces of nature (above, right) or absent entirely, leaving only the interaction and conflict of a few natural elements — the irresistible force of the sea and the immovable timeless rocks of the shore (left, below). The great Fox Hunt (right, below) is unique in its delicate outlines, flat forms, and sense of pattern. Here Japanese influences combine with a sense of the rugged battle for survival in nature. Homer was also a great watercolorist, whether applying the medium to the hunters of the Adirondacks or the richer, more colorful life of Florida and the Caribbean. Indeed, this period witnessed the birth of watercolor as an independent art form in America, and the nation was fortunate in having such great interpreters of the medium as Homer, Thomas Moran, and John Singer Sargent.

Albert Pinkham Ryder (1847–1917), Toilers of the Sea, *before* 1884, *oil on wood. The Metropolitan Museum of Art, George A. Hearn Fund,* 1915.

John LaFarge (1835–1910), Bridle Path, Tahati, *ca.* 1890, *watercolor. Courtesy of the Fogg Art Museum, Harvard University, Bettens Fund.*

The greatest of the solitary American painters of a fantasy world, Albert Pinkham Ryder certainly qualifies as a late-nineteenth-century romantic. Among his dark, glowing paintings, almost all small, his marines are the best known (above). Their sense of quiet simplicity and interest in abstract shapes brought Ryder the praise and admiration of many contemporary artists. If Ryder was the most individual of our visionaries, a number of others, such as John LaFarge, brought a more cultured, intellectual background to their religious and allegorical scenes. At the left, LaFarge exhibits his knowledge and understanding of Renaissance painting, particularly the art of Raphael and Titian. Indeed much American painting and sculpture in the late nineteenth century acknowledges a debt to the Italian Renaissance.

merican still-life painting of the late nineteenth century
ok on a radically different form from the bright and colorful
uit and flower painting of earlier years. William Michael
arnett, the most famous still-life specialist, always paints in a
ry masculine way, sometimes emphasizing trophies of the hunt
ight). His deceptively realistic style seems actually to project
rms into the viewer's space.

ht: William Harnett (1848–1892), After the Hunt, 1885, oil on
vas Courtesy, California Palace of the Legion of Honor, San
ncisco. Mildred Anna Williams Collection.

w: William Merritt Chase (1849–1916), In the Studio, not dated,
on canvas. The Brooklyn Museum. Gift of Mrs. C. H. De Silver in
ory of her husband.

Harnett received some of his training
in Munich which had superseded
Düsseldorf as the greatest German art
center. For American painters, Munich
stood primarily for dashing, dark,
vigorous figure painting, modeled after
Dutch seventeenth-century prototypes,
particularly the art of Franz Hals.
Frank Duveneck and William Merritt
Chase (left, below) were the greatest
and most influential of the Americans
who brought the Munich style back to
this country. Chase became the greatest
art teacher of the period. His fluidly
painted, scintillating views of his
famous studio, filled with antiques
and bric-a-brac, are among his most
charming and original works.

Above: James Abbott McNeill Whistler (1834–1903)
Nocturne in Black and Gold: The Falling Rocket, *ca.* 1874
oil on panel The Detroit Institute of Arts.

Left: James Abbott McNeill Whistler (1834–1903)
The White Girl, *1861–1862, oil on canvas*
National Gallery of Art, Washington, D.C. Harris Whittemore Colle

Right: John Singer Sargent (1856–1916)
Madame X (Mme Gautreau), *1884, oil on canvas*
The Metropolitan Museum of Art, Arthur H. Hearn Fund, 1916.

England and France have claimed with as much or more justification than America a number of the most important expatriate American painters of the late nineteenth century. One of these is Whistler, a most original artist who began working in the realistic manner of the Frenchman, Gustave Courbet (far left). In England, Whistler abandoned realism for his own form of Impressionism where the viewer's response to his effects became most important (near left). Whistler's interest in the formal relationships of artistic arrangements was in part inspired by his profound knowledge of Oriental art. To disclaim any interest in subject matter in his later work, Whistler often gave his paintings musical titles, such as symphony, nocturne, and so forth.

Perhaps more internationally famous than Whistler but primarily a society portraitist, John Singer Sargent worked with bravura brush work and scintillating colors. Sargent interpreted his often famous and prominent subjects with an emphasis on their positions in society and their elegant backgrounds (right), rather than on the incisive characterizations of Eakins.

Mary Cassatt (1845–1926), Caresse Enfantine, *1902, oil on canvas. National Collection of Fine Arts, Smithsonian Institution. Gift of William T. Evans.*

Impressionism — the investigation of the phenomena of light, color, and atmosphere, often at the expense of mass and space — had a more immediate and enthusiastic reception in America than in its native France, thanks to the support and activity of Mary Cassatt, probably the most famous American woman artist. Miss Cassatt, herself an American expatriate, allied herself with the French Impressionists, but particularly Edouard Degas; like him, she never abandoned her interest in solid figure painting, a phenomenon particularly evident in her often-repeated theme of the mother and child.

1877–1897 (1959). The best account of the Republican party in those years is George H. Mayer's *The Republican Party, 1854–1964** (1964). For administrative history, consult Leonard D. White's *The Republican Era, 1869–1901** (1958).

Some of the best insights into late-nineteenth-century politics can be obtained from the biographies of political leaders. Among the best are Harry Barnard's *Rutherford B. Hayes and His America* (1954); Allan Nevins's *Grover Cleveland* (1932); R. G. Caldwell's *James A. Garfield* (1931); G. F. Howe's *Chester A. Arthur* (1935); and H. J. Sievers's *Benjamin Harrison* (2 vols., 1952–1959).

On Southern politics, it is essential to consult C. Vann Woodward's *Origins of the New South, 1877–1913** (1951). See also Albert D. Kirwan's *Revolt of the Rednecks: Mississippi Politics, 1876–1925** (1951). Some of the best studies on the position of the Negro include Rayford W. Logan's *The Negro in American Life and Thought: The Nadir, 1877–1901* (1954); George B. Tindall's *South Carolina Negroes, 1877–1900** (1952); C. Vann Woodward's *The Strange Career of Jim Crow** (2d ed., 1957); and Daniel D. Smith's *The Negro in Congress, 1870–1901* (1945).

The presidential elections have been covered in Eugene H. Roseboom's *History of Presidential Elections* (rev. ed., 1964); Herbert J. Clancy's *The Presidential Election of 1880* (1958) and George H. Knoles's *The Presidential Campaign and Election of 1892* (1942) provide accounts of two elections.

On the main political issues of the period, see Ari Hoogenboom's *Outlawing the Spoils: A History of the Civil Service Reform Movement, 1865–1883** (1961); Edward Stanwood's *American Tariff Controversies in the Nineteenth Century* (2 vols., 1903); and Mary Dearing's *Veterans in Politics* (1952). The political and economic stability provided by the growing middle class has been brilliantly assessed by Robert H. Wiebe in *The Search for Order, 1877–1920* (1967).

On political conditions in the 1890s see H. U.

Faulkner's *Politics, Reform, and Expansion** (1959). J. Rogers Hollingsworth explains the difficulties within the Democratic party in *The Whirligig of Politics* (1963). Margaret Leech's *In the Days of McKinley* (1959) and H. Wayne Morgan's *William McKinley and His America* (1963) deal adequately with the winner in 1896. Paolo E. Coletta's *William Jennings Bryan, Political Evangelist, 1860–1908* (1964) is the best biography of Bryan and represents the first volume of a three-volume biography. Paul W. Glad's *McKinley, Bryan, and the People** (1964) is an excellent survey of the election of 1896 and the politics which preceded it. *The Presidential Election of 1896* (1964) by Stanley L. Jones is the most complete account of that important campaign and election.

Specialized studies on the Populists include Walter T. K. Nugent's *The Kansas Populists* (1963) and Norman Pollock's *The Populist Response to Industrial America** (1962), which contradict the stimulating but controversial interpretation found in Richard Hofstadter's *The Age of Reform** (1955). Other good local studies of populism are Robert P. Brooks's *The Agrarian Revolution in Georgia, 1865–1912* (1914) and R. C. Martin's *The People's Party in Texas* (1933). Among the best biographies of agrarian leaders are Francis B. Simkins's *Pitchfork Ben Tillman, South Carolinian** (1944); C. Vann Woodward's *Tom Watson, Agrarian Rebel** (1938); Martin Ridge's *Ignatius Donnelly* (1962); and Robert C. Cotner's *James C. Hogg: A Biography* (1959). No student should neglect the still standard *The Populist Revolt* (1931) by John D. Hicks.

The role of the Populists in 1896 has been well analyzed by Robert F. Durden in *The Climax of Populism: The Election of 1896** (1965). Most of the above works contain discussions of free silver, the leading political issue of the 1890s. On the money question in an earlier period consult Irwin Unger's excellent study, *The Greenback Era: A Social and Political History of American Finance, 1865–1879* (1964). *indicates availability in paperback.

American Cultural Life

America's remarkable economic expansion after 1865 stimulated significant social, cultural, and intellectual changes in the nation's life. Developments in the natural and social sciences, literature, education, religion, and the fine arts all testified to a vibrant cultural and intellectual environment. It was probably true, as foreign critics and many others charged, that Americans were excessively materialistic, but they did not live by bread alone; nor were they devoid of culture. As Lord Bryce wrote, "Manners are becoming in America more generally polished, life more orderly, equality between the sexes more complete, the refined pleasures more easily accessible than they have ever been among the masses of any people."

Understandably the intellectual and cultural changes of the late nineteenth century produced deep strains within American society. New urban conditions confronted people with unfamiliar ideas, changing institutional patterns, and strange forms of social behavior. The increasing emphasis on economic gain, the growing impersonality of city life, the greater mobility of the population, and reputedly declining moral standards convinced countless thousands that too many Americans were forsaking the ways of their forefathers. But this was generally the reaction of those who did not approve of change or the direction which the change was taking. And such critics are to be found in every generation.

Nothing upset the fundamental thought patterns of Americans or had such far-reaching intellectual influence as the evolutionary hypothesis of the British scientist Charles Darwin. In *The Origin of Species*, published in 1859, Darwin wrote that species had not been created independently and were not immutable. Rather, he said, "those belonging to what are called the same genera are lineal descendants of some other generally extinct species." Modifications were the results of natural selection. In conclusion, Darwin stated that probably all organic beings "which have ever lived on this earth have descended from some one primordial form, into which life was first breathed." Man, according to Darwin, was not the special creation of God but the product of millions of years of evolution.

Darwinism created controversy and furor in both scientific and religious circles. Its challenge to tradition was profound. In giving scientific support to the concepts of change, emergence, and evolution, Darwinism attacked supernaturalism and absolutes in every form. Absolutes could have no place in a thought system where everything changed in accordance with natural laws or principles. If man had evolved through natural selection from some animal form, supernaturalism with its ideas of special divine creation and intervention in the affairs of men could not be accepted.

Religion especially felt the impact of Darwin's writings, but evolutionary concepts affected law, history, education, economics, and most other aspects of American intellectual life. For instance, no longer were laws or the Constitution considered absolute and fixed; they were seen as growing and changing continually to meet the demands of the times. Oliver Wendell Holmes, Jr., wrote in *The Common Law* (1881) that "the law embodies the story of a nation's development through many centuries and that in order to know what it is, we must know what it has been, and what it tends to become." This new concept of law eventually produced a more liberal interpretation of the Constitution on social and economic matters.

In the field of history, the most prominent scholars came under the influence of evolutionary thinking. James Harvey Robinson of Columbia University saw human history evolving out of the struggle between the common people and the upper classes, while Frederick Jackson Turner of the University of Wisconsin and Harvard declared that American institutions had been changed and influenced chiefly by the country's physical environment, particularly the frontier. Economic institutions, too, came to be viewed not as something fixed but as responses to changes created by new conditions.

This application of evolutionary principles to society became known as "social Darwinism." Herbert Spencer, the great English philosopher, declared that the concepts of biological evolution, including natural selection and survival of the fittest, applied also to social systems. According to Spencer, man was improving constantly through the emerging social processes, and eventually a new human nature and an improved social structure would emerge. Among those who popularized Spencer's ideas in America were William Graham Sumner, a professor of social science at Yale, and the historian John Fiske. Nothing, wrote Sumner, could be done to improve society; men could only wait for the results of natural social processes. In proclaiming social Darwinism, Sumner played on the traditional American ideals of hard work, thrift, and virtue.

Social Darwinism provided a rationale for successful competition, but by the 1880s many Americans rejected the concept's negativism. People from many walks of life held that social abuses could be eliminated and improvements made through man's conscious effort. The late nineteenth and early twentieth centuries were alive with dissenters who refused to accept depression, violent labor-management disputes, slums, the unequal distribution of wealth, child labor, and other undesirable conditions without a search for correctives. Grangers, Populists, labor organizers, church leaders, and scholars insisted that social progress would come less through evolution than through positive human, even governmental, action.

Social Darwinism faced its major philosophical challenge in pragmatism. Among the leading pragmatists were Charles S. Peirce, perhaps the greatest philosopher this country has produced, and also a physicist; William James, a professor of philosophy and psychology at Harvard; and John Dewey, a leading philosopher and educator who settled at Columbia in 1904. In essence, pragmatism taught that the truth of ideas must be tested by experience. Truth was not absolute or final, but evolutionary and changing. It was not handed down by God, but discoverable by man through testing and experimentation. Rejecting all forms of Darwinian determinism, James attributed basic social progress to man's willingness to act on faith, to take risks, to subject beliefs to the test of experiment. Dewey carried this concept further and applied it to the group as well as to the individual. Ideas were to be judged by their results, not by some preconceived notions which had no practical or experimental basis. Reality grew out of experience. James's "philosophy of practicality" appealed strongly to Americans. Always a practical people, Americans found here a philosophy which gave meaning to their individual and national experience.

James H. Tufts, a social psychologist at the University of Chicago, well summarized the changes in late-nineteenth-century thought when he wrote: "My generation has seen the passing of systems of thought which had reigned since Augustus. The conception of the world as a kingdom ruled by God, subject to his laws and their penalties, which had been undisturbed by the Protestant Reformation, has dissolved. . . . The sanctions of our inherited morality have gone. Principles and standards which had stood for nearly two thousand years are questioned." Nowhere were the new scientific and philosophic currents more sharply felt than in religion.

Science and Religion

Most Americans claimed adherence to the Christian faith. As Alexis de Tocqueville wrote in the 1830s, "There is no country in the whole world in which the Christian religion retains a greater influence over the souls of men than in America." The people and their leaders professed a belief in the Bible as the revealed word of God, and in the Church, both Protestant and Catholic, as God's divine instrument through which Christ would speak to men. Although only some 15 to 20 percent of the people were church members in 1860, the influence of religion on the lives and conduct of the population was far greater than these numbers would imply.

But during the 1860s and 1870s, traditional religious thought and programs came under severe attack as a result of new ideas in natural science, biblical criticism, and philosophic concepts which emphasized man's role in the world.

Probably nothing disrupted accepted religious ideas so much as did Darwin's theory of evolution, new findings in geology, physics, and the other natural sciences. According to Darwin, God had not created the world in six days as recorded in Genesis; rather the world had evolved through eons of geologic time. Man had not been formed in the image of God; he had evolved from some unknown primordial form. Thus man was no special creation at all; he was simply the highest of the animal forms. An increasing number of intellectuals considered such widely held Christian beliefs as the virgin birth of Christ and Christ's death and resurrection as myths and illogical folktales beyond scientific verification. Moreover, scholars began to examine the Bible with the same critical approach that they applied to other historical texts or documents. These investigations seemed to prove that the Bible had been compiled over a period of centuries and that God had not moved the hands of those who wrote Holy Writ. These and other ideas challenged the very foundation of supernaturalism essential to Christian faith—a faith which held that man was a child of God, created in His image, and that God intervened in the affairs of His faithful followers through Christ and governed them through the Church.

During the 1870s, and to a greater extent in the 1880s, a sometimes highly emotional conflict emerged between science and religion. The popular controversy over evolution arose only after Darwin published his book *The Descent of Man* in 1871. While traditional Christianity was on the defensive, theologians and philosophers, and even some natural scientists, defended supernaturalism. In his *Systematic Theology* published in 1873, Charles Hodges upheld the infallibility of the Bible, and William G. T. Shedd supported many of the historic Christian beliefs in his book *Dogmatic Philosophy* (1888).

The picturesque attacks on religion by the well-known agnostic Robert G. Ingersoll both enlivened and embittered the controversy. According to Ingersoll, human progress did not depend on God, but on man in league with science. His Holy Trinity was not God, Christ, and the Holy Spirit but observation, reason, and experience, the trinity of science. He scoffed at miracles, lectured on such topics as "The Mistakes of Moses," and angered clergy and laity alike by attacking every vestige of religious faith and practice.

But Ingersoll represented an extreme point of view. Most intellectuals did not reject religion. Rather, they attempted to accommodate science and religion. Many liberal clergymen and theologians accepted evolution as the working out of God's magnificent plan for mankind. Others said that there could be no genuine conflict between science and religion because they were two different aspects of life. The Bible, after all, was not a scientific text; it was a guide to conduct and faith. An increasing number of ministers and laymen forsook religious fundamentalism with its emphasis upon personal salvation and adopted a liberal, humanistic gospel which found no conflict with evolutionism. Evolution and higher criticism affected Catholics less than Protestants inasmuch as the Vatican maintained the authority to determine truth. Still, no part of Christianity went untouched.

While natural science threatened some aspects of basic Christianity, critics attacked the programs and practices of the churches themselves. It was widely charged that the churches had failed to deal with social and economic problems and had made no effort to apply the Christian faith to practical affairs. Critics charged that the church had a duty to deal with such human problems as labor relations, poverty, war, minority rights, and political corruption. This was the social gospel—as contrasted with the gospel of individual salvation which had been the hallmark of Protestant Christianity.

Washington Gladden, a leading minister in Columbus, Ohio, was one of the most prominent clergymen to concern himself with broad social and economic issues. He was especially active in efforts to solve labor-management disputes. Josiah Strong, secretary of the Evangelical Alliance, emphasized social religion in his book *Our Country*, which sold hundreds of thousands of copies. In 1896, C. M. Sheldon, a Topeka, Kansas, minister, wrote a book entitled *In His Steps*, which eventually sold more than 20 million copies in the United States and abroad. Sheldon challenged Christians to live according to the principles of Jesus.

Several new organizations promoted religious teaching and social service. The Young Men's Christian Association arrived from England in 1851; the Young Women's Christian Association established its first branch in New York in 1858. The YMCA and YWCA were evangelically oriented but provided social benefits for young men and women in urban communities. The Salvation Army, another import from Great Britain, appeared in the United States in 1880. Besides its fundamentalist religious services, the Salvation Army provided low-cost rooming houses, food kitchens, employment bureaus, and other help to the urban poor.

Because of their missions and social service programs, Protestants made some gains in the cities. They generally were less successful, however, than the Roman Catholics. Beginning in the 1880s Catholic immigrants poured into urban centers from southern and eastern Europe, where they turned naturally to the Catholic Church. Moreover, Catholic parishes often served working-class districts whereas Protestant churches usually flourished in the middle- and upper-class neighborhoods. Parish priests gave help and comfort to the poor of all nationalities. This held Catholics in the church and won new converts. By the 1880s both Protestants and Catholics demonstrated a much higher degree of social consciousness than ever before.

But most churchmen still preferred fundamentalism, supernaturalism, and emphasis on personal salvation. Indeed, liberal theology and socialized religion did not greatly affect the general body of Christians. The popularity of evangelist Dwight L. Moody testified to the fact that the "old-time religion" was still very much

Mary Baker Eddy.   *The Granger Collection*

alive. Moody and his song leader, Ira D. Sankey, toured English and American cities, where thousands responded to Moody's vivid and moving sermons and to Sankey's emotional songs. Moody emphasized personal conversion, but he did not threaten his listeners with hellfire or eternal damnation. Rather, he stressed God's compassion for man. Fundamentalists stressed a literal interpretation of the Bible as God's word, the virgin birth of Christ, Jesus' death and resurrection, and the forgiveness of sin. The South was traditionally fundamentalist in religion; thus religious liberalism made less progress there than in other sections of the country.

One important new religious fellowship organized in the late nineteenth century was Church of Christ, Scientist, commonly known as Christian Science, with its special appeal to city dwellers. Christian Science was founded in 1875 by Mrs. Mary Baker Eddy, a New Englander who had been healed of a nervous disorder through a new theory of health. In *Science and Health with Key to the Scriptures* (1875) she proclaimed the belief that sin, sickness, and evil were God-created and therefore not real. Mrs. Eddy established the Mother Church in Boston in 1892; by 1906 her followers numbered some 85,000. Christian Science provided new opportunities for religious activity and leadership for women.

Church membership made striking gains in the United States during the half century after 1860. During that period, population more than tripled, while church membership increased more than sevenfold. Total membership rose from 4.8 million in 1860 to 21.7 million in 1890 and climbed to about 33 million in 1906. Of these communicants, 20 million were Protestant, about 12 million were Roman Catholic, and another 1 million were Jewish, Eastern Orthodox, and Mormon (Latter-day Saints). Protestantism was strongest in the South, Midwest, and West, especially among farmers and small-town people. Catholics had their greatest strength in the large cities of the Midwest and Northeast.

If Americans were less than fully committed to formal religion, their faith in education seemed quite beyond challenge. They accepted without question a direct relation between public education and national progress. Education for many was the best guarantee of expanding democracy, additional wealth, improved morals, increased individual opportunity, and the good society. William T. Harris, superintendent of the St. Louis school system (later United States Commissioner of Education from 1889 to 1906), wrote in 1871: "The spirit of American institutions is to be looked for in the public schools to a greater degree than anywhere else." Although there were serious inadequacies in educational administration, curriculum, financing, and state school laws, communities made great improvements in both the quantity and quality of education between the Civil War and the end of the nineteenth century. Except in the South, where public education did not become rooted before 1900, the country moved rapidly toward the dream of universal, public, tax-supported education.

During the post-Civil War years students entered schools at all levels in ever-increasing numbers. Between 1870 and 1910, public school enrollment rose from 6.9 to 17.8 million. Most of this growth occurred in the first eight grades, but the number attending public high schools increased from 80,000 to 915,000. Private schools taught thousands more. College enrollments revealed comparable gains, rising from only 52,000 in 1870 to 355,000 forty years later. Compulsory school attendance, typically for children between eight and fourteen, was an important factor in the growing enrollments. By 1898 thirty-one states and territories had laws setting minimum attendance requirements; unfortunately, these statutes were often poorly enforced. With more children in school, expenditures for education jumped sharply. The cost of public elementary and secondary education in the United States rose from $63.4 million in 1870 to $426 million in 1910.

Curriculum changes occurred at all levels of education, but particularly in the high schools and colleges. In the elementary schools, McGuffey's Readers, with their emphasis upon morality, thrift, industry, and patriotism, continued to be popular as late as 1900. Overall, teaching still emphasized the three R's, with some grammar, geography, and history added. The high schools introduced more courses in science and the humanities, along with some additional history and geography. Schools increased their emphasis on the vocational arts, with manual training as well as household and commercial subjects for non-college-bound students.

John Dewey was the foremost educational philosopher of the period. Dewey taught at the University of Chicago from 1894 to 1904, then moved to Columbia University. Thereafter Columbia became the fountainhead of new educational thought. Dewey looked upon education as a means of reforming society, but he believed that in achieving this end the school must create real life situations. In other words, he discounted knowledge acquired from memorization and insisted that children learned by playing together, expressing themselves, making things, and participating in group activities—in short, by doing and experiencing.

Higher education received strong impetus from the Morrill Land Grant Act of 1862 which granted to every state 30,000 acres of public land for each of its senators and representatives in Congress, to help it establish an agricultural and mechanical college. These colleges were intended to serve those, especially, who wanted practical education and had little or no opportunity to attend such institutions as Harvard or Yale.

No less than the land-grant colleges, the many technical schools reflected a growing emphasis upon practical education. These schools met the rising educational demands of a rapidly growing industrial and technical society. The Massachusetts Institute of Technology, which began operation in 1865, became the leading technical and scientific institution. Special women's colleges appeared after 1865. Henry F. Durant, who established Wellesley, said he wanted to "found a college for the glory of God by the education and culture of women."

Professional and graduate education rose sharply in the late nineteenth century. Harvard and the University of Virginia, among others, had established their famous law schools before the Civil War, but it was not until after 1870 that law schools expanded sufficiently to meet the need. Medical education followed a similar pattern, and by 1900 the nation's medical schools were turning out more than 5,000 trained doctors a year. Teacher training kept pace with other professional education.

Higher education benefited greatly from the distinctive leadership provided by a number of strong college and university presidents. Charles W. Eliot at Harvard (1869–1909), William Rainey Harper at Chicago (1891–1906), and Daniel Coit Gilman at Johns Hopkins (1875–1901) were among those who made major contributions. Eliot was a skilled administrator who worked for what he called the "new education." He introduced the elective system and emphasized the need for sciences, mathematics, and modern foreign languages. At Johns Hopkins, Gilman established the nation's first genuine graduate school.

Education for Blacks

American blacks had an insatiable appetite for learning. Viewing education as a lever to lift themselves out of dependency and poverty, they flocked to the schools established by Northerners after 1865. The Freedmen's Bureau and various religious denominations in the immediate post-Civil War South focused on the expansion of education for freed blacks. By 1870 the Freedmen's Bureau had spent some $5 million on Negro education; church and philanthropic groups had provided millions more.

At the same time, many Southerners demanded public, tax-supported education. Some Southern states passed laws in the 1860s and 1870s providing integrated public schools for both whites and blacks, but these laws were never satisfactorily implemented. The South lacked a tradition of public education. Many whites opposed taxes to educate blacks, and the absence of a strong tax base in most Southern communities retarded public education for the great majority of Southern youth, but especially for blacks. Education for blacks became even worse when the South established a complete separate school system for them. Segregation received legal approval in the separate-but-equal doctrine promulgated by the Supreme Court in *Plessy v. Ferguson* (1896), which applied to schools as well as to transportation and other public facilities. At the turn of the century, thousands of black children had no opportunity to attend school at all, and very rarely did a black youth attend college.

Still after 1865 a number of black colleges prepared blacks for educational and economic roles in an industrial society. In 1868 Samuel C. Armstrong, the son of American missionaries in Hawaii, established Hampton Normal and Agricultural Institute in Virginia. The leading black educator in the post-Civil War years, Booker T. Washington, a former slave and student at Hampton, became the first president of Tuskegee Institute in Alabama when it opened with thirty students in 1881. Other private colleges for blacks included Fisk University in Nashville, Howard University in Washington, D.C., and Atlanta University. Three Southern states established separate publicly supported colleges under the Morrill Land Grant Act of 1862, but these institutions were usually starved for funds.

George Washington Carver was another prominent black educator and scientist. Born in 1864, the son of slave parents, Carver received a master's degree in agriculture from Iowa State College and then settled at Tuskegee to teach and conduct research. His most famous work involved the search for industrial uses for the peanut. Despite such individual triumphs, discrimination, poverty, and lack of leadership held all levels of black education in the South to a minimum during the late nineteenth century.

The Natural Sciences

Advances in science reflected the improvements in American education. A number of American scholars made distinctive contributions to scientific advancement in the post-Civil War years. Most of the basic research was done in the nation's leading universities, such as Harvard, Yale, and Johns Hopkins. Some industries maintained chemists, physicists, and other scientists in their establishments, but these men usually concentrated on applying the results of scientific research to practical purposes rather than expanding the realm of theoretical knowledge.

J. Willard Gibbs, a quiet, reserved physicist at Yale, did basic research in thermodynamics which brought him international fame. His work provided the theoretical basis for the important area of science known as physical chemistry. In astronomy, Simon Newcomb greatly enlarged man's knowledge of the solar system. By the 1890s the United States had the most powerful telescopes in the world available for research in astronomy. Although American chemists failed to pursue much basic research compared with their European counterparts, they did apply new chemical knowledge to industry and agriculture on a broad scale. American scientists carried on extensive research in geology, zoology, and plant sciences. Medical science experienced great advances in surgical techniques and germ control. Appendectomies and similar operations, which had formerly been dangerous and often fatal, became quite routine. Dr. J. D. Bryant of New York performed one of the most famous operations of the period when he removed a malignant growth from President Cleveland's jaw in July 1893, thereby saving the President's life. Deaths from diphtheria and tuberculosis dropped substantially as sanitation and other public health measures improved.

Literary Currents

Between 1865 and World War I American letters were in an era of major transition, influenced by the industrial revolution and its effects on American life and culture. Romanticism and sentimentalism in literature declined in importance among intellectuals during the 1870s, to be followed by the rise of realism in the 1880s and a burst of realistic naturalism in the 1890s and early twentieth century.

Romantic, moralistic, and sentimental writings, however, persisted throughout the last third of the nineteenth century, revealing much about the tastes and intellectual level of the American reading public. Books with a moral, those which drew sharp contrasts between good and evil, and those with religious themes were far more widely read than novels dealing realistically with major social, economic, or political problems. Mary J. Holmes, who began her writing career in the 1850s, turned out her moralistic novels at a rate of nearly one a year well into the 1880s. Setting her stories in Virginia and Maryland, Mrs. E. D. E. N. Southworth wrote about beautiful heroines and ugly villains.

Novels with religious themes sold by the millions. It is not surprising that in a period of economic and social dislocation people were attracted to books which even in fictional form provided assurance and proved the ultimate triumph of right. Few books of fiction compared with Lew Wallace's religious novel of 1880, *Ben Hur.*

Success through self-help had always been a popular American theme and never more so than in the 1870s and 1880s. Playing on this deeply held notion, Horatio Alger (1834–1899) wrote more than 100 books for juveniles, including *Luck and Pluck* and *Tattered Tom.* Alger's poor heroes always achieved success through hard work, courage, and virtue.

Some of the best post-Civil War writing was achieved by a group of "local color" writers. These authors abandoned romanticism and presented a truthful, realistic portrayal of their

subjects and regions, but they did so in a sensitive and restrained manner. Their realism was confined largely to description and dialect; they gave little attention to analysis. Samuel Clemens ("Mark Twain," 1835–1910), one of the leading local colorists, wrote *Roughing It* (1872), *The Adventures of Tom Sawyer* (1876), *Life on the Mississippi* (1833), and *Huckleberry Finn* (1885)—all exciting works which brought him continuing national, and even international, fame. Edward Eggleston faithfully described aspects of mid-nineteenth-century rural life in Indiana in *The Hoosier Schoolmaster.* New England found an interpreter in Sarah Orne Jewett (1849–1909), who wrote *A Country Doctor* (1884) and *The Country of the Pointed Firs* (1896). These books placed her among the most creative artists in the local color group. The South produced strong local color writers. George W. Cable wrote about the Creole society in New Orleans in *The Grandissimes* (1880); the same year Joel Chandler Harris began to record authentic black stories in his Uncle Remus tales.

These local color novelists served as an effective intellectual bridge between the earlier romanticism and the realism of the 1880s, best exemplified in the work of William Dean Howells (1837–1920) and Henry James (1843–1916). Literary realism, Howells wrote, "is nothing more and nothing less than the truthful treatment of material." Henry James, the brother of the famous philosopher and psychologist William James, became disillusioned and unhappy with the lack of culture and intellectual sophistication in the United States and moved to London in 1876. From that vantage point, and drawing inspiration from such European realists as Balzac, Zola, and Tolstoy, James dealt frankly and directly with what he considered the provincialism of American culture in such novels as *The American* (1877), *Daisy Miller* (1879), and *The Portrait of a Lady* (1881).

Howells was generally considered the best American literary craftsman and man of letters in the late nineteenth century. Learning the printing and publishing business by working on his father's newspaper, he gradually turned to writing. Howells displayed his realism in *A Modern Instance* (1882) and *The Rise of Silas Lapham* (1884). In *The Rise of Silas Lapham*, he traced the troubled life of an uncultured, self-made Boston industrialist. This was the first attempt in American fiction to deal realistically with the price of self-made business success.

Fiercer and grimmer types of realism sprang out of the West from the pens of writers who viewed farm and small-town life as drab, barren, and depressing to mind and spirit. E. W. Howe, a Kansas newspaperman, described the shallow, petty, and unhappy existence in and around Atchison, Kansas, in *The Story of a Country Town* (1884). Better known were the works of Hamlin Garland (1860–1940), whose *Main-Travelled Roads* (1891), *A Son of the Middle Border* (1917), and other writings depicted the great gulf between the romantic ideal of happy farm life and the actual misery and cultural void of rural existence in the West.

This stark Western realism of Garland and Howe was soon matched by a group of young naturalists and social critics who pursued urban themes. One distinguishing mark of the new naturalism of the 1890s was a more open discussion of sex. Although not a contemporary success, Stephen Crane's *Maggie, A Girl of the Streets* (1892) exemplified the trend toward realistic naturalism. Here Crane described frankly the unhappy and futile life of a prostitute. Frank Norris, Theodore Dreiser, Upton Sinclair, and Jack London were other novelists who emphasized social criticism and increasingly found their themes in the influence of industrialism on American society.

Poets in the late nineteenth century found a wide reading public. James Whitcomb Riley achieved prominence in the 1880s with such well-known poems as "When the Frost Is on the Punkin" and "The Old Swimmin' Hole." Sidney Lanier, a Georgian, wrote dialect poems, including "Thar's More in the Man Than Thar Is in the Land" and "The Song of the Chattahoochee." Protesting drudgery and the exploitation of labor, Edwin Markham wrote "The Man with the Hoe" (1899), an exceptionally moving depiction of futility, and many other poems which became popular at the turn of the century.

Fine Arts and Architecture

Realism in literature paralleled a new emphasis upon realistic portrayal in painting. Though some artists continued the romantic treatment of their subjects, which had been so characteristic before the Civil War, a group of talented portrait and landscape painters raised their art to a new level of realism and excellence. Thomas Eakins (1844–1916) followed his own advice of peering deeply into American life and then portraying what he saw accurately and realistically. George Inness (1825–1894) painted some of the more powerful landscapes in the period, with special success in combining light, shadows, and color. Some of the more realistic and thoroughly American landscapes came from the brushes of Winslow Homer (1836–1910). Settling on the Maine coast, Homer painted scenes of his locality—the coast, the ocean, and fishermen. The paintings of Albert P. Ryder (1847–1917) remained largely unknown as he toiled in a tiny, cluttered New York studio between 1873 and 1898. In *Toilers of the Sea* and *Death on a Pale Horse*, he used heavy colors, blurred lines, and vague images. Besides painting landscapes and executing murals, John La Farge (1835–1910) made a unique artistic contribution by designing and manufacturing the best stained glass yet seen in America.

Two of the period's most significant artists were John Singer Sargent and James McNeill Whistler. Sargent (1856–1925) was an especially skilled and sensitive portrait painter, although his portraits of wealthy patrons were less realistic than those by Eakins and other contemporaries.

His portraits always had a luster, and his subjects reflected strength and elegance, qualities which were particularly evident in *The Wyndham Sisters*. Whistler (1834–1903) was one of America's most original artists. During his productive career, Whistler produced many paintings, scores of etchings, and about 150 lithographs. His most famous painting was *Portrait of the Artist's Mother*.

Italian neoclassicism dominated the form and spirit of American sculpture throughout the 1870s. Hiram Powers's popular statue *Greek Slave* was perhaps the best American example of this art form. After 1880 a number of younger American sculptors came under the influence of French naturalism. Foremost among the new generation of brilliant sculptors was Augustus Saint-Gaudens (1848–1907), who studied three years at the École des Beaux-Arts in Paris. His early triumph was a statue of Admiral David Farragut, first shown in Paris in 1880 and then brought to New York the following year. This work gave Saint-Gaudens quick and favorable recognition. Among his other famous works were *The Seated Lincoln* in Chicago and the statue called *Grief*, done for Henry Adams in memory of his wife. Almost entirely American-trained, Daniel Chester French (1850–1931) was another highly talented and sensitive sculptor. He produced many notable works, but his statue of Lincoln in the Lincoln Memorial in Washington, D.C., is probably his greatest artistic achievement. Slightly younger than French, Lorado Taft (1860–1936) was a native of Illinois who studied art in Paris and then returned to Chicago, where he did some of his best pieces. These included *The Blind* and *Solitude of the Soul*.

No less than other aspects of culture in the United States, American architecture drew heavily upon European forms. Indeed, it was a hodgepodge of Roman, Italian, and Gothic styles. One distinctive form of elegance in the 1870s was the Victorian Gothic in its numerous guises which ranged from the filigree jigsaw detail to the use of polychrome masonry; squat, pointed arches; high ceilings; and tall, arcaded windows. By the 1880s those who constructed expensive mansions for wealthy businessmen generally tried to emulate French chateaux or Italian villas. Such houses were built of heavy stone and had high, steep roofs, turrets, and towers. Although these European modes continued into the twentieth century, the dominant trend among American architects after 1870 was the achievement of concepts and forms which would suit modern industrial life, with emphasis upon function and environment.

Henry Hobson Richardson (1838–1886) brought some order out of architectural confusion when he returned from France, where he had studied at the École des Beaux-Arts. He introduced the French Romanesque style in Boston's Trinity Church, completed in 1879. He built the Marshall Field building in Chicago. While Richardson used heavy Romanesque forms, he moved toward less ostentation and more functional design. Richard Morris Hunt (1828–1895), also trained in Paris, introduced the more delicate French Renaissance style into the numerous houses which he built for merchant princes in New York and Newport, Rhode Island. McKim, Mead, and White, the famed architectural firm, created such outstanding public buildings at the turn of the century as the Pennsylvania Station, the Morgan Library, and the Columbia University Library—all in New York.

Lewis H. Sullivan (1856–1924) followed others to Paris. Upon his return he became a leading proponent of the Chicago school of architecture. His first important effort was the Chicago Auditorium. In his designs for the Wainright Building in St. Louis, the Schiller Building in Chicago, and the Prudential Building in Buffalo he evolved the design for the skyscraper with vertical steel skeleton construction. His most famous disciple was Frank Lloyd Wright (1869–1959). A young iconoclast, Wright developed another specifically American architecture. He emphasized the functional, or what he called the organic, style of construction; and in designing houses he lowered the roof to match the landscape, expanded the window space to increase natural lighting, and used more glass and new building materials. While Wright's unusual designs were ahead of their time in the 1890s, by 1910 he was having a marked influence upon architecture. The functional style finally prevailed in America, although classical and other European forms remained dominant during the nineteenth century.

Popular Culture

Although the nation produced a distinguished group of painters, sculptors, and architects during the late nineteenth century, there existed the usual gap between the higher forms of art and popular culture. The mass of Americans found intellectual and cultural satisfaction, as well as entertainment, in lectures, road shows, spectator sports, circuses, popular music, Currier and Ives prints, and photography. Cities provided the wealth and population to support expanded theater productions. Road companies played before audiences in hundreds of isolated communities. American drama in the postwar years generally avoided realism and relied on comic or sentimental situations.

To attend a circus was an unforgettable event in the lives of many postwar Americans. Country boys, small-town residents, as well as their city cousins, marveled at the human freaks, the clowns, the daring acrobats, and the wild animals. P. T. Barnum and James A. Bailey developed a three-ring circus, "the greatest show on earth," which after 1875 traveled throughout the United States.

Americans enjoyed minstrel shows, vaudeville, and light musicals. Minstrel shows, performed mainly by white men who blackened their faces with burnt cork, reached their height in the 1870s and 1880s. Composed of songs, dances, skits, and witty dialogue, these performances drew crowds everywhere. Some Negro groups added originality and authenticity to the minstrel shows. Theaters staging vaudeville, or variety shows, appeared in most major American cities in the late 1880s and soon pushed minstrel performances into the entertainment background. Motion pictures, introduced in the 1890s, and first shown as a part of vaudeville,

soon replaced vaudeville as the principal source of popular entertainment. The first regular movie theater opened in Pittsburgh in 1905, where patrons saw the first American story film, *The Great Train Robbery.*

Americans in the late nineteenth century had a passion for popular music, most of which was very sentimental, moralistic, and melodramatic. "After the Ball," "My Mother Was a Lady," and "O Promise Me" were typical hits during the 1890s. But the more distinctive American contributions to music were the blues, ragtime, and jazz. The "King of Ragtime" was Scott Joplin, a Negro who made history in 1899 with his "Maple Leaf Rag." Classical music found a rather limited appreciation in the United States, but symphony orchestras and grand opera were by no means absent. New York opened its Metropolitan Opera House in 1883.

Spectator sports found growing acceptance among urban residents who seemed increasingly less interested in their own physical exercise. Horse racing was extremely popular in the 1880s, but gambling around the racetracks alienated many of the "better element" from this sport. Prizefighting was brutal and sometimes bloody. Rules were almost nonexistent; participants hit, clawed, gouged, and wrestled until one man gave up. In 1882 John L. Sullivan won the world championship, which he held until 1892 when he lost to "Gentleman" Jim (James J.) Corbett. Skillful boxing was beginning to replace the earlier rough-and-tumble affairs. Baseball became professionalized shortly after the Civil War, and by the 1890s paid attendance at professional games reached several million annually.

Americans were characteristically "joiners." The various fraternal orders, college clubs, farm organizations, church groups, literary benefit societies, and professional associations attracted millions of members. The Masons, Odd Fellows, Knights of Pythias, Knights of Columbus, and Elks were among the scores of popular secret societies. Professional groups included the American Historical Association (1884), American Chemical Society (1876), American Bankers Association (1875), and the American Association of University Women (1882). It was a period of growing emphasis upon organization.

Some groups set out to achieve specific social and political reforms. The Women's Christian Temperance Union (1874) was an organized effort to oppose drinking and to fight the saloon. The American Equal Rights Association and the National Woman Suffrage Association, led by Susan B. Anthony and Elizabeth Cady Stanton, worked diligently for woman suffrage. But not all the organizations to which Americans flocked had such lofty motives. During the late 1880s and early 1890s, thousands of Americans joined the nativistic, anti-Catholic American Protective Association, formed in 1887 by an Iowan, Henry F. Bowers. The APA was a descendant of the Know-Nothings of the 1850s and fitted into the tradition of intolerance and bigotry which had come to the fore from time to time in American society. Strong among rural Americans who resented the Catholic immigrants flooding American cities, the APA demanded stricter naturalization laws, opposed Catholic political candidates, and fought to abolish parochial schools.

Newspapers, Magazines, Libraries, and the Chautauqua

Much of American cultural and intellectual development received its popularization in the nation's newspapers and magazines. The number of dailies increased from 971 to 2,226 between 1880 and 1900, giving urban readers and even the residents of smaller cities access to daily newspapers. There were thousands of weeklies and semiweeklies, read chiefly by farmers and small-town residents. After the establishment of rural free delivery in 1896, giving rural areas regular postal service, some farmers bought subscriptions to a city daily.

Major trends in newspaper publishing after the Civil War included growing sensationalism, a greater use of syndicated material, a heavier reliance on the news-gathering services, wider news coverage, the use of special features, and improved efficiency in production which resulted from such technological advances as the linotype machine.

Between the 1870s and 1890s new leadership arose in the American newspaper field. In 1872 two of the most famous men in journalism— Horace Greeley of the *New York Tribune* and James Gordon Bennett of the *New York* *Herald*—died. Among the new leaders in the newspaper world were Joseph Pulitzer, William Randolph Hearst, and Adolph S. Ochs. Pulitzer, a Hungarian-born immigrant, bought the *St. Louis Post-Dispatch* in 1878 and the *New York World* in 1883. Hearst, heir to a mining fortune, owned the *San Francisco Examiner* and later bought the *New York Morning Journal.* While both Pulitzer and Hearst emphasized sensationalism, which gave rise to the term "yellow journalism," Adolph S. Ochs, in 1895, purchased the sickly *New York Times* and set out to win readers by developing a reputation for public concern and comprehensive news coverage. Ochs soon pushed the *Times* to unquestioned primacy among American newspapers.

Magazines were available for readers of every level and interest; they contributed substantially to the country's general educational advance. *Harper's Magazine*, a monthly begun in 1850; the *Atlantic Monthly*, started in 1857; and *Scribner's*, which first appeared in 1871, appealed to intellectuals. These periodicals carried travel accounts, articles of historic interest, stories, and serious discussions of public questions. *Harper's*

Weekly, established in 1857 and later edited by George W. Curtis, had a wider appeal because of its spicy campaign against graft and dishonesty. E. L. Godkin founded the *Nation* in 1865. Largely a journal of opinion, its influence went far beyond its very limited and selective readership.

Ten- and fifteen-cent magazines, which were within the financial reach of a larger number of Americans, appeared in the 1890s. Samuel S. McClure founded *McClure's* in 1893 and set the price at 15 cents. Frank Munsey established *Munsey's* and set the price at 10 cents. Besides being cheap, these magazines carried more material of popular interest.

Libraries were another key to educational improvement. Most large cities had public libraries supported by taxation or private philanthropy, sometimes by both. By 1900 many smaller towns could boast the presence of one of those 9,000 public libraries in the United States. Andrew Carnegie contributed $60 million to the building of libraries in hundreds of American communities, and the "Carnegie Library" became one of the most familiar and influential institutions in many towns and cities. For people who had neither the desire nor the materials to read, public lectures played a significant educational role. The Chautauqua movement emerged from its humble beginnings in New York State in 1874 to become, during the next fifty years, a remarkably effective source of popular education and

THE HIGH PRIESTS OF THE SACRED FLAME.

"The High Priests of the Sacred Flame": A 1909 cartoon that took a jaundiced view of William Randolph Hearst and Joseph Pulitzer's "yellow journalism."   The Granger Collection

entertainment. Many prominent leaders traveled from place to place, lecturing on literature, politics, economics, travel, and other subjects.

Widening Opportunities for Women

Encouraged by expanding professional opportunities, women assumed an ever-increasing role outside the home. Besides teaching, women became active as writers and editors. Louisa May Alcott's children's books were immensely popular. Despite the resistance they faced, women by 1870 had gained admission to several medical schools. Nursing had even more attractions for middle-class women. Linda Richards, who graduated from the New England Hospital for Women and Children in 1873, was the nation's

first trained nurse. Marie Mahoney, who graduated six years later, was the first black nurse with formal training. Other women read law and were admitted to the bar. Myra Bradwell became a famous Chicago lawyer; she established and edited the *Chicago Legal News* with its national circulation. Women found professional opportunities in art, music, and library work. To create additional career opportunities for women, Ellen Richards led a movement to train women in "home sciences." This gave rise to home economics and the formation of the American Home Economics Association in 1908.

Women assumed leadership roles in religious, humanitarian, and reform activities. They taught Sunday School classes, ventured overseas as foreign missionaries, and occasionally preached in churches. Women organized charities and relief programs for the poor. The Women's Educational and Industrial Union provided assistance to women seeking employment or cultural involvement. Leaders of the Indian reform movement were largely women. Mary Bonney and Amelia Quinton formed the Women's National Indian Association to work for better treatment of the Indians, and Helen Hunt Jackson wrote the widely read *A Century of Dishonor*, a sharp indictment of federal Indian policy. Women played a leading role in the urban settlement house movement.

Women became more active in politics. Annie Diggs and Mary Lease proved effective Populist organizers and speakers in Kansas. Kate O'Hare won hundreds of supporters to the Socialist party. In 1907 Kate Barnard became Commissioner of Charities and Corrections in Oklahoma. In 1912 Jane Addams of Hull House fame, seconded Theodore Roosevelt's nomination for president at the Progressive party's convention. As women became more politically involved, their demands for suffrage increased. Carrie Chapman Catt, a dedicated woman suffragist, built strong support for the right of women to vote. The most active and vigorous women's organization was the Women's Christian Temperance Union. Besides opposing liquor, the WCTU was strongly committed to such reforms as woman suffrage, peace, and the elimination of prostitution.

Despite the widening opportunities for females in the late nineteenth century, the great majority of American women remained full-time homemakers. But the professional, humanitarian, and reform activities of women did play a major role in bringing about important social and political changes.

Conclusion

The powerful merchant and industrial elites of the late nineteenth century, in their single-minded pursuit of wealth, contributed little directly to the country's literary and artistic creativity, or even its educational achievements; yet the Gilded Age was not without its remarkable cultural advances. The increase in wealth and urban growth created unprecedented opportunities for writers, artists, sculptors, and architects. The late decades of the century, an age symbolized by materialism, produced books, both fictional and scholarly, paintings and sculptures, public and private buildings, the equal of any contemporary efforts in Europe in quality of design and execution. Only in music was the European lead beyond challenge. Even American universities approached the best of Europe in size and quality, with burgeoning libraries and superb scientific laboratories.

Although there was widespread criticism of American social and economic conditions among the less fortunate, with a concomitant demand for reform, most citizens appeared satisfied with their culture and society. They boasted of their economic gains and fully believed that American democracy was superior to any other form of government. They were proud of the nation's advances in science, education, literature, philosophy, social science, and law, whether these achievements had direct meaning for them or not. Americans considered themselves a religious people, and as most of them contemplated their country's material and cultural triumphs, they concluded that the United States had been especially blessed. Not even the reform demands of farm and labor groups in the 1890s could undermine the general mood of satisfaction.

Arthur M. Schlesinger's *The Rise of the City* (1933) and H. U. Faulkner's *The Quest for Social Justice, 1898–1914* (1931) treat the nation's social and cultural history between the 1870s and the First World War. Dealing more specifically with intellectual history are the pertinent chapters in Ralph Gabriel's *The Course of American Democratic Thought* (2d ed., 1956), *The American Mind** (1950) by Henry Steele Commager and Merle Curti's *The Growth of American Thought* (3d ed., 1964). The impact of Darwinism can be traced in the essays edited by Stow Persons, *Evolutionary Thought in America* (1950) and in Richard Hofstadter's *Social Darwinism in American Thought, 1860–1915** (1944).

On education see H. G. Good's *A History of American Education* (1956). One of the most important histories of education is Lawrence A. Cremin's *The Transformation of the School: Progressivism in American Education, 1876–1957** (1961). Horace Mann Bond's *The Education of the Negro in the American Social Order* (1934) is an excellent account of Negro education. Higher education can best be studied in the histories of individual institutions. S. E. Morison's *Three Centuries of Harvard* (1936) and Merle Curti and Vernon Carstensen's *The University of Wisconsin: A History* (2 vols., 1939) are both excellent. See also *Congress and Higher Education in the Nineteenth Century* by George N. Rainsforth (1972).

For an introduction to the period's religious history see the relevant sections of John T. Ellis's *American Catholicism* (1956) and Winthrop S. Hudson's *American Protestantism** (1961). Other general histories of religion in America include Edwin S. Gaustad's *A Religious History of America* (1966) and *A Religious History of the American People* (1972) by Sydney E. Ahlstrom. On the response of churches to social problems see Henry F. May's *Protestant Churches and Industrial America** (1949); A. I. Abell's *The Urban Impact on American Protestantism, 1865–1900* (1943) and *American Catholicism and Social Action** (1960); and Robert T. Handy (ed.), *The Social Gospel in America* (1966). Revivalistic faith can be studied in Stewart C. Cole's *The History of Fundamentalism* (1931); Christian Science is viewed favorably in Lyman P. Powell's *Mary Baker Eddy* (1950). On the Negro church see Carter G. Woodson's *The History of the Negro Church* (1921) and W. E. B. Du Bois's *The Negro Church* (1903).

The history of newspapers and magazines and their role in a democracy can be followed in F. L. Mott's *American Journalism* (2d ed., 1950) and volumes 3 and 4 of Mott's *History of American Magazines* (1938, 1957).

American literary developments in these years can best be traced in Vernon L. Parrington's *Main Currents in American Thought** (1930), vol. III, and Van Wyck Brooks's *The Confident Years, 1885–1915* (1952). Everett Carter's *Howells and the Age of Realism* (1954) considers perhaps the most important literary figure of the period. Studies dealing with some of the period's other outstanding writers include Bernard De Voto's *Mark Twain's America** (1951 ed.); Thomas Beer's *Stephen Crane: A Study in American Letters* (1923); and R. H. Elias's *Theodore Dreiser, Apostle of Nature* (1949).

Parts of the following studies contain valuable material on various phases of the fine arts, as well as architecture: Oliver W. Larkin's *Art and Life in America* (1949), especially parts 2 and 3; Samuel Isham's *The History of American Painting* (1942); Eugene Neuhaus's *The History and Ideals of American Art* (1931); Lorado Taft's *History of America's Sculpture* (1930); and James T. Flexner's *A Short History of American Painting* (1950). Lewis Mumford's *The Brown Decades: A Study of the Arts in America* (1931) deals mainly with painting and architecture. Gilbert Chase, in *America's Music* (1955), includes some excellent sections on music between the Civil War and World War I, while M. C. Hare's *Negro Musicians and Their Music* (1936) discusses the musical contributions of black Americans. Of special value to beginning students are the pertinent parts of *The Artists' and Writers' America* (2 vols., 1973) by Marshall B. Davidson and The Editors of American Heritage.

On the popular American idea of economic progress, see Irvin G. Wyllie's *The Self-made Man in America: The Myth of Rags to Riches** (1954) and John Tebbel's *From Rags to Riches: Horatio Alger and the American Dream* (1963).

*indicates availability in paperback.

22

The New American Empire

The American acquisition of Oregon and California in the 1840s was more than an isolated gesture designed to round out the nation's continental domain. It was part of the process of extending United States commercial and political interests ever westward toward the Orient. One of the guiding motivations of American continental expansion had been the quest for the three major harbors along the Pacific Coast—Puget Sound, San Francisco Bay, and San Diego Harbor—where large cities would emerge one day to propel American commercial, industrial, and naval power toward the great open ports of East Asia and the western Pacific.

Through half a century Boston merchants had laid the foundations for an expanding American interest in the Orient. Their established position at Canton prompted the John Tyler administration to negotiate the Treaty of Wanghia in 1844, an agreement guaranteeing American merchants the most-favored-nation treatment in China. This principle—the foundations of all United States commercial diplomacy—assured American merchants in any foreign port conditions of trade at least as advantageous as those enjoyed by the citizens of any other nation. After mid-century the United States continued to gain all commercial and extraterritorial rights in China which the British and French were wrenching by force of arms. Meanwhile the invasion of the northern Pacific by New England whalers and traders had gradually transformed Hawaii into an important outpost for Boston's commercial and missionary activity.

Increased traffic between California and China in the early fifties, added to the projection of a San Francisco–Shanghai steamship line, suddenly focused the attention of the United States government on the hermit nation of Japan. These important islands lay astride the "great circle route" from San Francisco to key ports along the north China coast. During 1854 Commodore Matthew C. Perry secured a treaty which destroyed Japanese isolation and established the foundation not only for increased American trade there but also for the legal, administrative, and economic modernization of that country. From the beginning, the American penetration of the Orient was devoid of the political and intellectual restraints that characterized this nation's relations with Europe. During the fifties William H. Seward termed the Pacific "the chief theater of events in the world's great hereafter." As Secretary of State he acquired Alaska in 1867 and began the process of opening new doors for American commerce in the Pacific.

Pacific Markets and Coaling Stations

China hung low on the American horizon largely because of its domestic infirmities. No event of the century so completely undermined China's power and prestige as did the Taiping Rebellion between 1850 and 1864. French and British victories against the rebels helped to save the ruling Manchu dynasty. But the Treaties of Tientsin, which these powers imposed on China in 1858, opened eleven additional treaty ports; established the right of diplomatic representation in Peking, the Chinese capital; and recognized the right of missionaries to proselytize freely in China. Several Western powers, moreover, secured control of border areas which the Chinese had regarded as vassal states. Russia gained a large region south of the Amur River and east of the Ussuri River in 1860. Between 1862 and 1867 France annexed Indochina. Britain occupied Burma, attached it to India, and imposed on China a new Indo-Chinese boundary favorable to India.

Anson Burlingame, the first American Minister to Peking (in 1861), embraced the growing American concern for China's independence and the protection of United States commercial interests in that country. During his years in China, Burlingame devoted himself to securing pledges from the great powers to preserve what remained of China's territorial integrity. He made his chief contribution to China, however, when, in 1867, he entered the service of the Chinese government to head its special mission to the Western world. In July 1868, he negotiated a special treaty with Seward in Washington, whereby the United States agreed formally to respect China's territorial and administrative integrity. Burlingame continued on to London, Paris, Stockholm, Copenhagen, The Hague, Berlin, and St. Petersburg. In none of these capitals could he negotiate treaties of self-denial toward China such as he had in Washington.

Korea, like Japan a hermit nation, likewise attracted Americans in search of trade. In 1871 the United States dispatched an expedition of five warships to negotiate a commercial treaty which would open that country to foreign commerce. Greeted with cannon shot and unable to communicate with Korean authorities, the Americans leveled several Korean forts and sailed away. It was left for the Japanese to break down Korean seclusion.

Behind America's accelerating involvement in the Pacific were intellectual, social, and economic developments of the first magnitude. Throughout the Western world, expansion had become the order of the day. By the eighties Britain, France, Belgium, Holland, and even Germany had inaugurated policies of partitioning Africa and the islands of the Pacific into colonies. Much of this new imperialistic spirit and the rivalries it generated resulted from the Darwinian notion of a competitive order in which only the fittest—whether individuals or nations—could survive. Such American writers as John Fiske and Josiah Strong urged the United States government to enter the race for empire, for no other nation's power, energy,

Minister Anson Burlingame and two aides with the first Chinese governmental delegation to the United States, 1868.

productivity, and institutions, they said, had better prepared it to bring backward and disorganized regions of the world under the protection of Western civilization. Fiske boasted in 1885 that the "work which the English race began when it colonized America is destined to go on until every land on the earth's surface that is not already the seat of an old civilization shall become English in its language, its religion, in its political habits and traditions, and to a predominant extent in the blood of its people." Religious groups entered this civilizing mission with enthusiasm, demanding the participation of government in carrying Christianity—the religion of the West—to the "barbarian" peoples of Asia, Africa, and the Southern Seas.

The more tangible incentive to American activity in the Pacific lay in the sometimes depressed state of the American economy. So speculative was most of the postwar railroad and industrial construction that it repeatedly toppled the national economy into periodic depressions, the worst of them blanketing the years 1873–1878 and 1893–1897. Each depression stimulated business consolidation and strengthened the hand of the strongest enterprises, but it also demonstrated the need of either expanded markets or a restructured American economy.

To secure the needs of American business abroad, the nation's leaders carefully limited official policy to the quest for markets, not acquisitions. Secretary of State James G. Blaine emphasized this distinction in August 1890. "Under the beneficent policy of protection," he said, "we have developed a volume of manufactures which, in many departments, overruns the demands of the home market. . . . Our great demand is expansion. I mean expansion of trade with countries where we can find profitable exchanges. We are not seeking annexation of territory."

Yet the opportunities for easy annexations

soon produced the appealing concept of "strategic bases." President Benjamin Harrison admitted to Blaine in 1891 that "as to naval stations and points of influence, we must look forward to a departure from the too conservative opinions which have been held heretofore." Such notions had been persuasively argued by Alfred T. Mahan in his *Influence of Sea Power upon History* (1890). This volume, based upon lectures delivered at the Naval War College, developed the theme that sea power—embracing commerce, naval vessels, bases, coaling stations, and even colonies—was essential for national greatness. England had pointed the way. Through additional books and articles Mahan's thesis reached an ever-widening audience, and in the Harrison administration his words began to bear fruit. Harrison's secretary of the navy, Benjamin F. Tracy, inaugurated a naval building program between 1890 and 1893, with the construction of the new steel battleships *Maine*, *Oregon*, and *Olympia*.

Samoa and Hawaii

Many Americans, inside and outside of government, shared a broad objective that included both an isthmian canal and several key bases in the Pacific. An American agent in the Pacific reported to the Secretary of State in December 1886: "It is now quite certain that an interoceanic canal across the Isthmus of Panama is one of the possibilities of the not very distant future, and it needs only a glance at the map to see that when that fact is accomplished the key of maritime dominance in the Pacific . . . will be held, not alone by Hawaii, but jointly by Hawaii and Samoa."

American interest in Samoa was not new. For over half a century, American navigators had called at these important South Pacific islands in search of items for the China trade. The Samoan Islands commanded several important sea lanes between San Francisco and Australia. In Pago Pago, on the island of Tutuila, the Samoans had one of the world's most beautiful and capacious harbors. In 1878 Secretary of State William M. Evarts negotiated with a representative of the Samoan chiefs a treaty which granted the United States a naval base at Pago Pago. But American rights in the Samoan Islands were not exclusive. Germany gained special privileges at Saluafata near Apia, while the British acquired the right to a naval base anywhere except at Saluafata or the United States site at Pago Pago. Thus Samoa became the center of a three-nation rivalry.

In 1884 Germany, through its representatives in Apia, made clear its intention to establish a protectorate over all the Samoan Islands. To secure a general agreement, Secretary of State Thomas F. Bayard invited British and German representatives to Washington in 1887, but Bayard could not persuade the Germans to drop their demand for a mandate over the islands; and the British, in exchange for German support in the Middle East, upheld the German position. Congress then appropriated special funds to strengthen American defenses at Pago Pago. Soon the President ordered three United States naval vessels to Apia, where the German base was located. There the Americans faced three German warships and one British warship with decks cleared for action. Suddenly a hurricane struck the harbor and wrecked all the German and American ships. This catastrophe cleared the air in Washington and Berlin, as well as in Samoa. Bismarck, the German chancellor, called a tripartite conference, which opened in Berlin late in April 1889. All three powers agreed to respect the independence of the islands, but the German-American rivalry continued. President Grover Cleveland declined to press the matter. In November 1898, during the presidency of William McKinley, the United States and Germany —Britain having withdrawn its interest— negotiated a permanent division of the Samoan Islands.

Hawaii could not escape the consequences of United States expansion into the Pacific. As early as midcentury, American traders, missionaries, and seamen had gained control of Hawaii's foreign commerce and converted the island economy to the production of sugar. The only lucrative outlet for Hawaii sugar lay in the United States, where Louisiana sugar interests controlled the national market. This raised the issue of annexation, for some Hawaiian planters preferred markets to independence. Few Americans shared their enthusiasm. During Hamilton Fish's incumbency as secretary of state in 1875, the government in Washington finally concluded a commercial treaty with the islands, which provided a free market for Hawaiian sugar in the United States in return for a pledge by Hawaii to maintain its independence. In the 1884 renewal, the United States secured the exclusive right to a naval base at Pearl Harbor.

Domestic sugar producers unwittingly reopened the annexation question. In the McKinley tariff of 1890, they added sugar to the free list and then gained a bounty of 2 cents per pound on the domestic product. Annexation alone would fully reopen the American market, but many of the leading Hawaiian planters opposed annexation for fear that United States contract-labor laws would eliminate from the islands their supply of cheap Oriental labor. Still the islands' political instability posed another threat. Queen Liliuokalani, who acceded to the throne in 1891, had made clear her dissatisfaction with the role of the foreign elite. John L. Stevens, the annexationist United States Minister at Honolulu, advised Washington in November 1892 that the impending crisis in the Hawaiian government would create a golden opportunity for annexation. Finally in January 1893, the Queen announced her decision to adopt a new constitution which would ensure native control of the islands. The foreign planters and merchants retaliated by establishing a provisional government and turning to Stevens for protection. Stevens promptly landed 150 marines from the warship *Boston*, recognized the provisional government as the *de facto* government of Hawaii, and proclaimed Hawaii a protectorate of the United States. The provisional government promptly offered a treaty of annexation; before the Senate could act, Cleveland entered the White House.

For Cleveland, these events in Hawaii were a serious reflection on American justice. He immediately dispatched James H. Blount, former congressman from Georgia, to Honolulu. Blount hauled down the American flag and ordered the marines back to their ship. But Cleveland could not restore the Queen to power. On July 4, 1894, the Americans in Hawaii established a republic, prepared either to maintain their independence or to accept annexation. In 1897 Japan dispatched a warship to Hawaii to underscore its anger at the decision of the Hawaiian government to bar some eleven hundred Japanese immigrants. Eventually the Hawaiian government relented. But in Washington the new McKinley administration reacted by negotiating an annexation treaty and sending it to the Senate for approval. The Senate rejected it overwhelmingly.

Latin America

United States policy toward Latin America was characterized far more by energy than direction. James G. Blaine, secretary of state in 1881, favored a greater American influence in the region both to expand this country's trade and to encourage Latin America's peace and stability. These purposes were laudable enough, but Blaine, in his pursuit of them, usually acted without calculating the American interest. He objected to European intervention even when it was harmless or when it was invited by Latin American governments—such as the Costa Rica–Colombia treaty to submit a boundary dispute to Belgian arbitration. When Colombia awarded a Panama canal contract to a French engineering firm, Blaine and others condemned the action as European intrusion and a threat to United States security. Ultimately the French company failed from lack of skills and resources.

Blaine's concern for hemispheric cooperation, even when exceedingly limited United States interests were at stake, faced a test in the so-called War of the Pacific in which Chile, in 1881, easily defeated Bolivia and Peru and demanded Peruvian territory along the Pacific. Blaine dispatched William H. Trescot, a former foreign service officer, to negotiate a peace which would enable Peru to retain its territory. Thus supported by the United States, Peru refused to negotiate. When it became obvious that the United States had no real interest in the conflict and would not use force, Chile also remained firm. Trescot, embarrassed by the futility of his position, asked for his recall. Eventually a more sober Peruvian government made peace on Chile's terms.

Another of Blaine's actions proved to be more successful. To encourage inter-American cooperation, he invited all Latin American countries to send delegates to a conference to be held in Washington in late 1882. Long before then he had left office. His successor, Fredrick T. Frelinghuysen, reversed his policies. But when Blaine returned to the State Department in 1889, he called the first Pan-American Conference in Washington to acquaint Latin American representatives with the variety and quality of American production.

President Cleveland's involvement in the Venezuela boundary dispute continued the American tendency to overreach in Latin America. The long-standing quarrel between Venezuela and British Guiana over their common frontier was of little concern to the United States. But when Britain rejected a series of arbitration proposals, Venezuela broke diplomatic relations in 1887 and launched a propaganda campaign in the United States to encourage intervention. Cleveland took up the Venezuelan cause, supported by an aroused Congress and public. In 1895 Secretary of State Richard Olney demanded that London submit to arbitration; otherwise Britain's policies of "virtual duress" would violate the Monroe Doctrine. In a delayed and thoughtful, but condescending, reply, Lord Salisbury rejected Olney's demand for arbitration. He reminded Washington that the United States, like other nations, had the right to defend its interests wherever they might be. But it could not assert special rights in any region merely because the region was American. The Monroe Doctrine, he made clear, had no standing in British or world diplomacy. Cleveland responded with a letter to Congress that bristled with war sentiment. Finally Britain, conscious of the need for more cordial relations with the United States, agreed to arbitration and gained generally the boundary that it had previously offered Venezuela.

The Spanish-American War

Cleveland had refused to consider the question of Samoan or Hawaiian annexation, and his successor McKinley had failed, in 1897, to push an annexation treaty through the Senate. But suddenly in 1898 and 1899 there no longer seemed to be any limit to American commitments in the Pacific. Oddly, the immediate occasion for the headlong thrust of American power into the Far East lay in Cuba, where the Cuban people had long been in revolt against Spain. Cuban revolutionaries well understood the American weakness for causes which could be represented as humanitarian, and the Spanish government, by continuing measures of extreme repression in Cuba, had unwittingly played into their hands.

By 1896, when the Spanish general, Valeriano Weyler, arrived in Cuba and instituted his *recon-*

centrado program to better control the population, the Cuban revolutionary *junta* in New York had launched a propaganda campaign to arouse and enlist the sympathies of the United States for Cuban independence. Spain complained that the United States, by permitting the *junta* to operate on American soil, was helping the revolution. To offset such charges, Cleveland, in both June 1895 and July 1896, issued proclamations of neutrality.

What assured the ultimate success of the Cuban cause was the overwhelming support it received from the American press. Editors throughout the East and the Midwest stressed the disruptive effect of the Cuban struggle on American trade and investments. At that time Americans had some $50 million invested in Cuba. William Randolph Hearst's *New York Journal* and Joseph Pulitzer's *New York World*, as well as other papers, charged the Spanish government with gross disregard for humanity in its abuse of Americans and Cubans alike. Much of the attack centered on ''Butcher'' Weyler and his policies. In time the press came to despise official American neutrality and to demand policies of intervention in behalf of Cuban independence. After McKinley's election such Republican newspapers as the *Chicago Tribune* boasted that the incoming administration would adopt a more humane, civilized, and patriotic policy. Still the nation's choices were limited. The United States could not resolve the Cuban dilemma through purchase, for Spain would not sell the island. Nor would the recognition of Cuban belligerency or independence terminate the chaos. Thus ultimately there could be no resolution to the Cuban question without the infusion of American military power.

McKinley entered the White House in March 1897, still hopeful of avoiding that choice. He had no greater desire than his predecessor to go to war. Yet he recognized the necessity to terminate the evident confusion in Cuba, and to that end he launched a diplomatic offensive against Spain. Convinced that Spain lacked the power to establish peace in Cuba, the President anchored his program to Spanish concessions. His new Minister to Madrid, Stewart L. Woodford, left Washington in the summer of 1897, armed with instructions which condemned the Spanish methods of warfare and demanded that Spain, in the interest of humanity, end the fighting on terms just to Cuba.

Spanish authorities in Madrid understood the President's demands clearly enough. The new Liberal Ministry in Spain, which gained power in October 1897, was determined to avoid a war which it could not win. It recalled Weyler and instructed his successor to revoke the oppressive policies. Then, in November 1897, the Liberal regime offered autonomy to the Cubans. Neither the Liberal Ministry nor the Spanish Queen, Woodford informed McKinley, could do more. The remaining hope for Spanish policy, therefore, lay in the possible decision of Cuban leaders to accept autonomy rather than demand full independence.

Few in Washington or Madrid believed a settlement possible. In his message to Congress in December 1897, McKinley asserted that Spain deserved every reasonable chance, but he warned that, if Spanish policy failed, the United States might be duty-bound to intervene with force. Woodford, like McKinley, questioned the sincerity of the Spanish proposals. But even more, he worried that the Cuban rebels would not accept them. The Ambassador's fears were justified. In January 1898, Havana rioted in defiance of Spain's decree of autonomy. McKinley dispatched the U.S.S. *Maine* to Havana to lend moral and material support to the American consul general there in his effort to protect United States citizens and property.

Spanish officials recognized the failure of their effort. But they also knew that it was American encouragement that stiffened the resistance of the Cuban insurgents to compromise. On January 17, the Queen informed Woodford that Cleveland had promised to sever all official American support for the rebels if Spain would grant autonomy. When McKinley refused to denounce the rebels, the Spanish government gave vent to its frustration by condemning the United States for its lack of neutrality. Spain now had no choice but to abandon Cuba completely, turn to Europe for moral and military support, or prepare to defend what remained of Spanish policy.

During February and March 1898, a series of incidents drove the United States and Spain toward war. The publication in the American press of a private letter critical of the President, written by Dupuy de Lôme, the Spanish Minister in Washington, forced the Minister's recall. Far more serious, however, was the destruction of the battleship *Maine* in Havana's harbor on February 15, with a heavy loss of life. No investigation ever established responsibility. Spanish behavior following the incident was impeccable; and officials in Washington, including the President, accepted the news with remarkable restraint. But widespread public opinion, whipped up by the press, demanded war. "Remember the Maine" became the new battle cry.

Congress, early in March, voted $50 million to assist the administration in strengthening the nation's defenses. On March 17, Senator Redfield Proctor of Vermont reported to Congress what he had seen on a recent tour of Cuba, describing in detail the suffering of an island people ravaged by thirty years of intermittent civil war, terrorism, and Spanish reprisals. Proctor's speech, because of the Senator's known temperance on the Cuban question, had a profound effect on American opinion. Then on March 28 the naval board of inquiry, appointed by McKinley to investigate the *Maine* tragedy, issued its report. With no attempt to fix responsibility, the board declared that the battleship had been destroyed by a mine. Congressional and public opinion reached a new level of intensity. The American Secretary of State urged Spain to make peace with Cuba, even at the price of independence.

As the crisis mounted in April, Republican congressmen and editors warned the President that if he did not lead the country into a popular war, others would. One Cabinet member criticized the President's hesitancy: "He is making a great mistake. He is in danger of ruining himself and the Republican Party by standing in the way of the people's wishes. Congress will declare war in spite of him. He'll get run over and his party with him." At last McKinley, in the interest of preserving both party unity and executive control of foreign policy, assumed responsibility for leading the nation to war. Woodford, still hopeful of peace, had reported on April 5 that the Queen had agreed to six months' unconditional suspension of hostilities in Cuba. Five days later he assured the President that by August 1 he could obtain peace by negotiation on the basis of either autonomy or independence for Cuba. Still, on April 11, 1898, McKinley sent his war message to Congress. Congress debated the message for a week and then adopted four resolutions which recognized Cuban independence, demanded a Spanish withdrawal, and authorized the President to employ the nation's military forces to achieve American purpose. Lastly, Congress asserted, in the famed Teller Resolution, its determination to leave the Cuban people free.

Despite the nation's lack of military preparedness in 1898, the conflict with Spain promised to be, as John Hay said, "A splendid little war." Spanish weakness, thoroughly anticipated by American officials, permitted the United States to enter the war with a standing Army of only 28,000 troops. Congress quickly authorized a force of 62,000, to be supplemented with 125,000 volunteers. In addition, the President could accept three volunteer cavalry regiments into the Armed Forces. One of these, the Rough Riders, transformed its commander, Theodore Roosevelt, into a popular war hero.

Of necessity the fighting centered in Cuba. There, in its initial phase, the United States Atlantic fleet, under Admiral William T. Sampson and Commodore W. S. Schley, blockaded the decrepit Spanish fleet in Santiago Harbor along Cuba's southern coast. Meanwhile, United States regular and volunteer units assembled amid indescribable confusion at Tampa, Florida,

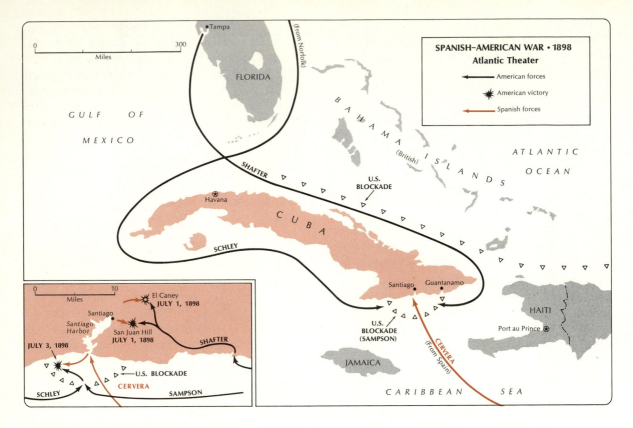

and Chattanooga, Tennessee. Rather than strike Havana, the commanding general of the Army, Nelson A. Miles, decided to send an American force (which included the Rough Riders) against Santiago. The force left Tampa and managed to stage a landing on Cuban soil. It moved toward Santiago, winning battles at El Caney and San Juan Hill, and yet seemed incapable of launching an attack on Santiago itself. But when the Spanish fleet steamed out of the harbor, only to be destroyed by the blockading American squadron, the garrison at Santiago capitulated. Spanish power in Cuba had collapsed in scarcely more than a month. Another American force had meanwhile occupied Puerto Rico. In July the Spanish government asked for the terms of peace.

Annexation of the Philippines

On May 1, 1898, Admiral George Dewey's United States squadron had sailed into Manila Bay and destroyed Spain's Pacific fleet at anchor. It was logical that the United States should strike Spanish power wherever it existed. Still, this sudden display of United States naval might in the distant Philippines and the possibilities which it opened for American empire building were not lost on a small but influential body of expansionists in Washington. Even at that early date such men as Roosevelt, Admiral Mahan, Senator Henry Cabot Lodge of Massachusetts, and Senator Albert J. Beveridge of Indiana had expansion in mind. It was Roosevelt who, as Assistant

Secretary of the Navy, had ordered Dewey to Manila. And on April 27, four days before Dewey's great victory, Senator Beveridge declared before a Boston audience: "In the Pacific is the true field of our earliest operations. . . . In the Pacific the United States has a powerful squadron. The Philippines are logically our first target." It is possible that McKinley, with an eye on the Philippines, had delayed his war message so that the fast cruiser *Baltimore* could reach Dewey with a special cargo of ammunition before Congress acted in favor of war.

With Dewey's victory, the McKinley administration moved quickly to establish American control of the Philippines. Spanish forces still held Manila, but a successful Filipino insurgency had already freed the islands of Spanish control and was closing in on the capital. Ignoring the clouded political status of the Philippines, McKinley, on May 11, ordered General Wesley Merritt to Manila. Merritt's forces, supported by Emilio Aguinaldo's insurgents, assaulted and occupied Manila on August 13. Next day American officials proclaimed Spain's capitulation.

This display of American power in the Pacific sealed the fate of Hawaii. Those who had vainly pushed Hawaiian annexation during 1897 had not allowed the issue to die. On May 4, three days after the battle of Manila Bay, the annexationists brought a joint resolution for Hawaiian annexation before Congress. Two months later the measure had gone through committees onto the floor of both houses. Requiring no more than a bare majority, the measure passed the House, on June 15, by a vote of 209 to 91, with 49 abstentions. The Senate concurred, 42 to 21. "We need Hawaii," McKinley wrote, "as much and a good deal more than we did California. . . . It is manifest destiny."

Unlike Samoa and Hawaii (two independent island groups), the Philippines, as Spanish territory, had been of necessity off limits to prewar American imperialist ambitions. Against the immediate background of the country's burgeoning

The Battle of Manila Bay, May 1, 1898.

The Granger Collection

interests in the Pacific, however, the reduction of Spanish power in the Philippines confronted the United States with an unanticipated dilemma. What was to be the disposition of the islands? At the outset the United States had four clear choices. It could return the islands to Spain, or it could grant them independence, as it had promised Cuba. It could transfer the islands to another power, or it could retain them. That this nation was drawn relentlessly toward annexation does not mean that it had no other choices. But the decision to destroy Spanish power in Manila had been crucial, for it closed all easy avenues of retreat.

Dewey's victory at Manila unleashed an expansionist drive among American editors, politicians, intellectuals, missionary societies, and businessmen toward the Philippines. Still, official United States policy toward the Philippines evolved slowly. Throughout May and June 1898, expansionists in Congress and the administration argued with the President on the necessity of acquiring the Philippines. Finally in June, Secretary of State William Day informed Lodge that perhaps the nation could not escape its destiny in the Pacific. Thereafter the President did not retreat. His directive to the American peace commission made clear his determination to acquire at least a portion of the Philippine archipelago. The task of defining the country's precise objectives in the Philippines the President entrusted to his peace commission.

Despite the magnitude of this distant commitment, McKinley made no effort to rationalize Philippine annexation except in terms of the nation's obligation to humanity. His persistent refusal to remind the American people of the price of empire became exceedingly pronounced during his tour of the Midwest in October 1898. In speech after speech, he dwelt on the accidental nature of this country's *de facto* possession of the Philippines and its special responsibility to the Filipinos which, he insisted, flowed from that possession. For example, he declared at Cedar Rapids, Iowa: "We accepted war for humanity. We can accept no terms of peace which shall not be in the interests of humanity." By attaching the issue of empire to humanitarian sentiment rather than national interest, McKinley assured himself a favorable public response; but in the process he deserted those principles of statecraft, expressed so well by John Quincy Adams, which had guided the nation through its first century of independence.

In Paris McKinley faced a divided peace commission. Four members—Whitelaw Reid, editor of the *New York Tribune*, Senators Cushman K. Davis of Minnesota and William P. Frye of Maine, and former Secretary of State Day, chairman of the commission—favored the annexation of all or part of the archipelago. But Senator George Gray of Delaware, the only Democrat, was absolutely opposed. He warned McKinley that annexation would invite trouble. Despite such advice, McKinley instructed the commission to claim the Philippines as indemnity. Late in November the commission framed its final demands on the Spanish government: the cession of Puerto Rico, Guam, and the entire Philippine archipelago to the United States in exchange for $20 million. Spain reluctantly accepted these terms in the Treaty of Paris, signed on December 10, 1898.

In Washington the treaty faced bitter opposition. In November a group of distinguished citizens, including former President Cleveland and industrialist Andrew Carnegie, formed the Anti-Imperialist League. Annexation, they charged, not only violated the nation's democratic and constitutional principles but also departed from America's traditional conservatism in foreign policy. The United States, wrote Carnegie, lacked not only the naval power to protect the Philippines but also the will to create it. Conservative Republican Carl Schurz feared that Philippine annexation would reduce the United States to absolute reliance on the British fleet. "If we do take the Philippines," Schurz concluded, "and thus entangle ourselves in the rivalries of Asiatic affairs, the future will be . . . one of wars and rumors of wars, and the time will be forever past when we could look down with condescending pity on the nations of the old world groaning under militarism and its burdens."

Stronger in argument than in organization, the anti-imperialists could not stem the tide of annexationism. Business interests, which envisioned the Philippines as a steppingstone to Chinese trade, insisted on holding the islands. Expansionist speeches in Congress were laden with visions of profit and glory—for commerce, industry, and religion. Even William Jennings Bryan, fresh from military service, argued in Washington that the Filipinos would benefit from the American investment in money, administration, and defense. He urged his fellow Democrats to approve the treaty. When the Senate, after a month of intense debate, settled down to vote, fifteen Democrats joined forty-two Republicans to carry the treaty against twenty-seven senators who opposed it. Two senators switching to the minority side would have assured its defeat. Lodge reported to Roosevelt, "The line of opposition stood absolutely firm. . . . [It was the] hardest fight I have ever known, and probably we shall not see another in our time where there was so much at stake."

Aguinaldo, the leader of the Philippine insurrection, had assumed that the islands, like Cuba, would receive their independence as a consequence of the Spanish-American War. Following the occupation of Manila, however, American officials ordered Aguinaldo to withdraw his Filipino insurgents from the city. Philippine disillusionment culminated with the announcement of the Treaty of Paris. On February 4, 1899, a clash outside Manila set off what soon evolved into a long, costly war for control of the islands. The insurrectionary government held almost all the islands in the archipelago and commanded an army of 20,000. The native forces, having general support among the people but lacking modern weapons, resorted to guerrilla warfare, which spread rapidly through the islands. To put down this insurgency, the United States spent millions of dollars, committed thousands of troops, and resorted to drastic antiguerrilla tactics such as burning villages and herding natives into enclosures to prevent sniping.

This struggle against a backward, native population challenged both the nation's principles and its prestige. Mark Twain attacked the American war in the Philippines, suggesting a new American flag "with the white stripes painted black, and the stars replaced by a skull and crossbones." The *Nation* complained that American repression was "bringing disgrace upon the American name and civilization." But other Americans demanded that the United States press on to victory to fulfill its obligations to civilization. Eventually the issue evolved into one of national prestige based on power, not principle. *Harper's Weekly* agreed with McKinley that, if the United States abandoned the Philippines under pressure, "we should be an object of derision to Europe and the Orientals would consider us of no account." Some insisted that antiwar protests in the United States encouraged the enemy and prolonged the war. Both the war and the protests continued unabated until April 1902, when the insurgents surrendered and recognized American rule.

The Open Door for China

As the nineteenth century neared its close, events in China drew the United States into even deeper commitments in the western Pacific. It became clear in 1894 that China was incapable of protecting its political and territorial integrity against external pressure. Japan, in a brief war, easily disposed of Chinese resistance, dispossessing China by treaty of Formosa, the Pescadores, and the strategic Liaotung Peninsula. Moreover, Japan forced China to recognize the independence of Korea and grant Japanese citizens the same trading privileges in China then enjoyed by citizens of the Western powers. Neither the United States nor Great Britain chose to interfere. But Russia, Germany, and France, at China's invitation, demanded successfully that Japan, in the interest of peace, return the Liaotung Peninsula to China. United States Minister Charles Denby warned Peking that the price of European assistance would run high.

Unfortunately China's troubles had only begun, for Russia's ambitions toward China were at least equal to Japan's. Having gained possession of Vladivostok and undertaken the construction of the Trans-Siberian Railway, Russia joined Germany and France in dividing China "like a melon" into spheres of influence. During March 1897, France gained control of the island of Hainan. In November German troops, employing the murder of two German Catholic priests as a pretext, seized Kiaochow, a port on the Shantung Peninsula, a seizure legalized in

March 1898, as a leasehold. Russia that month forced from the Chinese government a twenty-five-year lease to the fine harbor at Port Arthur. China seemed in danger of disappearing piecemeal. American business groups operating in China, especially the American-China Development Company, viewed these developments with grave concern. Left unopposed, the European powers would eventually wipe out the equal trading and investment privileges which Americans enjoyed in China.

British interests in China were far more extensive than those of the United States, for Britain had long dominated the foreign commerce of China through the British-operated Chinese Imperial Maritime Customs Service. Unwilling to use force to maintain its free access to all Chinese ports, the British government hoped to bring United States power into the Asian equation. In March 1898, the British government approached the McKinley administration for a cooperative policy "in opposing any action of foreign powers which would tend to restrain the opening of China to the commerce of all nations." McKinley, having been assured by Germany and Russia that they had no intention of defying the principle of open trade in China, informed the British that he saw no reason to depart from America's traditional policy of noninvolvement. That spring, moreover, the United States faced the immediate problem of Cuba. During 1898 the British government encouraged the United States to acquire the Philippines. Meanwhile it reversed its policies in China. Convinced that the Peking government was too weak to protect British interests, London officials acquired a lease of Weihaiwei on the Shantung Peninsula opposite Port Arthur. Next, they acquired special concessions in the Yangtze River Valley and at Kowloon, opposite Hong Kong. Britain thus retreated to the policy of leaseholds which it had earlier condemned.

When Secretary of State John Hay, in September 1899, issued the famous Open Door Notes, his action was largely unilateral. Britain's earlier concern for Chinese integrity was fully shared by the McKinley administration. William W. Rockhill, Hay's adviser on Far Eastern matters, hoped only that the United States, by restating its treaty rights in China, might encourage the other powers to maintain the principle of commercial equality in the ports which they controlled. Secretary Hay instructed Rockhill to prepare notes to be sent to the European powers.

The Open Door Notes, sent originally to Russia, Great Britain, and Germany (and later to Italy, France, and Japan) requested assurances from each nation that it would not interfere with the treaty rights of other countries within its sphere of influence. Hay asked, moreover, that each country involved in China allow the collection of existing Chinese tariffs, irrespective of spheres of influence, and that it treat its own citizens and other nationals alike in making such assessments as harbor dues. In his note to Britain, Hay seemed to oppose the spheres of influence themselves. The replies, especially from Britain and Russia, approved the commercial "Open Door" in principle; otherwise they were evasive. Yet the Secretary chose to announce to the world in March 1900 that his notes had brought favorable responses from all six nations. The acceptance of his proposals, Hay declared, was "final and definite." Some six months later, when China's Boxer Rebellion—a widespread antiforeign uprising across China—compelled the powers to dispatch troops to Peking to rescue their nationals from the besieged legations, the Secretary declared that American purpose in China included preserving Chinese territorial and administrative integrity.

Much of the American and European press took Hay's diplomatic exchanges at face value and praised the Secretary for his momentous success. Yet Hay's apparent achievements in behalf of China carried the seeds of disaster, for they, like the acquisition of the Philippines, confirmed an illusion that the United States could have its way in the Orient at little or no cost. Only the more realistic observers noted that Hay's diplomacy either had committed the United States to the use of force or had achieved

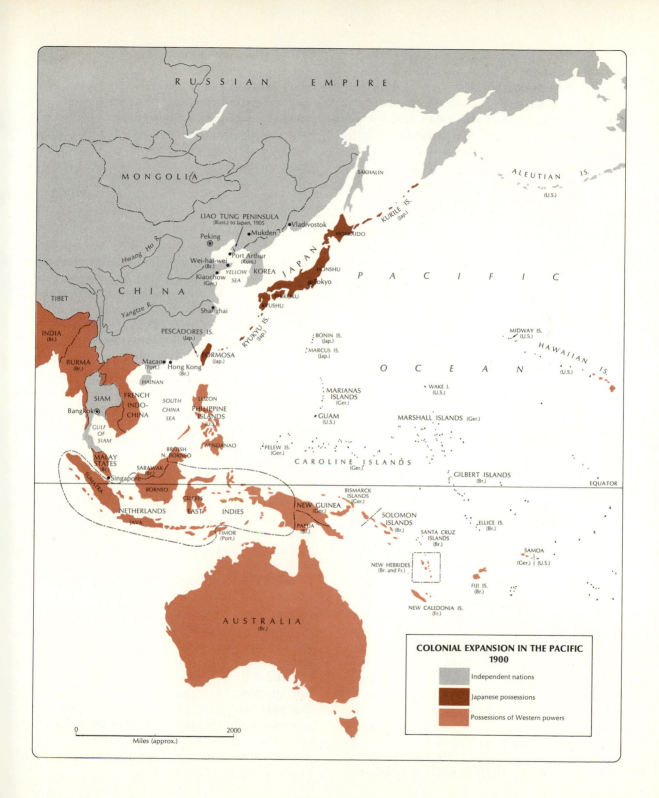

COLONIAL EXPANSION IN THE PACIFIC
1900

- Independent nations
- Japanese possessions
- Possessions of Western powers

THE NEW AMERICAN EMPIRE

[575]

nothing, for no nation would have compromised its essential interests in China merely at Hay's request. As Admiral Mahan wrote in December 1900, the United States could not "count upon respect for the territory of China unless we are ready to throw not only our moral influence but, if necessity arise, our physical weight into the conflict, to resist an expropriation, the result of which might be to exclude our commerce and neutralize our influence." Mahan observed that both Russia and Japan, the two dominant powers in the Far East, had far greater interests in China than the United States did. But the Open Door policy, by establishing a powerful and somewhat exaggerated American concern for the commercial and territorial integrity of China, rendered any nation which might challenge Chinese will the potential enemy of the United States.

Conclusion

By 1900 the United States had become a major Asiatic power, with colonies in the western Pacific some 7,000 miles from American shores. It had committed itself, at least morally and emotionally, to the commercial Open Door and the territorial integrity of China. Already American business anticipated increased markets and investment opportunities in China, especially in mining and railroads. Whatever the actual American interests in that country, official Washington would view any changes in the equilibrium of East Asia as a matter of vital concern. Thus the dramatic events of 1898 and 1899 had revolutionized the nation's attitudes toward the external world.

Editors, politicians, and businessmen looked confidently to the Far East as the new stage for American activity. In January 1900, Senator Beveridge dramatically acknowledged the new American interest in the Pacific: "The Philippines are ours forever. . . . And just beyond . . . are China's illimitable markets. We will not retreat from either. . . . The power that rules the Pacific is the power that rules the world. . . . That power will forever be the American Republic." The possible, even probable, consequence of such optimism was clear only to a minority of intellectuals, who warned that no American interest in the Pacific merited *carte blanche* commitments. Indeed, American expansion into the Pacific triumphed with such negligible national effort that it failed completely to challenge the American people's isolationist habits of mind. It never occurred to most citizens, or even to their leaders, that these new obligations in the Pacific might one day make exorbitant demands on the American Republic.

The Spanish-American War and its aftermath not only made the United States an Asiatic power; it also produced absolute American dominance in the Caribbean. Acquisition of Puerto Rico and *de facto* control of Cuba gave the United States special interests in that area which it would subsequently guard jealously. In time, the American people learned more, perhaps, than they cared to know about the world beyond their nation's continental borders; but once they were upon the road to world prominence, the logic of the course would not permit them to turn back. Nor did they immediately have any desire to do so. The war with Spain and subsequent expansion struck a responsive chord in America, feeding national and racial pride, promising lucrative trade, redeeming the traditional belief in the nation's mission, and incidentally redounding to the benefit of the Republican party which had been responsible for it all. The fact that the achievement of great power status—symbolized rather than caused by the "splendid little war"—had caught the imagination of most Americans in 1899 did not escape that perspicacious critic Mr. Dooley. "We're a gr-reat people," intoned his friend Mr. Hennessey. "We ar-re that," replied Finley Peter Dunne's Irish bartender. "We ar-re that. An' th' best iv it is, we know we ar-re."

Two older studies of the American penetration of the Pacific are Foster R. Dulles's *America in the Pacific* (1932) and Tyler Dennett's *Americans in Eastern Asia* (1922). Excellent discussions of United States interest in Hawaii can be found in Sylvester K. Stevens's *American Expansion in Hawaii, 1842–1898* (1945) and William A. Russ, Jr.'s *The Hawaiian Revolution, 1893–1894* (1959). G. H. Ryden ably treats the Samoan question in *The Foreign Policy of the United States in Relation to Samoa* (1933). Foster R. Dulles provides a highly useful background on expansionism in his *Prelude to World Power: American Diplomatic History, 1860–1900* (1965) and summarizes American empire building in *The Imperial Years** (1956). Walter LaFeber's *The New Empire: An Interpretation of American Expansion, 1860–1898** (1963) emphasizes economic forces in United States expansion. Thomas J. McCormick similarly stresses economic motivation in his *China Market: America's Quest for Informal Empire* (1967). Paul A. Varg analyzes interestingly the nonexistent nature of the China market in "The Myth of the China Market, 1890–1914," *American Historical Review*, LXXIII (February 1968).

For long the standard account of the background of the Spanish-American War was Julius W. Pratt's *Expansionists of 1898* (1936). E. R. May's *Imperial Democracy: The Emergence of America as a Great Power* (1961) and H. Wayne Morgan's *America's Road to Empire** (1965) are more recent and provide better balance. Walter Millis's *The Martial Spirit** (1931) presents a lively and generally critical account of United States policy toward Spain. J. E. Wisan's *The Cuban Crisis as Reflected in the New York Press, 1895–1898* (1934) treats well the role of newspapers in stirring up war sentiment, as does also M. M. Wilkerson's *Public Opinion and the Spanish-American War* (1932). Frank Freidel's *The Splendid Little War** (1962) is a short, dramatic, and pictorial history of the military and naval engagements. Robert L. Beisner's *Twelve against Empire* (1968) deals perceptively with the antiexpansionists. Henry F. Graff, editor of *American Imperialism and the Philippine Insurrection** (1969) has compiled an exciting and disturbing account of American behavior in the Philippine war.

On American policy toward China the standard account remains A. Whitney Griswold's *The Far Eastern Policy of the United States** (1938). Another excellent survey is A. L. P. Dennis's *Adventures in American Diplomacy, 1896–1906* (1928). Three highly useful accounts are Paul A. Varg's *Open Door Diplomat: The Life of W. W. Rockhill* (1952); C. S. Campbell, Jr.'s *Special Business Interests and the Open Door Policy* (1951) and M. B. Young's *The Rhetoric of Empire: America's China Policy 1895–1901* (1968). Samuel F. Bemis (ed.), *American Secretaries of State and Their Diplomacy* (1929), vol. IX, contains a study of John Hay. Foster R. Dulles has an essay on Hay in Norman A. Graebner (ed.), *An Uncertain Tradition: American Secretaries of State in the Twentieth Century** (1961). Both of these studies of Hay are favorable, as is Tyler Dennett's *John Hay: From Poetry to Politics* (1934).

*indicates availability in paperback.

23

Progressivism and Theodore Roosevelt

William McKinley's election in 1896 seemed to assure the continuation of the status quo politics which had characterized most of American political life since the Civil War. The defeat of the free-silver movement and the demise of the Populists appeared to remove the chief disruptive forces from the American scene. There were few, if any, clear predictions of major change. McKinley signed the Dingley tariff of 1897, which raised rates to the highest point in American history up to that time; in 1900 Congress passed the Gold Standard Act. In the presidential campaign of that year, McKinley defeated Bryan by an even larger majority than he had compiled four years earlier. The election returns offered proof that the nation approved of McKinley and his policies.

But such presumptions of widespread satisfaction were misleading. Demands for political, economic, and social change rumbled beneath the surface of an outwardly reassuring national consensus. The decade of the 1890s had been an especially restless period. Men and women had examined the nation's institutions and too often found them wanting. With time the reform urge became so general at the local, state, and national levels that it produced, after 1900, that massive effort to correct the evils of American society known as the "progressive movement."

Progressivism was an extremely complex phenomenon. It was not an integrated or unified quest for reform; rather it encompassed a wide variety of objectives and interest groups.

First it embraced political reform, which to most progressives meant creation of local, state and national governments fully responsive to the popular will. For many progressives democracy assumed the proportions of a panacea. Believing that the problems of democratic government could be solved by establishing more democracy, progressives favored granting the people a more direct voice in government. To that end they favored the direct primary method of nominating candidates; the direct election of senators,; the initiative and referendum; and, in some cases, the recall of judges.

Secondly, the progressive movement sought to reduce the political power of business and eliminate the "unholy alliance" between government and special interests. To that end reformers hoped to extend federal control over the nation's large industrial, financial, and transportation corporations. There was probably no other issue on which so many progressives agreed.

Thirdly, progressives hoped to improve the lives and increase the opportunities of the poor and underprivileged. They insisted that the government possessed both the power and the obligation to alleviate adverse social conditions with slum clearance, reduction of working hours, abolition of child labor, workmen's compensation laws, unemployment insurance, mothers' pensions, better care of prisoners, and other similar reforms. The progressives would place more responsibility on government in areas formerly neglected. Overall, the most notable aspect of the progressive movement was its underlying purpose of expanding the power and functions of government as a factor in American life.

Progressivism was truly a national movement. Reformers represented all sections and all classes, they existed in both major political parties, and they represented both urban and rural areas. Much of the strongest support centered in the growing cities. Many progressive leaders came from reasonably well-to-do families, had attended college, and they were often young. Although most social classes joined in the demand for reform, the backbone of the movement was found among the great middle class, including white-collar workers and professionals such as businessmen, lawyers, and publishers. But the urban middle class had no monopoly on either the leadership or the membership of the progressive movement. Robert M. La Follette in Wisconsin and Peter Norbeck in South Dakota were among the rural progressives who led their states into advanced programs of reform.

Although progressivism had a nature and character of its own, it grew out of the criticism and discontent so prevalent in American society in the late nineteenth century. Social critics such as Henry George, writers such as Henry D. Lloyd, and economists such as Richard T. Ely and Thorstein Veblen all had raised serious questions about American society. Moreover, the demands of the Grange, Greenbackers, and Populists, as well as some labor groups, emphasized the widespread discontent with political and economic conditions.

What concerned the progressives above all were the abuses and inequalities of opportunity which emanated from the power of the huge corporations. As businessmen achieved greater wealth, they turned to politics to protect their economic interests. The president of the sugar trust admitted candidly the practice and motives of large businesses in contributing campaign funds: "In the State of New York where the Democratic majority is between 40,000 and 50,000 we throw it their way. In the State of Massachusetts where the Republican majority is doubtful, they probably have the call . . . . "

What finally aroused millions of Americans to support reform were the dramatic revelations of

McCLURE'S MAGAZINE

NOVEMBER, 1903

The Labor Boss
The Trust's New Tool
By
RAY STANNARD BAKER

New York
By
LINCOLN STEFFENS

The Truth About Radium
By Cleveland Moffett

SIX SHORT STORIES

S. S. McCLURE CO. NEW YORK AND LONDON

Culver Pictures, Inc.

lished critical accounts of big business. Late in 1902 Ida Tarbell published her first article on the history of the Standard Oil Company. Ray Stannard Baker, the third of *McClure's* distinguished trio of writers, wrote on labor as well as conditions among blacks. Muckrakers thus exposed the evils of American society on a broad front; even the churches and the press came under attack.

Leading novelists in the early century joined the Muckrakers in placing the American economic system under sharp indictment. In *The Octopus* (1901) and *The Pit* (1903), Frank Norris sharply criticized the power of the railroads and grain speculators, respectively. Theodore Dreiser's *The Financier* and *The Titan* lashed out at greed and the lack of social responsibility among the rich. Jack London went even further in denouncing the American system. His novel *The Iron Heel* (1907) described class warfare between what he termed exploiting capitalists and the workers. Upton Sinclair's *The Jungle* was a detailed and sickening exposé of the meat-packing industry.

a group of journalists known as the "Muckrakers." This group of able writers received their special designation when Theodore Roosevelt once referred to them as people who were always raking in the muck. The Muckrakers investigated many undesirable aspects of American life and exposed these conditions in popular writings. The Muckrakers were specific in naming financiers, industrialists, and members of Congress who appeared to violate the public interest. *McClure's* topped the list of the highly successful muckraking magazines. Publisher S. S. McClure hired a competent staff of writers, which included Lincoln Steffens, Ida Tarbell, and Ray Stannard Baker. *McClure's* commanded national attention in October 1902, when it published the first of a series of articles by Lincoln Steffens on corruption in city government. In addition to articles on political dishonesty, *McClure's* pub-

Ida M. Tarbell.   *Library of Congress*

Many important reforms of the progressive period were inaugurated at the state and city level where progressives attempted to destroy the influence of powerful political bosses like Matthew Quay of Pennsylvania and Thomas C. Platt of New York. Ray Stannard Baker once wrote that local government had "become a government of the Bosses, by the Bosses, and distinctly for the Bosses." The power of such men as Quay and Platt was usually built on their connections with businesses, large and small, which required political favors. The railroads, insurance companies, public utilities, industrial corporations, and banks all exerted tremendous political pressure to obtain what they needed. Progressives could break the influence of such organizations only by placing government more directly in the hands of voters and extending the states' powers of regulation and control.

Robert M. La Follette brought progressivism to Wisconsin when that state elected him to the governorship in 1900. La Follette led and pushed Wisconsin lawmakers into a broad program of progressive reform. Before he went to the United States Senate in 1906, the Wisconsin legislature had passed a direct primary law, raised taxes on railroads and other corporations, brought the railroads under stricter control, passed a law to regulate lobbying, and inaugurated civil service in state employment. La Follette supported a state income tax which the state adopted after he left office. Moreover, while governor, La Follette called on specialists at the University of Wisconsin. University professors provided a "brain trust" for Wisconsin progressivism and set a pattern for the broader use of intellectuals in government service. Other Midwestern states as well enacted progressive laws. The South Dakota Legislature in 1898 adopted the initiative and referendum, and in 1907, that state's lawmakers passed a direct primary statute, legislation to prohibit free railroad passes, a measure requiring publication of campaign expenses, and one that forbade corporation contributions to campaign funds.

On the West Coast, Governor William S. U'Ren of Oregon set an outstanding example of progressive leadership; his reforms included the initiative and referendum as well as a direct primary. California's Governor Hiram Johnson defeated a powerful political machine backed by the Southern Pacific Railroad to establish a progressive administration. In the South, the election of Jeff Davis as governor of Arkansas (1901); James K. Vardaman of Mississippi (1903); and Hoke Smith of Georgia (1906) demonstrated that Southern reformers were throwing off the yoke of conservative, Bourbon rule. Although Southern legislatures enacted measures to control large corporations, they did not favor equal political rights for blacks.

Besides laws designed to give voters a more direct voice in government and to regulate big business, state legislatures enacted a wide variety of social legislation. Measures to prohibit child labor or to establish maximum hours and minimum wages in certain industries, safety legislation, and accident insurance all reflected a growing concern for industrial workers. Between 1909 and 1917, nineteen states passed laws regulating the hours of work for women; others strengthened existing legislation. New York passed a workmen's compensation act in 1910, and other states soon followed. This new emphasis on measures to protect workers reflected the social and economic problems growing out of a rapidly industrializing and urbanized society. Progressives at the state level worked for such far-reaching reforms as the direct election of senators, prohibition, and woman suffrage. All these objectives were achieved by 1920 with the approval of the Seventeenth, Eighteenth and Nineteenth Amendments to the Constitution.

There was fully as much need for political reform in the large American cities as in state governments. Josiah Strong observed in *The Challenge of the City* (1907) that in the large urban centers "maladjustments of society create the sorest friction. . . . It is chiefly in the city that the enormous powers of organization and of centralized wealth are wielded; and it is there that these powers must feel the wholesome restraint of righteous laws and of an enlightened popular conscience." There was little evidence of enlightened consciences or righteous laws in most American cities in the late nineteenth century.

The settlement house movement (see p. 480) gave strong impetus to urban reform. Middle-class volunteers such as Jane Addams moved into slum neighborhoods to provide help in housing, employment, and education; moreover, they demanded programs which would improve the entire urban environment. Settlement workers acquired information, applied political pressure, and communicated the needs of urban life and society to the general public. They played a key role in expanding the concept of social welfare—a major aspect of the progressive movement.

Without freedom from interference by state legislatures cities would achieve little reform. This realization stimulated the movement for so-called home rule to permit cities to determine the nature of their own governments. By 1914 twelve states had granted some degree of home rule to at least certain classes of cities. Many cities adopted the commission form of government, thereby placing government in the hands of a small group of qualified men who generally headed, in addition, the key city departments of police, fire, water, and sanitation control. One of the commissioners usually acted as mayor.

The commission system of city government brought improvements, but it lacked the executive and administrative authority to guarantee an efficient administration. From this secondary need grew the city-manager plan. Under this arrangement, the commission hired a trained administrator of city affairs and turned the executive functions of government over to him. Staunton, Virginia, first introduced the city-manager plan in 1908.

Blacks and Progressivism

Unfortunately, the widespread demand for increased democracy, together with social and economic reform, did not extend to blacks. Some Muckrakers discussed the plight of blacks, and concerned whites established centers and agencies to help them in the Northern cities, but black citizens found little more than sympathy. Progressivism generally did not challenge the second-class status of Negro citizenship. The Southern states persistently denied blacks the right to vote, and the political role of blacks in the North was almost as insignificant. Negroes suffered from social and economic discrimination as well. One New York official said in 1900 that "it's getting so the colored people have no rights in this city." Labor leaders denied them membership in unions; at times industrialists hired them as strikebreakers. State laws which segre-

gated Southern schools faced no threat from the courts after the Supreme Court upheld the doctrine of separate-but-equal accommodations in the case of *Plessy v. Ferguson* (1896). But the black schools were in almost every case grossly inferior. Whereas social segregation was almost absolute in the South, many Northerners were little more liberal in their attitude toward the Negro and his desire for equality. Northern hotels frequently denied accommodations to the prominent black leader Booker T. Washington.

Throughout the United States there was very little social intercourse between blacks and whites. President Theodore Roosevelt aroused a storm of protest when he invited Washington, then head of Tuskegee Institute, to have dinner with him on October 16, 1901. Southerners fumed at Roosevelt for what a Memphis newspaper called the "most damnable outrage ever."

Individual progressives spoke out on behalf of Negro rights, but they had little or no influence on public policy. During Woodrow Wilson's presidency, blacks lost ground in their drive for equal treatment. Federal departments on occasion segregated black employees, and the armed services barred them from all but the lowest ranks. The Virginia-born President accepted the removal of many blacks from federal employment without so much as a mild protest. After visiting the city of Washington in 1913, Booker T. Washington wrote: "I have never seen the colored people so discouraged and bitter as they are at the present time."

Among blacks themselves there was no agreement as to the means by which they could best improve their condition. Washington, spokesman for the older and more conservative black leaders, held that blacks must develop greater economic opportunities and then work to advance themselves. As president of Tuskegee Institute after 1881, Washington emphasized industrial education and believed that blacks could raise their economic status by learning trades and crafts. He did not press for intellectual leadership or social equality.

After a brief but highly popular speech in Atlanta, Georgia, in 1895, Washington emerged as the most widely accepted black philosopher of education and social action. For his race he championed self-help, thrift, hard work, acceptance of racial segregation, deemphasis of politics, and patience. By the early twentieth century, however, a group of young militant blacks broke with Washington and demanded the social, economic, educational, and political rights of full citizenship. They inaugurated a policy of fighting Jim Crowism, lynching, segregation, and every additional type of discrimination. Dr. W. E. B. Du Bois emerged as the principal leader of this group. He voiced his ideas in *The Souls of Black Folk* (1903) and later in a new militant periodical, the *Crisis,* which began publication in 1910. Especially after the terrible

W. E. B. Du Bois.   *Brown Brothers*

race riots in Springfield, Ohio, in 1904, in Atlanta, Georgia, and Brownsville, Texas, in 1906, and in Springfield, Illinois, in 1908, a minority of liberal whites gave support to black aims and objectives as expressed by Du Bois. In 1909 a group of blacks and whites founded the National Association for the Advancement of Colored People. Incorporated in 1910, the NAACP consisted primarily of intellectuals who set out to raise the Negro to *full* social, political, and economic equality. But progress was slow. The widespread terror and violence employed against blacks illustrated the intolerance of the early twentieth century.

Still there was continuous and positive action. In 1911 Eugene K. Jones and George E. Haynes, with others, founded the National Urban League, an organization for the uplift of urban blacks. Also, to win more respect for his race and to rectify its neglect in history, Carter Godwin Woodson, in 1915, organized the Association for the Study of Negro Life and History. The next year he began publication of the *Journal of Negro History* and, later, the *Negro History Bulletin.* Dr.

Woodson founded the Associated Publishers and took the lead in making "Negro History Week" a popular national celebration. Afro-Americans found satisfaction, moreover, in the distinguished inventions of such blacks as Jan Matzeliger, Elijah McCoy, John P. Parker, and Granville T. Woods, as well as in Jack Johnson's winning of the heavyweight boxing title and Matt Henson's sharing in the discovery of the North Pole in 1909.

Black ghettos became a rather common characteristic of Northern cities in the early years of the twentieth century. Previously blacks had lived in smaller, isolated communities—perhaps one, two, or three blocks surrounded by whites—but by 1914 large numbers of blacks became concentrated in New York's Harlem, on Chicago's South Side, and in older, crowded sections of other major cities. In many urban communities residential segregation soon had the sanction of local laws which specifically designated all-white and all-black blocks. But discriminatory pressures went far beyond the statutes. Initially some black areas such as Harlem contained much desirable housing. In time, however, blacks found it impossible to obtain acceptable housing. This gradual forcing of blacks into ghettos after 1900 resulted from increasing economic and social discrimination precisely when Americans were demanding reform in most other areas of national life.

Theodore Roosevelt: National Progressive Leader

On September 6, 1901, Leon Czolgosz, an anarchist, approached President William McKinley at a reception in Buffalo, New York, and shot him with a concealed weapon. The nation waited sorrowfully while the President lingered for eight days and then died. Upon taking the oath of the presidential office, Theodore Roosevelt promised to "continue, absolutely unbroken, the policy of President McKinley for the peace, prosperity and the honor of our beloved country." Long before he left office in 1909, however, Roosevelt had broken with much of the post-Civil War tradition in American politics. He became a vigorous exponent of progressive ideas.

Roosevelt was born of well-to-do parents in New York on October 27, 1858. Physically weak as a boy and bothered with asthma, he worked diligently to build up his body and became a strong advocate of physical fitness. He enjoyed all the advantages of an upper-class youth which then included travel abroad and a Harvard education. In 1881 he won election to the New York Legislature and served three terms in Albany. During the next few years he ranched in North Dakota, wrote history, including *The Winning of the West,* and served as United States Civil Service Commissioner as well as president of the Police Board in New York City. Following his resignation as police commissioner in 1897, he entered McKinley's administration as assistant secretary of the Navy. At the outbreak of war with Spain in 1898, Roosevelt obtained a commission as a lieutenant colonel and helped to organize the Rough Riders.

Roosevelt's return from Cuba coincided with Boss Thomas C. Platt's search for a respectable and prestigious candidate for the governorship of New York. Roosevelt seemed to fit the requirements. He campaigned hard and emerged victorious by a narrow margin. During his governorship, Roosevelt maintained his independence, but he made little effort to push for many reforms. But even his mild inclination toward reform displeased Platt, who sought to kick Roosevelt upstairs in 1900 by obtaining his nomination as the party's vice-presidential candidate. Roosevelt shunned the honor; he said that he would "rather be anything, say a professor of history." After his election he considered taking up law, but the death of McKinley rendered his plans irrelevant.

Theodore Roosevelt was a man of wide and varied interests. He was a strong advocate of, and participant in, the strenuous life. He liked sports and sometimes held boxing bouts in the White House. He traveled widely and frequently both in the United States and abroad. He liked all kinds and classes of people and was equally at home with kings, scholars, farmers, and workers. He enjoyed politics and became a skillful politician. Ambitious and competitive, Roosevelt appreciated power, but he desired to use power only for what he considered the public good. Like most progressives, he viewed issues in a moral light and held firm distinctions between good and evil. Overall, Roosevelt was a highly controversial and contradictory figure, but he was a leader. He was exceptionally adept at welding noncooperative, and sometimes conflicting, groups into a unit for political action. By education, experience, and temperament, Roosevelt was exceptionally well qualified to assume the presidency.

Roosevelt's Policies and Programs

Roosevelt moved cautiously during his first presidential term. His initial message to Congress was filled with generalities; there was nothing in it to frighten or worry conservatives. He emphasized the trust problem but urged caution in any action taken; he admitted that organized labor deserved protection but warned workers not to abuse their power. Roosevelt was realistic enough to know that he required congressional cooperation and that both House and Senate were ruled by conservatives. For Roosevelt to buck the congressional power structure directly would have been foolhardy.

Despite what may have seemed to be a lack of vigorous first-term leadership, Roosevelt took a number of actions and supported programs which firmly identified him with the surging demand for reform. In February 1902, the Attorney General revealed that the Department of Justice would commence an antitrust suit against the Northern Securities Company, a huge railroad combine. At about the same time, the President interfered in the anthracite coal strike and demonstrated a much fairer attitude toward organized labor than that displayed by his predecessors. Also in 1902 Roosevelt appointed Oliver Wendell Holmes to the Supreme Court. Holmes turned out to be one of the greatest liberal judges ever to sit on the high bench. Conservationists rejoiced when Roosevelt supported the Newlands Act in 1902, which provided federal funds for reclamation projects in the West.

Roosevelt confronted the issue of big business regulation. Here his attitudes and actions placed him squarely in the progressive mold. Roosevelt's campaign against monopoly secured for him the title of "trustbuster," although he accepted bigness in business as natural and therefore had no great interest in trustbusting. He did institute forty-two antimonopoly suits, but both of his successors, William Howard Taft and Woodrow Wilson, exceeded that number.

Roosevelt did not oppose all large corporations; he objected only to the abuses of corporate power. In other words, he made a distinction betweeen good and bad big business. Roosevelt had little faith in antitrust laws based on the nineteenth-century idea of competition. Rather, he preferred to preserve the efficiency and economic benefits of large business and industry but at the same time assure the public protection through strict government regulation. Roosevelt favored a federal administrative agency with power to investigate and control large corporations engaged in interstate commerce which violated or abused the public interest. He called for the regulation, not the destruction, of big business.

Thus Roosevelt gave strong support to the establishment of a Bureau of Corporations with power both to investigate industrial enterprises doing business in interstate commerce and to report its findings to the President for action. This Congress enacted, over strong protests, as a part of the bill which established a Department of Commerce in 1903.

But Roosevelt knew that he could not convince a conservative Congress to pass a law which would effectively regulate large corporations. So he turned to the Sherman Antitrust Act—which had been little used since its passage in 1890—as the only practical weapon at hand. A suit against the $400 million Northern Securities Company offered an ideal opportunity to test the authority of the Sherman Act to thwart the massive power of banking and railroad capital. Organized in 1901 by J. P. Morgan, Edward H. Harriman, and James J. Hill, the Northern Securities Company controlled either directly or indirectly most of the railroads west of the Mississippi. This large holding company appeared to exist in clear violation of the Sherman Antitrust Act. In 1904, two years after accepting the suit, the Supreme Court in a 5-to-4 decision held that the Northern Securities Company was an unlawful combination in restraint of trade. Meanwhile, Roosevelt had supported additional regulatory legislation. In 1903 Congress passed the Elkins Act, which compelled railroads to abide by their published rates.

Recent historical scholarship has shown that legislation to regulate big business received the support of important elements in the business community. Some businessmen and industrialists were tired of the cutthroat competition and saw government regulation and control as one way to restrain the activities and power of their rivals. Others viewed moderate regulation as a substitute for much stricter government control. The backing of some federal regulation by important segments of the business community added another dimension to progressivism and indicated how widespread the search for greater order in business had become.

Roosevelt and the Workingmen

Roosevelt demonstrated more understanding and sympathy for the problems and conditions of workingmen than his predecessors did. Like most progressives, Roosevelt believed that workers should receive justice and fair treatment. Although he approved of unions, Roosevelt did not give strong support to organized labor, in part because he rejected the idea of classes and feared that organized labor, like organized capital, might abuse its power. The test of Roosevelt's attitudes came in the anthracite coal strike of 1902.

In May, the United Mine Workers in northeastern Pennsylvania, under the leadership of John Mitchell, went out on strike. They demanded better pay, a shorter workday, more honest weighing of coal, and union recognition. The mine operators became adamant and refused any plan of arbitration or mediation. George F. Baer, head of the Philadelphia and Reading Coal and Iron Company, expressed their attitude when he said that "the rights and interests of the laboring men will be protected and cared for, not by the labor agitators, but by the Christian men to whom God in his infinite wisdom has given control of the property interests of the country." The strike dragged on, and by September coal shortages had created extensive suffering in some communities. The operators hoped that, as in the past, federal troops would be called out to maintain order until they broke the strike. Roosevelt, who became bitter over such displays of arrogance, warned that he might use troops to take over the mines and produce coal. This threat finally prompted the operators to accept mediation; the strikers returned to work late in October. Roosevelt appointed the Anthracite Coal Strike Commission, which heard hundreds of witnesses over the next several months. The Commission gave workers a 10 percent pay raise, some reduction in hours, and other reforms. But the workers did not win union recognition.

Roosevelt's dynamic leadership and action created enemies among the special interests, but the people as a whole admired and respected him. His personal popularity became clear in the campaign of 1904. No Republican could successfully contest his nomination; his party chose him unanimously as its standard-bearer. Unwilling to face certain defeat with another William Jennings Bryan nomination, the Democrats in 1904 sought a conservative candidate and nominated Judge Alton B. Parker of New York. But Parker was no match for the popular Roosevelt, who swept to victory with 7,628,000 votes, compared with only 5,084,000 for Parker. The Republicans won another smashing victory in Congress.

Roosevelt's sweeping victory gave him a new feeling of confidence. During his second term, at least until 1907, he demonstrated stronger leadership and an even greater commitment to progressive reform. He now concentrated on the problem of business regulation and control. In December 1905, he informed Congress that it was absolutely essential to give the federal government effective supervision over corporate power. Finally, in June 1906, after weeks of bitter debate and considerable compromise, Congress passed the Hepburn Act. This important law gave the Interstate Commerce Commission power to determine just and reasonable railroad rates, subject to court review. The act enlarged the ICC from five to seven members and extended its control to include express, sleeping-car, and pipeline companies. The Hepburn Act made the railroads one of the nation's more strictly regulated industries.

Although most progressives considered railroad legislation of prime importance, they also demanded greater national regulation of certain other industries, notably food and drugs. For years Dr. Harvey W. Wiley, chief of the Bureau of Chemistry in the United States Department of Agriculture, had campaigned for pure food and drug laws. Wiley had found that food processors preserved meat and milk with harmful chemicals and that dishonest labeling of patent medicines endangered the people's health. One of the most commonly used patent medicines was Lydia E. Pinkham's Vegetable Compound, which, according to the advertisements, was a remedy for all gynecological problems.

While it might seem strange that anyone would fight pure food and drug legislation, the opposition was strong. The *New York Sun* scoffed at Wiley's campaign for truthful labeling and gave him the title of "chief janitor and policeman of people's insides." Nonetheless, in June 1906, after Roosevelt had asked for action, Congress passed the Pure Food and Drug Act. This law prohibited the sale in interstate commerce of any misbranded or adulterated food or drugs, and provided means of enforcement and penalties for violations.

At the same time Congress moved to clean up the meat-packing industry. For years it had been known that much of the meat being processed came from unhealthy animals and was prepared under the most unsanitary conditions. The publication early in 1906 of Upton Sinclair's muckraking novel *The Jungle* created a public stir and aroused the President. Sinclair's book dealt with the nauseating conditions surrounding Chicago's meat-packing industry. Describing the production of sausage, Sinclair wrote: "These rats were nuisances, and the packers would put poisoned bread out for them, they would die, and then rats, bread, and meat would go into the hoppers together." Despite strong opposition from the packers and their political supporters, Congress, with Roosevelt's strong backing, passed the meat-inspection law in June 1906. This measure outlawed the sale of tainted meat in interstate or foreign commerce.

Many progressives were determined to preserve the nation's rapidly dwindling supply of natural resources. Loose and sometimes corrupt administration of the land laws had permitted corporate interests to gain control of waterpower sites and mineral, forest, grazing, and farm lands, and to exploit them for private gain. The movement for conservation took three forms. First, conservationists sought to arouse the general public in support of a national conservation movement. With Roosevelt's strong backing, they effectively publicized the need for conservation and organized support for specific policies. Roosevelt was greatly influenced and assisted by the knowledgeable and dedicated Gifford Pinchot, who in 1898 had become chief of the Bureau of Forestry in the Department of Agriculture. Secondly, conservationists believed that a broad survey of the country's natural resources was necessary to determine their best use on a scientific, planned basis. Finally, most conservation leaders insisted that the federal government withdraw large areas of forest, mineral, and other lands from public entry.

Conservation leaders were concerned primarily with the scientific management and efficient use of natural resources. They wanted policy making and administrative matters in the hands of qualified technicians rather than politicians or pressure groups. Roosevelt declared in 1908: "Let us remember that the conservation of natural resources . . . is yet but part of another and greater problem . . . the problem of national efficiency, the patriotic duty of insuring the safety and continuance of the Nation."

As noted earlier, Roosevelt gave presidential support to passage of the National Reclamation Act, or Newlands Act, in 1902. This law provided that funds from the sale of public lands in the West would be used to finance irrigation projects. Roosevelt was deeply interested in expanding the federal forest reserves. Previous Presidents had withdrawn some 46 million acres of forest lands under a law of 1891, but Roosevelt increased this figure to about 150 million

acres. He also withdrew coal, oil, and phosphate lands from public sale. Moreover, he established five new national parks and some game preserves. Roosevelt's calling of the Governors' Conference on conservation in May 1908 did much to publicize conservation programs and policies and led to the appointment of a National Conservation Commission later in the year.

Even the Panic of 1907 did not diminish Roosevelt's popularity among the masses. The year 1907 began on a prosperous note, but in early spring the prices of commodities and securities began to decline. By early fall, money was tight and credit scarce. On October 22 the Knickerbocker Trust Company of New York closed its doors; the next day panic selling struck the Stock Exchange. During the next few months bank and business failures plagued the economy. Fearing another catastrophe similar to that of the nineties, countless citizens, bankers included, demanded wholesale reform of the economy.

One direct result of the financial crisis was passage of the Aldrich-Vreeland Act in 1908. This law provided for a Monetary Commission to study credit and monetary problems. This investigation, under the leadership of Senator Aldrich, revealed the need for major improvements in the nation's financial structure. Some of these needs were finally met in the Federal Reserve Act of 1913. (See Chapter 24.)

Partly as a result of the Panic of 1907, Roosevelt became increasingly critical of big business. He declared on one occasion that the Panic had been caused by "the speculative folly and the flagrant dishonesty of a few men of great wealth." Indeed, during his last year in office, Roosevelt was much more outspoken against large, corporate enterprise than he had been earlier.

Roosevelt's Foreign Policy: Latin America

Roosevelt's training and sympathies qualified him to lead the country along the road of domestic reform, and he was equally well equipped to

deal with foreign affairs. He had not only observed European peoples and countries firsthand but also become personally acquainted with

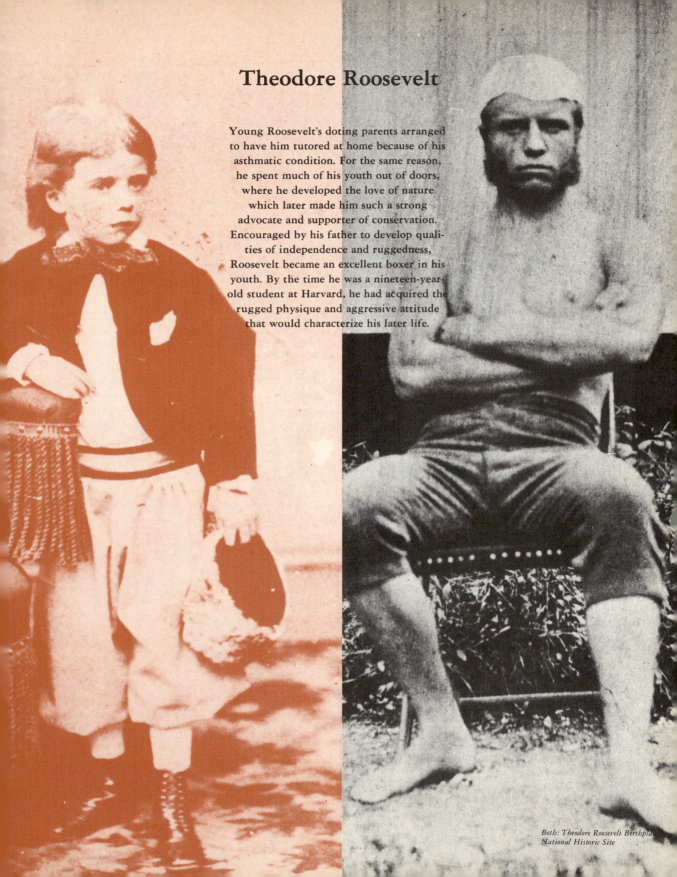

Theodore Roosevelt

Young Roosevelt's doting parents arranged to have him tutored at home because of his asthmatic condition. For the same reason, he spent much of his youth out of doors, where he developed the love of nature which later made him such a strong advocate and supporter of conservation. Encouraged by his father to develop qualities of independence and ruggedness, Roosevelt became an excellent boxer in his youth. By the time he was a nineteen-year-old student at Harvard, he had acquired the rugged physique and aggressive attitude that would characterize his later life.

Both: Theodore Roosevelt Birthplace National Historic Site

At the age of twenty-three, Theodore Roosevelt won his race for Assemblyman to the 21st District in New York. In Albany, he quickly earned a reputation as an intrepid reformer and in 1884 headed the state investigation of corruption in Tammany Hall. Attracting considerable attention in the press, this investigation established Roosevelt as a leader of the reform party. In all, he served three terms in the state capital.

In 1883, Roosevelt's passion for hunting, so contrary to his interest in conservation, took him West

Top: Theodore Roosevelt Birthplace, National Historic Site; above: New York Public Library, Picture Collection

to the Bad Lands, where he became so enamored of ranching life that he established the Elkhorn Ranch. That the picture of Roosevelt bringing criminals to justice (below) is posed should not detract entirely from its general authenticity.

In 1895, Roosevelt was appointed Police Commissioner of New York. Still energetically pursuing reform, he made many enemies. In particular he aroused the angry opposition of many citizens by enforcing the law forbidding sale of liquor on Sunday and closing saloons on that day, an action widely ridiculed by the press.

ELKHORN RANCH.
THEODORE ROOSEVELT, Proprietor.
SEAWALL & DOW, Managers.

P. O. address, Little Missouri, D. T. Range, Little Missouri, twenty-five miles north of railroad.

Above: Courtesy of the American Museum of Natural History; Below: Stefan Lorant Collection

In order to secure his renomination for the presidency, an office he stepped into after McKinley's assassination, Roosevelt toured the country in 1903. He achieved his goal, but only at the expense of his personal life, for he remained a devoted family man, and election to the presidency involved an invasion of family privacy. At top, his sons Archie and Quentin line up with the White House police.

Although born of a wealthy, aristocratic family, Roosevelt felt a moral responsibility to the common man. In interfering between capital and labor in the coal strike of 1902 he took an unprecedented presidential action, justified, however, by the conditions of the poor (above, waiting in line for coal). His ensuing battles against trusts made him an open target for cartoonists, and he came to be pictured as the man who swung a "big stick."

Although the Panama Canal remained unfinished until 1914, Roosevelt considered its construction his greatest achievement and in 1906 personally inspected its progress.

Underwood and Underwood

An active sportsman, Roosevelt expected his family, advisers, and associates to accompany him in his exercises. He and his family took long hikes at their Sagamore Hill estate (below), and he was a fierce rock climber in Washington's Rock Creek Park where reporters had a hard time keeping up (left). This love of the outdoors undoubtedly influenced his fight for conservation.

Left: Stefan Lorant Collection; below: Theodore Roosevelt Birthplace, National Historic Site

EEKL

FOR PRESIDENT

BULL MOOSE PARTY

Humpty Dumpty sat on the wall.
Humpty Dumpty had a bad fall.
All the ex-bosses
And Bully Moose men,
Can never put Humpty up again.

"MY BOY!"

DRAWN BY E. W. KEMBLE

As soon as his presidential term ended, Roosevelt left on an eleven-month hunting trip in Africa. When he finally returned to America, he found himself enthusiastically greeted by press and public alike, as the cartoon at far left demonstrates.

The rift between the conservatives and progressives in the Republican Party had become irreparable, and Roosevelt almost immediately jumped into the middle of the battle. Backed by the Progressives, he ran against Taft on the Bull Moose ticket and split the Republicans. The Bull Moose Party lived only briefly, however, ending effectively with the defeat of Taft and Roosevelt by Woodrow Wilson.

Despite deep disappointment after his defeat in the 1912 election, Roosevelt continued to work and travel. The death of his son Quentin, an aviator in France, came as a serious blow, and six months later Roosevelt himself died. One of his last photographs shows him with his granddaughter.

Far left: Library of Congress; left: Stefan Lorant Collection; inset: Brown Brothers; right: Theodore Roosevelt Birthplace, National Historic Site

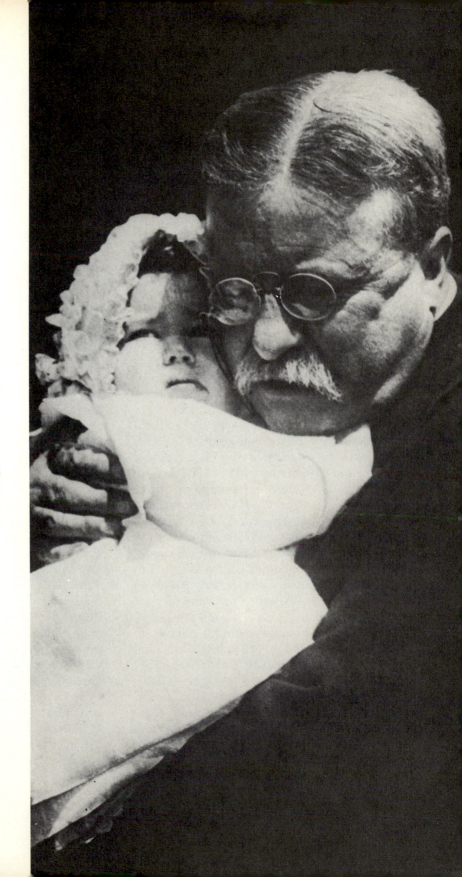

foreign political, diplomatic, and intellectual leaders. Moreover, Roosevelt had an internationalist outlook and believed that the United States should take a more active part in world affairs.

Roosevelt understood that international influence depended in large measure on national power. To sustain the worldwide responsibilities he believed essential, Roosevelt advocated, first, a larger and more efficient Navy. As President he argued incessantly for increased naval appropriations and displayed some of the nation's sea power when, in 1907, he sent sixteen warships around the world. Secondly, Roosevelt lent support to Secretary of War Elihu Root's Army reforms. In 1901 Root established the Army War College to provide special training for high command officers. Strongly nationalistic and even jingoistic at times, Roosevelt did not hesitate to use force against less developed peoples or countries in the Caribbean when he believed that nothing less would guarantee American interests in the region.

Roosevelt was concerned especially with the achievement of political stability in the Carribean area, where he considered the United States to have vital interests. After the Spanish defeat in 1898, United States military forces under General Leonard Wood ruled the island of Cuba; and during the period of occupation, which ended in 1902, American authorities worked hard to improve sanitation, education, and other social conditions on the island. But even after the military withdrawal, American sentiment and interest called for some form of continuing control.

The Platt Amendment offered a solution to the problem of retaining American influence and power in an independent Cuba. The Platt Amendment contained eight major provisions, of which two appeared essential. The United States acquired the right to intervene in Cuba both to protect life and property and to preserve Cuban independence. Secondly, the amendment required Cuba to lease or sell to the United States land necessary for coaling or naval sta-

tions. This stipulation led to the United States acquisition of the naval base at Guantanamo. Cuban leaders objected to the Platt Amendment, but they had no power to block it. Besides becoming part of the Cuban constitution, the articles of the Platt Amendment became the subject of a formal treaty signed in May 1903. For all practical purposes, Cuba became a protectorate of the United States.

Roosevelt sought the right to build an American-controlled canal across Central America, convinced that an interoceanic canal would solidify United States interests in that region. The need for such a water route seemed clear enough. During the Spanish-American War the U.S.S. *Oregon* required ninety-eight days to sail from the West Coast around South America to join the Caribbean fleet off Cuba. Acquisition of colonies in both the Caribbean and the Pacific in 1899 stressed even further the desirability of a direct water route connecting the two oceans.

Before the United States could obtain the necessary canal rights, it required an abrogation of the old Clayton-Bulwer Treaty, signed with Great Britain in 1850. This agreement provided for joint control of any isthmian canal which either nation might build. In November 1901, the Hay-Pauncefote Treaty ended the joint arrangement and thus opened the way for the United States to build and fortify its own canal.

Two routes, crossing either Nicaragua or Panama, were feasible. Initially, Roosevelt favored Nicaragua. The cost of building across Panama had been made prohibitive by the demands of the New Panama Canal Company, headed by Philippe Bunau-Varilla. This Frenchman had become chief engineer of the old French company that had attempted to dig a canal across Panama in the 1880s. By asking approximately $100 million for the French interests, Bunau-Varilla had boosted the total estimated price for digging across Panama to $60 million more than the cost of a canal through Nicaragua. But, realizing that United States construction across Nicaragua would destroy the value of his claim, Bunau-Varilla, in 1902, cut the price of the French assets to $40 million. In June 1902, the Spooner Amendment substituted Panama for Nicaragua, provided that Colombia (of which Panama was a part) would approve the transaction and that the French would sell their interests for $40 million.

Without difficulty, American diplomats negotiated the Hay-Herran Treaty with Colombia, which granted America permission to build a canal across Panama in return for a payment of $10 million outright, plus $250,000 a year in rental. But the Colombian congress rejected the treaty, chiefly because it thought the financial arrangements unsatisfactory. Rather than rely on further negotiation with the Colombian government, Roosevelt determined to move ahead unilaterally. He favored the seizure of Panamanian territory, but Bunau-Varilla's plotting rendered United States action unnecessary. The Frenchman arranged a so-called revolution, which took place in Panama on November 3, 1903. Aware of the approaching coup, Roosevelt had ordered United States naval vessels to be placed strategically where they could prevent Colombia from landing additional troops at Colon to put down the uprising. When Panama declared its independence from Colombia, the United States recognized the new government with indecent haste and, on November 18, signed a treaty with Panama. Bunau-Varilla represented the new republic. This treaty provided for payment to Panama of $10 million, plus $250,000 annually to begin after nine years, for a zone 10 miles wide. Moreover, the United States agreed to maintain the independence of Panama, thus reducing that country, in effect, to the level of a protectorate.

Canal construction began in 1904. When the canal was opened for traffic in 1914, it had cost some $400 million. Although the Canal Zone became an anchor in the American defense perimeter in the Caribbean and was a great boon to commerce, the methods by which Roosevelt achieved the American objectives aroused antagonism toward the United States throughout Latin America. Roosevelt never admitted that the United States had acted unethically. He believed firmly that his own actions, in securing the Canal Zone, were the correct ones.

During negotiations over the Panama Canal route, Roosevelt became involved in another diplomatic controversy, this time in Venezuela. For years the Venezuelans had contracted heavy debts to European and American creditors and had ignored demands for payment. In December 1902, Germany and England, two of the largest creditors, decided to collect their debts by force. They blockaded five ports and fired some shots into Venezuelan harbors. The previously arrogant dictator, Cipriano Castro, now called on the United States to arbitrate the debt problem. Roosevelt, who was primarily concerned over the possibility of a German challenge to the principle of the Monroe Doctrine, urged that the Venezuelan dispute be settled by arbitration. England quickly agreed, and shortly Germany did the same. A mixed commission and the Hague Permanent Court of Arbitration settled the claims of the creditors. Roosevelt had made it clear that the United States would not permit outside interference in the Western Hemisphere which might threaten the vital interests of the United States.

Roosevelt was extremely sensitive to the possibility of renewed foreign intervention in the Caribbean and Central American region. But only if the United States assumed the responsibility for maintaining political and economic stability in that area, he believed, could it prevent outside intervention. In May 1904, he wrote: "If a nation shows that it knows how to act with decency in industrial and political matters, if it keeps order and pays its obligations, then it need fear no interference from the United States. Brutal wrong-doing, or an impotence which results in a general loosening of the ties of civilized society, may finally require intervention by some civilized nation, and in the Western Hemisphere the United States might act as a policeman, at least in the Caribbean region." This statement became known as the "Roosevelt Corollary" to the Monroe Doctrine.

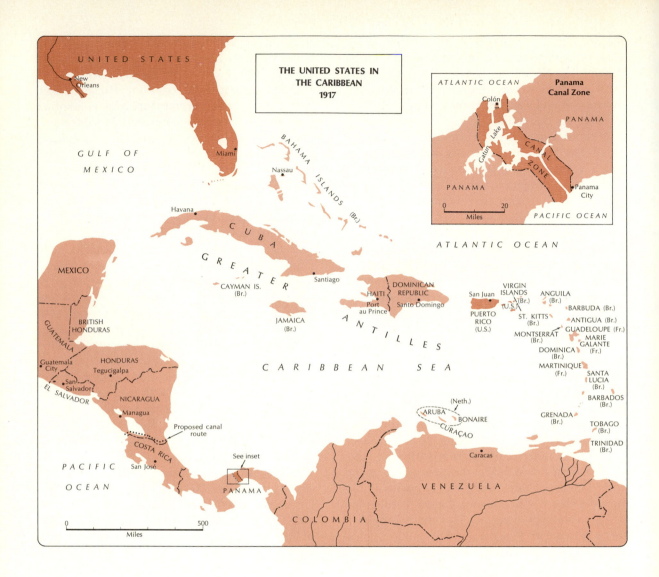

THE UNITED STATES IN
THE CARIBBEAN
1917

UNITED STATES

New
Orleans

GULF OF
MEXICO

Miami

BAHAMA ISLANDS (Br.)

Nassau

Havana

CUBA

GREATER

CAYMAN IS.
(Br.)

Santiago

ANTILLES

JAMAICA
(Br.)

HAITI

Port
au Prince

DOMINICAN
REPUBLIC

Santo Domingo

San Juan

PUERTO
RICO
(U.S.)

VIRGIN
ISLANDS
(Br.)
U.S.

ST. KITTS
(Br.)

MONTSERRAT
(Br.)

ANGUILA
(Br.)

BARBUDA (Br.)

ANTIGUA (Br.)

GUADELOUPE (Fr.)

MARIE
GALANTE
(Fr.)

DOMINICA
(Br.)

MARTINIQUE
(Fr.)

SANTA
LUCIA
(Br.)

BARBADOS
(Br.)

GRENADA
(Br.)

TOBAGO
(Br.)

TRINIDAD
(Br.)

MEXICO

BRITISH
HONDURAS

GUATEMALA

Guatemala
City

HONDURAS

Tegucigalpa

San
Salvador

EL SALVADOR

NICARAGUA

Managua

Proposed canal
route

COSTA RICA

San José

PACIFIC
OCEAN

See inset

PANAMA

CARIBBEAN SEA

ARUBA
(Neth.)

BONAIRE

CURAÇAO

Caracas

VENEZUELA

COLOMBIA

0   500
Miles

CARIBBEAN SEA

ATLANTIC OCEAN

Panama Canal Zone

ATLANTIC OCEAN

Colón

Gatún Lake

CANAL ZONE

PANAMA

PANAMA

Panama
City

PACIFIC OCEAN

0   20
Miles

Roosevelt soon had occasion to implement and test this policy in Santo Domingo. By 1903 that Caribbean nation had become virtually bankrupt and was heavily in debt to several major European powers. Foreign creditors from time to time had threatened to intervene. Roosevelt strongly opposed such a possibility and let it be known that, if any country intervened, it would be the United States. After an invitation from the Dominican president, Roosevelt did intervene early in 1905 and made an agreement whereby the United States would supervise the collection and disbursement of that country's customs receipts. Forty-five percent of the income was to be used for local government and 55 percent for the settlement of foreign debts. This arrangement worked satisfactorily, although the Senate refused to ratify it. In any event, the maintenance of political stability had become a basic objective of America's Caribbean and Canal diplomacy. The Roosevelt administration fulfilled this purpose in large measure by acquiring rights to the Panama Canal Zone, by maintaining a protectorate over Cuba, and by helping to guarantee order in small, unstable countries, including the colony of Puerto Rico.

Roosevelt's Foreign Policy: The Far East

Roosevelt was vitally concerned with American interests in the Far East. He supported the Open Door policy in China, although both he and Secretary of State John Hay feared privately that the policy contained the seeds of overcommitment, and thus embarrassment, for the United States. What Roosevelt sought above all in the Far East was a balance among China, Japan, and Russia which would prevent any single combination of forces in the Orient from challenging this country's limited, but growing, interests there. At the same time that the United States attempted to develop its trade and protect the interests of China, it faced the task of guarding the Philippines. Japan, the rapidly rising power of the western Pacific, loomed as the long-run threat to the Far Eastern balance of power. But in 1901 Russian expansion into Manchuria presented the immediate danger to peace in Asia and the territorial integrity of China.

Russian advances into Manchuria and finally into Korea challenged Japanese interests in that area; in 1904, after repeated warnings, Japan attacked the Russians. To Roosevelt Japan seemed to be defending the Open Door. He warned Germany and France that if they went to the aid of Russia, the United States would help Japan.

Roosevelt's central interest, however, lay in mediating the war. Aided by a major Japanese naval victory in May 1905, Roosevelt managed, in August, to bring representatives of Japan and Russia to Portsmouth, New Hampshire, for a peace conference. The Japanese arrived with a strong diplomatic position. Their military forces had won the battles. They had, moreover, an unseen ally in Great Britain, with whom they had signed the Anglo-Japanese Alliance in 1902. A few days before the peace conference opened, Secretary of War Taft, on his way to the Philippines, met with Count Katsura, Premier of Japan, and agreed to what became known as the Taft-Katsura Memorandum. In this agreement, fully supported by Roosevelt, the United States approved of Japan's control over Korea, while Japan declared that it had no "aggressive designs whatever on the Philippines."

The Japanese acquired almost everything they demanded at Portsmouth, except a large cash indemnity. Russia recognized Japan's predominant interests in Korea, granted concessions to the Japanese in Liaotung, and gave Japan the southern half of Sakhalin Island. Japanese influence replaced that of Russia in south Manchuria. But Roosevelt would not support the Japanese demand for a $600 million cash payment from Russia. Consequently, despite the fact that Japan made great gains, official and popular reactions to the treaty in Japan were extremely critical. The Japanese held the United States responsible for their failure to receive a cash indemnity. The Treaty of Portsmouth, by greatly strengthening Japan in the Far East, was a major step toward upsetting the balance of power. In the Root-Takahira agreement of 1908, the United States and Japan promised to maintain the status quo in the "region of the Pacific Ocean" and to respect the territorial possessions of one another in that area. This reflected again American concern for the Philippines, which lay outside the range of effective United States naval or military power.

During Roosevelt's administration, the United States worked out basic policies for governing the Philippines, its largest and most important colony. Most American officials, including Roosevelt, believed that before the Philippines could become self-governing or independent, they would require American tutelage for a long period. In 1901 Roosevelt appointed William Howard Taft as Governor

General of the Islands, and in July of the next year Congress passed the Philippine Organic Act. This law designated the Philippines an "unorganized territory," placing it under the control of a governor general and a commission, which had executive, legislative, and judicial powers. The commission arranged to redistribute some land to peasants—especially lands formerly held by the Catholic Church—sought to improve health and education, and inaugurated a variety of reforms.

Many Filipinos, however, wanted their freedom. When the United States permitted them an elective assembly in 1907, the Speaker of the House, Sergio Osmeña, pleaded for immediate independence. Manuel Quezon was among other nationalists who resisted continued United States domination. While the Filipinos gained some self-government under Roosevelt, and more under later presidents (they acquired an independent upper house in the Jones Act of 1916), it was not until the late 1920s that widespread support for Philippine independence developed in the United States.

Conclusion

As President, Theodore Roosevelt rode the crest of a massive reform movement that ultimately won the support of the majority of the American people. The movement was not his. Rather it was the creation of pervading economic and social problems, perceived with varying degrees of clarity and detail by observant citizens and publicized by an effective body of writers and reformers. By 1901, when Roosevelt entered the White House, the progressive movement embraced a widespread search for order to be supported by enforceable rules of fair play in the nation's economic affairs. The rules, when perfected, would govern the relationship of bankers, industrialists, and other possessors of major economic power to the country's natural resources, its laboring elements, and other segments of the business community itself. With objectives that broad, the program could be no more than a beginning.

Still Roosevelt, as President of the United States, left an indelible impression on the American consciousness. His administration was one of the three or four most active and dynamic in the country's experience before 1909. It led the nation, sometimes fumblingly, into a new course of governmental responsibility and economic reform at home and into new ventures abroad, especially in the Caribbean. Roosevelt's relations with the Far East, if unprecedented, revealed that he possessed a clear conviction that the ends and means of policy must be kept in balance. What guided Roosevelt generally was his acceptance of limits to his sphere of action. Early in his administration he agreed to demand nothing of the Republican party that would endanger its unity. He often needled the Republican Old Guard; he never defied it. He accepted, in large measure, what the Republican leadership in Congress would give him. He was a skillful and effective politician who accepted compromise as a necessity. At the same time, Roosevelt's reforms were considerable, and they pointed the direction toward greater reforms under future administrations.

SUGGESTED READINGS

George E. Mowry's *The Era of Theodore Roosevelt, 1900–1912** (1958) is the best survey of progressivism in the early twentieth century. *The Age of Reform: From Bryan to F.D.R.** (1955) by Richard Hofstadter finds much of the impetus for reform in what he calls "the status revolution."

Among the excellent books dealing with progressivism at the state level are George E. Mowry's *The*

*California Progressives** (1951); R. S. Maxwell's *La Follette and the Rise of the Progressives in Wisconsin* (1956); and H. L. Warner's *Progressivism in Ohio, 1897–1917* (1964). On some of the urban reformers see T. L. Johnson's *My Story* (1911) and F. C. Howe's *Confessions of a Reformer** (1925).

General economic and social conditions can be followed in H. U. Faulkner's *The Decline of Laissez Faire, 1897–1917* (1951) and *The Quest for Social Justice, 1898–1914* (1931). Evaluations of the role of the business community in reform can best be studied in Robert H. Wiebe's *Businessmen and Reform: A Study of the Progressive Movement* (1962) and Gabriel Kolko's *The Triumph of Conservatism: A Reinterpretation of American History, 1900–1916** (1963), which argues that business interests directed the course of events much along the lines they desired.

The Muckrakers have been interpreted by Louis Filler in *Crusaders for American Liberalism* (1939) and in C. C. Regier's *The Era of the Muckrakers* (1932). On specific reforms see James H. Timberlake's *Prohibition and the Progressive Movement, 1900–1920* (1963); Roy Lubove's *The Urban Community: Housing and Planning in the Progressive Era** (1967) and *The Progressives and the Slums: Tenement House Reform in New York City, 1890–1917* (1963); Aileen S. Kraditor's *The Ideas of the Woman Suffrage Movement, 1890–1920* (1965); and Allen F. Davis's *Spearheads for Reform: The Social Settlements and the Progressive Movement, 1890–1914* (1967). On the position of the Negro, see August Meier's *Negro Thought in America, 1880–1915; Racial Ideologies in the Age of Booker T. Washington** (1963); and F. L. Broderick's *W. E. B. Du Bois: Negro Leader in a Time of Crisis** (1959).

For biographical studies of Theodore Roosevelt see W. H. Harbaugh's *Power and Responsibility: The Life and Times of Theodore Roosevelt** (1961), which is comprehensive but friendly in tone; Henry Pringle's *Theodore Roosevelt** (1931), which was the standard biography for many years; and the short, lively interpretation by J. M. Blum, *The Republican Roosevelt** (1954). A brief, interesting survey of Roosevelt is David Henry Burton's *Theodore Roosevelt* (1972). See also Willard B. Gatewood, Jr., *Theodore Roosevelt and the Act of Controversy* (1970).

On the question of monopoly and business concentration during the Roosevelt administration see Charles R. Van Hise's *Concentration and Control: A Solution to the Trust Problem in the United States* (1912). Pure food and drug legislation has been well covered by O. E. Anderson in *The Health of a Nation: Harvey W. Wiley and the Fight for Pure Food* (1958). The *American Peace Movement and Social Reform, 1898–1918* (1973) treats an important topic well. Labor problems have been considered in the *Anthracite Coal Strike of 1902* (1957) by R. J. Cornell and Marc Karson's *American Labor Unions and Politics, 1900–1917* (1958). On conservation *The Gospel of Efficiency: The Progressive Conservation Movement, 1890–1920* (1950) by S. P. Hays is excellent, as is *The Politics of Conservation, Crusades and Controversies, 1897–1913* (1962) by E. R. Richardson. The best account of Roosevelt's foreign policy is Howard K. Beale's *Theodore Roosevelt and the Rise of America to World Power** (1956). His policies are also dealt with in H. C. Hill's *Roosevelt and the Caribbean* (1927); W. H. Callcott's *The Caribbean Policy of the United States, 1890–1920* (1942); D. C. Miner's *The Fight for the Panama Route* (1940); Dexter Perkins's *The United States and the Caribbean* (1947); and A. L. P. Dennis's *Adventures in American Diplomacy* (1928). *Theodore Roosevelt and the International Rivalries* (1970) by Raymond A. Esthus is an important contribution. On the Far East see A. W. Griswold's *The Far Eastern Policy of the United States** (1938); P. J. Treat's *Diplomatic Relations between the United States and Japan, 1895–1905* (1938); *Theodore Roosevelt and the Japanese-American Crises* (1934) by T. A. Bailey; and F. R. Dulles's *America's Rise to World Power, 1898–1954** (1955).

*indicates availability in paperback.

24

High Tide of Reform: Taft and Wilson

Republican strength and unity, so evident during and after the election of 1904, continued through the presidential campaign of 1908. The highly popular Roosevelt was in full command of the party and could have won another nomination had he wanted it. But following his thumping victory in 1904, he had announced that "under no circumstances will I be a candidate for or accept another nomination." Counting himself out as a candidate in 1908, Roosevelt nevertheless had no intention of permitting an open convention. Several months before the Republicans met, Roosevelt made clear his preference for his Secretary of War, William Howard Taft. With Roosevelt's backing, Taft captured the convention's vote on the first ballot.

Having lost heavily with a conservative candidate in 1904, the Democrats nominated William Jennings Bryan for a third time. Bryan's perennial strength within the Democratic party rested on his party loyalty, his large personal following, and his dramatic airing of national issues. Although the Democratic platform was more progressive than its Republican counterpart, the Republicans again won impressively. Taft's popular majority was 1.2 million; the electoral count was 321 to 162. The Republicans maintained their large majorities in the House and Senate. Despite Bryan's third defeat, the Democrats were in a stronger position than at any time since 1892, and continued Republican dominance depended upon Taft's skill in maintaining a reasonable degree of party harmony. But it was in his role as party chief that Taft experienced his greatest failure.

William Howard Taft brought not only unquestioned ability but also a wide variety of experience to the White House. Born in 1857 in Cincinnati, he graduated from Yale and then studied law. He held a number of judicial posts before McKinley selected him to head the Philippine Commission in 1900. The next year Taft became the first civil governor of the islands. In 1904 Roosevelt appointed him Secretary of War. Taft was a large, good-natured, easygoing, affectionate, modest, and tolerant man. He weighed 326 pounds in 1906 when he returned from a trip to the Philippines. Deliberate in thought and action, Taft preferred a calm, judicious approach to problems rather than a hasty impetuosity.

Many of Taft's troubles in the presidency stemmed from his personality. He had little interest in the hustle and bustle of politics; he once wrote his wife: "Politics, when I am in it, makes me sick." Taft's dislike of many activities expected of a president was a major handicap. But his chief shortcoming as president was his failure to respond to the country's progressive sentiment. He was basically conservative. His progressive ideas had reached their limit before his election, and his thinking on political principles and economic reform thereafter remained largely static. Unfortunately for Taft and his performance as president, a large faction within the Republican party, supported by many Democrats, was moving in 1909 toward more advanced progressivism.

In his inaugural address Taft pledged "the maintenance and enforcement" of the major Roosevelt reforms. Hewing close to the Republican platform, Taft called for regulation of big business and emphasized the need for conservation of natural resources. He promised reform of the banking laws to secure greater elasticity in the forms of "currency available for trade." Even a postal savings bank, he said, would "not be unwise or excessive paternalism." Taft suggested greater protection for workingmen against industrial abuses. He devoted considerable attention to the Negro question and demanded a downward revision of the tariff. Taft's address was a call for moderate progressivism along the lines already laid down by Roosevelt. At the close of the President's speech, Roosevelt grasped his hand and said: "God bless you, old man. It is a great state document." The two friends seemed as close as ever. A few days later, on March 23, 1909, Roosevelt sailed for an African hunting trip. By no means a Roosevelt fan, J. P. Morgan, it is reported, urged every lion to do its duty!

Never quite at home in the White House, Taft was left to implement a progressive program as leader of a party already showing signs of internal dissension. Differences between Taft and the

"Baby, kiss Papa good-by": This cartoon, which appeared on the cover of a 1909 issue of Puck, *predicts that Taft's policies will be a direct continuation of Theodore Roosevelt's. The bellhop is carrying Roosevelt's "big stick."*

The Granger Collection

HIGH TIDE OF REFORM: TAFT AND WILSON

progressive Republicans became evident in the fight over tariff revision, a troublesome political question which Roosevelt had studiously avoided, but which Taft had promised in his campaign. Introduced in the House by Representative Henry C. Payne, the new bill lowered tariff duties substantially. But in the Senate, lobbyists modified the proposed lower tariff schedules beyond recognition. Senator Aldrich accepted scores of amendments raising rates on such important products as lumber, iron, and textiles. Angered at the Aldrich proposals, a group of Midwestern progressives, including Senator La Follette, bitterly fought the amendments. More than tariff rates were at stake. To these insurgents Aldrich symbolized Eastern industrial and moneyed interests which were exploiting Western farmers.

The Senate fight over the tariff placed Taft in a difficult position. He could accept the views of Aldrich and the Senate majority, even though he opposed their rates; or he could support the insurgents and uphold his principles. But the President had nothing in common with the Westerners and really did not understand them. When the bill came to his desk, he signed it against the wishes of the Western progressives. Later he blundered badly when he told a crowd at Winona, Minnesota, that "on the whole . . . I think the Payne bill is the best bill that the Republican Party ever passed." Taft's praise of the law in a region which had opposed the measure indicated his lack of political judgment. Actually, the Payne-Aldrich tariff was more important politically than economically. It divided the Republican party. Western progressives fumed at Taft and accused him of siding with Eastern reactionaries and abandoning the Roosevelt policies.

To these progressive Republicans who were beginning to distrust Taft, the Ballinger-Pinchot controversy seemed to be clinching evidence that the President was betraying Roosevelt and progressive principles. Very shortly after Secretary Richard A. Ballinger took office as Secretary of Interior, he restored to private entry some of the Western lands which had been withdrawn during the last months of the Roosevelt administration, and placed them in the public domain. A Seattle lawyer with deep respect for the law, Ballinger claimed that his predecessors had set aside these lands illegally. Taft agreed. Many ardent conservationists, however, became skeptical of Ballinger's and Taft's devotion to conservation. Gifford Pinchot, Roosevelt's good friend and chief of the Forest Service, became especially critical of Ballinger.

When charges against Ballinger reached Taft, he rejected the idea that his Secretary of the Interior had done anything legally or morally wrong or that he was unfriendly to conservation. Pinchot, however, continued to attack the administration and called Ballinger "the most effective opponent the conservation policies have yet had." Taft was now faced with the difficult problem of dealing with an embarrassing fight within his official family. Siding with Ballinger, he dismissed Pinchot summarily early in 1910. The Ballinger-Pinchot controversy drove a wedge between the Taft administration and Roosevelt's followers. Taft regretted this and wrote that he hoped not to create a "rupture" with Roosevelt, but Pinchot hurried to Africa and told his former chief that Taft had betrayed conservation. At home some of Roosevelt's friends already contemplated passing up Taft in 1912 and again supporting Roosevelt for the presidency.

Despite the charges, Taft's record on conservation was in fact excellent. In some areas he even exceeded what Roosevelt had done. In 1909 he withdrew more than 3 million acres of oil land in California and Wyoming from all forms of public entry. The Withdrawal Act of 1910 gave the President specific authority to take back land from any private ownership; this provided the legal authority to do what Roosevelt had already done by executive action.

That event which best reflected the growing division in Republican ranks came early in 1910, when the insurgents challenged the power of the Speaker of the House, Joseph Cannon. Led by a young Republican from Nebraska, George W. Norris, the insurgents moved to amend the rules of the House to exclude the Speaker from the powerful Committee on Rules (which controlled the flow of legislation in the House), to enlarge the committee, and to make the committee elective rather than appointive by the Speaker. Cannon and his conservative backers tried every tactic and strategy to defeat the measures, but a coalition of insurgent Republicans and Democrats passed them after a hectic twenty-nine-hour session. This was a victory for legislative reform, but the bitter fight was to leave deep and lingering scars on the Republican party.

By 1910 it was obvious that Taft had failed as a political leader. No longer heading a united party, he now leaned openly toward the conservatives and ignored most of his progressive support. The midterm elections of 1910 were a disaster for the Republicans. Democrats swept to victory in the House of Representatives by a margin of 226 to 161. Champ Clark of Missouri became the new Speaker of the House in 1911.

Taft's decline as president resulted less from his failures than from his inability to dramatize his achievements. During his administration, progressivism continued unabated, but most people seemed to see only the President's mistakes. The Taft administration instituted more suits against industrial monopolies under the Sherman Antitrust Act than "trustbuster" Roosevelt had done. Suits against the American Tobacco Company and Standard Oil under Roosevelt were concluded in 1911. Taft supported the Mann-Elkins Act of 1910, which strengthened the power of the Interstate Commerce Commission by establishing a special Commerce Court to hear railway cases.

President Taft gave his backing to a variety of other reforms. The law establishing Postal Savings Banks, which had been advocated for many years, passed Congress in 1910. Establishment of a parcel post system in January 1913 was of special moment to farmers; thereafter they, with others, could have packages delivered with their other mail. In 1912 a Children's Bureau was established in the Department of Commerce and Labor to deal with "matters pertaining to the welfare of children and child life among all classes of our people." One of Taft's last acts as president on March 4, 1913, was to sign a bill creating a separate Department of Labor. Congress passed the Mann Act in 1910, which forbade the transportation of women across the state lines for immoral purposes. Also in 1910 Congress required representatives to publicize their campaign expenses; the next year Congress extended this obligation to senators. An important, but little-known, measure of 1911 stopped the use of white phosphorus in the manufacture of matches. This chemical had resulted in a high incidence of disease among workers in American match factories.

The Seventeenth Amendment to the Constitution, providing for the direct election of senators, was submitted to the states for ratification in 1912 and became effective the following year. New Mexico and Arizona entered the Union as the forty-seventh and forty-eighth states in 1912. Taft lent some support to the income tax amendment, the Sixteenth. This amendment became part of the Constitution in February 1913, a few days before Taft left the White House. In the long run, the federal income tax was of tremendous economic and social importance. It provided the revenue to meet the cost of expanding government services and endowed the federal government with the power to equalize income.

Foreign Affairs under Taft

When Taft became president in 1909, the jingoism and expansionism of the Spanish-American War period had largely disappeared. Although Taft had a deep interest in American affairs abroad, he intended to avoid crises and conflicts which would require the application of American power. There were occasions during his administration when he used American troops to implement foreign policy, but he preferred legal and diplomatic processes to any show of force. His secretary of state, Philander C. Knox, was an able lawyer who had served both McKinley and Roosevelt as attorney general.

American external relations remained generally calm and peaceful during the four Taft years. Believing that the United States should abstain from any political or diplomatic entanglements in Europe, Taft kept clear of the growing conflicts there which were driving the great powers toward war. Toward Asia and Latin America, however, where the gains from intervention promised to outweigh the costs, Taft's policies were scarcely isolationist at all. Taft and Knox were convinced that they could stimulate American overseas trade and investment without running any risks of conflict or war. Taft defined his fundamental objectives in 1910: "We believe it to be of the utmost importance that while our foreign policy should not be turned a hair's breadth from the straight path of justice, it may well be made to include active intervention to secure for our merchandise and our capitalists opportunity for profitable investment." In the Far East, Taft attempted to maintain and even to strengthen the Open Door policy, but he assumed he could achieve this goal by reliance on economic rather than military means. It was in the Caribbean–Central American area that the United States supplemented economic with military power to achieve its objectives. It was here that Taft implemented his so-called Dollar Diplomacy with positive action.

Taft, like Roosevelt before him, believed that political and economic stability in the region of the Caribbean was essential for the security of the United States. The building of the Panama Canal emphasized the strategic interest of the United States in that portion of the hemisphere. But American investments alone, Taft believed, would assure the stability which he sought. Furthermore, such investments would remove any threat of intervention by foreign creditors. After American bankers had made investments in any of these republics, the State Department could use its power and influence to protect the investors from revolution and possible default. If peace and order proved to be too elusive for diplomatic means alone, then the President could resort to actual armed intervention, but even then it would be limited to the support of governments friendly to American investments. Taft characterized this policy as one of "substituting dollars for bullets."

Despite outward appearances, Dollar Diplomacy did not represent simply the selfish use of a pliant State Department by United States investment bankers. In most cases government officials urged investors to make loans against their will to unsettled Latin American countries. Having succumbed to this pressure, the bankers expected, logically, that the State Department would support them by guarding their investments. Despite the general lack of formal treaty guarantees, United States capital flowed into Latin America in considerable volume during the early years of the twentieth century. In Latin America, the United States possessed the power to implement its policies, but in so doing it angered and alienated those Latin Americans who resented the resulting interference in their internal affairs.

Under the principle of Dollar Diplomacy, the Taft administration extended United States commitments in the Far East far beyond what the Roosevelt administration had regarded as acceptable. In 1908 Willard Straight, the American consul general at Mukden, Manchuria, had recommended to Elihu Root, Roosevelt's secretary of state, that the United States support a railroad project in Manchuria which would offer competition to the Japanese-controlled South Manchurian Railway. Root had recognized in this proposal a clear infringement on the Japanese sphere of interest and had refused to support it. Roosevelt and Root had no desire to give Japan a completely free hand in Manchuria, but neither did they intend to commit the United States to a crusade against Japanese expansion. Shortly before leaving the White House, Roosevelt advised his successor to avoid trouble with Japan "by preventing the occurrence of conditions that would invite war . . . ."

But in 1909 the Taft administration quickly converted the Open Door principle into an anti-Japanese weapon. As the representative of an American investment group, Straight now proposed the formation of a Chinchow-Aigun railway in Manchuria, again designed to offer direct competition to the Japanese line. For Taft this reliance on investment as a device to ease the Japanese out of Manchuria was a logical extension of Dollar Diplomacy. Already the project for applying Dollar Diplomacy to China was at hand. In 1909, a group of French, German, and English bankers, supported by their governments, arranged a loan to aid China in the construction of the Hukuang Railway in southern China. Knox insisted that the United States was equally concerned with the development of China and demanded that New York bankers be permitted to share in the China loan.

Then in November 1909, Secretary Knox extended this investment concept to a neutralization proposal which would place all Manchurian railroads under international control and thereby undermine Japan's growing economic interest in south Manchuria. Roosevelt warned Taft and Knox that their effort to commit the United States to a sharply anti-Japanese policy in Manchuria would either involve the nation in a policy of bluff or endanger Japan's interests so completely that it would lead to war. The neutralization proposal had the effect of driving the Japanese and Russians into one bloc, and in 1910 the two powers signed an agreement whereby they pledged to support one another in their spheres of influence.

With the collapse of the neutralization scheme, Knox turned to the bankers' consortium and, in 1911, negotiated a portion of a loan for American investors. But in 1912 Japan and Russia again undermined Knox's ambitions, when they entered the consortium and immediately ruled out all loans which would interfere with their economic interests in Manchuria. Taft's application of Dollar Diplomacy to China proved to be an immediate failure and an ultimate disaster. The United States did not have the power, or even the intent, to support the investment and commercial Open Door in Manchuria against the special and greater interests of other powers. Yet Taft and his advisers had committed the nation so completely to the principle of the Open Door in China that they, in effect, had placed the United States and Japan on a collision course from which neither could withdraw.

In his last annual message to Congress on December 3, 1912, Taft summarized the nation's foreign policy: "The relations of the United States with all foreign powers remain upon a sound basis of peace, harmony, and friendship." The United States, he continued, had given support to trade, had helped to preserve stability in Latin America, and had worked for peace. "We have emerged full grown as a peer in the great concourse of nations," he concluded. "We are now in a larger relation with broader rights of our own and obligations to others than ourselves."

But Taft's administration, despite its emphasis on peaceful processes, had planted the seeds of future trouble. His policies, set in open defiance of warnings by the nation's leading intellectuals, had cast American diplomacy in a dangerous Asia-first mold. Taft rejected the idea that an enduring European balance of power had given the American people a century of almost absolute security at little or no cost to themselves. That security, some said, would not survive a British defeat at the hands of Germany in Europe's approaching war. It was in Europe that the critical interests of the United States were at stake. But the Taft administration neglected the deeper, more critical challenge of Europe completely.

When Theodore Roosevelt returned from his world trip on June 18, 1910, a large and enthusiastic crowd welcomed him in New York. Republicans anxiously awaited his choice of position in the struggle between Taft and the progressives, but the former President carefully avoided any public commitments. It was clear that Roosevelt returned from abroad with a decided coolness toward his successor. Still Roosevelt tried to avoid an open break with the President. Republican disunity, he knew, would only help the Democrats, and Roosevelt detested Democrats.

Roosevelt's Western speaking tour in the summer of 1910 widened the growing gulf between him and Taft. In his numerous speeches and interviews he identified himself with the vanguard of progressivism. His views were best summarized in his noted speech entitled "The New Nationalism," delivered at Osawatomie, Kansas, late in August 1910. Roosevelt declared that he stood for "the square deal." He insisted that all groups must have justice but argued that "property shall be the servant and not the master of the commonwealth." The people, he said, must effectively control big business. He advocated both a graduated income tax and an inheritance tax. Turning to the problems of labor, Roosevelt declared that workmen's compensation and child-labor laws, as well as legislation to enforce better sanitary and safety conditions, were needed for workers. He demanded more extensive conservation measures and political reforms "to make our political representatives more quickly and sensitively responsive to the people." Roosevelt explained that he was not asking "for overcentralization; but I do ask," he said, "that we work in a spirit of broad and far-reaching nationalism when we work for what concerns our people as a whole." The interests of all the people, he said, could be effectively guarded only by the national government. These proposals reflected Roosevelt's earlier reading of

Herbert Croly's *The Promise of American Life* (1909).

By late 1910 many progressive Republicans had become firmly convinced that a strong progressive candidate must replace Taft in 1912. Senator La Follette gained some early support, but it soon became clear that most Republican progressives preferred Roosevelt. After the urging of his many friends, the former President responded to a request from eight governors on February 24, 1912, "My hat is in the ring." "I will accept the nomination for President," he wrote, "if it is tendered to me." Progressives now tumbled over one another to join the Roosevelt forces.

Although La Follette charged that Roosevelt had used him as a stalking horse to test the popularity of progressivism, in the states where people had a chance to express themselves on convention delegates, Roosevelt men won consistently. Roosevelt's critics, however, charged that he had destroyed party harmony in his mad quest for power. One detractor scoffed at Roosevelt in a parody on the Apostles' Creed:

> I believe in Theodore Roosevelt, maker of noise and strife, and in ambition his only creed (My Lord). He was born of the love of power and suffered under William Howard Taft, was crucified, died and buried. He descended into Africa. The third year he arose again from the jungle and ascendeth into favor and sitteth on the right hand of his party, whence he shall come to scourge the living and the dead.

Why did Roosevelt seek the nomination when his action was almost certain to divide the party and ensure victory for the Democrats? In the first place, his friends put enormous pressure on him. Too, he was motivated by his irritation with Taft, and it is possible that he was bored with private life. But most important, Roosevelt wanted to wield power in behalf of his objectives, and this required that he be president.

Roosevelt arrived at Chicago shortly before the Republican National Convention opened on June 18, to be on hand to direct his forces in the fight for the nomination. When a reporter asked him how he felt, Roosevelt replied, "I'm feeling like a bull moose." Subsequently, the bull moose became the symbol of the new Progressive party. A high degree of emotionalism and almost religious fervor imbued Roosevelt's followers. On the eve of the convention, Roosevelt addressed thousands of his loyal supporters and climaxed his remarks with the stirring words, "We stand at Armageddon, and we battle for the Lord."

When the convention officially opened the next day, Republicans were hopelessly split. The Taft forces were able to dominate the convention through the President's control of both the Republican National Committee and the Credentials Committee. However, when Taft's backers renominated the President on the first ballot, Roosevelt charged that Taft had stolen the nomination. The convention again chose John Sherman as the vice-presidential candidate. The platform called for a protective tariff, restrictions on monopoly, banking and currency reform, conservation of natural resources, restrictions on "undesirable immigration," economy and efficiency in government.

Even as the Republican Convention adjourned, a new party was emerging. That night in Orchestra Hall, Roosevelt told a madly cheering throng that he would accept the nomination of a new progressive party if it were offered to him. In August the progressives met again in Chicago for their formal convention. Grimly serious but highly emotional, the crowd listened to Roosevelt as he gave his "Confession of Faith." He attacked the two old parties, which, he said, were "boss-ridden and privilege-controlled" and represented only the rich. The delegates cheered wildly and sang:

Thou wilt not cower in the dust,
Roosevelt, O Roosevelt!
Thy gleaming sword shall never rust,
Roosevelt, O Roosevelt!

Thus the Progressive party, or Bull Moose party, was formally launched. The delegates named Roosevelt as their standard-bearer and Hiram Johnson, the progressive governor of California, as his running mate. Jane Addams's seconding of Roosevelt's nomination was an event which symbolized the increasing activity of women in public life.

In their platform the Progressives declared that the old parties had "become the tools of corrupt interests," and that the new party would "build a new and nobler commonwealth." The party pledged political reforms; legislation giving people the power to override certain court decisions; prohibition of injunctions in labor disputes; a wide variety of laws to protect workers; a strong federal administrative commission to control big business and monopoly; currency reform; conservation; and graduated federal income and inheritance taxes.

Optimistic Democrats watched the quarreling Republicans with deep satisfaction and enlivened hopes for victory. Their leading candidates were Champ Clark of Missouri, Speaker of the House; Woodrow Wilson, Governor of New Jersey; and Representative Oscar Underwood of Alabama. When the convention opened, Clark had more delegates than Wilson. But through the astute efforts of his managers and his identification with the progressive forces, Wilson finally received the nomination on the forty-sixth ballot.

Wilson's selection meant victory for the progressive forces within the Democratic party. The platform expressed Bryan-type progressivism and recommended "a tariff for revenue only"; control of big business both through strengthening the Sherman Antitrust Act and through passing additional restrictive laws; an income tax;

popular election of senators; a law to prohibit corporate contributions to campaign funds; new banking legislation and control of the "money trust"; additional regulation of railroads; rural credits to assist farmers; labor legislation; and conservation of natural and human resources.

Wilson and Roosevelt quickly dominated the contest of 1912. Taft conducted no real campaign, and few prominent people worked for his election. Roosevelt delivered speech after speech to explain his New Nationalism. Even after being wounded by a fanatic in Milwaukee on October 14, Roosevelt told his hushed audience that he would speak "as long as there is life in my body." Wilson, meanwhile worked hard to unite the Democrats and to popularize his New Freedom. He elevated the trust problem to major importance in his campaign, advocating strict government regulation to restore business competition.

With the Republican vote split, Wilson had only to win the normal Democratic vote to be assured of victory. In November, Wilson gained 6,293,019 votes; Roosevelt, 4,119,507; Taft, 3,484,956; and Debs, a Socialist candidate, 901,873. Wilson received a minority of the popular vote and polled fewer ballots than Bryan did in 1908, but his electoral college majority was overwhelming. He had 435 to Roosevelt's 88. Taft carried only two states with 8 electoral votes. The three progressive candidates— Wilson, Roosevelt, and Debs—had a combined vote of more than 11 million. Not all of these 11 million voters favored progressive principles, of course, but it seems clear that a large majority of the electorate in 1912 favored continued economic, social, and political reform.

Changing American Society

Wilson's America had lost much of its rural character and was becoming a nation of cities. By 1914 the country's population had reached nearly 100 million, but less than one-third of this number lived on farms. Increasingly, the urban areas set the pattern of national life, reflecting the nation's growing wealth. That wealth totaled some $186 billion in 1912, or eleven times what it had been a half century before. Compared with most peoples of the world, Americans had an enviable standard of living. Average annual per capita income reached almost $500 by 1914. This higher income provided better food, clothing, and shelter, as well as more money for education, leisure, and other purposes, than Americans had previously enjoyed. Many people did not share the advantages of private enterprise, but there was a growing concern for this minority. Indeed, one essential element in the progressive movement was the provision of greater care and better opportunities for the underprivileged.

The rapidity of social change was itself the most notable characteristic of American society. In the early years of the century Americans were more restless and mobile than in any previous period. Symbolic of their new energy and mobility was the automobile. In 1909 President Taft rode to his inauguration in a horse-drawn carriage; four years later the horsepower which conveyed Wilson to his inauguration was under the hood of an automobile. This change in a period of only four years was startling and fundamental. In 1900 automobiles had been regarded either as the playthings of the rich or as objects of interest for tinkering mechanics. In 1914 Henry Ford alone produced 258,356 units of his famous Model T.

This restlessness influenced American literature, social life, and the position of women. The hard-hitting novels of Frank Norris, Jack London, and Theodore Dreiser were beginning to replace the romantic fiction and religious novels

The Suffragettes

Until well into the twentieth century, women enjoyed only second- or third-class citizenship in most states. As pioneers and settlers of the West, women had labored alongside men to open up the country, but still they could not own property. They had campaigned ardently for the abolition of slavery, but when blacks received full citizenship—if only temporarily—women did not. In most states all a wife's possessions and earnings belonged to her husband. A woman could be divorced but could seldom sue for divorce. Her role was to keep the house, bear the children, and be respectful. For decades feminist leaders had protested these injustices.

Women's suffrage groups sprang up just after the Civil War; in 1890 they formed a national association. By then almost all women's organizations concentrated on a single goal: to get the vote. With the vote, they reasoned, would come the power to correct inequities, to create change. The suffragettes concentrated on public education. They had to convince the men who voted and governed that a great injustice existed. Public rallies, forums, speeches, discussion groups, articles, parades, pageants, demonstrations, and airship ascensions all constituted part of the effort.

Brown Brothers

The first International Convention of Women met in Washington in 1888. Among the leaders (right) were Elizabeth Cady Stanton (in front, right), who had organized the first woman's rights convention in 1848; Susan B. Anthony (fourth from left, front), America's most active and famous feminist and previously a temperance leader; and Frances Willard (left, standing), organizer and president of the Woman's Christian Temperance Union. Most feminists strongly opposed alcohol, and prohibition became law two years before woman suffrage.

Above, a terpsichorean pageant on the steps of the Treasury building in Washington depicted women's rights. Even tugboats bore the message.

Brown Brothers

Several territories, of which Wyoming was first, had granted suffrage to women before becoming states. By 1913 twelve such states had helped force the Nineteenth Amendment through Congress. Two-thirds of the states then had to ratify the amendment to put it into force. But many men vigorously opposed the idea. Their logic, as the storefront below indicates, led to the conclusion that women had the right to have no rights.

HEADQUARTERS NATIONAL ASSOCIATION OPPOSED TO WOMAN SUFFRAGE

VOTES FOR MEN

Brown Brothers

Women had the force of reason, justice, and morality backing their argument but the states proceeded slowly with ratification. The happy group above had just received word in 1919 that the Nineteenth Amendment had reached the half-way point with ratification by California. Then the pace increased; within a year Tennessee became the thirty-eighth state to ratify, and voting rights for women became law.

Brown Brothers

of the previous generation. These writers attempted to come to grips realistically with the problems emanating from rapid social and economic change. Americans were seeking new amusements and a faster social pace. City dwellers were beginning to frequent cabarets and enjoy late evening restaurant life. Young people, who found the waltz and the two-step far too slow for their generation, eagerly danced the faster fox-trot or the more acrobatic bunny hug, turkey trot, or grizzly bear. The words of an Irving Berlin song ran, "If they do that dance in heaven, Shoot me, 'hon,' tonight at seven." By 1914 most towns and cities had movie theaters.

Nowhere were the new and changing moods in America better expressed than in the expanding role of women. In the early years of the century there was a dramatic increase in the participation of women in public life. They engaged in a wide variety of welfare and reform work. Women lobbied for protective labor laws, participated in the peace movement, and organized clubs to promote welfare causes. Employment opportunities multiplied. As noted in Chapter 21, more and more women became librarians, entered the health professions, and assumed employment in social work, publishing, and education.

Changing female clothing and life-styles reflected the beginning of greater personal emancipation for women. Dress styles forsook rustling petticoats and raised the hemline above the ankle. By 1914 it was claimed that "of all the details and underraiment that belonged in a woman's wardrobe ten years ago, the only one that survives is the stocking." Those who considered women's hair their crowning glory were shocked and chagrined when Irene Castle, the famous dancer, set the style for bobbed hair in 1914. A few daring young ladies smoked an occasional cigarette, to the horror of most citizens. A New York policeman in 1904 told a woman in an automobile who was lighting a cigarette, "You can't do that on Fifth Avenue," and promptly arrested her.

Americans were rapidly becoming avid sports fans, mostly as spectators rather than as active participants. Boxing, baseball, and football contests drew hundreds of thousands of people annually. In 1913, some 151,000 persons watched Philadelphia defeat New York in baseball's World Series. Football crowds of more than fifty thousand were not uncommon.

But Americans were concerned also with the mind and the spirit. Free, tax-supported schools underlay the nation's educational system, and by 1914 more than 19 million students attended elementary and secondary schools. Education moved in new and important directions. Progressive educators such as John Dewey of Columbia University insisted that schools should be more child-centered and that students should have more freedom. At the same time, there were increased demands for education in the practical arts, agriculture, and homemaking. College enrollments rose very rapidly. It is both interesting and significant to note that Presidents Roosevelt, Taft, and Wilson all had college degrees from leading Eastern universities.

Judged by church membership, Americans seemed religious. About 40 percent of the population claimed church membership in 1914. But much of this membership was nominal and did not represent any deep or living religious faith. Biblical criticism and new developments in science continued to weaken the hold of traditional Christianity. Liberal churchmen emphasized the proper role of the church in social change and insisted that the task of Christians and the church was to improve life in this world. Puritanism and fundamentalism, with their emphasis on personal salvation, remained strong. The great majority of citizens continued to believe in the moral values of truth, justice, and loyalty; they were optimistic and had faith in progress. When Woodrow Wilson entered the White House in March 1913, most Americans could look at their society and find it satisfactory.

Thomas Woodrow Wilson was born in Staunton, Virginia, in 1856. Of Scotch-Irish ancestry, he was the son of Joseph R. Wilson, minister of the First Presbyterian Church in Staunton. Growing to manhood in the South, Wilson adopted Southern views on such economic questions as the tariff; he held the traditional Southern attitude toward blacks. In 1890, having earned a doctorate in history and political science at Johns Hopkins, he returned to his alma mater Princeton, where he taught and wrote until 1902, when he became president of the university.

Princeton's new president was of slender build and just short of 5 feet 11 inches tall. He had a narrow face, blue-gray eyes, and a prominent jaw which seemed to signify determination. Except among a few close friends, Wilson tended to be cold and distant. He often displayed stubbornness, for to him it was more important to cling firmly to principles than to take part in any compromise. Wilson had great confidence in his own judgement and expressed little tolerance for those who disagreed with him. At the close of an argument with him at Princeton, a faculty member said, "Well, Dr. Wilson, there are two sides to every question," to which Wilson replied sharply, "Yes, a right side and a wrong side." Wilson was deeply religious and, like his predecessors at Princeton, a loyal Presbyterian.

In 1910 the New Jersey Democrats needed a respectable candidate for governor—one who carried no mark of bossism. Wilson appeared to be the ideal man, and because of difficulties at Princeton, he was ready to leave the university. Campaigning on a reform program, he defeated his Republican opponent by a large majority. Until the election of 1910, Wilson had been known as a political conservative, but as gov-ernor of New Jersey he inaugurated a progressive administration. He demonstrated strong executive leadership in pushing through a direct primary law, a corrupt practices act to reduce dishonesty in elections, legislation to regulate public utilities, and a workmen's compensation law. By 1911 this program made him a national figure.

During the campaign of 1912, Wilson developed his New Freedom program. Like many other progressives, he viewed the power and influence of big business as one of the great unsolved questions facing Americans. Yet he was vague on the means required to resolve the problem of monopoly and industrial power. Eventually Wilson relied on Louis Brandeis, a brilliant and progressive lawyer from Boston, to develop his policies on trust control. Brandeis emphasized the need for legislation to control big business and enforce competition. Other aspects of Wilson's New Freedom included tariff reduction, labor legislation to protect workingmen, and political reform. Wilson opposed the protective tariff because, to him, it represented "governmental favoritism" to special groups and the reduction of competition.

Although Wilson relied on his Cabinet and other advisers, especially his good friend from Texas, Colonel Edward M. House, the new President himself was determined to head the new administration. Having expressed admiration for executive leadership and responsibility, he now had an opportunity to put his concept of government into practice at the national level. He once declared that "we have grown more and more inclined to look to the President as the unifying force of our complex system, the leader of both his party and his nation." Wilson, like Roosevelt, added strength to the presidency.

The New Freedom in Action

In his inaugural address on March 4, 1913, Wilson outlined a specific program which called for implementation. Lower tariffs, banking and currency reform, restrictions on industrial abuses, expansion of scientific services, better credit for agriculture, and conservation of natural resources were among his favorite reforms. Government, too, said Wilson, had a responsibility for safeguarding the health of the nation and protecting individual workers who could not, by themselves, obtain justice.

Wilson's first legislative objective was tariff reduction. Both he and the Democratic party were committed to this end. He believed that the protective tariff gave special advantages to certain big businesses, raised the cost of living, and was therefore an indirect and unjust tax on consumers. Tariff reduction, as a political issue, however, was complicated by the fact that a number of Democrats favored protection for special industries in their districts. Sugar producers in Louisiana, textile manufacturers in North Carolina, and wool growers in the West were among those who wanted some degree of protection. Confronted with opposition from Democrats as well as Republicans, Wilson had to exercise strong party leadership to obtain tariff revision.

In the House, Representative Oscar Underwood of Alabama prepared a tariff bill which lowered duties on many items. This passed by a large majority. In the Senate, where the measure was under the management of Senator F. M. Simmons of North Carolina, the opposition was tremendous. Only after the President publicly denounced the numerous lobbyists who were working against tariff revision and took a strong stand on behalf of the measure did the Underwood-Simmons bill pass on October 2. It lowered ad valorem rates, on the average, about 10 percent. This was the first major downward revision of the tariff since the Civil War. The final measure included the important income tax provision. This set normal income tax rates at 1 percent on incomes over $3,000 for a single person, with an additional tax (surtax) of 1 percent on net income from $20,000 to $50,000. The law graduated rates upward to a maximum of 6 percent on incomes in excess of $500,000. Referring to the lower tariff and the progres-

sive income tax, the jubilant Secretary of Agriculture, David F. Houston, declared, "I did not much think we should live to see these things."

For students of the nation's economy, banking and currency reform appeared far more essential than tariff revision. By 1912 political leaders had joined businessmen, bankers, farmers, economists, and others in demanding modification of the country's banking structure and relief from what was known as the "money trust." The two major weaknesses of the banking system were the inelasticity of the currency and the concentration of credit facilities. Under the National Banking Act of 1863, there was no provision for credit expansion or contraction to meet the needs of business and agriculture. For example, in rural areas farmers required credit in the spring during planting season, but the banks had no way of expanding their resources at that time to meet this special need. Furthermore, most of the credit was concentrated in the large banks of major cities such as Chicago, Boston, and New York. The National Monetary Commission, commonly known as the Aldrich Commission, set up under the Aldrich-Vreeland Act of 1908, recommended new legislation in 1912.

After months of debate, Congress passed the Glass-Owen bill in December 1913, which established the Federal Reserve System. The new law divided the country into twelve districts and established a Federal Reserve bank in each district. All national banks were required to become members of the system; state-chartered banks were urged to join. Member banks had to subscribe at least 6 percent of their capital stock and surplus to the capital stock of the Federal Reserve bank in their district. In other words, the Federal Reserve banks were bankers' banks, owned by the individual members. The bill provided for a new currency known as Federal Reserve notes. These were printed by the Treasury but held in custody of the Federal Reserve banks. The law required that Federal Reserve banks must keep a 40 percent gold reserve behind all Federal Reserve notes. A seven-man Federal Reserve Board, appointed by the President, supervised the system.

To increase the elasticity of the currency, member banks could rediscount commercial paper, such as notes and mortgages, with the Federal Reserve bank. This meant that the reserve bank loaned money to the local bank on this type of security. Expansion and contraction of credit would be regulated or controlled by what was known as the rediscount, or interest, rate. To expand credit, the Federal Reserve Board would reduce rediscount rates to bankers, who in turn could charge lower interest rates to local customers. To restrict credit, the Board could raise the discount rate, thus discouraging borrowing and possibly checking speculation and inflation. The Federal Reserve System supplied better credit facilities, a sounder currency, and greater national coordination of the country's monetary and banking systems. It also represented much greater intervention and responsibility by government in the economy, a fact of special importance.

Having achieved tariff and banking legislation, the new administration turned to antitrust problems. Wilson believed firmly that competition was the best regulator of business and favored

Woodrow Wilson and Samuel Gompers.
The Granger Collection

legislation which, he hoped, would guarantee competitive practices. Wilson's solution to the problem of monopoly was a revision of the Sherman Antitrust Act to spell out precisely what behavior was unlawful. Roosevelt and his followers still believed that strict regulation of big business by a strong federal commission was the best approach to the question of monopoly and business concentration.

Wilson finally accepted the idea of a strong regulatory commission; in September 1914, Congress enacted the Federal Trade Commission Act. This law established a Commission, composed of five members appointed by the President, authorized to prevent unfair methods of competition. If it found a business engaged in unfair or illegal practices, the Commission could issue "cease and desist" orders to eliminate such methods of competition. Businessmen could appeal the orders of the Commission to the courts. After passage of this law, Wilson lost interest in efforts to eliminate unfair competition by statute. Nevertheless, in October 1914, Congress passed the Clayton Antitrust Act, which made certain business actions unlawful. Among other provisions, the law forbade price discrimination between purchasers of commodities, and it outlawed discounts or price reductions made on condition that the purchaser not buy from another supplier.

The most controversial provisions in the Clayton Antitrust Act were those designed to exempt labor and farm organizations from prosecution under the antitrust laws and to abolish injunctions in labor disputes. Samuel Gompers, president of the American Federation of Labor, officials of the Farmers' Union, and other labor and agricultural leaders pressed hard for these reforms. Gompers wrote early in 1914 that immunity from injunctions "is the paramount issue before the working people of our land." But Wilson refused to support what he regarded to be undemocratic, class legislation. A final compromise declared that neither farm and labor organizations nor their members should be considered "illegal combinations or conspiracies in restraint of trade under the anti-trust laws.'' Another section declared that court injunctions could not be granted in any dispute between employees and employers ''unless necessary to prevent irreparable injury to property, or to a property right.'' Gompers declared happily that the anti-injunction provision was labor's Magna Charta. Actually, this section did not substantially alter labor's position under the law. Wilson had no intention of exempting labor unions completely from court orders or injunctions while other groups in society were subject to them.

In 1913 and 1914, Wilson and the Congress had concentrated on tariff, banking, and monopoly legislation. By the latter year some of Wilson's closest advisers urged him to give business a breathing spell, and the President made a conscious effort to prove that he was not, indeed, antibusiness. Moreover, the outbreak of war in Europe during August 1914 temporarily diverted Wilson from further reforms. Critical diplomatic questions now occupied most of his time and attention.

As the nation contemplated the presidential election of 1916, the political situation was discouraging for Wilson and his party. Greater Republican unity and strength, dissension within Democratic ranks, and the war issue all dimmed Democratic prospects. The best chance for victory seemed to lie in more advanced social reform. This need for issues which would bring wider political backing drove President Wilson further along the road of domestic reform. His appointment of Louis D. Brandeis to the Supreme Court in January 1916 indicated a revived and extended presidential progressivism.

Wilson in 1916 gave his support to a wide variety of agricultural and labor legislation. In July Congress, with hearty presidential blessing, passed the Federal Farm Loan Act. This new measure provided for twelve federal farm land banks, one in each of the Federal Reserve districts. Farmers could borrow up to 50 percent of the value of their land and 20 percent of the value of their improvements. Interest rates were kept low, and loans could run from five to thirty years, repayable in annual installments. Farmers at last had a law which would meet their particular needs for long-term credit. Congress that year also enacted other important agricultural legislation. The United States Warehouse Act permitted the issuance of receipts by licensed warehouses against properly stored farm produce. These receipts could be used as collateral for bank loans. Of significance to farmers with automobiles was the Rural Post Roads Act. This law inaugurated the expenditure of federal money to match state funds in the building of so-called rural post roads. In 1914 Congress passed the Smith-Lever Act to assist in ''giving education and practical demonstrations in agriculture and home economics to persons not attending'' land-grant colleges. In 1917 Congress passed the Smith-Hughes Act, which provided federal matching funds to encourage the teaching of vocational agriculture and home economics in the secondary schools.

Congress and the President devoted attention to the needs of labor as well as agriculture. In August 1916, lawmakers passed the Kern-McGillicuddy bill, which provided workmen's compensation for federal employees. The Keating-Owen child-labor bill became law a short time later only to be declared unconstitutional in the Supreme Court case of *Hammer v. Dagenhart* two years later. In 1916 Congress also passed the Adamson Act, which set eight hours as the standard workday on all railroad lines exceeding 100 miles.

Wilson's New Diplomacy

Wilson entered the White House surprisingly uninformed about the intricacies of diplomacy.

''It would be an irony of fate,'' he wrote to a friend shortly before his inaugural, ''if my administration had to deal chiefly with foreign affairs." As president, Wilson faced the termination of what had been, for his country, a century of security from Europe's dangers. But as he searched his mind and the past for ideas to guide the policies of the nation, which was rapidly losing its isolation, he accepted a body of thought and a set of purposes which denied the validity of almost every important element in the nation's diplomatic tradition from Washington to Cleveland.

Wilson and his first secretary of state, William Jennings Bryan, rejected emotionally and intellectually the necessity of war. Wilson sought to build a peace structure on two basic notions regarding human society. The first, rooted in his Presbyterian faith, assumed a just and sovereign God and a universe based on moral law. For Wilson the laws of righteousness applied to nations as well as to individual men. The essential task of leadership, therefore, was that of demanding high standards of conduct from people and nations and encouraging them to subordinate selfish interests to the greater interests of peace and human progress. The second of Wilson's basic postulates concerned method. The best agency for achieving moral progress, he believed, was democracy, the political embodiment of man's essential goodness and rationality.

U.S. Marines in Haiti.   *Brown Brothers*

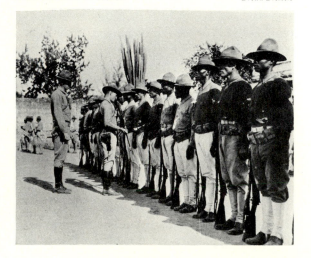

Wilson's world view, in short, looked to a moral order in which humankind, reasoning rightly and expressing its will through a worldwide democratic order, would compel aggressive, monarchical, or tyrannical rulers to avoid any unjust and irrational use of power.

It was completely fitting that Wilson's Secretary of State, the near-pacifist Bryan, negotiated during 1913 a series of bilateral treaties whereby the signatories agreed not to resort to war except at the end of a twelve-month period. It was thought that a year would be enough for tempers to cool and for diplomats to determine the superior legal and moral position in any conflict.

Wilson soon discovered occasions for putting his new diplomacy into effect. Convinced that the Taft policy of supporting the Six Power Consortium in China would undermine that nation's territorial and administrative integrity and thus constitute a form of imperialism, Wilson withdrew United States support.

But in Latin America, Wilson's moralism spelled intervention, not withdrawal, for the issues were different. The President, in March 1913, announced to the press that he intended to promote the interest of the common people in the Western Hemisphere. "We can have no sympathy," he said, "with those who seek to seize the power of government to advance their own personal interests and ambitions." Under this principle he denied recognition to Victoriano Huerta of Mexico, who assumed power in 1913 following the overthrow and murder of his predecessor. To rescue the Mexican population from such a dictator, the President encouraged the sale and shipment of arms to Huerta's political enemies. In April 1914, following the arrest of some American sailors at Tampico, United States forces occupied Veracruz. Ultimately Wilson's Mexican policies had the desired effect. Huerta, facing ever-stronger political and military opposition, fled to Spain, and in 1915 the United States recognized Venustiano Carranza.

With even greater confidence Wilson dispatched American marines to Haiti and Santo Domingo, two Caribbean republics, to restore order. These involvements again brought a measure of political stability to the two nations, but not because the Latin Americans accepted democracy or the legitimacy of Wilson's actions. They responded positively simply because they were powerless to challenge the will of an American president. Many educated Latin Americans, interested in law and order, lauded the President's purpose and hoped that his mission might eventually triumph. Many, however, objected strongly to United States interference in the affairs of independent states.

Conclusion

Even before Wilson's reelection in November 1916, the progressive movement had largely run its course. The ardor of some reformers had begun to cool as they saw many progressive objectives achieved. Moreover, the attention of the President and Congress was diverted increasingly toward international problems and the threat of war. But the changes wrought between 1900 and 1917 were of fundamental importance, and they left a permanent imprint upon the nation and its people. The American people had set out to solve problems emerging from unregulated industrialism by means of the positive state.

The progressive movement, which had begun at the turn of the century, continued to expand its influence during Wilson's first term. Progressivism marked the expansion of governmental powers at both the state and national levels. It expressed itself in greater government regulation, as well as in large increases in state and federal functions. Between 1900 and 1917 its innovations included primarily more protection for labor, control over money and banking, guarantees against impure food and drugs, credit for farmers, and conservation of natural resources. It was the income tax which, in the long run, provided the money to underwrite many of the new federal programs and to permit steps toward the social welfare state. Progressives had sought to make government more responsible to the people by adopting such measures as the primary, initiative and referendum, direct election of senators, and woman suffrage. But progressives also believed that political and economic reform went hand in hand—that one without the other would solve few problems. One of the greatest failures of the reformers was their unwillingness to insist on equal rights for blacks. Throughout the progressive era, blacks continued to suffer from discrimination in housing and employment, and in the exercise of their political rights. Only a few weak voices cried out against racial injustice.

It is true that the progressive movement did not solve all the political, economic, and social problems facing the United States, but it demonstrated how improvements could be brought about without revolution or radical change. As Frederick Lewis Allen, an observant chronicler of American life, wrote in *The Big Change*, the progressive movement showed "that when the ship of state was not behaving as it should, one did not need to scrap it and build another, but could, by a series of adjustments and improvements, repair it while keeping it running." In essence this was progressivism.

SUGGESTED READINGS

The best and most complete biography of William Howard Taft is Henry Pringle's *William Howard Taft* (2 vols., 1934). Paolo E. Coletta's *The Presidency of William Howard Taft* (1973) is also excellent. On Taft's political problems see K. W. Hechler's *Insurgency: Personalities and Politics of the Taft Era* (1940). George E. Mowry's *Theodore Roosevelt and the Progressive Movement** (1946) argues that Taft's difficulties in the presidency stemmed from his basic conservatism. A biography which throws further light on the Taft years is Richard Lowitt's *George W. Norris: The Making of a Progressive, 1861–1912* (1963). The election of 1912 has been most adequately discussed by Arthur S. Link in the first volume of his multivolume biography of Woodrow Wilson, entitled *Wilson: The Road to the White House** (1947). A briefer account of the election of 1912 can be found in Link's excellent volume *Woodrow Wilson and the Progressive Era, 1910–1917** (1954).

Besides consulting the standard texts in diplomatic history for Taft's foreign policy, see also the evaluation of Philander C. Knox in S. F. Bemis (ed.), *American Secretaries of State and Their Diplomacy* (1929), vol. IX, as well as the selection on Knox by Walter Scholes in Norman A. Graebner (ed.), *An Uncertain Tradition: American Secretaries of State in the Twentieth Century** (1961). Charles Vevier has dealt with America's China policy in *The United States and China* (1955).

The best study of Woodrow Wilson and the fullest account of his administration is Arthur Link's yet uncompleted multivolume biography. Up to 1974, Link had published *Wilson: The Road to the White House** (1947); *Wilson: The New Freedom** (1956); *Wilson: Struggle for Neutrality, 1914–1915* (1960); *Wilson: Confusions and Crises, 1915–1916* (1964); and *Wilson: Campaigns for Progressivism and Peace, 1916–1917* (1965). Good single-volume biographies of Wilson are H. C. F. Bell's *Woodrow Wilson and the People* (1945) and J. A. Garraty's *Woodrow Wilson* (1956), while John Blum's *Woodrow Wilson and the Politics of Morality** (1956) provides a critical interpretation of the Wilson presidency.

On specific major issues in Wilson's first administration, see the relevant parts of F. W. Taussig's *Tariff History of the United States** (8th ed., 1931), which deals with the Underwood-Simmons tariff. P. M. Warburg's *The Federal Reserve System* (2 vols., 1930) covers the origin and development of the new banking system. For a discussion of the income tax see the pertinent sections in D. R. Dewey's *Financial History of the United States* (1936) and W. J. Schultz and M. R. Caine's *Financial Development of the United States* (1937). Antitrust legislation has been discussed by Charles W. Dunn in *The Federal Trade Commission: An Experiment in the Control of Business* (1932). Books dealing with labor issues in the years just before World War I include volume III of *History of Labour in the United States* (1935) by John R. Commons and others, and Philip Taft's *The A. F. of L. in the Time of Gompers* (1957).

The sociological history of the period can be traced both in Walter Lord's *The Good Years** (1960) and in H. U. Faulkner's *The Quest for Social Justice* (1931).
*indicates availability in paperback.

25

The Great War and After

On June 28, 1914, a Serbian nationalist assassinated Archduke Franz Ferdinand, heir to the Austrian throne, at the Bosnian city of Sarajevo. That event proved to be a watershed in the history of the modern world, for it brought to an end a century of slow, but steady, progress toward liberalism and democracy and opened a new age of violence, revolution, dictatorship, and war. Assassinations were common enough in early twentieth-century Europe, but the murder of the Archduke brought into direct conflict two powerful, thoroughly armed alliances.

For most Europeans in 1914 war was unthinkable, eliminated supposedly by the destructiveness of modern weapons and the rationality of mankind. So secure seemed Europe's peace that the murder at Sarajevo created no premonition of disaster. Still the pressures for war in Europe had been accumulating for a generation. The rise of modern Germany to a commanding military and industrial position in Europe, added to the German-Austrian dual alliance of 1879, threatened Europe's equilibrium and its former security. German power, easily observable, would have been disturbing enough to Britain and France, the two major pillars of Europe's traditional order of power. But the German Kaiser, William II, made clear through the rhetoric of German nationalism that he intended to use his country's developing military and naval might to establish German primacy in world affairs. To offset the German threat, Britain and France formed the Entente Cordiale in 1904; they then joined Russia in the Triple Entente in 1907 to mass Europe's power in a final defense of the old order.

Imaginative diplomacy might still have prevented the impending war, but in the test of wills between two armed alliances time and inflexibility became the determinants of national action. Every country's military strategy demanded a first strike; this compelled almost immediate national decisions for or against war. Each alliance, moreover, convinced that firmness alone would prevent a general war, refused to compromise under pressure. Behind Serbia stood Russia, encouraging Serbian resistance; behind Russia—France and England. Germany extended equal guarantees to Austria. Mobilization, rapid and overwhelming, suddenly closed every avenue of retreat from disaster. With armies in motion and no offers of compromise forthcoming, each government in turn made its final decision for war.

Events of 1914 bore a significance beyond the world's immediate understanding. Yet those German and French soldiers who rushed into the Battle of the Marne were to touch the lives of American people as few, at that moment, could anticipate. For Europe, in the failure of its diplomacy to avoid war, had entered upon a suicidal struggle of sufficient magnitude to place its great stabilizing traditions in jeopardy. Indeed, so enormous was the ultimate power expended, so great the death toll, so balanced the forces locked in battle, that Europe could escape from its self-imposed catastrophe only by calling upon external power. It was the outside world with which Britain and France were aligned—Australia, New Zealand, eventually and most importantly, the United States—that brought final victory to the Allies. The Great War of 1914 demonstrated that Europe's balance of power, self-contained for three centuries, had become submerged in a worldwide balance in which Europe's destiny would henceforth be determined in large measure by power that lay outside the European continent.

Pressures on American Neutrality

In the view of most Americans, Europe's decision for war in 1914 exceeded rational limits. How could Europe, the most civilized of continents, terminate a century of unprecedented material and institutional progress by engaging in such self-destruction? For weeks editors had reassured their readers that war was impossible. The *New York Times* proclaimed as late as July 28, "That war is too dreadful for imagining and because it is too dreadful it cannot happen." When at last editors accepted the reality of conflict, they still could say with the *Independent*: "Luckily we have the Atlantic between us and Europe. It is their war, not ours." Most Americans applauded the President's proclamation of neutrality, as well as his appeal that they be "impartial in thought as well as in action." The war, Wilson said simply, is one "with which we have nothing to do, whose causes cannot touch us." Remaining neutral the United States would keep herself free "to do what is honest . . . and truly serviceable for the peace of the world."

Impartiality soon proved to be an illusion. The American people might want peace, but they could not remain neutral. "Hyphenated" Americans—immigrants and first-generation Americans—generally favored national policies that served the countries of their origin. Many of the nation's 12 million German-Americans and Irish-Americans openly supported the German cause. But overwhelmingly American sentiment favored the Allies. For old-line Americans, largely of English descent, the ties of culture, tradition, and interest were too firm to be broken. Indeed, pro-British editors, from August 1914 onward, warned the nation that German militarism and autocracy threatened the established European order. Could the United States remain neutral and permit the war to run its normal course? *Harper's Weekly* reminded its readers that it was the guardianship of the British navy which had permitted the United States to develop internally without carrying the burden of armaments. Germany could not become a major maritime power in the Atlantic without coaling stations or colonies in the Caribbean. Thus German ambitions on the high seas seemed to constitute a special threat to the Monroe Doctrine.

Washington officialdom, overwhelmingly representative of the country's Protestant, middle-class culture, was admittedly pro-British. Robert Lansing, first counselor in the State Department, and Walter Hines Page, United States ambassador to London, regarded German autocracy as a threat to American democracy. Wilson's trusted adviser, Colonel Edward House, warned the President in August 1914, "German success will ultimately mean trouble for us." This conviction—that American security demanded a British victory—really left no room for policies of genuine neutrality. Specific pressures militating against United States neutrality—the British propaganda campaign, the huge American financial investment in the Allied cause, and German submarine warfare—raised concrete issues which drove Washington and Berlin apart. But had the American people been thoroughly impartial, those issues would scarcely have existed or mattered.

British propaganda made a massive assault on American emotions. Having cut the transatlantic cable to Germany, the British and French governments were able to assure an Allied view of the war within the United States. They could expose the American people to only those aspects of the war which reflected adversely on Germany. German actions often reinforced British propaganda, for the invasion of Belgium, execution of British nurse Edith Cavell, long-range shelling of Paris, aerial bombardment of cities, use of the submarine against defenseless merchant and passenger vessels all had the effect of outraging the American mind. German propaganda, on the other hand, was clumsy and largely ineffective. To be effective, propaganda, like seeds, must fall on fertile ground; the very ease with which British propaganda provoked strong reaction in the United States demonstrated its general appeal to a thoroughly unneutral country.

Similarly the enormous financial commitment to Britain and France was less the cause of the ultimate American decision for war than evidence that the nation's financial and industrial leaders favored an Allied victory. The failure of neutrality came first. Had the country's industrialists been less partisan, they would not have retooled for war production to fill British and French orders with such enthusiasm. British control of the Atlantic merely coincided with their preferences. American business sentiments became even more pronounced when New York bankers pressed the Wilson administration for permission to finance Allied purchases in the United States. In August 1914, the President, on Secretary of State William J. Bryan's advice, had restricted private loans to belligerents in accordance with the official policy of neutrality. "Money," warned Secretary of State Bryan, "is the worst of all contrabands because it commands everything else." Still the State Department, to maintain Allied trade, permitted short-term Allied credit arrangements. And in 1915, when it became apparent that the Allies could no longer sustain their war effort—and hence their purchases in America—without additional credit, Wilson overruled Bryan and abandoned all restrictions on loans. This cleared the way for the public sale of Allied bonds. By April 1917, American investors had contributed in excess of $2 billion to the Allied war effort.

The Submarine Issue

Ultimately Berlin's reliance on the submarine to control British waters created the point of friction in United States–German relations that led to war. Again it was the absence of genuine neutrality that mattered. Had the outcome of the war been of no concern to Americans, this nation could have eliminated the submarine issue by either granting equal access for all belligerents to American production or terminating its war trade. Jefferson in his embargo had once made the latter choice. But after 1914, the United States insisted upon its right to ship food and

NOTICE!

TRAVELLERS intending to embark on the Atlantic voyage are reminded that a state of war exists between Germany and her allies and Great Britain and her allies; that the zone of war includes the waters adjacent to the British Isles; that, in accordance with formal notice given by the Imperial German Government, vessels flying the flag of Great Britain, or of any of her allies, are liable to destruction in those waters and that travellers sailing in the war zone on ships of Great Britain or her allies do so at their own risk.

IMPERIAL GERMAN EMBASSY
WASHINGTON, D. C., APRIL 22, 1915.

Brown Brothers

the German government was American willingness to accept this massive infringement on its maritime rights, for this demonstrated an unneutral attitude in Washington.

Germany retaliated with the only effective means available. On February 4, 1915, the German government informed Washington of its intention to establish a war zone around the British Isles. The refusal of countries to assert their neutral rights against Britain, the note complained, compelled Germany to impose a blockade. German vessels could not guarantee the safety of persons or cargoes belonging to neutrals; therefore the United States should keep its ships, goods, and citizens out of the war zone.

Wilson's response was predictable. Should German vessels attack a ship carrying an American flag and destroy American lives, he warned Berlin, the United States would view the attack as a violation of its neutral rights and would "hold the Imperial German Government to a strict accountability." The President, in short, would tolerate no German policy that impeded the flow of American goods and citizens to England. What aggravated Germany's dilemma was its reliance on the submarine. This frail and basically defenseless craft could not practice historic rules of "visit and search" without running the risk of destruction from ramming or, in the case of armed merchantmen, from a sudden, direct hit. In self-protection, a submarine commander had no choice but to launch his torpedoes and run, thereby deserting his obligation for the safety and welfare of survivors. This unprecedented moral and legal problem posed by the submarine, rather than its effectiveness as a commerce destroyer, determined Wilson's response to German policy.

German officials, seeking to avoid trouble with the United States, agreed to respect neutral flags and operate, as far as possible, under the traditional rules of maritime warfare. Within weeks after the announcement of the blockade, however, German torpedoes sank the British liner

munitions to Britain. Wilson's demand that Germany restrict its use of the submarine was simply his attempt to bridge the gap between his desire to secure a British victory and his intention to avoid war.

Britain, as early as August 1914, determined to use its naval power to impede the movement of goods into Germany and, more specifically, to control American shipping. British war vessels stopped American ships enroute to Germany, as well as to neutral ports, and examined them for contraband, broadly defined. In November, the British mined the North Sea so thoroughly that no ship could proceed without specific instructions from British officials. Finally, in March 1915, the British placed all trade with Germany under penalty of confiscation. What disturbed

Falaba, with the loss of one American crewman, and damaged the American tanker *Gulflight*. Shortly thereafter, the German ambassador placed a newspaper advertisement in the New York press, warning Americans to avoid travel on British vessels. On May 7, a submarine sank the giant British liner *Lusitania* off the Irish coast, with the loss of almost 1,200 persons, including 128 Americans. With a large segment of the American press demanding reprisal, Wilson on May 10 asserted: "There is such a thing as a man being too proud to fight. There is such a thing as a nation being so right that it does not need to convince others by force that it is right." The State Department's note of May 13 was mild, reminding Berlin that Germany had again broken the rules of maritime warfare and insisting that it take immediate steps to prevent a recurrence. The Germans replied that the *Lusitania* had been carrying munitions and guns and hence was no ordinary merchant vessel.

Wilson's advisers split over Germany's response. Some favored a second, more determined, warning to Berlin; others, led by Bryan, argued the legitimacy of the German position. The Secretary reminded the President early in June that he had not objected to the sinkings when American citizens were not involved. It was essential, Bryan said, to keep Americans out of the war zone. When the President rejected his advice and dispatched a second, more belligerent, *Lusitania* note, Bryan resigned. To succeed him Wilson named Lansing , already known for his extreme pro-British sympathies. Wilson viewed himself as the special protector of international law and morality. Preferring principle to expediency—at least in his relations with Germany—he refused to keep Americans at home or to relent in his opposition to German submarine practices. For the moment he had his way. Berlin, still hopeful of avoiding a break with the United States, instructed its U-boat commanders on June 6 not to sink passenger vessels, neutral or belligerent, without warning.

Twice within the next twelve months Germany and the United States were on the brink of war. After two Americans lost their lives on the torpedoed British liner *Arabic* in August 1915, Germany's moderate Chancellor Theobald von Bethmann-Hollweg soothed ruffled American feelings by offering apologies, indemnities for the dead, and the assurance that submarine attacks on merchant shipping were suspended. Again, in early 1916, when the sinking of the unarmed French passenger ship *Sussex* resulted in injury to several Americans, President Wilson's stern ultimatum extorted from Berlin the *Sussex* pledge that no submarine would sink unresisting merchant or passenger vessels without warning and without provisions for the safety of noncombatants. Wilson had now so fully committed America's honor and prestige on the issue of "strict accountability" that a renewal of German submarine warfare would almost inevitably lead to war.

Early in 1916 the President placed himself at the front of the burgeoning preparedness movement by proposing to Congress that the Army be drastically enlarged and the Navy undertake a building program which would make it second to none by 1925. He carried the fight to the American people in an extended speaking tour and, after a sharp struggle with pacifist groups and progressives, succeeded in pushing most of his program through Congress.

Wilson was acutely aware that the United States, with its amazing productivity, had become the key to the gigantic struggle raging in Europe. Germany, he knew, would not accept defeat without warring on American neutral rights in a final act of desperation. By 1916, Wilson concluded that this country's continued peace required a termination of the war. Early that year he supported Colonel House's mediation plan by dispatching him to Europe. In London, House negotiated with the British Foreign Minister the House-Grey Memorandum, a document which promised that the President, at some moment regarded opportune by the British and French governments, would propose a conference to end the war. Should Germany reject reasonable terms, the United States "would probably enter the war against Germany." When Wilson suggested after Germany's *Sussex* pledge that the time for a conference had arrived, London, now convinced that an Allied victory was possible, rejected the proposal outright. The British simultaneously tightened the blockade of the continent. Subsequent British censorship of United States mail and blacklisting of American firms regarded as pro-German embittered Wilson even more; he considered the drastic step of prohibiting loans and reducing exports to the Allies. Still he did neither, largely because he hesitated to endanger the Allied war effort.

With his mind on peace in 1916, Wilson entered his campaign for reelection. Unsure of his capacity to avoid war and desirous of running on his domestic record, the President hoped to avoid the foreign-policy issue. The Republican leadership, having broken the Progressive revolt, anticipated victory behind Charles Evans Hughes, distinguished former governor of New York and associate justice of the United States Supreme Court. The Republicans planned to capitalize on Wilson's alleged failure to protect the nation's honor in the Atlantic. Wilson hoped for a middle course which emphasized patriotism. Still the Democratic National Convention

could not resist the temptation to praise Wilson for keeping the nation out of war. With some reluctance, Wilson campaigned on his record of preserving American neutrality. This proved to be an attractive issue and encouraged the Democrats to identify Hughes with more bellicose Republicans and to accuse him of favoring war. Appealing to peace and progressivism, Wilson won a narrow victory, holding the South and capturing the major states of the West. His late surge in California was crucial.

Backed by the November victory, Wilson made a final peace effort on his own initiative. During December, he dispatched identical notes to all belligerent governments, requesting statements of war aims. Again the effort was doomed simply because the war's toll predisposed contestants to seek compensation that could come only with victory. None of the replies to Wilson's notes contained any offer of compromise. The President voiced another plea for peace without victory in his noted Senate speech of January 22, 1917. "Only a peace between equals can last," he warned. Again he was rebuffed. Peace without victory was peace without gain; this no nation at war dared to consider.

Committed to victory, the German high command now reached a crisis of decision. Powerful spokesmen for the German army, especially Field Marshal Paul von Hindenburg, demanded resumption of unrestricted submarine warfare in a drastic effort to stop the flow of food and munitions into England and France. Without such a policy he would no longer take responsibility for what occurred on the Western Front. In early 1917 the struggle behind the scenes between the cautious Bethmann-Hollweg and the impatient military chiefs came to a head. On January 8 the German government agreed to release U-boats on February 1. The German ambassador in Washington informed Lansing of the decision on January 31. Now every vessel afloat in English waters was subject to attack without warning. Wilson, following his

Sussex threat, severed diplomatic ties with Germany.

Thereafter the pressures for United States involvement in Europe's war were relentless. Reports from the Western Front placed the Allies on the verge of military collapse. American ship captains remained in port, unwilling to enter the war zone without armaments. On February 25, the destruction of the British liner *Laconia* demonstrated German determination to control English waters; on February 26, the President failed to wrest authority from Congress to arm merchant vessels. Two days earlier the White House had received a copy of the Zimmermann Telegram, intercepted by British intelligence, in which Alfred Zimmermann of the German Foreign Office proposed that Mexico enter an alliance with Germany in the event of an American declaration of war. Mexico, in return, would receive Texas, New Mexico, and California.

As the sinkings mounted during late February and March, the American press demanded war. On April 2, the President read his war message to Congress, committing the nation both to victory and to lasting peace. Congress responded quickly, the Senate adopting the war resolution on April 4 by a vote of 82 to 6; the House, two days later, 373 to 50. The United States was now at war.

Mobilization for War

America's declaration of war raised little for the Allies except their morale. German submarines continued to destroy Allied shipping at the rate of 900,000 tons per month. The U.S. Navy Department immediately assigned destroyers to antisubmarine duty in an effort to neutralize the German sea offensive. General Joseph Joffre, commander of the French army in 1916, had estimated that a half million Americans would be required to assure an Allied victory. But the War Department, under Secretary Newton D. Baker, proceeded to organize an army of 4 million men. What underwrote this effort was the Selective Service Act of May 18, 1917, a statute requiring all men between the ages of twenty-one and thirty (later forty-five) to register for the draft. So effective was the mobilization that within eighteen months the United States was able to transport an American Expeditionary Force of 2 million soldiers to France.

America's economic response to war began with Sarajevo. By 1917 Allied borrowing and the sale of Allied securities had pumped $5 billion of purchasing power into the American economy, enough to produce a major boom in the steel and munitions industries. Allied purchases of wheat, meat, and sugar had produced unprecedented prosperity in American agriculture as well. For a time the unregulated American economy responded to Europe's demands with considerable success, but during 1915 the competition for raw materials, labor, and limited railroad and port facilities shot prices upward, causing distress among American workingmen and European buyers alike.

Actually the federal coordination of industry was already under way. In August 1915, the decision to expand the Navy prompted the creation of a Committee on Industrial Preparedness to construct an inventory of American industries capable of producing munitions. The National Defense Act of June 1916 empowered the President to make demands on American industry in the interest of national defense. In August, the Military Appropriations Act established a Council of National Defense with an advisory commission to plan a large military force. After April 1917, the War Department still found it impossible to coordinate estimates of the various bureaus for the material required to equip an army. For that reason the Council of National Defense in July 1917 established the War Industries Board. Still it was not until after the appointment of Bernard Baruch to the Board's chairmanship in the spring of 1918 that the problems of materials allocation were finally brought under control.

The War Industries Board, having no authority to negotiate contracts, operated as an advisory and informational agency. Its authority and prestige lay in its accumulated knowledge and in the general recognition among officials and industrialists that the only alternative to cooperation was absolute chaos. Its decisions, once established, generally determined the behavior of others. To bring general efficiency to American production, as well as to conserve raw materials and transportation, the War Industries Board introduced standardization of products and a sharp decrease in the number of styles and designs. This made it possible for countless industries to contribute to the manufacture of rifles, artillery, and other military items. The Board curtailed the production of many commodities meant primarily for civilian consumption, permitting the automobile industry, for example, to operate at only 25 percent of capacity in 1918. Controlling prices by agreement, not law, the Board stabilized the prices of most basic raw materials. Consumer prices, however, inched upward throughout the war, bringing large profits to many producers and merchandisers. Unable to limit profits, the federal government, in October 1917, imposed a tax on those that exceeded the average of the immediate prewar years.

Europe's struggle exerted pressure on the nation's food as well as its industrial resources. The export of American food rose from a yearly average of 7 million tons during the years 1912 to 1914 to over 12 million tons in 1917–1918 and over 18.6 million in 1918–1919. Competitive bidding for raw and processed foods created both wild price increases and profiteering. The Lever Act of August 1917 established both the Food Administration and the Fuel Administration, the latter to govern the use of coal. To head the important Food Administration the President called on Herbert Hoover, the American mining engineer known for his brilliant success in handling Belgian relief during the early war years. Hoover's program as food administrator was similar to that of Baruch's for industry. Operating with a minimum of regulations and a staff of volunteers, Hoover managed to bring remarkable order to the marketing and distribution of grain. He encouraged the production of hogs and wheat, two essential commodities, by establishing prices that guaranteed a profit to both farmers and processors. He opposed retail price controls but asked the nation's women to practice restraint in their purchases of wheat and meat. By curtailing food consumption and the profit margins of food processors, Hoover reduced the gap between farm and retail prices.

United States shipments of food and equipment to Europe required a tremendous fleet of merchant vessels. In September 1916, Congress established the United States Shipping Board to direct the flow of goods across the Atlantic. With the declaration of war in April 1917, Congress chartered the United States Emergency Fleet Corporation to oversee the construction of a "bridge of ships" to the Allies. Under the direction of Edward N. Hurley, the Emergency Fleet Corporation succeeded in producing hundreds of vessels. The huge yard at Hog Island, near Philadelphia, demonstrated the efficacy of constructing ships by mass-production techniques, although the Hog Island yard did not deliver its first ship until December 1918, almost a month after the end of the war.

William G. McAdoo, Secretary of the Treasury, produced another triumph for federal regulation as chairman of the United States Railroad Administration. At the outbreak of the war, the railroad industry revealed all the ills of excessive competition, especially the duplication of terminal facilities, tracks, and rolling stock. Rail traffic became so congested from lack of coordination that it neared the point of breakdown. The Railroad Administration, gaining control late in 1917, assigned skilled engineers to the running of the trains, directed traffic by shorter routes, increased carloads, enforced the com-

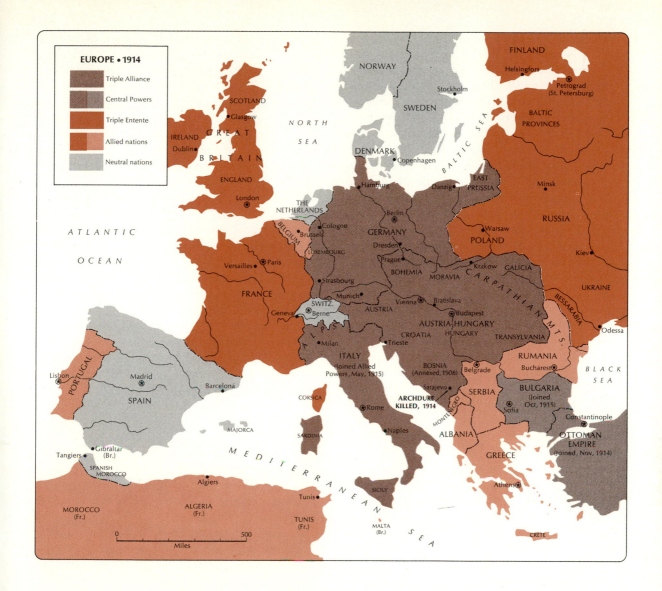

EUROPE · 1914

- Triple Alliance
- Central Powers
- Triple Entente
- Allied nations
- Neutral nations

FINLAND

Helsingfors

Petrograd
(St. Petersburg)

NORWAY

BALTIC
PROVINCES

SCOTLAND

Glasgow

Stockholm

SWEDEN

Minsk

IRELAND

GREAT

Dublin

BRITAIN

NORTH
SEA

DENMARK

Copenhagen

Hamburg

Danzig

EAST
PRUSSIA

BALTIC SEA

RUSSIA

ENGLAND

London

THE
NETHERLANDS

Cologne

Berlin

Warsaw

Kiev

BELGIUM

Brussels

GERMANY

POLAND

ATLANTIC

LUXEMBOURG

Dresden

OCEAN

Versailles

Paris

Prague

Krakow

GALICIA

UKRAINE

Strasbourg

BOHEMIA

MORAVIA

CARPATHIAN MTS.

FRANCE

SWITZ.

Munich

AUSTRIA

Vienna

Bratislava

Budapest

BESSARABIA

Odessa

Geneva

Berne

ALPS

Milan

Trieste

AUSTRIA-HUNGARY

CROATIA

HUNGARY

TRANSYLVANIA

BLACK
SEA

PORTUGAL

Lisbon

Madrid

Barcelona

SPAIN

CORSICA

ITALY
(Joined Allied
Powers, May, 1915)

Rome

BOSNIA
(Annexed, 1908)

Belgrade

RUMANIA

Bucharest

**ARCHDUKE
KILLED, 1914**

Sarajevo

SERBIA

BULGARIA
(Joined
Oct., 1915)

Constantinople

MAJORCA

SARDINIA

Naples

MONTENEGRO

Sofia

ALBANIA

OTTOMAN
EMPIRE
(Joined, Nov., 1914)

Tangiers

Gibraltar
(Br.)

GREECE

SPANISH
MOROCCO

Athens

MEDITERRANEAN

Algiers

SICILY

MOROCCO
(Fr.)

ALGERIA
(Fr.)

Tunis

MALTA
(Br.)

SEA

CRETE

TUNIS
(Fr.)

0   500
Miles

mon use of terminals, and coordinated railroad and ocean shipping. At war's end the railroads, despite their unprecedented volume of traffic, again had a surplus of 300,000 cars.

Economic Change

Ultimately the cost of the war had to be borne by the American people through loans and taxes. For the United States the cost of war from April 1917 to June 1920 was approximately $24 billion. Washington covered Allied demands on the American economy with loans totaling about

$9.5 billion. The nation met these expenditures with $10.7 billion in special wartime taxes and $23 billion in deficit spending. In August 1919, the war debt had reached $24.5 billion. It was this growing indebtedness that exerted the wartime pressures on price levels. By far the most important wartime tax was the excess profits tax which, in the year ending June 30, 1918, yielded over $2 billion. In its borrowing the government supplemented its reliance on bank credit with huge flotations of Liberty Bonds, of which 30 percent, totaling $7 billion, were purchased by citizens with annual incomes of $2,000 or less.

Responding to the demands of war, the American economy expanded astonishingly. But those responsible for the miracle of production did not share the rewards equally. Labor's experience was mixed. President Wilson's War Labor Board, established in April 1918, represented the interests of labor in wartime. It ruled out strikes and lockouts in the cause of industrial production, but it also encouraged unionization by recognizing the principle of collective bargaining. Union membership responded briskly. By 1919 Samuel Gompers's AF of L boasted a membership of 4.1 million as compared with 2.7 million in 1914. Labor's gains came largely from full employment rather than wage increases, for wages scarcely kept pace with the soaring cost of living. Those with fixed incomes suffered a comparative depression in the midst of wartime prosperity. The nation's farmers fared much better, for wartime food demands resulted in rapidly rising prices and a gain in farm income from $4 billion in 1914 to $10 billion in 1918.

By far the greatest profits, of course, went to giant corporations engaged in war production. Net incomes of large American corporations, as a whole, almost doubled between 1913 and 1916. Facing a heavy excess profits tax, corporations deflated their profit margins by paying large salaries and bonuses to their top officials. Thus the private income of business executives rose sharply. The number of those whose incomes ranged between $30,000 and $40,000 increased from 6,000 in 1914 to 15,400 in 1918.

The Quest for National Unity

Mobilization of the American economy proved much simpler than mobilization of the American mind. Thousands of Americans never accepted the necessity, much less the morality, of America's decision for war. A powerful and vociferous minority, convinced that the United States had no vital interest in a German defeat, attacked the Wilson administration openly and persistently. Conscious of the need for national unity, the President, on April 14, 1917, appointed his Committee on Public Information with a vigorous and dedicated chairman, George Creel. By appealing to patriotism and anti-German sentiment among the nation's intelligentsia, Creel managed to enlist artists, actors, writers, and educators, who flooded the country with propaganda pamphlets, posters, and carefully prepared newspaper editorials. Creel unleashed on the country thousands of public speakers who barraged movie audiences, public gatherings, schoolrooms, women's clubs, and even foreign language groups with a torrent of anti-German propaganda.

Wilson, in his conduct of the war, enjoyed the nonactive support of a vast majority of Americans. But the support which he required to silence his opposition came from a powerful minority of national leaders who believed that the government had the obligation to smother wartime dissent even with stern reprisal. Elihu Root delighted a crowd at the Union League Club in August 1917 by declaring that "there are men walking about the streets of this city tonight who ought to be taken out at sunrise tomorrow and shot for treason."

In accepting the Espionage Act of June 1917, Congress established a policy of wartime repression. The law was framed to discourage, by fines up to $10,000 and imprisonment up to twenty years, any "false reports or false statements" which might interfere with military operations or with recruitment and enlistment. The Espionage Act failed to quiet antiwar activities of radical and pacifist groups, so Congress broadened its definition of espionage in the Sedition Act of May 1918 to include anyone who might obstruct the sale of United States bonds or "willfully utter, print, write, or publish any disloyal, profane, scurrilous, or abusive language about the form of government of the United States, or the Constitution . . . or the flag of the United States, or the uniform of the Army or Navy, or bring the form of government . . . into contempt." The new law silenced more critics, but not all of them.

Armed with these two measures, federal officials proceeded to censor movies and the press. They ordered the motion picture industry to bury all pacifist films. What occupied the newspaper censors was not occasional major publications such as Oswald Villard's *New York Evening Post*, which opposed national policy, but the dozens of small radical and reform presses which never ceased to condemn the war. In August 1917, the government ordered the New York postmaster to bar *Masses* from the mails. In November 1917, it suppressed two Socialist papers, the *Milwaukee Leader* and the *New York Call*. Under the Trading with the Enemy Act of October 1917, the government put restrictions on the foreign language press, compelling most German language newspapers to drop their criticism of the war.

Ultimately the nation's drive for conformity centered on individuals. The most notable convicted under the espionage and sedition laws were Eugene V. Debs and Victor L. Berger, both leading Socialists. Debs, who defended the right of free speech at Canton, Ohio, in June 1918, and then for two hours attacked capitalism and predicted the ultimate triumph of socialism, was indicted for provoking resistance to government and sentenced to ten years in prison. Berger, editor of the *Milwaukee Leader*, was indicted in 1918 for his antiwar editorials, and in February 1919, with four other Socialists, received a twenty-year prison sentence. Later he won an appeal to the United States Supreme Court. The case of Charles T. Schenck, general secretary of the Socialist party, was noteworthy because it presented the occasion for Justice Oliver Wendell Holmes's opinion in *Schenck v. United States*. Holmes upheld the conviction on the grounds that the defendant's words had created "a clear and present danger" to the national security.

Wartime pressures for conformity were private and local as well as public and federal. In almost every community editors and patriotic groups exerted great moral, economic, and social pressure on those who disapproved of the war or its conduct. In many regions of the United States, German-Americans suffered untold abuse because of the general assumption that they favored a German victory. To assure orthodoxy in word and thought, many patriotic societies attempted to ban everything German: operas, symphonies, sauerkraut (renamed victory cabbage), even the German language. Whatever the exertions of the Wilson administration and its supporters to silence the war's critics, they never succeeded in convincing a significant minority of intelligent Americans that the nation's involvement was wise or just.

Wilson's Peace Program

Long before 1917 the President assigned the United States a peculiar role in history. This nation's political, social, and moral uniqueness, he believed, had given it a transcendent mission to serve humanity. America was born, he said, that all men might be free. In his inaugural of March 4, 1913, he asked that the government "be perfected so that it might be put to the service of humanity." After August 1914, he informed the nation repeatedly that Europe beckoned, not alone for material aid, but for guidance in creating a world of lasting peace and security. For him that world required, above all, establishment of free governments everywhere. Increasingly, Wilson's postulate for world peace and stability was the principle of self-determination. It was essential, he said, "that every people should be left free to determine its own polity . . . unhindered, unthreatened, unafraid, the little along with the great and powerful." As a logical extension of this purpose, he condemned imperialism, autocracy, aggression, and every other irrational use of force for the repression of populations. In his war message of April 1917, the President insisted that the United States would enter Europe's struggle to save the world from such misuse of power.

Wilson's crusade for humanity required a program capable of translating the nation's wartime purpose into a structure of lasting peace. Still his commitment to world organization came slowly. The Great War, with its unprecedented horrors, had driven thoughtful Europeans and Americans alike to the realization that the prevention of another war demanded a new world order. One group of concerned Americans had organized the League to Enforce Peace in 1915. The question which troubled it was clear: Could an effective system of collective security rest on world opinion rather than force? Leaders of the League to Enforce Peace generally believed that the mere existence of a worldwide sentiment against aggression, expressed in the votes of a world organization, would prevent the great majority of wars. Wilson no more than others could define the role of force and national obligation in a system of collective security, but events compelled him at last to endorse the league idea in principle. Addressing a meeting of the League to Enforce Peace in May 1916, he publicly favored American membership in a postwar international organization. In his noted speech before the Senate on January 22, 1917, he reaffirmed the American commitment to join a league of nations.

In September 1917, Wilson established The Inquiry, a group of experts chosen to frame specific war aims for the United States. During November the Bolsheviks drove the Russian provisional government from power and threatened to take Russia out of the war. Hesitant to face German negotiators alone, the Bolsheviks asked the Western Allies to enter the quest for peace by formulating a liberal peace program acceptable to Germany. Aided by a long memorandum from The Inquiry, the President now prepared his "Fourteen Points" address which he delivered to a joint session of Congress on January 8, 1918. Wilson argued for open diplomacy; self-determination for the alien peoples in the German, Austro-Hungarian, and Turkish empires; freedom of the seas; and the reduction of armaments. But, for Wilson, the fourteenth point was the one that mattered: "A general association of nations must be formed under specific covenants for . . . mutual guarantees of political independence and territorial integrity to great and small states alike." This speech elevated Wilson to a primary position among allied leaders and brought him the support of liberal sentiment throughout the world. Unfortunately there was little possibility that Wilson's peace program would survive the end of the fighting. Everyone favored the rights of humanity. Neither Americans nor Europeans, however, could agree on whose rights should be paramount, for no settlement could guarantee the rights of all. Wilson's phraseology raised every human, political, and territorial aspiration, but in practice the rights of people would be precisely what the spokesmen of the victorious powers chose to make them.

Wilson's peace program failed to keep Russia in the war. The Bolsheviks, securing no Western support that mattered to Germany, negotiated a peace with the Central Powers. This permitted the Germans to transfer massive forces from the Eastern to the Western Front for the 1918 offensive. The President balked at recognizing the undemocratic Bolshevik regime in Russia. Lansing worried less about its undemocratic nature than its militant ideology of world revolution. But if the Wilson administration denied recognition to the Bolshevik regime, it hesitated to commit the United States to the Allied effort to overthrow the Bolsheviks and restore the Eastern Front. In mid-1918 the President approved limited armed intervention in Siberia and northern Russia, but basically he believed that the Russian form of government was a matter of Russian self-determination.

Japan's Wartime Challenge

Even before 1917 Japan issued a warning that the President's concept of a just peace would have rough sailing in the real world of power politics. Late in August 1914, Japan declared war on Germany and occupied the German-held Shantung Peninsula in north China, as well as the German islands in the north Pacific—the Marianas, Carolines, and Marshalls. Then to strengthen their hand in China while Europe was still at war, Japanese officials confronted a weak Chinese government with twenty-one demands designed to give Japan extensive economic plus some administrative influence in China. With delaying tactics the Chinese managed to eliminate the six most stringent demands, but in May 1915, under a direct ultimatum, China agreed to the fifteen demands that remained. These included the recognition of Japanese rights in Shantung.

Washington watched Japan's aggression, determined to protect China but avoid direct involvement in the Far East. During March 1915, Secretary of State Bryan, to reassure Japan, acknowledged the fact "that territorial contiguity creates special relations between Japan and these districts." In May, however, he warned Japan that the United States would recognize no treaty imposed on China which impaired American treaty rights, Chinese integrity, or the principle of the Open Door. Facing a direct conflict with the United States over China,

the Tokyo government, in October 1915, joined the European alliance fighting Germany, and by 1917 had forced from its hard-pressed European allies an acknowledgment of Japanese claims to Shantung and the German islands north of the equator.

After April 1917, both the United States and Japan faced the prospect of a direct and bitter diplomatic confrontation at the peace table. In August the Japanese government sent a mission to the United States under Viscount Kikujiro Ishii. Ishii sought American recognition of Japan's "paramount interests" in China; Colonel House urged Wilson to accept the Japanese request. But the President made it clear to Ishii that the United States desired nothing less than Japanese observance of the Open Door principle. Both Lansing and Ishii wanted a formal agreement; to obtain it they employed the intriguing device of incorporating both the American and the Japanese viewpoints in the same document. The Lansing-Ishii Agreement of November 2, 1917, recognized "That Japan has special interests in China, particularly in that part to which her possessions are contiguous." At the same time the two nations agreed to adhere to the principle of the Open Door, or equal opportunity for commerce and industry in China. Such conflicting phraseology could be interpreted to mean anything or nothing, as individual Japanese, Chinese, and American officials preferred.

The European Armistice

Wilson faced the central challenge to his wartime leadership in Europe. He knew of the secret treaties whereby the Allied Powers had promised one another certain long-standing territorial

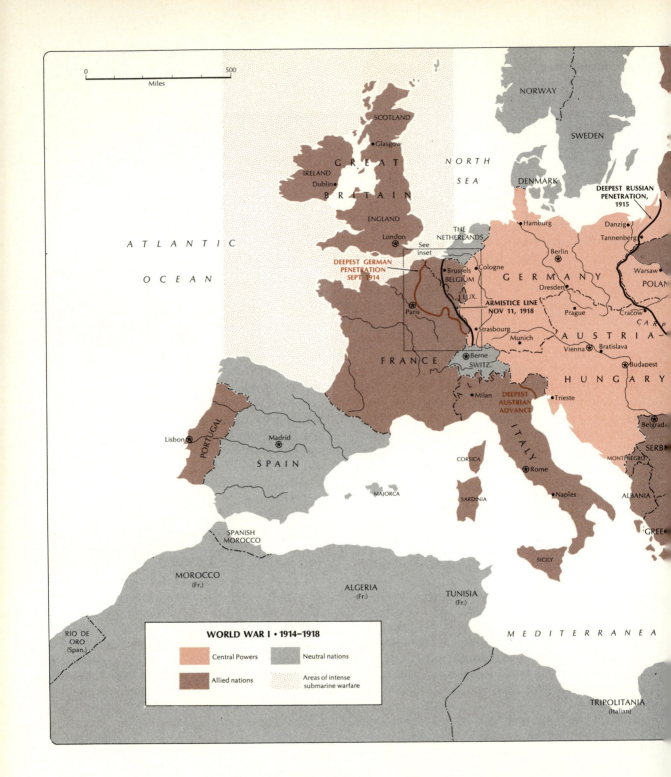

WORLD WAR I · 1914–1918

| Central Powers | Neutral nations |
| Allied nations | Areas of intense submarine warfare |

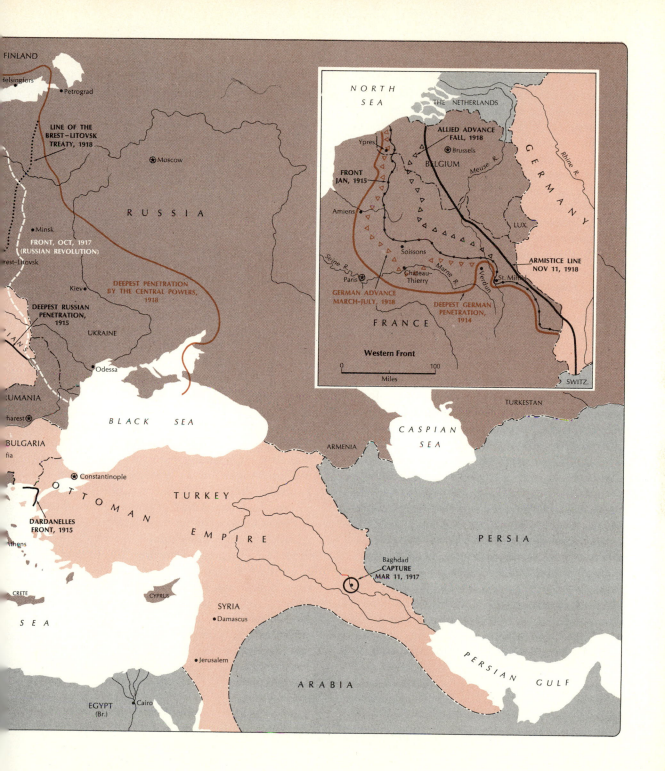

FINLAND

Helsingfors

Petrograd

**LINE OF THE
BREST–LITOVSK
TREATY, 1918**

Moscow

RUSSIA

Minsk

**FRONT, OCT, 1917
(RUSSIAN REVOLUTION)**

Brest-Litovsk

Kiev

**DEEPEST PENETRATION
BY THE CENTRAL POWERS,
1918**

**DEEPEST RUSSIAN
PENETRATION,
1915**

UKRAINE

Odessa

BLACK   SEA

RUMANIA

Bucharest

BULGARIA

Sofia

OTTOMAN

Constantinople

**DARDANELLES
FRONT, 1915**

Athens

TURKEY

EMPIRE

CASPIAN
SEA

ARMENIA

TURKESTAN

PERSIA

Baghdad
**CAPTURE
MAR 11, 1917**

SEA

CRETE

CYPRUS

SYRIA

Damascus

Jerusalem

ARABIA

PERSIAN   GULF

EGYPT
(Br.)

Cairo

Inset map:

NORTH
SEA

THE NETHERLANDS

Ypres

**ALLIED ADVANCE
FALL, 1918**

Brussels

BELGIUM

Meuse R.

GERMANY

Rhine R.

**FRONT
JAN, 1915**

Amiens

LUX.

Seine R.

Soissons

Château-
Thierry

Marne R.

Verdun

St. Mihiel

**ARMISTICE LINE
NOV 11, 1918**

Paris

**GERMAN ADVANCE
MARCH–JULY, 1918**

**DEEPEST GERMAN
PENETRATION,
1914**

FRANCE

SWITZ.

Western Front

0   100

Miles

THE GREAT WAR AND AFTER

objectives, but he refused to acknowledge their existence. He assumed that the war's end would find the Allies so dependent upon the United States for economic and military aid that he could impose on them his own conceptions of a proper peace. Wilson guarded his independence of action by refusing to enter a formal alliance with Britain and France, officially designating the United States only as an "Associated Power" in the Western coalition.

Wilson based his determination to control the postwar settlement on both his wartime diplomatic independence and the nation's military contribution to victory. To command the American Expeditionary Forces in France, Wilson chose General John J. Pershing, an able and imposing officer. So rapid and successful had been the American effort to create, train, and equip an army that Pershing's units began to arrive in France before the end of 1917. This raised a sharp controversy over their final training and commitment to battle. British and French commanders wanted American forces amalgamated with their own. Pershing opposed amalgamation, explaining to the President, "when the war ends, our position will be stronger if our army acting as such shall have played a distinctive and definite part." Wilson, recognizing the diplomatic advantage that would come with demonstrable American successes, upheld Pershing's decision. The American forces were kept intact and given their own sector on the Western Front.

In March 1918, Germany launched a desperate offensive. During June, American forces counterattacked, pushing the Germans back across the Marne at Chateau-Thierry and clearing Belleau Wood. The Germans, on July 15, made another drive toward Paris; but three days later their effort was finished. General Ferdinand Foch, Allied Supreme Commander, now ordered his counteroffensive. On August 8, the British broke through the Hindenburg Line, while French and American forces destroyed German resistance along the Aisne-Marne, St. Mihiel, and Argonne sectors. Then began the Allied move across France, with Pershing's command pushing forward along the Southern Front at Meuse-Argonne. In October, German army leaders, thoroughly demoralized, urged their government to seek armistice terms from President Wilson. American battle deaths of 48,000 were small compared with the 1,300,000 French and 900,000 British killed, but Pershing and the Americans had played a decisive role in the Allied victory of 1918.

On October 12, the German government, under Prince Max of Baden, agreed to an armistice based on Wilson's Fourteen Points. Wilson demanded the abdication of the Kaiser as a condition of peace. On October 20, Prince Max accepted the President's terms and promised sweeping political reforms based on democratic procedures. The President forwarded the German replies to Allied leaders only to discover that they anticipated a total German collapse and had no interest in an armistice based on the Fourteen Points. Wilson thereupon threatened to repudiate any Allied program that conflicted with his views. Under American pressure, the Allied Supreme War Council, on November 4, approved a prearmistice agreement, based largely on the Fourteen Points but with two qualifications concerning freedom of the seas and damages to civilians in German-occupied territory. On November 11, German representatives signed the Armistice, bringing the long, exhausting war to an end.

Wilson at Versailles

Unencumbered by wartime concessions, the President was confident that he could impose his peace on a stricken Europe. The opinions of people who, Wilson believed, had responded to his ideals, would crush those who stood in the way. "National purposes," he proclaimed in

September 1918, "have fallen more and more into the background and the common purpose of enlightened mankind has taken their place."

Wilson, accompanied by a large American delegation, crossed the Atlantic during December 1918, aboard the *George Washington*. His reception in Europe was tumultuous, reaffirming his impression that Europeans welcomed him as a savior of mankind. When the Versailles Peace Conference opened in Paris on January 12, 1919, delegations from thirty-two nations were present. It was clear that the issues at stake were too complex to be settled in general sessions. Of necessity, therefore, the Big Four—Wilson, Lloyd George of England, Georges Clemenceau of France, and Vittorio Orlando of Italy—took command of the Conference and conferred as a Council of Four. Newsmen who jammed Paris soon discovered to their dismay that the four leaders, despite the President's past condemnation of secret diplomacy, would conduct their business in absolute secrecy.

Wilson now learned to his sorrow that Europe's interest in his leadership lay in his capacity to produce men and material for victory, not in the nobility of his vision for humanity. Europe's spokesmen could propose no substitute for power politics. Wilson came to Paris to avoid any negotiation conducted within the framework of secret treaties. But his efforts to eliminate them with appeals to abstract principles such as self-determination fell on deaf ears. "God gave us the Ten Commandments," was Clemenceau's cynical comment, "and we broke them. Wilson gave us the Fourteen Points. We shall see." For such sarcasm Wilson was unprepared.

Fortunately for Wilson, the independence of Eastern Europe, so prominent an objective in his Fourteen Points, flowed easily from the collapse of the Central Powers. Even before the Versailles Conference, the peoples of Eastern and Southeastern Europe had established a new political order; the Conference had merely to recognize the change. Still this fulfillment of self-determination proved to be agonizingly difficult, for Wilson could not tidy up the map of Europe with a series of new nations, each representing a national grouping. Past migration and conquests condemned most boundary lines to bitter controversy, and the Conference did not hesitate to assign German territory to the new Slavic nations. Danzig, an important Baltic seaport in the German enclave of East Prussia, presented a special problem, for any Polish corridor to Danzig would not only attach a German population to Poland but also separate a body of East Prussians from the German nation. The Conference, however, granted Poland a corridor and designated Danzig as a free city, all in defiance of the principle of self-determination. For what seemed good strategic reasons, the Conference assigned the Germans of the Sudeten region to Czechoslovakia. Finally, it decreed Austria forever free of German control.

Italy, in accordance with the secret Treaty of London of 1915, claimed and received the Austrian Trentino to the Brenner Pass, as well as Trieste on the Dalmatian coast below the port of Fiume. Wilson accepted these arrangements despite their variance from the principle of self-determination. But Wilson rejected the Italian claims to Fiume, for this port constituted new Yugoslavia's only outlet to the sea. When Wilson, on April 23, 1919, appealed directly over the heads of the Italian delegation to the people of Italy on the question of Fiume, the Italians left the Conference. Returning two weeks later, Orlando managed to reserve this issue for later negotiation between Italy and Yugoslavia. Wilson's solution of applying plebiscites to troublesome areas had the effect of avoiding rather than solving the problems inherent in assigning territory. The President, moreover, never applied the doctrine of self-determination to the victors at all. The Versailles Conference did not touch the established empires of Britain, France, Belgium, Holland, or the United States. In practice, the principle of self-determination became a readily available device for punishing losers, especially in the region of Eastern Europe.

Germany confronted the Allies with questions equally demanding and far more divisive.

The "Big Four"—George, Orlando, Clemenceau, and Wilson—at Versailles, 1919.   *Brown Brothers*

France, through its spokesman Clemenceau, sought dismemberment of Germany through the creation of one or two Rhenish republics along the west bank of the Rhine. Wilson argued, in a series of long, violent debates, that French demands ignored both the prearmistice agreement and the principle of self-determination. When Clemenceau, in exasperation, accused Wilson of being pro-German, the President prepared to abandon the Conference. Clemenceau now yielded on the question of the Rhenish republics but gained the right to French occupation of the Rhineland and special guaranty treaties by which Britain and the United States promised to come to France's aid in the event of some unprovoked German attack. France gained as well permanent demilitarization of the west bank of the Rhine, limitation of the German ground forces to 100,000 men, and complete elimination of German naval and air forces. On the matter of reparations, Wilson faced both Clemenceau and Lloyd George. In the end Wilson agreed in principle to heavy, but undefined, German reparations and accepted a specific treaty article assigning to Germany and its allies full responsibility for the war.

During the war Britain and the dominions, along with Japan, had occupied German colonies in Africa and the Pacific, and they demanded at Paris that their possession be formally acknowledged. Eventually Wilson recognized the right of occupation for Britain and the dominions, although he held tenaciously that these colonies should come under a political mandate of the League of Nations for the protection of the native peoples. Under this new mandate system German islands in the Pacific north of the equator passed to Japanese control.

On the question of Shantung, Wilson was less successful. The Japanese based their case for retention on their nation's contribution to the Allied war effort in the Pacific, the Allied wartime guarantees, and the rights of conquest and occupation. Wilson argued that German rights in

Shantung reverted to China with the German defeat. At Wilson's insistence, V. K. Wellington Koo, Chinese ambassador to the United States and head of the Chinese delegation at Paris, addressed the Big Four, basing his appeal on American principles of self-determination and the Open Door. He reminded the delegates that China had signed its wartime agreements with Japan under duress. He terminated his argument by insisting that the Chinese people had the right to govern their own territory. Koo had won a moral victory, but he did not dissuade the British and French leaders from honoring their wartime pledges to Japan. Against the three Allies Wilson's principles had no chance. He agreed finally to a clause transferring Shantung to Japan on the latter's promise that the territory would be returned eventually to China. The Chinese delegation showed its chagrin by refusing to sign the treaty.

For Wilson one issue at Versailles outweighed all others—the establishment of the League of Nations. This question, if resolved satisfactorily, would in time permit some evolution toward a world that conformed to his vision. The French favored a league, but one that would underwrite a European balance of power and guarantee French security. The French plan, presented on February 3, 1919, proposed the creation of an international army and a general staff with power to make critical demands on the member states. Wilson, on the other hand, anticipated a league that would replace power politics with a universal alliance against war and the use of force. Underlying his league would be a general harmony of interest in peace and justice, reflected in a rational world opinion.

In presenting his Covenant to the Peace Conference on February 14, the President declared that its success would depend ultimately on the "moral force of the public opinion of the world." Wilson managed to embody his version of a League in the Treaty of Versailles. The Covenant provided for an Assembly in which all nations would be represented, a Council composed of the major powers, and a Secretariat. Wilson considered Article X, which guaranteed the "territorial integrity and political independence" of all members, to be "the heart of the covenant."

On May 17, 1919, the victors summoned German representatives to Paris to receive the treaty. They granted the Germans several days to study the terms and to propose modifications. Unable to introduce any significant changes without unwanted repercussion, the Germans accepted the treaty almost as presented. On June 28, German officials not associated with the wartime leadership signed the treaty in the Hall of Mirrors at Versailles.

The Great Debate

Treaty in hand, Wilson returned to Washington on July 8, 1919, prepared to battle the Senate for its approval. At that crucial moment he faced a powerful partisan challenge to his leadership at home as the result, in part, of his own decisions. Against the advice of Democratic friends, he chose, during the November 1918 elections, to make his success in Paris hinge on a Democratic congressional victory. The election of a Republican majority, he warned the nation, would be interpreted in Europe as a repudiation of his leadership. This permitted Republican congress-men to interpret their victories in 1918 as indeed a repudiation of the President's leadership. Wilson aggravated their resentment by failing to appoint a prominent Republican to the peace commission. Indeed, three of the men he named to join him on the commission—House, Lansing, and General Tasker H. Bliss—were associated with his administration. The fourth, Henry White, a noted diplomat, was only a nominal Republican. Despite the fact that he would face a Republican majority in the Senate, the President had made no effort to consult those

Republican leaders who would determine the ultimate fate of his treaty.

During the President's absence in Paris, Republican leaders in Washington, guided by Senator Henry Cabot Lodge of Massachusetts, chairman of the Senate Foreign Relations Committee, prepared their strategy of opposition. Lodge harbored both a deep personal dislike for Wilson and a profound distrust of his leadership. He had long been convinced, moreover, that the particular League plan proposed by Wilson would undermine the sovereignty of the United States. Finally, as Republican leader in the Senate he saw that Republican prospects in the 1920 presidential election hinged on that party's success in handling the League issue. Lodge suspected that the President controlled the Democratic party and much of the nation. Unless Republican leaders could unite on a moderate program of opposition and eventually win popular sentiment to their views, the party's chances in 1920 were less than promising. Lodge read his first warning to Wilson early in March 1919, when he circulated the so-called Round Robin resolution among Senate Republicans. This declared, in effect, that Wilson's League was unacceptable to the Senate. When Lodge presented the resolution, the presiding officer ruled him out of order, but Lodge proceeded nonetheless to read the names of the thirty-seven Republican signers. Clearly the President was in trouble.

To achieve a united Republican front against Wilson, Lodge required the support of Senators Hiram Johnson and William E. Borah, as well as other Republican irreconcilables who opposed any league. Lodge suggested to Borah that a number of amendments or reservations to the League Covenant might better defend the American interest than the Covenant unchanged. When Borah agreed to support this strategy, Lodge prevailed upon Republican elder statesman Elihu Root to draft a series of reservations. Among these was the principle that the United States would accept no mandate and employ no armed forces without permission of Congress. In addition, the Monroe Doctrine was to be considered "wholly outside the jurisdiction of the League of Nations." These and other reservations, Lodge insisted, were designed only to define more precisely American obligations to the League's security system. To strengthen his hand in the Senate, Lodge packed his Foreign Relations Committee with known opponents of Wilson's League.

On July 10, 1919, the President presented the treaty to the Senate, making it clear that he expected prompt and unqualified approval. To reject the League, he warned, would break the heart of the world. He concluded his speech with high emotion: "The stage is set, the destiny disclosed. It has come about by no plan of our conceiving, but by the hand of God who led us into this way. We cannot turn back. We can only go forward, with lifted eyes and freshened spirit, to follow the vision."

Much of the subsequent debate on the League revolved around Article X, which guaranteed against external aggression the territorial integrity and political independence of League members. Wilson insisted repeatedly that Article X, backed by the solemn promises of the world's leading nations, would stop aggressive war absolutely. Wilson skirted the question of national obligation to stop aggresssion, assuring Senators that each League member retained control over its own decisions. But, critics wondered, how could collective security be effective if no nation could be compelled, beyond its own interest, to support it? To stop aggression, said Lodge, the League would require such infringements on sovereignty that no one, not even the President, would favor it. "What will your league amount to," asked Borah, "if it does not contain powers that no one dreams of giving it?"

But Republican criticism of the League went deeper. Many saw in the League an agency for perpetuating the status quo with all its injustices. Elihu Root wrote of the League: "If perpetuated, it would be an attempt to preserve for all time unchanged the distribution of power and territory made in accordance with the views and exigencies of the Allies in this present juncture of affairs. It would necessarily be futile. . . . It would not only be futile; it would be mischievous. Change and growth are the law of life, and no generation can impose its will in regard to the growth of nations and distribution of power, upon succeeding generations.''

As the summer of 1919 dragged on, public sentiment ran hard toward the moderate Republican position which favored League membership, but with reservations. Tormented by Lodge's tactics of delay, Wilson decided to carry his case to the country. Against the advice of his doctor, he left Washington on September 3, 1919, opening his speaking tour in Ohio and moving slowly through the Middle West to the Dakotas. In this region he met with only partial success, for many of his isolationist audiences there were indifferent to the League. In both the Northwest and the great cities of California, however, he faced large and enthusiastic crowds. Finally, he turned eastward, speaking in Nevada, Utah, Wyoming, and Colorado. The President everywhere defended Article X as the guarantor of peace. Always his appeal centered on the American desire to avoid another war. Without the League, he said repeatedly, there would be no collective security; without collective security there would be no peace. Wilson's speech at Pueblo, Colorado, on September 25 ended his tour. Broken by the strain of one of the greatest forensic efforts in the nation's history, the President returned to Washington. On October 2 he had a major stroke, and during his final eighteen months in office, he was largely incapable of managing the duties and the functions required of the presidency.

In November 1919, the Republicans embarked on their final strategy to defeat Wilson's treaty. While the stricken President urged Senate Democrats to oppose any modification of the treaty, the Republican majority passed the reservations one by one. Thereafter the disposition of the treaty lay with Wilson. On November

THE ACCUSER

The Granger Collection

18, he instructed the Democrats to vote against the treaty as it contained the Lodge reservations. On the following day the Senate rejected the treaty with the reservations by the overwhelming vote of 55 to 39. Joining the Democrats were the irreconcilables who, in the colorful phrase of Senator Borah, wanted the League "twenty thousand leagues under the sea." The Democratic leadership then moved for approval of the treaty as Wilson wanted it. Again the treaty failed, this time by a vote of 53 to 39, with the Republican majority voting against it as a bloc. Many Democrats, believing it preferable to enter the League with the Lodge reservations than not at all, now broke ranks. When the Senate took its final vote in March 1920, enough Democrats voted for the Lodge reservations to produce a majority of 49 to 35, but still 7 votes short of the necessary two-thirds. Wilson's twenty-three unbending Democrats, joined by the Republican irreconcilables, had finally defeated the treaty.

Armistice negotiations had removed the danger of Germany but seemingly exposed the nation to the more insidious threat of Russian bolshevism with its declared program of world revolution. Newspapers reported the horrors of Bolshevik rule and warned the American people that their institutions were not immune to subversion. What gave credence to such fears was the tendency of American radicals to praise the Bolshevik Revolution in Russia and to disseminate the revolutionary doctrines emanating from the Third International of the world Communist movement.

In a general atmosphere of unease, specific events of 1919 set off the great Red Scare. It began in February when Mayor Ole Hanson, supported by the press, interpreted the general strike in Seattle as a Bolshevik-inspired assault on American values, rather than as a typical postwar labor-management dispute. Soon reports spread that unknown radicals had sent bombs to prominent officials. Most of the bombs never reached their destinations, but one damaged the house of Senator Thomas W. Hardwick of Georgia. Several May Day riots intensified the fear. On June 2 a series of explosions destroyed property in several cities. That day a bomb damaged Attorney General A. Mitchell Palmer's house in Washington. The Boston police strike of September 1919, vigorously attacked by Governor Calvin Coolidge, followed in November by the massive steel strike, again raised the specter of radical influence.

In Washington, Attorney General Palmer moved to curb the Reds with executive power. During November 1919, his agents rounded up hundreds of radicals, including dozens of officers and members of New York's Union of Russian Workers. During December 1919, the Justice Department deported, as radicals, over two hundred aliens.

During January 1920, the Senate passed a sedition law by voice vote. But in refusing to concur, the House terminated the movement toward a new era of repression. The excesses of hysteria and arrests without cause, culminating that month in the suspension of five Socialists from the New York Legislature, convinced responsible Americans that the witch hunt had gone too far. The *Literary Digest* reported on January 20 that the removal of the five Socialists produced almost universal condemnation by Republican, Democratic, and Socialist newspapers alike. In Washington, Louis F. Post, Assistant Secretary of Labor, canceled hundreds of Palmer's deportation orders when it became clear that the basis of deportation was generally no more than membership in some organization labeled subversive. While Palmer clamored for more drastic congressional legislation which would punish sedition, the nation generally regained its composure during the spring of 1920. Palmer's predicted Communist uprisings never occurred.

The crusade against radicalism effectively slowed the release of wartime offenders from state and federal prisons. In November 1918, many progressives joined the Socialists in demanding general amnesty for those held in prison because of their opposition to the war. As early as December 1918, Secretary of War Newton D. Baker received a petition with about fifteen thousand signatures recommending pardons for conscientious objectors. Much of the pressure for amnesty centered on the imprisoned Socialist leader Debs. Attorney General Palmer, in denying Debs's release, explained that he would be bitterly criticized by those who still considered Debs to be an extremely dangerous radical. Until Wilson left the White House in March 1921, he refused to support amnesty for political prisoners. In December 1921, a new president, Warren G. Harding, released Debs and almost two dozen other political prisoners. Two years later, President Calvin Coolidge, following the advice of a special commission, set free the remaining wartime prisoners.

To a nation recently at war, the peace of the early twenties seemed remarkably secure. At Versailles the Allies, by agreement among themselves, had assigned to Germany the sole responsibility for causing the Great War. From that reading of history emerged the welcome conclusion that postwar peace demanded little more than German adherence to the conditions imposed at Versailles. Thus the United States withdrew its power from Europe under the assumption either that the League would indeed maintain world peace or that, if it failed, nothing would occur to demand another massive military response from this country.

Such easy assumptions, not shared by all Americans, denied at least two inescapable lessons of the recent past. First, the refusal of the nation to forego the advantages of wartime trade, added to its ultimate unwillingness to accept British and French defeat, demonstrated that the American people could not escape a major European war, especially one that ventured onto the Atlantic. Second, Woodrow Wilson had not reordered the international system. In the future, as in the past, nations would perform in the international arena according to the traditional rules of diplomacy. Sound American policy, therefore, would avoid the extremes of denying the nation's interests in the politics of Europe and Asia and of identifying its concerns with the liberal aspirations of humanity everywhere. Instead, sound policy would recognize and protect a variety of specific national interests that had historically sustained the country's welfare and security. Unfortunately, Wilson's leadership drove American thought toward the very extremes against which the past had warned.

Isolationism—a state of mind denying the existence of any American political or military interests outside the Western Hemisphere—flowed logically from a deep postwar disillusionment with both Wilson and the war. The wartime President had promised the American people a new world order which he could not achieve; by ignoring the genuine gains that lay within the range of victory, he never adequately explained to his countrymen why their involvement had been both necessary and successful. It was not strange, therefore, that millions of Americans after 1919 concluded that the United States had gained little from its wartime experience. The noted journalist Oswald Garrison Villard concluded that it would have been better to take the lives of the American soldiers in cold blood on Broadway. Endlessly in the twenties Americans calculated the number of hospitals, libraries, and college buildings they could have constructed with the billions consumed to fight the war. With time the disillusionment became profound. Whatever its appeal, isolationism could hardly establish the foundations of policy for sustaining the world created at Versailles.

But internationalism was as oblivious of reality as isolationism was; both were strangers to the nation's nineteenth-century traditions. Indeed, isolationism and internationalism had more in common than the debates of the twenties would suggest. Both denied that the United States had a vital interest in any particular political and military configuration outside the Western Hemisphere. Whereas isolationism limited the nation's legitimate concerns to matters at home, internationalism asserted that American interests were universal—wherever mankind might be oppressed or in danger of aggression. Neither really focused on concrete issues which touched the nation's interests clearly and specifically. Isolationism stopped short of them; internationalism soared far beyond them. Whereas isolationism denied that the United States had any postwar role to play in world affairs, internationalism insisted that the United States play an active role. No more than isolationists, however, would internationalists accept the obligation that the country employ its power to enforce those arrangements in world politics that reflected its basic interests. Every internationalist scheme of the twenties emphasized the requirement, not of specific commitments abroad, but of agreements, declarations, and institutions which would confront any aggressor with a combination of international law, signed promises, or world opinion. In practice, all the new international agencies, such as the League of Nations and the World Court, embodied the effort of the favored nations—in the twenties, the victorious democracies—to establish the means whereby they might perpetuate a status quo which served their interests without the necessity of specific commitments or adequate defenses. Concepts of peace and peaceful change became the bulwark of the status quo, for as long as nations rejected the legitimacy of force, they denied themselves both the right and the power to alter the international order except in matters of little or no consequence.

Whatever their opposition to foreign commitments, Americans had no desire to escape the world of commerce and investment. Between 1922 and 1929 the net movement of capital out of the United States totaled some $3.6 billion. Businessmen demanded that their government sustain their privileged economic position everywhere on the globe. For a nation of worldwide business interests, peace was of the essence; therefore, it was not strange that many citizens insisted that the country accept a moral responsibility for peace. These generally conflicting objectives established the bounds of national behavior. United States external policies after 1920 varied from narrow nationalism to limited internationalism, all designed to serve the nation's specific interests in trade and progress as well as its general interest in the peaceful evolution of the postwar era.

The Postwar Challenge of Europe

The Great War had demonstrated that the old balance of power which had preserved Europe's stability—and with it, this nation's security—no longer existed. The Allied victory of 1918 had created the illusion of British and French supremacy, but this supremacy was viable only when underwritten by the full power of the United States. The Versailles Treaty established the conditions of postwar European stability. It provided for French military preponderance on which hinged the security of Europe. Second, it recognized the new Slavic states of East Europe. In a sense, these two essential elements of the post-Versailles order were related, for the independence of Eastern Europe would scarcely outlast the eclipse of French military dominance on the Continent.

For the moment neither of Europe's potential giants—Germany and Russia—loomed as a threat to the Versailles settlement. Germany's defeat temporarily removed any danger posed by that nation. Germans labored under a series of military limitations designed to curtail their

warmaking capacity. Still the Great War had broken neither the German military potential nor the determination of the German leadership to elevate that nation again to a major, perhaps dominant, role in European politics. Even in defeat, Germany remained potentially the most powerful and the most threatening country of Europe.

Russia emerged as an even greater problem, but one of unique character. For what made that nation loom as a special danger to the West and its traditions was less the power which it wielded than the ideology and long-range purpose which its rhetoric conveyed. Indeed, the Great War had produced two giant crusades against the evils of tyranny and war. Western ideology, embodied in Wilson's Fourteen Points, identified peace with the triumph of democracy and self-determination, all under the aegis of the League of Nations. Simultaneously Russia's Bolshevik leader, Nikolai Lenin, presented a peace program of his own, one based on world revolution and the classless society, all under the aegis of the Communist International. After 1920 this ideological conflict sustained America's policy of nonrecognition of the Russian government.

The easy and apparently successful isolation of Soviet Russia from the affairs of Europe after Versailles misled a generation of world leaders. For Russia, like Germany, possessed untold reserves of power and energy. Emerging from the Great War in economic and political chaos, the new Russia embarked on a massive program of general development intended to meet both the needs of public welfare and the requirements of national security. The Soviets' feeling of insecurity toward the West bordered on paranoia. Joseph Stalin, Lenin's successor, warned the Russian people in 1931 that "those who lag behind are beaten. . . . We are fifty or a hundred years behind the advanced countries. We must make good this lag in ten years. Either we do it or they crush us."

Long before the mid-twenties Russia had threatened the most vulnerable, and yet the most fundamental, territorial arrangements of the Versailles Treaty. In 1920 Russian armies invaded Poland, albeit in response to Western attacks on the Soviet Union, illustrating that country's contempt for the Eastern European settlement. Poland's successful resistance saved the Versailles frontiers, but the Western powers made no effort to protect their recent triumph for self-determination.

Britain, France, Germany, and the United States together might have guaranteed the political and territorial integrity of Eastern Europe. But they disagreed both in their intentions toward that region and in their attitudes toward one another. France, still fearful of Germany, made unrealistic demands for reparations and occupied the German Ruhr in 1923. For France the guarantee of Slavic independence was the key to European stability. Unlike France, Great Britain viewed Germany as an essential element in the reconstruction of postwar Europe. Lloyd George admitted in 1921 that England regarded Germany as a necessary bulwark against Russia. The Locarno Pact of 1925, marking the high point in postwar British, French, and German cordiality, reaffirmed Germany's boundaries on the west but pointedly failed to include any guarantees for the status quo in Eastern Europe. Britain simply entrusted the future of the Slavic states to Germany.

Still British faith in Germany's acceptance of the Versailles settlement was misplaced, for German ambition, no less than Russian, encompassed changes in the political structure of Slavic Europe. The Versailles Treaty's eastern provisions, especially those regarding Austria, Czechoslovakia, Danzig, and the Polish Corridor, focused German nationalist resentment on Eastern Europe, where the minimal interests of Britain and the United States, added to the internal weakness of the Slavic states, presented long-range opportunities for challenging the postwar settlement. Still any German effort to annex Austria or partition Poland and Czechoslovakia could result only in catastrophe.

Thus Britain and the United States, by their refusal to sustain their wartime alliance with France and their decision, whether purposeful or not, to cast Eastern Europe adrift, had consigned the Versailles system to eventual oblivion. For both nations this instability in the Versailles structure would eventually demand decisions either to use force in defense of the political integrity of Eastern Europe or to accept diplomatically whatever changes appeared consonant with their fundamental interests. For the moment such troublesome, yet inescapable, decisions appeared remote.

The Washington Treaties

Japan emerged from the Versailles Conference as one of its chief beneficiaries. But Japan, no less than Germany and Russia, entered the postwar era as a dissatisfied power. Not only were

Japan's designs on China still unrealized but also, as the dominant power of East Asia, Japan was now determined to substitute for the imperial structures of the West in Asia a Far Eastern hegemony of its own. To undermine Western influence in both Southeast Asia and the western Pacific Japan possessed two significant weapons: a remarkable expansive power, backed by an impressive navy; and the force of anticolonialism, deepened and augmented by the Versailles settlement. These two drives—Japanese expansionism and Asian anticolonialism—converged in their opposition to traditional Western dominance over the peoples and resources of the Orient. Confronted with this dual challenge, the Western nations in the Pacific faced choices neither broad nor promising.

Following Germany's defeat Wilson's projected naval program threatened to involve Britain, Japan, and the United States in a naval arms race which many isolationists regarded as unnecessarily dangerous and costly. On December 14, 1920, Senator Borah introduced a resolution asking the President to call a conference with England and Japan to arrange a holiday in naval armament. Borah's resolution won such widespread approval in the press and Congress that the new Republican administration of Warren G. Harding could not ignore it. Even editors who defended the need of United States naval supremacy agreed overwhelmingly that a multinational agreement on naval limitation would serve the dual American interest in external security and tax reduction.

To achieve such conflicting objectives as tax and naval reduction, the containment of Japan, and the abrogation of the Anglo-Japanese Alliance, which to Washington placed Britain on the side of Japan in the Far East, was a sizable order. Yet at the level of paper treaties and government propaganda Secretary of State Charles Evans Hughes gained all these objectives at the Washington Conference which opened on Armistice Day—November 11, 1921. Nine nations with interests in the Pacific had accepted the Secretary's invitation.

Hughes, in his keynote address, astonished delegates, naval experts, and newsmen alike with his sweeping proposal to halt battleship construction and to scrap sizable tonnage already in existence. He then proposed a 5-5-3 ratio in capital ships among the United States, Britain, and Japan, with ratios of 1.75 each for France and Italy. Knowing the British devotion to cruisers, Hughes omitted smaller vessels from his program. Japan refused to accept its assigned ratio of capital ships unless the United States, Britain, and France agreed not to fortify their possessions in the western Pacific—including American-owned Guam and the Philippines. Having no desire to fortify these distant islands anyway, Hughes readily agreed to the Japanese demands, and the five major naval powers put their names to the Five Power Pact.

Another agreement, the Four Power Pact, specifically terminated the Anglo-Japanese Alliance of 1902 and substituted for it a general declaration of respect for the status quo in the Orient and a promise to consult in response to any threat of aggression. It was signed by the United States, Great Britain, France, and Japan. The last of the Washington agreements, the so-called Nine Power Pact, reaffirmed the principles of the Open Door and pledged respect by all nations in attendance for the territorial integrity of China. Almost unnoticed, the United States achieved a settlement of the Shantung question, which the Japanese had promised Wilson at Versailles. On February 4, 1922, Chinese and Japanese delegates signed a treaty which restored Shantung to China and provided for China's purchase of the Japanese-controlled railway in Shantung with funds provided by Japanese bankers under a fifteen-year loan.

Harding submitted the treaties to the Senate with the assurance that they contained "no commitment to armed force, no alliance, no written or moral obligation to join in defense." Lodge, defending the Four Power Pact, denied that the principle of consultation implied a promise to rescue any Far Eastern victim from aggression. Even while they explained that the Washington

Treaties entailed no obligation or alliance, the internationalists proclaimed that the treaties would guarantee the stability of the Pacific region. It was not strange that measures which promised so much for so little won the overwhelming support of Congress. One Senator alone cast his vote against the Five Power Pact; Senate approval for the Nine Power Pact was unanimous. But the Four Power Pact, even with a reservation specifically disclaiming any obligation on the part of the United States to defend anyone, triumphed by a margin of only four votes. Isolationism and internationalism were indeed so similar as to be scarcely distinguishable.

Conclusion

After April 1917, the American people, under the leadership of Woodrow Wilson, chose to defend their interest in a British-led Europe with a major military effort. That involvement reestablished, at least on the surface, the traditional balance of power which had served so well the historic security interests of the United States. But if the United States had played an essential role in protecting British and French leadership in European affairs, then this country's continued involvement in the defense of those nations was necessary to maintain the European balance. Wilson had been unable to remake the world at Versailles. World affairs thereafter would *not* be governed by laws that transcended the policies and interests of individual nations, some of which had not accepted the provisions of the Versailles Treaty. Japan made clear its limited acceptance of the Versailles order as early as the Washington Conference.

Thus, the much-heralded achievements at Washington in 1922 were ephemeral. The Five Power Pact terminated all competition in capital ships, but it did not limit the building of cruisers, destroyers, submarines, and a wide variety of auxiliary craft. It made Japan the dominant naval power in the western Pacific. By agreeing to the nonfortification of Guam, the United States denied itself the only base in the Pacific from which it might protect the Philippines, for the latter islands lay well outside the effective range of vessels based in Hawaii. Without naval bases, Guam and the Philippines were hostages; with bases, they were a challenge to Japan. The Four Power Pact was totally without substance, for it conveyed no more than vague promises which, Harding and the Senate agreed, the United States never intended to fulfill. It was not clear, moreover, that the abrogation of the Anglo-Japanese Alliance served any useful purpose. It simply isolated Japan diplomatically and removed any restraining influence which Britain might have exercised within the alliance. And the Nine Power Pact did not offer China any genuine guarantees against Japanese expansionism. Secretary Hughes's subsequent negotiations with the Japanese over the cancellation of the Lansing-Ishii Agreement made it clear that the assertive spirit of that wartime agreement, not the Nine Power Pact, defined Japanese intentions toward China. Hughes had scarcely touched the Japanese problem.

SUGGESTED READINGS

On Wilson's role Arthur S. Link's *Wilson the Diplomatist** (1957) is brief, but highly judicious. Harley Notter has provided a good account of Wilson's foreign policies to 1917 in *The Origins of the Foreign Policy of Woodrow Wilson* (1937). On Wilson and the Far East see Tienyi Li's *Woodrow Wilson and Far Eastern Policy, 1913–1917* (1952).

Studies highly critical of Wilson's role in American intervention are C. H. Grattan's *Why We Fought* (1929); Walter Millis's *The Road to War* (1935); C. C.

Tansill's *America Goes to War* (1938); and Edwin Borchard and W. P. Lage's *Neutrality for the United States* (2d ed., 1940). Charles Seymour in his *American Neutrality, 1914–1917* (1935) defended Wilson's policies. Although he overemphasized the role of British propaganda, H. C. Peterson, in his *Propaganda for War* (1939), presents a superb account of the British effort to win American sympathy.

Several excellent studies of the neutrality period are Ernest R. May's *The World War and American Isolation, 1914–1917* (1959); Edward H. Buehrig's *Woodrow Wilson and the Balance of Power* (1955); and Daniel M. Smith's *The Great Departure: The United States and World War I, 1914–1920** (1965).

On American economic mobilization see W. F. Willoughby's *Government Organization in Wartime and After* (1919); Herbert Stein's *Government Price Policy in the United States during the World War* (1939); B. M. Baruch's *American Industry in the War* (1921); W. C. Mullendore's *History of the United States Food Administration, 1917–1919* (1941); and J. M. Clark's *The Costs of the World War to the American People* (1931). John Steuben's *Labor in Wartime* (1940) and Samuel Gompers's *American Labor and the War* (1919) trace labor's role in the war effort.

On molding public opinion see George Creel's *How We Advertised America* (1920) and J. R. Mock's *Censorship, 1917* (1941). H. C. Peterson and G. C. Fite's *Opponents of War, 1917–1918** (1957) reveals the wartime hysteria. American military policy is covered in E. M. Coffman's *The War to End All Wars: The American Military Experience in World War I* (1968).

Wilson's preparations for peace have received excellent treatment in Charles Seymour's *American Diplomacy during the World War* (1934); Lawrence E. Gelfand's *The Inquiry: American Preparations for Peace, 1917–1919* (1963); Selig Adler's *The Isolationist Impulse** (1957); Harry R. Rudin's *Armistice 1918*

(1944); and David F. Trask's *The United States in the Supreme War Council* (1961). On the impact of the Russian Revolution see George F. Kennan's *Russia Leaves the War** (1967) and N. Gordon Levin, Jr.'s *Woodrow Wilson and World Politics: America's Response to War and Revolution* (1968). On the Lansing-Ishii negotiations is Burton F. Beers's *Vain Endeavor: Robert Lansing's Attempt to End the American-Japanese Rivalry* (1962).

On Wilson at Versailles see Ray S. Baker's *Woodrow Wilson and World Settlement* (3 vols., 1922); Paul Birdsall's *Versailles Twenty Years After* (1941); and Thomas A. Bailey's *Woodrow Wilson and the Lost Peace** (1944). The Shantung question receives excellent treatment in Russell H. Fifield's *Woodrow Wilson and the Far East: The Diplomacy of the Shantung Question* (1952).

On the great debate over the League are T. A. Bailey's *Woodrow Wilson and the Great Betrayal** (1945); W. Stull Holt's *Treaties Defeated by the Senate* (1933); and John A. Garraty's *Henry Cabot Lodge: A Biography* (1953). The insecurity of the immediate postwar months has received excellent treatment in R. K. Murray's *The Red Scare: A Study in National Hysteria, 1919–1920** (1955).

Among the good introductions to Republican foreign policy after 1920 are L. Ethan Ellis's *Republican Foreign Policy, 1921–1933* (1968); Adler's *The Isolationist Impulse** (1957) and *The Uncertain Giant** (1965); and David F. Trask's *Victory without Peace: American Foreign Relations in the Twentieth Century** (1968).

On the Washington Conference see R. L. Buell's *The Washington Conference* (1922); Merlo J. Pusey's *Charles Evans Hughes* (2 vols., 1951); C. L. Hoag's *Preface to Preparedness: The Washington Conference and Public Opinion* (1941); and J. C. Vinson's *The Parchment Peace: The United States Senate and the Washington Conference, 1921–1922* (1956).

*indicates availability in paperback.

26

Politics and Society in the 1920s

The election of President Warren G. Harding in 1920 ushered in a period of political conservatism which continued throughout the decade. The reaction against President Wilson and his policies, opposition to the expanding role of government which was characteristic of the progressive movement, the influence of businessmen on governmental action, and the high degree of postwar prosperity all combined to strengthen the conservative position. Neither Harding nor Calvin Coolidge, the new vice president, believed in strong executive leadership. Indeed, one of the most significant aspects of the political history of the 1920s was the decline in the power and prestige of the presidency which had been so greatly enlarged by Theodore Roose-velt and Wilson. But the postwar generation did not demand strong presidential leadership. The American people were tired of reform and of great causes. They wanted to be left alone, to enjoy themselves and to grow rich.

At the same time rising standards of living, advances in science and improved technology, and new intellectual currents combined to produce rapid and profound social change in America. Life moved at a faster pace, and young people threw off personal restraints which they considered unacceptable. The 1920s were a time of reevaluation of popular standards and mores, a period of restlessness, confusion, and even conflict in social relations.

The election of 1920 was profoundly significant, not because of the issues which dominated the campaign, but because of those that were ignored. The sudden ending of the war, followed closely by the Red Scare and the great debate over the League of Nations, created an immediate collapse of wartime emotions. By 1920 the attacks on the Democratic leadership had shattered the spell of "the war to end all war." Boies Penrose, the Republican boss of Pennsylvania, observed accurately, "Any good Republican can be nominated for President and can defeat any Democrat."

The Republican Convention opened in Chicago on June 8. The front-running candidates for nomination were General Leonard Wood, a conservative nationalist and old associate of Theodore Roosevelt, and Frank O. Lowden, a distinguished businessman and governor of Illinois. From the opening speech, however, newsmen detected a strong undercurrent for a little-known senatorial backbencher named Warren G. Harding. When the balloting began, Wood and Lowden, running neck and neck, led the field by a wide margin, but neither could approach the required majority. Yet neither candidate found it possible to support the other. On the ninth ballot the Wood and Lowden forces, having demonstrated to their favorites that they could not win, bolted to Harding. The tenth ballot was a mere formality. For the vice presidency the party named Calvin Coolidge, the governor of Massachusetts.

Gathering at San Francisco, the Democratic party carried the full burden of Wilson's illness and declining popularity. Two members of the Cabinet, Secretary of the Treasury William G. McAdoo and Attorney General A. Mitchell Palmer, fought for the nomination for thirty-eight ballots until party leaders agreed, at last, on James M. Cox, former governor of Ohio. For the vice presidency they selected Wilson's assistant secretary of the Navy, Franklin D. Roosevelt. Wilson had predicted that the 1920 presidential campaign would be a "great and solemn referendum" on the League of Nations issue. Although the Democratic nominees agreed to accept reservations which would not impair the Covenant, they supported League membership sufficiently to sustain the enthusiasm of the Wilsonian intellectuals in the cities. But Cox and Roosevelt faced large defections among Western farmers and isolationists generally.

Harding had set the tone of his campaign as early as May 1920, when he declared in his uniquely florid style: "America's present need is not heroics, but healing; not nostrums, but normalcy; not revolution, but restoration; not agitation, but adjustment; not surgery, but serenity." Such speeches—described by McAdoo as "an army of pompous phrases moving over the landscape in search of an idea"—captured the national mood, for everyone desired an escape from crisis and a return to "normalcy." On the League issue, Harding, acting on Lodge's advice, remained especially vague. By alternating an occasional commitment to *some* international organization with outright rejection of the League, he delighted all elements in his party. To neutralize Cox's appeal on the League issue, thirty-one leading Republicans, including Elihu Root, Charles Evans Hughes, and William Howard Taft, signed a statement which promised that Harding, if elected, would favor United States membership with reservations in the League of Nations. Harding could scarcely be called a strong candidate, yet so overwhelming was the reaction against Wilson and the war that he received over 16 million votes, representing 61 percent of the total cast, to approximately 9 million for Cox. Eugene Debs, running as the Socialist candidate from an Atlanta prison, received over 900,000 votes. The American people had agreed with Republican leaders that the United States did not require an intellectually and physically demanding foreign policy.

Harding was a friendly, easygoing politician who had none of the qualities essential for the American presidency. His career in Ohio politics had been mediocre; his record in the United States Senate had been no improvement. He was a poor judge of men; he permitted friendship and political cronyism to dictate many key appointments. He knew little about economics; and he viewed the presidency as an honor, not a responsibility. He had some serious shortcomings of character. For a time he engaged in extramarital love affairs and had a daughter born out of wedlock. But despite his glaring weaknesses, the American people responded warmly to this handsome, democratic, congenial man who in many ways seemed like one of them.

Important political and economic problems faced the new administration. Partly because of the postwar depression which began in 1920, Congress and the President faced various groups demanding special legislation. Veterans wanted a bonus; businessmen demanded higher tariffs and tax reduction; labor unions insisted on tighter immigration restrictions; and hardpressed farmers turned to Congress for legislative relief.

With the support of both businessmen and farmers, Congress passed the Emergency Tariff Act in May 1921. It was followed a little more than a year later by the Fordney-McCumber tariff law which raised rates to their highest point in American history up to that time. This measure increased duties on such farm commodities as wheat, wool, and sugar; and on chemical products, chinaware, textiles, and other industrial goods. The Fordney-McCumber Act answered the growing economic nationalism of the postwar period, but it encouraged foreign countries to increase their tariffs and almost eliminated the possibility that European nations would pay their war debts to the United States.

Another reflection of the strong postwar nationalism was the demand for immigration restriction. World War I had effectively reduced immigration, but following the Armistice large numbers of foreigners again arrived in the United States. Many citizens opposed this new influx of immigrants because, as one writer explained it, "these newcomers were far removed in speech, customs, habits of thought, and appearance from the original stock of this country." Workingmen opposed increased immigration because of its threat to United States wage scales; businessmen and others favored restriction in the hope of barring radical political doctrines which, they said, were imported by foreigners. In 1921 Congress passed the Emergency Quota Act which provided that only 3 percent of a nationality resident in the United States in 1910 could come to the United States in any one year. This law was less restrictive against Southern and Eastern Europeans than many people wished. After Coolidge became president, Congress in 1924 enacted a new immigration act which permitted only 2 percent of any nationality residing in the United States in 1890 to be admitted each year. By setting the date back to 1890 the law was much more discriminatory against Southern and Eastern Europeans. At that time very few people from that part of Europe had settled in the United States. The 1924 law also excluded the Japanese. In 1927 immigration was limited to an annual quota of only 150,000. The quota assigned each country was determined by multiplying the total by the percentage of that nationality living in the United States in 1920. The United States had thus adopted a plan of restrictive immigration and had abandoned its historic policy of admitting generally all those who desired to enter the United States.

Republican policy of reduced government spending and large tax cuts had won Harding's enthusiastic support, and Secretary of the Treasury Andrew W. Mellon took the lead in achieving these goals. Congress in 1921 repealed the excess profits tax and lowered surtaxes on large incomes from a wartime high of 65 percent to 50

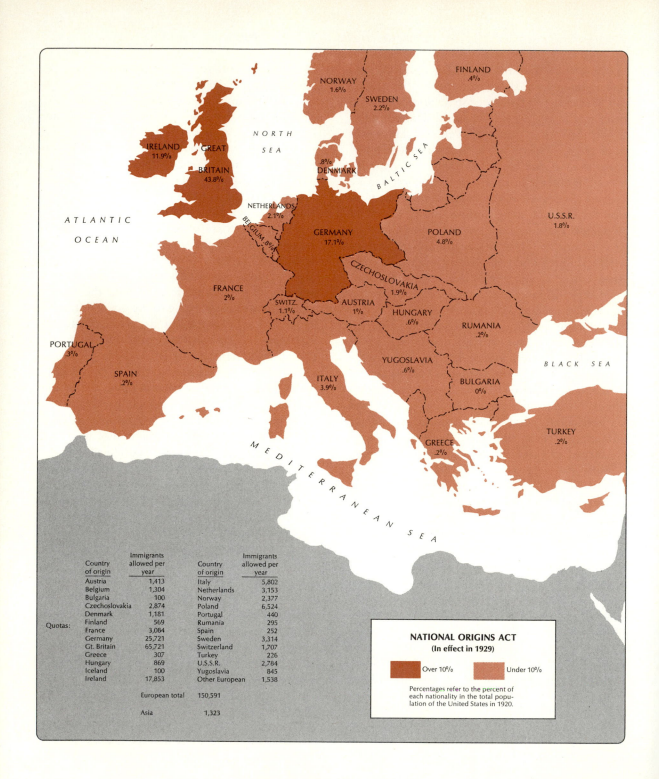

| NORWAY 1.6% |
| SWEDEN 2.2% |
| FINLAND .4% |

| IRELAND 11.9% | GREAT BRITAIN 43.8% |
| DENMARK .8% |
| NETHERLANDS 2.1% |
| BELGIUM .8% |
| GERMANY 17.1% | POLAND 4.8% |
| U.S.S.R. 1.8% |
| FRANCE 2% |
| CZECHOSLOVAKIA 1.9% |
| SWITZ. 1.1% | AUSTRIA 1% | HUNGARY .6% |
| RUMANIA .2% |
| PORTUGAL .3% | SPAIN .2% |
| YUGOSLAVIA .6% |
| ITALY 3.9% | BULGARIA 0% |
| GREECE .2% | TURKEY .2% |

N O R T H   S E A

B A L T I C S E A

A T L A N T I C   O C E A N

B L A C K   S E A

M E D I T E R R A N E A N   S E A

Quotas:

Country of origin	Immigrants allowed per year	Country of origin	Immigrants allowed per year
Austria	1,413	Italy	5,802
Belgium	1,304	Netherlands	3,153
Bulgaria	100	Norway	2,377
Czechoslovakia	2,874	Poland	6,524
Denmark	1,181	Portugal	440
Finland	569	Rumania	295
France	3,084	Spain	252
Germany	25,721	Sweden	3,314
Gt. Britain	65,721	Switzerland	1,707
Greece	307	Turkey	226
Hungary	869	U.S.S.R.	2,784
Iceland	100	Yugoslavia	845
Ireland	17,853	Other European	1,538
		European total	150,591
		Asia	1,323

NATIONAL ORIGINS ACT
(In effect in 1929)

Over 10%   Under 10%

Percentages refer to the percent of
each nationality in the total population of the United States in 1920.

percent. This was only the onset of a series of Republican tax reduction measures in the 1920s chiefly helpful to those with large incomes.

Policies of tax reduction dictated Harding's opposition to adjusted compensation for veterans. Men who had fought in the Great War believed strongly that their country owed them more than the $30 a month which most of them had received for their military service while those at home earned high wages. When Congress convened in April 1921, it became evident that the lawmakers were determined to pass some form of bonus legislation. Supported by the American Legion, which had been organized in 1919, Congress voted an adjustment compensation bill. Harding killed it with a veto.

Harding did support one basic administrative reform—the Budget and Accounting Act of 1921. With the growth of federal receipts and expenditures, it had become increasingly clear that the country needed an improved budgetary system. The law provided for a Director of the Budget and a Comptroller General. These officials, appointed by the President with Senate approval, worked as an arm of the executive branch. Over the years, the Director of the Budget became one of the most powerful men in government; he determined how much money Congress should be asked to appropriate for each governmental agency.

Scandal in High Places

Harding's term in Washington was more plagued by major scandal and petty graft than any administration since that of U. S. Grant. Although honest himself, the President's loose morals did not command respect from his associates and subordinates and may even have encouraged some of them to treat law and morality lightly. The "Ohio Gang," as his followers from back home were commonly known, engaged in a variety of corrupt activities. Some of them used their official positions and friendship with Harding to enrich themselves. Before Jess Smith, a close friend of Attorney General Harry Daugherty, shot himself in Daugherty's apartment in May 1923, he had engaged in such illicit activities as selling pardons, paroles, and liquor permits. When someone asked Smith if he planned to take a government job, he reportedly answered that he could make more money working for nothing! "My God, how the money rolls in," he once remarked. In the Veterans' Bureau, headed by Charles R. Forbes, officials practically gave away surplus war goods in return for financial benefits. Forbes was convicted of bribery. Another scandal involved Thomas R. Miller's Alien Property Custodian's office.

Harding's old friend Albert B. Fall, whom he had named Secretary of the Interior, turned out to be the administration's major crook. Fall became deeply involved in the Teapot Dome scandal. The Teapot Dome affair arose out of controversy between East and West over federal conservation policies and from conflicts between the Navy and Interior Departments over leasing of oil reserves which had been set aside earlier by Presidents Taft and Wilson. In May 1921, control of the oil reserves was transferred from the Navy Department, headed by Edwin Denby, to the Interior Department, where they came under Fall's administration. Less than a year later Fall leased Teapot Dome in Wyoming to Harry F. Sinclair and subsequently the Elk Hills reserve in California to Edward L. Doheny. These agreements were made without public bids. Doheny indicated the value of these leases when he later testified, "We will be in bad luck if we do not get $100,000,000 profits." But Sinclair and Doheny were not the only ones to turn a profit. An investigation revealed that Fall, who resigned in 1923, had received nearly $500,000 from those who stood to gain from the oil reserves. In 1929, after a long court battle, Fall was convicted of accepting a bribe. He was fined $100,000 and sentenced to one year in jail. Such scandals left a permanent mark on Harding's presidency; the low level of morality and national concern reflected the degree of public indifference to the honest and efficient conduct of national affairs.

But corruption and immorality were not the worst features of the Harding administration. Harding did not know the meaning of leadership; he did not believe in executive responsibility; and he permitted the nation to drift when it needed firm direction. He died on August 2, 1923, in San Francisco during a return trip from Alaska. People mourned the death of this kind, generous President who had freed Eugene V. Debs from prison and supported the eight-hour day for steelworkers, but Americans had lost a friend, not a leader.

"A Puritan in Babylon"

Harding's successor, Calvin Coolidge (1872–1933), came from a diligent family in rural Vermont. He was graduated from Amherst, attended law school, and began to practice in Northampton, Massachusetts, in 1898. Coolidge held a series of minor offices in Massachusetts before he became successively a member of the state legislature, lieutenant governor, and then governor. He gained national attention in 1919 when he received credit for ending the Boston police strike. Coolidge was a shy, taciturn puritan who believed in the traditional values of hard work, industry, thrift, and morality.

Coolidge was a dedicated economic and political conservative, well qualified to carry on the policies associated with normalcy. In his first annual message, he instructed Congress that government expenditures and taxes must be reduced and that the tariff schedules should not be changed. These policies, he believed, would benefit business and industry—those elements he considered responsible for the nation's economic progress. Fearful of governmental powers, he maintained that "there is an inescapable personal responsibility for the development of character, of industry, of thrift, and of self-control. These do not come from the government, but from the people themselves."

When Coolidge took office much was known about malfeasance in the Harding administration. Consequently, one of the President's first tasks was to restore integrity and morality in government. He did this by forcing from office those who had discredited Harding. Besides cleaning up the administration, Coolidge gave attention to the principal measures then before Congress. These included immigration restriction, tax reduction, a bonus for veterans, and agricultural legislation. Coolidge enthusiastically supported the Immigration Act of 1924 and was equally devoted to lower taxes. The Revenue Act of 1924 reduced income taxes from 8 to 6 percent and lowered maximum surtaxes from 50 to 40 percent. Coolidge's opposition to a cash bonus could not defeat an adjusted compensation measure for veterans. This law provided for payments to veterans of $1 for each day of service in the United States during the war and $1.25 for each day spent outside the country. On the agricultural question, Coolidge took a position unpopular among many Midwestern Republicans when he opposed every attempt by the federal government to raise farm prices.

Progressivism and the Campaign of 1924

Despite the political conservatism of the Harding and Coolidge administrations, a rather strong undercurrent of progressivism existed during the 1920s. But lacking national leadership, effective organization, and attractive policies, the postwar progressives were little more than bothersome critics of the conservative Republican majority. In 1924 Senator George W. Norris and a number of other progressives came out in favor of federal operation of hydroelectric plants and equipment constructed at Muscle Shoals in northern Alabama during the war. They hoped to expand the generating capacity to produce cheap electricity and low-cost fertilizer for farmers. Many conservatives preferred the assignment of these facilities to private enterprise and supported Henry Ford, who had offered $5 million for a ninety-nine year lease of Muscle Shoals. However, Congress rejected Ford's proposal. Progressives kept the dam sites open for later development by the Tennessee Valley Authority. Still this was at best a negative victory.

Much of the progressive strength centered in the agricultural Midwest, where farmers suffered from heavy debts, low prices, and inadequate incomes. By 1922 both rural and urban progressives decided to challenge the national administration. In February 1922, representatives of agriculture and labor, some Socialists, and miscellaneous reformers met in Chicago to form the Conference for Progressive Political Action. During the next two years these groups discussed the formation of a third party. Meeting in Cleveland on July 4, 1924, they nominated Senator Robert La Follette for president. After lashing out at the corrupting power of private monopoly, the new Progressive party called for public power, government ownership of railroads, effective farm relief, labor legislation which would guarantee the right of collective bargaining, and more liberal payments to veterans. This inclination to solve problems by expanding the role of government placed the new party strictly in the progressive tradition.

While the Progressives were organizing for 1924, most Republicans rallied behind the renomination of Calvin Coolidge, who had announced late in 1923 that he would seek a full term. When the delegates met in Cleveland on June 10, 1924, Coolidge received a first-ballot nomination. Most Republicans apparently agreed with Henry Ford, who said, "The country is perfectly safe with Coolidge. Why change?" Charles G. Dawes won the vice-presidential nomination. The Republican platform expressed the prevailing conservatism and called for "rigid economy in government," tax reduction, high tariffs, and farm relief.

While the Republican Convention was brief and quiet, the Democratic 1924 gathering was long, loud, and controversial. The leading candidate appeared to be William G. McAdoo, Wilson's secretary of the Treasury. McAdoo had considerable support throughout the South and West, but Eastern Democratic leaders favored Governor Alfred E. Smith of New York. A product of New York City's lower East Side and Tammany Hall, Smith had won the governorship in 1918. As governor he had achieved a number of social and administrative reforms. Smith was a Roman Catholic; he argued that prohibition—that great experiment of the twenties—should be repealed. For both reasons his chief opposition came from the "dry" Protestants of the Midwest and South. The Democratic Convention soon split over a resolution denouncing the Ku-Klux Klan. Thereafter neither McAdoo nor Smith could win the nomination. As a result, the convention turned to a compromise candidate and chose John W. Davis, a handsome, conservative lawyer of West Virginia and New York. To offset Davis's conservatism, the convention named Governor Charles W. Bryan of Nebraska, brother of William Jennings Bryan, for vice president. The Democratic platform demanded lower tariffs, aid for farmers, conservation, and government operation of Muscle Shoals.

Since Coolidge—scarcely an orator—abstained from personal campaigning, much of the Republican effort fell to Dawes. Believing that Davis was no threat, Dawes directed his campaign largely at La Follette, whom he pictured as a flaming radical. He urged people to "keep cool with Coolidge." The dominant issue, Dawes said, was "whether you stand on the rock of common sense with Calvin Coolidge, or upon the sinking sands of socialism with Robert M. La

Follette." The result was another sweeping Republican victory as Coolidge piled up more votes than Davis and La Follette combined. The President won 15,817,000 popular votes, while Davis and La Follette received 8,385,000 and 4,832,000 respectively. Judged by the outcome of the election, Coolidge pursued precisely those policies desired by a majority of the people.

More Normalcy

Coolidge accepted the election of 1924 as a mandate to continue the program which Harding had begun. In his annual message to Congress, the President declared that "rigid economy in public expenditures" was the lasting remedy for economic ills. Reduced taxes, he explained, had been largely responsible for the country's general prosperity. He recommended further tax cuts and argued that lower surtaxes on high incomes would actually produce more revenue by encouraging business expansion. He told Congress that operations at Muscle Shoals were "better suited to private enterprise" and urged that the properties there be sold or leased. Although he hoped something might be done to restore agricultural prosperity, Coolidge warned again that "the government cannot successfully insure prosperity or fix prices by legislative fiat." He insisted that prosperity came "from the natural working out of economic laws."

Tax reduction and farm relief emerged as the dominant political issues in the second Coolidge administration. Although taxes had been slashed in 1921 and again in 1924, Secretary Mellon wanted even larger cuts. He advanced the idea that tax reduction "increases the amount of capital which is put into productive enterprises, stimulates business, and makes more certain that there will be more $5,000 jobs to go around." Mellon saw a direct relation between monetary and fiscal policy—in this case low taxes—and full employment. Responding to the demand for lower taxes, Congress reduced rates in 1926 and again in 1928.

Despite lower taxes, the federal government was able to maintain a Treasury surplus throughout the 1920s. By opposing new government programs and cutting expenditures to about $3 billion a year, the Treasury enjoyed an annual average surplus of about $1 billion from 1923 to 1929. This enabled Congress to reduce the national debt (which had jumped to some $24 billion by 1920) to about $16 billion in 1929. Praising these policies, Coolidge told Congress in 1928: "Four times we have made a drastic revision of our internal revenue system, abolishing many taxes and substantially reducing almost all others. Each time the resulting stimulation to business has so increased taxable incomes and profits that a surplus has been produced." The President exaggerated the economic benefit of his tax laws, but the obvious business boom seemed to justify his policy.

Farm relief was more controversial politically. By 1925 farm groups, especially those in the normally Republican Midwest, were well organized and pushed hard for the McNary-Haugen bill, a plan which would involve the federal government in achieving higher farm prices. But Coolidge, in vetoing McNary-Haugen bills in 1927 and 1928, said that farmers must solve their own problems.

Despite his alienation of many farmers, Coolidge's popularity remained exceedingly high. By 1928 increasing farm prosperity had even reduced discontent in the rural regions. The great majority of Americans applauded Coolidge. The President's negativism became a virtue, his conservatism a blessing. Three months later Coolidge left the White House amidst glowing praise from his countrymen. The *New York Times* editorialized that Coolidge had "fitted exactly into the needs and inarticulate desires of the American people when he became president."

In August 1927, President Coolidge announced, "I do not choose to run for president in 1928." Although Coolidge's withdrawal opened the way for an open race, when the Republicans met in Kansas City in June 1928, Herbert Hoover had a commanding lead among the convention delegates. Closely identified with the exuberant prosperity of the 1920s, he had won high praise from the business community for his efficient administration of the Department of Commerce. Despite some opposition from farm leaders, the convention nominated Hoover on the first ballot. Charles Curtis of Kansas won the vice-presidential nomination. The platform called for continued tariff protection, tax reductions, government economy, farm relief without "putting the government in business," and support for prohibition.

One month later the Democrats met in Houston, Texas. Alfred E. Smith, who had been denied the nomination four years earlier, was clearly the leading candidate. Again he faced the opposition of the "dry" South and Midwest which did "not choose to vote for booze." But this time Smith won the nomination on the first ballot. To give the ticket geographical and religious balance, the convention named Senator Joseph T. Robinson of Arkansas, a dry and a Methodist, for vice president. Even though Smith's position on prohibition repeal was clear, the Democratic platform pledged an honest effort to enforce the Eighteenth Amendment. This contradiction between the position of the candidate and the platform did nothing to help the Democrats.

The campaign of 1928 occurred amid booming prosperity, labor peace, almost full employment, and improved conditions among farmers. Under these circumstances it is not surprising that the Republicans emphasized the alleged connection between their policies and good times throughout the nation. Hoover talked freely about the prospect of a chicken in every pot and two cars in every garage.

No Democrat could have won the presidency in 1928, but Smith had special liabilities which assured his defeat. No Catholic had ever been elected president, and millions of people believed that such an event should never happen. Although Hoover expressed no religious prejudice, many of his supporters warned against a Catholic president. "If Smith is elected will the Pope of Rome rule the United States?" asked one Missouri voter. Hoover won by a landslide. He polled 21,392,000 votes, while Smith gained only 15,016,000. Republicans had convinced a majority of the voters that victory for their party was the key to continued prosperity. Despite what appeared to be a political catastrophe for the Democrats, they had done better than the returns indicated. Smith ran well in many large cities; he reduced the Republican majorities in some of the strongest Republican agricultural states. The overall political trend was clearly favorable to the Democratic party.

American Society in the 1920s

The 1920s have been called the "jazz age" and the "roaring twenties," terms which imply that people were primarily interested in having fun and ignoring more serious matters. It is true that many people danced the Charleston, made bathtub gin, and read sexy novels, but the picture of a whole nation going mad in pursuit of pleasure is highly distorted. The period's deeper meaning can be found in the urban-rural conflict. Rural Americans attempted to preserve their old ideals and values against the threat of urban thought and behavior. The conflicts over prohibition, the

Ku-Klux Klan, and the teaching of Darwinism illustrated the intellectual and moral divide between urban and rural America.

Urbanization continued to have a profound effect on American life. Although cities had been growing rapidly for a century, the nation had remained predominantly rural. But in 1920 the census bureau found 51.4 percent of the people in towns and cities of 2,500 or more. By the end of the decade 56.2 percent of the population was urban. Urbanization developed so swiftly that at the end of the 1920s no more than 25 percent of Americans still resided on farms. Urban influences spread to every crossroads and village in the country. Cities not only produced most of the wealth, but also set the patterns of action and conduct for a great majority of citizens.

Most metropolitan areas had large numbers of recent immigrants. Moreover, thousands of blacks moved to Northern cities during and after the Great War. By the 1920s, most of the nation's big cities had a polyglot population of different races and nationalities, a condition which caused many white Americans to fear for the country's future stability and progress.

The 1920s was a highly nationalistic period. Most Americans believed that their institutions were clearly superior to anything found in foreign countries, and they were intolerant of any criticism of the American way of life. The demand for conformity which had been forced on citizens during the war, and then again during the Red Scare, continued throughout the decade, although to a much smaller extent. High-tariff laws, restrictions on immigration, strong opposition to any brand of radicalism—communism, socialism, or the IWW—were all reflections of intense nationalism.

The dramatic case of Nicola Sacco and Bartolomeo Vanzetti raised doubts that radicals could obtain a fair trial in the United States. Sacco and Vanzetti were accused of killing a paymaster and guard at a shoe factory in South Braintree, Massachusetts, during April 1920. They were convicted in July 1921 on what appeared to be insufficient evidence. After a seven-year legal battle, marked by public demonstrations in their behalf, they were again found guilty. To the end many Americans believed that the two men died because of their admitted radicalism and not because of convincing proof of their guilt.

Nothing illustrated better the raucous and intolerant quality of nationalism than the organization and growth of the Ku-Klux Klan. Formed again in 1915 by William J. Simmons and a few followers in Georgia, the Klan proposed to "unite white male persons, native born gentile citizens . . . who owe no allegiance of any nature to any foreign government, nation, institution, sect, ruler, or people." The Klan opposed black rights and insisted on white supremacy in the South. It attacked Jews and Catholics. In 1923 a Klan leader equated Roman Catholicism with "foreign idealism" and infidelity. The Klan denounced Jews because they supposedly had foreign financial connections. At first the Klan grew slowly, but after 1920, it experienced phenomenal expansion and by 1924 it had 4 or 5 million members.

While many Klan members came from the small towns of the South, Midwest, and Far West, cities had their quota of Klansmen. Both rural and urban white Americans feared the blacks, suspected the Catholics, and disliked recent immigrants. In Oklahoma, Texas, Indiana, and a few other states, the Klan became a strong political force in the early 1920s, but its influence declined after 1924 because of poor leadership and lack of generally acceptable objectives.

Blacks and Normalcy

Klan attitudes toward the black man were not unlike those held by a majority of white Americans, in both North and South. Despite the fact that thousands of blacks had fought gallantly in

Prejudice and Progress

The revival of the Ku Klux Klan seemed just one more symptom of the struggle between the ideas of rural America and those of the new urban and technological culture in the 1920s. The original Klan was organized in 1865 by former Confederate general Nathaniel B. Forrest. Its tactics of terror having prevailed in the South, the Klan quieted down, only to be reactivated in 1915. During the 1920s membership grew to four or five million. Now, however, the Klan operated in the North as well. Not merely against equal rights for blacks, now it came out against a host of other things: Catholics, Jews, immigrants, liquor. By 1925 the Klan was so strong it held a mass parade down Pennsylvania Avenue past the White House.

In a time of change the Klan appealed to certain native-born, rural, Protestant Americans. In its publications it proclaimed the virtues of a free press, the ballot, law enforcement, 100 percent Americanism, and the Holy Bible. Some of its Klaverns distributed baskets of food to the poor at Thanksgiving and Christmas. But in the atmosphere it created vigilantism too often replaced the process of law. From 1920 through 1925, for example, 225 lynchings took place in the United States.

While government did little to advance the economic welfare or civil rights of blacks during the 1920s, the Negro himself made an increasingly important impact on the cultural scene, particularly in entertainment and the arts. During this decade, jazz, a form developed largely by blacks, won widespread and enthusiastic acceptance. Great jazz artists of the period include Louis Armstrong, fourth from left in King Oliver's Band (center piece); Duke Ellington (above); Jelly Roll Morton, Thomas "Fats" Waller, J. P. Johnson, and W. C. Handy. On Broadway a series of musicals featured black stars like Florence Mills (right, above), Ethel Waters, Bill Robinson, and Josephine Baker.

A figure of special importance in the entertainment world was Paul Robeson, who established himself as a singer of spirituals on the concert stage where other black performers, including Marion Anderson (right) and Roland Hayes sang both classical and operatic arias. Robeson also became a leading actor in such plays as *All God's Chillun Got Wings* by Eugene O'Neill (right, below). Other important black actors in the 1920s included Charles Gilpin, Rose McClendon, and Richard Harrison.

Above: Brown Brothers; below: Culver Pictures, Inc.

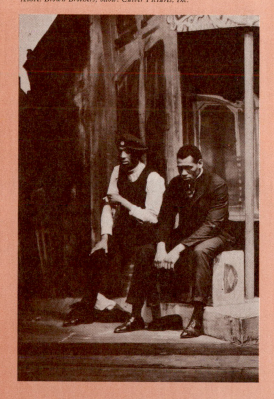

Walter White   *Underwood and Underwood*

Langston Hughes

The 1920s also saw a flowering of black literary talent. A man who popularized black writers was Dr. Alain Locke, professor of philosophy at Howard University, critic, and essayist, who in 1925 published an anthology, *The New Negro.* Important black poets of the period were Claude McKay, author of *Harlem Shadows* and several novels; Countee Cullen, who wrote *Color* and *The Black Christ;* and Langston Hughes, whose *Weary Blues* was the first of his many books. Among fiction writers were Walter White, author of the novels *The Fire in the Flint* and *Flight;* short-story writer Nora Zeale Hurston, and Jean Toomer, Wallace Thurman, Nella Larsen, and Jessie Fausset. The NAACP's *The Crisis* and *Opportunity,* a magazine founded for the Urban League by sociologist Charles S. Johnson, encouraged literary talent. Less well-known than the writers, a number of blacks distinguished themselves in other fields, including the historians Rayford W. Logan and Carter Woodson, sociologist E. Franklin Frazier, biologist Ernest Just, economist Abram Harris, a number of medical scientists, and many painters.

A. Philip Randolph

Nora Zeale Hurston   *Brown Brothers*

In 1925, A. Philip Randolph organized the Brotherhood of Sleeping Car Porters and became an increasingly important labor leader and spokesman for Negro rights. When many industries having government contracts at the outbreak of World War II would not hire blacks, Randolph's call for a march on Washington forced government action. In 1960 Randolph led in forming the Negro American Labor Council to fight prejudice in organized labor.

...de McKay   *Brown Brothers*

Countee Cullen

Schomburg Collection, New York Public Library

Alain Locke

National Association for the Advancement of Colored People

Leading groups in the struggle for black progress during the 1920s included the NAACP and the National Urban League, but a new, more colorful, and more radical group, the Universal Negro Improvement Association, also had a following. The NAACP, with more than four hundred branch offices across the nation, fought for black rights in the courts and

Brown Brothers

sought support for legislation such as the Dyer antilynching bill. The Urban League worked against discrimination in hiring practices. The UNIA, however, through its dynamic leader Marcus Garvey (above) held that blacks could prosper only by returning to Africa. The Ku Klux Klan approved Garvey's scheme and most black intellectuals denounced it, but between 1917, when it was organized, and 1923, the "Back to Africa" movement received some $10 million from its black supporters—Garvey rejected white aid. With these funds Garvey established The Black Star Line for transporting blacks to Africa and supported his African Legion which wore uniforms of green, black, and red. In 1921 the UNIA convention in New York drew 25,000 delegates and named Garvey "Provisional President General of Africa." In 1923 Garvey was sentenced to five years in prison on a charge of using the mails to defraud, and in 1927 he was deported to his native Jamaica.

the Great War—171 members of the black 369th Infantry were decorated by the French government—they came home to the same old economic, social, and political discrimination. Blacks resented more than ever the position of inferiority forced upon them. Many had left the South during the war and migrated to the Northern cities where they obtained jobs in industry and, like returning black veterans, were not prepared for the intolerant attitudes of Northern whites. As blacks sought better housing, improved education, and equal accommodations in public conveyances, they ran into a wall of resistance in the North just as they had in the South.

National tensions and the revival of the Ku-Klux Klan carried the bitter tradition of riots and lynchings into the postwar period. Between 1919 and 1921 there were violent race riots in Chicago, Tulsa, and other American cities. Earlier, Southerners had murdered thousands of blacks in the process of restoring exclusive white rule in the South. Although the nation experienced almost four thousand lynchings from 1889 to the end of the 1920s, Congress passed no antilynching legislation and no president acted vigorously against this practice.

Throughout the 1920s, the National Association for the Advancement of Colored People and the National Urban League assaulted bigotry and battled for greater social, economic, and educational rights for blacks. But discrimination gave way slowly, if at all. Marcus Garvey's Universal Negro Improvement Association, which emphasized race pride, had a substantial following in the early 1920s. Many blacks had been taught to despise Africa and blackness and to exalt things European. Garvey made heroic efforts to combat this. But his only solution for the "race problem" was the emigration of black Americans to Africa. No plan or organization did much to change the unequal position of blacks in American society. They continued, in general, to remain second-class citizens.

Blacks, however, did gain recognition in literature and the arts. So many able Afro-American writers and artists were active during the 1920s, and after, that the movement with which they were consciously associated became known as the Negro or Harlem Renaissance. What characterized the work of the group was great technical skill, race pride, and a certain militancy. Among the leaders were Langston Hughes, Claude McKay, Countee Cullen, James Weldon Johnson, Jessie Redmond Fauset, Walter White, Noble Sissle, Catherine Dunham, and Richard Wright. Johnson published *The Book of American Negro Poetry* in 1922; that year McKay, an immigrant from Jamaica, wrote a book of verse, *Harlem Shadows,* which expressed bitter resentment toward the treatment of blacks in America. Seven years later Countee Cullen's *The Black Christ* appeared. Both Jessie Redmond Fauset's *There Is a Confusion* (1924) and Walter White's *Fire in the Flint* (1924) dealt with some of the problems facing blacks in their effort to establish a place in American society. White's *Rope and Faggot: A Biography of Judge Lynch* was a well-researched study of lynching. George Schuyler wrote a great deal of critical commentary on American life. Much of this creative effort seemed to culminate in the appearance of Richard Wright's novel *Native Son* in 1940.

On the stage, Paul Robeson played in Eugene O'Neill's *All God's Chillun Got Wings* (1924); in 1930 Richard B. Harrison performed in *The Green Pastures.* Negro musical revues were well attended in the 1920s; and Louis Armstrong became one of the premier jazz artists of all time, and other black musicians took the lead in solidifying the jazz culture.

Eubie Blake and Noble Sissle produced the music for "Shuffle Along," one of the more popular musicals of the period. Solid achievements such as these were valid indications that blacks had abundant talent; unfortunately what they lacked was the opportunity to demonstrate that talent on a broader front.

Prohibition as a moral and political issue deeply divided Americans in the 1920s. When the Eighteenth Amendment went into effect on January 16, 1920, it represented the culmination of a long campaign to outlaw the manufacture and sale of intoxicating liquor. The Prohibition party; the Woman's Christian Temperance Union, organized in 1874; and the Anti-Saloon League, formed in 1893, had been highly effective in winning support for prohibition. Moreover, prohibition became a major progressive reform which gained support especially from old-stock middle- and upper-class reformers. During the war people argued that grain should be used for food instead of liquor. In 1917 Congress passed the prohibition amendment by large majorities, and by 1919 enough states had ratified the amendment to make it a part of the Constitution. Once the Constitution had prohibited the manufacture and sale of intoxicating liquor, Congress had to interpret the term "intoxicating." Later in 1919 Congress passed the Volstead Act, which defined intoxicating liquor as any drink containing over one-half of 1 percent alcohol.

Enforcement proved difficult, although in the early years of prohibition the law was quite effective throughout much of the nation. The amount of liquor consumed dropped sharply, and alcoholism and alcohol-related diseases declined substantially. However, by 1923 enforcement was breaking down. Congress never provided sufficient money to hire the agents needed to enforce the law, and in communities which opposed prohibition little was done to abolish the liquor trade. Moreover, crime and corruption fed on the illicit liquor traffic. Al Capone, Chicago's leading racketeer in the late 1920s, controlled much of the liquor business, as well as other illegal activities in that city, and his gang killed those who tried to infringe on his business.

What rendered prohibition embarrassing to politicians and law-enforcement agencies alike was the refusal of many wealthy citizens to alter their drinking habits. Never had drinking been so fashionable. It was largely the rich who made crime and racketeering profitable. President Hoover became so concerned about the whole problem that in 1929 he appointed a commission headed by George W. Wickersham to study that "great social and economic experiment." Reporting in 1930, the commission recommended continued prohibition but offered few constructive suggestions on law enforcement. By that time, however, it was becoming clear that an increasing number of Americans were having serious doubts about prohibition as a national social policy.

Manners and Morals

Society is always changing, but in the 1920s social change seemed to be swifter and more dramatic than in previous generations. People had more leisure and money, the automobile provided them with greater mobility, and radios and movies furnished them a new, passive form of entertainment. Restlessness surged through the country. Youth demanded more freedom and rebelled at customary social restraints. Women sought to escape the restrictions placed on them by law and tradition.

No single development had a more profound effect on American society than the automobile. "Why on earth do you need to study what's changing this country?" asked one observer. "I can tell you what's happening in just four letters: A-U-T-O!" The automobile age had started before World War I, and by 1920 the number of passenger cars registered in the United States had reached more than 8 million. But this was only the beginning. By 1930 some 23 million automobiles were traveling on American streets and highways. Expanded use of the automobile not only gave people much more mobility, but also affected courtship, vacation travel, employment, and recreation. By the 1920s the automobile had become a distinct part of the American way of life.

Commercial radio broadcasting began in Pittsburgh in 1920. Seven years later millions of Americans listened regularly to music, drama, and sports. Some 40 percent of the nation's families owned radios by 1930. Movie theaters attracted crowds of anxious entertainment seekers in towns and cities from New York to San Francisco. Silent pictures had given way to sound films by 1929.

The constant search for excitement and amusement reflected the deep restlessness in American society. Spectator sports such as baseball, football, and prizefighting attracted millions of fans. Babe Ruth of the New York Yankees was baseball's idol, and in 1927 the "king of swat" hit sixty home runs to establish a record not broken until the 1960s. Harold "Red" Grange of the University of Illinois, one of the greatest football players of all time, packed spectators into the Big Ten university stadiums. Prizefighting had two of history's greatest champions in Jack Dempsey and Gene Tunney. Dempsey defeated Jess Willard in 1919 and held the heavyweight crown until 1926, when he lost to Tunney.

The music and dances of the 1920s were a further expression of the national mood. The most popular dances, at least among the younger people, were the fast and acrobatic Charleston and Black Bottom. Such songs as "The Love Nest," "Hot Lips," and "I Gotta Have You" indicated the popularity of songs stressing love and sex. The black influence on music was seen in jazz and blues songs such as "St. Louis Blues" and "Memphis Blues."

The new youth cult deeply worried and alarmed older Americans. Short, above-the-knee dresses, the new dances, necking parties, and the frank discussion of sex by the country's young people all demonstrated that they were bent on

Dancing the Charleston in the 1920s.

The Granger Collection

freedom. The antics of youth convinced many citizens that degeneracy had displaced decency and that carnality had destroyed morality.

It was not easy to bridge the marked and agonizing generation gap which existed between the young and their elders. Many spokesmen for the younger generation were frankly critical of the society which they had inherited from their parents, a society which most mature Americans looked upon as the best in the world. "The older generation has certainly pretty well ruined this world before passing it on to us," wrote one youthful observer in 1920. "They give us this thing, knocked to pieces, leaky, red-hot, threatening to blow up; and then they are surprised that we don't accept it with the same attitude of pretty decorous enthusiasm with which they received it, way back in the 'eighties.'" To be sure, only a minority of the nation's youth threw off the restrictions of the past and the standards of their parents, but the visible change indicated a new social day had dawned.

Some women embarked on a crusade for personal emancipation. They demanded equality in manners and morals. They assumed such male prerogatives as drinking, smoking, and sexual freedom. But prewar progressive crusades in which women had been so active stagnated or declined in the postwar decade. Although a few women such as Belle Moskowitz were active in politics and others supported an Equal Rights Amendment to the Constitution and a birth control program, except for regular employment there was actually some decline in the number of activities women were involved in outside the home.

Literary Currents

Restlessness, desire to break from the past, and distaste for American culture all received expression in the popular literature of the 1920s. F. Scott Fitzgerald shocked thousands of readers with his novel *This Side of Paradise*, published in 1920. His leading character, Amory Blaine, engaged in a variety of drinking and loving bouts which purportedly represented the actions of many young people of that time. During the next few years scores of novels exploited the themes of alcohol and sex without coming to grips with anything of much social importance except the idea of youthful revolt against the restricting puritanism of their forebears.

Works of serious social criticism also captured the spirit of the 1920s. Sinclair Lewis pictured the mean, dull life of a small Midwest town in *Main Street* (1920). Of Gopher Prairie he wrote: "It is negation canonized as the one positive virtue. It is the prohibition of happiness. It is slavery self-sought and self-defended. It is dullness made God." Two years later Lewis analyzed what he considered the petty commercialism of an American small-town businessman in *Babbitt*. Lewis's novel *Elmer Gantry* was a vitriolic attack on the revivalist preacher. In *Winesburg, Ohio* (1919) Sherwood Anderson told a series of stories which described the frustration, shallowness, and loneliness of life in a small American community. Theodore Dreiser's *An American Tragedy* (1925) related the story of a young man who ruined his life and finally met death because of his unrestrained desire for wealth and position. Ernest Hemingway became a self-conscious member of the critical generation with his *The Sun Also Rises*. Lewis, Dreiser, Anderson, and Hemingway personified the writers who were cynical and defeatist about America. They were part of the so-called lost generation, many of whom spent much of their time in Paris complaining about their native land, but living off its fruits. Perhaps the sharpest critic of white, middle-class, Protestant society was H. L. Mencken. Through the columns of the *American Mercury* he attacked almost every aspect of American life. But Americans generally believed theirs to be the best society man had ever created.

Most popular fiction in the 1920s, however, did not follow sex themes or stress the undesirable aspects of American life and culture. The writings of Zane Grey, Harold Bell Wright, Willa Cather, Booth Tarkington, and Edna Ferber provided no break from the past and were much more widely read than the works of Fitzgerald or Lewis. Ferber's *So Big*, which won a Pulitzer prize, and *Cimarron* caught the excitement and drama in the settlement of the Southwest. Zane Grey's Westerns sold by the millions.

Religion and Education

Although Americans considered themselves a religious people, traditional Christianity experienced some trying times in the years between the Great War and the Great Depression. In the first

Art in America: 1905–1940

In the early twentieth century, the more progressive elements in American
art took two directions. The first, in a native idiom, led toward a new and
vigorous interpretation of the contemporary scene, particularly the world of
urban America. The group of artists concerned with this theme were dubbed
"The Ashcan School" because of their nonidealizing tendencies, or "The
Eight," because the major New York group exhibition of their work in 1908
included eight painters. Even this group, however, included only five artists
devoted to depicting the contemporary urban world and its inhabitants in
broad, slashing brush strokes—Robert Henri, John Sloan, George Luks, Everett
Shinn, and William Glackens. Glackens would shortly abandon the dramatic
approach of these early years for an American version of Renoir's Impressionism. The other members of "The Eight"—Ernest Lawson, an Impressionist
landscapist, Arthur B. Davies, an idealizing dreamer, and Maurice
Prendergast, who developed a very personal form of Post-Impressionism—
allied themselves with the urban realists only in sympathy against the
entrenched academics.

Meanwhile, in the first two decades of the century a progress of American
painters found their way to Europe, studying and absorbing the new,
revolutionary movements of Cubism, Orphism, Futurism, and Abstraction—

such men as Marsden Hartley, Max Weber, Joseph Stella, Alfred Maurer, and others whose works were greeted, on their return to America, with complete incomprehensibility and hostility. Indeed, Modernism aroused the greatest aesthetic controversy of the early twentieth century when pictures in this style appeared at Alfred Stieglitz' New York Gallery, "291," at such exhibitions as the 1913 Armory Show which presented the first comprehensive survey of advanced European tendencies, and the Forum Exhibition of American Modernism of 1916.

Among those in partial retreat from Modernism, Marsden Hartley, in this crude but powerfully expressionistic treatment of the Maine landscape, for example, was among the most original as he emphasized solid massiveness in depicting mountains, trees, water, and clouds.

Marsden Hartley (1877–1943)
Mt. Katahdin, Autumn No. 1, 1939–40, oil
F. M. Hall Collection, University of Nebraska Art Galleries.

The isolationism which set in after World War I and affected American political life had its cultural counterpart in the arts. Many of the leading American Modernists abandoned their progressive tendencies and fell back upon a form of modified realism. Weber returned to a new exploration of his first great inspiration, Cézanne; Stella turned to a form of exotic mysticism, and Hartley painted expressionistic landscapes and figure studies in New Mexico and then Maine. Only Stuart Davis and Charles Demuth continued to explore and develop later forms of Cubism. That geometric concentration and sharpness of form, however, was applied to an interpretation of American industrialism in the work of the "Immaculate" or "Precisionist" artists, such as Charles Sheeler, who came to be called "Cubist-Realists."

The reaction against European Modernism also gave birth to the Regionalist school which advocated the denial of advanced foreign influences and a return to native American subject matter. A group of Midwestern artists, Grant Wood, John Stewart Curry, and Thomas Hart Benton, found even the Eastern cities too contaminated by foreign ideas. In the 1920s and 1930s, both realism and regionalism received new impetus, and regional schools of different degrees of conservatism and modernism developed throughout the nation. One form of realism had particular significance and attracted a large number of talented painters. "Social Realism" involved artists such as Ben Shahn, Jack Levine, and others who were concerned with the problems of war, refugees, workers, and urban ills and corruption.

During these years, the most original tendencies in American sculpture did not parallel painting, and neither urban realism nor abstraction and other forms of modernism found much of a sculptural counterpart. Rather, a stylized linearism, as personified in the work of Paul Manship and later given a powerful, expressionist interpretation by Manship's pupil, Gaston Lachaise, constituted the most striking sculptural development. The 1920s also saw a return to direct carving of wood, alabaster, and stone by such sculptors as William Zorach, John Flannagan, and José de Creeft, who made use of the unique color, texture, grain, and even shape of their basic materials.

Gaston Lachaise followed his master, Manship, in retaining an emphasis on simple, curvilinear outlines and sleek surfaces, but he endowed his gigantic figures with such a sense of voluptuousness and sensuousness that they seem almost to grow and expand before us.

Gaston Lachaise (1882–1935), Standing Woman, 1912–1927, bronze.

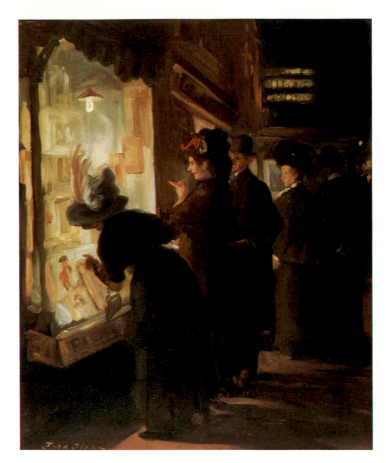

Of "The Eight," or "Ashcan School,"
John Sloan was the foremost painter
of the urban scene itself and the
life of the people in the cities. He
matched these vivid scenes with an
equally vivid technique.

John Sloan (1871–1951)
Shop Window, 1901, *oil*
The Newark Museum. Gift of Mrs. Felix Fuld,
1925.

Robert Henri was the leading spirit
of "The Eight." Primarily a figure
and portrait painter, he chose sympathetic, appealing subjects which
he interpreted with vivid brush
work and dramatic and rich color.

Robert Henri (1865–1929)
Laughing Child, 1907
Collection Whitney Museum of American Art, New York

Until about 1911 or 1912 William
Glacken's work was devoted to similar themes
(right). His technique finds its ancestry in
the painterly heritage of the Frenchman,
Manet, and the Americans who studied in
Munich—Frank Duveneck and particularly
William Merritt Chase. A number of other
painters did share a devotion to contemporary
realism with "The Eight," however, including
Jerome Myers, Glenn Coleman, and best-
known and most successful of all, George
Bellows. Bellows' outstanding figure painting
is best seen in his powerful, expressive prizefighting scenes with their emphasis upon
action and ruggedness (below).

William Glackens (1870–1938)
Park on the River, 1905
The Brooklyn Museum, Dick S. Ramsay Fund.

George Bellows (1882–1925), Both Members of This Club, 1909, *oil on canvas*
National Gallery of Art, Washington, D. C. Gift of Chester Dale.

Top: Marsden Hartley (1877–1943), Portrait of a German Officer, 1914, oil on canvas. The Metropolitan Museum of Art, Alfred Stieglitz Collection, 1949. Above: Max Weber (1881–1961), Chinese Restaurant, 1915, oil on canvas. Collection Whitney Museum of Art, New York. Right: Stanton MacDonald-Wright (1890–   ), Synchromy #3, 1917. Collection of Mr. and Mrs. Milton Lowenthal.

ile the painters of the Ashcan School
sued their realistic art at home, other
ists went to Europe and studied the
olutionary Modernism of the young
asso, Matisse, and Kandinsky. In
rmany at the beginning of World
r I, Marsden Hartley created vivid,
i-abstract, geometric patterns based
n military flags, banners, and
ignia (left, above). Max Weber in-
ed first by Matisse and the Fauve
ement, worked with raw color and
d chromatic contrasts; later he turned
he flat, geometric and kaleidoscopic
ns of Cubism and Futurism applied
Jew York subjects (left, below).
ph Stella, was even more inspired by
ian Futurism, which found its most
d American interpretation in the
ntings Stella did of the Brooklyn
dge (right), then considered a symbol
dvanced technology. Weber and Stella
ight these new movements back to
erica; Stanton MacDonald Wright,
g with Morgan Russell, founded a
ement in Paris known as Synchrom-
which, like the native French
hism, consituted a coloristic, dy-
ic rebuttal (below) to the monochro-
ic, static character of Cubism
ough both shared an interest in
-abstraction and the use of
ietric shapes.

Joseph Stella (1877–1946), The Bridge, 1922, gouache.
The Newark Museum. Purchase 1937, Felix Fuld Bequest.

Arthur G. Dove (1880–1946), Fog Horns, 1929, *oil.*
Colorado Springs Fine Arts Center.

John Marin (1870–1953), Maine Islands, 1922, *watercolor.*
The Phillips Collection.

Hartley, Weber, Stella, and MacDonald Wright were American followers and counterparts of Europe's leading Modernists. Arthur Dove's oils, watercolors, and collages, some among the earliest American abstractions, made up a more individual contribution, evocative paintings often with loose naturalistic associations based upon the suggestiveness of shapes and sounds (left, above).

John Marin developed a very individual, shorthand calligraphy in his vivid watercolors of Maine. The fragmentation of forms (left, below) is based upon Cubism, but the sense of movement, and his recreation of structure with interior frames, is his own. While the reaction against Cubism set in in both America and Europe after 1920, Stuart Davis continued to investigate the breaking-up of forms in flat, two-dimensional patterns. His dynamic conjunctions and interweaving of color areas have often been likened to the rhythms of contemporary jazz (below).

*uart Davis (1894–1964), Report from Rockport, 1940, oil. Collection of Mr. and Mrs. Milton Lowenthal.

One of the most strikingly original and distinctly American
movements of the 1920s and 1930s was called "Precisionism";
its practitioners were referred to as "The Immaculates" because
of their use of sharply defined, precise forms. Charles Sheeler best
characterizes these artists who often devoted their talents to the
depiction of the industrial landscape (right, above). Devoid of
irregular shapes and outlines, these paintings omit any trace of
the accidental. This emphasis upon geometric regularity is a
Cubist heritage perhaps most clearly seen in the work of Charles
Demuth, where the flat patterns and linear overlays never destroy
the recognizability of the subject (below).

Charles Demuth (1883–1935), My Egypt, 1927, oil on composition board. Collection, Whitney Museum
of American Art, New York.

Charles Sheeler (1883–1965), American Landscape, 1930. *Collection, The Museum of Modern Art, New York, Gift of Abby Aldrich Rockefeller*

Precisionist clarity of form found its most original interpretation in the flower and leaf studies of Georgia O'Keeffe. Here the magnification of the object and the elimination of everything accidental transmits an effect on the one hand nearly abstract, and on the other, seemingly pulsating with a sense of growth and life.

Georgia O'Keeffe (1887–   )
The White Flower, 1931, *oil*
Collection, The Whitney Museum of Art, New York.

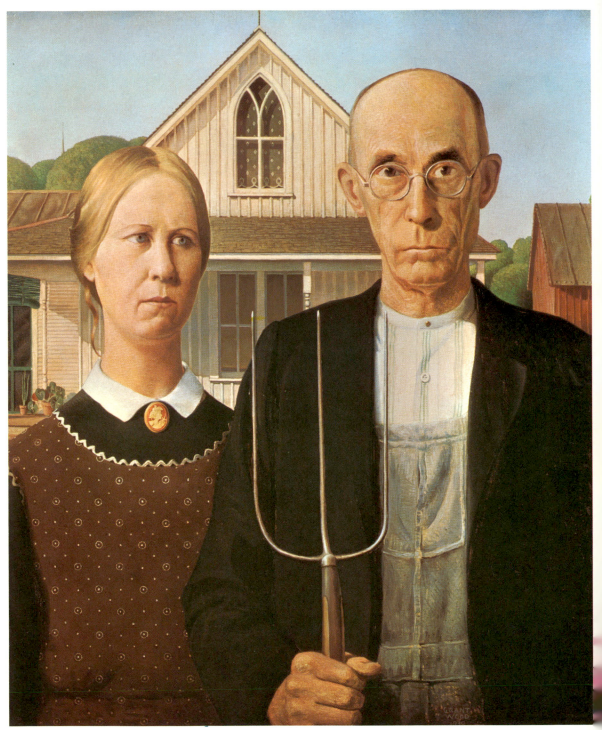

Grant-Wood (1892–1942), American Gothic, 1930, *oil on beaver board. Courtesy of the Art Institute of Chicago, Friends of American Art Collection.*

The reaction to European Modernism found its highest expression in the work of those artists who depicted the world of the rural Midwest. The most original talent among these Regionalists was Grant Wood, who revived a meticulous technique to satirize the grim smugness of the people of his region (left). Charles Burchfield interpreted the Victorian heritage of America's towns in Surrealist, dream-like fashion. In these monumental watercolors, Burchfield gives an anthropomorphic character to his old buildings, with their window-eyes, door-mouths, and haunted, alive expressions (right). A more straightforward melancholy appears in the old structures and their lonely inhabitants depicted in Edward Hoppers's urban scenes (below). These paintings are quiet descendants of the urbanism of the Ashcan School, but they gain in structure and monumentality from a subtle overlay of Cubist logic and geometry.

p: Charles E. Burchfield (1893–1967), Church Bells Ringing, Rainy Winter Night, 1917, watercolor on paper. The Cleveland Museum of t. Gift of Mrs. Louise M. Dunn in Memory of Henry G. Keller. Above: Edward Hopper (1882–1967), Early Sunday Morning, 1930, oil on vas. Collection, Whitney Museum of American Art, New York.

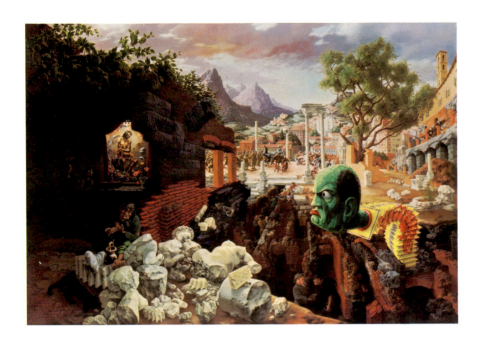

Nearly all of the advanced American Modernists of the decade between 1910–1920 retreated to more conventional, certainly more realistic artistic styles in subsequent years. Hartley's later style has already been discussed. Among other painters, Peter Blume is probabl[y] America's best known Surrealist creating dreamlike images in a meticulous and minute style. In "The Eternal City," his most famous canvas, he used this approach to caricature the impact of Mussolini and Fascism.

Both Jack Levine and Ben Shahn acknowledged their involvement with the problems of the period in their art, and they are appropriately known as "Social Realists." Jack Levine often depicted gangsters and corrupt politicians in a biting, satirical manner (left, below), while Ben Shahn is perhaps best known for his much shared sympathy with the executed Sacco and Vanzetti, his artistic protest expressing outrage against social injustice (right). Both artists utilized expressionist techniques, that is, they make use of distortions of natural forms for emotional, dramatic effects: Shahn's approach is very linear; Levine concentrates upon broad, fluid masses of rich paint.

The major innovation in American sculpture of the early twentieth century, combined a simplification of form with sharp, sleek linearism and the suggestion of movement stemming from the Art Nouveau movement and constituting a reaction to the historical monuments and generalized allegories of such artists as Saint Gaudens and French. Paul Manship was the most outstanding sculptor to take this direction. He was also one of the leading teachers of the following generation of sculptors.

Paul Manship (1885–1966)
Diana
Museum of Art, Carnegie Institute, Pittsburgh, Pa.

Stone carving in the mid-nineteenth century involved only the sculptor preparing the design and hired workmen executing the carving. The return to carving by artists such as William Zorach and others came about 1920. The subjects of such representational sculpture are usually quite conservative, but the artists often allowed the shape of the block to determine the final form, and they often chose special, exotic woods, marbles, or other stones to take advantage of peculiar colors, variations in the grain of the material, and other qualities intrinsic to the medium.

William Zorach (1887–1966)
Mother and Child, 1927–1930, Spanish marble
The Metropolitan Museum of Art, Fletcher Fund, 1952.

place, the increasing emphasis upon science and the acceptance of newer theological views tended to cast doubt on some basic Christian beliefs. For example, one survey of 500 ministers revealed that only forty-six of them thought it was necessary to believe in the virgin birth of Christ to be a Christian. Such ideas shook many church members and left them confused and uncertain.

Churches came under the influence of the prevailing business philosophy of the prosperous 1920s. Indeed, some church and lay leaders pictured Jesus as a successful businessman and attempted to sell Christianity much as they would soap or cigarettes. The most popular nonfiction book in the middle 1920s was Bruce Barton's *The Man Nobody Knows*. Barton presented Jesus not as a man of sorrows, but as a skilled executive who "picked up twelve men from the bottom of business and forged them into an organization that conquered the world."

Competition from sports, the movies, and the automobile was a third factor which influenced organized religion. By the 1920s millions of nominally faithful Christians were finding other things to do on Sunday. Instead of going to church they took a drive in the country, played golf, watched a baseball game, or went to a movie.

Despite these conditions, the number of churches and church membership grew in the postwar decade. The country had some 232,000 churches and synagogues with a total membership of 54.5 million in 1926, an increase of nearly 13 million members during the previous ten years. There were some 32 million Protestants, divided into more than 200 separate denominations; 18.6 million Catholics; and approximately 4 million of the Jewish faith. The rate of increase among Catholics was slackening off because of the drop in immigration. By 1926, some 55 percent of the American people over thirteen years of age were church members, a higher percentage than at any previous time in American history.

The trend toward liberalism and modernism in theology continued, especially in the larger denominations and those affiliated with the Federal Council of Churches. Many, although not all, of these religious leaders demonstrated a keen interest in the social gospel, believing that the church was an agency to remake society here and now. But fundamentalists were still strong. They held firmly to the Bible as the absolute word of God and insisted that one could not be a true Christian without believing in the virgin birth, the physical resurrection of Jesus, and the second coming of Christ. "Billy" Sunday, the great revivalist of the day, drew huge crowds as he denounced sin and called for repentance.

Many fundamentalists favored laws designed to protect the thought and action of the public. The court case which challenged the Tennessee law forbidding the teaching of evolution illustrated the conflict between science and religion, between liberals and fundamentalists. In 1925, John T. Scopes was arrested for teaching evolution at Dayton, Tennessee. Clarence Darrow, a brilliant, atheistic criminal lawyer, defended the young biology teacher while William Jennings Bryan, conservative Presbyterian and elder statesman of the Democratic party, assisted the prosecution. The antievolutionists won the case, but Scopes later gained freedom on a technicality. The strain of defending his fundamentalist views in the terrible July heat contributed to Bryan's death a short time later. Despite Bryan's evident ignorance of science, religious conservatives believed that he had given an admirable defense of the true faith. However, the case had no great effect on science teaching in the schools.

For many years, most Americans had been committed to public, tax-supported education, at least through high school. Moreover, by 1914 progressive educators had generally accepted John Dewey's ideas of the child-centered school. For a number of years fewer classical subjects such as Greek and Latin had been offered, and high schools were adding what were considered more practical courses, such as agriculture and business arithmetic. To a large extent, the trends

Darrow and Bryan at the Scopes trial.   *Brown Brothers*

in education in the 1920s were a continuation of changes which had been in progress for at least a generation.

Rapidly growing enrollments and school expenditures at all levels reflected the faith of the American people in education. The total number of children in school from kindergarten through the twelfth grade rose from 23.2 million in 1920 to 28.3 million a decade later. By 1920 more than 81 percent of the nation's children between five and seventeen years of age were in school. While total enrollment advanced 21 percent in the 1920s, the number of students going to high school jumped more than 100 percent. This emphasized the increasing importance being attached to high school education, not only as preparation for college but as training for life. The number of college students nearly doubled during the decade, reaching more than a million in 1930.

Educational opportunities still varied greatly in different regions of the United States and between urban and rural communities. There were still thousands of one-room, ungraded country schools where a minimum amount of learning occurred. In the South, educational opportuni-

ties for blacks and many poor whites were extremely inadequate, in some cases nonexistent. Hundreds of thousands of black children received no preparation to attend high school or college, or to live in an increasingly technological society.

Science received strong emphasis both inside and outside the universities. Although much of the commentary on science was poorly prepared and sometimes inaccurate, newspapers, magazines, and books kept people informed of the latest scientific developments. Widespread discussion of evolution made many people aware for the first time that scientists had placed man in the animal kingdom, and this realization contributed measurably to the conflict between religion and science. Psychology was among the newer and most popular branches of science. The ideas of Sigmund Freud, the famous Austrian physician who developed the form of psychotherapy called psychoanalysis, commanded widespread attention. In other areas, Arthur H. Compton of the University of Chicago won a Nobel prize in 1927 for his contributions to x-ray research. Almost every field of natural science showed progress during the 1920s, but the average citizen was interested chiefly in its practical application to his living standards. Plastics and rayon were only a few of the products which grew out of the new discoveries.

Many people received much of their education from newspapers and magazines. Every large city had one or more daily newspapers, and most small towns published a weekly. As newspapers after 1920 became increasingly uniform in appearance and content, people in all parts of the country read the same Associated Press news stories, the same syndicated columnists, and even the same comic strips. Two of the most notable developments in magazine publishing were the founding of *Reader's Digest* by Dewitt Wallace in 1922 and the establishment of *Time* by Henry R. Luce the following year. Both *Time* and *Reader's Digest* became huge successes because the magazines filled a need for people who wanted their reading condensed and digested.

Conclusion

President Harding caught the spirit of the times when he called for normalcy. To most Americans this meant maintaining things much as they had been in prewar America. In the 1920s there was a strong reaction against further expansion of governmental powers to promote the general welfare such as that which had characterized the progressive movement. By sensing this mood and acting on it, the Republicans were easily able to win the presidency and to control Congress by large majorities. As long as prosperity continued, the Republican administrations seemed to be acting in the national interest and received commensurate popular endorsement.

At the same time, American social and cultural life underwent some basic changes. Rapid urban growth, greater mobility emphasized by growing use of the automobile, greater freedom for youth, and new intellectual currents combined to produce major innovations in American society. Although some observers charged that Americans in the postwar years were purposeless and lacked serious aims and objectives, the twenties produced enduring contributions in literature, history, education, science, and the fine arts.

SUGGESTED READINGS

There are several excellent surveys of the 1920s. These include W. E. Leuchtenburg's *The Perils of Prosperity, 1914–1932** (1958); John D. Hicks's *Republican Ascendancy, 1921–1933** (1960); H. U. Faulkner's *From Versailles to the New Deal* (1950); and Arthur M. Schlesinger, Jr.'s *The Crisis of the Old Order, 1919–1933** (1957).

The best biographies of Harding are Andrew Sinclair's *The Available Man: Warren Gamaliel Harding* (1965) and Francis Russell's *The Shadow of Blooming Grove: Warren G. Harding and His Times* (1968), and Randolph C. Downes, *The Rise of Warren Gamaliel Harding.* (1970). On the Harding administration see Robert K. Murray, *The Harding Era* (1969). The best study on Coolidge is D. R. McCoy's *Calvin Coolidge: The Quiet President* (1967). Biographies of other leaders prominent in the 1920s add a great deal to a better understanding of the politics of the period. These include William H. Harbaugh's *Lawyer's Lawyer: The Life of John W. Davis* (1973); Oscar Handlin's *Al Smith and His America** (1958); J. A. Garraty's *Henry Cabot Lodge* (1953); and Richard Lowitt's *George W. Norris* (1971). On the presidential elections see Wesley Bagby's *The Road to Normalcy: The Presidential Campaign and Election of 1920* (1962); K. C. MacKay's *The Progressive Movement of 1924* (1947); R. V. Peel and T. C. Donnelly's *The 1928 Campaign* (1931); and E. A. Moore's *A Catholic Runs for President* (1956), an account of Al Smith's campaign to reach the White House.

The scandals of the Harding administration have been treated in a lively fashion by S. H. Adams in *The Incredible Era* (1939). On the background of Teapot Dome, see J. Leonard Bates's *The Origins of Teapot Dome* (1963); for a full account consult Burl Noggle's *Teapot Dome: Oil and Politics in the 1920s* (1962).

American society in the 1920 has drawn an unusually large number of writers and interpreters. The most perceptive contemporary account is F. L. Allen's *Only Yesterday** (1931). Volume VI of Mark Sullivan's *Our Times, The Twenties* (1935) contains a wide variety of material on American life and culture, but it lacks unity and organization. P. W. Slosson's *The Great Crusade and After, 1914–1928* (1930) is a good survey of the period's cultural history. Some of the social changes which were occurring in America are shown in the study of Muncie, Indiana, published in 1929 by R. S. and H. M. Lynd in *Middletown** . On urban growth and influence see George E. Mowry, *The Urban Nation, 1920–1960** (1965).

The Red Scare has been most fully treated by R. K. Murray in *Red Scare: A Study in National Hysteria, 1919–1920** (1955). On the Ku-Klux Klan see *The Ku Klux Klan in American Politics* (1962) by A. S. Rice, as well as C. C. Alexander's *The Ku Klux Klan in the Southwest** (1965). A satisfactory history of prohibition is Andrew Sinclair's *Era of Excess: A Social History of the Prohibition Movement** (1962). The position of Negroes in the 1920s has been treated by J. H. Franklin in part of his *From Slavery to Freedom** (2d ed.,

1956) and in Stephen H. Bronz, *Roots of Negro Racial Consciousness: The 1920's* (1964). The Harlem renaissance is best treated by Nathan Huggins (1971) in *Harlem Renaissance.*

Generally critical contemporary evaluations of American culture have been summarized in *Civilization in the United States: An Inquiry by Thirty Americans* (1922), edited by Harold E. Stearns. On religion see the relevant sections in Norman Furniss's *The Fundamentalist Controversy, 1918–1931* (1954); Paul A. Carter's *The Decline and Revival of the Social Gospel,* 1920–40 (1956); and *American Catholicism and Social Action* * (1960) by A. I. Abell. Educational trends may be followed in Lawrence A. Cremin's *The Transformation of the School: Progressivism in American Education, 1876–1957* * (1961.

Literary trends are well treated in Lloyd Morris's *Postscript to Yesterday: American Life and Thought, 1896–1946* * (1947) and J. Hoffman's *The Twenties* * (1955). *The Woman Citizen: Social Feminism in the 1920s* (1973) by J. Stanley Lemons is excellent on that topic.
*indicates availability in paperback.

27

Prosperity, Hoover, and the Great Depression

Except for the short-lived depression of 1921 and 1922, the decade after the Great War was unusually prosperous. Increased industrial efficiency, expanded production, high profits, almost full employment, and a rising standard of living characterized those postwar years. Gross national product, or the total production of goods and services in the United States, increased from $74.2 billion to $104 billion between 1919 and 1929, and annual per capita income rose from $710 to $857 in dollars of the same purchasing power. Greater production and wider distribution of goods meant better living standards for millions of Americans.

To be sure, many citizens, including those in urban slums, the uneducated and untrained, the handicapped, and tenants and sharecroppers on the farm, did not earn enough to maintain what might be considered a decent standard of living, but overall there was no place in the world where so many had so much. In accepting the presidential nomination in 1928, Herbert Hoover said: "We in America today are nearer to the final triumph over poverty than ever before in the history of any land." Indeed, no president in the twentieth century took office under what appeared to be more favorable circumstances than Herbert Clark Hoover did. The stock market boom which followed his inauguration on March 4, 1929, seemed to reflect business confidence and the prospect of even brighter days ahead. Yet within six months a severe stock market panic precipitated a major depression. The optimism so prevalent before 1929 soon receded before the realities of hard times. By 1932 the country was looking for new, more flexible leadership. Already most Americans had repudiated both Hoover and his policies.

Postwar prosperity merely accelerated the major trends already established in American business and industry. These included larger units of production, technological advances, mass output of goods, increased labor efficiency, and improved management practices. The continued growth of large-scale, corporate enterprise resulted in the domination of leading industries by a few giants. By the end of the 1920s, for example, Ford, Chrysler Corporation, and General Motors produced 83 percent of the automobiles; two companies, General Electric and Westinghouse, manufactured the bulk of the nation's electrical equipment.

Increased industrial efficiency and mass production relied on advancing technology: the use of new sources of power, chiefly electricity; better planning; scientific management; and industrial research which led to improved techniques and new products. As a result of these changes, industrial productivity rose sharply during the 1920s. In manufacturing the annual rate of growth averaged about 5.4 percent, one-fifth above that of the prewar period. Because of increased efficiency, a wide variety of low-cost

consumer goods—automobiles, household commodities, chemical products, etc.,—flowed from American factories in a steady stream.

To a large extent the prosperity of the 1920s rested on a group of newer, expansive industries, such as motor vehicles, as well as on extensive construction. Production of automobiles, trucks, and buses not only provided an abundance of jobs and a market for numerous raw materials, but also created a whole group of related economic activities from road building to service stations. By 1929 the value of motor vehicles produced reached $5.3 billion, and the industry employed 447,000 workers, or about 5 percent of all the wage earners in manufacturing. Between 1920 and 1929 the annual sales of automobiles, trucks, and buses jumped from 2,227,000 to 5,337,000. The output of so many automobiles created a huge demand for steel, glass, paint, leather, and other products, and their operation provided the foundation for another major industry—oil.

Henry Ford set the pattern for the expanding automobile industry. A machinist and later an engineer for the Edison Illuminating Company of Detroit, Ford invented his first car in 1896. Seven years later he founded the Ford Motor Company, and in 1909 he began selling the famous Model T. Through mass production Ford strove for greater efficiency and lower prices. By 1924 some models of the famed Model T could be bought for less than $300. To provide ample purchasing power for the increased flow of commodities, he favored good wages. Ford raised wages to $5 a day in 1914, far above the going figure in manufacturing. Other rapidly expanding industries included petroleum, radios, household appliances, chemicals, and public utilities.

Construction likewise stimulated the economy and created new jobs. Total expenditures on private building reached more than $11 billion in 1926 and never fell below $7 billion in any year between 1922 and 1930. Increasingly prosperous

Brown Brothers

Ford RUNABOUT

$265 *f.o.b. Detroit*

Starter and Demountable Rims $85 Extra

The Lowest Priced Two-Passenger Car

The Ford Runabout is the most economical car for personal transportation known.

Priced lower than any other motor car, its maintenance and running expenses are in keeping with its present low cost.

To salesmen and others who average a high daily mileage in business, the Runabout has a special appeal both for its operating economy and its convenience in making city and suburban calls.

families purchased hundreds of thousands of new private homes, and businessmen built thousands of new commercial establishments.

American foreign trade contributed further to postwar prosperity. During the war the United States had shifted from a debtor to a creditor nation—that is, it had greater investments abroad than foreigners had in this country. By 1919 America's creditor position in the private sector amounted to about $3.7 billion. This situation occurred at least partly because the United States maintained a favorable balance of trade, selling more goods and services overseas than it imported. In 1928, America's favorable balance reached more than $1 billion. The United States exported an increasing number of manufactured goods, especially automobiles, machinery, electrical supplies, and gasoline, as well as farm commodities.

Not all businesses were prosperous. Some of the older, more competitive industries such as bituminous coal, shoes, shipping, and textiles were among those which experienced difficult times. During the decade, coal production declined and hundreds of mines closed down. Coal, still required for some basic industries, faced increasing competition from gas and electricity as a source of power. Long before 1929 the coal industry bordered on depression. Textiles also suffered during the 1920s. Increasing competition from rayon and silk injured the cotton and woolen industries. Cotton textile manufacturers continued to move southward to take advantage of the proximity of raw materials as well as the cheaper labor, cheaper power, and tax benefits offered by Southern states to attract industry.

Both ocean shipping and railroads faced difficult problems in the postwar years. At the close of the war the United States had a large excess of merchant ships, of which some 60 percent was owned by the government. In line with the philosophy of getting the government out of business, Congress passed the Jones Act in 1920, which provided for the sale of government-owned ships on generous terms. But the ship-

ping industry was so depressed that sales went slowly. The Jones-White Act of 1928 granted shippers increased subsidies for carrying the mail and permitted government loans to buyers of government vessels. But nothing seemed to revive the industry.

Although railroads invested billions of dollars in the 1920s to improve their operations and services, they were not prosperous. They faced too much competition from automobiles and trucks. The Transportation Act of 1920 ended wartime government operation of the railways and then authorized the consolidation of the railroads into a limited number of large, integrated systems. In this manner Congress hoped to encourage efficiency and permit a higher return on investment. The Interstate Commerce Commission considered 6 percent a fair return, but railroad profits generally did not reach that point in the 1920s.

American industry demonstrated during the twenties that most problems of production had been solved. Plants and factories, using mass-production methods, turned out an ever-increasing quantity and variety of goods. But what about distribution? An economy based on mass production cannot function without mass consumption. Consequently, businessmen developed and improved their marketing and sales techniques to encourage consumers to buy the commodities which existed in such abundance. Installment credit, changing styles, and advertising were among the means employed to increase demand. Although consumer credit had been used for many years, it reached unprecedented proportions in the 1920s. People bought automobiles, radios, furniture, jewelry, clothing, and many other commodities on the installment plan. In 1927, for example, some 75 percent of the automobiles and an equal percentage of radios were purchased on credit. An abundant supply of money provided the necessary funds for a rapid expansion of purchases on time payments.

Advertisers appealed to every human want and emotion in their efforts to create demand. Certain products, they claimed, would make people happy or healthy, give them popularity or prestige. Packard advertised that "a man is known by the car he keeps." If a woman failed in love, perhaps she had halitosis, which could be cured by using Listerine. Newspapers, magazines, billboards, direct mail, and the radio bombarded consumers with slogans and appeals to buy this or that product. Advertising itself became big business, and by 1927 industry spent some $1.5 billion to create consumer preference.

Business and industry reaped untold benefits from a friendly public and a sympathetic government. Americans agreed overwhelmingly that business was the backbone of the nation, that what was good for business was good for the entire country. It was considered good economics to give governmental support to the wants and needs of businessmen. The *Wall Street Journal* reported that "never before, here or anywhere else, has a government been so completely fused with business." President Coolidge added his observation that "the business of America is business."

Not surprisingly, many federal policies were designed specifically to assist business and industry. The Fordney-McCumber tariff of 1922 raised duties on a number of manufactured goods specifically to reduce the competition from foreign producers and thus permit higher prices for domestic products. Tax policies were geared to help big business. In 1926 Congress approved the depletion allowance for certain minerals which provided a tax benefit to investors in those industries. This was especially helpful to the oil industry.

Secretary of Commerce Hoover helped business both by improving the Department's statistical services and by promoting greater foreign trade and commerce. The federal government indirectly helped business by abandoning any serious attempts to enforce the antitrust laws.

Wage Earners in Prosperity

Most wage earners benefited from the growing industrial prosperity of the 1920s. Jobs were plentiful, and wages more than kept pace with the cost of living. The average earnings of employed wage earners (adjusted to changes in prices) increased about 24 percent between 1921 and 1928. Not all workers enjoyed the same economic progress, but overall, wage earners enjoyed a rising standard of living. Between 1921 and 1928, annual income to wage earners advanced about $200. The income of workers in trade, the service industries, transportation, and construction also rose. Meanwhile, hours of work declined. Between 1890 and 1914 the average workweek in manufacturing dropped from sixty to fifty-four hours; by 1926 the usual workweek was about fifty hours. Higher wages and shorter hours reflected the increased efficiency and productivity of labor. In manufac-

turing, output per worker rose more than 20 percent between 1923 and 1929.

Although labor generally shared in the prosperity of the 1920s, not all workers achieved a decent standard of living. Many low-paid employees in the service industries, personal servants, migrant workers, and especially members of minority groups such as Spanish-Americans and blacks were bypassed by the good times. For these millions the United States was still no land of opportunity. In 1929 the bottom 10 percent of the nation's families received only 2 percent of the national income. This figure had not changed measurably during the previous decade. But whatever problems some workers faced in the 1920s, labor as a whole was better off than in any previous peacetime period. Hundreds of thousands of wage earners moved to the suburbs and joined middle-class America.

Improved labor conditions did not result from the power or influence of unions. Organized labor actually declined during the 1920s. Indeed, membership in unions fell from about 5 million in 1920 to about 3.6 million ten years later. Most union members were affiliated with the American Federation of Labor, and a majority of these were in the skilled crafts. Workers in the large, mass-production industries such as steel, farm machinery, textiles, and chemicals were not organized at all.

Although unions had made substantial gains during the Great War, it soon became clear that American industry had accepted labor organization only because of government pressure and as a patriotic gesture. As soon as the war ended, industrial leaders proceeded to fight the principle of unionization. Management discharged men who attempted to organize unions, hired espionage agents to gather information on labor leaders, employed strikebreakers, and charged that some labor leaders were radical, unAmerican, and even communistic.

Some businessmen fought trade unions by resorting to "welfare capitalism." Workers who were treated well, ran the principle, would not be attracted to union leaders. Practically, this meant more pleasant working conditions, with drinking fountains and recreational facilities as well as group insurance, bonuses, and even stock sales to workers at reduced prices. Businessmen sponsored company unions. These unions gave workers the appearance of representation and bargaining power with management; but since company unions were always financed and controlled by the company, their leaders could not speak freely and independently for the workers.

Unions suffered from the lack of vigorous and aggressive leadership. Samuel Gompers, president of the AF of L until his death in 1924, and his successor, William Green, were conservative trade union leaders who showed little interest in organizing the great mass-production industries or in opposing national policies. Even John L. Lewis, head of the more militant United Mine Workers, voted for Coolidge in 1924.

Agriculture and Farm Problems

Agriculture's position in the American economy continued to decline in the postwar years. By 1930 agriculture was responsible for only about 10 percent of the gross national product. At the end of the 1920s, farm operators had an average annual net operating income of only $943. On a per capita basis, this was less than $300 a year for people in agriculture, compared with $775 for all Americans.

Low farm income did not stem from lack of efficiency or poor productivity. Throughout the decade American farms became larger and more efficient. In 1920 American farming was still geared to the horse and mule, but during the following decade tractors and tractor-drawn machinery transformed and modernized most agricultural production. Farmers also planted improved seeds, used more fertilizer, bred better livestock, and developed better management. This increased efficiency resulted in productivity that far outran demand. Economists explained the low farm income by pointing out that farmers invested too much land, labor, and capital in agricultural production.

The postwar farm depression began in the summer of 1920 and remained especially severe until 1923. Within eighteen months after June 1920, wheat prices fell from more than $2.50 a bushel to less than $1; cotton dropped to as little as 13 cents a pound after having brought 35 cents in 1919. Between 1919 and 1921 net farm income declined from $9 billion to about $3.3 billion. By 1921 farm products had lost one-fifth of their purchasing power. This postwar decline in prices and income resulted from continued heavy production, lack of purchasing power in foreign countries, and loss of some export markets to competitors such as Canada and Australia.

No domestic question plagued the Harding and Coolidge administrations more than the depression in agriculture. By 1921 friends of the farmers proposed a variety of relief measures. Some favored outright government price-fixing for farm products, while others believed that cooperative marketing, more liberal credit, tariff protection, and regulation of the commodity and livestock exchanges would solve the price problem. In 1921 a group of Western and Southern senators organized the Farm Bloc to push farm legislation through Congress. This bloc secured the Packers and Stockyards Act (1921) and the Capper-Tincher Grain Futures Act (1922), which placed livestock and grain marketing under federal control, and the Capper-Volstead Cooperative Marketing Act of 1922, which exempted processing and marketing cooperatives from the antitrust laws. In 1923 Congress also passed the Intermediate Credits Act, which established twelve intermediate credit banks to provide money for banks and agricultural corporations which could then extend credit to farmers.

But none of these measures reached the heart of the farm problem—surpluses, low prices, and the disparity between the prices of farm and nonfarm commodities. In 1922 George N. Peek, president of the Moline Plow Company, and his associate Hugh Johnson developed a plan which they called "equality for agriculture." Peek and Johnson advocated segregating the surplus and disposing of it abroad for whatever it would bring. With the surplus removed, they believed that agricultural tariffs would raise commodity prices on the domestic market to a "fair exchange value" or parity.

In the spring of 1924, Senator Charles L. McNary of Oregon and Representative Gilbert N. Haugen of Iowa introduced a bill incorporating Peek's ideas. The first McNary-Haugen bill sought to raise the prices of eight basic agricultural commodities—wheat, flour, corn, cotton, wool, cattle, sheep, and swine—to a point where they would have the same purchasing power as they had between 1909 and 1914, when prices were considered fair to farmers. To raise prices, the government would establish a corporation with an appropriation of $200 million to purchase and sell abroad any market-depressing surpluses of these basic commodities. If the corporation bought products at the higher domestic price and then sold them abroad at the lower world price, it would lose money. To pay these losses, farmers were to be taxed on each bushel or pound of a commodity sold. This was known as the equalization fee. Corporation officials would calculate the losses on their foreign sales and then assess farmers of that particular crop enough to make up the deficit. But the farmer would benefit. For that part of his production sold on the domestic market he would receive a considerably higher price, increasing his total income even after he paid the equalization fee. The McNary-Haugen bill, in establishing the principles of government responsibility and parity prices, was a sharp break from tradition.

Although Congress defeated the McNary-Haugen bill in 1924, its supporters organized, lobbied, and continued to push for enactment. Congress finally passed a McNary-Haugen bill in 1927. Coolidge still opposed this approach to agricultural relief, and he killed the measure with a stinging veto. After another strong campaign in Congress, lawmakers enacted a modified McNary-Haugen bill the following year. Coolidge also vetoed this measure. There was little for the advocates of farm relief to do but await whatever action President-elect Herbert Hoover might take. Nevertheless, the campaign for farm relief in the 1920s demonstrated that many farmers, in addition to economists and political leaders, had come to realize that without a governmental program for crop limitation agriculture would never achieve much prosperity. It established as well the parity-price concept, which came to be the major goal of farm groups.

When Hoover became president in March 1929, general economic conditions appeared excellent. Even the agricultural situation had improved. Properly impressed with what he saw around him, Hoover declared in his inaugural address that "ours is a land rich in resources; stimulating in its glorious beauty; filled with millions of happy homes; blessed with comfort and opportunity."

Hoover's inauguration climaxed a highly successful career in business, philanthropy, and public service. Born in 1874 at West Branch, Iowa, Hoover was graduated from Stanford University with a degree in geology. His employment after 1897 with an English mining firm took him to many parts of the world. By the outbreak of the Great War he had made a substantial fortune. From 1914 to 1928 he devoted himself largely to public service. He served as director of Belgian relief in 1914, became head of the United States Food Administration in 1917, and then directed American postwar relief efforts in Europe. By 1920 Hoover had become a national figure with the reputation of a good administrator. As Secretary of Commerce, he held a prominent place in both the Harding and the Coolidge administrations.

Hoover's basic philosophy determined his actions as president. He had a very strong belief in individualism, personal initiative, individual liberty, and equality of opportunity. In his view, economic progress rested on competition, free enterprise, and minimum governmental regulation. Hoover objected strongly to extensive federal power over the economy because, he said, "You cannot extend the mastery of government over the daily working life of a people without at the same time making it the master of the people's souls and thoughts."

During the six months of his administration prior to the stock market crash, Hoover dealt with two principal issues—agricultural relief and the tariff. Addressing a special session of Congress on April 16, 1929, the President outlined the farmers' difficulties but warned that they could not be cured by legislation or "by the Federal government alone." Hoover believed that an effective tariff, some advice to farmers on production, and the creation of agricultural marketing cooperatives would be of sufficient help to farmers.

The widely heralded Agricultural Marketing Act, which became law on June 15, allegedly placed agriculture "on a basis of equality with other industries." It provided for a Federal Farm Board, which would encourage the formation of national marketing associations for farm commodities. Congress appropriated $500 million to supply needed credit to assist the cooperatives in holding crops and marketing them in a more orderly fashion. The new law permitted the Federal Farm Board to form stabilization corporations to buy farm commodities in the open market as a means of maintaining prices in periods of unusual price-depressing surpluses.

Although the Federal Farm Board was successful in encouraging the formation of agricultural marketing associations, general economic conditions created problems which the cooperatives were unable to meet. Prices slipped badly in 1930 in the wake of the stock market crash. When the wheat, cotton, and other cooperatives found themselves unable to maintain prices, the Board created stabilization corporations, which bought wheat and cotton on the open market in the hope of stopping the dangerous price decline. But large production continued even in the face of lower prices, and the Board soon found that it could not support prices without considerably more money. By the fall of 1931, after two years of operation, the Board held millions of bushels of wheat and large quantities of cotton. Ultimately it lost some $345 million on its transactions.

For Hoover the tariff was an accurate measure of the nation's economic welfare. In asking

Congress to make "limited changes" in the tariff, he argued that both agriculture and industry would benefit from higher import duties which would protect the domestic market. Congressman Willis C. Hawley of Oregon introduced a tariff bill, which passed the House in May 1929. Although this measure raised duties on minerals, textiles, dyestuffs, and other commodities, most of the upward revisions were modest. Strong pressure for greatly increased rates developed in the Senate, where representatives of high protection were firmly entrenched.

As finally passed after a year of bitter debate, the Hawley-Smoot bill made some 890 upward revisions in the tariff. It raised rates an average of about 7 percent over those of the Fordney-McCumber law, thus bringing duties to the highest level in American history. Congress accepted the flexible provision insisted on by the President. This section permitted the Tariff Commission to recommend a rate increase or decrease of as much as 50 percent to equalize the cost of production in the United States and abroad.

The Great Crash

Unfortunately for Hoover's popularity and his place in history, the exuberant prosperity of the 1920s had almost run its course. Still the general optimism prevailed until the time of the stock market crash. Political leaders, businessmen, and economists agreed generally that the future was bright. Early in October, Charles E. Mitchell, chairman of the National City Bank of New York, stated that "the industrial situation of the United States is absolutely sound." But these

and other encouraging predictions proved terribly wrong. Stock prices had broken sharply on September 5 and then followed an erratic course during the next several weeks. Conditions reached a crisis on October 29 when frantic stockholders offered 16,410,000 shares for sale at ruinously low prices; some stocks found no takers at any figure. While the crash affected the stock market and financial community immediately and severely, it heralded the beginning of a long and cruel depression.

What caused the Great Depression? The stock market crash was less the cause of the Depression than a reflection of basic weaknesses in the economy. Despite favorable surface conditions, there were throughout the 1920s underlying defects in the American economy. First, some major industries did not experience the general prosperity which characterized most of the economy. Meager farm income meant that farmers lacked purchasing power to buy their share of the increasing output of goods and services. Coal, textiles, and shoes were among other industries which suffered from low profit margins. Moreover, while employment rose during the 1920s, the biggest gains were in the low-paid service trades rather than in those industries where earnings were high. Furthermore, the condition of American foreign trade was not as healthy as it appeared. American exports were

Variety's October 30, 1929, headline about the Great Crash was typically irreverent, but its lead story gave a more somber perspective: "The most dramatic event in the financial history of America is the collapse of the New York Stock Market. . . ."
The Granger Collection

heavy but foreigners paid for large quantities of imports with dollars derived from American investments in foreign securities. In some measure Americans paid for their own exports. This was dangerous, for if United States citizens reduced or stopped their lending overseas, the country's exports would decline. After 1928, when Americans curtailed their loans abroad, exports dropped rather sharply.

Much of the economic expansion in the 1920s resulted from heavy investments in new plants and equipment. These expenditures created demand for capital goods and provided additional jobs. But the building of more productive facilities was predicated on an expanding consumer market to buy the goods flowing out of the new factories. Although demand by consumers was generally strong before 1929, it could not equal the growing output of goods and services. Without enough earned income to purchase the production of American farms and factories, people resorted to large-scale credit buying. Any curtailment in credit would reduce consumer purchases, which in turn would discourage capital investment and create unemployment. By 1929 the American capacity to produce had far outrun the capacity to consume at current prices.

Unequal distribution of income was a big factor in creating economic maladjustments. Too much of the nation's income went to upper-income groups in the form of huge profits and dividends. In 1929 the top 10 percent of the families received 39 percent of the total income. Since people in this income bracket had little need for more consumer goods, they invested their money in more productive facilities, or, in many cases, speculated on the stock market. Farmers and workers could have consumed more but were unable to do so because of low incomes. About 42 percent of American families in 1929 earned less than $1,500 a year. High prosperity in a consumer-oriented economy required high consumer expenditures. Too few Americans had sufficient income to keep the economy functioning at full capacity.

Credit buying, added to heavy stock market speculation, sustained a level of selling which far exceeded purchasing power from wages and salaries. Prosperity became increasingly artificial. Stock prices began to rise sharply in 1924. The speculative mania, based on a boom psychology, continued until the October 1929 crash. The price of many stocks went to fantastic heights. During the summer of 1929 alone Westinghouse stock shot up from 151 to 286 on the stock exchange. But the values were artificial, and a loss of confidence which turned buyers into sellers could, and indeed did, set off a panic.

By the fall of 1929 all the weaknesses in the American economy had combined to bring the "new economic era" to an end. Lack of prosperity in certain basic industries such as agriculture; an export trade which depended heavily on American loans abroad; the poor distribution of income; a bad corporate structure which permitted promoters and grafters to bleed company assets and take advantage of innocent investors; and stock speculation and manipulation all played a part in the economic conditions that brought on the tragic Depression.

The Depression

Initial reaction to the stock market crash was not one of general panic or discouragement. Hoover assured the nation on October 25 that "the fundamental business of the country, that is, production and distribution of commodities, is on a sound and prosperous basis." For Robert P. Lamont, Secretary of Commerce, there existed "none of the underlying factors which have been associated with or have preceded the declines in business in the past."

President Hoover wanted desperately to avoid an economic slump with its unemployment, farm foreclosures, and business failures. The danger was that any additional drop in consumer purchasing power would cause producers to reduce output and discharge unneeded workers. Unemployment would restrict demand for agricultural and industrial commodities even further, causing more layoffs. To prevent this vicious downward cycle from gaining any momentum Hoover accepted the need for sustaining prices, wages, employment, and investment at or near current levels. If this could be achieved, the stock market crash would not be the forerunner of depression. Hoover intended to secure these objectives through voluntary action.

At a series of White House meetings, Hoover urged businessmen to maintain wage rates and employment, to increase spending on new plants and equipment, and to avoid price cuts. He advised labor to avoid demands for higher wages. The President called for expanded federal public works and requested governors to enlarge expenditures for state construction. After Hoover recommended easier credit, the New York Federal Reserve Bank reduced the rediscount rate from 5 to 4½ percent. Explaining these actions to Congress on December 3, the President declared that he had instituted "systematic . . . cooperation with business" in order to sustain wages and employment and to prevent economic decline and individual hardships.

Despite optimistic predictions that voluntary business-government cooperation would assure continued prosperity, it soon became evident that the country was sliding into a depression. By the spring of 1930, some 4 million people were jobless. Despite Hoover's urging, businessmen could not maintain employment and wages in the face of weakening demand. Conditions went from bad to worse. By early 1933 every aspect of the economy seemed depressed. Farm prices had declined to disastrous levels, and net agricultural income had dropped to only one-third of what it had been in 1929. Unemployment rose to at least 12 million in early 1933, when approximately one-fourth of the labor force was without work. Thousands of industrial, financial, and other business firms went broke, and the Dow-Jones index of fifty leading industrial stocks fell from an average of 364 to 62 between 1929 and 1933. More than 2,000 banks, some of them large institutions, closed their doors in 1931 alone, wiping out billions in deposits. Everywhere in 1932 Americans faced want, distress, and bankruptcy. Bread and soup lines lengthened as cities and counties faced heavy demands for relief. Men, looking for work, increasingly found signs which read, "No Help Wanted Here."

The Administration Program

Meanwhile, the President struggled to create a program which would inaugurate a return to better times. Hoover was not callous or indifferent to the needs of suffering people. Indeed, much of his reputation rested on his earlier humanitarian and relief work in Europe. But in devising plans and programs to fight the growing Depression, he held that economic recovery depended on the actions of private industry and that the needy must find relief in local or state agencies. The federal government, he insisted, must avoid direct relief. Despite these firmly held views, Hoover attempted more programs to combat the Depression than had any previous

president in similar circumstances. But his policies were either too limited or fundamentally wrong. Hoover failed to understand that the Depression following 1929 was not another historic decline in the business cycle in which recovery would be largely automatic.

As the Depression deepened, critics demanded some use of federal funds to finance job-creating public works as well as direct relief for the unemployed. Hoover favored a modest increase in federal projects to help relieve unemployment and to increase purchasing power, but he never viewed such spending as a major attack on the Depression. He believed that the basic fight against hard times must come from the private sector. Nevertheless, Hoover stepped up expenditures for roads, federal buildings, and other public projects. Work began on the Hoover Dam on the Colorado River in 1930, and by 1932 the federal government was spending about $500 million a year on public works.

By late 1930 the problem of relief for the needy became a matter of pressing national concern. Private agencies and local communities, which had historically supplied help for destitute citizens, faced demands that greatly exceeded their limited resources. Growing numbers of political leaders insisted that federal funds alone could provide sufficient relief. But Hoover held that reliance on the federal Treasury would break down the "sense of individual generosity" and strike "at the roots of self-government." In October 1930, the President appointed Colonel Arthur Woods to head the Emergency Committee for Employment, created to coordinate and stimulate the nation's voluntary relief agencies. Special relief committees appeared in most large cities during the winter of 1930–1931, but they lacked the needed funds. Even as conditions grew worse, Hoover clung to his principles. He declared in December 1931 that "the federal government must not encroach upon nor permit local communities to abandon that precious possession of local initiative and responsibility."

Hoover continued to believe that economic recovery depended primarily on the actions of private enterprise. To assist business, he favored the private expansion of credit. But this attempt failed. Meanwhile, Eugene Meyer, head of the War Finance Corporation under Wilson, sought to develop a federal credit agency. In December 1931, Hoover gave the proposal token backing; in January 1932, Congress established the Reconstruction Finance Corporation. While hardly an administration measure, the RFC was the most important antidepression legislation enacted during Hoover's presidency. The new law authorized the RFC to lend up to $2 billion to banks, insurance companies, railroads, and other large businesses to stave off bankruptcy or expand operations.

By the winter of 1931–1932 some 10 million Americans were unemployed. Desperation stalked the land. Children cried from cold and hunger, mothers wept, and fathers cursed their misfortunes. Entire families in some cities lived on as little as $2 and $3 a week for food, and millions in rural areas, especially the South, received no relief at all. Men pawed through garbage cans and fought over scraps of food. Such pitiful conditions brought increasing demands for federal appropriations for direct assistance. The La Follette–Costigan bill called for an appropriation of $375 million in relief, but it went down to defeat in February 1932, as other relief measures did. Confronted with growing demands for federal aid, Hoover in March supported a congressional authorization to distribute through the Red Cross some 40 million bushels of wheat and 5 million bales of cotton held by the Federal Farm Board. But such limited relief again failed to meet the burgeoning needs. Finally, in June 1932, Hoover approved a loan from the Reconstruction Finance Corporation of up to $300 million for direct relief. Although the amount was clearly insufficient, the federal money was a boon to hard-pressed state relief agencies. The same bill permitted the RFC to lend up to $1.5 billion to the states for self-liquidating works.

In July 1932, Congress created a Home Loan Bank System to assist homeowners facing foreclosure. The RFC made available $125 million to supply funds for twelve new rediscount banks which could furnish additional credit to banks, savings and loan associations, and other financial institutions which held home mortgages. However, the law came too late to save many homes.

Despite some expansion of public works, the creation of the RFC and the Home Loan Banks, and loans to the states for relief, to many Americans Hoover's program seemed timid and inadequate. By the winter of 1931–1932 cries from many quarters demanded a much broader federal attack on the Depression. At the same time the public mood underwent a noticeable change. As people lost their homes and farms through foreclosure, as unemployment increased and men tramped the streets looking for work, as bread and soup lines lengthened, and as hopelessness gripped the nation, some citizens advocated radical revolution. One Oklahoma rancher, who had lost his land and cattle by foreclosure, declared, "We have got to have a revolution here like they had in Russia." An unemployed Detroit worker with four children argued that the Soviet system was "a better system than we've got" because the Russians provided work for all. In his book *Toward Soviet America* (1932), William Z. Foster, a leading Communist, wrote that the only hope for American workers was "the revolutionary way."

Although genuine revolutionaries were few even at the depth of the Depression, the bitter criticism of the American economic system revealed deep and widespread frustration and discontent. Why, many asked, need there be starvation amidst plenty? Americans were hungry while wheat surpluses filled grain elevators; they were naked while warehouses bulged with surplus cotton; they needed manufactured goods while the factories stood idle. In other words, all of the means of production were at hand—land, labor, capital, technology, and raw materials—but the masses were in dire want. As the famed British economist John Maynard Keynes wrote in 1932, it was "not a crisis of poverty, but a crisis of abundance." Yet no one seemed to know how to attack economic stagnation and utilize abundance.

Hoover's repeated predictions that conditions would soon improve, his call for personal and national restraint, and his devotion to economy and a balanced budget could not deter the angry demands for action. During the summer of 1932 there were unusual manifestations of discontent as veterans marched on Washington and hundreds of Midwestern farmers went on strike. As the Depression steadily deepened, veterans of the Great War insisted on full payment of the bonus which Congress had voted them in 1924. Under pressure from the American Legion and other spokesmen for the veterans, Congress passed a bill over Hoover's veto in February 1931, permitting a veteran to borrow up to 50 percent of his total bonus. This did not satisfy the veterans, who believed that they deserved all their bonus money. In May and June 1932, hundreds of veterans marched on Washington to lobby for the Patman bill, then before Congress. Although Patman's measure, which called for total payment of the bonus, passed the House, it died in the Senate. After Congress adjourned in July, many veterans returned home, but several thousand stayed on. As tensions rose, conflicts occurred between veterans and the police; two veterans were shot and mortally wounded. Federal troops under General Douglas MacArthur finally drove out the Bonus Expeditionary Force. Hoover believed that Communist agitators had made this action necessary, but critics charged that the President had acted hastily and unwisely.

Almost simultaneously, trouble erupted in the Middle West as farmers resorted to direct action in their effort to raise agricultural prices. In May militant farmers under Milo Reno organized the National Farmers' Holiday Association at Des Moines, Iowa. The farm strike began in August when farmers around Sioux City and Council Bluffs, and some near Des Moines, picketed the highways and blockaded attempts to deliver milk and livestock to market.

The Election of 1932

The continuing depression added up to trouble for the Republican party as the 1932 election approached. The bases of Republican strength four years earlier—business and industrial prosperity and Hoover's personal popularity—had been shattered beyond recognition. Many faithful Republicans had no hope that Hoover would be reelected, but practical politics dictated his renomination. In June a dreary and pessimistic convention in Chicago mechanically named Hoover and Curtis the party's standard-bearers.

In contrast, the Democrats met in Chicago on June 27 with high expectations. Governor Franklin D. Roosevelt of New York had emerged as the leading Democratic candidate. His strongest support existed among the more progressive elements of the party in the South and West who resented the conservative, business-oriented control which John J. Raskob, national party chairman, and Alfred E. Smith had exerted over the party since 1928. Elected governor in 1928 during a Republican landslide, Roosevelt had demonstrated unusual political talents, and he had informed himself in detail of the problems facing his state and the nation. During his governorship he supported public power, conservation, labor legislation, and a large program of unemployment relief. His outstanding political record, plus a familiar name, a successful fight against poliomyelitis contracted in 1921, and a pleasant personality, placed Roosevelt in a commanding position. Roosevelt won the nomination on the fourth ballot, after California and Texas swung to his support. The convention chose John Nance Garner of Texas, Speaker of the House after the Democrats won control in 1930, as the vice-presidential candidate. Shattering precedent, Roosevelt flew immediately to Chicago to deliver his acceptance speech to an excited and expectant crowd. He attacked the Republicans, declared that the Democratic party was "the bearer of liberalism and of progress," and promised relief, public works, the repeal of prohibition, farm legislation, and tariff reduction. The delegates cheered madly when Roosevelt pledged "a new deal for the American people."

There was nothing to encourage the Republicans as they entered the campaign. A number of leading progressives, including Senators Norris and La Follette, deserted the party and supported Roosevelt. Hoover protested that

Hoover and Roosevelt riding to Roosevelt's inauguration, March 4, 1933. The Granger Collection

Republican policies had nothing to do with causing or continuing the Depression, but the President and his party could not disassociate themselves from that responsibility.

If people in 1932 failed to react favorably to Hoover, they responded warmly and enthusiastically to his opponent. Roosevelt could not stand or walk without braces on his legs, but he campaigned so vigorously that people hardly realized that he was handicapped. He traveled more than 25,000 miles and spoke to scores of audiences. His so-called brain trust, composed of advisers such as Raymond Moley and Rexford G. Tugwell of Columbia University, and M. L. Wilson of Montana State College, supplied him with ideas and materials for his speeches. Roosevelt directed his campaign toward the "forgotten man." He promised a vigorous federal assault on the Depression. He also urged economy and a balanced budget. On these last points Hoover and Roosevelt seemed to agree.

Although Roosevelt described his objectives only in general terms, Hoover charged that such proposals "would destroy the very foundations of our American system." But people were interested in bread and jobs, not in philosophies of government. They wanted a change in Washington. Roosevelt won a resounding victory, carrying all but six states. His popular majority was 22,809,636 to only 15,758,901 for Hoover.

The Democrats swept Congress, 310 to 117 in the House of Representatives; 60 to 35, with one independent, in the Senate. The Republican rout was complete.

Conclusion

The Hoover administration started under seemingly favorable circumstances. But Hoover had hardly become adjusted to the White House when a stock market crash signaled the beginning of a terrible depression. Still he continued to regard the economy as basically sound; he believed that recovery depended principally upon the action of business and industrial leaders. But when it became evident that private interests could not or would not turn the economic tide, he supported a modest program of government action. The federal government did more to fight depression under Hoover than it had under any previous president. But, even so, many people regarded the President's programs as inadequate, and demanded greater government action to achieve recovery. When Hoover continued to disagree, the voters elected a new leader who promised a broad attack on the Depression.

SUGGESTED READINGS

The best survey of the economy in the 1920s is George Soule's *Prosperity Decade: From War to Depression, 1917–1929** (1947). However, the works by Hicks, Leuchtenberg, and Faulkner cited in the *Suggested Readings* at the end of Chapter 26 all contain material on economic developments. On business and industry see *America's Capacity to Produce* (1934) by E. G. Nourse and associates; and *America's Capacity to Consume* (1934) by Maurice Level and associates. For the important automobile industry see R. C. Epstein's *The Automobile Industry* (1927) and Allan Nevins and F. E. Hill's *Ford: Expansion and Challenge, 1915–1933* (1957). Industrial concentration has been well analyzed by A. A. Berle, Jr., and Gardiner C. Means in *The Modern Corporation and Private Property* (1933). J. W. Protho considers the business mind in *The Dollar Decade: Business Ideas in the 1920's* (1954).

*The Lean Years: A History of the American Workers, 1920–1933** (1960) by Irving Bernstein is an excellent account of labor and its problems during those years. Another important work is *Republicans and Labor, 1919–1929* (1969) by Robert H. Zieger. There are also good chapters in Joseph Rayback's *A History of American Labor** (1958). On income and the standard of living after World War I see Simon Kuznets's *National Income and Its Composition, 1919–1938* (1941).

Books dealing with farm problems include pertinent chapters in M. R. Benedict's *Farm Policies in the United States* (1950); and Theodore Saloutos and John D. Hicks's *Twentieth Century Populism: Agricultural Discontent in the Middle West, 1900–1939** (1951). James H. Shideler provides an excellent discussion of the approaches to farm problems in *Farm Crisis, 1919–1923* (1957), while G. C. Fite traces the McNary-Haugen bills in *George N. Peek and the Fight for Farm Parity* (1954).

A good biography of Herbert Hoover yet remains to be written. However, for uncritical and adulatory accounts see Eugene Lyons's *The Herbert Hoover Story* (1959) and David Hinshaw's *Herbert Hoover, American Quaker* (1950). The best account of Hoover's administration is H. G. Warren's *Herbert Hoover and the Great Depression** (1959).

Several good general works which include valuable material on the Hoover years are A. M. Schlesinger, Jr.'s *The Crisis of the Old Order** (1957); Broadus Mitchell's *Depression Decade: From New Era to New Deal, 1929–1941** (1947); Dixon Wecter's *The Age of the Great Depression, 1929–1941* (1948); and F. L. Allen's *Since Yesterday: The Nineteen-thirties in America, September 3, 1929–September 3, 1939* (1940).

On the causes of the Depression see J. K. Galbraith's *The Great Crash, 1929** (1955). A. U. Romasco is critical of Hoover's handling of the Depression in *The Poverty of Abundance: Hoover, the Nation, the Depression** (1965), while Murray N. Rothbard criticizes government efforts to solve depression problems in *America's Great Depression* (1963).

The failure of Hoover's farm program is well covered in Saloutos and Hicks's *Agricultural Discontent in the Middle West* and Murray Benedict's *Farm Policies of the United States, 1790–1950*, both cited above. Financial and tax policies can be traced in Paul Studenski and H. E. Krooss's *Financial History of the United States* (1952). Jesse J. Jones, first head of the Reconstruction Finance Corporation, has traced the history of that agency in *Fifty Billion Dollars: My Thirteen Years with the RFC, 1932–1945* (1951). A good brief analysis of the election of 1932 can be found in R. V. Peel and T. C. Donnelly's *The 1932 Campaign: An Analysis* (1935), but the best account of Roosevelt's victory in 1932 is Frank Freidel's *The Triumph*, vol. II of his *Franklin D. Roosevelt* (1956).

*indicates availability in paperback.

28

Franklin D. Roosevelt and the New Deal

By the winter of 1932–1933 a mood of despair and hopelessness stalked the land. Hoover's promises of economic recovery had become increasingly absurd in the light of depressed conditions in business, agriculture, banking, and employment. Citizens generally shared the belief that something basic was wrong in a society where millions went hungry and ill clothed in the midst of plenty. By early 1933 passive resignation gave way to demands that the national leadership tackle those problems whose solutions were beyond the capabilities of individuals or local and state governments. Some called for a complete change in the system, but the great majority of people intended to solve their prob-

lems within the established framework of government. They agreed that the federal government was the only agency with sufficient power and resources to meet the immediate crisis.

But what precisely could or would the new administration do to revive national confidence and to restore economic recovery? Although Roosevelt had promised a New Deal, he had not indicated the precise content of his intentions. During the next six years, however, the President, supported by Congress and the country, developed a broad program of relief, recovery, and reform. Roosevelt demonstrated that, with proper leadership, democracy could work successfully in time of extreme emergency.

Franklin Delano Roosevelt (1882–1945) was extraordinarily well prepared to assume leadership in 1933. Experienced in both state and national political affairs, he possessed a flexible mind, a buoyant and optimistic spirit, a sensitivity to the needs of people, and a dedication to the American democratic tradition. Roosevelt was not restricted by tradition or hampered by a rigid economic philosophy. He was an innovator; he held no brief for old remedies unsuited to new problems. He declared in 1931 that "a new economic and social balance calls for positive leadership and definite experiments which have not hitherto been tried." "It is common sense to take a method and try it," he said later. "If it fails admit it frankly and try another. But above all try something." Roosevelt insisted that the government had a responsibility to meet the needs of its citizens and to solve the problems caused by the Great Depression. Such demands on government, he believed, required vigorous executive leadership.

The New Deal which began to emerge in March 1933 was largely pragmatic. It was the outcome of many ideas, with roots in the New Nationalism of Theodore Roosevelt, the New Freedom of Woodrow Wilson, and the trade association movement of the 1920s. But the New Deal was not entirely devoid of an underlying philosophy or plan. The mainstream of New Deal thought was directed toward both restricting the abuses of financial and business power and advancing the welfare of farm and labor groups. Critics damned some aspects of the New Deal as socialistic and un-American, but Roosevelt was no radical. He believed in a middle course of action. Basically, the New Deal sought to preserve and strengthen the capitalistic system by distributing its benefits more broadly.

In his first inaugural address, Roosevelt exuded confidence and hope. Turning the neat phrase for which he became so famous, the President said, "The only thing we have to fear is fear itself." But, he continued, the country had fallen on evil days because of the "unscrupulous money changers." He called for a restoration of social values. He asked for a strict supervision of banking and credit, a program to put people to work, a balance between income and expenditures, and a "good neighbor policy" in world affairs. The President's talk of discipline, duty, and recovery of "precious moral values" struck a popular mood among citizens who felt that somehow the nation had lived riotously and then fallen upon difficult times.

Banking Reform and Abandonment of the Gold Standard

Meanwhile, crisis had piled upon crisis. The banking collapse had become so serious by inauguration day that Roosevelt and his advisers gave its solution first priority. Between 1930 and March 1933, some 5,504 banks had ceased operation. As banks closed, people rushed to withdraw their funds from those which still remained open. The banking situation had become so critical by the fall of 1932 that in October the Governor of Nevada closed the banks of his state to stop withdrawals by panicky depositors. Other governors soon took similar action.

When Roosevelt took office, most of the nation's banks had been closed by state action. Roosevelt and his advisers considered it imperative to restore confidence in the banking system. Following a weekend of confusion and worry, Roosevelt proclaimed a national four-day bank holiday on Monday, March 6, and suspended all banking functions. This gave the administration time to work out legislation to place before the special session of Congress, called for March 9. When Congress met, Roosevelt urged "immediate action" on the Emergency Banking Act.

Within eight hours both houses had passed the measure and it had been signed by the President. The new law permitted the Reconstruction Finance Corporation to provide additional capital for state and national banks, the Federal Reserve to issue greater quantities of notes to relieve any shortage of currency, and the Secretary of the Treasury to call in all gold coins and gold certificates. Finally, the law provided for the appointment of "conservators" to examine the conditions of closed banks and to make arrangements for their reopening. There was nothing radical about this legislation. The government acted to save the private banking system, not to nationalize the banks. "Capitalism," wrote Raymond Moley, "was saved in eight days."

One important aspect of the Emergency Banking Act was the removal of the United States from the gold standard. On March 10 Roosevelt issued an order forbidding the export of gold except where demanded by business requirements. Then on April 5 another executive order directed all persons to turn over their gold to the Federal Reserve banks by May 1. A joint resolution of Congress on June 5 completely destroyed the gold standard by outlawing clauses in public and private contracts which required payment in gold.

As business continued to stagnate in the summer of 1933 and pressure mounted for effective inflationary policies, Roosevelt and his advisers, notably Professor George F. Warren of Cornell University, agreed that price levels could be raised by lowering the gold content of the dollar, thereby creating more dollars against gold reserves. In practical terms this meant raising the price of gold above the current figure of $20.67 an ounce. The President on January 31, 1934, finally set the new price at $35, which devalued the dollar to 59.06 cents. A day earlier Congress had passed the Gold Reserve Act, which made Federal Reserve notes redeemable in "lawful money" instead of gold. With the coinage of gold prohibited, the nation abandoned the gold standard completely. The President's monetary policies had no noticeable effect upon prices or recovery.

Once the banking crisis had been brought under control, Congress proceeded to inaugurate some basic reforms in the banking system. The Glass-Steagall Act of June 16 placed tighter federal controls on the national banks, separated commercial from investment banking, and permitted branch banking under specific circumstances. The law's most popular feature, however, was the provision which guaranteed bank deposits. It authorized the new Federal Deposit Insurance Corporation to insure deposits in member banks up to $5,000 initially.

Passage of the Emergency Banking Act was the beginning of a dramatic period of New Deal history commonly referred to as the First Hundred Days. Congress and the people appeared willing to follow the President without serious question. Humorist Will Rogers declared that "if he burned down the capital we would cheer and say 'well, we at least got a fire started anyhow.'" Roosevelt took advantage of this popular psychology to push through a broad program of antidepression legislation.

Early Relief Efforts

Beyond the immediate banking crisis the most serious problem facing the nation was unemployment. States and local communities had nearly exhausted their relief funds. Reports of extreme suffering flooded state and federal agencies. A Philadelphian explained that "one woman said she borrowed 50 cents from a friend and bought stale bread for 3½ cents per loaf, and that is all they had for eleven days except for one or two meals." In response to such conditions, Roosevelt declared on March 21 that it was essential for Congress to enact measures "aimed at unemployment relief."

Ten days later Congress established the Civilian Conservation Corps to help young men between the ages of seventeen and twenty-five who could not find jobs. These young men lived in camps and planted trees, beautified parks, built dams, and performed other useful tasks, for which they received $30 a month. By 1942 more than 2 million youths had been given work on CCC projects.

Congress passed the Federal Emergency Relief Act on May 12. This law at last recognized that relief was a national problem. The lawmakers approved $500 million for grants to the states to help relieve distress among the unemployed. Roosevelt placed administration of the law in the hands of Harry L. Hopkins, who had headed relief work in New York State during Roosevelt's governorship. By the summer of 1933, FERA was sponsoring a wide variety of work relief projects employing approximately a million persons; but the resources and activity of the FERA were entirely inadequate to meet relief needs as the fourth winter of the Depression approached. Consequently, President Roosevelt created the Civil Works Administration on November 9, 1933. The CWA quickly expanded the work relief program. By January 1934, about 4,260,000 workers found employment on gov-

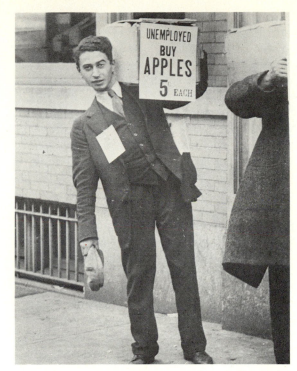

Brown Brothers

ernment projects. The CWA was abandoned in July 1934, and the whole relief load fell back on the still inadequate FERA.

Help for Farmers

Relief, however necessary, was no solution to unemployment. The answer to unemployment lay in a revival of the entire economy. Much of the agrarianism in the economic thinking of the period held that the return of general prosperity depended upon improved agricultural purchasing power.

Conditions among farmers were critical. Huge surpluses and poor demand for food and fiber both at home and abroad had driven prices down to disastrous levels. Wheat brought as little as 25 cents a bushel, chickens 4 cents a pound, eggs 8 cents a dozen, and hogs $2 and $3 a hundred pounds. Considering 1909–1914 prices as equaling 100, the prices of agricultural products had

fallen to 65 by 1932. Consequently, debts became a crushing burden and thousands of farmers lost their homes through foreclosure. In this atmosphere of crisis, Congress passed the Agricultural Adjustment Act in May.

The central purpose of the AAA was the elevation of farm prices to a level which would give agricultural commodities the same purchasing power which they had enjoyed in the 1909–1914 period. This was the principle of parity, or "equality of purchasing power," for which farmers had been striving for over a decade. To achieve this price objective, production and consumption had to be brought into balance by reducing output through production controls.

Farmers who signed agreements to cut acreage were to receive benefit payments directly from the federal government. Funds for these payments were to come from a special tax paid by processors of farm commodities. Thus, farmers would not only receive higher prices as a result of reduced production but they would also receive checks from the Treasury. Growers of eight basic commodities—wheat, cotton, corn, tobacco, rice, hogs, milk, and milk products— were eligible for benefit payments in exchange for reduced production.

It became imperative to implement the AAA quickly. Consequently, Administrator George N. Peek and his staff slashed red tape and within a few weeks had signed 1,032,000 cotton growers to contracts designed to reduce acreage by more than 10 million acres. Since the cotton was already planted, it became necessary to plow up part of the growing crop. Cotton farmers received $178 million in benefit payments in 1933; in addition, the price of cotton advanced from about 5 to 8 cents a pound. Widespread drought in the Wheat Belt in 1933 greatly reduced production and made it unnecessary to plow up growing wheat. Nonetheless, adjustment payments went to farmers who agreed to cut their acreage in 1934 and 1935. To raise hog prices, the AAA killed 6.1 million pigs and 222,000 sows in the latter part of 1933. The next year corn-hog farmers received benefit payments to reduce pig litters and corn acreage.

The AAA was an extensive experiment in national planning. Never before had the federal government developed such a comprehensive program to bring relief to a depressed sector of the economy. But many recognized that farmers were in an unfavorable bargaining position with other economic groups and that they needed "the centralizing power of government" to improve their position. Then, on January 6, 1936, the Agricultural Adjustment Act ceased to exist. In *United States v. Butler et al.*, the Supreme Court, in a 6-to-3 decision, held that processing taxes were unconstitutional and that Congress had no power to control agricultural production.

The Supreme Court decision, outlawing processing taxes and benefit payments to farmers who curtailed their acreage, left agriculture without any relief program. Congress closed the gap promptly when it passed the Soil Conservation and Domestic Allotment Act. Under the new legislation farmers were to be paid not for withdrawing land from production but for soil conservation practices. Those who substituted "soil-conserving" for "soil-depleting" crops— the principal crops in surplus such as cotton, corn, and wheat—became eligible for direct government payments.

The Agricultural Adjustment Act of 1938, commonly referred to as the second AAA, replaced the Soil Conservation and Domestic Allotment Act. The new law retained the necessary soil conservation features, but it granted the Secretary of Agriculture more authority to control surpluses. If acreage restriction failed to control price-depressing surpluses, the Secretary could establish marketing quotas to regulate the amount of each basic commodity which a producer could sell. If the farmer exceeded his quota or allotment, he was subject to a penalty tax. Moreover, the new law authorized the Secretary to make loans against commodities stored in government warehouses, expanding the activities of the Commodity Credit Corporation established in 1933 for this purpose. Despite efforts to restore a favorable condition between supply and demand, farm surpluses continued to accumulate; agricultural income remained low throughout the 1930s.

Benefit payments for acreage reduction and price-support legislation provided little or no help for the poorer tenants, sharecroppers, and migratory farm workers. By 1935 these very low-income farmers became a pressing issue for such New Dealers as Secretary of Agriculture Henry A. Wallace and Rexford Tugwell. In April, President Roosevelt established the Resettlement Administration, which sought to retire millions of acres of submarginal land and to resettle occupants on better land. The New Deal made a further attempt to rehabilitate low-income farmers when Congress in 1937 passed the Bankhead-Jones Farm Tenancy Act. This measure authorized loans to tenants, laborers, and sharecroppers to enable them to buy farms. Again the Farm Security Administration of 1937 assisted the poorest class of farmers. It provided rehabilitation loans, established migratory labor camps, and formed FSA cooperative communities. These programs for farmers revealed concern but achieved few constructive goals.

As early as June 1933, the Farm Credit Act abolished or reorganized some of the older farm credit agencies while creating new ones. Debt-burdened farmers received further relief in the Frazier-Lemke Farm Emergency Act of June 1934. This law permitted a farmer who could not meet his mortgage debt and was in danger of foreclosure to appeal to a federal district court for relief. On demand of the indebted farmer the court would allow him to remain on the farm for five years and to pay the creditor a rent set by the judge. This five-year moratorium the Supreme Court declared unconstitutional in May 1935 because it denied creditors their property rights. A revised measure, passed in August, met Court objections.

The National Industrial Recovery Act

Without industrial recovery the country's jobless workers would never find regular employment. On June 16, 1933, Congress passed the National Industrial Recovery Act, which incorporated the administration's program to bring about industrial recovery. It was to remain in effect for two years. Hugh S. Johnson, who had been associated with the War Industries Board in the Great War, was appointed administrator.

Many business leaders believed that industry's chief trouble came from excessive competition which reduced profits, forced wage reductions, and increased unemployment. Before 1933 a number of businessmen recommended intelligent planning which would reduce competition and bring supply into line with demand. But who should do the planning? Eventually, the principle of government-business cooperation won the day.

The stated purpose of the NIRA was to promote cooperation among businessmen, to eliminate unfair competition, to increase consumption of agricultural and industrial products with expanded purchasing power, to reduce unemployment, and to improve labor standards. To achieve these elusive objectives, representatives of major industries and government were to frame "codes of fair competition." These codes included minimum prices, production controls, specific credit terms, particular service standards, and many other provisions. Once an industrial code had been drawn up and approved by the President, its provisions became legally binding on all business in that industry. This was industrial self-government under federal supervision.

Section 7a of the law guaranteed employees the right to organize and to bargain collectively, and it required employers to comply with minimum-wage and maximum-hour provisions in the codes. The minimum-wage figure varied in different geographic areas and in different industries, but it was generally 40 cents an hour. A maximum workweek of forty hours appeared in 85 percent of the codes and covered approximately half of the employees of industries under the National Recovery Administration (NRA). Some codes prohibited labor by children under sixteen. The Blue Eagle of the NRA became the symbol of industrial recovery. The goal of spreading employment was promoted with the pageantry of wartime.

By shortening the workweek and reducing child labor, the new industrial program extended jobs to more than 2 million workers in 1933. But the overall contribution of the NRA to recovery was meager at best. Dividing up available employment among more workers may have been temporarily beneficial, but it did not solve the problem of creating new jobs. Moreover, despite the President's plea to hold the line, prices went up as fast as, or faster than, wages. Thus there was no substantial increase in purchasing power. Nor after the initial boomlet was there any marked increase in employment or in the volume of production. Like the AAA, the NRA was basically a program of scarcity. The NRA did not stimulate recovery, but it did encourage such permanent reforms as minimum wages, maximum hours, the elimination of child labor, and the establishment of collective bargaining for workers as a national policy.

Title II of the NRA created a Public Works Administration. The PWA was designed to supplement other provisions of the basic law by expanding employment with public works. About half of the cost of these projects was to be furnished by PWA, the other half by states and municipalities. Besides supplying new employment, the public projects, through increased purchases of cement, lumber, steel, and other products, would supposedly stimulate the entire economy. This was part of the New Deal's pump-priming program, designed to increase employment, expand purchasing power, and swell capital investment.

Besides key relief and recovery legislation, Congress passed other important measures during and after the First Hundred Days. On May 18, 1933, Senator George W. Norris finally realized his dream when Congress approved the Tennessee Valley Authority. The Securities Act of May 1933, followed in 1934 by a broader and more permanent measure, the Securities Exchange Act, represented governmental efforts to prevent any recurrence of the stock market debacle of 1929. The latter measure required stock exchanges to register with the Security and

Two 1935 views of the New Deal.

The Trojan Horse at Our Gate
—Orr in the Chicago Tribune

Still Pecking Away
—Talburt in the Washington Daily News

Exchange Commission, and required brokers to present information about the companies whose stock they sold. The Commission sought to prevent misrepresentation in the sale of securities. Of major benefit to farmers was the Rural Electrification Act of 1935. By the end of the decade this act brought electricity to millions of farms.

Despite its apparent successes, the New Deal by 1935 faced determined opposition. Businessmen were apprehensive and critical. One manufacturer declared that he intended to take a year off from his business and work for Roosevelt's defeat. "So many businessmen have been so deeply engrossed in their private business that they have permitted half-wits to seize the Government," he said. Roosevelt's call for higher taxes on business in 1935, his attack on what he called "the royalists of the economic order," and the passing of an undistributed profits tax aroused bitterness and anger among conservatives.

The Supreme Court, moreover, became a major barrier to economic planning as it outlawed several New Deal measures. In 1935 the Court declared the National Industrial Recovery Act and the Frazier-Lemke Bankruptcy Act unconstitutional; in January 1936, it struck down the Agricultural Adjustment Act. The court killed the NRA by a unanimous decision in the case of *Schechter Poultry Company v. United States.* The Schechter Poultry Company of New York, convicted in the circuit court of violating the live poultry code, appealed to the Supreme Court. The Supreme Court held that the authority granted by Congress to the President for code making was an unconstitutional delegation of legislative power. Furthermore, said the Court, the defendants were not engaged in interstate commerce, and, therefore, the enactment of the law was an unconstitutional federal invasion of areas that had been reserved for the states specifically.

The Second New Deal

During 1935 the New Deal shifted its emphasis from relief and recovery to social and economic reform. In what came to be known as the Second Hundred Days, ending in August 1935, Congress enacted a wide variety of banking, labor, social security, and other reform laws. Some historians have pointed to 1935 as the dividing point between the first and the second New Deals. Still it is easy to overemphasize the differences between the outlook and accomplishments of the New Deal before and after 1935. Most of the reform measures adopted between 1935 and 1938 had been under consideration for many years. But in 1935 Congress ushered the United States finally into the position of a welfare state. The New Deal's early relief efforts, although helpful, had by late 1934 and 1935 proved to be both insufficient and morally undesirable. After abandoning the CWA in July 1934, the relief program was little more than a federal dole, which Harry Hopkins called "the

most degrading" kind of relief. By January 1935, some 5 million families and individuals were on emergency relief rolls. After studying the problem, Roosevelt declared, on January 4, that the federal government should quit the business of relief and provide work for able but destitute workers.

Congress responded to the President's request for a work relief program by passing the Emergency Relief Appropriation Act in April 1935. This law appropriated $4.88 billion for "relief, work relief, and to increase employment by providing useful projects." On May 6, the Works Progress Administration began to function with Harry Hopkins as administrator. Hopkins moved quickly; within a few months the WPA had organized thousands of work relief projects, which included the construction of airports, schools, highways, libraries, playgrounds, and parks for public use. WPA projects were developed to employ musicians, artists, and other professional persons who could not find regular employment. Between 1936 and 1941, the WPA employed an average of about 2 million workers per month. The Federal Emergency Appropriation Act also authorized the National Youth Administration. This program provided part-time work for high school and college students to enable them to continue their education.

Expenditures for direct relief and work projects increased the federal deficits after 1933. Between 1933 and 1940, the various national relief agencies spent approximately $15 billion, more than half of which was expended by the WPA. In return, several million people gained employment, and the nation profited from better school buildings, parks, roads, and other physical assets. Despite these large outlays, the Depression held on stubbornly.

Labor and the New Deal

Following the Schechter case, the administration faced the task of salvaging the benefits extended to labor in the NRA. On August 5, 1935, the President signed the National Labor Relations Act, commonly called the Wagner Act. This law gave workers the right to form unions and to bargain collectively "through representatives of their own choosing." The law established a National Labor Relations Board, which was empowered to investigate and issue cease-and-desist orders as a means of preventing unfair labor practices.

Having guaranteed collective bargaining, Congress in June 1938 passed the Fair Labor Standards Act, which established minimum wages and maximum hours. This law set minimum wages for employees producing goods for interstate commerce at 25 cents an hour and limited the regular workweek to forty-four hours. The law prohibited children under sixteen from working in most industries, making unnecessary a child labor amendment. Many workers such as those in agriculture were exempt from provisions of the law. In any event, the New Deal had gone far by 1938 in providing decent wages, more leisure time, and the abolition of child labor, all of which had been historic aims of workingmen.

Meanwhile, a fundamental split occurred in the ranks of organized labor. The conflict resulted from disagreement over the best means to organize the millions of workers in the great mass-production industries such as steel, auto-

mobiles, and rubber. The American Federation of Labor, which claimed more than 80 percent of union membership, had historically organized its members on a craft, or trade union, basis. However, during the early 1930s the AF of L came under increasing attack from leaders within its own ranks who wanted to organize the mass-production workers in industrial unions. John L. Lewis, president of the United Mine Workers, headed a group of aggressive labor leaders who argued that workers in a particular industry such as steel should be organized in a single large industrial union instead of on the basis of crafts and trades. In November 1935, Lewis and other unionists formed the Committee for Industrial Organization to organize industrial unions.

In 1936 the CIO began an aggressive campaign to organize steelworkers. Within a few months it extended its organizing efforts to the automobile, glass, rubber, and other mass-production industries. By the end of 1937 the CIO claimed a total of 3.7 million members. This was approximately 300,000 more than were affiliated with the AF of L, which had been active for more than a half century. The great industries such as steel and automobiles fought unions and collective bargaining with every weapon at their command, including strikebreakers, lockouts, violence, discriminatory hiring, and aid from the local police. But Ford's recognition of the United Auto Workers in June 1941, some four years after General Motors recognition, symbolized a victorious climax for organized labor. Overall, New Deal legislation was a major factor in strengthening labor's bargaining position and economic welfare.

Social Security

Perhaps the most fundamental New Deal reform was the Social Security Act, approved by the President on August 5, 1935. Here the Roosevelt administration broke sharply with the past. Most citizens had accepted the idea that people should care for their own needs, through individual savings, both in old age and in periods of unemployment. Local and state governments had historically provided some direct relief. Church and charitable organizations had also helped the needy.

As the Depression wore on, various individuals and organizations proposed visionary schemes to aid the elderly. Dr. Francis E. Townsend of California won millions of supporters for his old-age pension plan, which called for federal payments of $200 per month to every man and women over sixty years of age. By 1935 Townsend claimed 5 million backers. Huey P. Long of Louisiana advocated a Share-Our-Wealth program, in which he recommended providing every family the necessities of life with income derived from heavy taxes on high incomes. Father Coughlin, a Detroit priest, won millions of followers with his plan for inflation, nationalization of certain industries, and a living wage for all industrial labor.

The popularity of such schemes undoubtedly increased Roosevelt's interest in more workable measures. The demands of Father Coughlin and others undoubtedly hastened passage of the Social Security Act of 1935. A broad and comprehensive measure, the law provided for old-age insurance, federal aid to the states for old-age pensions, unemployment insurance, aid to dependent children, and support for various public health programs. The old-age insurance provision, commonly called social security, was the only part of the law administered solely by the federal government. A federal tax on both employees and employers provided funds from which payments could be made to qualified people over sixty-five. Many workers, including agricultural and casual laborers, state employees, and domestic servants, were exempt from benefits of the original law. Later amendments extended coverage to millions of additional workers.

Title I of the law was designed to encourage a more uniform system of old-age pensions among the states and to aid people who were not covered by old-age insurance. Of basic importance to labor was the law's provision for unemployment insurance. To acquire the funds for payments to unemployed workers, the law placed a federal tax on employer payrolls.

Utility Regulation, Tax Revision, Conservation, and Public Power

Another New Deal reform passed in August 1935 was the Public Utility Holding Company Act. The purpose of this law was to reduce the abuses of holding company control in the field of public utilities. That reform faced strenuous opposition, but it was not as controversial as Roosevelt's 1935 tax revision. In a special message to Congress on June 19, the President called for "progressive taxation of wealth and of income" and "a wider distribution of wealth." Specifically, Roosevelt recommended higher income and inheritance taxes and a graduated corporate income tax. What created deep consternation was the President's frank desire to use taxation as a means of checking economic power. Congress refused to give the President every-

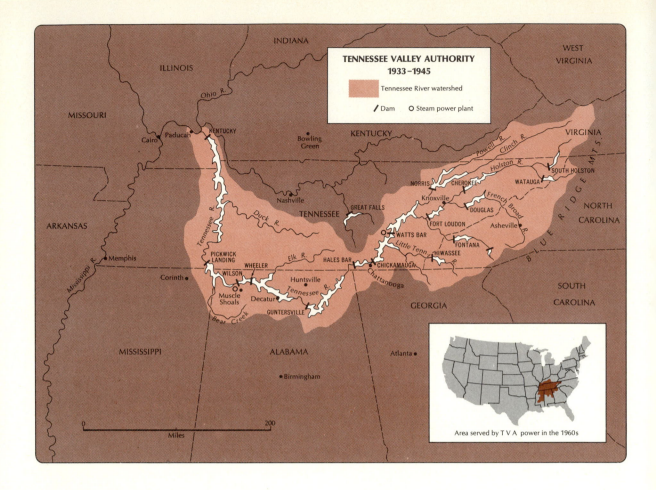

Area served by T V A power in the 1960s

thing he requested, but it did raise rates on large estates and high incomes and levied an excess profits tax on corporations.

Conservation of natural resources was another broad area of reform in which the President had shown personal interest for many years. From the beginning of his administration, Roosevelt gave strong support to soil conservation and flood control. The Department of Agriculture, working through the Soil Erosion Service and later the Soil Conservation Service, carried on an aggressive program after 1933 in an attempt to reclaim millions of acres of land eroded by wind and water. In 1934 Congress enacted the Taylor Grazing Act, which authorized the Secretary of the Interior to establish grazing districts and to institute improved land practices on ranges which had been nearly ruined by overuse.

Conservation was one of the major objectives of the Tennessee Valley Authority, approved in May 1933. Most of the subsequent controversy surrounding TVA dealt with electric power development. The law itself listed navigation, flood control, and the development of agricultural resources as the program's prime objectives. To control floods, aid navigation, and generate electricity, the TVA built thirty principal dams on the Tennessee and tributary rivers. Nine of the high-level dams created huge reservoirs, often referred to as "the Great Lakes of the South." They created river navigation from Paducah, Kentucky, to Knoxville, Tennessee—a distance of some 630 miles. The production of fertilizer and the planting of trees, grass, and soil-conserving crops curbed erosion and restored soil fertility in an area where farm income was very low. Basically TVA brought an economy of abundance to an entire region.

The Tennessee Valley Authority authorized the sale of power, with preference given to "states, counties, municipalities and cooperative organizations." The TVA increased the use of electricity on farms in the region through lower charges. Thus the Authority played a major role in rebuilding the economy of the Tennessee Valley. Other federal power projects included those on the Columbia River at Bonneville, Oregon, and at Grand Coulee in Washington.

Reelection in 1936

As the election of 1936 approached, the President came under severe attack from those whom the New Deal had alienated. Some of the most vocal Roosevelt-haters had formed the American Liberty League in 1934 to combat what they considered to be dangerous and un-American trends in the Roosevelt policies. They intended to block the President's renomination and reelection. But when the Democrats met in convention at Philadelphia late in June, they renominated Roosevelt and Garner on the first ballot. The Democratic platform praised the New Deal and promised additional reforms along lines already marked by the administration.

So shattered had been the Republican party by defeats in 1932 and 1934 that it approached the campaign with neither a program nor a leader. In searching for a man to challenge Roosevelt, the Republicans finally agreed on Governor Alfred M. Landon of Kansas. Landon had withstood the earlier Democratic landslide and had given his state an efficient and moderately progressive administration. Warning that "America is in peril," the platform sharply castigated the New Deal for dishonoring American traditions and betraying its pledges to the people. The Demo-crats, according to official Republican doctrine, were guilty of waste and extravagance.

Besides the Republican opposition Roosevelt faced a conglomeration of leftish critics such as Dr. Francis Townsend, Father Coughlin, and the followers of the late Huey P. Long, who had been assassinated in 1935. These forces combined in June to organize the Union party. They named Representative William Lemke of North Dakota as their candidate for the presidency.

Landon had no chance despite his energetic campaigning and a *Literary Digest* poll which predicted a Republican victory. James A. Farley, who directed the Democratic campaign, declared that the Kansan would carry only two states. Farley was right. Roosevelt received over 11 million more votes than Landon and won all the electoral votes except those of Maine and Vermont. Congress continued heavily Democratic. The result was a smashing personal victory for Roosevelt, who by that time had begun to weld a variety of economic, social, and ethnic groups into an effective political organization. Farmers, workers, urbanites, intellectuals, recent immigrants, Jews, and millions of blacks made up a coalition which the Republicans did not challenge successfully until 1952.

The Court Fight

Roosevelt's popular victory in 1936 and the return of a strong Democratic Congress strengthened his determination to change the complexion of the Supreme Court. Following Court decisions in 1935 and 1936 which outlawed several basic New Deal measures, the President became increasingly critical of the Court's conservatism. In February 1937, he presented to Congress his plan of reform. He requested that the number of Supreme Court justices be increased from nine to a possible fifteen. An essential feature of the plan would permit the President to appoint a new justice (up to a total of fifteen) for each one over seventy who chose to remain on the Court.

The President's proposal raised a storm of protest. Critics labeled his plan a "court-packing" scheme which would permit the Executive to run roughshod over the Constitution. Leading Senators, including such stalwart Democrats as Burton K. Wheeler and Joseph C. O'Mahoney, organized to defeat the President's formula. Republicans quietly followed the liberal Democratic lead, forcing Roosevelt to battle

congressional Democrats openly. Joseph T. Robinson of Arkansas, the majority leader and a loyal party man, led the contest for the administration until July, when he died. After weeks of bitter struggle, Congress rejected Roosevelt's Court plan.

Even before Congress turned down this so-called judicial reform, the Supreme Court handed down a number of decisions upholding New Deal laws. In March and April 1937, the Court declared the Railway Labor Act, a revised Frazier-Lemke farm mortgage law, and the Wagner Act (in *National Labor Relations Board v. Jones and Laughlin Steel Company*) constitutional. These decisions, especially that upholding the Wagner Act, convinced many that the President's move to enlarge the Court was unnecessary. As one wag declared, "A switch in time saved nine."

Recession and Fiscal Policies

While Congress wrestled with proposed Court changes, the recession which began in 1937 dealt the New Deal's recovery program a harsh blow. During the last quarter of 1936, it appeared that genuine prosperity was at last returning. Although there were still 8 to 10 million unemployed, nonfarm employment was picking up, and industrial output, corporate profits, and real income were all increasing. But in the first part of 1937 the economy leveled off, and by September the country slipped back into a full-fledged state of depression (Democrats preferred the term "recession"). The economic decline between September 1937 and June 1938 was one of the most drastic in American history. What caused this sharp economic reversal?

Perhaps the substantial cut in government expenditures was the major cause. Between January and March 1937, monthly net federal outlays declined by some $300 million. This had the effect of reducing personal incomes and the purchasing power necessary to sustain production. Furthermore, at a time when increased private investment was needed to offset reduced

government spending, the Federal Reserve system restricted credit. Finally, the poor outlook for profits tended to discourage private investment.

The 1937–1938 recession forced Roosevelt and his advisers to examine more intensively than before questions dealing with budget and fiscal policies. By early 1938 the role and function of government spending had become a vital issue. Basically, Roosevelt favored a balanced budget and promised to recommend it as soon as business and agriculture recovered. Yet he regarded large-scale spending and federal loans as one essential means of restoring prosperity. In other words, Roosevelt accepted the concept of pump priming—that government spending would stimulate private investment. But the recession of 1937 gave the pump-priming theory a rude shock. When the government, after four years of deficit financing, finally reduced its expenditures, private funds did not fill the investment gap. Why had the economic pump not remained primed?

One group of economists maintained that the

United States had reached a point of economic maturity. This meant that industrial expansion had permanently slowed down to the point where private investment could not absorb the accumulated savings. To compensate for this, they said, heavy government expenditures, another name for public investment, were necessary to keep the economy operating at a high level. The famous British economist John Maynard Keynes developed this theme in his book *The General Theory of Employment, Interest, and Money,* published in 1936. Keynes stressed the need for public spending to stimulate economic expansion when private investment was insufficient to provide full employment. There is no evidence, however, that Keynes, who visited the United States in 1934, had any direct influence on New Deal fiscal policies after 1937. But practical politicians who were in a position to influence the President's thinking strongly urged greatly enlarged federal expenditures and deficit financing.

In a special message on April 14, 1938, President Roosevelt declared that "today's purchasing power . . . is not sufficient to drive the economic system at higher speed. Responsibility of government requires us . . . to supplement the normal processes and . . . to make sure that the addition is adequate." Congress rejected some Roosevelt recommendations, but in 1938 it increased appropriations for federal relief and other purposes by some $3 billion. The national deficit jumped from $1.4 billion in 1938 to $3.6 billion in 1939. Although most Americans, including the President, clung to the principle of balanced budgets, the New Deal established the pattern of federal taxing, borrowing, and spending to help direct and govern the economy. Between 1933 and 1940 the federal debt rose from $19.5 billion to nearly $43 billion.

Life in the Depression

For most Americans life in the Depression was a struggle for the bare necessities of existence. In the mid-1930s more than 40 percent of the nation's families lived on less than $1,000 a year; millions of them earned less than $500 annually. Southern sharecroppers and migrant workers received as little as $100 a year. Most people remembered the scarcity of money. They had not only to watch their dollars, but to guard their nickels and pennies as well.

Money shortages produced important changes in the daily lives of people. Car owners often ran their automobiles until they simply defied repair. Children's college educations were postponed because parents could not pay even modest tuition charges of less than $100 in state-supported institutions. Trips to the doctor and dentist were delayed until a major emergency forced a family to seek medical attention. Even with federal food distribution after 1933, millions of families had inadequate diets. What made the lack of money and resulting poverty tolerable was that the condition was so widespread.

Joblessness instilled widespread restlessness and rootlessness in American life as people wandered about in search of more promising conditions. Hitchhikers lined the highways; railroad boxcars were filled with men who drifted aimlessly from place to place. An unusually large migration left the Great Plains which, because of severe droughts between 1934 and 1936, became a Dust Bowl. Thousands of Oklahoma, Kansas, western Texas, and eastern Colorado farmers left their homes and headed toward California in old jalopies piled high with personal belongings. John Steinbeck caught the spirit and dealt with the problems of this migration in his best seller *The Grapes of Wrath* (1939).

With the inauguration of the five-day week in many industries—to say nothing of those without work—people had more leisure time in the 1930s than ever before. They spent hours before their radios listening to sports, news, music, and drama. Among the most popular radio programs were "Amos 'n' Andy" and "The Lone Ranger," which first appeared in 1933. Movies became increasingly popular. Walt Disney produced full-length, animated pictures, of which *Snow White and the Seven Dwarfs* (1938) was the most famous. *The Good Earth* (1937), *Gone with the Wind* (1939), and the big musical extravaganzas, many of which featured the dancing of Fred Astaire, all drew huge crowds. Those who enjoyed dancing or listening were treated to remarkable sounds by the big-name bands. Benny Goodman, Guy Lombardo, Tommy Dorsey, and Count Basie were among the most popular bandleaders; the trumpeter Louis Armstrong won great acclaim as an individual performer.

Several writers attempted to deal specifically with the Depression, but most popular novelists offered their readers an escape from their day-to-day troubles. In this class were Pearl Buck's *The Good Earth* (1931), a story set in China; Margaret Mitchell's *Gone with the Wind* (1936); and Kenneth Roberts's *Northwest Passage* (1937). Searching for happiness and contentment, millions of readers enjoyed such books as Walter B. Pitkin's *Life Begins at Forty* (1933) and Dale Carnegie's *How to Win Friends and Influence People* (1937). However, William Faulkner, Ellen Glasgow, and James T. Farrell wrote powerful and relevant novels during the Depression years, and both Erskine Caldwell, in *Tobacco Road* (1932),

and John Steinbeck, in *Grapes of Wrath* (1939), dealt meaningfully with the effect of harsh environments on people.

Although people were discouraged and uncertain, they did not turn to religion for solace or direction. Both Protestant and Catholic churches added members, but growth was slow and much of the membership showed little interest. Yet people continued to search for answers. Referring to social and economic reform, one youth declared in 1932: "If someone came along with a line of stuff in which I could really believe, I'd follow him pretty nearly anywhere." People wanted some kind of social salvation, but they were uncertain how to detect or achieve it. The old certainties were gone. As Archibald MacLeish wrote: "We don't know—we can't say— we're wondering." Surveying college youth in 1936, *Fortune* magazine reported: "The present-day college generation is fatalistic . . . the investigator is struck by the dominant and pervasive color of a generation that will not stick its neck out. It keeps its shirt on, its pants buttoned, its chin up, and its mouth shut. . . . Security is the summum bonum of the present college generation." Despite widespread discouragement and uncertainty about the future, most Americans continued to believe that they would somehow solve their problems. Some joined the Communist party. But programs to achieve social salvation outside the capitalistic system and by undemocratic means did not attract many adherents.

Minority Groups in the New Deal

Franklin D. Roosevelt showed greater interest in the welfare of blacks, Mexican-Americans, Indians, and other citizens outside the mainstream of American society than had any president before his time. Not only did he sympathize personally with their second-class economic and social position, but also he brought a number of people into his administration who harbored a genuine concern for these groups. Harold Ickes, who had been president of the local NAACP chapter in

Chicago, Rexford Tugwell, Harry Hopkins, officials in the Farm Security Administration, as well as Mrs. Roosevelt, were among the New Deal leaders who fought for the rights and welfare of underprivileged minorities.

Blacks suffered severely during the Depression. Unemployment among blacks was about double that of whites, as white workers replaced blacks in even the lowest and most menial jobs. Blacks frequently met discrimination in the dis-

The Depression

The depression of the 1930s affected virtually every family in the nation and caused such drastic dislocations for many that it became to millions of Americans an emotional as well as a financial depression. Between twelve and fifteen million workers—about one quarter of the labor force—were out of work by 1933, and by the middle 1930s more than 40 percent of the nation's families lived on less than $1,000 a year. Some, like the migrant workers in the Dorothea Lange photograph below, did not see much more than $100 in cash in a year. Those who had saved their money were not spared. Bank failures—5,504 of them between 1930 and 1933—wiped out the life-savings of millions.

As the months of joblessness rolled into years, thousands of workers felt an increasing sense of personal powerlessness. Self-confidence, and confidence in the traditional American values of initiative, thrift, and competition wavered. And so it happened that the nation elected to follow Franklin Delano Roosevelt, a leader who radiated self-assurance and energy and who told the people, "The only thing we have to fear is fear itself."

otograph by Dorothea Lange, Library of Congress

Growing up on a great Hudson River estate in Hyde Park, New York, Roosevelt's upbringing insured the self-assurance that constantly marked his outward personality. This quality shines out in most of his photographs—missing, perhaps, in the picture of him as a boy at the wheel of his grandfather's yacht (above) but very apparent in the view of him in his riding outfit taken when he was eleven (left). Roosevelt went to the "best" schools—Groton, Harvard, and Columbia Law, ran successfully for the New York State Senate, and served as Assistant Secretary of the Navy during the Wilson administrations. In 1920 the Democrats nominated him as their candidate for Vice-President. Projecting his characteristic verve, he campaigned with the Presidential candidate, James M. Cox (right, above).

In 1921, at the age of thirty-nine, Roosevelt was stricken with infantile paralysis. Rebuilding his physical strength forced him into relative political inactivity for seven years. He maintained his political ties, however, and received the nomination for governor of New York by acclamation at the State Democratic Convention in 1928. He won by a small margin and in the same year helped Santa Claus at the Beekman Street Hospital in New York (right, center). Two years later he was reelected by a margin of around 725,000 votes—the highest ever bestowed on a New York state candidate—and the victory helped him to secure the presidential nomination in 1932. In the final days of the campaign (right, below) he appeared with Al Smith, unsuccessful Democratic presidential candidate in 1928, at his side.

Left and above: Franklin D. Roosevelt Library; right, all pictures: United Press International

In 1933, as breadlines lengthened and banks closed, local governments and banks issued scrip money of their own, like the "Young Plan" dollar (above). By Roosevelt's inauguration on March 4, state governments had ordered most of the nation's banks closed. In his address Roosevelt promised action and immediately declared a national bank holiday for March 6. By March 9, his banking legislation was in Congress. Thus began the famous "first hundred days," during which the executive branch fed Congress an unprecedented volume of proposals for programs to restore the country's economic health.

Perhaps most unusual was the National Industrial Recovery Act. Under the NRA, businessmen were asked to set up industry-wide codes which would set minimum prices, production controls, credit terms, encourage minimum wages and maximum hours, provide for collective bargaining, and eliminate child labor. Some businessmen, however, felt the law gave too much power to labor. Some liberals thought price-setting against the consumer's interest. The Supreme Court invalidated the NRA in May, 1935, but the law established the administration's support for collective bargaining and minimum wages and maximum hours.

In another early move, Roosevelt created the Tennessee Valley Authority. The TVA would provide electric power for four and a half million people, as well as improved navigation, nitrate production, industrial power, flood and erosion control, and recreation facilities. Other New Deal power projects included dams on the Columbia River in Oregon, on the Missouri River at Fort Peck, Montana, and the Grand Coulee Dam in Washington state.

The Works Progress Administration, one of the best known of the New Deal projects, did not begin until 1935, after the government had tried other systems for putting the unemployed to work. The WPA built airports, schools, highways, libraries, playgrounds, and parks and provided work projects for writers, musicians, artists, and actors. Between 1936 and 1941, an average of 2,000,000 workers per month earned an average monthly wage of $56. One of the many murals painted under this program (far right, below) depicts the concert given by Marion Anderson at the Lincoln Memorial in Washington, D.C., after she had been denied the right to sing in Constitution Hall.

Left: The Chase Manhattan Bank Money Museum; above: Dorothea Lange, The Oakland Museum Collection

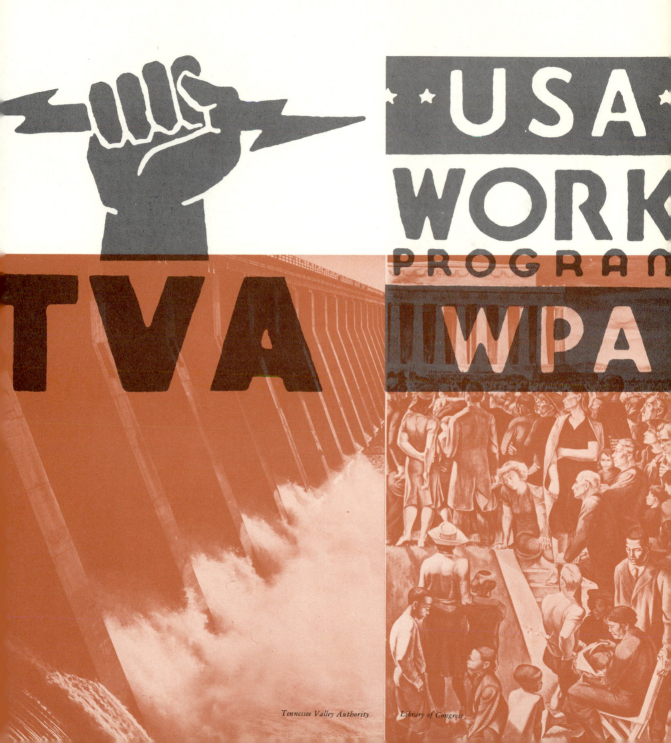

TVA

USA WORK PROGRAM WPA

Tennessee Valley Authority   *Library of Congress*

The Agricultural Adjustment Act (AAA) sought to increase farmer income by paying him to decrease production, a move which also served to keep up the prices for what the farmer did produce. In 1936 the Supreme Court voided the Agricultural Adjustment Act of 1933, but Congress passed a substitute law which accomplished largely the same purposes while meeting the court's objections. In the meantime, the Roosevelt administration had turned some of its attention to helping a section of the farm population which did not receive checks for keeping land out of production—the poor tenants, sharecroppers, and migratory workers—and the farmers who held small acreages.

Designed to help the poorest farmers, the Farm Security Administration provided rehabilitation loans, camps for migrant laborers, and cooperative communities, and in many ways the agency had a useful if not notable impact. One project of the FSA, however, did leave a lasting impression—the photographic project. Under the direction of Roy Stryker, a small team of talented photographers took hundreds of thousands of pictures, creating an emotional documentary report on rural America during the Depression which conveys a human meaning that no statistics can. From the FSA collection at right, above, is Arthur Rothstein's famous dust bowl picture taken in Cimmaron County, Oklahoma. The other pictures here, by the late Dorothea Lange, show, below, a class-conscious sign in a gas station in Kern County, California; right, below, two families from Missouri looking for work in California; and at far right, a migrant mother, about whom Miss Lange wrote: "She sits under a shelter on the edge of the pea fields, with no work because the crop froze. On this morning the family sold the tires from their automobile, for food."

Top: FSA Photograph by Arthur Rothstein, Library of Congress; all other pictures: FSA Photographs by Dorothea Lange, Library of Congress

Encouraged by a sympathetic Democratic administration and inspired by dynamic leadership, organized labor rose to prominence in the 1930s. The gain did not come, however, without bitter struggles, both within the labor movement and in conflicts with management. The new unions worked for gains in wages or shorter hours but particularly for the principles of the closed shop and exclusive representation in collective bargaining. Management of some of the industries, including some steel and auto companies, fought the unions with strikebreakers, lockouts, and aid from the local police. In one of the most violent strikes, at the Republic Steel Company in Chicago in 1937, police killed ten strikers and strike sympathizers. At left, police battle striking truck drivers in Minneapolis in 1937. Below, labor leader Walter Reuther comforts a fellow unionist beaten up in a struggle at the Ford Dearborn plant in 1937.

During the Roosevelt years Congress passed legislation which has benefited organized labor ever since. After the Supreme Court invalidated the NRA, important measures included the National Labor Relations Act and the Fair Labor Standards Act.

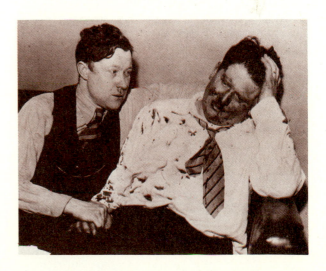

tribution of relief. Moreover, the NRA codes did not really protect black workers because most of their jobs were not covered by wage and hour agreements. To many NRA meant "Negroes Ruined Again." The AAA hurt blacks throughout the rural South. As Southern landowners received payments to take land out of production, they dismissed thousands of farm tenants and sharecroppers.

Some New Deal programs, however, provided opportunities for blacks. About 200,000 black youths served in the CCC, although generally on a segregated basis; many thousands received educational assistance through the NYA. The Resettlement Administration and the Farm Security Administration helped many rural black families improve their position. But more important than specific programs was the fact that some blacks received responsible positions in the Roosevelt administration. For example, Robert L. Vann of Pittsburgh served as Special Assistant to the Attorney General, and William H. Waite, dean of the Howard University Law School, became Assistant Solicitor in the Department of the Interior. Roosevelt was not an activist in extending civil rights, but he did become a symbol for justice and equality. Consequently, blacks rapidly shifted their political loyalty to Roosevelt and the Democratic party.

The Great Depression intensified the already unsatisfactory conditions among America's Indi-

an population. Designed to create independent farmers through allotments of individual landholdings, the Dawes Act of 1887 had failed miserably. In some cases Indians had sold their land; in other instances, holdings became fragmented through inheritance. Without productive land, education, or job skills, thousands of Indians lived in poverty and disease. During the 1920s a number of reformers, notably John Collier, secretary of the Indian Defense Association, called for a new approach to Indian policy. Rather than attempting to force Indians into the ways of white men, he recommended the preservation of Indian culture. In 1934 Congress passed the Wheeler-Howard Act, which provided for tribal self-government, loans for Indian business ventures, and funds to educate Indian youth. This approach to Indian problems was at best only partially successful.

Migrant workers, often Mexican-Americans, constituted yet another group of underprivileged citizens who failed to make any substantial gains under the New Deal. Living always on the edge of disaster, these cotton, fruit, and vegetable pickers, who followed the harvest from one part of the country to the other, experienced difficult and often tragic times. Working for extremely low wages, living in huts scarcely fit for animals, and often unable to send their children to school, the migrants drifted about the country in search of a minimum existence. New Deal programs failed to reach the hard-core poor.

Conclusion

Despite the quantity and variety of New Deal legislation, it required the impact of World War II to bring complete economic recovery to the United States. New Deal efforts to aid employment were partially successful at best. In 1939, after six years of New Deal programs, agricultural prices were still below parity; manufacturing production was slightly lower than a decade earlier; corporate profits had not reached the level of 1929; and unemployment still totaled

about 9 million. However, advances from 1932 could be noted in almost every aspect of economic life. Corporate profits were up; farm prices were higher; unemployment was down; and per capita income after taxes (in dollars of constant buying power) had risen from $679 in 1933 to $925 in 1939.

The New Deal fell short of restoring full prosperity, but it reestablished faith and confidence in the American system. Moreover, the reform measures were of fundamental importance. Labor benefited from the right to bargain collectively as well as from minimum wages and maximum hours. Laws regulating banking and security sales protected bank depositors and investors alike. Cheaper electricity had been introduced into millions of homes. Old age had been brightened by the prospect of social security.

Expansion of government functions and responsibilities was the most meaningful aspect of the New Deal. Although government powers had been growing for many years, they developed more rapidly after 1933 and moved in the direction of social welfare. The government intervened extensively in the economy to help farmers and industrial laborers especially.

By the eve of World War II Americans were living in a "mixed economy." Private enterprise continued to be the mainspring of economic activity, but government had assumed a partnership role in which it assumed responsibility for individual and national economic welfare. Franklin Roosevelt's role in bringing about these changes had been crucial. His personal magnetism, his identification with millions of forgotten Americans, his skillful political leadership, and his ability to discover practical and possible alternatives to seemingly insoluble problems accounted for his achievements in social and economic reform. He accepted the American tradition of compromise and gradual change. Therein lay his strength—and perhaps the underlying reason for his success.

SUGGESTED READINGS

The best-balanced, but still incomplete, biography of F. D. Roosevelt is Frank Freidel's *Franklin D. Roosevelt* (1952–   ), four volumes of which had appeared by 1973. *The Lion and the Fox* (1956) by James M. Burns is a serious, well-researched study. For Roosevelt's prepresidential career see *FDR: The Beckoning, 1882–1928* (1972). On Roosevelt's thought see D. R. Fusfeld's *The Economic Thought of Franklin D. Roosevelt and the Origins of the New Deal* (1956). The intellectual impact of the New Deal has been covered in *Ideologies and Utopias; the Impact of the New Deal on American Thought* by Arthur A. Ekirch (1969). On the continuing worldwide depression see Charles P. Kindleberger, *The World in Depression, 1929–1939* (1973).

By far the most meaningful general survey of the New Deal is W. E. Leuchtenberg's *Franklin D. Roosevelt and the New Deal** (1963). The economic history of the period has been given detailed treatment by Broadus Mitchell in *Depression Decade* (1947), while Dixon Wecter has emphasized the social history of the period in *The Age of the Great Depression* (1948). One of the earliest and still useful surveys of the New Deal is Basil Rauch's *A History of the New Deal, 1933–1938** (1944), which stresses the differences between the first and second New Deals. In *The Coming of the New Deal** (1958), A. M. Schlesinger, Jr., provides a detailed and stimulating account of the

major issues during the first two years of the New Deal. Early New Deal activities can best be followed in *Franklin D. Roosevelt: Launching the New Deal* (1973) by Frank Freidel.

Many of Roosevelt's associates have written about the President and New Deal policies. Among the best accounts is that by Secretary of Labor Frances Perkins, *The Roosevelt I Knew* (1946); Raymond Moley's *The First New Deal* (1966). See also Rexford G. Tugwell's *F.D.R., Architect of an Era* (1967) and *In Search of Roosevelt* (1972).

On the question of agriculture and farm relief see G. C. Fite's *George N. Peek and the Fight for Farm Parity* (1954); J. L. Shover's *Cornbelt Rebellion: The Farmer's Holiday Association* (1965); D. E. Conrad's *The Forgotten Farmers: The Story of Sharecroppers in the New Deal* (1964); and *Three Years of the Agricultural Adjustment Administration* (1937) by E. G. Nourse and others. Van L. Perkins has presented an excellent account of the AAA's first year in *Crisis in Agriculture* (1969).

Attempts to achieve business recovery have been given detailed treatment by L. S. Lyon and others in *The National Recovery Administration* (1935). The authors argue that the NRA may have retarded rather than stimulated recovery. H. S. Johnson's memoir, *The Blue Eagle from Egg to Earth* (1935), points up many of the problems and conflicts within the NRA.

Among the best books on monetary and fiscal policies is G. G. Johnson, Jr.'s *The Treasury and Monetary Policy, 1933–1938* (1939).

The basic work on federal relief is J. C. Brown's *Public Relief, 1929–1939* (1940). D. S. Howard's *The WPA and Federal Relief Policy* (1943) is also excellent. Help for America's youth has been discussed by B. G. and E. K. Lindley in *A New Deal for Youth: The Story of the National Youth Administration* (1938) and John A. Salmond's *The Civilian Conservation Corps, 1933–1942* (1967).

George Wolfskill has written an excellent account of the growing political opposition to Roosevelt in *The Revolt of the Conservatives: A History of the American Liberty League, 1934–1940* (1962). Some of the best material on the election of 1936 can be found in D. R. McCoy's excellent biography of the Republican candidate, *Landon of Kansas* (1966), and *The Politics of Upheaval** (1960) by Arthur M. Schlesinger, Jr.

The shift in the New Deal toward greater emphasis on reform has been well covered in Schlesinger's *The Politics of Upheaval*. An excellent brief account can be found in Paul Conkin's *FDR and the Origins of the Welfare State** (1967). On social security see E. E. Witte's *Development of the Social Security Act* (1962) and Lewis Meriam's *Relief and Social Security* (1966) and Arthur J. Altmeyer, *The Formative Years of Social Security* (1966). Activities of the old-age groups can be followed in Abraham Holtzman's *The Townsend Movement: A Political Study* (1963). On Huey Long see T. H. Williams, *Huey Long: A Biography* (1969). Charles J. Tull provides a good account of the Detroit radio priest in *Father Coughlin and the New Deal* (1965). *Radical Visions and American Dreams: Culture and Social Thought in the Depression Years* (1973) by Richard H. Pells is excellent.

Joseph Rayback's *A History of American Labor** (1959) and Philip Taft's *The A.F. of L. from the Death of Gompers to the Merger* (1959) contain useful chapters on labor during the New Deal period. The conflict within the labor movement has been well described by James V. Morris in *Conflict within the AFL: A Study of Craft versus Industrial Unionism, 1901–1938* (1959). See also Charles K. McFarland, *Roosevelt, Lewis and the New Deal, 1933–1940* (1970). A first-rate study of agriculture in the later New Deal is C. T. Schmidt's *American Farmers in the World Crisis* (1941). Sidney Baldwin's *Poverty and Politics: The Rise and Decline of the Farm Security Administration* (1968) shows how the New Deal failed to solve the problems of the rural poor.

On the TVA see J. S. Ransmeier's *The Tennessee Valley Authority: A Case Study in the Economics of Multiple Purpose Stream Planning* (1942). W. H. Droze has dealt with the TVA in terms of resource planning in *High Dams and Slack Waters: TVA Rebuilds a River* (1965).

On increased government expenditures, taxation, and the expanding role of government, see A. E. Burns and D. S. Watson's *Government Spending and Economic Expansion* (1940) and L. H. Kimmel's *Federal Budget and Fiscal Policy, 1789–1958* (1959). The best account of the recession of 1937–1938 is *The Economics of Recession and Revival* (1954) by K. D. Roose. On the regulation of business see R. F. de Bedts' *The New Deal's SEC, 1933–1938* (1964).

On society in the Depression see Wecter, cited above. Dealing with the quality of life in more detail is W. F. Ogburn (ed.), *Social Changes during the Depression and Recovery* (1935) and the more useful study by R. S. and H. M. Lynd, *Middletown in Transition** (1937), which carries their study of Muncie, Indiana, into the 1930s. The position of the Negro in the New Deal period can be traced in Gunnar Myrdal's *An American Dilemma: The Negro Problem and Modern Democracy** (2 vols., 1944); and the pertinent sections of the *Negro American: A Documentary History** (1967) by Leslie H. Fishel, Jr., and Benjamin Quarles; and *Black Protest Thought in the Twentieth Century** (1965) by August Meier, Elliott Rudwick, and Francis L. Broderick. An excellent source is Raymond Wolters, *Negroes and the Great Depression* (1970).

*indicates availability in paperback.

29

The Challenge of Global Politics: The 1930s

When Franklin D. Roosevelt entered the White House in March 1933, world events had already exploded the illusion of permanent peace. So promising had been the experience of the twenties, however, that not even the Japanese assault on Manchuria in 1931 could disturb the democracies' general faith in the world's peace structure. Unfortunately the peace which postwar Americans had accepted as their special dispensation had always been ephemeral, because that peace reflected less a general acceptance of the Versailles settlement (symbolic of the status quo) than the temporary weakness of the dissatisfied nations. Still as long as no powerful nation resorted to force, nothing could shatter the easy conclusion that all wars had been fought and all issues resolved. So completely did Britain, France, and the United States dominate the immediate postwar world that key American officials mistakenly attributed the globe's apparent stability to a universal acceptance of Western democratic leadership and Western no-

tions of proper international behavior. Edwin L. James of the *New York Times* questioned this assumption in October 1930: "America's great world political position is not due primarily to our moral leadership but primarily to our wealth and economic position. If we were a poor and weak nation the world would today care no more about what we thought than did the world before the Great War."

For both European and American proponents of peace and the status quo during the twenties, world opinion was the controlling element in international affairs. That opinion, they believed, would compel any would-be aggressor to limit change to what was peaceful. Still, they might have recalled the words of Lord Cecil, spoken in defense of the League of Nations Covenant in 1919: "For the most part there is no attempt to rely . . . upon force to carry out a decision of the Council or the Assembly of the League. . . . What we rely upon is public opinion . . . and if we are wrong about it, then the whole thing is wrong." Manchuria had demonstrated that the entire concept was wrong. But the illusion that opinion controlled the world and that it always favored peace had continued unchallenged for so long that Western leaders behaved as if their rhetoric of peaceful change was in itself a genuine barrier to war. "I cannot recall any time," declared Winston Churchill in 1932, "when the gap between the kind of words which statesmen used and what was actually happening in many countries was so great as it is now." The international crises of the thirties would merely demonstrate again and again the uselessness of any system that relied on the force of world opinion to maintain the peace.

The Republican Heritage

The reliance of Americans in the 1920s on paper—on stocks and bonds at home and treaties without obligations abroad—culminated in the Kellogg-Briand Peace Pact of 1928. Eventually this effort to outlaw war won the overwhelming support of internationalists, isolationists, and pacifists—all those Americans, indeed, who placed their faith in agreements and agencies designed to focus the supposedly crippling power of international law and world opinion on any nation that dared to break the peace. Still the movement to outlaw war developed slowly. During April 1927, on the tenth anniversary of the United States declaration of war against Germany, Aristide Briand, the French foreign minister, addressed a message to the American people proposing a Franco-American agreement to outlaw war between the two nations.

While the State Department, angered at Briand's decision to approach the American public rather than the government in Washington, continued to avoid the issue, a crusade to outlaw war began to sweep the country. Leading Eastern and Midwestern newspapers gave the issue enthusiastic coverage. Jane Addams of Hull House, Chicago, presented the President a petition with 30,000 signatures encouraging him to take the initiative. When the League of Nations Assembly convened in September 1927, the Polish representative introduced a resolution asking the League to renounce all wars of aggression. Briand reminded the Assembly that the universal conscience of mankind constituted a perfect tribunal to prevent aggressive war. On Septem-

ber 27, the Assembly unanimously adopted the Polish resolution, branding wars of aggression an international crime. This League action sent President Coolidge and his secretary of state, Frank B. Kellogg, in search of some antiwar formula that would mollify both Briand and the American peace advocates.

Kellogg found the answer to Briand's bilateral proposal in a multilateral treaty to outlaw war. Assured of national support, Kellogg in December submitted the idea of a multilateral pact to the French government. Paris's response, though affirmative, was less than enthusiastic. French officials saw immediately that a multilateral treaty, designed to eliminate the danger of war everywhere, would expand the international commitment to the status quo so completely that it would destroy all sense of specific obligation among the major powers for world peace. But the American press, oblivious of the fundamental issue raised by outlawry—that of obligation—generally responded to Kellogg's proposal with unbounded enthusiasm. "Oh, the miracle of it!" exclaimed Salmon O. Levinson of Chicago, a leading outlawry advocate. Coolidge passed judgment on the proposal: "It holds a greater hope for peaceful relations than was ever before given to the world."

Kellogg joined Briand and dozens of other leading diplomats in Paris late in August 1928. The signing of the Kellogg-Briand Peace Pact was magnificent. Some diplomats remained skeptical of the treaty's value, but officially, at least, sixty-four nations eventually consigned war to oblivion. Some Americans were jubilant. The *Boston Herald* declared: "It is a thing to rejoice over, it is superb, it is magnificent." For Carrie Chapman Catt the world was moving unmistakably toward biblical ploughshares and pruning hooks. But Rabbi Stephen S. Wise of New York labeled the pact the wishbone rather than the backbone of peace.

In the Senate the treaty faced little opposition. Kellogg reassured the Foreign Relations Committee that the pact was devoid of commitment except the commitment not to make aggressive war. "[Other nations] knew perfectly well," he said, "that the United States would never sign a treaty imposing any obligation on itself to apply sanctions or come to the help of anybody." Some senators dismissed the question of means as nonessential. Senator Robert Wagner of New York hailed the treaty "as a great and lasting crystallization of the human will to peace." Amid such oratory the Senate, on January 15, 1929, endorsed the treaty by a vote of 85 to 1. So painless was the nation's involvement in another impressive peace effort that isolationists and internationalists alike could share the apparent triumph.

By the late twenties Republican foreign policy had achieved such visible success that it had won the overwhelming endorsement of the American people. So expansive had been America's share of world trade, so reassuring the Europe of the twenties, so apparent the contributions of the League to international stability, that countless Americans viewed the Versailles peace structure with increasing satisfaction.

President Hoover hoped to continue the work of peace begun by the Washington Treaties and the Kellogg-Briand Peace Pact. At his suggestion Prime Minister Ramsay MacDonald of Great Britain issued invitations to the London Naval Conference in October 1929.

In January 1930, Great Britain, the United States, France, Italy, and Japan began discussions in London on the issue of naval disarmament. The two continental powers, France and Italy, were too distrustful of one another to

accept significant naval reductions without special security guarantees from the United States. When Washington failed to offer guarantees, Italy and France refused to sign the more important articles of the treaty. Britain, the United States, and Japan negotiated an agreement limiting cruisers on a ratio of 10-10-6, and submarines and other auxiliaries at 10-10-7. Britain was permitted an escape from these provisions in the event of a threat from France or Italy. The treaty did little to limit the world's navies. The United States would have required a major naval building program even to approach the treaty's rather generous quotas.

Hoover attempted to resolve the vexing questions of war debts and reparations, but without much success. With economic crises both at home and abroad, in June 1931, the President suggested a one-year moratorium, or standstill arrangement, on the payment of intergovernmental debts. Both debtors and creditors agreed. In the summer of 1932 the concerned European powers, at Lausanne, Switzerland, agreed to scale down German reparations payments to a mere $750 million, provided that the United States would reduce its claims for war debts proportionately. This the Hoover administration refused to do. Thus the entire question of war debts and reparations remained open at the end of the Hoover years. Early in 1933 Adolf Hitler terminated German reparations. Meanwhile, war debt payments to the United States all but stopped; except for Finland, no country paid its full account.

That internationalism which found its ultimate expression in the Nine Power Pact, the Kellogg-Briand Peace Pact, and the movement for naval limitation constituted the essence of Republican foreign policy. Thus it required no more than an armed clash outside Mukden, Manchuria, in September 1931, to shatter the peace of Asia and challenge all the assumptions upon which the West had erected its elaborate peace structure. Behind the struggle for Manchuria lay a network of unequal treaties which had given Japan a variety of special privileges in Manchuria, including the right to station troops along the South Manchurian Railway. Chinese nationalism and antiforeignism directed much of China's energy toward the elimination of Japanese influence in Manchuria. Finding Japan's investments as well as its favored positions in South Manchuria in jeopardy, Japanese militarists exploded the Mukden incident to establish total military and political sway over Manchuria.

Japanese action exposed the gap between the ends and means of United States Far Eastern policy. This nation's primary objectives in the Orient were embodied in the Nine Power Pact of 1922. To avoid the necessity of either accepting diplomatically the changes wrought by Japan in Manchuria or undoing the Japanese aggression with counterforce, the Hoover administration resorted to the doctrine of nonrecognition. In January 1932, Secretary of State Henry L. Stimson informed both the Chinese and Japanese governments that the United States would recognize no territorial changes on the Asian mainland which resulted from the use of force. The League of Nations, lacking the firm support of the great democracies, was powerless to act. Still its mild rebuke of Japan, based on the Lytton Commission's report which in general supported the American principle of nonrecognition, prompted the Japanese to withdraw dramatically from the world body in 1933. Confronted by no opposition of significance in Asia, the Japanese reorganized Manchuria into the puppet state of Manchukuo. Yet Stimson, in his praise of American action, insisted that nothing had occurred in Manchuria to challenge the applicability of either the Nine Power Pact or the Kellogg-Briand Pact.

Japanese aggression did not destroy the peace system of the 1920s; it merely exposed obvious weaknesses. Western diplomacy after 1919 amounted to a massive effort to reinforce the Versailles treaty structure with additional guarantees. As long as all signatories of the Nine Power Pact and the Kellogg Pact accepted the principles those documents embodied, the structure would be stable indeed. The fact that some countries—notably Germany, Russia, and Japan—had made clear their rejection of fundamental elements in the Versailles Treaty, especially with regard to Eastern Europe and China, was not in itself a measure of diplomatic failure. No major treaty could establish a worldwide political and territorial arrangement which would satisfy all peoples over a long period of time. Throughout history it was the endless minor adjustments, whether wrought by force or not, which had given a measure of longevity to prominent historic settlements.

But after 1919 change to be legitimate had also to be peaceful, its limitations to be prescribed by world opinion. The new diplomacy of the twenties contained no provision for acceptance of even minor shifts in the world's political and territorial structure unless underwritten by general agreement. The great democracies based their hopes for peace on the assumption that in a rational world peace would always take precedence over ambition or aggression. But the Japanese had demonstrated in Manchuria that the necessary harmony of interest in peace and peaceful change did not exist. World opinion, Japan made clear, was either impotent or wrong-minded. Nor was this the end of the Western dilemma. Governments with the power to make war continued to harbor objectives which exceeded the limits of peaceful change. For the democracies, after 1932, the choices were clear. Either they would accept alterations in the status quo created by force or they would fight another major war to sustain inviolate the world which they had designed at Versailles.

Challenge of the Dictators

Even as Roosevelt led his country through the famed Hundred Days of 1933, Adolf Hitler was consolidating his power in Germany. Without the support of a powerful democratic tradition, the Weimar Republic, symbol of Germany's acceptance of the Versailles Treaty, failed to answer the challenge of economic despair. President Paul von Hindenburg, in January 1933, invited Hitler to become chancellor. Possessed of a powerful voice and an elite guard—the notorious *Schutz Staffel*—and preaching defiance of Versailles, Hitler had built his National Socialist party into a formidable political force. The conservative industrialists, aristocrats, army officers, and editors who joined Hitler to control their country's future discovered too late that they had underestimated Hitler's passion for personal power. During the summer of 1934, following the death of Hindenburg, Hitler purged his party of disloyal elements and established himself as dictator. He then moved to direct the considerable industrial might and energy of Germany toward the satisfaction of his ambitions. In his book *Mein Kampf* ("My Struggle"), published in 1924, Hitler had clarified his intention of tearing the Versailles Treaty to shreds. Whether he could fulfill his promises to himself and the German people depended on the response of England and France, the two European guarantors of the status quo.

For two years Hitler moved cautiously in foreign affairs while he consolidated his power and converted Germany into a highly nationalistic, totalitarian, anti-Semitic state. By 1935 he was prepared to challenge the military restrictions imposed on Germany at Versailles. On March 9 the German government announced its decision to build an air force. A week later Hitler, assuring Europe of his peaceful intentions, informed the world that henceforth the German army would be based on national compulsory service and increased immediately to 550,000 men, over five times the number authorized by the Versailles Treaty. Britain sanctioned German rearmament further by consenting to a German navy 35 percent of the size of Britain's. Finally in March 1936, Hitler sent German troops into the Rhineland, repudiating the Locarno Pact of 1925 and the Versailles clauses which had set Germany's western front-

iers. France, lacking its former confidence, did not threaten retaliation. The League Council condemned Germany's violation of the treaty system but could not formulate a concrete response.

Endangered by German power, France turned to the Soviet Union and signed a mutual assistance pact with the Kremlin in May 1935. When this accord antagonized France's Eastern European allies, notably Poland and Yugoslavia, France turned to Italy. During the twenties, Mussolini's domestic and foreign policies had been less than commendable, but by the mid-thirties Italy had again become a respectable member of the international community. Hitler's abortive attempt to annex Austria in July 1934 sent a wave of fear through Italy, for the possible extension of German authority to the Brenner Pass threatened Italian security. Hitler's Austrian venture drove Mussolini toward a fearful France and simultaneously provided him with an unparalleled opportunity for mischief-making with little danger of Western retaliation. Mussolini, in October 1935, sent his black-shirted legions into Ethiopia. French Premier Pierre Laval nodded assent. Britain refused to countenance this aggression, but lacking French support, hesitated to push economic sanctions to the point of possible effectiveness. Unaided by Western diplomacy, but unopposed by Western power, Mussolini, armed with modern weapons and mustard gas, completed his conquest of Ethiopia.

During 1936 Britain and France paid the price of indecision and disunity. Their refusal to prevent Italian aggression demonstrated the League's ineffectiveness; their refusal to recognize Mussolini's gains in Africa drove him into the arms of Hitler. When Hitler in July 1936 extorted an agreement from the Austrian government which opened the way for Nazi penetration, Mussolini acquiesced and thereby laid the foundation for the Rome-Berlin Axis, the very alignment that French and British diplomacy had sought to prevent. The triumphant Italy now followed Japan and Germany out of the League. The Western democracies, Hitler surmised, would not defend the Versailles Treaty with policies that threatened their interest in peace. After 1936 Hitler's indulgence, not the will of the democracies, sustained what remained of European stability.

Isolationism at High Tide

If President Roosevelt detected the aggressive designs of Hitler and Mussolini during his first term, he refused to exert any effective leadership to control them. He had, under extreme isolationist pressure, avoided questions of foreign commitment during his victorious campaign. After March 1933, his public statements reassured an isolationist America of his determination to avoid foreign commitments. As late as October 2, 1935, he promised the American people that whatever happened abroad, the United States would "remain unentangled and free." Roosevelt's foreign policy made no break with the Republican past, for neither his words nor his actions included any precise definition of the American stake in the Versailles system.

Roosevelt's recognition of the Soviet Union in November 1933 evinced new attitudes toward Moscow's Bolshevik regime but no commitment to European politics. Joseph Stalin, in a move which made the post-Lenin Soviet regime more acceptable in the West, had gradually downgraded the Marxist-Leninist notion of "world revolution." The specter of Bolshevik terror had not been entirely erased from Western minds, but somehow it no longer seemed threatening. There were practical reasons as well for bringing Russia fully into the family of nations. Businessmen detected possibilities for commerce with a friendly Russia. Diplomats hoped that a Soviet Union active in world councils might serve as a counterweight to German and Japanese aggressiveness. Roosevelt, in October 1933, communicated to the Kremlin his desire to discuss the question of diplomatic recognition. Maxim Litvinov arrived in Washington shortly thereafter, prepared to pledge that the Kremlin would "refrain from interfering in any manner in the internal affairs of the United States."

A month later, Roosevelt announced the establishment—after some sixteen years—of United States diplomatic relations with the Soviet Union.

Roosevelt's so-called Good Neighbor policy meant improved United States–Latin American relations. But this was scarcely an innovation. Throughout the twenties American interventionism had been on the wane. President Harding had withdrawn American troops from Santo Domingo. President Coolidge, through his able ambassador Dwight Morrow, had vastly improved United States relations with Mexico. Former Secretary Hughes assured the Pan-American Conference at Havana in 1928 that the United States would intervene in Latin America only when its national security demanded such action. Under Hoover the United States had returned to its traditional policy of recognizing *de facto* governments in Latin America, whatever their methods of achieving and maintaining power. In the spring of 1931 Secretary of State Stimson ordered United States marines out of Nicaragua and prepared to terminate the American occupation of Haiti.

FDR merely continued this trend toward anti-imperialism and mutual respect, launching his Good Neighbor policy in his first inaugural. "In the field of world policy," he declared, "I would dedicate this nation to the policy of the good neighbor—the neighbor who . . . respects the sanctity of his agreements in and with a world of neighbors." In subsequent speeches the President made clear that American obligations under the Monroe Doctrine were limited to hemispheric defense. Secretary of State Cordell Hull, at the Pan-American Conference which met in Montevideo during 1933, supported a Latin American declaration which asserted that "no state has the right to intervene in the internal or external affairs of another." True to his pledge, Roosevelt refused to sanction the dispatch of American troops to stabilize Cuban internal conditions in 1933 during another of the island's many revolutions, despite a number of precedents and much advice to do so. In May 1934, Sumner Welles negotiated a treaty with the *de facto* Cuban government which recognized that country's full national sovereignty. Three months later, United States troops left Haiti.

During 1934 congressional isolationists moved to the center of the stage. The thicker the clouds heralding the coming storm in Europe, the more the American people, through their representatives in Congress, sought to insulate themselves from its effects. The Johnson Act of 1934 forbade United States citizens or corporations to lend money to, or buy securities from, any foreign government which was in default on its debts to the United States.

Congressional isolationists next disposed of the World Court issue. During the Hoover years, Elihu Root, with the cooperation of the League Council, had devised the "Root Formula" whereby, if the United States joined the World Court, it would gain equal right with League members to oppose advisory opinions and to withdraw from the Court if its demands were denied. For several years isolationists kept the plan in committee while the Court itself, because of its conservative decisions, became increasingly unrealistic and unpopular. Then in January 1935, Roosevelt submitted the Root proposal to the Senate, where the top-heavy Democratic majority promised the needed two-thirds majority. Before the Senate could vote, however, the nation's isolationist forces closed in. Father Charles E. Coughlin, Detroit's ultra-isolationist "radio priest," urged his listeners to warn their senators against Court membership; William Randolph Hearst advised his readers: "The way to keep America out of the League of Nations trap . . . is to keep America out of the League Court. Telegraph your senators." The resulting cascade of letters and telegrams ap-

"The radio priest," Father Charles E. Coughlin, on the air around 1935. The Granger Collection

parently changed some senatorial minds. By 7 votes the United States declined to enter the World Court.

The year 1935 brought congressional isolationists their supreme triumph of the decade. The stage was well set. In early 1934 two disturbing books, Helmuth C. Engelbrecht's *Merchants of Death* and George Seldes's *Iron, Blood, and Profits*, "proved" what many Americans had long believed: that American involvement in the Great War resulted from the pressures of financiers and munitions manufacturers who feared for their investments and profits if Britain and France should fall.

The Senate, disturbed by such exposés, ordered an inquiry into the matter of war profits, placing at the head of its investigating committee Senator Gerald P. Nye of North Dakota. Nye's Munitions Investigating Committee, during a period of almost two years, published seven reports totaling 1,400 pages. The testimony on the 1914–1917 period revealed a pattern of lobbying, questionable business practices, and huge wartime profits. The evidence was almost wholly circumstantial and by no means proved that Woodrow Wilson had been the dupe of avaricious bankers and manufacturers. But in the atmosphere of the middle thirties, with the reputation of businessmen in eclipse and with Hitler and Mussolini threatening the peace of Europe, the lessons of history seemed clear enough. From Nye's discoveries millions of Americans, including members of Congress, concluded that merely to guarantee the profits of a few "merchants of death" the United States had entered into a costly and unnecessary war.

In April 1935, Senator Nye introduced in the Senate a set of resolutions designed to keep the United States out of the next European war. After a tortuous legislative history, the Neutrality Act of 1935 emerged from the congressional mill. It was thought that the concept of an impartial arms embargo, plus the restrictions on wartime travel which the bill contained, would eliminate precisely those pressures which had undermined American neutrality in the days of Wilson. Although Roosevelt would have preferred a measure requiring an arms embargo only against aggressors, he reluctantly accepted Congress's formula for guaranteeing the nation's peace. Roosevelt promptly invoked the Neutrality Act against both parties in the Ethiopian war, but many commodities not within its purview, such as oil, continued to flow into Italy. In 1936 Congress again rejected Roosevelt's request for a discretionary embargo, choosing instead to extend the life of existing legislation and its prohibition of loans and credits.

Events in Spain soon put the new neutrality legislation to the test. In July, 1936, a revolt by army chiefs under the leadership of Francisco Franco in Spanish Morocco developed into a general struggle for control of the central Span-ish government at Madrid. In the protracted civil war which followed, a number of European powers became involved—Hitler's Germany and Mussolini's Italy on the side of the Franco rebels, Russia on the side of the duly elected Madrid government. Great Britain and France favored the International Nonintervention Committee in London.

Washington pursued a dual objective—to protect American neutrality and to limit the civil war to Spanish territory. Roosevelt persistently viewed the conflict not as a rebel assault on a legitimate government but as a war between two belligerents. This permitted him to announce a moral embargo of munitions to both sides. When American exporters demanded the right to ship arms to the Madrid Loyalists, Congress extended the Neutrality Law to include the Spanish Civil War. American neutrality denied the Loyalists needed arms—Hitler and Mussolini gave Franco not only weapons but also fighter pilots and planes—and thus, in a negative way, contributed to their defeat.

Even as the Spanish Civil War raged, Congress perfected its neutrality program. Previous acts had not touched the issue of wartime trade in noncontraband goods. The Third Neutrality law of May 1937 gave the President discretionary power to prohibit the export of nonmilitary goods to belligerents unless paid for in advance and carried in foreign ships. This cash-and-carry principle would permit Americans a profitable wartime trade in nonmilitary items. The act declared illegal American loans to belligerents and travel on the ships of warring nations. The neutrality laws represented isolationism at high tide.

War in the Far East

Civil war in Spain, except for the limited involvement of Mussolini and Hitler, was an internal affair which threatened the destruction of an elected government but not necessarily the stability of Europe. Unfortunately events in China permitted no such easy rationalization. On July 7, 1937, Japanese forces clashed with Chinese units at the Marco Polo Bridge, several miles west of Peking. Within six months Japanese troops occupied Peking, Shanghai, Nanking,

Canton, and Hankow. China's president, Chiang Kai-shek, having transferred his capital to Chungking in China's far west, adamantly refused to yield. Chinese Communists in the north under Mao Tse-tung, increasingly adept at guerrilla warfare, prevented Japanese successes in the hinterland which they controlled. Japan was thus trapped in a war which had become excessive in its demands but from which Tokyo dared not retreat. At stake in the Sino-Japanese War was not only the Far Eastern balance of power but also the treaty arrangements which had permitted an uneasy coexistence between American and Japanese objectives in China. Japan's assault on China left Washington only two realistic choices. The United States could either accept changes in the Far East at China's expense or face a rapid deterioration in American-Japanese relations, possibly ending in war.

Cordell Hull responded to the Japanese challenge with a formula which conveyed the notion of resistance but actually avoided all responsibility for dealing with specific infringements on the established treaty structure. His statement of principles, announced on July 16, 1937, embodied the essence of United States official policy toward change. "We advocate," he said, "adjustments of problems in international relations by processes of peaceful negotiation and agreement. We advocate faithful observance of international agreements. Upholding the principle of the sanctity of treaties, we believe in modification of provisions of treaties, when need therefore arises, by orderly processes carried out in a spirit of mutual helpfulness and accommodation." Unfortunately, Hull's principles, as a guide for national policy, were scarcely helpful. His insistence that change rest only on agreement meant in practice that there could be no change. Such an approach to world affairs served the interests of the "have" powers magnificently, inasmuch as it placed all legitimacy in international conflict on the side of those who possessed what they wanted. But it presented the "have-not" nations with the extreme choice of either accepting the status quo or defying it

without benefit of negotiation or compromise.

For a time in 1937 it appeared that President Roosevelt would break new ground. His "Quarantine Speech," delivered at Chicago on October 5, contained phraseology which struck terror into the hearts of isolationists. For the first time the President openly recognized the existence of war and suggested that peace-loving nations quarantine aggressors as they would an epidemic. "The peace-loving nations," he said, "must make a concerted effort in opposition to those violations of treaties . . . which today are creating a state of international anarchy and instability from which there is no escape through mere isolation or neutrality." Editors and politicians took seriously this apparent appeal for sanctions. The *Wall Street Journal* had apoplexy, advising the President: "Stop foreign meddling; America wants peace." Actually Roosevelt had not inaugurated any dramatic shift in the nation's official outlook. In his address he named no specific interests which the nation would defend. Like Hull, he condemned "aggressors," not because they wanted what they did not have, but because they chose to employ force to gain their objectives. At his subsequent press conference, newsmen pointed to the discrepancy between Roosevelt's veiled threat to aggressors and his official adherence to the Neutrality Act. Under pressure, the President admitted that he had devised no concrete plan of action for halting any aggression anywhere. This became doubly clear in November 1937, when the United States avoided every stand at the Brussels Conference, which had been specifically called to formulate a joint response to Japanese expansionism.

Nevertheless, Roosevelt searched for some course of action through which he might exert leadership. In January 1938, belatedly responding to a suggestion of Undersecretary of State Sumner Welles, the President proposed to Hull that the major powers invite representatives of nine minor nations to draw up an agreement which might answer the Axis demands. Hull agreed, but the new British prime minister, Neville Chamberlain, was determined to pursue

Secretary of State Cordell Hull in 1938, announcing that the United States would follow a "middle of the road" foreign policy.

King Features

injustices of the Versailles Treaty he might keep Hitler's and Mussolini's ambition within reasonable bounds. Chamberlain's policy of appeasement might have succeeded had the dictators not seen every Western concession as cowardice rather than a sincere effort to sustain peace.

Symptomatic of the difficulties Roosevelt faced on the domestic front was the reintroduction in 1938 of the Ludlow Resolution. Sponsored by Representative Louis Ludlow of Indiana, this proposed amendment to the Constitution stated that, except in the event of actual invasion of the United States or its territories, the question of war should be submitted to a national referendum. Roosevelt, in a letter to the Speaker of the House on January 6, warned that such a measure would render the President impotent in his conduct of the nation's foreign relations and do a great disservice to American security. Representative Hamilton Fish of New York expressed the isolationist position when he declared that Congress "could do nothing better or greater for world peace than to give the American people the right to vote to stay out of war." White House pressure defeated the Ludlow amendment in the House, but not without a struggle and by only 21 votes, eloquent testimony of the isolationist sentiment in Congress.

his own course in European affairs and rejected the Roosevelt plan. Chamberlain hoped that by recognizing the Axis efforts to terminate the

German Expansionism

Facing no determined opposition in the West, Hitler stripped his Ministry and officer corps of their cautious elements and prepared for his final challenge to the territorial provisions of the Versailles Treaty. Chancellor Kurt von Schuschnigg of Austria, although under German pressure, refused early in 1938 to appoint an Austrian Nazi to a key cabinet post, and called instead for an immediate Austrian plebiscite on the question of union with Germany. Thereupon Hitler forcefully annexed that country, the land of his birth, to Germany. This annexation, the so-called *Anschluss*, he announced on March 12,

1938. France, in the throes of a cabinet crisis, was not prepared to respond. For Chamberlain in London the consolidation of two German populations was not unreasonable. Washington kept studiously quiet.

Hitler immediately planned his next move— the annexation of some 3 million Sudeten Germans assigned to Czechoslovakia by the Versailles Treaty. While Nazi agitators churned the pro-German emotions of the Sudetenland, the Czech government, backed by a good army and strong Czech nationalism, prepared to fight. Chamberlain, unsure of Russian and French support, had no interest in committing British forces to the defense of Czechoslovakia. At Munich, a place-name which was to become synonymous with appeasement, Chamberlain, on September 30, 1938, gave away vital Czech territory, extracting from Hitler in exchange certain unenforceable guarantees for Czech minorities. On October 5, Roosevelt expressed to Chamberlain his "hope and belief that there exists today the greatest opportunity in years for the establishment of a new order based on justice and on law." Instead, Nazi Germany's annexation of the Sudetenland inaugurated a reign of terror which swept into the heart of Czechoslovakia. Long before March 1939, when Hitler's armies added this Slavic nation to the Third Reich, Czech resistance had been totally destroyed. Czechoslovakia thus became the West's first sacrifice to peace.

Throughout the critical year that followed the *Anschluss* of Austria, Hull continued to condemn international lawlessness and reminded the aggressor nations that their leaders, too, had signed the Kellogg Peace Pact. In his message of January 1939, the President pointed to both the continued buildup of German power and the refusal of the dictators to negotiate reasonably with the democracies. Again he hinted at possible sanctions against disturbers of world peace. He admitted freely that the United States had no desire to use force, but he suggested that "there are many methods short of war, but stronger and more effective than mere words, of bringing home to aggressor governments the aggregate sentiments of our own people." Once more the President searched for a means to bridge the gap between American isolationism and the requirements of a policy which could stop aggression. What he wanted, he said, was a revision of the neutrality laws before a possible outbreak of war in Europe would force him to invoke a national embargo to the detriment of the victims of aggression. In mid-April 1939, after the German seizure of Czechoslovakia had sparked another period of rising tensions, Roosevelt appealed to both Hitler and Mussolini to bring their problems to the negotiating table. The Italian government ignored, and Berlin ridiculed, the President's overture.

Congressional isolationists fought bitterly to keep the policy of enforced neutrality in operation. Such Republican leaders as Senators Robert A. Taft of Ohio and Arthur H. Vandenberg of Michigan, joined by former President Hoover and the historian Charles A. Beard, argued for the concept of "fortress America." Taft declared that the United States was in no danger of attack, for Hitler could not dispose of his enemies even in Europe. While the debates raged in Congress, the President, according to some reports, insisted before the Senate Committee on Military Affairs that the frontier of America was on the Rhine. Although he publicly condemned these reports as "a deliberate lie," the damage had been done. When Key Pittman, serving as administration spokesman, introduced a bill to repeal the arms embargo and place all goods, military and nonmilitary, on a cash-and-carry basis, so powerful was the opposition that Pittman could not even bring the measure out of committee. The President declared at a White House conference that the repeal of the arms embargo might actually deter the Axis from a possible attack on the West. Isolationist Senator Borah replied that he had superior sources of information which assured him that Europe was in no danger of war. Congress adjourned on August 5 without taking action.

Perhaps it mattered little. On August 24 Hitler purchased needed Russian neutrality with a nonaggression pact. Unable to rely on the West for defense against Hitler, Stalin had bought time to improve his western defenses. In the bargain he gained German recognition of a Soviet sphere of influence in Latvia, Estonia, Finland, and Eastern Poland. Hitler, having neutralized Russia in the east, was free to venture elsewhere. Late in August he demanded British cooperation in compelling Poland to satisfy German territorial demands by negotiation. When Warsaw rejected a German ultimatum, in September 1, 1939, Hitler sent his *Panzer* divisions swarming into Poland. Thereupon, Britain and France reluctantly declared war on Germany. American neutrality now faced its ultimate test.

The Decline of American Neutrality

On September 3, 1939, President Roosevelt framed his official response to the outbreak of war in Europe. "This nation will remain a neutral nation," he assured the American people, "but I cannot ask that every American remain neutral in thought as well. Even a neutral cannot be asked to close his mind or his conscience." At the same time he promised that, within the limits of his power, there would "be no blackout of peace in the United States." Already the President had placed the nation's isolationist hopes on the altar of its preference for an Allied victory. It was ultimately Roosevelt's refusal to accept a British defeat that placed United States policy on its course of total commitment to the struggle for Europe. What varied after September 1939 were merely the American policies and resources demanded by a final Allied victory.

Initially Roosevelt looked to the country's defenses. He prodded the nations of the Western Hemisphere to call a conference, which met at Panama on September 23, 1939. This conference, in one dramatic move, adopted the Declaration of Panama, which established a 300-mile zone around the hemisphere, excluding Canada and other undisputed possessions of the European countries. This zone was designated off limits to marauding vessels of any non-American belligerent. Time would demonstrate, however, that nations can more easily declare a defense zone than patrol it.

Roosevelt next renewed his assault on the neutrality laws. Appealing to the nation's isolationist sentiment, he assured a special session of Congress in September that a repeal of the embargo would guarantee the peace of the United States better than the existing legislation. Following six weeks of vigorous debate and backstage maneuvering, Congress on November 2 voted for repeal. The Neutrality Act of 1939 authorized export of arms and munitions to the belligerents on a cash-and-carry basis. The restrictions of the 1937 act on loans and travel remained in effect. The new act was nondiscriminatory: in theory all belligerents were permitted to buy arms in the United States provided they paid cash and carried the goods in their own ships. But Britain's control of the sea decreed that Britain and France alone would benefit. Again America would become the arsenal of democracy.

For six months the contradiction between the goal of increased Allied trade and the avoidance of conflict was scarcely apparent, for in the absence of any Nazi thrusts against Western Europe the price of Allied success seemed limited enough. Then early in 1940 Hitler's *Wehrmacht* invaded Denmark and Norway. Denmark's fall made the future of its two possessions, Iceland and Greenland, a matter of deep American concern. In May 1940, the United States opened a consulate on Greenland to better observe developments in the northern Atlantic. That month the British occupied Iceland. During May the German *Blitzkrieg* (lightning war) made possible by superbly trained, highly motivated troops organized in well-supplied armored divisions led by tank spearheads—struck Holland and Belgium. German forces quickly pushed the British forces stationed on the Continent against the coast at Dunkirk, where a miraculous evacuation rescued them. Mussolini chafed to enter the war and reap the rewards of an easy Axis victory. This Washington was powerless to prevent. Perhaps the threat of an American declaration of war might have influenced the Italian *Duce*, but in June 1940, neither Roosevelt nor the American people were prepared for such drastic action.

On June 10, five days after German tanks smashed into France and on the same day Mussolini entered the war, Roosevelt, speaking at the University of Virginia, irrevocably committed the United States to an Allied victory. America was convinced, he said, "that military and moral victory for the gods of force and hate would endanger the institutions of democracy in the Western world." The United States, he declared, would pursue two courses: extend to the "opponents of force" this nation's material resources, and speed up military production so that the United States would be prepared to meet any emergency.

On June 13, the day before German troops entered Paris, causing the French government to transfer to Bordeaux, Premier Paul Reynaud appealed to Roosevelt: "The only chance of saving the French nation, vanguard of democracies, and through her to save England . . . is to throw into the balance, this very day the weight of American power." Winston Churchill, now prime minister of England, urged the President a day later, "A declaration that the United States will if necessary enter the war might save France." Such a declaration Roosevelt could not, or would not, make. He had committed the material resources of the United States to Allied victory; without congressional approval he could not commit manpower. But what Roosevelt could achieve with executive action he would do. In September 1940, he negotiated a destroyer deal whereby the United States transferred to England fifty surplus destroyers in return for bases on British territory in the Americas. By giving Britain the wherewithal to combat German submarines, the United States declared in unmistakable terms its support of England in the war against Germany.

Even so, every new crisis in Europe seemed to widen the chasm in American opinion between isolationism and interventionism. One group of interventionists, led by editor William Allen White of Kansas, formed the Committee to Defend America by Aiding the Allies. By July 1940, this organization had 300 branches, and by the end of the year the Century Group of the New York chapter was advocating the immediate declaration of war on Germany. In Congress the majority support for larger appropriations and the peacetime draft measured Hitler's burgeoning impact on the country's emotions. Leading isolationists exerted their influence through the America First Committee. Beginning in September 1940 as a decidedly conservative movement, the America First Committee advocated the building of an impregnable Western Hemisphere defense system as the most hopeful means of avoiding involvement in the broils of Europe. It soon attracted the support of most pro-German or anti-British elements in the country, including the Ku-Klux Klan and Father Coughlin's Christian Front. Colonel Charles A. Lindbergh, Jr., the noted American aviator, was the committee's leading spokesman. In a series of influential speeches, beginning as early as September 1939, Lindbergh argued that this nation's destiny and interests could be served better at home than in Europe and that the policy of aiding the Allies would lead the United States into war and disaster. Meanwhile Roosevelt pursued his own course, using the power and influence of his office to extend the nation's commitment to Britain, now facing Germany alone.

By nominating Wendell Willkie in 1940, the Republican party foreclosed any effective interparty debate on the question of foreign involvement. Early in the campaign Willkie, chief executive of a large utilities corporation, criticized Roosevelt's pro-British attitudes and actions. "If his promise to keep our boys out of foreign wars is no better than his promise to balance the budget," he warned, "they're already almost on the transports." Yet Willkie no less than the President favored support for England. For his part, Roosevelt insisted that he had no intention of carrying the United States into war. On November 2, for example, he promised a Buffalo audience: "Your President says this country is not going to war." Throughout the campaign of 1940 both candidates remained well within the American consensus; both favored aid to Britain while denying that such a program was a commitment to war. This general agreement on policy permitted the President, despite Republican accusations that he was edging the country toward war, to sustain his personal quest for an ultimate British victory. Roosevelt won by nearly 5 million votes, and the Democrats retained a strong majority in Congress.

From Aid to Full Commitment

On December 8, 1940, Britain's Prime Minister Churchill solemnly informed the newly reelected American President that Britain's heavy purchases of arms and munitions in the United States had exhausted English monetary resources. The doughty Churchill, son of an American mother, expressed confidence that the United States would find the means to sustain Britain's war effort. In lend-lease, Roosevelt discovered a formula which, while relieving Britain's financial difficulties, was still acceptable to

Lend-lease: A huge outpouring of war material from the "arsenal of democracy" to its beleagured allies.

the vast majority of Americans. In his annual message of January 6, 1941, he declared bluntly that the nation's security had never been more seriously threatened. Reminding Congress that the United States was committed to both victory for the democratic cause and security for the United States, he reiterated his claim that increased aid to England, now to be underwritten with American dollars, was the best means for this country to avoid active belligerency. "They do not need manpower," he said of the British. "They do need billions of dollars' worth of the weapons of defense."

For two months Congress debated the President's proposal incorporated in H.R. 1776; at issue was the whole question of the nation's future relation to the European war. Outside Congress the America First Committee condemned the heavy financial commitment embodied in the proposed program, but to no avail. On March 11, 1941, Congress passed the Lend-Lease Act by a substantial margin, stipulating only that Britain take sole responsibility for the transportation of American goods across the Atlantic. The new law gave the President the power to procure articles of defense and "to sell, transfer title to, exchange, lease, lend, or otherwise dispose" of them to any country "whose defense the President deems vital to the defense of the United States." This was lend-lease. By placing control of war production in the hands of the federal government, it converted the nation fully into "the arsenal of democracy."

One problem remained—that of guaranteeing delivery of American production to Britain in the face of the increasing effectiveness of German submarine warfare. During the spring of 1941, the President committed the United States to a final pro-British measure short of actual American belligerency. In April he informed Churchill that the United States would unilaterally extend its Atlantic security zone to the line of 25° west longitude. The United States, the President promised, would now use its aircraft and naval vessels to patrol the Atlantic from bases in Greenland, Newfoundland, the United States, Bermuda, and the West Indies. In his message announcing the new policy to the nation, the President concluded by proclaiming the existence of an "unlimited national emergency."

Roosevelt's undeclared war in the Atlantic brought United States vessels increasingly into direct conflict with German submarines. The U.S.S. *Greer* was fired upon and returned fire in September 1941. In October the destroyer U.S.S. *Kearny* took a torpedo in its side. Later that month the U.S.S. *Reuben James*, while escorting a convoy west of Ireland, was destroyed by a torpedo. An aroused Roosevelt took to the air on October 27 and committed the United States to the total destruction of Nazi power.

The fulfillment of that pledge still required a declaration of war, and Congress was in a resistant mood. Only a major crisis could bring that body to accept total involvement. It remained for events in the Pacific to destroy what remained of isolationism's moral and political influence on national policy.

Crisis in the Pacific

In the four years following the Marco Polo Bridge incident United States–Japanese relations had gone from bad to worse. In December 1937, Tokyo offered apologies and an indemnity for the damages and loss of life incurred when Japanese aircraft sank the American gunboat *Panay* on the Yangtze River in China. Japan, its armies now deep in China, declared the Open Door "inapplicable" to Asian conditions and in 1938 proclaimed a "New Order" in the Far East, which rejected former treaty arrangements outright and asserted Japanese hegemony in Chinese and Asian affairs. Secretary of State Hull reminded Tokyo that it too had signed the treaties which established the existing order in the Far East and was therefore no less obligated than the United States to honor them.

Japanese vulnerability to United States economic coercion gave Washington a powerful diplomatic weapon. Yet economic sanctions were never systematically enforced before 1941. During the summer of 1938 the State Department inaugurated an informal embargo on the shipment of aircraft and parts to Japan. Then in July 1939, tired of unavailing protests and remonstrances, the State Department announced that in six months the United States would terminate its 1911 commercial treaty with Japan, thereby placing Japanese-American trade on a day-to-day basis. As an additional warning to Japan, FDR transferred the Pacific fleet from San Diego to Pearl Harbor. Meanwhile, Japan, turning its attention from its stalemated war in China, moved into the vacuum in Southeast Asia left by German victories in Holland and France. After penetrating French Indochina and Thailand, the Japanese signed the Tripartite Pact with the European Axis in September 1940. With this pact the three signatories—Germany, Italy, and Japan—divided up much of the world on paper.

During the winter of 1940–1941, the United States slowly tightened its economic vise. Aviation gasoline, then scrap iron and steel, iron ore, pig iron, copper, brass—all came under the embargo. Hurt by the gradual squeeze, Tokyo hoped for a settlement with the United States. In his initial conversations with the new Japanese representative, Admiral Kichisaburo Nomura, in April 1941, Secretary Hull repeated his conditions for improved United States–Japanese relations: "Nondisturbance of the status quo in the Pacific except as the status quo may be altered by peaceful means." What Tokyo wanted, it made clear in its response of May 12, was a settlement with China. To achieve this, however, the Japanese needed a promise that the United States would discontinue assistance to the Chinese if they refused to negotiate realistically. For Hull the conditions were inadmissible, for they implied negotiations based on force. Washington refused to grant Japan a free hand in China. Yet, as Ambassador Joseph C. Grew wrote Hull from Tokyo, the only alternative to a compromise settlement in China was general war in the Pacific.

In Tokyo the Japanese government was torn between the moderates, led by Premier Prince Fumimaro Konoye, who favored a settlement with the United States, and the uncompromising pro-German element under Foreign Minister Yosuke Matsuoka. In late June the Matsuoka faction gained ascendancy. On July 2 the cabinet agreed that Japan would pursue a course in Southeast Asia preparatory to establishing its Greater East Asia Co-Prosperity Sphere. Although the extremist Matsuoka was eased out of office in late July, the Imperial Japanese government moved massive forces into southern Indochina. Roosevelt, on July 26, responded by freezing all Japanese assets in the United States. The Dutch and British followed the American lead.

As the freezing order of July gradually developed into a full-fledged embargo ending all Japanese-American trade, the moderate Prince Konoye resumed his search for an agreement with the United States. On August 3 Nomura conveyed to Washington his appeal for a private conference with Roosevelt. Against the advice of Ambassador Grew, who knew the political situation in Tokyo, Secretary Hull demanded that the Japanese agree in advance to deal with China openly and fairly. This destroyed any possibility of a summit conference; Konoye gave way in October to the Japanese military. General Hideki Tojo, the new premier, put in motion a dual policy aimed at an early resolution of the United States–Japanese conflict. First, he pushed forward the Japanese plans for war. Second, he dispatched Saburo Kurusu, an experienced diplomat, to Washington to manage what would be final negotiations. On November 5, an Imperial conference in Tokyo gave Kurusu until November 25 to achieve agreement; thereafter the issue of war would go before the Emperor. From Tokyo, Ambassador Grew warned Washington that time was running out.

When Kurusu arrived to begin his negotiations with Hull, he came armed with two proposals. Proposal A asked Washington to give its approval to a Japanese-dominated Asia; Hull rejected it promptly. On November 20 the Japanese diplomat presented Hull with Proposal B. In exchange for a free hand in settling accounts with China and the resumption of normal United States commercial relations with Japan, Tokyo would withdraw its troops from southern, perhaps from all, Indochina. Acceptance of the Japanese proposal would require a compromise of principle; rejection might spark a war for which the United States was ill prepared. Both Hull and Roosevelt endorsed a counterproposal calling for a truce in the Sino-Japanese War, Japanese troop withdrawals from southern Indochina, and conditional termination of the United States freezing order on trade. Chinese opposition prompted Hull to shelve this plan without presenting it to the Japanese. On November 26, Washington replied formally to Japanese Proposal B. Hull demanded that Japan withdraw its forces from China and Indochina and in the place of the Asian New Order accept the benefits of renewed American trade. Hull understood clearly that Tokyo officials would never accept his proposals. On the morning of November 27, he phoned Secretary of War Henry Stimson: "I have washed my hands of it and it is now in the hands of the Army and the Navy." That same day the Army and the Navy flashed war warnings to American outposts in the Pacific.

On December 6 Tojo informed his representatives in Washington that they would soon receive a message in fourteen parts, terminating diplomatic relations with the United States. The Navy Department in Washington received the first thirteen parts of the intercepted message at noon on that day. By nine o'clock that evening the department had decoded the message and had prepared it for distribution. When Roosevelt read the document at the White House, he reportedly observed, "This means war." The United States would stand on its record, again permitting Japan to make the next move. Even then the President made no mention of the intended attack on Pearl Harbor; nor did he suspect that the Japanese attack would come immediately. Not until 7:30 in the morning of December 7 did Washington officials see the final part of the Japanese message. Herein Tokyo informed the United States government that further negotiations could achieve no useful purpose. Another decoded message, received later that morning, instructed the Japanese dip-

lomats in Washington to present the fourteen-part message at 1 P.M.

Attaching some significance to that hour, Washington dispatched its final warning to Pearl Harbor through Western Union to San Francisco, and from there to Hawaii by RCA radio. The warning arrived at the RCA office at 7:33 A.M., Hawaii time. A messenger was en route to Fort Shafter when the Japanese attack on Pearl Harbor began. Because of their own decoding problems, Nomura and Kurusu did not arrive at the White House until shortly after two. As they entered the waiting room, Hull received an unconfirmed report that the Japanese had struck Pearl Harbor. The Secretary, after leafing through the Japanese message, told the diplomats bitterly that he had never seen a document "more crowded with infamous falsehoods and distortions." Japan's sudden and devastating attack on Pearl Harbor drew from the American people at last what Roosevelt had been unable to achieve—a total commitment to war.

Conclusion

Pearl Harbor shattered the isolationist defense against American involvement in Europe's war so completely that it soon raised suspicions among Roosevelt's critics that the President and his administration had plotted the Pacific disaster. These charges, which proliferated with the passage of time, flowed from the dual assumption that Washington had received warnings of the Japanese attack and that, to make the disaster profound, had purposely delayed the December 7 message to Hawaii so that the garrisons there could not establish an adequate defense. It had been clear that the Japanese task force was moving after late November toward some target, but correspondents throughout the Pacific anticipated the assault in the region of Southeast Asia. There is no conclusive evidence, therefore, that Washington expected the attack at Pearl Harbor before it actually occurred. The Pearl Harbor tragedy was merely a logical projection of the

general failure of policy in the thirties. For too long the country and its leaders had refused to come to grips with the challenge of the dictators, either by means of diplomacy or by war. Washington officials had assumed falsely that they need not take the Japanese problem seriously. It was the suddenness, and especially the unexpectedness, of the Pearl Harbor attack that created the traumatic response of the American people.

Neither Tokyo nor Washington could escape responsibility for the collapse of peace in Asia. Japan had embarked on aggressive war against China and should not have expected the United States, with its long tradition of paternalism toward China, to accept readily the notion of an imposed treaty. Still the American response scarcely served the cause of peace. It was never made clear what Washington expected of its economic sanctions against Japan. The final message of December 7 did not render Japan blameless for its abuse of China, but it did explain why those who, like Secretary Hull, chose to interfere in the conflicts of other nations under the principle of peaceful change must expect to pay a price. "The American Government," it said, "advocates in the name of world peace those principles favorable to it and urges upon the Japanese Government the acceptance thereof. The peace of the world may be brought about only by discovering a mutually acceptable formula through recognition of the reality of the situation and mutual appreciation of one another's position." Traditionally, international politics had rested on the rights of the stronger; by the new morality of the interwar years, it rested on the rights of possession. In their refusal to accept the conditions imposed on them by the Versailles settlement, the aggressors of the thirties simply rejected the Western notion that possession gave special rights. The result was tension and finally war.

SUGGESTED READINGS

Two excellent volumes on the Kellogg-Briand Pact are D. H. Miller's *The Peace Pact of Paris* (1928), and especially Robert H. Ferrell's *Peace in Their Time: The Origins of the Kellogg-Briand Pact* (1952). L. Ethan Ellis's *Frank B. Kellogg and American Foreign Relations, 1925–1929* (1961) is a general study of the Kellogg years. On the crisis of 1931–1932 in Manchuria see S. R. Smith's *Manchurian Crisis, 1931–1932* (1948). H. L. Stimson has described his role in *The Far Eastern Crisis: Recollections and Observations* (1936), as well as in Stimson and McGeorge Bundy's *On Active Service in Peace and War* (1947). Richard N. Current has contributed *Secretary Stimson: A Study in Statecraft* (1954) and "The Stimson Doctrine and the Hoover Doctrine," *American Historical Review*, LIX (April 1954). Another excellent study is Armin Rappaport's *Henry L. Stimson and Japan, 1931–1933* (1963).

Two excellent surveys of American foreign policy between Manchuria and Pearl Harbor are Robert A. Divine's *The Reluctant Belligerent: American Entry into World War II** (1965) and John E. Wiltz's *From Isolation to War, 1931–1941** (1968). Also of great value for the thirties are Selig Adler's two volumes *The Isolationist Impulse** (1957) and *The Uncertain Giant** (1965). For Roosevelt's policy toward Latin America see E. O. Guerrant's *Roosevelt's Good Neighbor Policy* (1950) and Bryce Wood's *The Making of the Good Neighbor Policy** (1961). United States relations with Russia are given adequate treatment in William A. Williams's *American-Russian Relations, 1781–1947* (1952); R. P. Browder's *The Origins of Soviet-American Diplomacy** (1954); and Edward M. Bennett's *Recognition of Russia** (1970).

Two excellent studies of American isolationism are Donald Drummond's *The Passing of American Neutrality, 1937–1941* (1955) and R. A. Divine's *The Illusion of Neutrality** (1962). On liberal isolationism see Wayne S. Cole's *Senator Gerald P. Nye and American Foreign Relations* (1962). Cole's *America First: The Battle against Intervention, 1940–1941* (1953) is an able study of the America First Committee. Two excellent volumes on the late thirties are W. L. Langer and S. E. Gleason's *The Challenge to Isolation, 1937–1940* (1952) and *The Undeclared War, 1940–1941* (1953).

The evolution of United States policy toward Japan can be traced in Dorothy Borg's *The United States and the Far Eastern Crisis of 1933–1938* (1964); Herbert Feis's *The Road to Pearl Harbor: The Coming of the War between the United States and Japan** (1950); and Paul W. Schroeder's *The Axis Alliance and Japanese-American Relations, 1941* (1958). Highly critical of Roosevelt are C. C. Tansill's *Back Door to War: The Roosevelt Foreign Policy, 1933–1941* (1952) and C. A. Beard's *President Roosevelt and the Coming of the War* (1948). On Japanese policy in the thirties see S. E. Morison's *The Rising Sun in the Pacific* (1948); R. J. C. Butow's *Tojo and the Coming of the War* (1961); and F. C. Jones's *Japan's New Order in East Asia* (1954). Roberta Wohlstetter's *Pearl Harbor: Warning and Decision** (1962) is a superb study of the Pearl Harbor crisis. See also *Roosevelt and Pearl Harbor* (1970) by Leonard Baker.

*indicates availability in paperback.

30

Victory over the Axis

As early as April 1939, five months before the outbreak of war in Europe, the Joint Planning Committee of the United States Armed Forces had agreed that the United States, if involved in a two-front war, would fight a defensive action in the Pacific and concentrate its efforts on the destruction of the German *Wehrmacht*. The Combined Staff Conference of British and American officers, held in Washington during February and March 1941, reaffirmed this basic strategy. Then in June the Nazi invasion of Russia brought that continental power into the war. Roosevelt no less than Churchill recognized the Soviet Union as an ally and directed immediate aid to that beleaguered country. When the United States entered the war in December,

military planning could proceed with the assurance of ultimate Allied success.

Still the imperatives behind a Europe-first strategy remained valid enough. Germany was the strongest of the Axis countries, deeply entrenched in Europe. In time its industrial and scientific genius would multiply its destructive force, possibly, some feared, to the point of invincibility. Britain and the U.S.S.R. were reeling under the offensive thrusts of Nazi power on the ground and in the air. Without the total effort of these two nations, the United States could not hope to break the German resistance. It was essential, therefore, that American reinforcements appear in Europe as quickly as possible to bolster the efforts and the morale of those fighting Germany.

Prime Minister Winston Churchill crossed the Atlantic on December 22, 1941, and opened informal discussions with President Roosevelt to establish their joint leadership in the conduct of the war. From this Arcadia Conference came the Declaration of the United Nations, signed on January 1, 1942, in which all enemies of the Axis powers agreed to fight the war to a satisfactory conclusion. The Arcadia Conference established the Combined Chiefs of Staff, composed of British and American military officers, and instituted an ever-increasing flow of lend-lease aid to the European theater of war.

Western leaders, under pressure from Moscow, accepted the need for a second front. Beyond that their disagreements were profound. British officials made clear as early as August 1941 their preferences for a tight naval blockade of the Continent, the bombing of German cities and industries, the encouragement of opposition to Hitler in Nazi-occupied countries, limited strikes along the periphery of German power, and finally a massive assault against Germany itself. With these proposals the American Joint Chiefs of Staff were in general agreement. But the issues on which they differed were fundamental and centered on peripheral attacks, especially those which could delay the massive invasion of Western Europe.

Britain had been at war for two years. Its army, if small, was prepared for action. The British navy still controlled the seas. Unable to contest German power on the Continent, England had either to engage the Germans with light raids in the Mediterranean or remain inactive. The United States, on the other hand, was not immediately prepared to engage the Germans on any front. General George C. Marshall, Chief of Staff of the Army, argued for a rapid buildup of Allied equipment and manpower in England for a cross-channel attack to relieve the Russians. In March 1942, Roosevelt sent Marshall and Harry Hopkins, his personal emissary, to London to press the matter of a second front

to be launched late in 1942. The British agreed readily to a second front for 1943, but only the threatened fall of Russia, they declared, would justify such a decision in 1942.

Still the two Western Allies, whatever the state of their readiness, could not postpone until 1943 their active participation in the war. Again in July, Roosevelt sent Marshall, Hopkins, and Ernest J. King, Chief of Naval Operations, to raise the question of the second front with Churchill. The Prime Minister, opposed to an early cross-channel attack, countered with Operation Torch, an invasion of North Africa to check the German drive into the eastern Mediterranean. Churchill, supported by Roosevelt, had his way; British and American leaders prepared for the North African invasion with landings scheduled for November 1942. The Roosevelt-Churchill decision to postpone the second front in Europe produced anger and dismay in Moscow.

Ultimately Torch proved to be a brilliant success. The Germans, misled by their extensive triumphs of 1941 and 1942 in North Africa and determined to gain control of Suez, gradually overextended their lines of communication and supply. In May 1942, Erwin Rommel's *Afrika Korps*, composed of both German and Italian troops, launched an offensive, took Tobruk, and drove the British forces back to El Alamein, 70 miles west of Alexandria. There the two armies remained poised for four months while their commanders considered matters of supply and strategy. Rommel was an outstanding officer— intelligent, popular, and candid. Facing him was General Bernard Law Montgomery—capable, overbearing, and resourceful. Supported by new shipments of heavy equipment, Montgomery's troops broke through the German lines, and by early November had put Rommel's forces to flight across North Africa. By the time that the Germans reached Mersa Matruh, they had lost 60,000 men and 500 tanks. That month the British recaptured Tobruk and Benghazi.

Rommel now faced trouble from another direction—Operation Torch. On November 8, 1942, British and American forces under General Dwight D. Eisenhower conducted the first major amphibious landings in the Mediterranean with three major beachheads at Casablanca in Morocco and at Oran and Algiers in Algeria. For Hitler, Torch proved to be an irretrievable disaster. By mid-November Allied troops entered Tunisia. Tripoli fell to the British in January 1943. In May the British occupied Tunis; the Americans entered Bizerte. The German forces, now without Rommel, who had fled, retreated into the Cape Bon peninsula. Here the Germans on May 13 surrendered everything they had in North Africa—250,000 troops, plus stores and equipment. Torch reopened the way to Suez and the Middle East.

During the months of 1942 and 1943 Hitler's armies met even greater disaster on the Russian front. The German summer offensive of 1942 had brought startling successes at Sevastopol, Voronezh, and Rostov. By September, Nazi forces had moved through the Crimea into the Caucasus toward the Baku oil fields. During August they reached Stalingrad and entered the city in September. Hitler wanted Stalingrad desperately, but the Russians were equally determined to hold it. The *Wehrmacht* had been stopped at Leningrad and Moscow, but it was still powerful, enjoying superiority in everything but numbers. The battle for Stalingrad, one of the largest and most terrible battles of all time, raged through October and November 1942. Thousands died every day. Russian General Georgi Zhukov described the battle well: "I would not have believed such an inferno would open up on this earth. Men died, but they did not retreat."

During November Hitler admitted the German failure, but he refused to pull his troops away from the Volga. Zhukov launched a powerful counterattack, closing the ring around twenty German divisions, already suffering a terrible Russian winter without access to supplies. In January 1943, what was left of the German forces surrendered. This wasteful battle of Stalingrad demanded much of Germans and Russians alike. The U.S.S.R. lost more men in that one battle than the United States lost in the entire war; but Germany lost more—its dominance of the European Continent.

The Mediterranean Campaign

During January 1943, Roosevelt and Churchill met at Casablanca to plan the next stage in their war against Hitler. Again British and American officials quarreled over questions of priority. The United States Chiefs of Staff still preferred the concentration of Allied equipment, landing craft, and manpower in England in preparation for a cross-channel invasion in 1943. But the logic of the military situation favored Sir Alan Brooke's strategy of attacking the Axis forces in the Mediterranean. American leaders at Casablanca agreed to the invasion of Sicily, in July, to be followed in September by a thrust at Italy itself. Thus the ultimate Allied strategy against Germany was a compromise between those who wanted to attack hard at the edge of Axis power, principally Southern Europe, and those who favored a 1943 cross-channel invasion of France. Churchill agreed to Overlord, the name assigned to the cross-channel invasion, while General Eisenhower promised support for the invasion of Italy. At the Teheran Conference of November 1943, Stalin, long bitter over the West's failure to establish a major second front, endorsed Overlord enthusiastically, promising at the same time a strong Russian offensive to coincide with the cross-channel attack. Roosevelt now decided to keep Marshall in the United States and placed Eisenhower in charge of Overlord.

In the great debate over strategy, American

officials thought primarily, if not exclusively, of a military victory with the least possible loss of American life. Their concern was the rapid and efficient destruction of German power. Churchill's objectives were both political and military. He believed it essential that the Western Allies occupy as much of the Balkans and Slavic Europe as possible ahead of the advancing Soviet troops. As late as 1944 he still favored a major invasion of the Balkans. Churchill rationalized this strategy in terms of military victory, but he hoped ultimately to prevent the establishment of Russian power in the heart of Europe.

Measured by subsequent Allied victories, the military compromises appeared sound enough, producing a steady collapse of German positions. Even at that, progress through Italy from the Salerno beachhead proved to be difficult. The invasion of the peninsula soon drove Italy out of the war, but the flood of German soldiers sent to fill the vacuum turned Italy into a major battleground. The hoarding of American power in England deprived Allied commanders in Italy of some available strength and forced them to engage in prolonged heavy fighting, always against strategic odds. The slowness of the Italian campaign measured the frustration of those who placed their faith in operations in the Mediterranean.

Planning for Germany

Russia's success in stabilizing the Eastern Front, added to the anticipated Western triumphs in the Mediterranean, raised the central issue of Germany's future. What concerned Roosevelt as early as 1943 was the need to reassure the Kremlin that the Western Allies, though still unable to open a second front, were determined to fight on to total victory over Germany. To that end the President read the following statement at a press conference at Casablanca on January 24: "Peace can come to the world only by the total elimination of German and Japanese war power. The elimination of German, Japanese and Italian war power means the *unconditional surrender* by Germany, Italy, and Japan."

Thus was born the controversial concept of unconditional surrender. What effect did it have on the course of the war? Churchill denied that it prolonged the war or played into Hitler's hands by undermining the idea of revolt or conspiracy within Germany. Nothing short of military victory, ran his argument, would have compelled the Germans to stop the war. Critics of this decision charged that the policy helped to unify Germany and induced the Axis countries to fight with increased determination.

Discussions at Casablanca raised, but did not settle, the question of postwar Germany. At their meeting in Moscow during October 1943, however, the Foreign Ministers of the United States, Britain, and Russia created a European Advisory Commission to draft a German surrender document and an agreement for the Allied military government of Germany. At Teheran in November 1943, Roosevelt and Churchill granted Stalin a Soviet zone in central Germany extending westward to within 100 miles of the Rhine. This preliminary agreement placed Berlin well within the Soviet zone, but the city itself remained a separate entity to be occupied jointly.

Another question posed by Germany was more fundamental. What disposal were the Allies to make of Germany's power to wage war? Secretary of the Treasury Henry Morgenthau, Jr., favored stripping Germany of its major industries and reducing it to an agricultural nation. But War Department officials, who were busily planning the postwar occupation and control of Germany, challenged Morgenthau's views. These men anticipated the rapid postwar reconstruction of the German economy. Hull and Secretary of War Henry L. Stimson believed both that a strong and productive Germany was essential for the economic health of Europe and that a punitive policy was incompatible with the American liberal tradition. Directive 1067, issued by the Joint Chiefs of Staff in October 1944, embodied the principles toward postwar Germany which were to guide American military leaders. It accepted the zones of occupation defined by the European Advisory Commission and declared that Germany was to be occupied "as a defeated enemy nation." Nazism and militarism would be destroyed and Germany required to pay reparations and make restitution to countries devastated by Nazi aggression.

Victory in Europe

Only a scientific miracle could have saved Germany after 1943. On both the Mediterranean and Eastern fronts the German positions were collapsing with continuing regularity. As early as January 1944, the Western Allies established a beachhead at Nettuno-Anzio, 30 miles south of Rome. During the spring they completed their assault on Cassino, a key position in the German defense of central Italy. On June 1, the United States Fifth Army liberated Rome.

Meanwhile, by late 1942 and 1943, strategic air bombing of German targets from bases in Britain had become terribly effective. New radar sighting devices made feasible huge night raids over German cities. The British, relying on incendiary bombs, launched massive air attacks which destroyed large parts of major German cities. On May 30, 1942, the first 1,000-bomber run over Cologne killed more than 10,000 civilians and established the pattern of subsequent British night raids. During July 1942, the first units of the United States Eighth Air Force under General Ira C. Eaker arrived in England to join the air assault against Germany. The assigned mission of the Eighth Air Force was to strike at key German industries, such as aircraft and electrical power plants, transportation centers, submarine bases, and petroleum and synthetic rubber industries, through daylight high-altitude precision bombing.

General Eisenhower arrived in England during January 1944, to assume supreme command of the Allied Expeditionary Forces. Thereafter the preparations for the cross-channel invasion proceeded rapidly. On June 6 the Allied forces concentrated in southern England struck the mainland on a 60-mile front along the Normandy coast. This assault was the largest amphibious operation in history. In the initial landing were 176,000 troops, carried by 4,000 landing craft and supported by 600 warships and 11,000 aircraft. General Montgomery commanded the ground forces in the invasion; General Omar Bradley led the American land contingents. German units, rushed into the area, were no match for Allied power.

During the summer of 1944 Allied forces began the final assault against the German continental defenses. In Operation Dragoon, on August 15, British and American forces—including the United States Seventh Army under General Alexander M. Patch—landed in southern France between Marseilles and Nice. This invasion gave the Allies control of the large port of Marseilles and brought additional troops into France for the final push into Germany. Now numbering 2 million, the rapidly advancing Allies on the Western Front closed in on the retreating Germans, liberating Paris on August 25 and Brussels, Antwerp, and Luxembourg in September. United States forces entered Germany near Eupen and Trier. One Allied setback was the famous Battle of the Bulge which in December 1944 cost 77,000 American casualties. Also in 1944 the Germans retaliated against Britain with jet-propelled, pilotless V-1 aircraft. The V-1 offensive reached its climax in July and August. In September the first supersonic V-2 German rockets reached London. German rockets were no more destructive than bombers.

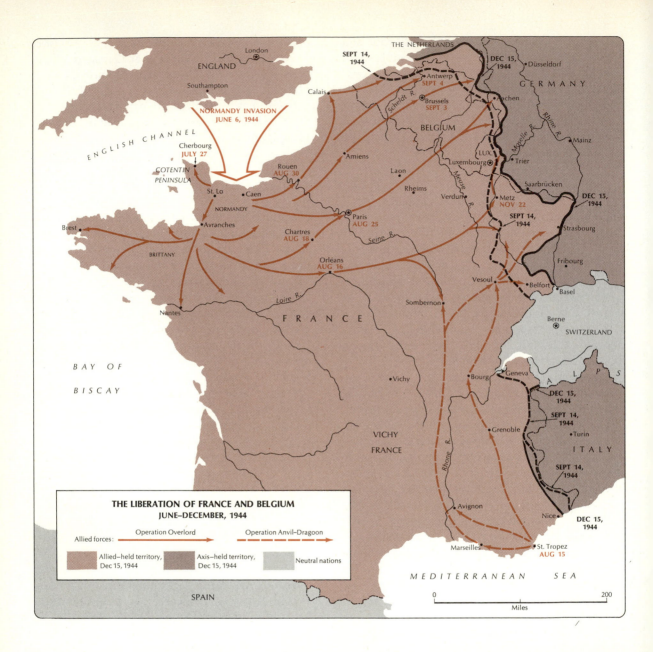

THE LIBERATION OF FRANCE AND BELGIUM
JUNE–DECEMBER, 1944

Allied forces:
Operation Overlord →
Operation Anvil–Dragoon →

Allied–held territory, Dec 15, 1944
Axis–held territory, Dec 15, 1944
Neutral nations

Unable to prevent the launching of such weapons, the British and American bomber forces, now almost free of *Luftwaffe* opposition, resumed their bombing of German cities and industrial targets.

At the Malta Conference of January 1945, Allied leaders assumed that Germany would attempt to send armies eastward to support its crumbling forces on the Russian front. To hamper this movement, the Allies agreed to bomb such major east German transportation centers as Berlin, Leipzig, and Dresden. On February 3 nearly a thousand B-17s bombed Berlin, killing or injuring 25,000 civilians. Such bombing, however, did not play the major role in the German defeat. What crippled Germany's power were the Allied victories on the battlefronts. The destruction of German cities did not seriously curtail, much less destroy, German productivity. Even a city as thoroughly damaged as Hamburg recovered 80 percent of its production in three months. Key German industries were dispersed widely and generally defended with strong aircraft and antiaircraft installations. Many basic German industries, such as that of machine tools, were never seriously damaged. Nevertheless, the bombing of German cities greatly injured German morale; by late 1944 most Germans regarded the war as lost, but those who had been subjected to heavy bombing were the first to acknowledge that conviction.

After January 1945, the collapse of the Ger-man positions came with conspicuous regularity. During February, British forces moved rapidly through Holland toward the German border; to the south United States troops, on March 7, entered both Düsseldorf and Cologne. Meanwhile the Russians had crossed East Prussia, had seized both Belgrade and Budapest late in 1944, had taken Warsaw, and in January had reached the Oder River. Early in April 1945, they launched their attack on Berlin and entered the city on April 24 to begin their deliberate reduction of the German capital. On May 1 the provisional German government under Admiral Karl Doenitz announced Hitler's death. The next day Berlin fell; and on May 7, Field Marshal Alfred Jodl signed the instrument of unconditional surrender at Reims. May 8—VE Day—signaled the end of the struggle for Europe.

The War in the Pacific

By the summer of 1942 the task of deflating the Japanese empire seemed almost insuperable. In the six months following the destruction of the United States fleet at Pearl Harbor, Japan's land and naval forces, with superb planning and modern techniques, subjugated a vast area of the Pacific. The Japanese had captured the American outposts of Guam and the Philippines; the British island of Hong Kong; the entire Malay Peninsula with its base of Singapore, the great British bastion guarding the entrance to the Indian Ocean; British Burma with its tributary islands in the Indian Ocean; the whole East Indian Archipelago belonging to the Dutch; Attu and Kiska islands near the western extremity of the Aleutians.

But Japan had failed to penetrate India and the Indian Ocean and to break the line which barred its passage to Australia and New Zealand. On the Chinese mainland, moreover, Japan still faced the resistance of Chiang Kai-shek's Chinese armies. Japan, like Germany, had moved into a power vacuum and had overextended its military commitments. Japan, like Germany, failed to strike at the genuine sources of United States power within the United States itself, thus permitting this nation to rebuild its power in the Pacific for the slow and deliberate destruction of Japan's far-flung bases. As early as May and June 1942, in two remarkable naval engagements—the battles of the Coral Sea and of Midway—United States naval forces stalled the Japanese offensive in the South Pacific.

Oceans are formidable barriers only to those who do not control them. For a nation possessing naval superiority they become the highroad of invasion. The American counteroffensive against Japan in the Pacific began at Guadalcanal in the Solomon Islands in August 1942. Subsequently, the combined sea, air, and land forces of the United States hopped from island to island northwestward toward the Philippines. In June 1943, General Douglas MacArthur launched an assault on the highly strategic Japanese positions in the Bismarck Archipelago. Admiral William F. Halsey, under MacArthur's command, took Munda airfield in the central Solomons and in November established an airfield at Empress

Augusta Bay, Bougainville, from which the United States could strike Rabaul, 234 miles distant. MacArthur's forces swept around New Guinea and proceeded by a series of envelopments to attack where the Japanese were weakest and bypass strong Japanese positions in difficult terrain. By February 1944, United States forces had broken the Bismarck's Barrier by bypassing Rabaul. MacArthur's troops pushed on into the Admiralties, where they established a huge base at Manus. Next, in a leapfrogging advance of 400 miles, they captured Hollandia on the coast of Netherlands New Guinea, with its excellent airfields. In little over twelve months American forces, with Australian units, had pushed 1,300 miles closer to the heart of the Japanese empire.

Admiral Chester Nimitz launched his movement across the central Pacific in November 1943, with a successful amphibious infantry attack on Makin Island in the Gilberts. That month marines landed and destroyed the Japanese garrison on Tarawa in one of the bloodiest battles of the Pacific war. Bypassing several Japanese bases, the Navy swung its power into the Marshalls, where infantry captured the Kwajalein Atoll in another fierce battle, giving the United States a huge anchorage. During February 1944, American forces converted the Eniwetok Atoll into another powerful base in the Marshalls. These successes permitted the Navy to give Truk in the eastern Carolines the blast-and-bypass treatment and continue on into the Marianas. There the United States fleet faced a Japanese squadron, which had steamed from the Philippines to cut off the American advance. In the first Battle of the Philippine Sea, on June 20, 1944, the American forces drove the Japanese back into the shelter of the Philippines. Meanwhile United States forces had reoccupied Guam. Before the end of November 1944, United States aircraft began the bombing of Japan from bases in the Marianas.

On October 19, two massive assault forces, carrying General Walter Krueger's Sixth Army, appeared off the coast of Leyte in the Philip-

pines. The armada stretched across the vast Pacific horizon. Out at sea, Admiral William Halsey's carrier task force awaited a possible Japanese naval attack. Japan's Singapore fleet, which made up the bulk of Japan's remaining naval strength, moved against the American fleet. Between October 23 and 25 the greatest sea battle of all time was fought for Leyte Gulf. American landing forces required a month of fighting to gain control of Leyte. Samar, a large neighboring island, offered little resistance. The long-awaited invasion of Luzon began on January 9, 1945, and in February the advance units of the Sixth entered Manila. By the late spring of 1945, Japanese strength on the mainland of China was also collapsing.

During February 1945, the United States Navy and Marine Corps captured Iwo Jima in the Bonin Islands. Then on April 1, under cover of an intense naval bombardment, Army and Marine units established a beachhead on the west coast of Okinawa in the Ryukyus. United States fighters from Iwo Jima swept the air over Japan, while B-29 Superfortress heavy bombers based in the Marianas averaged 1,200 sorties a week. The Third Fleet sailed into Japanese waters and hammered the coastal cities, unopposed. Meanwhile in the Philippines, MacArthur's command prepared two invasions of Japan.

These invasions never occurred, for three events of August 1945 brought the war to an immediate end. At Yalta in February 1945, Stalin promised again, in exchange for the return to Russia of all Japanese territory taken from that nation in 1905, to terminate his country's official neutrality in the Pacific and declare war on Japan three months after victory in Europe. On August 6 the United States, with British concurrence, dropped an atomic bomb on Hiroshima, completely leveling most of the city and creating havoc among the population with fire and radioactivity. Two days later Russia declared war on Japan and occupied Manchuria. On August 9, the Strategic Air Command loosed a second, more powerful atomic bomb on Nagasaki. The next day the Japanese government, having suf-

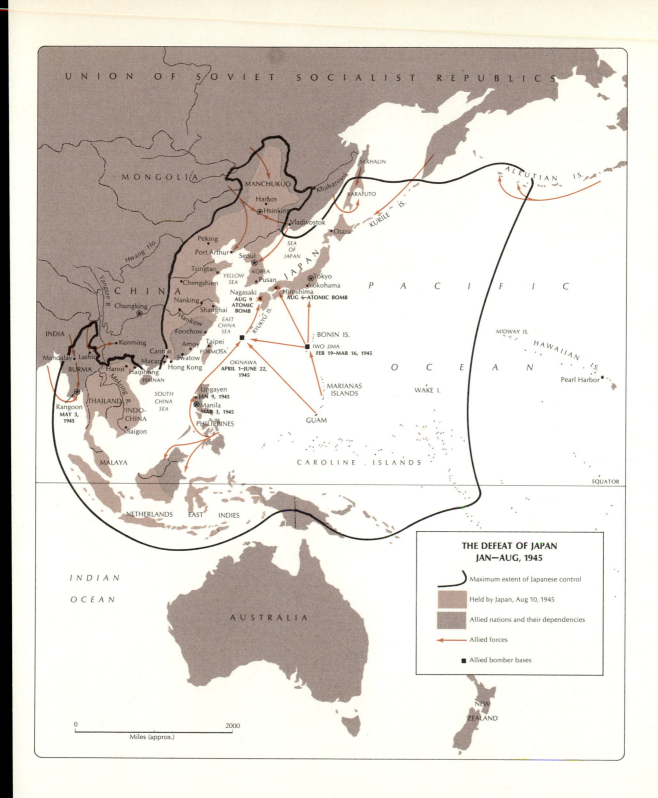

UNION OF SOVIET SOCIALIST REPUBLICS

MONGOLIA

MANCHUKUO

Harbin

Hsinking

Khabarovsk

SAKHALIN

Vladivostok

KARAFUTO

Peking

Otaru

KURILE IS.

Port Arthur

SEA
OF
JAPAN

Seoul

KOREA

Tsingtao

YELLOW
SEA

Pusan

Tokyo

Yokohama

Chengshien

CHINA

Hiroshima

AUG 6–ATOMIC BOMB

Hwang Ho

Nanking

Nagasaki

AUG 9

ATOMIC

BOMB

PACIFIC

Chungking

Shanghai

Yangtze R.

Hankow

EAST
CHINA
SEA

Foochow

RYUKYU IS.

MIDWAY IS.

HAWAIIAN IS.

INDIA

Kunming

Amoy

Taipei

BONIN IS.

OCEAN

Mandalay

Lashio

Canton

FORMOSA

IWO JIMA

FEB 19–MAR 16, 1945

Pearl Harbor

BURMA

Macao

Swatow

OKINAWA

APRIL 1–JUNE 22,

1945

Hanoi

Haiphong

Hong Kong

WAKE I.

Mekong R.

HAINAN

THAILAND

SOUTH
CHINA
SEA

Lingayen

JAN 9, 1945

MARIANAS
ISLANDS

Rangoon

MAY 3,
1945

INDO-
CHINA

Manila

MAR 3, 1945

GUAM

Saigon

PHILIPPINES

MALAYA

CAROLINE ISLANDS

EQUATOR

NETHERLANDS EAST INDIES

INDIAN

OCEAN

**THE DEFEAT OF JAPAN
JAN–AUG, 1945**

Maximum extent of Japanese control

Held by Japan, Aug 10, 1945

Allied nations and their dependencies

Allied forces

Allied bomber bases

AUSTRALIA

NEW

ZEALAND

0   2000

Miles (approx.)

VICTORY OVER THE AXIS

[761]

fered unanticipated and unbearable disaster, surrendered.

Writers have criticized the decisions both to invite Russia into the war against Japan and to drop the two atomic bombs, for these eleventh-hour applications of force appeared unnecessary to bring the war to an immediate conclusion. The employment of atomic bombs gave the United States the dubious distinction of being the first nation in history to loose such weapons on civilian populations. Some

American scientists recommended that the first bomb merely be exploded in the presence of Japanese observers to demonstrate the destructive power thereafter available to the United States. President Truman decided otherwise, convinced that the new weapon would end the war quickly and thus save lives. Japan was already defeated, but whether the Emperor would have ended Japanese resistance short of the atomic explosions was then, and remains still, a matter of doubt.

Victory on the Home Front

Allied success in World War II required astonishing triumphs on the home front as well as on the battlefront. Not only did the United States supply its own troops and civilian population, but it provided billions of dollars' worth of commodities, including military equipment, to Russia, England, and other Allies. The evolution of the United States into democracy's arsenal was at times slow, halting, and inefficient, but ultimately the organization of the country's human and physical resources for war was nothing less than phenomenal. Hitler's threat to American security seemed so clear that few questioned the war's costs.

The battle of production and distribution demanded strong government controls over industry, transportation, agriculture, and manpower. Never before in American history had the federal government assumed so much control of the nation's economy or so much direction of its scientific and technological development.

In the summer of 1940 there were fewer than a half million men in the American Army, Navy, and Marine Corps. But on September 16 Congress passed the Selective Training and Service Act, the first peacetime draft law in American history. All young men between the ages of twenty-one and thirty-six were to register; those who qualified were to serve one year. After Pearl Harbor Congress changed the age limits to include all men between eighteen and forty-five,

and lengthened the time of service. However, late in 1942 the upper age limit for active service was reduced to thirty-eight. Local selective service boards administered the law, and before the end of the war had drafted more than 10 million men. During 1945 the total number in the Armed Forces reached 12,123,455.

Still, modern war had become as much a struggle between factories as between battalions. Late in May 1940, shortly before France fell, the President appointed a Council of National Defense patterned on the World War I experience. Soon afterward he named a National Defense Advisory Committee to assist the Council in directing and organizing various phases of the economy. Already United States and British demands had created problems of allocation and priority. Bernard Baruch, head of the War Industries Board during World War I, favored more centralized economic mobilization. Roosevelt, however, continued to rely on committees and agencies which did not have the power to organize the country's defense needs.

In January 1941, less than a year before Pearl Harbor, the President created the Office of Production Management and appointed William Knudsen of General Motors to head it. The job of the OPM was to fix priorities for scarce goods, stimulate defense output, and coordinate the government's purchasing program.

With American entry into the war Roosevelt

established the central government control over the economy which many people had long regarded as necessary. In January 1942, he created the War Production Board and named Donald Nelson of Sears, Roebuck to head the new agency. WPB's purpose was to "determine the policies . . . of the several Federal departments, establishments, and agencies in respect to war procurement and production." President Roosevelt had already outlined the productive task ahead when he called for 60,000 planes and 45,000 tanks in 1942; 125,000 planes and 75,000 tanks the year following.

Congress established other agencies to deal with the economic problems of war. The Office of Defense Transportation bore the responsibility for making the most efficient use of the country's transportation; the War Shipping Administration organized and supervised the shipping industry; the Combined Production and Resources Board integrated American efforts with those of England.

Besides setting production goals, the government loaned money to companies to build and expand their plants. In some cases the government built factories and leased them to private operators; sometimes it both constructed and operated the plants. In producing synthetic rubber the federal government developed a whole new wartime industry. It built rubber plants at Baton Rouge, Houston, and Los Angeles; by 1944 the country's synthetic rubber output had reached 700,000 tons a year.

By the end of 1942 the United States economy had been converted to war. What occurred in the automobile industry was characteristic of the general shift to military production. The number of passenger cars produced in 1941 was 3,779,682, but this figure dropped to 222,862 in 1942 and to only 610 in 1944. Instead of producing automobiles, the powerful auto industry manufactured tanks, jeeps, aircraft, machine guns, and other heavy military equipment.

Guided by the Maritime Commission, the shipbuilding industry performed productive feats thought to be impossible in the prewar period. In 1941 it required seven months to complete a moderate-size merchant vessel, but by 1944 Henry J. Kaiser and other shipbuilders were constructing the famous Liberty ship in as little as two weeks. Many people considered Kaiser a miracle man as his shipyards at Portland, Oregon, and Richmond, California, sent hundreds of vessels down the ways in record time. By 1944 American yards launched almost fifty merchant ships a day. Aircraft production was perhaps even more amazing. In March 1944 alone, United States factories built 9,117 military airplanes.

Actually the United States reached the peak of its war production in 1943, when war consumed about 35 percent of the gross national product. During the war period United States factories produced about 300,000 aircraft, 87,000 tanks, 70,000 landing craft, 5,600 oceangoing merchant ships, vast quantities of arms and ammunition, and other needed supplies and equipment—all of which proved overwhelming in battle.

More money and effort went to science and technology during World War II than ever before, and scientific triumphs contributed markedly to American and Allied military success. Among the prominent innovations based on science were radar, sonar to detect underwater objects, the proximity fuse, bombsights, improved explosives, and the atomic bomb.

To organize and administer scientific work relating to defense and war, President Roosevelt, in June 1940, established the National Defense Research Committee. That year British and American scientists began to exchange data on explosives, radar, and detection devices. In 1941 the President placed the country's wartime scientific efforts in the hands of a new agency, the Office of Scientific Research and Development, headed by Vannevar Bush, president of the Carnegie Institution. The OSRD recruited many leading physicists, chemists, and engineers, and arranged for the assistance of hundreds of outstanding scientists in universities and private industry.

Ultimately the most important new weapon developed during World War II was the atom bomb. Basic data on nuclear fission had been accumulating since the 1890s, especially after 1929, when E. O. Lawrence built the first cyclotron. As war approached in 1941, American scientists turned their attention to the development of atomic power. In 1942 Roosevelt established the Manhattan Project, headed by General Leslie R. Groves, to develop the atomic bomb. In two years the government spent $2 billion to build the new weapon. On July 16, 1945, authorities tested the first atomic bomb on an isolated spot some 120 miles southeast of Albuquerque, New Mexico, to inaugurate a new age in history.

Manpower needs rose dramatically after America's entry into the war. The War Manpower Commission, created in April 1942, had the responsibility for securing enough workers to fill defense jobs. There were still 5.5 million unemployed in 1941; these provided a reservoir for the expanding war industries. Migration from the farm to urban communities added to the industrial labor force. Moreover, younger and older people took jobs, and millions of women went to work in defense plants. To assure uninterrupted production, President Roosevelt called a conference of labor and industry to develop means of settling labor disputes. Labor and management agreed on a no-strike, no-lockout policy. On January 12, 1942, the President established the National War Labor Board with members from labor, business, and the public. These agencies held some employees in key positions by threatening them with military service. In April 1943, the War Manpower Commission froze workers in certain important jobs.

American farm production during World War II was little short of phenomenal. Despite the tremendous demands for food by Allied armed forces, United States civilians enjoyed more abundance than in prewar years. Oversupply had plagued farmers in the 1930s; after 1941 the United States was fortunate to have substantial surpluses of farm products on hand. Thereafter

the nation had merely to shift from a policy of restricted output to one of full production. Total output rose about 23 percent between the 1935–1939 period and 1945, although cultivated acreage increased only 5 percent. Thus the gain came largely from better farming practices and a series of favorable crop years. Organized in 1943, the War Food Administration, headed by Chester C. Davis, encouraged production and regulated the distribution of food.

Despite price controls, agricultural prices rose to 113 percent of parity by 1944; with increased production, farmers experienced unprecedented prosperity. Total net farm income jumped from $6.6 billion to $12.4 billion between 1941 and 1945. Tenancy declined to the lowest level since 1910. Farmers reduced their debts and generally improved their financial position and standard of living.

Beginning in 1941, the huge wartime demand for goods unleashed strong inflationary pressures on the economy. In August the President created the Office of Price Administration. But not until October 1942 did Congress pass the Stabilization Act, which gave the President authority to control wages, salaries, and prices. Roosevelt established the Office of Economic Stabilization to coordinate the wage and price stabilization effort. He named James F. Byrnes of South Carolina, then on the Supreme Court, to head this office.

Still inflation continued. In April 1943, President Roosevelt issued his famous "hold-the-line" order. He instructed the Office of Price Administration "to place ceiling prices on all commodities affecting the cost of living . . . to authorize no further increases in ceiling prices except to the minimum extent required by law." The OPA now had both the power and the will to enforce price controls rigorously. The fact that consumer prices rose only 4.2 percent between April 1943 and August 1945, a period of twenty-eight months, indicated the success of this policy. At the same time the War Labor Board enforced rigid wage and salary controls.

To supplement the price control program, the

government inaugurated a system of rationing. Besides restraining prices, rationing provided a more even distribution of scarce commodities. Starting with tires in January 1942, OPA soon added gasoline, sugar, meat, and other products in short supply to the list. Some 5,600 local boards administered the program through a system of certificates and coupons. Before the war ended, however, black market operations existed in many communities; that is, rationed commodities entered the market illegally and at higher-than-ceiling prices. But overall, most Americans accepted the imposition of price controls and rationing as a necessary wartime sacrifice.

Americans found that modern, mechanized warfare required tremendous sums of money. The United States not only financed its own military machine but also spent billions on lend-lease. Between 1940, when defense costs began to increase, and the end of the war in 1945, federal expenditures rose from about $9 billion to nearly $100 billion annually. Taxes provided some 44 percent of the wartime receipts. The remainder came from borrowing—a considerably better record than that which the government achieved in World War I. Congress passed higher income taxes in 1942 and 1944. The 1944 measure raised the maximum tax rates to 94 percent, the highest in the nation's history. One new and lasting development in tax policy was the resort to payroll deductions. This eased the payment of tax obligations and assured the government a steady income.

Since taxes provided less than half the needed revenue, the government borrowed heavily from individuals and corporations. In 1941 the national debt stood at about $48 billion, more than double what it had been at the beginning of the New Deal. During the following four years it jumped to $258 billion.

Nationalism and Civil Rights

Most Americans supported the war wholeheartedly from Pearl Harbor until the Japanese surrender in August 1945. That opposition which had troubled Woodrow Wilson did not exist after 1941, largely because the Pearl Harbor attack seemed to substantiate the rightness of the American cause. The Office of War Information, headed by the witty and perceptive Elmer Davis, stimulated nationalism and support for the war. The OWI used radio programs, newspapers, and pamphlets to publicize the government's point of view. Songs like "God Bless America" and "Praise the Lord and Pass the Ammunition" aroused patriotic emotions.

The Office of Censorship placed some restrictions on wartime expression. News correspondents, moreover, often withheld information voluntarily, although they did not usually hide defeats and mistakes from their readers. Hansen Baldwin, military writer for the *New York Times*, wrote critical articles dealing with military inefficiency and civilian blunders; and Ernie Pyle revealed the horrors of war in his intensely human accounts from the front.

Civil liberties did not escape some restrictions. The Smith Alien Registration Act of 1940 gave the federal government power to curb those who tried to interfere with the "loyalty, morale, or discipline" of the military forces or who advised disloyalty or overthrow of the government by force or violence. This was the first peacetime sedition law since 1798. There were several convictions under this legislation during the war, including that of the American Nazi William Dudley Pelley. The Postmaster General restricted circulation of Father Coughlin's *Social Justice* and a Communist paper, the *Militant*, by withdrawing mailing privileges.

Japanese residing in the western part of the United States suffered the worst civil rights violations. In February 1942, President Roosevelt ordered restrictions against certain people in prescribed military areas of California, western Arizona, Oregon, and Washington. Persons of Japanese ancestry, regardless of whether or not they were American citizens, were subjected to curfew and later excluded from those areas. The War Relocation Authority established ten inland detention centers for Japanese resettlement.

This action was a gross infringement of the civil rights of people who had been convicted of no crime. Still in *Hirabayashi v. United States* the Supreme Court upheld the executive order which required Japanese in the prescribed areas to remain in their homes between 8 P.M. and 6 A.M. "as a protection against espionage and against sabotage."

Blacks in Wartime

Blacks had made some gains in education, employment, and social position during the New Deal years, but progress against discrimination had been spotty and slow. There were, for example, very few blacks in any branch of the Armed Forces in 1940. The Selective Service Act of September 1940 forbade racial discrimination in the drafting and training of soldiers, but many local draft boards ignored this order and accepted only whites. Black leaders complained about discrimination and segregation in the Armed Forces, but again concessions and reform came slowly. Blacks even found it difficult to obtain jobs in the expanding defense industries.

As black frustrations grew early in 1941, A. Philip Randolph, president of the Brotherhood of Sleeping Car Porters, urged Negroes to march on Washington and demand equal rights. Alarmed at this possibility, Roosevelt issued an order on June 25, shortly before the projected march, declaring that "there shall be no discrimination in the employment of workers in defense industries or Government because of race, creed, color or national origin." The President appointed a Fair Employment Practices Committee to deal with the problem. These measures met bitter resentment in the South. One Southern writer warned that "all armies of the world . . . could not force upon the South the abandonment of racial segregation."

About 1 million blacks served in the American Armed Forces during World War II—some 700,000 in the Army, and thousands more in the Navy, Air Force, and Marines. Hundreds

received commissions. It was not until 1945 that blacks, as individuals, entered white units and fought side by side with whites against Hitler's legions in Germany. At most military camps and in the surrounding communities, black servicemen faced discrimination in theaters, post exchanges, and even in officers' clubs. In July, 1944, a War Department order banned racial segregation in transportation and recreation facilities at army posts, but it was never enforced. Not even the high military honors which many blacks won could overcome the continuing discrimination.

Pressure from the FEPC and other government agencies gradually opened up new employment opportunities for blacks in defense industries. Thousands entered aircraft, shipbuilding, steel, and rubber plants. Defense-related employment drew an increasing number from the rural South into Northern and Western cities. The black population of Los Angeles doubled between 1940 and 1945; thousands went to Detroit, Chicago, and other cities. Tension over discrimination opened the way for several race riots. The most serious conflict occurred in Detroit in June 1943, when a fistfight set off rumors and rioting which ended only after twenty-five blacks and nine whites had been killed. It took 6,000 troops to restore order. Although blacks made some notable social and economic gains, by 1945 an increasing number expressed open resentment at fighting for a society which professed democratic principles but refused to grant them first-class citizenship.

America became fully involved in World War II on December 7, 1941, when Japan staged its disastrous air attack on Pearl Harbor causing damage so extensive that details were kept secret for a year. The core of the American fleet in the Pacific was destroyed, and over two thousand sailors, soldiers, and civilians were killed.

Congress declared war against Japan on the next day, and Germany and Italy did the same against the United States three days later. On December 9 President Roosevelt delivered a message of hope for the postwar world: "We are now in the midst of a war, not for conquest, not for vengeance, but for a world in which this nation, and all that this nation represents, will be safe for our children. . . . We are going to win the war and we are going to win the peace that follows."

Navy Department, The National Archives

World War II

After Pearl Harbor official policy placed 112,000 Japanese-Americans, or Nisei, living in California, Arizona, Oregon, and Washington under a curfew from 8 PM until 6 AM. Subsequently shipped to ten detention centers, they lived as prisoners behind barbed wire for most of the war. About two-thirds of these people were American-born citizens, and some of the Japanese-American mothers had sons in the United States Army. The pictures on these pages come from an exhibition of Dorothea Lange's photographs prepared by Richard Conradt and presented at the Oakland Museum.

Far left and below: War Relocation Authority, The National Archives; near left and both right: Dorothea Lange, War Relocation Authority, The National Archives

-STOP-
AREA LIMITS
FOR PERSONS OF
JAPANESE ANCESTRY
RESIDING IN THIS
RELOCATION CENTER
SENTRY
ON DUTY

A special photographic unit headed by Captain Edward Steichen created an extensive visual document of the Navy's role in the war. Here air crewmen aboard the *U.S.S. Saratoga* prepare for a strike against Rabaul in November, 1942; left, center, one of the men wounded in the strike is helped from his plane; left, bottom, a view of the battle for Saipan in June, 1944.

Wayne Miller for Navy Dept., The National Archives

Wayne Miller for Navy Dept., The National Archives

No documentation of World War II caught its human meaning—the terror and suffering—more powerfully than the photographs taken by W. Eugene Smith in the Pacific. A selection of Smith's work from his book, *Photographer*, appears here. Below, men wait at a medical-aid station on the Iwo Jima beachhead in February, 1945; above, a Marine demolition team detonates a charge to blast Japanese troops out of an Iwo Jima cave; right, above, a flamethrower in action on Okinawa.

mericans became aware of the horror of the
ar through photographs such as those at
eft of concentration camps where officers of
he Third Reich murdered an estimated six
hillion Jews in a deliberate program of
enocide.

The United States dropped an atomic
omb 28 inches in diameter and 120 inches
ong, with an explosive power of 20,000 tons
f TNT, on the city of Hiroshima on August
, 1945. Exploding 2,000 feet above the city,
obliterated an area of more than 4 square
hiles and killed an estimated 80,000 people
nd injured at least as many more. Three
ays later another atomic bomb fell on
agasaki. On August 14 Japan surrendered.
elow is a view of Hiroshima after the bomb
ad been dropped; at far right, a victim of
adiation burns.

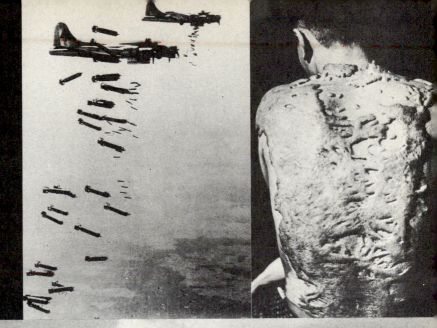

Officially ending World War II, Japanese representatives signed the surrender document on September 2, 1945, aboard the battleship *Missouri*.

Despite the need for national unity, partisan politics continued with little change. People retained their faith in the ordinary democratic processes; they held elections as usual; and conflicts between Congress and the President existed much as in peacetime. About all that united Democrats and Republicans was the desire for military victory.

The drive for domestic reform had slackened long before the United States entered the war; thereafter the concentration on wartime issues provided added occasions to attack the philosophy and programs of the New Deal. Roosevelt himself declared that "Dr. New Deal" had been replaced by "Dr. Win-the-War." In the midterm elections of November 1942, the Republicans made substantial gains by attacking the New Deal. When Congress met in January 1943, the Democrats had their narrowest margin in years: 218 seats compared with 208 for the Republicans. Even in the Senate increased numbers of Republicans, added to conservative Democrats, gave Congress a decidedly conservative outlook.

By 1944 the Republicans had a number of hopeful candidates, including Wendell Willkie, who had run well in 1940, and Harold Stassen, former governor of Minnesota. By convention time, however, Governor Thomas E. Dewey of New York had emerged as the party's leading prospect. Dewey had made a national reputation as a crime fighter when he served as New York City's district attorney. After nominating Dewey on the first ballot, the delegates named Governor John W. Bricker of Ohio, a strong conservative, to run with the moderately progressive Dewey.

Many Democrats who had objected to Roosevelt's third term were even more opposed to a fourth-term nomination. Former Vice President John Nance Garner wrote in 1943, "I think it would be a terrible thing to have Roosevelt elected again." But no one could successfully challenge the President, and too many Democrats feared that only Roosevelt could carry the party to victory in 1944. Roosevelt received the nomination on the first ballot. After considerable skirmishing over the vice-presidential choice, the delegates chose Senator Harry S. Truman of Missouri. Truman had emerged as a national figure through his investigations of national defense problems. Still the Missourian had other assets: he came from a border state; powerful Democrats considered him conservative; and, as one observer said, he was "an approximation of everybody."

Dewey campaigned against "the tired old men" of the Roosevelt administration and accused the Democrats of lethargy and inefficiency. He emphasized the country's need of new leadership and more effective administration. Speculation about the President's health

The strain of the depression years, the years of World War II, and age itself all took their toll on Franklin Roosevelt—as this photograph, taken during the election campaign of 1944, so clearly shows.

(United Press International)

forced Roosevelt to abandon his plans not to engage in a personal campaign. He made several major speeches, generally speaking from a seated position. Organized labor, especially the Political Action Committee of the CIO, established in 1943, campaigned vigorously for the President. Liberals in general still supported him. The result was a landslide victory for Roosevelt in the electoral college—432 to 99—although his popular margin was scarcely 2.5 million votes. Republicans gained a higher percentage of the votes than at any time since 1928, but organized labor, minority groups including blacks and Jews, federal employees, and intellectuals made up a coalition which was still loyal to Roosevelt and the Democratic party.

Roosevelt's health, which had been a subject of comment during the campaign, grew steadily worse after the election. By January 1945, he looked ill. His face was drawn, he appeared thin and tired, his hands trembled, and his voice sometimes faltered. Despite his worsening condition, he continued to perform his heavy duties and even made a trip to Yalta in February. Then on April 12 he died suddenly of a cerebral hemorrhage at his Warm Springs, Georgia, home. A shocked and sorrowful nation could scarcely believe that the man who had led it through depression and war was gone.

Life on the Home Front

Little in American society remained untouched by war. Family ties loosened as millions of men left their homes for military duty and women moved from the household to the factory. The housing shortage became critical in many areas, especially near military installations. Gasoline rationing sharply reduced travel in private automobiles. As one observer remarked, "You could have fired a bazooka down any Main Street in the country without hitting a vehicle." Colleges and universities were deeply affected. Faculty members joined the armed services; student enrollments dropped sharply as only women and young or physically disqualified men remained. The government used college and university facilities for some training programs. But in 1944 the nation's institutions of higher learning granted only 141,582 degrees, as compared with 216,521 in 1940. Higher education suffered because of the war, but religion flourished. Churches were filled with worshipers, and between 1940 and 1946 membership in all religious bodies rose by some 6 million. Moreover, religion became more personal and emotional as wives and parents prayed for their loved ones abroad.

Another important influence on American life was the enlarged role of the federal government. The powers and responsibilities of government had been increasing for many years, but neither the regulatory actions of the progressive era nor the New Deal legislation matched the extent to which the national government affected the lives of people during World War II. The draft; wage, rent, and price controls; and rationing touched every citizen. Taxing and spending policies of the federal government influenced the economy far beyond anything previously known. Wartime budgets outstripped WPA's meager resources. Eventually most wartime restrictions disappeared, but the increased role of government in the nation's economic and social life continued. The war accentuated the trend toward "big government."

Americans emerged from World War II more prosperous than at any time in their history. The gross national product, in dollars of constant purchasing power, increased from $230 billion in 1940 to $360 billion in 1945, a rise of 56 percent. Per capita income climbed 30 percent. Businessmen regained some of the reputation they had lost during the Depression. Although people complained of scarcities and hardships, morale on the home front was excellent throughout the war.

For a time in 1945 it seemed to Americans that the nation's wartime effort had laid the foundation for a new era of international cooperation. Three wartime allies—Britain, Russia, and the United States—had rendered Germany powerless. American diplomacy had sustained the great coalition and, through careful wartime planning, had apparently created the basis for continuing world peace. As long as Allied diplomacy produced mutually profitable agreements on military strategy, American officials could encourage the assumption that Big Three relations were sound. But with Nazi Germany's demise in 1945 it became clear that the world held little more assurance of tranquillity than it had in 1939.

On August 14, 1941, President Roosevelt and Prime Minister Churchill, meeting in the North Atlantic, officially proclaimed their joint political objectives in the famed Atlantic Charter. The Charter declared that the United States and Great Britain sought "no aggrandizement, territorial or other," and that they desired "to see no territorial changes that [did] not accord with the freely expressed wishes of the people concerned." In a London broadcast ten days later, Churchill praised the Atlantic Charter as an Anglo-American declaration of unity and purpose. Yet the Charter, so thoroughly attuned to American and British aspirations, ignored completely the already-expressed purposes of the third major wartime partner, the Soviet Union. The United States and Britain entered the war as powers seeking nothing in victory but the reestablishment of the older Versailles order. The Soviets, however, were neither creators nor beneficiaries of that order. Reeling under the Nazi assault, the Russians made it increasingly clear after 1941 that they would insist upon a strong Soviet voice in Eastern Europe. Russian leaders, moreover, would take the necessity for Germany's utter defeat far more seriously than would Britain or the United States, for Germany had invaded Russia twice in one long generation. Stalin was unprepared to settle for a postwar world based solely on the principle of self-determination.

Soviet ambivalence toward the question of postwar reconstruction became manifest early in the war. Once Hitler turned on them, the Russians were in no position to antagonize their Western Allies. Eventually they signed the Atlantic Charter. Even then Stalin made clear his determination to maintain control of all the areas granted to Russia by the Nazi-Soviet Pact of August 1939. For Roosevelt and Hull, Soviet territorial demands created a cruel dilemma. The Atlantic Charter ruled out any compromise with the Soviets on postwar spheres of influence. Yet without the full military effort of the U.S.S.R., the United States and Great Britain would have been hard pressed to defeat the Axis at all. Hull discovered an answer to this quandary in the critical decision to postpone until the end of the war all territorial decisions potentially in defiance of the Charter. When on December 4, 1941, three days before Pearl Harbor, the British Foreign Office informed Washington that the Soviet Union was suspicious of Western intentions and that Foreign Secretary Anthony Eden would shortly visit Moscow to allay Soviet doubts, Hull warned the British against any secret arrangements regarding the future of Eastern Europe. United States postwar policies, he wrote, "have been delineated in the Atlantic Charter which today represents the attitude not only of the United States but also of Great Britain and of the Soviet Union."

The Charter did not, of course, express the attitude of the Soviet Union. Thus the decision to postpone territorial settlements simply kept hidden from public view the ultimately inescapable elements of future discord among the Big Three. Any rhetoric which promised publicly a postwar triumph for the principles of self-determination in vast and important areas where American and British power would have little influence could lead only to eventual embarrassment and disillusionment for all concerned. Yet at no time in the course of the victorious campaigns against the Axis powers did the Roosevelt leadership attempt to escape this self-imposed dilemma. The policy of postponing all essential political decisions in the interest of wartime unity might have been realistic and possibly successful had Roosevelt and Hull prepared themselves and the nation for some hard bargaining with the Soviets at the termination of hostilities. But to the end of the war they based all United States postwar policy toward liberated Europe on the principles of the Atlantic Charter without either pondering the means required to compel the Kremlin to accept such principles or preparing the people of the United States and Europe for their predictable failure.

Divided Europe

At the Yalta Conference of February 1945, Roosevelt could scarcely hide the impending clash between Western and Soviet purpose in Eastern Europe. In January, the State Department had intimated to the President that the time when the West could influence the politics of Eastern Europe was gone. London, Paris, and Washington had lost that prerogative when they failed to protect Czechoslovakia and Poland from German and Soviet power in 1939.

Already events in liberated Poland had put the wartime alliance to a stern test. Early in January 1945, Moscow announced the Soviet Union's recognition of the Russian-controlled Lublin Committee as the provisional government of Poland. At Yalta, Roosevelt and Churchill refused to accept the Lublin Committee as representative of the Polish people. Stalin, facing still-powerful Nazi resistance on the Eastern Front and desiring for the moment to avoid a break with the West, accepted both the Declaration on Poland and the Declaration on Liberated Europe, which provided for free elections on the basis of universal suffrage and the secret ballot in the Slavic states. Russia received the eastern portion of Poland's prewar territory; Warsaw was to accept the old Curzon Line for its eastern border and be compensated in the west at the expense of a defeated Germany. Again the wartime policy of postponement had dominated the actions of the Big Three.

Confronted both with Western reluctance to negotiate a general agreement on boundary questions, as well as with continued political resistance within the Slavic states themselves, Stalin in 1945 proceeded unilaterally to turn Eastern Europe into a Soviet sphere of influence. In February he dispatched Soviet diplomat Andrei Vishinski to Bucharest to force King Michael to appoint the Soviet puppet Petra Groza as head of the new Communist-dominated government in Romania. Early in March, Foreign Minister V. M. Molotov demanded that the Lublin regime form the core of the provisional government of Poland promised at Yalta. The pattern of Kremlin policy was thus established. Using military, political, and ideological leverage, Stalin established a series of Communist-led governments in regions occupied by the Red troops. In this way Stalin fulfilled his wartime objective of preventing the reestablishment of unfriendly states along Russia's western frontier.

This pattern of Soviet behavior, whatever its logic and necessity from the Russian viewpoint, became deeply disturbing—indeed unacceptable—to Washington officialdom. The Ambassador to Moscow, Averell Harriman, reminded the new president, Harry S. Truman, burdened by Roosevelt's death in April 1945 with full responsibility for United States foreign policy, that Soviet domination of Eastern Europe was intolerable. He urged the President to adopt a strong stand toward the Kremlin and make it clear that the United States expected the U.S.S.R. to live up to the Yalta agreements. The power to force compliance, believed Harriman, lay in the American economy; the Soviets would yield "because they needed our help in their reconstruction program.'' Washington officials generally favored a hard line. When Foreign Minister Molotov called at the White House on April 23, Truman warned him that no longer would United States–Soviet agreements be a ''one-way street.'' Shortly thereafter the President, without warning, terminated lend-lease aid to Russia. The action disturbed the Soviets, but not enough to alter their established purposes for Slavic Europe. Even as the war in Europe drew to an end, the Soviets gave the United States three clear choices: agreement in defiance of principle, continued postponement of all political settlements, or war. Washington pushed postponement into the postwar era, preferring not to recognize diplomatically any political and territorial arrangements which defied self-determination.

Later, revisionist historians of the 1960s criticized the Truman leadership both for its unwillingness to recognize Soviet security interests in Eastern Europe and for its assumption that a hard-line policy, whether anchored to economic or atomic power, would compel a satisfactory adjustment in Soviet behavior. They charged not only that the hard line failed to achieve its objectives but, even worse, that it revealed an American aggressiveness toward the U.S.S.R. which eventually broke up the Big Three alliance.

By the late spring of 1945 the differences between United States and Soviet purpose in Eastern Europe were moving rapidly beyond the point of reconciliation. At this critical juncture, President Truman dispatched Harry Hopkins to confer with Stalin on the matter of Poland's future. In Moscow, Hopkins warned the Russian leader that Kremlin policy toward liberated Europe and especially Poland was fast destroying the sympathy of the American people for the Soviet Union. Stalin was unmoved, reminding Hopkins of the vital importance of Poland to Russia's security. Ambassador Harriman commented, ''I am afraid that Stalin does not and never will fully understand our interest in a free Poland as a matter of principle. The Russian Premier is a realist in all of his actions, and it is

hard for him to appreciate our faith in abstract principle. It is difficult for him to understand why we should want to interfere with Soviet policy in a country like Poland which he considers so important to Russia's security unless we have some ulterior motive.''

From April until June 1945, continuing Big Three disagreements over postwar reconstruction focused on the question of German occupation, including the future of Berlin. Churchill argued that the occupation zones agreed upon at Yalta need not influence military operations and that Berlin, Prague, and Vienna could be occupied by whatever power reached them first. It seemed essential to Churchill that Western forces reach Berlin ahead of the Russians. If Soviet troops took Berlin, he wrote to Roosevelt, it might make Stalin even more arrogant and intractable. Churchill did not have his way. General Eisenhower, Supreme Commander of the Western forces in Europe, operated under a general directive that called for military action against the German army. Eisenhower believed it more important to capture the Nazi forces opposing him than to compete with the Russians for the capture of Berlin. And the Allies did not come to a general understanding with Russia, as Churchill thought they should, before retiring to the agreed-upon zones of occupation. Truman, backed by advisers who argued that Churchill was too concerned with Britain's continental interests, decided to pull American forces back without a previous settlement with the Kremlin.

In June 1945, the President announced the satisfactory settlement of the Polish question, concluding with a benediction to Soviet-American friendship. The question of Western access to Berlin, an international island in the Soviet German Zone, remained open. Though Stalin insisted that Western access to Berlin through Soviet-controlled territory was a privilege, not a right, the Soviets granted limited access both by road and by air. Thereafter the Western allies—bereft of political and military leverage in the Soviet zone—had no choice but to trust in the cooperative spirit of the Kremlin.

During the war Roosevelt and Hull had given leadership and expression to the growing conviction that any postwar order which guaranteed peace and self-determination would require an international organization that included both the United States and the U.S.S.R. At the Moscow Conference of October 1943 Hull extracted from the Soviets an agreement regarding membership in such a world body; thereupon Roosevelt committed the United States to the creation of the United Nations. By the summer of 1944 State Department planning demanded a further exchange among representatives of the Big Three. When conversations opened at Dumbarton Oaks in Washington, on August 21, 1944, the Soviet delegate submitted two distracting requests: first, that each of the Soviet Republics receive individual membership in the new body, and, second, that the permanent members of the projected UN Security Council possess the power of absolute veto. At Yalta, in February 1945, Roosevelt agreed that three UN seats should go to the Soviet Union (the Congress could claim a like number for the United States if it desired) and that each of the permanent members of the Security Council—the United States, Soviet Russia, Great Britain, France, and China—should have a veto over all matters except those in which they were themselves a party.

On April 25, 1945, President Truman welcomed delegates of fifty nations gathered at San Francisco to formally establish the United Nations. At that moment the one major unresolved issue was the veto, for now the Soviets insisted that the veto power be extended to include even the *discussion* of a dispute. The British and American delegations demurred, and the Latin Americans, viewing this as a means whereby one of the major powers could silence a smaller nation, threatened to bolt the conference. For eleven days the debate raged while the Russian delegation stood fast. Finally, upon receipt of

specific instructions from Stalin, the Russians relented. It was thus decided that, although any permanent member could block action by the Council with a veto, there would be no veto of discussion. Among other issues, the conference accepted the trusteeship system of administering dependent territories, placing it under the supervision of the Security Council. At the demand of the Latin American and Arab nations, Secretary of State Edward Stettinius introduced a proposal, endorsed overwhelmingly by the small nations and accepted by the U.S.S.R., which provided that a country could invoke regional alliances to defend itself when the Security Council failed to act.

As established at San Francisco, the United Nations was to be similar to the defunct League of Nations in its overall organization. This organization included a General Assembly for all members, a Security Council in which the major powers would always have membership, and a Secretary-General to handle administrative matters. China joined Britain, France, Russia, and the United States as a permanent member of the Security Council simply because Roosevelt insisted on assigning China big power status. The Security Council, by design, wielded controlling influence until Soviet vetoes rendered it ineffective. The UN Charter provided for numerous committees and councils to deal internationally with various political, economic, and social problems: the United Nations Economic and Social Council, the Trusteeship Council, the International Monetary Fund, and the International Court of Justice.

Truman concluded the two-month-old conference on June 26, 1945, with a note of optimism and warning: "It has already been said by many that this is only the first step to a lasting peace. That is true. The important thing is that all our thinking and all our actions be based on the realization that it is only a first step. Let us all have it firmly in mind that we start today from a good beginning and, with an eye always on the final objective, let us march forward.'' The United States Senate ratified the Charter by the overwhelming vote of 89 to 2. The nation's mood was scarcely isolationist.

Potsdam to London

During May 1945, Churchill had pressed Truman for the earliest possible negotiation with Stalin of a general European settlement. The settlement, he had declared, should come before the Allies lost their bargaining power through the withdrawal of their forces from their advanced positions. Russia's attitude toward the Yalta agreements, Churchill saw, forecast trouble along the entire spectrum of postwar issues. The common interest in victory, which had sustained the wartime alliance, had evaporated with Germany's defeat. Obligated now to transfer the gains of war to a new order of peace and stability, the wartime Allies faced a range of political questions on which they had never agreed, but which nevertheless demanded settlement if the wartime alliance was to continue.

When Truman, Churchill, and Stalin met at Potsdam in mid-July 1945, the Western leaders had either to accept the new Soviet presence in East-Central Europe as the basis of negotiation, to push the Soviets back by force or negotiation, or again to postpone the key issues in dispute. Unfortunately, any postponement would expose all the fundamental disagreements between the East and West and automatically subject the world to a new era of tension. On the concrete issues of Germany and Eastern Europe, Stalin employed every possible device to maintain a maximum degree of Soviet prestige, power, and maneuverability. When he failed to win concessions, he pushed for postponement. The Big Three at Potsdam agreed eventually that Germany should be demilitarized, denazified, and democratized. For reparations each occupying power was authorized to remove property from its own zone and to seize German assets abroad. The conference implemented the Yalta declaration by agreeing that only those states of Eastern Europe with ''recognized democratic governments'' would be permitted to sign the peace treaties or apply for membership to the United Nations. But what was the meaning of democracy? Secretary of State James F. Byrnes insisted on the American interpretation. ''The will of the majority of the people,'' he said, ''can be determined only if all the people are able to vote free from force and intimidation.'' Such a definition the Russians would not accept. Still the Soviet control of Eastern Europe was far from absolute.

At the London Conference of September 1945, Allied foreign ministers again acknowledged their commitment to the peacetime reconstruction of Europe. But the schism in the Grand Alliance was now profound. The victors no longer shared fundamental purposes in Germany. For months that country had been in Allied hands, and if the occupying powers could

Stalin, Truman, and Churchill at Potsdam, July 1945.   (Brown Brothers)

not agree on the treatment of the defeated enemy, they could agree on nothing fundamental. The great divergence between East and West in their attitudes toward German industry measured the rift in the wartime alliance. Lord Nathan, British Undersecretary of War, observed before the House of Lords, "We must be careful to safeguard against a breakdown of German industry." Russia, by contrast, proceeded under the Potsdam Agreement to drain Germany's eastern zone of its factories and resources and even to demand additional German assets located in the western zones. Slowly the Kremlin organized its zone into another satellite. When Secretary of State Byrnes proposed in September 1946 that the zones of Germany be reunited both politically and economically, Moscow made it clear that the unification of Germany would be accomplished on Soviet terms or not at all.

Although the Soviets, and sometimes France, questioned the wisdom of British and American moderation toward Germany, they readily joined those two nations in bringing German Nazis to the bar of justice. The trials, conducted at Nuremberg, Germany, sought to establish a body of international law under which leaders designated as war criminals might be punished for the aggressive actions of their nations. There was some condemnation of the decision to prosecute leaders of the defeated enemy, partly because the body of law governing the trial did not exist at the time the alleged crimes were committed. Nevertheless, the trials went forward, and in October 1946 an international tribunal condemned twelve prominent Nazis to death. Thereafter the trials of lesser Nazi officials continued quietly, free from the glare of publicity, for some years.

Soviet and American purposes continued to clash as violently over the future of Eastern Europe as they did over Germany. Again the basic conflict raised the issues of Russian security and Western principle. Byrnes assured Molotov at the London Conference that the United States desired pro-Soviet governments along Russia's western borders; the Soviets, because of their magnificent war effort, deserved nothing less. Byrnes insisted only that they be free. Molotov responded that any government of Slavic Europe that was free would not be pro-Soviet; therefore these governments would not be free. The dilemma was as insoluble in diplomacy as it was simple in concept. United States–Soviet negotiations over the future of Eastern Europe had reached the dead end.

Conclusion

Five years earlier the United States had demonstrated its limited concern for Slavic Europe when it permitted Hitler to uproot the entire Versailles order in that region without any threat of reprisal. Yet in 1945, even while it recognized the legitimacy of the Soviet security interest in East-Central Europe, Washington avoided the recognition of any Soviet sphere of influence. It preferred to quarrel over issues totally under Russian control, even to the disruption of the wartime alliance, rather than desert the principle of self-determination. For this unprecedented interest in the welfare of the Slavic peoples the reasons were clear enough. The wartime experience itself had reawakened not only an American interest in world affairs but also a widespread commitment to the liberal-democratic principles of Woodrow Wilson now embodied in the Atlantic Charter. If the Roosevelt and Truman administrations admitted privately the virtual elimination of Western influence from Eastern Europe, the actual record of Soviet repression, reported in detail by American diplomats throughout the autumn of 1945, rendered the recognition of the Soviet hegemony increasingly difficult. Soviet behavior, moreover, challenged deep American preferences for an open world to which Americans, as well as citizens of all nations, would have access. Whatever the commercial and investment opportunities existing in Slavic Europe, some Americans insisted on the right to share them with the U.S.S.R. Soviet ideology merely encouraged the growing distrust of Kremlin policy among United States officials.

Finally, the Democratic administrations faced domestic political pressures which reduced their freedom of action. Many Eastern European minorities, especially Polish Americans, threatened political retribution against those who refused to support European self-determination. Much of the Catholic and conservative Republican press took up their cause. By autumn 1945, congressional Republicans demanded of Truman what Roosevelt had promised and failed to achieve: a world of justice built on the Atlantic Charter. On

December 5, 1945, a committee of House and Senate Republicans issued a policy statement chiding the administration's Eastern European policy for its desertion of principle. Unfortunately, such pressures amounted to declarations of hope, not plans for action. Republican criticism, which provided for no more than a change in rhetorical style, created an illusion that the nation had choices which really did not exist. The new "get tough" attitude gave nothing away; nor did it assure any settlement on American terms. Unable to drive the Soviets back to their 1939 boundaries, yet unwilling to accept the Soviet sphere of influence, American officials could only retreat to a new, more promising, and more determined phraseology.

SUGGESTED READINGS

For the role of the United States in World War II see A. R. Buchanan's excellent *The United States and World War II** (2 vols., 1964) and K. S. Davis's *An Experience of War: The United States in World War II* (1965). Winston Churchill's monumental six-volume history of the war has been abridged into one volume: *Memoirs of the Second World War* (1959). On Roosevelt's role in the war years see James MacGregor Burns, *Roosevelt: Soldier of Freedom** (1970). S. E. Morison has summarized his vast researches on the war at sea in *The Two-Ocean War* (1963).

On the military decision to use the atomic bomb the best general accounts are Herbert Feis's *Japan Subdued: The Atomic Bomb and the End of the War in the Pacific* (1961) and Walter S. Schoenberger's *Decision of Destiny* (1970).

United States strategy and management of the war are analyzed in Ray G. Cline's *Washington Command Post: The Operations Division* (1951); Kent Robert Greenfield's *American Strategy in World War II: A Reconsideration* (1963); Anne Armstrong's *Unconditional Surrender: The Impact of the Casablanca Policy upon World War II* (1961); S. E. Morison's *Strategy and Compromise* (1958); Hansen W. Baldwin's *Great Mistakes of the War* (1950); and Sumner Welles's *Seven Decisions That Shaped History* (1951).

On economic mobilization see Eliot Janeway's *The Struggle for Survival: A Chronicle of Economic Mobiliza-*

tion in World War II (1951); Francis Walton's *Miracle of World War II: How American Industry Made Victory Possible* (1956); H. C. Murphy's *National Debt in War and Transition* (1950); L. V. Chandler's *Inflation in the United States* (1951); W. W. Wilcox's *The Farmer in the Second World War* (1947); and Joel Seidman's *American Labor from Defense to Reconversion* (1953).

Roland Young's *Congressional Politics in the Second World War* (1956) shows the growing political conservatism of Congress during World War II. On American society in wartime see Jack Goodman's *While You Were Gone: A Report on Wartime Life in the United States* (1946). On blacks see Louis Harris's *The Negro Revolution in America* (1964); E. F. Frazier's *The Negro in the United States* (rev. ed., 1957); and Ulysses Lee's *United States Army in World War II: Special Studies: The Employment of Negro Troops* (1966).

On the wartime origins of the rift in the Grand Alliance, the standard works are Herbert Feis's *Churchill, Roosevelt, Stalin: The War They Waged and the Peace They Sought** (1957) and William H. McNeill's *America, Britain, and Russia: Their Cooperation and Conflict, 1941–1946** (1953). Two briefer accounts are John L. Snell's *Illusion and Necessity: The Diplomacy of Global War** (1963) and Gaddis Smith's *American Diplomacy during the Second World War** (1965). For Yalta see John L. Snell (ed.), *The Meaning of Yalta**

(1956); Edward R. Stettinius, *Roosevelt and the Russians: The Yalta Conference* (1949); and Diane Shaver Clemens, *Yalta** (1970).

For the American role in the creation of the United Nations Organization see R. B. Russell's *A History of the United Nations Charter: The Role of the United States, 1940–1945* (1958) and Leland M. Goodrich's *The United Nations* (1959).

On the beginnings ·of the Cold War see John Lukacs's *A History of the Cold War** (1961); Martin F. Herz's *Beginnings of the Cold War* (1966); John W. Spanier's *American Foreign Policy since World War II** (1960); Norman A. Graebner's *Cold War Diplomacy, 1945–1960** (1962); Hugh Seton-Watson's *Neither War nor Peace: The Struggle for Power in the Postwar World** (1960); Herbert Feis's *Between War and Peace: The Potsdam Conference** (1960); Louis J. Halle's *The Cold War as History* (1967); Wilfrid F. Knapp's *A History of War and Peace* (1967); and Adam Ulam's *Expansion and Coexistence: The History of Soviet Foreign Policy, 1917–1967** (1968).

Leading revisionist works are W. A. Williams's *The Tragedy of American Diplomacy** (1959); D. L. Fleming's *The Cold War and Its Origins, 1917–1960* (2 vols., 1961), a massive and important contribution to revisionist writing; Frederick L. Schuman's *The Cold War: Retrospect and Prospect** (1962); Gar Alperovitz's *Atomic Diplomacy: Hiroshima and Potsdam** (1965); David Horowitz's *The Free World Colossus** (1965); and Walter LaFeber's *America, Russia, and the Cold War** (1971).

*indicates availability in paperback.

31

Truman and Eisenhower: The Postwar Years at Home

Peace came as a great relief to the American people in 1945. Weary of sacrifice and the strains of war, they welcomed the opportunity to pursue their individual desires. Yet the transition from war to peace was not without its problems. Government officials had developed plans for converting the economy from war to peace, but these were not ready for implementation when the war ended. What rendered the situation more difficult was the absence of agreement on what policies the government should follow. Consequently, the immediate postwar period was one of confusion and controversy over domestic as well as foreign affairs. Inflation, labor-management disputes, dissatisfaction with the speed of military demobilization, scarcity of consumer goods, and general unrest all created serious problems for the new President, Harry S. Truman.

Republican victories in the midterm elections of 1946, added to the public's growing discontent with the Democrats, aroused hope among GOP leaders that they might capture the White House in 1948. For sixteen years the Democratic party had controlled the presidency; now the Republicans would have their day. But Truman upset the pollsters and won reelection. He then went ahead and pushed for his Fair Deal, a broad reform program which extended and amplified the New Deal. At first many people could not determine where President Truman stood politically but by the end of his presidency his programs and policies placed him in the tradition of twentieth-century reform. He no less than Franklin D. Roosevelt believed in the extension of federal powers and functions to solve the problems of an industrialized society.

Harry S. Truman

No president in the history of the Republic had ever faced a greater variety of difficult domestic and international issues than Harry S. Truman did at the close of World War II. Furthermore, Truman was not well prepared by formal education, training, or experience to deal with such complex national problems. Recognizing his inadequacies, Truman displayed an uncharacteristic humility when, talking to reporters shortly after Roosevelt's death, he said: "Please boys, give me your prayers. I need them very much." Still the new President gained confidence quickly.

Truman's career was typical of many American politicians. Born on a Missouri farm in 1884, he served in World War I, engaged in an unsuccessful clothing venture, and then entered politics. Supported by the Kansas City boss Thomas J. Pendergast, Truman won the judgeship of the Jackson County Court in 1922. This was an administrative, rather than a judicial, post and one in which he learned much about the art of politics. He was elected to the United States Senate in 1934 and reelected in 1940. His service in the Senate was adequate but not distinguished. He was selected for the vice presidency in 1944 largely because he held moderate views and came from a key border state. His record before 1945 was no better or worse than that of many other loyal Democrats who had served in the Senate.

Truman approximated the stereotype of the average American; he seemed neighborly—the typical resident of an American town. He enjoyed the simple things of life—his family, a drink, a game of poker with friends, a turn at the piano, or an occasional history book. But more

Senator Harry S. Truman was all smiles when he was nominated as Democratic vice-presidential candidate in 1944. This "average American's" own rendezvous with destiny was less than nine months away.
(UPI photo)

than most people he liked and understood party politics. To Truman, the Democratic party was the only true representative of the people and the only agency capable of governing the country. Moreover, he had the courage of his convictions and did not hesitate to take unpopular stands. In 1945, however, most Americans agreed that Truman was an unpromising successor to Roosevelt. No one questioned Truman's loyalty to the New Deal, but some wondered whether he would administer Roosevelt's policies, press for more advanced reforms, or retreat to a more conservative position.

Demobilization

Of all the questions before the American people in the late summer and early fall of 1945 none seemed so important as demobilization. In September 1944, authorities announced a point system under which the men who had served longest would be released first. Although this plan worked equitably, demobilization did not proceed as fast as most civilians and military personnel desired.

Lack of transportation created a major bottleneck. Troops demonstrated in Manila, Frankfurt, and other cities when ships were not available to take them home quickly. A campaign at home of "no boats, no votes" gained widespread popular attention. Nevertheless, rapid demobilization quickly reduced the world's strongest military power to a shadow of its former strength. In September 1945, the Army discharged 597,000 men; in December the number reached 1,112,000. President Truman later referred to the policy as disintegration rather than demobilization. From a high of more than 12 million in 1945, the nation's Armed Forces were cut to only 1,582,000 by 1947. In late 1945 President Truman urged that the United States maintain a strong Army, Navy, and Air Force to meet American responsibilities throughout the world, but most citizens preferred a reduction in taxes and military spending.

Opposition to the President's request for universal military training (UMT) was further evidence of the popular postwar outlook. Congress ignored Truman's recommendation for UMT in October 1945 and permitted the Selective Service Act to expire on March 31, 1947. Thereafter the Armed Forces depended entirely upon voluntary enlistments until the lawmakers enacted another Selective Service law in 1948. The President did succeed, however, in securing legislation designed to unify the armed services. In July 1947, Congress passed the National Security Act, which provided for a Department of Defense. Although the Army, Navy, and Air Force (which was now placed on an equal basis with the older services) continued as separate Departments, they all came under the new Secretary of Defense. This measure established the Central Intelligence Agency, the National Security Council, and the Joint Chiefs of Staff. Meanwhile, by the Atomic Energy Act of 1946, Congress placed postwar atomic development in the hands of a five-man civilian commission.

Economic Reconversion

During the war Americans had anticipated the reconversion of industry to peacetime production. Good wages and salaries during a period of rationing and price controls had left millions with accumulated savings, now available to purchase consumer goods such as automobiles, refrigerators, and washing machines. But what economic policies would best fulfill the needs and desires of the American people? How could the change-over from the production of war supplies to civilian goods be carried out most efficiently? How could widespread unemployment be avoided during the period of reconversion? Some authorities, recalling the record of 1920–1921, predicted a postwar economic slump with unemployment reaching 8 million by early 1946.

National leaders argued over the speed and the degree to which wartime rules and regula-

tions should be repealed. Many Americans, restless under three years of economic controls, argued that price, wage, and other restrictions should be abandoned immediately. Admitting that prices would rise in the short run, these advocates of the free market declared that businessmen, once freed from regulations, would soon produce enough to meet the demand and send prices again into decline. Others, including President Truman, believed that government controls over prices, wages, and rents must be continued until production caught up with demand. Otherwise, a large surplus of money seeking a limited supply of goods would create high prices and harmful inflation.

Immediately after Japan's defeat President Truman relaxed government controls over the economy. In August he ordered the end of rationing of gasoline, tires, fuel oil, processed foods, and other commodities. He gave labor more freedom to seek higher wages through bargaining with employers. Moreover, between August 14 and October 1, the government canceled $23 billion in war contracts and reduced the number of orders and regulations dealing with production from 650 to 79. On October 15, officials lifted all restrictions on construction. Despite these relaxations, the President reminded people that the Stabilization Act would be in force until June 20, 1946, and that some controls over prices, wages, and rents were still required.

Reconversion was complicated by the perennial conflict between industry and labor. While labor wanted higher wages and no increase in prices, businessmen demanded higher prices and stable wages. Labor received at least partial backing from the administration when President Truman declared on October 30 that "there is room in the existing price structure for business as a whole to grant increases in wage rates." Industrialists rejected this view. When General Motors refused to grant the United Auto Workers a 30 percent wage increase in November 1945, some 180,000 men walked off their jobs. This action inaugurated a series of strikes in major industries when people were complaining of the continued shortages. After weeks of negotiations the UAW accepted a General Motors proposal for a wage increase of $18\frac{1}{2}$ cents an hour. The strike ended on March 13, 1946.

In January, two months earlier, some 750,000 steelworkers went on strike after the industry refused their demand for a $2-a-day wage boost. The steel firms declared that they could not raise wages unless the Office of Price Administration would permit higher prices. To settle the issue, OPA allowed the companies to increase steel prices as much as $5 a ton. The steelworkers, too, agreed to an $18\frac{1}{2}$-cents-an-hour boost in wages. Coal and railroad workers, as well as those in some other major industries, also struck in the spring of 1946. Most of the controversies ended with wage increases of $18\frac{1}{2}$ cents an hour.

Despite growing pressure to remove price controls, the OPA kept the cost of living reasonably stable until the spring of 1946. By that time the government had permitted so many price changes that the cost of living began to rise steeply.

During the early summer of 1946 the conflict between those who favored continued controls and those who opposed them became intensely bitter. Since the Stabilization Act was scheduled to expire on June 20, the arguments over the role of government in reconversion now focused on the continued necessity of that wartime legislation. President Truman had requested the extension of price controls, but Congress passed a law late in June which permitted general price increases. Calling the bill "a sure formula for inflation," Truman gave it a stinging veto on June 29, only one day before the old law would expire. He criticized the bill because it sustained "the Government's responsibility to stabilize the economy and at the same time it destroys the Government's power to do so."

Congress sustained the President's veto and several weeks later passed a somewhat stronger measure which Truman signed "with reluctance." During the period when no controls were in effect—July 1 to July 25—the price index of 900 commodities jumped more than 10 percent; wholesale prices of farm products rose 24 percent and retail food prices nearly 14 percent.

Pressures to remove government controls from prices, wages, and rents continued unabated. Unable to resist longer, the President ended meat controls in October; the following month he abandoned most other price controls and wage regulations. During the last half of 1946, consumer prices increased some 15 percent; food price increases doubled that figure. The administration had lost its war against inflation.

Despite inflation, labor-management disputes, and strikes, the reconversion of the economy from war to peace was remarkably successful. The postwar depression simply did not occur. Civilian employment reached 55.2 million in 1946—nearly 7 million above that of 1940—and unemployment was only 2.3 million, less than that of the first year of war in 1942. Gross national product, in dollars of constant purchasing power, rose about one-third between the good year of 1929 and 1946. Average annual per capita income was about $500 higher in 1946 than in 1929, although inflation subsequently reduced these gains temporarily. Not only did the industrial sector enjoy nearly full employment at good wages, but farmers, too, were unusually prosperous. Heavy demand for agricultural products both at home and abroad drove farm prices up to exceptionally high levels. Net farm income rose to $15.5 billion in 1947, the highest point to that time in American history. Within a short period following the war an increasing number of Americans were enjoying prosperity and a rising standard of living.

Postwar prosperity rested, first, on the huge demand for goods and services which had grown during the war. People wanted new houses and all the standard commodities which had been unavailable or in short supply. Moreover, in 1945 individuals had $37 billion in savings to help buy the things they wanted. Buyers snapped up automobiles as fast as they rolled off the assembly lines in 1946 and 1947. The nearly 4 million passenger cars manufactured in 1948 failed to supply the demand, but production continued upward until in 1950 auto makers turned out 6.6 million units. The demand for new housing was equally strong and inflationary. By 1949 more than a million new nonfarm residences were started. The Federal Housing Administration supported much of the housing boom by guaranteeing long-term loans to buyers.

Large expenditures by industry for new plant and equipment stimulated the economy even more. In 1948 American businessmen spent about $22 billion on capital outlays—some two and one-half times more than the figure for 1945. Moreover, government spending continued high. Those who believed that the federal budget could be cut to approximately its prewar figure—$9 billion in 1940—were sadly mistaken. Annual federal expenditures declined drastically from their wartime peak of almost $98 billion, but needs at home and commitments around the world kept appropriations at record peacetime levels. The federal budget declined to $33 billion in 1948, but it increased again thereafter. Altogether, large individual, corporate, and government spending provided the purchasing power needed to keep the consumer-oriented economy advancing at a rapid pace.

Congress under the New Deal had accepted some responsibility for the condition of the economy, but not until after World War II did it assume major responsibility for maintaining general prosperity. The Employment Act of 1946 was a landmark in national economic policy. The law declared that "it is the continuing policy and responsibility of the Federal Government to use all practicable means," in cooperation with private industry and state and local governments, to afford "useful employment opportunities, including self employment, for those able, willing, and seeking to work, and to promote maximum employment, production, and purchasing power." This act did not specify how the federal government would achieve these objectives, but it implied that Washington could and would control the business cycle through government spending, taxing, and other fiscal policies. The law provided for a Council of Economic Advisers to study economic trends and recommend to the President which policies would best serve the economy.

Postwar Politics

Although a great majority of Americans rallied to President Truman when he assumed office, his personal popularity, as well as that of his party, soon declined. Truman appeared indecisive and uncertain about the direction of his leadership. For months his responses to postwar issues seemed to lack purpose. Then on September 6, 1945, Truman delighted loyal New Dealers when he outlined a liberal program which went beyond even that of Roosevelt. He called for expanded unemployment insurance, a higher minimum wage, full employment legislation, a Fair Employment Practices Commission to deal with racial discrimination, housing legislation, and federal aid for slum clearance.

In Congress, however, the tide of conservatism was running strong—a continuation largely of the conservative trend evident during the war years. Now that peace had arrived, lawmakers were anxious to regain some of the powers which they had given up to the Executive during the war. Congress, one observer wrote, was "in a mood to test its own power." And a coalition of Southern Democrats and conservative Northern Republicans had preferences of its own. This group insisted on lower taxes, reduced federal expenditures, greater controls over labor, and policies which would take the federal government out of business. By the spring of 1946 the country as a whole seemed content with what had already been done in the field of social security and welfare legislation.

Already the Democratic party was in trouble. Democrats carried the blame for the inflation, strikes, and general unrest. By April, the number of voters who believed that the President was incapable of handling his job had jumped to 34 percent, a sharp rise from previous months. The popular image of President Truman and his party was scarcely flattering. Moreover, critics charged that some of the people around Truman, the so-called Missouri Crowd, were engaged in immoral, if not illegal, activities. Some insisted that Truman was soft on communism and that radical labor leaders influenced or controlled his administration. As the 1946 midterm elections approached, Republican posters asked: "Had Enough? Vote Republican."

Most political analysts concluded early that the Republicans would gain control of the House; what surprised them was the size of the victory in November—246 to 188. However, many Democrats were stunned when the Republicans also won a majority of 51 to 45 in the Senate. For the first time since 1930, Republicans controlled both houses of Congress. The voters apparently favored a greater conservatism in government and a return to some form of Republican normalcy.

The Eightieth Congress

One prime objective of the Republican-controlled Eightieth Congress was the amendment of the Wagner Act of 1935. For several years conservatives had argued that this law gave organized labor an undue advantage over management. When John L. Lewis, in November 1946, led his coal miners out on strike for the second time that year, many people were furious. And they were not satisfied when the court levied a heavy fine on the United Mine Workers' president for having violated a restraining order. As one writer said, "a veritable typhoon of public opinion" was developing against organized labor, especially against union leadership.

This growing antilabor sentiment expressed

itself in passage of the National Management Relations Act in June 1947. Sponsored by Senator Robert A. Taft and Congressman Fred A. Hartley, the Taft-Hartley Act gave employers more freedom to propagandize against unions, outlawed the closed shop, permitted suits by employers to recover losses in jurisdictional disputes, forbade union campaign contributions, and required union officials to sign affidavits that they were not Communists. The law required unions to give a sixty-day notification before modifying or terminating a contract, during which time they were not to strike. Moreover, in case a projected strike threatened the national health or safety, the Attorney General could obtain an eighty-day injunction which would render a strike unlawful and compel negotiators to end the dispute. For President Truman the Taft-Hartley Act went much too far in the attempt to restore the balance of economic power between labor and management. In a sharp veto message, he declared that the law "would contribute neither to industrial peace nor to economic stability and progress." Congress promptly overrode the President's veto by large majorities.

Truman also found himself in sharp disagreement with the Republican Congress over tax policy. Spokesmen for business, industry, and high-income groups argued that heavy taxes discouraged enterprise and retarded economic expansion. By 1947 these groups insisted that the time for tax cuts had arrived. Truman favored some tax reduction, but he declared in January 1947, that "we should maintain tax revenues at levels that will not only meet current expenditures but also leave a surplus for retirement of the public debt." By the end of 1946, the federal debt stood at about $269 billion. The President believed that whatever reductions were voted should go chiefly to low-income groups.

Ignoring the President, Congress passed a bill in May 1947 which cut taxes between 10 and 30 percent. Truman vetoed the measure, arguing that it was "the wrong kind of tax reduction" and came "at the wrong time." He argued that the bill favored the rich. Congress passed another tax reduction law in July, but it met a similar fate at the hands of the President. Finally, in April 1948, Congress passed a tax reduction bill which relieved some 7.4 million low-income citizens from any tax liability, and raised exemptions from $500 to $600. Truman vetoed this bill, too, but Congress overrode his objections.

The President and Congress disagreed sharply over civil rights. In a special message of February 2, 1948, Truman recommended antilynching and anti-poll tax laws as well as the establishment of a permanent Fair Employment Practices Commission. The President said that "all men are entitled to equality of opportunity." Southerners, especially, reacted strongly to Truman's civil rights program.

Confronted with determined opposition in Congress, Truman not only failed to achieve civil rights legislation, but also divided the Democratic party, an especially important matter in a presidential election year. Truman further angered conservatives by proposing a broad social welfare program calling for national health insurance, federal aid to education, higher minimum wages, housing legislation, and a significant expansion of social security. On few domestic fronts did Truman have his way.

The Election of 1948

Early in 1948 Democratic prospects appeared almost hopeless. The President's popularity and leadership seemed completely eroded. During the Eightieth Congress, lawmakers had followed their own independent paths, ignoring and frustrating the President and his program. Southerners opposed Truman for his civil rights stand; many old New Dealers questioned his devotion to social reform. Some anti-Truman liberals rallied behind Henry A. Wallace, who had announced on December 29, 1947, that he would seek the presidency as head of a new Progressive party.

Some Democrats searched frantically for a strong leader to replace Truman as the party's nominee. They attempted to interest General Dwight D. Eisenhower and Justice William O. Douglas, but without success. Truman's announcement, on March 8, that he would seek another term produced nothing but despair in Democratic ranks. One Democratic governor declared, "We don't want to run a race with a dead Missouri mule." Some jokes circulating in Washington were: "I wonder what Truman would do if he were alive" and "To err is Truman." But the party was saddled with the

Truman delivering a "whistle stop" campaign speech in Waco, Texas, 1948. Television and travel by jet plane have virtually eliminated this mode of electioneering.

(Brown Brothers)

Missourian, and when the convention met in Philadelphia it nominated him on the first ballot. The delegates chose Senator Alben W. Barkley of Kentucky as the vice presidential nominee in an effort to attract discontented Southerners. The Democratic platform called for higher minimum wages, repeal of the Taft-Hartley Act, federal aid to education, expansion of social security, flexible farm price supports, and a strong civil rights act.

The convention was apathetic when the President appeared to deliver his acceptance speech. The hour was late and delegates were tired, but Truman aroused considerable enthusiasm by his defense of the New Deal and his attack on the "do-nothing Eightieth Congress." As Truman attacked his opponents, elements in his own party moved to assure his defeat. Anti-Truman Democrats met at Birmingham on July 17 and nominated Governor J. Strom Thurmond of

South Carolina and Governor Fielding Wright of Mississippi on a Dixiecrat ticket. This Southern party sought support among anti-civil rights groups. Shortly thereafter the Progressive party formally nominated Henry Wallace and Senator Glen Taylor of Idaho as its standard-bearers. The Progressives advocated a socialistic domestic program and closer relations with the Soviet Union. Now the Democratic party seemed to be hopelessly split.

Meanwhile, the Republicans again nominated Governor Thomas E. Dewey and gave him a strong running mate in Governor Earl Warren of California. The Republicans promised greater efficiency and honesty in government, a campaign against domestic communism, and lower taxes. Besides tacitly accepting most of the New Deal, the Republicans proposed some social reforms of their own.

Dewey campaigned in a conservative, restrained fashion. Supported by the public opinion polls and most political prognosticators, he behaved as if he had already won the election. He voiced platitudes about inefficiency in government and accused the Truman administration of crime, corruption, and softness toward communism. He failed to come to grips with national issues and tended to remain aloof from the people.

Truman, on the other hand, entered the race in a fighting mood. In his acceptance speech he had accused the Republicans of subservience to the special interests. His call for repeal of the Taft-Hartley Act brought most of organized labor into his camp. The CIO's Political Action Committee and the AF of L's Labor's League for Political Education worked hard for Truman's reelection. Truman also charged that the Republican Eightieth Congress had ignored the needs of agriculture by failing to provide enough storage for surplus farm crops. Besides dwelling on specific issues, Truman skillfully played on lingering fears that the Republican party was the party of depression and hard times. The President carried on a 31,000-mile whistle-stop campaign where he proved to be at his best. People responded enthusiastically to his barbs and jibes at the opposition, and shouts of "Give 'em hell" and "Atta boy, Harry" frequently punctuated his off-the-cuff and formal talks. Despite the appearance of growing Democratic support, scarcely an analyst believed that Truman could win.

Still Truman won a stunning upset victory. He gained 24 million votes to 22 million for Dewey, while Thurmond and Wallace trailed far behind with 1,169,000 and 1,156,000 votes respectively. Truman did not win a majority of the popular vote, but he carried the key states and held a majority in the electoral college of 303 to 189. The Democrats regained control of both houses of Congress. Republicans ready to occupy the White House suddenly discovered that they had been rejected.

There were fundamental reasons for Truman's surprising victory. The labor and the farm vote had made the difference in such key states as Ohio and Iowa. Moreover, the Democrats benefited from the general prosperity and the fear of many that a Republican administration might undermine the good times and the social and economic gains made since 1933. On their part the Republicans committed some serious blunders. Too many overconfident party members failed to vote, and the conservative tone of the Republican-controlled Eightieth Congress lost the independent voter support. In the final analysis Truman demonstrated that the coalition of workers, farmers, minority groups, and intellectuals which Roosevelt had put together was still a winning combination.

The Fair Deal

Once elected in his own right, President Truman placed his administration fully behind a broad program of social and economic reform. In his message to Congress on January 5, 1949, he reviewed past Democratic achievements and called for additional welfare programs. Specifically Truman recommended repeal of the Taft-Hartley Act, an increase in minimum wages to 75 cents an hour, higher taxes on corporations and middle- and upper-income groups, stronger antitrust laws, parity income for farmers, broader coverage and increased payments under social security, a system of medical insurance, federal aid to education, slum clearance, and low-cost housing. The President perhaps unwittingly labeled his own administration when, near the end of his address, he said: "Every segment of our population and every individual has a right to expect from our Government a fair deal."

Truman's fair deal message aroused heated discussion over the question of big government and state socialism. One *Washington Evening Star* writer termed the President's address "the most frankly socialistic ever presented by a president of the United States." Another critic charged

that Truman had swung far to the left and that his program would "flatter and bribe every pressure group in the country." Other Americans were less fearful and believed that the President was moving in the right direction. According to the *New York Times*, social reforms such as Truman advocated were "all proper objectives of a democratic people, and the proper concern of a democratic government in this modern age."

Truman soon discovered that Congress was less than enthusiastic about his domestic program. The perennial coalition between Southern Democrats and conservative Northern Republicans rendered the Democratic majorities almost meaningless. Still Truman and his labor supporters moved quickly against the Taft-Hartley Act. While union spokesmen and some Democratic leaders criticized the so-called "Slave Labor Law," a majority of Congress agreed that the law was working well and not injuring the unions.

Truman, however, did achieve some parts of his program. In 1949 Congress approved an increase in the minimum wage from 40 to 75 cents an hour. The next year Congress increased social security benefits and broadened the law to cover more than 10 million additional people, including self-employed workers, farm laborers, and domestic servants. The Housing Act of 1949 set as a national goal "a decent home and a suitable living environment for every American family." The law provided federal aid for slum clearance and the construction of about 800,000 public housing units. On the other hand, Congress refused to establish a permanent Fair Employment Practices Commission and ignored Truman's request for federal aid to education, compulsory health insurance, as well as antilynching and anti-poll tax legislation.

By 1949 the farm problem had become a major issue, partly because of a sharp decline in agricultural income. In 1948 the Eightieth Congress had postponed, rather than settled, the farm problem by passing the bitterly contested Hope-Aiken bill. This act committed the federal government to maintain prices on basic agricultural commodities at 90 percent of parity until June 1950. This goal would be achieved by loans to producers at a set rate through the Commodity Credit Corporation. Much of the debate over the Hope-Aiken bill centered on the issue of whether the federal government should continue to guarantee high, fixed price supports. Senator Aiken proposed that price supports vary from 60 to 90 percent of parity, depending on the supply of a particular commodity. While Truman and a majority in Congress favored the principle of flexible price supports, spokesmen for Southern and Midwestern farm groups wielded enough political influence to defeat the idea and to continue high, rigid supports.

Sharp agricultural price declines in 1949 again placed the farm issue before Congress. Truman's new secretary of agriculture, Charles F. Brannan, stirred up new controversy by proposing a different approach to the farm problem. Brannan explained that he wanted to reduce the production of commodities such as wheat and cotton, which had flowed into government storage, and at the same time expand the consumption of fruit, milk, vegetables, meat, and other

perishable products. To achieve these goals, Brannan proposed high, fixed price supports for most commodities, but only on a limited portion of a farmer's production. Government loans would still support the price of storable products. But in the case of perishable commodities, prices would be permitted to fall to whatever price the market dictated, and the difference between the market price and the predetermined price-support figure would be covered by a direct cash payment to the farmer by the government. Brannan argued that his plan would guarantee farmers a good income and at the same time assure low prices to consumers.

Labor groups, the National Farmers' Union, and consumer spokesmen quickly rallied behind the Brannan Plan. Strong opposition arose among those who believed the scheme too expensive and an excessive infringement of government control over farming. Most farm organizations, except the Farmers' Union, opposed the plan; conservatives, who claimed that it would "socialize" agriculture, fought it bitterly. Brannan's opponents successfully substituted a measure which simply extended price supports on basic commodities at 90 percent of parity through 1950. Several other crops would be supported at from 60 to 90 percent of parity. Congress again found it difficult to abandon high, fixed supports to which farmers had become accustomed during and immediately after World War II. Increased farm prices occasioned by the Korean war in 1950 reduced the pressure on Congress for new legislation during the remainder of the Truman administration. Between 1949 and 1951 net agricultural income rose from less than $13 billion to $16.3 billion. War had again rescued the farmers.

Tax policies produced additional controversies in Truman's second term. In 1949 the President asked Congress to raise tax rates in order to reduce inflationary pressures on the economy and to permit payments on the national debt, which stood at some $252 billion. That year Congress refused to enact any major new tax law, but following the outbreak of the Korean

War, the lawmakers raised taxes on corporations, increased the excess profits tax, and levied additional excise duties. In 1951 Congress again raised both individual and corporate income taxes and added more excise taxes.

Despite the perennial executive-legislative conflict of the Truman years, Congress and the President made important changes in governmental organization and administration. The Legislative Reorganization Act of 1946 reduced the number of standing committees in the House from forty-eight to nineteen, in the Senate from thirty-three to fifteen. These changes, it was hoped, would improve the speed and efficiency of Congress. To improve the federal administration, Congress established two commissions, both under the chairmanship of former President Herbert Hoover, to study the organization of the executive branch of the government. Some resulting reforms included the institution of better accounting and budgeting practices, the removal of the government from some business, and the development of a career service in the federal government. Even more important was the Twenty-second Amendment to the Constitution, which limited the tenure of future presidents to two terms. The amendment went into effect in 1951.

Communism: National Danger or "Red Herring"?

During most of his White House years Truman suffered from the charge that his administration was soft on communism. In March 1947, Truman formed a Loyalty Review Board to screen federal employees; he instructed the Attorney General to designate subversive organizations. But these actions did not satisfy those who attributed postwar troubles both at home and abroad to Communist subversion. The House Un-American Activities Committee condemned what it considered the President's indifference to Communist infiltration. In June 1948, the Mundt-Nixon bill, designed to control Communist and Communist-front organizations, passed the House but died in the Senate. A few months later, in August 1948, Elizabeth Bentley and Whittaker Chambers, admitted former Communists, charged that several former government officials were either Communists or Communist sympathizers. Chambers created a national sensation when he named Alger Hiss, a career government employee who had worked in both the Agriculture and State Departments, as a Communist spy. Hiss denied the charge, and Truman referred to the investigation as a "red herring." Hiss's first trial ended in a "hung" jury. Later Hiss went to prison, convicted of perjury.

In February 1950, about a month after the Hiss conviction, Senator Joseph McCarthy of Wisconsin declared that the State Department was full of Communists and fellow travelers. He produced no evidence, but many chose to believe him. They pointed to Communist gains around the world—the Russian explosion of an atomic bomb and the victory of the Chinese Communists in 1949—and concluded that domestic Communists were somehow responsible. In September 1950, Congress approved the Subversive Activities Contol Act, generally known as the McCarran Act after its author, Senator Pat McCarran of Nevada. This law declared illegal any conspiracy to form a totalitarian dictatorship in the United States. It gave the government power to deport certain aliens. Congress passed the McCarran Act over Truman's veto and thereby added fuel to the charges that the President was not a strong anti-Communist. In the midterm elections of 1950, Republicans argued that the Truman administration was riddled with Communist spies. This issue undoubtedly contributed to the Democrats' loss of twenty-eight House and five Senate seats.

The McCarran-Walter Act in June 1952 was another direct result of the growing fear of communism. Speaking on behalf of the bill,

Senator McCarran declared that those who opposed his measure "would wittingly or unwittingly lend themselves to efforts which would poison the blood stream of the country." This law, passed over Truman's veto, provided broad grounds for deporting or denying entrance to those who were thought to be security risks.

While the McCarran-Walter Act completely revised and updated the Immigration Act of 1924, it continued to favor the immigration of Northern and Western Europeans. This obvious discrimination against many peoples of the world seemed to Truman undesirable and undemocratic.

Eisenhower and the Election of 1952

By 1952 the nation was in a mood of anger and frustration. The Korean conflict had produced wide divisions within the country. Americans were deeply concerned over the threat of domestic communism; they complained that inflation was eating away their incomes and savings. To deal with the uncertainties abroad and the frustrations at home, voters looked for a strong leader. Their choice was General Dwight D. Eisenhower.

Eisenhower's candidacy attracted wide attention not only because of the general's remarkable personality and distinguished military career, but also because his known views on United States diplomatic and military policy seemed to agree with the national consensus. At the Republican Convention Eisenhower received the full support of the East and enough from other sections to assure his nomination on the first ballot. For vice president the convention named Senator Richard M. Nixon, a Californian who for six years had exploited the Communist issue to the fullest. Nixon was completely acceptable to Senator Robert A. Taft's conservative faction of the party. Truman's Republican adviser, John Foster Dulles, wrote the platform which strongly attacked Roosevelt and Truman for losing the dearly won peace at Teheran, Yalta, and Potsdam. In Asia, declared the platform, a Democratic administration had denied Chiang the support he required and thereby substituted in the Pacific a murderous enemy for a proven ally. It had invited the Korean War and then refused to push on to victory. Finally, Dulles promised a program that would "mark

the end of the negative, futile and immoral policy of 'containment' which abandons countless human beings . . . [and] enables the rulers to forge the captives into a weapon for our destruction."

Whatever Eisenhower's initial intent, he soon turned to foreign policy as the chief Republican weapon in the campaign. This appeared strange inasmuch as he had been Chief of Staff under the Truman administration and one of the architects of NATO. Dulles, too, had served the Truman administration and had negotiated the Japanese treaty. But both men were driven by political necessity. On domestic issues the Republican party could offer the country little except promises that it would halt the trend toward socialism. Eisenhower promised honesty in government and an end to inflation. But it was on the Korean issue that Eisenhower showed his supreme effectiveness as a campaigner. In a climactic appeal to the nation, he promised at Detroit on October 25 that, if elected, he would go to Korea to seek an early and honorable end to the war. He appealed skillfully to the frustrations and dissatisfactions which had developed around this inconclusive conflict.

With President Truman's announcement in March 1952 that he would not run for reelection, Senator Estes Kefauver of Tennessee stumped the country in an effort to fill the leadership vacuum in the Democratic party. At the same time a well-organized group of Northern Democrats moved to draft Governor Adlai Stevenson of Illinois. Hesitant to the end, Stevenson finally accepted the party's nomination and in an appealing acceptance speech charmed millions of television viewers with his unusual wit and style. "Let's talk sense to the American people," he said. "Let's tell them the truth, that there are no gains without pains." For its vice-presidential nominee the party selected Senator John J. Sparkman of Alabama.

Through the ensuing campaign Stevenson delighted the country's intellectuals with his eloquence and candor. He made no effort to escape the Truman record. In Europe he promised only containment, and that at great expense. He condemned those who promised victory in Europe because, he said, there were no means available to achieve it. He upheld the Korean action as a successful example of collective security which, if it had not produced victory, had at least frustrated aggression. For Eisenhower's promise to go to Korea, Stevenson had no answer. "Rather than exploit human hopes and fears, rather than provide glib solutions and false assurances," he explained, "I would gladly lose this Presidential election."

Against Eisenhower's personal popularity Stevenson had no chance. The November balloting gave the Republican nominee 33,800,000 votes to Stevenson's 27,300,000. The Republicans gained control of both houses of Congress, although by very narrow margins. The Republican party scored heavily on Eisenhower's personal appeal, on the charges of Democratic failure, and on the popular belief that Eisenhower could end the Korean War.

Eisenhower the President

Dwight D. Eisenhower was the first top-ranking general to occupy the White House since U. S. Grant. Except for two years as president of Columbia University from 1948 to 1950, his had been exclusively a military career. Born in Texas in 1890, he grew up in Abilene, Kansas, and then entered West Point, where he graduated in 1915. He moved steadily up the officer ranks; during 1942 Roosevelt placed him in charge of the Allied invasion of North Africa. The next year Eisenhower became Commander in Chief of the Allied forces in Western Europe, and in June 1944 directed the invasion of Normandy. By the end of World War II he had become an international hero. Sixty-two at the time of his election, Eisenhower was honest, dignified, sociable, and modest. His personal warmth and friendly smile inspired trust and confidence. People called him "Ike," showing their feeling of friendship and intimacy for him.

Although Eisenhower lacked practical political experience, he intuitively provided a type of leadership which satisfied most Americans. Recognizing that much of the demand for change and reform which had been so strong under the New Deal and Fair Deal had subsided during the prosperous 1950s, he followed the path of "moderate progressivism" in federal policies. Eisenhower explained his basic approach as one "that preserves the greatest possible initiative, freedom and independence of soul and body of the individual but that does not hesitate to use government to combat cataclysmic economic disasters." Republican divisions rendered moderation difficult and forced Eisenhower to rely on Democratic support to achieve most of his programs.

During the campaign Eisenhower had promised that, if elected, he would bring "the best brains in the country" to Washington. As it turned out, the first Republican Cabinet in twenty years represented the usual array of professional and political interests and varied little in caliber from previous Cabinets. The top post of Secretary of State went to John Foster Dulles, a successful New York lawyer and State Department adviser. The President's closest adviser on domestic policy was Secretary of the Treasury George Humphrey of the M. A. Hanna Company of Cleveland. Another wealthy and conservative adviser was Charles E. Wilson, president of General Motors, who became Secretary of Defense. Wilson's blunt and untactful statements sometimes embarrassed the administration and opened the way for sharp criticism. Discussing self-reliance he remarked: "I've always liked bird dogs better than kennel-fed dogs myself—you know, one who'll get out and hunt for food rather than sit on his fanny and yell."

One Eisenhower appointment had extremely important implications for the future. During his first year in office the President named Governor Earl Warren of California as Chief Justice of the United States Supreme Court. Fred Vinson, a Truman appointee to the Supreme Court, died in September 1953, and Eisenhower gave his position to the noted liberal Republican.

Old Issues and New Leadership

In his State of the Union address on February 2, 1953, Eisenhower defined his general approach to economic and social problems. He called for an end to "planned deficits," a reduction of federal expenditures, lower taxes, and curbs on inflation. Fluctuations in prices, he said, should be dealt with by "sound fiscal and monetary policy, and . . . the natural workings of economic law." He promised that the administration would not ask for renewal of the price or wage controls scheduled to expire April 30. The President also recommended new farm legislation, as well as modifications of the Taft-Hartley Act. On social issues, Eisenhower declared that he would strive to achieve "civil rights and equality of employment opportunity," an extension of social security, and some betterment of the nation's schools. "There is . . . ," he concluded, "a middle way between untrammeled freedom of the individual and the demands for the welfare of the whole Nation. This way must avoid government by bureaucracy as carefully as it avoids neglect of the helpless." This was a clear statement of Eisenhower's "middle way."

For most Republicans the first order of business was tax reduction. The President favored this course, but he opposed reductions before federal expenditures could be lowered. He did not want to endanger the nation's defenses or add to the public debt. Despite strong pressure, Eisenhower successfully resisted congressional efforts to lower taxes in 1953. During 1954 the

President and Secretary Humphrey curtailed both military and civilian expenditures; they reduced federal outlays and trimmed the deficit to $3.1 billion. Thereafter they agreed to widespread tax reductions. Congress lowered a wide range of excise taxes in April 1954. In another law, passed in August, the lawmakers permitted faster tax write-offs for businessmen. Altogether, the annual tax savings amounted to about $7.4 billion, but most of the advantages went to high-income groups.

This controversy over tax policy was tied closely to the economic recession which began in the summer of 1953. A drop in defense spending, increased inventories, and a slowdown in private investment all combined to bring on the recession. Manufacturing production dropped and unemployment rose sharply by the winter of 1953–1954. Faced with a lagging economy, Democrats and labor leaders called for massive federal spending to stimulate the economy and create jobs. But Eisenhower refused to "go into any slambang emergency program" unless it was necessary. He obviously did not think such action necessary. The President preferred to encourage private investment with lower taxes. Genuine economic prosperity, he believed, rested primarily in the private sector rather than in federal spending. By the late spring of 1954 a rise in both consumer and capital expenditures, accompanied by increased public outlays for social security, unemployment insurance, and welfare payments, pushed the economy upward.

Eisenhower faced his first major controversy over public power in 1954, when the Atomic Energy Commission approved an agreement with Edgar H. Dixon and Eugene Yates to construct a plant at West Memphis, Arkansas. Supporters of public power, especially the friends of TVA, charged loudly that the government was favoring the private power trust against the public interest. Eisenhower defended the contract and argued that the government had no reason to provide electricity for Memphis. Following months of controversy, the AEC canceled the contract, but only after the revelation that a conflict of interests existed between a government official and the firm which handled some of the Dixon-Yates financing.

Another example of Eisenhower's opposition to what he called "the implacable expansionism of the federal government" was his support of the Submerged Lands Act. This law sought to solve the controversy between the federal government and the states, particularly California, Texas, and Louisiana, over control of submerged coastal lands rich in oil. In 1947 the Supreme Court had decided that California was "not the owner of the three-mile belt along its coast" and that the federal government owned the underwater resources, including oil. Those who favored federal control of the submerged coastal lands argued that the underlying oil belonged to all the people and that state ownership would result in a "giveaway" to a few favored oil companies. Congress passed the Submerged Lands Act in May 1953. This law transferred offshore oil lands along the Gulf and California coasts to the states.

Communism and Internal Security

Even after his own party came to power in 1953, Senator Joseph McCarthy continued to charge that the federal government was infiltrated with Communists. Indeed, McCarthy not only insisted that the Truman administration had been soft on communism but also charged that President Eisenhower had failed to rid the government of security risks. He accused government departments, the colleges and universities, and even the churches of harboring Communists or supporting what he called the "Communist apparatus." People who dared to speak out against his rash charges McCarthy labeled "Communists" or, at best, "fellow travelers." A Red Scare, not unlike that which followed World War I, was in full swing.

Many people hoped that Eisenhower would destroy McCarthy's growing influence with a direct attack upon the Senator and his methods. But the President believed that the best way to defeat McCarthyism was to ignore the Senator. Finally, in 1954, McCarthy overreached himself—as Eisenhower had believed he would—when he accused the Army of shielding a disloyal Army dentist, Major Irving Peress. During April a Senate subcommittee investigated the Army as millions watched on television. McCarthy's unsubstantiated attacks on Secretary of the Army Robert Stevens revealed that he was an arrogant, ignorant, and intolerant bully. Disgusted with this performance, as well as with other McCarthy activities, the Senate passed a condemnatory resolution in December 1954, declaring that McCarthy's actions were "contrary to senatorial traditions." Already the general fear of communism had declined and McCarthy's public support had disintegrated. He died three years later, in May 1957.

Although the fear of internal Communist subversion subsided, it never completely disappeared. Throughout the decade, Congress and the Executive took firm action to eliminate security risks and people of questionable character from government service. In 1953–1954 security officials dismissed about 3,000 federal employees under Eisenhower's security program. In one celebrated case involving internal security the Atomic Energy Commission, in June 1954,

G. David Schine, Senator Joseph McCarthy, and McCarthy's aide Roy Cohn in 1954, when the names of all three were household words across the land.

(United Press photo)

withdrew the security clearance of the atomic scientist J. Robert Oppenheimer. The Commission accused him of associating with known Communists and of ignoring the needs of domestic security. Nine years later the AEC reversed itself and honored Oppenheimer with a $50,000 prize for his contributions to nuclear physics.

The Election of 1956

Despite the many controversial issues which faced Eisenhower, nothing seemed to dim his personal popularity. What columnist Ernest K. Lindley wrote in 1953 was equally true in 1956. The President's popularity, said Lindley, was personal and reflected "affection, confidence in his integrity, and the feeling that he graces the office of Chief Executive." Beyond this, Lindley said, "one senses confidence in his judgment about the overriding questions of defense and foreign policy in a dangerous world." Moreover, by 1955 and 1956 the country was enjoying a high level of prosperity. Despite the recession in 1953–1954, gross national product in stable prices had risen from $381 billion to $412 billion. In the same period, annual per capita income increased from $1,592 to $1,705. And by 1956 unemployment was down to only 2.2 million workers. Business was booming almost every-

where. Under these circumstances, Republicans could understandably boast of "peace, progress and prosperity."

Although political conditions appeared favorable to Republicans in 1956, they were understandably disturbed when the President in September 1955 suffered a severe heart attack at Denver. Fortunately, he made an excellent recovery and announced on February 29, 1956, that he would seek a second term. For Republicans this settled the issue. When the party met at the Cow Palace in San Francisco in August, delegates renominated Eisenhower and Nixon on the first ballot. Convention orators emphasized the twin Eisenhower achievements of prosperity and peace.

Meanwhile, the Democrats had again nominated Adlai Stevenson. A more vigorous contest developed over the vice presidential choice.

Ultimately Senator Estes Kefauver of Tennessee defeated Senator John F. Kennedy of Massachusetts. The keynote speaker, Governor Frank Clement of Tennessee, delivered a hard-hitting, emotional attack on the Eisenhower administration, calling it a "sordid record of broken promises and unredeemed pledges." As the campaign got under way, Stevenson struck harder and took a less lofty and intellectual position than he had in 1952. But neither Stevenson nor the Democratic party had anything to offer which could equal the Republican appeal of peace, progress, and prosperity. Eisenhower won another smashing victory as he gained 57.4 percent of the popular vote and carried all but seven states.

Despite Eisenhower's campaigning, both houses of Congress went Democratic in the midterm elections of 1954. In the Senate the narrow Democratic majority was 48 to 47, with one independent; in the House the Democrats led 232 to 203. In 1956 Congress remained Democratic, revealing that the President was considerably more popular than his party. In the House the Democrats achieved a lead of 234 to 201; in the Senate they held a slight margin of 49 to 47. In the Eighty-fifth Congress, which opened in January 1957, congressional leadership still rested in the hands of two powerful Texans—Lyndon B. Johnson, Majority Leader in the Senate, and Sam Rayburn, Speaker of the House.

Second-Term Issues

Soon after the beginning of Eisenhower's second term, the boasted prosperity suddenly ended. By the fall of 1957 the country had fallen into another sharp recession. Consumer spending leveled off, manufacturing output declined, private investment fell, and by December unemployment had risen to 5.2 percent of the labor force. It went even higher in early 1958. Not until the late spring of 1958 did conditions improve significantly.

Once again there were loud demands for increased government spending to stimulate the economy and provide employment. But the President opposed pump-priming schemes; the talk of turning to government, he said, "evidences lack of faith in the inherent vitality of our free economy." In denouncing some spending ideas, he declared that they would lead to "the wholesale distribution of the people's money in dubious activities under federal direction."

Despite Eisenhower's conservative-sounding public statements, he moved quickly to use the antidepression tools available to the federal government. These were the so-called stabilizers which concerned the economists. The Defense Department speeded up military procurement and expanded military construction. This helped conditions in industrial centers such as Detroit where unemployment was high. The administration increased grants-in-aid for new hospitals and other public facilities and spent more on the interstate highway program. The Federal Housing Administration lowered down payments on FHA-insured housing loans, and the Federal Reserve Board lowered interest rates. Thus Eisenhower did not hesitate to use a wide variety of government programs, involving huge expenditures, to aid the economy. The President achieved his objectives of a balanced budget in fiscal 1956 and 1957, but the deficit rose to $2.8 billion in the year ending June 30, 1958, and jumped to a whopping $12.4 billion the following year. As it turned out, government spending was still the most effective antidote for depression.

This recession was a major cause of a growing disillusionment with the Eisenhower administration. Still other developments plagued the Republicans as the 1958 midterm elections approached. The Eisenhower administration's professions of purity were seriously refuted when Sherman Adams, the President's chief assistant, admitted taking gifts from a Boston textile firm which was seeking favors in Washington. Adams resigned on September 22, but his actions continued to embarrass the Republicans. Moreover, Southerners had become embittered at Eisenhower when he sent troops to Little Rock in 1957 to enforce the Supreme Court's decision on school integration. Republicans lost labor support when they backed state right-to-work laws so strongly opposed by organized labor. The Russian Sputnik in 1957 caused some to wonder if the Republicans had permitted the country to fall behind in the space race. Finally, the Democrats capitalized on farmers' dissatisfaction with Secretary Ezra Taft Benson and the Republican farm program.

The Republicans, especially Vice President Nixon, attempted in vain to answer the Democratic critics. In 1958, the Democrats gained their most spectacular congressional victory since the 1930s. They picked up 48 seats in the House to give them a majority of 282 to 154. In the Senate they added 15 seats, making a division there of 64 Democrats to only 34 Republicans. Republican losses were heavy in the Midwest farm belt and in industrially depressed areas.

Agriculture and Labor

On farm policy the Republican party was committed to change. In the campaign of 1952 it opposed high price supports and restricted production. Eisenhower believed that farmers deserved parity prices—indeed, during the campaign he advocated 100 percent of parity—but he said parity prices must be found in the marketplace and not in federal price supports. Secretary of Agriculture Benson was particularly critical of Democratic farm policies and argued that farmers had become too dependent on the government for price and income.

There was little that Eisenhower and Benson could do to change farm policy immediately. Congress in 1952 had extended price supports on basic commodities at 90 percent of parity through the 1953 and 1954 crop years. In August 1954, however, the Republican Congress enacted a new price-support law which permitted the Secretary of Agriculture to guarantee prices to cooperating farmers at between 82.5 and 90 percent of parity in 1955, and between 75 and 90 percent in 1956. This reflected the principle of flexible price supports which had been under discussion since 1947. The price-support figure under the new law would be determined by production. Higher output would dictate lower support prices. It was hoped this formula would discourage production.

Secretary Benson used his discretionary powers to loosen production controls. Consequently, surpluses mounted and large quantities of farm commodities flowed into storage, which in turn increased government costs for the program. Total net farm income dropped from $15.3 billion in 1952 to $13.3 billion in 1953 and to $12.6 billion in 1954. It went even lower in 1955 and 1956. Uneasy over the possible political consequences of decreasing agricultural prices, Congress, in April 1956, passed the administration's soil-bank plan, which provided payments to farmers for taking farmland out of production.

Surplus production continued to be the essence of the farm problem. Reduced acreage, increased exports, and higher home consumption could not guarantee prices favorable to farmers. In July 1954, Congress passed the Agricultural Trade Development and Assistance Act, informally known as P.L. 480, which permitted the sale of surplus farm commodities abroad for foreign currencies instead of dollars. Food could be bartered or even given away. The law encouraged domestic consumption through school lunch and welfare programs. Surpluses and low prices still prevailed. To make matters worse for farmers, prices of nonfarm commodities continued to rise, giving farm products a low exchange value.

Postwar Problems

The United States inherited a seemingly endless series of skirmishes after the second great world conflict. Yet the crises in Korea, Suez, Syria, Iraq, Jordan, and Lebanon might have been weathered with more aplomb and less internal wrangling had not the dreadful spectre of "the bomb" loomed so large.

The Korean War originated in the chaos left over from World War II. Japanese troops had surrendered there to American forces in the south and to the Russians in the north. A line to facilitate military administration was drawn at the 38th parallel, but in June, 1950, North Korean forces crossed it to invade the Republic of Korea to the south. Worried about stability in the Pacific, the United States took the matter to the United Nations which promptly asked its members to resist this aggression and asked the United States to command the necessary troops. Below, street-fighting in Seoul raged repeatedly. The capitol of South Korea changed hands four times during the war.

Then Wisconsin Senator Joseph McCarthy began to move. Something called an "international Communist conspiracy" hovered behind every palm tree, underlay every nationalistic squabble. McCarthy's notion was that American Communists, especially in the State Department, had let China go Communist. Now the Chinese, their every action dictated by Moscow, threatened the American sphere of influence in the Pacific. The nation hesitated, then common sense broke through. Officially censured by the Senate, McCarthy died not long after the ruin of his career.

Two Presidents saw the country through the 1950s. Truman, the snappish ex-enlisted man and former Missouri politician, shouldered his responsibilities gamely. Eisenhower, the famous general and master tactician, satisfied the country's demand for stability in an insecure world.

"Say, What Ever Happened To 'Freedom-From-Fear'?"

One effective spokesman for the liberal viewpoint during the 1950s, as he was for the 1960s, was the syndicated cartoonist Herbert Block. This sampling of his work reflects some of the main concerns of the American people during the decade that ended in 1960. The atom bomb, the hydrogen bomb, and other nuclear refinements continued to terrify the country. In his *Herblock Book* (Beacon Press, 1952), the cartoonist pointed out that "even when we had a monopoly on the atomic bomb, that didn't make us feel secure because it created new fears about what big secrets might get out. And within a couple of years after the first atomic blasts we already had the security shakes so bad that anyone who missed out on recent history might have supposed we were the only country in the world that *didn't*

"Well, Goodness—We Can't Investigate Everybody!"

All drawings: Herblock

"Somebody From Outside Must Have Influenced Them"

"Want To See Me Blow Out Everything
With One Puff?"

have the bomb instead of being the only one that had it. . . . Some secrets did get out, and it takes only one or two espionage cases to create general talk about 'all those fellows' giving away 'all our secrets'."

This national absorption with fear over "security" appears over and over again in these cartoons. Among the other problems looming large during the Eisenhower years, equal rights for black citizens and the ever-present Cold War against the Soviet Union, its satellite states, and Communist China received continuing attention. American chagrin at being beaten by the Soviet Union in launching the first earth satellites subsequently stimulated vast government outlays for scientific education and research.

"What Is This—A Game?"

"Don't Mind Me—Keep Right On Working"

United Press International

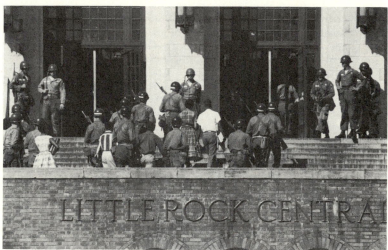

Burt Glinn, Magnum

Two developments of the 1950s significantly advanced the cause of black
equality: the Supreme Court decision that segregation in the public schools
is, *per se*, unconstitutional, and the appearance of new black leadership.
Above, long lines gather in the corridor of the Supreme Court Building
several hours before the Court opened its first hearing on the school issue
in 1952, hoping to share the fewer than fifty seats available to the public.
Below, Eisenhower sent Federal troops into Little Rock, Arkansas, in 1957,
five years after the decision, to insure the safety of the first black students
to attend Little Rock High School. Right, above, Martin Luther King, Jr.,
was arrested in Montgomery, Alabama, while leading a Negro boycott
against city bus service in 1955. King's ideal of passive, nonviolent resistance and his goal of ultimate integration dominated much of the black
movement during the 1950s.

President Eisenhower took one of the best remembered of his public stands during his farewell address on January 17, 1961, when he warned the nation to beware of the growing power of the "military–industrial complex."

Above: Charles Moore, Black Star; below: United Press International

Strong farm opposition to strict acreage and production controls prevented Congress from inaugurating firm restrictions on output. Throughout the last years of the Eisenhower administration the President and Congress sparred over farm policy, but none of the makeshift and piecemeal legislation reached the heart of the problem.

Both 1953 and 1954 were peaceful on the labor front. Some union leaders continued to demand repeal of the Taft-Hartley Act, but Congress refused to respond. In his annual economic report of January 1955, President Eisenhower recommended an increase in the minimum wage from 75 cents to 90 cents an hour and additions to the number of workers covered by the minimum-wage law. Despite strong opposition from the United States Chamber of Commerce and the National Association of Manufacturers, Congress in 1955 raised the minimum wage to $1 an hour. In 1954 unemployment compensation benefits were extended to approximately 4 million additional workers.

After 1956 the movement for greater regulation and control of labor unions became more demanding. Indeed, labor officials now battled to keep Congress from passing stronger antiunion measures. The hearings of the Select Senate Committee under Senator John L. McClellan of Arkansas scarcely served the cause of labor at all. Beginning in 1957, the Committee disclosed examples of bribery, graft, racketeering, illegal expense accounts, deals between union leaders and employers to hold wages down, and other abuses in the top levels of union leadership. Many lawmakers concluded that union members needed protection against their own leaders. In 1958 Congress passed the Welfare and Pension Plans Disclosure Act, which permitted public scrutiny of union pension and welfare funds to safeguard workers' contributions.

By 1959, Congress was prepared to restrict union power. After seven months of controversy, it passed the Labor Management Reporting and Disclosure Act, commonly called the Landrum-Griffin Act. This was the first major legislation in the field of labor-management relations since Taft-Hartley in 1947. The legislation required unions to file financial reports with the Secretary of Labor, banned convicts from holding union office, and established additional controls over secondary boycotts and picketing. Some features of the Landrum-Griffin Act received labor support, but unions generally considered it antilabor and opposed it. The new law measured the growing influence of government in the entire field of labor-management relations.

Unions continued to grow, though less rapidly than earlier. In 1955 the American Federation of Labor and the Congress of Industrial Organizations merged into one giant union with some 15 million members. By the late 1950s much of the old militancy had disappeared. Critics charged that the big unions were rich, smug, and complacent. Several factors may have accounted for the change—the conservatism of national labor leaders, high wages (the average weekly wage in manufacturing was $91 in 1960), and a primary interest in security. Unions now worked for job protection, pensions, sick leave, and paid vacations.

Trade and Aid

Much of America's postwar economic strength and prosperity rested on a thriving foreign trade. Presidents Truman and Eisenhower both worked to reduce trade barriers. When Eisenhower entered the White House, however, protectionist sentiment was growing in many quarters. Conservative Republicans who had traditionally favored high tariffs, and certain businessmen who suffered domestically from foreign competition advocated more protection for domestic industries.

Congress had periodically extended the Trade

Agreements Act of 1934, which had provided for lower tariffs and trade restrictions on a reciprocal basis, during both the Roosevelt and Truman administrations. Although Eisenhower faced somewhat stronger pressure from protectionists, Congress followed his recommendations and extended the Trade Agreements Act in 1953, 1954, 1955, and 1958. The President, under pressure, raised tariffs on watch movements and a few other products, but generally he fought for measures which would expand international trade. One of his major concerns was the balance-of-payments deficit which by the late 1950s caused a serious drain on American gold reserves. Large military expenditures overseas, private foreign investments, tourist outlays, and foreign aid, as well as spending for imports, produced the deficit. Expanded international trade, believed Eisenhower, would increase American exports and curtail the outflow of gold. The surplus of exports over imports remained large during the Eisenhower years—usually ranging from $4 billion to $6 billion a year—but even this was not enough to compensate for the United States expenditures and investments abroad.

Some of the drain on American resources was due to the foreign aid program begun in the Truman administration. The purpose of foreign aid had been twofold: first, to assist in the reconstruction of shattered economies in the war-torn countries of Western Europe and to help underdeveloped nations improve their living standards; second, and more negatively, to blunt the appeal of communism and thwart Russian expansion. Foreign aid, in short, was one means by which the United States fought the Cold War.

Eisenhower sought to maintain both his pledge of economy and his defense of American interests abroad. In most years during the 1950s the final appropriations for foreign aid varied from a low of $2.7 billion to a high of about $6 billion. Foreign aid took many forms. It included military and economic assistance, educational and technical aid, and long-term loans. Critics argued that the United States was squandering money, that waste and inefficiency were rampant, and that foreign aid did not win friends in the Cold War struggle. In the absence of any consensus on this issue, the President followed a middle course by urging increased economy and efficiency in the program while at the same time requesting enough money to accomplish the objectives which he thought necessary.

Economic Growth

No economy in the world could match the agricultural and industrial productivity of the postwar United States. Americans had solved their problems of production much earlier; still important developments in the 1950s greatly accelerated industrial efficiency. Some of the more significant technological advances grew out of the electronics revolution, particularly the development of the computer and the linkage of these electronic devices with automated machinery. This permitted programming and continuous-flow production which greatly increased industrial efficiency in those plants which adopted the new techniques.

American industry produced a flood of new products—electronic equipments, plastics, foods, detergents, medicines—all based on research and development programs. Large companies spent millions of dollars on both basic and applied research in their own laboratories and in grants to scientists in the nation's universities. By 1960 industry's expenditures for research and development amounted to some $4 billion annually and provided employment for nearly 765,000 scientists and engineers. National defense programs also relied heavily upon scientists working for large corporations and universities.

Americans had scarcely become accustomed to

the military and peacetime implications of atomic energy—the Atomic Age—before they were confronted with an equally startling development—the launching of vehicles into outer space. Following the Russian launching of two satellites in the autumn of 1957 (one of which carried two dogs), the United States inaugurated an intensive effort to equal and surpass the Russian feats in space. In April, 1958, President Eisenhower recommended that all of America's space activities, except "for those projects primarily associated with military requirements," be turned over to a new federal agency. Congress promptly passed the National Aeronautics and Space Act. This law directed the President to proceed with a "comprehensive program" for space development. The nonmilitary aspects of the program were assigned to the National Aeronautics and Space Administration (NASA), headed by a civilian. Meanwhile, on January 31, 1958, the United States placed its first satellite in orbit.

The longtime trend toward larger and larger corporate giants continued in the postwar years. The multibillion-dollar company became increasingly common in manufacturing, insurance, banking, and utilities. By 1960 corporations with assets in excess of $1 billion—less than one hundred of them—owned almost half the country's corporate wealth. The American Telephone and Telegraph Company was the nation's largest private corporation, with assets of $24.6 billion; General Motors was the largest industrial company, with assets of $12.7 billion. To hedge against shifting markets, many large corporations created conglomerates whereby they added businesses engaged in totally unrelated activities. Increasingly by 1960 mergers assumed the conglomerate form. Some corporations in control of

abundant capital resources extended their operations to foreign countries in the form of mammoth multinational corporations. Long before 1970 the sales of American-controlled foreign corporations exceeded the total national output of England and France. Backed by sophisticated technology, these giants wielded immeasurable economic and political influence in many countries.

Several major industries including electronics, automobiles, chemicals, and aircraft, relied heavily upon government defense contracts. Hundreds of thousands of workers depended on government defense spending for their jobs. The implications of this development became so serious by the end of Eisenhower's administration that the President warned: " . . . we must guard against the acquisition of unwarranted influence, whether sought or unsought, by the military-industrial complex. The potential for the disastrous rise of misplaced power exists and will persist. We must never let the weight of this combination endanger our liberties or democratic processes."

Americans produced abundantly, but neither government nor private industry had solved the need for more equitable distribution of goods and services and sufficient economic growth to absorb the growing labor force. An economic growth of about 2.9 percent annually during the 1950s could not provide jobs for everyone who wanted to work. Indeed, by the latter part of the decade, unemployment rates persisted at around 6 percent of the labor force. Even though per capita income rose to $1,968—about $180 in dollars of constant purchasing power over 1953—poverty remained a significant national phenomenon and a matter of continuing concern to national leaders.

Cultural Trends after Mid-Century

American culture reflected the restrictive pressures of technology and affluence on national thought and behavior. In *The Lonely Crowd*

(1950), sociologist David Riesman suggested that people responded to a wide variety of impersonal mass values. Vance Packard explained in

The Hidden Persuaders (1957) how experts manipulated public thinking through mass communications and motivational research. Indeed, nothing affected American cultural life as did the mass media—television, radio, movies—and its all-pervasive advertising. Television became the ultimate master of the public's attention. The three networks—NBC, CBS, and ABC—undoubtedly wielded a powerful influence for uniformity in national thought and behavior. Life styles varied, but patterned vacations and travel, superhighways and automobiles, billboards and filling stations, and motels and roadside restaurant chains added to the similarities of existence in the suburbs and lesser cities and created a pervading sameness through much of American society.

But the outward conformity was deceiving. The United States remained a remarkably open society, tolerating diversity and innovation even as it encouraged conformity. The result was a varied texture of restricted and permissive behavior which left many in a futile search for identity and place. Even for the economically successful acceptance, respect, and self-esteem often remained elusive, creating a multitude of mental and physical disabilities. In 1967 nearly 27 percent of American marriages were ending in divorce, a measure of social tension. More than 6 million Americans were classed as alcoholics. Hospitals and outpatient clinics were clogged with disturbed and worried people. Those who preferred suicide to coping with life were legion.

American attitudes toward sex demonstrated the new permissiveness. Biologist Alfred Kinsey first subjected American sex habits to objective scrutiny in his *Sexual Behavior in the Human Male* (1948) and his *Sexual Behavior in the Human Female* (1953). Later William Masters and Virginia Johnson, in their *Human Sexual Response* (1968), examined in detail biological reactions to a variety of sexual experiences. That public and private attitudes toward sex underwent change in postwar America was evident everywhere in the general decline of inhibitions. Films such as the blatantly pornographic *Deep Throat* and the more

seriously artistic *Last Tango in Paris*—duplicated by countless others—featured nudity, eroticism, and sexual violence. Classic pornography such as John Cleland's *Fanny Hill* became readily available; new novels were even more explicit. Hugh Hefner, editor of *Playboy* magazine, converted visual sex into a financial empire. The terms "hard-core porn" and "soft-core porn" entered the national vocabulary. Through twenty years of growing sexual license the Supreme Court searched for a definition of obscenity that all could understand. Finally in *Miller v. California* (1973) the Court noted that obscenity was not protected by the First Amendment and that community, not national, standards were the only proper test of what was obscene.

Some authorities insisted that the open depiction of nudity and sex did not necessarily alter the country's sexual behavior. Still the new permissiveness broadened the acceptability of premarital relations; the birth-control pill encouraged both promiscuity and trial marriages. Many admitted that cohabitation demanded its price. Relationships without love remained emotionally sterile; those with love became emotionally binding. As Karen Durbin once expressed it, "Married or single, there's no such thing as a free divorce."

Much of postwar American literature focused on the tensions within society, especially the struggle to achieve identity against impersonal forces. Leading writers presented their characters as pawns controlled by circumstances, wallowing in self-pity, and seeking nothing beyond immediate gratification or escape through death. Some earlier masters lived on into the postwar era. Ernest Hemingway wrote one successful postwar novel, *The Old Man and the Sea* (1953), before his death in 1961. John Dos Passos continued to write into the 1960s, but he failed to recapture his earlier literary power. William Faulkner turned out important works until his death in 1962. Centering his stories on Southern social problems and race relations, Faulkner became, to some critics, the nation's foremost novelist. Robert Penn Warren achieved special distinction with his novel, *All the King's Men* (1946), based on the career of Huey Long.

World War II provided the themes for some of the younger novelists. Norman Mailer's *The Naked and the Dead* (1948) and James Jones's *From Here to Eternity* (1951) dealt with the everlasting conflict between the individual soldier and the impersonalized command structure. Saul Bellow, J. D. Salinger, and Philip Roth were sensitive Jewish novelists who dealt variously with the search for identity among minorities. Bellow's *Herzog* (1964) and *Mr. Sammler's Planet* (1970), Salinger's *Franny and Zooey* (1961), and Roth's *Portnoy's Complaint* (1969) were highly representative of their work. Postwar novelists relied heavily on descriptions of violence, sex, drunkenness, dope addiction, and perversion to uncover the frailties of human society. In his *Tropic of Cancer* Henry Miller carried erotic realism beyond American literary precedents to express a completely nihilistic view of life.

Few playwrights achieved distinction. Eugene O'Neill continued his successes with such plays as *The Iceman Cometh* (1946) and *Long Day's Journey into Night* (1956). Tennessee Williams and Arthur Miller, two young dramatists, won national acclaim. Williams developed plots around violence, sex, and degeneracy in his *A Street Car Named Desire* (1947) and *Cat on a Hot Tin Roof* (1955). Miller's *Death of a Salesman*, a magnificent portrayal of human weakness, enjoyed long runs in the late forties and successful revivals thereafter. Among the poets, Wallace Stevens and Robert Frost achieved high levels of excellence.

All forms of painting experienced change. In the 1950s abstract expressionism became the principal art form, best exemplified perhaps by the work of Jackson Pollock. By the 1960s painters such as Kenneth Noland and Frank Stella went even further in abandoning representation and emphasized bold and flashy colors painted in no special pattern or design. Pop art included visual exhibits of unprecedented variety. By the 1960s many wondered what art had become. Any object, it seemed, was art if the critics and buyers so decreed. Of course, Picasso and his contemporaries had earlier faced similar criticism and bewilderment, but many argued—perhaps rightly—that history would deal less favorably with most innovators of the sixties.

Education offered opportunity as never before in the history of the United States. Between 1950 and 1966 elementary, secondary, and college enrollments jumped from 29.7 million to 55.9 million. While expansion occurred at all levels, the greatest relative increase occurred in the colleges. The number of college students more than doubled between 1950 and 1967, reaching nearly 7 million. During those years expenditures for elementary, secondary, and higher education rose from approximately $8 billion to almost $49 billion. Education became big business with some 2.5 million persons directly employed.

Following World War II the federal government greatly expanded its support of public education. The Servicemen's Readjustment Act of 1944 ("GI Bill of Rights") helped to finance the education of millions of veterans. Although Congress defeated general school-aid bills during the Truman administration, lawmakers established the National Science Foundation in 1950. This agency controlled funds for scientific research and for improvements in university instruction, especially in the natural sciences and mathematics. President Eisenhower proposed modest programs of federal aid to education, but controversies over integration, opposition to assistance for private schools, and fear of national control helped to defeat his measures. However, in 1958 Congress responded to the launching of the Russian satellite by passing the National Defense Education Act. The NDEA provided loan funds for college students and money for graduate fellowships. It authorized programs to improve the teaching of science, mathematics, and foreign languages. In 1963 Congress authorized funds for the construction of higher education facilities; two years later it added assistance for a wide range of educational programs. By

1965 the federal government was spending nearly $6 billion annually for education.

Most Americans found consolation and hope in religion as well as education. A Gallup Poll of 1968 indicated that 98 percent of the population believed in God, that almost two-thirds were church members, and that 45 percent generally attended church. In 1967 there were nearly 70 million Protestants, 46 million Catholics, and about 5 million Jews. But numbers belied the true state of religion in postwar America. Many members had only a nominal interest in church affiliation; their level of participation remained low. Secularism and materialism, science and technology, the desires and demands of modern life limited deep religious commitment to the comparative few. Still church membership remained a mark of respectability, and for some a necessary insurance for the hereafter.

Religion's limited influence reflected internal doubts and divisions as well. Dissentions within Protestantism and Catholicism as well as disputes over the precise role of the church in modern society created undeniable confusion. Among Catholics were those who clung to the Church's ancient forms while liberal communicants advocated basic changes, such as the substitution of English for Latin in the Mass. Thomas J. J. Altizer and William Hamilton produced a storm of protest from both conservative and liberal Christians with their book, *Radical Theology and the Death of God* (1966). They made clear the chasm that separated radical theologians from most churchmen.

Liberal Protestants meanwhile urged their churches to undertake broad programs of social action. Churches provided much of the leadership for social reform at both and local and national levels. Ministers and lay leaders worked for peace, campaigned for civil rights, and battled for social justice. Catholic Archbishop Patrick A. O'Boyle, Methodist Bishop John Wesley Lord, and other churchmen insisted that the voice of the church be heard on the great issues of the time. The ecumenical movement, responding to the growing liberalism and social concern, became a positive force in Protestantism. It encouraged unprecedented cooperation between Protestants and Catholics and effected mergers among a number of Protestant denominations.

Conclusion

Both the Truman and the Eisenhower administrations contributed significantly to the expanding welfare state. Truman's leadership in the field of minimum wage legislation, social security, housing, and social welfare placed his achievements in the mainstream of twentieth-century political, social, and economic reform. Although there was growing criticism of "big government" and the "welfare state" by many conservatives, Eisenhower did little to curb the trend toward greater governmental functions and powers. In fact, Eisenhower consolidated the reforms of the New Deal and Fair Deal.

While the nation was not without its problems, the gross national product and the standard of living showed good gains in the Truman-Eisenhower years. In dollars of constant purchasing power, between 1945 and 1960 annual per capita disposable income grew from $1,696 to $1,968. In other words, there was a substantial increase in the real standard of living for the majority of Americans. To most citizens the late 1950s seemed an especially good time for themselves and the nation.

SUGGESTED READINGS

There is no satisfactory biography of Truman, but consult Frank McNaughton and Walter Hehmeyer's *Harry Truman: President* (1958); Alfred Steinberg's *The Man from Missouri: The Life and Times of Harry*

S. *Truman* (1961); Cabell B. Phillips, *The Truman Presidency* (1966); and Bert Cochran, *Harry Truman and the Crisis Presidency* (1973), all of which provide useful insights into his character and administration. Also students should see Louis W. Koenig's *The Truman Administration: Its Principles and Practice* (1956); and Barton J. Bernstein and Allen J. Matusow's *The Truman Administration: A Documentary History** (1966). A general account by Eric Goldman, *The Crucial Decade—and After: America, 1945–1960** (1961), provides a lively introduction to the period. Truman's *Memoirs* (2 vols., 1955) gives a good account of his administration.

On postwar economic reconversion see Bert Hickman's *Growth and Stability in the Postwar Economy* (1961); and *United States Fiscal Policy, 1945–1959* (1961) by A. E. Holmans.

Labor problems are discussed in Joel Seidman's *American Labor from Defense to Reconversion* (1953); R. Alton Lee's *Truman and Taft-Hartley* (1966); and Arthur F. McClure, *The Truman Administration and the Problems of Postwar Labor, 1945–1948* (1969). Agricultural trends appear in *Farm Policies and Politics in the Truman Years* (1967) by Allen J. Matusow.

Politics in the Truman years are discussed by Samuel Lubell in *The Future of American Politics* (1952). On the exciting campaign of 1948 see Irwin Ross, *The Loneliest Campaign; The Truman Victory of 1948* (1968). There are several good books on other aspects of the Truman years. Housing has been considered by Richard Davies in *Housing Reform during the Truman Administration* (1966); and civil rights are discussed by Eleanor Bontecou in *The Federal Loyalty and Security Program* (1953). Other important books include Susan M. Hartmann's *Truman and the 80th Congress* (1971); William C. Berman's *The Politics of Civil Rights in the Truman Administration* (1970) and Donald R. McCoy and Richard T. Ruetten's *Quest and Response: Minority Rights and the Truman Administration* (1973).

Eisenhower presents his first administration in a favorable light in his memoirs, *Mandate for Change, 1953–1956* (1963). Many of the key historical documents relating to Eisenhower's administration are conveniently located in *The Eisenhower Administration, 1953–1961* (2 vols., 1971), edited by Robert L. Branyan and Lawrence H. Larsen. An excellent analysis of Eisenhower's political appeal can be found in Samuel Lubell's *Revolt of the Moderates* (1956). Emmet John Hughes, a speech writer for Eisenhower, discusses some of the main developments of Eisenhower's White House years in *The Ordeal of Power* (1963). See also the survey by Herbert S. Parmet, *Eisenhower and the American Crusades* (1972).

Kenneth S. Davis has written on Eisenhower's two-time opponent in *A Prophet in His Own Country: The Triumphs and Defeats of Adlai Stevenson* (1957). One of the better books on the Vice President is Earl Mayo's *Richard Nixon* (1959). Secretary of Agriculture Ezra T. Benson discussed the problems of his post in *Crossfire: The Eight Years with Eisenhower* (1962). On Eisenhower's second election see Charles A. H. Thomson's *The 1956 Presidential Campaign* (1960).

The best general survey of economic trends during the Eisenhower years is Harold G. Vatter's *The U.S. Economy in the 1950's** (1963). Another essential source is *The Economic Report of the President* published each January. On farm problems and the administration's farm policy see Ezra T. Benson's *Freedom to Farm* (1960). For brief discussions of labor's problems and advances see the pertinent parts of Joseph G. Rayback's *A History of American Labor* (1966) and Sidney Lens's *The Crisis of American Labor** (1961). On other important aspects of the economy see John Kenneth Galbraith's *The Affluent Society** (1958); Leonard S. Silk's *The Research Revolution* (1960); and *Regions, Resources, and Economic Growth** (1960) by H. S. Perloff and others.

*indicates availability in paperback.

32

The Course of Containment, 1947-1965

What gave substance to the unchanging structure of European politics in 1945 and 1946 was the military division of Europe. Against the hard fact of Russian occupation Western diplomatic efforts to free Eastern Europe were inconsequential. The Soviet Union had demonstrated both its power and its determination to manage the postwar reconstruction of those regions relieved of Nazi forces by the westward-moving Russians. It was the unchallengeable Soviet dominance throughout Eastern Europe that underlay Henry A. Wallace's growing criticism of the Truman posture of hostility toward the U.S.S.R. In his Madison Square Garden speech of September 1946, Wallace, then secretary of Commerce, urged the administration to recognize the Soviet sphere as a necessary step toward Big Three unity and peace. Truman had approved the speech beforehand, but accepted Wallace's resignation when members of Congress and the administration complained. Ultimately the continuing quarrel over Germany and Eastern Europe produced a total breakdown of the wartime alliance and a series of Western responses based on fear and insecurity.

The reasons for the disintegration of Western confidence were many. For Western members of the Grand Alliance the intensifying and apparently unending conflict with Europe's most powerful nation was scarcely reassuring, even if that conflict was confined to words. Whether the Kremlin had designs on regions beyond its immediate control was never certain, but both Soviet action and Soviet rhetoric suggested an aggressive intent. If the U.S.S.R., in solidifying its control over East-Central Europe, had chosen to defy one important body of wartime agreements, of what value would Kremlin assurances be on other questions? By 1947 the declarations of Soviet officials not only proclaimed the superiority of the Communist system and predicted its ultimate triumph but also recognized the division of the world into two ideological camps. That year Russia resurrected its world propaganda organ, the Cominform. While Britain and the United States had demobilized precipitously after the war, the U.S.S.R. had maintained a large army and air force. Now only the American monopoly of atomic weapons gave the West a military capability equal to that of Russia.

To the Truman administration the question of Soviet intentions toward the non-Soviet world became a matter of increasing concern. Churchill warned the nation in his famed Fulton, Missouri, speech of March 1946 of the need for vigilance and increased power to meet the challenge of Russian imperialism. Churchill urged a new alliance of the English-speaking peoples to offset Soviet strength. He condemned "the police governments" of Eastern Europe. An "Iron Curtain," he said, had been rung down across the center of Europe.

Already American experts in Soviet affairs had begun their examination of the Russian past for clues which might expose that nation's long-range objectives. George F. Kennan wrote from Moscow in February 1946: "The Kremlin's neurotic view of world affairs is the traditional and instinctive Russian sense of insecurity.... Russian rulers ... have learned to seek security only in patient but deadly struggle for the total destruction of rival power, never in compacts and compromises with it." No longer could the West escape a long-term struggle for power and prestige with the Soviet Union. Concluding his analysis anonymously in the July 1947 issue of *Foreign Affairs,* Kennan recommended an American policy of "long-term, patient but firm and vigilant containment of Russian expansive tendencies."

Magnifying American doubts regarding Soviet intentions was Europe's apparent inability to recover from the ravages of war. Western Europe's economic stagnation had created such a vast dollar gap by 1947 that the leading European nations were on the verge of bankruptcy. Agricultural production was low; food shortages threatened. Soviet plans for Western Europe were unknown, but Russian military preparedness, enhanced by flourishing Communist parties in France and Italy and the weakness of Western Europe itself, seemed to demand some Western response.

By 1947 Greece was in the throes of a Communist-led revolution, and Turkey, militarily weak and lying at Russia's borders, appeared especially vulnerable to Soviet encroachment. When Great Britain informed Washington that it could no longer carry the burden for eastern Mediterranean stability, President Truman decided to respond promptly. In March 1947, he asked Congress for military and economic assistance totaling $400 million for Greece and Turkey. Congress quickly voted the funds, thereby implementing the Truman Doctrine.

The Greek-Turkish aid program, which established Washington's determination to support nations and governments resisting Communist pressure, led logically to the Marshall Plan. Secretary of State George C. Marshall announced this program at Harvard University in June 1947 and secured Congressional acceptance in the Foreign Assistance Act of 1948. Aimed at the long-range economic rehabilitation of Europe, the new program placed the responsibility for economic planning on the recipient nations themselves. Secretary Marshall, as advised by the State Department's Policy Planning Staff under Soviet expert Kennan, excluded all ideological implications from his goals and offered aid to all nations which would cooperate in the program, including Russia and its satellites. Yet the Marshall Plan, though designed to blur the division of Europe, because of Soviet rejection assumed the appearance of having an anti-Soviet purpose—building centers of strength in Western Europe as part of a general American policy of containment. Between 1948 and 1952 the United States granted economic and military assistance of more than $17 billion. So beneficial was Marshall aid that the Western European economies soon surpassed their productivity of the prewar years.

Events of 1948 deepened the East-West conflict across Europe. A Communist coup in Czechoslovakia during February carried that neutral nation into the Soviet orbit. Many Americans regarded the coup as another Russian at-

Art in America: 1945–1970

Deriving his art from that of Surrealists such as Joan Miro and Yves Tanguy, Arshile Gorky developed a style in which personal forms dredged up from his mind were transcribed in paint on canvas, exhibiting representational elements but conceived in an abstract, spontaneous fashion.

Arshile Gorky (1904–1948)
The Liver is a Cock's Comb, *1944, oil on canvas*
Albright-Knox Art Gallery, Buffalo, New York.
Gift of Seymour H. Knox

During and immediately following World War II, American art emerged as the primary aesthetic force on the international art scene. Artists in Europe and later in the Orient followed the trends set by leading American painters and sculptors, a tendency that still prevails.

The vital force in American art of the 1940s and 1950s was abstraction. The investigation and exploration of abstract art took many exciting forms during the second decade of the twentieth century in Europe in the hands of painters such as Kandinsky, Malevich, and others, and many Cubist works approached abstraction in their concern for formal elements. These movements also included American followers, and a number of artists, Arthur Dove and Stanton MacDonald-Wright among them, produced counterparts of European abstraction. Nevertheless, abstraction in American art did not become really vital until its resurgence in the revolutionary work of Arshile Gorky in the mid-1940s, and at the end of that decade in the painting of Willem de Kooning, Jackson Pollock, and others. The phenomena which inspired this turn to abstraction were manifold and complex, ranging from the dream imagery of the Surrealists to the formalized, two-dimensional simplifications of Picasso, with much reinforcement by other European artists who came to America.

The dominant trend in American abstraction of this period has been termed "Action Painting" or "Abstract Expressionism." Stylistically, the movement involved the use of broad, slashing strokes, with color laid on either with brilliant, kaleidoscopic chromatic ar-

Robert Motherwell (1915–   )
Elegy to the Spanish Republic XXXIV, 1953–1954, *oil*
Albright-Knox Art Gallery, Buffalo, New York. Gift of Seymour H. Knox.

The sombreness of Robert Motherwell's eloquent series of "elegies" to the Spanish Republic reflects both the dramatic nature of Spain and a reaction to the melancholy drama of the Spanish Civil War. The alternating verticals and ovals from a rhythmic procession across the canvas. All these works share a repudiation of three-dimensional illusionism, exhibiting instead a respect for the flat canvas and picture plane.

rangements or in deeply dramatic contrasts, sometimes only of bla and white. Recognizable form all but disappeared, and the ve activity of the artist and his emotional involvement with his m dium became the message. The paint medium itself received prima emphasis, with the elimination of any suggestion of three-dime sional space and the appearance on the canvas of thick, paint i pasto, often directly applied from the tube, the obvious appeara of the shape and stroke of the paint brush, sometimes the trickle wet paint down the canvas, and in the case of Jackson Pollock, use of direct flow and dripping of paint. Not all abstraction t this form, of course; the many varieties of abstract approach cluded more lyrical works by artists such as *William Baziotes*, as well as "*Abstraction Impressionism*," geometric abstraction, and other tendencies. Contemporary sculpture also shared the abstract predilections of the painters: a new concern for open space and the relationships of solid form with this space emerged along with the introduction of movement and even sound into sculpture, particularly in the work of *Alexander Calder*.

Abstract Expressionism is still a major art form, but by the late 1950s, a reaction had set in, a reaction which took many forms. Still abstract is the work of the "color" artists who are concerned only with the effects of color, not the nature of the paint medium itself, and who often emphasize sharp, hard-edged color areas with an emphasis upon the optical, eye-jarring qualities of color relationships and contrasts, a movement known as "*Op Art*." Other artists deliberately reacted against abstraction, returning to visually recognizable images. "*Pop Art*" is perhaps the most famous of such reactions, emphasizing in sometimes witty and always cynical terms the mundane aspects of American middle-class culture—the advertisements, the billboards, the comic strip images with which we are all so familiar—taken out of context and monumentalized. Figure painting too, has once again reappeared as a major art form today, whether influenced by the vigorous brush work and color of the action painters, as in the West Coast school of *Richard Diebenkorn*, or continuing in the now classically realistic approach of *Andrew Wyeth*.

...ndy Warhol (1931–)
...ampbell's Soup Can with Peeling Label, 1962
...urtesy, The Leo Castelli Gallery, New York.

The best put-ons are those of Andy Warhol—painter, sculptor, film-maker, and celebrity—with his images of soup cans, coca-cola bottles, movie stars, and the like presented to us in a cynical, humorous way as "high art."

In the late 1940s, Willem De Kooning abandoned his semirepresentational figurative approach and created a series of black and white abstractions (left, above). The shapes and formal organizations of these works developed out of Cubism, but they exhibited a freedom, a painterly quality, and a dramatic richness alien to Cubist art. Subsequently De Kooning reacted against the elimination of color and created both abstractions and figurative paintings of slashing brush work and rich chromatic power. In the most famous of these, his series of "Women," he created a barbaric, horrific image of a monumental female (left, below). The ferociousness of the image is equivalent to that of his technique.

Above: Willem de Kooning (1904–   )
Painting. 1948
Collection, The Museum of Modern Art, New York. Purchase.
Below: Willem de Kooning
Woman, I, 1950–1952
Collection, The Museum of Modern Art, New York. Purchase.

Until the last years of his life, Franz Kline remained within the limits of black and white abstraction. Here, even more than with De Kooning, the breadth and power of the paintbrush is apparent, as the artist builds up an architecture of black monolithic strokes against a white background.

anz Kline (1910–   )
ahoning, 1956, oil on canvas
llection, Whitney Museum of American Art, New York.

Jackson Pollock is probably the most internationally famous
American artist of the mid-century. Like De Kooning,
Kline, and Motherwell, he too at times worked only with
black and white tones. In his most famous works, he
poured and splattered the paint directly on the canvas,
weaving endless rhythyms back and forth, creating a
complex web involving the eye in a labyrinth of strands,
basically controlled but with some accidental elements.
Many of these paintings are enormous, and Pollock is one
of the first artists to create environments which surround
and incorporate the viewer in an intriguing, unfamiliar
world.

Above: Jackson Pollock (1912–1956)
Autumn Rhythm, 1950, *oil on canvas*
The Metropolitan Museum of Art, George A. Hearn Fund, 1957.
Below: Jackson Pollock
Portrait and a Dream, 1953, *enamel on canvas*
Dallas Museum of Fine Arts. Gift of Mr. and Mrs. Algur H. Meadows and the Meadows Foundation, Inc.

Not all the Abstract Expressionists eschewed color: Hans Hofmann, for instance, expressed joy through the use of all the colors in the spectrum. His pictures have been likened to a lush garden in their coloration, but Hofmann is essentially an abstract humanist whose love of life is expressed in terms of the painter's medium—raw color, vigorous brush work, flat canvas.

Adolph Gottlieb forsook his earlier, mysterious hieroglyphs for a series of depictions of circular forms and bursts of color juxtaposed to one another. Still they are symbolic in some enigmatic way—of male and female, of cosmic entities, or of other possible meanings.

Above: Hans Hofmann (1880–   )
The Pond
Collection, Richard Brown Baker, New York.
Right: Adolph Gottlieb (1903–   )
Transfiguration #2, 1958, *oil*
Collection of Mrs. Harriet Weiner.

Softer, more diffuse color radiates from the paintings of Mark Rothko who creates walls of color, like Pollock's canvases environmental, but totally non-linear. The glow of color in Rothko's work foreshadowed the color painters of the last ten years.

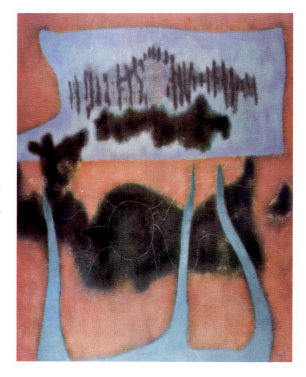

William Baziotes is one of several artists who created abstractions which sometimes took on archaeological, sometimes aquatic connotations. But instead of using dynamic action in his paint application, he creates a soft, poetic, and lyrical mood.

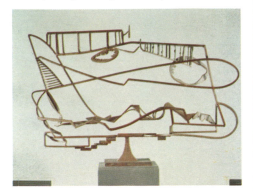

David Smith (1912–   )
Hudson River Landscape, 1951, *steel*
Collection, Whitney Museum of American Art, New York.

The Abstract Expressionist painters had their sculptural equivalents and the most famous among them has been David Smith. Smith's earlier abstractions involve interwoven linear patterns, equivalent to those in the paintings of Pollock, where lines not only constantly change but where these lines define contrasting abstract forms in space (above). Later, Smith moved on to monolithic, totemic images of powerful, solid masses of metal, in brilliant and powerful block form (right). Smith's work clearly demonstrates that in the last twenty years, sculpture has moved beyond its traditional range to incorporate landscape and still-life subjects.

David Smith, Cubi XXVII. *The Solomon R. Guggenheim Museum Collection.*

Until recently wood has been the major medium of Louise Nevelson. Her brooding and mysterious images created from both accidentally broken and found machine-made pieces, have gained new meanings as she has juxtaposed them. Diverse parts are sometimes harmonized by the application throughout of a soft, matte black black paint.

With Alexander Calder's work, movement and sound join the expected properties of sculpture. The juxtaposition of fragile lines and flat color elements in his mobiles suggests a sculptural equivalent of Miro's fantasies.

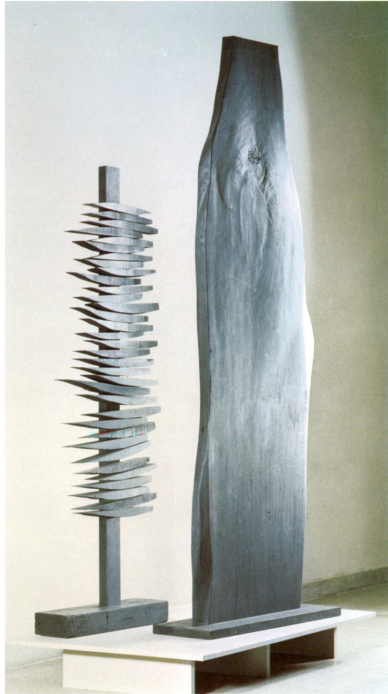

Louise Nevelson (1904–   ), First Personage, 1956 or 1957, wood. The Brooklyn Museum, Dick S. Ramsay Fund.

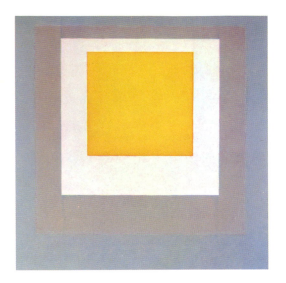

The more cerebral work of the geometric abstractionists, whose simplification of form and elimination of the nonessential belies a profound psychological and emotional effect, descends directly from Cubism. Josef Albers has created hundreds of paintings entitled "Homage to the Square" (left) in which the colors of three or four squares react upon one another and at the same time create the illusion of regression or of forward motion. A logical next step appears in the work of his pupil, Richard Anuskiewicz, the leading optical artist in America, whose rigidly geometric but daring color juxtapositions and mergings seem to accomplish impossible three-dimensional movements of colors back and forth from the picture plane.

Above: Josef Albers (1888–   ), Homage to the Square: "Ascending," 1953, oil on composition board. Collection, Whitney Museum of American Art, New York. Right: Richard Anuskiewicz (1930–   ), Manipest, 1965, liquitex on board. The Newark Museum. Purchase 1966, Wallace M. Scudder Bequest.

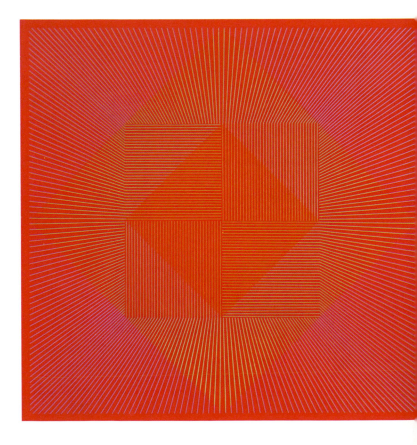

Anuskiewicz's color patterns
re complex, Ellsworth Kelly has
ken color to the other extreme
d monumentalized it by mag-
fying large, color areas of
illiant hue enshrined for their
n sake (right, above). He
hieves power through mini-
alization. Another approach
color appears in the work of
e Washington Color School
d its finest practitioner,
orris Louis (right, below).
haracteristically this group of
tists uses stripes, bands, or
ils, sometimes opaque, some-
nes transparent, vertically in-
relating with each other.

ve: Ellsworth Kelly (1923–   ), Green,
e, Red, 1964, oil on canvas. Collection,
itney Museum of American Art, New York.
ht: Morris Louis (1912–1962), Capricorn,
o–1961. Private Collection, Courtesy of
re Emmerich Gallery.

Although Abstract Expressionism reached its peak in the late 1950s, the color artists, the minimalists, and the optical painters proved that abstraction could be investigated in many new ways. On the other hand, one can also speak of a reaction to abstraction, though not, certainly, a "return" to the figure if that would suggest a recurrent traditionalism. Rather, representational art took on a new face, particularly among the "Pop" artists who, in fact, were influenced by the Abstract Expressionists in their raw color, the flatness of their images, and the power of the shapes that make up these images. A transitional figure, Jasper Johns presents us with everyday, familiar forms—targets, flags, maps, numerals—but uses a painterly approach which is exciting and amusing, at once familiar and yet mysterious (left). James Rosenquist is heir to commercial advertising but his strangely mixed images, blurred edges, and magnified scale suggest something hallucinatory and surreal (above). Roy Lichtenstein, the master of the magnified comic strip with his giant ben-day dots, is never so effective as when he parodies the Abstract Expressionists and their brush work (left, below).

Left: Roy Lichtenstein (1923–   ), Little Big Painting, 1965. Collection, Whitney Museum of American Art, New York. Left, above: Jasper Johns (1930–   ), Target with Four Faces, 1955, mixed media. Collection, The Museum of Modern Art, New York. Gift of Mr. and Mrs. Robert C. Scull. Top: James Rosenquist (1933–   ), Silver Skies, 1962. Courtesy, The Leo Castelli Gallery, New York. Collection, Mr. and Mrs. Robert C. Scull.

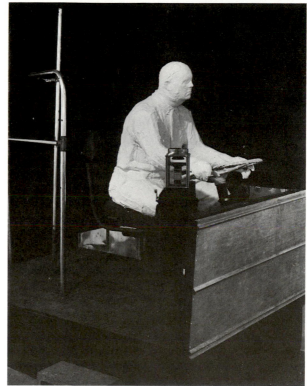

"Pop" sculpture also exists, notably at the hands of Claes Oldenburg, whose garishly colored giant hamburgers (below) take on a new reality while preserving the humor of "Pop." Of late, he has moved on to soft, vinyl, everyday images—typewriters, electric fans—and to monuments so gigantic that they almost equal "Pop" architecture. Not really an artist of this movement but often related to it, George Segal creates white, plaster Everyman images, figures engaged in mundane, everyday activities (right). Segal is divorced from "Pop" in the sense of loneliness and melancholy he achieves: part of this inheres in his medium, part in his subjects, and part in his compositions and interpretations.

Above: George Segal (1924–) Bus Driver, 1962, figure of plaster over cheesecloth, bus parts, Collection, The Museum of Modern Art, New York, Philip Johnson Fund. Below: Claes Oldenburg (1929–), Dual Hamburgers, 1962, painted plaster. Collection, The Museum of Modern Art, New York, Philip Johnson Fund.

Once a highly able and successful West Coast Abstract Expressionist, in the late 1950s Richard Diebenkorn divorced himself from that movement to paint figurative works while still utilizing the expressive techniques of his earlier style (left). In fact, along with David Park and Elmer Bischoff, he was and is one of the leaders of a whole new group of West Coast figure painters. Throughout the artistic revolutions of the last twenty years, however, more traditional, detailed, and realistic approaches to painting have by no means disappeared. In fact, the haunting emotionalism of Andrew Wyeth (below), certainly the most famous and best-loved living American painter, reminds us not only of the heritage of American painting but of its incredible diversity.

Richard Diebenkorn (1922–), Girl With Cups, 1957, *oil on canvas*
Collection, Richard Brown Baker, New York.

Andrew Wyeth (1917–), Christina's World, 1948, *tempera on gesso pa*
Collection, The Museum of Modern Art, New York, Purchase.

tempt to move the Iron Curtain westward. In June a Soviet blockade of the Western land routes into West Berlin, designed especially to counter the Western decision to organize the British, French, and American zones of occupation into a West German state, only confirmed that judgment. Britain and the United States responded with the famed Berlin airlift which supplied the beleaguered city until Stalin, early in 1949, called off the blockade.

Such apparent Soviet aggressiveness convinced many Americans and Europeans that the paramount issue was no longer that of recovering influence in Eastern Europe but of preserving Western Europe's independence. From this fear evolved the North Atlantic Treaty, signed on April 4, 1949, by representatives of the United States, Canada, England, France, Italy, Portugal, the Netherlands, Denmark, Norway, Belgium, Luxembourg, and Iceland. Under this defense agreement, an attack against one of the signatories would be considered an attack against all members. Ratified by an overwhelming Senate majority on July 21, the pact, which provided for joint NATO forces headquartered in Paris, went into effect during August.

NATO transformed American occupation forces in Germany into defenders of Western Europe against a possible Soviet attack. Under newly appointed Secretary of State Dean Acheson's direction, the European aid program shifted from economic to military assistance. United States policy now sought to provide Western Europe the defense behind which it could move on to full economic recovery. By bringing political and economic stability to Western Europe, the United States would guarantee both its own security and the cause of peace. The Kremlin, responding to the defection of Yugoslavia in 1948, the failure of the Berlin blockade, and the creation of NATO, established the East German regime, strengthened its control over the satellites, and ultimately formed the Warsaw Pact.

Every phase of the Truman administration's economic and military program for Europe won the overwhelming support of Congress and the public. Yet powerful intellectual and political minorities questioned the wisdom of the new emphasis on military preparedness. In the absence of any clearly defined danger to America's security, some Republicans questioned the costly commitment of United States men and material to Western Europe's defense. "Just as a nation can be destroyed by war," admonished Senator Robert A. Taft, the acknowledged leader of the administration's conservative critics in Congress, "it can also be destroyed by a political and economic policy at home which destroys liberty or breaks down the financial and economic structure."

Other critics were concerned less with the expense than with the ultimate purpose of containment. Was the American effort designed to stabilize Europe and to establish the foundations for future negotiations with Russia? Or was it to underwrite an anti-Soviet crusade aimed at terminating both the Kremlin's influence in Eastern Europe and its attempt to spread communism elsewhere? For Acheson Western power would serve the laudable cause of negotiating from strength.

Still the acceptable goals of future negotiation remained unclear. To Washington officials the struggle between Russia and the United States had become ideological. As Secretary Acheson declared before the American Society of Newspaper Editors in April 1950: "We are faced with a threat . . . not only to our country but to the civilization in which we live and to the whole physical environment in which that civilization can exist. This threat is the principal problem that confronts the . . . United States in the world today." Clearly a struggle defined in such terms provided little hope for future settlements. Soviet danger, so defined, made necessary the defense of Western society, but no American leader could explain how military containment in Europe might resolve the ideological threat or dismantle the Iron Curtain. United States effort could stabilize and contain the Soviet forward position; short of war, it could not do more.

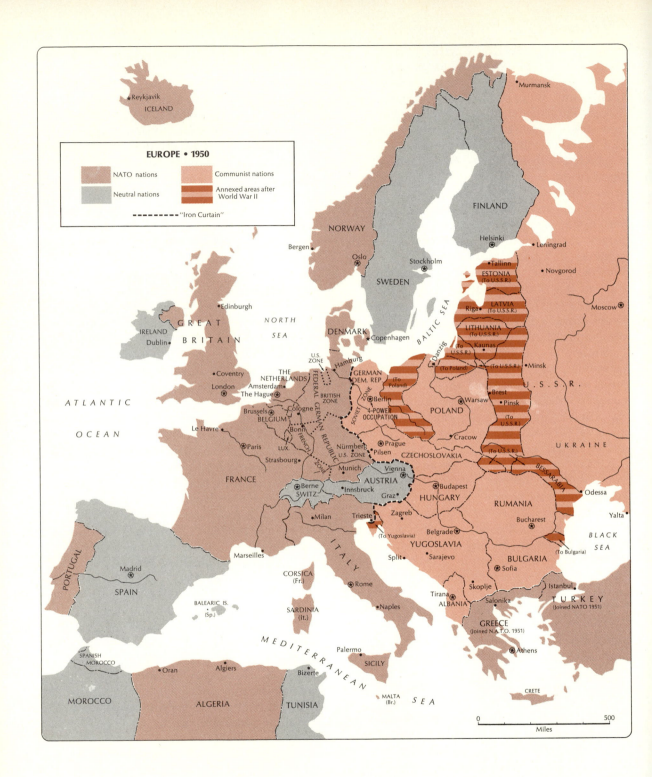

EUROPE • 1950

NATO nations

Neutral nations

Communist nations

Annexed areas after
World War II

- - - - - "Iron Curtain"

ICELAND
★Reykjavik

• Murmansk

FINLAND

NORWAY
Bergen•
Oslo⊛

• Helsinki
Leningrad•

SWEDEN
Stockholm

Tallinn
ESTONIA
(To U.S.S.R.)

• Novgorod

Riga•
LATVIA
(To U.S.S.R.)

Moscow⊛

GREAT
BRITAIN
Edinburgh•

NORTH
SEA

DENMARK
Copenhagen•

LITHUANIA
(To U.S.S.R.)
Kaunas•

IRELAND
Dublin•

BALTIC SEA

Danzig
(To
U.S.S.R.)

(To U.S.S.R.)

Minsk•

IRELAND

Coventry•

THE
NETHERLANDS
Amsterdam•
The Hague⊛

U.S.
ZONE
Hamburg•

GERMAN
DEM. REP.
(To
Poland)

(To Poland)

U.S.S.R.

London•

BRITISH
ZONE

Berlin⊛

Warsaw⊛

Brest•
Pinsk•

Brussels•
BELGIUM

Cologne•

SOVIET
ZONE

4-POWER
OCCUPATION

POLAND

(To
U.S.S.R.)

ATLANTIC

Le Havre•

Bonn⊛
FRENCH
ZONE

UKRAINE

OCEAN

Paris•

LUX.

Nürmberg•
U.S. ZONE

Pilsen•
Prague•

Cracow•

(To U.S.S.R.)

Strasbourg•

CZECHOSLOVAKIA

BESSARABIA

FRANCE

Munich•

Vienna⊛
AUSTRIA

Berne⊛
SWITZ.

Innsbruck•

Graz•

Budapest⊛

HUNGARY

Odessa•

Yalta•

Milan•

Trieste•
(To Yugoslavia)

Zagreb•

RUMANIA

Bucharest⊛

BLACK

PORTUGAL

Madrid⊛

Marseilles•

CORSICA
(Fr.)

Rome⊛

Belgrade⊛

YUGOSLAVIA

SEA

Split•

Sarajevo•

BULGARIA

SPAIN

BALEARIC IS.
(Sp.)

SARDINIA
(It.)

Naples•

Tirana•
ALBANIA

Sofia•

Skoplje•

Salonika•

Istanbul•

TURKEY
(Joined NATO 1951)

SPANISH
MOROCCO

Palermo•

SICILY

GREECE
(Joined N.A.T.O. 1951)

CRETE

MEDITERRANEAN

Athens⊛

MOROCCO

Oran•

Algiers•

Bizerte•

SEA

MALTA
(Br.)

ALGERIA

TUNISIA

0   500
Miles

Events in Asia soon disturbed the strong foreign policy consensus in Washington. During 1949, increasingly significant victories by Mao Tsetung's Red Army in China shook the American people emotionally and politically as had few other issues in the country's history. In 1945 Japan's capitulation alone appeared sufficient to establish the foundation for political and military stability throughout the Orient. But Japanese power and aggressiveness had not been the only threats to a stable, Western-oriented Asia. For generations South and Southeast Asia had been the exclusive domain of the European imperial nations, and it was the massive presence of the Occident which gave the region its political stability. Japan's initial success in driving the Western Powers out of the Pacific had changed all that; Tokyo had fostered and strengthened a feeling of increasing significance to modern Asia: nationalism. Indeed, so successful was Japan's deliberate effort to incite anti-Western sentiment in lands which came under its control that by 1945 the old Western-dominated order could not be resurrected at reasonable cost.

Franklin D. Roosevelt, who took the Atlantic Charter seriously, had strongly urged the Allies to apply self-determination universally. Roosevelt was concerned especially that the French give independence to Indochina, but he also urged the reluctant Churchill to promise freedom to England's Asian colonies. If the United States was prepared to withdraw from the Philippines (as it did in 1946), England and France, he declared, should do no less in areas under their control. Britain gave way to the inevitable. Beginning in 1947 London granted independence to India, Pakistan, Burma, and Ceylon. The Dutch, facing determined nationalist opposition, granted self-determination to Indonesia in 1948. Meanwhile, France's decision to remain in Indochina subjected that colony, after 1946, to a bitter civil war. Washington, requiring French cooperation in Europe, did not press France to dismantle its empire in the Far East.

Such vast changes incident to nation building tended to produce violence and turmoil where there had been political stability. Power may abhor a vacuum, but this seemed to matter little, for the Pacific war had reduced Japan, Asia's traditional aggressor, to an enfeebled state. The United States occupation of Japan, commencing in September, 1945, had placed every aspect of that nation's economic and political life under the severest scrutiny and control. Directed by General Douglas MacArthur, Supreme Commander of the Allied Powers (SCAP), occupation policy methodically erased the sources of Japanese expansionism and political repression. A multinational tribunal tried the top wartime Japanese officials, including two former premiers, and sentenced them to death as war criminals, thus breaking the influence of Japan's former leadership. Occupation policy did not seek to destroy the Japanese economy but rather to limit the economic and political power of the mammoth prewar industrial combines. As a further precaution, Japan's 1946 constitution limited that country's military forces to those required for domestic security. Later, when Washington recognized the power vacuum created by Japan's military weakness, it would foster the expansion of the Japanese economy.

The Chinese Debacle

During the critical days of November–December 1941, the United States had chosen war with Japan rather than compromise at China's expense. Thereafter the United States had the power to save the Chinese central government of Chiang Kai-shek from its external enemies; after 1943, as the war with Japan raged on, it was not certain that American arms could save Chiang from the Chinese Communists who fought the Japanese from their strongholds in the North. So extensive was the wartime corruption in the central government that by 1944 United States officials readily predicted Chiang's ultimate failure to hold China. When the global war ended in 1945, the United States, as the dominant Pacific power, faced the task of reconciling the two ancient and implacable enemies in China—Chiang and the Communist Mao Tsetung.

Roosevelt's chief postwar goal in the Far East had been the development of a strong, united, and democratic China, which might serve as a stabilizing force throughout Asia. President Truman, adopting this goal, dispatched the recently retired General George C. Marshall to China in December 1945 to arrange a truce and, if possible, mediate the establishment of a coalition government. Although it seemed for a time that Marshall might succeed, his mission simply delayed for a moment an irrepressible war—irrepressible because neither the Communists nor the Nationalists would trust the other side or compromise on essential points. When Marshall abandoned his mission in early 1947, aiming a parting blast at Nationalists and Communists alike, the civil war resumed on an ever-wider scale.

Throughout 1948 the Nationalists' position deteriorated rapidly. Incompetence and corruption, inflation, and other problems had left the Nationalist party—the Kuomintang—greatly weakened. For too long the regime had been bound to the landlord and banker-merchant interests and had ignored the desperate plight of most Chinese. Lacking honesty, efficient organization, and understanding, it was unable to compete successfully for popular support with the highly integrated, disciplined, and land-reform-oriented party of Mao Tse-tung. The Kuomintang's military debacles were compounded by Chiang's strategic blunders. Ignoring his American advisers, he overextended his defense lines by invading northern China. There his armies assumed positions within Chinese cities and lost all options for maneuver or retreat. Harried and battered by Mao's evergrowing and highly motivated Red Army, Chiang's army was disastrously defeated. He withdrew with remnants of his following to Formosa in December 1949. Meanwhile, in October, Mao established the People's Republic of China, decreed his government's devotion to communism, established ties of friendship with the Soviet Union, and commenced a great crusade against American presence in the Far East.

China and the Great Debate

Nationalist China's debacle fell heavily on the Truman leadership. To explain Chiang's failure, the State Department, in August 1949, published the famed China White Paper, a 1,000-page document which sought to prove that the Chinese revolution was indigenous in its causes and almost totally beyond American power to control. The more than $2 billion in grants and credits which the Kuomintang had received from the United States, ran the official argument, represented far greater economic and military resources than those available to the Chinese Communists. Chiang, the victim of a genuine and widespread revolution, failed because of

poor leadership and a woeful lack of will to fight among his soldiers. The Communist victory, although unwanted, was not necessarily a danger to American interests. The Chinese revolution represented internal pressures, not an international conspiracy. If nationalism in India or Burma aimed at liberation from alien rule, that of China sought the strength and unity needed to solidify Chinese sovereignty against foreign encroachment and exploitative treaties.

Arguments that attributed Chiang's defeat to the failures of the Nationalist regime itself did not survive the bitter debate that followed. Those who regarded any Communist-led uprising as part of a global conspiracy could only regard the Communist victory in China as a stupendous triumph for international communism, centered in Moscow, in its course of world domination. To many Americans it was inconceivable that a country as powerful as the United States could not have saved Chiang. The State Department, and with it the Democratic administration, were especially vulnerable to attack because the Department had not taken Congress (or the American people) into its confidence. It had neglected to commit its potential critics publicly to the idea that, short of committing the United States to a land war in Asia, the Washington government could not save Chiang. Thus in August 1949, Republican Senator Styles Bridges could dub the White Paper "a 1,054-page whitewash of a wishful, do-nothing policy which has succeeded only in placing Asia in danger of Soviet conquest."

Such charges of failure won the immediate support of many "old China hands"—officials, missionaries, merchants, students, and travelers who had spent time in China and who hoped for the return of Chiang Kai-shek to the mainland. But it was left for Senator Joseph McCarthy of Wisconsin to submerge the China issue almost irretrievably in the mire of politics and emotions. In a sensational Wheeling, West Virginia, speech of February 1950, McCarthy captured the nation's attention with the charge that the State Department was thoroughly infested with communists. This unsubstantiated accusation not only inaugurated another phase in the growing partisanship over Far Eastern policy but also provided an explanation for the collapse of Chiang Kai-shek. If the United States had failed to sustain his regime (went the new explanation), the answer lay not in Chinese Nationalist failures

or the limits of American influence in Asia, but rather in the treason of State Department officials. Supported by an argument that not only explained past failures but also promised Chiang's return to power on the mainland, McCarthy rapidly gained an unshakable influence over both American attitudes toward Asia and the Republican party, which he had given a winning cause. Still few Americans harbored any desire to fight the major war in the Pacific which alone would achieve Chiang's return.

During 1950 official American appraisal of events in the Far East underwent a revolutionary change. Behind this change lay the fundamental assumption—shared by many citizens—that an international conspiracy centered in the Kremlin had been responsible for all Communist-led pressures on the status quo in East and Southeast Asia. The Sino-Soviet Pact of February 1950 convinced official Washington that the U.S.S.R. had enlisted China's millions in Russia's program of global expansion. The Truman administration, following this line of reasoning, quickly committed the United States to the support of the French in Indochina. In May 1950, Secretary Acheson explained in Paris that "the United States government, convinced that neither national independence nor democratic evolution exist in any area dominated by Soviet imperialism, considers the situation to be such as to warrant its according economic aid and military equipment to the Associated States of Indochina and to France in order to assist them in restoring stability and permitting these states to pursue their peaceful and democratic development." Thus the early months of 1950 were critical in the development of global containment policy to prevent Soviet expansion in the Far East.

The Korean War

Korea became a potentially crucial area of Cold War conflict in August 1945, when General Douglas MacArthur received instructions from

the United States Joint Chiefs of Staff to accept the surrender of all Japanese forces in Korea south of the 38th parallel. Russian forces were then pouring into Manchuria and Korea, and Secretary of State Byrnes concluded that the United States would do well to maintain jurisdiction over the southern portion of the peninsula. What was occurring in Germany that year became the example for Korea. The division of Korea as a matter of administrative convenience quickly evolved into a firm division based on military power. Yet the United States, with no interest in maintaining a large military force in that country, began to withdraw its troops in November 1947. General MacArthur and the National Security Council endorsed this decision; Congress in 1949 and again in 1950 generally opposed appropriations for an American presence in Korea. In his speech of January 1950, Acheson pointedly excluded both Korea and Chinese Nationalist-held Formosa from the American defense perimeter.

Scarcely six months later, on June 25, a well-prepared North Korean army struck deep into South Korea, sending poorly trained South Korean troops reeling in disorderly retreat. Having already accepted the Communist pressures in China and Indochina as part of a global conspiracy, the Truman administration viewed the North Korean aggression across the 38th parallel as the beginning of a new Moscow-based assault upon the free world. "The attack upon the Republic of Korea," said the President, "makes it plain beyond all doubt that the international Communist movement is prepared to use armed invasion to conquer independent nations." Truman immediately ordered United States air and sea power to the assistance of the South Korean government of Syngman Rhee. When it became clear that such limited support was not enough to turn back the North Korean thrust, two divisions of American land forces under General MacArthur moved into the breach. Truman simultaneously neutralized Formosa, placing the United States Seventh Fleet in position to prevent any movement of troops between the island and the Chinese mainland. Overnight Formosa acquired a new strategic significance as part of an enlarged United States defense system in the

Pacific. The United States had meanwhile appealed to the United Nations for support and the international body sanctioned what came to be called an "international police action." Some members sent token forces to Korea. Still Washington's military restraint resulted as much from limited capability and fear of direct Soviet involvement as from the UN's desire to limit the war to Korea and terminate the fighting at an early date.

Throughout the autumn months of 1950 both objectives appeared readily achievable. By September MacArthur had demonstrated his capacity to hold South Korea and had begun operations to throw back the North Korean armies. MacArthur's landing at Inchon on September 15 met no air or ground resistance, and as American troops moved inland, they soon put the North Korean troops to flight. During October, Truman met MacArthur on Wake Island. There the two men agreed to pursue the objective of occupying the entire Korean peninsula and securing its political unification. Yet early in October the Indian Ambassador to Peking, K. M. Panikkar, advised the world that Chinese forces would enter the struggle if United Nations troops crossed the 38th parallel. Truman explained his refusal to take this warning seriously in his *Memoirs*. The problem, he wrote, "was that Mr. Panikkar had in the past played the game of the Chinese Communists. . . . It might . . . be no more than a relay of Communist propaganda. There was also then pending in . . . the General Assembly . . . a clear authorization for the United Nations commander to operate in North Korea." At Wake, moreover, MacArthur had assured the President that the Chinese would not enter a war in which they would face certain defeat.

MacArthur was wrong. As Allied troops pushed northward to within 50 miles of the Korean-Manchurian border, thousands of Chinese "volunteers" were thrown into battle. By the end of November, MacArthur's advance had been blunted by numerically superior Chinese–North Korean forces; by January 1951,

United Nations troops had grudgingly given ground to a line below the 38th parallel. Clearly the United States faced a series of momentous decisions. American officials may have rationalized the necessity of United States involvement in Korea in terms of an international Communist conspiracy, but they had no interest in a general war against China, much less the U.S.S.R. On the other hand, Washington's official explanation of the enemy demanded a victory in Korea if the United States hoped to prevent the repetition of aggression elsewhere. Clearly, the Truman administration was in serious intellectual and military trouble.

During its initial phases, the Korean War had produced no conflict in American politics. As long as the limited United States action in Korea promised perfect but inexpensive success, no Republican spokesman was moved to be critical. But once Chinese intervention had transformed the war into a long, costly stalemate, Republicans charged that Korea was another consequence of the Truman administration's basic incompetence and even "softness" on communism. Specifically, they charged, the United States government had made two blunders. First, it had not provided South Korea with an army capable of resisting the North Korean attack; second, it had publicly shunted Korea and Formosa outside the American perimeter of defense. "They knew that we had permitted the taking over of China by the Communists," declared Senator Taft, "and saw no reason why we should seriously object to the taking over of Korea. The Korean War and the problems which arise from it are the final result of the continuous sympathy toward communism which inspired American policy."

Such partisan attacks helped to drive Truman and Acheson toward a tougher policy in Asia. Blanket charges of treason leveled at the State Department forced Secretary Acheson to prove that he was as rampantly anti-Communist as his critics. In February 1951, the United States engineered a UN resolution branding Communist China an aggressor in Korea. During the spring of 1951, Acheson emphatically stated that

he would neither recognize the Peking regime nor permit the United Nations to do so. At the same time the Secretary never altered his earlier explanation for Chiang's failure—that it was the result of an internal revolution largely unrelated to Soviet policy in Asia.

General MacArthur's recall from his command in Korea, in April 1951, set off a new debate on American goals in Asia. MacArthur, temperamentally unable to accept the concept of "limited war," had become openly critical of the administration's circumspection in the conduct of the stalemated war in Korea, and called for a war to defeat communism totally in Asia. "We must win," he said. "There is no substitute for victory." The General's strategy for victory called for a blockade of the China coast, heavy air and sea bombardment of the Chinese mainland, and support for a Nationalist Chinese invasion from the island of Formosa. Truman thought the strategy exceedingly dangerous. Wearied at length with the popular general's virtual insubordination, Truman relieved MacArthur of his command. Acclaimed by millions of Americans upon his return to the United States, MacArthur defended his views before a joint session of Congress. In May 1951, before a joint congressional committee, he argued his program for victory with the chiefs of the three armed services.

MacArthur, despite triumphal tours across the nation, failed to reverse Truman policy. If the pursuit of limited war was inconsistent with the official explanations for American involvement in Korea, the President nonetheless continued to hold the line against those who took the doctrine of global conflict seriously. General Omar Bradley later summarized the administration's quarrel with MacArthur when he declared that the adoption of the MacArthur strategy would have led to a general war with Red China—"the wrong war, at the wrong place, at the wrong time, and with the wrong enemy." In October 1951, peace negotiations began in Korea at Panmunjom, although intermittent fighting continued.

Eisenhower, Dulles, and Liberation

In January 1953, President Dwight D. Eisenhower and his secretary of state, John Foster Dulles, entered office committed to goals abroad which they could not achieve. Partisan criticism of previous years had convinced too many Americans, among them key Republican leaders, that Communist influence should be not only contained but also rolled back. Yet this could be done only at the price of war—a war which not even the hard-line anti-Communists wanted. Dulles, long experienced in foreign affairs, was himself an advocate of policies which called for meeting the Communists at every point and sending them into retreat. But whatever the Secretary's desires and promises, available American power limited the Eisenhower-Dulles actions essentially to those adopted by the Truman administration. The thrust of United States policies after 1953 grew out of the same assumptions and enjoyed the same broad national support that it did earlier, and it made no substantial difference whether the government was under the control of the Republican or Democratic party. What changed in 1953 was style and rhetoric, not the substance of policy.

Soviet purpose in Europe still gave the United States only two realistic choices: either to bring overwhelming power to bear on the U.S.S.R. and force compliance with the principle of self-determination, probably at the cost of a general war, or to accept the Soviet position in East-Central Europe as the fulfillment of Russia's historic security needs and acknowledge Russia's forward position as a basis of future negotiations. President Truman, unable to make this choice, sought to stabilize the lines of demarcation while official rhetoric suggested, first, that the United States had no intention of recognizing any Soviet hegemony in Eastern Europe and, second, that successful containment would ultimately roll the Russians back to their prewar boundaries. Dulles set out to create the image of a foreign policy that would dispose of the Communist menace more effectively and completely than the Truman approach had. In his article "A Policy of Boldness," published in *Life* magazine during May 1952, Dulles rejected as inadequate the Truman-Acheson reliance on long-range containment. Democratic policy, Dulles declared, had been conceived less to eliminate the Soviet peril than to live with it, "presumably forever." The time had come, he asserted, to develop a *dynamic* foreign policy that conformed to *moral* principles. American policy must move beyond "containment"; it must anticipate the "liberation" of those who lived under compulsion behind the Iron Curtain. Dulles emphasized that liberation demanded above all that the United States avoid any European settlement recognizing Soviet control of alien peoples. At no time, however, did he suggest the means by which the United States could achieve the liberation of Eastern Europe without war.

Liberation for Eastern Europe could have no

President Eisenhower and John Foster Dulles enjoy a light moment in 1953.   (UPI photo)

relation to actual United States policies for the reason that no issue between the Soviet Union and the satellite countries was vital to American interests. Clearly any revolt behind the Iron Curtain would lead not to United States intervention but to pure embarrassment. Thus in 1956, when Russian tanks smashed a general uprising in Hungary, Dulles, though extremely distressed, refused to act. He had either to employ military force to free Hungary or to admit that events behind the Iron Curtain were, after all, outside the area of basic American concern. Rejecting both courses as too costly, Dulles voiced a futile protest and turned to the United Nations for condemnatory resolutions. These he received often and overwhelmingly. Moscow ignored these declarations and proceeded to impose a thoroughly pro-Soviet regime on the Hungarians. Yet if the Soviets had proved their power and determination (and simultaneously the inability of Dulles's words to accomplish much against Soviet tanks), they had also discovered that their interference in the affairs of the Slavic states engendered widespread opposition and resentment. Beginning with Hungary, Soviet control over the eastern European states began to weaken.

China

With the accession of Eisenhower to the presidency, the Nationalist China bloc, composed largely of Old Guard Republicans, gained full command of America's China policy. After 1953 such men as Admiral Arthur W. Radford, chairman of the Joint Chiefs of Staff; Walter S. Robertson, Assistant Secretary of State for Far Eastern Affairs; and Senator William F. Knowland of California, chief spokesman for Nationalist China in Congress; as well as Dulles himself, determined the nation's attitudes toward China and created the rationales to support them. What this new leadership hoped to achieve in China was, in large measure, a reestablishment of the Open Door. This objective necessitated a government amenable to the goodwill and paternalism of the United States, one willing in its foreign relations to behave in a manner compatible with American interests and desires. Such a government might become, as both the Roosevelt and Truman administrations had anticipated, a core of stability in Eastern Asia and the protector of the traditional balance of power. Chiang Kai-shek's return to power on the mainland, it was assumed, would fulfill this magnificent dream.

Too responsible to follow its Far Eastern advisers into military ventures against Red China, yet too fearful of public opinion to reduce its public support of the Nationalists, the Eisenhower administration adopted a phraseology which promised the eventual destruction of the Chinese Communist government. In February 1953, the President created the impression that he was "unleashing" Chiang Kai-shek when he issued instructions that the Seventh Fleet no longer shield the mainland. Nonrecognition of the mainland regime perpetuated the illusion of Chiang's eventual triumph; at the same time, it pacified most friends of Chiang in the United States. Eisenhower no more than Truman seriously considered military ventures against the Communist Chinese. He followed instead the Truman precedent of limiting Nationalist China's activities to the defense of Formosa, pointedly writing this limitation into the bilateral defense agreement negotiated with Nationalist China in December 1954.

After American officials had made the basic decision to remain involved in the China struggle, it was only a matter of time before the offshore islands of Quemoy and Matsu would become a vexing subject in American foreign policy. Nationalist forces had occupied the islands on their retreat from the mainland to Formosa in 1949, but not until the fall of 1954 did the Chinese Communists move sufficient military equipment into the coastal areas to threaten the islands with bombardment. When Peking issued a verbal threat against Formosa in January 1955, Secretary Dulles assured Chiang that the Republic of China would not "stand alone" against invasion from the mainland. Then came the bombardment of the offshore islands. Congress promptly authorized the President to defend these islands if it appeared that any attack on them would be preliminary to an attack on Formosa itself. Although there was little or no strategic connection between the offshore islands and Formosa, the tiny islands hugging the China coast symbolized for the Kuomintang government-in-exile its eventual return to the mainland. By identifying the issue of China's future with the defense of Quemoy and Matsu, Chiang Kai-shek forced the Eisenhower administration to develop a formula which would reassure Nationalist China and yet not commit the United States to a strategically impossible position.

The Formosa Resolution of January 1955 permitted the Republican leadership to postpone any determination of policy on the offshore island issue. But when the mainland Chinese suddenly subjected these islands to a merciless shelling in September 1958, it seemed that the moment of decision had arrived. During the crisis it became evident that Chiang was the controlling element in American action. In October, Washington suggested partial demobilization of the offshore islands as a basis for negotiation, but Chiang adamantly opposed compromise. Flying to confer with the Nationalist leader, Dulles issued a communiqué at Taipei restating the American intention: "The United States recognizes that the Republic of China is the authentic spokesman for Free China and of the hopes and aspirations entertained by the great mass of the Chinese people. . . . The foundation of this mission [to return to the mainland] resides in the minds and hearts of the Chinese people." The crisis passed when Mao's forces made no effort to storm the islands. But the dream of Chiang's return to the mainland—presumably without force—still determined official American attitudes.

The New Look

President Eisenhower inherited from his Democratic predecessor a long-range military program designed to maintain a balance among the Army, Navy, and Air Force. Beginning in 1950, Truman had gradually increased the country's military production to support a higher level of American and Allied preparedness. This anticipated buildup amounted to a doubling of the nation's ground and naval strength and a tripling of its air power. During the 1952 campaign, Republican orators pledged not only a stronger defense against Communist aggression but also a reduction in federal expenditures. "Our problem," said Eisenhower, "is to achieve military strength within the limits of endurable strain upon our economy."

In a determined effort to make good the Republican campaign pledge, Eisenhower and his Secretary of Defense, the industrialist Charles E. Wilson, proceeded to reduce the military budget for 1954 from $44 billion to $34 billion, distributing the savings rather evenly among the Army, Navy, and Air Force. Termed the "New Look," the resulting military posture acquired precise meaning when the President declared in January 1954 that United States defense policy would emphasize air-atomic power, an innovation permitting the nation to wield maximum destructiveness at minimum cost. Economy-minded Republicans were delighted. Yet even with the novel emphasis on air power, the Eisenhower level of military preparedness remained considerably above that which existed before 1950.

In a New York address of January 12, 1954, Secretary Dulles attempted to elevate the New

Look into a broad strategic concept. The United States, he warned, would henceforth "depend primarily upon a great capacity to retaliate, instantly, by means and at places of our own choosing." Dulles's words implied retaliatory bombing of areas near the source of any Communist aggression, presumably the key cities of Russia and China. Although many took the new doctrine of "massive retaliation" at face value, believing that it represented a new, inexpensive, and sure method of stopping all aggression, Dulles's critics feared that the new reliance on atomic and nuclear weapons would limit the American choice in any conflict either to total inaction or to nuclear war. And it was not clear how bombing in Asia would terminate a guerrilla war; guerrillas, operating independently, would merely scatter under such attacks and resume their operations elsewhere. These doubts, expressed fully and often, compelled the administration to explain its policies so repeatedly that Walter Lippmann, in March 1954, declared official explanations of the new look so voluminous that it had become "almost a career in itself to keep up with them." As time wore on, it became clear that what had appeared initially as a novel and momentous decision really amounted to no change in policy at all. What was new in the program, declared the *Manchester*

Guardian, was Dulles's effort to convince the American people that the official strategy followed in 1954 was superior to that advanced in 1953.

At the level of actual policy, the Eisenhower administration sustained, and even extended, the Truman commitment to Europe's stabilization. Eisenhower accepted Acheson's judgment that West Germany should be rearmed and brought into the Western defense system. What prevented the resolution of this question before 1954 was the French fear of a large German military force. In this context Dulles had warned the French in December 1953 that Paris's refusal to accept German rearmament "would compel an agonizing reappraisal of the basic United States policy," the implication being that the United States would leave Western Europe to its own devices. When the French government responded to Dulles's preachments by rejecting membership in the European Defense Community, London broke the impasse by committing several British divisions to the Continent as a special guarantee to France. Thereafter, negotiations among the Western powers swiftly completed the military organization of Western Europe. West Germany entered NATO in 1955 and began to rearm in fulfillment of its obligations to Western defense.

Korea and Indochina

By the mid-fifties Europe was militarily stable. Whether that stability resulted from the economic and military reconstruction of Western Europe or from the limited intentions of Soviet policy, the United States could view Europe with supreme satisfaction. It was in Asia that United States military policies appeared incapable of bringing clear victories or permanent solutions. NATO was a reasonable military system because the Soviet threat to which it responded could be defined in general military terms. In Asia the military challenge was not well defined. Washington, it is true, had indicated that the threat to

Asia was Soviet aggression. In practice however, the United States could not react to Communist pressure in Asia as if it really emanated from the U.S.S.R. for the simple reason that Soviet power was not in evidence. And to the extent that danger came not from the Kremlin but from indigenous forces existing within Asia itself, the sources of Asian instability were more political than military. To meet such a challenge the Dulles doctrine of "massive retaliation" was worse than useless. Not even the alliances negotiated in 1951 with Australia, New Zealand, the Philippines, and Japan were very promising.

Eisenhower's first order of business in Asia was the termination of the long, enervating war in Korea. Settlement came hard. Soviet propaganda, accusing the United States of crimes against the Korean peoples, kept the situation tense. But what specifically stalled the truce negotiations even during the Truman days was the prisoner-of-war issue. When enemy prisoners in UN camps learned that the Panmunjom truce negotiations might soon terminate the war and return them to North Korea and China, several thousand indicated that they would kill themselves rather than return home. The problem of repatriation produced a deadlock in the armistice talks, as the Communist side rejected the Western view that prisoners of war be given a choice in the matter.

Suddenly, when the situation in Korea appeared utterly hopeless, the truce negotiations began to succeed. Whether the change resulted from Stalin's death or Eisenhower's alleged threat of full-scale war is not clear. Late in March 1953 the Chinese and North Koreans accepted an American suggestion that both sides exchange sick and wounded prisoners of war. Several days later the Communist negotiators agreed to the principle of voluntary repatriation. When it became clear that the Korean settlement would continue that country's division, Syngman Rhee, the president of South Korea, ordered the release of thousands of enemy prisoners who were allowed to lose themselves in the South Korean population. Washington and London disclaimed Rhee's action, and the negotiations continued. On July 27, 1953, Korean hostilities formally ended. The armistice left a divided Korea, demonstrating again a worldwide balance of power too stable to permit significant changes in areas contested by the antagonists in the Cold War.

Whatever its relationship to an international Communist conspiracy, the war in Korea had been fought in a conventional manner. In Korea nationalism had been less an issue than pure military aggression. In Indochina, however, where the United States had become equally committed to the containment of Communist influence, the struggle was primarily a guerrilla war against a remnant of European imperialism. By 1950 Ho Chi Minh, the Marxist leader of Indochinese independence, had submerged all competing nationalist groups in that region later called Vietnam into a solid anti-French phalanx. French attempts to divert the nationalistic sentiment of Indochinese to native leaders of France's choice failed. Supported by little more than the Catholic minority among their former colonists, the French suffered an endless succession of disasters in northern Indochina.

For the United States, still convinced that Ho's campaign represented less a civil war than another Moscow-directed Communist aggression, the French carried the burden of containment in Southeast Asia. Washington underwrote the French effort with shipments of material valued at more than $2 billion and by 1953 was financing 80 percent of the war costs. Despite all, Ho's guerrillas continued to inflict merciless punishment on the French troops. By February 1954, the French made it clear that they were ready to negotiate their total withdrawal from Indochina. Washington was more tenacious, for it insisted that the West avoid any compromise with Ho Chi Minh. As the *New York Times* reported early in February 1954: "The official view in Washington is that any deal with the Vietminh [the Communist-led forces of Indochina] would probably result in a Communist conquest of the whole peninsula, followed by increasing Communist pressure on the entire Southeast Asia area." The American concept of global danger would not permit a French defeat. Yet no one explained how the United States intended to achieve Ho's defeat without direct American involvement. To avoid their dilemma, Washington officials simply denied until April that the French were losing.

During the early summer of 1954, while the French went down to defeat at Dienbienphu, representatives of fourteen nations directly concerned with Far Eastern matters met at Geneva, Switzerland, to resolve the problems of Korea and Indochina. There Britain and France searched for a compromise that would permit a graceful French withdrawal. Dulles, still under extreme pressure from Americans who feared any settlement with Ho, lectured the Communist delegates at Geneva on the question of Korean unification and then returned to the United States, permitting Under Secretary Walter B. Smith to carry the burden of American diplomacy. The final Geneva agreement divided Indochina into the independent states of Laos, Cambodia, and Vietnam, the latter separated temporarily at the 17th parallel until elections, to be held in 1956, should determine the nature of its general government. Ho Chi Minh settled for the immediate control of North Vietnam under the assumption that he would soon gain South Vietnam through the peaceful agency of the ballot. Although Washington declined to sign the Geneva accords, it assured the signatories that the United States would not directly challenge the settlement.

Having been compelled to accept another Communist gain in Asia in defiance of the American doctrine of falling dominoes (the belief that the loss of one region would result automatically in the loss of others), Dulles now announced that the domino theory no longer applied. The United States, he said in July 1954, was in the process of establishing a new alliance committed to the defense of the status quo in Southeast Asia. This new pact, signed at Manila in September, brought into being the eight-nation Southeast Asia Treaty Organization, consisting of Britain, France, the United States, Australia, New Zealand, the Philippines, Thailand, and Pakistan, with headquarters at Bangkok, Thailand. Underwriting the alliance was American striking power. At Manila, Dulles let it be known that the United States would fight no more conventional wars in Asia. It would, he said, grant logistic, naval, and air support to Asian armies, but if that proved insufficient to halt Communist aggression—the only kind of aggression that Dulles recognized—the United States would resort to its weapons of massive destruction.

Meanwhile the United States assumed responsibility for South Vietnam and selected Ngo Dinh Diem, a pro-Western Catholic who had spent the civil war years in Japan and the United States, to lead the new state. Surrounded with American equipment and advisers, Diem faced an almost impossible task: competing successfully with Ho Chi Minh, his country's revered liberator, for the support of the Vietnamese people. Even Eisenhower predicted an overwhelming victory for Ho in the promised elections. When Diem called off the elections scheduled for 1956, thus thwarting Ho's dream of plucking South Vietnam without firing a shot, a renewal of the struggle for power in South Vietnam became inevitable. Thereafter Southeast Asia's stability rested, politically, on Diem's success in nation building and, militarily, on the American success in creating a defense structure in the Philippines, Thailand, Pakistan, South Vietnam, and Laos that could, singly or multilaterally, match the demonstrated power for Ho.

By the late 1950s it was clear that neither purpose was succeeding. Because Diem carried the essential burden of containment in Southeast Asia, United States officials praised his leadership as if it were performing miracles. Unfortunately those miracles were nonexistent, as was effective military power among the nation's Asian allies. Still if neither program to guarantee the political stability of Southeast Asia succeeded, the United States would one day accept a further extension of Ho's influence on the Asian mainland or attempt to prevent that extension with direct military involvement.

Crisis in the Middle East

The Middle East, like southern Asia, had become important in American diplomacy only after 1945. During 1947 President Truman, against the advice of State Department career officials, committed the United States publicly to the formation of an independent Jewish nation in the British mandate of Palestine. When in 1948 Jews established the state of Israel (and thus displaced a large number of Arabs who had long lived there), the President urged immediate recognition against the warning of Secretary Marshall, who feared that such action would alienate the entire Arab world. Only a few minutes after the Jews proclaimed their new country, on May 14, 1948, Truman's press secretary announced that the President had extended *de facto* recognition. Despite this extreme show of partisanship, United States relations with the Arab countries of the Middle East did not deteriorate measurably.

The oil-rich, Western-dominated lands rimming the southern and eastern Mediterranean emerged late as a battleground of the Cold War. It was Colonel Gamal Abdel Nasser, ruler of Egypt after 1952, who was instrumental in bringing big-power rivalry into the Middle East. A spokesman for both Egyptian nationalism and Pan-Arabism, Nasser early inaugurated a persistent propaganda campaign against the British and Western presence in the Middle East. During 1954, after managing to eliminate British control of the Suez Canal, he launched grandiose plans for the economic rehabilitation of Egypt through a vast irrigation project—the Aswan Dam. For this purpose, Nasser received pledges of loans from Britain, the United States, and the International Bank. Suddenly the promising situation exploded in the Egyptian's face. Nasser had accepted aid and promises of aid from Europe and America at the same time that the controlled Cairo press reviled the West, extolled Russia, and challenged Israel. When Nasser, playing both sides of the street, turned to the Soviet bloc for arms and a large loan, Secretary of State Dulles, in July 1956, announced that he was withdrawing the American offer to finance the Aswan Dam. When both Britain and the International Bank followed the American lead, Nasser retaliated on July 26 by seizing the privately operated Suez Canal.

Then followed three months of tense negotiations among interested parties. Nasser agreed to compensate the owners of canal stock, but what disturbed the British and French was Egyptian control of a waterway that for them possessed great strategic significance. Though Nasser pledged not to interfere with free navigation, neither Britain nor France was prepared to accept such assurances from a man they considered untrustworthy. They would not, as Britain's Anthony Eden said, allow such a leader "to have his thumb at our windpipe." Convinced that Nasser would respond only to force, Britain and France quietly prepared for direct military action. On October 29, 1956, the Israeli government, after consulting with the British and French, sent its armies across the Egyptian border in ostensible retaliation for Egyptian raids on its territory. Britain and France then demanded that both sides in the ensuing Sinai war keep away from the canal. When Nasser ignored them, Anglo-French planes bombed Egyptian airfields. On November 5 and 6 British and French troops landed at Port Said and advanced southward along the canal. Nasser, in an act of desperation, scuttled ships at the canal's mouth to deny its use to the invaders.

Informed world opinion ran heavily against Britain, France, and Israel. The United States led the movement for condemnatory resolutions in the United Nations. On November 2 the General Assembly adopted an American resolution asking all parties to observe a truce and to pull back behind the 1949 armistice lines. Isolated diplomatically, Britain and France complied with the United Nations request in December. The Soviet Union, which emerged from the crisis as the defender of Arab nationalism, alone gained from the crisis.

American policy in the Middle East required some reassessment. President Eisenhower's message of January 5, 1957, was addressed to that need. The President requested a congressional grant of authority to employ necessary means to blunt the extension of Soviet power in the area of the Mediterranean. After vigorous debate, Congress, on March 7, empowered the President to inaugurate a program of economic and military aid in the area. The joint resolution declared America's determination "to use armed forces to assist any such nation or group of nations requesting assistance against armed aggression from any country controlled by international communism." Whether Congress and the President assumed that threats to the status quo could emanate only from the Kremlin or whether they simply employed the concept of Russian aggression to rationalize any costly policy they chose to undertake was not clear. In any event, the so-called Eisenhower Doctrine rested on two insecure foundations, one intellectual and one military. It obscured the role of Arab nationalism in Middle Eastern instability; and because it viewed the problem of the Middle East in ideological terms, the doctrine committed the United States to stability in a region where there were few strong or stable states.

The years after Suez were troubled ones for the Middle East, and in one way or another the United States was caught up in its broils. The Arab states and Israel were locked in an arms race; the Arabs squabbled among themselves, dividing into shifting alignments. Nasser's Egypt and Syria, avowedly neutralist but in reality virulently anti-American, were amalgamated into the United Arab Republic in 1958. Turkey, Iran, and Iraq—all states of the northern tier—were generally pro-Western. These three states Dulles had tied to Britain and Pakistan to form the largely ineffective Central Treaty Organization in 1955. Lebanon, Saudi Arabia, and Jordan vacillated between the extremes. In 1957 King Hussein of Jordan, bolstered by the dispatch to the eastern Mediterranean of the United States Sixth Fleet, was able to survive an attempted coup and move his regime a step closer diplomatically to the United States and Great Britain. Scarcely a year later, hitherto pro-Western Iraq moved in the opposite direction after a successful palace revolution. Nevertheless the new Iraqi government received prompt American recognition.

By mid-1958, pro-Nasser terrorists and insurrectionists threatened the governments of Lebanon and Jordan. Both nations complained to the United Nations. When that organization, largely because of Soviet obstructionism, was unable to act, Lebanon and Jordan appealed to the United States and Britain. An American Army brigade, flown into Lebanon from West Germany, and a regiment of British paratroopers, dropped into Jordan, saved the two pro-Western regimes. For the United States the Lebanon landing was as daring as it was significant in aiding Middle Eastern stability. Again the pressures were only obliquely Communist-inspired, but the American commitment to stability in the Middle East was almost absolute, threatening Washington with permanent involvement in Arab politics. Fortunately, the region now entered an era of relative stability. But Pan-Arabism of the Nasser variety—highly nationalistic and anti-Western—did not die.

The Changing Cold War

Under the Eisenhower-Dulles leadership the Cold War progressed at two levels. The innumerable crises of the mid-fifties, whether directly attributable to the Soviet Union or not, had the effect of sustaining a high level of Soviet-American rivalry. Inured to the idea that Soviet ambition was insatiable and its machinations omnipresent, Dulles tended to confront every Kremlin action with uncompromising opposition, even at the price, he said, of going to the brink of war. It is doubtful whether any postwar crisis actually brought the United States and the U.S.S.R. to the brink, for in no single confrontation did both countries have interests at stake which were worth the risk of a general war.

Dulles's notion of a sharply divided world, characterized by endless and deadly conflict, became increasingly difficult to sustain. Developments in the 1950s contradicted this simple notion. At the level of negotiation the West achieved a peace treaty for Austria in 1955. By the mid-fifties, Russia had shattered the American monopoly in nuclear weapons; the search for military superiority ended in a stalemate. At the same time, America's increasing vulnerability to direct nuclear attack undermined Western European confidence in the deterrent effect of America's nuclear arsenal, especially when a conventional European war might again spare the territory of the United States. After 1958 President Charles de Gaulle of France opted for a French nuclear deterrent. Under conditions of nuclear stalemate, NATO's continued reliance on weapons of massive destruction, all under United States control, produced strains in matters of defense and diplomacy. Europeans who had no interest in living dangerously believed the time had arrived to negotiate a détente with the Soviet Union. Confidence born of economic recovery and the perennial experience of successful coexistence with the Soviet bloc contributed to the growing spirit of European independence.

Soviet policies contributed to the further erosion of Cold War insecurity. The death of Stalin in 1953 promised to free Soviet policy of the hard and seldom-reassuring behavior of the previous years. After 1956 the Kremlin's new "collective leadership," headed by Marshal N. A. Bulganin and Nikita Khrushchev, removed Stalinist elements from positions of authority and adopted foreign-policy statements which suggested new, imaginative, and hopeful approaches to world problems. Conceding the irrationality of nuclear war, Russia now officially adopted the doctrines of "peaceful coexistence" and the "noninevitability of war."

Soviet policies of economic competition and coexistence undoubtedly permitted the Kremlin to establish wider and more satisfactory relations with much of the Afro-Asian world. Yet they produced no substantial change in the diplomatic stalemate with the West. The Big Four Geneva Summit Conference of July, 1955, established a mood of cordiality. The spokesmen of Britain, France, Russia, and the United States agreed that, whatever their differences, they would not resort to war to resolve them. Beyond that no agreements were possible. Again in 1957, buoyed by the prestige of launching the first earth satellites, the Soviets pressed for a new summit meeting to discuss disarmament and diplomatic détente, emphasizing their campaign with a public exchange of letters with Western heads of state. During the Middle East crisis of 1958 the Kremlin was noticeably more restrained than it had been two years earlier in the Suez affair. Immediately thereafter the Kremlin veered sharply back toward the Stalinist path. When Khrushchev managed finally to arrange the Paris Summit Conference of 1960, he chose to terminate it abruptly by demanding—but not receiving—a public apology from Eisenhower. Francis G. Powers and his U-2 spy plane, shot down over Russia, were pretexts for the conference's disruption; the essential cause lay in the unwillingness of either side to compromise any of its long-established positions.

Such failures of diplomacy produced little concern. Somehow the issues of the 1940s no longer had any real significance. The areas of direct conflict had become so stabilized that it did not matter whether the precise issues they raised were settled or not. Not even the Berlin crisis of November 1958 could disturb the pattern. Russian Premier Nikita S. Khrushchev started the row over divided Berlin when he demanded that the West accept the city's neutralization within six months. If the West refused, he said, the Soviet Union would turn its zone over to East Germany and thus force Great Britain, the United States, and France to deal with a regime and a country whose existence they did not officially recognize. When the Western powers demurred, making clear their determination to resist such a unilateral policy, Khrushchev silently permitted the day of reckoning to pass.

Europe's very stability forced the Cold War

into the Afro-Asian world where third parties could initiate the moves which sustained the Soviet-American rivalry. In the more fluid trouble spots of Asia and Africa native leaders enjoyed a tactical independence which empowered them to embarrass both Russia and the West, even when they did not cause a direct confrontation. Khrushchev announced repeatedly that the Kremlin regarded its support for "wars of national liberation" totally legitimate, although he failed to explain what form that support would take. Still it was the Kremlin's apparent support of change that drove United States actions outside Europe increasingly into a counterrevolutionary mold. With Dulles's death in the summer of 1959, United States policy passed largely under Eisenhower's direct control.

Headline issues of the late 1950s seldom originated in the Soviet-American competition. United States diplomacy was troubled more by disagreements within the Western alliance or with the countries of Latin America than by quarrels with the U.S.S.R. Similarly, the Kremlin found its relations with China and Eastern Europe more trying and enervating than its exchanges with the West. Ideological alignments no longer had their former relevance. The struggle for power and prestige between the United States and the U.S.S.R. continued to be an important fact of international life, but it was no longer the only one of importance. By 1960 there were few fundamental decisions in world politics which either the United States or the Soviet Union could control. The Cold War was not dead. Europe was still divided. But the old East-West struggle had been consigned to narrow limits by the growing independence of nations whose leaders refused to identify their national purposes and interests with those of either of the two superpowers.

Kennedy and the Eisenhower Legacies

There was little significant disagreement on American foreign policy between John F. Kennedy and Richard M. Nixon in the presidential contest of 1960. Kennedy's narrow victory placed a Democrat back in the White House, but his record in foreign affairs could scarcely be innovative. Few of his appointments went to men who had favored a critical review of established policies. Dean Rusk, Kennedy's choice for Secretary of State, was a former Rhodes scholar, professor of political science, and, under Truman, Assistant Secretary of State for Far Eastern Affairs. Compared to Dulles, he appeared calm and self-effacing, but his association with Asian policy in 1951 and the positions he had then assumed suggested that his views toward the Communist world were as distrusting as those of his Republican predecessor. Kennedy himself forthrightly warned in his inaugural that the United States would "pay any price, bear any burden, meet any hardship, support any friend, oppose any foe to assure the survival and the success of liberty." Yet he reminded his audience that the instruments of war had far outpaced the instruments of peace.

Abroad the challenge to Kennedy was clear, yet largely unrecognized. The policies he had inherited from Eisenhower were popular because they gave the assurance of success without defining success or establishing its price. Kennedy faced the difficult, perhaps unpopular, necessity of revising many of the nation's postwar commitments, especially in Asia, which had expanded during the Eisenhower years when American purpose was largely unchallenged. The nation's capacity to control foreign events had deteriorated markedly in the 1950s, not because of American failures but because of the accretion of Russian power, the recovery of Europe, and the explosive force of nationalism in Asia and Africa.

Kennedy's initial moves were promising enough. On March 1, 1961, he announced the formation of a Peace Corps, an ingathering of generally young men and women who, as volunteers, would help to carry American technology, energy, leadership, and goodwill to the underdeveloped world. The program evoked an astonishingly favorable response both in Congress and among the nation's college students. Scarcely two weeks later, on March 13, the President proposed his Alliance for Progress to the Latin American ambassadors assembled at the White House. This program he instituted to implement the Act of Bogotá, signed by nineteen nations in September 1960, which established a cooperative program—including a ten-year American commitment of $20 billion—for Latin American economic development. The Alliance for Progress attached to the promise of aid the demand for Latin American economic and political reform. The doubtful willingness of established Latin American elites to exchange their power for United States dollars doomed the program from the beginning. But in 1961 this was not apparent.

At this promising stage disaster struck. For more than a year Fidel Castro's Cuba had confronted the United States with an embarrassing hemispheric problem. Castro's dictatorial methods, his nationalization program, his clear ties with the Soviet bloc, his support of burgeoning revolutionary movements elsewhere in Latin America, and his constant and intemperate denunciations of United States "imperialism" brought Cuban-American relations to the breaking point. Kennedy as president inherited a carefully planned counterrevolutionary movement, organized and designed by the United States Central Intelligence Agency, to overthrow the Cuban regime. By early 1961 there were from 2,000 to 3,000 rebel Cuban soldiers training in the United States for an invasion of Cuba. Other units were being organized in Guatemala.

Kennedy doubted the wisdom of the invasion planned for the spring of 1961, but so insistent were his advisers upon its feasibility that he granted a grudging consent. On April 17, 1961, some 1,300 assault troops struck the Cienaga de Zapata swamps of Las Villas Province (Bay of Pigs) in Cuba. The anticipated popular uprising did not occur. Castro's regulars demolished the invading forces, establishing the Cuban government more solidly in power than ever before. The President accepted full blame for the fiasco with good grace, but it had been a sobering experience for the new administration.

Eisenhower bequeathed Kennedy a still more dangerous challenge in Southeast Asia. Here the issues had never been clearly defined, and the United States had no such strategic advantage as it possessed in Cuba. During his final months in the White House, Eisenhower had faced the impending collapse of pro-Western regimes in both Laos and South Vietnam. The pro-Western Laotian government had no chance against the pro-Communist Pathet Lao guerrilla forces, representing the anti-Western revolutionary pressures unleashed initially by Ho Chi Minh. In August 1960, a Laotian paratroop captain, Kong Le, seized Vientiane, the capital of Laos, and proclaimed a neutralist government under Prince Souvanna Phouma. Encouraged by the United States, rightist Prince Boun Oum put Souvanna Phouma to flight. The result was to bring the Pathet Lao and the Soviet Union to the deposed Prime Minister's aid. Having inherited this explosive situation, Kennedy, in March 1961, warned Moscow, Peking, and Hanoi via television that the United States would not tolerate a Communist conquest of Laos. But during April, he followed the British and Soviet lead in calling a fourteen-nation conference in Geneva which quickly instructed Souvanna Phouma to form a coalition government including representatives of the right, center, and left in Laotian politics. The new coalition government assumed office in June 1962. By 1963 the Pathet Lao elements had deserted, driving the neutralist middle into a coalition with the right and subjecting the jungle country again to the throes of civil war.

In South Vietnam both Ngo Dinh Diem in Saigon and the Asian SEATO allies had failed to contain Ho Chi Minh. By 1961 South Vietnam faced an expanding guerrilla movement, aided and abetted by North Vietnam. Rather than desert or even modify Eisenhower's commitment to Diem, the Kennedy administration offered additional military aid and advisers. Yet Kennedy issued a stern warning to Diem on May 25, 1961: "Military pacts cannot help nations whose social injustice and economic chaos invite insurgency and penetration and subversion."

In recommitting the nation to Saigon's ultimate victory, Washington again rejected the view of Far Eastern experts that the struggle against Diem was fundamentally a civil war and thus beyond American capacity to control. To Secretary Rusk there was no civil war—only external aggression. Early in October 1961, Diem announced that he now faced regular army units. Kennedy responded by dispatching General Maxwell D. Taylor and State Department adviser Walter W. Rostow on a fact-finding mission to South Vietnam. General Taylor recommended that Washington make clear its intention to retaliate against North Vietnam, suggesting an initial force of 10,000 ground troops to guard South Vietnam's northern frontier. Kennedy clarified the United States position. "Let me assure you again," he informed Diem, "that the United States is determined to help Vietnam preserve its independence, protect its people against Communist assassins, and build a better life through economic growth."

In pursuit of this policy, the President in 1962 stepped up military aid to South Vietnam, promising victory without any resort to United States combat forces. Defense Secretary Robert S. McNamara reported optimistically that "every qualitative measurement we have shows that we're winning this war." During the summer of 1963, Diem's repression of the Buddhists produced renewed political opposition to his regime. In Washington, an embarrassed Kennedy now criticized Diem openly. In October, dissident rightist South Vietnamese generals assassinated the Vietnamese leader, encouraged by official American behavior. By the autumn of 1963, the United States had 16,000 troops in Vietnam, with a continuing commitment to an anti-Communist victory and without a plan of escape. Like Eisenhower, Kennedy had misconstrued and underestimated the enemy. The prospect of a costly American involvement continued to mount.

Kennedy and Europe

Despite his distrust of the Soviet Union, Kennedy entered the White House hopeful of discovering a more positive approach to the Cold War. He discovered quickly, however, that he had little room to maneuver within the context of established American policy. So complex, interrelated, and extensive were the nation's commitments and relationships that he felt constrained to move cautiously, reacting to situations as they developed. Kennedy no more than his predecessors would accept the status quo in Europe as the basis of negotiation. In July 1961, he proclaimed "Captive Nations Week" and urged the American people to recommit themselves to the support of the just aspirations of all peoples. He reassured the Bonn government that the United States goal in Europe was German reunification under the principle of self-determination. But he had also announced as early as January 1961 that he intended "to explore promptly all possible areas of cooperation with the Soviet Union."

Nothing had occurred to deflate the President's optimism when early in June 1961 he journeyed to Vienna to exchange views with Premier Nikita Khrushchev. For Kennedy the confrontation with the blustering Khrushchev was utterly disillusioning. "I tell you now," he said later, "that . . . was a very sober two days." Besides declaring the Soviet Union's intention to support so-called "wars of national liberation," the Soviet leader handed Kennedy a note warning the West that unless it accepted the conversion of West Berlin into a free city, the Soviet Union would sign a treaty with East Germany and turn over to that country the control of access routes into West Berlin. Kennedy reminded Khrushchev that the West was in Berlin legally and intended to remain, even at the risk of war.

Kennedy and his advisers recoiled at this demonstration of Soviet animosity. During the weeks following the new Soviet ultimatum, Democratic and Republican leaders in Congress assured the administration of their support of any policy required to protect Western access to Berlin. The President announced on July 25 an increase in United States forces through a larger draft and the call-up of some reserves. Meanwhile, East German refugees flooded through Berlin into West Germany; during August the number reached a thousand a day. Obviously the Soviets and East Germans could not permit this drain of manpower from Communist rule. On the night of August 12, the Communists sealed the border between East and West Berlin. Eventually they completely closed the Iron Curtain by erecting the Berlin Wall. Although the crisis

Drawing the line on October 22, 1962: As millions anxiously watched their TV screens, President Kennedy announced a "strict quarantine"—a naval blockade—of Russian military equipment to Cuba.

(UPI photo)

subsided, the future of West Berlin remained the key to the East-West struggle in Europe. For the Soviets the city was the pawn to compel formal Western acceptance of a divided Germany. For the United States West Berlin remained a symbol of Europe's will to hold the line against communism.

During Kennedy's second year in office, Fidel Castro and Khrushchev combined to create the most serious crisis of the Kennedy years. In January 1962, Secretary Rusk secured the expulsion of Cuba from the Organization of American States. In his news conference of September 13, 1962, the President acknowledged a steady movement of Soviet technical and military personnel onto the island. Should Cuba become an offensive military base, Kennedy warned, the United States would adopt any necessary course to protect its security. During October, members of Congress and the press clamored for a more vigorous stand. Meanwhile, secret governmental surveillance revealed the construction of offensive missile bases on Cuba. During October, administration advisers wrestled with the question of alternatives, most recommending an immediate United States attack on the island. The President, however, selected a more moderate course of action.

On October 22, 1962, in an emergency broadcast, Kennedy informed the nation of the Cuban missile threat and proclaimed "a strict quarantine on all offensive military equipment under shipment to Cuba." He called upon Khrushchev to "halt and eliminate this clandestine, reckless, and provocative threat to world peace." Any missile launched from Cuba against any nation of the Western Hemisphere, the President warned, would bring immediate retaliation against the Soviet Union itself. As a United States war fleet moved into the Atlantic to intercept Soviet cargo vessels headed for Cuba, Khrushchev agreed to dismantle the Cuban missile bases in exchange for the removal of analogous NATO weapons in Turkey. This offer Kennedy rejected, countering with the promise to lift the blockade and rule out any future invasion of Cuba provided the

Russians removed their weapons under inspection. Kennedy's action, determined as it had been, left Khrushchev with the necessary escape. The Russian leader accepted the guarantees against invasion and ordered the bases dismantled.

Unrelenting tension in Europe induced Kennedy to inaugurate a program designed to strengthen the North Atlantic Treaty Organization. At the heart of his so-called Grand Design for Europe was the laudable concept of Atlantic unity. Kennedy hesitated to define the kind of Atlantic partnership he contemplated, but he made clear his two preferences on Allied defense policy. First, he opposed French President Charles de Gaulle's effort to build an independent European nuclear deterrent, urging rather that Europe rely on the nuclear arsenal of the United States. Second, he hoped to broaden NATO's defense options by stressing the need for a "wider choice than humiliation or all-out nuclear action." This accent on flexible strategy did not rule out the development of more efficient and accurate nuclear weapons systems.

Late in 1962 Britain forced a showdown on Kennedy's design for Europe. British military planners had earlier organized their nation's nuclear defense around the United States Skybolt air-to-ground missile system. Now the Kennedy administration, having developed an alternative in the Polaris submarine missile, canceled the expensive Skybolt program. The move provoked sharp reactions in London. In an effort to soothe ruffled British feelings, Kennedy conferred with British Prime Minister Harold Macmillan at Nassau in December 1962. There he agreed to provide Britain with Polaris missiles. In addition, the two leaders, in an effort to meet the requirements of joint nuclear control, devised a multilateral defense force of nuclear-armed naval vessels manned by mixed NATO crews. At the same time, Kennedy promised American support for British entrance into the European Common Market to further cement European unity.

France's Charles de Gaulle, in a caustic January 1963 press conference, brought Kennedy's Grand Design crashing to the ground—vetoing British membership in the Common Market, rejecting membership for France in any multinational defense force, and insisting that France, no longer able to trust the United States, would develop its own nuclear deterrent.

Even as de Gaulle consigned the Grand Design to the category of lost causes, the President embarked on his final effort to reach an understanding with the U.S.S.R. In the Cuban missile crisis, Kennedy and Khrushchev had walked to the brink of disaster and recoiled with a new appreciation for the burdens which they shared. In his address at American University on June 10, 1963, Kennedy reminded Americans and Russians alike of their joint responsibility for the Cold War and of their common interest in a more rational world. This speech led directly to Kennedy's second and last major foreign-policy success. Late that summer he negotiated with Russia the Test Ban Treaty limiting nuclear testing to underground sites. Congress, responding to an upsurge of favorable public opinion, approved the treaty in September by a vote of 81 to 19. This proved to be the last major foreign policy action of Kennedy's thousand days.

Lyndon Johnson's Policies

President Johnson no more than Kennedy cared to question the assumptions and purposes of the country's foreign policies. He informed a joint session of Congress, "This nation will keep its commitments from South Viet-Nam to West Berlin." Addressing a meeting of the Associated Press in New York during April 1964, he reaffirmed the country's commitment to the Geneva agreement on Laos and to the defense of South Vietnam. Johnson, like Kennedy, accepted the validity of the domino theory. "I am not going to be the President," he said, "who saw Southeast Asia go the way China went." Symbolic of the basic continuity between the Johnson and Kennedy administrations was the new president's retention of Dean Rusk, Robert McNamara, and Walt Rostow.

Like Eisenhower and Kennedy, the new President underestimated the enemy in Vietnam. He optimistically assumed that the Saigon government, with additional American advisers, would strike a telling blow for containment in Southeast Asia. He assured the nation on February 23, 1964, that "the contest in which South Vietnam is now engaged is first and foremost a contest to be won by the Government and the people of that country for themselves." In May, Secretary of Defense McNamara predicted that the major portion of the United States military task would be completed in 1965. During August, 1964, following an alleged North Vietnamese attack on American naval vessels in the Gulf of Tonkin, Congress, at the President's request, adopted a resolution which seemed to commit it to any future action required for victory in Southeast Asia. The resolution declared that the United States was "prepared, as the President determines, to take all necessary steps, including the use of armed forces, to assist any protocol state of the Southeast Asia Collective Defense Treaty requesting assistance in defense of its freedom." At the end of 1964, when Johnson had already won reelection, the United States had stationed 23,000 members of the Armed Forces in Vietnam, and Congress had given full authorization to the use of American power in any manner necessary to secure victory.

Conclusion

Although President Eisenhower talked of new initiatives and directions in American foreign policy, he followed the same basic course laid down by Truman—the policy of containment. Eisenhower and Dulles sought to strengthen the North Atlantic Treaty Organization as a bulwark against Communist expansion in Europe, but they made no real effort to "roll back" the Iron Curtain. By 1955, Europe had achieved a balance either of interests or of nuclear deterrence. This neutralized major threats to the peace in that quarter. American attempts to apply containment to Asia were less successful. The Southeast Asia Treaty Organization, conceived as an Asian counterpart to NATO, lacked any effective military power other than that which the United States might provide. Indeed, nowhere were the alliances capable of meeting the dangers which rationalized their existence except through the largely unilateral employment of United States retaliatory power. Although the United States was able to avoid involvement in a land war in both Asia and the Middle East in the 1950s, threats to American objectives and to area stability were imminent.

After 1961 the Democratic national leadership remained wedded to policies established in the late 1940s, policies which had now hardened into dogma. Cognizant of the fact that the Cold War had changed, John F. Kennedy, in his tragically shortened presidential term, attempted—though not consistently—to establish "bridges" between East and West and to reduce the danger that miscalculation or a misunderstanding might escalate into war. Recurrent crises associated with Cuba, Berlin, and Vietnam placed Kennedy and his successor, Lyndon B. Johnson, under severe pressure to respond to what appeared to be an extension of Communist—hence Soviet and Chinese—power. Like Eisenhower, the two Democratic presidents, both intelligent and humane men, defined the Communist threat in global terms. A source of trouble in the past, this state of mind in 1964–1965 was to lead to even greater national dilemmas in the future.

On the formulation of the Truman Doctrine and the Marshall Plan see Joseph M. Jones, *The Fifteen Weeks** (1955); W. Reitzel, M. A. Kaplan, and C. G. Coblenz, *United States Foreign Policy, 1945–1955** (1956); Walter Lippmann, *The Cold War* (1947); George F. Kennan, *Memoirs, 1925–1950* (1967); Dean G. Acheson, *Present at the Creation* (1971); and John Gaddis, *Origins of the Cold War** (1972). The decision to resist Russian pressures on Berlin in 1948 can be studied in L. D. Clay's *Decision in Germany* (1950) and W. P. Davison's *The Berlin Blockade* (1958). Three excellent studies of NATO are Robert Osgood's *NATO: The Entangling Alliance* (1962); B. T. Moore's *NATO and the Future of Europe* (1958); and Klaus Knorr (ed.), *NATO and American Security* (1959). Coral Bell in *Negotiation from Strength* (1962) investigates the question of the objectives of Western foreign policy, as does Hans J. Morgenthau in his *In Defense of the National Interest* (1951).

For the China problem during and immediately after the war, see Herbert Feis's *The China Tangle: The American Effort in China from Pearl Harbor to the Marshall Mission** (1953); C. F. Romanus and Riley Sunderland's *Stilwell's Mission to China* (1953); Barbara W. Tuchman's *Stilwell and the American Experience in China, 1911–1945* (1971); Tang Tsou's *America's Failure in China, 1941–1950** (2 vols., 1967); John F. Melby's *The Mandate of Heaven: Record of a Civil War: China, 1945–1949* (1969); Akira Iriye's *Across the Pacific: An Inner History of American–East Asian Relations* (1967); and Russell D. Buhite's *Patrick J. Hurley and American Foreign Policy* (1973). On United States occupation policy in Japan see E. O. Reischauer's *The United States and Japan** (1957); Kazuo Kawai's *Japan's American Interlude* (1960); E. J. L. Van Aduard's *Japan from Surrender to Peace* (1954); F. S. Dunn's *Peace Making and the Settlement with Japan* (1963); and Russell Brines's *MacArthur's Japan* (1948). For the Truman-MacArthur controversy see J. W. Spanier's *The Truman-MacArthur Controversy and the Korean War** (1959) and Trumbull Higgins's *Korea and the Fall of MacArthur* (1960).

Books on Dulles include John R. Beal's *John Foster Dulles: A Biography* (1959); Louis L. Gerson's *John Foster Dulles* (1967); Richard Goold-Adams's *John Foster Dulles* (1962); Roscoe Drummond and Gaston Goblentz's *Duel at the Brink: John Foster Dulles' Command of American Power* (1960); and Paul Peeters's *Massive Retaliation: The Policy and Its Critics* (1958).

Books on the United States and Asia since midcentury are A. T. Steele's *The American People and China** (1966); A. Doak Barnett's *Communist China and Asia: A Challenge to American Policy** (1960); Donald S. Zagoria's *The Sino-Soviet Conflict** (1962); E. O. Reischauer's *Wanted: An Asian Policy* (1955); Ronald Steele's *Pax Americana** (1967); and Richard J. Barnet's *Intervention and Revolution: America's Confrontation with Insurgent Movements around the World* (1968). Two excellent accounts of the early postwar struggle for Vietnam are Ellen J. Hammer's *The Struggle for Indochina** (1954) and Robert Shaplen's *The Lost Revolution: The U.S. in Vietnam, 1946–1966** (1966). Two basic studies by Bernard B. Fall are *Street without Joy: From the Indochina War to the War in Viet-Nam* (4th rev. ed., 1964) and *The Two Viet-Nams: A Political and Military History* (5th rev. ed., 1965).

On the Middle East and Suez crisis of 1956 see J. C. Campbell's *Defense of the Middle East* (1958); Guy Wint and Peter Calvocoressi's *Middle East Crisis* (1957); Lionel Gelber's *America in Britain's Place* (1961); and Herman Finer's *Dulles over Suez* (1964). On the challenges of Europe during the Eisenhower years see Gerald Freund, *Germany between Two Worlds* (1961); Hans Speier, *Divided Berlin: The Anatomy of Soviet Blackmail* (1961); Stephen D. Kertesz (ed.), *The Fate of East Central Europe: Hopes and Failures of American Foreign Policy* (1956); Leon Epstein, *Britain: Uneasy Ally* (1954); and Stanley Hoffman (ed.), *In Search of France** (1963).

*indicates availability in paperback.

33

The Troubled Sixties

Having controlled the White House for eight years, the Republican party anticipated the 1960 election with misgivings. Dwight D. Eisenhower's personal luster had scarcely dimmed. Whatever the inadequacies of his administration—and amid the conditions of peace and prosperity, they were not immediately apparent—none had injured his popularity. But it was clear that the Republican party had failed to turn the President's image into any genuine political gains. Republican Governor Theodore R. McKeldin of Maryland had reminded a Republican audience in February 1957 that the party ''hasn't a thing the country wants'' except Eisenhower. The Eisenhower policies reflected the preferences of the moderates in American society. But those middle-of-the-road policies which seemed to answer the requirements of Eisenhower's huge consensus did not belong alone to the President or his party. They had been guided through Congress more by such Democratic leaders as Lyndon Johnson and Walter George than by Congressional Republicans. Whatever Eisenhower's parliamentary successes, they belonged to the Democratic party as well as the Republican. The American people had elected and sustained Eisenhower as a national, not a party, leader. Now millions who had lauded him would not hesitate, with his retirement, to return the White House to the Democratic party.

Richard M. Nixon had moved into a commanding position of leadership within the Republican party during his second term as vice president. His office had provided him with experience as well as news coverage as he attended high-level conferences and embarked on official tours of the Far East, Latin America, and Europe. Perhaps no American had conversed with so many of the world's political and diplomatic leaders. His willingness to carry the campaign burden in 1954, 1956, and 1958, moreover, had won the approval of Republican party managers. Throughout his years in Eisenhower's shadow, Nixon had performed as an able and active public figure. By early 1960, Republican spokesmen agreed generally that Nixon not only merited the party's nomination but also offered the greatest promise of electoral success in November. At Chicago in July, Nixon gained the nomination on the first ballot with scarcely an opposing vote.

Republican strategists at the convention made clear the pattern of campaigning which they intended to pursue. Congressman Walter Judd's keynote address recounted the alleged failures of the Democratic party in foreign affairs. Former New York Governor Thomas E. Dewey, continuing the assault on the Democratic past, lauded Nixon for his major contribution in shaping the Republican policies "which brought victory after victory for freedom in Iran, in Trieste, in Austria, in Lebanon, in Jordan, in Laos, in West Berlin, yes, and in Quemoy and Matsu and Formosa." This studied effort to gear the Republican campaign to foreign affairs found confirmation in the nomination of Henry Cabot Lodge, Eisenhower's representative at the United Nations, for the vice presidency.

The Democratic party entered the campaign in its usual state of disarray. In part this reflected its majority status and its many divergent elements; in part it reflected the party's custom of engaging in open and vigorous internal struggle to determine its choice of candidate. Among the front-running Democratic contestants in 1960 were four senators—John F. Kennedy of Massachusetts, Lyndon B. Johnson of Texas, Hubert H. Humphrey of Minnesota, and Stuart Symington of Missouri—as well as Adlai Stevenson, the still-popular Democratic nominee of 1952 and 1956. Kennedy's costly and well-organized campaign, managed effectively by his younger brother Robert, was already four years old. When the Massachusetts Senator formally announced his candidacy in early 1960, he was clearly in the lead with pledged support and a large, energetic, and dedicated political organization. At the opening of the Democratic Convention in Los Angeles early in July, Kennedy enjoyed a commanding lead; he won on the first ballot. To placate the South on the issues of civil rights and his own Catholicism, Kennedy selected Senator Lyndon B. Johnson as his running mate.

Kennedy faced Nixon with one notable advantage—7 or 8 million more registered Democrats than Republicans. His task, therefore, consisted in casting the campaign as a struggle between parties on such traditional New Deal issues as farm policy and social security. He declared, "It is not a fight between Mr. Nixon and myself. We lead two parties, two forces, two sources of energy." At St. Louis, Kennedy accused Nixon of attempting to hide from his party's record. In short, Kennedy attempted to reconstitute, as completely as possible, the old Roosevelt coalition of Northern liberals and Southern conservatives, of farmers and laborers. Johnson attempted to keep the South in line on civil rights. Facing the issue of his Catholicism frankly, Kennedy hoped to offset any losses on that score by capturing the many Catholics who had strayed into the Republican camp.

Republican success hinged on Nixon's ability to turn the campaign into a contest of personalities, not parties. Hence, Nixon asked the nation to ignore party labels and to seek the best man for the Presidency. Throughout his campaign he concentrated on building an image of himself as a devoted, fearless, patriotic leader who could guide the nation through perilous times. Nixon was equally anxious to capitalize on his close association with the popular Eisenhower, eventually promoting the "Ike and Dick" theme. To enlarge this latter asset Nixon dwelt often and long on the Republican successes of the fifties.

Foreign affairs dominated much of the early campaigning, figuring prominently in the four television "debates" which the candidates staged before audiences estimated at 70 million viewers. These encounters were damaging to Nixon. Having anchored his campaign to personality, he engaged Kennedy in an arena where Kennedy's own quite remarkable personality and ready grasp of domestic and foreign affairs could neutralize Nixon's primary assets. Kennedy emphasized the central theme in foreign affairs at St. Louis early in October: "If we are to protect our heritage of freedom, if we are to maintain it around the world, we must be strong—militarily, educationally, scientifically, and morally." Thereafter Kennedy pointed continuously to the alleged decline of American power and prestige around the world. He spoke freely of the "missile gap." Because neither candidate dared inform the country that it could not choose its own world, both Kennedy and Nixon came eventually to support most of the uncompromising United States postures of the past.

Throughout the campaign the attitudes of the American voter remained a mystery. Religion and personality are imponderables that do not lend themselves to precise measurement. Many voters influenced by religion refused to be questioned at all. Secondly, the TV debates tended to lessen party ties and caused people to think of competing personalities—not to Nixon's advantage. Thirdly, the increase and migration of population challenged established voting patterns and rendered prophecy almost impossible. Ultimately, Kennedy triumphed in a very close election because, like Roosevelt and Truman before him, he was able to capture the large cities by wide margins. He gained as much as 75 to 80 percent of the urban black vote, as well as a heavy majority among labor, minority, and Catholic groups.

The New Frontier

Kennedy, in accepting the party nomination in July, had told the nation: "The New Frontier is here whether we seek it or not . . . uncharted areas of science and space, unsolved problems of peace and war, unconquered pockets of ignorance and prejudice, unanswered questions of poverty and surplus." The Kennedy team was young. The average age of his Cabinet was less than forty-eight years, compared with fifty-seven for that of Eisenhower. Many of the Kennedy appointees were new to Washington. Whether recruited from the leading universities or from business, their outlook was intellectual. Besides Rusk as Secretary of State, Kennedy selected former Ford Motor Company president Robert McNamara as Secretary of Defense; Douglas Dillon, a wealthy and able Republican banker, as Secretary of the Treasury; Arthur J. Goldberg, a distinguished lawyer and labor negotiator, as Secretary of Labor. After some hesitancy, the President named his brother Robert to the Cabinet as Attorney General. Demanding much of those around him, Kennedy created an administration noted for its energy and enthusiasm.

Kennedy, no less than Lincoln, was determined to assume primary responsibility for the decisions of his administration. The Cabinet, he thought, had grown too powerful; his predecessors too often had deferred to it as an institution and permitted its more ambitious members to assume excessive control of policy. The President, Kennedy believed, should govern with the advice, but not the consent, of his Cabinet. To expedite decisions, Kennedy abandoned many of the formal instruments of government, such as the full meetings of the Cabinet and the

National Security Council; instead he worked with small groups of experts on policy questions.

In his inaugural address the President asked for congressional cooperation to get the nation moving again. During his first weeks in the White House he flooded Congress with messages outlining an ambitious legislative program which ranged from aid to depressed areas and expanded health insurance to foreign aid and defense. Normally such a program for social and economic betterment might have slipped quickly and easily through Congress. The Democratic majority in the Senate was 67 to 33; in the House, 257 to 178. But a bloc of conservative Northern Republicans and Southern Democrats was powerful enough to sidetrack legislation in committee or on the floor. Congress passed administration requests for foreign aid, defense, and space exploration, as well as for some minor poverty and housing measures. But the record of the first session of the Eighty-seventh Congress was spotted less with successes than failures. Columnists criticised the President for limiting his leadership to rhetoric and proposals. During 1962 the President fared little better. In the spring an angered Kennedy forced U.S. Steel to rescind price increases, incurring the wrath of business leaders and sending the stock market into a sharp decline. But the President secured one major legislative triumph late that year—the Trade Expansion Act, which clothed the administration with powers to manipulate the tariff in the interest of freer trade with Europe.

What silenced many of Kennedy's potential detractors was the business recovery of the early sixties. Kennedy entered the White House amid a minor recession, with over 8 percent of the labor force unemployed. Increased public expenditures reduced unemployment in 1961. Following several months of sluggishness in the economy early in 1962, the country suddenly moved into a new era of prosperity, with the GNP reaching an annual rate of almost $600 billion. Still unemployment remained high at 5½ percent, and in June 1962, Wall Street suffered a disastrous selling spree. Those who advocated a Keynesian approach to economic expansion now had their way. In 1963 the President confronted Congress with a deliberately planned budget deficit of $12 billion. The economy moved into another record year. To control inflation under conditions of rapid economic growth, Kennedy established some wage-price guideposts which defined the standards of noninflationary wage and price changes in private business. The capstone of Kennedy's Keynesian program was his proposed $10-billion tax cut, which Congress adopted in 1964. These measures inaugurated the longest period of continuous economic expansion in the nation's history.

Unfortunately Kennedy's successful efforts at business stimulation scarcely touched the nation's structural poverty at all. The new prosperity bypassed millions of citizens. Because of a multitude of welfare programs, the poor were not as destitute as they had been during the Great Depression. But they simply did not share in the nation's economic expansion. Among the hard-core poor were blacks and Puerto Ricans jammed into urban ghettos, whites in Appalachia, Indians and Spanish-Americans, farm families in the South, migrant workers, and many of the elderly. Some 25 million Americans were mired in poverty with incomes below the official poverty line. Perhaps double this number lived precariously near the poverty line. These people were part of what Michael Harrington called "the other America."

Among those who existed at the fringes of national life were the 16 million rural poor, concentrated overwhelmingly in the broad strip of the Appalachian Mountains stretching from southern New York to central Alabama. Here in Appalachia lived the remnants of the poor whites, trapped in permanent poverty, filth, and degradation. Late in 1963 a CBS editor reported his reaction to a trip through Clay County, Kentucky: "Drive through [the county seat] a couple of miles and you come to Horse Creek and Crawfish Holler. Here is the worst living . . . and the lowest form of human existence I have seen anywhere in the United States. . . .

Some of the shacks were windowless, there were shuffling women in filthy sacks—not old but relatively young—and garbage and junk." In the teeming urban ghettos poverty meant dirty, substandard housing, with rats far more numerous than people. It meant unemployment or at best low-paid, unskilled jobs such as dishwashing, domestic service, or day labor. Even those who worked forty hours a week, fifty-two weeks a year, at the 1960 minimum wage of $1 an hour grossed only $2,080 annually.

Kennedy acknowledged the existence of the nation's hard-core poverty but found it preferable politically to pursue tax cuts rather than social legislation. The New Frontier offered little to the rural and urban poor. Still by 1963 the President realized that beyond tax reduction, which brought benefits only to those with adequate incomes, the country required a positive war on poverty.

Blacks and Civil Rights

In the twenty-five years after 1940 the black population of the United States rose from 12.8 million to about 22 million. At the same time much of the black population shifted from the rural South to northern cities. As blacks moved northward during and after World War II, they were jammed into the growing urban slums of such cities as New York, Philadelphia, Cleveland, Detroit, and Chicago. Having suffered from generations of segregation and discrimination in the South, they hoped to find conditions better in the North. Instead, they found themselves confronted with *de facto*, if not legal, segregation in housing. Those blacks who could afford better houses and tried to move into the suburbs usually met stiff resistance. Blacks likewise faced discrimination in their search for employment. Problems of motivation and unemployment trapped countless urban blacks in a hopeless cycle of poverty, crime, and failure. But southern blacks as well continued to exist without equal political rights, adequate education, social equality, and economic opportunity. Blacks across the nation became increasingly militant in their demands for equality and justice, ably supported by whites who believed that the social and legal status of blacks was inexcusable.

Strict school segregation, which existed in seventeen states in 1945, began to crumble as blacks sought entrance to the professional schools of southern universities in the late 1940s.

After winning a case in the federal district court in 1948, George W. McLaurin entered the College of Education at the University of Oklahoma, although not until 1950 did he gain full equality of treatment. Also in 1950, the previously all-white University of Oklahoma Law School admitted Ada Lois Sipuel. The Universities of Texas, Missouri, and North Carolina, all traditionally segregated institutions, shortly thereafter admitted blacks for graduate study. But the Supreme Court destroyed the main bastions of legal segregation in education in the case of *Brown v. Board of Education of Topeka* in 1954. The Court held that "segregation of children in public schools solely on the basis of race" denied children of minority groups equal educational opportunities. This latter-day decision overthrew the historic "separate but equal" doctrine established in 1896 by *Plessy v. Ferguson*.

Meanwhile blacks made notable gains on other fronts. In 1948 President Truman had ordered that segregation be terminated in the Armed Forces; the Defense Department demanded that landlords around military bases treat all service personnel equally in accepting their applications for housing. In 1953 the Supreme Court ruled that restrictive covenants in real estate transactions could not be enforced; two years later the Interstate Commerce Commission banned segregation on all interstate trains and buses and in public waiting rooms.

Southern states had found many ways to deny

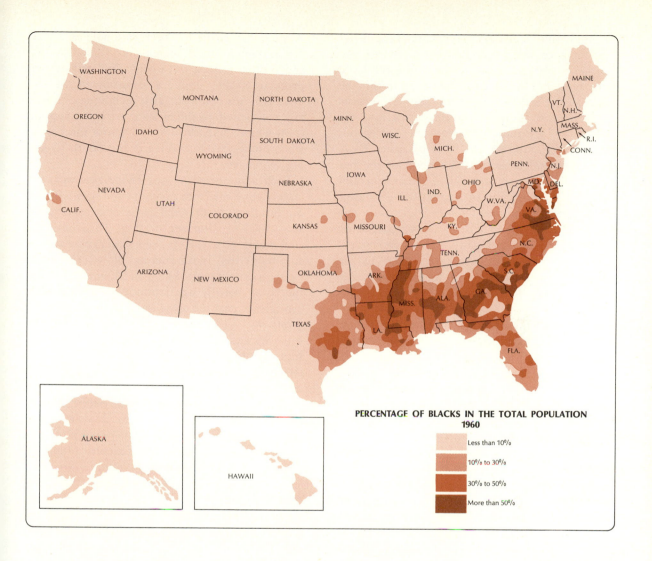

WASHINGTON
MONTANA
NORTH DAKOTA
MAINE
OREGON
MINN.
VT.
N.H.
IDAHO
SOUTH DAKOTA
WISC.
N.Y.
MASS.
WYOMING
MICH.
R.I.
CONN.
NEVADA
IOWA
PENN.
N.J.
UTAH
NEBRASKA
OHIO
MD.
DEL.
CALIF.
ILL.
IND.
W.VA.
COLORADO
VA.
KANSAS
MISSOURI
KY.
N.C.
ARIZONA
TENN.
S.C
OKLAHOMA
ARK.
GA.
NEW MEXICO
MISS.
ALA.
TEXAS
LA.
FLA.

ALASKA

HAWAII

PERCENTAGE OF BLACKS IN THE TOTAL POPULATION
1960

Less than 10%

10% to 30%

30% to 50%

More than 50%

blacks the franchise, permitting whites to control local politics even in areas where blacks were in the majority. It was not until 1957 that Congress, over the strong objections of Southerners, finally enacted broad legislation designed to guarantee blacks the right to vote. This law provided for a Commission on Civil Rights, authorized an additional Assistant Attorney General to deal with civil rights matters, and declared illegal any threat or intimidation designed to prevent anyone from exercising his right to vote. Although the Civil Rights Act of

1957 appeared a major advance in protecting the constitutional rights of blacks, the tactic of barring registration continued to keep many away from the polls. In 1960 Congress passed legislation which, under certain conditions, permitted judges to appoint referees to assist blacks to register and vote. But the huge gap between what the laws provided and the conditions experienced by blacks persisted.

Earlier, in December, 1955, the struggle for equality had assumed a new, more promising form when Mrs. Rosa Parks, a black seamstress in Montgomery, Alabama, refused to give up her seat in a crowded city bus and went to jail. Formerly any such defiance of white rules had been rendered ineffective by passivity within the ranks of the blacks themselves. But in this racial confrontation over an old Jim Crow law, the blacks, led by the intelligent and courageous young black minister Dr. Martin Luther King, Jr., conducted a successful boycott of the bus system. After a year of walking, blacks won their fight for the abolition of segregation on buses. By the time that the United States Supreme Court, late in 1956, had declared segregation on municipal buses unconstitutional, the movement had spread to other southern cities. In the Montgomery crisis, King perfected his strategy of civil disobedience through peaceful resistance.

Black students, adopting this new strategy, now attacked segregation in southern restaurants and public facilities. They resorted to sit-ins, marches, picketing, and boycotts. In February, 1960, four students from the black Agricultural and Technical College at Greensboro, North Carolina, sat down at a lunch counter restricted for whites with the determination to remain until the management either served them or shut down. The sit-in, added to the picket lines and economic boycotts, soon brought a wide variety of private segregated business to terms. This assault on segregation invited the support of such black organizations as the National Association for the Advancement of Colored People (NAACP), the Congress of Racial Equality (CORE), King's new Southern Christian Leadership Conference (SCLC), as well as the Student Nonviolent Coordinating Committee (SNCC). These organizations instructed young blacks in nonviolent techniques.

Still the price of success came high, for many businessmen fought back with toughs and police; some preferred bankruptcy to concession. Then in May 1961, James Farmer, national director of CORE, took a group of "freedom riders" by bus through Virginia, the Carolinas, Georgia, and Alabama to challenge segregation in interstate bus terminals. In Alabama they faced violence and mob reprisals, but eventually, with federal protection, they ended segregation in the Birmingham bus terminal. This technique of invading segregated facilities soon attracted support from white sympathizers throughout the North, who joined freedom rides in the South to face jail sentences.

Each summer after 1961 civil rights workers, largely students from northern colleges, entered the South to further the cause of desegregation and to aid in voter registration. This continued civil rights pressure sparked violence in several southern cities. In the summer of 1964 three civil rights workers were killed in Mississippi. Later the local sheriff, his deputy, and others were brought to trial for these slayings. Several of the group received long prison sentences. Despite setbacks and the generally slow pace of change, the civil rights movement revealed increasing strength. During the summer of 1963 the March on Washington brought over 100,000 blacks and whites to that city in the largest public demonstration in the nation's history. Martin Luther King addressed the huge throng as it stretched down the mall from the Lincoln Memorial toward the Washington Monument.

So massive had become the civil rights movement, so pervading its implications, that the Kennedy administration could not ignore the South's program of resistance. Despite the 1954 decision on desegregation, the South had experienced no more than token integration. White Citizens Councils and the Ku-Klux Klan continued to determine the status of race relations in many southern communities. Although President Eisenhower had sent federal troops to Little Rock in 1957 to enforce integration, his dramatic action had little long-range effect. In 1964 only 2.1 percent of black students in eleven southern states attended integrated schools. Most Southern communities responded to special court orders, but to nothing else.

President Kennedy, in September 1962,

backed by his brother as Attorney General, made his first decisive move in behalf of racial integration when he placed the full power of the federal courts behind the registration of black veteran James H. Meredith at the University of Mississippi. Throughout the spring of 1963 such southern communities as Birmingham, Alabama, were torn by racial violence. In May Kennedy told a news conference, "As it is today, in many cases they [the blacks] do not have a remedy, and therefore they take to the streets." By July the battle over civil rights had entered Congress, where the Senate Judiciary Committee opened its hearings on the President's new civil rights legislation. Despite the new urgency, it was clear that the President's civil rights bill would not pass during that session of the Eighty-eighth Congress.

The Kennedy Leadership

Critics laid much of the responsibility for congressional inaction at the feet of the President. James Reston had complained in June, "There is something wrong with his leadership on the home front. Something is missing in his speeches, his press conferences, his trips and his timing. He is not communicating his convictions effectively." Not long after, the President prepared a message for delivery in Dallas: "In a world of complex and continuing problems, in a world full of frustrations and irritations, America's leadership must be guided by the lights of learning and reason—or else those who confuse rhetoric with reality and the plausible with the possible will gain the popular ascendancy with their seemingly swift and simple solutions to every world problem." The words would remain unspoken. On November 22, 1963, the day the speech would have been given, the President, in Dallas to mend a rift in the Texas Democratic party, was cut down by an assassin.

The handsome young President's tragic death created an instant cult which made him appear different in death from what he had been in life. He had promised to get the country moving again, but Congress, in November 1963, was scarcely moving at all. His legislative program lay strangled in committee. Even his popularity had dropped in October to 57 percent—still high, but nothing compared to the eulogies which followed his assassination. Yet the dichotomy between the Kennedy image and the Kennedy record had been apparent long before his death. Kennedy possessed personal attributes which permitted his image to transcend his box score either in Congress or in his handling of foreign affairs.

Much of the world had come to trust Kennedy instinctively as a man whose immediate failures and shortcomings would give way ultimately to triumphs at home and abroad that reflected his high intelligence, his rational appraisal, and his decent intentions. Kennedy harbored a noble vision of the nation and the world, and it was this high expectation that created the void when he died. He had not occupied the White House in a time of crisis, but in a time of change. He sought to understand that change and to adjust the nation's policies to it. Yet the conditions of American and international life imposed narrow limits on his statesmanship; despite the brilliance of his administration, it was incapable of extensive innovation. Many of its judgments in foreign affairs were considerably less than sound. But Kennedy had given Washington a rebirth of vitality and made it more than ever the center of world attention. The emotions unleashed across the globe by his death, often among those who had never really approved of his leadership, attested to the hope he had carried for a better future.

The political ascent of Lyndon Johnson, who now assumed the mantle of the fallen President, had been long and difficult. Possessing only the special advantage of his own capacity, he had achieved remarkable success. Entering the House of Representatives from Texas in 1937, he had served there for eleven years as a loyal Democrat, finally moving to the Senate in 1948. Four years later, he served the first Eisenhower Senate as Minority Leader. With the Democratic landslide of 1954, he emerged as Majority Leader and for six years devoted his skills to steering the Eisenhower legislative program through the Senate. When Kennedy had been merely another member of the Senate, Johnson was, next to the President, the most important man in American political life. In 1960, he had gone to Los Angeles with 300 delegate votes. Unable to stop Kennedy's bandwagon, however, he settled for the vice presidency.

As President, Johnson scarcely resembled Kennedy at all. He was determined, resourceful, and experienced, but he lacked certain of Kennedy's assets. Kennedy represented urban, industrial New England; Johnson represented the rural, agricultural Southwest. Kennedy represented the new and the novel; Johnson represented the traditional. Johnson was not a good speechmaker as John Kennedy had been. Unlike Kennedy, moreover, the new President had difficulty in laughing at himself. He was unable to establish a close rapport with the Washington press corps. His favorite motto, from Isaiah, was, "Come now, let us reason together." By reasoning, coaxing, compromising, and arm twisting, he set out to win where it mattered—in his relations with Congress.

Johnson entered the White House with an enormous reserve of congressional respect and goodwill. Southern Senators especially—those who had paralyzed the Kennedy program—harbored an emotional commitment to Johnson's success. On November 27, in his first presidential address, Johnson reminded Congress: "For 32 years, Capitol Hill has been my home. I have shared many moments of pride with you, pride in the ability of the Congress of the United States to act, to meet any crisis, to distill from our differences strong programs of national action." The President listed the important measures before Congress, indicating that he assigned top priority to the civil rights bill. "I urge you," he said, "to eliminate from this nation every trace of discrimination and oppression that is based upon race or color." The President in late 1963 had the political advantage over Congress, and he knew it. A *Newsweek* public opinion poll revealed not only a 2-to-1 vote of no-confidence against the Eighty-eighth Congress but also overwhelming approval for the administration's proposed domestic program.

During the spring of 1964 Congress and the nation began to respond favorably to Johnson's special brand of leadership. By promising to reduce the proposed Kennedy budget, Johnson managed to coax the tax bill out of the Senate Finance Committee. The House had passed the measure as early as the previous September. The Senate concurred after a brief debate on February 7, 1964. The President forced the civil rights bill into the House at the end of January. This measure would outlaw racial discrimination in most hotels, restaurants, and theaters; authorize the Attorney General to initiate suits in behalf of aggrieved persons in desegregation or discrimination cases; and permit the halting of funds to federal projects which tolerated the existence of racial discrimination. The measure passed the House in February by a vote of 290 to 130. The Senate finally passed the bill in June.

The President, meanwhile, declared his long-anticipated "war on poverty" during March in the form of the Economic Opportunity Act of 1964. Despite vigorous Republican opposition, the bill passed the Senate on July 23, and the House two weeks later. It provided for work experience and training, for community action programs to combat poverty, and for a domestic peace corps known as Volunteers in Service to America (VISTA). On matters of domestic legislation the second and final session of the Eighty-eighth Congress, which opened in January and adjourned in October, 1964, had proved to be the most productive in many years. The Johnson style of getting things done had become a national phenomenon. During the critical weeks of debate on the key bills before Congress, President Johnson had bombarded doubtful members with phone calls and invitations to breakfasts, luncheons, dinners, and informal exchanges. The Johnson techniques were effective, but they often demanded compliance and subservience to the point of irritation.

Amid such triumphs Johnson faced the challenge of the 1964 Presidential campaign. Senator Barry Goldwater of Arizona, spokesman of traditional Republican conservatism, was his party's leading candidate. Governor Nelson Rockefeller of New York tried to outdistance Goldwater, but he failed. Subsequently, Governor William Scranton of Pennsylvania, like Rockefeller a liberal, sought to head off Goldwater's nomination, again without success. Goldwater easily won his party's nomination at San Francisco. The convention selected William E. Miller, a Catholic Representative from New York, for the vice presidency.

Goldwater's views, expressed simply and directly in his book, *The Conscience of a Conservative* (1960), conformed to the pre-New Deal Republican philosophy of "rugged individualism." The nation's salvation, he believed, lay in states' rights. He opposed federal aid programs as a threat to individual freedom; he emphasized morality and traditional values of competition and hard work. In foreign affairs, he popularized assumptions and goals at odds with containment. Goldwater recognized no limits to either American power or Communist perfidy and greed. From these two conclusions flowed his insistence that the United States must accept nothing less than "total victory" in the Cold War. The Senator's specific proposals demanded unrelent-

ing hostility toward the U.S.S.R. and China. In his view, negotiations with the Kremlin were dangerous and useless. The way to win in Vietnam, he said in May 1963, was to drop "a low-yield atomic bomb on Chinese supply lines in North Vietnam." Goldwater's campaigning was based on the assumption that the American people were tired of the complexities and uncertainties of international life and demanded clear-cut solutions. Yet he failed signally to set forth what he would do differently.

Meanwhile the Democratic party projected a mood of confidence and relaxation. Johnson faced only one internal party challenge to his nomination—that of Governor George Wallace of Alabama. This Southern proponent of states' rights attempted to build support for his candidacy among low-income white Americans, North and South, who experienced most directly the pressures of desegregation. Goldwater's nomination abruptly removed him from the race. Thus the Democrats could meet at Atlantic City, New Jersey, on August 24 and proclaim unity. The Johnson-dominated convention nominated Senator Hubert H. Humphrey of Minnesota as Johnson's running mate and presented a moderate platform, including a civil rights plank on which the party could agree. The platform accused Goldwater of recklessness in his varied proposals for victory in the Cold War.

In the campaign, Johnson concentrated on the twin themes of peace and prosperity. Problems remained, he admitted, but the record of achievement in the years after 1947 had been extensive, even profound. Along with Democratic spokesmen, he hammered at the notion that the Republican candidate could not be trusted with the nation's leadership. By election day, every political yardstick presaged a Johnson sweep. On November 3, Johnson's popular vote of 61 percent in fact set an all-time record—over 43 million to 27 million for Goldwater. Winning forty-four states, Johnson lost only Arizona and five states of the deep South. In the North there was little "white backlash" against the Civil

Rights Act. Outside the South, Johnson carried almost everything—cities, suburbs, rural areas, blacks, Roman Catholics, and even doggedly Republican Vermont. Congress remained under Democratic control by margins in both houses of over 2 to 1.

The Great Society

During his campaign the President had sketched out a new program for the nation—the "Great Society." "We are only at the beginning of the road to the Great Society," he said in January 1965, adding: "No longer are we called upon to get America moving. We *are* moving." The goals of the Great Society included the beautification of the country; the elimination of urban blight, as well as air and water pollution; medical aid for the aged; help for education; a more vigorous war on poverty; and new suffrage guarantees for blacks.

Johnson wasted little time. By July 1965, the Eighty-ninth Congress had written enough of the Great Society program into law to emerge as the most productive since Roosevelt's Second New Deal of 1935. First, Congress approved the President's request for $1.1 billion to help the eleven-state poverty region of Appalachia. Second, agreeing to aid the children of the poor regardless of whether they were attending public or private schools, Congress skirted the traditional church-state issue and passed a $1.3 billion general education bill. Third, Medicare, an especially dramatic breakthrough for the Great Society, provided the elderly with two months of low-priced hospital care and allowances for other medical costs. Fourth, a $7.5 billion omnibus housing bill, including a revolutionary plan to provide rent subsidies for persons whose income was low enough to qualify for public housing, provided for the construction of 60,000 units of low-rent public housing over a period of four years. President Johnson's voting rights bill of 1965, having received a special impetus from a civil rights crisis in Selma, Alabama, that spring, moved swiftly through Congress. It eliminated discriminatory literacy tests, anticipated the lawsuits which would soon terminate state poll taxes, and provided for federal registrars to assist blacks in registering to vote. Congress also repealed $4.5 billion in excise taxes to stimulate the economy.

Behind these achievements was not only the Johnson landslide of 1964 but also the full support of the business community. The booming economy had convinced increasing numbers of business leaders that big government was a boon, not a threat, to economic expansion. If Congress lost some of its momentum during 1966, it wrote a proud record nevertheless. It created the Department of Transportation as the twelfth department in the Cabinet, giving it full responsibility for the development of a coordinated national transportation system. It passed a $1.2 billion "demonstration cities" program to create models for urban development. For the first time in history, it established safety standards for all highway vehicles. It broadened the regulations for the labeling and packaging of foods, drugs, cosmetics, and household supplies. Finally, Congress appropriated $3.7 billion to help clean up the country's rivers and lakes and $186 million to fight air pollution.

Yet the Great Society, for all its legislative triumphs, had barely scraped the surface of the nation's essential problems of poverty and civil rights. "The walls of the ghettos are not going to topple overnight," editorialized the *New York Times* in retrospect, "nor is it possible to wipe out the heritage of generations of social, economic, and educational deprivation by the stroke of a Presidential pen." Nor was it clear that the federal government would win its war against poverty even along established lines of action. The complex program would not succeed without imaginative and effective administrators. Normal bureaucratic inertia and inefficiency could quickly sink the whole Great Society into an administrative quagmire. The President had managed to place both poverty and civil rights programs on the books; he had not demonstrated the capacity to make either program effective.

Financing was the second barrier to the creation of the Great Society. Though stupendous, the nation's wealth was not unlimited. During 1966 Congress declined to fund the President's domestic program. Nor would the congressional situation improve. Democratic setbacks in 1966 reduced the President's majority in the House by forty-seven seats and pushed the membership toward conservatism. Again in 1967 Congress passed several important bills; but it ignored many vital issues facing the nation. Eventually Congress extended the poverty program for two additional years with appropriations of approximately $2 billion per year. Yet, despite the size of the federal effort, the Johnson years—like the Kennedy or Eisenhower years—did not help the poor to any significant degree.

Actually the country invested comparatively little in the Great Society. The entire war on poverty between 1964 and 1967 cost the American people only $6.2 billion—less than 1 percent of the annual gross national product. By 1967 Congress had reduced the annual budget for the poverty program to less than one quarter of 1 percent of the GNP. Such expenditures, added to the rhetoric of hope which accompanied them, could raise expectations, pay the salaries of federal officials, create some new jobs, and build some highways and public structures. They could not do much more. The country's ills, its basic human dilemmas, became more, rather than less, apparent with the passage of time.

The Warren Court

Even more, perhaps, than the executive-based proponents of the New Frontier and the Great Society, the United States Supreme Court emerged in the sixties as the conscience of the nation. Following the school desegregation decision of 1954, the Supreme Court became so aggressive and wide-ranging in its defense of civil and minority rights that it too left an unmistakable mark on the nation's history. The Chief Justice, in fact as well as name, was Earl Warren. Thirty years of public life, including a stint as Governor of California and a run for the vice presidency in 1948, had shaped him into a pragmatist. If he lacked the philosophical nature of Justice Hugo Black or the critical intellectuality of Justice Felix Frankfurter, he harbored a highly developed sense of justice and fair play. After his appointment in 1953 Earl Warren embodied the spirit of the Court.

The Court's remarkable string of decisions began in 1962. Over Frankfurter's last dissent, the Court ruled in *Baker v. Carr* (1962) that federal courts had the right to review the fairness of legislative districting. In most states at this time small towns and rural districts enjoyed disproportionate power in state legislatures; rural and small-town majorities had no desire to engage in redistricting that would reflect the increasing shifts in population from rural areas to the cities. In the *Baker* case the Supreme Court agreed that unequal apportionment deprived many voters of equal protection of the laws under the Fourteenth Amendment.

Other decisions revolutionized the electoral process. In *Gray v. Sanders* (1963) the Court invalidated the Georgia county unit system which assigned each county a certain number of unit votes and declared the candidate securing the largest number to be the victor in a primary election. The old system had given rural areas a preponderant control over state elections. In *Harper v. Virginia State Board of Elections* (1966), the Court held that the poll tax violated the equal protection clause of the Fourteenth Amendment. That same year in *South Carolina v. Katzenbach* the Court ruled out all literacy tests to determine voting qualifications for those who had completed the sixth grade. Clearly the Warren Court was determined to give every American equal rights to participate in the nation's democratic processes.

In its 1961–1962 session, the Supreme Court took up the difficult problems of civil rights. Although the Constitution bans only official segregation, not private prejudice, the Court in 1961 accepted several "sit-in" cases for review. In *Thompson v. City of Louisville,* the Court decided that the "due process" clause of the Fourteenth Amendment upheld the right of the S. H. Kress Company to ask blacks to leave the lunch counter as required by a local ordinance providing for a racial separation at eating facilities. In *NAACP v. Button,* on the other hand, the Court overturned a Virginia law denying minority groups the right to institute integration cases when those instituting the suits had no direct pecuniary interest or liability.

For many years, Justice Black had argued that the rights granted a defendant in federal criminal courts applied equally to criminal defendants in state courts. In *Hamilton v. Alabama* (1962) the Court held that a state must provide counsel in a capital case even when it was not evident that failure to do so would prejudice the defendant. Previously the Supreme Court had not required that states provide lawyers for indigent persons except in special cases. But in *Chewning v. Cunningham* (1963), the Warren Court voided a conviction on grounds that an indigent defendant had been denied counsel. In a similar case, *Gideon v. Wainright* (1963), the Supreme Court decreed unanimously that in the interest of fairness every person accused of a crime was entitled to counsel. In *Escobedo v. Illinois* (1964), the Court ruled further that counsel must be present at criminal interrogations leading to a confession. These Supreme Court decisions met continuous dissent, for a minority of the Court argued vigorously that they undermined the effectiveness of police activity.

On issues of censorship and obscenity the Warren Court generally assumed a position of extreme tolerance. In *Bantam Books Incorporated v. Sullivan* (1963) the Court overturned a Rhode Island procedure for restricting the dissemination of obscene literature. The majority found the Rhode Island commission's power to warn dealers and wholesalers regarding the sale of certain books and magazines as, in effect, a system of censorship without the necessary safeguards from state regulation. In *Jacobellis v. Ohio* (1964) the Court overturned the conviction of the defendant for showing an allegedly obscene movie, *The Lovers,* on the grounds that the Constitution defends all forms of expression except hard-core pornography, which no one could define. Yet the Court drew limits to the extent of obscenity and free speech that it would tolerate. In *Ginzburg v. United States* (1966) it upheld Ralph Ginzburg's conviction and prison sentence on the ground that the advertising of his magazine *Eros* and the newsletter *Liaison* featured "the leer of the sensualist." If the Court still hesitated to examine the content of material to determine whether it was "dirty" or "worthless," it would at least protect the public from advertising of a highly suggestive nature.

So pervasive were such decisions on civil rights and civil liberties, criminal procedures, and censorship that the Court by the 1960s had greatly expanded the latitude of the individual for self-expression, self-fulfillment, and equality of status. Applauded by liberals, the trend was damned by conservative critics who desired more—not less—social and governmental control. Some conservatives across the country urged Warren's impeachment.

The Price of Vietnam

Washington's well-established goal of sustaining anti-Communist governments threatened by Communist-led revolutionaries, operating allegedly as part of a Moscow-based international conspiracy, had forced United States containment policies into a decidedly counterrevolutionary pattern. It had done so in Vietnam; it would do so again in the Dominican Republic. In April 1965, rebel forces favoring the return of deposed former president Juan Bosch staged a revolt which prompted the right-wing Dominican forces to establish a counterrevolutionary junta. Thomas C. Mann, chief advisor to the Johnson administration on Latin American affairs, declared that the rebels were Communist-led. As the rioting continued, President Johnson landed over 20,000 United States military personnel, announcing his dual objective on May 2: to protect American lives and property and "to help prevent another Communist state in this hemisphere." Privately he supported the narrow-based junta. Soon it became clear, however, that United States policy was such a massive infringement on the principle of self-determination that it had no chance of success. Thereafter Washington, with the support of the Organization of American States, arranged a provisional government which, in turn, prepared the Dominican Republic for another election. This permitted the President to escape his self-imposed dilemma. But in Vietnam the United States commitment to Saigon was too deep to permit any escape through compromise.

From the beginning of its involvement in Vietnam, Washington had pursued one clear objective—the protection of the Saigon regime from Communist-led assaults. Whether the enemy resided south or north of the 17th parallel—the initially temporary but increasingly permanent line separating North from South Vietnam—was of no consequence. United States policy had been based on the assumption that limited American aid could guarantee Saigon's total military and political success. During 1964, however, it became obvious that Diem's successors in Saigon were incapable of disposing of the Communist-led forces bearing down heavily on what remained of South Vietnam's political and military structure. Thus, Johnson faced the disturbing choice of either liquidating the war largely on Hanoi's terms or converting the struggle for Vietnam into an American war. With little hesitation he made the latter choice.

What the President required to place Hanoi under the direct pressure of United States military superiority was some dramatic incident. That event came on February 7, 1965, when the Vietcong attacked Pleiku, an outpost in the central highlands, and killed eight American advisers. Four hours later Johnson authorized an air attack on Dong Hoi, 40 miles north of the demilitarized zone in North Vietnam, at the same time reassuring the nation, "We seek no wider war." Behind this decision lay the assumption, firmly held in Washington as official dogma, that the bombing of the north would bring Ho Chi Minh to the negotiating table in six—at most ten—weeks.

Even as he predicted early successes, the President committed the country to a course of military escalation. As Hanoi adjusted its defenses to withstand assaults from the air, the President simply extended the bombing to more targets. When the situation continued to deteriorate, Johnson dropped the "advisory role" designation of United States military personnel in Vietnam and authorized General William Westmoreland to use the 50,000 men in his command for ground action against the enemy. On July 28, 1965, the President announced that the United States personnel in South Vietnam would be increased from the 75,000 already there to 125,000. "If we are driven from the field in Vietnam," he warned, "then no nation can ever again have the same confidence in American protection." Having accepted that rationale of the struggle, the President was prepared to increase the military escalation to any level required for victory. The troop buildup reached 200,000 in 1966 and continued upward until it exceeded 500,000 in 1967. Meanwhile the volume of bombs dropped on enemy targets north and south of the 17th parallel reached stupendous proportions. During 1968 the bomb tonnage gradually exceeded that in both the Pacific and European theaters during the Second World War. By then the war had cost more than 200,000 American casualties—over 30,000 dead—and $30 billion a year.

Yet the fighting went on. Hanoi, now fully committed, matched each new American increment with a countering escalation of its own. By 1967 McNamara admitted that the bombing had not interdicted the infiltration and flow of supplies from the North. As the war continued, moreover, the ability of the enemy, whether Vietcong or North Vietnamese regulars, to move freely through the countryside, striking anywhere and everywhere, suggested the difficulty of the struggle. In the absence of established battle lines, United States forces measured success, not by territory captured and held, but by the number of enemy killed. By 1968 that body count exceeded 400,000—more than the entire North Vietnamese army—and yet the enemy continued to strike.

At home, opposition to the war kept pace with its escalation. The unleashing of such large quantities of destructiveness against an Asian people injured the moral sensibilities of millions of Americans and gradually divided the nation. Those who challenged United States policy in Southeast Asia agreed generally that the Vietnamese conflict was a civil war to be resolved by

the Vietnamese people themselves. They regarded it as an overcommitment of American resources and manpower in an area where United States security interests were, at most, secondary. Among the outspoken opponents of the war were retired Generals James Gavin and Lauris Norstad, many of the country's leading Far Eastern experts, and both Democratic and Republican members of Congress. In domestic matters, also, the effects of the war effort began to be felt. By 1967, expenditures on the war had overheated the economy, weakened the dollar, contributed to an international monetary crisis, and unleashed inflationary pressures necessitating tax increases.

As the political, economic, and emotional costs of the war continued to climb, Washington officials—thinking thus to justify the costs—enlarged the consequences of victory and defeat. Never had a limited encounter carried so completely in theory the burden of the world's future. According to the official rationale, the effort in South Vietnam would not only save that country and all Southeast Asia from aggression; it would at last eliminate the danger of a great war. As President Johnson assured the American people in 1967, "I am convinced that by seeing this struggle through now we are greatly reducing the chances of a much larger war—perhaps a nuclear war." If peace was indeed indivisible—if war anywhere endangered the peace everywhere—then world stability did hinge on the United States ability to counter successfully any forcible Communist-led challenge to the status quo. In short, the Johnson administration promised to contain Communist expansion everywhere and save liberty for all mankind by fighting and winning in Vietnam.

The Election of 1968

Normally the incumbent Johnson, completely in command of his office and his party's machinery, would have anticipated both renomination and reelection as a matter of course. As the new year

broke, the President expected no less. He entered the campaign, moreover, determined to stand firm on matters of Vietnam, poverty, and civil rights, and to hold the center of American

Robert F. Kennedy, March 29, 1968.

(Central Press Association)

Meanwhile, President Johnson's campaign slowly disintegrated under the pressures of politics and war. The Vietcong Tet offensive against the cities of Vietnam early in 1968 broke the illusion of impending victory and plunged the President's popularity into a sharp decline. McCarthy's showing in New Hampshire disturbed the White House staff, for it was evident that McCarthy would take the forthcoming Wisconsin primary. Kennedy's candidacy posed an even greater threat, for a Gallup Poll of early March rated Kennedy and Johnson about equal in strength among Democrats and independents. Still the President's announcement of March 31 that under no circumstances would he accept another nomination caught the country by surprise.

Robert Kennedy now emerged as the leading Democratic contender. On April 2, McCarthy gained an easy victory in Wisconsin, but already

Robert F. Kennedy, June 5, 1968.   (UPI photo)

politics. But 1968 was no ordinary year, and no longer would such purposes command even the support of all Democrats. In the Senate, the outspoken opponents of administration policy included such key Democrats as J. William Fulbright of Arkansas, Mike Mansfield of Montana, Eugene J. McCarthy of Minnesota, Robert Kennedy of New York, and George McGovern of South Dakota—men who were prepared to force an intraparty debate on the burning issue of Vietnam. During November, 1967, McCarthy announced his own candidacy for the Democratic presidential nomination. His campaign, starting slowly, had picked up little momentum by the time he entered the New Hampshire primary in February 1968. Johnson was entered as a write-in candidate with the full support of the state's Democratic leaders. McCarthy's vote of 42.4 percent (to Johnson's 49.5) suggested the extent of opposition to the war, broke the nation's political logjam, and within days brought Robert Kennedy into the race as an active presidential candidate.

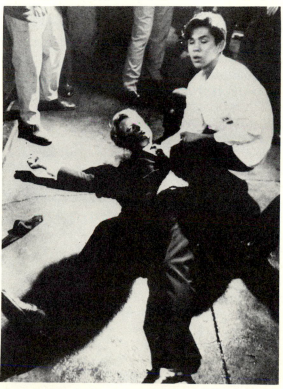

the Kennedy machine, backed by the Kennedy millions and the bulk of the party's literary talent, cast a shadow over the remaining Democratic primaries. Distinguishing Kennedy and McCarthy were their styles and appeals rather than the issues.

Kennedy's first major victory came on May 7 in the Indiana primary. The two Democratic candidates pointed toward their final showdown in the June 4 California primary. There, after a strenuous and sometimes bitter campaign, Kennedy emerged victorious again. Shortly after midnight on June 5, with victory assured, Kennedy thanked his cheering supporters in the ballroom of Los Angeles' Ambassador Hotel. Moments later he lay mortally wounded in the kitchen corridor—like his brother, the victim of an assassin's bullet.

When the Democratic campaign resumed later in June, the field still did not belong to McCarthy. Somewhat earlier, on April 27, Vice President Hubert H. Humphrey had announced his candidacy. Humphrey had ignored the primaries, for his strength lay in the Democratic organization—in the White House and the federal bureaucracy, among state and local Democratic leaders, with the spokesmen of organized labor, and in the South. So tight was the Humphrey organization that it quickly rendered the primaries irrelevant. The McCarthy candidacy had no chance.

Election year 1968 held clear advantages for the party out of power. The Republican leadership could place the full burden of overcommitment abroad, riots, inflation, higher taxes, and internal tensions on the ruling Democratic party. Long identified with the war in Vietnam, the Republicans could continue to demand victory by attributing past failure not to elusive ends but to the gradualism and vacillation of Johnson's military policies.

The front-running Republican was Richard Nixon, former Vice President and Republican presidential nominee of 1960. Nixon had protected his well-established reputation as a Republican regular by supporting Goldwater in 1964 and by campaigning hard and successfully for Republican congressional candidates two years later. By February 1968, when Nixon announced that he would enter the New Hampshire primary, he had already dispelled the notion, created by his debacle in the 1962 California governor's race, that he was a loser. Nixon swept the New Hampshire primary and then went on to other primary victories. Long before convention time, Nixon, like Humphrey, held what proved to be an insurmountable lead for his party's nomination.

McCarthy's so-called new politics challenged the established political structure on matters of foreign policy and the quality of American life. After February 1968, politics-as-usual faced a second serious challenge in the states' rights candidacy of former Alabama Governor George C. Wallace. Wallace's appeal spoke to the discontent of conservative citizens, rich and poor, who believed their welfare endangered by high taxes, court decisions, and federal interference in local and state affairs. Wallace's program revealed his single-minded concern for property rights and freedom of local and individual decision, both threatened, he said, by the federal bureaucracy.

Nixon won the Republican nomination on the first ballot at Miami, Florida. The platform promised both a victory for self-determination and the "de-Americanization" of the war in Vietnam. After his flawless triumph, Nixon, in an effort to placate the party's conservative leadership in both the South and the important border states, selected largely unknown Governor Spiro T. Agnew of Maryland for the vice presidency. He entered the final race for the White House with superb advantages, possessing the freedom not only to remind the nation of its troubles but also to hold the Democratic party solely responsible for them.

With Humphrey's nomination assured, the Democrats, meeting in Chicago during August, focused their attention on the party platform. Rejecting compromise with the dissidents, Humphrey accepted a Vietnam plank reflecting the official views of the State Department. Thus, despite the long crusade against the war—much of it centering in Democratic ranks—the Democrats' Vietnam plank was almost identical to that of the Republicans. Having swept to victory on the first ballot, Humphrey chose as his running mate the highly regarded but little-known Senator Edmund S. Muskie of Maine. Neither of the major parties had nominated a popular hero; neither offered programs which might be expected to end the Vietnam war or to meet the problems of poverty and racial discrimination.

Exploiting his political advantages to the utmost, Nixon fastened his campaign to criticism of Democratic failures. Promising a "new leadership for the American people," he pledged an honorable end to the war in Vietnam, clear-cut military supremacy over Russia, and a cut in foreign aid. On domestic issues he asserted that he would take personal charge of the battle against crime, that he would bring inflation under control, and that he would either eliminate or improve the administration of many federal programs.

Humphrey's nomination in Chicago had resulted in a badly split party. Antiwar Democrats refused to march with him in New York's Labor Day parade. Sparse crowds, unimaginative scheduling, merciless heckling by antiwar demonstrators, and the continued alienation of McCarthy and Kennedy followers haunted Humphrey's footsteps. What kept him running and hoping was the simple conviction that in November the American people would reject a Nixon Presidency. Although he eventually veered away from Johnson's hard-line position on Vietnam and called for a reassessment of United States policies, his precise intentions, if elected President, remained unclear.

During the closing weeks of the race, Humphrey's aggressive, underdog campaigning began to tell. In part, his larger and increasingly enthusiastic crowds reflected dissatisfaction with the Nixon strategy. Lower-middle-class voters, for thirty years the bulwark of Democratic power, began to sense that the GOP candidate was dodging the issues. Campaigning on the economic achievements of successive Democratic administrations, Humphrey gradually solidified what remained of the old Roosevelt coalition. Unlike Nixon, Humphrey invaded the core of the big cities, appealing to traditional party loyalties. Nearly 100 percent of voting blacks supported him. During October much of the McCarthy faction returned to the Democratic fold.

Suddenly the promise of peace in Vietnam gave the Humphrey campaign a shot in the arm. On March 31, simultaneously with his withdrawal from the presidential race, President Johnson ordered a halt in United States bombing north of the 20th parallel and invited North Vietnam to enter talks with American representatives. Late in April, the President announced that talks would shortly open in Paris with Averell Harriman serving as the chief United States negotiator. As the Paris talks opened in May, Hanoi repeated its demand that successful negotiations could proceed only after the United States had halted the bombing of all North Vietnam. Washington insisted, in return, that Hanoi give some formal assurance that a full bombing halt would be met with a deescalation of its own effort in South Vietnam.

Then on November 1 the President dramatically announced that new (albeit unexplained) developments had permitted him to halt completely the bombing of North Vietnam. Simultaneously he declared that within a week the conversations in Paris would be broadened to include both the Saigon government and the National Liberation Front (NFL) of South Vietnam. Ahead, however, were more weeks of wrangling over procedural matters, including the shape of the conference table. Not until January 25, 1969, did the first substantive session of the renewed Paris talks convene at the Hotel Majestic. Thus the political impact of the President's announcement proved to be negligible.

Still, by November, Nixon and Humphrey were coming down the homestretch neck and neck. The Gallup Poll declared the popular vote a tossup between Nixon's predicted 43 percent and Humphrey's 42, with Nixon still holding a larger advantage in the electoral college. These final predictions proved to be accurate. Humphrey dominated the Northeast, adding Michigan, Minnesota, Texas, and Washington, and gained approximately 43 percent of the national vote. States' rights candidate George Wallace captured five states of the South: Arkansas, Louisiana, Mississippi, Alabama, and Georgia. Nixon, often by a narrow margin, took the remaining states, again with 43 percent of the popular vote. His final margin over Humphrey was less than 500,000 out of more than 70 million votes cast. Republican strategy was successful only in the presidential race. Congress remained safely Democratic.

Johnson in Retrospect

Lyndon Johnson had been a "lame duck" President since renouncing another term in March; the election merely determined his successor.

During his last days in the White House it was clear that his troubles had flowed not from the avoidance of responsibility but from his attempts to accomplish too much. He accepted without question the notion of American omnipotence, believing that he could perform in accordance with the longings and myths of the country. His goal was to fulfill the dreams of all Americans, including the underprivileged, and to maintain all the nation's foreign commitments. At times, his domestic triumphs were astonishing, for he presided over an age of progressivism unmatched since the New Deal. He signed forty pieces of legislation in support of education alone. He expanded the nation's health programs, achieved greater protection for consumers, and advanced the cause of conservation. He instituted vast programs to answer the needs of the poor, both black and white. The years 1963–1969 were not unproductive.

Vietnam proved to be Johnson's white whale. He had chased it through turbulent seas for four years; he was still in pursuit when he left office. His Vietnam policies resulted finally in far more division at home than victory in Asia. The reason is clear. Those policies were anchored to words and emotions—to high promises of success and dire warnings of the consequences of failure—and not to a body of clearly recognizable circumstances, such as those created by Hitler in 1941, which carried their own conviction and recommended their own responses. It was not strange that the country divided sharply between those who took the rhetoric and admonitions seriously and those who did not. To defend his Vietnam intervention with a half million men, the President was compelled to exaggerate the importance of that region to the United States and the rest of the world until he had committed more in cost and destruction than the results could justify. Thus Johnson's ultimate tragedy was his refusal to admit error—error which in part he had inherited from previous administrations—and to acknowledge the limits of his power to reorder human existence simultaneously in the slums of American cities and the far-off jungles of Vietnam.

Urban Violence and Black Power

As the decade of the sixties approached its midway point, it was nowhere apparent that the country's simmering discontent would soon explode into open violence. The civil rights movement of the early sixties, culminating in the great march on Washington in 1963, demonstrated the frustrations and injustices of American society. The urban, poverty, and civil rights programs of the New Frontier and the Great Society had given the nation's outcasts some hope for an improving future. Yet those programs were ultimately too inadequate to matter. Those seeking justice and opportunity for blacks or an end to the Vietnam war recognized the limits of their influence in the face of a determined administration in Washington and an uninformed and unconcerned public. Convinced that their grievances merited positive governmental responses which were never forthcoming, ghetto and campus minorities gradually turned to demonstrations, marches, riots, and destruction to dramatize their concerns. The ghettos erupted first.

Many black slum dwellers, finding most legitimate avenues to economic security blocked, lived by their wits. Mark Battle, an expert on black urban culture, once described the varieties of existence in the slums. "Walk with a Negro youth in his ghetto environment," he wrote, "and . . . you'll quickly get a taste for the components of his life: a drug addict nodding in a doorway; a drunk vomiting or urinating in a hallway; a sex party on a rooftop; seven-year-olds scampering over fences with stolen jars of pigs' feet; a floating crap game in an alley; bars full of prostitutes; fights in which the strong pick on the weak; merchants who overprice their shoddy goods and charge one dollar to cash a Government allotment check.'' What mattered to most urban blacks was less an avenue of escape from the ghettos than the conversion of the ghettos into promising areas of human existence. For many New York blacks Harlem had an appealing quality; whatever its problems, it offered a known environment and the promise of a better life.

During the mid-1960s the generally restrained black discontent gave way to violence. The first serious outburst occurred in Los Angeles during August 1965. For six days, blacks rampaged through the streets of Watts on Los Angeles' south side, destroying 200 buildings and damaging 600 others by burning and looting. The riot produced thirty-four deaths, over 1,000 injuries, and almost 4,000 arrests, as well as $140 million in property damage. Subsequent summers witnessed major outbreaks in Los Angeles, San Francisco, Chicago, New York, Newark, and Detroit. Before the Detroit riot of July 1967, was brought under control, 14,000 paratroopers, National Guardsmen, and state and local police, using tanks and machine guns, were called into action. The riot toll in Detroit reached thirty-eight deaths, 2,000 injuries, and 3,200 arrests. Property damage reached a half billion dollars. Altogether between 1965 and 1967, riots struck seventy-six cities, killing twelve policemen and 118 civilians.

These riots, in their formlessness and violence, lacked any clear plan, purpose, or philosophy. For some they seemed an expression of blind reaction against general conditions in the ghetto; for others, including some youngsters, they were a lark and an opportunity to pick up free merchandise. Following the 1967 riots, President Lyndon B. Johnson appointed a high-level commission to study civil disorders in American cities, but events cried for action, not investigation. Most knowledgeable authorities already knew the basic, if not the immediate, causes of riots—racism, discrimination, poor housing, joblessness, and the absence of hope.

Moderate black leaders, led by Dr. Martin Luther King, condemned the destruction. But amid the riots black leadership passed into the hands of "black power" advocates. The movement toward "black consciousness" was an amalgam of deep frustration among black leaders and the black nationalist philosophy of Malcolm X, before his assassination a militant spokesman of the Black Muslims. Stokely Carmichael, leader of the Student Nonviolent Coordinating Committee (SNCC), emerged as one of the most articulate black nationalists. To Carmichael it seemed clear that American blacks would never overcome their disadvantages of poverty and "blackness" as long as they accepted programs and standards created by white leadership. If the power structure in American society remained concentrated in the hands of whites, blacks could achieve their goals only by creating positions of strength.

Black power advocated solidarity among Afro-Americans as the surest means of achieving economic and political influence commensurate with their numbers. It demanded as well that blacks hold top positions in institutions where their numbers and interests were predominant. Its adherents rejected the term "Negro" as a creation of the white race and demanded the simple designation "black." At the level of action, black power was never a single movement, but varied in program according to the immediate preferences of those who advocated it—Carmichael, Floyd McKissick, Rap Brown, Eldridge Cleaver, or Ron Karenga. Veteran civil rights leader James Farmer, chairman of the Congress of Racial Equality (CORE), agreed with many of the more militant that black separatism, as a method of building black solidarity, was a phase through which the nation must pass before it achieved full racial equality. But not all black leaders accepted the black power rationale. Following the Detroit riot, four black moderates asserted: "Killing, arson, looting are criminal acts and should be dealt with as such." Roy Wilkins, executive director of the NAACP, applauded Vice President Humphrey when he declared, "Racism is racism—and there is no room in America for racism of any color."

National leaders reacted variously to both the riots and the black militancy. Conservatives tended to view the riots as conspiratorial, perhaps even Communist-inspired, or at best the inevitable result of the civil rights movement which had destroyed the traditions of custom and restraint hitherto holding blacks in check. For them the answer lay in strengthening the nation's law enforcement agencies. Others believed the riots the result of historic black disadvantages, some going back to slavery. The President's special Advisory Commission on Civil Disorders (headed by Governor Otto Kerner of Illinois), submitting its findings in late February 1968, recommended a sweeping program to alleviate social ills. The nation, it warned, was moving toward two societies, one black and one white, separate and unequal. The commission recommended the creation of 2 million new jobs and 6 million new homes.

During March 1968, the liberals in the Senate moved toward an open housing law, still searching for a compromise that would make the measure palatable for millions of sensitive white homeowners. It required the assassination of Martin Luther King in Memphis, Tennessee, early in April 1968, to galvanize Congress into action. Despite the continued opposition to open housing, Congress passed the President's final civil rights measure, with its promise of general open housing by 1970.

Despite continued discrimination in employment and segregation in housing and education, many blacks made substantial social and economic gains in the postwar generation. In sports, entertainment, higher education, government, business, and the armed services, the walls of discrimination cracked if they did not crumble. Blacks starred in professional baseball, football, and basketball; others achieved national recognition in music, literature, art, education, and public service. Jackie Robinson, Willie Mays, and Henry Aaron were three of the greatest of postwar baseball players. Ralph Bunche was a successful mediator for the United Nations in the Middle East. For his efforts Bunche received the Nobel Peace Prize. In 1967 President Johnson appointed Thurgood Marshall as the first black ever to sit on the Supreme Court. Gwendolyn Brooks became a Pulitzer prize-winning poetess; Sidney Poitier won fame as an actor; Leontyne Price gained recognition as one of the true greats of opera; John Hope Franklin emerged as one of the country's leading historians; James Baldwin and Ralph Ellison achieved distinction as writers. It was not that blacks made no progress; the continuing problem as late as 1970 was that progress and change did not keep pace with rising economic expectations and the growing demands for equality and social justice.

The Student Revolt

Students entered the vanguard of national dissent. Previous generations had given voice to the nation's ideals of freedom, justice, and equal opportunity without examining the inapplicability of those ideals to millions of their fellow citizens. For many sensitive college-aged youths, the crisis-laden 1960s destroyed the optimism which had sapped the social concern of their elders; the tensions in American society demonstrated that the country had not responded well to its challenges in the cities, in the areas of civil rights, in matters of equal opportunity, or in the aesthetic quality of national life. More than any previous generation of American students, those of the sixties adopted a social orientation. Not satisfied with simple criticism, students set out to participate in the process of human betterment. They worked and marched for civil rights, helped in black registration drives, worked in the slums, and joined the Peace Corps.

That same prosperity which gave thousands of students the freedom and security to challenge established ways also built the modern univeristy system. During the five years from 1960 to 1965 enrollment in American colleges and universities increased by more than one-half. American universities became not only larger but also better, evolving into places of immense intellectual stimulation. The result was nothing less than a revolution in standards and performance; the academic community became both more active and better informed than ever before.

Writers quickly identified the central object of student criticism as the so-called establishment. Student critics contended that change came too slowly, that the country's institutions had become too large, too cumbersome, and too dedicated to established policies and attitudes. Attacks on the establishment brought students into direct conflict with university administrators. Disturbances on the University of California's Berkeley campus in late 1964 disrupted normal academic work and resulted finally in the dismissal of President Clark Kerr. Thereafter the attack on university administrations, often supported openly and vigorously by faculty members, swept the country from California to New England. Students rebelled at the dehumanization of life in the large universities, where they found themselves computerized, mass-produced, and ignored. They complained of disinterested instruction, of professors too busy in travel and research to conduct classes, of their inability to participate in university decisions that affected them and determined the quality of their educational experience. To counter such practices they demanded a degree of control over the curricula and, in some cases, the hiring and firing of faculty. Student warfare on university establishments culminated in the riots at Columbia University in the spring of 1968 and at Cornell University a year later.

Campus reaction to the broader challenges of the sixties was never monolithic. The majority of students revealed far more concern over preparation for industry, football, fraternities, dating, and automobiles than with social and university reform. At the other extreme the nation's unanswered challenges drove a minority of students into open rebellion. Rejecting orderly processes and majority rule, demanding above all free and open discussion, and condemning established institutions generally, they insisted that the American system be uprooted. On campuses the radical student movement often became associated with the Students for a Democratic Society (SDS), founded in 1962 and claiming by 1968 a membership reaching into the thousands. As philosopher of the new radicalism, Herbert Marcuse, in his *One Dimensional Man* (1964), argued that social salvation would come, not from the welfare state, but from the outsiders, the exploited and oppressed, to whom he assigned the right to use violence if legal means proved inadequate. In time radical student dissent focused on Vietnam and became so unrestrained that it produced disorders, parades, draft-card burning, and riots. By 1967 the Vietnam issue had created a merger between the antiwar and civil rights movements, both tending that year toward violence. On the campuses themselves the radicals attacked ROTC programs and all university connections with defense industries.

Frequently writers and critics failed to distinguish between the campus radicals and the vast number of students in the center of the spectrum who were neither disinterested nor violent. Here were the tens of thousands of students who gave new hope to American life. They were deeply concerned over national policies which they considered less than intelligent. But they were not in the streets or heckling speakers. These students were the true adherents of the new politics. As such, their anti-Vietnam convictions carried them logically into the camps of Eugene McCarthy and Robert Kennedy during the 1968 campaign. Humphrey's nomination at Chicago terminated their totally laudable antiwar political activity.

During 1968 an important segment of the student rebellion became identified with the concerns of black students. In large measure this new phase combined the student and black power movements into a massive effort to transform a portion of American higher education to satisfy the specific interests and needs of blacks. Black demands centered on curriculum; subsidies; more black teachers, coaches, and other personnel in predominantly white schools; and a lowering of admission standards. In part, black student leaders sought an education that would prepare them specifically for service in black communities. But even more, they wanted a program that recognized their uniqueness as blacks, that stopped attempting to fit them for life in a white, middle-class society. To assert their blackness, such students began to eat separately in mixed dining halls, wear natural hair styles, and demand separate dormitories and separate social functions. Ultimately, the search for relevance led to demands for black studies programs, developed from the perspective of black ethnocentrism. Early in 1969 a Harvard University faculty committee recommended a degree program in Afro-American studies. The demands for special courses, special programs, and, in most cases, even autonomous black departments spread rapidly across the nation.

Confrontation

The five-year Presidency of Lyndon B. Johnson might well be termed an "era of confrontation." A principal "confronter" was Johnson himself, who used his legislative expertise to attack most of the major problems faced by American society. In his zeal to come to grips with the country's problems, he also escalated the war in Vietnam, hoping to terminate it quickly. This attempt, however, failed, proving the undoing of much of his domestic program. The War on Poverty between 1964 and 1967 cost $6.2 billion—less

Bernie Boston, Washington Evening Star Photo

than 1 percent of the gross national product, whereas the Vietnam war, by 1968, cost nearly five times that much each year.

Meanwhile other confrontations occurred. Blacks escalated their own war against racial injustice by nonviolent efforts at first, later, new black-nationalist movements shunned white participation. Youth also emerged on the American scene as students and student organizations sought greater influence in campus affairs, worked for civil rights, and, especially, protested the war in Vietnam. The youth shown above was photographed during the confrontation at the Pentagon, the two-day Peace March in Washington in 1967.

Direct and often violent confrontations between those who believed in black equality and those who held with the entrenched institutions of segregation also characterized Johnson's years. One of the most dramatic civil-rights demonstrations involved a mass march of 25,000 from Selma to Montgomery, Ala., protesting illegal barriers against voter registration. Two white supporters, a Detroit housewife and a Boston minister, were murdered, their deaths recalling those of others who had lost their lives in this struggle for basic rights during the preceding years of the decade.

President Johnson used the Selma March as the occasion for an address to a joint session of Congress in which he urged a new law—later passed—intended to eliminate discriminatory literacy tests, obviate poll taxes, and supply federal registrars to help Negroes in the South register to vote.

Photographs on these pages, taken during the course of the Selma march, and those on the next four pages are from the book *America in Crisis*, (Holt, Rinehart & Winston, 1969) with photographs by Magnum and text by Mitchel Levitas, and from an exhibit based upon the book.

The attitudes of American leaders toward the strife in Vietnam (next two pages) gradually edged toward greater involvement during the 1960s and escalated sharply after the election of President Johnson in 1964. From a force of 4,000 advisors in 1962 an Army of more than 500,000 troops had grown by 1968. By 1970 more than 40,000 Americans had been killed, and well over 100,000 had been seriously wounded. Some 400,000 of the enemy were "counted" dead. Estimates of South Vietnamese civilian casualties ran between 100,000 and 150,000 a year.

Following page: left, Donald McCullin, Magnum; both right, P. J. Griffiths, Magnum

"The time has come to put our bodies on the machine and stop it," Mario Savio, student protest leader at Berkeley, had said early in the decade. During the 1960s, the disaffected young threw themselves into a variety of confrontations with the Establishment, but no fight unified them more than their opposition to the Vietnam war. Student protest, long a tradition in Europe, Latin America, and Japan, engaged American students as never before.

Demonstrations, marches, sit-ins, opposition to on-campus ROTC training, interference with career recruitment by companies producing war materiel, antiwar literature and theater, draft-card burning—all gave evidence of student involvement. The Peace Movement peaked once in October, 1967, when at least 100,000 demonstrators staged a two-day march on Washington (below), ending in a vigil at the Pentagon. Violence, tear gas, and mass arrests marked the conclusion of the event, as they have punctuated many others since.

Disappointed by the failure of the Peace Movement in the Democratic Party—a failure seemingly caused by Senator Eugene McCarthy's lack of organizational support and by the assassination of Senator Robert Kennedy —many young activists moved on the Democratic Convention in Chicago to protest. Mayor Daley had mobilized a 12,000-man force at the convention hall—6,000 National Guardsmen and 6,000 regular Army troops. Four nights of rioting ensued, bringing charges, as the Walker report mentions, of lawlessness by the demonstrators and gratuitous brutality and violence by the police (near left).

Far left and spread: Charles Harbutt, Magnum; near left: Roger Malloch, Magnum

While no President since Reconstruction signed more civil rights legislation than President Johnson, his administration was beset by violent riots growing out of the alienation of the black community. These photographs were taken in the Watts area of Los Angeles, in Detroit, and in Washington, D.C., only three of the nearly one hundred cities where festering ghettos have erupted since 1964.

This or similar alienation also fathered "black power" movements in various styles, the most vocal and notable being the Black Panthers. In the 1950s and 1960s blacks did make gains, but gains inhumanly slow in reaching the mass of the black population.

Both left: United Press International; both right: Burt Glinn, Magnum

President Nixon and his vice-president inherited an unpopular war and an inflationary economy. Even the glorious success of man's first moon landing was somewhat dimmed by the knowledge that the money used for the space program might have been better spent elsewhere—for poverty programs, urban renewal, ecological blight, education.

Elliott Erwitt, Magnum

Some youths gave up completely on American society. They dropped out of college, forsook jobs, and abandoned all responsibility. Even more than those on the campuses they attacked competitiveness, status, conformity, educational and religious institutions. Many of these young dropouts objected to what they considered fundamental contradictions, double standards, and hypocrisies in both personal and national life. A multitude of underground newspapers blossomed across the country to articulate their attack on American values. Many of the young shared a deep sense of immediacy. As one university president declared, "This generation has no utopia. Its idea is the Happening. Let it be concrete, let it be vivid, let it be personal. Let it be *now*."

Eventually, disillusionment drove thousands of young radicals into a counterculture, reflected in new and strange forms of political expression, as well as in drugs, communal pads, street theaters, dashikis, astrology, and scientology—all evidencing a sharp break with established social norms. The first stage of the youthful retreat centered in the "beatnik" movement of the fifties. The dissent from the smugness of that decade found its vindication in Allen Ginsberg's *Howl* (1955) and Jack Kerouac's *On the Road* (1957), as well as in various forms of verse, usually beyond the comprehension of the uninitiated. The "beat generation" gathered in such cities as New Orleans and San Francisco, but more often moved about aimlessly in their escape from responsibility. No less than the Bohemians of previous generations, they discarded the confining standards of middle-class American society. The beatniks sought individualism in their appearance—long hair, beards, old clothes, and sandals. By the sixties this early phase of the so-called bearded rebellion had disappeared.

But the beatniks set the pattern and style of the much larger youth defection of the sixties—the hippie movement. Again distinguishable by their beards, beads, shaggy hair, and unkempt attire, the hippies congregated in such places as the Haight-Ashbury district of San Francisco and New York's East Village. In time their unstructured existence created a conformity of its own. In keeping with their intense opposition to the Vietnam war, the hippies disdained authority and regimentation and emphasized the qualities of gentleness and nonviolence. Thousands of hippies joined available communes. Many of these existed in urban centers, but in time they invaded the countryside. If the communes varied in organization, rules, and philosophy, they tended to embody some form of communal existence which included the sharing of responsibility, property, love, and children. To sustain their simple, often squalid, existence, members secured outside employment or contributed money received from home.

As if to emphasize their separation from straight society, the hippies turned to drugs. Federal anti-drug measures had little effect on the postwar use of drugs in the United States. By the sixties the drug scene corresponded largely to the hippie scene, although eventually the use of drugs spread across the campuses and into the high schools. So common became the use of "pot" (marijuana) among the young that some authorities advocated a new look at the laws governing its sale and use. Heroin and other mentally repressive drugs moved gradually from the ghettos into the hippie culture. Despite the possibility of mental and emotional damage, many young drug users experimented with such hallucinatory drugs as speed and LSD. These, they said, expanded their sensitivity, deepened their emotions, and sharpened their imagination. One patron saint of the drug culture was former Harvard Professor Timothy Leary, a frequent user of LSD, who told the young to "turn on, tune in, and drop out."

As the hippie culture disintegrated in the late sixties, it spawned a tougher, more violent street culture which resorted to trashing, stealing, and

Woodstock, 1969.   (Magnum Photo)

even murder. Some groups, notably the motor-cycle gangs, lived for a time by terror and destruction. The radical student movement terminated in the Youth International Party (Yippies), a semiserious political movement which advocated drugs and violence. The Yip-pies, led by Abbie Hoffman and Jerry Rubin, played the central role in the mammoth antiwar confrontation in Chicago during the 1968 Demo-cratic convention.

At the decade's end Charles Reich's *The Green-ing of America* (1970) gave the youth movement both its historical rationale and its ultimate pur-pose. Reich's Consciousness I and II reflected earlier American ideals of enterprise and man-agerial success and the concomitant acceptance of the corporation in American life. His Con-sciousness III rejected corporate society and emphasized the individual living in a genuine community. Individuals, sharing their values, experiences, and wisdom in an organic relation-ship, would create a new American culture. Reich's attack on corporate society and the price it exacted from a rich and beautiful environment

was too graphic to ignore. His book created sympathy for, if not full understanding of, the rebellious generation. But even as Reich pre-dicted a new age based on Consciousness III, the youth movement lost its force. Faced with de-clining income and opportunity in a more restric-tive economy, the young retreated to the tradi-tional protections of home, work, and education, determined again to enter the American system on its terms. In time the campuses recaptured their former quiet without producing additional learning.

Rock music characterized the 1960s much as jazz had done in the 1920s. Rock was a national phenomenon, never limited in its appeal to any specific elements in American society. Still its embodiment of new sounds, hard-driving rhythm, unprecedented noise levels, lyrics of protest, and psychedelic effects to heighten emo-tions identified much of rock music with the youth revolt. Such artists as Chuck Berry had introduced rhythm and blues, better known as rock and roll, in the fifties, but it was the English influence of the Beatles and the Rolling Stones that led America into the furtively creative musi-cal era of the sixties. The Beatle formula—electrical amplification, heavy bass work, and novel chord structures—permeated the Ameri-can musical scene. For a time the earlier styles of Elvis Presley and country western music could scarcely survive the impact. As Aaron Copland, the composer, said, ''When people ask to re-create the mood of the sixties, they will play Beatle music.'' When the Beatles appeared on the Ed Sullivan TV show in 1964, their innova-tions had already triumphed.

Groups such as the Beatles, the Rolling Stones, the Doors, the Mothers of Invention, and Blood, Sweat and Tears drew thousands to their concerts; recording companies sold mil-lions of their records. The folk songs of Joan Baez and the intonations of philosopher-singer Bob Dylan were especially popular among the rebellious. The three-day rock music festival at Woodstock, New York, during August 1969, became the supreme moment of the hippie movement. There some 400,000 young men and women of Woodstock Nation reacted with shouts and anguish to the heavy beat and the lyric obscenities of the music. When the sound finally ended, the thousands drifted away as quietly as they came.

Conclusion

Of the many social problems facing postwar America, three were of overriding importance: civil rights, a persistent hard-core poverty, and the special challenge of urban decay. During the 1950s, these matters received some attention from politicians, social scientists, lawyers, and the concerned generally. While they seemed serious, those problems produced no national crisis during the "placid" fifties. By the 1960s, however, the urban and civil rights issues had become explosive. Tired of continued discrimination, blacks lost patience with the slowness of change. They became increasingly militant in their demands for full civil and economic rights. The central city, which had gradually come to be populated by a variety of minority groups, presented an array of problems—persistent unemployment, poor housing, inadequate services, and lack of income—which seemed almost insurmountable. In the 1960s riots broke out in the ghetto sections of scores of cities where unemployment was high and the poor were alienated from the mainstream of American society. The restless and belligerent sixties found at least a few critics calling for radical revolution. The war in Vietnam merely deepened the frustrations and social anxieties.

Much of the nation's unrest scarcely touched that generation of Americans which had come through the Great Depression and World War II to achieve a reasonably affluent, comfortable existence. Those who had been poor in the 1930s and had become prosperous in the 1950s and 1960s identified their success with adherence to traditional values—hard work and careful atten-

tion to job, business, or profession. Having escaped poverty, they were not ashamed of their comfortable circumstances. For them security was more important than challenge or experimentation. Many of the restless and dissatisfied sons and daughters of these middle-, upper-middle-, and upper-class homes had never known want or poverty. Consequently, they could not understand their parents' emphasis upon money, status, and work. Parents, on the other hand, could not understand how some of their children could be indifferent, even hostile, to such practical things as formal education and preparation for work. The generation gap was not without precedent, but never had it ever been so great as in the 1960s.

Yet despite all the attention given to restless and nonconformist youth in the 1960s—college dropouts, drug users, revolutionaries, and critics generally—their number was relatively small. Perhaps the radical appeal was limited even on college campuses, because American society was better than many critics would admit. New technology had freed men from the drudgery of labor and given them more leisure; rising educational levels permitted men to escape the darkness and conformity of ignorance; and expanding economic opportunity and higher incomes gave people a greater choice of work and recreation. Indeed, there were more opportunities for personal fulfillment than ever before. Still the youthful critics had claimed correctly that the quality of American life had scarcely approached the possibilities embodied in the nation's wealth, its intelligence, its vast and expensive educational system.

SUGGESTED READINGS

John F. Kennedy's Presidency is related in detail in two outstanding volumes written by members of his

White House staff: A. M. Schlesinger, Jr.'s *A Thousand Days: John F. Kennedy in the White House* (1965)

and Theodore C. Sorenson's *Kennedy** (1965). Far more critical are Henry Fairlie's *The Kennedy Promise* (1973) and Nancy Gager Clinch's *The Kennedy Neurosis* (1973). Two remarkably perceptive volumes on presidential election politics in the sixties are Theodore H. White's *The Making of the President, 1960** (1961) and *The Making of the President, 1964** (1965). Undoubtedly the most ambitious contemporary effort to arrive at some understanding of Lyndon B. Johnson is Eric F. Goldman's *The Tragedy of Lyndon Johnson* (1969). Tom Wicker's *JFK and LBJ: The Influence of Personality upon Politics* (1968) sees Kennedy as a man in pursuit of excellence and Johnson as a man concerned with power and responsibility.

Edward Quinn and P. J. Dolan (eds.), *The Sense of the Sixties** (1968), and Howard Zinn, *Postwar America: 1945–1971* (1972), discuss the decade's critical issues—war, students, radical movements, the blacks, religion, and science. For the thought of the sixties see Ronald Berman's *America in the 1960s: An Intellectual History* (1968). Another volume of value is Ben J. Wattenberg and R. M. Scammon, *This U.S.A.: An Unexpected Family Portrait of 194,067,296 Americans Drawn from the Census* (1965). On poverty in America are Michael Harrington, *The Other America** (1963), and H. M. Caudill, *Night Comes to the Cumberlands** (1963). On the changing South see Avery Leiserson (ed.), *The American South in the 1960s** (1964) and Charles O. Lerche, Jr.'s *The Uncertain South: Its Changing Patterns of Politics in Foreign Policy* (1964).

On the status of blacks in the sixties see James W. Silver's *Mississippi: The Closed Society** (1964); Charles E. Silberman's *Crisis in Black and White** (1964); Malcolm X's *Autobiography** (1965); and James Baldwin's *The Fire Next Time** (1963). Two volumes which trace desegregation in the United States since 1954 are Reed Sarratt's *The Ordeal of Desegregation: The First Decade* (1966) and Benjamin Muse's *Ten Years of Prelude: The Story of Integration since the Supreme Court's 1954 Decision* (1964). Analyzing various phases of the black pressures on American society are Louis E. Lomax's *The Negro Revolt** (1962); Robert Goldston's *The Negro Revolution* (1968); Benjamin Muse's *The American Negro Revolution from Nonviolence to Black Power, 1963–1967* (1968); and August Meier and Elliott

Rudwick's *CORE: A Study of the Civil Rights Movement* (1973). Two books on Martin Luther King appeared shortly after his assassination in 1968: Lionel Lokos's *House Divided: The Life and Legacy of Martin Luther King* (1968) and William Robert Miller's more sympathetic *Martin Luther King, Jr.* (1968).

For a general evaluation of Johnson's foreign policies see Philip L. Geyelin's *Lyndon B. Johnson and the World* (1966). Books which deal with the Vietnam issue during the Johnson years are Richard M. Pfeffer (ed.), *No More Vietnams?** (1968), a symposium containing contributions from seven well-known students of American Far Eastern relations; Mary McCarthy's *Hanoi** (1968); Frances Fitzgerald's *Fire in the Lake** (1972); David Halberstam's *The Best and the Brightest** (1972); and Telford Taylor's *Nuremburg and Vietnam** (1970). Five volumes concerned specifically with the globalism in United States foreign policy are Ronald Steel's *Pax Americana** (1967); Edmund Stillman and William Pfaff's *Power and Impotence** (1966); Theodore Draper's *Abuse of Power** (1966); J. William Fulbright's *The Arrogance of Power** (1966); and Richard J. Barnet's *Intervention and Revolution** (1968).

For the election of 1968 see Richard H. Rovere's *Waist Deep in the Big Muddy: Personal on 1968* (1968). Three British journalists, Lewis Chester, Godfrey Hodgson, and Bruce Page, produced the first major study of the 1968 campaign in their *An American Melodrama: The Presidential Campaign of 1968* (1969). Joe McGinniss's *The Selling of the President: 1968* (1969) is a highly critical account of the Nixon campaign. More favorable to Nixon is Theodore White's *The Making of the President, 1968** (1969).

For the campus revolt see especially Alan Adelson, *S.D.S.* (1971); Paul Jacobs and Saul Landau (eds.), *The New Radicals** (1966); Tom Hayden, *Trial** (1970); Carl Oglesby (ed.), *The New Left Reader** (1969); and Herbert Marcuse, *One Dimensional Man** (1964). Describing the counterculture are Theodore Roszak, *The Making of a Counter-Culture* (1969); R. S. Gold (ed.), *The Rebel Culture** (1970); D. B. Louria, *The Drug Scene** (1968); Keith Melville, *Communes in the Counter Culture* (1972); and Charles A. Reich, *The Greening of America** (1970).

*indicates availability in paperback.

34

After Two Centuries

Richard M. Nixon assumed his presidential duties in January 1969, in an atmosphere of quiet confidence. He had surrounded himself with men of distinction and broad outlook. For Secretary of State he had chosen William P. Rogers, an urbane New York lawyer and one-time Attorney General under Eisenhower. Melvin R. Laird, former Wisconsin representative, entered the cabinet as Secretary of Defense. For Presidential Assistant for National Security Affairs, Nixon selected Dr. Henry A. Kissinger, a distinguished Harvard scholar who had migrated from Germany as a boy. To head the important Council of Economic Advisers he chose Paul W. McCracken, a University of Michigan economist. Daniel P. Moynihan, a recognized expert on problems of the city, joined the administration as Presidential Assistant for Urban Affairs.

Nixon confronted a still-divided nation. As presidential candidate he had neither sought nor gained the allegiance of the blacks, the poor, or the alienated. Indeed, where the nation's stability was most vulnerable, his support was almost nonexistent. In such areas the policies he advocated promised few rewards. The surest approach to a stronger Republican future, therefore, lay in a more determined assault on the center of the political spectrum at the price of alienating even further the disaffected in American life. For Nixon's supporters, this mattered little. "It is time," argued Vice President Spiro T. Agnew, "for the preponderant majority, the responsible citizens of this country, to assert their rights. . . . If, in challenging, we polarize the American people, I say it is time for a positive polarization."

By any standard of measurement the American economy was a modern miracle. Long before the 1970s the standard of living of most Americans had reached levels undreamed of before Pearl Harbor. The gross national product (GNP) rose from somewhat over $284 billion in 1950 to over $850 billion in 1968. By 1973 the GNP had zoomed to $1,285 billion. Median family income advanced from $3,319 in 1950 to more than $8,000 in 1968. Five years later it exceeded $10,000. Inflation cut deeply into the buying power of these rising incomes, but the genuine economic gains were significant nevertheless. Real income or purchasing power climbed some 66 percent during the first twenty postwar years. Economic growth reserved its special benefits for the very rich. Many old families—the Rockefellers, Mellons, and Vanderbilts—retained and expanded their fortunes, but thousands of the new-rich entered the multimillionaire class. By the 1960s there were approximately 100,000 millionaires in the United States; of these 646 declared a gross annual income of more than $1 million for tax purposes in 1965. The new fortunes were made largely in oil, insurance, and real estate.

Americans surpassed all others in the universal quest for comfort and convenience. Multitudes of them acquired new houses or inhabited attractive apartments laden with electrical appliances and other expensive furnishings. By 1967 about 22 percent of all American families owned two or more automobiles. Americans spent billions on sports, as both spectators and participants. With domestic travel included, Americans in the mid-1960s spent more than $40 billion a year on recreation and another $3 to $4 billion on foreign travel.

Perhaps the most striking difference between the postwar era and those which preceded it was the pace of scientific and technological change. The most dramatic advances in science occurred in atomic energy, space exploration, oceanography, molecular biology, and the health sciences. A host of new processes and products flowed from the country's scientific achievements—atomic energy for peaceful uses, synthetic fibers, new medicines, and electronic equipment. The digital computer, first invented in 1944, was able to perform amazing feats of memory and calculation. Transistors replaced vacuum tubes in the late 1950s, making possible more powerful yet smaller computers with a far greater range of applicability. By the 1960s computers made possible scientific computations that would otherwise have required thousands more man-hours of effort by mathematicians and engineers. These machines now guide spaceships, keep track of plane reservations, and check federal income tax returns. Linked to automatic machinery, they determine production levels; they order materials and write checks to pay for them; they control billing, warehousing, and shipping. Automation threatens segments of the industrial labor force with unemployment although it also creates thousands of new jobs.

Nowhere did technology assume the role of mission so completely as it did in the development of atomic power. This achievement symbolized the success of American industrialization. Yet, oddly enough, the new power created less a mood of triumph than a sensation of doom. Eventually scientists questioned the processes in which they were engaged, but they were overwhelmed by the growing force of momentum—the seemingly uncontrollable thrust in the direction which previous decisions had charted. Some became horrified and bewildered at their handiwork, but they could no longer change direction or even judge the wisdom of their endeavor. As historian Daniel Boorstin has written, "In the end, all the voices urging caution and second thoughts about long-term consequences were barely audible above the roaring, crushing momentum of the gargantuan organized effort." The same sense of momentum captured the space program, which, in July 1969, achieved the first moon landing. Technologically the feat was astounding, but many questioned the human value of the effort.

That momentum, demonstrated so clearly by the atomic and space programs, came to dominate many aspects of life in the United States. Industrial development responded less to demonstrable needs than to previous investments, available technology, and anticipated profits. After midcentury it seemed impossible to stem the momentum in automobile production, highway construction, urban and university expansion. Between 1945 and 1970 the number of automobiles in the United States increased from 35 million to 95 million, an advance of well over 200 percent for a population which increased only 40 percent. Automobiles became increasingly larger, more powerful, and expensive, not because such changes served any national (or even rational) requirement but because larger automobiles could be manufactured, advertised, and sold at greater profit than smaller ones. Under the assumption that efficient power in the form of gasoline would remain cheap and plentiful, the public permitted the automobile industry to kill off other forms of transportation— railroads, streetcars, and electrical interurban lines. Thus it required only the gasoline shortage of late 1973 to create a national energy crisis and push the price of fuel to unprecedented levels. That crisis, moreover, raised the cry for self-sufficiency to be achieved through expanded use of coal and nuclear power.

Urban change likewise had a momentum of its own. On November 20, 1967, the population of the United States passed the 200 million mark, an increase of 50 million since 1950. The social significance of this population growth was less its rapidity than its burgeoning concentration in the large cities of America: by 1970 the nation was more than 70 percent urban. That year only 5 percent of the people lived on farms, compared with 23 percent in 1940. Yet these population shifts did not represent the full impact of urbanization. Cities engulfed entire geographical areas; great ''megalopolises''—areas of almost continuous urban density—emerged between Washington, D.C., and Boston, along the Great Lakes, and in both northern and southern California. Affluence produced major changes within the metropolitan areas themselves. Millions of citizens deserted the inner cities and moved to the suburbs; minority groups, principally blacks, replaced them. The settlements around Washington, D.C., were typical examples of the new trend. Between 1960 and 1968 the population gain in the central city was only 5.2 percent compared with 64 percent in the adjoining Virginia and Maryland suburbs. By 1970 some 37 percent of all Americans lived in suburbs while 31 percent lived in the central cities. New schools, churches, theaters, restaurants, shopping centers, and even light industries sprang up in the new suburbias. For most suburban dwellers the central business districts ceased to be vital cores of employment, shopping, and entertainment.

Actually the cities were in serious trouble even before the flight to the suburbs began. To achieve a minimum level of efficiency, comfort, and safety, these vast concentrations of population required community spirit—a willingness to engage in planning that would commit public funds to the well-being of all inhabitants, not merely the affluent. What little planning evolved, however, was designed to serve the needs of commerce and industry, not the broader requirements of human existence. Business leaders might favor better transportation to facilitate the movement of workers and buyers to their places of business, but they had no interest in expanding resources at their command on nonprofit poverty, welfare, slum clearance, or beautification programs. What the private market could do for the cities it did magnificently; the cities became the nation's great producers of wealth and profit. Where the financial community failed through neglect, no public agency could succeed.

In time the urban centers succumbed to the decades of neglect. In deep financial trouble after midcentury, they relied on state and federal programs to combat their mounting physical disabilities. Housing—the chief victim of inner-city poverty—remained their most conspicuous evidence of deterioration. Business districts as well suffered from degeneration and decay. Crime surged through the city streets, making fear and indeed physical danger a fact of life for most urban dwellers. The automobile took its toll, demanding ever-wider streets and more expansive parking lots, creating unbelievable congestion, and encouraging the deterioration of the inner cities.

Uncontrolled industrial and business expansion damaged the American environment. Much of the country's natural beauty suffered from the encroachments of highways, land developers, and the urban sprawl. Land use, generally planless, resulted in staggering waste and destruction that only a rich country would tolerate. Housing subdivisions, designed to attract urban dwellers to the countryside, encouraged speculation and polluted lakes and streams with mud and debris. Urban areas created an avalanche of trash that threatened to bury them. Americans, thriving on technology, discarded over 400 billion pounds of solid waste a year. With no curtailment of trash production in sight, cities were rapidly running out of burial space. Many would face acute crises in the seventies.

Industrial pollution comprised another assault on the environment—more dangerous because more deadly. At times smog blanketed Los Angeles as well as major cities along the Atlantic coast. Automobile exhaust was the major offender, followed closely by a variety of smoke- and fume-producing industries. Altogether American factories shared in the creation of 142 million tons of smoke and fumes each year. Every city of 500,000 people or more dumped at least 50 million gallons of sewage a year into the nation's streams, rivers, and lakes. Leakage from offshore oilwells or tankers polluted large areas of ocean; gummed up wharves and beaches; killed fish and wildlife; and contaminated oysters, scallops, and soft-shell clams.

Industrial growth offered jobs, opportunities, profits, and comforts. That it levied exorbitant social and economic costs seemed equally apparent. But perceptions of these costs and the means to control them varied. Conservative economists insisted that government and the free market, responding to public preferences, would exert the necessary restraints on corporate behavior and the uses of technology. Not even the control of pollution and energy use lay outside the normal operation of the free market, they argued; for what generated pollution was not growth but the failure of society to levy the necessary charges against such abuses. Optimists still believed that technology itself possessed the power to eliminate most physical challenges to human well-being. Proponents of growth argued, finally, that scarcity, not abundance, governed the lives of millions of the nation's poor. They believed that growth alone would create enough goods to satisfy the needs of all.

Environmentalists argued that the country had already entered an ecological crisis which demanded a government responsive to the challenges of scarcity and a new creed that most Americans could share. Some writers wondered how the free market could resolve questions of pollution and ecological catastrophe, of resource and energy depletion, when supply and demand were geared to the gratification of immediate wants. What troubled this minority especially was not the underconsumption of the poor but the overindulgence of the many. The United States, with a mere 6 percent of the world's population, consumed one-third of the world's energy. At established growth rates the country's energy needs would double in the seventies alone. Such exploitation of the earth's ecosystem, warned Barry Commoner in *The Closing Circle* (1971), would cause it to collapse. Eventually, he believed, the limitations of air, water, land, energy, and resources would demand a no-growth condition. Thus the new creed assumed that growth and technology were subject to social control, and that human existence based on restrained tastes could be rewarding. As William Ophuls observed in the April 1974 issue of *Harper's*: "A sophisticated and economically sound technology could bring us a life of simple sufficiency that would yet allow the full expression of the human potential. Having chosen such a life, . . . we might find it had its own richness."

The Underside of American Life

Success is an elusive condition, never easily attributable to individuals or to any social class. Still by the American standard of success—the ability to get ahead—there were countless millions in the seventies who had not achieved it. The most common rationale for unlimited economic growth was the country's self-assigned obligation to provide greater opportunities for its economically depressed. Without economic growth any general improvement in the lot of the poor would require a corresponding loss of wealth and status elsewhere in American society. The bitter resistance of the affluent to programs of economic redistribution was understandable enough. But it was equally clear that no conceivable level of economic production would resolve the needs of those millions who remained relatively unaffected by the astonishing economic expansion of previous decades. The barriers to wider distribution were historical, social, and political as well as economic. There remained a chasm between affluence and the power of the economy to drag even the marginal poor above the official poverty line. Capital expenditures of $100 billion in 1973 could not produce full employment.

In 1970 the nation's poor still numbered over 10 percent of the population. Many of the poor resided in the cities, but the incidence of poverty was far higher in the rural areas, especially in the backcountry extending from West Virginia southward into the Gulf States. Migrant farm laborers—several hundred thousand of them—worked their way northward from Georgia to the Canadian border each summer, living in appalling conditions, clearing perhaps a thousand dollars or often nothing at all. For tenant farmers of the deep South the antipoverty programs were often of limited value. Federal subsidies for cotton saved plantations but not the field hands. Federal programs poured billions of dollars into Appalachia; what they achieved was not clear. There were new roads, airfields, and dams; these, unfortunately, did little for the poor. In one four-county area of Kentucky 40 percent of the families had incomes of less than $1,000 a year. Most new jobs belonged to the expanded federal bureaucracy.

In urban America, poverty programs were not less successful than in rural areas; their failures were only more conspicuous. Much of the direct urban effort had not distinguished between central cities and suburbs. Federal expenditures for highways, airports, water and sewage systems brought greater returns to the middle-class suburbs than to the crowded tenements of the inner cities. President Johnson's Community Action Program (CAP) assumed that the poor, supported by the federal government, could design and carry out their own programs. Ultimately Congress appropriated over $6 billion for approximately one thousand programs. These generally lacked the necessary cooperation of local agencies. The limited gains against urban poverty after the midsixties resulted less from federal programs than from the glacial encroachments of prosperity.

Blacks made substantial economic gains after 1965, but they failed to share proportionally in the nation's prosperity. Median incomes for black families reached $6,860 in 1972, but that median remained pegged at about 59 percent of the median income of white families. The absolute gap in income widened. Measured by the official poverty line of $4,275 for a nonfarm family of four, the number of poor blacks increased in 1972 to 7.7 million—no less than one-third of all blacks residing in the United

States. The black middle class—sophisticated, well dressed, well housed—remained a small minority of the black population. The ratio of black unemployed remained twice that of whites through 1972 and 1973. Among urban black teenagers unemployment was over 35 percent.

Despite two decades of court victories for integration, the schools of the nation remained overwhelmingly segregated. Still in 1973, 46 percent of black pupils in eleven Southern states were in school with white majorities, compared to only 2 percent in 1964. Only 9 percent were in all-black schools. In the North 28 percent of blacks attended white majority schools; 11 percent were in all-black schools. In the North desegregation had scarcely begun. No plan, including busing, could overcome the reality of segregated housing. Increasingly black leaders appeared willing to settle for segregation provided that all-black schools received improved facilities, equipment, and instruction.

César Chavez addressing a crowd in San Rafel, Calif.

In Northern urban centers the elevation of blacks to high office became commonplace; in the South black political gains were less conspicuous but no less significant. Over 67 percent of Mississippi blacks were registered to vote in 1970; in 1965, only 8.3 percent. Such increases were typical of the entire South. In many Southern communities blacks controlled local governments and school boards, generally offering a superabundance of goodwill to help the whites adjust to the new order. Improved black-white relationships often reflected necessity rather than enlightenment. Still the foundation of self-interest was promising enough, especially when racial cooperation paid off in economic progress.

Spanish-speaking Americans, the nation's second largest minority group, suffered from poverty and discrimination no less than blacks. In 1973 over 10 million residents of the United States claimed Mexican, Cuban, Puerto Rican, or other Latin backgrounds. The Puerto Ricans, numbering some 750,000, lived largely in New York. Although they represented no more than 8 percent of the city's population, they accounted for one-third of all welfare recipients and a third of all inhabitants of substandard housing. More important numerically were the more than 6 million Mexican Americans of the five Southwestern states—California, Arizona, New Mexico, Texas, and Colorado. Unemployment among them ranged from 8 to 13 percent, twice the national average. The unemployed, underemployed, and unskilled who had given up the quest for employment varied from 42 to 47 percent. Many struggled as migrant laborers, living in poverty, filth, and disease. In New Mexico they faced the special problem of land titles. One authority estimated that Mexican Americans, following the American acquisition of New Mexico in 1848, lost over 5.5 million acres of private and communal property to Anglo-Americans. Those lands, declared New Mexico's Reies López Tijerina, would bring the Mexican American minority the jobs, food, and educational opportunities required to overcome racial and economic discrimination.

Increasingly Mexican Americans, in the pattern of the black civil rights movement, adopted the term "Chicano" to establish their cultural identity. Preaching a form of ethnic nationalism, Chicano leaders set out to develop a sense of community, a pride in their subculture, a renewed interest in Mexico's cultural heritage. In their quest for cultural recognition Chicanos demanded bilingual education for their Spanish-speaking children. The absence of Chicano language and culture in the schools sustained a cycle of underachievement. Chicano children averaged five years less schooling than whites, two less than blacks. Almost none reached college. To assert their economic and political interests against school boards and employers, Chicanos turned to collective action. César Chávez, above all a product of his culture, organized the National Farm Workers Association in 1962 and conducted a series of successful strikes to raise the wages of Chicano agricultural workers in California. His movement faltered in the 1970s as the Teamsters Union won more and more contracts with growers.

American Indians occupied the nation's bottom economic rung. Indian unemployment was the highest in the United States, exceeding 50 percent on most reservations. Half the nation's Indian families lived on $3,000 a year or less. The Oglala Sioux of South Dakota were 70 percent unemployed. The Navajo of Arizona endured hardships beyond the imagination of most Americans. They lived in tarpaper shacks and one-room hogans scattered over the desert, without adequate food or income. Almost half of Navajo children died before they reached their first birthday. Federal appropriations supported masses of bureaucrats but contributed little to the welfare of the country's special wards. Indians who deserted the reservations for the cities experienced little advantage; they still faced discrimination and unemployment. The Interior Department's Bureau of Indian Affairs (BIA) drowned the Indians in regulations. Reservation schools confirmed the Indians' sense of powerlessness and encouraged reliance on the BIA. Repeatedly the Interior Department leased reservation lands to corporations which tore up the earth, cut the timber, and polluted the waters—all under the argument that Indian lands were private property.

For some Indians this scarcely mattered. Those who favored the Indian Reorganization Act of 1934 demanded no more than recognition as the legal successors to the aboriginal tribes. This permitted them to control the reservations in cooperation with BIA officials. Opposed to them were the "treaty Indians" whose more ambitious purposes included the recovery of ancestral lands, the reestablishment of communal forms of economic life, and the perpetuation of Indian culture. This group organized the radical American Indian Movement (AIM) which condemned national policies and reservation officials alike. In October 1972, members of AIM closed in on Washington, eventually occupying the Bureau of Indian Affairs building and inflicting over $2 million in damage before they left the city with cartons of documents highly damaging to the BIA. Then from March until May 1973, AIM occupied and held the hamlet of Wounded Knee at the Oglala Pine Ridge reservation of South Dakota, all in defiance of federal authority. At issue in this confrontation was the allegedly corrupt Indian government at Pine Ridge; the deeper roots of the struggle lay in the continuing rivalries within the Indian community and the plight of some 800,000 Indians trying to come to terms with a vanishing past and an unpromising future.

Women's Liberation

Women—more than half the nation's inhabitants—had not, by many standards, acquired a status of equality in American life. Militants among them regarded their sex as another oppressed element in need of liberation. The women's liberation movement of the sixties encompassed basically middle-class housewives and college women who rebelled at the thought that their contribution to a male-dominated society lay chiefly in their sex. Betty Friedan's *The Feminine Mystique* (1963) gave the women's liberation movement both form and purpose. Friedan's middle-class associates formed the National Organization for Women (NOW) in 1966. To create the necessary legal base for the liberation of women, NOW sponsored the equal rights amendment which met its chief opposition from women who feared the loss of special legislative advantages which protected women in commerce and industry. To encourage female participation in politics, the women's movement formed the National Women's Political Caucus in 1972. Gloria Steinem's *Ms* was the movement's leading periodical.

Behind new militancy were three factors which held women to their traditional status—male supremacy, marriage, and the structure of the economic system. Those who sought liberation condemned the notion of male biological superiority which assigned women—even the most intelligent of them—the roles of motherhood, sexual partnership, family martyrdom, intellectual and economic dependence. For them marriage merely encouraged the tradition of economic exploitation and psychological mutilation. Women tolerated marriage, they said, only because it satisfied their economic and social requirements. Lacking independent social status, women could measure their worth only by identification with their husbands and children.

Whatever their educational level and competence, women faced job and pay discrimination. In every profession they held few of the top positions. In 1970 only 4.8 percent of the country's over three million managers and administrators were women. A *Fortune* magazine survey revealed that in one group of 6,500 corporate executives earning $30,000 a year or more only eleven were women. Like blacks, women in industry comprised a reserve army of workers, forced out by white males when labor was plentiful. In June 1974, the Supreme Court challenged pay discrimination when it ruled that employers must pay men and women equally for essentially equal work. The implications of that decision were beyond calculation. Measured by the pervading disadvantages facing women in American life, however, such gains seemed marginal. Women in increasing numbers cast off their inhibitions and expressed rage at the inferior status which society assigned them. Roxanne Dunbar expressed the cry of many women for liberation: "We are damaged and we have the right to hate and to have contempt and to kill and to scream. But for what? . . . Do we want the oppressor to admit he is wrong, to withdraw his misuse of us? . . . That does not make up for what I have lost, what I have never had. . . . Nothing will compensate for the irreparable harm it has done to my sisters. . . . How could we possibly settle for anything remotely less . . . than total annihilation of a system which systematically destroys half its people?"

Nixon's Progress Abroad

Friends of the Nixon administration gave it a year to wind up the American involvement in Vietnam. Yet the countdown began as early as March 1969. Over 10,000 Americans had died since the start of the Paris peace talks, 1,100 of them during the first three weeks of March. Upon his return from Saigon that month Secretary of Defense Laird informed Congress that the United States would increase South Vietnam's fighting capacity until the South Vietnamese forces could replace American units in an ultimately successful war. By promising both victory and the eventual Vietnamization of the war, Laird had created the foundations of Republican

Vietnam policy. Thereafter the administration repeated its warning that it would measure troop withdrawals by the capacity of the South Vietnamese army to assume the full military burden.

Recognizing the national aversion to more Vietnams, Nixon searched for a new formula which would assign the essential responsibility for Asian security to the Asians themselves. Early on his Pacific tour of July 1969 the President informed reporters at Guam that in the future the United States would defend the Asian nations against a nuclear threat, but that the Asians must confront internal subversion themselves. Nixon repeated this message in Manila and Jakarta. In Bangkok, Thailand, however, he appeared to reverse himself when he assured the Thais that the United States would stand shoulder to shoulder with them in resisting aggression both from within and from without. The new "Nixon Doctrine" left Asian as well as American observers puzzled. It reduced no American commitments; it repudiated no past agreements. Its intent, rather, was to uphold established goals without submerging the United States in another Asian war.

Neither Vietnamization nor the Nixon Doctrine silenced the war's critics. The nationwide moratorium of October 15, 1969, comprised the largest demonstration of antiwar sentiment during four years of direct American involvement. Antiwar leaders next planned the giant mobilization in Washington for November 15. The President met the challenge head-on with a carefully planned television address. On November 3 he gave the nation two choices—a precipitate withdrawal of all Americans from Vietnam with its predicted disaster for South Vietnam, the Middle East, Berlin, and even the Western Hemisphere, or the continued implementation of his Vietnamization program with its promise of eventual withdrawal and victory. Faced with that choice, the silent majority— those to whom the President directed his words —responded with anticipated approval. But the President had skirted the alternatives posed by the war's critics—a modification of the Saigon

regime or a war without foreseeable end. On November 15, some 250,000 converged on Washington to make their dissatisfaction known, but the President had already blocked their appeal to the nation's masses.

During the spring of 1970 North Vietnamese sanctuaries just over the Cambodian border some 35 to 50 miles west of Saigon seemed to endanger the Vietnamization program. In March an anti-Communist military coup in Cambodia drew additional North Vietnamese forces into that country. Finally on April 30 the President announced an American invasion of Cambodia to assure the success of his withdrawal program, destroy Communist supply centers, establish the conditions for successful negotiations, and protect American prestige. The United States, he warned, dared not behave like a "pitiful, helpless giant." The reaction was violent. Antiwar demonstrations disrupted 400 college campuses; at Kent State University in Ohio four students died in a confrontation with National Guardsmen. Militarily the Cambodian operation achieved some limited successes. With few casualties the American troops unearthed massive supply dumps, more extensive and better stocked than any previously found in the war.

Beyond the destruction of food and munitions the gains from the Cambodian venture were not clear. Cambodia now emerged as an active theater of war. The new display of force did not enhance the prospects for peace. The administration's repeated truce proposals avoided Hanoi's minimum demand for a negotiated political settlement. Critics who rejected the possibility of a military solution argued for the withdrawal of all American troops by an established deadline; in the Senate the Hatfield-McGovern amendment recommended the end of December 1971. This proposal failed, 55 to 39. With solid congressional support the President pursued his program of Vietnamization, spurred on by declining morale in the American forces. Already he had reduced American troop levels in Vietnam to 425,000; he promised another 150,000-man cut by April 1971. In reducing the American presence in Vietnam, the President had either to divorce his goals from those of Saigon or to entrust his pursuit of victory to other, more acceptable, sources of power. Beginning in November 1970, Nixon unleashed American air power against North Vietnam in what became the most massive air war in history. Having stabilized American policy in Vietnam at acceptable levels of expenditure, the President turned to other diplomatic fronts which promised greater successes.

So complete was Nixon's control of Vietnam policy that Daniel Ellsberg's release of the top-secret Pentagon Papers to the *New York Times* and the *Washington Post* in the early summer of 1971 scarcely challenged it. Still by revealing much of the shallowness of thought behind the American involvement, the publication of this massive document, completed in 1968, threatened to embarrass the administration. The Justice Department quickly obtained an injunction to prevent further publication of excerpts. The Supreme Court, with three justices dissenting, held in *New York Times Company v. United States* that the government had failed to show justification for the imposition of "prior restraint" against publication. The Court's majority, in upholding freedom of the press, argued that the publication of the Pentagon Papers did not endanger the security of the United States.

For twenty years United States policy toward China had been based on a carefully sustained rejection of the mainland regime as the legitimate government of China. Peking's excesses during the Cultural Revolution of the midsixties isolated that regime and reinforced Washington's program of opposition. Suddenly in 1971 the older perception of China as a dangerous, revolutionary force in Asia, meriting every American effort to isolate it, evaporated under Nixon's leadership. That year Peking made clear its desire for better relations with Washington. China's new pragmatism responded to the pervading realities of the Sino-Soviet rift which had brought fifty Russian divisions to the Chinese frontier, the re-emergence of Japan as a major

Soviet Party Leader Brezhnev and President Nixon during Nixon's historic visit to the U.S.S.R.

United Press International

factor in Asian life, and the expectation of peace in Vietnam.

Nixon responded to the prospects of normalized United States–Chinese relations by dispatching adviser Henry Kissinger to Peking in July 1971 to arrange a summit meeting. These tendencies toward détente culminated in the President's trip to Peking in February 1972. The communique which ended the historic week-long visit recognized that Taiwan, where Chiang Kai-shek still ruled, was part of China. The island's future would be determined by the Chinese themselves. That the President's diplomacy toward China enjoyed widespread acclaim was not strange. Nixon's own anti-Communist past allayed many conservative doubts. For other Americans the older attitudes, defended with such flamboyant rhetoric, never made much sense. In 1971 the Peking government replaced the Republic of China in the UN without producing distress among the American people—or damage to the UN.

Nixon's dramatic journey to Moscow in May

1972 again responded to changing circumstances. Behind the march to that summit was a half-decade of accumulating conviction that the Cold War drift had ceased to serve the interests of either the United States or the U.S.S.R. The overriding concern of the two superpowers was the avoidance of nuclear war; beyond that, the mutual desire to curtail the ruinously expensive arms race. During the early seventies the two nations expended some $130 billion for defense annually. Both countries possessed over one thousand missile launchers, a far larger number of nuclear warheads, and nuclear-armed submarine fleets. In addition, the United States maintained a large long-range bomber force. The Russians, moreover, desired American technology, especially computers and machine tools, as well as trade agreements backed by ample American credits. The Sino-Soviet rivalry demanded the dispersal of Soviet military forces and raised the prospect of a two-front confrontation. For the United States, conditions had also changed. West German Chancellor Willy Brandt's *Ostpolitik* (Eastern policies) of 1970 opened the way for all-European accommodation by recognizing, in treaties with Warsaw and Moscow, the postwar frontiers of Central Europe. Thereafter Washington could no longer regard the Soviet domination of East-Central Europe as the central issue in the East-West conflict.

Soviet leader Leonid Brezhnev's speech before the Communist Party Congress in March 1971 formally announced the Kremlin's desire for improved Soviet–United States relations. Nixon responded cautiously, determined to work on the broadest possible range of issues. When negotiations in Washington and Moscow during the spring of 1971 settled a series of minor questions, the President, on October 12, announced his plans for a trip to Moscow in May 1972. Thereafter Kissinger, in confidential negotiations, completed the final preparations. The presummit agreements were essential for the success of the summit itself. The documents signed at Moscow amid continuous displays of cordiality were not overwhelming but they were impressive enough. Unable to agree on the Middle East where the Soviets and Americans continued to supply arms to Israel and the Arab states, Nixon and Brezhnev bound their two countries together with a variety of joint committees and projects. They signed two nuclear arms pacts, one limiting defensive missiles to two sites, the other freezing offensive weapons to current levels for five years. Nixon and Brezhnev agreed to a second summit, to be held in Washington during June 1973.

The basis of the Nixon-Kissinger approach to Russia and China was the conviction that both countries had become *status quo* powers, and thus part of a new international equilibrium. As the President confided to *Time* magazine in January 1972: "[T]he only time . . . we have had any extended periods of peace is when there has been a balance of power. So . . . I think it would be a safer world and a better world if we have a strong, healthy United States, Europe, Soviet

President Nixon and Secretary of State Henry Kissinger during the Mideast crisis (1973)

United Press International

Union, China, and Japan, each balancing the other. . . ." Still the changes in American purpose were more apparent than real. The Nixon Doctrine did not reduce the nation's official demands on Asia. Détente established the foundation for Soviet-American cooperation in areas of tension, but always under the imperative that Russia not alter any situation to its advantage.

Following the Middle East crisis of October 1973, Kissinger warned that the United States could permit no Soviet victories against American arms. Fundamentally the Nixon approach attempted to multilateralize the burden of maintaining world stability without compromising any established American objective in areas of United States–Soviet competition.

Nixonian Politics: Divisiveness at Home

That national consensus which supported the President's policies abroad existed for none of the country's major challenges at home. The unresolved questions of American society were too complex, too potentially expensive, to permit easy calculations of public interest in either continuity or change. Political and economic pressure groups aggravated the national dilemma by drowning the country with facts and arguments designed to protect their specific interests. Strong leadership might have clarified perceptions of public need and generated sufficient unity to encourage forthright governmental responses. But the President identified his administration with the so-called silent majority of Middle America which hoped only to solidify social and economic gains already achieved. He was scarcely in communication with the disaffected minorities, especially the blacks, at all.

Throughout his first presidential year Nixon dominated the Democratic-controlled Congress. Even on social and economic policies—areas traditionally in the Democratic preserve—he kept his congressional opponents off balance. As President, Nixon could scarcely ignore the poverty issue, for the country's ill-conceived, often demeaning, and generally inadequate programs for social improvement were costing the American taxpayers billions of dollars. In 1969 approximately 10 million Americans were on welfare rolls. The program of Aid to Families with Dependent Children (AFDC) brought the number of children receiving welfare to more than half the total. President Johnson's Commission

on Income Maintenance proposed a minimum annual income for every family. Nixon adopted the commission's formula in his wide-sweeping Family Assistance Program of 1969 which would provide cash payments of $1,600 plus food stamps valued at $820 to a family of four on relief. The Philadelphia Plan, which established quotas for black workers on federal construction projects, permitted the President to make an important gesture toward blacks. Nixon preempted the environmental issues by investing rhetoric and little else. When Congress met in January 1970, it faced an administration-sponsored program carefully designed to neutralize the most important issues before the nation: pollution, inflation, crime control, and welfare. Democratic strategists admitted that in Nixon they faced the most consummate politician since FDR.

Unfortunately the President could not translate his command of the Washington scene into genuine gains against inflation—one issue on which he asked voters to measure his success. From the outset Nixon hoped to control inflation without paying the normal price of unemployment. Rejecting direct wage and price controls, he agreed with his economic advisers that the answer lay in restrictions on the money supply. To curtail spending, the Federal Reserve System restricted credit and sent interest rates to record levels. But the President refused to depress the economy by controlling federal spending. So heavy were the expenditures for defense, the space program, and the Vietnam war that the federal government ran an $18 billion deficit in the fiscal year of 1971. The mixed Nixon program stifled sales, pushed some corporations to the point of bankruptcy, and increased unemployment. But it failed to suppress inflation.

Nixon avoided open confrontation with his detractors. Yet beneath the surface the anger and resentment of the Johnson years continued to seethe, sustained largely by the continuing war in Vietnam. Republican strategists, approaching the 1970 elections, prepared to exploit the alienated minority in their effort to transform the Republican Party into the normal majority party of the United States. To broaden its solid minority base the G.O.P. required defections from both George Wallace's Southern white supporters and the increasingly conservative Democrats of Middle America. Thus Nixon's so-called Southern strategy of 1970 aimed at the separation of the Democratic Party's liberal, antiwar leadership from the Southern and labor-ethnic elements that comprised the older Roosevelt coalition. By pinning the issues of violence and permissiveness on Democratic liberals, the President hoped to drive conservative Democrats into the G.O.P.

During September Vice President Agnew, who carried the Republican campaign burden, opened his alliterative war on the Democratic "vicars of vacillation," "nattering nabobs of negativism," and "hopeless, hysterical hypochondriacs of history." He defined the Democratic leadership as the "radiclib elite." Gradually he identified Democratic leaders with the rebellious youth. Would the nation, he asked, follow an elected President or a disruptive,

radical minority? During October the President himself entered the campaign, using campus disorders to turn the election into a referendum on students. On election eve he called on all Americans "to stand up and be counted against the appeasement of the rock throwers and obscenity shouters of America." Somehow the effort failed. On November 3 the Democrats lost two Senate seats, but gained nine House members and eleven governorships. Only eighteen of the fifty-two senate and gubernatorial candidates for whom Nixon and Agnew campaigned won their elections.

Throughout 1971 the nation's economy continued to suffer from "stagflation"—stagnation and inflation. Critics proposed price and wage controls, especially where corporations were not subject to open market operations. Finally, on August 15, the President deserted his earlier opposition to controls and announced a ninety-day price-wage freeze during which the administration would establish a new program for price and wage stability. To increase American sales abroad the President suspended the established ratio of dollars to gold, thereby permitting dollar devaluation against other currencies. This terminated the international monetary system created in July 1944 at Bretton Woods, based on dollar-gold convertibility. Many economists still insisted that the free market alone could establish long-term economic stability. That the President and his advisers shared this view presaged their eventual desertion of controls. On January 11, 1973, the President announced Phase III of his economic program which relaxed most federal regulations.

The Presidential Campaign of 1972

Democratic leaders, contemplating the 1972 presidential campaign, were determined to avoid the chaos of the 1968 Chicago convention. By March 1970, the party had adopted new guidelines whereby women, young voters, and minorities would receive delegate representation in

the 1972 convention roughly proportional to their numbers in the general population. This reform assured an open convention but it effectively broke the control of Old Guard Democrats over the Democratic Party. For the moment this mattered little, for Edmund Muskie of

Maine, choice of most Democratic regulars, was clearly the party's front-runner. Yet he scarcely survived the New Hampshire primary in March. Senator George McGovern of South Dakota, the party's chief spokesman for the New Politics— and thus the potential beneficiary of the new party rules—won 37 percent of the votes.

Thereafter McGovern, capturing state conventions, winning some primaries, losing others to George Wallace and Hubert Humphrey, moved ahead of the pack. Victories in California and New York during June assured his nomination at the Miami convention in July. But McGovern did not capture the Democratic Party. Without the party reforms he would not have won at all. To the end he ran poorly in the opinion polls; his primary votes totaled less than those of Humphrey. He was a minority candidate in his own party. Disaster almost leveled the McGovern campaign in late July when Senator Thomas F. Eagleton of Missouri, his choice for the vice presidency, admitted that he had undergone psychiatric care. Eagleton withdrew under pressure. McGovern selected R. Sargent Shriver, former head of the Peace Corps and ambassador to France, to join him on the ticket.

Nixon's nomination at Miami Beach in August came quickly and overwhelmingly—1,347 to 1 on the first ballot. The White House-controlled platform endorsed the Nixon record. The powerful Committee for the Re-election of the President (CRP), working independently of the Republican Party, collected an estimated $60 million to finance the Nixon campaign. Polls made the President a 2-to-1 choice over McGovern. Thus assured of victory, Nixon refused to debate the issues. Throughout the campaign Nixon avoided the press; he authorized no aide to speak for him.

But if the Republican Party could avoid the issues, it could not escape charges of corruption. During March the country learned that the International Telephone and Telegraph Company (ITT) had agreed to finance the Republican national convention in San Diego at the same time that the Justice Department pulled back

from a major antitrust case involving ITT. In September a federal grand jury indicted two former White House aides, plus five accomplices, on eight counts of stealing documents and bugging the Democratic headquarters at Washington's Watergate complex on June 17. Never before in the nation's history had White House aides been indicted for crime.

President Nixon and his former Attorney General, John Mitchell, now heading his re-election effort, denied that anyone "presently employed" in the administration was involved in the Watergate affair. Still the fact that former aides had access to funds collected by CRP continued to implicate the administration. Gradually it appeared from an accumulation of evidence even then available that the Watergate raid was only part of an elaborate Republican attempt at disruption and sabotage to spread confusion throughout the Democratic campaign effort. This activity, it seemed, had extended to forging letters, seizing confidential files, disrupting campaign schedules, and seeking information on the private lives of Democratic campaign workers. For some writers—even Republicans—this evidence of wrongdoing was deeply alarming. Still every McGovern effort to capitalize on the Watergate affair proved ineffective. Many Americans no longer expected much efficiency and honesty in government. Others simply wrote off McGovern's charges as "politics" and hence probably untrue.

McGovern's campaign never recovered from the Eagleton episode. Americans generally did not regard him as a serious candidate. He spoke fervently but few listened. By October McGovern faced rejection everywhere, even among old-line Democrats. Unions representing 11 million voters refused to endorse him. Nixon's victory in November was as overwhelming as the polls predicted. His popular vote topped 60 percent; his 49 states (he lost only Massachusetts and the predominantly black District of Columbia) gave him a towering 521 to 17 advantage in the electoral college. He carried New York City—the first Republican to do so since 1924. He splintered the old New Deal coalition, breaking completely the traditional Democratic hold on the South. Yet Nixon's victory reflected less the majority's approval of his leadership than its antipathy toward McGovern. Nixon's noncampaign and McGovern's apocalyptic rhetoric brought only 54 percent to the polls, the lowest turnout in 24 years. The Democrats fared far better on other fronts, gaining two seats in the Senate and losing only 12 in the House. They also won 11 of the 18 governorships at stake.

The Second Term

Fresh from his landslide victory, Nixon admitted to newsmen: "The tendency is for an administration to run out of steam after the first four years, and then to coast, and usually coast downhill. This is particularly true when there is what you call a landslide victory. . . ." His purpose, he said, was to change that historical pattern. By January 1973, he had purged his top administrative staff, placing in key positions a new group which shared his concern for economy, efficiency, and unquestioned loyalty. Backed by new advisers and the mandate of 1972, the President set out to trim the programs of the Democratic past. "America was not built by government," ran the theme of his second inaugural, "but by people—not by welfare, but by work." A leaner government that demanded more of its citizens would nurture a new spirit of independence, self-reliance, and pride. Whether the President's new austerity program embodied the national will was irrelevant; within a year his administration was fighting for its life in the face of new Watergate revelations.

Throughout the 1972 campaign Nixon effectively neutralized the Vietnam issue by warning his Democratic opponents that any public criticism of the war would damage his peace negotiations in Paris. On election eve Kissinger, the chief negotiator, proclaimed that "peace is at hand." Yet it required additional talks and two weeks of saturation bombing of North Vietnam to accomplish the ceasefire of late January 1973. This agreement provided for the return of all American prisoners of war and the withdrawal of all United States military personnel within sixty days. The President claimed "peace with honor"

but inspired no public outburst of joy. Whatever emotions the nation could arouse it reserved for the returning prisoners of war.

Nixon responded to the continued insurgency in Cambodia with another massive air offensive. By late April 1973, the United States had bombed the Cambodian countryside for fifty successive days. But the administration's war policies were now doomed. In May a Gallup Poll revealed that 60 percent of the American people opposed the bombing, that 75 percent believed congressional approval necessary. During June Congress acted, attaching riders which denied the use of federal funds in Cambodia to increasingly essential financial legislation. Ultimately the administration had to either capitulate or see the whole government deprived of operating funds. The House and Senate agreed to the President's proposal of a bombing cutoff on August 15 to bring the American war in Southeast Asia to an end. Cambodia demonstrated that a united Congress was still the commanding force in the American constitutional system. Another, more potent, demonstration of that lesson lay ahead.

In mid-June 1973, Leonid Brezhnev arrived in Washington for the second Nixon-Brezhnev summit. After two days of talks at the White House, which began on June 19, Nixon and Brezhnev signed agreements for cooperation in oceanography, agriculture, transportation, and cultural exchange. The two leaders then retired to Camp David, the presidential retreat in Maryland, returning to Washington to sign key accords on arms limitation and peaceful uses of atomic energy. On June 22 the two leaders signed an agreement pledging mutual efforts to avoid military confrontations that could lead to a nuclear war; that accord climaxed over a year of secret negotiations. Later Nixon and Brezhnev flew to the President's estate at San Clemente, California, and terminated their working sessions by completing a seventeen-page communiqué calling for further détente between the two countries. Again the summit was characterized by pomp, pageantry, and exhibitions of cordiality and good humor. Some critics regarded it as a public relations performance, pointing to the continuing ideological conflict underneath, the immensity of Soviet conventional armed forces, and the narrow focus of the agreements themselves. But reaction in general was very favorable.

Beginning with the October 1973 Arab-Israeli war, Kissinger, now Secretary of State, focused the American diplomatic effort on the search for a permanent Middle East settlement. By January 1974, his peripatetic diplomacy had gained a truce between Egypt and Israel; it had established the foundations for Middle East peace talks at Geneva. Then in May and June 1974, Kissinger capped one of the greatest displays of personal diplomacy on record in securing an agreement between Israel and Syria over the disputed Golan Heights. For twenty-eight days he flew back and forth between Jerusalem and Damascus to arrange the Israeli withdrawal and the return of Israel's prisoners of war. To ratify this new United States relationship with the Arab world, President Nixon in June embarked on a triumphal tour of Egypt, Saudi Arabia, Syria, Israel, and Jordan. Everywhere his cordial receptions broadened his image as a maker of peace.

By early July Nixon was in Moscow for his third summit meeting with Soviet leader Brezhnev. His agreements were modest and failed to include the desired arrangement on offensive nuclear weapons, but they kept the United States–Soviet détente on course. As Nixon and Brezhnev agreed to a fourth summit in 1975, the President attributed the success of détente to the personal friendship he had developed with Brezhnev. Public opinion polls registered the country's general satisfaction with Nixon's accomplishments abroad.

By the summer of 1974 inflation overshadowed all other issues before the nation. Analysts predicted a severe money crisis which could injure banks and corporations alike. Phase IV of the President's economic policy had in effect phased out all remaining controls by early 1974, freeing major companies to announce extensive price increases. As the GNP declined in 1974, the consumer price index bolted upward toward an annual rate of almost 15 percent. This produced suspicion and resentment not only among low- and middle-income families, but also among more affluent Americans who found that incomes in excess of $20,000 a year were insufficient to meet family requirements. Inflation redistributed income, overturned social priorities, and misallocated resources.

Experts on the economy were not helpful. Those who had applied the available economic tools—tax cuts and heavy governmental expenditures—to expand production in the 1960s had applied them not to a depressed economy but to one already performing at a high level of employment and consumption. Thereafter Vietnam could easily overheat the economy. The economic managers who had once claimed unlimited powers over the state of supply and demand seemed powerless to control the resulting inflation. World pressures aggravated the dilemma. The oil embargo and high oil prices, world food shortages, and expanding economies everywhere created global demand in excess of supply. Liberal economists advocated tax cuts plus greater outlays to overcome shortages of food and fuel. Conservatives generally upheld the administration's program of tight money and moderate fiscal restraint, with reliance on the free market to establish ultimate price stability. Still others favored controls on prices and profits to stop the lockstep raising of prices by large corporations. For businessmen the answer lay in industrial expansion, with Washington encouraging new investment with special tax incentives. Meanwhile continuing inflation fell disproportionately on the American people, undermining faith in the fairness of national policy.

The Lengthening Shadow of Watergate

For Americans generally, Nixon's triumph of November 1972 buried the Watergate issue beyond resurrection. During September and October 1972, *Washington Post* reporters Carl Bernstein and Bob Woodward had disclosed CRP's secret funds and White House connections, its eavesdropping and bugging, its political espionage. White House denials sustained the public's overwhelming disinterest. But on January 8 the trial of the "Watergate Seven" opened in Judge John J. Sirica's U.S. District Court in Washington. Shortly thereafter five of the defendants, including former White House employee E. Howard Hunt, pleaded guilty to conspiracy, eavesdropping, burglary, and bugging. On January 30 the jury found the other two defendants—G. Gordon Liddy and James W. McCord, Jr.—guilty on all counts. Despite Sirica's questioning, the trial failed to implicate the White House or the President's re-election committee. Already it was known that Jeb Stuart Magruder, deputy director of CRP, had ordered Liddy to establish a political intelligence operation, and that Hugh W. Sloan, Jr., a CRP finance officer, had turned over large sums of money to Liddy. But Sloan denied that he or any CRP official knew that Liddy had planned the Watergate break-in.

Sirica conditioned the sentencing of McCord and Liddy on their willingness to cooperate with the new Senate Watergate Committee, headed by North Carolina's Sam Ervin. On March 19 McCord sent a letter to Sirica declaring that political pressure had been brought on all the defendants to plead guilty and remain silent, that perjury had been committed during the trial, and that others, not identified, had been involved in the Watergate affair. Shortly thereafter McCord told the Ervin committee that former Attorney General Mitchell, White House counsel John W. Dean III, White House staffer Charles Colson, and Magruder had either approved or personally knew of CRP's wiretapping, bugging, and espionage operations.

Meanwhile federal prosecutors had become convinced that Watergate involved a massive White House conspiracy; on April 15 that evidence reached the President. Magruder and Dean, both deeply troubled by the long cover-up, implicated themselves as well as Mitchell and Nixon's two top White House aides, H. R. (Bob) Haldeman and John Ehrlichman. On April 17 the President made his first public admission that the Watergate scandal might reach into the White House. He cited March 21 as the date on which he first learned the details of the cover-up. Then on April 30, in a major television address, Nixon accepted full responsibility for the Watergate affair, but denied any personal involvement in either the break-in or the cover-up. His associates, he said, had kept the facts from him. When he discovered the facts, he had instituted a new probe. The President announced the resignations of Haldeman, Ehrlichman, Attorney General Richard Kleindienst, and Dean. He replaced Kleindienst with Elliot L. Richardson. Strangely the President refused to condemn those around him whose actions now endangered his presidency. He even called Haldeman and Ehrlichman "two of the finest public servants it has been my privilege to know."

During May the government's case against Daniel Ellsberg for his release of the Pentagon Papers on the Vietnam war during the summer of 1971 ended in a mistrial. The White House revealed that Hunt and Liddy, two members of the White House investigations unit—the so-called plumbers—had broken into the office of Ellsberg's psychiatrist, Dr. Lewis Fielding, during September 1971, in search of derogatory information. In a 4,000-word Watergate statement, released on May 22, the President explained that he had established the special intelligence unit and authorized wiretapping in the interest of national security. Those who undertook illegal activities without his knowledge, he said, may have "felt justified in engaging in specific activities that I would have disapproved."

Beginning in May 1973, the televised Senate Watergate hearings revealed the siege mentality which had gripped the White House. As staffer Dwight Chapin reminded young Herbert L. Porter, who testified in June, "One thing you should realize early on, we are practically an island here." The chief task of the White House team was that of protecting the President from the hostile forces that surrounded the island. Mitchell testified that he would have gone to almost any length in covering up the scandals as long as Nixon's re-election seemed to require it. Colson admitted later that he and others regarded themselves above the law while working in the White House. Amid such assumptions any action, even burglary, was a necessary—and justifiable—act of national defense.

Nixon's survival rested on his argument that his aides had betrayed him and that he himself was innocent of the cover-up. Magruder's key testimony in June implicated both CRP and the White House in the Watergate cover-up. As he told the committee: "The cover-up began that Saturday when we realized there was a break-in. I do not think there was ever any discussion that there would not be a cover-up." Subsequent testimony established the pattern of payments to buy the silence of the Watergate burglars. Dean challenged the President's defense directly when he charged that the President knew of the cover-up almost from the beginning. It was not until Nixon faced a Senate investigation in March 1973, recalled Dean, that he became concerned with Watergate. At the critical March 21 meeting Dean revealed details of the cover-up. "I began by telling the President," he said, "that there was a cancer growing on the Pres-

idency and that if the cancer was not removed that the President himself would be killed by it." Dean charged that the President discussed clemency for the Watergate Seven and even a payment of $1 million to buy the defendants' silence. Subsequent testimony failed to corroborate Dean's accusations. Indeed, in their testimony Mitchell, Ehrlichman, and Haldeman argued that the President knew nothing of the cover-up before March 21. When the televised Watergate hearings ended in August the Ervin committee had failed to break the Watergate case.

What proved to be crucial testimony came in July when Alexander P. Butterfield, a former White House operations man, revealed that a secret, highly sophisticated White House electronics system had recorded all the office and telephone conversations of the President after its installation in the spring of 1971. This revelation inaugurated a giant test of wills between the President and all government investigators. To prepare the Justice Department's legal case against White House officials charged with wrongdoing, Attorney General Richardson had appointed Harvard law professor Archibald Cox. Cox demanded nine tapes as necessary evidence for his staff. The President, claiming executive privilege, refused to release the tapes. By October Cox had obtained two court rulings which upheld his right to subpoena the tapes. Nixon offered Cox a compromise. Cox rejected it and Nixon ordered him fired. Both Richardson and the Deputy Attorney General, William Ruckelshaus, refused to carry out the order and resigned. Finally newly-appointed Solicitor General Robert Bork removed Cox from his position; the staff continued, unchanged. Early in November Nixon named Leon Jaworski, a prominent Texas lawyer, as Watergate prosecutor.

Meanwhile disaster struck the Nixon administration on another front. Weeks of grand jury testimony into alleged kickbacks which Vice President Agnew had received both as a Maryland official and as Vice President, raised the issue of criminality and tax evasion. Late in

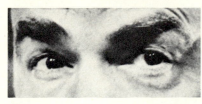

1972

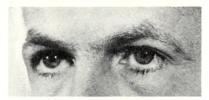

The arrest on June 17 of (left to right) James W. McCord, Jr., Bernard L. Barker, Eugenio R. Martinez, Frank Sturgis, and Virgilio R. Gonzalez for the break-in at Democratic headquarters had little effect on the landslide victory of Nixon in November. Nixon, insulated from the public, saw the Watergate drama unfold through the eyes of staff members like (top to bottom) John D. Ehrlichman, John W. Dean III, H. R. Haldeman, and Jeb Stuart Magruder.

WATERGATE

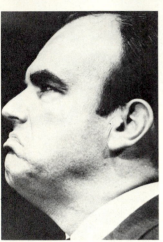

On October 20 Special Prosecutor Archibald Cox was fired for refusing to comply with a presidential proposal for turning over taped material to the Senate Watergate Committee, and Attorney General Elliot Richardson resigned in protest (top). This so-called Saturday Night Massacre provoked a public outcry against the whole Watergate affair that had been building up during the preceding months' hearings conducted by Senator Sam Ervin's committee. The testimony of former Nixon staff members like John D. Ehrlichman, John M. Mitchell, and John W. Dean III had greatly increased the controversy.

Top: The New York Times; all others on this page: United Press International Photo

1974

Top and right: Wide World Photos; left: United Press International Photo

The House Judiciary Committee (top) in its final sessions voted on five articles of impeachment: On July 27 it passed by a vote of 27–11 an article charging Nixon with obstruction of justice; on July 29 by a vote of 28–10 it charged abuse of power; on July 30 it passed 21–17 an article charging the President with unconstitutionally defying its subpoenas and defeated two other articles—concealing the Cambodian bombing (26–12) and willful income tax evasion (26–12). On July 24 the Supreme Court ruled 8–0 that Nixon must turn over tapes of 64 conversations related to Watergate trials; on July 30 White House attorney James St. Clair and a Secret Service agent (left) turned over the first 20 tapes to Judge John J. Sirica (right).

On August 8, 1974, Richard M. Nixon announced his resignation, the first president to do so in the history of the United States. The next day White House guards rolled up the red carpet as he left the White House as President for the last time, shortly before the swearing-in of Gerald R. Ford as 38th President. On September 8 Ford granted Nixon a full pardon for any crimes committed by him while in office. At the time of the pardon 28 of Nixon's associates—including a vice-president, 4 Cabinet officers, White House aides, and high Republican Party officials—were involved in criminal charges. The controversy surrounding Watergate would continue for years.

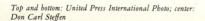

October, after numerous denials of wrongdoing, the Vice President resigned, accepting a $10,000 fine and immunity from further criminal prosecution.

President Nixon misjudged the public reaction to Cox's dismissal. Thousands of telegrams poured into Washington demanding the President's impeachment. Nixon quickly turned over the subpoenaed tapes. This spurred demands for his removal, for the public soon learned that two of the subpoenaed tapes were missing. During October twenty-eight House members supported the move toward impeachment. The annual convention of the AFL-CIO approved a resolution demanding Nixon's resignation or impeachment. By early November the Gallup Poll reported a dip in support for the President from 68 to 27 percent during the course of the year. In December the House Judiciary Committee appointed John M. Doar, a Republican lawyer who had served in the Justice Department under Robert Kennedy, to direct its investigation of the charges against the President.

Nixon struck back at his detractors with his so-called Operation Candor, in which he argued his cause before appreciative audiences. On November 20 he assured the nation's nineteen Republican governors that there would be no further disclosures. But on the following day the White House admitted that one of the requested tapes—covering a Nixon-Haldeman Watergate conversation three days after the break-in—had an 18-minute gap which experts later attributed to deliberate erasure. On December 6 Republican Congressman Gerald Ford of Michigan was sworn in as Vice President of the United States. In the final gesture of "Operation Candor" the President, on December 8, released a massive financial statement to answer mounting allegations of irregularity in his personal finances.

Late in February 1974, the second Watergate grand jury, impaneled in April 1973, indicted seven White House officials on charges of covering up the Watergate burglary by destroying evidence, lying to investigators, buying silence with large sums of money, and offering clemency. Those accused included Haldeman, Ehrlichman, Mitchell, and Colson. The jury also delivered to Judge Sirica a sealed briefcase of evidence reportedly dealing with the President's role in the Watergate conspiracy. Not until June 1974, did the country learn that the grand jury, by a vote of 19 to 0, had named Nixon as an unindicted co-conspirator in the Watergate cover-up. Jaworski had argued that an incumbent president could not be indicted by a grand jury. Meanwhile concurrent reports of the Internal Revenue Service and the special congressional investigative unit found the President some $432,000 shy in back taxes and interest for his first four years in the White House. Shortly thereafter a House report set the federal expenditure on the President's San Clemente and Key Biscayne houses at $17.1 million. Even the White House admitted that over $200,000 went into house improvements.

Throughout the early spring of 1974 Nixon assured the nation that Jaworski and the grand jury possessed all the information they needed to bring the Watergate investigation to a conclusion. But in April the Judiciary Committee voted unanimously to subpoena tapes of forty-two presidential conversations. The showdown came on April 30 when Nixon announced in a televised address that he was delivering to the committee—and making available to the American people—transcripts of most of the subpoenaed conversations, totaling some 1,200 pages. He gambled that the transcripts would encourage his supporters, divide his critics, and shake the bipartisan unity of the Judiciary Committee. Only by a narrow 20 to 18 vote did the committee remind the President that he had not complied with the committee's request.

On the central question of the President's involvement in Watergate the transcripts were ambivalent. But other revelations were not helpful. Even after March 21, 1973, it was clear that the President had made no effort to stop the payments of hush money or extend the inquiry into the cover-up. Nor did he ever encourage his subordinates to answer the grand jury forthrightly. Not once did the President condemn his associates for defying what should have been the minimal standards of his administration. The transcripts revealed no White House concern for the presidency, for national security, or for the operations of government. Even with the deletions of unprintable language, the transcripts were the most self-incriminating document ever published by an American president. Pennsylvania's Republican Senator Hugh Scott termed the White House performance "shabby, disgusting, immoral." Many Republican regulars again asked the President to resign.

Amid such demands the House Judiciary Committee, backed by a 410-to-4 vote to subpoena anything it required, began its formal, secret impeachment hearings. The committee's large staff had been gathering evidence and preparing its presentation since January. House transcripts of key tapes differed significantly from those of the White House. In one segment of the committee's transcript, Nixon, on March 22, 1973, told John Mitchell, "I want you to stonewall it, plead the Fifth Amendment, cover up or anything else" when called before the grand jury. James D. St. Clair, who headed the President's legal staff, rested his defense largely on the claim that Nixon did not approve the hush money payments, but acted rather as an interested spectator.

Whatever the quality of the staff effort, committee members could not, as a group, simply weigh the evidence. Prejudices, party affiliations, and uncertainties of constituent opinion would influence decisions. The polls revealed that at least three out of four Americans distrusted the President. Still a majority seemed to oppose impeachment, although public opinion polls in May and June registered a clear majority in favor of the President's removal. To reinforce public doubts Nixon used every occasion to emphasize the notion that the presidency itself was in danger. A strong United States and a strong presidency, he declared repeatedly, were the most powerful guarantees of world peace.

What were proper grounds for impeachment? In February 1974, the Judiciary Committee's staff released a report, replete with English precedents, which declared that in an impeachment proceeding a president was indictable not only for criminality but also for dereliction of public duty and the abuse of presidential powers. For legal historians the issue was not criminality or due process but simply whether a president had conducted himself properly in office. St. Clair argued that a president could be impeached only for criminal acts "of a very serious nature," committed in his official capacity. Thus the President's future rested on the extent of agreement among Congressmen that such questions as obstruction of justice, the misuse of power, and failure to prevent illegal actions by subordinates were indeed impeachable offenses.

The Storm Breaks

During July the impeachment pressures closed in on the President. St. Clair, facing another subpoena deadline, threatened to appeal Judge Sirica's ruling which ordered the White House to turn over sixty-four tapes. To bypass the Court of Appeals, Jaworski took the question directly to the Supreme Court. Late in July the Court, by a vote of 8 to 0, declared that the President could not withhold conversations and tapes that contained evidence required for a criminal trial. The ninth member of the Court, Associate Justice William Renquist, had removed himself from the case because he had once worked in the Justice Department under John Mitchell. Within hours Nixon agreed to comply with the decision.

With the lines of argument tightly drawn, Judiciary Committee chairman Peter W. Rodino of New Jersey and the committee staff had moved slowly week after week, presenting the evidence in detail. The committee's accent on privacy encouraged leaks to the press which, the White House charged, were designed to tear down the President's reputation. Such accusations undermined the bipartisanship which Rodino's caution had sought to sustain. The release of the committee's massive evidence further damaged the bipartisan mood. Then in July the public announcement of the staff's impeachment charges, based on a broad definition of impeachable offenses, provoked rage in the White House. Press secretary Ronald L. Ziegler called the House committee a "kangaroo court." Vice President Ford charged that anti-Nixon Democrats were using impeachment to reverse the national decision of 1972. Meanwhile the President regarded himself the innocent victim of a conspiracy perpetrated by his political enemies.

All White House efforts to hold House Republicans in line failed. Late in July the Judiciary Committee, in televised debate, voted its first article of impeachment, charging the President with obstruction of justice. Six Republicans joined the twenty-one Democrats to create a 27-to-11 majority. Then by a vote of 28 to 10 the committee charged the President with misuse of power. A third article charged the President with disobeying House subpoenas for tapes. One week later—on August 5—the President's defense collapsed. In releasing transcripts of three June 23, 1972, conversations with Haldeman, Nixon admitted that he had used the CIA to stall an FBI investigation of Watergate. Thus ended

two years of presidential claims to innocence. The ten Republican stalwarts on the House committee, joined by top Republican House and Senate leaders, now defected. On August 8, with his Senate minority evaporating, the President announced his resignation before a national television audience. At noon on the following day Chief Justice Warren Burger administered the presidential oath to Gerald Ford. Watergate had dragged on for two years, but ultimately its resolution reaffirmed the supremacy of Congress and the rule of law. The American constitutional system again prevailed. With Ford's elevation one question dominated all others: Would presidential responsibility undermine the essentially conservative, partisan, anti-civil rights positions which Ford had upheld throughout his long congressional career? Analysts predicted that the new President's modesty and accessibility would permit him to reduce alienation and renew confidence in government.

Still the expectations that Nixon's resignation would resolve the problems of national leadership were tinged with illusion. The mere transferral of presidential power would not clarify the country's political beliefs nor terminate its ideological conflicts. Nor would it unify and strengthen the parties or revitalize the processes of government. Had the country's leadership answers for inflation, economic adjustment, tax and election reform, or environmental control, it could have acted despite Watergate. The unfinished business before the nation was sufficient to torment any future administration.

Conclusion

For two hundred years the American people had pursued a dream which combined freedom and opportunity into a body of limitless expectations. But it was a dream reserved for the industrious and those who faced no barriers to the full exertion of mind and body. The great land with its ample resources and its inviting possibilities never ceased to beckon. Eventually millions in

every generation responded, seeking their fortunes in business, speculation, or clearing the wilderness. It was a great vision of free, independent, self-reliant people doing great things for themselves and for others. Each generation in turn could assume that it would be richer, perhaps even happier, than the one which preceded it. For the successful it was a dream of equal opportunity and justice come true. Possessed of a civilization with such possibilities for self-fulfillment, Americans shared a messianic urge to make a better world, whether through the welcoming of immigrants, the dispatching of missionaries, the acquisition of new territories, the extension of foreign aid and investment, or the waging of war. With good reason, most Americans accepted the notion of a special destiny for the United States.

Unfortunately the dream was laden with self-deception. With wealth came violence and crime, the squandering of resources, the pollution of streams and air, industrial piracy, political bossism, reeking cities with ghettos and slums. From the beginning the dream ignored the millions without a chance as if they scarcely existed. The old American dream never belonged to all, especially not to blacks and Indians. And it was the gap between the old dream and the reality that alienated so much of the nation's responsible youth and even some of their elders. Still the main challenge lay not in rejection of the old vision but in its redefinition to give hope, encouragement, and opportunity to those millions of forgotten Americans who had never shared in the nation's fundamentally middle-class culture.

America's unanswered challenges required, above all, a drastic restructuring of priorities. For too long the nation had attempted to live under inflated commitments which compelled it to spend beyond its income and promise beyond its capabilities. In foreign affairs, succeeding administrations had refused to limit national goals to what was humanly reasonable. Woodrow Wilson had led the country to war, not to defend the Atlantic community against German aggression, but to make the *world* safe for democracy. Franklin Roosevelt promised not only the defeat of the Axis powers but also a postwar world free of want and fear. Harry S. Truman promised to defend the opponents of Communism anywhere on the globe. Lyndon Johnson promised to win freedom for everyone by fighting in Vietnam. Richard Nixon did not compromise the country's global quest for order; his new multilateralism attempted only to achieve that goal with reduced involvement abroad. Whatever the objective national interest in any conflict, some Americans believed the country powerful enough to win any involvement merely through unstinted fighting and spending.

Commitments limited to the essentials of national security would remain expensive enough, but the reduction of excessive obligations elsewhere could well provide the means to create a healthier, safer, and more promising environment at home and the possibilities of enduring national greatness. When and how the nation would convert its technological and productive superiority into genuine triumphs over its human and physical disabilities remained uncertain. For none of the great challenges to human existence—wars of mass destruction, overpopulation, pollution, and the depletion of resources—provoked sufficient interest or unity of purpose to command the needed attention of those charged with the responsibility of governing.

Why the nation would spend $25 billion to place a man on the moon while neglecting the crushing and inescapable problems of congestion, defacement, and decay on earth was obvious enough. Technological feats challenged no private interests and required no expressed consensus; an administration could pursue them undisturbed by Congressmen, lobbyists, or non-existent people on the moon. If older standards of national performance no longer met the needs of society, new ones remained elusive. The American people were too divided in purpose, in ideology, and in expectation to accept either a more demanding concept of national purpose or the price required to achieve it. Still they had demonstrated a capacity to respond positively and energetically to challenges which they could understand. Perhaps a sensitive national leadership could yet create a popular consensus around a new, more inspiring vision of America in time to permit the necessary human and environmental reconstruction at bearable cost.

On the postwar American economy see A. H. Hansen's *The Postwar American Economy: Performance and Problems** (1964). More optimistic is *America in the Sixties: The Economy and Society* (1960) by the editors of *Fortune*. For an analysis of the corporation in American life see W. L. Warner's *The Corporation in the Emergent American Society* (1962); J. K. Galbraith's *The New Industrial State** (1971); A. A. Berle's *Power without Property: A New Development in American Political Economy** (1959); the highly favorable D. E. Lilienthal's *Big Business: A New Era* (1953); and the critical R. J. Barber's *The American Corporation** (1970). On the impact of technology see Nathan Rosenberg's *Technology and American Economic Growth* (1972).

Most writing on the cities and urban planning has not been hopeful. See Jane Jacobs's *The Death and Life of Great American Cities** (1961); Jean Gottman's *Megalopolis** (1961); F. R. Harris and J. V. Lindsay's *The State of the Cities* (1972); and R. C. Wood's *Suburbia: Its People and Politics** (1959). Concern for the environment is clear in Rachel Carson's classic, *Silent Spring** (1962); Barry Commoner's *The Closing Circle** (1971); Nancy Wood's *Clearcut: The Deforestation of America** (1971); Ben Kelley's *The Pavers and the Paved* (1970) on the impact of automobiles and superhighways; and Katie Kelly's *Garbage* (1973). For pessimistic evaluations of industrial momentum see V. C. Ferkiss, *Technological Man** (1969); Alvin Toffler, *Future Shock** (1970); and Robert L. Heilbroner, *An Inquiry into the Human Prospect* (1974). Less concerned is Peter Passell and Leonard Ross's *The Retreat from Riches: Affluence and Its Enemies* (1973).

Any evaluation of the underside of American society begins with poverty. Four books that describe the nation's poverty are Michael Harrington's influential *The Other America: Poverty in the United States** (1962); B. H. Bagdikian's *In the Midst of Plenty: A New Report on the Poor in America** (1964); H. P. Miller's *Rich Man, Poor Man** (1964); and the Conference on Economic Progress's *Poverty and Deprivation in the U.S.: The Plight of Two-Fifths of the Nation* (1962). Ferdinand Lundberg's *The Rich and the Super-Rich* (1968) analyzes the other end of the economic spectrum.

Basic studies of the Chicanos are Joan W. Moore and Alfredo Cuéllar, *Mexican Americans* (1970), and Matt S. Meier and Feliciano Rivera, *The Chicanos: A History of Mexican Americans** (1972). Renato Rosaldo, Robert A. Calvert, and Gustav L. Seligmann's (eds.), *Chicano: The Evolution of a People** (1973), is an impressive anthology. On the Indian see A. M. Josephy's (ed.), *Red Power* (1971). Betty Friedan's *The Feminine Mystique** (1963) and Kate Millett's *Sexual Politics** (1970) are standard works on women's liberation. Also important is Eva Figes's *Patriarchal Attitudes* (1970). Two useful anthologies are Robin Morgan's (ed.), *Sisterhood Is Powerful** (1970), and Jean E. Friedman and William G. Shade's (eds.), *Our American Sisters** (1973).

James Chace's *A World Elsewhere: The New American Foreign Policy* (1973) comprises a basic evaluation of the Nixon foreign policies. Critical of Nixon's Cambodian venture is Malcolm Caldwell and Lek Tan's *Cambodia in the South-East Asian War* (1973). On Kissinger's thought see Stephen R. Graubard's *Kissinger: Portrait of a Mind* (1973). Studies on the Nixon presidency are John Osborne's *The Nixon Watch* (1970); Rowland Evans, Jr. and Robert D. Novak's *Nixon in the White House: A Critical Portrait* (1971); Walter Hickel's *Who Owns America?* (1971); and Leonard Silk's *Nixonomics* (1972). The politics of the Nixon years are analyzed in Samuel Lubell's *The Hidden Crisis in American Politics** (1970); R. M. Scammon and B. J. Wattenberg's *The Real Majority* (1970); and David Broder's *The Party's Over* (1972). On the 1972 election see R. S. Anson's *McGovern* (1972), and Theodore H. White's *The Making of the President: 1972** (1973).

J. Anthony Lukas outlined the basic history of Watergate in the *New York Times Magazine*, July 22, 1973, and January 13, 1974. For the early exposure of the Watergate affair see Carl Bernstein and Bob Woodward's bestseller, *All the President's Men** (1974). Jeb Stuart Magruder revealed his involvement in the scandal in *An American Life: One Man's Road to Watergate* (1974).

*indicates availability in paperback.

Appendix

Supplementary Bibliography

Students may find it useful for particular purposes to be able to refer to topical histories, guides, atlases, historical dictionaries, and other such works. As these works generally have not been mentioned in the "Suggested Readings" following each chapter and are not always easy to find, the authors have put together the following recommendations.

For an invaluable introduction to the study of history as well as for bibliographical purposes, the student should consult the *Harvard Guide to American History* (2 vols., 1974) edited by Frank Freidel.

Topical histories of great value abound, especially in the more traditional fields of history. Among these Daniel M. Smith's *American Diplomatic Experience* (1972)* is a reliable survey. For a neo-Marxist or "revisionist" interpretation of American diplomacy, see Lloyd Gardner and others, *The Creation of the American Empire* (1973). The best overview of American military history is Russell F. Weigley's *The American Way of War* (1973). The best comprehensive account of the American army is Weigley's *History of the United States Army* (1967). The best survey of American constitutional history is Alfred H. Kelly and W. A. Harbison's, *The American Constitution* (4th ed., 1970). For economic history, see Gilbert C. Fite and Jim E. Reese, *An Economic History of the United States* (3d ed., 1973). Ray A. Billington's *Westward Expansion* (4th ed., 1974) is outstanding in its field.

In social and intellectual history good topical studies are also available. No one volume on American intellectual history has yet surpassed Merle Curti's *The Growth of American Thought* (3d ed., 1964). On religion Sidney Mead's *The Lively Experiment* (1963) is a thoughtful essay. Much more detailed is Sydney L. Ahlstrom's *A Religious History of the American People* (1972). John Hope Franklin's *From Slavery to Freedom* (4th ed., 1974) is the most authoritative work on the history of American blacks. For works on the Indians, see the "Suggested Readings" for Chapter 1. For American social history generally, Nelson M. Blake's *A History of American Life and Thought* (1963) is useful. Gilbert Chase's *America's Music* (2d ed., 1966) has a strong popular music bias. The most detailed work on American architecture is William H. Pierson and William Jordy's *American Buildings and Their Architects* (4 vols., 1973). On American literature one should still consult Robert E. Spiller's (ed.), *A Literary History of the United States* (3 vols., 1966). The best single volume on American art is Daniel M. Mendelowitz's *A History of American Art* (1970).

Reference works of value are more and more numerous. The best single volume of statistical information is a Department of Commerce publication, *Historical Statistics of the United States to 1957* (1960). Biographical data can be found in the *Dictionary of American Biography* (22 vols., 1946) or more briefly in J. G. E. Hopkins' (ed.), *Concise Dictionary of American Biography* (1964). For political figures the student may also find the *Biographical Directory of the American Congress, 1774–1971*, and Robert Sobel's *Biographical Directory of the United States Executive Branch, 1774–1971*, useful. Recent interest in women's history has produced a distinguished biographical dictionary of *Notable American Women, 1607–1950* (3 vols., 1971). Topical chronologies distinguish R. B. Morris's *Encyclopedia of American History* (3d ed., 1970). Brief essays on historical events appear in the *Dictionary of American History* (2d ed., 5 vols, 1942; vol. VI, 1961).

Several publications provide data on politics. For party platforms, see Kirk H. Porter and D. B. Johnson's *National Party Platforms, 1840–1972* (1973). Essays and documents appear in A. M. Schlesinger's (ed.), *American Presidential Elections, 1789–1968* (4 vols., 1971) and in his *History of United States Political Parties, 1789–1972* (4 vols., 1973). Key presidential messages appear in Fred L. Israel, *The State of the Union Messages of the Presidents, 1790–1966* (3 vols., 1966).

Historical geography is the subject of a number of excellent works. Ralph H. Brown's *Historical Geography of the United States* (1948) surveys the subject usefully, supplementing the pioneering study by

Ellen C. Semple, *American History and Its Geographic Conditions* (1933). Excellent maps appear in J. T. Adam's (ed.), *Atlas of American History* (1943), W. R. Shepherd's (ed.), *Historical Atlas* (1964), and *The American Heritage Pictorial Atlas of the United States* (1966).

Publications of historical documents abound, but the most useful is H. S. Commager's *Documents of American History* (8th ed., 1969).

In a class by itself with authoritative essays on a wide variety of topics is the *International Encyclopedia of the Social Sciences* (17 vols., 1968).

The Declaration of Independence

WHEN IN THE COURSE OF HUMAN EVENTS, it becomes necessary for one people to dissolve the political bands which have connected them with another, and to assume the Powers of the earth, the separate and equal station to which the Laws of Nature and of Nature's God entitle them, a decent respect to the opinions of mankind requires that they should declare the causes which impel them to the separation.

We hold these truths to be self-evident, that all men are created equal, that they are endowed by their Creator with certain unalienable rights, that among these are Life, Liberty, and the pursuit of Happiness. That to secure these rights, Governments are instituted among Men, deriving their just powers from the consent of the governed. That whenever any Form of Government becomes destructive of these ends, it is the Right of the People to alter or to abolish it, and to institute new Government, laying its foundation on such principles and organizing its powers in such form, as to them shall seem most likely to effect their Safety and Happiness. Prudence, indeed, will dictate that Governments long established should not be changed for light and transient causes; and accordingly all experience hath shown, that mankind are more disposed to suffer, while evils are sufferable, than to right themselves by abolishing the forms to which they are accustomed. But when a long train of abuses and usurpations, pursuing invariably the same Object evinces a design to reduce them under absolute Despotism, it is their right, it is their duty, to throw off such Government, and to provide new Guards for their future security.—Such has been the patient sufferance of these Colonies; and such is now the necessity which constrains them to alter their former Systems of Government. The history of the present King of Great Britain is a history of repeated injuries and usurpations, all having in direct object the establishment of an absolute Tyranny over these States. To prove this, let Facts be submitted to a candid world.

He has refused his Assent to Laws, the most wholesome and necessary for the public good.

He has forbidden his Governors to pass Laws of immediate and pressing importance, unless suspended in their operation till his Assent should be obtained; and when so suspended, he has utterly neglected to attend to them.

He has refused to pass other Laws for the accommodation of large districts of people, unless those people would relinquish the right of Representation in the Legislature, a right inestimable to them and formidable to tyrants only.

He has called together legislative bodies at places unusual, uncomfortable, and distant from the depository of their public Records, for the sole purpose of fatiguing them into compliance with his measures.

He has dissolved Representative Houses repeatedly, for opposing with manly firmness his invasions on the rights of the people.

He has refused for a long time, after such dissolutions, to cause others to be elected; whereby the Legislative powers, incapable of Annihilation, have returned to the People at large for their exercise; the State remaining in the mean time exposed to all dangers of invasion from without, and convulsions within.

He has endeavoured to prevent the population of these States; for that purpose obstructing the Laws of Naturalization of Foreigners; refusing to pass others to encourage their migrations hither, and raising the conditions of new Appropriations of Lands.

He has obstructed the Administration of Justice, by refusing his Assent to Laws for establishing Judiciary powers.

He has made Judges dependent on his Will alone, for the tenure of their offices, and the amount and payment of their salaries.

He has erected a multitude of New Offices, and sent hither swarms of Officers to harass our People, and eat out their substance.

He has kept among us, in times of peace, Standing Armies without the Consent of our legislature.

He has affected to render the Military independent of and superior to the Civil Power.

He has combined with others to subject us to a jurisdiction foreign to our constitution, and unacknowledged by our laws; giving his Assent to their Acts of pretended Legislation:

For quartering large bodies of armed troops among us:

For protecting them, by a mock Trial, from Punishment for any Murders which they should commit on the Inhabitants of these States:

For cutting off our Trade with all parts of the world:

For imposing taxes on us without our Consent:

For depriving us in many cases, of the benefits of Trial by jury:

For transporting us beyond Seas to be tried for pretended offences:

For abolishing the free System of English Laws in a neighbouring Province, establishing therein an Arbitrary government, and enlarging its Boundaries so as to render it at once an example and fit instrument for introducing the same absolute rule into these Colonies:

For taking away our Charters, abolishing our most valuable Laws, and altering fundamentally the Forms of our Governments:

For suspending our own Legislatures, and declaring themselves invested with Power to legislate for us in all cases whatsoever.

He has abdicated Government here, by declaring us out of his Protection and waging War against us.

He has plundered our seas, ravaged our Coasts, burnt our towns, and destroyed the lives of our people.

He is at this time transporting large armies of foreign mercenaries to compleat the works of death, desolation, and tyranny, already begun with circumstances of Cruelty & perfidy scarcely paralleled in the most barbarous ages, and totally unworthy the Head of a civilized nation.

He has constrained our fellow Citizens taken Captive on the high Seas to bear Arms against their Country, to become the executioners of their friends and Brethren, or to fall themselves by their Hands.

He has excited domestic insurrections amongst us, and has endeavoured to bring on the inhabitants of our frontiers, the merciless Indian Savages, whose known rule of warfare, is an undistinguished destruction of all ages, sexes, and conditions.

In every stage of these Oppressions We have Petitioned for Redress in the most humble terms: Our repeated Petitions have been answered only by repeated injury. A Prince, whose character is thus marked by every act which may define a Tyrant, is unfit to be the ruler of a free people.

Nor have We been wanting in attentions to our British brethren. We have warned them from time to time of attempts by their legislature to extend an unwarrantable jurisdiction over us. We have reminded them of the circumstances of our emigration and settlement here. We have appealed to their native justice and magnanimity, and we have conjured them by the ties of our common kindred to disavow these usurpations, which, would inevitably interrupt our connections and correspondence. They too must have been deaf to the voice of justice and of consanguinity. We must, therefore, acquiesce in the necessity, which denounces our Separation, and hold them, as we hold the rest of mankind, Enemies in War, in Peace Friends.

WE, THEREFORE, the Representatives of the UNITED STATES OF AMERICA, in General Congress, Assembled, appealing to the Supreme Judge of the world for the rectitude of our intentions, do, in the Name, and by Authority of the good People of these Colonies, solemnly publish and declare, That these United Colonies are, and of Right ought to be FREE AND INDEPENDENT STATES; that they are Absolved from all Allegiance to the British Crown, and that all political connection between them and the State of Great Britain, is and ought to be totally dissolved; and that as Free and Independent States, they have full Power to levy War, conclude Peace, contract Alliances, establish Commerce, and to do all other Acts and Things which Independent States may of right do. And for the support of this Declaration, with a firm reliance on the Protection of Divine Providence, we mutually pledge to each other our Lives, our Fortunes, and our sacred Honor.

The foregoing Declaration was, by order of Congress, engrossed, and signed by the following members:

John Hancock

NEW HAMPSHIRE
Josiah Bartlett
William Whipple
Matthew Thornton

MASSACHUSETTS BAY
Samuel Adams
John Adams
Robert Treat Paine
Elbridge Gerry

RHODE ISLAND
Stephen Hopkins
William Ellery

CONNECTICUT
Roger Sherman
Samuel Huntington
William Williams
Oliver Wolcott

NEW YORK
William Floyd
Philip Livingston
Francis Lewis
Lewis Morris

NEW JERSEY
Richard Stockton
John Witherspoon
Francis Hopkinson
John Hart
Abraham Clark

PENNSYLVANIA
Robert Morris
Benjamin Rush
Benjamin Franklin
John Morton
George Clymer
James Smith
George Taylor
James Wilson
George Ross

DELAWARE
Caesar Rodney
George Read
Thomas M'Kean

MARYLAND
Samuel Chase
William Paca
Thomas Stone
Charles Carroll, of Carrollton

VIRGINIA
George Wythe
Richard Henry Lee
Thomas Jefferson
Benjamin Harrison
Thomas Nelson, Jr.
Francis Lightfoot Lee
Carter Braxton

NORTH CAROLINA
William Hooper
Joseph Hewes
John Penn

SOUTH CAROLINA
Edward Rutledge
Thomas Heyward, Jr.
Thomas Lynch, Jr.
Arthur Middleton

GEORGIA
Button Gwinnett
Lyman Hall
George Walton

Resolved, That copies of the Declaration be sent to the several assemblies, conventions, and committees, or councils of safety, and to the several commanding officers of the continental troops; that it be proclaimed in each of the United States, at the head of the army.

The Constitution

PREAMBLE

We, the people of the United States, in order to form a more perfect Union, establish justice, insure domestic tranquillity, provide for the common defence, promote the general welfare, and secure the blessings of liberty to ourselves and our posterity, do ordain and establish this Constitution for the United States of America.

ARTICLE I

Section 1. All legislative powers herein granted shall be vested in a Congress of the United States, which shall consist of a Senate and House of Representatives.

Section 2. (1) The House of Representatives shall be composed of members chosen every second year by the people of the several States, and the electors in each State shall have the qualifications requisite for electors of the most numerous branch of the State Legislature.

(2) No person shall be a Representative who shall not have attained to the age of twenty-five years and been seven years a citizen of the United States, and who shall not, when elected, be an inhabitant of that State in which he shall be chosen.

(3) Representatives and direct taxes[1] shall be apportioned among the several States which may be included within this Union according to their respective numbers, which shall be determined by adding to the whole number of free persons, including those bound to service for a term of years, and excluding Indians not taxed, three-fifths of all other persons.[2] The actual enumeration shall be made within three years after the first meeting of the Congress of the United States, and within every subsequent term of ten years, in such manner as they shall by law direct. The number of Representatives shall not exceed one for every thirty thousand, but each State shall have at least one Representative; and until such enumeration shall be made, the State of New Hampshire shall be entitled to choose 3; Massachusetts, 8; Rhode Island and Providence Plantations, 1; Connecticut, 5; New York, 6; New Jersey, 4; Pennsylvania, 8; Delaware, 1; Maryland, 6; Virginia, 10; North Carolina, 5; South Carolina, 5, and Georgia, 3.

(4) When vacancies happen in the representation from any State, the Executive Authority thereof shall issue writs of election to fill such vacancies.

(5) The House of Representatives shall choose their Speaker and other officers, and shall have the sole power of impeachment.

Section 3. (1) The Senate of the United States shall be composed of two Senators from each State, chosen by the Legislature thereof,[3] for six years and each Senator shall have one vote.

(2) Immediately after they shall be assembled in consequence of the first election, they shall be divided as equally as may be into three classes. The seats of the Senators of the first class shall be vacated at the expiration of the second year, of the second class at the expiration of the fourth year, and of the third class at the expiration of the sixth year, so that one-third may be chosen every second year; and if vacancies happen by resignation or otherwise, during the recess of the Legislature of any State, the Executive thereof may make temporary appointment until the next meeting of the Legislature, which shall then fill such vacancies.[3]

(3) No person shall be a Senator who shall not have attained to the age of thirty years, and been nine years a citizen of the United States, and who shall not, when elected, be an inhabitant of that State for which he shall be chosen.

(4) The Vice President of the United States shall be President of the Senate, but shall have no vote unless they be equally divided.

(5) The Senate shall choose their other officers, and also a President pro tempore, in the absence of the Vice President, or when he shall exercise the office of the President of the United States.

(6) The Senate shall have the sole power to try all impeachments. When sitting for that purpose, they shall be on oath or affirmation. When the President of the United States is tried, the Chief Justice shall preside; and no person shall be convicted without the concurrence of two-thirds of the members present.

(7) Judgment in cases of impeachment shall not extend further than to removal from office, and disqualification to hold and enjoy any office of honor, trust, or profit under the United States; but the party convicted shall nevertheless be liable and subject to indictment, trial, judgment, and punishment, according to law.

Section 4. (1) The times, places and manner of holding elections for Senators and Representatives shall be prescribed in each State by the Legislature thereof; but the Congress may at any time make or alter such regulations, except as to places of choosing Senators.

(2) The Congress shall assemble at least once in every year, and such meeting shall be on the first Monday in December, unless they shall by law appoint a different day.[4]

Section 5. (1) Each House shall be the judge of the elections, returns, and qualifications of its own members, and a majority of each shall constitute a quorum to do business; but a smaller number may adjourn from day to day, and may be authorized to compel the attendance of absent members in such manner and under such penalties as each House may provide.

(2) Each House may determine the rules of its proceedings, punish its members for disorderly behavior, and with the concurrence of two-thirds expel a member.

(3) Each House shall keep a journal of its proceedings, and from time to time may publish the same, excepting such parts as may in their judgment require secrecy; and the yeas and nays of the members of either House on any

---

[1] Changed by 16th amendment.

[2] "Other persons" meant slaves. This was changed by the 14th amendment.

[3] Changed by 17th amendment.

[4] Modified by 20th amendment.

question shall, at the desire of one-fifth of those present, be entered on the journal.

(4) Neither House, during the session of Congress shall, without the consent of the other, adjourn for more than three days, nor to any other place than that in which the two Houses shall be sitting.

Section 6. (1) The Senators and Representatives shall receive a compensation for their services to be ascertained by law, and paid out of the Treasury of the United States. They shall in all cases, except treason, felony, and breach of the peace, be privileged from arrest during their attendance at the session of their respective Houses, and in going to and returning from the same; and for any speech or debate in either House they shall not be questioned in any other place.

(2) No Senator or Representative shall, during the time for which he was elected, be appointed to any civil office under the authority of the United States which shall have been created, or the emoluments whereof shall have been increased during such time; and no person holding any office under the United States shall be a member of either House during his continuance in office.

Section 7. (1) All bills for raising revenue shall originate in the House of Representatives, but the Senate may propose or concur with amendments, as on other bills.

(2) Every bill which shall have passed the House of Representatives and the Senate shall, before it becomes a law, be presented to the President of the United States; if he approve, he shall sign it, but if not, he shall return it, with his objections, to that House in which it shall have originated, who shall proceed to reconsider it. If after such reconsideration two-thirds of that House shall agree to pass the bill it shall be sent, together with the objections, to the other House, by which it shall likewise be reconsidered; and if approved by two-thirds of that House it shall become a law. But in all such cases the votes of both Houses shall be determined by yeas and nays, and the names of the persons voting for and against the bill shall be entered on the journal of each House respectively. If any bill shall not be returned by the President within ten days (Sundays excepted) after it shall have been presented to him, the same shall be a law in like manner as if he had signed it, unless the Congress by their adjournment prevent its return; in which case it shall not be a law.

(3) Every order, resolution, or vote to which the concurrence of the Senate and House of Representatives may be necessary (except on a question of adjournment) shall be presented to the President of the United States, and before the same shall take effect shall be approved by him, or being disapproved by him, shall be repassed by two-thirds of the Senate and the House of Representatives, according to the rules and limitations prescribed in the case of a bill.

Section 8. (1) The Congress shall have power:

To lay and collect taxes, duties, imposts, and excises to pay the debts and provide for the common defense and general welfare of the United States; but all duties, imposts, and excises shall be uniform throughout the United States.

(2) To borrow money on the credit of the United States.

(3) To regulate commerce with foreign nations, and among the several States and with the Indian tribes.

(4) To establish a uniform rule of naturalization and uniform laws on the subject of bankruptcies throughout the United States.

(5) To coin money, regulate the value thereof, and of foreign coin, and fix the standard of weights and measures.

(6) To provide for the punishment of counterfeiting the securities and current coin of the United States.

(7) To establish post-offices and post-roads.

(8) To promote the progress of science and useful arts by securing for limited times to authors and inventors the exclusive rights to their respective writings and discoveries.

(9) To constitute tribunals inferior to the Supreme Court.

(10) To define and punish piracies and felonies committed on the high seas, and offences against the law of nations.

(11) To declare war, grant letters of marque and reprisal and make rules concerning captures on land and water.

(12) To raise and support armies, but no appropriation of money to that use shall be for a longer term than two years.

(13) To provide and maintain a navy.

(14) To make rules for the government and regulation of the land and naval forces.

(15) To provide for calling forth the militia to execute the laws of the Union, suppress insurrections, and repel invasions.

(16) To provide for organizing, arming, and disciplining the militia, and for governing such part of them as may be employed in the service of the United States, reserving to the States respectively the appointment of the officers, and the authority of training the militia according to the discipline prescribed by Congress.

(17) To exercise exclusive legislation in all cases whatsoever over such district (not exceeding ten miles square) as may, by cession of particular States and the acceptance of Congress, become the seat of Government of the United States, and to exercise like authority over all places purchased by the consent of the Legislature of the State in which the same shall be, for the erection of forts, magazines, arsenals, drydocks, and other needful buildings.

(18) To make all laws which shall be necessary and proper for carrying into execution the foregoing powers and all other powers vested by this Constitution in the Government of the United States, or in any department or officer thereof.

Section 9. (1) The migration or importation of such persons as any of the States now existing shall think proper to admit shall not be prohibited by the Congress prior to the year one thousand eight hundred and eight, but a tax or duty may be imposed on such importation, not exceeding ten dollars for each person.

(2) The privilege of the writ of habeas corpus shall not be suspended, unless when in cases of rebellion or invasion the public safety may require it.

(3) No bill of attainder or ex post facto law shall be passed.

(4) No capitation or other direct tax shall be laid, un-

less in proportion to the census or enumeration herein-before directed to be taken.[5]

(5) No tax or duty shall be laid on articles exported from any State.

(6) No preference shall be given by any regulation of commerce or revenue to the ports of one State over those of another, nor shall vessels bound to or from one State be obliged to enter, clear, or pay duties to another.

(7) No money shall be drawn from the Treasury but in consequence of appropriations made by law; and a regular statement and account of the receipts and expenditures of all public money shall be published from time to time.

(8) No title of nobility shall be granted by the United States. And no person holding any office of profit or trust under them shall, without the consent of the Congress, accept of any present, emolument, office, or title of any kind whatever from any king, prince, or foreign state.

Section 10. (1) No State shall enter into any treaty, alliance, or confederation, grant letters of marque and reprisal, coin money, emit bills of credit, make anything but gold and silver coin a tender in payment of debts, pass any bill of attainder, ex post facto law, or law impairing the obligation of contracts, or grant any title of nobility.

(2) No State shall, without the consent of the Congress, lay any impost or duties on imports or exports, except what may be absolutely necessary for executing its inspection laws, and the net produce of all duties and imposts, laid by any State on imports or exports, shall be for the use of the Treasury of the United States; and all such laws shall be subject to the revision and control of the Congress.

(3) No State shall, without the consent of Congress, lay any duty of tonnage, keep troops or ships of war in time of peace, enter into agreement or compact with another State, or with a foreign power, or engage in war unless actually invaded, or in such imminent danger as will not admit of delay.

ARTICLE II

Section 1. (1) The Executive power shall be vested in a President of the United States of America. He shall hold his office during the term of four years[6] and together with the Vice-President, chosen for the same term, be elected as follows:

(2) Each State shall appoint, in such manner as the Legislature thereof may direct, a number of electors equal to the whole number of Senators and Representatives to which the State may be entitled in the Congress; but no Senator or Representative or person holding an office of trust or profit under the United States shall be appointed an elector.

The electors shall meet in their respective States and vote by ballot for two persons, of whom one at least shall not be an inhabitant of the same State with themselves. And they shall make a list of all the persons voted for, and of the number of votes for each, which list they shall sign and certify and transmit, sealed, to the seat of the Government of the United States, directed to the President of the Senate.

The President of the Senate shall, in the presence of the Senate and House of Representatives, open all the certificates, and the votes shall then be counted. The person having the greatest number of votes shall be the President, if such number be a majority of the whole number of electors appointed, and if there be more than one who have such a majority, and have an equal number of votes, then the House of Representatives shall immediately choose by ballot one of them for President; and if no person have a majority, then from the five highest on the list the said House shall in like manner choose the President. But in choosing the President, the vote shall be taken by States, the representation from each State having one vote. A quorum, for this purpose, shall consist of a member or members from two-thirds of the States, and a majority of all the States shall be necessary to a choice. In every case, after the choice of the President, the person having the greatest number of votes of the electors shall be the Vice-President.[7] But if there should remain two or more who have equal votes, the Senate shall choose from them by ballot the Vice-President.

(3) The Congress may determine the time of choosing the electors and the day on which they shall give their votes, which day shall be the same throughout the United States.

(4) No person except a natural born citizen, or a citizen of the United States at the time of the adoption of the Constitution, shall be eligible to the office of President; neither shall any person be eligible to that office who shall not have attained to the age of thirty-five years and been fourteen years a resident within the United States.

(5) In case of the removal of the President from office, or of his death, resignation, or inability to discharge the powers and duties of the said office, the same shall devolve on the Vice-President, and the Congress may by law provide for the case of removal, death, resignation, or inability, both of the President and Vice-President, declaring what officer shall then act as President, and such officer shall act accordingly until the disability be removed or a President shall be elected.

(6) The President shall, at stated times, receive for his services a compensation which shall neither be increased nor diminished during the period for which he shall have been elected, and he shall not receive within that period any other emolument from the United States or any of them.

(7) Before he enter on the execution of his office he shall take the following oath or affirmation:

"I do solemnly swear (or affirm) that I will faithfully execute the office of President of the United States, and will, to the best of my ability, preserve, protect, and defend the Constitution of the United States."

Section 2. (1) The President shall be Commander-in-Chief of the Army and Navy of the United States, and of the militia of the several States when called into the actual service of the United States; he may require the opinion,

---

[5] Modified by 16th amendment.
[6] The 22d amendment limited President to two terms.

[7] Changed by 12th amendment.

in writing, of the principal officer in each of the executive departments upon any subject relating to the duties of their respective offices, and he shall have power to grant reprieves and pardons for offences against the United States except in cases of impeachment.

(2) He shall have power by and with the advice and consent of the Senate to make treaties, provided two-thirds of the Senators present concur: and he shall nominate and by and with the advice and consent of the Senate shall appoint ambassadors, other public ministers and consuls, judges of the Supreme Court, and all other officers of the United States whose appointments are not herein otherwise provided for, and which shall be established by law; but the Congress may by law vest the appointment of such inferior officers as they think proper in the President alone, in the courts of law, or in the heads of departments.

(3) The President shall have power to fill up all vacancies that may happen during the recess of the Senate by granting commissions, which shall expire at the end of their next session.

Section 3. He shall from time to time give to the Congress information of the state of the Union, and recommend to their consideration such measures as he shall judge necessary and expedient; he may, on extraordinary occasions, convene both Houses, or either of them, and in case of disagreement between them with respect to the time of adjournment, he may adjourn them to such time as he shall think proper; he shall receive ambassadors and other public ministers; he shall take care that the laws be faithfully executed, and shall commission all the officers of the United States.

Section 4. The President, Vice-President, and all civil officers of the United States shall be removed from office on impeachment for and conviction of treason, bribery or other high crimes and misdemeanors.

ARTICLE III

Section 1. The judicial power of the United States shall be vested in one Supreme Court, and in such inferior courts as the Congress may from time to time ordain and establish. The judges, both of the Supreme and inferior courts, shall hold their offices during good behavior, and shall at stated times receive for their services a compensation which shall not be diminished during their continuance in office.

Section 2. (1) The judicial power shall extend to all cases in law and equity arising under this Constitution, the laws of the United States, and treaties made, or which shall be made, under their authority; to all cases affecting ambassadors, other public ministers and consuls; to all cases of admiralty and maritime jurisdiction; to controversies to which the United States shall be a party;[8] to controversies between two or more States, between a State and citizens of another State, between citizens of different States, between citizens of the same State claiming lands under grants of different States, and between a State, or the citizens thereof, and foreign states, citizens, or subjects.

(2) In all cases affecting ambassadors, other public ministers, and consuls, and those in which a State shall be a party, the Supreme Court shall have original jurisdiction. In all the other cases before mentioned the Supreme Court shall have appellate jurisdiction both as to law and fact, with such exceptions and under such regulations as the Congress shall make.

(3) The trial of all crimes, except in cases of impeachment, shall be by jury, and such trial shall be held in the State where the said crimes shall have been committed; but when not committed within any State the trial shall be at such place or places as the Congress may by law have directed.

Section 3. (1) Treason against the United States shall consist only in levying war against them, or in adhering to their enemies, giving them aid and comfort. No person shall be convicted of treason unless on the testimony of two witnesses to the same overt act, or on confession in open court.

(2) The Congress shall have power to declare the punishment of treason, but no attainder of treason shall work corruption of blood or forfeiture except during the life of the person attainted.

ARTICLE IV

Section 1. Full faith and credit shall be given in each State to the public acts, records, and judicial proceedings of every other State. And the Congress may by general laws prescribe the manner in which such acts, records, and proceedings shall be proved, and the effect thereof.

Section 2. (1) The citizens of each State shall be entitled to all privileges and immunities of citizens in the several States.

(2) A person charged in any State with treason, felony, or other crime, who shall flee from justice, and be found in another State, shall, on demand of the Executive authority of the State from which he fled, be delivered up, to be removed to the State having jurisdiction of the crime.

(3) No person held to service or labor in one State, under the laws thereof, escaping into another shall in consequence of any law or regulation therein, be discharged from such service or labor, but shall be delivered up on claim of the party to whom such service or labor may be due.[9]

Section 3. (1) New States may be admitted by the Congress into this Union; but no new State shall be formed or erected within the jurisdiction of any other State, nor any State be formed by the junction of two or more States, or parts of States, without the consent of the Legislatures of the States concerned, as well as of the Congress.

(2) The Congress shall have power to dispose of and make all needful rules and regulations respecting the territory or other property belonging to the United States; and nothing in this Constitution shall be so construed as to prejudice any claims of the United States, or of any particular State.

Section 4. The United States shall guarantee to every State in this Union a Republican form of government, and shall protect each of them against invasion, and, on application of the Legislature, or of the Executive (when the

[8] Changed by 11th amendment.

[9] Became irrelevant after passage of 13th amendment abolishing slavery.

Legislature cannot be convened) against domestic violence.

ARTICLE V

The Congress, whenever two-thirds of both Houses shall deem it necessary, shall propose amendments to this Constitution, or, on the application of the Legislatures of two-thirds of the several States, shall call a convention for proposing amendments, which in either case, shall be valid to all intents and purposes, as part of this Constitution, when ratified by the Legislatures of three-fourths of the several States, or by conventions in three-fourths thereof, as the one or the other mode of ratification may be proposed by the Congress, provided that no amendment which may be made prior to the year one thousand eight hundred and eight shall in any manner affect the first and fourth clauses in the Ninth Section of the First Article; and that no State, without its consent, shall be deprived of its equal suffrage in the Senate.

ARTICLE VI

(1) All debts contracted and engagements entered into before the adoption of this Constitution shall be as valid against the United States under this Constitution as under the Confederation.

(2) This Constitution and the laws of the United States which shall be made in pursuance thereof and all treaties made, or which shall be made, under the authority of the United States, shall be the supreme law of the land, and the judges in every State shall be bound thereby, anything in the Constitution or laws of any State to the contrary notwithstanding.

(3) The Senators and Representatives before mentioned and the members of the several State Legislatures, and all executives and judicial officers, both of the United States and of the several States, shall be bound by oath or affirmation to support this Constitution; but no religious test shall ever be required as a qualification to any office or public trust under the United States.

ARTICLE VII

The ratification of the Conventions of nine States shall be sufficient for the establishment of this Constitution between the States so ratifying the same.

The Amendments to the Constitution

ARTICLE I

Congress shall make no law respecting an establishment of religion, or prohibiting the free exercise thereof; or abridging the freedom of speech or of the press; or the right of the people peaceably to assemble and to petition the Government for a redress of grievances.

ARTICLE II

A well-regulated militia being necessary to the security of a free State, the right of the people to keep and bear arms shall not be infringed.

ARTICLE III

No soldier shall, in time of peace, be quartered in any house without the consent of the owner, nor in time of war but in a manner to be prescribed by law.

ARTICLE IV

The right of the people to be secure in their persons, houses, papers, and effects, against unreasonable searches and seizures, shall not be violated, and no warrants shall issue but upon probable cause, supported by oath or affirmation, and particularly describing the place to be searched, and the persons or things to be seized.

ARTICLE V

No person shall be held to answer for a capital or other infamous crime unless on a presentment or indictment of a Grand Jury, except in cases arising in the land or naval forces, or in the militia, when in actual service, in time of war or public danger; nor shall any person be subject for the same offence to be twice put in jeopardy of life or limb; nor shall be compelled in any criminal case to be a witness against himself, nor be deprived of life, liberty or property, without due process of law; nor shall private property be taken for public use without just compensation.

ARTICLE VI

In all criminal prosecutions, the accused shall enjoy the right to a speedy and public trial, by an impartial jury of the State and district wherein the crime shall have been committed, which districts shall have been previously ascertained by law, and to be informed of the nature and cause of the accusation; to be confronted with the witnesses against him; to have compulsory process for obtaining witnesses in his favor, and to have the assistance of counsel for his defence.

ARTICLE VII

In suits at common law, where the value in controversy shall exceed twenty dollars, the right of trial by jury shall be preserved, and no fact tried by a jury shall be otherwise re-examined in any court of the United States than according to the rules of the common law.

ARTICLE VIII

Excessive bail shall not be required, nor excessive fines imposed, nor cruel and unusual punishments inflicted.

ARTICLE IX

The enumeration in the Constitution of certain rights shall not be construed to deny or disparage others retained by the people.

ARTICLE X

The powers not delegated to the United States by the Constitution, nor prohibited by it to the States, are reserved to the States respectively, or to the people.[10]

ARTICLE XI
The judicial power of the United States shall not be construed to extend to any suit in law or equity, commenced or prosecuted against one of the United States, by citizens of another State, or by citizens or subjects of any foreign state.[11]

ARTICLE XII
The Electors shall meet in their respective States and vote by ballot for President and Vice-President, one of whom at least shall not be an inhabitant of the same State with themselves; they shall name in their ballots the person voted for as President, and in distinct ballots the person voted for as Vice-President; and they shall make distinct lists of all persons voted for as President, and of all persons voted for as Vice-President, and of the number of votes for each, which list they shall sign and certify, and transmit, sealed, to the seat of the Government of the United States, directed to the President of the Senate; the President of the Senate shall, in the presence of the Senate and House of Representatives, open all the certificates and the votes shall then be counted; the person having the greatest number of votes for President shall be the President, if such number be a majority of the whole number of Electors appointed; and if no person have such majority, then from the persons having the highest number, not exceeding three, on the list of those voted for as President, the House of Representatives shall choose immediately, by ballot, the President. But in choosing the President, the votes shall be taken by States, the representation from each State having one vote; a quorum for this purpose shall consist of a member or members from two-thirds of the States, and a majority of all the States shall be necessary to a choice. And if the House of Representatives shall not choose a President, whenever the right of choice shall devolve upon them, before the fourth day of March next following, then the Vice-President shall act as President, as in the case of the death or other constitutional disability of the President. The person having the greatest number of votes as Vice-President shall be the Vice-President if such number be a majority of the whole number of Electors appointed, and if no person have a majority, then, from the two highest numbers on the list the Senate shall choose the Vice-President; a quorum for the purpose shall consist of two-thirds of the whole number of Senators, and a majority of the whole number shall be necessary to a choice. But no person constitutionally ineligible to the office of President shall be eligible to that of Vice-President of the United States.[12]

ARTICLE XIII
Section 1. Neither slavery nor involuntary servitude, except as a punishment for crime whereof the party shall have been duly convicted, shall exist within the United States, or any place subject to their jurisdiction.

Section 2. Congress shall have power to enforce this article by appropriate legislation.[13]

ARTICLE XIV
Section 1. All persons born or naturalized in the United States, and subject to the jurisdiction thereof are citizens of the United States and of the State wherein they reside. No State shall make or enforce any law which shall abridge the privileges or immunities of citizens of the United States, nor shall any State deprive any person of life, liberty, or property, without due process of law; nor deny to any person within its jurisdiction the equal protection of the laws.
Section 2. Representatives shall be apportioned among the several States according to their respective numbers, counting the whole number of persons in each State, excluding Indians not taxed. But when the right to vote at any election for the choice of Electors for President and Vice-President of the United States, Representatives in Congress, the executive and judicial officers of a State, or the members of the Legislature thereof, is denied to any of the male inhabitants of such State, being twenty-one years of age and citizens of the United States, or in any way abridged, except for participation in rebellion or other crime, the basis of representation therein shall be reduced in the proportion which the number of such male citizens shall bear to the whole number of male citizens twenty-one years of age in such State.
Section 3. No person shall be a Senator or Representative in Congress, or Elector of President and Vice-President, or hold any office, civil or military, under the United States, or under any State, who, having previously taken an oath, as a member of Congress, or as an officer of the United States, or as a member of any State Legislature, or as an executive or judicial officer of any State, to support the Constitution of the United States, shall have engaged in insurrection or rebellion against the same, or given aid or comfort to the enemies thereof. But Congress may, by a vote of two-thirds of each House, remove such disability.
Section 4. The validity of the public debt of the United States, authorized by law, including debts incurred for payment of pensions and bounties for services in suppressing insurrection or rebellion, shall not be questioned. But neither the United States, nor any State shall assume or pay any debt or obligation incurred in aid of insurrection or rebellion against the United States, or any claim for the loss or emancipation of any slave; but all such debts, obligations, and claims shall be held illegal and void.
Section 5. The Congress shall have power to enforce, by appropriate legislation, the provisions of this article.[14]

ARTICLE XV
Section 1. The right of the citizens of the United States to vote shall not be denied or abridged by the United States or by any State on account of race, color, or previous condition of servitude.
Section 2. The Congress shall have power to enforce the provisions of this article by appropriate legislation.[15]

[10] The first 10 amendments were ratified in 1791.
[11] Ratified January 8, 1798.
[12] Ratified September 25, 1804.

[13] Ratified December 18, 1864.
[14] Ratified July 28, 1868.
[15] Ratified March 30, 1870.

ARTICLE XVI

The Congress shall have power to lay and collect taxes on incomes, from whatever sources derived, without apportionment among the several States, and without regard to any census or enumeration.[16]

ARTICLE XVII

The Senate of the United States shall be composed of two Senators from each State, elected by the people thereof, for six years; and each Senator shall have one vote. The Electors in each State shall have the qualifications requisite for Electors of the most numerous branch of the State legislatures.

When vacancies happen in the representation of any State in the Senate, the executive authority of such State shall issue writs of election to fill such vacancies: Provided, That the legislature of any State may empower the executive thereof to make temporary appointments until the people fill the vacancies by election as the legislature may direct.

This amendment shall not be construed as to affect the election or term of any Senator chosen before it became valid as part of the Constitution.[17]

ARTICLE XVIII

Section 1. After one year from the ratification of this article the manufacture, sale or transportation of intoxicating liquors within, the importation thereof into, or the exportation thereof from the United States and all territories subject to the jurisdiction thereof for beverage purposes is hereby prohibited.

Section 2. The Congress and the several States shall have concurrent power to enforce this article by appropriate legislation.

Section 3. This article shall be inoperative unless it shall have been ratified as an amendment to the Constitution by the legislatures of the several States, as provided in the Constitution, within seven years from the date of the submission hereof to the States by Congress.[18]

ARTICLE XIX

Section 1. The right of citizens of the United States to vote shall not be denied or abridged by the United States or by any State on account of sex.

Section 2. Congress shall have power, by appropriate legislation, to enforce the provisions of this article.[19]

ARTICLE XX

Section 1. The terms of the President and Vice-President shall end at noon on the 20th day of January, and the terms of Senators and Representatives at noon on the 3rd day of January, of the years in which such terms would have ended if this article had not been ratified; and the terms of their successors shall then begin.

Section 2. The Congress shall assemble at least once in every year, and such meeting shall begin at noon on the 3rd day of January, unless they shall by law appoint a different day.

Section 3. If, at the time fixed for the beginning of the term of the President, the President elect shall have died, the Vice-President elect shall become President. If a President shall not have been chosen before the time fixed for the beginning of his term, or if the President elect shall have failed to qualify, then the Vice-President elect shall act as President until a President shall have qualified; and the Congress may by law provide for the case wherein neither a President elect nor a Vice-President elect shall have qualified, declaring who shall then act as President or the manner in which one who is to act shall be selected, and such person shall act accordingly until a President or Vice-President shall have qualified.

Section 4. The Congress may by law provide for the case of the death of any of the persons from whom the House of Representatives may choose a President whenever the right of choice shall have devolved upon them, and for the case of the death of any of the persons from whom the Senate may choose a Vice-President whenever the right of choice shall have devolved upon them.

Section 5. Sections 1 and 2 shall take effect on the 15th day of October following the ratification of this article (Oct., 1933).

Section 6. This article shall be inoperative unless it shall have been ratified as an amendment to the Constitution by the legislatures of three-fourths of the several States within seven years from the date of its submission.[20]

ARTICLE XXI

Section 1. The eighteenth article of amendment to the Constitution of the United States is hereby repealed.

Section 2. The transportation or importation into any State, Territory, or Possession of the United States for delivery or use therein of intoxicating liquors, in violation of the laws thereof, is hereby prohibited.

Section 3. This article shall be inoperative unless it shall have been ratified as an amendment to the Constitution by convention in the several States, as provided in the Constitution, within seven years from the date of the submission hereof to the States by the Congress.[21]

ARTICLE XXII

Section 1. No person shall be elected to the office of the President more than twice, and no person who has held the office of President, or acted as President, for more than two years of a term to which some other person was elected President shall be elected to the office of the President more than once. But this Article shall not apply to any person holding the office of President when this Article was proposed by the Congress, and shall not prevent any person who may be holding the office of President, or acting as President, during the term within which this Article becomes operative from holding the office of President or acting as President during the remainder of such term.

Section 2. This article shall be inoperative unless it shall

[16] Ratified February 25, 1913.

[17] Ratified May 31, 1913.

[18] Ratified January 29, 1919. Repealed by the 21st amendment.

[19] Ratified August 26, 1920.

[20] Ratified January 23, 1933.

[21] Ratified December 5, 1933.

have been ratified as an amendment to the Constitution by the legislatures of three-fourths of the several States within seven years from the date of its submission to the States by the Congress.[22]

ARTICLE XXIII
Section 1. The District constituting the seat of Government of the United States shall appoint in such manner as the Congress may direct:
A number of electors of President and Vice President equal to the whole number of Senators and Representatives in Congress to which the District would be entitled if it were a State, but in no event more than the least populous State; they shall be in addition to those appointed by the States, but they shall be considered, for the purposes of the election of President and Vice President, to be electors appointed by a State; and they shall meet in the District and perform such duties as provided by the twelfth article of amendment.
Section 2. The Congress shall have power to enforce this article by appropriate legislation.[23]

ARTICLE XXIV
Section 1. The right of citizens of the United States to vote in any primary or other election for President or Vice President, for electors for President or Vice President, or for Senator or Representative in Congress, shall not be denied or abridged by the United States or any State by reason of failure to pay any poll tax or other tax.
Section 2. The Congress shall have power to enforce this article by appropriate legislation.[24]

ARTICLE XXV
Section 1. In case of the removal of the President from office or of his death or resignation, the Vice President shall become President.
Section 2. Whenever there is a vacancy in the office of the Vice President, the President shall nominate a Vice President who shall take office upon confirmation by a majority vote of both Houses of Congress.[25]
Section 3. Whenever the President transmits to the Presi-

[22]Ratified March 1, 1951.
[23]Ratified March 29, 1961.
[24]Ratified January 23, 1964.
[25]Ratified February 10, 1967.

dent pro tempore of the Senate and the Speaker of the House of Representatives has written declaration that he is unable to discharge the powers and duties of his office, and until he transmits to them a written declaration to the contrary, such powers and duties shall be discharged by the Vice President as Acting President.
Section 4. Whenever the Vice President and a majority of either the principal officers of the executive departments or of such other body as Congress may by law provide, transmit to the President pro tempore of the Senate and the Speaker of the House of Representatives their written declaration that the President is unable to discharge the powers and duties of his office, the Vice President shall immediately assume the powers and duties of the office as Acting President.

Thereafter, when the President transmits to the President pro tempore of the Senate and the Speaker of the House of Representatives his written declaration that no inability exists, he shall resume the powers and duties of his office unless the Vice President and a majority of either the principal officers of the executive department or of such other body as Congress may by law provide, transmit within four days to the President pro tempore of the Senate and the Speaker of the House of Representatives their written declaration that the President is unable to discharge the powers and duties of his office. Thereupon Congress shall decide the issue, assembling within forty-eight hours for that purpose if not in session. If the Congress, within twenty-one days after receipt of the latter written declaration, or, if Congress is not in session, within twenty-one days after Congress is required to assemble, determines by two-thirds vote of both Houses that the President is unable to discharge the powers and duties of his office, the Vice President shall continue to discharge the same as Acting President; otherwise, the President shall resume the powers and duties of his office.

ARTICLE XXVI
Section 1. The right of citizens of the United States, who are eighteen years of age or older, to vote shall not be denied or abridged by the United States or by any State on account of age.
Section 2. The Congress shall have power to enforce this article by appropriate legislation.[26]

[26]Ratified July 1, 1971.

Amendments at Present before the States

Section 1. The Congress shall have power to limit, regulate and prohibit the labor of persons under eighteen years of age.
Section 2. The power of the several States is unimpaired by this article except that the operation of State laws shall be suspended to the extent necessary to give effect to legislation enacted by Congress.
    Submitted to the legislatures of the several States June 2, 1924.

Section 1. Equality of rights under the law shall not be denied or abridged by the United States or by any State on account of sex.
Section 2. The Congress shall have the power to enforce, by appropriate legislation, the provisions of this article.
Section 3. This amendment shall take effect two years after the date of ratification.
    Submitted to the legislatures of the several States in 1972.

The Presidents, Vice Presidents, and Cabinet Members, 1789–1974*

THE WASHINGTON ADMINISTRATION (FEDERALIST)

	Name	Dates Served
President	George Washington	1789–1797
Vice President	John Adams	1789–1797
Secretary of State	Thomas Jefferson *(Republican)*	1789–1793
	Edmund Randolph	1793–1795
	Timothy Pickering	1795–1797
Secretary of the Treasury	Alexander Hamilton	1789–1794
	Oliver Wolcott	1794–1797
Secretary of War	Henry Knox	1789–1794
	Timothy Pickering	1794–1796
	James McHenry	1796–1797
Attorney General	Edmund Randolph	1789–1793
	William Bradford	1793–1795
	Charles Lee	1795–1797
Postmaster General	Samuel Osgood	1789–1791
	Timothy Pickering	1791–1794
	Joseph Habersham	1794–1797

THE ADAMS ADMINISTRATION (FEDERALIST)

	Name	Dates Served
President	John Adams	1797–1801
Vice President	Thomas Jefferson *(Republican)*	1797–1801
Secretary of State	Timothy Pickering	1797–1799
	John Marshall	1799–1801
Secretary of Treasury	Oliver Wolcott	1797–1800
	Samuel Dexter	1800–1801
Secretary of War	James McHenry	1797–1799
	John Marshall	1799–1800
	Samuel Dexter	1800–1801
	Roger Griswold	1801
Attorney General	Charles Lee	1797–1801
	Theophilus Parsons	1801
Postmaster General	Joseph Habersham	1797–1801
Secretary of Navy	Benjamin Stoddert	1798–1801

THE JEFFERSON ADMINISTRATION (REPUBLICAN)

	Name	Dates Served
President	Thomas Jefferson	1801–1809
Vice President	Aaron Burr	1801–1805
	George Clinton	1805–1809
Secretary of State	James Madison	1801–1809
Secretary of Treasury	Samuel Dexter *(Federalist)*	1801
	Albert Gallatin	1801–1809
Secretary of War	Henry Dearborn	1801–1809
Attorney General	Levi Lincoln	1801–1804
	Robert Smith	1804–1805
	John Breckinridge	1805–1806
	C. A. Rodney	1806–1809
Postmaster General	Joseph Habersham *(Federalist)*	1801
	Gideon Granger	1801–1809
Secretary of Navy	Benjamin Stoddert *(Federalist)*	1801
	Robert Smith	1801–1804
	Jacob Crowninshield	1804–1809

THE MADISON ADMINISTRATION (REPUBLICAN)

	Name	Dates Served
President	James Madison	1809–1817
Vice President	George Clinton	1809–1813
	Elbridge Gerry	1813–1817
Secretary of State	Robert Smith	1809–1811
	James Monroe	1811–1817
Secretary of Treasury	Albert Gallatin	1809–1813
	G. W. Campbell	1814
	A. J. Dallas	1814–1815
	W. H. Crawford	1815–1817
Secretary of War	William Eustis	1809–1812
	John Armstrong	1812–1813
	James Monroe	1814–1815
	W. H. Crawford	1815–1817
Attorney General	C. A. Rodney	1809–1811
	William Pinkney	1811–1814
	Richard Rush	1814–1817
Postmaster General	Gideon Granger	1809–1814
	R. J. Meigs, Jr.	1814–1817
Secretary of Navy	Paul Hamilton	1809–1813
	William Jones	1813–1814
	B. W. Crowninshield	1814–1817

THE MONROE ADMINISTRATION (REPUBLICAN)

	Name	Dates Served
President	James Monroe	1817–1825
Vice President	D. D. Tompkins	1817–1825
Secretary of State	J. Q. Adams	1817–1825
Secretary of Treasury	W. H. Crawford	1817–1825
Secretary of War	Isaac Shelby	1817
	George Graham	1817
	J. C. Calhoun	1817–1825
Attorney General	Richard Rush	1817
	William Wirt	1817–1825
Postmaster General	R. J. Meigs, Jr.	1817–1823
	John McLean	1823–1825
Secretary of Navy	B. W. Crowninshield	1817–1818
	Smith Thompson	1818–1823
	S. L. Southard	1823–1825

THE ADAMS ADMINISTRATION (NATIONAL REPUBLICAN)

	Name	Dates Served
President	John Quincy Adams	1825–1829
Vice President	J. C. Calhoun *(Republican)*	1825–1829
Secretary of State	Henry Clay	1825–1829
Secretary of Treasury	Richard Rush *(Republican)*	1825–1829
Secretary of War	James Barbour *(Republican)*	1825–1828
	P. B. Porter *(Republican)*	1828–1829
Attorney General	William Wirt *(Republican)*	1825–1829
Postmaster General	John McLean *(Republican)*	1825–1829
Secretary of Navy	S. L. Southard *(Republican)*	1825–1829

THE JACKSON ADMINISTRATION (DEMOCRAT)

	Name	Dates Served
President	Andrew Jackson	1829–1837
Vice President	John C. Calhoun	1829–1833
	Martin Van Buren	1833–1837
Secretary of State	Martin Van Buren	1829–1830
	Edward Livingston	1830–1832
	Louis McLane	1833–1834
	John Forsyth	1834–1837
Secretary of Treasury	S. D. Ingham	1829–1830
	Louis McLane	1830–1832
	W. J. Duane	1833
	R. B. Taney	1833–1834
	Levi Woodbury	1834–1837
Secretary of War	J. H. Eaton	1829–1831
	Lewis Cass	1831–1837
	B. F. Butler	1837
Attorney General	J. M. Berrien	1829–1831
	R. B. Taney	1831–1833
	B. F. Butler	1833–1837
Postmaster General	W. T. Barry	1829–1835
	Amos Kendall	1835–1837
Secretary of Navy	John Branch	1829–1831
	Levi Woodbury	1831–1834
	Mahlon Dickerson	1834–1837

THE VAN BUREN ADMINISTRATION (DEMOCRAT)

	Name	Dates Served
President	Martin Van Buren	1837–1841
Vice President	R. M. Johnson	1837–1841
Secretary of State	John Forsyth	1837–1841
Secretary of Treasury	Levi Woodbury	1837–1841
Secretary of War	J. R. Poinsett	1837–1841
Attorney General	B. F. Butler	1837–1838
	Felix Grundy	1838–1840
	H. D. Gilpin	1840–1841
Postmaster General	Amos Kendall	1837–1840
	J. M. Niles	1840–1841
Secretary of Navy	Mahlon Dickerson	1837–1838
	J. K. Paulding	1838–1841

THE HARRISON ADMINISTRATION (WHIG)

	Name	Dates Served
President	William H. Harrison	1841
Vice President	John Tyler	1841
Secretary of State	Daniel Webster	1841
Secretary of Treasury	Thomas Ewing	1841
Secretary of War	John Bell	1841
Attorney General	J. J. Crittenden	1841
Postmaster General	Francis Granger	1841
Secretary of Navy	George Badger	1841

THE TYLER ADMINISTRATION (WHIG AND DEMOCRAT)

	Name	Dates Served
President	John Tyler	1841–1845
Vice President	None	

	Name	Dates Served
Secretary of State	Daniel Webster (Whig)	1841–1843
	H. S. Legaré (Whig)	1843
	A. P. Upshur (Whig)	1843–1844
	J. C. Calhoun (Democrat)	1844–1845
Secretary of Treasury	Thomas Ewing (Whig)	1841
	Walter Forward (Whig)	1841–1843
	J. C. Spencer (Whig)	1843–1844
	George Bibb (Whig)	1844–1845
Secretary of War	John Bell (Whig)	1841
	John McLean (Whig)	1841
	J. C. Spencer (Whig)	1841–1843
	J. M. Porter (Whig)	1843–1844
	William Wilkins (Whig)	1844–1845
Attorney General	J. J. Crittenden (Whig)	1841
	H. S. Legaré (Whig)	1841–1843
	John Nelson (Whig)	1843–1845
Postmaster General	Francis Granger (Whig)	1841
	C. A. Wickliffe (Whig)	1841
Secretary of Navy	G. E. Badger (Whig)	1841
	A. P. Upshur (Whig)	1841
	David Henshaw (Whig)	1843–1844
	T. W. Gilmer (Whig)	1844
	J. Y. Mason (Whig)	1844–1845

THE POLK ADMINISTRATION (DEMOCRAT)

	Name	Dates Served
President	James K. Polk	1845–1849
Vice President	G. M. Dallas	1845–1849
Secretary of State	James Buchanan	1845–1849
Secretary of Treasury	R. J. Walker	1845–1849
Secretary of War	W. L. Marcy	1845–1849
Attorney General	J. Y. Mason	1845–1846
	Nathan Clifford	1846–1848
	Isaac Toucey	1848–1849
Postmaster General	Cave Johnson	1845–1849
Secretary of Navy	George Bancroft	1845–1846
	J. Y. Mason	1846–1849

THE TAYLOR ADMINISTRATION (WHIG)

	Name	Dates Served
President	Zachary Taylor	1849–1850
Vice President	Millard Fillmore	1849–1850

	Name	Dates Served
Secretary of State	J. M. Clayton	1849–1850
Secretary of Treasury	W. M. Meredith	1849–1850
Secretary of War	G. W. Crawford	1849–1850
Attorney General	Reverdy Johnson	1849–1850
Postmaster General	Jacob Collamer	1849–1850
Secretary of Navy	W. B. Preston	1849–1850
Secretary of Interior	Thomas Ewing	1849–1850

THE FILLMORE ADMINISTRATION (WHIG)

	Name	Dates Served
President	Millard Fillmore	1850–1853
Vice President	None	
Secretary of State	Daniel Webster	1850–1852
	Edward Everett	1852–1853
Secretary of Treasury	Thomas Corwin	1850–1853
Secretary of War	C. M. Conrad	1850–1853
Attorney General	J. J. Crittenden	1850–1853
Postmaster General	N. K. Hall	1850–1852
	S. D. Hubbard	1852–1853
Secretary of Navy	W. A. Graham	1850–1852
	J. P. Kennedy	1852–1853
Secretary of Interior	A. H. Stuart	1850–1853

THE PIERCE ADMINISTRATION (DEMOCRAT)

	Name	Dates Served
President	Franklin Pierce	1853–1857
Vice President	W. R. D. King	1853–1857
Secretary of State	W. L. Marcy	1853–1857
Secretary of Treasury	James Guthrie	1853–1857
Secretary of War	Jefferson Davis	1853–1857
Attorney General	Caleb Cushing	1853–1857
Postmaster General	James Campbell	1853–1857
Secretary of Navy	J. C. Dobbin	1853–1857
Secretary of Interior	Robert McClelland	1853–1857

THE BUCHANAN ADMINISTRATION (DEMOCRAT)

	Name	Dates Served
President	James Buchanan	1857–1861
Vice President	J. C. Breckinridge	1857–1861
Secretary of State	Lewis Cass	1857–1860
	J. S. Black	1860–1861
Secretary of Treasury	Howell Cobb	1857–1860
	P. F. Thomas	1860–1861
	J. A. Dix	1861
Secretary of War	J. B. Floyd	1857–1861
	Joseph Holt	1861
Attorney General	J. S. Black	1857–1860
	E. M. Stanton	1860–1861
Postmaster General	A. V. Brown	1857–1859
	Joseph Holt	1859–1861
Secretary of Navy	Isaac Toucey	1857–1861
Secretary of Interior	Jacob Thompson	1857–1861

THE LINCOLN ADMINISTRATION (REPUBLICAN)

	Name	Dates Served
President	Abraham Lincoln	1861–1865
Vice President	Hannibal Hamlin	1861–1865
	Andrew Johnson (Unionist)	1865
Secretary of State	W. H. Seward	1861–1865
Secretary of Treasury	S. P. Chase	1861–1864
	W. P. Fessenden	1864–1865
	Hugh McCulloch	1865
Secretary of War	Simon Cameron	1861–1862
	E. M. Stanton	1862–1865
Attorney General	Edward Bates	1861–1863
	T. J. Coffey	1863–1864
	James Speed	1864–1865
Postmaster General	Horatio King	1861
	Montgomery Blair	1861–1864
	William Dennison	1864–1865
Secretary of Navy	Gideon Welles	1861–1865
Secretary of Interior	C. B. Smith	1861–1863
	J. P. Usher	1863–1865

THE JOHNSON ADMINISTRATION (UNIONIST)

	Name	Dates Served
President	Andrew Johnson	1865–1869
Vice President	None	
Secretary of State	W. H. Seward (Republican)	1865–1869
Secretary of Treasury	Hugh McCulloch (Republican)	1865–1869
Secretary of War	E. M. Stanton (Republican)	1865–1867
	U. S. Grant (Republican)	1867–1868
	Lorenzo Thomas (Republican)	1868
	J. M. Schofield (Republican)	1868–1869
Attorney General	James Speed (Republican)	1865–1866
	Henry Stanbery (Republican)	1866–1868
	W. M. Evarts (Republican)	1868–1869
Postmaster General	William Dennison (Republican)	1865–1866
	A. W. Randall (Republican)	1866–1869
Secretary of Navy	Gideon Welles (Republican)	1865–1869
Secretary of Interior	J. P. Usher (Republican)	1865
	James Harlan (Republican)	1865
	O. H. Browning (Republican)	1865–1869

THE GRANT ADMINISTRATION (REPUBLICAN)

	Name	Dates Served
President	Ulysses S. Grant	1869–1877
Vice President	Schuyler Colfax	1869–1873
	Henry Wilson	1873–1877

	Name	Dates Served
Secretary of State	E. B. Washburne	1869
	Hamilton Fish	1869–1877
Secretary of Treasury	G. S. Boutwell	1869–1873
	W. A. Richardson	1873–1874
	B. H. Bristow	1874–1876
	L. M. Morrill	1876–1877
Secretary of War	J. A. Rawlins	1869
	W. T. Sherman	1869
	W. W. Belknap	1869–1876
	Alphonso Taft	1876
	J. D. Cameron	1876–1877
Attorney General	E. R. Hoar	1869–1870
	A. T. Ackerman	1870–1871
	G. H. Williams	1871–1875
	Edwin Pierrepont	1875–1876
	Alphonso Taft	1876–1877
Postmaster General	J. A. J. Creswell	1869–1874
	J. W. Marshall	1874
	Marshall Jewell	1874–1876
	J. N. Tyner	1876–1877
Secretary of Navy	A. E. Borie	1869
	G. M. Robeson	1869–1877
Secretary of Interior	J. D. Cox	1869–1870
	Columbus Delano	1870–1875
	Zachary Chandler	1875–1877

THE HAYES ADMINISTRATION (REPUBLICAN)

	Name	Dates Served
President	Rutherford B. Hayes	1877–1881
Vice President	William A. Wheeler	1877–1881
Secretary of State	William B. Evarts	1877–1881
Secretary of Treasury	John Sherman	1877–1881
Secretary of War	George W. McCrary	1877–1879
	Alex Ramsey	1879–1881
Attorney General	Charles Devens	1877–1881
Postmaster General	David M. Key	1877–1880
	Horace Maynard	1880–1881
Secretary of Navy	R. W. Thompson	1877–1881
	Nathan Goff, Jr.	1881
Secretary of Interior	Carl Schurz	1877–1881

THE GARFIELD ADMINISTRATION (REPUBLICAN)

	Name	Dates Served
President	James A. Garfield	1881
Vice President	Chester A. Arthur	1881
Secretary of State	James G. Blaine	1881
Secretary of Treasury	William Windom	1881
Secretary of War	R. T. Lincoln	1881
Attorney General	Wayne MacVeagh	1881
Postmaster General	T. L. James	1881
Secretary of Navy	W. H. Hunt	1881
Secretary of Interior	S. J. Kirkwood	1881

THE ARTHUR ADMINISTRATION (REPUBLICAN)

	Name	Dates Served
President	Chester A. Arthur	1881–1885
Vice President	None	
Secretary of State	F. T. Frelinghuysen	1881–1885
Secretary of Treasury	Charles J. Folger	1881–1884
	Walter Q. Gresham	1884
	Hugh McCulloch	1884–1885
Secretary of War	Robert T. Lincoln	1881–1885
Attorney General	Benjamin H. Brewster	1881–1885
Postmaster General	Timothy O. Howe	1881–1883
	Walter Q. Gresham	1883–1884
	Frank Hatton	1884–1885
Secretary of Navy	William E. Chandler	1881–1885
Secretary of Interior	Henry M. Teller	1881–1885

THE CLEVELAND ADMINISTRATION (DEMOCRAT)

	Name	Dates Served
President	Grover Cleveland	1885–1889
Vice President	T. A. Hendricks	1885–1889
Secretary of State	Thomas F. Bayard	1885–1889
Secretary of Treasury	Daniel Manning	1885–1887
	Charles S. Fairchild	1887–1889
Secretary of War	William C. Endicott	1885–1889
Attorney General	Augustus H. Garland	1885–1889
Postmaster General	William F. Vilas	1885–1888
	Don M. Dickinson	1888–1889
Secretary of Navy	William C. Whitney	1885–1889
Secretary of Interior	Lucius Q. C. Lamar	1885–1888
	William F. Vilas	1888–1889
Secretary of Agriculture	Norman J. Colman	1889

THE HARRISON ADMINISTRATION (REPUBLICAN)

	Name	Dates Served
President	Benjamin Harrison	1889–1893
Vice President	Levi P. Morton	1889–1893
Secretary of State	James G. Blaine	1889–1892
	John W. Foster	1892–1893
Secretary of Treasury	William Windom	1889–1891
	Charles Foster	1891–1893
Secretary of War	Redfield Proctor	1889–1891
	Stephen B. Elkins	1891–1893
Attorney General	William H. H. Miller	1889–1891
Postmaster General	James Wanamaker	1889–1893
Secretary of Navy	Benjamin F. Tracy	1889–1893
Secretary of Interior	John W. Noble	1889–1893
Secretary of Agriculture	John M. Rusk	1889–1893

THE CLEVELAND ADMINISTRATION (DEMOCRAT)

	Name	Dates Served
President	Grover Cleveland	1893–1897
Vice President	Adlai E. Stevenson	1893–1897
Secretary of State	Walter Q. Gresham	1893–1895
	Richard Olney	1895–1897
Secretary of Treasury	John G. Carlisle	1893–1897
Secretary of War	Daniel S. Lamont	1893–1897
Attorney General	Richard Olney	1893–1895
	James Harmon	1895–1897
Postmaster General	Wilson S. Bissell	1893–1895
	William L. Wilson	1895–1897
Secretary of Navy	Hilary A. Herbert	1893–1897
Secretary of Interior	Hoke Smith	1893–1896
	David R. Francis	1896–1897
Secretary of Agriculture	John S. Morton	1893–1897

THE MC KINLEY ADMINISTRATION (REPUBLICAN)

	Name	Dates Served
President	William McKinley	1897–1901
Vice President	Garret A. Hobart	1897–1901
	Theodore Roosevelt	1901
Secretary of State	John Sherman	1897
	William R. Day	1897–1898
	John Hay	1898–1901
Secretary of Treasury	Lyman J. Gage	1897–1901
Secretary of War	Russell A. Alger	1897–1899
	Elihu Root	1899–1901
Attorney General	James McKenna	1897
	John W. Griggs	1897–1901
	Philander C. Knox	1901
Postmaster General	James A. Gary	1897–1898
	Charles E. Smith	1898–1901
Secretary of Navy	John D. Long	1897–1901
Secretary of Interior	Charles N. Bliss	1897–1899
	Ethan A. Hitchcock	1899–1901
Secretary of Agriculture	James Wilson	1897–1901

THE ROOSEVELT ADMINISTRATION (REPUBLICAN)

	Name	Dates Served
President	Theodore Roosevelt	1901–1909
Vice President	Charles Fairbanks	1905–1909
Secretary of State	John Hay	1901–1905
	Elihu Root	1905–1909
	Robert Bacon	1909
Secretary of Treasury	Lyman J. Gage	1901–1902
	Leslie M. Shaw	1902–1907
	George B. Cortelyou	1907–1909
Secretary of War	Elihu Root	1901–1904
	William H. Taft	1904–1908
	Luke E. Wright	1908–1909
Attorney General	Philander C. Knox	1901–1904
	William H. Moody	1904–1907
	Charles J. Bonaparte	1907–1909

	Name	Dates Served
Postmaster General	Charles E. Smith	1901–1902
	Henry C. Payne	1902–1904
	Robert J. Wynne	1904–1905
	George B. Cortelyou	1905–1907
	George von L. Meyer	1907–1909
Secretary of Navy	John D. Long	1901–1902
	William H. Moody	1902–1904
	Paul Morton	1904–1905
	Charles J. Bonaparte	1905–1907
	Victor H. Metcalf	1907–1908
	Truman H. Newberry	1908–1909
Secretary of Interior	Ethan A. Hitchcock	1901–1907
	James R. Garfield	1907–1909
Secretary of Agriculture	James Wilson	1901–1909
Secretary of Labor and Commerce	George B. Cortelyou	1903–1904
	Victor H. Metcalf	1904–1907
	Oscar S. Straus	1907–1909
	Charles Nagel	1909

THE TAFT ADMINISTRATION (REPUBLICAN)

	Name	Dates Served
President	William H. Taft	1909–1913
Vice President	James S. Sherman	1909–1913
Secretary of State	Philander C. Knox	1909–1913
Secretary of Treasury	Franklin MacVeagh	1909–1913
Secretary of War	Jacob M. Dickinson	1909–1911
	Henry L. Stimson	1911–1913
Attorney General	George W. Wickersham	1909–1913
Postmaster General	Frank H. Hitchcock	1909–1913
Secretary of Navy	George von L. Meyer	1909–1913
Secretary of Interior	Richard A. Ballinger	1909–1911
	William L. Fisher	1911–1913
Secretary of Agriculture	James Wilson	1909–1913
Secretary of Labor and Commerce	Charles Nagel	1909–1913

THE WILSON ADMINISTRATION (DEMOCRAT)

	Name	Dates Served
President	Woodrow Wilson	1913–1921
Vice President	Thomas R. Marshall	1913–1921
Secretary of State	William J. Bryan	1913–1915
	Robert Lansing	1915–1920
	Bainbridge Colby	1920–1921
Secretary of Treasury	William G. McAdoo	1913–1918
	Carter Glass	1918–1920
	David F. Houston	1920–1921
Secretary of War	Lindley M. Garrison	1913–1916
	Newton D. Baker	1916–1921
Attorney General	James C. McReynolds	1913–1914
	Thomas W. Gregory	1914–1919
	A. Mitchell Palmer	1919–1921
Postmaster General	Albert S. Burleson	1913–1921
Secretary of Navy	Josephus Daniels	1913–1921
Secretary of Interior	Franklin K. Lane	1913–1920
	John B. Payne	1920–1921
Secretary of Agriculture	David F. Houston	1913–1920
	Edwin T. Meredith	1920–1921

	Name	Dates Served
Secretary of Commerce	William C. Redfield	1913–1919
	Joshua W. Alexander	1919–1921
Secretary of Labor	William B. Wilson	1913–1921

THE HARDING ADMINISTRATION (REPUBLICAN)

	Name	Dates Served
President	Warren G. Harding	1921–1923
Vice President	Calvin Coolidge	1921–1923
Secretary of State	Charles E. Hughes	1921–1923
Secretary of Treasury	Andrew Mellon	1921–1923
Secretary of War	John W. Weeks	1921–1923
Attorney General	Harry M. Daugherty	1921–1923
Postmaster General	Will H. Hays	1921–1922
	Hubert Work	1922–1923
	Harry S. New	1923
Secretary of Navy	Edwin Denby	1921–1923
Secretary of Interior	Albert B. Fall	1921–1923
	Hubert Work	1923
Secretary of Agriculture	Henry A. Wallace	1921–1923
Secretary of Commerce	Herbert C. Hoover	1921–1923
Secretary of Labor	J. J. Davis	1921–1923

THE COOLIDGE ADMINISTRATION (REPUBLICAN)

	Name	Dates Served
President	Calvin Coolidge	1923–1929
Vice President	Charles G. Dawes	1925–1929
Secretary of State	Charles E. Hughes	1923–1925
	Frank B. Kellogg	1925–1929
Secretary of Treasury	Andrew Mellon	1923–1929
Secretary of War	John W. Weeks	1923–1925
	Dwight F. Davis	1925–1929
Attorney General	Henry M. Daugherty	1923–1924
	Harlan F. Stone	1924–1925
	John G. Sargent	1925–1929
Postmaster General	Harry S. New	1923–1929
Secretary of Navy	Edwin Denby	1923–1924
	Curtis D. Wilbur	1924–1929
Secretary of Interior	Hubert Work	1923–1928
	Roy O. West	1928–1929
Secretary of Agriculture	Henry A. Wallace	1923–1924
	Howard M. Gore	1924–1925
	William M. Jardine	1925–1929
Secretary of Commerce	Herbert C. Hoover	1923–1928
	William F. Whiting	1928–1929
Secretary of Labor	James J. Davis	1923–1929

THE HOOVER ADMINISTRATION (REPUBLICAN)

	Name	Dates Served
President	Herbert C. Hoover	1929–1933
Vice President	Charles Curtis	1929–1933
Secretary of State	Henry L. Stimson	1929–1933
Secretary of Treasury	Andrew Mellon	1929–1932
	Ogden L. Mills	1932–1933
Secretary of War	James W. Good	1929
	Patrick J. Hurley	1929–1933
Attorney General	William D. Mitchell	1929–1933
Postmaster General	Walter F. Brown	1929–1933
Secretary of Navy	Charles F. Adams	1929–1933
Secretary of Interior	Ray L. Wilbur	1929–1933
Secretary of Agriculture	Arthur M. Hyde	1929–1933
Secretary of Commerce	Robert P. Lamont	1929–1932
	Roy D. Chapin	1932–1933
Secretary of Labor	James J. Davis	1929–1930
	William N. Doak	1930–1933

THE ROOSEVELT ADMINISTRATION (DEMOCRAT)

	Name	Dates Served
President	Franklin D. Roosevelt	1933–1945
Vice President	John Nance Garner	1933–1941
	Henry A. Wallace	1941–1945
	Harry S. Truman	1945
Secretary of State	Cordell Hull	1933–1944
	E. R. Stettinius, Jr.	1944–1945
Secretary of Treasury	William H. Woodin	1933–1934
	Henry Morgenthau, Jr.	1934–1945
Secretary of War	George H. Dern	1933–1936
	Henry A. Woodring	1936–1940
	Henry L. Stimson	1940–1945
Attorney General	Henry S. Cummings	1933–1939
	Frank Murphy	1939–1940
	Robert H. Jackson	1940–1941
	Francis Biddle	1941–1945
Postmaster General	James A. Farley	1933–1940
	Frank C. Walker	1940–1945
Secretary of Navy	Claude A. Swanson	1933–1940
	Charles Edison	1940
	Frank Knox	1940–1944
	James Forrestal	1944–1945
Secretary of Interior	Harold L. Ickes	1933–1945
Secretary of Agriculture	Henry A. Wallace	1933–1940
	Claude R. Wickard	1940–1945
Secretary of Commerce	Daniel C. Roper	1933–1939
	Harry L. Hopkins	1939–1940
	Jesse Jones	1940–1945
Secretary of Labor	Frances Perkins	1933–1945

THE TRUMAN ADMINISTRATION (DEMOCRAT)

	Name	Dates Served
President	Harry S. Truman	1945–1953
Vice President	Alben W. Barkley	1949–1953
Secretary of State	James F. Byrnes	1945–1947
	George C. Marshall	1947–1949
	Dean G. Acheson	1949–1953
Secretary of Treasury	Fred M. Vinson	1945–1946
	John W. Snyder	1946–1953
Secretary of War	Robert H. Patterson	1945–1947
	Kenneth C. Royall	1947

	Name	Dates Served
Attorney General	Tom C. Clark	1945–1949
	J. Howard McGrath	1949–1952
	James P. McGranery	1952–1953
Postmaster General	Frank C. Walker	1945
	Robert E. Hannegan	1945–1947
	Jesse M. Donaldson	1947–1953
Secretary of Navy	James V. Forrestal	1945–1947
Secretary of Interior	Harold L. Ickes	1945–1946
	Julius A. Krug	1946–1951
	Oscar L. Chapman	1951–1953
Secretary of Agriculture	Clinton P. Anderson	1945–1948
	Charles F. Brannan	1948–1953
Secretary of Commerce	Henry A. Wallace	1945–1946
	W. Averell Harriman	1946–1948
	Charles W. Sawyer	1948–1953
Secretary of Labor	Lewis B. Schwellenbach	1945–1948
	Maurice J. Tobin	1948–1953
Secretary of Defense	James V. Forrestal	1947–1949
	Louis A. Johnson	1949–1950
	George C. Marshall	1950–1951
	Robert A. Lovett	1951–1953

THE EISENHOWER ADMINISTRATION (REPUBLICAN)

	Name	Dates Served
President	Dwight D. Eisenhower	1953–1961
Vice President	Richard M. Nixon	1953–1961
Secretary of State	John Foster Dulles	1953–1959
	Christian A. Herter	1959–1961
Secretary of Treasury	George M. Humphrey	1953–1957
	Robert B. Anderson	1957–1961
Attorney General	Herbert Brownell, Jr.	1953–1957
	William P. Rogers	1957–1961
Postmaster General	Arthur E. Summerfield	1953–1961
Secretary of Interior	Douglas McKay	1953–1956
	Fred A. Seaton	1956–1961
Secretary of Agriculture	Ezra T. Benson	1953–1961
Secretary of Commerce	Sinclair Weeks	1953–1958
	Lewis L. Strauss	1958–1959
	Frederick H. Mueller	1959–1961
Secretary of Labor	Martin P. Durkin	1953
	James P. Mitchell	1953–1961
Secretary of Defense	Charles E. Wilson	1953–1957
	Neil H. McElroy	1957–1959
	Thomas S. Gates, Jr.	1959–1961
Secretary of Health, Education, and Welfare	Oveta Culp Hobby	1953–1955
	Marion B. Folsom	1955–1958
	Arthur S. Flemming	1958–1961

THE KENNEDY ADMINISTRATION (DEMOCRAT)

	Name	Dates Served
President	John F. Kennedy	1961–1963
Vice President	Lyndon B. Johnson	1961–1963
Secretary of State	Dean Rusk	1961–1963
Secretary of Treasury	C. Douglas Dillon	1961–1963
Attorney General	Robert F. Kennedy	1961–1963
Postmaster General	J. Edward Day	1961–1963
	John A. Gronouski	1963
Secretary of Interior	Stewart L. Udall	1961–1963

	Name	Dates Served
Secretary of Agriculture	Orville L. Freeman	1961–1963
Secretary of Commerce	Luther H. Hodges	1961–1963
Secretary of Labor	Arthur J. Goldberg	1961–1962
	W. Willard Wirtz	1962–1963
Secretary of Defense	Robert S. McNamara	1961–1963
Secretary of Health, Education, and Welfare	Abraham A. Ribicoff	1961–1962
	Anthony J. Celebrezze	1962–1963

THE JOHNSON ADMINISTRATION (DEMOCRAT)

	Name	Dates Served
President	Lyndon B. Johnson	1963–1969
Vice President	Hubert H. Humphrey	1965–1969
Secretary of State	Dean Rusk	1963–1969
Secretary of Treasury	C. Douglas Dillon	1963–1965
	Henry H. Fowler	1965–1969
Attorney General	Robert F. Kennedy	1963–1964
	Nicholas Katzenbach	1964–1967
	Ramsey Clark	1967–1969
Secretary of Interior	Stewart L. Udall	1963–1969
Postmaster General	John A. Gronouski	1963–1965
	Lawrence F. O'Brien	1965–1968
	Marvin Watson	1968–1969
Secretary of Agriculture	Orville L. Freeman	1963–1969
Secretary of Commerce	Luther H. Hodges	1963–1964
	John T. Connor	1964–1967
	A. B. Trowbridge	1967–1969
Secretary of Labor	W. Willard Wirtz	1963–1969
Secretary of Defense	Robert F. McNamara	1963–1968
	Clark Clifford	1968–1969
Secretary of Health, Education, and Welfare	Anthony J. Celebrezze	1963–1965
	John W. Gardner	1965–1968
Secretary of Housing and Urban Development	Robert C. Weaver	1966–1969
Secretary of Transportation	Alan S. Boyd	1966–1969

THE NIXON ADMINISTRATION (REPUBLICAN)

	Name	Dates Served
President	Richard M. Nixon	1969–1974
Vice President	Spiro T. Agnew	1969–1973
	Gerald R. Ford	1973–1974
Secretary of State	William P. Rogers	1969–1973
	Henry A. Kissinger	1973–1974
Secretary of Treasury	David M. Kennedy	1969–1970
	John B. Connally	1970–1972
	George P. Shultz	1972–1974
	William E. Simon	1974–1974
Attorney General	John N. Mitchell	1969–1972
	Richard G. Kleindienst	1972–1973
	Elliot L. Richardson	1973–1973*
	William B. Saxbe	1973–1974
Postmaster General	William M. Blount	1969–1971**

*Mr. Richardson served both as Attorney General and Secretary of Defense at different times.

**The Postal Reorganization Act of 1970 provided for replacement of the Post Office Department by a new U.S. Postal Service, an independent Federal Agency. Its head, retaining the title of Postmaster General, is no longer a member of the Cabinet.

	Name	Dates Served		Name	Dates Served
Secretary of Interior	Walter J. Hickel	1969–1971	Secretary of Health, Education and Welfare	Robert H. Finch	1969–1970
	Rogers C. B. Morton	1971–1974		Elliot L. Richardson	1970–1973
				Casper W. Weinberger	1973–1974
Secretary of Agriculture	Clifford M. Hardin	1969–1971			
	Earl L. Butz	1971–1974	Secretary of Housing and Urban Development	George Romney	1969–1973
				James T. Lynn	1973–1974
Secretary of Commerce	Maurice H. Stans	1969–1972			
	Peter G. Peterson	1972–1973	Secretary of Transport-ation	John A. Volpe	1969–1973
	Frederick B. Dent	1973–1974		Claude S. Brinegar	1973–1974

THE FORD ADMINISTRATION (REPUBLICAN)

	Name	Dates Served
Secretary of Labor	George P. Shultz	1969–1970
	James D. Hodgson	1970–1973
	Peter J. Brennan	1973–1974
President	Gerald R. Ford	1974–

As of September 1, 1974, President Ford had made no changes in the Nixon cabinet.

	Name	Dates Served
Secretary of Defense	Melvin R. Laird	1969–1973
	Elliot L. Richardson	1973–1973
	James R. Schlesinger	1973–1974

Justices of the United States Supreme Court, 1789–1974*

Name and Residence	Service Term	Years	Dates	Name and Residence	Service Term	Years	Dates
John Jay, N.Y.	1789–1795	5	1745–1829	Ward Hunt, N.Y.	1873–1882	9	1810–1886
John Rutledge, S.C.	1789–1791	1	1739–1800	*Morrison R. Waite*, Ohio	1874–1888	14	1816–1888
William Cushing, Mass.	1789–1810	20	1732–1810	John M. Harlan, Ky.	1877–1911	34	1833–1911
James Wilson, Pa.	1789–1798	8	1742–1798	William B. Woods, Ga.	1881–1887	6	1824–1887
John Blair, Va.	1789–1796	6	1732–1800	Stanley Matthews, Ohio	1881–1889	7	1824–1889
Robert H. Harrison, Md.	1789–1790	–	1745–1790	Horace Gray, Mass.	1882–1902	20	1828–1902
James Iredell, N.C.	1790–1799	9	1751–1799	Samuel Blatchford, N.Y.	1882–1893	11	1820–1893
Thomas Johnson, Md.	1791–1793	1	1732–1819	Lucius Q. C. Lamar, Miss.	1888–1893	5	1825–1893
William Paterson, N.J.	1793–1806	13	1745–1806	*Melville W. Fuller*, Ill.	1888–1910	21	1833–1910
John Rutledge, S.C.	1795–†	–	1739–1800	David J. Brewer, Kans.	1890–1910	20	1837–1910
Samuel Chase, Md.	1796–1811	15	1741–1811	Henry B. Brown, Mich.	1891–1906	15	1836–1913
Oliver Ellsworth, Conn.	1796–1799	4	1745–1807	George Shiras, Jr., Pa.	1892–1903	10	1832–1924
Bushrod Washington, Va.	1798–1829	31	1762–1829	Howell E. Jackson, Tenn.	1893–1895	2	1832–1895
Alfred Moore, N.C.	1799–1804	4	1755–1810	Edward D. White, La.	1894–1910	16	1845–1921
John Marshall, Va.	1801–1835	34	1755–1835	Rufus W. Peckham, N.Y.	1896–1909	13	1838–1909
William Johnson, S.C.	1804–1834	30	1771–1834	Joseph McKenna, Calif.	1898–1925	26	1843–1926
Brockholst Livingston, N.Y.	1806–1823	16	1757–1823	Oliver W. Holmes, Mass.	1902–1932	30	1841–1935
Thomas Todd, Ky.	1807–1826	18	1765–1826	William R. Day, Ohio	1903–1922	19	1849–1923
Joseph Story, Mass.	1811–1845	33	1779–1845	William H. Moody, Mass.	1906–1910	3	1853–1917
Gabriel Duval, Md.	1811–1835	24	1752–1844	Horace H. Lurton, Tenn.	1910–1914	4	1844–1914
Smith Thompson, N.Y.	1823–1843	20	1768–1843	Charles E. Hughes, N.Y.	1910–1916	5	1862–1948
Robert Trimble, Ky.	1826–1828	2	1777–1828	Willis Van Devanter, Wyo.	1911–1937	26	1859–1941
John McLean, Ohio	1829–1861	32	1785–1861	Joseph R. Lamar, Ga.	1911–1916	5	1857–1916
Henry Baldwin, Pa.	1830–1844	14	1780–1844	*Edward D. White*, La.	1910–1921	11	1845–1921
James M. Wayne, Ga.	1835–1867	32	1790–1867	Mahlon Pitney, N.J.	1912–1922	10	1858–1924
Roger B. Taney, Md.	1836–1864	28	1777–1864	James C. McReynolds, Tenn.	1914–1941	26	1862–1946
Philip P. Barbour, Va.	1836–1841	4	1783–1841	Louis D. Brandeis, Mass.	1916–1939	22	1856–1941
John Catron, Tenn.	1837–1865	28	1786–1865	John H. Clarke, Ohio	1916–1922	6	1857–1945
John McKinley, Ala.	1837–1852	15	1780–1852	William H. Taft, Conn.	1921–1930	8	1857–1930
Peter V. Daniel, Va.	1841–1860	19	1784–1860	George Sutherland, Utah	1922–1938	15	1862–1948
Samuel Nelson, N.Y.	1845–1872	27	1792–1873	Pierce Butler, Minn.	1922–1939	16	1866–1939
Levi Woodbury, N.H.	1845–1851	5	1789–1851	Edward T. Sanford, Tenn.	1923–1930	7	1865–1930
Robert C. Grier, Pa.	1846–1870	23	1794–1870	Harlan F. Stone, N.Y.	1925–1941	16	1872–1946
Benjamin R. Curtis, Mass.	1851–1857	6	1809–1874	*Charles E. Hughes*, N.Y.	1930–1941	11	1862–1948
John A. Campbell, Ala.	1853–1861	8	1811–1889	Owen J. Roberts, Pa.	1930–1945	15	1875–1955
Nathan Clifford, Maine	1858–1881	23	1803–1881	Benjamin N. Cardozo, N.Y.	1932–1938	6	1870–1938
Noah H. Swayne, Ohio	1862–1881	18	1804–1884	Hugo L. Black, Ala.	1937–	–	1886–1971
Samuel F. Miller, Iowa	1862–1890	28	1816–1890	Stanley F. Reed, Ky.	1938–1957‡	19	1884–
David Davis, Ill.	1862–1877	14	1815–1886	Felix Frankfurter, Mass.	1939–1962	23	1882–1965
Stephen J. Field, Calif.	1863–1897	34	1816–1899	William O. Douglas, Conn.	1939–	–	1898–
Salmon P. Chase, Ohio	1864–1873	8	1808–1873	Frank Murphy, Mich.	1940–1949	9	1890–1949
William Strong, Pa.	1870–1880	10	1808–1895	*Harlan F. Stone*, N.Y.	1941–1946	5	1872–1946
Joseph P. Bradley, N.J.	1870–1892	22	1813–1892	James F. Byrnes, S.C.	1941–1942‡	1	1879–1972

Name and Residence	Service Term	Years	Dates	Name and Residence	Service Term	Years	Dates
Robert H. Jackson, N.Y.	1941–1954	13	1892–1954	Arthur J. Goldberg, Ill.	1962–1965	3	1908–
Wiley B. Rutledge, Iowa	1943–1949	6	1894–1949	Abe Fortas, Tenn.	1965–1969	4	1910–
Harold H. Burton, Ohio	1945–1958	13	1888–1964	Thurgood Marshall, N.Y.	1967–	—	1908–
Fred M. Vinson, Ky.	1946–1953	7	1890–1953	*Warren C. Burger*, Minn.	1969–	—	1907–
Tom C. Clark, Tex.	1949–1967‡	18	1899–	Harry A. Blackmun, Minn.	1970–	—	1908–
Sherman Minton, Ind.	1949–1956	7	1890–1965	Lewis F. Powell, Jr., Va.	1972–	—	1907–
Earl Warren, Calif.	1953–1969	16	1891–1974	William H. Rehnquist, Ariz.	1972–	—	1924–
John Marshall Harlan, N.Y.	1955–	—	1899–				
William J. Brennan, Jr., N.Y.	1956–	—	1906–				
Charles E. Whittaker, Mo.	1957–1962	5	1901–1973	* Chief Justices in italic.			
Potter Stewart, Ohio	1958–	—	1915–	† Rejected December 15, 1795.			
Byron R. White, Colo.	1962–	—	1917–	‡ Retired.			

Admission of the States, 1787–1959

Delaware	December 7, 1787	Michigan	January 16, 1837
Pennsylvania	December 12, 1787	Florida	March 3, 1845
New Jersey	December 18, 1787	Texas	December 29, 1845
Georgia	January 2, 1788	Iowa	December 28, 1846
Connecticut	January 9, 1788	Wisconsin	May 29, 1848
Massachusetts	February 6, 1788	California	September 9, 1850
Maryland	April 28, 1788	Minnesota	May 11, 1858
South Carolina	May 23, 1788	Oregon	February 14, 1859
New Hampshire	June 21, 1788	Kansas	January 29, 1861
Virginia	June 25, 1788	West Virginia	June 19, 1863
New York	July 26, 1788	Nevada	October 31, 1864
North Carolina	November 21, 1789	Nebraska	March 1, 1867
Rhode Island	May 29, 1790	Colorado	August 1, 1876
Vermont	March 4, 1791	North Dakota	November 2, 1889
Kentucky	June 1, 1792	South Dakota	November 2, 1889
Tennessee	June 1, 1796	Montana	November 8, 1889
Ohio	March 1, 1803	Washington	November 11, 1889
Louisiana	April 30, 1812	Idaho	July 3, 1890
Indiana	December 11, 1816	Wyoming	July 10, 1890
Mississippi	December 10, 1817	Utah	January 4, 1896
Illinois	December 3, 1818	Oklahoma	November 16, 1907
Alabama	December 14, 1819	New Mexico	January 6, 1912
Maine	March 15, 1820	Arizona	February 14, 1912
Missouri	August 10, 1821	Alaska	January 3, 1959
Arkansas	June 15, 1836	Hawaii	August 21, 1959

Index